Economic Report
of the President

Together with
The Annual Report
of the
Council of Economic Advisers

March 2019

Contents

---

*For a detailed table of contents of the Council's *Report*, see page 23.

Economic Report of the President

Economic Report of the President

To the Congress of the United States:

For the past two years, my Administration has been focused on strengthening the United States economy to enable greater opportunity and prosperity for all Americans.

During my first year in office, we began by building a foundation of pro-growth policies. We initiated sweeping regulatory reform—issuing 22 deregulatory actions for every new one added—and signed into law the Tax Cuts and Jobs Act, the biggest package of tax cuts and tax reform in our country's history. Consumer and business confidence skyrocketed as we reversed incentives that had driven away businesses, investment, and jobs for many years. With these cornerstones of a robust economy in place, we restored enthusiasm for doing business in America. This has achieved enormously positive results for American workers and families.

The United States economy has created 5.3 million jobs since I was elected to office. Wage growth continued in 2018, with the lowest-earning workers experiencing the strongest gains. By the fourth quarter of 2018, real disposable personal income per household was up more than $2,200 from the end of 2017. The national unemployment rate reached a nearly 50-year low of 3.7 percent in September 2018, hovering at or below 4 percent for 11 consecutive months—the longest streak in nearly five decades. Opportunity is expanding so fast that there are more job openings in our economy than there are current job seekers. These positions will be filled as more Americans join the labor force or rejoin it after years of discouragement and pessimism. In January 2019, more than 70 percent of workers entering employment were previously out of the labor force, and the labor force participation rate reached 63.2 percent—the highest since 2013. For the second consecutive year, economic growth has either matched or surpassed my Administration's forecast, and the economy has grown at a 3.1 percent rate over the last four quarters.

This progress is remarkable. It is a victory for all Americans now benefiting from a strengthened economy. But the greatest triumph of all is this: we have created an era of opportunity in which Americans left behind by previous Administrations are finally catching up and even getting ahead.

An Economic Agenda for the Success of Every American

An economic agenda that enables struggling Americans to succeed begins with the creation of opportunities. Years of misguided policies, however, diminished opportunity, disregarded the importance of American workers for our country's success, and turned millions of our hard-working citizens into collateral damage. On a massive scale, jobs were lost as unfair trade deals gutted American manufacturing and a backward tax code drove away businesses and investment. The American people suffered the consequences of past leaders' unalloyed aspirations for global trade; which enriched other nations and impoverished our working families, as we increasingly imported goods formerly made here by American workers. Those seeking hope from Washington received dismissive explanations. They were told that low growth and meager opportunity were the "new normal"—that nothing could be done to stop the damage. Meanwhile, economic hardship derailed families and communities: Hopelessness deepened, and drug abuse and other maladies spread.

Our country could not achieve its highest economic potential with a workforce hollowed out by the mistaken policies of the past—policies that treated our citizens as an afterthought, hurt our most vulnerable workers, and crippled our economy. Over the past two years, my Administration has implemented a pro-growth policy agenda that puts Americans first and creates conditions that enable all our citizens to succeed.

By strengthening the United States economy, we have empowered many groups that historically have had a harder time getting ahead. Unemployment among those without a high school degree is the lowest in nearly 30 years. In the past year, the unemployment rate among women fell to 3.3. percent, matching its lowest rate since 1953. Teenage unemployment reached its lowest rate in nearly 50 years. My Administration has presided over the lowest unemployment rates for people with disabilities on record. Poverty rates for both black Americans and Hispanic Americans reached record lows in 2017. Homelessness among veterans fell by 5.4 percent in the past year. The bottom 10 percent of earners are experiencing the highest wage growth on record, and we have lifted nearly 5 million Americans off food stamps since my election. Revitalized American manufacturing—something once thought impossible—has restored opportunities for American blue-collar workers. In the first two years of my Administration, we have created manufacturing jobs at six times the pace of the previous Administration's last two years, for a total of nearly half a million jobs. Blue-collar workers, on average, are on track to see almost $2,500 more in annual wages.

The success of America's workers is essential to the success of our country. We will continue to prioritize workforce development in the years ahead, and we will keep fighting on behalf of all Americans seeking opportunities to contribute. In establishing the National Council for the American Worker, my Administration is emphasizing the importance of results-driven job training and reskilling programs; we must equip our students and workers with competitive skills adapted to our rapidly changing economy. This initiative has already secured commitments from the private sector to invest in over 6.5 million retraining opportunities.

An economic agenda that lifts all Americans must also address the destructive effects that over-incarceration has on our families and our communities. With the enactment of the First Step Act of 2018, we have achieved a bipartisan victory for criminal justice reform. The First Step Act modifies sentencing for less serious crimes and prioritizes rehabilitation to enable former prisoners to reenter society as productive, law-abiding citizens. Well-designed prison programs that help bring families together and give reformed prisoners the tools to find work are crucial for reducing the costs of crime and our over-incarceration.

Finally, we remain committed to encouraging self-sufficiency and advocating for work as the best way to foster human dignity and escape poverty. In our strengthened economy, long-awaited job opportunities have become available to millions of Americans who are eager to support themselves. Although help must be accessible to those who are struggling, expanding work requirements can further reduce both poverty and dependency among those able to work. Over half of all nondisabled, working-age adults receiving food stamps are not working. By finding ways to put their talents to productive use, we would both enrich our society and help them live more fulfilling lives. My Administration values the capabilities of all Americans, and we will continue to implement a pro-growth, pro-opportunity agenda that puts self-sufficiency within reach.

Investing in Innovation and the Future of American Greatness

To maintain economic momentum and expand opportunity in our Nation, we will continue to champion American innovation and entrepreneurship. Smart deregulation and technological advances have unleashed American energy dominance, and made American energy the way of the future. The United States is now the world's single largest producer of crude oil and natural gas. Our strength in the energy sector has invigorated our economy, created jobs, and reduced our dependence on energy from countries that do not share our values.

The instinct to invent and create has driven America forward since its founding and has enabled our country to export ideas that have rapidly improved the world. To do right by our researchers and inventors, we must hold foreign nations to account for stealing our intellectual property and forcing technology transfers. To do right by American taxpayers and consumers, we must continue fighting for lower pharmaceutical drug prices and end global free-riding on Americans' transformative research. And to bolster growth, we must continue to unleash the power of possibility by revolutionizing our Nation's technological capabilities within the industries of the future, including artificial intelligence, advanced manufacturing, and 5G technology.

By reducing the costs and confines of oppressive, growth-killing regulation, we have improved the ability of American entrepreneurs to start and expand their businesses. Many aspiring entrepreneurs, however, live in areas of our country that are starved of the capital that entices business investment and creates jobs. The Investing in Opportunity Act, part of our historic tax reform law, is addressing this problem. It is using tax incentives to draw investment into Opportunity Zones, areas struggling with higher unemployment and poverty. These areas are experiencing increases in commercial real estate transactions, as investors seize on the potential for Opportunity Zones to reignite the American Dream for those who have been left behind.

Our dedication to investing in a brighter future must be paired with a commitment to fixing past mistakes. We have made significant strides to reverse the damage of trade policies that harmed our country for many years. We renegotiated the destructive North American Free Trade Agreement and reached a new agreement, the United States–Mexico–Canada Agreement. We also negotiated a revised United States–Korea Free Trade Agreement. At the time of this *Report*'s publication, we are conducting negotiations with China, the European Union, and Japan. In addition, we intend to begin negotiations with the United Kingdom as soon as it leaves the European Union. With these historic achievements, we have begun an era of trade policy that finally puts the interests of the United States and our hard-working families first.

To improve the welfare of our Nation and its citizens, we are redoubling our efforts to fix an immigration system that has been broken for decades. The chaos at our Southern Border comes at an intolerable cost to American citizens, who deserve peaceful, prosperous communities. We cannot tolerate the crime, drug smuggling, illegal entry, and human trafficking enabled by a porous border. The current system that allows dangerous gang members into our society, strains public services, and rewards those who ignore our laws over those who respect our citizenship process is simply unsustainable for our Nation. We must have an orderly immigration system that honors United States citizenship as the unrivaled privilege we all know it to be.

As shown in the *Report* that follows, we are ushering in an era of renewed dedication to our citizens. It is my great honor to champion the American people and to make their success and well-being my top priority. This pro-growth, pro-opportunity agenda celebrates the irreplaceable value of America's working families and embraces the extraordinary possibilities for American ingenuity to improve the human condition. It is an economic agenda that lays the foundation for the future of American greatness.

The White House
March 2019

The Annual Report

of the

Council of Economic Advisers

Letter of Transmittal

Council of Economic Advisers
Washington, March 19, 2019

Mr. President:

The Council of Economic Advisers herewith submits its 2019 Annual Report in accordance with the Employment Act of 1946, as amended by the Full Employment and Balanced Growth Act of 1978.

Sincerely yours,

Kevin A. Hassett
Chairman

Richard V. Burkhauser
Member

Tomas J. Philipson
Member

Council of Economic Advisers
Washington, March 19, 2019

Mr. President:

In the 10 chapters that constitute this *Report* the Council of Economic Advisers provides a detailed account of the U.S. economy in 2018, and offers analysis of the Administration's economic policy agenda for the years ahead.

In preparing the *Economic Report of the President* the Council strives to incorporate the most recent data available at the time of the *Report's* statutorily mandated transmittal to Congress, and to ensure through internal processes that our analysis of these data adheres to the strictest standards of verification and replication. Due to delayed data releases owing to a partial government shutdown from December 22, 2018, to January 25, 2019, it was not possible for the Council to incorporate preliminary estimates of gross domestic product and personal income and outlays in the fourth quarter of 2018 while upholding our replication procedures and a production schedule required to comply with the statute.

However, I am pleased to report in this letter that the data confirm and reinforce the findings of this *Report* and do not materially alter its conclusions.

Sincerely yours,

Kevin A. Hassett
Chairman

Introduction

In accordance with the Employment Act of 1946, the purpose of this *Report* is to provide the U.S. Congress with "timely and authoritative information concerning economic developments and economic trends" for the preceding year and, prospectively, for the years ahead. As required by the Employment Act, the *Report* also sets forth the Administration's program for achieving the chartered purpose of:

> Creating and maintaining, in a manner calculated to foster and promote free competitive enterprise and the general welfare, conditions under which there will be afforded useful employment opportunities, including self-employment, for those able, willing, and seeking to work, and to promote maximum employment, production, and purchasing power (79th U.S. Congress, 1946).

In the 10 chapters that constitute this *Report*, we present evidence that the Trump Administration's policy actions and priorities are thus far delivering economic results consistent with the 1946 mandate.

For the second consecutive year, the U.S. economy outperformed expectations and broke from recent trends by a substantial margin. In June 2017, the Congressional Budget Office projected that during the four quarters of 2018, real gross domestic product (GDP) would grow by 2.0 percent, the unemployment rate would decline by 0.1 percentage point, to 4.2 percent, and employment growth would average 107,000 jobs per month. Instead, real GDP in the first three quarters of 2018 grew at a compound annual rate of 3.2 percent—above the Trump Administration's own fourth quarter–over–fourth quarter forecast for the second successive year—the unemployment rate declined by 0.4 percentage point, to a near-50-year low of 3.7 percent, and employment growth averaged 223,000 jobs per month. Growth in labor productivity, which averaged just 1.0 percent between 2009:Q3 and 2016:Q4, doubled to 2.0 percent in 2018. Capital expenditures by nonfinancial businesses rose 13.9 percent at a compound annual rate through 2018:Q3.

Figures I-1 through I-4 show that the strong economic performance in 2017 and 2018 was not merely a continuation of trends already under way during the postrecession expansion, but rather constituted a distinct break from the previous pace of economic and employment growth since the start of the current expansion in 2009:Q3. The figures depict observed outcomes before (blue) and after (red) the election, with the dotted lines representing the projected trend estimated on the basis of preelection data. Consistent with conclusions in the 2018 *Economic Report of the President*, investment, manufacturing employment, worker compensation, and new startups have all risen sharply in the two years since the 2016 election.

Figure I-1. Real Private Nonresidential Fixed Investment, 2012–18

Dollars (billions, 2012)

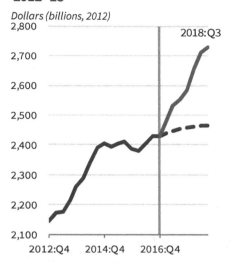

Figure I-2. Durable Goods Manufacturing Employment, 2012–18

Employment (thousands)

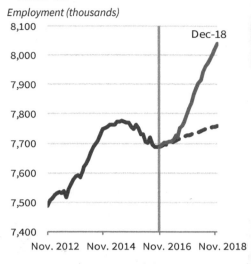

Figure I-3. New Business Applications, 2012–18

Number of applications

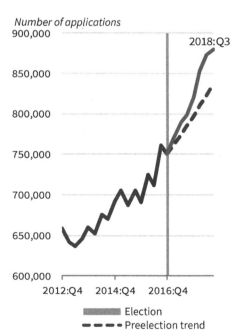

Figure I-4. Average Weekly Earnings of Goods-Producing Employees, 2012–18

Dollars per week

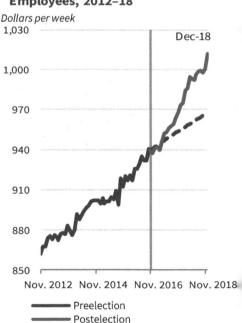

Sources: Bureau of Economic Analysis; Bureau of Labor Statistics; U.S. Census Bureau; CEA calculations.
Note: All trends are estimated over a sample period covering the entire preelection expansion from 2009:Q3 (2009, July) to 2016:Q4 (2016, November). Figure I-4 represents the average nominal weekly earnings of goods producing production and nonsupervisory employees in nominal dollars. Trends are estimated on compound annual growth rates and levels reconstructed from projected rates.

In addition, overall economic output by the third quarter of 2018 was $250 billion, or 1.3 percent, larger than projected by the 2009:Q3–2016:Q4 trend, with the compound annual growth rate up 1.2 percentage points over trend. Higher output growth was driven by a marked rise in real private investment in fixed assets, which was 10.6 percent over the projected trend as of the third quarter. In the first three quarters of 2018, the contribution of real private nonresidential fixed investment to GDP growth rose from 0.6 percentage point, the average of the preceding expansion, to 1.0 percentage point, while investment as a share of GDP rose to its second-highest level for any calendar year since 2001. Real private nonresidential fixed investment by nonfinancial businesses rose 8.3 percent at a compound annual rate through 2018:Q3, climbing to a level 14.7 percent above that projected by the 2009:Q3–2016:Q4 trend. As of December 2018, average nominal weekly earnings of goods producing production and nonsupervisory workers had risen $2,300 above trend on an annualized basis.

In the chapters that follow, we demonstrate that these departures from the recent trend are not accidental but rather reflect the Trump Administration's deliberate measures to create and maintain conditions under which the U.S. economy can achieve maximum employment, production, and purchasing power. Specifically, a unifying theme throughout this *Report* is that these conditions are generally achieved by providing maximum scope for the efficiency of free enterprise and competitive market mechanisms, and ensuring that these mechanisms are operative in both domestic and global markets.

Beginning with chapter 1, "Evaluating the Effects of the Tax Cuts and Jobs Act," we use currently available data to examine the Tax Cuts and Jobs Act's (TCJA's) anticipated and observed effects, with particular attention to the relative velocities of adjustment along each economic margin. We find that by lowering the cost of capital, the TCJA had an instant and large effect on business expectations, with firms immediately responding to the TCJA by upwardly revising planned capital expenditures, employee compensation, and hiring. We also observe revised capital plans translating into higher capital expenditures and real private investment in fixed assets, with nonresidential investment in equipment, structures, and intellectual property products growing at a weighted average annual rate of about 8 percent from 2017:Q4 through 2018:Q3, climbing to $150 billion over the pre-TCJA expansion trend of 2009:Q3 through 2017:Q4. (Equipment investment trends are calculated through 2017:Q3, because the TCJA's allowance of full expensing of new equipment investment was retroactive to September 2017.) In addition to tallying more than 6 million workers receiving bonuses directly attributed to the TCJA, with an average bonus size of $1,200, we also estimate that real disposable personal income per household rose to $640 over the trend by the third quarter of 2018, or 16 percent of the CEA's estimated long-run effect of $4,000 per household. In real terms, median usual weekly earnings of all full-time wage and salary workers were up $805 over trend on an annualized basis.

We also report evidence of a reorientation of U.S. investment from direct investment abroad to investment in the United States, as the TCJA attenuated incentives to shift productive assets and profits to lower-tax jurisdictions. Specifically, in the first three quarters after the TCJA's enactment, U.S. direct investment abroad declined by $148 billion, while direct investment in eight identified tax havens declined by $200 billion. In the first three quarters of 2018, U.S. firms repatriated almost $600 billion in overseas earnings. Based on extensive evidence from a large body of corporate finance literature, we conclude that shareholder distributions through share repurchases are an important margin of adjustment to a simultaneous positive shock to cash flow and investment, constituting the primary mechanism whereby efficient capital markets reallocate capital from mature, cash-abundant firms without profitable investment opportunities to emerging, cash-constrained firms with profitable investment opportunities.

In chapter 2, "Reducing the Burden of Regulatory Costs," we examine the Administration's important deregulatory efforts, which have also led to improved performance over the previous two years. We develop a framework to analyze the cumulative economic impact of regulatory actions on the U.S. economy. As the first Administration to use regulatory cost caps to reduce the cumulative burden of Federal regulation, the Trump Administration in 2017 and 2018 issued more deregulatory actions than regulatory actions and reversed the long-standing trend of rising regulatory costs. By raising the cost of conducting business, regulation can prevent valuable business and consumer activities.

More important, however, we also stress that regulations in one industry affect not only the regulated industry or sector but also the economy as a whole. We find that this implies that official measures understate regulatory costs and therefore also understate the regulatory cost savings of the Trump Administration's regulatory reforms because they do not account for relevant opportunity costs, especially those accruing outside the regulated industry. The official data show that from 2000 through 2016, the annual trend was for regulatory costs to grow by an average of $8.2 billion each year. In contrast, in 2017 and 2018 Federal agencies took deregulatory actions that resulted in costs savings that more than offset the costs of new regulatory actions. The official data show that in fiscal year 2017, the deregulatory actions saved $0.6 billion in annualized regulatory costs (with a net present value of $8.1 billion); and in fiscal year 2018, the deregulatory actions saved $1.4 billion in annualized regulatory costs (with a net present value of $23 billion). Looking at just three important deregulatory case studies, the CEA calculates that the three actions will reduce annual regulatory costs by an additional $27 billion.

Chapter 3, "Expanding Labor Force Opportunities for Every American," discusses the dramatic effect the revival of the economy has had on labor markets. Consistent with the robust pace of economic growth in the United States, the labor market is the strongest that it has been in decades, with an unemployment rate that remained under 4 percent for much of 2018. Employment is expanding and wages are rising at their fastest pace since 2009. Whenever both quantity and price go up in a market, this must be partly driven by a rise in demand. This suggests that an important change in the labor market has been an increase in the demand for labor, induced potentially by a supply-side expansion enabled by tax reform and deregulation. Although the low unemployment rate is a signal of a strong labor market, there is a question as to whether the rapid pace of hiring can continue and whether there are a sufficient number of remaining potential workers to support continued economic growth. This pessimistic view of the economy's potential, however, overlooks the extent to which the share of prime-age adults who are in the labor market remains below its historical norm.

As is explored in chapter 3, potential workers could be drawn back into the labor market through Administration policies designed to reduce past tax and regulatory distortions and to encourage additional people to engage in the labor market. Policies examined in this chapter that intend to increase labor force participation include reducing the costs of child care, working with the private sector to increase employer training and reskilling initiatives, and pursuing criminal justice reform to increase labor force engagement among affected communities. We also highlight the potential benefits of reducing occupational licensing, and incentivizing investment in designated Opportunity Zones to improve economically distressed areas, as provided for in the TCJA.

In chapter 4, "Enabling Choice and Competition in Healthcare Markets," we seek to address the 1946 mandate for this *Report* to analyze how to "foster and promote free and competitive enterprise" to a greater extent in the U.S. healthcare sector. We discuss the rationales commonly offered for government intervention in healthcare and explain why such interventions often, and unnecessarily, restrict choice and competition, demonstrating that the resulting government failures are frequently more costly than the market failures they attempt to correct. In light of recent public proposals to dramatically increase government intervention in healthcare markets, such as "Medicare for All," we also analyze how these proposals eliminate or decrease choice and competition. As a result, we find that these proposals would be inefficient, costly, and likely reduce, as opposed to increase, the population's health. Funding them would create large distortions in the economy, with the universal nature of "Medicare for All" constituting a particularly inefficient way to finance healthcare for lower- and middle- income people.

We contrast such proposals with the Trump Administration's actions that are increasing healthcare choice and competition for healthcare. We focus on the elimination of the Affordable Care Act's individual mandate penalty, which will enable consumers to decide for themselves what value they attach to purchasing insurance and which we project will generate $204 billion in value over 10 years. Expanding the availability of association health plans and short-term, limited-duration health plans will increase consumer choice and insurance affordability. We find that taken together, these three sets of actions will generate a value of $453 billion over the next decade. On the pharmaceutical front, the Food and Drug Administration is increasing price competition by streamlining the drug application and review process at the same time that record numbers of generic drugs are being approved, price growth is falling, and consumers have already saved $26 billion through the first year and a half of the Administration. In addition, the influx of new, brand name drugs resulted in an estimated $43 billion in annual benefits to consumers in 2018.

Chapter 5, "Unleashing the Power of American Energy," discusses the important role of energy markets in the new economic revival and the Administration's goal of stimulating free market innovation to enable U.S. energy independence. Coal production stabilized in 2017 and 2018 after a period of contraction in 2015 and 2016. The United States is now a net exporter of natural gas for the first time in 60 years, and petroleum exports are increasing at a pace that suggests positive net exports by 2020. Taking advantage of America's abundant energy resources is a key tenet of the Trump Administration's plan for long-term economic growth as well as national security. This is best achieved by recognizing that price incentives and the role of technological innovation—which is guided by the price incentive in a market economy like that of the United States—are critical for understanding the production of both renewable natural resources and nonrenewable natural resources like petroleum.

By enabling domestic production, the Administration seeks to facilitate the evolution of the U.S. economy's role in global markets. Since the President took office, the U.S. fossil fuels sector has set production records. These were led by technological improvements, tax changes that lowered the cost of investing in mining structures, elevated global prices, and deregulatory actions that raised the expected returns of energy projects. Chapter 5 documents 65 deregulatory actions affecting the energy sector that were completed through the end of fiscal year 2018, with projected present value savings of over $5 billion.

In chapter 6, "Ensuring a Balanced Financial Regulatory Landscape," we revisit the causes and consequences of, and responses to, the financial crisis of 2008. In particular, we identify that the absence of actuarially fair pricing of implicit government guarantees of financial institutions and markets was a major factor exacerbating the crisis. Unfortunately, we also find that the salient legislative response to the crisis—the 2010 Dodd-Frank Act—not only failed to resolve this flaw but also excessively raised regulatory complexity, with the increased cost of compliance falling disproportionately on small and midsized financial institutions, which account for a disproportionate share of commercial and industrial lending to small and medium-sized enterprises.

In addition to articulating the Administration's approach to achieving the Seven Core Principles for financial regulation, established by Executive Order 13772, chapter 6 also demonstrates how the Economic Growth, Regulatory Relief, and Consumer Protection Act of 2018 released small and medium-sized banks from the more restrictive provisions of Dodd-Frank, while preserving heightened regulatory oversight of genuinely systemically important financial institutions.

Again reflecting the CEA's 1946 mandate to evaluate "current and foreseeable trends in the levels of employment, production, and purchasing power," chapter 7, "Adapting to Technological Change with Artificial Intelligence while Mitigating Cyber Threats," analyzes how technological change in information technology is likely to affect future U.S. labor markets. We begin by reviewing the latest developments in artificial intelligence (AI) and automation, concluding that a narrow, static focus on possible job losses leads to a misleading picture of the likely effects of AI on the Nation's economic well-being. Technological advances might eliminate specific jobs, but they do not generally eliminate work, and over time they will likely greatly increase real wages, national income, and prosperity.

For example, technological change enabled many agricultural economies to transition from having a majority of the economy being devoted to food production to a small percentage of the economy being able to better feed its population than before. Automation can complement labor, adding to its value, and even when it substitutes for labor in certain areas, it can lead to higher employment in other types of work and raise overall economic welfare. That appears likely to be the case as AI applications diffuse through the economy in the future, though important new challenges will arise concerning cybersecurity. Indeed, AI appears poised to automate or augment economic tasks that had long been assumed to be out of reach for automation.

Despite the economic resurgence of the past two years, there has been a rise in interest in vacating the free enterprise principles that have been instrumental to that recovery, and in turning instead to more socialized production methods that have generally been abandoned in countries that have tried them. Consistent with the 1946 mandate for this *Report*, we therefore turn, in chapter 8, "Markets versus Socialism," to reviewing the empirical evidence on the economic effects of varying degrees of socialization of productive assets and the income generated by those assets. Hayek (1945) argued that the essential role of a competitive market price mechanism is to communicate dispersed and often incomplete knowledge, whereby firms will expand and consumers contract activity when prices are high and vice versa when prices are low, with both sides of the market thereby being guided by prices to equate demand with supply. We find that experiences of socialism that do not use prices to guide production and consumption this way have generally been characterized by distorted incentives and failures of resource allocation—in some extreme instances, on a catastrophic scale.

In addition to quantifying the human and economic costs of highly socialist systems, we also estimate the effects of more moderate degrees of socialization. We find that even among market economies, average income and consumption are lower in those with relatively high levels of government taxes and transfers as shares of output—such as Denmark, Sweden, Norway, and Finland—than in the United States. This is because the relatively high average tax rates on middle incomes that finance this "Nordic model" also disincentivize generating income in the first place. Finally, we estimate that if the recent U.S. proposals for socialized medicine in terms of "Medicare for All" were implemented and financed by higher taxes, GDP would decline by 9 percent, or about $7,000 per person, in 2022.

In chapter 9, "Reducing Poverty and Improving Self-Sufficiency in America," we discuss the impact of the revival of the economy, more specifically on low-income households, and the Trump Administration's approach to escaping poverty through economic growth and work-based public policies. President Lyndon B. Johnson declared a War on Poverty in January 1964. When using a full-income measure of poverty that is capable of capturing success in the War on Poverty, we find that poverty declined from 19.5 percent in 1963 to 2.3 percent in 2017. This far exceeds the decline from 19.5 to 12.3 percent according to the Official Poverty Measure. However, victory was not achieved by making people self-sufficient, as President Johnson envisioned, but rather through increased government transfers. A new war on poverty should seek to further reduce material hardship based on modern standards, but should do so through incentives to achieve work and self-sufficiency. We discuss the Trump Administration's important actions along these lines: expanding work requirements for nondisabled, working-age welfare recipients in noncash welfare programs; increasing child care assistance for low-income families; and increasing the reward for working by doubling the Child Tax Credit and increasing its refundability.

Finally, in chapter 10, "The Year in Review and the Years Ahead," we analyze important macroeconomic developments in 2018 and present the Trump Administration's full, policy-inclusive economic forecast for the next 11 years, including risks to the forecast. Overall, assuming full implementation of the Trump Administration's economic policy agenda, we project real U.S. economic output to grow at an average annual rate of 3.0 percent between 2018 and 2029. We expect growth to moderate, from just over 3.0 percent in 2018 and 2019, as the capital-to-output ratio asymptotically approaches its new, postbusiness tax reform steady state and as the near-term effects of the TCJA's individual provisions on the rate of growth dissipate into a permanent level effect.

Partially offsetting this moderation are the expected contributions of the supply-side effects of the Trump Administration's current and future deregulatory actions, as discussed in chapter 2; the permanent extension of the personal income tax provisions of the TCJA, as discussed in chapter 1; and the Administration's infrastructure proposal, as analyzed in the 2018 *Economic Report of the President*. In chapter 10, we also explore potential downside risks to the forecast, including nonimplementation, or repeal, of the Trump Administration's economic policy agenda, slowing economic growth in major economies outside the United States, and the possible adverse economic effects of recent public proposals for "Medicare for All" and a top marginal income tax rate of 70 percent.

Collectively, the 10 chapters that constitute this *Report* demonstrate that the strong economic performance in 2017 and 2018 constituted a sharp break from the previous pace of economic and employment growth since the start of the present expansion, reflecting the Administration's reprioritization of economic efficiency and growth over alternative policy aspirations that subordinated growth. We further demonstrate that a unified agenda of tax, regulatory, labor, healthcare, financial, and energy market reforms that enhance the role of market prices is a more efficient and effective approach to unleashing the growth potential of the U.S. economy. The CEA's mandate under the Employment Act of 1946 is to advise on how best to achieve "maximum employment, production, and purchasing power." To this end, this *Report* provides evidence supporting the CEA's endorsement of free, competitive enterprise relying on market prices to guide economic activity over alternatives demanding increased socialization of productive assets and a consequently diminished role for market prices.

Contents

Appendixes

Figures

Tables

Boxes

Chapter 1

Evaluating the Effects of the Tax Cuts and Jobs Act

The 2018 *Economic Report of the President*, citing an extensive literature of over 80 peer-reviewed studies, provided evidence that before the Tax Cuts and Jobs Act (TCJA), the U.S. economy and U.S. workers had been adversely affected by the conjunction of rising international capital mobility and increasingly uncompetitive U.S. business taxation relative to the rest of the world. The *Report* concluded that the results of the convergence of these two trends were deterred capital formation in the United States, an absence of capital deepening, and consequently stagnant wage growth. Considering the weight of evidence in support of these observations, the *Report* projected that the business and international provisions of the TCJA would raise the target U.S. capital stock, reorient U.S. capital away from direct investment abroad in low-tax jurisdictions and toward domestic investment, and raise worker compensation and household income through both a short-run bargaining channel and long-run capital deepening channel. Finally, the *Report* noted that reductions in effective marginal personal income tax rates could be expected to induce positive labor supply responses.

In this chapter, we evaluate each of these anticipated effects of the TCJA on the basis of currently available data, and with particular attention to the relevant time horizons of each margin of adjustment to the positive tax shock. We find that firms responded immediately to the TCJA by upwardly revising planned capital expenditures, employee compensation, and hiring. We further find that real private investment in fixed assets rose at an annual rate of about 8 percent from the fourth quarter of 2017 through the third quarter of 2018, to $150 billion (about 6 percent) above the level reconstructed from the projected trend of the preceding expansion, during which fixed investments grew at an annual rate of about 5 percent. In addition to reporting a tally of over 6 million workers receiving an average bonus of nearly $1,200, we also estimate that, as of the third quarter of 2018, real disposable personal income per household was up $640 over the trend. Expressed as a perpetual annuity, this corresponds to a lifetime pay raise of about $21,000 for the average household—a $2.5 trillion boost to total real disposable personal income across all households.

Finally, we report that the flow of U.S. direct investment abroad declined by $148 billion, while U.S. direct investment in eight identified tax havens declined by $200 billion, as U.S. multinational enterprises redirected capital investment toward the domestic economy. Applying insights from a large body of corporate finance literature, we then discuss channels—particularly shareholder distributions—through which we expect repatriations of past corporate earnings previously held abroad in low-tax jurisdictions to be efficiently reallocated by capital markets from cash-abundant to cash-constrained firms.

On December 22, 2017, President Trump signed into law the Tax Cuts and Jobs Act (TCJA). With an estimated $5.5 trillion in gross tax cuts accompanied by $4 trillion in new revenue over 10 years, and with fundamental changes to itemization and a movement toward a territorial system of corporate income taxation, the TCJA arguably constituted the most significant combination of tax cuts and comprehensive tax reform in U.S. history. The TCJA was motivated by four principal objectives: tax relief for middle-income families, simplification of the personal income tax code, economic growth through business tax relief and increased domestic investment, and repatriation of overseas earnings.

First, accordingly, in the personal income tax code, the standard deduction was approximately doubled by the TCJA, thereby exempting a greater share of middle-class incomes from Federal income tax liability altogether, and simplifying tax filing for millions of American taxpayers who would previously have had to itemize deductions. The law also lowered marginal personal income tax rates across nearly all brackets, and raised and expanded eligibility for the Child Tax Credit. Second, the law eliminated certain deductions that disproportionately benefited higher-income households, while capping others—such as the Mortgage Interest Deduction and State and Local Tax Deduction—that similarly skewed toward the highest-income tax filers.

Third, to address the previous relative international uncompetitiveness of U.S. business taxation, the TCJA lowered the top marginal Federal statutory corporate tax rate from 35 percent—the highest in the developed world—to 21 percent. In addition, the TCJA introduced a 20 percent deduction for most owners of pass-through entities and generally allowed for immediate full expensing of new equipment investment. Fourth, to encourage repatriation of past overseas earnings of U.S. multinational enterprises previously held abroad in low-tax jurisdictions, and to prevent future corporate profit shifting through the mispricing of intellectual property products and services, the TCJA applied a low 8 or 15.5 percent tax on previously untaxed deferred foreign income and introduced a trio of new mechanisms to deter artificial corporate profit shifting.

In the 2018 *Economic Report of the President*, the Council of Economic Advisers estimated that these provisions of the TCJA would:

1. Raise real capital investment by lowering the user cost of capital and thus raising the target steady-state flow of capital services.
2. Raise the growth rate of U.S. output—in the short run, through both supply- and demand-side channels; and in the long run, through a supply-side channel.
3. Raise worker compensation and household income, both through a short-run profit-sharing channel and a long-run capital deepening channel, raising the steady-state level of capital per worker.
4. Incentivize higher labor force participation.
5. Reorient U.S. capital investment away from direct investment abroad and toward domestic investment.
6. Induce large-scale repatriation of past overseas earnings of U.S. multinational enterprises previously held in low-tax jurisdictions.

In this chapter, we evaluate these estimates and projections utilizing data available since the TCJA became law, and with particular attention to the relevant time horizons of different margins of adjustment to a positive tax shock. Consistent with projections reported in the 2018 *Economic Report of the President*, we find that output and investment accelerated in response to the reduction in the user cost of capital, and more importantly rose substantially above the trend. Real gross domestic product (GDP) growth rose 1.0 percentage point above the recent trend, while capital expenditures by nonfinancial businesses were up 12.1 percent over the trend.

We also find that real disposable personal income rose above the trend, especially as forward-looking firms raised near-term compensation to retain similarly forward-looking workers in a tightening labor market. As of 2018:Q3, we estimate that real disposable personal income per household was up about $640 over the trend, while real median usual earnings of full-time wage and salary workers were up $805 on an annualized basis. We furthermore report survey data indicating that these margins of adjustment were immediately anticipated by marked shifts in business expectations in response to the TCJA.

In addition, we report that in the first three quarters of 2018 alone, $570 billion in overseas corporate dividends, including earnings previously reinvested abroad, were repatriated to the United States, out of an upper-bound estimated total stock of as much as $4.3 trillion, and that U.S. direct investment abroad declined by $148 billion as U.S. multinational enterprises redirected capital investment toward the domestic economy. We then discuss how repatriation affects the distribution of corporate earnings to shareholders, and how efficient capital markets utilize shareholder distributions to reallocate capital from established, cash-abundant firms without profitable investment opportunities to more dynamic, cash-constrained firms with profitable investment opportunities. Finally, we also report the results of several simple simulations estimating the implied effects on long-run Federal government tax revenues of the higher economic growth that has thus far been observed since the TCJA's enactment.

In summary, we find that the U.S. economy is responding auspiciously to the positive tax shock of the TCJA along multiple margins, and in patterns that are both broadly and specifically consistent with projections reported in the 2018 *Economic Report of the President*. Looking ahead, we suggest that making permanent the TCJA provisions that are currently scheduled to expire would improve the long-run potential growth of the U.S. economy.

Output and Investment

Changes in corporate income tax rates and depreciation allowances can induce large investment effects through their effect on the user cost of capital—as demonstrated by Cummins and Hassett (1992); Auerbach and Hassett (1992); Cummins, Hassett, and Hubbard (1994, 1996); Caballero, Engel, and Haltiwanger (1995); Djankov and others (2010); and Dwenger (2014). Essentially, the user cost of capital is the rental price of capital, corresponding to the minimum return on investment required to cover taxes, depreciation, and the opportunity costs of investing in physical capital accumulation versus financial alternatives. By increasing (or decreasing) the after-tax rate of return on capital assets, a decrease (increase) in the tax rate on corporate profits decreases (increases) the before-tax rate of return required for the marginal product of new physical assets to exceed the cost of producing and using these assets, thereby raising (lowering) firms' demand for capital services.

As documented in the 2018 *Economic Report of the President*, early empirical estimates of the user-cost elasticity of investment (e.g., Eisner and Nadiri 1968) were much smaller than the neoclassical benchmark of unit elasticity (Jorgenson 1963; Hall and Jorgenson 1967), and were often outperformed by simple accelerator models of investment. However, subsequent studies (e.g.,

Goolsbee 1998, 2000, 2004; and Cummins, Hassett, and Oliner 2006) demonstrated that estimates likely suffered from considerable omitted variable bias owing to (1) unobserved firm heterogeneity; (2) mismeasurement of investment fundamentals, resulting in attenuation bias; and (3) the correlation of statutory changes in corporate income tax rates, depreciation allowances, and tax credits with cyclical factors.

Studies that successfully achieve identification—particularly by exploiting plausibly exogenous variation in the user cost of capital in the cross section of asset types (e.g., Cummins and Hassett 1992; Auerbach and Hassett 1992; Cummins, Hassett, and Hubbard 1994, 1996; and Zwick and Mahon 2017), or by utilizing micro-level panel data (e.g., Caballero, Engel, and Haltiwanger 1995; Dwenger 2014; and Zwick and Mahon 2017)—accordingly estimate much higher user-cost elasticities of investment. Indeed, Dwenger (2014) is unable to reject the null hypothesis that the user-cost elasticity is not statistically different from the neoclassical benchmark of –1.0. This implies that a tax change that lowers the user cost of capital by 10 percent would raise demand for capital services by up to 10 percent.

Following Devereux, Griffith, and Klemm (2002) and Bilicka and Devereux (2012), and assuming a consensus estimated user-cost elasticity of investment of –1.0, in the 2018 *Economic Report of the President*, the CEA calculated that the corporate income tax provisions in the TCJA would, on average, lower the user cost of capital, and thus raise demand for services, by approximately 9 percent. Using the Multifactor Productivity Tables from the Bureau of Labor Statistics in a growth accounting framework to increment the Congressional Budget Office's June 2017 10-year GDP growth projections by the additional contribution to output from a larger target capital stock, and assuming constant capital income shares, the CEA then calculated that the steady-state U.S. economic output would be between about 2 and 4 percent higher in the long run.

More formally, DeLong and Summers (1992) derive the adjustment dynamics by beginning with this identity:

$$\Delta Y_t = (r + \delta)\Delta K_t$$

where Y is output, r is the social net rate of return, δ is the economic depreciation rate, and K is the capital stock. The gross increase in Y produced by an increase in K is the gross rate of return on capital multiplied by the increase in K. The capital stock of an economy initially in the steady state that receives a permanent boost, I, to its gross investment therefore evolves according to:

$$\Delta K_t = I - \delta K_{t-1}$$

That is, the increase in the capital stock is equal to new gross investment minus depreciation of the preceding period's capital stock.

In the first period, the entire increase in investment translates into an increase in the capital stock: $\Delta K_t = I$, such that $\Delta Y_t = (r + \delta)I$. In the second period, investment will still be higher by I, but because $K_1 > K_0$, depreciation will also be higher. The increase in the capital stock will therefore be smaller: $\Delta K_2 = (I - \delta K_1)$ = $(I - \delta I) = (1 - \delta)I$, and $\Delta Y_2 = (r + \delta)(1 - \delta)I$. Successive increases in the capital stock will accordingly diminish, with the sum of changes gradually converging to a steady-state value ΔK^*:

$$\Delta K^* = I/\delta$$

And the cumulative change in output converges to a new steady-state level:

$$\Delta Y^* = I(r + \delta) / \delta$$

An increase in investment equal to 1 percentage point of output can therefore induce up to a $(r + \delta) / \delta$ percentage-point increase in the steady-state level of output, and up to a $(r + \delta) / \delta t$ increase in the growth rate of output over a period of t years.

In the absence of capital adjustment costs, the standard neoclassical model therefore predicts an immediate jump in investment in the first period, though with no effect on the rate of growth of investment thereafter. The level effect, however, is permanent, such that the capital-to-output ratio and the ratio of the flow of new investment to the outstanding capital stock gradually approach their new, steady-state levels, as illustrated with a hypothetical example in figure 1-1.

Economic research (e.g., Hartman 1972; Abel 1983; Caballero 1991; and Bar-Ilan and Strange 1996), suggests that the costs associated with adjusting capital stocks may result in short-run adjustment lags. Consequently, we would expect the first margin of adjustment to a positive tax shock to capital investment to be expectations, which, unlike capital and labor market contracts, are instantaneously flexible. Consistent with this anticipated effect, figure 1-2 reports the percentage of businesses in the National Federation of Independent Business's (NFIB's) monthly survey reporting plans to raise capital expenditures in the next 3 to 6 months, reported as a 3-month centered moving average to smooth out random noise.

Figure 1-2 shows two marked upward shifts in the percentage of firms reporting planned increases in capital investment—first, at the moment of Donald Trump's election to the U.S. Presidency; and second, at the moment of the TCJA's passage. These increases followed two years during which the percentage of firms reporting plans to raise capital expenditures was essentially flat. Reinforcing this pattern, figure 1-3 reports the percentage of NFIB respondents reporting that now is a good time to expand. Once again, the survey data reveal two marked spikes—first, after the election of President Trump; and second, after the TCJA's passage. After the TCJA's passage, the percentage of respondents reporting that now was a good time to expand broke the survey's previous 1984 record to set a new all-time high.

Meanwhile, in 2018:Q1, the Business Roundtable (2018) survey of CEOs reported record highs for their capital spending index and the percentage

Figure 1-1. Adjustment Dynamics to a New Steady-State Capital Output Ratio

I_t / K_{t-1}

Percentage of the capital stock per year

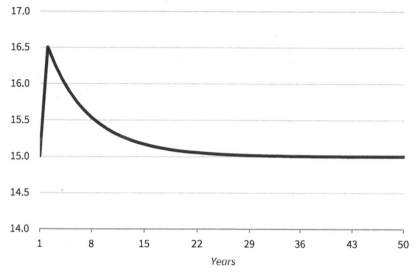

Years

K / Y

Years of I to build K

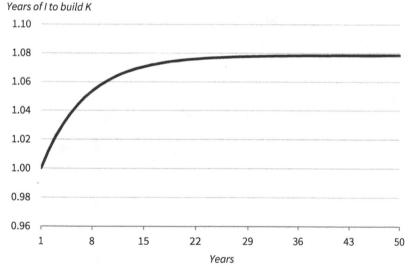

Years

Source: CEA calculations.
Note: Adjustment to a new steady state after a 10 percent decline in the user cost of capital, assuming $r = 0.05$, $\delta = 0.15$, and an initial capital-output ratio of 1.0.

Figure 1-2. Percentage of NFIB Survey Respondents Planning Capital Expenditures in the Next 3 to 6 Months, 2016–18

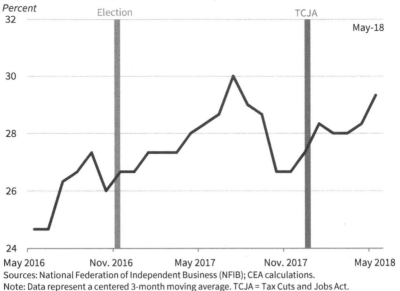

Sources: National Federation of Independent Business (NFIB); CEA calculations.
Note: Data represent a centered 3-month moving average. TCJA = Tax Cuts and Jobs Act.

Figure 1-3. Percentage of NFIB Survey Respondents Reporting That Now Is a Good Time to Expand, 2016–18

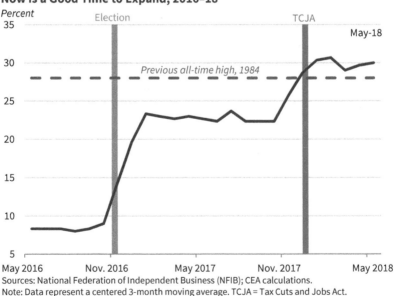

Sources: National Federation of Independent Business (NFIB); CEA calculations.
Note: Data represent a centered 3-month moving average. TCJA = Tax Cuts and Jobs Act.

reporting rising capital spending in the next 6 months. Through 2018:Q3, both series remained higher than at any point since 2011:Q2. Also in 2018:Q1, the percentage of respondents to a National Association of Business Economists (2018) survey reporting rising capital expenditures on information and communication technology hit a record high, and has remained well above the previous average since the question entered the survey.

Broader survey results reflect the same pattern. Figure 1-4 reports the centered 3-month moving average of Morgan Stanley's Planned Capital Expenditures (Capex Plans) Index, which tracks what business firms will probably spend in coming months. Again, after two years of decline, we observe two marked spikes after the election of President Trump and the TCJA's passage. Indeed, at the start of 2018, the index set its all-time high. Over time, as actual investment begins to reflect investment plans, we would expect these indices, as well as other survey responses, to edge back, as more respondents report plans to leave investment unchanged once the new, higher level of investment is attained.

An additional, short-run margin of adjustment—succeeding the adjustment of expectations but preceding the adjustment of actual physical capital stocks—is new capital goods orders, as reported by purchasing managers. Figure 1-5 reports core capital goods orders, in billions of dollars, from January 2012 through November 2018. Once again, after two years of declines, we observe two sharp spikes in capital goods orders within months of investment-relevant events—first, after President Trump's election; and second, after the TCJA's passage.

Despite expected adjustment costs and investment lags in the transition to a higher-target capital stock, the first three quarters after the TCJA's passage saw a notable acceleration in investment. Figure 1-6 reports growth in real private nonresidential fixed investment from the time of the TCJA's passage until the third quarter of 2018, both for nonresidential investment overall and for the major subcomponents of structures, equipment, and intellectual property products, expressed as compound annual growth rates to smooth substantial quarterly volatility, with investment being the most volatile component of GDP.

On a downward trend since 2014, we again observe a marked reversal, with private nonresidential fixed investment overall, as well as investment in each subcomponent of investment, up over preelection and pre-TCJA trends. Indeed, if we regress the compound annual growth rate of private nonresidential fixed investment on a linear time trend over the sample period 2009:Q3–2017:Q4 (2017:Q3 for equipment), and we project this trend into 2018 and reconstruct levels from forecasted growth rates, we find that as of 2018:Q3, overall private nonresidential fixed investment was up $150 billion (5.8 percent) over the trend. Among nonfinancial businesses, overall capital expenditures were up 12.1 percent over the trend.

Figure 1-4. Morgan Stanley's Capex Plans Index, 2016–18

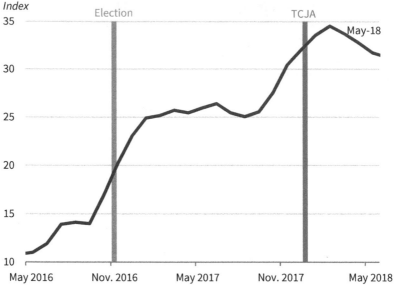

Sources: Bloomberg; CEA calculations.
Note: Morgan Stanley's Planned Capital Expenditures (Capex Plans) Index tracks what firms plan to spend in coming months. TCJA = Tax Cuts and Jobs Act. Data represent a centered 3-month moving average.

Figure 1-5. Core Capital Goods Orders, 2012–18

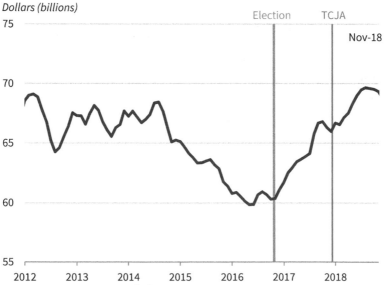

Sources: Census Bureau; CEA calculations.
Note: Core goods include nondefense capital goods, excluding aircraft. Data represent a centered 3-month moving average, truncating in November 2018. TCJA = Tax Cuts and Jobs Act.

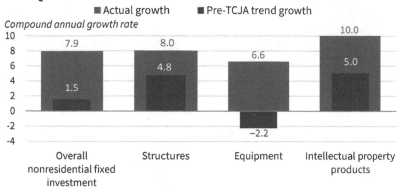

Figure 1-6. Growth in Real Nonresidential Fixed Investment, 2017:Q4–2018:Q3

■ Actual growth   ■ Pre-TCJA trend growth

Compound annual growth rate

Sources: Bureau of Economic Analysis; CEA calculations.
Note: The structures and intellectual property products pre-TCJA trends are calculated on the sample 2009:Q3–2017:Q4. The equipment pre-TCJA trend is calculated on the sample 2009:Q3–2017:Q3, because full expensing was retroactive to September 2017. The data for structures and intellectual property products represent a 3-quarter compound annual growth rate. Equipment data represent a 4-quarter compound annual growth rate. The overall rates for the nonresidential fixed investment trend and actual compound annual growth are calculated based on a weighted average of the structures, equipment, and intellectual property product components.

Equipment investment, in particular, exhibited a pronounced spike in the fourth quarter of 2017, as both the House and Senate versions of the TCJA bill, which were respectively introduced on November 2 and November 9, stipulated that full expensing for new equipment investment would be retroactive to September 2017. This created a strong financial incentive for companies to shift their equipment investment to the fourth quarter of 2017, so as to deduct new equipment investment at the old 35 percent statutory corporate income tax rate. After the initial spike in the rate of growth in fixed investment, standard neoclassical growth models would predict a return of the *rate* of growth to its pre-TCJA trend, but from a higher, post-TCJA *level*, with the capital-to-output ratio thereby asymptotically approaching its new, higher steady-state level.

More revealingly, considering higher-resolution data at the detailed asset level, we observe that asset types exhibiting larger residuals from an $AR(n)$ step-ahead forecast of the user cost of capital also experienced larger forecast errors for real investment in 2018. Following Cummins, Hassett, and Hubbard (1994), figure 1-7 reports autoregressive forecast errors for each disaggregated equipment investment series against forecast errors for the detailed asset-level user cost of capital, assuming equity financing. As can be observed in the figure, there is a negative correlation between forecast errors for the user cost of capital and investment, consistent with larger declines in the user cost of capital inducing larger increases in demand for capital services.

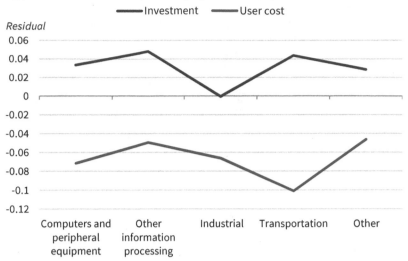

Figure 1-7. Forecast Errors for Equipment Investment and Price

Investment — User cost

Residual

```
 0.06
 0.04
 0.02
    0
-0.02
-0.04
-0.06
-0.08
 -0.1
-0.12
```

Computers and peripheral equipment | Other information processing | Industrial | Transportation | Other

Sources: Bureau of Economic Analysis; CEA calculations.
Note: Residuals from autoregressive forecasts of growth rates of each disaggregated equipment investment series are plotted against residuals from autoregressive forecasts of the percent change in the simplified user cost of capital by asset type.

Finally, though the projected increase in steady-state output is predominantly a long-run effect deriving from a higher flow of capital services as the economy transitions to a higher steady-state target capital stock, already in 2018 we observe the effects on growth of higher investment demand after corporate tax reform and robust consumer spending followed the enactment of the TCJA's individual provisions. During the 34 quarters between the start of the current expansion in 2009:Q3 and the TCJA's enactment in 2017:Q4, the average contribution of real private nonresidential fixed investment to GDP growth was 0.6 percentage point. But in the first three quarters after the TCJA's passage, the contribution of real private nonresidential fixed investment to GDP growth rose to 1.0 percentage point. As a share of GDP, private nonresidential fixed investment in the first three quarters of 2018 attained its second-highest level since 2001.

As documented in the 2018 *Economic Report of the President*, the principal challenge for estimating the effect of changes in corporate and personal income tax rates on economic growth is that the timing of tax changes tends to correlate with cyclical factors. Specifically, legislators tend to lower tax rates during periods of economic contraction and raise rates during periods of economic expansion, which can negatively bias estimates of the effects of changes in marginal tax rates on investment and output.

Two recent empirical approaches to addressing this threat to identification are structural vector autoregression (SVAR) and the use of narrative history to identify exogenous tax shocks; both approaches were reviewed in the 2018 *Report*, and estimates from this literature were applied to the TCJA. The SVAR approach, which was pioneered by Blanchard and Perotti (2002), identifies tax shocks by utilizing information about fiscal institutions to distinguish between discretionary and automatic or cyclical tax changes. Meanwhile, the narrative approach, which was initiated by Romer and Romer (2010), relies on a textual analysis of tax debates to identify exogenous tax changes with political or philosophical, rather than economic, motivations. More recently, Mertens and Ravn (2013) have developed a hybrid of both approaches that utilizes Romer and Romer's narrative tax shock series as an external instrument to identify structural tax shocks.

Using the estimated revenue effects of the TCJA from the Joint Committee on Taxation (JCT 2017), Mertens (2018) applies estimated coefficients from the SVAR and narrative approaches to a tax cut of the TCJA's magnitude. He calculates that effects based on aggregate tax multiplier estimates—by Blanchard and Perotti (2002), Romer and Romer (2010), Favero and Giavazzi (2012), Mertens and Ravn (2012), Mertens and Ravn (2014), and Caldara and Kamps (2017)—imply a cumulative effect on GDP between 2018 and 2020 of 1.3 percent. Applying estimated impacts based on responses to individual marginal tax rates from Barro and Redlick (2011) and Mertens and Montiel Olea (2018), he calculates a cumulative effect by 2020 of 2.1 percent. Finally, applying estimated effects of disaggregated individual and corporate tax multipliers from Mertens and Ravn (2013), he calculates the cumulative effect on GDP between 2018 and 2020 of individual tax reform to be 0.5 percent, and the cumulative effect of business tax reform to be 1.9 percent.

As shown in figure 1-8, actual GDP growth in 2018 was consistent with these estimated effects. Between 2012:Q4 and 2016:Q4, the compound annual growth rate of real GDP averaged just 2.3 percent, slowing to 2.0 and 1.9 percent in 2015 and 2016, respectively. After increasing to 2.5 percent in 2017, GDP was on pace in the first three quarters of 2018 to grow by 3.2 percent over the four quarters of the calendar year, for the first time since 2004. Moreover, this growth represented a sharp divergence from the trend. Regressing the compound annual growth rate of GDP on a time trend over a pre-TCJA expansion sample period 2009:Q3–2017:Q4, projecting this trend into 2018, and reconstructing levels from forecasted growth rates, we find that as of 2018:Q3, GDP growth in 2018 was up 1.0 percentage point over the trend. Although it is difficult to empirically disentangle the TCJA's effects on growth from the effects of the Trump Administration's other economic policy initiatives to date, particularly deregulatory actions, the estimates reported in chapter 2, "Deregulation That Frees the Economy," of the 2018 *Economic Report of the President* suggest that these actions likely contributed less than 0.1 percentage point to growth in 2018.

We also estimate the TCJA's effect on 2018 growth by calculating the divergence of observed growth from a 2017:Q3 baseline forecast, as discussed in chapter 10 of this *Report* and chapter 8, "The Year in Review and the Years Ahead," of the 2018 *Economic Report of the President*. To construct this baseline, we treat the TCJA as an unanticipated shock arriving in the fourth quarter of 2017. Adapting the approach of Fernald and others (2017), we then decompose pre-2017:Q4 growth rates into trend, cyclical, and higher-frequency components—using Okun's law and a partial linear regression model with a frequency filter—to estimate the long-run growth rate. We then estimate an unrestricted vector autogressive model (VAR) on detrended growth rates through 2017:Q3 of real GDP, the unemployment gap, the labor force participation rate, real personal consumption expenditures, and the yield spread of 10-year over 3-month Treasuries. We determine optimal lag length by satisfaction of the Akaike and Hannan-Quinn information criteria. Postestimation and VAR forecasting, we then add the estimated long-run trend. Relative to this baseline forecast, observed output growth was up 1.4 percentage points at a compound annual rate as of 2018:Q3. Figure 1-9 compares these two estimated effects of the TCJA to the SVAR and narrative estimates reported by Mertens (2018).

Another approach to evaluate the TCJA's effect on growth is to compare the Congressional Budget Office's (CBO) final, pre-TCJA 10-year economic projection with the post-TCJA actuals. In June 2017, the CBO forecasted real GDP growth of 2.0 percent in 2018, with real private nonresidential fixed investment growing by just 3.0 percent. If GDP growth during the four quarters of 2018 was instead 3.2 percent, as the U.S. economy was on pace to achieve through 2018:Q3, and if it were to then immediately revert to the CBO's June 2017 forecast, in 2027 economic output would be 1.2 percent higher than projected. If GDP were to simply grow by 3.2 percent in 2018, by the CBO's upwardly revised August 2018 forecast of 2.8 percent in 2019, and if it were to then revert to the pre-TCJA projection, in 2027 economic output would be 2.5 percent higher than projected, in line with the CEA's initial estimates.

Data available through 2018:Q3 therefore suggest that estimates from the Tax Policy Center (0.0), Penn-Wharton Budget Model (0.6–1.1 percent), JCT (0.7 percent on average over 10 years, implying a 10-year level effect of 1.2 percent), and Tax Foundation (1.7 percent) may constitute lower bounds. The preliminary evidence is, however, consistent with a more recent analysis by Lieberknecht and Wieland (2018), who employ a two-country dynamic stochastic general equilibrium model to estimate a long-run GDP effect of 2.6 percent.

An important implication of higher-than-projected growth is Federal government revenue. The JCT estimated the TCJA's conventional revenue cost at $1.5 trillion over 10 years, and a dynamic estimate of $1.1 trillion, after accounting for higher revenue due to economic growth, net of increased interest payments. If the TCJA's effect on economic growth exceeds the JCT's estimate, the actual long-run revenue cost may be lower.

Figure 1-8. Growth in Real GDP, 2012:Q4–2018:Q3

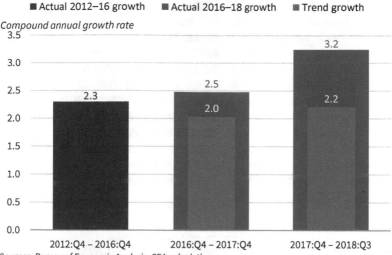

Sources: Bureau of Economic Analysis; CEA calculations.
Note: Data represent a compound annual growth rate over the given quarters. The 2016:Q4–
2017:Q4 preelection trend projection is calculated for 2009:Q3–2016:Q4. The 2017:Q4–2018:Q3
pre-TCJA trend projection is calculated for 2009:Q3–2017:Q4.

The cumulative effect of higher near-term growth on revenue can be illustrated by calculating the difference between the CBO's final, pre-TCJA (June 2017) 10-year projections of growth and revenue, advancing from 2017:Q4 actuals, and the CBO's final, pre-TCJA 10-year economic projections updated with 2018 actual GDP data and April 2018 CBO revenue projections. Fiscal year revenue-to-GDP projections are converted to calendar years by assigning 25 percent of the subsequent fiscal year to the current calendar year. First, we assume that actual nominal GDP growth in the four quarters of 2018 achieved its 2018:Q1–2018:Q3 annualized pace of 5.6 percent. Second, we assume that actual nominal GDP growth in 2019 achieves the Administration's current projection of 5.3 percent. Third, we assume that, thereafter, growth reverts to the pre-TCJA trajectory projected by the CBO. Fourth, we assume that the ratio of revenue to GDP was as projected by the CBO in April 2018. In this simulation, Federal tax revenue would be about $500 billion higher over the 10 years through 2027. This macroeconomic feedback alone would thereby offset more than one-third of the conventional cost of the law.

Because increased growth in calendar year 2018 was likely augmented by other legislative and Administration policies, as well as nonpolicy economic factors, we also estimate the likely macroeconomic feedback of higher growth by applying the estimated coefficients from Romer and Romer (2010) and Mertens (2018) to GDP growth in 2018, 2019, and 2020, and assuming April 2018 revenue-to-GDP projections. This approach yields an estimated cumulative revenue effect of between $140 and $190 billion over 3 years, or between $480

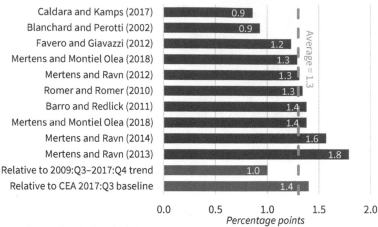

Figure 1-9. Structural VAR and Narrative Estimates versus Actual

Caldara and Kamps (2017)   0.9
Blanchard and Perotti (2002)   0.9
Favero and Giavazzi (2012)   1.2
Mertens and Montiel Olea (2018)   1.3
Mertens and Ravn (2012)   1.3
Romer and Romer (2010)   1.3
Barro and Redlick (2011)   1.4
Mertens and Montiel Olea (2018)   1.4
Mertens and Ravn (2014)   1.6
Mertens and Ravn (2013)   1.8
Relative to 2009:Q3–2017:Q4 trend   1.0
Relative to CEA 2017:Q3 baseline   1.4

Average = 1.3

0.0   0.5   1.0   1.5   2.0
Percentage points

Sources: Mertens (2018); CEA calculations.
Note: VAR = vector autoregression. The 2009:Q3–2017:Q4 trend is estimated on compound annual growth rates and levels reconstructed from projected rates. The CEA's 2017:Q3 baseline is estimated using a VAR and statistical frequency filter, as described in chapter 10 of this *Report*. Mertens (2018) compiles references to 10 estimates from other papers (these other estimates are shown in this figure). Mertens and Olea (2018) provide two estimates from the same paper.

and $640 billion over 10 years if the level effect persists. Excluding Mertens's (2018) international estimations, which treat deemed repatriation—an effective reduction in the implicit tax liability of U.S. multinational enterprises—as a tax increase, the approach suggests a cumulative revenue feedback over 10 years of $810 billion. Because these empirically estimated growth effects only extend for three years, whereas the increased flow of capital services as the economy transitions to a higher steady-state capital-to-labor ratio is a long-run effect, the corresponding revenue effects may constitute a lower bound (box 1-1).

Because the TCJA was passed by Congress under the budget reconciliation process, the bill's conventional revenue cost, as estimated by its official scorer, the JCT, could not exceed $1.5 trillion over 10 years. As a result, several provisions of the TCJA are scheduled to expire by the end of fiscal year 2027. Specifically, many of the provisions affecting the personal income tax code are due to expire on December 31, 2025, whereas among corporate income tax provisions, bonus depreciation, particularly for equipment investment, is set to begin phasing out on January 1, 2023, and to fully phase out on December 31, 2026.

Using a neoclassical growth model, Barro and Furman (2018) estimate that making the TCJA's temporary business provisions permanent would raise long-run GDP by 2.2 percentage points above their baseline, law-as-written estimate, and by 0.8 percentage point over 10 years. Using a more

Box 1-1. The Mortgage Interest Deduction and the Tax Cuts and Jobs Act

Before the passage of the Tax Cuts and Jobs Act, discussions of potential changes in the mortgage interest deduction (MID) raised concern about possible future effects on home value and homeownership (NAR 2017). The National Association of Realtors commissioned a study that forecasted a 10.2 percent decline in home prices in the short run resulting from proposals in the TCJA that included, at the time, changes to the MID (PwC 2017). The TCJA did not eliminate the MID, but it did reduce the maximum mortgage eligibility by $250,000 (CEA 2018). In addition, the TCJA included a doubling of the standard deduction, which was projected to reduce taxable units claiming the MID and increase tax units utilizing the standard deduction (CEA 2017b).

The MID is a regressive subsidy with greater benefit for those with mortgages on more expensive homes, in part because individuals with higher incomes are more likely to itemize their deductions rather than opt for the standard deduction. The incentive provided by the MID for more expensive homes has ramifications for the housing market. Earlier CEA analyses and reviews of the literature note that the MID is not associated with higher home ownership rates, even though that was a central goal for maintaining the policy (CEA 2017b). Furthermore, given the incentive for larger and/or more expensive home purchases, the MID inflates housing prices.

The impact of the MID on housing prices is found to vary across different housing markets, depending on the elasticity of housing supply. A market with a more inelastic supply would face greater downward pressure on housing prices than a market with elastic supply as a result of an elimination of the MID. Furthermore, earlier CEA analyses comparing home ownership rates in the United States with those in Canada and other countries belonging to the Organization for Economic Cooperation and Development found the MID to be "neither necessary nor sufficient" for relatively higher home ownership rates (CEA 2017b, 7).

The final TCJA legislation, which was signed into law in December 2017, did not eliminate the MID—though, as noted above, both the change in the amount of mortgage debt for which interest can be deducted and the doubling of the standard deduction would result in fewer tax filers utilizing itemized deductions and the MID. Given this policy change, examining the reaction of both homeownership rates and housing prices across the country and across different markets can provide insight into the predicted effects detailed above. In the first 11 months of 2018, though housing prices contin-ued to increase, the pace of housing price growth ticked slightly down. In the first three quarters of 2018, homeownership rates slightly increased.

Housing prices, measured by a number of housing price indices, have increased nationally since 2012. In the first 11 months of 2018, real house price indices continued to increase, though the pace of annual growth slowed slightly. The 12-month percentage change among three of the four real house price indices displayed in figure 1-i decreased in 2018, though they have remained positive.

At the city level, the reaction of housing prices varied in the first three quarters of 2018. As noted above, how housing prices respond to a change in use of the MID is dependent on the elasticity of housing supply. In markets where housing supply is less responsive, such as San Francisco, housing prices would be expected to react more to changes in use of the MID versus a housing market with a less-regulated supply, such as Dallas. Though the real housing price indices in both San Francisco and Dallas continued to increase in the first three quarters of 2018, the annual change in Dallas's real housing price indices continued on the downward trend that was evident before the TCJA's passage. The pace of annual change in San Francisco, however, quickened in the first three quarters of 2018 after the TCJA's passage (figure 1-ii).

Contrary to a report commissioned by the National Association of Realtors in May 2017, which predicted that MID reforms similar to that ultimately enacted by the TCJA would cause a short-run decline in national home prices of 10.2 percent, housing prices have increased in some markets (PwC 2017).

Homeownership rates nationally had trended down for several years, though they saw a reversal in 2016, when rates began to move upward for the first time since 2004. After the TCJA's passage, homeownership continued to increase nationally through the first three quarters of 2018 (figure 1-iii). Faster

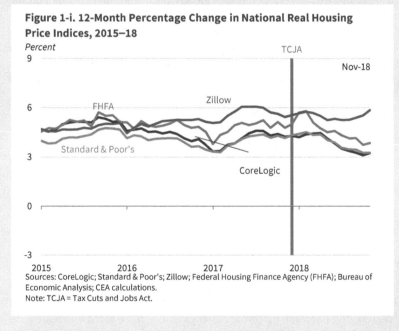

Figure 1-i. 12-Month Percentage Change in National Real Housing Price Indices, 2015–18

Sources: CoreLogic; Standard & Poor's; Zillow; Federal Housing Finance Agency (FHFA); Bureau of Economic Analysis; CEA calculations.
Note: TCJA = Tax Cuts and Jobs Act.

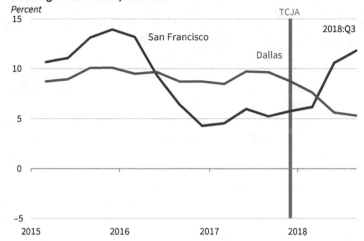

Figure 1-ii. Four-Quarter Percentage Change in Regional Real Housing Price Indices, 2015–18

Percent

San Francisco

Dallas

TCJA

2018:Q3

Sources: Federal Housing Finance Agency; Bureau of Economic Analysis; CEA calculations.
Note: TCJA = Tax Cuts and Jobs Act.

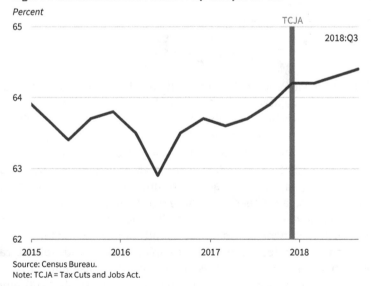

Figure 1-iii. National Home Ownership Rate, 2015–18

Percent

TCJA

2018:Q3

Source: Census Bureau.
Note: TCJA = Tax Cuts and Jobs Act.

economic growth resulting from the TCJA would be expected to shift the demand curve for housing outward.

U.S. fiscal policy continues to implicitly subsidize owner-occupied housing by excluding imputed rental income from income taxation and through direct and indirect financial support of government-sponsored mortgage enterprises, as discussed in chapter 6 of this *Report*. User cost calculations reported by Poterba and Sinai (2008) suggest that the implicit subsidy of untaxed imputed rent is 1.5 times that of the MID, with the magnitude of the differential impact increasing in household income. Feldman (2002) and Passmore, Sherlund, and Burgess (2005), meanwhile, find that government sponsorship of the Federal National Mortgage Association and Federal Home Loan Mortgage Corporation lower mortgage rates by 7 to 50 basis points.

richly specified, two-country dynamic stochastic general equilibrium model, Lieberknecht and Wieland (2018) find that making the temporary provisions permanent would raise the long-run growth effect from 2.6 to 5.7 percent.

We can also estimate the effect on output of making permanent the TCJA's provisions currently set to expire in 2025 by calculating the static budget impact in 2026 and 2027 and applying the estimated impact multipliers reported by Mertens (2018). Specifically, calculating the change from 2025 in the JCT's (2017) static revenue estimate for 2026 and 2027, dividing by the Administration's projection for GDP in 2026 and 2027, reversing the sign, and applying the estimated tax multipliers indicate a cumulative impact of up to 0.4 percentage point by the end of 2027.

Labor Market Effects

In the 2018 *Economic Report of the President*, the CEA demonstrated that due to the high mobility of capital relative to labor, the incidence of corporate income taxation is increasingly borne by labor, though there is an important distinction between short- and long-run economic incidence. In the short run, increases (or decreases) in corporate income taxation are largely borne by current owners of corporate capital, through a decline (rise) in asset values, and by investors, through lower (higher) after-tax rates of return. However, the CEA estimated that in the long run, labor bears a majority of the burden of corporate income taxation, as an increase (decrease) in the effective tax rate on capital income from marginal investment lowers (raises) steady-state demand for capital services. The consequent decline (rise) in the capital-to-labor ratio lowers (raises) labor productivity and thus depresses (lifts) labor compensation.

Consistent with this investment channel, Giroud and Rauh (2018), employing Romer and Romer's (2010) narrative approach to estimate the effects of State-level corporate income tax changes, find short-run statutory corporate tax elasticities of both employment and establishment counts of about –0.5, and elasticities of –1.2 over a 10-year horizon. Moreover, a broad survey of empirical studies of the incidence of corporate income taxation, reported in the 2018 *Economic Report of the President*, indicates that workers ultimately bear between 21 and 75 percent of the economic burden of corporate taxation, with more recent studies generally constituting the upper bound of this range, reflecting growing international capital mobility. The studies that were cited suggest a corporate income tax elasticity of wages of between –0.1 and –0.5, with estimated tax semielasticities from –0.4 to as large as –2.4.

Applying these estimated elasticities to the TCJA, the CEA calculated that a permanent 14-percentage-point reduction in the Federal statutory corporate tax rate would raise average annual household income by between $2,400 and $12,000 in the long run, with an average estimate of $5,500. Dropping the two lowest and two highest estimates suggests a tighter range, between $3,400 and $9,900.

Although these are long-run, estimated wage effects resulting primarily from a gradual transition to a new steady state with a higher capital-to-labor ratio, even in the short term, we would expect to observe forward-looking firms revising their labor market expectations. Models of rent sharing indicate that, in the short run, workers stand to benefit from increased profits accruing to their parent employer through a bargaining channel. This model does not make any predictions about changes in employment levels. Arulampalam, Devereux, and Maffini (2012) present a model of rent sharing in which changes in the corporate tax rate, expensing provisions, and overall marginal tax rates (from various and sundry other tax provisions) all serve to affect the wage. The model supposes a single union representing all wage earners. How the model's predictions would change under different bargaining arrangements is not clear, though in each case, the signs of the first derivative on corporate tax rates, longer depreciation schedules, and overall marginal tax rates are all negative, such that the TCJA is predicted to unambiguously increase workers' wages through the bargaining channel.

This theory accords with the empirical evidence, first noted by Krueger and Summers, that "more profitable industries tend to use some of their rents to hire better quality labor, and share some of their rents with their workers" (Krueger and Summers 1968, 17; also see 1988). More recent studies of intra-industry wage differentials confirm that rent sharing remains a feature of the U.S. labor market (Barth et al. 2016; Card et al. 2016; Song et al. 2019).

In the results of the research by Arulampalam, Devereux, and Maffini (2012), the wage is roughly equal to the weighted average of the outside wage option of the employer and some share of the firm's location-specific profit. Changes in expensing provisions affect the profits over which employers and employees bargain, even in the absence of changes in the target capital stock—as do other adjustments outside the corporate income tax rate that serve to affect the firm's tax liability. Arulampalam and her colleagues note that if cost reductions induced by the tax law are fully passed on to consumers in the output market, the profits over which to bargain are unchanged. Finally, Arulampalam and colleagues' result highlights the role of the corporate tax rate itself, τ, in the wage bargain. Higher values of τ raise the value of the firm's outside option (here, relocation to another tax jurisdiction) and lower bargained wages. Lowering τ reduces the value of the firm's outside option (in this case, another tax jurisdiction) and, thus, increases worker wages.

Each of these effects is "immediate," manifesting in higher worker wages as soon as the impact of changes in corporate taxes on firm profits is known with some certainty. Thus, the spate of bonus and increased wage announcements immediately after the TCJA's enactment, reported in box 1-2, is consistent with the rent-sharing model of worker wages. It is also consistent with survey data that were gathered immediately after the TCJA's passage. Figures 1-10 and 1-11 report the net percentage of NFIB survey respondents reporting plans to raise worker compensation and increase employment over the next three months, expressed as a three-month centered moving average to smooth random monthly volatility. As with planned capital expenditures, the survey results indicate two marked upward shifts in compensation and hiring plans—the first after the election of President Trump, and the second after the TCJA's passage. In August 2018, the net share of independent businesses reporting plans to increase employment in the next three months set a new all-time record, whereas in October 2018, the net share of independent business reporting plans to raise worker compensation in the next three months broke a 28-year record to set a new all-time high.

Reinforcing the private survey data, and consistent with the research of Giroud and Rauh (2018), data from the Bureau of Labor Statistics' Job Openings and Labor Turnover survey also show a sharp uptick in labor demand after the TCJA's passage. Figure 1-12 reports total private job openings from 2014 through 2018. After leveling off in 2016 at between about 5 and 5.5 million, private job openings surged after the TCJA's passage, topping 6.5 million by August 2018. In addition, during the entire pre-TCJA expansion, real nonproduction bonuses per hour grew at a compound annual rate of 5.4 percent. Since the TCJA came into effect, they have risen $150 per worker on an annual basis, or by 9.3 percent.

Available labor earnings data are also consistent with the CEA's projections. Relative to a time trend estimated over the entire pre-TCJA expansion sample period (2009:Q3–2017:Q4), as of 2018:Q3, real disposable income per household was up $640 over the trend. Expressed as a perpetual annuity, this corresponds to a lifetime pay raise of about $21,000 for the average household, assuming the real discount rate currently implied by Shiller's cyclically adjusted earnings-to-price ratio for the Standard & Poor's (S&P) 500 of 3.1 percent. Across all households, this constitutes a $2.5 trillion boost to household

Box 1-2. Corporate Bonuses, Wage Increases, and Investment since the TJCA's Passage

In a dynamic, competitive economy, like that of the United States, firms compete for workers. And a robust academic literature, pioneered by one of President Obama's CEA chairs, Alan Krueger, shows that more profitable employers pay higher wages. Why? Because a firm that attempts to pay a worker less than he or she is worth will quickly lose the worker to a competitor. In a tight labor market, wage bargaining models predict that firms will respond to a profits windfall by raising wages and bonuses to attract and retain talent.

The CEA has already tallied 645 companies that have offered bonuses, and/or increased retirement contributions, since the TCJA was enacted. The total number of workers receiving a bonus or increased retirement contribution now stands at over 6 million, with an average bonus size of $1,154 (figure 1-iv). Additional workers are seeing higher take home pay, given that nearly 200 companies have announced increases in wages, with 102 of these firms announcing minimum wage increases.

Walmart, the Nation's largest private employer, has announced an increase in the starting wage of its workers of $2 an hour for the first six months and $1 thereafter. For a full-time employee working 40 hours a week, this means up to $3,040 a year in additional pay. These pay increases are for those earning Walmart's minimum wage, so, as a share of income, the gains are substantial—at least 16 percent.

Many other employers have done the same as Walmart—including BB&T, the 11th-largest bank by assets in the United States, where full-time workers who are paid the bank's minimum wage will see a $6,000 increase in their annual income. Nearly 15 percent of firms announcing minimum wage hikes have provided increases of at least $4,000.

Hard-working Americans are also seeing savings in their electricity bills thanks to the TCJA. More than 130 companies have pledged to pass tax savings on to their customers in the form of reduced tax rates—a practice that will pass savings on to millions.

The President's promise to lower corporate taxes and reduce red tape has led American businesses to a surge in investment, and since the TCJA became law, the CEA has tallied over $220 billion in new corporate investment announcements attributable to it. Likewise, the March 2018 Morgan Stanley composite Planned Capital Expenditures (Capex Plans) Index marked a record high in a series that began 13 years ago. As discussed earlier in this chapter, the official investment statistics show that this investment boom is already taking hold. This is welcome news; according to the CEA's calculations, a return to the historical rate of capital deepening in the United States would give households a boost of $4,000 in annual wage and salary income by 2026.

The bottom line is that the TCJA's enactment in December 2017 gave a much-needed boost to American workers, who in recent years have endured

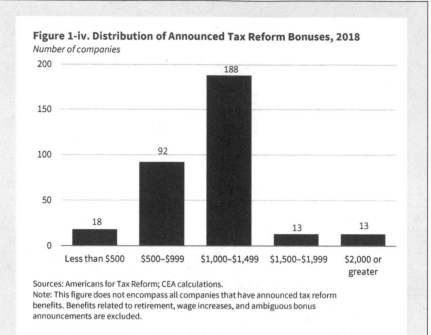

Figure 1-iv. Distribution of Announced Tax Reform Bonuses, 2018
Number of companies

Sources: Americans for Tax Reform; CEA calculations.
Note: This figure does not encompass all companies that have announced tax reform benefits. Benefits related to retirement, wage increases, and ambiguous bonus announcements are excluded.

chronic underinvestment due to a corporate tax code that discouraged domestic capital formation. With investment growth now accelerating in response to the corporate tax cuts, we should consider the recent spate of bonus and wage hike announcements as merely a down payment on a long-overdue raise for American households.

income. As discussed above, this effect is expected to grow over time through increased capital deepening, raising capital per worker, labor productivity, and wages. Though long-run capital deepening is expected to further raise real disposable personal income, this effect will be partially offset if the personal income tax cuts currently scheduled to expire after 2025 are not extended or made permanent through new legislation.

Figure 1-13 reports compound annual growth rates in real median weekly earnings of full-time wage and salary workers and real average weekly earnings of production and nonsupervisory employees in manufacturing since the TCJA's enactment, relative to the recent trend. On an annualized basis, real median usual earnings for full-time wage and salary workers were up $805 over the trend, while real average earnings for production and nonsupervisory employees in the manufacturing sector specifically were up $493 (box 1-2).

In the longer run, as articulated by the CEA (2017a) and in the 2018 *Economic Report of the President*, we expect wage gains to be driven primarily by increased investment raising the target capital stock, and thus the

Figure 1-10. Net Percentage of NFIB Survey Respondents Planning to Raise Worker Compensation in the Next 3 Months, 2016–18

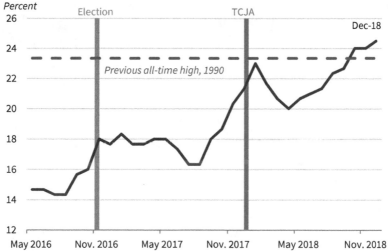

Sources: National Federation of Independent Business (NFIB); CEA calculations.
Note: Data represent a centered 3-month moving average, truncating in December 2018.
TCJA = Tax Cuts and Jobs Act.

Figure 1-11. Net Percentage of NFIB Survey Respondents Planning to Increase Employment, 2016–18

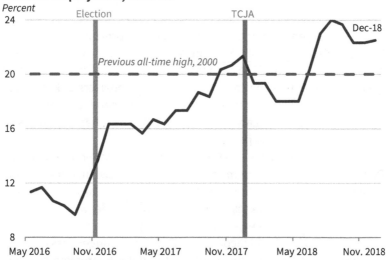

Sources: National Federation of Independent Business (NFIB); CEA calculations.
Note: Data represent a centered 3-month moving average, truncating in December 2018.
TCJA = Tax Cuts and Jobs Act.

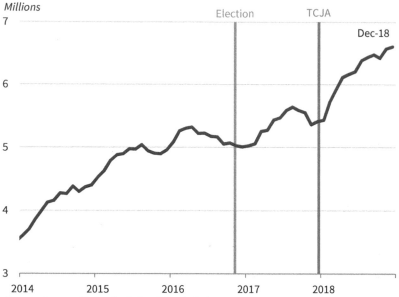

Figure 1-12. Total Private Job Openings, 2014–18

Millions

Sources: Bureau of Labor Statistics; CEA calculations.
Note: Data represent a centered 3-month moving average, truncating in December 2018.
TCJA = Tax Cuts and Jobs Act.

steady-state level of capital per worker and, consequently, labor productivity. Already in 2018, we observe evidence of this mechanism operating. During the pre-TCJA expansion in 2009:Q3–2017:Q4, growth in business sector labor productivity averaged 1.0 percent, compared with a pre-2008 postwar average of 2.5 percent. Growth in nonfarm business sector labor productivity averaged 1.1 percent during the pre-TCJA expansion, compared with a pre-2008 postwar average of 2.3 percent. In contrast, in the first three quarters of 2018, business sector labor productivity grew at an annual rate of 2.0 percent—double the rate of the pre-TCJA expansion. Labor productivity in the nonfarm business sector grew at an annual rate of 1.8 percent.

Finally, as noted in the 2018 *Economic Report of the President*, Keane and Rogerson (2012, 2015) demonstrate that because incremental human capital acquired through employment raises expected future earnings—the net present value of which varies inversely with age—older and relatively more experienced workers can be expected to have larger labor supply responses to changes in marginal personal income tax rates than younger, less experienced workers. Indeed, we observe this effect in the data. Regressing the employment-to-population of over-55-year-olds on a linear time trend fully interacted with a binary variable for post-TCJA over a sample period July 2009–December 2018, we estimate a positive coefficient on the interaction term, and we can reject the null hypothesis of no slope change with 95 percent confidence. In

Figure 1-13. Above-Trend Real Labor Compensation and Wage Growth, 2018

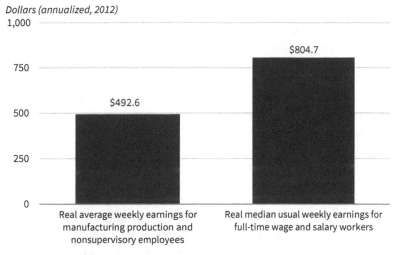

Dollars (annualized, 2012)

Sources: Bureau of Labor Statistics; Bureau of Economic Analysis; CEA calculations.
Note: The trend is calculated for 2009:Q3 (September 2009 for monthly data) through 2017:Q4 (December 2017 for monthly data). Annualized 2012 dollars assume a 52-work-week year.

contrast, we cannot reject the null hypothesis with a similar level of confidence for other age cohorts, which suggests that the TCJA may have had a specific, positive effect on labor force participation among near-retirement and retirement-age workers at the margin.

Although there is some evidence (e.g., Blau and Robins 1989; Whittington 1992; and Haan and Wrohlick 2011) that expansion of the Child Tax Credit may positively affect the long-run potential labor supply through the fertility channel, the data that are currently available do not permit evaluation of this hypothesis. However, there is also evidence (e.g., Blau and Robins 1989; Whittington 1992; Averett, Peters, and Waldman 1997; and Haan and Wrohlick 2011) of positive labor supply responses among females to decreases in the effective cost of child care through public subsidies. Consistent with this literature, female labor force participation among those age 25–34 years rose 0.9 percentage point in 2018—2.1 percentage points above the trend during the period 2009:Q3–2017:Q4. In contrast, overall female labor force participation rose 0.5 percentage point (1.3 percentage points over the trend), while male labor force participation among those age 25–34 rose just 0.3 percentage point (0.7 percentage point above the trend). The elimination of personal exemptions may have partially offset any maternal-specific labor supply effects of the Child Tax Credit's expansion, though this offsetting effect would have been mitigated by the near doubling of the standard deduction.

International Developments

In the 2018 *Economic Report of the President*, the CEA reported that an additional margin along which changes in corporate income tax rates can affect economic growth is through the propensity for multinational enterprises to engage in profit shifting across international tax jurisdictions. One technique for effecting such profit shifts is the use of international transfer pricing of intellectual property assets between U.S. multinational enterprises and their subsidiaries in lower-tax jurisdictions.

Though transfer pricing is intended by tax authorities to be conducted on an "arm's length," transactional basis, in practice the pricing of relatively untraded or otherwise illiquid proprietary intellectual property is often opaque, with the result that firms may systematically underprice the value of the transferred asset. Guvenen and others (2017) estimate that such profit shifting by multinational enterprises results in substantial U.S. economic activity being imputed to overseas affiliates, and therefore has been understating the United States' GDP, particularly since the 1990s. These researchers correct for this mismeasurement by reweighting the consolidated firm profits that should be attributed to the United States by apportioning profits according to the locations of labor compensation and sales to unaffiliated parties. Applying these weights to all U.S.-based multinational enterprises and aggregating to the national level, the authors calculate that in 2012, about $280 billion in official foreign profits could have been properly attributed to the United States.

Importantly, the 2018 *Economic Report of the President* documented that the propensity to engage in international profit shifting is highly responsive to effective marginal corporate income tax rate differentials. For example, Hines and Rice (1994), estimate a tax semielasticity of profit shifting of –2.25, indicating that a 1-percentage-point decrease in a country's corporate tax rate is associated with an increase of 2.25 percent in reported corporate income.

Before the TCJA, the United States had one of the highest statutory corporate income tax rates among the countries that belong to the Organization for Economic Cooperation and Development, and U.S. multinational enterprises therefore faced strong incentives to report profits in lower-tax jurisdictions. Hines (2010), Phillips and others (2017), and Zucman (2018) each rank the top 10 jurisdictions they quantitatively identify as tax havens. In these rankings, 8 economies—Bermuda, Hong Kong, Ireland, Luxembourg, the Netherlands, Singapore, Switzerland, and the U.K. Caribbean islands—appear on all three lists. As of 2017, these 8 jurisdictions, with a combined population of just 0.6 percent (44 million) of the world's population and 3.2 percent of global output, accounted for 43 percent of the United States' direct investment abroad position, on a historical cost basis. After the TCJA's passage, in the first two quarters of 2018, U.S. direct investment in these 8 jurisdictions declined by $200 billion (box 1-3).

The "Deemed Repatriation" of Accumulated Foreign Earnings

In addition to reduced incentives to shift corporate earnings on a flow basis, the TCJA also included provisions designed to incentivize the repatriation of past earnings previously held abroad. In particular, the TCJA imposed a one-time tax, which it termed "deemed repatriation," on past, post-1986 earnings that were being held abroad, regardless of whether these earnings are repatriated. With a tax of 15.5 percent on earnings representing liquid assets such as cash and 8 percent on earnings representing illiquid, noncash assets, payable over eight years, deemed repatriation was intended to incentivize the reallocation of past corporate earnings from investment in low-yield assets in low-tax jurisdictions to real investment in U.S.-based fixed assets. Indeed, on a directional basis, outbound U.S. direct investment consequently declined by $148 billion in the first three quarters of 2018, as U.S. multinational companies redirected investment toward the domestic economy.

Although the precise volume of total accumulated U.S. corporate earnings held abroad is difficult to estimate, we can calculate an approximation by summing the net flow of earnings reinvested abroad since 1986—as reported in table 6.1 of the Bureau of Economic Analysis' International Transactions Accounts—through 2017. This calculation suggests that a maximum cumulative total of $4.3 trillion was held abroad by U.S. multinational enterprises as of 2017:Q4. Of this sum, $571 billion, or 13 percent, was repatriated in the first three quarters of 2018 alone, including both the flow of current earnings and the distribution of past earnings. The trend in the volume of quarterly repatriations through 2018:Q3 suggests that this pace can be expected to abate in 2019.

Although the distribution of past earnings between cash and noncash investments abroad is similarly difficult to assess, Credit Suisse (2015) recently estimated that 37 percent of overseas earnings of nonfinancial S&P 500 companies were held in the form of cash. The share, 43 percent, of the U.S. direct investment position accounted for by the eight small jurisdictions identified by Hines (2010), Phillips and others (2017), and Zucman (2018) as tax havens is therefore consistent with the Credit Suisse estimate. Assuming a 37 percent cash share of a $4.3 trillion stock, deemed repatriation could raise as much $460 billion in additional tax revenue by 2026, before reduced credits for foreign taxes are paid.

This constitutes an extreme upper-bound estimate of potential revenue from deemed repatriation, because the cumulated flow of reinvested earnings may include defunct firms and/or firms that have since been acquired by other foreign-based firms. But there are also reasons to expect that the JCT and the Bureau of Economic Analysis's (BEA's) estimates of $340 and $250 billion, respectively, may be conservative. Specifically, data revisions since the JCT and BEA estimations, as well as the inclusion of reinvested earnings in 2017:Q4, yield a substantially larger tax base for the deemed repatriation tax. Second, private sector estimates (Credit Suisse 2015) suggest calculations based on the

Box 1-3. The TCJA's Provisions Shift the United States toward a Territorial System of Taxation

Accompanying the substantial reduction in the U.S. corporate tax rate as part of the Tax Cuts and Jobs Act were provisions that shifted the United States away from a worldwide system of taxation and toward a territorial system. The provisions of the Global Intangible Low-Tax Income (GILTI), the Foreign Derived Intangible Income (FDII), and the Base Erosion and Anti-Abuse Tax (BEAT) aim to address the incentives for U.S. firms to shift profits abroad. Profit-shifting has become increasingly costly in recent decades, with estimated revenue loss increasing 2.5 times between 2005 and 2015, rising by an estimated $93 to $114 billion, or 27 to 33 percent of the U.S. corporate income tax base (Clausing 2018). A total of 80 percent of the profit shifted abroad by U.S. firms in 2015 was to tax haven countries. The previous worldwide system taxed U.S. firms on their global profits, though most profits earned abroad by U.S. firms were only taxed once they were repatriated to the United States. Evidence from surveyed U.S. tax executives indicated that U.S. firms exposed themselves to nontax costs to avoid taxes on repatriated income (Graham, Hanlon, and Shevlin 2010). The United States was one of just 6 nations among 35 countries belonging to the Organization for Economic Cooperation and Development with a worldwide tax system before the TCJA's passage. As a result, U.S. firms were left at a potential competitive disadvantage to other OECD-country firms competing in overseas markets that were generally not subject to home-country taxes on profits earned abroad (Pomerleau 2018). The inclusion of the GILTI, FDII, and BEAT in the TCJA shifted the United States toward a hybrid territorial system, lowering incentives for U.S.-based firms to shift profits out of the country.

The GILTI and FDII are complementary provisions that address the tax system's treatment of intangible income. The GILTI is a tax at a reduced rate on the foreign profits of a U.S. firm earned with respect to activity of its controlled foreign corporations in excess of a 10 percent return, where 10 percent is the rate of return attributable to depreciable tangible assets in a competitive market. A rate of return in excess of 10 percent is attributed to mobile income from intellectual property or other intangible assets. The FDII also addresses profits from intangible assets, including intellectual property, but with respect to U.S. firms' excess returns related to foreign income earned directly. The FDII provides for a reduced tax rate on foreign-derived U.S. income in excess of the 10 percent rate of return associated with tangible assets (Pomerleau 2018). Together, the GILTI and FDII are intended to neutralize the role that tax considerations play in choosing the location of intangible income attributable to foreign market activity.

The BEAT establishes a tax on U.S. firms with revenue of $500 million or more and base erosion payments generally in excess of 3 percent of total deductions. Base erosion payments are generally certain deductible payments that a U.S. firm makes to related and controlled foreign corporations.

The BEAT discourages firms from profit-shifting to lower-tax foreign jurisdictions by applying the 10 percent BEAT tax rate generally to both taxable income and base erosion payments made by the firm (Pomerleau 2018). The 10 percent rate started phasing in from 5 percent in 2018, and will end up rising to 12.5 percent in 2025.

The BEAT, GILTI, and FDII contribute to reshaping the incentives the firms face in determining the location of assets as well as new investment when considering after-tax income. When coupled with the notable reduction in the corporate tax rate, this shift toward a territorial system of taxation may contribute to the TCJA's supply-side effect on changing the growth rate of U.S. output. The growth in the intellectual property component of real nonresidential business fixed investment is above the recent trend (see figure 1-6 in the main text). Investment in real intellectual property products grew at the fastest pace since 1999 in the first three quarters after the TCJA's passage, at a compound annual rate. Further, by disincentivizing profit shifting, the provisions could have a positive impact on the corporate income tax base. The GILTI, modeled with the reduction of both the corporate income tax rate and the rate for repatriated income, is estimated to increase the corporate tax base by $95 billion, resulting in $19 billion in additional U.S. revenues (Clausing 2018).

cash share of total assets less equity of U.S.-majority-owned foreign affiliates, as reported in the BEA's Activities of U.S. Multinational Enterprises accounts, may substantially underestimate the share of cumulated reinvested earnings liable for the deemed repatriation taxation at the 15.5 percent rate. During the temporary two-year repatriation holiday introduced by the Homeland Investment Act (HIA) of 2004, U.S. multinational firms repatriated $400 billion, of which about $300 billion, or 27 percent of the about $1.1 trillion in then-accumulated overseas earnings, is attributed to the HIA (Redmiles 2008; Herrick 2018).

However, though many authors have attempted to draw comparisons between the HIA and the TCJA (e.g., Gale et al. 2018; and Herrick 2018), aside from introducing an incentive to repatriate, the two laws are otherwise generally incommensurable. Most importantly, the comparison is invalid because the TCJA, in addition to deemed repatriation, also permanently lowered the user cost of capital, whereas the HIA, a temporary tax cut on past earnings, did not. Though the Jobs and Growth Tax Relief Reconciliation Act of 2003 had expanded first-year depreciation allowances for certain properties, increased Section 179 expensing, and cut the dividend tax rate for individual shareholders, these provisions were all temporary, expiring, respectively, in December 2004, December 2005, and December 2008. Thus, the bonus depreciation introduced in 2003 expired before the HIA came into effect, while Section 179 expensing applied for only half the duration of the repatriation holiday, and the dividend tax cut applied to no more than three or four years of the lives of assets newly installed during the HIA repatriation holiday.

In addition, under the "new view" of dividend taxation, the tax advantage of financing marginal investment out of retained earnings or low-risk debt exactly offsets the double taxation of subsequent dividends. As a result, among firms financing marginal investment out of retentions and paying dividends out of residual cash flows, taxes on dividends have no impact on investment incentives (King 1977; Auerbach 1979; Bradford 1981; Auerbach and Hassett 2002; Desai and Goolsbee 2004; Chetty and Saez 2005; Yagan 2015). This contrasts to the "traditional view," in which marginal investment is financed through variations in the level of new shares. Under the "new view" of dividend taxation, we would therefore expect the impact of the HIA on U.S. domestic investment to have been limited to cash-constrained firms.

Consistent with the "new view," Dharmapala, Foley, and Forbes (2011) find that the HIA had no significant effect on domestic investment, employment, or research and development, in part because most U.S. multinationals were not financially constrained at the time, and because repatriated earnings were generally distributed to shareholders through share repurchases, particularly among firms with stronger corporate governance. Among firms with low investment opportunities and high residual cash flows, stronger corporate governance would indeed predict higher shareholder distributions, given that weakly governed managers may face incentives to raise executive compensation or embark on risky or otherwise low-return acquisitions. Blouin and Krull (2009) also find that, on average, firms that repatriated in response to the HIA had lower investment opportunities and higher free cash flows than nonrepatriating firms, and relatively increased share repurchases by about $60 billion, though this had no significant effect on dividend payments.

In contrast to Dharmapala, Foley, and Forbes (2011), but consistent with the "new view," Faulkender and Petersen (2012) find that the HIA had a large, positive effect on domestic investment by previously capital-constrained firms, though unconstrained firms accounted for the majority of repatriations. Faulkender and Petersen's findings suggest that domestic and foreign internal funds are not perfectly fungible, and that lowering the cost of repatriating foreign income reduces the cost of financing marginal investment with internal foreign funds. Consistent with the imperfect fungibility of domestic versus foreign internal funds, Desai, Foley, and Hines (2016) find that high corporate tax rates encourage borrowing through trade accounts, with U.S. multinational firms employing trade credit to reallocate capital between locations with differing tax rates. These researchers conclude that the additional corporate borrowing through trade accounts is comparable in magnitude to the additional borrowing through bank loans and debt issuance associated with higher corporate tax rates.

Reinforcing Faulkender and Petersen's results and in contrast to Dharmapala, Foley, and Forbes (2011), Dyreng and Hills (2018) find that employment increased in the geographic region surrounding the headquarters of repatriating multinational enterprises in the three years immediately after the HIA's inception, and that the effect of repatriation on employment was increasing in the amount repatriated. Dyreng and Hills observe that the positive employment effect was strongest when the geographic region is defined as a 20-mile radius around the headquarters of repatriating firms, with estimates indicating that employment rose by more than three employees for every $1 million repatriated in response to the HIA.

Share Repurchases and Capital Distributions

Research conducted by the Federal Reserve shows that, coinciding with repatriated earnings in the first quarter in 2018, there was a substantial increase in share repurchases conducted by U.S. multinational firms (Smolyansky, Suarez, and Tabova 2018). This analysis further shows that the increase in share repurchases was concentrated in the top 15 firms in terms of total cash held abroad. Figure 1-14 shows the elevated level of real repatriated earnings by U.S. firms coincident with an increase in real share repurchases relative to total assets.

The large positive shock to share repurchases, centralized in the top cash-held-abroad U.S. firms, after the TCJA's enactment has garnered an extensive discussion on the impact of share repurchases. As noted in more recent research, "a common critique is that each dollar used to buy back a share is a dollar that is not spent on business activities that would otherwise stimulate economic growth," though "people seem to forget some of the very basic lessons of financial economics when it comes to share repurchases" (Asness, Hazelkorn, and Richardson 2018, 2).

Jensen's (1986, 323) free cash flow hypothesis outlined the agency conflicts that arise between shareholders and corporate managers when firms have substantial "cash flow in excess of that required to fund all projects that have positive net present values when discounted at the relevant cost of capital." Jensen notes that managers of a firm with large free cash flows may use those excess flows to pursue low-return acquisitions rather than distributing residual cash to shareholders. He further suggests that agency conflicts between managers and shareholders are greater within firms with larger free cash flows as "the problem is how to motivate managers to disgorge the cash rather than investing it at below the cost of capital or wasting it on organization inefficiencies" (Jensen 1986, 323). Jensen's seminal hypothesis informs the later literature by underscoring how excess or free cash flows, if unable to be invested in projects with a positive net present value, may incur economic costs and lead to agency conflicts.

Dittmar and Mahrt-Smith (2007) find evidence in support of Jensen's hypothesis. Consistent with Dharmapala, Foley, and Forbes's (2011) observation

Figure 1-14. Real U.S. Repatriated Earnings and Share Repurchases, 2015–18

■ Total real repatriated earnings (left axis)

■ Ratio of real nonfinancial corporate share repurchases to total assets (right axis)

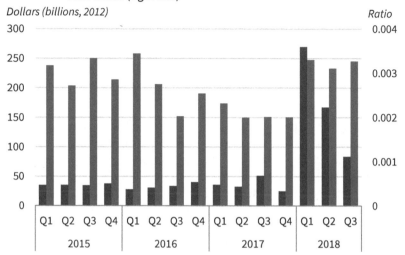

Sources: Federal Reserve Board; Bureau of Economic Analysis; CEA calculations.

that share repurchases in response to the HIA were particularly pronounced among repatriating firms with stronger corporate governance, Dittmar and Mahrt-Smith estimate that investors value $1.00 in cash in a poorly governed firm at only $0.42 to $0.88. Contrary to popular myth, this is the primary mechanism whereby share repurchases may raise share prices; repurchases otherwise have no mechanical effect on share price. For example, following Cochrane (2018), suppose a company with $100 in cash and a factory worth $100, and with two outstanding shares, each valued at $100, uses that $100 in cash to repurchase one of the two outstanding shares. The company now has one asset—a factory worth $100—and one outstanding share, worth $100. There has been no change in share price or shareholder wealth. However, if investors had previously worried that there was a 40 percent chance that corporate management would squander the $100 in cash on excessive executive compensation or loss-making investment projects or acquisitions, then the two shares would have been valued at $80 each. If the company then repurchased one of the two outstanding shares, it would have $20 in cash, a factory worth $100, and one outstanding share valued at $112, assuming that investors still attach a 40 percent probability to mismanagement.

Grullon and Michaely (2004) also provide empirical evidence that supports Jensen's free cash flow hypothesis, finding, among other results, that the market reaction to firms announcing share repurchases is more robust if the firm is more likely to overinvest, and that repurchasing firms experience substantial reductions in systematic risk and the cost of capital relative to nonrepurchasing firms. Their findings support Jensen's hypothesis that share repurchases are a firm's value-maximizing response when they do not have investments to make that have a positive net present value. Grullon and Michaely (2004, 652) further note that "repurchases may be associated with a firm's transition from a higher growth phase to a lower growth phase. As firms become more mature, their investment opportunity set becomes smaller. These firms have fewer options to grow, and their assets in place play a bigger role in determining their value, which leads to a decline in systematic risk."

Though share repurchases and dividend payments constitute alternative mechanisms for distributing earnings, they are imperfect substitutes. First, dividends are subject to personal income tax when received, but capital gains are not taxed until realized, and therefore many investors prefer share repurchases over dividends because they allow the shareholder to determine when he or she incurs the tax liability. Second, in open market repurchases, firms do not have to commit to repurchase. Third, there is no expectation that distributions through share repurchases will recur on a regular basis, in contrast to dividends (Dittmar 2000). In practice, market participants view changes in the amount of dividends paid to be a signal of management's view of the firm's prospects. Because dividend decreases are viewed negatively, firms tend not to raise dividend payments unless management believes they can be maintained. Dividends thus tend to exhibit "stickiness," increasing when management believes the firm's prospects are sustainably good and decreasing only when absolutely necessary (Brav et al. 2005).

Brennan and Thakor (1990), Guay and Harford (2000), and Jagannathan, Stephens, and Weisbach (2000) accordingly find that since the Securities and Exchange Commission legalized share repurchases in 1982, they have become firms' preferred method for distributing "transient," nonoperating residual cash flows, whereas dividend payments are the preferred method for distributing "permanent," operating residual cash flows. Thus, theory and empirical evidence suggest that, among cash-unconstrained firms, a large, positive shock to cash flow, such as from a lowered cost of accessing the accumulated stock of past residual cash flows abroad, is likely to be distributed via share repurchases. Among previously cash-constrained firms, any profit windfall in excess of positive expected return investment opportunities is also likely to be distributed via share repurchases.

Figure 1-15 reports a pronounced increase in corporate share repurchases after the TCJA's passage, with repurchases rising above the recent trend by $200 billion as of 2018:Q3. In contrast, figure 1-16 reports that though corporate net dividend payments rose slightly after the TCJA's passage, the increase was modest, and net dividends were only $15 billion above the recent trend.

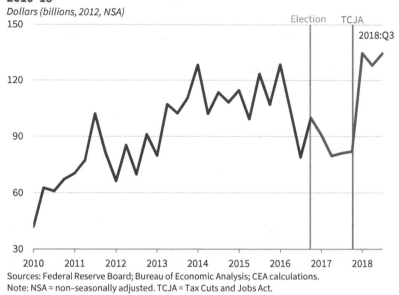

Figure 1-15. Real Nonfinancial Corporate Share Repurchases, 2010–18

Dollars (billions, 2012, NSA)

Sources: Federal Reserve Board; Bureau of Economic Analysis; CEA calculations.
Note: NSA = non-seasonally adjusted. TCJA = Tax Cuts and Jobs Act.

Observed share repurchases may be substantially smaller in volume relative to repatriations because under the "new view" of dividend taxation, a simultaneous positive shock to cash flow and investment generates an ambiguous effect on shareholder distributions, depending on the relative magnitudes of the coincident shocks. Though the has TCJA created a positive financial windfall—both for past residual earnings and future cash flow—it has also substantially and permanently lowered the break-even rate of return on marginal investment. Auerbach and Hassett (2002) find that though the probability of share repurchases is higher among firms with a greater cash flow, the probability of repurchase activity is lower among firms with more investment, and the estimated coefficients on cash flow and investment are of the same absolute magnitude. Indeed, a Wald test that the sum of the estimated coefficients on two lags of investment equals (in absolute value) the sum of the estimated coefficients on two lags of cash flow is accepted at all standard levels of significance, and for every specification estimated, and the simple correlation is very close to –1.0.

Auerbach and Hassett (2002) further observe that the probability of repurchase activity is highest among large firms with strong capital market access—as indicated by high bond ratings and coverage by multiple analysts. Consistent with these results, Hanlon, Hoopes, and Slemrod (2018), analyzing corporate actions in response to the TCJA, find that observed increases in share repurchases after the TCJA's passage were extremely concentrated among a

Figure 1-16. Real Corporate Net Dividends, 2010–18

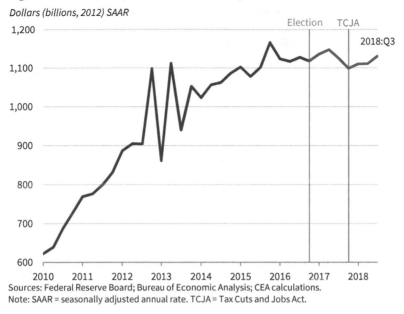

Sources: Federal Reserve Board; Bureau of Economic Analysis; CEA calculations.
Note: SAAR = seasonally adjusted annual rate. TCJA = Tax Cuts and Jobs Act.

very small subset of cash-abundant firms—particularly Apple, Amgen, Bank of America, Pfizer, and JPMorgan Chase. Excluding already-cash-unconstrained Apple alone from the sample, these researchers find that the value of shares repurchased in 2018:Q1 were no higher than the value of shares repurchased in 2016:Q1. The concentration of the increase in the volume of repurchase activity among such a small subset of firms suggests that though these firms may have been cash-unconstrained, many other firms faced binding financing constraints.

The corporate finance literature therefore strongly suggests that repurchase activity is an integral margin of adjustment to a positive cash flow–cum– investment shock, constituting the primary mechanism whereby efficient capital markets reallocate capital from mature, cash-abundant firms without profitable investment opportunities to emerging, cash-constrained firms with profitable investment opportunities. For example, Alstadsaeter, Jacob, and Michaely (2017) find that a 10-percentage-point cut in Sweden's dividend tax rate in 2006 improved efficiency by inducing capital reallocation from established, cash-rich firms to cash-constrained firms.

Similarly, Fried and Wang (2018) find that non-S&P 500 public firms— which are generally younger and faster growing than S&P 500 firms—were net importers of equity capital for every year between 2007 and 2016, with net shareholder inflows into these firms equal to 11 percent of net shareholder distributions by S&P 500 firms. These researchers further observe that a

Figure 1-17. Real Private Nonresidential Fixed Investment by Noncorporate Businesses, 2012–18

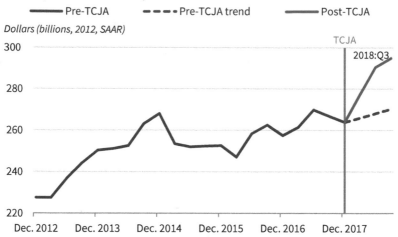

Sources: Federal Reserve Board; Bureau of Economic Analysis; CEA calculations.
Note: SAAR = seasonally adjusted annual rate. The trend is calculated for 2009:Q3–2017:Q4. Nominal values are deflated using the chain price index for private nonresidential fixed investment. TCJA = Tax Cuts and Jobs Act.

Figure 1-18. Real Venture Capital Investment, 2012–18

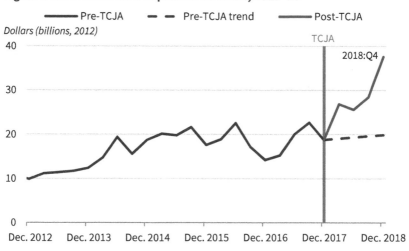

Sources: National Venture Capital Association; Bureau of Economic Analysis; CEA calculations.
Note: The trend is calculated for 2009:Q3–2017:Q4. To deflate the real value in 2018:Q4, it is assumed that the GDP chain price index grew at the same compound annual rate in 2018:Q4 as in 2018:Q1–Q3. TCJA = Tax Cuts and Jobs Act.

Figure 1-19. Gross Foreign Sales of U.S. Corporate Stocks, 2013–18

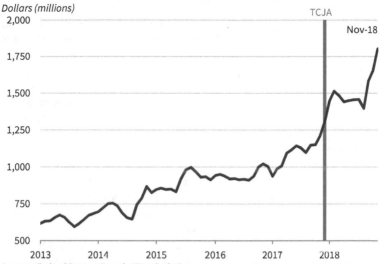

Sources: Federal Reserve Board; CEA calculations.
Note: Data represent a centered 3-month moving average, truncating in November 2018.
TCJA = Tax Cuts and Jobs Act.

substantial fraction of net shareholder distributions by all public companies is reinvested in initial public offerings by newly listing companies, as well as in nonpublic firms through venture capital and private equity vehicles. They additionally note that these firms account for more than 50 percent of private nonresidential fixed investment, employ nearly 70 percent of U.S. workers, and generate almost half of corporate profits. As shown in figures 1-17 and 1-18, real private investment by noncorporate businesses and private equity firms rose sharply in 2018. Among noncorporate firms, in the first three quarters of 2018, real nonresidential fixed investment rose 16.0 percent at a compound annual rate, which would constitute the fastest calendar-year growth in noncorporate business investment since 1993 if sustained through the fourth quarter (see box 1-4 for a discussion of the TCJA and family farms).

Asness, Hazelkorn, and Richardson (2018, 4) echo Fried and Wang's (2018) findings. In particular, they address the "myth" that "share repurchases have come at the expense of profitable investment." They note that funds obtained by the shareholder after a repurchase are often invested elsewhere. This "redirection of available capital" ensures that capital flows to new investment opportunities. They do note that "there is always the possibility for agency issues to create incentives for corporate managers to engage in suboptimal share repurchase decisions," though the literature on agency theory finds positive value in paying back free cash flows as much as it does negative ones.

Box 1-4. Estate Taxes and Family Farms

A total of 98 percent of U.S. farms are family businesses. Succession planning, successfully passing the farm to the next generation, is a critically important issue for farm families. The Tax Cuts and Jobs Acts reduced the effective tax rate for family farm households by 3.3 percent. Williamson and Bawa (2018), researchers at the Department of Agriculture, estimate that if the TCJA's estate tax provisions had been in place in 2016, family farm households would have faced an average effective tax rate of 13.9 percent that year instead of 17.2 percent. The TCJA also doubled the estate value that could be excluded from an individual's estate taxes to $11.18 million. A large portion of a farm's assets are illiquid, most often with land as the largest category, equaling millions of dollars. Without a significant estate tax exemption, farms would sometimes need to be liquidated to meet estate tax liability.

President Trump was clear that he wanted to spare farm families from the punitive effects of estates taxes when passing the farm to the next generation. The TCJA achieves this objective by virtually eliminating the need for farms to pay estate taxes. Williamson and Bawa (2018) estimate that if the TCJA's estate tax provisions had been in place in 2016, then 0.11 percent of all farm estates would have had to pay estate taxes, and only 0.58 percent would have had to file an estate tax return. And Williamson and Bawa also estimate that the aggregate tax liability of all farm estates in 2016 would have been

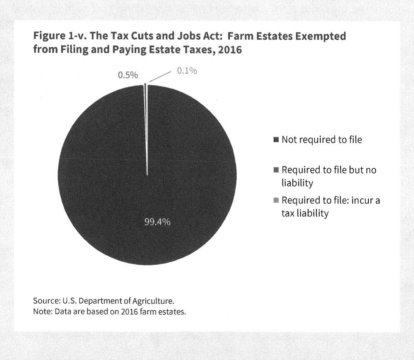

Figure 1-v. The Tax Cuts and Jobs Act: Farm Estates Exempted from Filing and Paying Estate Taxes, 2016

0.5%   0.1%

99.4%

■ Not required to file

■ Required to file but no liability

■ Required to file: incur a tax liability

Source: U.S. Department of Agriculture.
Note: Data are based on 2016 farm estates.

reduced from $496 million under the previous estate tax rules to $104 million under the TCJA (figure 1-v).

By doubling the estate tax threshold, introducing a 20 percent deduction for pass-through income, and extending and expanding bonus depreciation for equipment investment, the TCJA may also positively affect investment by independent farms. Poterba (1997) demonstrates that the estate tax is effectively a tax on capital income and thus lowers after-tax investment returns—particularly, as mortality risk is increasing in age, among older proprietors. Kotlikoff and Summers (1981, 1988) and Gale and Scholz (1994) also highlight the substantial contribution of intergenerational transfers to aggregate capital formation. Especially if the TCJA's provisions that are currently scheduled to expire are made permanent, the TCJA can therefore be expected to incentivize new capital formation among independent farms, thereby raising productivity and steady-state output.

Finally, an additional second-order effect of increased repurchase activity in response to repatriation is the impact of share repurchases on measured foreign direct investment. The BEA (2018) defines foreign direct investment as the ownership or control, directly or indirectly, by a single foreign individual or entity, of "10 percent or more of the voting securities of an incorporated U.S. business enterprise, or an equivalent interest in an unincorporated U.S. business enterprise." Consequently, given that U.S. multinational enterprises employ some fraction of repatriated funds to repurchase outstanding shares, some of these shares may have been previously held by foreign entities. Accordingly, figure 1-19 reports the three-month centered moving average of gross foreign sales of U.S. corporate stocks. Consistent with repatriating firms repurchasing shares, including shares previously held by foreign entities, we observe a substantial spike in gross foreign sales immediately after the TCJA's enactment.

Conclusion

In the 2018 *Economic Report of the President*, the Council of Economic Advisers demonstrated that before the TCJA's enactment, the U.S. economy and labor market were adversely affected by the conjunction of rising international capital mobility and increasingly internationally uncompetitive U.S. business taxation, with adverse consequences for domestic capital formation, capital deepening, and wages. Drawing on an extensive academic literature, the *Report* concluded that the TCJA's business and international provisions would raise the target U.S. capital stock, reorient U.S. capital away from direct investment abroad in low-tax jurisdictions and toward investment in the United States, and raise household income through both a short-run bargaining channel and a long-run capital deepening channel. The *Report* also documented that reductions in effective marginal personal income tax rates by the TCJA were expected to induce positive labor supply responses.

In this chapter, we have used the available data to examine each of these anticipated effects of the TCJA, with particular attention to the relative velocities of adjustment along each margin. We find that the TCJA had an immediate and large effect on business expectations, with firms immediately responding to the TCJA by upwardly revising planned capital expenditures, employee compensation, and hiring. We also observe revised capital plans translating into higher private investment in real fixed assets, with nonresidential fixed investment growing at an annual rate of about 8 percent in the period 2017:Q4–2018:Q3, to a level $150 billion over the recent trend. In addition to tallying more than 6 million workers receiving bonuses that could be directly attributed to the TCJA, with an average bonus of $1,200, we also estimate that as of September 2018, real disposable personal income per household had risen $640 over the trend during calendar year 2018 thus far. As a perpetual annuity, this increase in compensation corresponds to a lifetime pay raise of about $21,000 for the average household, or $2.5 trillion across all households.

Finally, we also report evidence of a reorientation of U.S. investment from direct investment abroad, particularly in low-tax jurisdictions, to investment in fixed assets in the United States. Specifically, in the first three quarters after the TCJA's enactment, U.S. direct investment abroad declined by $148 billion, while the U.S. direct investment position in eight identified tax havens declined by $200 billion. Citing a large body of corporate finance literature, we conclude that shareholder distributions through share repurchases is an important margin of adjustment to a simultaneous positive shock to cash flow and investment, constituting the primary mechanism whereby efficient capital markets reallocate capital from mature, cash-abundant firms without profitable investment opportunities to emerging, cash-constrained firms with profitable investment opportunities.

Chapter 2

Deregulation: Reducing the Burden of Regulatory Costs

When appropriate, well-designed regulatory actions promote important social purposes, including the protection of workers, public health, safety, and the environment. At the same time, complying with regulations increases the cost of doing business and results in opportunity costs—business and consumer activities that are forgone due to regulation. For decades, the regulatory state has expanded and imposed an ever-growing burden of regulatory costs on the U.S. economy.

The Trump Administration has taken major steps to reverse the long-standing trend of rising regulatory costs. In 2017 and 2018, Federal agencies issued many times more deregulatory actions than new regulatory actions. From 2000 through 2016, the annual trend was for regulatory costs to grow by $8.2 billion each year. In contrast, in 2017 and 2018 Federal agencies took deregulatory actions that resulted in cost savings that more than offset the costs of new regulatory actions; in fiscal year 2017, deregulatory actions saved $8.1 billion in regulatory costs (in net present value), and in 2018, they saved $23 billion.

In this chapter, we develop a framework to analyze the cumulative economic impact of regulatory actions on the U.S. economy. Regulation affects productivity, wages, and profits in the regulated industry and in the economy as a whole. Economics tells us that the regulatory whole is greater than the sum of its parts. However, Federal regulations have traditionally been considered on a stand-alone basis. The Trump Administration's reform agenda uses regulatory cost caps to reduce the cumulative burden of Federal regulation. In addition to regulation-specific cost-benefit tests, the cost caps induce agencies to view all their regulations as a portfolio, which is more congruent with the experiences of the households and businesses subject to them.

Small business owners, consumers, and workers gain when less regulation means lower business costs, lower consumer prices, more consumer choice, and higher worker productivity and wages. The chapter discusses a number of notable deregulatory actions during the Trump Administration, and gives detailed information about the association health plan rule; the short-term, limited-duration insurance rule; and the joint employer standard.

G overnment regulation is ubiquitous in modern economies. When appropriate, well-designed regulatory actions promote important social purposes, including the protection of workers, public health, safety, and the environment. As business owners and managers are aware, complying with regulations often increases the cost of doing business. Moreover, regulatory actions also result in opportunity costs: business and consumer activities forgone due to regulation. Ultimately, consumers and workers bear much of the burden, because business-entry barriers, higher costs, and lower productivity are reflected in higher prices, limited consumer choice, and lower real wages. For decades, the regulatory state has expanded and imposed an ever-growing burden of regulatory costs on the U.S. economy.

In 2017 and 2018, the Trump Administration took major steps to reverse the long-standing trend of rising regulatory costs. In fiscal year 2017, there were 15 significant deregulatory actions and 3 new significant regulatory actions, saving $8.1 billion in regulatory costs (in net present value), according to official measures (OMB 2017a). In fiscal year 2018, there were 57 significant deregulatory actions and 14 new significant regulatory actions, saving $23 billion (OMB 2018).

The Trump Administration's regulatory reform agenda uses regulatory cost caps to seek to reduce the cumulative burden of federal regulation. Economics tells us that the regulatory whole is different from the sum of its parts. Households and businesses are required to comply with new regulations along with old ones. Nevertheless, Federal regulations have traditionally been considered on a stand-alone basis. Under the Trump administration, agencies are now also given regulatory cost caps for the upcoming year. In addition to regulation-specific cost-benefit tests, the cost caps induce agencies to view all their regulations as a portfolio, which is more congruent with the experience of the households and businesses subject to them. While pursuing their agency-specific missions—for example, the Environmental Protection Agency's (EPA) mission to protect human health and the environment—the regulatory cost caps provide the framework for agencies to evaluate regulatory costs, to consider deregulatory actions, and to set priorities among new regulatory actions. Moreover, when the executive branch sets the regulatory cost caps across all federal agencies, the caps reflect the priorities and trade-offs imposed by the cumulative regulatory burden on the U.S. economy.

The Trump Administration has sought to lift the burden of unnecessary regulatory costs while encouraging Federal agencies to preserve important protections of workers, public health, safety, and the environment. The regulatory reform agenda is guided by cost-benefit analysis—a systematic way to balance the benefits of regulatory actions, including the value of these important protections, with the costs. The regulatory cost caps require prioritization among costly rules. An agency cannot meet its cost cap simply by eliminating costly regulatory actions; it eliminates regulatory actions when the benefits do not justify the costs.

Last year, we discussed the impact of deregulation on aggregate economic growth (CEA 2018). Based on the evidence reviewed, we concluded that if the United States adopted product market regulatory reforms, over the next decade gross domestic product (GDP) could be 1.0 to 2.2 percent higher (CEA 2018).

In this chapter, we report on progress and dig deeper into the economic effects of regulation and deregulation. We develop a framework to analyze the cumulative economic impact of regulatory actions on the U.S. economy. Regulation affects the regulated industry and the economy as a whole. Consider the effects of a regulation—such as the expansive joint employer standard featured at the end of this chapter—that discourages specialization and encourages centralized decisionmaking along an industry's supply chain. Productivity and competition are often greater when separate businesses can specialize in the various tasks required to produce the final consumer good (Becker and Murphy 1992). For example, some businesses specialize in handling raw materials, others in branding and intellectual property, others in performing the clerical work, and still others in regional retail. But the regulation incentivizes a number of these supply-linked businesses to act as a single large business and as a result forgo many of the productivity gains from specialization and decentralized decisionmaking (see also chapter 8 of this *Report*). Productivity is further sacrificed as capital moves out of the industry. In certain circumstances (discussed below), one result can be lower pay for workers—even workers outside this sector—because the work done in the sector is made less productive due to the regulation, and because fewer employers are competing for workers in the sector. Consumers also will pay higher prices due to the regulation's effect on costs and diminished competition in the retail market.

Although estimating the benefits and costs of Federal regulatory and deregulatory actions might appear to be a technocratic exercise, the principles that underlie the exercise are democratic. To complete an evidence-based cost-benefit analysis requires expertise not only in economic analysis but often also in scientific areas relevant to the regulated industry. Career public servants in the agencies provide the needed expertise; career public servants in the Office of Information and Regulatory Affairs (OIRA) within the Office of Management and Budget (OMB) review the completed analyses. A previous OIRA Administrator, Cass Sunstein (2018), proclaimed the process as the "triumph of the technocrats." However, the goal of economic analysis is to estimate the benefits and costs based on the preferences of the people affected by the regulatory actions. Cost-benefit analysis is "an attempt to replicate for the public sector the decisions that would be made if private markets worked satisfactorily" (Haveman and Weisbrod 1975, 171). Cost-benefit analysis uses the information revealed in market transactions to guide public sector decisions. For example, a regulatory cost-benefit analysis places a high value on improving health and safety based on empirical evidence that people are willing to pay a great deal to reduce the risks of injury and death. The empirical evidence captures the public's preferences for health and safety, not the analyst's. The Trump Administration recognizes that the public—including workers, consumers, and small business owners—are key stakeholders in deregulation and actively seeks their feedback on proposed regulatory and deregulatory actions.

In the next section, we use our economic framework to discuss different types of regulatory actions and when they are needed to improve the economy. We then survey the current regulatory landscape and provide information on the number and costs of Federal regulatory actions, and on how the regulatory cost caps are reducing the regulatory burden on the U.S. economy. Following that, we use our framework to analyze the cumulative economic impact of regulatory actions. We then discuss lessons from our framework.

The chapter concludes with a set of three case studies that illustrate the value of meaningful regulatory reform. The case studies explore different aspects of how Federal deregulatory actions improve productivity and reduce costs for small businesses and their workers. The first case study is about a rule that allows more small businesses to form association health plans to provide lower-cost group health coverage to their workers. The second case study is about a rule that expands consumer options to purchase short-term health coverage. And the third case study is about the reform of the joint employer standard. Regulatory costs, and therefore the regulatory cost savings of the Trump Administration's regulatory reforms, are understated by the official measures in all three cases because the official measures did not include all the relevant opportunity costs, especially those accruing outside the regulated industry. The case studies provide guidance on how to strengthen the regulatory analysis of deregulatory actions.[1]

Principles of Regulation and Regulatory Impact Analysis

Although there are tens of thousands of regulatory actions, a fairly simple economic framework helps organize their effects. Regulation affects productivity, wages, and profits in the regulated industry. Then, as capital and labor move in response to the compliance costs and incentive effects of the regulation, regulation affects productivity, wages, and profits in the economy as a whole. The effects of regulatory actions, taxes, and other market distortions accumulate multiplicatively within the industry and along that industry's supply chain, through what economists call "convex deadweight costs." The concept of convex deadweight costs is a well-established result in the economic analysis of taxation (Auerbach and Hines 2002). Taxes impose a burden on the economy in excess of the tax revenues collected; the excess burden is also known as the deadweight cost, the deadweight loss, or the welfare loss due to taxation. The deadweight cost function is convex; if the tax is increased by 10 percent, the deadweight costs of the tax increase by more than 10 percent. As we discuss in detail below, the regulatory deadweight cost function is also convex. A new regulatory action that increases regulatory costs by 10 percent increases the cumulative regulatory cost burden by more than 10 percent. As we discuss below, even though in many cases most of the burden of a regulatory action is outside the regulated industry, the burden can be quantified, primarily with information about the regulated industry alone.

Public Goods and Private Markets

The economic framework distinguishes public goods (and services), such as clean air, from private goods, such as automobiles and health insurance. The economic term "public good" refers to a good of which one person's consumption does not reduce the availability of the good for other consumers and of which it is difficult or impossible to exclude those consumers who do not pay for the good from using it. Due to these properties, households and businesses have insufficient incentives to purchase and produce public goods in private markets. For example, consumers tend to free-ride on other people's purchases rather than purchase the good for themselves. Although private goods are not necessarily free from market failures, individual households and businesses have significant incentives to engage in these activities, and they are situated in a chain of economic activity that is critical for understanding

---

[1] The CEA previously released research on topics covered in this chapter. The text that follows builds on the following research paper produced by the CEA: "Deregulating Health Insurance Markets: Value to Market Participants" (CEA 2019).

the cumulative effect of regulatory actions. A number of regulatory actions are designed to enhance public goods, even while the opportunity cost of such actions includes the loss of the output from private goods. Other regulatory actions are designed to increase the total value of private good production by correcting failures in the markets for private goods. Regulatory actions sometimes combine both these elements; but even in these cases, it helps to examine the economic functions separately.

Environmental regulatory actions are an important type of regulatory actions that trade private goods for public goods, where environmental quality is the public good. A number of employment regulatory actions are also examples, when they restrict employers' practices in order to promote, say, fairness. Regulations of public goods typically, although not always, involve a loss of private good output, usually when these regulations reduce productivity in the process of producing these goods.[2] The productivity loss is not by itself an argument against regulations of public goods, because the value of the public goods needs to be part of the cost-benefit analysis; but of course the amounts of losses and gains need to be accurately assessed.

Regulations to enhance productivity are assessed on the basis of their productivity effects; they may reduce productivity in some activities so as to increase it overall. For example, regulations designed to prevent a financial crisis enhance productivity. Chapter 6 discusses the Dodd-Frank Act, which established a wide range of regulatory mandates to reduce the likelihood and severity of future systemic financial crises. The Trump Administration's financial regulatory approach balances the benefits of preventing financial crises and the regulatory costs that Dodd-Frank imposed on the banking industry, on other financial providers, and on the public.

The Process of Doing Regulatory Impact Analysis

Regulatory actions promote important societal goals, but not without opportunity costs. Since President Reagan's Executive Order 12291 was issued in 1981, most Federal agencies have been required to use cost-benefit analysis to strike an appropriate balance in rulemaking (White House 1981). Early in their first terms, Presidents Clinton, Obama, and Trump each signed Executive Orders that continued to require most Federal agencies to conduct Regulatory Impact Analyses (RIAs) of new and existing rules. Each RIA includes a cost-benefit analysis. Federal independent regulatory agencies—such as the Consumer Financial Protection Bureau, the Securities and Exchange Commission, and the Federal Reserve—are not required to conduct RIAs (OMB 2017b).

---

[2] Sometimes a regulation prohibits certain types of labor from engaging in private-good production, in which case the output effect would come from fewer production inputs rather than less productivity. Some measures of productivity could even be enhanced if the prohibitions apply to the less productive inputs, but in this chapter we refer to productivity in the more specific multifactor sense (BLS 2018b).

Federal regulatory cost-benefit analyses are grounded in welfare economics, the branch of economics that studies questions about the well-being of a society's members. In principle, regulatory cost-benefit analyses should help guide Federal agencies to adopt the set of regulatory actions that net the largest societal benefits over regulatory costs. Key concepts in estimating benefits and costs are willingness to pay and opportunity costs. Federal agencies draw on extensive bodies of economic research that provide estimates of societal willingness to pay for beneficial regulatory outcomes, including improvements in health, safety, and the environment. The agencies also develop estimates of the opportunity costs of regulatory actions.

Cost-benefit analyses of deregulatory actions are guided by the same principles of applied welfare economics that guide cost-benefit analyses of regulatory actions. In particular, opportunity costs and willingness to pay continue to be the key concepts. The economic concept of sunk costs can also play an important role in analyzing a deregulatory action. Some firms' and consumers' responses to regulatory actions involve sunk costs that cannot be recovered, even if the action is subsequently modified or eliminated. As a result, the costs savings from a deregulatory action might be less than the costs of the original regulatory action. However, the existence of large sunk costs might point to an important source of opportunity cost savings from deregulatory actions. Sunk costs to comply with a regulatory action can serve as a barrier to entry that gives market power to established firms (Aldy 2014). Although these firms cannot recover their sunk costs, a deregulatory action that removes costly requirements can promote the entry of new firms, increase competition, and decrease prices.

The Current Regulatory Landscape

This section examines the current regulatory landscape. First, it explores current Federal regulatory and deregulatory actions. Then it explains how the Trump Administration's regulatory cost caps are reducing costs.

Federal Regulatory and Deregulatory Actions

Last year, we discussed the various approaches that researchers have taken to the difficult task of quantifying the extent of Federal regulation (CEA 2018). One approach is to count the number of pages in the *Federal Register* or the *Code of Federal Regulations*. Another approach is to use an index based on textual analysis of keywords in these publications, like "shall" or "must," that indicate restrictions on the economy. In this subsection, we review evidence on the number of rules and estimates of the regulatory costs. From 2000 through 2018, Federal agencies published over 70,000 final rules in the *Federal Register*—an average of more than 10 a day. OMB reviews those rules that are considered significant. Figure 2-1 shows the number of economically

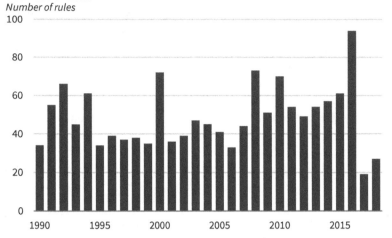

Figure 2-1. Economically Significant Final Rules, Presidential Year 1990–2018

Number of rules

Sources: Office of Information and Regulatory Affairs; George Washington University Regulatory Studies Center.

Note: A presidential year begins in February and ends in January of the subsequent year. The final rule count includes all interim final rules and final rules.

significant rules—including both regulatory and deregulatory actions—that OMB reviewed in each presidential year (February of the given year through January of the next year). Throughout this chapter, we use "regulatory and deregulatory actions" as umbrella terms, but we use more precise terms when needed (see box 2-1).

Federal regulatory and deregulatory actions cover a wide range of economic activity. Above, we make the distinction between regulations to enhance productivity and regulations of public goods. Earlier discussions made a similar distinction between economic and social regulations (Joskow and Rose 1989). With the deregulation movement of the 1970s, Federal efforts shifted away from economic regulatory actions that restricted entry and regulated prices (see box 2-2). State and local economic regulation of sectors such as electricity remain common. Currently, many Federal agencies issue regulatory actions designed to promote social purposes, including the protection of workers, public health, safety, and the environment. Other Federal regulatory actions are designed to improve the functioning of specific sectors of the economy. This *Report* discusses the economics of sector-specific developments and policies, including regulatory and deregulatory actions, in its other chapters; chapter 1 discusses taxes, chapter 3 discusses the labor market, chapter 4 discusses healthcare, chapter 5 discusses energy, and chapter 6 discusses banking. In this chapter, we focus on crosscutting issues in regulatory and deregulatory actions that are independent of the specific industry being regulated.

Box 2-1. The Terminology of Federal Regulatory Actions

Agencies in the executive branch issue regulatory actions, also called rules, to implement Federal legislation passed by Congress. Executive Order 12866 established the process for the Office of Information and Regulatory Affairs (OIRA) within the Office of Management and Budget (OMB) to review proposed and final rules. Under this Executive Order, rules may be categorized as "significant" or "economically significant." OIRA coordinates the reviews of all the rules that it deems significant, which are specifically defined as rules that are anticipated to

1. "Have an annual effect on the economy of $100 million or more or adversely affect in a material way the economy, a sector of the economy, productivity, competition, jobs, the environment, public health or safety, or State, local, or tribal governments or communities;

2. Create a serious inconsistency or otherwise interfere with an action taken or planned by another agency;

3. Materially alter the budgetary impact of entitlements, grants, user fees, or loan programs or the rights and obligations of recipients thereof; or

4. Raise novel legal or policy issues arising out of legal mandates, the President's priorities, or the principles set forth in this Executive Order."

Economically significant rules are a subcategory of significant rules that meet requirement 1 above of having an annual effect on the economy of $100 million or more or having other adverse effects. If a rule is deemed economically significant, an assessment of its economic benefits and costs is typically required before it is finalized.

The Congressional Review Act (1996) introduced the term "major rule" to the U.S. Code to categorize certain rules regulated by congressional action. A major rule is essentially an economically significant rule—one that is determined by OIRA to likely result in significant adverse economic effects or an annual effect on the economy of $100 million or more (U.S.C. Section 804[2]). However, not all economically significant rules are deemed to be major.

OIRA formally defined the terms "regulatory action" and "deregulatory action" when describing rules to better implement and track the Trump Administration's regulatory reform agenda under Executive Order 13771, which requires Federal agencies to issue two deregulatory actions passed for each new regulatory action. Under this Executive Order, a "regulatory action" is a finalized significant rule or guidance document that imposes total costs greater than zero. A "deregulatory action" can include any agency action that has been finalized and has total costs less than zero (including significant and nonsignificant rulemaking; guidance documents; some actions related to international regulatory cooperation; and information collection requests that repeal or streamline recordkeeping, reporting, or disclosure requirements).

Box 2-2. Economic Regulation and Deregulation

Economic regulation refers to the regulation of prices and entry into specific industries. Economic regulation has been used in industries with economies of scale, including electricity, telephone service, and cable television (Joskow and Rose 1989). In industries such as these, in theory it can make sense to restrict entry to a single firm to take advantage of economies of scale and lower production costs. To prevent the single firm from exploiting its market power and charging higher prices, prices are regulated so the firm earns a normal return. Economic regulation has also been used in multifirm industries, including airlines, banking, and trucking. Depending on the industry, economic regulations are implemented at the local, State, and national levels.

Although the principles of economic regulation are grounded in economic theory, in practice it has not always led to good economic results. In 1970, the Council of Economic Advisers described the "disappointing" performance of economic regulation: "Entry is often blocked, prices are kept from falling, and the industry becomes inflexible and insensitive to new techniques and opportunities for progress" (CEA 1970, 107). Amid other economic and political developments in the 1970s, the failures of economic regulation helped lead to the deregulation movement.

Perhaps the most dramatic success story is the deregulation of the airline industry. Rose (2012, 376) refers to it as "one of the greatest microeconomic policy accomplishments of the past fifty years" and credits deregulation as generating "lower average fares; greater numbers of flights, non-stop destinations, and passengers; dramatically different network structures; and increased productivity." Borenstein and Rose (2014) provide a brief history. In 1925, the U.S. government began regulating the airline industry with the Air Mail Act (43 Stat. 805). This legislation (and its amendments) allowed the Post Office to award contracts and created subsidies for mail delivery by private airlines. After mismanagement by the Postmaster General and a desire to regulate a chaotic marketplace, Congress passed legislation, including the Civil Aeronautics Act of 1938, that established the precursor to the Civil Aeronautics Board (hereafter the "Board"), to oversee economic regulation of the nascent industry (52 Stat. 977).

With the Board setting airfare and routes, airlines competed on in-flight quality, schedule convenience, and seat availability. The lack of price competition encouraged airlines to offer more frequent flights with fewer passengers and more amenities. Regulation also encouraged airlines to purchase new aircraft regularly to offer the latest technology, rather than allow assets to depreciate, because the Board did not allow airlines to charge lower prices for flights on older aircraft (Borenstein and Rose 2014). The ratio of passengers to seats available declined with the number of route competitors and route distance (Douglas and Miller 1974). The Board tried to maintain the industry's profitability by raising airfares, but the airlines responded by increasing flight frequency, which further decreased passengers per available seat and raised costs closer to the price set by the Board.

President Carter appointed the economist Alfred Kahn as chair of the Board in 1977, with a mandate to deregulate the airline industry. With rising airfares in regulated markets, the Airline Deregulation Act of 1978 dismantled the Board and eliminated price controls, entry restrictions, and regulated networks. After 1978, load factors soared and profit yields fell as the airlines began to compete on price. Instead of comparing prederegulation and post-deregulation loads, profits, and prices, ideally researchers would compare the outcomes under deregulation to outcomes in a hypothetical counterfactual world where airline deregulation never occurred. Borenstein and Rose (2014) suggest that the Standard Industry Fare Level (SIFL)—created by the Board to determine airfares prior to deregulation and updated based on input cost and productivity changes—provides a useful counterfactual. Compared with the SIFL, in 2011 actual airfares were 26 percent lower. Using the SIFL coun-terfactual, in 2011 airline deregulation created $31 billion (in 2011 dollars) in benefits for consumers (Borenstein and Rose 2014).

In addition to the Airline Deregulation Act of 1978, the deregulation movement under President Ford and President Carter included the Railroad Revitalization and Regulatory Reform Act of 1976, the Motor Carrier Act of 1980, and the Depository Institutions Deregulation and Monetary Control Act of 1980. Alfred Kahn (1988) argued that airline deregulation helped make possible the deregulation of these other major industries.

Most of the Federal regulatory actions tabulated in the figures in this chapter are not economic regulations but instead are social regulatory actions designed to protect workers, public health, safety, and/or the envi-ronment, or to promote other social goals. OMB (2003) advises the Federal agencies issuing these regulatory actions that, in competitive markets, there should be a presumption against price controls, production or sales quotas, mandatory uniform quality standards, or controls on entry into employment or production. In this way, the lessons learned in the deregulation movement of the 1970s continue to shape current Federal regulatory practices.

Federal regulatory actions range from simple housekeeping to actions that change manufacturing processes, business practices, and ultimately the prices and availability of consumer goods and services. Between January 2000 and November 2018, OMB reviewed over 4,000 significant final rules. The Department of Health and Human Services accounted for 16 percent of the final rules reviewed by OMB, followed by the Environmental Protection Agency, with 11 percent, and the Department of Agriculture, with 8 percent. The Department of Transportation and Department of Commerce round out the top five agencies with the most final rules since 2000. Together, these top five rulemaking agencies accounted for almost half the significant rules reviewed this century, while 44 other Federal agencies issued the remainder of the final rules (figure 2-2). It needs to be noted that an OMB review is currently not required for actions issued by Federal independent regulatory agencies. Until 2018, an OMB review was also not generally required for tax regulatory actions taken by the Department of the Treasury.

In its annual *Reports to Congress*, OMB provides an accounting of the benefits and costs of selected major rules published in the preceding fiscal year. Figure 2-3 shows the regulatory costs created by the new rules included in OMB's *Reports* each year from 2000 through 2018, and the planned costs from the OMB Regulatory Budget for 2019. Figure 2-4 shows the simple accumulation—ignoring interactions—of the costs of Federal regulatory actions. Regulatory costs are measured in constant, inflation-adjusted 2017 dollars and are on an annualized basis to show the ongoing costs that the rules will continue to impose on the economy. We report the midpoints of OMB's ranges of estimated costs. From 2000 through 2016, the annual trend was for regulatory costs to grow by $8.2 billion each year. If regulatory costs continued to grow at that rate, cumulative costs would reach over $163 billion by 2019 (figure 2-4).

However, the regulatory landscape changed in 2017 and 2018. From 2000 to 2018, the simple accumulation of regulatory costs totaled $138 billion, which is just over 11 percent lower than what would have been predicted based on the trend from 2000 to 2016 (figure 2-4; also see box 2-3 on small businesses' perspectives on regulatory costs). The growth in regulatory costs did not just slow down; it reversed. In fiscal years 2017 and 2018, deregulatory actions resulted in regulatory cost savings that more than offset the costs of new regulatory actions. Since 1981, Federal agencies have used a systematic general framework to estimate the costs of new regulatory actions, but over time there have been differences in methodologies and assumptions (OMB 2006). With this caveat in mind, from 1981 through 2016, cost savings from deregulatory actions more than offset new regulatory costs in only three years—in 1981 and 1982, which were the first two years of the Reagan Administration; and in 2001 when the Congressional Review Act was used to repeal a costly rule about workplace repetitive-motion injuries (OMB 2006).[3]

In this chapter, we define "deregulation" as any action by the government that reduces its control over business and consumer decisions. There are several ways to deregulate. Federal agencies' deregulatory actions account for most of the cost savings shown in figure 2-3. Deregulatory actions include revising regulatory processes, modifying existing rules, and eliminating existing rules. Deregulatory actions also include periodic updates of rules, such as fishing quotas or medical reimbursement rates, that save regulatory costs. For

---

[3] Because the rule about repetitive-motion injuries was repealed, later OMB reports do not include the rule's estimated costs in 2000 or the cost savings from its repeal in 2001. OMB also revises its estimates when needed. In figures 2-3 and 2-4, we use the later reports, which do not show a net cost savings in 2001.

Figure 2-2. OMB-Reviewed Final Rules, by Agency, 2000–2018

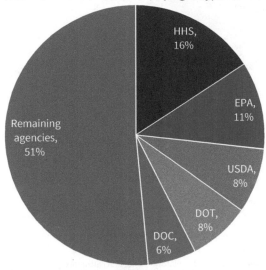

Sources: Office of Management and Budget (OMB); CEA calculations.
Note: HHS = Department of Health and Human Services; EPA = Environmental Protection
Agency; USDA = Department of Agriculture; DOT = Department of Transportation; DOC =
Department of Commerce. The percentage calculation includes all the final rules reviewed
by OMB per agency from January 1, 2000, to October 31, 2018.

Figure 2-3. Real Annual Costs of Major Rules, Fiscal Years 2000–2019

Dollars (billions, 2017)

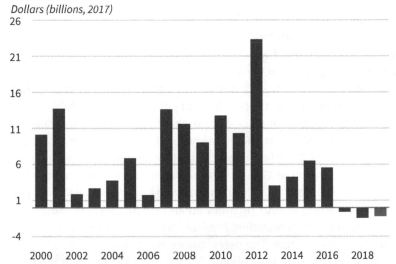

Sources: Office of Information and Regulatory Affairs (OIRA); CEA calculations.
Note: The cost estimates for years 2000–2016 are taken from the most recent *OIRA Report
to Congress* with an estimate for that year. The real cost estimate for 2019 is a projected
estimate from the OIRA Regulatory Budget for fiscal year 2019. Annual cost estimates
include all major rules for which both benefits and costs have been estimated.

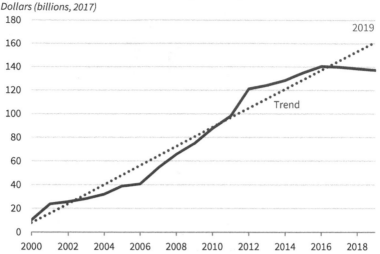

Figure 2-4. Cumulative Costs of Major Rules, Fiscal Years 2000–2019

Dollars (billions, 2017)

Sources: Office of Information and Regulatory Affairs; CEA calculations.
Note: Cumulative costs begin in 2000, assuming there are no costs from before fiscal year 2000.
Data from figure 2-3 were used to determine the yearly cumulative costs. The trend is calculated
for 2002 through 2016.

example, the National Oceanic and Atmospheric Administration is required by law to periodically review designations and protections of essential fish habitats. The 2018 revision of essential fish habitat designations opened large areas off the coast of New England to commercial sea scallop harvesting, resulting in a net economic benefit of $654 million.

Congress can deregulate by passing legislation that alters the statutory regulatory requirements. The economic deregulation movement of the 1970s involved major legislative actions to deregulate the trucking and airline industries (see box 2-2). More recently, the Tax Cuts and Jobs Act of 2017 included a provision that removed the tax penalty that enforced the Affordable Care Act's (ACA) mandate that individuals had to purchase health insurance (see chapter 4). The 2018 Economic Growth, Regulatory Relief, and Consumer Protection Act modified regulation of the banking industry (see chapter 6). Congress can also use its authority under the 1996 Congressional Review Act to eliminate Federal regulatory actions. From 1996 through 2016, the Congressional Review Act had only been used once, in 2001 (mentioned above). In 2017, Congress used the act to overturn 15 rules, including the Fair Pay and Safe Workplaces rule and the Stream Protection rule. The deregulatory action for those two rules alone resulted in total cost savings of about $500 million. In 2018, Congress used the

Box 2-3. Small Businesses and the Regulatory Burden

Owners of small businesses have their own perspective on regulatory costs. The National Federation of Independent Business (NFIB 2001) regularly conducts monthly surveys of small business owners. One monthly NFIB survey question asks small businesses to identify the "single most important problem facing [their] business." They are given a list of common small business burdens and allowed to write in responses. Between 2012 and the election of President Trump, the NFIB reported that government regulation was the most frequently cited top concern for small businesses, at about 45 percent of the time. (The last report before the election was in October 2016. Survey responses do not distinguish between concerns about Federal regulations versus State or local regulations.) Since the election, regulation has never been the most frequently cited top concern of small businesses. NFIB also conducts monthly surveys assessing small business optimism. Figure 2-i shows an upward recent trend in the NFIB index of small business optimism. Small business optimism began to sharply increase after the November 2016 election and has now reached record highs.

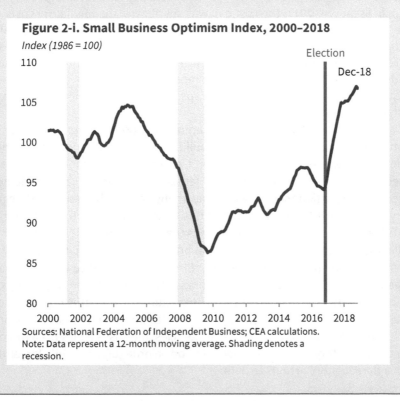

Figure 2-i. Small Business Optimism Index, 2000–2018

Index (1986 = 100)

Sources: National Federation of Independent Business; CEA calculations.
Note: Data represent a 12-month moving average. Shading denotes a recession.

act to overturn guidance issued in 2013 by the Bureau of Consumer Financial Protection.[4] Finally, deregulation can also result from litigation.

The Trump Administration's Regulatory Cost Caps Are Reducing Costs

The turnaround in the growth of regulatory costs is the direct result of the regulatory cost caps that were established early in the Trump Administration. In fiscal year 2017, there were 67 deregulatory actions and 3 new significant regulatory actions (22-for-1), saving in net present value $8.1 billion in regulatory costs. Of the deregulatory actions in fiscal year 2017, 15 were significant (5-for-1; see box 2-1 for a definition of significant actions). In fiscal year 2018, there were 176 deregulatory actions and 14 new significant regulatory actions (12-for-1), saving in net present value $23 billion in regulatory costs. Of the deregulatory actions in fiscal year 2018, 57 were significant (4-for-1). This turnaround reflects President Trump's January 30, 2017, Executive Order 13771, "Reducing Regulation and Controlling Regulatory Costs." This Executive Order requires Federal agencies to eliminate, on average, two regulatory actions for each new regulatory action and, for the first time, to meet a regulatory cost cap. In fiscal year 2017, the cost cap was set at zero; the regulatory costs created by any new regulatory actions had to be at least offset by deregulatory actions. In 2018, across all agencies, the cap was set at a $9.8 billion (present value) reduction in regulatory costs. In the first two years under Executive Order 13771, Federal agencies have more than met both the two-for-one requirement and the regulatory cost caps. See box 2-4 for more discussion of notable deregulatory actions.

Deregulation has been faster than many experts thought possible. The notice-and-comment requirements build a lot of inertia into the Federal rulemaking process for regulatory and deregulatory actions. Shortly after Executive Order 13771 was issued, Potter (2017) cautioned that to undo existing regulatory actions could take "many, many years." The record of deregulatory actions in 2017 and 2018 allays this concern. Looking to the future, for 2019 Federal agencies have adopted caps that, when met, will save another $18 billion in projected regulatory costs (net present value). In addition, in 2019 the Department of Transportation and the EPA expect to finalize a proposed rule regarding corporate average fuel economy. The $18 billion in regulatory cost savings in 2019 (net present value) do not include the potential regulatory cost savings from this rule. The Administration notes the impact separately in order to highlight ongoing reform across all agencies; the cost savings from this one-time deregulatory action are expected to be an order of magnitude larger than other deregulatory actions to date.

---

[4] The act states that Congress has 60 days after the rule is submitted to overturn it; because the 2013 policy guidance had not been submitted to Congress in 2013 for review, the 2018 Congress could overturn it.

Box 2-4. Notable Deregulatory Actions

Previous administrations have issued costly regulatory actions affecting markets for labor, energy, insurance, education, and credit—to name a few. These regulatory actions were imposing a large cumulative cost, and they reduced economic growth for the reasons examined in this chapter. Many of these actions have been overturned during the Trump Administration. And some of these overturned regulations were also notable, even when viewed in isolation.

In the labor area, the National Labor Relations Board (NLRB) had expanded the definitions of joint employer and independent contractor that would have reduced competition and productivity in labor markets, as discussed at the end of this chapter. The NLRB had also permitted "micro-unions," which means that subsets of employees could organize even if the majority of employees did not want to be represented by a labor union.

Several notable regulations from the previous Administration substantially added to employers' compliance costs. Its Overtime Rule required employers to track hours worked by a wider range of employees, including a number of white-collar workers, even though the rule would not substantially increase workers' pay as shown by basic economics (Trejo 1991) and as verified empirically by an economist at the Department of Labor (Barkume 2010). Furchtgott-Roth (2018) details the Trump Administration's changes in these rules, as well as changes to other notable rules affecting employers such as the Persuader Rule, the Fiduciary Rule, and Fair Pay and Safe Workplaces Executive Order.

The Federal Communications Commission's Open Internet Order (commonly called the Net Neutrality rule) restricted pricing practices by Internet service providers. Like price controls more generally, the rule would have resulted in a less productive allocation of resources. The commission repealed the rule in 2017.

Regulations may be increasing entry barriers and reducing competition in higher education, including Gainful Employment Regulations and the Borrower Defense Rule. The Trump Administration's Department of Education is currently reviewing these and other notable regulations.

Chapter 5 of this *Report* discusses how energy productivity has been enhanced by repealing or revising notable prior rules, including the Clean Power Plan, the Waters of the United States, the Waste Prevention Rule, the Stream Protection Rule, and the closure of an area on the coastal plain of the Arctic National Wildlife Refuge. The Safer Affordable Fuel Efficient (SAFE) Vehicles rule is also discussed below.

Notable health insurance deregulations include the setting of the ACA's individual mandate penalty to zero, giving small businesses more flexibility to join associated health plans, and eliminating previous restrictions on the sales of short-term, limited duration insurance (see the end of this chapter and chapter 4 of this *Report*).

Regulations had also hindered productivity and competition in the financial and banking sector. Chapter 6 of this *Report* discusses the Trump Administration's actions to reform implementation of the Dodd-Frank Act, nullify the Consumer Financial Protection Bureau's Arbitration Rule, and revise the National Credit Union Administration's Corporate Credit Union Rule.

The regulatory cost caps establish an incremental regulatory budget and create new incentives for Federal agencies. Rosen and Callanan (2014) provide a useful history and discussion of the idea of a regulatory budget. In 1980, the CEA described a regulatory budget "as a framework for looking at the total financial burden imposed by regulations, for setting some limits to this burden, and for making trade-offs within those limits" (CEA 1980, 125). Instead of establishing a budget limit on total regulatory costs—which, as the CEA mentioned, are hard to measure—Executive Order 13771 establishes a budget in terms of the incremental costs added or reduced by new actions; this Executive Order builds on earlier efforts to encourage retrospective regulatory review (see box 2-5).

Within each agency, the caps create internal incentives to prioritize costly regulations, to limit the compliance costs of new regulatory actions, and to remove outdated or inefficient existing actions. Breyer (1993, 11) argued that agencies often suffer from tunnel vision and pursue "a single goal too far, to the point where it brings about more harm than good." The cost caps help expand an agency's focus of vision. To pursue its agency-specific mission—for example, the EPA's mission to protect human health and the environment; under Executive Order 13771, the EPA now also has internal incentives to pay greater attention to regulatory costs. For example, Rosen (2016, 53) pointed out that given a regulatory budget, "an excessively costly regulation would come at an opportunity cost to the agency, because it would require the agency to forgo other regulatory initiatives." For the same reason, the regulatory budget gives the agency incentives to consider deregulatory actions, including the removal of outdated or inefficient rules. Although an agency that suffers from tunnel vision might tend to look mainly for opportunities to expand its regulatory portfolio, the cost caps shift the agency's focus to how it might alter its regulatory portfolio toward more cost-effective actions.

By creating an incremental regulatory budget, the cost caps serve a function similar to private businesses' accounts and to the Federal government's fiscal budget. Demski (2008) described the managerial uses of business accounting information as focusing on two questions—What might it cost? and Did it cost too much? The private sector business manager uses the information in the accounts to judge how well the management of each company division

Box 2-5. Retrospective Regulatory Review

In addition to conducting reviews of new regulatory actions, the Executive Orders issued by Presidents Reagan, Clinton, and Obama instructed Federal agencies to conduct retrospective reviews of currently effective regulatory actions (respectively, Executive Orders 12291, 12866, and 13563). The GAO (2007, 2014) and Aldy (2014) discuss the history of these efforts in detail.

In his 2012 State of the Union Address, President Obama highlighted the retrospective review of an EPA rule that, since the 1970s, had defined milk as an "oil" and forced some dairy farmers to spend $10,000 a year to prove that they could contain an oil spill. The elimination of this requirement was estimated to result in $146 million (in 2009 dollars) annually in regulatory costs savings. But it is perhaps more notable that the requirement was in place for over three decades. A report for the Administrative Conference of the United States assessed the broader impact of President Obama's emphasis on retrospective review (Aldy 2014). The study examined all major rules listed in the 2013 and 2014 OMB *Reports to Congress*. In 2013 and 2014, the ratio of deregulatory actions to new regulatory actions was 1 to 10, compared with the ratio of 4 to 1 achieved in 2018. (Including nonmajor deregulatory actions, the 2018 ratio was 12 to 1.)

A retrospective review yielded cost savings from 2012 to 2016. However, as shown above in figures 2-3 and 2-4, the total regulatory costs of major rules grew especially rapidly in 2012 and more slowly in the years 2013–16; by comparison, total regulatory costs fell in 2017 and 2018. Raso (2017) concluded that retrospective reviews were a "credible but small component of the Obama administration's rulemaking efforts."

DeMenno (2017, 8) studied public participation in agencies' retrospective review processes initiated in 2011. She found 3,227 comments across the 10 agencies in her sample, which she described as "significantly lower than agencies often receive for rulemakings." The EPA received somewhat over 800 comments and the Department of Education received 30 comments, compared with the 63,000 and 16,300 comments, respectively, that these agencies received about the Trump Administration's deregulation initiative.

and how well each division's strategy have performed. In a similar way, the executive branch can use the information in the incremental regulatory budget to judge how well each agency has performed—that is, how well each agency uses regulatory actions to improve societal welfare. A key difference between a private business and a Federal agency is that regulatory actions impose unreimbursed costs on private parties to comply with the actions. Because regulatory costs are like a hidden tax, the incremental regulatory budget also plays a similar role as the Federal government's fiscal budget. Without a regulatory budget, agencies might tend to treat private resources as a "free good" (Rosen

2016). Moreover, like the Federal budget, the regulatory budget strengthens political accountability and transparency (Rosen and Callanan 2014).

OIRA sets the regulatory cost caps that will be allowed for each agency. The cost caps may allow an increase or require a net reduction in regulatory costs. The cost caps impose a discipline on Federal agencies but allow for flexibility when agencies identify important new regulatory opportunities to better protect the public. OMB's guidance also allows agencies to accumulate cost savings. Otherwise, agencies would have an incentive to enact new regulatory actions at the end of the year so as to use up any regulatory cost savings that exceeded that year's cap.

The general public—including workers, consumers, owners of small businesses, and other interested parties—also contribute to the deregulatory reform process. The Administrative Procedures Act sets out the steps that Federal agencies must follow to take new regulatory and deregulatory actions (Garvey 2017). In the first step of the most common notice-and-comment process, the agency proposes a rule and invites public comment through a Notice of Proposed Rulemaking. Sometimes, public comment is solicited even earlier before issuing a prospective rule, through an Advance Notice of Proposed Rulemaking. These notices are published in the *Federal Register*. The public can also view and comment on proposed regulatory and deregulatory actions online via the website regulations.gov. The Trump Administration encourages public input on its deregulation initiatives. The Administration's Executive Order 13777 requires Federal agencies to establish Regulatory Reform Task Forces, and many agencies' task forces issue specific requests for public comment. For instance, in response to its request, the EPA received more than 460,000 public comments. After taking into account identical or nearly identical form letters, the EPA received 63,000 unique comments. The Department of Education received over 16,300 comments in response to its request. The workers, consumers, and business owners who participate in the regulated markets provided information from their own experiences about the likely effects of deregulation.

Several other countries have used regulatory caps similar to the Trump Administration's approach to deregulation (Gayer, Litan, and Wallach 2017; Renda 2017). Some countries have placed caps on regulatory requirements or actions, while others have placed caps on regulatory costs. In 2001, the Canadian province of British Columbia required that for every new regulatory requirement, two regulatory requirements must be eliminated. After having reduced regulatory requirements by 40 percent by 2004, the requirement was changed to a cap of no net increase in regulatory requirements. The provincial government reports that since 2001, these steps have reduced regulatory requirements by 49 percent (British Columbia 2017). In 2012, the Government of Canada (2015) required that for every new regulation (which are much less numerous than regulatory requirements), one regulation must be eliminated.

The Netherlands, Denmark, Norway, and the United Kingdom have adopted targets for net reductions in regulatory costs—that is, regulatory cost caps (Renda 2017).

Although Executive Order 13771 requires U.S. Federal agencies to estimate reductions in opportunity costs broadly defined, other countries focus on narrower measures, such as administrative burdens, compliance costs, or direct costs imposed on businesses (Renda 2017). Using narrower measures can have unintended consequences. For example, in the United Kingdom, requiring large retailers to charge for plastic bags was counted as a reduction in the net costs to businesses, even though this cost reduction was exactly offset by the increase in consumer costs (Morse 2016).

The Trump Administration's deregulatory process, established by Executive Order 13771, is crafted to achieve significant and sustained progress toward reducing the regulatory burden on the U.S. economy. After reviewing the recent history in the United States and other countries, Gayer, Litan, and Wallach (2017) note the potential of the Administration's deregulation efforts but caution that these efforts might not go far enough, or might go too far. The deregulatory actions in 2017 and 2018, and those planned for 2019, show that these efforts are overcoming the inertia built into the Federal rulemaking notice-and-comment process. At the same time, the requirement that deregulatory actions must be subject to the same rigorous cost-benefit analysis required of new regulatory actions helps ensure that deregulation will not go too far.

Why More Deregulation?

This section seeks to answer the question of why there needs to be more deregulation. First, it examines estimates of the aggregate cost of regulation. And second, it considers the need to level the playing field for deregulation.

Estimates of the Aggregate Cost of Regulation

Up to this point, we have focused on studies of the burden or costs of Federal regulatory actions. Of course, State and local regulatory actions also impose costs. State and local actions are too diverse to easily summarize, but examples help illustrate their range. Chapter 3 of this *Report* describes the extent and variation across States in occupational licensing. In the first half of 2018, just under one-quarter of all workers reported that they had an active professional certification or license, usually because it is required for employment. As another example, State laws regulating the beer industry are so inconsistent that it leads industry leaders to describe the domestic market as "like selling in fifty different countries almost" (Morrison 2013). State regulatory actions often prevent brewers from selling directly to customers. Although there is no conclusive evidence that these laws limit craft beer entrepreneurship, statistical associations show that there are more breweries in places that provide easier access to markets for small producers (Malone and Lusk 2016).

Local regulatory actions add to the cumulative regulatory burden. Last year, we discussed the impact of local land use regulations, including an estimate that with decreased zoning restrictions in three cities—New York, San Jose, and San Francisco—the growth rate of aggregate output between 1964 and 2009 could have increased enough to increase GDP in 2009 by 8.9 percent (CEA 2018). Turning to other local regulations, the U.S. Chamber of Commerce Foundation (2014b, 11) ranks 10 U.S. cities on their regulatory environment for small businesses. The study uses the World Bank's Doing Business framework and compiles publicly available information from official U.S. sources (World Bank 2018). According to this measure, "Dallas and Saint Louis impose the lightest regulatory burdens on small businesses," whereas New York, San Francisco, and Los Angeles impose heavy burdens. For example, in New York starting a business requires 7 procedures, dealing with construction permits requires 15 procedures, and registering property requires 7 procedures. In another study, the U.S. Chamber of Commerce Foundation (2014a) examined regulations for food trucks. Boston and San Francisco, for example, require 32 procedures to open a new food truck, compared with Denver's 10 required procedures.

Some efforts have been made to estimate the total costs of regulatory actions in the United States. One approach is to build the total cost estimate from the bottom up, using regulatory action- and industry-specific estimates of regulatory costs. Taking this approach, the costs of Federal social regulation (i.e., actions designed to promote social purposes, including the protection of workers, public health, safety, and the environment) were estimated to be $198 billion in 1997 (in 1996 dollars) (OMB 1997). The 1997 estimate was built up from earlier studies, and then added OMB estimates of the costs of new regulatory actions from 1987 to 1996. OMB continued to use this approach through 2000, when it estimated that the total regulatory costs were in the range of $146 billion to $229 billion (in 1996 dollars). We updated the estimated total regulatory costs to 2018 by adding OMB's estimates of the costs of new regulatory actions after 2000 to the 2000 estimate. This exercise yields a midrange estimate that the total regulatory costs in the U.S. in 2018 were $421 billion (all costs adjusted to 2017 dollars). Taking the same general approach but using additional sources, a study published by the Competitive Enterprise Institute estimated the total costs of social regulations in the U.S. in 2018 were $1.2 trillion (Crews 2018).

OMB and a report by the Congressional Research Service noted important limitations for bottom-up estimates of regulatory costs. First, estimated costs are available for only a small fraction of all regulatory actions. Second, there are difficult questions about the quality of the original underlying data and analyses (OMB 2002; Carey 2016). Moreover, at a conceptual level, the simple sum of action-specific costs does not necessarily provide an accurate measure of total regulatory costs. A major theme of this chapter is that the cumulative burden of multiple regulatory actions exceeds the simple sum of costs when each action is considered one by one. In light of these limitations, OMB (2002) deemphasized estimates of total costs, and subsequent OMB *Reports* no longer included them. Instead, the current practice is to focus on the last 10 years of major Federal regulatory actions (OMB 2017b).

Cross-country comparisons provide a different perspective on the extent of U.S. regulatory actions and on these actions' potential to improve economic performance. Cross-country comparisons from a number of different studies suggest that in the recent past, the regulatory burden in the United States was lower than in many, but not all, other countries. The cross-country rankings are not sufficiently current to reflect the Trump Administration's deregulatory actions. In the most recent data, the United States was 8th out of the 190 rated economies in the Ease of Doing Business ranking, lagging behind New Zealand, Singapore, Denmark, Hong Kong, South Korea, Georgia, and Norway (World Bank 2018). The United States is 27th out of 35 countries in the product market regulation ranking by the Organization for Economic Cooperation and Development (OECD) (CEA 2018).[5] A total of 3 of the top 4 OECD ranked countries have adopted regulatory caps—the Netherlands, ranked first; the United Kingdom, second; and Denmark, fourth. In last year's *Report*, we estimated that if the United States adopted structural reforms and achieved the same level of product market regulation as the Netherlands, U.S. real GDP would be 2.2 percent higher over 10 years (CEA 2018). In the Economic Freedom of the World overall ranking, the United States is sixth, trailing Hong Kong, Singapore, New Zealand, Switzerland, and Ireland.

These cross-comparisons also provide the basis for top-down estimates of total U.S. regulatory costs. The Congressional Research Service (Carey 2016) describes a prominent example of a top-down estimate from a report for the National Association of Manufacturers (Crain and Crain 2014). Crain and Crain use the World Economic Forum's Executive Opinion Survey to develop a proxy measure of the amount of regulation in each of 34 OECD member countries from 2006 to 2013. (The proxy measure is not the same as the OECD product market regulation index or the other cross-country indices discussed above.) They estimate a regression model that shows GDP per capita as a function of the regulation index and a set of control variables that capture other influences on GDP. They find a statistically significant association between their index of

---

[5]As noted in chapter 8 of this *Report*, the OECD product market survey was limited to the State of New York, and therefore may not be representative of the rest of the country. The data show that the United States is suffering from relatively high regulatory protection of established firms, due to exemptions from antitrust laws for publicly controlled firms (OECD 2018). In addition, the OECD notes that U.S. product market regulation is more restrictive than that of other OECD economies due to the prevalence of State-level ownership of certain enterprises, particularly in the energy and transportation sectors.

low regulatory burden and GDP per capita. They also compared the U.S. score on the regulation index with the average score on the regulation index in five benchmark countries with the lowest regulatory burdens. On the basis of this comparison, they estimate that if the burden of regulation in the United States were as low as in the benchmarks, U.S. GDP would be $1.4 trillion higher. This estimate forms one component of their estimate of the total regulatory costs in the United States (Crain and Crain 2014).

The Congressional Research Service notes that there have been a number of criticisms of this top-down estimate of regulatory costs (Carey 2016). It would be useful for policymakers to know the impact of different broad regulatory programs on the value of goods and services that the U.S. economy can produce. Comparing GDP per capita achieved by different countries that have taken different regulatory approaches mimics this thought experiment. In principle, the top-down approach should capture the cumulative burdens of regulatory actions. However, there are fundamental methodological challenges regarding how to measure regulatory burden across countries and on the validity of drawing causal inferences from the estimated statistical associations. Further econometric specification issues include the selection of the dependent and independent variables and the correct functional form of the relationship between the dependent and independent variables.

To sum up, total regulatory costs in the United States are difficult to estimate with precision. However, the cost estimates—which range from almost half a trillion to over a trillion dollars—are sufficiently large to justify the argument that deregulatory actions should be considered as a priority to help sustain U.S. economic growth. The cross-country comparisons of regulatory burdens also suggest that there is room to reduce the burden in the United States.

The Need to Level the Playing Field for Deregulation

If regulatory review worked perfectly, it might seem that deregulation would never be needed. Each deregulatory action is subjected to the same cost-benefit analysis required for new regulatory actions (OMB 2017a). Regulatory review thus requires that a deregulatory action's benefits (the regulatory costs saved) must justify the action's costs (the benefits forgone when the original regulatory action is modified or eliminated). The original regulatory review should have ensured that the benefits of the original regulatory action justified its costs. If the results of the original regulatory review were correct and unchanging, a deregulatory action should never be needed, and indeed should not pass regulatory review itself.

However, until the use of regulatory cost caps, the regulatory process was likely to have been tilted toward the benefits of expanding the regulatory state. Because regulatory actions address agencies' core missions—such as protecting workers, public health, safety, and the environment—there is a natural tendency for the analyses to emphasize benefits over costs. In the past, some agencies' regulatory analyses came across like advocacy documents "to *justify* a predetermined decision, rather than to *inform* the decision" (Broughel 2015, 380); emphasis in the original). OMB's OIRA regulatory review process provides a check on this tendency. In the extreme, the focus on agency-specific missions leads to tunnel vision, causing regulators to go too far in pursuing their agencies' missions (Breyer 1993). The economic theory of regulation and public choice economics provide additional insights into the functioning of government bureaucracies. Regulatory actions can serve the interests of established firms in the industry—for example, by creating barriers that prevent the entry of new firms (Stigler 1971). Chapter 3 of this *Report* reviews evidence that State professional licensing requirements serve as barriers to entry rather than promoting the public interest. In addition to altruistic support for an agency's mission, Niskanen (1971) argues that self-interested regulators pursue actions that expand the scope and size of their agency.

Several examples illustrate the possible tilt in agencies' past analyses toward the benefits of regulatory actions over the costs.[6] Dudley and Mannix (2018) criticize RIAs of air-quality regulations. More generally, Dudley and Mannix (2018, 9) argue that agencies do not appear to search for benefits and costs objectively but instead focus on benefits and "quantify or list every conceivable good thing that they can attribute to a decision to issue new regulations." Gayer and Viscusi (2016) provide a detailed discussion of the controversial question of whether Federal agencies should measure the benefits of climate change policies from a domestic or global perspective. The "Circular A-4" guidance document (OMB 2003) instructs Federal agencies to focus on regulatory benefits and costs to citizens and residents of the United States. When a regulatory action has effects beyond the borders of the United States, agencies are told to report those effects separately (OMB 2003). However, previous analyses have compared the global benefits of major environmental regulatory actions with domestic compliance costs. For example, the EPA estimated that the proposed Clean Power Plan would yield global climate benefits in 2030 worth $30 billion (in 2011 dollars) (79 *FR* 67406). Gayer and Viscusi (2016) find that this estimate falls to $2.1 to $6.9 billion (in 2011 dollars), counting only domestic climate benefits. In contrast, Pizer and others (2014) argued that the global perspective is appropriate given the distinctive nature of the climate change problem and the need for global solutions.

---

[6] The tilt toward benefits does not hold across the board. For example, Department of Homeland Security's RIAs are often unable to quantify the benefits of safety rules that address high-consequence / low-probability events. However, the lack of quantified benefits does not necessarily avoid, and might even exacerbate, the tilt toward benefits. Under Executive Order 12866, when benefits and/or costs are unquantified, RIAs discuss whether the benefits of a regulatory action "justify" the costs. The subjective judgment about whether unquantified benefits justify the costs might allow more room for an intentional or unintentional tilt toward benefits.

Whether intentionally or not, other analyses have downplayed costs. For example, a regulatory analysis concluded that a 2016 rule that placed limits on consumers' options to purchase short-term health insurance would have no effect on the majority of consumers who purchased such coverage, but did not provide quantified evidence for this conclusion. In 2018, an analysis of a deregulatory reform of the 2016 rule discussed the potential for regulatory cost savings and concluded that the deregulatory action was likely to be economically significant and have an annual impact of over $100 million. The Congressional Budget Office (CBO 2018) projected that the 2018 deregulatory reform will lead to 2 million additional enrollees in short-term insurance. The 2018 deregulatory action did more than just remove the 2016 rule's restrictions. There is also uncertainty about the effects of the 2016 regulatory action and the 2018 deregulatory action. Despite these caveats, however, it is hard to reconcile the finding that the 2016 rule was not economically significant with the CBO's projections and with further analysis, which estimated that the 2018 deregulatory action of the short-term health insurance market will provide cost savings worth $7.3 billion in 2021 (CEA 2019).

A body of research compares the results of agencies' prospective regulatory analyses conducted before the rules were passed with the results of retrospective analyses conducted afterward (Harrington, Morgenstern, and Nelson 2000; OMB 2005; Morgenstern 2018). These comparisons of prospective and retrospective analyses have focused on the accuracy of the original estimates. However, the prospective/retrospective comparisons do not address the problem that important categories of costs were omitted entirely in the original analysis (Harrington, Morgenstern, and Nelson 2000). Moreover, the prospective/retrospective comparisons do not shed light on the magnitude of the omitted costs or how including them might have changed the results of the prospective analyses.

Whether intentionally or not, omitting important categories of costs will result in systematic underestimation of costs. Regulatory analyses typically focus on compliance costs, which are the most obvious source of opportunity costs. For example, Belfield, Bowden, and Rodriguez (2018) reviewed 28 RIAs of education regulatory actions from 2006 to 2015. They found that the education RIAs only calculated the paperwork costs of documenting compliance with regulatory actions—what Belfield, Bowden, and Rodiguez call the administrative compliance costs. Opportunity costs include, but are not limited to, administrative and other compliance costs. When a firm hires workers and purchases new capital equipment to comply with a regulatory action, for example, society gives up the value of the other goods and services that those workers and capital could have produced. Aggregate paperwork costs of regulation are substantial; if the 9.8 billion hours devoted to regulatory paperwork in 2015 instead were used by employees to create output equal to their average hourly earnings, it would total $245.1 billion, an amount equal to 1.35 percent of that year's GDP (CEA 2018). But other sources of opportunity costs can be more subtle and difficult to see (see box 2-6). For example, when the intended or unintended consequence of a regulatory action is to prevent a purchase, the action prevents a mutually beneficial exchange. The buyer's potential gain is measured by the consumer's surplus—the difference between the maximum the consumer is willing to pay and the amount actually paid. The seller's potential gain is measured by producer's surplus—the difference between the minimum the producer is willing to accept and the amount actually received. The losses of consumer and producer surpluses are part, and potentially a large part, of the regulatory action's opportunity costs.

Federal agencies' analyses do not always measure consumer and producer surpluses because to do so would require estimates of the elasticities of demand and supply. OMB (2000, 13) argues that estimating consumer and producer surpluses "requires data that [are] usually not easily obtained and assumptions that are at best only educated guesses." The difficulty of measuring opportunity costs has often been discussed in subsequent OMB *Reports*, although different Administrations have given it different emphases (Fraas and Morgenstern 2014).

Even without a preceding tilt toward the benefits of the regulatory state, there are several other reasons deregulation will be needed and can lead to regulatory cost savings that more than offset the forgone benefits of the original regulatory action. First, in a dynamic economy, new products and technological developments will often require new approaches. For example, as the drone industry took off, the Federal Aviation Administration amended its rules to allow small, unmanned aircraft systems in airspace, and it changed the certification requirement of drones' remote pilots (81 *FR* 42063). Small, unmanned aircraft do not raise the same safety concerns as manned aircraft. The flight training and other requirements for pilots of manned aircraft imposed high regulatory costs and created few benefits when applied to pilots of drones. The development of automated vehicles poses similar challenges for the Department of Transportation (DOT). As a first step, DOT now interprets the definitions of "driver" and "operator" as not referring exclusively to a human but also to an automated system. And DOT (2018) encourages the developers of automated driving systems to adopt voluntary technical standards as an effective nonregulatory approach.

Second, new information can emerge that requires the reevaluation of regulatory actions. For example, after the Food and Drug Administration (FDA) issued a rule to implement the Food Labeling Act, companies and trade associations told the FDA about the difficulty of updating labels within the required time frame. The industry's concerns included the need for new software, the need to obtain additional nutritional information about its products, and the possible need to reformulate its products. In a deregulatory action, the FDA extended the compliance date by 1.5 years (83 *FR* 19619). The cost savings

Box 2-6. Opportunity Costs, Ride Sharing, and What Is Not Seen

The opportunity cost of a regulatory action is the value of the activities forgone because of the action. In a classic essay, the 19th-century French economist Frédéric Bastiat argued that taking into account not only that which is seen but also that which is not seen is the difference between a "good economist" and a "bad economist." His parable of the broken window is an example of opportunity costs. The "bad economist" concludes that the broken window is good for the economy; when the shopkeeper pays the glazier to repair the window, it encourages the glazier's trade. But the "good economist" recognizes that which is not seen; because the window needs to be repaired, the shopkeeper loses the enjoyment from the forgone opportunities to make other purchases. Likewise, in addition to the more easily seen compliance costs, regulatory actions often involve substantial opportunity costs.

Measuring the opportunity costs of regulatory actions can be difficult; they are not easily seen. The development of ride sharing provides an example where the opportunity costs of regulating the taxi industry can be estimated. Most major U.S. cities restrict entry into the taxi industry. A typical regulatory approach is to require taxi medallions, which are transferrable permits required to operate a taxi (Cetin and Deakin 2017). The restriction on entry drove up the price of taxi rides and created monopoly profits for the owners of medallions, which could be worth hundreds of thousands of dollars. Ride-sharing services including Uber and Lyft provide a close substitute for the services provided by taxis. The competition from ride-sharing services eroded medallion holders' market power and led to sharp decreases in medallion prices. Cohen and others (2016) analyze data on almost 50 million individual-level observations of users of the UberX service. The researchers exploit the richness of the data to estimate that in 2015, the UberX service generated about $2.9 billion in consumer surplus in the four cities studied. The gain in consumer surplus from UberX sheds light on the opportunity costs of the cities' regulation of taxis. The "bad economist" might conclude that restricting the number of taxis was good for the economy because it increased taxi owners' profits. But the "good economist" recognizes that which was not seen: the value consumers gain when ride-sharing services compete with taxis.

Reviews of deregulatory actions should attempt to account for as much of the opportunity costs as possible. Current guidance already stresses the importance of measuring opportunity costs (OMB 2003). Economic theory sometimes does not provide a simple formula to extrapolate the unseen opportunity costs from more easily observed regulatory compliance causes. Nevertheless, careful analysis and consideration of the likely consequences of regulatory actions will shed light on the opportunity costs savings that are possible from deregulatory actions. Public input into the deregulatory process is likely to be helpful in this exercise.

from the delay offset the benefits forgone because of the delay. The extension of the compliance dates does not prevent companies from revising their labels sooner, and data show that over 29,000 products have already adopted the new Nutrition Facts label (83 *FR* 19619). The extension reduces compliance costs while still promoting public health by helping consumers make better decisions about their food choices.

Another example of an agency using new information to reduce regulatory costs is the Federal Aviation Administration's (FAA) revision of a rule to allow ground tests of helicopters to demonstrate compliance for night operations. The FAA's airworthiness standards for helicopters require that each pilot compartment must be free of glare and reflection when operated at night. In the past, this aspect of airworthiness was evaluated by night flight tests, which cost, on average, about $37,000. The FAA determined that ground tests are equally effective to demonstrate compliance and cost only about $4,400 per test. The compliance cost savings for the entire industry were estimated to be about $277 million (in present value).

The Cumulative Economic Impact of Regulation

This section discusses the cumulative economic impact of regulation. First, we explore how the effects of regulation are transmitted through markets. Then we describe the cumulative regulatory burden—both its basic aspects and its costs along the supply chain.

The Effects of Regulation Are Transmitted through Markets

Even when the costs of regulations of public goods and regulations to enhance productivity might appear to fall primarily on a single industry, it is important to interpret productivity broadly for the economy as a whole because the industry's costs affect the movement of capital and labor between the regulated industry and the rest of the economy. Take the occupation of barbers. Their production technology—scissors, chair, sink, and a shop—has hardly changed in a century, even though their inflation-adjusted wages have grown by about a factor of five (Mulligan 2015b). The development of safety and disposable razors has helped consumers substitute toward the home production of shaves, but not haircuts. Nevertheless, barbers' wages grew even while their technology was static, mainly for two simple reasons: (1) Productivity grew in farming, manufacturing, information, and many other industries; and (2) barbers have a choice of occupation and industry, which means that either the wages of barbering keep up with the rest of the economy or barbering disappears as an occupation. Barbering is not special; every occupation has its wage determined by productivity elsewhere in the economy. Wages in any occupation and industry are determined by the industry's supply of and demand for labor, which in turn are determined by productivity elsewhere in the economy.

For example, the labor supply of barbers reflects their productivity in their next best alternative occupation and industry. Given the intimate relation between regulation and productivity, regulation will therefore usually have a significant economic impact beyond the regulated industry.

A regulated industry with price-elastic customer demand yields the more obvious result that higher costs increase the prices charged to customers, reduce production, and reduce industry employment and revenue. But the results of regulatory actions are less obvious, to the extent that industries like barbering face relatively price-inelastic customer demand. Consider a perfectly competitive market with constant unit costs. When a regulatory action drives up the unit cost of production, the change in industry revenues equals the change in consumer expenditures on the product. Given relatively inelastic demand, the increase in unit cost results in higher consumer expenditures and higher revenues. The higher revenues cover the costs of production and regulatory compliance. As Becker, Murphy, and Grossman (2006) pointed out, the paradoxical result is that more capital and labor are drawn into the industry, even though production and consumption are reduced. In other words, the opportunity costs in the price-inelastic case accrue primarily outside the industry because the rest of the economy must produce with less capital and labor.

Policymakers sometimes emphasize the potential impact of regulatory actions on jobs (i.e., the use of labor). Under Executive Order 12866, one of the criteria for when a cost-benefit analysis is required is if the action is likely to have a material effect on jobs. Under Executive Order 13777, agencies' Regulatory Reform Task Forces are required to prioritize repealing or modifying regulatory actions that eliminate jobs or inhibit job creation. However, for the reasons explained above, in some industries it can be misleading, both for magnitude and direction, to assess the benefits of a regulatory action solely on the basis of the jobs created or destroyed in the regulated industry (a strength of the current practice of regulatory cost-benefit analysis is that agencies do not assess benefits this way). Our framework also emphasizes that it is important to consider the effects—including job effects—outside the regulated industry.

Regulatory actions that affect the degree of competition in an industry are also cases in which productivity needs to be understood broadly. For example, a monopoly withholds production, and therefore its use of capital and labor, in order to extract higher prices from its customers. Its capital and labor are used elsewhere, where they are less productive, or are not used at all. Either way, the result of a monopoly is—all else being the same—less total output, and the result of competition is more total output.

We examine these effects in an economic framework similar to that of Goulder and Williams's (2003) model of excise taxes, where the primary difference is that an excise tax delivers its revenue to the public treasury, whereas regulatory action may use up the revenue in less efficient production.[7] The framework has a composite commodity reflecting the value produced by the economy's many industries combined. The industries use capital and labor with efficiency that depends on regulation, either because regulation discourages certain types of production or, as with the monopoly example, because it distorts the interindustry composition of production. In the aggregate, therefore, both regulations of public goods and regulations to enhance productivity have many of the same consequences as aggregate "productivity shocks," which have been studied extensively in economics (Gray 1987; Crafts 2006).

The Cumulative Burden I: Within Industry

According to a former OIRA Administrator, "Cumulative burdens may have been the most common complaint that I heard during my time in government. Why, people asked, are agencies unable to coordinate with one another, or to simplify their own overlapping requirements, or to work together with State and local government, so that we do not have to do the same thing two, five, or ten times?" (Sunstein 2014, 588). The NFIB's surveys of the owners of small businesses confirm the OIRA Administrator's experience. The NFIB conducted regulation-specific surveys in 2001, 2012, and 2017. When asked which best describes the source of their regulatory problems, the majority of small business owners consistently responded that it was the total volume of regulations coming from many government agencies, as opposed to a few specific regulations coming from one or two agencies (in this question, respondents were not asked to identify specific regulations). In 2001, 50 percent of respondents identified the volume of regulations as the problem, compared with 47 percent of respondents identifying specific regulations. In 2012, the number of respondents citing the problem of the volume of regulations jumped to 62 percent. In 2017, this number dropped to 55 percent. This subsection analyzes how businesses experience cumulative burdens, and it uses the economics of convex deadweight costs and supply chains to assess these burdens and show how they have sometimes been neglected in cost-benefit analyses.

Figure 2-5 begins to illustrate cumulative burdens by focusing on a specific "regulated" industry that, like any other industry, has a downward-sloping factor demand curve that reflects the diminishing marginal value of what that industry produces. Factors refer to the labor, capital, and materials used in the production process. The industry factor supply curve represents the marginal opportunity costs: holding constant the total factors of production, when more factors are used to produce in the regulated industry, fewer are available to produce in the other industries.

---

[7] It is also possible that part of the "revenue" associated with a regulation's distortions goes to some of the market participants. A monopoly is an example where the industry output price is distorted and the revenue from that "tax" takes the form of a monopoly rent (Harberger 1954).

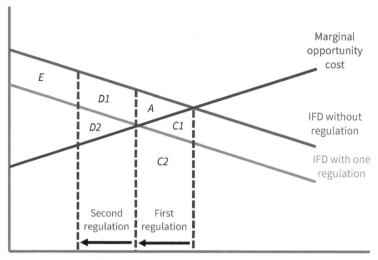

Figure 2-5. Distorted Allocation of Resources Among Industries

Marginal value product

Marginal opportunity cost

IFD without regulation

IFD with one regulation

Factor usage in the regulated industry

Note: IFD = Industry factor demand.

The value of production combined across all industries is maximized when the regulated industry is producing a quantity exactly at the intersection of the two curves shown in figure 2-5, where the marginal value product of the factors of production are equalized between industries. For the sake of illustration, we consider first one regulatory action, and then later add a second regulatory action that has the same size impact on factor usage in the regulated industry. Each action reduces the degree of competition in the regulated industry, for example by added legal or technological barriers to entering the industry. As noted above for the case of monopoly, a less competitive industry has less factor demand and therefore uses less of the factors of production. The first regulatory action therefore reduces the value of the regulated industry's output by the combination of areas *A*, *C1*, and *C2*. As a result of the reduction in the regulated industry's output, factors of production shift to other industries. Areas *C1* and *C2* represent the resulting gain in output value in the other industries. The value of the output loss combined across all industries is triangular area *A* shown in figure 2-5.

Because it is assumed for the moment that an important effect of regulation is competition, as emphasized at the end of this chapter with the joint employer standard, the part of the output represented by combined areas *E* and *D1* is retained by the industry's producers as economic profit rather than competitive factor incomes (i.e., competitive payments to labor and capital). For other regulatory actions, such as the two health insurance regulatory actions examined at the end of this chapter, areas E and $D1$ are output losses rather than a transfer of income.[8]

In this chapter, we use the public finance concept of deadweight cost to describe cumulative effects of regulation. If a regulatory action depresses an industry's resource usage by 1 percent, the lost transactions are likely those that were creating the least surplus, which is why these transactions disappear merely because of just one regulatory action. But when the second regulatory action comes along, the transactions of least value are already gone, so that the next 1 percent depression of the industry must eliminate relatively higher-value transactions than the first 1 percent did. This is shown in figure 2-5; even though the first and second actions have the same-size impact on factor usage in the regulated industry, the second action has a larger cost in terms of aggregate output. That is, combined areas $D1$ and $D2$, which show the incremental cost of the second regulatory action in terms of aggregate output, are greater than area A, which is the corresponding cost of the first regulatory action. The field of economics usually refers to such costs as "convex"—given that doubling the regulatory action more than doubles the costs of regulation. The other side of the coin is that assessing the incremental costs of regulation requires an estimate of how much the industry has already been distorted.

In addition to showing how regulatory costs accumulate, figure 2-5 also shows why a regulatory action's effect on industry employment is not entirely a cost. Note that the value of the regulated industry's output is the area under the "without regulation" factor demand curve (colored red in the figure) up to the equilibrium factor usage for the industry. The impact of regulatory action on the value of the regulated industry's output is therefore the impact on that area due to the change in the amount of factor usage. Areas $C1$ and $C2$ therefore capture the value created by labor and capital that switch to other industries, which admittedly is less than the combined values A, $C1$, and $C2$ that they would have created in the regulated industry. To the extent that the regulatory action causes capital and labor to cease employment entirely, we need to look at the aggregate factor markets, as we do in the next subsection.

The Cumulative Burden II: Costs along the Supply Chain

The interindustry cumulative cost shown in figure 2-5 is commonly considered in traditional cost-benefit analyses, but it is incomplete because the typical industry is surrounded by public policy distortions. The labor and capital used

---

[8] Even when the two areas reflect a lack of competition, they may ultimately prove to be output losses to the extent that market participants use their capital and labor in order to increase their share of the economic profits at the expense of others (Tullock 1967; Dougan and Snyder 1993). When the two areas reflect an output loss, it is possible that the industry factor demand curve is rotated counterclockwise (Mulligan and Tsui 2016), rather than shifted down as shown in figure 2-5, which corresponds to the case in which the final demand for the regulated industry's output is locally price elastic.

in the regulated industry, and elsewhere, are taxed. We show the accumulation of taxes and regulatory actions in figure 2-6, which shows the aggregate, economy-wide, long-run supply and demand curves for capital. For the same reason that the area under the "without regulation" industry demand curve in figure 2-5 is the value of industry output, the area under the corresponding demand curve in figure 2-6 is the value of long-run aggregate output. The aggregate capital demand curve is the sum of the capital demands of the regulated and other industries, and therefore the regulatory action shifts it down according to the regulated-industry shift shown in figure 2-5.[9]

Figure 2-6 shows how the industry-specific regulation has a second effect on output by reducing the aggregate amount of capital in the economy. The amount of output lost due to less capital is equal to combined areas B1, B2, and F. As discussed below, output is reduced still further, to the extent that the regulatory action shifts down the aggregate labor demand curve and thus reduces the aggregate amount of labor.

Output is not necessarily the same as welfare, because increasing output with additional labor and capital comes at the cost of supplying the additional inputs—for example, the cost of delaying consumption in order to build up the capital stock. If the aggregate capital supply curve fully reflected the marginal cost of capital, then the only social loss to be found in figures 2-5 and 2-6 would be area A, representing the net loss of value created in the regulated and other industries. However, to the extent that the supply of capital is itself distorted— say, due to taxes on capital income—the marginal cost curve for capital is below the supply curve as drawn in figure 2-6, by a proportion equal to the tax rate for capital income.[10] The overall cost of regulatory action therefore includes not only area A in figure 2-5 but also the deadweight cost associated with the reduction in capital, shown as combined areas B1 and B2 in figure 2-6. As found by Goulder and Williams (2003), the deadweight cost and loss of output associated with reduced aggregate factor usage often significantly exceeds the loss of output that comes from distorting the composition of

---

[9] The quantitative relationship between combined areas A, D1, and E in figure 2-5 and combined areas B1 and B2 in figure 2-6 depends on what is also happening in the aggregate labor market, which for brevity is not shown in this chapter, and the degree to which economic profits are created or destroyed by the regulatory action. A regulation that affected only consumer goods industries and had no effect on economic profits might not shift the demand curve in figure 2-6.

[10] If capital were subsidized, then the marginal cost curve would be above the supply curve. In macroeconomics, the opportunity cost of capital is often referred to as the "rate of time preference" or the "rate of impatience," reflecting the fact that the opportunity cost of capital in the future is less consumption in the present (Romer 2011; Fisher 1930). If the regulation were increasing the value of output rather than decreasing it, then area A in figure 2-5 would be negative (an increase in productivity), so that the regulation increases the use of capital and areas B1 and B2 in figure 2-6 would be an additional benefit.

Figure 2-6. How Industry Regulation Affects the Aggregate Factor Market

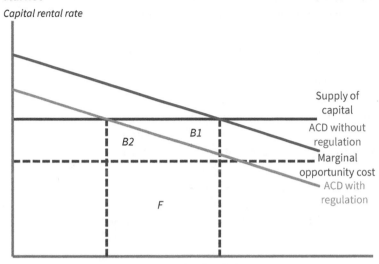

Capital rental rate

Supply of capital

ACD without regulation

B1

B2

Marginal opportunity cost

ACD with regulation

F

Aggregate quantity of capital

Note: ACD = Aggregate capital demand.

activity among industries.[11] A regulatory cost imposed on a specific industry can add substantial excess burdens to the capital and labor markets. The case studies at the end of this chapter are such examples.

The aggregate labor market has a diagram analogous to figure 2-6, with the gap between labor supply and marginal labor cost due to taxes on labor income and other distortions of the labor market. In a small, open economy where wages are primarily determined in international markets, the picture would be quite similar, including a horizontal supply curve and a horizontal opportunity cost curve. Otherwise, we would draw the labor supply curve sloping upward and would also shift it due to the income effects of the productivity change (Ballard and Fullerton 1992). Either way, the labor market has an additional factor cost, analogous to figure 2-6's areas *B1* and *B2*. Moreover, to the extent that labor and capital are complementary production factors and regulatory action reduces their aggregate employment, there are further reductions in the aggregate demand for capital and labor and therefore further reductions in aggregate output and aggregate surplus.

Although not shown in figure 2-6, another possible effect of regulating an industry is to shift up the supply curves for capital and labor. For example, suppose the regulated industry has its capital taxed at lower rates than other industries. Then the cost-benefit analysis would commonly recognize that

---

[11] Goulder and Williams (2003) examined excise taxes rather than regulations, but the aggregate analysis is the same, as long as figure 2-5's areas *D1* and *E* are a transfer rather than an aggregate output loss.

additional capital tax revenue is a benefit of a regulation that induces capital to move out of the industry. But we must also count the costs associated with the reduced aggregate supply of capital due to the fact that the regulation raises the average marginal tax rate on capital. Those costs include lower wages (resulting from less capital investment) and a loss of capital tax revenue that potentially offsets the revenue gain reflected in the usual analysis.[12]

The cumulative cost of regulation can nonetheless be estimated in practice, primarily with information from the regulated industry. Specifically, only information from the regulated industry is required to estimate lost factor incomes A, E, and D1, which are the result of the regulatory actions holding constant the aggregate amounts of labor and capital. Because areas B1 and B2 (and their analogues in the labor market) are the result of the lost factor incomes shown in figure 2-6, their magnitude can be included by rescaling the industry-specific effects according to the "marginal deadweight cost of government revenue," as estimated in the field of public economics (Feldstein 1999; Saez, Slemrod, and Giertz 2012; Weber 2014).[13]

The additional factor costs of regulation have different implications for cost-benefit analyses, depending on whether a regulatory action is a regulation of public goods or a regulation to enhance productivity. The additional factor costs are associated only with industries that produce private goods using the factors of production and experience a net cost from the regulatory action. Take, for example, a regulation of a public good that improves environmental quality at the expense of reduced manufacturing output. Figure 2-5's area A measures costs (associated with a reduced value of production in manufacturing and the other industries) but not necessarily net costs, because it does not include the environmental benefit. Area A generates additional factor costs, such as those shown by areas B1 and B2 in figure 2-6, because capital and labor are used in the production of private goods. There is no additional factor cost (or benefit) associated with the environmental benefit because that is a public good. In other words, recognizing the additional factor costs can change the sign of the net benefit of regulations of public goods because they are associated with the output losses but not the environmental benefits.

Regulations to enhance productivity are different in this regard because their costs and benefits both accrue in industries that are producing private goods with the factors of production. In this case, if figure 2-5's areas A, D1, and E measure net costs, then areas B1 and B2 in figure 2-6 cannot change the

---

[12] Another example is the proposal to shift health insurance from employers to the individual market where taxation is greater. The shift has a benefit reflected in the additional tax revenue (Gruber 2011), but the shift also reduces the aggregate supply of labor because, holding tax policy constant, it raises the average marginal tax rate on work.

[13] The CEA (2019) followed this practice in its analysis of health insurance deregulatory actions, taking the rescaling factor to be 1.5: for every $1 of deadweight loss in the health insurance industry, it added another 50 cents of factor market distortion costs.

sign of the net cost; they only increase its magnitude.[14] To be more general, we note that to the extent a public good contributes to private production, some regulatory actions will be combinations of regulations of public goods and regulations to enhance productivity.

Our application of Goulder and Williams's (2003) framework has a rather simple supply chain where final goods markets ("the industries") draw directly from capital and labor markets, so that the cumulative cost of regulation is simply the combination of costs in final goods markets (represented in figure 2-5) and costs in factor markets (represented in figure 2-6). But in reality, multiple industries can be situated in a vertical supply chain, in which case there would be more than two sets of costs to consider. The cumulative costs can be especially large when individual industries in the chain pass on their costs more than one for one, which is a result known in the industrial organization field as "double marginalization" (Tirole 1988). The specification of the joint employer standard, discussed at the end of this chapter, is an example of how the Trump Administration's deregulatory actions have improved efficiency along supply chains.

Lessons Learned: Strengthening the Economic Analysis of Deregulation

This section considers lessons learned vis-à-vis strengthening the economic analysis of deregulation. First, it looks at how to diagnose market failure. Second, it describes the costs of regulatory actions that are correct on average. Third, it explores examples of the excess burdens of regulatory actions. Fourth, it looks at the burdens of nudge regulatory actions. Fifth, it describes how to expand the use of regulatory impact analysis.

Diagnosing Market Failure

Regulatory review should be careful to not overdiagnose market failure. The first step in a regulatory cost-benefit analysis is to identify the problem the action is intended to address: a market failure or other social purpose, such as promoting privacy and personal freedom (OMB 2003). In many circumstances, competitive markets tend to successfully guide the use of society's resources to their highest value. In economic terminology, markets fail when resources are not achieving their most highly valued use. A typical regulatory impact analysis should compare the benefits of correcting a market failure with the opportunity costs of the regulatory action. For example, an environmental regulatory action might address the market failure created by the negative

---

[14] For the purposes of the analysis in this chapter, the CEA assumes that the various industries affected by regulation are equally substitutable or complementary with the supplies of capital and labor. This assumption could be relaxed by examining the more general framework of Goulder and Williams (2003).

externalities when a manufacturing plant pollutes the air. Other market failures include a lack of market competition, inadequate consumer information, and when consumers and producers have asymmetric information.

Because the cumulative regulatory burden is large, when diagnosing market failures, the burden of proof should be high. The possibility of a market failure does not by itself mean that a Federal regulatory action is appropriate. Regulatory actions are costly and, like markets, government bureaucracies are imperfect (Kahn 1979). Federal regulatory actions are more likely to be appropriate when they correct market failures that result in large misallocations of resources. OMB (2003) guidance for RIAs tells Federal agencies to focus on significant market failures and, when feasible, to describe the market failure quantitatively. The burden of proof should be high, because a claim that there is a market failure must mean that something blocks mutually beneficial exchanges from taking place. In the example given above of a polluting plant, the potential exchanges are between the public, which values cleaner air, and the manufacturer, which could take costly steps to reduce air pollution (and the consumers of the product that is now more expensive).

Minor symptoms in which markets do not work perfectly should not lead to the diagnosis of a significant market failure. In situations where exchanges fail to take place, the Nobel laureate Ronald Coase (1960) identified the lack of clearly defined property rights and transaction costs as the root causes of market failure. All markets face transaction costs, so the question is not whether there is a market failure, but whether the transaction costs are a major barrier that prevents many beneficial exchanges (Zerbe and McCurdy 1999). In the polluting plant example, it is reasonable to expect that high transaction costs create a significant market failure. However, in other cases the potential market failure can be less clear. For example, indoor air pollution from second-hand cigarette smoke might seem to fit the definition of a market failure of an externality. But because the ownership of the airspace within their properties was both established and relatively easy to police, many hotel chains and some restaurant chains enacted smoking bans long before State or local laws required them to (Institute of Medicine 2009). In spite of some transaction costs—enforcement of the bans within their airspace—these voluntary bans were market successes. Hotel and restaurant owners could increase their profits by guaranteeing more valuable, clean air unpolluted by cigar and cigarette smokers to their nonsmoking customers who were willing to pay for access to it. However, voluntary bans might not go far enough to meet all social goals. In cases like this, a careful empirical analysis is required to determine the quantitative significance of the market failures that may remain.[15]

---

[15] As long as all parties (consumers, workers, and so on) can make voluntary transactions, it might be profit- and welfare-maximizing to allow smoking in certain establishments.

The Costs of Regulatory Actions That Are Correct on Average

In a market economy that is too complex for any regulator or scholar to fully understand, regulators are bound to make mistakes. Decades ago, Friedrich Hayek (1945, 524) insisted that centralized economic planning is impossible, even when regulators have access to much statistical information about the economy, because statistical information "by its nature cannot take direct account of these circumstances of time and place, and that the central planner will have to find some way or other in which the decisions depending on them can be left to the 'man on the spot.'"

At best, central planning is highly imperfect, and, as we illustrate with some important examples below, closely watched attempts to fine-tune industries with regulation have suffered costly failures. Remarking on the deregulation of the airline industry, Kahn (1979, 1) observed that "the prime obstacle to efficiency has been regulation itself, and the most creative thing a regulator can do is remove his (and her) body from the market entryway." One reason why Executive Order 13771 places great importance on receiving public input on proposed regulatory actions is that the households and businesses that will be burdened with the costs—Hayek's "man on the spot"—are in a better position to identify them.

The convex deadweight cost approach also complements Hayek's observation that planning is highly imperfect. Once we acknowledge that regulation involves errors of magnitude or even direction, the fact that the costs are convex means that optimal regulation is necessarily cautious because the benefit of pushing the market one unit in the direction of efficiency is less than the cost of (accidentally) pushing the market one unit in the direction of inefficiency. Regulation that is correct on average can nonetheless have a negative expected net benefit.[16]

Consider figure 2-5 again. The regulator identifies, say, an environmental benefit that justifies imposing a productivity cost equal to area A. This benefit would be obtained by contracting the industry by the increment shown in figure 2-5. If the regulator were perfect and the industry were contracted by that amount, the actual cost, A, would be equal to the environmental benefit. But if the regulator were imperfect—say, by having a 50 percent chance of contracting the industry by twice as much and a 50 percent chance of not contracting it at all—the expected cost of the regulatory action would be $(A + D1 + D2)/2$, which is greater than A because of the convex deadweight costs discussed above. This example shows how regulation would have costs equal to benefits when the regulation is exact, but expected costs exceeding benefits when the

---

[16] For a more extensive analysis, see Mulligan (2015a). Milton Friedman (1953) makes a related argument for cautious monetary policy. The Friedman model has macroeconomic variance as the cost rather than deadweight costs, but delivers a similar conclusion—that even monetary policy that leans against the wind on average can nonetheless make the business cycle more volatile—because variance is also a convex function.

regulatory action is correct only on average. When acknowledging that the effects of regulation are uncertain, it follows that the best estimate from a decision perspective is one that is pessimistic as to net benefits relative to the statistical expectation (Hansen and Sargent 2008).

Examples of the Excess Burdens of Regulatory Actions

Regulatory reviews of deregulatory actions should routinely account for the excess burdens of regulation. Accounting for excess burdens is consistent with current guidance, but it appears to be uncommon. Current guidance for regulatory reviews stresses the need to look beyond the direct costs of a regulatory action and to examine "countervailing risks," which are defined to include "an adverse economic . . . consequence that occurs due to a rule and is not already accounted for in the direct cost of the rule" (OMB 2003). The excess burdens of regulatory actions in other markets, such as the capital market shown in figure 2-6, fit the definition of an adverse economic consequence.

One lesson from research on taxation is that the excess burden depends on the existence and levels of preexisting distortions—taxes and subsidy programs—in the economy. A standard example from taxation is the excess burden of a new tax on a certain good (e.g., restaurant food), when there is a preexisting tax on a good that consumers see as a complement (e.g., gasoline used to drive to the restaurant). The new restaurant tax further reduces gasoline sales and magnifies the distortion created by the preexisting gasoline tax. The reduction in gasoline tax revenues measures the excess burden (Harberger 1964). The source of the excess burden is the misallocation of resources due to the preexisting gasoline tax; the new restaurant tax magnifies the resource misallocation in the market for gasoline. In the same way, a new regulatory action that increases costs in the restaurant business magnifies the preexisting resource misallocation in the market for gasoline and generates an excess burden that could be measured by the reduction in gasoline tax revenues.

To illustrate the potential magnitude of the regulatory excess burden due to a preexisting tax, suppose a hypothetical regulatory action increases the cost of producing a restaurant dish by $2. As a result of the price increase, suppose that the typical consumer reduces his or her purchases from 10 to 9 dishes a month. Because the restaurant dish and the gasoline are complements (due to the need to drive to the restaurant), further suppose that the restaurant regulatory action causes him or her to spend $10 less on gasoline per month. If the market for restaurant food is competitive with constant unit costs of production, the standard measure of the opportunity cost of the regulatory action is $19 per month: $18 in compliance costs ($2 for each of the 9 dishes still consumed) plus a consumer surplus loss of $1 a month. Assuming that taxes account for 30 percent of the price of gasoline (which is about true in Pennsylvania, where in 2018 the State gasoline tax of $0.587 a gallon is added to the Federal tax of $0.184 a gallon), the reduction in gasoline tax revenues from this consumer—which measure the regulatory excess burden—is $3 a month. In this example, the total cost of the restaurant regulatory action is correctly measured to be $22. Failing to include the excess burden omits $3 in costs, or almost 14 percent of the total costs.[17] The share of the total costs accounted for by the excess burden depends on the strength of the demand-complementarity and the size of the preexisting tax (Goulder and Williams 2003). If the good with a preexisting tax is a substitute for the good produced by the regulated industry, the excess burden is negative—that is, the excess burden of the preexisting tax is reduced.

Moving from the hypothetical example to a real-world regulatory action, the 2010 Affordable Care Act required chain restaurants to post calories of menu items. Major cost elements in the RIA of this requirement included collecting and managing records of nutritional analysis, revising or replacing menus, and training employees (79 *FR* 67406). The FDA estimated that the compliance costs are $84.5 million (in 2011 dollars, annualized at a 7 percent discount rate). Based on an analysis that the labels will shift consumers toward healthier foods and reduce obesity, the FDA estimated that the annualized benefits are $595.5 million (in 2011 dollars). A more complete analysis of the calorie-posting rule would not exactly parallel the hypothetical example. Unlike the hypothetical example, the calorie-posting rule mainly creates fixed costs of compliance. However, if the fixed costs restrict entry and competition, the rule would still reduce consumption of restaurant food and of the complementary good, gasoline. Although the RIA's estimated compliance costs did not include an estimate of the excess burden imposed in the market for gasoline, in this case correcting the omission is unlikely to change the conclusion that the benefits of the regulatory action exceeded the costs. A more complete analysis could also consider other preexisting distortions that affect the chain restaurant industry, such as agricultural subsidies and the joint employer standard (discussed below). The potential complications illustrate a common challenge in RIAs—the need to include the most important distortions without making the analysis overly long and complex.

A cost-benefit analysis should account for changes in tax revenues when they measure the excess burdens that regulatory actions impose in the presence of preexisting distortions (Harberger 1964). The standard economic analysis of a tax increase measures the tax revenues generated and the excess burden imposed on the economy, known as the deadweight cost of taxation (Auerbach and Hines 2002). In a cost-benefit analysis of a tax increase, the change in revenues from that tax is merely a transfer payment that leaves

---

[17] In practice, an RIA of the restaurant regulatory action might fail to account for the reduction from 10 to 9 dishes per month. The approximation that assumes no reduction would lead the RIA to overestimate the compliance costs to be $20. The approximation in estimating compliance costs could offset part of the mistake of ignoring the $3 excess burden. In general, approximations and mistakes need not cancel each other out.

social benefits unchanged; the tax revenues represent a monetary payment from one group (the consumers who pay the tax) to another group. But the point of the example given above was to evaluate the hypothetical regulatory action that imposed new costs on the restaurant industry and also shifted consumer demand for gasoline when there already was a preexisting gasoline tax. Because of the preexisting tax, consumers have already given up the lower-value purchases of gasoline. Consumers' marginal willingness to pay for gasoline exceeds—by the amount of the tax—the marginal opportunity costs of the factors of production used in the gasoline industry. The preexisting gasoline tax results in the misallocation of resources to the market for gasoline. When the regulatory action increases the price of restaurant dishes and shifts the demand for the complementary good, gasoline, the resource misallocation due to the preexisting distortion is magnified. As a result, the regulatory action creates an excess burden, which is measured by the change in tax revenues.

By the same reasoning, a cost-benefit analysis should account for changes in subsidy expenditures when they measure excess burdens created by regulatory actions. Again, the common case where subsidy expenditures are treated as transfer payments does not apply. For example, chapter 4 discusses the costs and benefits of setting the Affordable Care Act's individual mandate penalty to zero. The CBO (2017) projected that setting the penalty to zero will reduce federal expenditures on ACA subsidies by $185 billion over 10 years. The ACA premium subsidy is properly treated as a transfer when the task is evaluating the effects of the subsidy. But the analytical task in chapter 4 is to evaluate removing the mandate penalty, not to evaluate changing the ACA subsidy rules. The reduction in subsidy expenditures measures the benefits of setting the penalty to zero. Parallel to the analysis of a preexisting tax, the preexisting ACA subsidy results in the misallocation of resources, and the mandate penalty magnifies the resource misallocation. A consumer who voluntarily gives up his or her subsidy when the mandate penalty is removed is not, by comparison with his or her situation with the penalty in place, harmed because the Treasury no longer provides a subsidy. Instead, the consumer has received a benefit by no longer being constrained by the tax penalty, and at the same time taxpayers benefit by no longer having to finance the ACA subsidy. As in the case for taxation, whether the regulatory excess burden is positive or negative depends upon whether the goods are substitutes or complements, as well as on whether the regulatory action decreases or increases subsidy expenditures.[18]

In practice, taking into account all the adverse economic consequences of a regulatory action might seem a daunting task. To estimate the costs of the Clean Air Act and the Clean Water Act, Hazilla and Kopp (1990) constructed an

---

[18] Self-paid treatment would also be provided in the absence of insurance enrollment and would, in the absence of behavioral considerations, be reflected in the height of the health insurance demand curve. The shapes of both the demand and supply curves would determine the discrepancy between surplus changes and federal budget effects.

econometric general equilibrium model that included 36 producing sectors on the supply side and a complete model of consumer behavior on the demand side. If the general equilibrium approach is taken, it is important that the models include the preexisting taxes and subsidies that drive the excess burdens of regulation. Murray, Keeler, and Thurman (2005) evaluated a possible rule of thumb that, to capture excess burdens, the direct costs of environmental regulatory actions should be adjusted upward by 25 to 35 percent. Their analysis showed that the rule of thumb is not necessarily a good approximation and concluded that whenever possible, estimates of regulatory costs should be based on the specific nature of the regulatory actions and likely interactions between the tax and regulatory systems.

In many circumstances, instead of a rule of thumb, an implementable formula provides a good approximation of the excess burden that a tax or regulatory action imposes in the labor market (Goulder and Williams 2003). The formula captures general equilibrium interactions that are often left out. The use of this approximation—and, when needed, extending it to include other important sources of excess burdens—allows reviews of new regulatory and deregulatory actions to be based on more complete estimates of total regulatory costs.

The Burdens of Nudge Regulatory Actions

Regulatory reviews should take a cautious approach to so-called nudge regulatory actions. The relatively new field of behavioral welfare economics suggests that policy nudges can help people make better decisions (Chetty 2015). The typical definition of a policy nudge is that it changes behavior, although it is easy to avoid and has a low cost (Thaler and Sunstein 2008). For example, employers can nudge their workers to save more for retirement by making enrollment in a 401(k) retirement plan the default option (Madrian and Shea 2001). Because it was easy for the workers to opt out of the 401(k) plan, changing the default option fit the definition of a nudge. Advocates argue that nudges help consumers make choices—in this case, saving more for retirement—that are in the best interests of the consumers themselves. However, behavioral welfare economics poses a number of challenges for regulatory reviews. Behavioral economics arguments might tend to exacerbate the tilt in the regulatory process toward the benefits of expanding the regulatory state. In addition, although some nudge regulatory actions may yield important benefits, they also may involve easy-to-overlook opportunity costs.

The basic challenge is whether "individual failures" should be added to the standard list of market failures as potential justifications for new regulatory actions. The logic in favor of adding them is the argument that policy nudges help people avoid making predictable mistakes—decisions that the individuals themselves would agree are not in their own best interest. The mistakes can be called "internalities"; individuals impose costs on themselves that they fail to consider when making decisions. The main guidance document for regulatory review, "Circular A-4" (OMB 2003), does not discuss individual failures or internalities. OMB's (2003) guidance emphasizes that when possible, benefits should be estimated based on consumers' revealed preferences. In contrast, behavioral welfare economics emphasizes that because consumers make systematic mistakes, their revealed preferences are not a reliable guide for estimating benefits. For example, if consumers mistakenly fail to take into account future savings from more energy-efficient products, their revealed preference for inefficient products should not be used to measure the benefits of regulatory actions to promote energy efficiency. OMB's guidance and behavioral economics thus place different emphases on the role of revealed preferences in benefit estimation. However, OMB's guidance does not explicitly exclude methods of behavioral economics; nor does it exclude the argument that individual failures might provide the rationale for new regulatory actions. Executive Order 13707—issued September 15, 2015—encourages Federal agencies to apply insights from behavioral economics and, following Britain's example, a "nudge unit" (officially, the Social and Behavioral Sciences Team) was established to explore policy options. Increasingly, in practice RIAs discuss individual failures as providing a rationale for regulatory action.

In the past, Federal agencies have claimed that regulatory actions were needed because consumers and businesses failed to take into account the future savings from buying more energy- and fuel-efficient products (Gayer and Viscusi 2013). The arguments in the regulatory analyses echo long-standing claims about energy conservation policies (Allcott and Greenstone 2012). Much of the evidence for the claims came from engineering estimates of energy conservation cost curves. The engineering studies often concluded that energy can be conserved at a negative net cost—that is, that investing in energy conservation more than pays for itself. The apparently unexploited gains from investing in conservation might be viewed as evidence that many consumers and businesses make mistakes about energy conservation. However, engineering estimates typically omit opportunity costs and may fail to properly account for physical costs and risks. The shortcomings of engineering studies make the estimates "difficult to take at face value" (Allcott and Greenstone 2012, 5).

The opportunity costs of investing in energy conservation can take many forms. Allcott and Taubinsky (2015) conducted two randomized experiments to estimate the effect of providing consumers with more information about the energy efficiency of lightbulbs. In both experiments, even after efforts to inform consumers and call attention to the energy savings, large shares of consumers continued to purchase incandescent lightbulbs rather than compact fluorescents. The experimental results suggest that a regulatory action that bans incandescent lightbulbs creates significant opportunity costs for those consumers who simply prefer the lighting provided by incandescents. In principle, the benefits (or costs) of a ban on incandescent lightbulbs could be estimated in two steps: First, complete an engineering estimate of the value of the energy savings; and second, adjust the engineering estimate downward to account for lost consumer surplus. An analogous approach has been used to estimate the value of reducing consumption of a good that harms health (Ashley, Nardinelli, and Lavaty 2015). The practical difficulty of implementing this approach has been called "a tall order" (Levy, Norton, and Smith 2018, 26).

In another important example of regulatory policy to conserve energy, the National Highway Traffic and Safety Administration (NHTSA) and the EPA set Corporate Average Fuel Economy (CAFE) standards for passenger cars and light trucks. The rule, which was finalized in 2012, increased the stringency of the fuel economy standards, which were estimated to then require manufac- turers to achieve a fleet-wide standard of 40.3 miles per gallon for the 2021 model year. This rule would have increased to 48.7 miles per gallon for the 2025 model year, if the NHTSA had the statutory authority to set standards that far into the future in a single rulemaking. The 2012 NHTSA regulatory impact anal- ysis concluded that the benefits of the standards substantially exceeded the regulatory costs. In the analysis, future fuel savings for consumers accounted for 77 percent of the estimated benefits (Gayer and Viscusi 2013). In fact, the analysis estimated that the fuel savings for consumers would exceed the addi- tional costs they would incur in the form of higher-priced vehicles. In contrast, holding everything else being constant, the regulatory actions cannot make a rational consumer better off and might make them worse off.[19] Some rational consumers might make the same fuel economy choices that the NHTSA's analysis estimated were "right," in which case the regulatory action would not change their behavior and thus would not create any benefits for them. Some rational consumers might instead decide that other car features are more desirable than future fuel economy, in which case the regulatory action makes them worse off. For example, under the standards, consumers might not be able to purchase cars they prefer with more powerful but less fuel-efficient engines. If the results of the 2012 analysis are accurate, one must believe that consumers who make such choices are not acting in their own self-interest. The standards also created environmental benefits, which played a "largely

---

[19] The regulatory actions reduce choices, and in general more choices are better than fewer choices. More technically, the fuel economy regulatory actions impose additional constraints on the consumer's optimization problem. The solution to a more constrained optimization problem cannot lead to an outcome that is preferred over the solution to a less constrained optimization problem. The regulatory actions might mean that everything else is not constant. For example, if there are economies of scale in producing more fuel-efficient cars, the CAFE regulatory actions could decrease the average cost. The cost reduction would benefit consumers who prefer more fuel efficiency. However, if there are also economies of scale in producing less fuel-efficient cars, there would be an offsetting cost increase for consumers who prefer other attributes, such as more powerful engines. Of course, all consumers can also be made better off by the reduction in externalities. The RIA measured those benefits separately. The question of consumer rationality is whether there are net private benefits for consumers from future fuel savings.

incidental role" in the cost-benefit analysis (Gayer and Viscusi 2013, 19). If the analysis were corrected so that consumers behaved self-interestedly, the estimated costs of the standards would have been greater than the estimated benefits (Gayer and Viscusi 2013; Allcott and Knittel 2019).

Recently, a 2018 NHTSA and EPA preliminary regulatory impact analysis of the proposed Safer Affordable Fuel Efficient (SAFE) Vehicles Rule concluded that a deregulatory action—in the form of retaining the 2020 standards through model year 2026—would reduce regulatory costs by between $335 billion (in 2016 dollars; 3 percent discount rate) and $502 billion (in 2016 dollars; 7 percent discount rate) over the lifetime of the vehicles (NHTSA and EPA 2018). The regulatory analysis is complex and runs over 1,600 pages. It considers eight regulatory alternatives and multiple conceptual and empirical modeling issues. Our discussion focuses on its treatment of the question of whether consumers undervalue fuel economy when making car purchases. New empirical evidence suggests that buyers undervalue fuel economy only slightly, if at all (Busse, Knittel, and Zettelmeyer 2013; Allcott and Wozny 2014; Sallee, West, and Fan 2016). The studies analyze data on the sales of different models of cars to identify the impact of higher fuel economy on the selling price. In addition, the studies use rich data to control for the influence of other attributes—for example, more engine power—that also influence the selling price. Holding these other factors constant, the studies find that consumers are willing to pay higher prices for more efficient cars that reduce their future fuel costs. The studies compare the estimated willingness to pay for higher fuel economy with estimates of the expected fuel savings. The estimated fuel savings depend not only on the car's fuel economy but also on future gasoline prices and the extent to which future savings are discounted. Depending on different assumptions about future fuel prices and discount rates, the studies estimate that when purchasing cars, consumers incorporate from 55 percent to over 100 percent of future fuel costs. Although the precise degree of undervaluation (if any) is difficult to know, the empirical evidence is inconsistent with the 2012 cost-benefit analysis implying that most consumers mistakenly ignore fuel economy.

When a regulatory analysis argues from behavioral economics that a regulatory action corrects individual failures, the RIA should apply the same evidence standards used when evaluating standard market failures. As mentioned above, OMB's (2003) guidance tells Federal agencies to determine that the market failure is significant, and that they should describe the failure both qualitatively and, when feasible, quantitatively. The discussion in the 2018 preliminary regulatory impact analysis of whether consumers undervalue fuel economy is a good example of an evidence-based and quantified description; the analysis suggests that the individual failure of undervaluation is probably not significant. In other cases, behavioral economics research on individual failures might sometimes fail to meet the standard of providing strong evidence for quantification. To a large extent, empirical evidence on individual failures comes from experiments in economic laboratories. Although carefully designed and controlled experiments provide tight tests of specific behavioral hypotheses, it is problematic to try to extrapolate experimental results to predict how people make real-world decisions in markets.

Even with empirical support that a nudge is needed, measuring the costs of a regulatory nudge is difficult. This difficulty arises in part from the issue of how to precisely define what constitutes a nudge. The criteria that a nudge is easy to avoid and has a low cost are not precisely quantified (Thaler and Sunstein 2009). Some policies that correct supposed consumer mistakes are not nudges. For example, fuel economy standards are not a nudge; the standards are not easily avoided and impose opportunity costs because they limit the availability of cars with desirable features. In contrast, the Motor Vehicle Fuel Economy Label rule is a nudge designed to correct the same consumer mistakes. If this nudge worked, fuel economy standards would be unnecessary (Gayer and Viscusi 2013). Glaeser (2006) points out that other common nudge policies essentially create a psychic tax—even though the nudges do not require explicit payments, consumers bear a real cost. Cost-benefit analyses should account for the fact that stigmatizing behavior imposes real costs, regardless of whether the behavior is in the consumers' own best interest. More research is needed to develop empirical estimates of the costs of stigmatization and the willingness to pay to avoid it. Promising approaches include revealed and stated preference methods that have been developed to estimate the willingness to pay for other commodities that are not directly traded in markets (OMB 2003).

Expanding Use of Regulatory Impact Analysis

Another priority to strengthen the regulatory review process is to expand the number of complete and quantified regulatory cost-benefit analyses. Because the time, personnel, and resources available for regulatory reviews are limited, Federal agencies are only required to conduct cost-benefit analyses of significant regulatory actions. As a result, from 2000 through 2018, about 70,000 final rules were published in the *Federal Register*, and fewer than 6,000 of these rules were deemed significant under Executive Order 12866. Because the unreviewed rules were anticipated to not have economic effects greater than $100 million annually or other significant adverse effects, in principle they might account for a small share of total regulatory costs. However, given the volume of unreviewed rules, the uncounted regulatory costs might add up to a significant share. OMB should continue to carefully review agencies' analyses of whether the regulatory action is significant in the first place.

For a large fraction of significant rules discussed in OMB's *Reports to Congress*, the agencies were not able to completely quantify the benefits and/or costs. Furchtgott-Roth (2018) examines a number of important Federal labor market regulations, including the joint employer standard case study at the end of this chapter, that were not evaluated with cost-benefit analyses when they were issued.[20] Unlike 1981 Executive Order 12291, which explicitly required an analysis of whether the potential benefits exceeded the potential costs, the current regulatory review Executive Order 12866, which was enacted in 1993, requires only that the potential benefits "justify" the potential costs. Although at other points this Executive Order still refers to maximizing net benefits, the wording might leave the door partly open for an unquantified cost-benefit analysis. In many cases, regulatory analyses have been incomplete (Hahn and Tetlock 2008). Studies of the U.S. regulatory review process have found that over the past 30 years, in only about one-third to one-half of the cases was the regulatory analysis able to conclude that the benefits exceeded the costs (Hahn and Dudley 2007). In most of these cases, the original analysis was simply unable to quantify the benefits and/or the costs. After reviewing OMB's *Reports on the Benefits and Costs of Federal Regulations* across different administrations, Fraas and Morgenstern (2014) concluded that the Obama Administration placed more emphasis on difficult-to-measure benefits such as the value of dignity and equity. Sunstein (2018) argues that as a general principle, regulatory cost-benefit analyses should try to measure the willingness to pay to honor moral commitments. Even when it is difficult to place a dollar value on a regulatory action's benefits, quantifying its costs makes the trade-offs involved more transparent.

Improving cost-benefit analyses of a set of regulatory actions known as "budgetary transfer rules" is another priority. Budgetary transfer rules involve changes in receipts or outlays, such as Medicare funding. An important principle of cost-benefit analyses is that lump-sum transfers that do not change economic behavior but simply transfer income from group A to group B do not yield net benefits or net costs. The benefits for group B are exactly offset by the costs imposed on group A. However, budgetary transfer rules are not lump-sum transfers and thus cause people to change their behavior. For example, a regulatory action that changes Medicare payments is not simply a transfer from taxpayers to healthcare providers. Taxpayers and healthcare providers will respond to the changed incentives created by the regulatory action. The transfer rule has a budgetary impact and also has effects on private sector behavior. As discussed above, a cost-benefit analysis should measure all the changes in consumer and producer surplus that result when regulatory actions change private sector behavior. In the past, most agencies typically reported only the estimated budgetary effects of the transfer rules and sometimes the direct compliance costs. Recognizing that "transfer rules may create social benefits or costs," OMB encourages agencies to report them "and will consider incorporating any such estimates into future *Reports*" (OMB 2017b, 22). The framework

---

[20] Some were issued by independent agencies, or were issued as informal guidance, or were considered economically insignificant.

we develop above provides guidance for more complete cost-benefit analyses of transfer rules.

A complete cost-benefit analysis of transfer rules also requires consideration of preexisting distortions—namely, subsidies and taxes. By the nature of transfer rules, the actions often change behavior that is already affected by government subsidies. For example, a Medicare transfer rule might increase or decrease coverage for healthcare services. A transfer rule might also increase or decrease total Federal expenditures that need to be financed through taxes. In many cases, one component of the costs of a transfer rule will be the rule's budgetary impact, rescaled by an estimate of the marginal deadweight cost of government revenue.

Until 2018, the OIRA review process generally excluded two important sets of regulatory and deregulatory actions: tax regulatory actions taken by the Department of the Treasury, and regulatory actions taken by independent agencies. Just as with the regulatory actions that are currently subject to cost-benefit analysis, these regulatory actions promoted important goals, but at an opportunity cost. A regulatory cost-benefit analysis is thus still needed to help strike the right balance.

On April 11, 2018, the Department of the Treasury and OMB signed a memorandum of agreement that outlines a new process for OMB to review tax regulatory actions under Executive Order 12866 (White House 2018). This agreement reflected Treasury's and OMB's shared commitment to "reducing regulatory burdens and providing timely guidance to taxpayers," particularly guidance necessary to unleash the full benefits of the Tax Cuts and Jobs Act. Under the agreement, a tax regulatory action will be subject to OIRA review if it has an annual nonrevenue effect on the economy of $100 million or more. Many tax regulatory actions are focused on improving the collection of tax revenues, and there is a long-standing process to review the revenue effects of the Department of Treasury's regulatory actions. However, similar to other agencies' regulatory actions, some tax regulatory actions are designed to change incentives so as to promote social goals. For example, the Department of the Treasury issued tax regulatory actions that clarify which transactions would quality for beneficial tax treatment for investments in Opportunity Zones, such as equity investments made in Qualified Opportunity Funds that invest in the Opportunity Zones. The proposed rule is expected to qualify as a deregulatory action because it will reduce taxpayers' planning costs. By reducing taxpayers' uncertainty, the rule should promote the goal of encouraging investments to flow into Qualified Opportunity Funds. (The Opportunity Zone initiative is discussed in more detail in chapter 3.)

Regulatory and deregulatory actions continue to be issued by independent agencies are not subject to the OMB regulatory review process. The economic framework we develop above is broad enough to encompass independent agencies' actions. The principles of regulatory cost-benefit analysis apply equally well to these actions, although of course they will need to be applied to the specific contexts of the independent agencies. Several independent agencies have created groups to conduct economic analyses internally. In 2009, the Securities and Exchange Commission created the Division of Economic and Risk Analysis. In recent developments, the Consumer Financial Protection Bureau has established its own Office of Cost-Benefit Analysis, and the Federal Communications Commission is in the process of establishing an Office of Economics and Analytics. There remains an unmet need for cost-benefit analyses of the regulatory actions taken by the independent agencies. Coglianese (2018) discusses three proposed policy options for improving independent agencies' regulatory analyses: through the courts, through the OMB process, or through a required analysis undertaken outside OMB.

Case Studies of Deregulatory Actions and Their Benefits and Costs

This section presents three case studies of deregulatory actions and their benefits and costs. The first case study describes association health plans. The second study examines short-term, limited-duration insurance plans. And the third study discusses the specification of the joint employer standard.

Case Study 1: Association Health Plans

A major theme of this chapter is that the burdens of regulatory actions accumulate, which means that the cumulative costs of a set of actions will be larger than the sum of the costs of each regulatory action analyzed one by one. Case studies 1 and 2 illustrate the process in reverse: The cost savings from deregulatory actions also accumulate. The CEA's (2019) analysis used CBO projections and other evidence to conduct prospective cost-benefit analyses of two deregulatory actions taken in 2018 that expanded consumer health coverage options: the association health plan (AHP) rule; and the short-term, limited-duration insurance (STLDI) rule. These deregulatory reforms restore and expand options in health insurance markets within the existing statutory frameworks, including the Affordable Care Act. We discuss the benefits and costs of each action separately, but the analysis accounts for the cumulative nature of the deregulatory actions.

Specifically, the CBO (2018) projected the combined impact of the AHP and STLDI rules. The CBO's projections also incorporated the fact that the Tax Cuts and Jobs Act of 2017 had already set the individual mandate penalty to zero owed by consumers who did not have Federally-approved coverage or an exemption. (Chapter 4 provides a more detailed analysis of the individual mandate penalty.) Taking into account the zero-mandate penalty, the CBO (2018) projected that by 2023, the AHP and STLDI rules will lead to 4 million more AHP enrollees and 2 million more STLDI enrollees.

Before 2018, under Title I of the Employee Retirement Income Security Act (known as ERISA), the Department of Labor had adopted criteria in subregulatory guidance that restricted the establishment and maintenance of AHPs. On June 21, 2018, the Department of Labor issued the AHP deregulatory action to establish an alternative pathway to form AHPs that modified some of the criteria. The AHP rule is an example of how deregulation does not always involve the elimination of an existing rule, but can instead involve revising subregulatory guidance through notice-and-comment rulemaking.

The AHP rule's removal of regulatory burden expands the ability of small businesses and working owners without other employees to join AHPs. AHPs allow small businesses and certain working owners to group together to self-insure or purchase large group insurance. AHPs allow small businesses to offer their workers more affordable and potentially more attractive health coverage. Summing up over the groups of consumers whose health coverage options are expanded by the AHP rule, the CEA (2019) estimated that in 2021, after consumers and markets have had time to adjust, removing the regulatory burden will yield net social benefits worth $7.4 billion. In addition, these savings are estimated to reduce regulatory excess burdens by $3.7 billion.

Many uninsured Americans today work for small businesses. The ACA subjected health insurance coverage for small businesses to mandated coverage of essential health benefits and price controls (in the form of restrictions on how premiums are set) that are not required for large businesses. Under the ACA, AHP coverage provided to employees through an association of small businesses and certain working owners is regulated the same way as coverage sold to larger businesses. Interpreting ERISA, the AHP rule provides a new pathway to form AHPs that modified the earlier subregulatory restrictions. New AHPs will be able to form by industry or geographic area (e.g., for metropolitan areas and States).[21] Fully insured AHPs could be established beginning on September 1, 2018, while self-funded AHPs needed to wait until early 2019.

Two studies provide estimates of the effects of the AHP rule on insurance coverage and ACA premiums. The CBO (2018) projects that after the rule is fully phased in, it will expand AHP enrollments by about 4 million people. Also, the CBO projects that consumers who switch to AHP coverage will be healthier than average enrollees in small group or individual plans. Based on the CBO's projections, the CEA (2019) estimated that the AHP rule will cause gross (of subsidy) premiums in the nongroup market to increase by slightly more than 1 percent. Another study estimated that the proposed rule on AHPs will cause

---

[21] The AHP rule expands organizations' ability to offer AHPs on the basis of common geography or industry. For example, existing organizations such as local chambers of commerce could offer potentially large AHPs. According to the Association of Chamber of Commerce Executives, local chambers of commerce range in size from a few dozen firms to more than 20,000 firms. Depending upon the number of workers per chamber member, the potential group size of chambers of commerce-based AHPs range from the hundreds to the tens of thousands.

3.2 million enrollees to leave the individual and small group markets and enter AHPs by 2022 (Avalere 2018).

The AHP rule will allow small businesses to offer their workers more affordable health coverage by reducing the administrative cost of coverage through greater economies of scale. The share of the premium accounted for by administrative costs falls with insurance group size; the share is 42 percent for firms with 50 or fewer employees, compared with 17 percent for firms with 101 to 500 employees and 4 percent for firms with more than 10,000 employees (Karaca-Mandic, Abraham, and Phelps 2011). The AHP rule allows the average group size to expand, which reduces the average cost of AHP coverage—a significant advantage for many small and medium-sized businesses.

The AHP rule also gives small businesses more flexibility to offer their workers health coverage that is more tailored to their needs. At this point in time, it is speculative whether AHPs will provide relatively comprehensive coverage or more tailored coverage. Providing more choices over tailored coverage options could have substantial value for consumers. An analysis of choices made in the employment-related group market found that offering more preferred plan choices was as valuable for the median consumer as a 13 percent premium reduction (Dafny, Ho, and Varela 2013). The CEA's (2019) analysis did not include a separate estimate of the value of more tailored plan options. In some circumstances, there may be a trade-off between AHP group size and the extent of tailoring, because the more tailored plan might not be attractive to all potential AHP members. In this context, the estimate of the benefits of reduced administrative costs provides a lower bound for benefits; consumers who do not take advantage of the lower administrative costs of larger AHPs do so because they value tailored coverage more highly than the cost savings.

The AHP rule affects four groups of people: consumers who move out of ACA-compliant individual coverage in the nongroup market to ACA-compliant group coverage through an AHP; consumers who move out of small-group coverage; consumers who would have AHP coverage with or without the rule; and consumers who would have been uninsured without the rule. To estimate the effects of the AHP rule, the CEA (2019) used data from the CBO's (2018) projections and estimates of administrative costs. The AHP rule's addition of a new pathway to form AHPs, which modified the criteria for the creation of AHPs, decreased costs and thus increased the consumer surplus for AHP enrollees. The CEA's (2019) estimates include changes in the consumer surplus, and the reductions in the excess burden of regulatory costs. As discussed above, the consumer surplus and excess regulatory burden are often omitted. The CEA's (2019) analysis of the AHP rule provides a useful case study and guide to estimate these important aspects of regulatory costs.

The first step is to estimate the benefits that flow from consumers moving out of ACA-compliant individual coverage in the nongroup market. Based on differences in administrative costs of ACA-compliant coverage in the individual market versus AHPs' ACA-compliant coverage in the group market, the CEA estimated that each enrollee who shifts from ACA-compliant individual coverage to ACA-compliant group AHP coverage saves $619 in administrative costs and enjoys $309 in net surplus from the cost reduction. In addition, the CEA estimated that after accounting for the loss of cross-subsidies and their effects on ACA-compliant premiums and subsidies in the nongroup market, each enrollee who shifts from ACA-compliant individual coverage into ACA-compliant AHP group coverage reduces third-party expenditures by $1,933. Aggregated over the 1.1 million enrollees who shift, in 2021 these effects of the AHP regulatory reform yield benefits worth $2.5 billion.

The second step is to estimate the benefits that flow from the roughly 2.5 million consumers who respond to the rule by moving out of small-group coverage into AHP coverage. By allowing enrollees to switch to AHPs that are larger than their existing small group plans, the CEA estimated that the AHP rule will on average reduce insurance administrative costs by $1,924, so each enrollee enjoys $962 of surplus from this cost reduction. The CEA assumed that the reduction in administrative costs also reduces Federal tax expenditures on health insurance by an average $349 per enrollee. Aggregated over the 2.5 million enrollees who make this shift, these effects of the AHP rule yield benefits worth $3.3 billion.

The third step is to estimate the benefits that the AHP rule generates for the consumers who would have AHP coverage with or without the rule. Due to the increase in average AHP group size, the CEA estimated that the rule reduces administrative costs by $335 per enrollee. The CEA assumed that the reduction in administrative costs also reduces Federal tax expenditures on health insurance by an average $61 per enrollee. The aggregate benefits from this effect of the AHP rule are worth $1.7 billion.

The fourth step is to estimate the benefits the AHP rule generates for consumers who would have been uninsured without the rule. The CBO (2018) projected that the AHP regulatory reform will reduce the number of uninsured consumers by 400,000. Because they are responding to a reduction in administrative costs that averages $619 per enrollee (as above), each newly insured AHP enrollee enjoys a consumer surplus of $309 from their purchase. The CEA (2019) also estimated that third-party costs of uncompensated care fall by $989 for each newly insured AHP enrollee. Offsetting these benefits, Federal tax expenditures on health insurance increase by an estimated $1,519 per newly insured AHP enrollee. The aggregated net costs of these effects of the AHP rule are $0.1 billion.

Summing up over the four groups of consumers whose insurance options are expanded by the AHP rule, the CEA (2019) estimated that in 2021, the rule yields social benefits worth $7.4 billion. The estimate of social benefits takes into account both the benefits and costs, including the possibility that the AHP rule imposes new costs on a subset of enrollees in the nongroup market who pay higher insurance premiums.

Case Study 2: Short–Term, Limited–Duration Insurance Plans

The second case study considers an August 2018 deregulatory action that expanded short-term, limited-duration insurance (STLDI) plans. The 2018 STLDI rule revised a rule issued by the previous Administration in 2016. At the time of the enactment of the ACA and until the 2016 rule, STLDI plans had longer durations than allowed by the 2016 rule. The 2016 rule expressed a concern that consumers were purchasing STLDI plans as their primary form of coverage to avoid ACA requirements. The 2016 rule therefore shortened the total duration of STLDI plans from less than 12 months to less than 3 months (81 *FR* 75316).

The 2018 STLDI rule removed the restrictions created by the 2016 rule, which allows consumers more flexibility to purchase short-term insurance. On August 3, 2018, the Department of the Treasury, Department of Labor, and Department of Health and Human Services published a final rule that extended the length of the initial STLDI contract term to less than 12 months and allowed for the renewal of the initial insurance contract for up to 36 months, which is the same as the maximum coverage term required under COBRA continuation coverage (U.S. Congress 1985). Because the administrative costs and hassles of purchasing health insurance can now be spread out over a longer period of coverage, the STLDI rule also has the effect of lowering the average costs consumers pay for insurance. The CEA (2019) estimated that in 2021, the STLDI rule will yield benefits worth $7.3 billion. In addition, the savings in costs were estimated to reduce excess burdens by $3.7 billion.

Because STLDI plans are not considered to be individual health insurance coverage under the Health Insurance Portability and Accountability Act and the Public Health Service Act, STLDI coverage continues to be exempt from all ACA restrictions on insurance plan design and pricing. This allows STLDI plans to offer a form of alternative coverage to those who do not seek permanent individual health insurance coverage. The STLDI rule requires that STLDI policies must provide a notice to consumers that these plans may differ from ACA-compliant plans and, among other differences, may have limits on preexisting conditions and on health benefits, and have annual or lifetime limits.[22] Insurers were allowed to begin issuing STLDI plans on October 2, 2018—60 days after publication of the final rule.

Four studies provide estimates of the effects of the STLDI rule on insurance coverage and ACA premiums. The CBO projects that the STLDI regulatory reform will result in an additional 2 million consumers in STLDI plans by 2023 (CBO 2018). Based on CBO projections, the CEA (2019) estimated that the STLDI

---

[22] ACA-compliant coverage, including coverage offered on the exchange, continues to have no limits on preexisting health conditions.

rule will increase gross premiums by slightly more than 1 percent in the same time frame. The Centers for Medicare & Medicaid Services (CMS) project that by 2022, 1.9 million consumers will have STLDI policies and that, as a result, gross premiums for ACA coverage could increase by up to 6 percent (CMS 2018). A study published by the Urban Institute in 2018 predicts that the rule could increase STLDI enrollment by 4.2 million, but does not provide an estimate of the impact on gross ACA premiums (Blumberg, Buettgens, and Wang 2018). A 2018 study published by the Commonwealth Fund estimates that the rule could increase STLDI enrollment by 5.2 million and could increase gross ACA premiums by 2.7 percent (Rao, Nowak, and Eibner 2018).

Under both the 2016 and 2018 rules, STLDI plans are exempt from ACA requirements, including the mandated coverage of the 10 essential health benefits (CCIIO 2011). The 2016 STLDI rule limited the duration of an STLDI contract to less than 3 months. The 2016 rule's restrictions on the duration of an STLDI contract exposed potential STLDI enrollees to the risk of losing their STLDI coverage at the end of three months, or if they could obtain a new STLDI policy, having their deductibles reset, among other things. The CEA (2019) therefore modeled both the renewability restriction and the limited terms as an addition to the load costs and hassle of STLDI plans associated with applying for coverage every 3 months rather than every 36 months, which are hereafter referred to as "loads."[23] Assuming no tax penalty on the uninsured, the CEA compared high-loaded STLDI plans (2016 rule) with low-loaded STLDI plans (new rule), and took the difference to be the impact of the new rule.

Allowing for STLDI plans under the 2016 rule makes the CEA's analysis different from some others (e.g., Blumberg, Buettgens, and Wang 2018) that assume that no STLDI plan is available under the 2016 rule, and fundamentally changes some of the results. According to the CEA's approach, even under the 2016 rule, there would be little reason for consumers paying premiums far in excess of their expected claims to continue with ACA-compliant individual coverage, because at least they have the expensive but not impossible option of reapplying for STLDI coverage every three months. The marginal STLDI enrollees must instead be those who receive either an exchange subsidy or a cross-subsidy from other members of the ACA-compliant individual market risk pool.[24] The CEA's approach also does not permit adding an additional benefit to STLDI enrollees from relief from the essential health benefits mandate, because they already had that relief under the previous rule, albeit with higher loads.

[23] The CEA notes that, under the 2016 rule, a consumer having difficulty continuing STLDI coverage could turn to ACA-compliant plans, which in a sense is a choice with extra loading to the extent that the applicable regulations deviate from the consumer's preferences.

[24] It is possible that the 2017 ACA-compliant risk pool included a number of consumers with a low ratio of expected claims to net premiums, but this *Report* is looking at plan years 2019 through 2028, when the individual mandate penalty is zero and market participants have had time to adjust to the reality of high premiums for ACA-compliant plans.

Lower premiums result from smaller loads because premiums finance both claims and loads. But, with the exemption from ACA regulations, STLDI plans also have more freedom to control moral hazard and to dispense entirely with loads associated with unwanted services by excluding those services from the plan. These are some of the reasons why premiums for STLDI coverage are often less expensive than premiums for ACA-compliant individual market insurance plans (CMS 2018; Pollitz et al. 2018).

Many health insurance simulation models treat consumer choice as a negative- or zero-sum game. A person who reduces his or her net premium spending by $1,000 when he or she forgoes unneeded coverage merely increases by $1,000 the premiums that must be collected from those who retain that coverage. This assumption is unrealistic because of moral hazard, administrative costs, and the fact that the exchanges cap and means-test premiums. For example, this person's gross premium for the forgone coverage may have been $1,500 (he receives premium subsidies on the exchange), $300 of which goes to administrative costs, and another $1,200 goes to the person's own claims that were of little value but are made as long as he or she is forced to have the coverage. This person's enhanced choice saves taxpayers $500, and imposes no cost on the risk pool. As demonstrated in the CEA's 2019 report, a broader and more realistic range of insurance market frictions, and thereby more reliable conclusions, are possible without unduly complicating the analysis.

The STLDI rule affects three groups of consumers: consumers who move out of ACA-compliant individual coverage and into STLDI coverage; consumers who would have chosen STLDI coverage with or without the rule; and consumers who would have been uninsured without the rule. To estimate the effects of the STLDI rule, the CEA (2019) used data from the CBO's (2018) projections, estimates of the elasticity of demand for health insurance, and estimates of the administrative and time costs of STLDI coverage. Before the 2018 rule, the 2016 rule's restrictions on STLDI coverage increased costs and thus reduced consumer surplus for STLDI enrollees. The CEA's (2019) estimates include changes in the consumer surplus, and reductions in the excess burden of regulatory costs. As discussed above, the consumer surplus and excess regulatory burden are often omitted. The CEA's (2019) analysis of the STLDI deregulatory action provides a useful case study and guide to estimate these important aspects of regulatory costs.

The first step is to quantify the benefits that the STLDI rule generates for consumers who move out of ACA-compliant coverage into STLDI coverage. The CBO projects that the rule will result in 2 million new enrollees in STLDI plans. The CEA (2019) estimated that over 1 million of these are consumers who shift from ACA-compliant individual coverage to STLDI coverage. The CMS projects that the average STLDI premium in 2021 will be $4,200. Assuming that the elasticity of demand for STLDI coverage is –2.9, the CEA estimated that by removing the combined effects of the limits on renewability, the limited term, and the administrative costs and hassles, the STLDI rule reduces the load by $1,218. On average, each enrollee who switches from ACA-compliant individual coverage to STLDI coverage thus enjoys a consumer surplus of $609. (The average net surplus equals one-half the total cost savings of $1,218.) After accounting for the loss of cross-subsidies, we estimate that each enrollee who shifts from ACA-compliant individual coverage to STLDI coverage reduces third-party expenditures by $3,459. Aggregated over the 1.3 million enrollees who shift, in 2021 these benefits of the STLDI rule are worth $5.3 billion.

The effects of the STLDI rule depend upon how many consumers shift from ACA-compliant individual coverage to STLDI coverage, and of those, how many received ACA premium subsidies. The CEA (2019) used the CBO's (2018) projections that over 1 million consumers will switch from ACA-compliant individual coverage. The economic analysis in the STLDI rule assumes that in 2021, 600,000 enrollees will switch from ACA exchange plans to STLDI coverage, and another 800,000 will switch from off-exchange plans. In terms of how many switchers received ACA premium subsidies, we assume that the STLDI switchers will be on average similar to the enrollees projected to respond when the tax penalty is set to zero (CBO 2018). This assumption is uncertain. The CMS (2018) projects that mostly unsubsidized enrollees will switch to STLDI coverage. Similarly, the economic analysis in the STLDI Final Rule anticipates that most consumers who switch to STLDI coverage will have incomes that make them ineligible for ACA premium subsidies. The CEA (2019) conducted a sensitivity analysis that estimated the benefits from the STLDI rule under different assumptions about the number of consumers who switch from ACA-compliant individual coverage and the number of unsubsidized switchers.

The second step is to quantify the benefits that the STLDI rule generates for consumers who would have chosen STLDI coverage with or without the new rule. The CEA (2019) assumed that 750,000 consumers would have chosen STLDI coverage with or without the new rule. Each of these consumers gains the $1,218 in reduced load costs (as noted above). Aggregating over 750,000 consumers, the STLDI rule yields an additional $0.9 billion in benefits.

The third step is to quantify the benefits that the STLDI rule generates for the consumers who would have been uninsured without the rule. The CBO (2018) projects that the STLDI deregulatory reform will reduce the number of uninsured consumers by 0.7 million people, each of whom also enjoys a consumer surplus of $609 from their purchases (as noted above). The CEA (2019) also estimated that third-party costs of uncompensated care will fall by $989 for each newly insured STLDI enrollee. Aggregated over 0.7 million, the benefits for previously uninsured consumers who move into STLDI plans add another $1.1 billion.

Summing up over the three groups of consumers whose insurance options are expanded by the STLDI rule, the CEA (2019) estimated that in 2021, the rule yields benefits worth $7.3 billion. The estimate of social benefits takes into account both the benefits and costs, including the possibility that the STLDI rule imposes new costs on a subset of enrollees in the nongroup market who pay higher insurance premiums.

Case Study 3: Specifying the Joint Employer Standard

During the Obama Administration, a new, expansive standard for determining joint employers dramatically changed the landscape of labor regulation for the employers of millions of American workers. This new standard especially burdened franchising, which is a large and rapidly growing part of retail, technology, and other sectors. This subsection explains why returning to the previous—narrow—standard, as the Trump Administration is doing, enhances productivity, competition, and employment in labor markets, with a net annual benefit likely exceeding $5 billion. These results occur in large part because the expansive standard increased entry barriers into local labor markets and discouraged specialization along the supply chain.

The working conditions of many of the Nation's employees are "affected by two separate companies engaged in business relationship."[25] A joint employer standard specifies when two or more companies are simultaneously the employer for legal purposes, and therefore both joint and severally liable "for unfair labor practices committed by the other." The definition of a joint employer is pertinent to legal liability in Fair Labor Standards Act litigation, enforced by the Department of Labor, and to collective bargaining rules overseen by the National Labor Relations Board. The NLRB established a common law standard by deciding various cases over the years, although that standard was volatile between 2014 and 2018. In 2018, including a board member appointed by President Trump, the NLRB issued its Notice of Proposed Rulemaking proposing to follow the standard before 2015, which was that "to be deemed a joint employer under the proposed regulation, an employer must possess and actually exercise substantial direct and immediate control over the essential terms and conditions of employment of another employer's employees in a manner that is not limited and routine."[26]

In August 2015, a decision by the NLRB established a more expansive standard that did not require the control to be direct or to be actually exercised. The NLRB's shift to a more expansive standard became apparent to the business community no later than July 2014, when the NLRB Office of the General Counsel asserted that McDonald's was a joint employer (NLRB 2014; Greenhouse 2014). The Department of Labor had also, in 2016, provided

---

[25] The quotations in this section are from 83 *FR* 46681–82.

[26] In addition to issuing the Notice of Proposed Rulemaking in 2018, the NLRB issued a December 2017 decision returning to the earlier (narrower) standard, although that decision was vacated in 2018 "for reasons unrelated to the substance of the joint-employer issue" (83 *FR* 46685).

informal guidance specifying a more expansive standard, and then during the Trump Administration withdrew that guidance.

Consider a few examples. Company ABC retains a temporary agency TMP for some clerical staffing that needs to be performed at ABC's location. If TMP has no supervisor at ABC's location and ABC is selecting and supervising the temporary employees, then by both standards ABC is a joint employer of those employees. The determination would, under the narrower standard, be the reverse if TMP was doing the supervision without detailed supervisory instructions from ABC.

Company FRA is a franchisee for company XYZ, which specifies the daily hours that FRA stores are open for business but does not involve itself with individual scheduling assignments. XYZ would not be a joint employer under the narrower standard but probably would be under the expansive standard.[27] Under the expansive standard, the NLRB charged McDonald's, which has the vast majority of its restaurants owned and operated by independent franchisees, as a joint employer for its franchisees' actions (Elejalde-Ruiz 2016). The McDonald's case was settled in 2018, with McDonald's no longer designated as a joint employer (Luna 2018), although an administrative judge rejected the settlement, which may be headed back to the NLRB for approval.

From an economic perspective, a joint employer determination prohibits the division of management responsibility that normally coincides with the assignment of management tasks along a supply chain. By restricting the allocation of responsibility along the supply chain, the chain will be less productive and involve less division of tasks (Becker and Murphy 1992). As an important example, franchisers may need to abandon their franchise status and either abandon the company assets or deploy them in a less productive corporate (nonfranchise) structure, where all the workers in the chain are employed by the franchiser.

Franchising, which is "a method of distributing products or services, in which a franchiser lends its trademark or trade name and a business system to a franchisee, which pays a royalty and often an initial fee for the right to conduct business under the franchiser's name and system," is by itself a ubiquitous business practice—about half of retail sales in the United States involve franchised operations (83 *FR* 46694; Norton 2004). About 9 million workers are employed by franchises (Elejalde-Ruiz 2016; Gitis 2017). Temporary help services is another important business model affected by the joint employer

---

[27] The NLRB's expansive standard is more speculative to apply and derives from a single NLRB decision, *Browning-Ferris*; two dissenting NLRB members found it to be "impermissibly vague." Franchisers can be joint employers under the narrower standard if, e.g., they specify that franchisees provide specific fringe benefits to franchisee employees.

standard, with 266,006 firms in 2012 obtaining about 2.5 million employees from 13,202 supplier firms.[28]

An expansive joint employer standard affects the competitiveness of the markets for labor as well as the productivity of the affected industries. The NLRB's Office of the General Counsel, advocating the expansive standard, stated that such a standard is needed to give workers additional market power (Phillips 2014). To the extent that the expansive standard causes franchises to be absorbed by the franchiser, the monopsony market power of employers would be increased.[29] Either of these adverse competition effects of the expansive standard are represented by areas D1 and E in figure 2-5 above, with the "regulated industry" understood to be franchised supply chains or the temporary help industry. In order to quantify the annual amounts contained in these areas, we first estimate that employment in these businesses is about 8 percent of total employment. Because their average pay is lower, we estimate that total wages for 2017 are about $386 billion for franchisees and temporary help services.[30] The monopsony power created by the expansive standard reduces the wages paid by these businesses. For each 1 percent that wages are reduced, the aggregate wedge between wages paid and marginal productivity is about $7.7 billion in 2017 and $11 billion a year on average for the years 2020–29.[31]

Krueger and Ashenfelter (2018) estimate that increasing the market power of employers by fully eliminating competition for labor among those franchisees associated with the same franchiser would create a labor wedge equal to about one-sixth of the inverse of the wage elasticity of industry labor supply. At an industry supply elasticity of 1 (or 4), this means that worker's wages are depressed by 8 (or 2) percent, respectively. Assuming that some franchising would have continued even with the expansive standard, these are upper bounds but suffice to show that the 1 percent effect hypothesized above is plausible.

The $11 billion per year is a transfer, but it also represents a reduction in the aggregate demand for labor. Given that labor is already significantly taxed,

---

[28] The number of firms is from 87 *FR* 46694; and the number of employees is from FRED (2018). Temporary help employment has now exceeded 3 million.

[29] Consolidation on the worker side of the market (that is unionization) may offset the wage effect of consolidation on the employer side. However, the two are reinforcing in terms of the amount of labor and therefore inefficiency because each side with market power tends to reduce quantities (demanded or supplied, as applicable) in order to squeeze the other side of the market (Williamson 1968; Farrell and Shapiro 1990; Whinston 2006).

[30] The Bureau of Labor Statistics finds that the annual mean wage of temporary help service workers was $37,090 in May 2017. We proxy franchisee workers' wages using the annual mean wage of workers in retail trade, i.e., $32,930. We then create an annual mean wage of both groups by taking a weighted average of the two groups' wages.

[31] This assumes wage elasticities of labor supply and demand that are approximately equal in magnitude, so that a 1 percent movement down the labor supply curve is associated with about the same movement up the labor demand curve. To convert a 2017 amount to an average for 2020 through 2029, we assume 5 percent annual growth.

there is a social cost of reduced labor demand for the reasons discussed in connection with figure 2-6. Using the same 50 percent deadweight cost factor used for the health insurance case studies, that makes an annual net social loss of about $5.5 billion from the anticompetitive aspects of the expansive standard. A similar cost calculation would result if it were assumed instead that the expanded standard creates a similar-sized wedge in the labor market due to additional unionization.

Any productivity effects need to be added to the anticompetitive aspects. The CEA has not yet been able to quantify these effects, aside from noting above the number of workers employed by franchisees and in the temporary help industry. Nevertheless, the productivity effects may be important because franchisers view the franchise system as essential for them to be innovative and adaptive to changing market conditions (Hendrikse and Jiang 2007). McDonald's is a major franchiser, and its annual reports show how it has increased the number of franchisee stores while decreasing the number of company stores. Its goal is to have 95 percent of its stores be franchise stores.

Related subregulatory guidance issued in 2015 by the Department of Labor proposed a revised test for independent contractor status. Independent contractors account for about 7 percent of U.S. employment (BLS 2018a; Furchtgott-Roth 2018) and are important in the relatively new sharing economy. The 2015 test shares many of the same economic issues with the expansive joint employer standard: specialization, competition, innovation, and so on. But potentially unique to independent contractors is the direction of the "tax gap"; the expansive independent contractor standard may increase revenues from employee and business taxation, whereas the expansive joint -employer standard may reduce it.[32] The additional labor or capital tax revenue resulting from the regulation is reflective of a benefit, although there is also a cost in the other direction due to a reduction in the aggregate supplies of labor and capital (recall figure 2-6).

In summary, the recent decisions by the NLRB and the Department of Labor to return to the narrow joint employer standard will create an annual net benefit of billions of dollars in the forms of added competition and productivity in low-skill labor markets. A rough estimate suggests that the net annual benefit will probably exceed $5 billion.

Conclusion

Regulation involves trade-offs. Many regulatory actions have helped protect workers, public health, safety, and the environment. However, ever-growing

---

[32] One issue, not yet resolved by the CEA, is whether business income franchisers are taxed at a lower marginal rate than business income of franchisees, especially now that the statutory corporate income tax rate has been cut. Regarding the employee / independent contractor tax gap, for varying conclusions see Bauer (2015) and Eisenbach (2010).

cumulative regulatory costs have burdened the U.S. economy. In 2017 and 2018, the Trump Administration's regulatory cost caps turned around the growth in regulatory costs. Small business owners, consumers, and workers gain when less regulation means lower business costs, lower consumer prices, more consumer choice, and higher worker productivity and wages that exceed any reduction in the regulations' benefits. Guided by cost-benefit analyses, Federal agencies are eliminating and revising regulatory actions when the benefits do not justify the costs and to improve the cost-effectiveness of regulatory actions in accomplishing their important goals.

This chapter has used an economic framework to analyze the need for, and potential of, the Trump Administration's deregulatory agenda. The framework emphasizes what small-business owners have long known—that regulatory costs accumulate and multiply. When an industry is regulated, the effects are felt across the U.S. economy. Starting in 2017 and 2018, the economy has started to grow stronger as the cost savings from deregulatory actions have begun to accumulate. Deregulation is improving the country's fundamental productivity and incentives to enable sustained economic growth.

Chapter 3

Expanding Labor Force Opportunities for Every American

Consistent with the robust pace of economic growth in the United States, the labor market is the strongest that it has been in decades, with an unemployment rate that remained under 4 percent for much of 2018. Although this low unemployment rate is a sign of a strong job market, there is a question whether the rapid pace of hiring can continue and whether there are enough remaining potential workers to support continued economic growth. This pessimistic view of the economy's potential overlooks the extent to which the share of prime-age adults who are in the labor market remains below its historical norm. It also fails to capture the extent to which these potential workers could be drawn back into the labor market by increasing worker productivity and wages as well as by correcting labor market distortions from past tax and regulatory policies. This chapter explores trends in employment and wages as well as the positive effects of the Trump Administration's policies on increasing the returns to work and encouraging additional adults to engage in the labor market.

Fundamentally, when people opt to neither work nor look for work it is an indication that the after-tax income they expect to receive in the workforce is below their "reservation wage"—that is, the minimum value they give to time spent on activities outside the formal labor market. For some, this reflects the low wages that they expect to earn through formal work—either because they lack the education and skills desired by employers or because firms lack the physical capital necessary to enhance their productivity. Reskilling programs can prepare these individuals for higher-wage jobs. Similarly, the reduction in corporate income tax rates, the expensing of businesses' investment in equipment, and the creation of the Opportunity Zones provided by the Tax Cuts and Jobs Act each makes it less costly for firms to invest in the necessary physical capital to increase worker productivity, which results in higher wages. Consistent with strong economic growth, wages continued to increase through 2018, and this wage growth has been particularly strong among the lowest-earning workers. This wage growth has the potential to give more people incentives to begin looking for work.

For others who remain outside the formal labor market, this decision reflects the tax and regulatory distortions that limit the after-tax return that they would receive from formal work. Some regulations, such as occupational licensing, directly raise the costs of entering the labor market and therefore reduce the number of people seeking work. The high cost of child care, in part driven by regulatory and other requirements, provides a disincentive to work in the formal labor market and an incentive to take care of one's own children rather than hire others to do so. This Administration's deregulatory policies have reduced these labor market distortions, thereby drawing some prime-age workers back into the labor market.

This chapter outlines recent labor market trends, both for the adult population as a whole and for key population subgroups. It also considers policies that could further remove government distortions and increase the after-tax return to formal work, thereby increasing work incentives for potential entrants into the labor market. These policies will encourage additional workforce growth and further expansion of the U.S. economy.

For adults (age 16 years and over) who are working or looking for work, the current labor market is among the strongest in recent decades. The economy is in the midst of its longest consecutive streak of monthly job creation in at least 80 years. The national unemployment rate sat at 3.9 percent in December 2018, after reaching a near 50-year low in November. Since 1970, the national unemployment rate has reached a rate below 4 percent during only 13 months, with 8 of these months occurring in 2018. Additionally, for the first time since the Bureau of Labor Statistics (BLS) began tracking job openings in 2001, there are more job openings than unemployed workers, suggesting that firms still seek to hire more people.

Despite the strong job market and the surplus of open positions, millions of adults are neither employed nor seeking work. Because these individuals are not actively looking for work, they are considered to be out of the labor market and are not counted as unemployed, even though many of them are in their prime working years and could be working. In fact, the share of prime-age (25–54 years) adults who are working remains below the share seen at the peaks of the previous two economic expansions. The availability of these prime-age adults who currently remain outside the labor force creates the potential for continued increases in employment, despite the historically low unemployment rates. Doing so, however, necessitates a better understanding of the reasons these adults are currently not working and the development of economic policies and workforce training opportunities to draw them into the labor market.

A key component of efforts to draw additional workers into the labor market is increasing the potential wages that they could receive. This is because, when jobs are available and plentiful, the decision to remain out of the labor force signals a belief among those individuals that the wage they could receive is below the value they place on their time outside the labor market. Among those who are employed, there is evidence that wages are rising for the typical worker. Real hourly earnings based on the Personal Consumption Expenditures (PCE) Price Index, which is a measure of inflation, rose by 1.5 percent for all workers and by 1.7 percent for nonsupervisory workers. This is the sixth consecutive year of positive real hourly earnings growth for nonsupervisory workers and the longest streak since the eight years of consecutive earnings growth from 1995 through 2002.

Encouragingly, wage growth is accelerating, as real hourly earnings increases for both all workers and for nonsupervisory workers in 2018 exceeded those in either 2016 or 2017. Wage gains in 2018 have also been particularly strong among the lowest-earning workers. These wage gains are an indication that policies designed to increase the productivity of workers, such as the corporate tax rate reductions in the Tax Cuts and Jobs Act, are translating into higher paychecks. But despite these recent improvements, there is still room for further wage growth, both from new policies designed to enhance productivity and from the effects of recent policies to reaching additional workers.

With the dual goals of further growing the workforce and increasing the wages of those who are working, in this chapter we consider labor market trends in recent decades, both for the population as a whole and for key demographic subsets. While recognizing that most adults engage in productive nonwork activities, we also explain how potential distortions caused by taxes and regulations can lead some adults whose most productive use of time is in the formal labor market to instead engage in other activities. Furthermore, we consider the reasons that the potential wage rates for some workers on the sidelines are below their reservation wages, and what could be done to enhance their productivity and increase their potential after-tax earnings if they entered the labor market. Finally, we discuss this Administration's policies to increase economic opportunities for a diverse range of adults to enable them to engage more fully in the growing economy.[1]

Long-Run Trends in Adult Employment, Labor Force Participation, and Wage Earnings

What do long-run trends in the labor market tell us about the economy? This section considers these trends, focusing on adult employment, labor force participation, and wage earnings.

Employment and Labor Force Participation

From 1960 through 2001, there was a marked increase in adult (age 16 and older) labor force participation (i.e., the share of all adults who are working or unemployed and looking for work) in the United States (see figure 3-1). Largely driven by more adult women entering the workforce, it rose by over 8 percentage points, from 58.5 percent in March 1960 to 67.1 percent in February 2001.[2] Since 2001, however, the trend in participation rates has reversed and has been in decline. By the end of 2015, the 62.7 percent participation rate was more than 4 percentage points below its 2001 peak. Earlier in 2015, participation rates had reached their lowest since 1977. This decline can only be partially attributed to the Great Recession, as participation rates also fell before the recession from 2001 through 2007 and after the recession from 2009 through 2015. From 2015 through 2018, the participation rate stabilized, and as of December 2018, it remained at 63.1 percent.

The share of all adults who are working—the employment-to-population ratio—shows a similar long-run pattern, but has additional business cycle volatility because unemployment rises during recessions and falls during expansions. In recent years, as the labor force participation rate has stabilized and the unemployment rate has fallen, the share of all adults who are working has risen. In December 2018, 60.6 percent of adults were working, which is more than 2 percentage points above where it stood seven years ago, in 2011. But it still remains considerably below where it stood at the turn of the 21st century.

---

[1] The CEA previously released research on the topics covered in this chapter. The text that follows builds on these research papers produced by the CEA: "Returns on Investments in Recidivism-Reducing Programs" (CEA 2018e); "Addressing America's Reskilling Challenge" (CEA 2018a); "Military Spouses in the Labor Market" (CEA 2018d); and "How Much Are Workers Getting Paid? A Primer on Wage Measurement" (CEA 2018c).
[2] These dates reflect the final month before the official start of each recession, according to the National Bureau of Economic Research (NBER 2010).

Figure 3-1. Labor Force Participation Rate and Employment-to-Population Ratio, 1950–2018

Source: Bureau of Labor Statistics.
Note: Shading denotes a recession.

In part, the decline in both the labor force participation rate and the employment-to-population ratio since 2001 was to be expected, due to the aging of the population. For over 30 years, from the late 1960s through the late 1990s, the share of the population over age 55 was nearly unchanged, making up between 26 and 28 percent of all adults. But since then, as members of the Baby Boom generation have aged, this stability has dissipated, with those over age 55 growing as a share of all adults. In 2018, more than 35 percent of the adult population was over age 55—with 19 percent over age 65 (see figure 3-2). As those who are of traditional retirement age account for a larger share of the total adult population, participation rates will decline if rates for workers at any given age remain unchanged. The effects of the aging population on overall employment and participation rates have been partially offset by rising participation of those at or near traditional retirement age (see figure 3-3). As discussed in chapter 3 of the *2018 Economic Report of the President*, this increase in participation rates among older adults is partially attributable to improved health statuses relative to earlier cohorts (CEA 2018b). The increase is also consistent with policy changes that reduce the incentives to retire early, including the delayed full retirement age for Social Security and encouraging the use of defined contribution retirement plans, which do not have built-in incentives for early retirement. But even as the most recent cohorts of adults

Figure 3-2. Adult Population by Age (Years), 1950–2018

Share of adult population (percent)

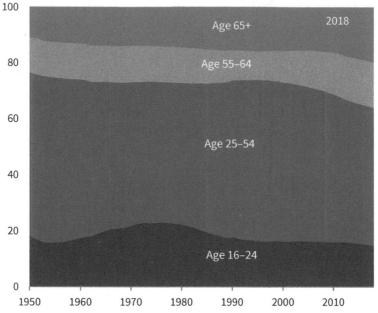

Sources: Bureau of Labor Statistics; CEA calculations.

Figure 3-3. Labor Force Participation Rate by Age, 1950–2018

Percent

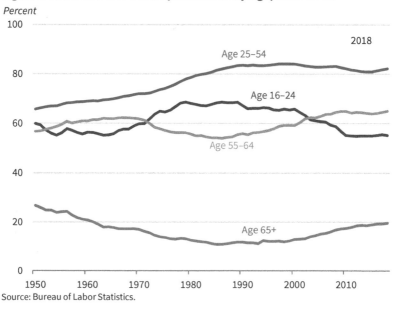

Source: Bureau of Labor Statistics.

reaching older ages are working more than those of similar ages did in the past, those over age 65 still work at substantially lower rates than younger age groups. Hence, the higher-than-traditional participation rates of these older adults are not sufficient to fully offset the loss in participation associated with the aging population.

To separate out the effects of aging, economists often focus on prime-age adults, who are age 25–54 years. This group is of particular importance because they generally are neither in school nor retired. Thus, they represent those adults who are most expected to be working.

Among prime-age adults, labor force participation rates fell from a high of 84.1 percent in 1999 to a 30-year low of 80.9 percent in 2015. This decline in prime-age participation accounted for between 35 and 40 percent of the overall decline in participation over this period—indicating that the falling overall participation rates among the adult population over the past 20 years cannot be attributed to aging alone.

However, the last three years have been more positive with regard to prime-age participation. In both 2016 and 2017, the labor force participation rates of prime-age adults rose by 0.4 percentage point, offsetting some of the declines over the previous 15 years. In 2018, the growth in participation of prime-age adults continued, suggesting that recent progrowth policies are encouraging more businesses to hire and more people to enter the labor force.

Although it is common to consider prime-age employment as a whole, embedded within both the long-term decline in employment rates and improvements over the past few years are diverse population groups with occasionally differing trends. These trends have been markedly different for males and females as well as for married and single individuals, and for those who do and do not have children. Although all races and ethnicities have seen increases in their employment rates in recent years, the relative increases among African Americans and Hispanics have been particularly strong, and the employment rate among working-age adults with a high school degree or less grew faster in 2018 than for those with more education. Although employment in rural areas still lags far behind that in urban areas, recent employment growth in manufacturing and other sectors that are disproportionately located in rural communities offers hope for employment recovery in those communities. To the extent that employment trends differ across population groups or geographies, there is an opportunity to both explore the source of these divergences and to consider targeted policies to address specific challenges and further increase labor market participation, as is done later in this chapter.

Wages and Labor Earnings

The wages that workers earn in the labor market are of similar importance to employment trends for determining the financial well-being of American households. Economists have long understood that increases in wages, as well as increases in the demand for labor, are driven by rising worker productivity (Hellerstein, Neumar, and Troske 1999). In a competitive labor market, firms pay workers a wage that is equal to the value of their marginal product. As worker productivity increases, the value of each hour of labor to firms will rise.[3] Consequently, wages will subsequently rise as well, because firms that do not increase their pay will see their workers go to other, higher-paying, firms. Hence, policies that increase workers' skills, such as additional education or training, increase the amount firms are willing to pay for their now-more-productive labor. Policies that increase the amount of capital that workers have at their disposal to produce goods and services will also increase their productivity and, subsequently, increase their wages. For example, because high corporate taxes act as a disincentive for firms to invest in the capital that would make workers more productive, numerous researchers have found that workers bear much of the burden of corporate taxes. Consequently, reductions in the corporate income tax rate lead to increases in the wages paid to workers (Hassett and Mathur 2006; Desai, Foley, and Hines 2007; Felix 2007, 2009). (For a more detailed discussion of this relationship with respect to the Tax Cuts and Jobs Act, see chapter 1.)

Although the BLS and other Federal agencies report several different wage measures, each of which has its own advantages, we focus here on wage trends from the Census Bureau's Current Population Survey (CPS). (For a comparison of the 12 surveys and programs administered by the BLS, with information on pay and benefits, see BLS 2018.) The statistics reported by the BLS using CPS data focus on full-time workers and do not capture the value of fringe benefits and bonuses—whose growth has contributed to total compensation growth among workers in recent decades.[4] They also do not directly capture the changing composition of the workforce, including the education and skill levels of those who are working.[5] In addition, these statistics focus on wages for all working adults (age 16 and older), and not just those of prime working-age. However, these data are particularly useful for understanding the full distribution of wage trends, given that researchers can use them to consider wages at different points in the distribution.

Figure 3-4 shows the trend in nominal wage growth among all adult, full-time workers in the CPS data. In the fourth quarter of 2018, median nominal weekly wages grew by 5.0 percent over the previous year. Under any measure

---

[3] Labor productivity affects wages regardless of whether the labor market is competitive, "monopsonistic," or "monopolistic."

[4] From 1982 through 2018, total compensation growth in the BLS Employment Cost Index grew about 0.3 percent per year faster than wages alone from the same survey.

[5] For a broader discussion of these composition effects, see CEA (2018b). Some researchers, including Daly and Hobijn (2017) and the Federal Reserve Bank of Atlanta (2018), attempt to correct for these composition effects by controlling for worker characteristics or following the same workers over time.

Figure 3-4. Nominal Weekly Wage Growth Among All Adult Full-Time Wage and Salary Workers, 2010–18

Percent (year-over-year)

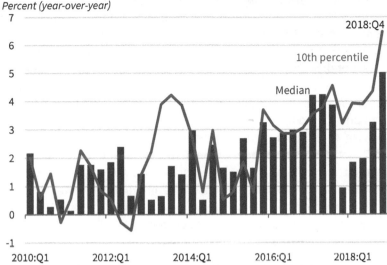

Sources: Bureau of Labor Statistics; Current Population Survey; CEA calculations.
Note: Data are non–seasonally adjusted.

of inflation, this suggests that real wages are growing. Based on the Consumer Price Index for all Urban Consumers (CPI-U), which the BLS traditionally uses to track inflation, real median weekly wages of full-time workers grew by 2.7 percent from the fourth quarter of 2017 through the fourth quarter of 2018. And on the basis of the Chained Consumer Price Index (Chained CPI), which academics consider a more accurate reflection of cost of living adjustments than the CPI-U and is now used for indexing tax brackets, real median weekly wages of full-time workers grew by 3.0 percent during this time. Moreover, based on the PCE Price Index, which is the inflation measure preferred by the Congressional Budget Office (2018) and the Federal Reserve Board of Governors (2000), real median weekly wages of full time workers grew by 3.1 percent over this time.

In addition, recent wage growth has been the fastest for those at the bottom of the wage distribution. Over the past two years, (from the fourth quarter of 2016 through the fourth quarter of 2018), nominal wages for the 10th percentile of the full-time wage distribution have increased by an annual average of 4.8 percent. Looking just at the past year (from the fourth quarter of 2017 through the fourth quarter of 2018), wage growth at the 10th percentile was an even stronger 6.5 percent. This wage growth at the 10th percentile over the past two years outpaces the 3.0 percent annual growth in median nominal wages among full-time workers and the 3.5 percent annual growth at the 90th percentile.

The trend under this Administration for wage gains of the full-time wage distribution's 10th percentile to exceed the growth rate for the distribution's middle and top stands in sharp contrast to that seen in the 2001–7 business cycle. During that period, wage growth for the 10th percentile was frequently the slowest of these three measures. Year-over-year wage growth for the 10th percentile only outpaced wage growth for the 90th percentile in six quarters over the six-year period, and even then only did so by more than 0.4 percentage point once. Although the bottom of the distribution has since experienced rapid wage growth, in 2013, this growth followed 2012, when there were nearly no wage increases at the bottom of the distribution, and this growth was not sustained into future years. If the trend under this Administration continues, with the most rapid earnings gains occurring among those lower in the wage distribution, it would be consistent with that seen in the late 1990s, when unemployment was similarly low and the bottom of the distribution also experienced several years of robust wage growth (Ilg and Haugen 2000).

Although the most recent quarter saw the nominal weekly wages at the 10th percentile and at the median of full-time workers grow at their fastest year-over-year pace since at least 2001, some economists question why wage growth has not been faster in recent decades. In addition, given the current strong labor market and low unemployment rate, one could have expected even larger wage gains in recent years.

The primary factor in understanding wage growth relates to the productivity growth of workers, given the close link between productivity and wages. During the period from the official end of the Great Recession in June 2009 through the end of 2016, productivity growth averaged just 0.9 percent a year.[6] This is dramatically slower than the productivity growth during the previous two expansions (figure 3-5). During both the 1991–2001 and 2001–7 business cycle expansions, as reported by the National Bureau of Economic Research (NBER), productivity growth exceeded 2 percent a year, on average.

Economists disagree on the long-term potential for high productivity growth. Fernald (2015) notes that a productivity slowdown predated the Great Recession and believes that the period of strong productivity gains in the mid-1990s and early 2000s was the exception. Others, including Yellen (2016), are more optimistic about potential productivity improvements. This view is supported by Borio and others (2015), who found that the credit boom and subsequent financial crisis misallocated labor to sectors with low productivity

---

[6] The BLS uses the Implicit Price Deflator when tracking productivity growth. This deflator shows slower productivity growth than the CPI-U, Chained CPI, and PCE inflation indexes. Consequently, research comparing productivity growth with wage growth must have caution in using the same inflation measures. Failing to do so results in an artificial gap between compensation growth and productivity growth (Brill et al. 2017).

Figure 3-5. Nonfarm Business Sector Real Output per Hour, 1980–2018

Percent (year-over-year change)

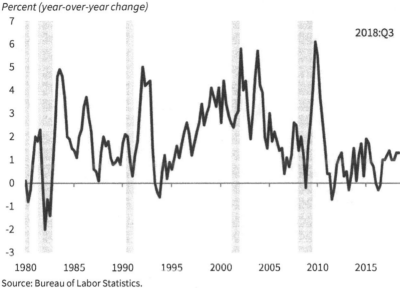

Source: Bureau of Labor Statistics.
Note: Shading denotes a recession.

growth, suggesting that the recent period of low productivity growth is not reflective of the economy's future potential. Between 2017 and 2018, productivity growth ticked up, averaging 1.3 percent a year through the third quarter of 2018. Although this remains below the productivity gains during previous expansions, these improvements are consistent with the optimistic perspective that there is still a potential for faster productivity growth. Moreover, the changes in the Tax Cuts and Jobs Act intending to boost productivity by encouraging capital investment were just recently enacted, so their full effect on productivity has likely not yet been realized. These changes include the reduction in corporate tax rates discussed in chapter 1 and the creation of Opportunity Zones discussed later in this chapter.

Although productivity growth is the most important driver of wage gains, some economists have also debated nonproductivity factors that affect wage growth. Much of this discussion relates to the bargaining power among workers. One reason for this lack of bargaining power is the possibility that the economy remains in a relatively elastic range of the labor supply curve, meaning that there are still more potential workers who would be willing to work without a substantial increase in the wage rate. Historically, the current low unemployment rate would suggest that firms desiring to hire additional workers would need to increase wages (Leduc and Wilson 2017). However,

Figure 3-6. Share of Adults Starting Work Who Were Not in the Labor Force Rather Than Unemployed, 1990–2018

Percent

Sources: Bureau of Labor Statistics; Current Population Survey; CEA calculations.
Note: Shading denotes a recession.

focusing exclusively on the unemployment rate ignores the lower prime-age employment-to-population ratio than in earlier decades as well as the growing share of older workers in good health who could be drawn into the labor market. These potential workers who are not currently in the labor market contribute to the elasticity of the labor supply. For this reason, Ozimek (2017) recently suggested that the ratio of employment to population is more relevant than the unemployment rate for understanding wage growth trends.

In support of this theory, researchers can use CPS data (which track individuals over several months) to observe the prior-month labor force status of those who find employment in any given month. These data include both adults who are starting work for the first time and those who are starting a job after a period of not working. In the fourth quarter of 2018, 73.1 percent of all adults who started working had been out of the labor force in the previous month—compared with just 26.9 percent who had been unemployed (figure 3-6). This is the largest share coming from out of the labor force since tracking of labor flows began in 1990. It suggests that firms are finding workers who are not currently in the labor force and that these adults who are currently out of the labor force remain relevant for understanding both wage growth and the potential for further increases in employment.

An additional hypothesis that some have recently considered for the slower-than-expected wage growth in recent decades is that firms are exercising monopsony power in the labor market. Under this hypothesis, if the number of firms competing for workers decreases, the remaining firms have increased market power and can depress wages (Webber 2015; Muehlemann, Ryan, and Wolter 2013; Ashenfelter, Farber, and Ransom 2010; Twomey and Monks 2011). Although it does appear that higher industry concentration can result in lower wages, recent research suggests that this has not exacerbated a reduction in wage growth during this period. This is because increases in concentration have not been sufficiently large to play a meaningful role. Bivens, Mishel, and Schmitt (2018) find that increased concentration may have reduced wage growth by just 0.03 percent a year between 1979 and 2014. In addition, recent research by Rinz (2018) observes that when looking at industry concentration measured at a local level where firms are competing for workers, rather than at the national level, industry concentration has actually declined over the past four decades, which is counter to the claims of rising concentration slowing wage growth.

Prime-Age Employment by Gender

Shifting from considering labor market trends for the entire adult population to those for specific demographic groups, figure 3-7 shows the labor force participation rate and the ratio of employment to population among prime-age men and women over the past 58 years. Individuals who are neither working nor looking for work are out of the labor force. The gap between the participation rate and the employment-to-population ratio reflects unemployed workers, so as unemployment falls, the gap between these two series will decline.

From 1950 until the early 1970s, over 95 percent of males age 25 to 54 were in the labor force every month. In the late 1960s, the combination of a strong labor market and a lack of young males looking for work in the civilian labor market due to the Vietnam War led to historically low unemployment rates. Consequently, in 1968 not only were just over 95 percent of prime-age males in the labor force but nearly 95 percent were working.

Fifty years later, in December 2018, the employment rate for these prime-age males was nearly 10 percentage points lower, as just over 86 percent of these males were employed. This reflects a long-term secular decline in prime-age male employment. Although employment rates rise during economic expansions and fall during recessions, when looking at the peak employment rate across business cycles (based on NBER definitions), the peak employment rate of prime-age males in each business cycle since 1968 has failed to reach the peak achieved in the previous business cycle.[7] During the current expansion, only in 2017 did the employment rate for prime-age males reach the trough of the previous business cycle from 2003.

---

[7] Employment in 1989 recovered to above the peak in 1981 between the double-dip recessions. However, it did not reach the 1979 peak before this pair of recessions.

Figure 3-7. Labor Force Participation Rate and Employment-to-Population Ratio for Prime-Age Adults by Gender, 1950–2018

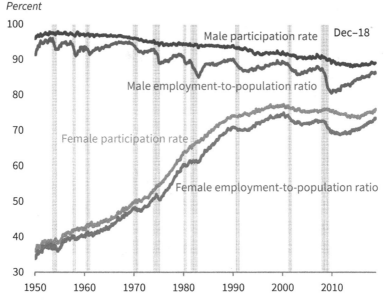

Percent

Source: Bureau of Labor Statistics.
Notes: Prime-age adults are those age 25–54 years. Shading denotes a recession.

Although the prime-age male labor force participation rate has also fallen over this period, from nearly 95 percent in 1968 to 88.2 percent in December 2015, it appears to have leveled off in the past three years, and was at 89.0 percent in December 2018. As a result of the rising employment rate and flat participation rate for prime-age males since 2015, the gap between these two series (which reflects the share of prime-age males who are unemployed) has declined. If the male participation rates had not stabilized since 2015, the continued growth in male employment that occurred would not have been possible without reaching an even lower rate of unemployment.

Nonetheless, this long-term decline in the employment and labor force participation rates of prime-age males represents a substantial decline in the size of America's workforce. The gap of 1.1 percentage points between the current prime-age male employment-to-population ratio and that from November 2007 at the peak of the previous business cycle reflects about 700,000 prime-age men who are not working. And the gap of 2.7 percentage points between the current employment-to-population ratio and that from February 2001 at the peak of the previous business cycle reflects 1.7 million prime-age males who are not working. Some of these nonworkers are unemployed, while others remain out of the labor force. Because the number of prime-age males who are out of the labor force exceeds that seen in earlier business cycles, this represents an opportunity to further increase employment even while the unemployment rate remains near historical lows.

Despite the well-established decline in prime-age male labor force participation rates and employment-to-population ratio over the past 50 years, the precise reasons for the decline remain unclear. One explanation for the recent weakness of male participation rates is the rise in opioid-related disorders (see box 3-1). The longer-term decline is also consistent with patterns finding that employment growth over the past 40 years has been weakest in male-dominated industries, including the decline of manufacturing that was occurring until recent years. Since the late 1960s, over two-thirds of all manufacturing workers have been males, including 72 percent of manufacturing workers in 2018. However, over the course of the 50 years from 1966 to 2016, the number of manufacturing jobs declined by over 5.5 million, despite an increase in total employment of 80 million jobs. Consequently, the share of males working in manufacturing jobs fell from 30 to 12 percent. Similarly, mining and logging as well as construction, whose workforces are each nearly 90 percent male, both saw slower employment growth than the workforce as a whole. However, since the fourth quarter of 2016, employment in manufacturing has increased by 3.6 percent, in construction by 8.5 percent, and in mining and logging employment by 16.1 percent. Each of these exceeds the 3.3 percent growth in total employment over this period.

In considering whether the long-term decline in male employment and labor force participation rates can be reversed, it is useful to look back to the 1960s, which is the last time when the unemployment rate was below 4 percent for a longer consecutive stretch of months than in 2018. The strength of the labor market during that 1960s business cycle resulted in the prime-age male employment rate increasing from peak to peak. No business cycle since then has accomplished this feat. There is some early, limited evidence that the current strong labor market may at least be limiting the continued decline of participation among prime-age males, and perhaps increasing it slightly. In 2018, the average monthly participation rate of prime-age males was up 0.4 percentage point relative to 2017 and up 0.5 percentage point relative to 2016. 2018 was also the fourth consecutive year where the average monthly male prime-age participation rate increased—the first time that this has happened for four consecutive years since at least the 1950s. This indicates that more prime-age males are entering or staying in the labor force.

Standing in sharp contrast to the employment patterns of prime-age males over this period, the labor force participation rates and employment rates of prime-age females, as shown in figure 3-7, rose nearly continuously for nearly 40 years from the late 1950s through the late 1990s. In the early 2000s business cycle, however, the consistent increases abated. The period from 2001 through 2007 saw the first peak-to-peak decline in either female employment or female participation rates in 50 years. Hence, the continued decline in

Box 3-1. The Opioid Epidemic and Its Labor Market Effects

The opioid epidemic that is affecting communities throughout the United States has resulted in a decline in the health of Americans and the health of the economy. Over the past decade, the number of opioid-related deaths in the United States per year has more than doubled, from 19,000 in 2007 to 49,000 in 2017 (NIH 2018). Life expectancy has fallen for the third year in a row, in part due to more frequent opioid and drug overdoses.

This opioid crisis has important economic repercussions. Ghertner and Groves (2018) find a correlation between substance use measures and economic measures, including unemployment rates and poverty. Although the Federal Reserve Board of Governors (2018a) does not find a similar correlation with objective economic outcomes, it does observe a correlation between opioid exposure and subjective perceptions of the local economy. The CEA (2017) found that the total cost of the opioid crisis was $504 billion in 2015; and several researchers, including Krueger (2017), have suggested that opioid usage has exacerbated a decline in labor force participation among prime-age males.

Krueger (2017) notes that 47 percent of prime-age males who are out of the labor force report using pain medication, with almost two-thirds of them using prescription pain medication on a given day. He finds a strong association between county-level opioid prescriptions in 2015 and declines in labor force participation between 2000 and 2015, with opioid prescriptions potentially accounting for a decline of 0.6 percentage point in prime-age male participation during this period. Other recent research has also documented a strong link between opioid prescriptions and lower participation, using more detailed data on prescribing practices or including additional areas or years of data (Aliprantis and Schweitzer 2018; Harris et al. 2018). Although its applicability to the U.S. context is uncertain, Laird and Nielsen (2016) find evidence that such a link may be causal, at least in Denmark. They observe that when people who move their place of residence wind up with a doctor who tends to prescribe more opioids, they are more likely to drop out of the labor force. However, Currie, Jin, and Schnell (2018) do not find evidence that higher rates of prescription opioids reduce participation in the United States. Ultimately, more research is needed to determine what impact illicit opioid use may have on labor market activity. Nonetheless, the strong link suggests that the fatal costs of the opioid epidemic may not capture its full cost to society.

In response, President Trump has mobilized the Administration to confront this crisis. In October 2017, the President declared a national public health emergency, which directed all executive branch agencies to employ every appropriate resource to combat the opioid epidemic (White House 2018b). By enlisting the aid of the executive agencies, the President has expanded access to services while also seeking to limit the availability of prescription and illicit opioids.

In March 2018, President Trump launched the Initiative to Stop Opioid Abuse and Reduce Drug Supply and Demand, which seeks to negate the epidemic through primary prevention, evidence-based treatment, and recovery support services. This includes implementing the Safer Prescribing Plan, which supports State prescription drug monitoring programs, and calls for all federally employed healthcare providers and nearly all federally reimbursed opioid prescriptions to follow best practices within five years. It also targets overprescription and illicit drug supplies by enlisting the Department of Justice to crack down on illegal supply chains in U.S. communities.

With help from Congress, the President has signed into law the SUPPORT for Patients and Communities Act, which is a step forward in fighting the opioid epidemic. This legislation improves access to treatment and recovery services, improves the inspection capabilities of mail-handling facilities to detect controlled substances entering the United States, and authorizes grants to States for their work monitoring substance use. The President and Congress allocated $6 billion in new funding in the Budget Resolution for 2018 and 2019 to further the fight against the opioid epidemic. With more resources, executive branch agencies are now be able to scale up their efforts to contain the effects of opioid misuse while providing more resources to Americans seeking help and treatment.

By counteracting the damaging health effects of the opioid crisis, the labor market will continue to improve, as more Americans leave the sidelines and enter the workforce. The Administration's commitment to American workers goes beyond a prosperous and booming economy; it also includes encouraging healthy and productive lives.

prime-age male employment rates along with the plateau of prime-age female employment rates resulted in the overall decline in the share of prime-age adults who were working in the early 2000s. More recently, the employment rate of prime-age women, which was 73.4 percent in December 2018, finally surpassed the previous business cycle peak of 72.7 percent. In addition, the labor force participation rate of prime-age women increased, from 73.9 percent in December 2015 to 75.9 percent in December 2018. As a result of the rapid growth in female employment and slower growth in female participation, the gap between these two series (which reflects the share of prime-age females who are unemployed) has declined. As was the case for males, if the female participation rate had not increased since 2015, the continued growth in female employment that occurred would not have been possible without reaching an even lower rate of unemployment.

Nevertheless, female prime-age employment remains more than 10 percentage points below that for prime-age males. This suggests that policies that remove remaining barriers to working have the potential to further increase employment rates among these prime-age females. These include paid family leave policies discussed in chapter 3 of the 2018 *Economic Report of the President* (CEA 2018b), the transfer program policies discussed in chapter 9 of this *Report* to encourage self-sufficiency among low-income females, as well as the policies we discuss below that target middle-income females who bear the primary responsibility for child care.

Barriers to Work from Child Care Expenses

One potential reason for lower labor force participation rates among prime-age females than prime-age males is the division of child care and home production responsibilities across genders, especially among families with young children.[8] The relationship between child care responsibilities and employment patterns among females can be seen in figure 3-8, which shows the participation rates among prime-age females based on their marital status and the presence and age of children in the household.

As discussed above, during the 1980s the employment rates and the labor force participation rates of females rose sharply. From figure 3-8, we see that the increase participation in the 1980s came primarily among married females. The participation rates of married mothers of young children under age 6 (the green line), married mothers of older children (the light blue line), and married females without children at home (the yellow line) all increased by at least 7 percentage points over the decade between 1982 and 1992. No similar increases were seen during the 1980s among single females with children (the gray and red lines) or without children (the dark blue line). Consequently, by the early 1990s, the participation rates for mothers of young children were similar across marital statuses, as were the rates for mothers of older children. However, participation rates still differed based on the age of the child, because the rates for both married and single females with young children were substantially below those for females with either no children or older children.

The similarity in levels of labor force participation rates among married and single mothers of young children in the early 1990s was only temporary, however. Starting in the mid-1990s, there was a dramatic increase in the participation rates for single mothers with young children, which rose by over 15 percentage points between 1994 and 2001, while their unemployment rate also declined. As discussed in greater detail in chapter 9, this increase has largely been attributed to the success of social assistance programs and welfare reforms that have brought these single mothers with children into the labor

---

[8] An increasing share of fathers also indicate that they are not working because they are taking care of their family. In the March 2018 CPS, 1.6 percent of prime-age fathers of young children (under age 6) said they were not working because they were taking care of their family—up from 0.2 percent in 1989. This trend could be an exacerbating factor in the broader decline in prime-age male employment over this period. Nevertheless, the fewer than 2 percent of prime-age fathers of young children who are not working to take care of their family is far below the 28 percent of prime-age mothers of young children who were not working to take care of their family.

Figure 3-8. Labor Force Participation Rates Among Prime-Age Females by Marital and Parental Status, 1982–2018

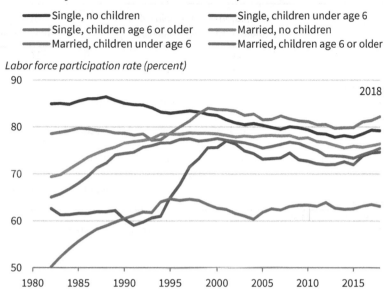

Sources: Current Population Survey; CEA calculations.
Notes: Data represent an annual average across all months. Data for 2018 are the average through July. Prime-age females are those age 25–54 years.

market (Juhn and Potter 2006; Meyer 2002). Similar increases did not occur among married mothers of young children, whose participation rate reached a plateau in the early 1990s. In contrast to that seen for single mothers, the current 63.1 percent participation rate among married mothers with children under age 6 in 2018 is slightly below where it was in 1994. The participation rates among married mothers of young children is also well below that for all other prime-age females.

Prime-age married females with young children are less likely to be working or looking for paid work than are other married females, and they make up a disproportionately large share of all prime-age married females who are out of the labor force. Although married mothers with young children represent 27 percent (10.1 million / 36.9 million) of all married prime-age females, they make up 37 percent (3.7 million / 10.2 million) of all married prime-age females who are out of the labor force (table 3-1). These married mothers of young children who are out of the labor force are evenly distributed across the educational spectrum, although on average they have somewhat less education than married mothers of young children as a whole. About 35 percent of married mothers of young children who are out of the labor force have a high school degree or less, whereas 39 percent have at least a bachelor's degree. This

Table 3-1 Number of Prime-Age Females by Marital and Parental Status, 2018

Category	Employed (thousands)	Unemployed (thousands)	Not in labor force (thousands)	Total (thousands)
Single, no children	13,249	524	3,610	17,382
Single, children under age 6	2,435	218	901	3,554
Single, children age 6 or older	4,855	258	1,107	6,220
Married, no children	9,695	258	3,068	13,021
Married, children under age 6	6,238	170	3,744	10,152
Married, children age 6 or older	10,110	259	3,379	13,748

Sources: Current Population Survey (CPS); CEA calculations.
Note: Average across monthly CPS data through July 2018. Prime-age females are those age 25–54 years.

compares with 24 percent of all prime-age married mothers of young children who have a high school degree or less.

Supporting this conclusion that child care responsibilities are important for the labor force participation decisions of parents with young children, the Federal Reserve's "Survey of Household Economics and Decisionmaking" finds that among nondisabled prime-age females age 25–54 who are not working or working part time and have a child in their home under age 6, over 60 percent say that child care plays a role in this decision (Federal Reserve Board of Governors 2018b). Among nondisabled, prime-age females whose youngest child is between the ages of 6 and 12, half of those who are not working and one-third of those working part time say that child care contributed to their decision. This suggests that there remain females who are taking care of children rather than engaging in the formal labor market due to child care responsibilities. However, the survey does not differentiate between child care costs and other reasons that parents of young children may be less likely to pursue formal employment, such as a preference for working at home and investing directly in their children's well-being.

In some instances, parents opting to engage in child care activities may reflect an efficient allocation of resources if this is a more efficient use of these parents' time than working in the formal labor market. However, several distortions of the child care market caused by tax and regulatory policies could prevent this from being the case. One such distortion occurs because labor market activities are taxed, whereas time spent on home production activities is not. Consequently, some females may decide that their after-tax wage is too low to justify formal work, even though they might have chosen formal work if it had not been for the taxes. However, some programs exist to help offset this distortion. For example, the child and dependent care tax credit offsets this distortion by providing a tax credit of 20 to 35 percent of the first $3,000 of child care expenses for one child (and $6,000 for two or more children). However, this tax credit will not fully offset the distortion for those whose required expenses for basic child care exceed these amounts.

A second distortion of the child care market occurs because regulation can raise the costs of child care.[9] Although some regulation is necessary for the safety and well-being of children, other regulations and requirements can raise the costs of this care, thereby reducing access to child care and discouraging parents from engaging in formal labor market activities.

According to data from ChildCare Aware of America (2018), the average annual cost of child care nationwide for a four-year-old is about $9,000, whereas the average annual cost for an infant is about $11,500.[10] The cost for toddlers typically falls between the higher infant cost and the lower four-year-old cost. For comparison with earnings from employment, these costs can be converted to hourly terms by dividing the cost of full-time care for each State by 2,000 hours (50 weeks multiplied by 40 hours per week). Based on these data, the hourly child care costs for a four-year-old and an infant are respectively about $4.50 and $5.75. At the State level, these hourly costs range from $2.34 for a four-year-old and $2.65 for an infant in Mississippi to $9.33 for a four-year-old and $11.83 for an infant in the District of Columbia.

When considering the net returns to employment and whether to enter the labor market after having a child, these costs can offset any wages earned

---

[9] Although this section focuses on the high cost of child care and labor force participation rates, it is also the case that these costs can act as a disincentive to have children. Milligan (2005) and LaLumia, Sallee, and Turner (2015) find small increases in fertility in response to increased child tax benefits, although Crump, Goda, and Mumford (2011) suggest that this response is small and only in the short term, and Baughman and Dickert-Conlin (2009) find no relationship between child-based tax credits and fertility rates among the targeted population. To the extent that fertility decreases as the costs of raising a child increases, high child care costs may also lead some people to forgo having children or to have fewer children. Though increased fertility rates are beneficial for long-run economic growth, exploring the relationship between child care costs and fertility rates is outside the scope of this chapter.

[10] ChildCare Aware of America (2018) offers three separate methodologies for calculating the national average that produces a range of average cost for infants between $11,314 and $11,959. These estimates are broadly in line with estimates from other sources. In 2015, the National Survey of Early Care and Education found that the price for center-based child care for an infant was $4.40 an hour at the median and $7.80 an hour on average (HHS 2015). For 40 hours per week of care year round, this reflects $9,152 (median) to $16,224 (mean) of expenses for the year. A separate survey of parents by Care (2018) found that the average cost of infant care paid by parents was $211 per week, or $10,972 for a year. Knop and Mohanty (2018) found in the 2014 Survey of Income and Program Participation that working mothers who paid for child care and whose youngest child is under age 6 paid an average of $240 per week on child care for all their children, although their analysis of the 2014 CPS found lower estimates.

through employment. Figure 3-9 therefore shows the average hourly cost for center-based child care for four-year-old children and infants in each State as a share of the median before-tax hourly wage in the State. In every State, the hourly cost of care for one young child represents at least 15 percent of the median hourly wage in the State. Parents with two or more young children in child care will have a larger financial burden. Similarly, lower-income adults may also pay a larger share on child care if they are unable to find lower-cost providers (see chapter 9 for a discussion of work and child care decisions for lower-income adults who are potentially eligible for welfare programs). Across all States, the hourly cost of child care for a single four-year-old is on average 24 percent of the State median wage, while the cost of child care for an infant is 30 percent of the State median wage. Including commuting times, when a child is with a paid caretaker but his or her parent is not paid for working, the financial burden is even greater.[11]

Given that a decrease in the cost of child care essentially means an increase in the effective wage rate for those who use child care to go to work, one way to determine the potential labor supply response to a reduction in the cost of child care is by considering estimates of the response of labor supply decisions to wages. If work increases when wages go up, then work should also increase when child care costs go down. Based on their extensive literature review, McClelland and Mok (2012) conclude that for every 1 percent increase in the wage rate, there is a 0.1 percent increase in the number of people who work, and a 0.1 percent increase in hours worked among those who were already working.[12] For workers (or potential workers) earning $20 an hour facing child care costs of $5 an hour (about the national average cost for one child in center-based care), a 20 percent decrease in child care costs (from $5 to $4) would increase the effective wage by 7 percent. For workers (or potential workers) earning $20 an hour with two children in child care, the effective wage would rise by 20 percent (from $10 an hour, after $10 an hour of child care costs, to $12 an hour after including the now-reduced child care costs). Applying the labor supply elasticities from McClelland and Mok (2012), a 7 percent increase in the effective wage would increase the number of workers and hours worked among current workers by 0.7 percent each. A 20 percent increase in the effective wage would lead to an increase of 2 percent each. However, such calculations are only illustrative, because they do not account for the actual hours of child care purchased relative to hours worked, the number of children each family has in child care, or the wage distribution of people who might use child care. McClelland and Mok (2012) also conclude from their

---

[11] Based on data from the American Community Survey, workers who commute 5 days a week spend an average of about 4 hours a week commuting to and from work.

[12] McClelland and Mok (2012) report a range of 0 to 0.2 for both the elasticity with regard to the decision to work and the decision regarding how many hours to work. Here we use the middle value of 0.1.

Figure 3-9. Child Care Costs as a Percentage of States' Median Hourly Wage, 2017

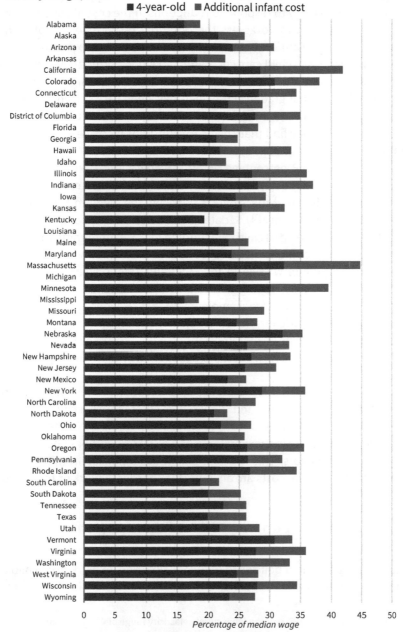

Sources: ChildCare Aware of America (2018); Bureau of Labor Statistics; CEA calculations.
Notes: Child care costs per hour are obtained by dividing the cost of full-time, center-based child care for 4-year-olds by 2,000 hours. Montana's child care costs are for 2016. Infant care costs are not available for South Dakota, so these costs are computed as the toddler care costs scaled up by the national average percent difference between costs for infant and toddler care.

literature review that the labor supply elasticity of married females (about 0.2) is larger than that for unmarried females (about 0.05), suggesting that married females are more likely to respond to reductions in the cost of child care.[13]

An alternative way to assess the potential responsiveness of work to reductions in child care costs is to consider studies that explicitly test how previous reductions in child care costs affected work. Fortunately, a number of studies have explored this question. Baker, Gruber, and Milligan (2008) study a policy in Quebec that gradually provided new child care subsidies requiring parents to pay at most $5 a day for each child age four and under, regardless of family income. They find that child care subsidies increased the use of care by almost 15 percentage points, and increased labor force participation among mothers by close to 8 percentage points. Lefebvre and Merrigan (2008) find similar effects of Quebec's child care subsidies; and Lefebvre, Merrigan, and Verstraete (2009) find that these effects persist in the medium and long terms. Herbst (2017) uses historical U.S. data to estimate the impact of the Lanham Act of 1940, which provided child care funding to U.S. communities in response to the deployment of many males to World War II. He finds substantial effects on the labor supply of women in the 1950 and 1960 Census years. Outside North America, studies looking at Spain and Norway find mixed effects of child care subsidies on maternal employment (e.g., Havnes and Mogstad 2011; Nollenberger and Rodríguez-Planas 2015). In a review of the literature on the effects of child care costs on maternal labor supply, Morrissey (2017) concludes that a 10 percent decrease in costs increases employment among mothers by about 0.5 to 2.5 percent.

Altogether, the empirical evidence on the responsiveness of labor supply decisions to wages in general and to child care costs more specifically suggests that a reduction in the cost of care could lead to increases in the number of people who participate in the workforce and also the number of hours worked among current workers. This is consistent with responses from survey data showing that child care costs are an important barrier to work or to additional work.[14]

Policies to Reduce Barriers to Work Resulting from Child Care Expenses

In considering potential policies to reduce the barriers to work from child care expenses among married mothers, it is useful to first consider how existing

---

[13] McClelland and Mok (2012) report a labor supply elasticity range of 0 to 0.3 for married women and 0 to 0.1 for men and single women.

[14] Although we focus in this chapter on the labor supply effects of child care, the effect on child outcomes are also an important consideration. Here the effects of child care subsidies are mixed, with Herbst and Tekin (2016) finding that children receiving subsidized early child care score lower on cognitive ability tests in kindergarten and Havnes and Mogstad (2011) finding that subsidized care had strong positive effects on children's educational attainment and labor market outcomes.

policies may result in the divergent employment outcomes for single and married mothers of young children discussed above. Some programs focus on reducing employment disincentives among both single and married parents. These include the child and dependent care tax credit, which provides a tax credit for a portion of child care costs when working; the child care development fund, which provides assistance through block grants for people attending job training or educational programs; and dependent care flexible spending accounts, which allow parents to pay for child care expenses using pretax dollars.

Nevertheless, as discussed in greater detail in chapter 9, many of the public policies targeted at increasing employment in the 1990s were focused on families living in poverty, often without a worker in the family. These included the Earned Income Tax Credit (EITC), which provides substantial incentives to enter the labor market for single parents and parents without a working spouse. Hence, the EITC effectively increases the average hourly compensation of low- and middle-income parents who are entering the workforce, as long as there is no other working parent in the family, which can offset these child care expenses.

However, among married women with a working spouse, the EITC typically has either no effect or a negative effect on after-tax hourly wages. This is because policymakers structured the EITC to incentivize work among low-income individuals who would represent the first worker in a family, rather than encouraging both parents to work. For example, consider the EITC that a married couple with two children with at least one full-time worker receives (table 3-2). The maximum EITC benefits of $5,716 is reached with just one full-time, year-round worker making the federal minimum wage ($7.25 per hour) in the family; and if this worker makes $15 per hour, the couple will be in the phase-out region of EITC benefits without any earnings from the second parent. This means that once one family member is working full time, adding a second worker to the family cannot increase EITC benefits and will frequently result in a reduction of these benefits.

Without the offsetting EITC benefits, the combination of child care expenses and tax liabilities can offset nearly all the financial benefits from work, even for relatively well-paid workers. Consider a married mother with one child whose spouse earns $20 per hour and who is considering starting to work full time herself at an hourly wage of $20. If her child requires care that costs $5 per hour each, these expenses would offset 25 percent of her pretax hourly wage. Based on the Urban Institute's (2012) "Net Income Change Calculator"—which incorporates any Federal, State, local, and payroll tax liabilities—the combined expenses from child care and taxes could constitute half of her pretax wages. If she had two children that require care, the combination of additional taxes and child care expenses could represent about three-fourths of her pretax wages. These substantial child care expenses act as a similar burden for a single

Table 3-2. EITC Benefits for a Married Couple with Two Children, Based on the Additional Earnings from a Second Full-Time Worker, 2018

First full-time worker's hourly wage (dollars)	Second full-time worker's hourly wage (dollars)				
	0.00	7.25	10.00	15.00	20.00
7.25	5,716	4,737	3,578	1,472	–
10.00	5,716	3,578	2,420	314	–
15.00	4,526	1,472	314	–	–
20.00	2,420	–	–	–	–
25.00	314	–	–	–	–

Sources: Internal Revenue Code; Internal Revenue Service (2018); CEA calculations.
Note: EITC=Earned Income Tax Credit. Assumes both workers are working full-time, year-round (40 hours per week and 50 weeks per year). The maximum possible EITC benefits that a parent of two children can receive is $5,716.

female considering work, but the additional EITC benefits for which she qualifies through work will partially offset these expenses associated with entering the labor market.

One way to reduce the financial burdens of child care for both single and married females considering working is to reduce the direct costs of care. Given the high costs of care relative to wages, it is important to consider how government policies may drive up these costs. Regulations that impose minimum standards on providers can decrease the availability and increase the cost of obtaining care, thus serving as a disincentive to work.

Because staff costs constitute the majority of child care costs, regulations that constrain the number, characteristics, and required activities of staff members can greatly affect costs (National Center on Early Childhood Quality Assurance 2015). Although States differ on which facilities are exempt from licensing requirements, all States license child care facilities and require a minimum ratio of staff members to children (for details on licensing regulations and exemptions from these requirements, see HHS 2014). For 11-month-old children, minimum staff-to-child ratios ranged from 1:3 in Kansas to 1:6 in Arkansas, Georgia, Louisiana, Nevada, and New Mexico in 2014. For 35-month-old children, they ranged from 1:4 in the District of Columbia to 1:12 in Louisiana. For 59-month-old children, they ranged from 1:7 in New York and North Dakota to 1:15 in Florida, Georgia, North Carolina, and Texas. Assuming an average hourly wage of $15 for staff members (inclusive of benefits and payroll taxes paid by the employer), the minimum cost for staff per child per hour would range from $2.50 in the most lenient State to $5 in the most stringent State for 11-month-old children, from $1.25 to $3.75 for 35-month old-children, and from $1.00 to $2.14 for 59 month-old children. Figure 3-10 shows the distribution of States over minimum staff-to-child ratios, as well as the average

Figure 3-10. Number of States and Average Center-Based Child Care Cost by Minimum Staff-to-Child Ratio and Age Group

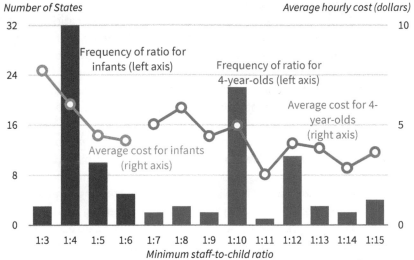

Sources: Childcare Aware of America; Early Childhood Training and Technical Assistance System.
Note: Infants are up to 11 months for maximum staff ratios and 12 months for average annual cost. Maximum ratio data are for 2014. Annual cost data are for 2017.

hourly cost of center-based care in each State. For both Infants and 4-year-old children, costs tend to fall as fewer staff members are required. Of course, minimum ratios are likely correlated with other State-level factors that determine costs, including demand from residents for different quality levels of child care. Still, these ratios may be binding constraints for many families, especially for low- to moderate-income families in States with high minimum ratios.

In addition to the number of staff members required, the wages they are paid add to the overall cost of child care. Wages are based on the local labor market demand for the employees' skills and qualifications, as well as the availability of workers in the field. Regulations that require higher-level degrees or other qualifications drive up the wages required to hire and retain staff, increasing the cost of child care. Though recognizing that some facilities are exempt from these requirements, all States set requirements for minimum ages and qualifications of staff, including some that require a bachelor's degree for lead child care teachers. Other staff-related regulations that can drive up costs include required background checks and training requirements. In addition to standards regarding staff, many States set minimum requirements for buildings and facilities, including regulating the types and frequency of environmental inspections and the availability of indoor and outdoor space.

Also, most States set a maximum number of children who can be included in a given care group, which can require additional building space.

These regulations are often beneficial for the health and safety of the children (Hotz and Xiao 2011). To the extent that these regulations increase safety and reduce injuries in child care settings, they have measurable societal benefits. Nevertheless, some regulations likely have little effect on children's well-being or the quality of care being provided while acting as a barrier to entry that can limit competition and increase prices (Gorry and Thomas 2017). As discussed later in this chapter, this concern exists for a range of licensed occupations in addition to child care workers.

Consistent with this concern, research generally finds that child care regulations increase the cost and reduce the supply of care options. Hotz and Xiao (2011) study how changes in regulations over time affect the number of center-based care establishments. They estimate that decreasing the maximum number of infants per staff member by one (thereby increasing the minimum staff-to-child ratio) decreases the number of center-based care establishments by about 10 percent. Also, each additional year of education required of center directors decreases the supply of care centers by about 3.5 percent. Similarly, Currie and Hotz (2004) find that when States adopt more stringent education requirements for child care center directors, increase minimum staff-to-child ratios, and require more frequent inspections, the number of children enrolled in center-based care falls. Other studies focus on variation in regulations at a point in time within States across age groups—for example, determining whether States with relatively more stringent regulations for four-year-old children than infants have relatively higher costs of care for four-year-old children compared with infant care. With this approach, Blau (2007) finds that tighter regulations do not necessarily increase costs, while Gorry and Thomas (2017) find some evidence that they do increase costs.

Ultimately, the regulation of child care is designed to increase the quality of care provided to children. These quality improvements may benefit children who remain in care, but they may also increase the costs paid by parents beyond their willingness or ability to pay. Evidence for this can be seen in the shift away from center-based care and toward family care providers (also known as home-based care) after regulations on care centers are increased (Hotz and Xiao 2011). These family care providers, where children are cared for in the provider's home rather than at a center, are typically subject to less regulation and offer care at a lower cost than at a center. The National Survey of Early Care and Education found that the median cost of home-based infant care was 28 percent below that for center-based care and 19 percent lower for a four-year-old (HHS 2015). For some parents, family care centers reflect a more cost-effective way to obtain care and may offer a preferred environment for the children or greater convenience for the parent. However, to the extent that regulations are shifting more parents from center-based to home-based care, this may indicate that regulations are distorting the market and parents are not willing or able to pay for the resulting higher costs. Furthermore, regulations designed to increase the average quality of care may not do so if parents forgo the more tightly regulated market as a result.

In addition, regulations designed to increase the quality of child care centers may not actually do so if centers respond by reducing other inputs, such as teacher training, that also affect quality (Blau 2007). Thus, by loosening regulations that do not substantially affect the safety or quality of care, States may be able to reduce the cost of formal child care and increase parental work effort.

Prime-Age Employment by Race, Ethnicity, and Education

A key concern in evaluating the economy and the labor market is the extent to which certain demographic groups are consistently left behind. In particular, black and Hispanic employment rates have consistently fallen short of those of whites. This is apparent in figure 3-11, which shows the prime-age ratio of employment to population by race. To reduce the noise in the series, we use quarterly average employment rates. Since this series began in 1994, the white prime-age employment rate has consistently been at least 4 percentage points above that for blacks, and at least 3 percentage points above that for Hispanics.

Although there is further progress to be made in closing the racial and ethnic employment gaps, it is apparent that the economic growth during the current business cycle is having the largest positive effect on the employment of blacks and Hispanics. The average difference of 4.6 percentage points between the prime-age employment rates of blacks and whites in 2018 and of 3.5 percent between Hispanics and whites are each the smallest annual gaps ever recorded since the BLS began publishing prime-age employment-to-population ratios by race in 1994.

Although prime-age employment-to-population ratios are not available by race before 1994, prime-age labor force participation rates are available for earlier years (see figure 3-12). The gaps in participation rates across races and ethnicities have not closed as rapidly as have employment-to-population ratios, as figure 3-11 shows. This is because unemployment rates for prime-age blacks and Hispanics have both declined more rapidly than the unemployment rate declined for whites. Nevertheless, the average gap of 2.6 percentage points in prime-age participation rates between whites and blacks in both 2017 and 2018 were the smallest since 1983. As discussed in box 3-2, the current disparity in employment and participation rates between white and black prime-age adults is almost completely attributable to a racial employment gap among males rather than females.

Similar results are apparent when considering the recent trends in prime-age employment-to-population ratios by education level, because those with

Figure 3–11. Employment-to-Population Ratio for Prime-Age Adults by Race, 1994–2018

Percent (non–seasonally adjusted)

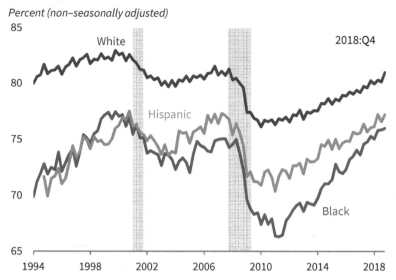

Source: Bureau of Labor Statistics.
Note: Prime-age adults are those age 25–54 years. The series for Hispanics starts in 1994:Q4. The BLS does not publish prime-age employment-to-population ratios for any race before 1994. Shading denotes a recession.

Figure 3-12. Labor Force Participation Rate for Prime-Age Adults by Race, 1972–2018

Percent (non–seasonally adjusted)

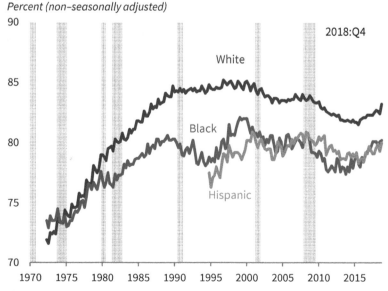

Source: Bureau of Labor Statistics.
Note: Prime-age adults are those age 25–54 years. The series for Hispanics starts in 1994:Q4. Shading denotes a recession.

Box 3-2. Employment Rates among Black Men

The ratio of employment to population is an important measure of the share of the civilian noninstitutional population who are employed and allows us to combine information from both the labor force participation and unemployment rates. As figures 3-i and 3-ii show, there has historically been a wide gap in employment rates between black and white prime-age adults.

However, a notable aspect of this disparity in employment rates is that it currently appears to be driven primarily by the employment disparity for males across the two races, rather than females. For instance, while the employment-to-population ratio for prime-age white males in the fourth quarter of 2018 was 87.7 percent, for prime-age black males it was 9.4 percentage points lower, at 78.4 percent. For females, conversely, the prime-age employment-to-population ratio had been higher for black females than white females from September 2016 until the fourth quarter of 2018. In the fourth quarter of 2018, the prime-age employment-to-population ratio for black females was within 0.3 percentage point of that for white females.

Numerous researchers have explored the black/white employment disparity, trying to better understand the factors driving this gap. This research suggests that the employment gap results from multiple sources (Bound and Freeman 1992), with common explanations including differences in education or skills (Wilson 2015; Moss and Tilly 1996; Neal and Johnson 1996), labor mar-

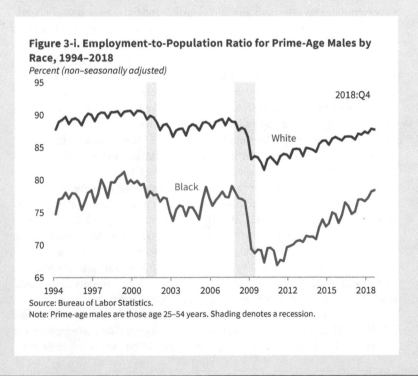

Figure 3-i. Employment-to-Population Ratio for Prime-Age Males by Race, 1994–2018
Percent (non–seasonally adjusted)

Source: Bureau of Labor Statistics.
Note: Prime-age males are those age 25–54 years. Shading denotes a recession.

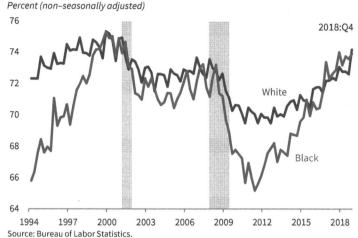

Figure 3-ii. Employment-to-Population Ratio for Prime-Age Females by Race, 1994–2018

Percent (non–seasonally adjusted)

2018:Q4

White

Black

Source: Bureau of Labor Statistics.
Note: Prime-age females are those age 25–54 years. Data are non–seasonally adjusted. Shading denotes a recession.

ket discrimination (Bertrand and Mullainathan 2004; Darity and Mason 1998; Shulman 1987), and the "first fired, last hired" phenomenon, which asserts black workers are hit much harder by recessions and take a longer time to recover from economic downturns, as noted by Couch and Frailie (2010) and Weller (2011). (Couch and Fairlie observe, however, that the decline in unemployment late in a business cycle comes more from a reduction in the rate of job losses rather than actually being the last hired.) Especially because the racial disparity is driven by male, rather than female, employment, an additional explanation is the lasting effects of higher incarceration rates among black males (Western and Pettit 2000, 2005; Holzer, Offner, and Sorensen 2005; Pager, Western, and Sugie 2009; Neal and Rick 2014).

In 2016, close to 70 percent of people incarcerated were racial or ethnic minorities, with over one-third being black (Carson 2018). Black males are six times more likely to be incarcerated than white males (figure 3-iii). According to the Sentencing Project (2018), about 1 in 12 black males in their 30s is in prison or jail every day. Those who are incarcerated are not included in employment statistics; but if those with a criminal record are less likely to find employment after their release, these high incarceration rates could exacerbate the lower employment rates among black males.

Previous research has found that this is the case. Bhuller and others (2016) find that spending time in prison has a negative effect on employment outcomes after release. They assert that incarceration may result in depreciated human capital and limit employment opportunities due to societal stigma. Western and Pettit (2000) observe that individuals with criminal records have significantly fewer employment opportunities and lower earnings. They go on to say that it is impossible to truly understand patterns of employment without also considering incarceration rates.

Criminal justice reform has been a leading priority of the Trump Administration. In March 2018, the President issued an Executive Order (White House 2018a) that would bring numerous Federal agencies together, helping to identify ways to improve the reentry of formerly incarcerated individuals into the labor force, in addition to reducing recidivism and improving public safety overall. The Administration has also worked with Congress to pass the FIRST STEP Act, which the President signed into law on December 21, 2018. This legislation will help strengthen reentry programs for federal prison inmates while reducing recidivism. For further discussion on recidivism reducing programs in the United States see the 2018 report released by the CEA (2018d).

The Trump Administration has also emphasized policies that further the period of economic growth, recognizing that the "first fired, last hired" phenomenon suggests that the black workers who are less likely to find work early in economic expansions disproportionately benefit from extended periods of hiring. Consistent with this philosophy, the disparity in the black and

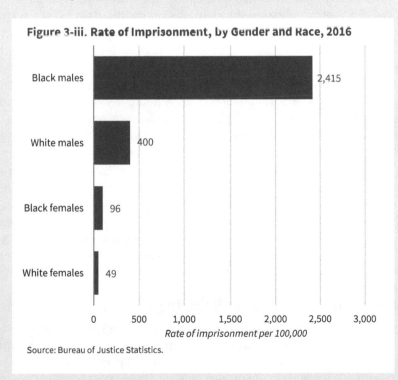

Figure 3-iii. **Rate of Imprisonment, by Gender and Race, 2016**

Rate of imprisonment per 100,000

Source: Bureau of Justice Statistics.

white employment-to-population ratios has been steadily declining. In 2018, the average black/white employment gap among prime-age adults reached 4.6 percentage points, a historical low since BLS began publishing prime-age employment-to-population ratios by race in 1994. Among individuals of all ages, the average gap in 2018 was an even lower, at 2.4 percentage points, also representing a historical low.

less education who traditionally were the least likely to be working have made the greatest gains in employment over the past two years. In the fourth quarter of 2016, 86.2 percent of prime-age adults with at least a bachelor's degree were employed, relative to 69.5 percent of those with a high school degree or less (figure 3-13). But since the end of 2016, gains in prime-age employment have been most prevalent among those with less education. As of the third quarter of 2018, the employment rate of those with a bachelor's degree is essentially unchanged, falling by 0.1 percentage point, while the employment rate for those with a high school degree or less has risen by 2.3 percentage points and the employment rate for those with some college, but no bachelor's degree, has risen by 0.4 percentage point.

The relative rise in employment rates for those with less education and the rise among prime-age black adults mirror the rises from the latter years of the late 1990s business cycle, when there were notable increases in employment rates among these groups. This is consistent with research that lower-skilled and marginalized workers are often hit hardest during economic downturns (Kaye 2010; Elsby, Hobijn, Sahin 2010) and that unemployment gaps between black and white workers narrow late in expansions near business cycle peaks (Couch and Fairlie 2010). This historical pattern illustrates the importance of continued progrowth policies that increase the productivity of workers and encourage further hiring of these workers.

Despite these recent improvements, the substantial gap in employment rates between those with a bachelor's degree and those with a high school degree or less highlights the need to rethink and improve our approaches to training workers so that more adults can gain the skills desired by employers in the current economy. This includes both improving the alignment of workers' skills with those sought by employers and evaluating regulations that mandate additional training for workers that employers may not otherwise require.

Increasing Workers' Skills and Closing Skill Mismatches

Even during periods with a strong labor market, some low-skill workers will be unable to find work if they lack the skills currently required by hiring firms. Other workers may simply opt against even looking for work if they perceive a skills mismatch between their current skills and those employers seek.

Figure 3-13. Employment-to-Population Ratio for Prime-Age Adults by Education Level, 1992–2018

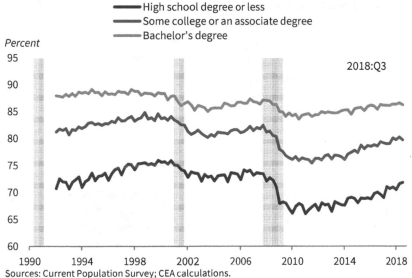

Percent

Sources: Current Population Survey; CEA calculations.
Note: Prime-age adults are those age 25–54 years. Data are non–seasonally adjusted. Shading denotes a recession.

For some workers, the skills mismatch occurs purely because they lack skills required across a range of industries. According to an international survey on adult skills conducted by the Organization for Economic Cooperation and Development (OECD 2013), a somewhat larger share of adults in the United States have lower mathematics and problem-solving skills than in other OECD member countries, while literacy skills in the United States are similar to those in other countries.

For others, however, skill mismatches occur because they were trained in an industry where the growth in employment has failed to keep up with the overall population. Figure 3-14 shows employment growth by industry since 1979, relative to the total adult population change. During this period, although several primarily service occupations—including education and health services as well as professional and business services—have expanded faster than the U.S. population has grown, others have exhibited slower growth. For workers trained in these slower-growing industries, improvements in their employment prospects necessitate either a revitalization of their current industry or retraining to allow them to transition to industries where employment is growing more rapidly. This is also consistent with the latest data on job openings from the BLS, which found that the industries with the highest vacancy rates in 2018

Figure 3-14. Employment Growth by Industry Relative to Total Adult Population Growth, 1979–2018

■ Female employment ■ Male employment
– – – Total population growth

Mining and logging
Construction
Manufacturing
Wholesale trade
Retail trade
Transportation and warehousing
Utilities
Information
Financial activities
Professional and business services
Education and health services
Leisure and hospitality
Other services
Government

–2   –1   0   1   2   3   4
Average growth per year (percent)

Sources: Bureau of Labor Statistics; CEA calculations.

were largely the industries that have been exhibiting the fastest employment growth in recent decades (figure 3-15).

In some instances, employers may address any skills gaps among their workers by offering training to new employees. This is especially true in a tight labor market, when there are relatively few people looking for work with the skills necessary to do the job. However, employers may be reluctant to undertake this investment if they are concerned that after training a worker, the firm will lose him or her to a rival firm.

In considering these concerns about "poaching," economists often distinguish between general and specific human capital. General human capital includes the set of skills workers obtain that can be applied to multiple firms, whereas specific human capital is more narrowly applicable to a single firm or a narrow set of firms. For example, learning to operate a proprietary computer system would be specific human capital, but capabilities to write in a ubiquitous programming language would constitute general human capital. From an employer's perspective, spending on specific human capital is a safer investment, because it is less likely to give workers who receive the training increased opportunities for outside jobs. However, not all skill gaps can be bridged with specific human capital, which suggests that employers individually may not

Figure 3-15. Job Opening Rates by Industry, 2018:Q4

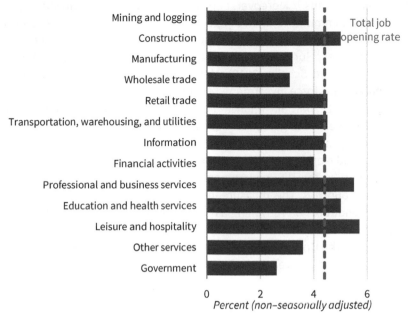

Source: Bureau of Labor Statistics.

have the financial incentive to bridge the gap between the skills they require to be globally competitive and the skills the U.S. workforce possesses.

If employers will not pay to train workers in new skills, workers may engage in training themselves. According to the OECD (2013), although the United States does better than most countries in employing low-skill workers, the returns to additional skills are particularly strong in the United States. This suggests that it would be advantageous for many workers to increase their own skills, even in the absence of employer-provided training.

There is evidence that Americans do engage in more adult learning than is seen in many other countries—although adult learning rates in the United States are much higher for those who already have at least basic levels of skills than among the lowest-skilled adults. According to the OECD (2013), 40 percent of low-skilled adults participated in adult education in the year before their study, compared with 70 percent of higher-skilled adults who did so.

Although most of the benefits from reskilling programs accrue to workers and their employers, in some instances public participation in the reskilling of workers may be appropriate, for several reasons. First, although work-ers who are successfully reemployed will reap the majority of the resulting financial benefits, these benefits do not accumulate solely to workers. The public also stands to benefit from successful reemployment, both because it increases public tax revenues and because it reduces reliance on social safety net programs.[15] Moreover, persistent unemployment can subsequently affect local communities, including a potential link to opioid use, and have intergenerational effects (e.g., decreased income) on the children of displaced workers (Charles, Hurst, and Schwartz 2018; Oreopoulos, Page, and Stevens 2008; Stevens and Schaller 2010). Many of these same considerations drive other public workforce investments: ensuring access and funding for students through grade 12, partially financing postsecondary education, and providing high-quality metrics to guide students to successful postsecondary programs. Skills training, in some ways, fits nicely into a portfolio of public investments in education and workforce development already in place. Figure 3-16 illustrates the spending by the U.S. government on labor market programs compared with other countries. This measure includes other labor market policies (e.g., public expenditures on retraining as well as on job counseling and job search assistance, as defined by the OECD) and not just skills training. Nonetheless, it suggests that the United States spends relatively little on these programs relative to that by most developed countries, especially as measured as a share of GDP.[16]

That adult learning rates are higher in the United States than in many other countries, and that public expenditures on adult education are lower suggests that much of the adult learning results from private sector expenses. Figure 3-17 shows that this is the case. During childhood, public education constitutes the majority of education spending. Education spending among adults is lower overall than it is for children. But this is especially true for public education spending, given that most of the spending on education for those age 30 and older comes from either private sources or from training paid for by employers. The Trump Administration has emphasized the need to redouble the private sector's involvement in increasing the skill levels of the American workforce. Through the Pledge to America's Workers, the President has secured pledges from American businesses to create enhanced career and training opportunities for 6.5 million workers. Additionally, through the National Council for the American Worker, the Administration intends to develop a national workforce strategy that increases the efficiency and effectiveness of Federal workforce programs and better cooperates with the private sector to equip workers with the skills desired by employers (see box 3-3).

---

[15] However, we note that workers forgo earnings as they acquire skills, which means that for a time the Treasury forgoes tax revenue and might spend more on safety net programs. This also means that minimum (cash) wage laws may act as a barrier to skill acquisition (Hashimoto 1982; Neumark and Wascher 2003).

[16] Of course, funding decisions should be made based on cost-benefit assessments as well as an understanding of the gaps in private labor market expenditures, and researchers have found that several European training programs do not pass the cost-benefit test (Kluve 2010; Card, Kluve, and Weber 2010).

Figure 3-16. Public Expenditures on Active Labor Market Programs, 2016

Percentage of GDP

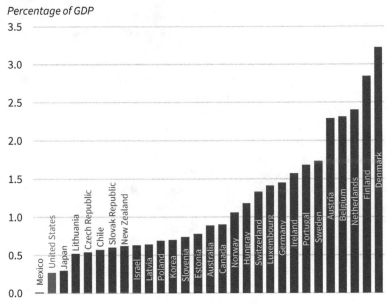

Source: Organization for Economic Cooperation and Development.

Figure 3–17. Expenditures on Education and Skills Training by Age and Source, 2017

■ Public education spending   ■ Private education spending

■ Employer costs, formal training   ■ Employer costs, informal training

Expenditures per capita

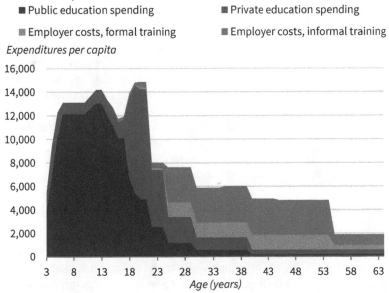

Sources: Organization for Economic Cooperation and Development; Census Bureau; Bureau of Economic Analysis; Georgetown Center on Education and the Workforce; CEA calculations.

Box 3-3. The President's National Council for the American Worker

As technology advances and the economies around the globe become more interconnected, the skills demanded by employers change. This may in part explain why there are 1 million more job openings than job seekers in the U.S. economy. As such, it is vital for workers to keep pace with change and adapt and/or update their skill sets to meet the needs of the labor market, enabling the employment of every American who desires to work.

In July 2018, the President signed an Executive Order establishing the President's National Council for the American Worker. This council's goal is to develop a national strategy to ensure that American workers have access to innovative education and job training or retraining opportunities that will equip them to succeed in the global economy. The Federal government currently has over 40 grant programs that support workforce development. The new council seeks to make these programs more effective, innovative, and results-driven.

Another crucial aspect of the council is that it helps promote working partnerships between American businesses, workers, and educational institutions. Information gaps can hinder the economy and limit the opportunities for American workers; therefore, the council intends to link all participants in the economy, informing them about what jobs are available, where they are located, what skills are required to succeed, and how best to obtain these skills.

The Executive Order also provides for the formation of an advisory board made up of leaders in education, philanthropy, state government, and the private sector. Together with the Administration, these leaders are working toward implementing successful job-training programs, including both formal and informal educational opportunities. The Administration has also established the Pledge to America's Workers, which calls upon businesses to commit to investing in America's workers. Companies have pledged to create enhanced career and training opportunities for more than 6.5 million Americans through a variety of tried-and-true methods, such as apprenticeship programs and on-the-job training.

The President's National Council for the American Worker is devoted to helping every American worker obtain the skills necessary to succeed and to ensure that every business's needs are met, guaranteeing that every American benefits from the prosperous and booming economy that American ingenuity has built.

In considering how to encourage more Americans to seek additional skills training, it is important to consider why some individuals may not seek out further training, despite the positive financial returns it is likely to provide. In some instances, the lack of information about jobs available in the local labor market, the skills required for these jobs, and training programs that can best equip them with these skills may be to blame. The expansion of online job aggregators has greatly eased the search for job openings, but it has not necessarily assisted workers in determining the skills required for these jobs and the specific training steps that are needed. Closely related to this problem is the uncertainty about which skills will be necessary to remain competitive in the labor market of the future.

Another reason some workers may not engage in skills training is the real or perceived costs of postsecondary education, which serves as a barrier to individuals who are not already successful in the labor market. This is a particular concern for those who are budget constrained and unable to fund training efforts while maintaining the financial stability of their households. Yet without making this investment, the likelihood that these individuals will find a way into the labor market is reduced. Predictions about the growth in jobs linked to automation, which require advanced programming and information technology skills, suggest that workers with fewer years of education (who are likely to have lower incomes) may have fewer job opportunities in the future (Manyika et al. 2017; OECD 2018b; PwC 2018). Those who are unemployed may find it even harder to reenter the job market if they do not have technological skills, although several State and Federal programs are targeted to assist them to develop the necessary skills. The State of New Jersey, for example, allows unemployment benefits to be extended to individuals who are working to complete training programs after they would have otherwise expired. Additionally, the Reemployment Services and Eligibility Assessment Program at the Department of Labor, which was funded through the Bipartisan Budget Act of 2018, provides States with funding for programs that provide reemployment services to help unemployed adults develop marketable job skills and reenter the job market more quickly.

For individuals who cannot engage in skills training programs due to financial constraints, some low-cost or no-cost models support training and retraining without imposing additional financial burdens. In particular, apprenticeships and other on-the-job learning opportunities provide a financial bridge so workers can earn a wage during their training and do not face the personal expenditure outlays and lost income associated with enrolling in formal education. Apprentices and those participating in other types of earn-and-learn opportunities undertake productive work for an employer, earn wages, receive training primarily through supervised earn-and-learn training models, and engage in related classroom instruction. Moreover, apprenticeships reduce the need for individuals to figure out on their own which skills are most desired by employers because employers help design these programs based on in-demand knowledge and skills. Additionally, apprenticeships have been shown to provide a strong boost to workers' future labor market outcomes (Neumark and Rothstein 2005; Lerman 2014). Despite these advantages, apprenticeships make up less than 0.5 percent of the U.S. labor force, compared with roughly 2 to 4 percent in Australia, Britain, Canada, and Germany.

The President highlighted the benefits of apprenticeships and work-based learning in his June 2017 Executive Order to expand apprenticeship, including by establishing new Industry-Recognized Apprenticeship Programs (IRAPs) developed by third parties. This Executive Order also directed Secretary of Labor Alexander Acosta, in partnership with the Secretary of Commerce and the Secretary of Education, to establish the Task Force on Apprenticeship Expansion (2018) "to identify strategies and proposals to promote apprenticeships, especially in sectors where apprenticeship programs are insufficient." The task force met for almost a year, and in May 2018 published its report, which makes a number of recommendations. The Department of Labor is now actively working to implement the task force's recommendations and set up a new IRAP system, and other Federal agencies are doing their part to support these recommendations as well.

Another approach to increasing access to reskilling programs includes increasing the flexibility of unemployment insurance (UI) benefits for those seeking additional skills. Because UI benefits are conditional on a displaced worker not being rehired, they may discourage some recipients both from quickly finding new ·employment opportunities and from enrolling in an apprenticeship program, which also must pay wages. Apprenticeship programs include well-planned work-based and classroom learning. For this reason, it may be appropriate to allow apprentices to continue receiving a portion of the UI benefits they would otherwise receive to offset lost earnings while they are learning. This would further incentivize individuals to seek and participate in apprenticeships to learn new skills after a layoff.

Despite the logic of extending some or all UI benefits during periods of retraining, there is scant empirical evidence on the benefits of these programs. The State of Georgia launched a now-defunct program called GeorgiaWorks, which allowed workers to receive full UI benefits while participating in unpaid apprenticeship programs. The success of GeorgiaWorks, however, is unclear because it did not include a well-designed evaluation component. The Trade Adjustment Assistance Program, however, uses a similar model to allow for the collection of UI benefits while receiving job training and was found to be largely unsuccessful (Schochet et al. 2012; Decker and Corson 1995). This highlights the importance of ensuring that any apprenticeships are structured so workers do not only learn new skills but also that those skills will be valued in the workforce and lead to successful employment opportunities and careers.

Reforming Occupational Licensing

For a substantial share of positions, many low-skill workers must not only demonstrate to an employer that they have the requisite skills for a job but also obtain a professional license. In the first half of 2018, just under one-fourth of all workers reported that they have an active professional certification or license. These licenses are often a requirement for employment, as over 80 percent of those with a license say that this license is required for their job. The share of jobs requiring occupational licensing has risen sharply since the 1950s, when only 5 percent of all jobs were covered by licensing laws (Kleiner and Krueger 2010).

The traditional justification for occupational licensing is to protect consumer health and safety, especially in occupations where the quality of a service provider cannot be easily evaluated by consumers (Akerlof 1970; CEA, Department of the Treasury, and Department of Labor 2015; Kleiner 2000; Shapiro 1986). Given this, it is perhaps unsurprising that healthcare practitioners are the most frequently licensed, with about three-fourths of workers reporting that they have a license. Nevertheless a sizable share of workers in a wide-range of non-healthcare occupations report having a professional license—including two-thirds working in legal professions; over 30 percent of financial specialists; and over 20 percent of installation, maintenance, and repair workers (figure 3-18). These licenses are also not limited to highly skilled workers within each occupation. As illustrated in figure 3-18, in many occupations the share of workers who have a professional license is similar when considering only those workers without a bachelor's degree.

If all these licenses were necessary for the health and safety of consumers, one would expect some uniformity of occupations requiring licenses across States. However, a 2012 study showed that the share of low-wage occupations requiring licenses ranged from 24 percent in Wyoming to 70 percent in Louisiana (Carpenter et al. 2012). One potential explanation for the difference in licensing requirements is that States are simply weighing the relative risks of unlicensed workers differently. If this were the case, then States with greater licensing requirements would license the same occupations as less regulated States while simply adding additional occupations. Instead, however, there are idiosyncrasies in the occupations that States license. For example, despite having the lowest share of low-wage occupations requiring a license, Wyoming is just one of 21 States to have licensing requirements for travel guides (Carpenter et al. 2012). Although it is possible that state-specific needs lead to these idiosyncratic licensing requirements, this suggests that other factors are likely contributing to which occupations States choose to license.

These occupational licenses come at a significant cost to the U.S. labor market by acting as a barrier to entry for new workers seeking to join a profession and, in turn, artificially raising wages in the occupation for incumbent workers. It has also been found that some state licensing boards have engaged in practices that result in unfair competition and antitrust activities. For example, in the case of *North Carolina State Board of Dental Examiners v. Federal Trade Commission* (2015), the lack of oversight by the State of North

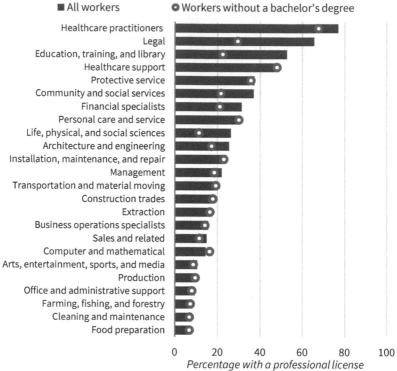

Figure 3-18. Workers with a Professional License or Certification, by Occupation and Education Level, 2017

■ All workers ● Workers without a bachelor's degree

Healthcare practitioners
Legal
Education, training, and library
Healthcare support
Protective service
Community and social services
Financial specialists
Personal care and service
Life, physical, and social sciences
Architecture and engineering
Installation, maintenance, and repair
Management
Transportation and material moving
Construction trades
Extraction
Business operations specialists
Sales and related
Computer and mathematical
Arts, entertainment, sports, and media
Production
Office and administrative support
Farming, fishing, and forestry
Cleaning and maintenance
Food preparation

0   20   40   60   80   100
Percentage with a professional license

Sources: Current Population Survey; CEA calculations.

Carolina allowed dentists to successfully lobby to prevent nondentists from participating in tooth-whitening procedures, despite the relatively low risk of such procedures for patients. Though there is no clear consensus on the precise effect of licenses on compensation, recent estimates suggest a wage premium for licensed workers ranging from about 7.5 percent (Gittleman and Kleiner 2016; Gittleman, Klee, and Kleiner 2018) up to 15 percent (Kleiner, Krueger, and Mas 2011). If the wage premium from occupational licensing is entirely due to economic rents, Kleiner, Krueger, and Mas (2011) estimate that with a labor demand elasticity of 0.5, the 15 percent wage premium would reflect 2.8 million fewer jobs in these occupations due to licensing. Applying a similar calculation with the lower-end estimate for the wage premium, a 7.5 percent wage premium would reflect about 1.4 million fewer jobs if the licenses are not reflecting additional human capital and increased productivity among these workers.

State occupational licensing also reduces worker mobility because many licenses cannot be transferred from one State to another. Recognizing that high migration is seen as a strength of the U.S. labor market relative to other countries and reflects a key way that workers can adjust to labor market shocks, economists have expressed concerns about declines in geographic mobility in the United States in recent decades (for an overview of these concerns, see Molloy, Smith, and Wozniak 2017). These declines are documented by Molloy, Smith, and Wozniak (2011) and by Kaplan and Schulhofer-Wohl (2017), who each find that interstate mobility has reached a 30-year low.[17] Johnson and Kleiner (2017) suggest that occupational licensing has exacerbated this decline. On the basis of their estimates, interstate migration is 36 percent lower for those working in occupations with State-specific licensing relative to other occupations. They also estimate that the rise in licensing from 1980 to 2015 can explain between 3 and 13 percent of the overall decline in interstate mobility over this time. The effects of licensing on interstate mobility observed by Johnson and Kleiner are consistent with a 2015 report by the CEA that observed substantially lower interstate mobility rates for workers in highly licensed occupations relative to those in less licensed ones (CEA, Department of the Treasury, and Department of Labor 2015).

Occupational licenses also impose an additional burden on military spouses, who move much more frequently than the general population and potentially face relicensing requirements with each interstate move. The 2016 American Community Survey indicated that working-age military spouses were seven times as likely to move across State lines in the United States as the civilian noninstitutionalized working-age population in general (CEA 2018d). Also, though the 690,000 military spouses represent a relatively small share of the overall working population, military spouses are more likely than the general population to work in an occupation requiring a license, given that 35 percent of military spouses in the labor force worked in occupations requiring a license or certification (DOD 2016; Department of the Treasury and DOD 2012).

Employment Experiences in Rural Areas

Beyond differences in employment patterns by demographic characteristic, differences in employment patterns appear across geographies, including whether the community is in an urban or rural environment. Although there are several ways that communities can be defined as urban or rural, for the purposes of this chapter we do so based on whether or not the county is located in a metropolitan statistical area.

In general, from the early 1980s through the early 2000s, the prime-age employment patterns in urban and rural areas largely followed similar trajectories. Between the fourth quarter of 1980 and the fourth quarter of 2007, rural

---

[17] Using CPS data, for example, Kaplan and Schulhofer-Wohl (2017) find that about 1.5 percent of people moved across State lines in 2010, down from closer to 3 percent in 1980 and over 3 percent in 1990.

employment rates for prime-age adults rose by 5.3 percentage points—which is just slightly higher than the rise of 5.1 percentage points in urban employment rates during this time (figure 3-19). The similarities in employment patterns across these communities diverged, however, after the Great Recession. Though both urban and rural employment fell sharply in the Great Recession, prime-age urban employment rates experienced a nearly complete recovery, and are approaching their prerecession level from the end of 2007. This is despite the fact that some urban areas have restrictive zoning, which increases the costs of housing and real estate and limits employment growth (OECD 2018a).

In contrast to the experience in urban areas, prime-age rural employment rates have not shown the same level of recovery. In rural areas, as of the third quarter of 2018, the prime-age employment-to-population ratio has only risen by 2.9 percentage points since the end of 2011, and remains 2.4 percentage points below where it was at the end of 2007. This divergence is actually even greater if one looks at all adults, rather than only those of prime working age, due to the faster aging of the labor force in rural areas (USDA 2017c).

There are several reasons why employment patterns in urban and rural area may diverge. One is a purely technical explanation: that every 10 years, the Census Bureau reclassifies nonmetropolitan counties that have grown as large as metropolitan ones. Goetz, Partridge, and Stephens (2018) show that population growth in counties considered rural in 1950 is more than double that of counties considered urban in 1950. The supposedly slow historical population growth of rural areas results from the reclassification of fast-growing counties as urban—so, using definitions of urban and rural, it appears that rural areas have grown more slowly. They note that one analyst likened this to taking the best team out of a sports league each year and then wondering why the remaining teams are not performing as well as before. Although the reclassifications are based on population growth, they could also influence observed economic trends if the rural areas with stronger economic performance are more likely to undergo reclassification. However, these reclassifications only result in an implicit trend break once each decade (when the reclassification occurs) and thus should not alter trends within decades, when the definitions are stable. Hence, this cannot explain why the employment of prime-age adults has lagged in rural areas since the Great Recession after decades of similar prime-age employment rates in these two types of communities.

A second reason relates to the industry compositions across urban and rural areas. Although manufacturing represents only 6.2 percent of all urban employment, it constitutes a much larger share, 10.8 percent, of employment in rural areas. In fact—after wholesale and retail trade, education and health services, and public administration—manufacturing is the fourth-largest industry for rural employment (figure 3-20). As such, the declines in manufacturing

Figure 3-19. Employment-to-Population Ratio for Prime-Age Adults by Geography, 1976–2018

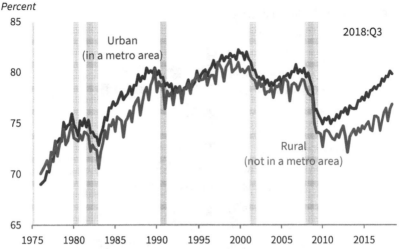

Percent

Sources: Current Population Survey (CPS); CEA calculations.
Note: Prime-age adults are those age 25–54 years. These data aggregate monthly CPS surveys within a quarter. Metro area definitions are subject to change over time. Data are non-seasonally adjusted. Shading denotes a recession.

employment in recent decades have had a disproportionate effect on rural communities.

A third potential explanation relates to the differences in the characteristics of urban and rural populations. For example, education levels in rural areas have historically been lower than in urban areas, and this gap has been growing. In 2016, 19 percent of adults in nonmetropolitan areas had a bachelor's degree versus 33 percent in urban areas—a gap of 14 percentage points (USDA 2018c). Earlier, in 2000, this gap was somewhat smaller, at 11 percentage points; 26 percent of adults in urban areas had bachelor's degrees, versus 15 percent in rural areas (figure 3-21).[18] Recognizing that there are substantial differences in employment rates by education level, as discussed earlier in this chapter, the growing educational divide between urban and rural adults can further exacerbate their divergent employment trajectories.

One potential reason for the growing education divide is the out-migration of young adults. The exit of college-educated young adults is often identified by policymakers as an important concern for rural areas. This indicates

---

[18] One potential reason for the growing education divide is that education seems to earn a higher return in urban areas versus rural ones. A recent analysis by the U.S. Department of Agriculture (USDA 2017e) found that adults in urban areas with a bachelor's degree earn $70,146, versus $51,996 in rural areas.

Figure 3-20. Industry Employment by Geography, 2017

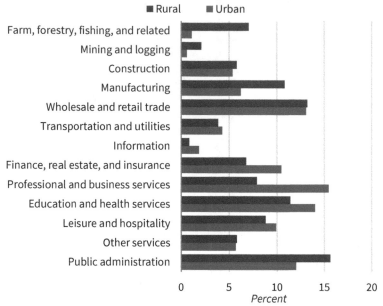

Sources: Bureau of Economic Analysis; CEA calculations.
Note: Metroplitan area definitions are subject to change over time.

that the problem may not be so much the education level of rural youth but their retention once they complete higher education. Reichert, Cromartie, and Arthun (2014) found that geographically challenged rural areas are particularly dependent on young adults who decide to move back to their rural communities. Fiore and others (2015) found that the cost of living and strength of the local economy were of primary importance in persuading rural youth in Iowa to return. In a survey of young adults from a sampling across the rural United States, Reichert, Cromartie, and Arthun (2014) find that deciding to return to the rural community of their raising is tied closely to place and personal ties maintained with their home community. Returnees sometimes were able to return because they were able to work remotely. They also returned to become part of both farm and nonfarm family businesses.

Finally, though not directly related to the growing employment gap between urban and rural areas, an important component of rural economies that cuts across many sectors is self-employment or entrepreneurship. Numerous analyses have shown the importance of entrepreneurship for the economic health of rural areas. Rupasingha and Goetz (2013) provide strong empirical evidence that higher self-employment rates in rural counties are associated with increases in income and employment and with reductions in poverty rates. Self-employment is also particularly important for rural

Figure 3-21. Educational Attainment in Rural versus Urban Areas

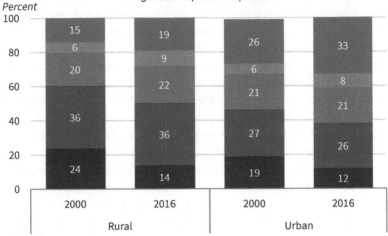

Source: Department of Agriculture.
Note: Metro area definitions are subject to change over time. Data may not sum to 100 due to rounding. For full details, see USDA (2018c).

communities, because the rate of self-employment in rural areas exceeds that in urban environments (Wilmoth 2017).

Goetz and Rupasingha (2009) found that greater self-employment growth was associated with higher shares of construction and services employment. Also, self-employment and entrepreneurship are enhanced when rural areas are close to growing, small metropolitan areas (Tsvetkova, Partridge, and Betz 2017). Larger increases in self-employment growth were also associated with more females in the labor force. But more retail employment in a county was associated with smaller increases in self-employment over time. Goetz and Rupasingha (2009) also used the Economic Freedom of North America Index to evaluate the effect of government policies on proprietorships. This index measured the extent of restrictions on economic freedom. Not surprisingly, more economic freedom is associated with higher rates of business formation.

Self-employment opportunity goes hand in hand with the return of young adults who left to pursue higher education. Reichert, Cromartie, and Arthun (2014) report that those who return to rural communities contribute to economic growth, often through entrepreneurship. Policies that promote small businesses and self-employment could encourage the return of young adults to their home communities. Their return then enhances economic growth and

Expanding Labor Force Opportunities for Every American | 187 strengthens rural economies, which can further encourage the return of more young adults.

Farming employs a shrinking share of the labor force in rural areas. In 2015, 6 percent of rural employment was directly in the farming sector. Agriculture and related industries made up 11 percent of U.S. employment in 2017, but not all in rural areas. With just over 2 million farms, many rural residents live on farms (USDA 2018b). Small family farms, often with a nonfarming occupation, make up nearly 90 percent of the 2 million farms but only produce about one-fourth of the output (Burns and Macdonald 2018).

Though farming reflects a smaller share of the rural labor force than it once did, the rural manufacturing advantage in part comes from closer proximity to raw materials, including those grown or raised on farms. For example, food manufacturing is prevalent in rural areas because of the proximity of raw products to process—making up 18 percent of all rural manufacturing employment. Similarly, 7 percent of wood products manufacturing is in rural areas, which is consistent with the closer proximity to inputs into this manufacturing process. However, between 2001 and 2015, the decline in rural manufacturing employment was widespread across manufacturing sectors. During this period, employment in every manufacturing sector except for tobacco and beverage manufacturing declined in rural areas (USDA 2017d). This highlights the importance of policies targeted at revitalizing manufacturing generally for the economic health of rural communities.

Policies to Enhance Rural Communities

Recent policies of the Trump Administration have been particularly beneficial to these rural communities. These policies include efforts to revitalize industries that are disproportionately located in rural communities; supporting small businesses and entrepreneurship; and promoting economic development in less developed areas through Opportunity Zones, including in many rural communities.

One component of revitalizing rural areas involves restoring the manufacturing industries that have been languishing and losing jobs in recent decades. Although manufacturing jobs are important for both urban and rural communities, the larger share of rural employment that is in manufacturing industries means that these jobs are particularly important for rural communities (USDA 2017a). Reflecting the priority that this Administration has placed on revitalizing manufacturing, over the past two years manufacturing has experienced substantial growth. As seen in figure 3-22, in 2018 manufacturing employment grew by just over 2 percent, the fastest annual growth since 1994. And this acceleration of growth in manufacturing is part of a broader increase in employment in goods-producing industries generally. Goods-producing employment grew by at least 1 percent each year from 2011 until 2015, but in 2016 this growth stalled and the industry only grew by 0.4 percent. In 2017,

Figure 3-22. Manufacturing Employment Growth, 1980–2018

Percent (annual change)

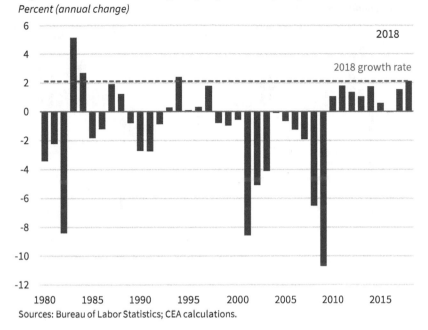

Sources: Bureau of Labor Statistics; CEA calculations.

goods-producing employment gains accelerated again, and this acceleration continued into 2018 (figure 3-23). In 2018, goods-producing employment rose by 3.2 percent—its second-fastest annual growth rate since 1984.

A second set of policies that benefits many areas, but especially rural economies, is the existence and facilitation of entrepreneurship through pro-prietorships and self-employment. One-sixth of all self-employed adults live in rural communities, and a larger share of the rural population (6.7 percent in 2016) is self-employed than is the case in suburbs (6 percent) or center cities (5.7 percent) (Wilmoth 2017). Consequently, policies that encourage the growth of small businesses and benefit self-employed entrepreneurs have the potential to disproportionately benefit rural communities.

A major objective of the Tax Cuts and Jobs Act of 2017, as discussed in chapter 2, is to facilitate the success of entrepreneurs. Self-employed workers and pass-through entities, which make up the majority of small businesses, benefit from the act's lower individual tax rates. Most also qualify for the new 20 percent deduction for pass-through entities and will further benefit from the expanded Section 179 deduction for the purchase of business equip-ment. A 2018 survey of small business owners by the National Federation of Independent Businesses (NFIB 2018b) indicates that 87 percent of small

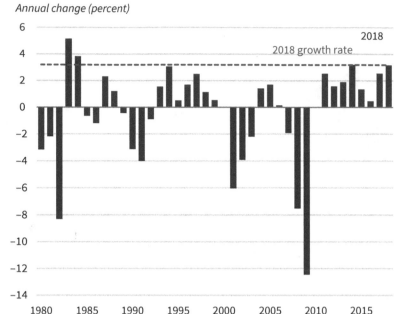

Figure 3-23. Goods-Producing Employment Growth, 1980–2018

Annual change (percent)

Sources: Bureau of Labor Statistics; CEA calculations.

business owners recognize that the Tax Cuts and Jobs Act will have a positive impact on the economy.

Given the finding that less restrictive business environments help entrepreneurs, reducing regulatory burdens is similarly important. According to the NFIB's (2018a) survey of small businesses, its Small Business Optimism Index has remained at near-record high levels since the Trump Administration came into office. The NFIB includes the unburdening of small businesses from taxes and regulations as factors in this surging optimism.

In addition to incentivizing small businesses by removing regulatory barriers and reducing the marginal tax rates of the self-employed and pass-through businesses, the Trump Administration is also incentivizing improvements in rural infrastructure. One such investment that can enhance growth in rural areas is increased high-speed, high-capacity Internet access (USDA 2017b). Kim and Orazem (2016) found that rural firms are 60 to 101 percent more likely to locate in ZIP codes with good broadband access. Their study, which focuses on start-up firms in rural areas, emphasizes the importance of providing adequate infrastructure to enhance the location and success of entrepreneurs. Although improved Internet access can benefit a range of communities, their study suggests that good broadband access benefits most rural areas that are close to urban areas or that have higher populations. Good broadband access enables

Box 3-4. Strengthening Local Economies through Opportunity Zones

The Tax Cuts and Jobs Act of 2017 included a provision that offers tax incentives for private investment in distressed areas designated by State governors as Opportunity Zones. Under the law, taxpayers who invest their unrealized capital gains in Opportunity Zones, via so-called Opportunity Funds, can defer taxes on these gains for as long as they remain in Opportunity Funds (but no later than the end of 2026). In addition, taxpayers can avoid paying a portion of the original capital gains tax depending on how long they keep these gains in an Opportunity Fund. They can avoid all taxes on capital gains accrued based on investment in the Opportunity Fund (above the original capital gain) if they keep these funds in the Opportunity Fund for at least 10 years.

Governors designated Opportunity Zones in their States in early 2018, with their choices finalized by the U.S. Treasury in June 2018. Out of about 75,000 census tracts in the United States (each designed to contain about 1,200 to 8,000 residents), over half were eligible and over 8,700 were chosen. Among eligible census tracts, governors tended to designate as Opportunity Zones those with higher poverty rates and lower median incomes. The average poverty rate among Opportunity Zones in 2016 was 29 percent, compared with an average of 25 percent in all eligible census tracts, and an average of 15 percent across all census tracts in the country (Gelfond and Looney 2018). In addition, rural areas make up almost a quarter of tracts designated as Opportunity Zones (Economic Innovation Group 2018), exceeding the overall share of the population living in rural communities.

Although the scale and flexibility offered by Opportunity Zones are new, place-based policies to encourage investment in distressed areas are not. State and Federal Enterprise Zone programs generally offered tax incentives for businesses that located in certain areas or employed people who lived in such areas. Most studies found that Federal Empowerment Zone programs tended to increase employment and wages in designated areas, although there were no similar positive effects of State-based programs on employment (e.g., Neumark and Kolko 2010; Busso, Gregory, and Kline 2013). Another Federal initiative, the New Markets Tax Credit, is more similar to Opportunity Zones, in that it targets census tracts with low incomes and high poverty rates, and offers tax incentives for investment made in designated areas. Unlike Opportunity Zones, however, eligible investments are more restricted and must be preapproved by public authorities. The New Markets Tax Credit led to increased investment in targeted industries with some evidence of positive effects in reducing unemployment and poverty (Gurley-Calvez et al. 2009; Harger and Ross 2016; Freedman 2012).

Bernstein and Hassett (2015) suggest that the effectiveness of previous place-based policies was limited by weak or misaligned incentives for investment, overly burdensome bureaucratic requirements, and limited scope for the types of investments that could be made. Opportunity Zones offer a means of flexibly investing in distressed areas without encumbrance by bureaucratic requirements. The scope of potential investment is large, with trillions of dollars in unrealized capital gains that could be harnessed. In addition, State and local governments have signaled their own efforts to complement Federal incentives in Opportunity Zones. At the Federal level, President Trump signed Executive Order 13853 on December 12, 2018, which establishes the White House Opportunity and Revitalization Council and directs Federal agencies to streamline Federal programs and offer greater flexibility to States to target public investment in Opportunity Zones whenever possible under current law. The large potential scale of the Opportunity Zone investment, complemented by public efforts, could unleash substantial economic growth in communities that have been most left behind throughout the United States.

people to work remotely from rural areas who would otherwise need to live closer to urban areas. With the importance of broadband access in mind, in January 2018 President Trump signed Executive Order 13821, which streamlines the process to expand broadband to rural areas (White House 2018c).

An additional priority of the Administration is encouraging private investment in areas that previously lacked private capital spending so economic growth can be spread more widely. A key component of this approach is through the creation of Opportunity Zones in the Tax Cuts and Jobs Act, which encourages a wide spectrum of investment in infrastructure in rural areas and other communities where economic growth could be enhanced through this influx of capital (see box 3-4).

Policies beneficial to rural communities are further promoted by the Strengthening Career and Technical Education for the 21st Century Act, which the President signed in July 2018, and by the Task Force on Agriculture and Rural Prosperity, which the President established in April 2017. The Strengthening Career and Technical Education for the 21st Century Act specifically benefits rural areas by allowing States to designate up to 15 percent of allocated funds to a reserve for targeted rural education and training needs. The task force similarly promotes rural development by identifying and recommending policy changes that ensure good broadband access, improve the quality of rural life, support the rural workforce, harness technological innovation, and enhance economic development (White House 2017).

Conclusion

Given the historically low unemployment rates that were achieved in 2018, it is clear that maintaining the recent rapid pace of employment growth necessitates a better understanding of the reasons that some adults, and particularly those of prime working-age, remain outside the formal labor market. Especially because there are already more job openings than unemployed people looking for work, continued growth of the workforce requires overcoming the barriers that have kept some adults outside it.

Fundamentally, if people voluntarily remain outside the labor market when there is a surplus of available jobs, it is an indication that they value their time spent on other activities above the amount that employers are willing to pay. As a result, central to expanding the number of people engaged in the labor force are policies that increase workers' wages, decrease the fixed costs of entering the labor force, or remove distortions that cause some whose most productive use of time is in the formal labor market to instead engage in other activities.

As outlined in this chapter, policies of the Trump Administration focus on each of these areas. The corporate tax rate reductions and expensing of business investment in equipment in the Tax Cuts and Jobs Act incentivized additional capital spending by employers, which in turn leads to higher productivity and larger wage gains. The individual tax cuts in the act similarly mean that workers keep a larger share of any wage earnings, and more potential workers will find it worthwhile to seek employment. Increased investments in human capital, along with physical capital, also increase the returns to work. There is strong evidence that wages are higher and unemployment is lower among those with higher levels of education. Efforts to increase the education and skill levels of the American workforce, including the pledges from businesses secured by the Trump Administration to train or retrain over 6.5 million workers, should raise the potential wages and employment prospects for the recipients of this training.

Further removing regulatory distortions can also increase the likelihood that the returns to work are sufficiently high to draw additional adults into the labor market. These deregulatory efforts include reducing occupational licensing, which imposes a fixed cost on potential labor market entrants, and reducing regulations on paid child care activities, which raise the costs of child care and discourage parents from seeking formal employment.

Although many policies to remove distortions and enhance workers' productivity and wages are nationally focused, there has been a clear disparity in the recovery from the Great Recession in urban compared with rural areas. This geographic divide necessitates policies focused on industries that are prevalent in rural communities so there are more employment opportunities for potential workers in rural areas throughout the country. The Administration's focus on industries, including manufacturing and mining, that are disproportionately located in rural areas, as well as place-based policies such as the creation of Opportunity Zones, have the potential to broaden the scope of the Nation's economic expansion to areas that did not experience strong employment gains in earlier years.

Although the labor market faces headwinds as members of the Baby Boom generation reach traditional retirement age, these demographic trends do not dictate that the United States will face secular stagnation brought on by slow employment growth in the coming years. Through the policies of this Administration, as discussed in this chapter, there is the potential to increase economic opportunities for all Americans by increasing the wages of those who are working and by drawing more people into the labor market than has been the case in recent years.

Chapter 4

Enabling Choice and Competition in Healthcare Markets

America is unique in both the extent to which it employs private markets to deliver and fund healthcare and in the quality of care provided. While there is substantial government involvement in healthcare regulation and funding, government payers often utilize private market mechanisms in their programs, and most Americans obtain their healthcare through private markets. The delivery of high-quality, innovative care in the United States is the result of market forces that enhance patients' welfare by allowing parties to act in accord with their own, self-determined interests. Nevertheless, the ability of markets to provide affordable, high-quality care for the entire population and the value of government interventions in healthcare markets have been debated for decades.

This chapter discusses the rationales commonly offered for the government's intervention in healthcare and explains why such interventions often, unnecessarily, restrict choice and competition. The resulting government failures are frequently more costly than the market failures they attempt to correct. Though some features of healthcare—such as uncertainty, third-party financing through insurance, information asymmetry, barriers to entry, and inelastic demand—interfere with efficient market function, we argue that these features are neither unique to healthcare markets nor so disruptive that they mandate extensive government interventions. We contend that competitive markets for healthcare services and insurance can and do work to generate affordable care for all.

Current proposals to increase government involvement in healthcare, like "Medicare for All", are motivated by the view that competition and free choice cannot work in this sector. These proposals, though well-intentioned, mandate a decrease or elimination of choice and competition. We find that these proposals would be inefficiently costly and would likely reduce, as opposed to increase, the U.S. population's health. We show that funding them would create large distortions in the economy. Finally, we argue that the universal nature of "Medicare for All" would be a particularly inefficient and untargeted way to serve lower- and middle-income people.

We contrast such proposals with the Trump Administration's actions that are increasing choice and competition in healthcare. In the health insurance arena, we focus on the elimination of the Affordable Care Act's individual mandate penalty, which will enable consumers to decide for themselves what value they attach to purchasing insurance and generate $204 billion in value over 10 years. Expanding the availability of two types of health insurance—association health plans; and short-term, limited-duration health plans—will increase consumers' choices and insurance affordability. We find that, taken together, these three sets of actions will generate a value of $453 billion over the next decade. For biopharmaceuticals, the Food and Drug Administration has increased price competition by streamlining the process for drug application and review. Record numbers of generic drugs have been approved, price growth has fallen, and consumers have already saved $26 billion during the first year and a half of the Administration. In addition, the influx of new, brand name drugs resulted in an estimated $43 billion in annual benefits for consumers in 2018. Data through the end of 2018 show that, for the first time in 46 years, the Consumer Price Index for prescription drugs fell in nominal terms—and even more in real terms—during a calendar year.

The dominant theory in economics for centuries in the Western world has been the efficiency of the free market system. For a free market to be efficient, free choice and competition must exist in the market to allow consumer demand to be met by suppliers. In markets, prices reveal economically important information about costs and consumers' needs, and send signals to both sides of the market to facilitate an efficient allocation of resources. Centrally set prices undermine the important allocative role of prices in the economy.

Of course, many markets deviate in substantial ways from the conditions under which markets are perfectly efficient. Market failures occur to a greater or lesser extent throughout the economy. The important question is what to do about them. Market failures may be less damaging than the distortions and costs introduced by various interventions intended to correct them.

Following the research of Kenneth Arrow (1963), many economists and policymakers have argued that unique features of healthcare make it impossible for competition and markets to work. They claim that uncertainty in the incidence of disease and in the effectiveness of treatment, information asymmetry between providers and consumers of healthcare, barriers to provider entry, and the critical importance of and inelastic demand for health services all interfere with market function and justify government intervention in—or even its takeover of—healthcare markets. Some members of Congress have proposed nationalizing payments for the healthcare sector (which makes up more than a sixth of the U.S. economy) through the recent "Medicare for All" proposal. This policy would distribute healthcare for "free" (i.e., without cost sharing) through a monopoly government health insurer that would centrally set all prices paid to suppliers such as doctors and hospitals. Private insurance would be banned for the services covered by the "Medicare for All" program.

This chapter begins by critically examining the rationales offered for the government's intervention in healthcare. We find that though some characteristics of healthcare may present obstacles to a perfectly functioning market, these are not insurmountable problems that mandate the government's intervention in healthcare and can be overcome by market and nonmarket institutions. Moreover, these problems also occur in markets for many other goods without calls for government takeovers and the suppression of consumer choice and competition. Government intervention in healthcare is only clearly warranted where the political process has made a determination that some level of healthcare for low-income people is a merit good—a beneficial good that would be underconsumed, justifying replacing consumer sovereignty with another norm—so that government redistribution programs to provide healthcare in kind for low-income people might enhance efficiency.

We next critique the "Medicare for All" proposal. This plan would eliminate choice and competition—everyone would be forced to participate in the same insurance, with mandatory premiums set through tax policy and without the option of choosing an alternate insurance if they dislike the government's plan. Our analysis shows that the proposal would reduce longevity and health in the U.S., decrease long-run global health by reducing medical innovation, and adversely affect the economy through the large tax burden required to fund the program.

In contrast to proposals that diminish health and damage the economy by curtailing market forces, the next section of this chapter details the Trump Administration's efforts to improve choice and competition in health insurance markets so as to help them better serve low- and middle-income people. The Administration has reduced the penalty associated with the Affordable Care Act's (ACA's) individual mandate to zero, so consumers can decide for themselves the value of purchasing health insurance. We analyze this deregulatory reform and find that it will generate $204 billion in value over 10 years. In addition, the administration has increased the choices and affordability of available health insurance plans by expanding association health plans and extending the available terms and renewability of short-term, limited-duration insurance plans. As opposed to sabotaging healthcare markets, conventional incidence analysis by the CEA implies that these three deregulations of health insurance markets together will benefit Americans by $453 billion during the next decade.

Finally, the last section discusses the Administration's reforms to enhance choice and competition in biopharmaceutical markets by streamlining the drug application and review process in a way that effectively lowers barriers to entry while ensuring a supply of safe and effective drugs. This deregulatory effort is contributing to a record number of generic drug approvals since January 2017, resulting in slower price growth and savings of $26 billion over the first year and a half of the Administration. In addition, the influx of new, brand name drugs since January 2017 has induced price reductions, resulting in an estimated $43 billion in annual benefits for consumers in 2018, even though the methods currently being used to estimate changes in drug prices do not reflect this. For the first time in 46 years, the Consumer Price Index for prescription drugs fell in both nominal and real terms during a calendar year.

We conclude that the market for health insurance and healthcare should be supported through increased choice and competition, not hampered by increased government intervention. Competitive markets for healthcare services and insurance—whether privately or publicly funded—can and do work to provide high-quality care for people at all income levels.[1]

---

[1] The CEA previously released research on topics covered in this chapter. The text that follows builds on the following research papers produced by the CEA: *The Opportunity Costs of Socialism* (CEA 2018c), *The Administration's FDA Reforms and Reduced Biopharmaceutical Drug Prices* (CEA 2018a), and *Deregulating Health Insurance Markets: Value to Market Participants* (CEA 2019).

Rationales for the Government's Healthcare Interventions That Restrict Competition and Choice

This section reviews the specific rationales for the government's intervention in healthcare markets and argues that they are often exaggerated; are not unique to healthcare; and, when present in markets for other types of goods and services, have not been used to call for government control.

In a market economy, free choice among competing suppliers generally leads to an efficient allocation of resources and maximizes consumer welfare. In the market system that predominates in the United States, people are mostly free to spend their own money and are therefore more careful in deciding how much to spend and on what the money is spent compared with when money is spent by governments on their behalf. Fiscal and regulatory policies that limit choice and competition distort allocations and reduce consumer welfare from what it would be in the absence of these policies.

Unfortunately, every market has features that deviate from it working perfectly, and healthcare is no exception. Some argue that specific features of healthcare make it unsuitable for the market mechanisms that we employ in the rest of the economy. Fifty-six years ago, the economist Kenneth Arrow published a seminal article identifying ways in which healthcare deviates from perfectly competitive markets and thus could generate an inefficient allocation of resources (Arrow 1963). The primary factors he identified included:

1. Uncertainty in the incidence of disease and in the effectiveness of treatment, and hence the likelihood of recovery.
2. Information asymmetry between providers of medical services and patients who lack an understanding of disease processes and treatments.
3. Barriers to entry that limit the supply of providers, including the need to attend selective medical schools and state licensing standards that include educational and training requirements. These barriers can be imposed by the government (licensing) or by private parties who often have a financial interest in limiting the supply of their service (limited admission to medical school, residency and fellowship training programs and specialty board society certification which is often needed to obtain hospital privileges).

Arrow (1963, 947) pointed out that these features lead to inefficient markets, and "when the market fails to achieve an optimal state, society will, to some extent at least, recognize the gap, and nonmarket social institutions will arise attempting to bridge it. . . . The medical-care industry, with its variety of special institutions, some ancient, some modern, exemplifies this tendency."

This section discusses the healthcare features that Arrow pointed out, the adaptations to them that can create problems of their own, and additional factors that some claim justify government intervention, either through public financing or public production in healthcare. We find that many of the arguments for the value of intervention have been exaggerated and that the costs of market failures in healthcare are often lower than the costs of government interventions undertaken to remedy them.

Uncertainty, Third–Party Payments, and the Problem of Moral Hazard

The primary institution that has arisen in response to the uncertainty inherent in healthcare is private healthcare insurance or third-party payments. Insurance mitigates the financial risk of getting sick and allows risk-averse individuals to pool the risk. This pooling of risk across the population enhances welfare by reducing the financial risk of uncertain illness events for each individual. Nevertheless, some have argued that the widespread adoption of third-party insurance in healthcare creates its own problems that warrant government intervention.

It has long been recognized that there is a trade-off between risk reduction through insurance and appropriate incentives at the time of care (Zeckhauser 1970). Payment after the time of service via third parties, such as private or public insurance plans, mutes the incentives of patients to shop based on quality and price, and therefore negates market mechanisms, which leads to the problem of overconsumption relative to production costs or moral hazard.

Normally, the risk against which insurance is purchased should be out of the individual's control. In healthcare, costs largely depend on the choice of a doctor and the willingness of this doctor and the patient to use medical services. Health insurance can increase the risk that is insured against: medical costs. Moreover, because medical insurance limits considerations of cost as services are consumed, "widespread medical insurance increases the demand for medical care" (Arrow 1963, 961). By inserting third-party control over payments, "insurance removes the incentive on the part of individuals, patients, and physicians to shop around for better prices for hospitalization and surgical care" (Arrow 1963, 962). Healthcare insurance reduces the price that an individual faces to zero or, if there is a copay or coinsurance, to greater than zero, but still less than the cost of the service as reflected by the market price. This is a recipe for wasteful spending and a welfare loss to society.

The primary way insurers deal with moral hazard is through cost sharing—deductibles, copayments, and coinsurance—to discourage overutilization by moving consumers up the demand curve. The Rand Health Insurance Experiment of the 1970s and early 1980s randomly assigned patients to health plans with different levels of cost sharing. It showed that higher consumer cost-sharing leads to lower utilization, with little discernible impact on health (Newhouse 1993). Cost-sharing provisions have become far more common and burdensome for patients over the past few years. Nevertheless, unless cost sharing is quite high, it cannot eliminate moral hazard.

However, moral hazard is less of a problem than it at first appears to be, and it has important lessons to impart about the proper role of health-care insurance. Although seeking extra medical care because of insurance is rational economic behavior for an insured individual who gets to spread the cost over all other insured people, the presence of moral hazard suggests that "some uncertain medical care expenses will not and should not be insured in an optimal situation" (Pauly 1968, 537). The problem presented by moral hazard only clearly applies to items where we would expect zero (or very low) prices to lead to overuse—things like "routine physician's visits, prescriptions, dental care, and the like"—but not necessarily to serious illnesses (Pauly 1983, 83). In the case of invasive surgeries, painful treatments and tests, and medications with serious side effects, patients would be unlikely to overutilize them, regardless of how low the costs were (Nyman 2004). No one would have their gallbladder or pancreas removed, undergo chemotherapy, or endure a bowel preparation for a colonoscopy simply because the services were free—they would only utilize these services to treat or diagnose serious illnesses.[2] In other words, moral hazard is predominantly a problem when insurance covers routine or nonessential, discretionary services (e.g., cosmetic surgery) that most economists think should not be covered by insurance. It is not a problem for medical expenditures for the serious, costly, and unpredictable illnesses and treatments that most economists would agree should be covered by health insurance. For serious illnesses, insurance may promote additional spending that is likely to enhance welfare because the patient would have purchased it himself or herself if insurance had given them cash instead of directly paying for the service (Nyman 2004).

The interposition of third-party payment seems less problematic when we consider that insurers must compete to attract enrollees. In the process, they will act as agents for those enrollees in selecting and contracting with high-quality providers through networks or other means and negotiating favorable prices with these providers. The rigors of the market, perforce, help align private, third-party payers' actions with buyers' preferences. But the same cannot be said for third-party public payers. Unlike private insurers, which must compete on price, public payers do not need to compete. This makes private payers more likely than public payers to act as agents for patients.

---

[2] The incidence of disease may respond to costs in the long run (see the comparisons of short- and long-run factors below). For example, the price of treating a disease may affect people's behaviors or treatment of antecedent conditions so that the incidence of the disease ultimately changes.

Asymmetric Information

A common argument for the government's intervention in healthcare markets is that there is asymmetric information—that is, sellers know more than buyers about the nature and quality of the service that is being sold. Although this is true in virtually any market, in industries ranging from legal services to automobile repair, academics and policymakers often single out healthcare for government intervention. This is despite the fact that market and nonmarket mechanisms have developed to deal with such information issues, usually at far lower costs than government alternatives.

A nonmarket institution that Arrow (1963) identified as developing to deal with information asymmetry was professional medical ethics and the trust that physicians would be more motivated by fiduciary obligations to their patients than by profits. Trust is particularly important because patients are prone to rely on their physician's advice regarding what care is needed and where to obtain it (Chernew et al. 2018). Whether ethical and professional standards always succeed is a matter of debate, but it is likely that they—in combination with legal obligations to the patient—do alleviate the problem of information asymmetry. The advent of the Internet as a readily available information source—and the push for healthcare providers to provide medical information to patients through the now-universal legal requirement for informed consent—has decreased the asymmetry problem since Arrow (1963) wrote 56 years ago.

In addition, because 90 percent of healthcare spending is on patients with chronic conditions (Buttorff, Ruder, and Bauman 2017), these patients have the opportunity to gain knowledge from experience and to be highly informed relative to other markets. They learn which treatments work best for them and which have intolerable side effects, which providers are most knowledgeable and responsive, and where care can be most readily and cheaply obtained. Moreover, most people care deeply about healthcare. They are far more likely to seek out and utilize knowledge about healthcare than about, for instance, buying a vacuum cleaner.

The information asymmetry problem has also been mitigated by the fact that third-party payers, rather than patients, are often the real buyers of healthcare. Employers in their roles as insurers and purchasers of healthcare and third-party insurers pay for most of the care received, and they are far more informed than buyers in most markets. Indeed, they often know as much as the sellers about the set of products or services they are considering buying. Many payers explicitly quantify the costs and benefits of what they buy before actually paying for it—for example, through so called cost-effectiveness analysis. These buyers act as agents for patients by excluding providers or products that do not meet quantitative cost-benefit criteria from networks or formularies. The utilization of quantitative purchasing metrics creates a more informed demand side in healthcare.

Barriers to Market Entry

Arrow (1963, 966) posited that though trust and delegation "are the social institutions designed to obviate the problems of informational inequality," licensing and educational certification standards were developed to reduce consumers' uncertainty "as to the quality of the product insofar as this is possible." Arrow acknowledged that this adaptation to market imperfection creates its own problems for the efficient function of the healthcare market—barriers to entry, which, among other problems, inefficiently limit the supply of healthcare providers.

Licensing and educational certification standards are not unique to healthcare; our society is awash in licensing and education requirements, from those for lawyers to those for hairdressers, that restrict market entry. What makes healthcare unique is the pervasiveness of these requirements and the fact that they are imposed by both public (licensing) and private parties, which often have a financial interest in limiting the supply of their service. Medical schools and residency training programs, run by physicians and medical institutions, select their enrollees; and graduation is a prerequisite for licensing. Moreover, certification by privately run, specialty board societies is often needed to obtain hospital privileges.

Licensing and minimum-quality standards can control entry, can assure quality in markets where there is information asymmetry between providers that know the quality of their service and consumers who do not, or can entail some combination of both (Stigler 1971; Leland 1979). Although they undoubtedly interfere with market efficiency, licensing and quality standards seem far more reasonable in medicine than they do for hairdressers. The reason is that trial and error works well when you can recover from the errors, but not when the provider's errors can result in irrevocable harm. Arrow (1963) suggested that there are three approaches to dealing with uncertainty about a provider's qualifications and licensing: (1) Allow licensing and exclude nonqualified entrants; (2) certify or label entrants as qualified without compulsory exclusion; and (3) do nothing and allow consumers to make their own choices. In an often–incorrectly cited statement about these alternatives for licensing—not, as some have mistakenly maintained (Reinhardt 2010), a statement about the need for government-provided health insurance—Arrow (1963, 967) wrote, "It is the general social consensus, clearly, that the *laissez-faire* solution for medicine is intolerable."

The Inelastic Demand for Healthcare

Some argue that the importance of medical care and the often-emergent nature of the care make it impossible for healthcare markets to work efficiently. Patients have neither the time nor the inclination to shop on the basis of price and quality. In circumstances like a trip to the emergency room after a car accident or a heart attack, choice is often impossible. Patients may also have little choice when, after their initial choice of hospital and physician for elective procedures, they become captive to a host of other services and providers that they cannot effectively choose. Thus, the context in which the service is provided, rather than the nature of the service itself, often determines whether consumers have the opportunity to make choices. For example, a computerized axial tomography (CT) scan of the head as part of a workup for an ongoing neurological problem allows making a choice between different service providers, but a similar CT scan for an acute head trauma does not. Or patients considering surgery for an aortic aneurysm can consider which surgeon and hospital best suits their needs but do not have the luxury of choice when their aneurysm is rupturing.

This issue is reflected in the price elasticity of demand for healthcare services—how much the quantity demanded changes in response to changes in price. Although the range of estimates for the price elasticity of demand for healthcare is relatively wide, it tends to center on –0.17, meaning that it is relatively price inelastic (Ringel et al. 2002). Studies of the price elasticity of demand for medical services, however, suggest that cheaper, more routine purchases—for example, preventive care and pharmacy benefits—have larger price elasticities than expensive, emergent care. Similarly, the demand for outpatient services is more price sensitive than the demand for hospital stays (elasticities, respectively, of –0.31 and –0.14); and unlike the situation for adults, price changes have no effect on the quantity of inpatient services demanded for children. It is reasonable to assume that treatment for serious or emergency care—for example, treatment for a trauma or for newly diagnosed cancer—is very inelastic. This is consistent with the basic economic observation that the price elasticity of demand becomes more elastic over time. In the short run (e.g., in an emergency), demand may be relatively inelastic because there may be few substitutes and consumers do not have time to look for alternatives. But elasticity increases in the longer term, as substitutes become available and consumers have time to shop.

A related way to assess the possibility of healthcare choice and competition is to determine whether healthcare services are "shoppable"—that is, whether patients can schedule when they will receive care, compare and choose between multiple providers based on price and quality, and determine where they will receive services.

Despite the issues presented by emergency care, people can shop for most healthcare services. A study of people under 65 with employer-provided insurance found that 43 percent of healthcare services are potentially shop-pable by consumers (Frost and Newman 2016). But the study failed to include spending on prescription drugs, which are generally shoppable as well. When the 11 percent of healthcare spending that goes to prescription drugs is added in, a majority of healthcare spending (43 + 11 = 54 percent) is shoppable.

In a study of 2011 claims by auto workers, shoppable services were reported as accounting for 35 percent of total healthcare spending, with inpa-tient shoppable services accounting for 8 percent of total spending and out-patient shoppable services accounting for 27 percent of total costs (White and Eguchi 2014). Yet this study, like the one cited above, also counted prescription drugs as part of total spending but did not include them in the shoppable cate-gory. When drugs are added in, shoppable goods and services accounted for 56 percent of healthcare spending. The study found that shoppable services are common and constitute a high percentage of the inpatient services provided, even though inpatient care is considered less shoppable than outpatient care. Of the 100 highest-spending diagnosis-related groups (i.e., categories of medi-cal problems that determine payment for hospital stays) for inpatient care, 73 percent were shoppable; of the 300 highest-spending diagnosis-related groups for outpatient care, 90 percent were shoppable. The implication is that nonshoppable services, though a minority of services provided, are much more expensive and therefore represent a larger percentage of spending.

The literature is mixed on whether patients consider information on price and quality in making healthcare choices. Many reports find that patients do not utilize current price information tools to shop for healthcare. In a recent study of one shoppable service (lower-limb magnetic resonance imaging scans, MRIs), few patients consulted a free price transparency guide (less than 1 percent), and they did not select their provider based on overall prices or their out-of-pocket costs (Chernew et al. 2018). This is consistent with other studies showing that though a majority of plans now provide pricing information to their enrollees, only 2 to 3.5 percent of enrollees look at it (Frakt 2016). A study of employee behavior in the year before and after an online price transpar-ency toll was introduced at two large companies operating in multiple market areas found that only a small percentage of employees used the tool, and it was not associated with a decrease in healthcare spending (Desai et al. 2016). Nevertheless, a study of enrollees in Medicare Part D prescription drug plans indicates that they will respond to a choice of low-cost options by switching from expensive to less expensive plans (Ketchum, Lucarelli, and Powers 2015). Experiments with reference pricing—a system of payment where an employer or insurer pays with usual coinsurance and copay provisions up to a maximum "reference" price for a nonemergency health service, and patients are respon-sible for all costs above that price—have found that consumers will shift to lower-price providers (Robinson, Brown, and Whaley 2017).

Similarly, a systematic review of the literature found limited evidence about the effect of quality information on patient choice and concluded that current attempts to provide comparative data have a limited impact (Faber et al. 2009). Nevertheless, there is evidence—based on a study of three conditions (heart attacks, heart failure, and pneumonia) and two common surgical procedures (hip and knee replacements) that together account for a fifth of Medicare hospitalizations and hospital spending—that higher-quality hospitals (as measured by rates of risk-adjusted survival, readmissions, and adherence to practice guidelines), attract a greater market share at a point in time and also grow more over time (Chandra et al. 2016a). This positive correlation between hospital quality and market share was strongest for patients who were not emergency admissions and therefore had more scope for choice. The reported failure of patients to consider available price and quality information may reflect the quality and ease of access of the information tools assessed rather than the willingness of patients to shop based on price and quality.

A confounding factor in assessing healthcare shoppability is the way healthcare consumers shop. After selecting their physician, they are prone to rely on his or her advice regarding what care is needed and where to obtain it. In the study of lower-limb MRIs described above, the referring physician was the primary determinant of where patients received their MRI, and most physicians referred to a narrow group of providers—each orthopedist sent, on average, 79 percent of their referrals to a single radiologist (Chernew et al. 2018). This referral pattern could be problematic in the current wave of health system consolidation, particularly in vertical integration. Referring physicians who work for hospitals within vertically integrated networks were far more likely to refer to providers within that hospital network, and the MRIs performed by hospital-based providers are generally more expensive than MRIs performed by out-of-hospital providers. Having a vertically integrated referring physician raised the cost of an MRI by 36.5 percent and the amount paid by the patient by 31.9 percent.

Concentration in provider markets leads to market power that interferes with patients' ability to shop for insurance and medical services. It is standard economic theory that monopolies and oligopolies lead to an inefficient allocation of resources and to waste. But the government has standard approaches for dealing with this problem, like antitrust enforcement and regulatory changes, that encourage competition and discourage unfair business advantages. These methods are the appropriate solution for the concentration of market power in healthcare markets, not government financing or a takeover. The Administration's report, *Reforming America's Healthcare System Through Choice and Competition* (HHS 2018), discusses the important role played by the antitrust divisions of the Federal Trade Commission and the Department of Justice.

Healthcare Is Not Exceptional

Healthcare is not unique in having features that lead to the departures from market efficiency that Arrow outlined 56 years ago, or that others have since espoused. Most people know far less about the workings of their car than their auto mechanic does. And there is uncertainty about when a person will have an accident or suffer a car breakdown and whether the mechanic's intervention will successfully restore the car's functions. Barriers to market entry in the form of licensing and education requirements cover hundreds of different professions and service providers, often with little demonstrable gain. And healthcare is not the only market where there is relatively inelastic demand.

The question for healthcare, as well as for every sector of the economy, is: What is the optimal way to deal with market inefficiencies? Government intervention is not the only, or even an obvious, answer, and it can be as inefficient and costly as private market failures—often even more so. Market failure is ubiquitous, in the sense that all the conditions for perfect competition are rarely achieved, so failure occurs to a greater or lesser extent throughout the economy. Various types of failures can be thought of as externalities—that is, as "nonmonetary effects not taken into account in the decisionmaking process"—when parties engage in transactions (Zerbe and McCurdy 1999, 561). The question then becomes how to minimize the transaction costs to eliminate or minimize the externalities.

The relationship between hospital quality and market share described above suggests that competition and market forces—which would normally exert pressure on low-productivity firms to become more efficient, shrink, or exit the market—are playing a role in healthcare services (Chandra et al. 2016a). Another study found that, despite the conventional wisdom that idiosyncratic features of the healthcare sector—like consumer ignorance of quality, and the lack of price sensitivity resulting from health insurance—would lead to wide variation in healthcare productivity, the dispersion of productivity across hospitals treating heart attacks is similar to or smaller than the productivity dispersion across a large number of U.S. manufacturing industries (Chandra et al. 2016b). Because productivity dispersion has been shown both theoretically and empirically to decrease with greater competition, this suggests that healthcare may not be more insulated from demand-side competitive pressures than other sectors. Taken together, these studies "suggest that, contrary to the long tradition of 'healthcare exceptionalism' in health economics, the healthcare sector may have more in common with 'traditional' sectors subject to standard market forces than is often assumed" (Chandra et al. 2016b, 102).

Redistribution and Merit Goods

Although less often discussed by economists, a legitimate justification for the government's intervention in healthcare is that healthcare is a merit good whose consumption is not only valued by patients who consume it but also by the third parties that finance this consumption. Broadly speaking, a merit good is one for which society has made a judgment that the merits (or demerits) of a particular good or service require superseding consumer sovereignty with an alternative norm (Durlauf and Blume 2008). This occurs when society makes a judgment that the good will be underconsumed in a free market economy because of a divergence between the private benefits individuals take into account and the actual benefits to the public. Such goods should be subsidized so that consumption does not entirely depend on ability and willingness to pay.[3]

Virtually every high-income country, including the United States, has made a collective judgment that healthcare and health insurance provide greater utility than some consumers can afford. American society, through the political process, has therefore been willing to redistribute income to subsidize healthcare for low-income people, with the efficient level of distribution determined by the preferences of the population. Under such merit motives, providing healthcare in kind through programs like Medicaid, rather than through cash transfers to people who make purchases based on their own preferences, is optimal and efficiency enhancing. This creates the reverse situation from the moral hazard problem, where pricing below cost decreases efficiency by inducing beneficiaries to consume more healthcare than they normally would. "Under merit motives such pricing below cost does not create moral hazard and, indeed, enhances efficiency" (Mulligan and Philipson 2000, 22). However, this sort of paternalistically motivated merit good transfer program may be far less progressive than a conventional analysis of lump sum income transfers would suggest.

Despite international agreement that governments have a role in funding, to a greater or lesser extent, health insurance, few countries (the United Kingdom being the notable exception) actually pay for and provide healthcare for all. And a survey of 19 countries, including both developed and developing ones (i.e., China and India), shows that they all allow private funding and provisions of healthcare and private health insurance (Mossialos et al. 2017). Budgetary constraints and societal priorities and preferences for how to utilize limited resources impose a practical limit on merit motives. Several States— after enacting legislation (Vermont, in 2014), having failed ballot initiatives

---

[3] Merit goods should not be confused with public goods, which must be provided by the government because the private market will not supply them. Public goods differ from private goods (including merit goods) because they are nonexcludable—i.e., the supplier of the good cannot prevent people who do not pay for it from consuming it—and they are nonrival—i.e., consumption by one person does not make the good unavailable to others (Durlauf and Blume 2008). The classic example is national defense. In protecting the Nation from attack for one person, we cannot easily exclude others from being protected, even if they are unwilling to pay. One person's consumption of protection does not lessen the amount of protection others can consume. Healthcare, in contrast, is both excludable and rival.

(Colorado, in 2016), or experiencing stalled legislation (California, in 2017)—have not followed through on single-payer healthcare initiatives because of financing concerns (Weiner, Rosenquist, Hartman 2018).

Current Proposals That Decrease Choice and Competition

This section discusses current proposals to increase the government's involvement in healthcare that are partly motivated by the view that competition and free choice cannot work in healthcare. Here, we assess the proposals by many members of Congress for "Medicare for All" that would nationalize payments for the healthcare sector, which makes up more than a sixth of the U.S. economy.

Some claim that only the government can take advantage of economies of scale in healthcare and that a government healthcare monopoly will be more productive by avoiding "waste" on administrative costs, advertising costs, and profits and by using its bargaining power to obtain (i.e., dictate) better deals from healthcare providers. A recent proposal sponsored or cosponsored by 141 members of Congress (S. 1804; H.R. 676), titled "Medicare for All" (M4A), would distribute healthcare for "free" (i.e., without cost sharing) through a monopoly government health insurer that would centrally set all prices paid to suppliers such as doctors and hospitals. This proposal would make it unlawful for a private business to sell health insurance or for a private employer to offer health insurance to its employees. Although President Obama promised, contrary to fact, that consumers could keep their health insurance plan under the ACA, M4A takes the opposite approach: All private health insurance plans will be prohibited after a four-year transition period.

Instead of relying on competition and individual choice to control prices, M4A would lower them by fiat. M4A's ban on private competition would be even more restrictive than healthcare plans in other countries and other government programs in the United States. For example, the government does not ban private schools, even though it collects taxes to run a public school system. Education providers—a.k.a. teachers—can still work at private schools, and parents can forgo free public education and pay private school tuition. Under the M4A bill, patients would have no insurance alternatives. Health providers, though not government employees, would have no choice but to receive their income and instructions from the Federal government or from the relatively few people who could afford to purchase expensive medical services without insurance.

A major issue for M4A is the low productivity of government programs in translating tax revenues into outputs valued by participants, such as improved health. This problem is common with in-kind programs like government-provided healthcare, where beneficiaries often do not value the healthcare that is provided as much as the money that is spent on it. According to the Centers for Medicare & Medicaid Services (CMS 2017), in 2016 about $7,590 was spent per U.S. Medicaid beneficiary. If Medicaid beneficiaries were given this spending to allocate as they see best, most would not spend it all on health insurance. In the Oregon Medicaid expansion experiment, Finkelstein, Hendren, and Luttmer (2015) found that Medicaid enrollees only valued each additional $1 of government Medicaid spending at $0.20 to $0.40 (also see Gallen 2015). Similarly, a study of Medicaid-like coverage provided through Massachusetts' low-income health insurance exchange found that most enrollees valued their coverage at less than half its cost (Finkelstein, Mahoney, and Notowidigdo 2017).

A second issue is inefficient financing. The price paid to this government monopoly in health insurance, the analogue to the revenue received by private plans, would be determined through tax policy.

M4A will be neither more efficient nor cheaper than the current system, and it could adversely affect health. As we show below, evidence on the productivity and effectiveness of single-payer systems suggests that M4A would reduce longevity and health, particularly among the elderly, while only minimally increasing the fraction of the population with health insurance. In the near term, it would lead to shortages and decreased access to care. And in the long-run, M4A could decrease quality by decreasing innovation. A smaller economy would be another likely adverse effect, due to M4A's disincentives to work and earn. The CEA has calculated that if M4A were financed solely through higher taxes, it would reduce long-run gross domestic product (GDP) by 9 percent and household incomes after taxes and health expenditures by 19 percent (see chapter 8 of this *Report* for further discussion).

Implications for the Value of the Program and Health Outcomes

M4A would replace the existing private and public system for financing healthcare insurance—which includes private, group insurance for about half the population; government insurance for lower-income households, with essentially zero out-of-pocket expenses, in the Medicaid program covering 21 percent of the population; Medicare for the elderly and nonelderly disabled covering 14 percent of the population, including traditional Medicare that has cost sharing in the form of deductibles and coinsurance, privately run Medicare Advantage plans that compete against other advantage plans and traditional Medicare for enrollees and insure about a third of Medicare recipients, and privately run Medicare Part D plans for prescription drug coverage; and the individual, nongroup market covering 7 percent of the population, consisting of the ACA exchanges and nonexchange plans (Kaiser Family Foundation 2017a, 2017b). The existing system also provides uncompensated emergency care—because the 1986 Emergency Medical Treatment and Labor Act requires hospitals to treat anyone coming to their emergency departments, regardless of their insurance status or ability to pay—and uncompensated nonemergency care delivered by various providers. Therefore, changing the financing of health would leave limited room to improve health among U.S. citizens by expanding insurance coverage. The current system includes some non–Medicaid eligible citizens who remain uninsured, but by all estimates they are healthy people, which is why they choose not to purchase an ACA plan (CBO 2017).

M4A would determine quality and productivity through centrally planned rules and regulations. As opposed to a market with competition, if a patient did not like the tax charged or the quality of the care provided by the government monopoly, he or she would have no other insurance options. In addition, price competition in healthcare itself, as opposed to health insurance, would be eliminated because all the prices paid to providers and suppliers of healthcare would be set centrally by the single payer.

Despite its name of "Medicare for All", the proposed plan differs from the currently popular Medicare program by eliminating cost sharing; by preventing private health plans from competing, as in the Medicare Advantage and Part D programs; by preventing private markets from supplementing the public program; and, according to the bill in the House of Representatives, by prohibiting provider institutions from participating in the program unless they are public or not-for-profit entities. Moreover, even if M4A made no changes to Medicare operations, it still would have the problem of taking a program that functions reasonably well for about a sixth of the population and making it work on a vastly larger scale.

Under the existing system, the primary financial limits on healthcare utilization are copayments, coinsurance, and deductibles, which keep premiums lower by discouraging overconsumption of free healthcare at the time of service. M4A would eliminate these out-of-pocket expenses for everyone. If the aggregate supply of healthcare were held unchanged, M4A would reduce health and longevity by reallocating healthcare from high-value uses to lower-value ones. In addition, M4A would reduce the aggregate supply of healthcare by reducing payments to providers, by discouraging innovation, and by using a centralized bureaucracy to allocate resources. We expect that healthcare for the elderly people who are currently covered by Medicare would be especially adversely affected by decreased access to care and decreased longevity.

Here, we illustrate the evidence for the relationship between single-payer programs, healthcare, and health outcomes, including short-run effects, assuming that it has no impact on medical innovation, as well as long-run effects that incorporate changes in incentives for innovation and the resulting impact on future health.

Economies of Scale and Administrative Costs in Insurance

Many M4A advocates argue that the major benefit of adopting single-payer healthcare would be that the costs of producing health insurance by a state monopoly would be lower than under competition. Some evidence on this comes from the literature on the so-called administrative costs of health insurance that do not directly go toward paying for care for beneficiaries. In order to hold regulation constant, Sood and others (2008) analyzed administrative costs within a single State, California. They considered administrative costs and profit levels as the residual of the premium revenue spent directly on beneficiaries' healthcare. They found that in 2006, private plans spent about 12 percent on administrative costs and had profit levels that were significantly below the average for all Standard & Poor's 500 companies (5 vs. 7.5 percent), which, given the existence of government plans, makes profits of only 2 or 3 percent of overall health spending. The CBO (2016) found that private plans spent 13 percent of their premium revenues on administrative expenses and that 2 percent were profits. In contrast, Sood and others (2008) found that Medicare costs were 5 percent, plus the administrative costs of intermediaries that collect premiums and process Medicare claims.

However, the putative efficiency of Medicare administration by the CMS compared with private insurers may simply be a product of inadequate accounting. Medicare patients—the elderly, the disabled, and patients with end-stage renal disease—are sicker and costlier than the younger enrollees in private plans. Medicare's administrative costs as a share of medical spending are smaller mainly because medical spending is higher for the Medicare population compared with the population below 65 that is privately insured—nearly two and a half times higher per person (Book 2009). In addition, insurers' administrative costs do not rise proportionally with total health claim costs—most administrative expenses are fixed per program or are incurred on a per-beneficiary basis, and claims processing costs represent a very small share of administrative costs. If we look at administrative costs *per enrollee*, we find that Medicare is more *inefficient* than private insurers (Kessler 2017). Sood and others (2008) found that Medicare spends $471 per enrollee on administrative costs, close to the $493 in for-profit plans, and actually above the $427 spent across all California health plans. Similarly, Book (2009) found that as a proportion of total costs in 2005, Medicare's administrative costs were 5.8 percent, compared with 13.2 percent for private insurance; but Medicare's administrative costs per person were $509, compared with $453 for private insurance. An additional reason that administrative spending by private insurers artificially appears higher than that by the CMS for Medicare is that private insurers' administrative costs include State premium taxes, from which the CMS is exempt, and directly provided medical services—such as disease management services and nurse consultation telephone lines—that are not counted as paid medical claims (Book 2009).

Philipson (2013) found that the focus on administrative costs omits other important costs, and forgone opportunities, of the state monopoly approach. Under a government monopoly health insurer, the plan is financed with taxes rather than voluntarily paid premiums. As is discussed below, the economic cost of taxes is not merely the revenue that arrives in the Treasury but also the distortions of household and business decisions induced by taxes. This applies to administrative costs as well, so that $1.00 in administrative costs in the private sector is equivalent to about $1.50 in administrative costs in the public sector.

In addition, claims of Medicare superiority ignore the vital role that private "administrative" expenses—such as marketing, profits, and utilization controls—play in driving competition and innovation in the marketplace. Administrative costs also help prevent fraud and improper payments, which are estimated to be about 8 and 10 percent of Medicare and Medicaid spending, respectively (HHS 2018).[4] Furthermore, private plans reduce overall costs by aggressively reviewing healthcare utilization. As a result of competition among plans, lower overall expenses are passed on to consumers as lower premiums, even though a greater percentage of those expenses may be administrative. In contrast, a public program does not engage in premium competition. Beneficiaries, workers, and shareholders of private plans would not tolerate the higher premiums or lower wages or dividends that would be the result of lax utilization controls or high levels of fraud.

Healthcare providers, as distinct from health plans, also spend significant time and resources on administrative costs (Woolhandler, Campbell, and Himmelstein 2003; Himmelstein 2014). Some of these costs serve the economic functions noted above, such as controlling fraud and overutilization; but others are specifically related to billing. It has been asserted (Weisbart 2012) that a single-payer system would eliminate many billing-related expenses, but these savings may not materialize, because providers would likely need to struggle with voluminous new Federal regulations issued to deal with the myriad different circumstances that could arise among the 325 million people who would be on the single government plan.

It is unlikely that a government-run monopoly's efforts to lower healthcare costs by eliminating profits and marketing would be any more effective than government monopoly efforts in other sectors of the economy. In many other industries, economists have generally found that production costs under a monopoly are higher than with competition. Monopolies that are owned in whole or in part by the government incur higher costs than private corporations that operate competitively. The seminal research by Boardman and Vining (1989) found robust evidence that government-owned and mixed enterprises are less efficient than private corporations. More recent work has examined the inefficiencies and higher costs incurred by public monopolies in the education

---

[4] Overpayments were about $32 billion in Medicare Fee-for-Service and $36 billion in Medicaid. Underpayments only accounted for 3 percent and 1 percent respectively of the programs. The Medicaid Fraud Control Unit reports (Murrin 2018) that over the last five years, fraud has accounted for nearly 75 percent of all its convictions.

and corrections sectors (Hoxby 2014; Gaes 2008). Once these factors are taken into account, Medicare's efficiency advantage becomes illusory, even if abnormal profits and marketing were eliminated from the private sector.

Cross–Country Evidence on the Effects of Universal Healthcare on Health Outcomes and the Elderly

Proponents of M4A often refer to European-style programs of socialized medicine as their role model, but the European programs appear to deliver less healthcare to the elderly and result in worse health outcomes for them.[5] Many of these programs ration older patients' access to expensive procedures directly or through waiting times (Cullis, Jones, and Propper 2000). Such age discrimination in coverage occurs because there is no competition between plans under a monopoly. If there were, presumably private plans—which would be outlawed under M4A—would emerge to offer the care not adequately covered by the government monopoly.

Current Medicare beneficiaries would likely be hurt by M4A's expansion of the size of the eligible program population. The evidence for a trade-off between universal and senior healthcare is supported by both the European single-payer experience that limits care for the elderly compared with the U.S., along with the recent domestic U.S. reforms under the ACA that reduced projected Medicare spending by $802 billion to help fund expansions for younger age groups (CBO 2015).

The United States' all-cause mortality rates relative to those of other developed countries improve dramatically after the age of 75 years. In 1960—before Medicare—the U.S. ranked below most EU countries for longevity among those age 50–74, yet above them among for those age 75 and higher. This pattern persists today. Ho and Preston (2010) argue that a higher deployment of life-saving technologies for older patients in the U.S. compared with other developed countries leads to better diagnosis and treatment of diseases of older people and greater longevity.

The availability and utilization of healthcare are particularly important for cancer longevity. Cancer is the leading cause of death in many developed countries, especially among older individuals, and it constitutes an important component of overall U.S. healthcare spending. Philipson and others (2012) found that U.S. cancer patients live longer than cancer patients in 10 EU countries, after the same diagnosis, due to the additional spending on higher-quality cancer care in the U.S. Figure 4-1 shows the results for life expectancy after diagnosis.[6] Ho and Preston (2010) point out that in Europe, where the proportion of surgically treated patients declines with age, five-year survival

---

[5] Note that a number of European countries—including Belgium, Germany, and Switzerland—have universal healthcare without having a single-payer system.
[6] Between the two continents, difference not attributable to a different propensity to screen for cancer in the U.S.

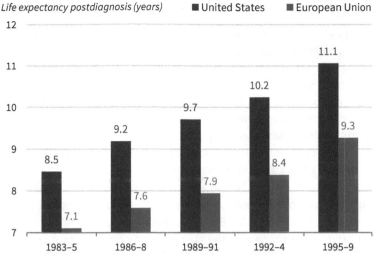

Figure 4-1. Average Survival from a Cancer Diagnosis, 1983–99

Life expectancy postdiagnosis (years) ■ United States ■ European Union

Source: Philipson et al. (2012).
Note: The results are standardized by age, gender, and cancer site. EU countries for which survival data were consistently available over the analysis period are included: Finland, France, Germany, Iceland, Norway, Slovakia, Slovenia, Scotland, Sweden, and Wales.

rates for colorectal cancer are lower for elderly patients than younger patients. But in the United States, where utilization of surgery does not decline with age, colorectal cancer survival rates do not decline for elderly patients.

This effect is not confined to cancer treatment. For ischemic heart disease—the world's leading cause of death—the use of cardiac catheterization, percutaneous coronary angioplasty, and coronary artery bypass grafting declines with patients' age, but declines more steeply in other developed countries than in the United States. Compared with these developed countries, the U.S. has a lower case fatality rate for acute myocardial infarction (the acute manifestation of ischemic disease) for older persons but not for younger persons age 40 to 64 (Ho and Preston 2010).

This disease-specific evidence is more informative about the benefits of healthcare than often-discussed cross-country comparisons of nationally aggregated outcomes, such as overall population longevity and aggregate healthcare spending. There are many determinants of overall population health other than healthcare—such as diet, exercise, genes, and violence—that differ across countries (CEA 2018b). These factors may lead to lower U.S. longevity even while U.S. healthcare is of higher quality. The fact that many wealthy foreigners who could afford to obtain care anywhere in the world come to the U.S. for specialized care is perhaps the strongest indication of its superior quality. The general pattern of medical tourism is that the United States exports high-quality care while importing low-cost care (Woodman 2015).

The Lower Quality of Universal Coverage, in Terms of Reduced Availability

Another major quality attribute of healthcare is how long one must wait to receive it. The highest-quality care may be ineffective if there are delays in diagnosis or treatment. For example, delays in diagnosing or treating cancer will cause decreased survival and increased suffering, regardless of how good the care is. This major dimension of the quality of care may fall with government expansions of care as they generate excess demand, and thereby may induce queues with waiting times to access care.

Because it is "free" at the time of service, the single-payer, universal-coverage system gives consumers more reason to consume healthcare (Arrow 1963; Pauly 1968). The Rand Health Insurance Experiment documented that as the amount of coinsurance decreased, utilization of medical care rose (Newhouse 1993; Brook et. al. 2006). M4A cuts the out-of-pocket expenses that people in private insurance and the current Medicare system pay (about 70 percent of the insured population) to zero (Kaiser Family Foundation 2017a). In addition, when it cuts provider reimbursement rates, a single-payer system gives the healthcare industry less reason to supply it.[7] Something must determine who gets the scarce provider resources, and quality degradation is the typical way that markets make this determination when prices are unable to do so (Mulligan and Tsui 2016). The quality degradation may take the form of shorter appointment times, longer patient travel times, or longer waiting times to receive care.

Waiting times for nonemergency or elective surgery were shorter for adults (18 and older) in the U.S. than in 10 other developed countries, especially those with a single-payer system. Table 4-1 shows that 61 percent of Americans waited less than 1 month after being advised that they needed surgery. The comparable figures for Canada and the United Kingdom, two countries frequently cited as models by M4A advocates, were 34.8 percent and 43.4 percent, respectively. Similarly, table 4-2 shows that only two countries (Germany, at 71.2 percent; and Switzerland, at 73.2 percent) had a slightly higher percentage of patients able to see a specialist within 4 weeks of referral than the U.S. (69.9 percent), and neither of these countries has a single-payer system (Mossialos et al. 2017). The figure for Canada was 38.0 percent, and that for the U.K. was 48.6 percent.

In a recent report, the CEA (2018c) pointed out that waiting times for seniors to see a specialist in the U.S. were shorter than in single-payer countries (figure 4-2). Some argue that this shows that Medicare, and thus its distant cousin "Medicare for All", works and should be extended to everyone. This is a misinterpretation.

---

[7] M4A reduces payments to providers (subtitle B of Title VI of the Senate "Medicare for All" Act of 2017).

Table 4-1. Adult Waiting Times for Nonemergency or Elective Surgery, 2016

Country	Less than one month (percent)	Between one and four months (percent)	Four or more months (percent)	Do not know or decline to answer (percent)	Total (count)
Australia	56.8	28.3	8.4	6.6	683
Canada	34.8	44.0	18.2	3.0	557
France	51.4	47.0	1.6	0.0	173
Germany	39.0	58.1	0.0	2.9	124
Netherlands	48.9	39.8	4.5	6.9	99
New Zealand	43.3	38.6	14.9	3.2	141
Norway	37.0	41.9	15.3	5.8	208
Sweden	37.3	46.8	11.8	4.1	1,015
Switzerland	59.3	32.8	6.5	1.5	219
United Kingdom	43.4	31.8	12.0	12.8	87
United States	61.0	31.7	3.6	3.7	268

Source: Commonwealth Fund Survey.

Note: Respondents answered the survey question, "After you were advised that you needed surgery, how many weeks did you have to wait for the non-emergency or elective surgery?"

Table 4-2. Adult Waiting Times for Specialist Appointments, 2016

Country	Less than four weeks (percent)	At least four weeks (percent)	Do not know or decline to answer (percent)	Total (count)
Australia	54.7	39.3	6.1	2,156
Canada	38.0	58.5	3.5	2,228
France	60.2	39.8	0.0	639
Germany	71.2	27.4	1.4	459
Netherlands	64.0	28.9	7.1	580
New Zealand	49.3	47.3	3.3	404
Norway	36.9	55.5	7.7	605
Sweden	48.1	44.7	7.2	3,251
Switzerland	73.2	25.9	0.9	810
United Kingdom	48.6	42.5	8.9	371
United States	69.9	25.3	4.8	1,019

Source: Commonwealth Fund Survey.

Note: Respondents answered the survey question, "After you were advised to see or decided to see a doctor in specialist health care/specialist (or consultant), how many weeks did you have to wait for an appointment?"

Figure 4-2. Seniors Who Waited at Least Four Weeks to See a Specialist during the Past Two Years, 2017

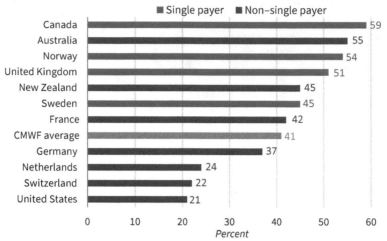

Sources: Canadian Institute for Health Information; Ghanta (2013); Commonwealth Fund survey.
Note: Single-payer systems were compiled by Ghanta (2013) from World Health Organization sources. CMWF average refers to the average of the 11 countries in the Commonwealth Fund survey. Results exclude respondents who never attempted to get an appointment.

All that figure 4-2 shows is that the current Medicare system, which mixes public and private elements—including competition between hundreds of Medicare Advantage plans and between hundreds of Medicare Part D drug plans and public and private financing—is superior to foreign, single-payer systems (see chapter 8 for more discussion). It does not indicate that Medicare is superior to the insurance currently available for the non-Medicare U.S. population. And it has little bearing on what to expect from M4A. M4A is not simply an expansion of Medicare. It is a completely different program that bans private insurance and competition, and that anticipates a system-wide lowering of reimbursement levels below private insurance rates. According to the CMS Actuary, lowering private provider rates to current Medicare rates would lead to a drop of about 40 percent for hospitals' reimbursements and 30 percent for physicians' reimbursements by 2022, decreases that are scheduled to grow even greater over time, due to statutory Medicare payment restraints enacted as part of the ACA and the Medicare Access and CHIP Reauthorization Act of 2015 (CMS 2018; Blahous 2018b). These lower reimbursement rates will undoubtedly prolong waiting times and worsen access to care because providers respond to reimbursement levels. In a study of Medicaid fees, every $10 change up or down led to a 1.7 percent change in the same direction in the proportion of patients who could secure an appointment with a new doctor (Candon et al. 2017). Even more worrisome, Medicare's hospital payment rates are, on average, so far below hospitals' reported costs of providing services that the CMS Actuary projects that by 2019, over 80 percent of hospitals will lose money treating Medicare patients. If this projection is correct, M4A would force 80 percent of hospitals to lose money when treating *all* their patients (Blahous 2018b).

One does not need to go abroad to see the problems with single-payer medicine. The Veterans Health Administration (VHA) is a publicly funded, single-payer system to provide care to military veterans. Its government-employed providers, particularly medical specialists, are underpaid compared with the private market and lack the motivation to provide the care that market competition to produce profits generates. In 2014, it was widely reported that the Phoenix VHA facility, along with several other facilities, had kept large numbers of veterans waiting inordinate amounts of time to receive treatment and that some had died while waiting (Farmer, Hosek, and Adamson 2016). Many of the facilities had falsified records in order to meet the VHA's target of providing appointments within 14 days. Using the VHA's own data, outside researchers found tremendous variation in waiting times across VHA facilities. Although most veterans get care within 2 weeks of their preferred appointment dates, a significant number wait more than 60 days, and only half reported getting care "as soon as needed" (Farmer, Hosek, and Adamson 2016, 9). The Veterans Access, Choice, and Accountability Act of 2014 created a temporary plan—the Choice Program—to give veterans the option of receiving care from a private, community-based provider when timely care is unavailable from a VHA facility. Unfortunately, the program had limited success—veterans were still experiencing lengthy actual waiting times for appointments in 2016 (GAO 2018). In June 2018, President Trump signed the VA MISSION Act of 2018 to extend funding for the Choice Program and to improve it by consolidating it over the next year with six other programs offering community-based care into the single Veterans Community Care program. This statute aims to minimize the inconsistent experience that veterans receive by requiring the VHA to standardize access to care, assess the system's capacity to provide the care required, establish a high-performing national network of providers to offset capability gaps, and transition the VHA to an integrated healthcare system.

A U.S. Single–Payer System Would Have Adverse Long–Run Effects on Global Health through Reduced Innovation

There has been much theoretical and empirical economic analysis concluding that lowering prices for innovative industries often has short-run benefits that are dominated by long-run costs. Lowering prices by having a single payer for innovative healthcare technologies is analogous to reducing patent terms, for both reduce the return to medical research-and-development (R&D) investments. Both have short-term benefits, lowering prices for *existing* technologies—but at the cost of reducing the flow of *new* technologies that ultimately lower the real price of healthcare.

The value of healthcare generated by innovation over time exceeds its additional costs (Cutler 2004). The lower premiums of the 1970s bought lower-quality care than is available today—no one today would settle for a 1970s level of care. Forty years of innovations have raised prices, but they have raised the value of healthcare even more. Some innovations are very expensive—for example, today's specialty drugs—and others are relative bargains—such as antibiotics, new treatments for heart attacks that cost $10,000 in real terms but add a year of life expectancy (Cutler and McClellan 2001), and new cancer treatments in the 1980s and 1990s that cost an average of only $8,670 per year of life gained (Philipson et al. 2012). Other innovations add little value. Though it is often impossible to know in advance which innovation will be a good value, it is imperative to preserve the incentive to innovate so there will continue to be new, high-value innovations.

Because worldwide innovation relies so heavily on the U.S. market to support it, adopting an M4A program would likely adversely affect innovation because the global market for new innovations would shrink. A large body of literature looks at the effects of market size on innovation. For example, using the passage of the Medicare Prescription Drug, Improvement, and Modernization Act of 2003 as a source of variation, Blume-Kohout and Sood (2013) find an elasticity with respect to market size of between 2.4 to 4.7 for Phase 1 clinical trials. These estimates are well within the range of the work of Acemoglu and Linn (2004), who find an elasticity of 3.5 for approved new molecular entities. Moreover, these results are consistent with evidence on the impact of public policy on market size.[8] Although these long-run effects on a reduced pace of innovation are more difficult to quantify, they may well be more important than the short-run effects of spending less on elder care.

U.S. patients and taxpayers alike have financed the returns on R&D investments to innovators. Unlike other developed countries with single-payer systems, which nearly all impose some sort of price controls, the U.S. market has less public sector financing and is therefore more open to market forces. In a free market, prices of products reflect their value, as opposed to prices in government-controlled markets, which reflect political trade-offs. Among the nations that belong to the Organization for Economic Cooperation and Development, more than 70 percent of patented pharmaceutical profits come from sales to U.S. patients, even though the United States only represents 34 percent of the organization's GDP at purchasing power parity (CEA 2018a).

Empirical research on pharmaceutical innovation and other industries has shown that R&D investments are positively related to market size. For

---

[8] For example, Finkelstein (2004) finds a 2.5-fold increase in the number of new vaccine clinical trials for affected diseases following the adoption of three public health policies aimed at raising vaccination rates, and Yin (2008) finds that the introduction of the Orphan Drug Act raised the flow of new clinical trials for rare diseases by 182 percent in the three years following the passage of the policy.

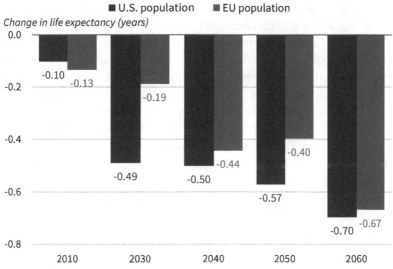

Figure 4-3. Effect of U.S. Drug Price Controls on Global Longevity, Among Those Age 55–59, 2010–60

■ U.S. population ■ EU population

Change in life expectancy (years)

-0.10
-0.13
-0.19
-0.49
-0.50
-0.44
-0.57
-0.40
-0.70
-0.67

2010   2030   2040   2050   2060

Source: Lakdawalla et al. (2009).
Note: Data were estimated by the author based on the Global Pharmaceutical Policy Model.

the case of medical innovation, evidence suggests that a 1 percent reduction in market size reduces innovation—defined as the number of new drugs launched—by as much as 4 percent (Acemoglu and Linn 2004).

Given that future profitability drives investment in this way, Lakdawalla and others (2009) examined the impact on medical innovation of the U.S. adopting European-style price controls. The study examined patients over the age of 55 and considered the reduction in R&D and new drugs approved that these price controls would cause. The paper found resulting increases in mortality due to heart disease, hypertension, diabetes, cancer, lung disease, stroke, and mental illness. Given that innovations are financed by world returns that are mostly earned in the U.S., the mortality effects on health were substantial, both in the U.S. and in Europe (figure 4-3).

If M4A would lead to the same below-market pharmaceutical prices that other countries have imposed through government price controls, it would reduce the world market size and thereby medical innovation, and ultimately mean that future patients would forgo the health gains that would have come from these forgone innovations.

Financing "Medicare for All"

Apart from M4A's effects on the amount and quality of healthcare provided, there is the issue of how it would be financed and what impact this decision would have on the overall economy. The CMS, which administers most government-financed healthcare, projects that in 2022 the private sector will spend $1.47 trillion on private health insurance and $0.46 trillion in out-of-pocket health expenses, in an economy with a total GDP of $24.35 trillion (National Health Expenditure Accounts projections; CEA 2018c).

Because healthcare is free at the time of service to users under M4A, and otherwise would not be "free" for those not enrolled in government programs, M4A would increase healthcare utilization at the Federal government's expense. Blahous (2018a) predicts that there would be extra utilization of $0.44 trillion in 2022. Adding this figure to the private health insurance and out-of-pocket expenses it would replace would lead to a total addition to Federal spending of $2.37 trillion in 2022. Without M4A, $2.37 trillion would be 9.7 percent of GDP, or 11.7 percent of consumption, or an average about $18,000 per household (CEA 2018c). An even larger amount of Federal health spending would occur if the most comprehensive list of covered services were adopted in reconciling the Senate and House M4A bills.

The CEA (2018c) found that paying for M4A solely with uniform spending cuts across all existing Federal programs would require 53 percent across-the-board cuts in 2022. Without additional taxes, all other Federal programs would need to be cut by more than half. This would imply cuts to Social Security of about $0.7 trillion, to (the existing part of) Medicare of about $0.4 trillion, and to the Defense Department's budget of about $0.4 trillion. If Medicare were exempted, 79 percent of Social Security (about $1.0 trillion per year) would need to be cut, and annual Defense cuts would need to be about $0.6 trillion.

Alternatively, M4A could be financed solely with taxes. Some argue that the population would be no worse off because these new taxes would simply replace the cost of premiums paid to private sector insurers. This argument ignores the fact that taxation distorts economic activity so that the cost of tax revenues is larger than the revenues. The excess burden, or "deadweight loss," reflects the decreased economic efficiency and product output that exceeds the tax revenue collected. To illustrate, if the government imposed a per-passenger tax of $100,000 on air travel, it would collect virtually no revenue because almost no one would fly, but it would impose a large burden on the population in excess of the revenue collected by replacing air travel with less efficient cars and other types of ground transportation. The existing empirical literature finds that this burden is about 50 cents on the dollar, so that the cost of collecting the taxes to fund M4A in a year would be about 1.5 times the additional revenue needed to fund the larger program (Feldstein 1999; Saez, Slemrod, and Giertz 2012; Weber 2014).[9]

Between the two extreme funding scenarios—funding M4A entirely by cuts in spending or entirely by tax increases—lies a middle ground of using

---

[9] The excess burden rate is larger, and potentially infinite, when considered particularly large increases in revenue, as with M4A. Also see chapter 8 of this *Report* for additional perspective on the excess burden of M4A.

a combination of both spending cuts and tax increases. This approach was followed in the recent Federal healthcare expansion under the ACA, whereby funding was split between tax increases and spending cuts to Federal healthcare programs (CBO 2009). It is unclear whether sufficient tax revenue could be collected for the much larger proposed M4A program, given the existence of tax avoidance behavior, particularly by the higher-income populations that provide the largest share of total Federal tax revenues. If the amount of maximum revenue collected, the height of the so-called Laffer curve, were below what would be required in new funding, then spending cuts would be required, regardless of whether lawmakers would prefer to finance the entire program with taxes.

The Administration's Actions to Increase Choice and Competition in Health Insurance

In contrast to policies curtailing market forces advocated in "Medicare for All" proposals, this section details the Trump Administration's efforts so far to improve choice and competition in health insurance markets in order to help them better serve lower- and middle-income people.

As part of its broader policy agenda to deregulate markets, the Trump Administration has completed three deregulatory reforms that expand consumers' health insurance options: (1) reducing, through the Tax Cuts and Jobs Act of 2017, the ACA's individual mandate penalty to zero; (2) a June 2018 rule expanding the ability of small businesses to form association health plans (AHPs) to provide low-cost group health insurance to their employees; and (3) an August 2018 rule expanding the term, renewability, and usefulness of short-term, limited duration insurance (STLDI) plans. As discussed above, several market failures are relevant to health insurance. Taking the relevant market failures into account, we use the standard methods of welfare economics to assess the potential efficiency gains to affected consumers and taxpayers. We find that these deregulatory actions will generate benefits to Americans worth about $453 billion over the next 10 years (CEA 2019). The reforms will benefit lower- and middle income consumers and all taxpayers, but leave small premium increases on some middle- and higher-income consumers. The benefits of giving a large group of consumers more insurance options far outweighs the projected costs imposed on the smaller group that will pay higher premiums. These reforms do not sabotage the ACA; they provide a more efficient focus of tax-funded care to those in need.

In this section, we examine in depth the most productive of the reforms, elimination of the individual mandate penalty, which will benefit Americans by $19 billion, including the deadweight cost of taxation in 2021 (when the markets will have largely adjusted to the reform) and $204 billion between

2019 and 2029. Though we will briefly mention the other two reforms, AHPs and STLDIs, they are discussed at length in chapter 2.

The Stability of the Nongroup Health Insurance Market

The ACA's proponents argued that three key components of the statute were essential and had to work together for the act to be economically viable—the so-called three-legged stool (see Gruber 2010). The first leg of the stool is guaranteed issue and community rating, whereby consumers must be offered coverage without the premium varying because of preexisting condition or health status.[10] The second leg of the stool is the individual mandate penalty on the remaining uninsured population, so that healthy consumers do not wait until they are ill to sign up. The third leg of the stool is a system of subsidies, so that lower- and middle-income consumers can afford coverage. Under this view, deregulatory reforms that expand health insurance options beyond the ACA's insurance markets risk destabilizing the ACA insurance markets. The relatively healthy consumers who might best respond to expanded options are seen as critical sources of ACA insurance-market revenue because their premiums are expected to exceed their healthcare claims.[11]

However, several features of the insurance market undermine this argument. Most important, the claim that the individual mandate is indispensable is flawed, due to the large ACA premium subsidies that most ACA exchange enrollees receive. The view that deregulation sabotages the ACA is based on the assumption that the premiums paid by unsubsidized healthy consumers are a critical source of exchange revenue.[12] Federal subsidies are far more important. Figure 4-4 displays the annual premiums on the exchanges as a function of family income and composition. Only consumers who are ineligible for premium subsidies—those with incomes above 400 percent of the Federal poverty line on the exchanges and everyone with ACA-compliant coverage off the exchanges—actually pay the entire premium. There were 14.4 million people in the nongroup market in the first quarter of 2018, 10.6 million on the exchanges, and only 3.8 off the exchanges in both ACA-compliant and noncompliant plans (Kaiser Family Foundation 2018). In 2018, only 13 percent of consumers (1.4 million) who purchased insurance on the ACA exchanges

---

[10] Premiums are allowed to vary within a narrow range based upon age (3:1 adjustment) and smoking status.

[11] When it adopted the ACA, Congress itself evidently believed that the individual mandate was necessary to a regulatory system that included guaranteed issue and community rating. Congress expressly found that the individual mandate was "essential to creating effective health insurance markets in which improved health insurance products that are guaranteed issue and do not exclude coverage of preexisting conditions can be sold" and that "the absence of the [individual mandate] would undercut Federal regulation of the health insurance market" (42 U.S.C. § 18091).

[12] This is closely related to "adverse selection": The departure of a healthy person from a risk pool is purported to be adverse in terms of reducing plan premium revenue more than it reduces claims. Due to the ACA subsidies, adverse selection will operate differently, in that subsidized healthy persons will have less incentive to leave the ACA exchanges.

did not receive subsidies and therefore paid the full premium.[13] The other 87 percent of exchange consumers (9.2 million) received subsidies through the ACA's premium tax credits and so paid just a fraction of the full premium. Many of these subsidized people also received cost-sharing reduction subsidies to reduce their out-of-pocket costs if their income was between 100 and 250 percent of the Federal poverty line and they purchased a Silver exchange plan. ACA-compliant coverage is sold both on and off the ACA's exchanges, but subsidies are only available for coverage purchased on the exchanges. Including the two types of ACA-compliant individual market coverage (on and off exchanges) that share a common risk pool and have the same premiums, about 38 percent of consumers who purchased ACA-compliant, individual insurance paid the full premium in 2017. The percentage of unsubsidized consumers in the individual market has fallen every year from 2015 to the present as premiums have risen.

The regulatory reforms expand insurance options. To the extent that the consumers who leave the ACA exchanges for these options are healthier than average, their departure will somewhat raise gross premiums for those who remain on the exchanges. But for subsidized consumers who remain on the exchanges, the premium increases will be mainly paid by taxpayers, not the consumers themselves. Although the CBO projects that setting the individual mandate tax penalty to zero will encourage healthier-than-average enrollees to leave the ACA exchanges, the CBO also projects that their departure will reduce Federal expenditures on ACA premium subsidies from 2018 through 2027 by $185 billion (CBO 2017; Gruber 2010).[14] Of course, the CBO's projections of Federal expenditures are uncertain. But figure 4-4 shows the origin of these projections: For consumers with family incomes less than 400 percent of the Federal poverty line, the individual mandate penalty taxes them for turning down large amounts of government assistance.

The role of the ACA premium subsidies in stabilizing the exchanges has been acknowledged by others, including the previous Administration (CEA 2017; Sacks 2018; Collins and Gunja 2018). The premium subsidies' stabilizing role is consistent with the experience of the past few years, in which rising premiums did not curtail demand. ACA exchange premiums have almost doubled in just a few years (figure 4-5), though there has been hardly any change in

---

[13] "Grandfathered" plans that were in effect when the ACA was passed are exempt from some of the ACA's provisions. The fraction of workers with employer-sponsored insurance enrolled in grandfathered plans decreased from 56 percent in 2011 to 16 percent in 2018 (Kaiser Family Foundation 2018). During the transitional period, another set of "grandmothered" plans have also been exempt from certain ACA provisions.

[14] Taking into account all the effects of setting the individual mandate penalty to zero, the CBO projects a $338 billion reduction in Federal expenditures from 2018 through 2027, $179 billion of which will be a reduction in Federal expenditures on Medicaid (CBO 2017).

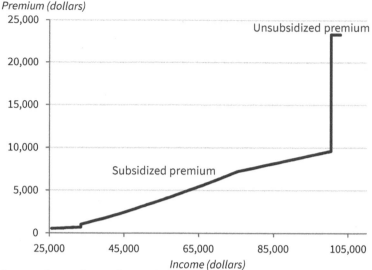

Figure 4-4. Premium Costs as a Function of Household Income, 2018

Premium (dollars)

Unsubsidized premium

Subsidized premium

Income (dollars)

Source: Kaiser Family Foundation Subsidy Calculator.
Note: Data represent the national average premium for a family of four with two 50-year-old adults and two teenagers with no tobacco use.

exchange enrollment.[15] Figure 4-5 demonstrates that the U.S. Treasury (i.e., taxpayers) shouldered almost the entire premium increase for ACA plans.

Even though gross premiums almost doubled between 2014 and 2018, lower- and some middle-income consumers were insulated from the effects of these increases by the subsidies. Although there may also have been other factors at work, these trends are consistent with the CBO's (2017, 2018) projections that further increases in the full exchange premiums (usually referred to as "gross" premiums) will not destabilize the ACA exchange markets. Between 2018 and 2019, benchmark ACA premiums dropped by 1.5 percent.

The individual mandate penalty adds an unnecessary leg to the ACA stool, resulting in economic inefficiencies. Comprehensive insurance, particularly with extremely low cost sharing, could cause patients to overconsume healthcare that provides little benefit relative to the cost—the moral hazard problem discussed above.[16] The significant decline in premium subsidies as income rises also distorts labor markets by taxing income and some types of

---

[15] Figure 4-5 does not include cost-sharing reduction payments or reinsurance payments. Fiedler (2018) calculates that cost-sharing reduction payments were equivalent to about 9 percent of average exchange premiums in 2017. Part of the premium increase between 2017 and 2018 was attributable to the nonpayment of cost-sharing reduction payments in 2018.

[16] The 2018 *Economic Report of the President* (CEA 2018b) discusses the large body of evidence that health insurance coverage, and presumably the additional healthcare consumed by consumers as a result of it, provides little health benefit.

Figure 4-5. Nominal Gross Premiums per Member per Year for Subsidized Enrollees, 2014–18

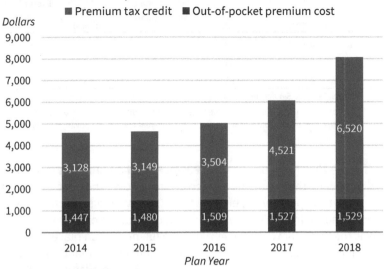

Source: Kaiser Family Foundation Subsidy Calculator.
Note: Data represent the average national premium for a single, nonsmoking 50-year-old at 200 percent of the Federal poverty line with no children.

full-time employment and introduces another marriage penalty in the tax code (Mulligan 2015). Consumers have heterogeneous preferences for risk, smooth cash flow, and range of coverage. As such, it is wasteful to use a tax penalty to coerce people to purchase insurance that does not meet their needs (Mulligan and Philipson 2004). Many "health insurance simulation models" ignore moral hazard and any effect of health insurance policy on labor market equilibrium. Those simulations therefore rule out by assumption many of the benefits of allowing consumers to voluntarily leave ACA-compliant plans (Gallen and Mulligan 2018).

In sum, the three-legged-stool justification for the individual mandate tax penalty is not consistent with the basic facts of how the ACA works in practice. The penalty and other restrictions on consumer choice are not needed to support the guaranteed issue of community-rated health insurance to all consumers, including those with preexisting conditions. The ACA premium subsidies stabilize the exchanges.

Setting the Individual Tax Mandate Penalty to Zero

The ACA's individual mandate imposed a monetary penalty on nonexempt consumers who did not have ACA-compliant coverage. The Tax Cuts and Jobs Act of 2017 involved a tax cut on the uninsured as well as on people purchasing noncompliant ACA coverage by setting the individual mandate penalty to zero,

Table 4-3. IRS Reporting of Individual Mandate Payments, 2014–16

Tax year	Returns paying IM penalty (millions)	IM revenue (billions of dollars)	Mean penalty paid (dollars)	Minimum penalty (dollars)	Exemptions (millions)
2014	8.1	1.69	210	95	12.4
2015	6.7	3.11	465	325	12.7
2016	4.0	2.83	708	695	10.7

Sources: Internal Revenue Service (IRS); Busch and Houchens (2018); CEA calculations.

Note: IM = individual mandate. The minimum penalty is the minimum statutory penalty per person-year. The uninsured per penalty paid is the uninsured person-years per return paying penalty.

effective in the 2019 tax year (131 Stat. 2054). Part of our analysis is the amount of penalty revenue that would have been collected over the next 10 years if the act had not set the penalty to zero. We took the revenue projections from the CBO, and noted their consistency with the actual collections for tax year 2016, which was the first year when the ACA put the full penalty in place. In that year, about 4 million Federal tax returns included individual mandate payments, down from 6.7 million for tax year 2015 (table 4-3). The average 2016 penalty paid per household return was $708. The mandate tax penalty is a regressive tax that falls more heavily on relatively low-income people—the majority of those who paid the tax penalty in 2015 were lower- and middle-income consumers with incomes less than 400 percent of the Federal poverty line.

Analyses of removing the individual mandate penalty provided a range of estimates of the impact on the number of insured consumers and on gross ACA premiums. The estimates refer to increases in the full ACA premiums (gross of subsidies), not the out-of-pocket (net) premiums enrollees pay after taking into account the premium subsidies they receive. The CBO (2017) has projected that setting the mandate tax penalty to zero will result in 3 million fewer consumers with ACA-compliant nongroup insurance coverage in 2019, 4 million fewer in 2020, and 5 million fewer each year from 2021 through 2027.[17] Because the enrollees who leave ACA-compliant individual coverage are projected to be healthier than those remaining, the CBO has also projected that gross premiums would rise by an average of 10 percent.

Nevertheless, the CBO (2017) projects that the 2018–27 budgetary impact of setting the mandate penalty to zero will be to reduce the Federal deficit by $338 billion, which includes a $185 billion reduction in Federal expenditures on ACA premium subsidies. A Commonwealth Fund study analyzed the impact of setting the individual mandate penalty to zero under 10 scenarios (Eibner and Nowak 2018). Each scenario reflected different assumptions about how people respond to financial and nonfinancial factors. In this study's baseline scenario,

---

[17] The CBO also projects voluntary reductions in Medicaid enrollment and enrollment in employment-based coverage. The CEA is still studying these effects, which were not included in the analysis.

setting the mandate penalty to zero was estimated to reduce enrollment in the nongroup market by 3.4 million in 2020 and increase the gross premium for bronze plans on the ACA exchanges by 7 percent. We use the CBO's estimates, which involve a larger change in enrollment (5 million fewer enrollees) and a larger increase in premiums (10 percent) than the baseline scenario that the Commonwealth Fund estimates.

A Cost–Benefit Analysis of Setting the Individual Mandate Tax Penalty to Zero

Setting the ACA's individual mandate penalty to zero benefits society by allowing people to choose not to have ACA-compliant health coverage without facing a tax penalty, and by saving taxpayers money if fewer consumers purchase subsidized ACA coverage. We estimate that in 2021, when the CBO (2017, 2018) projects that markets will have largely adjusted to the changes, setting the mandate penalty to zero will yield net benefits worth $19 billion, including the excess burdens of taxation. The total net benefit of the reform over the period 2019 through 2029 comes to $204 billion. The benefits grow over time, so the benefits in 2021 are estimated to be lower than average annual benefits over the 10-year horizon.

Without the tax penalty, consumers will likely reduce their ACA-compliant coverage, which refers in this section to coverage purchased on the ACA exchanges and coverage obtained outside the exchanges as long as it complies with the provisions of the ACA. Our analysis recognized that consumers place some value on the ACA-compliant coverage they give up.[18] To the extent that these consumers are healthier than average, including them in the insurance pool also benefits others in the pool by reducing the premium needed to cover the pool's average healthcare expenditures. At the same time, society incurs costs to provide health insurance coverage. Providing insurance to those who value it most highly nets large social benefits. Insuring more and more of the population nets progressively smaller social benefits, because it covers enrollees who do not value the coverage as highly. When insuring even more of the population requires providing insurance to enrollees who value the insurance at less than what it costs society, on net the social benefits become negative. This is captured in figure 4-6 by the downward-sloping net marginal social benefits (MSB) schedule, which shows that as enrollment increases, net social benefits decline and eventually become negative. The MSB schedule is the

---

[18] In keeping with much of the cost-benefit literature, the CEA used the Kaldor-Hicks criterion, which means that all citizens' benefits and costs are measured in dollars, with all citizens' totals getting the same weight. In accord with this focus on Kaldor-Hicks economic efficiency, our analysis estimated the value of health insurance coverage to the consumers themselves.

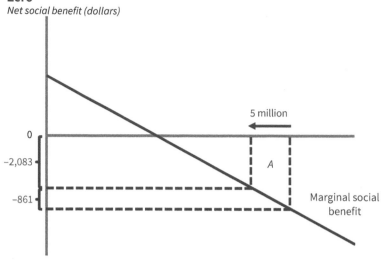

Figure 4-6. Benefits of Setting the Individual Mandate Penalty to Zero

Net social benefit (dollars)

5 million

0

−2,083

A

−861

Marginal social benefit

Enrollees whose coverage is compliant with the Affordable Care Act

cumulative distribution of net social benefits; for illustrative purposes only, the MSB schedule in figure 4-6 is linear.[19]

Our cost-benefit analysis, summarized by the MSB schedule portrayed in figure 4-6, uses the standard methods of welfare economics. Consumers' decisions about whether to have ACA-compliant coverage reveal the value consumers place on this coverage. The value consumers place on insurance reflects their expected healthcare expenditures and the value they place on reducing their financial risk. Some consumers who choose not to have ACA-compliant coverage might have higher healthcare expenditures than they expected and lack coverage. This would not necessarily mean that these consumers were unwise in their choice of insurance; they were unfortunate.

Although the MSB schedule shown in figure 4-6 reflects the value that consumers place on their own health insurance, our analysis took into account all the benefits and costs, including the costs imposed on third parties. First, some consumers who lack insurance coverage and then fall ill or have an accident receive uncompensated care from providers. The providers might bear some or all of the costs of uncompensated care; or they might pass some costs along to third parties, such as privately insured patients, through higher prices. Garthwaite, Gross, and Notowidigdo (2018) analyzed confidential hospital

---

[19] As noted below, our triangle analysis assumes that the MSB schedule is approximately linear in the portion of the distribution that responds to the removal of the tax penalty. We also assume zero economic profits for insurers, in that premium revenues are exhausted by claims and loads. Loads, in turn, reflect competitive payments to labor and capital employed in the insurance industry.

financial data and concluded that, on average, each additional uninsured person costs hospitals about $800 each year. We use this result to estimate the third-party effects of uncompensated care provided to consumers who do not have ACA-compliant coverage. Second, to the extent that the enrollees who leave the market are healthier than average, their health insurance decisions will increase insurance premiums charged to those who remain in ACA-compliant coverage. The CBO (2017) projects the zero tax penalty will increase premiums in the nongroup market by about 10 percent. This 10 percent forecast is likely to be too high, because the CBO did not expect the decline in benchmark premiums that occurred from 2018 to 2019.

Nevertheless, our analysis used the 10 percent estimate and accounts for the third-party effects on Federal expenditures for premium subsidies and on premiums paid by nonsubsidized enrollees. Most of the enrollees who remain in ACA-compliant coverage receive premium subsidies, which means that the increased premiums will be largely financed by increased Federal subsidy expenditures. A subset of enrollees who do not receive subsidies will pay higher premiums. Our empirical implementation of the MSB schedule incorporates the third-party effects on uncompensated care, on Federal expenditures for premium subsidies, and on premiums paid by nonsubsidized enrollees.

We concluded that setting the individual mandate penalty to zero benefits society by reducing inefficient coverage in the market for ACA-compliant health insurance. The ACA premium subsidies are the first source of inefficiency. The premium subsidies make health coverage more affordable to lower- and middle-income consumers; but on net, the subsidies reduce the social benefits from health insurance because they result in many enrollees who value the insurance at less than its cost. Pauly, Leive, and Harrington (2018) also estimated that many uninsured consumers experience financial losses due to ACA coverage.[20] The tax penalties that enforced the individual mandate are the second source of inefficiency and exacerbate the inefficiency due to the premium subsidies.

Setting the individual mandate penalty to zero may reduce some ACA premium subsidy payments and, if it does, will generate a social gain. In cost-benefit analyses, a reduction in subsidy payments is often merely a transfer that leaves social benefits unchanged—the benefits to taxpayers are exactly offset by the costs to the recipients who lose the subsidy. When comparing the ACA with premium subsidies to a hypothetical ACA without subsidies, the ACA premium subsidy is properly treated as a transfer. But the purpose of this analysis is to evaluate the effect of relaxing restrictions on consumer choice,

---

[20]Some might question the judgment of consumers for whom a large subsidy is not enough by itself to induce them to purchase ACA-compliant insurance. Features of the ACA exchanges—administrative loading fees, price controls, moral hazard, premium subsidies that distort labor markets, and heterogeneous preferences—make it reasonable, and consistent with economic efficiency, for a risk-averse person to remain uninsured when his or her risk is low enough.

not changing the ACA premium subsidy rules. The subset of individuals who may only have subsidized ACA coverage due to the mandate penalty is shown in figure 4-6. To illustrate: If (as we calculate below) the average net subsidy in 2021 would be about $2,083 and the average penalty about $861, an individual who voluntarily gives up his or her $2,083 subsidy when the $861 penalty is removed is not harmed by losing the Treasury subsidy. Instead, the individual has received a benefit by no longer being constrained by a penalty at the same time that taxpayers benefit by no longer having to finance the subsidy. The CEA's application of standard welfare economics to this situation is proper but unfamiliar because of the complicated design of the ACA and its related regulations.[21]

The CBO (2017, 2018) projected that setting the tax penalty to zero would decrease enrollment in ACA-compliant coverage in 2021 by 5 million enrollees. We estimated that after accounting for the average premium assistance received and the other third-party effects, each of these 5 million enrollees reduces third-party expenditures by $2,083 (CEA 2019). If it had not been set to zero, the average tax penalty would have been $861 in 2021.[22] As a result of these two market frictions, we estimated that each of these enrollees valued their coverage by $2,514 less than what it cost society, a figure arrived at by adding the deadweight loss per person induced to take coverage by the penalty to the subsidy amount (CEA 2019).[23] In figure 4-6, the social benefits of repealing the mandate are given by the base of area A (5 million) multiplied by its average height, which measures the value gap ($2,514). Aggregated over the 5 million enrollees, setting the individual mandate tax penalty to zero will yield social benefits of about $13 billion in 2021, plus reducing the excess burden of taxation by another $6 billion.[24] (See box 4-1 for overviews of two important additional deregulatory healthcare reforms.)

---

[21] Following Goulder and Williams (2003), our analysis accounts for important general equilibrium interactions between the deregulatory reforms and preexisting distortions created by the premium subsidies and labor market taxation. The reduction in the subsidy payments are part of the social benefits created by the tax penalty repeal.

[22] From table 4-1, the average tax penalty paid in 2016 was $708. We assume that the tax penalty would have grown at an annual rate of 4 percent.

[23] The tax penalty averages $861 per enrollee, so the triangular area of deadweight loss per person induced to take compliant coverage equals half of $861, which is $431. This is added to the $2,083 net subsidy to arrive at an average gap of $2,514.

[24] One aspect of the projected benefits of the Administration's deregulatory reforms is that they reduce Federal expenditures on ACA premium subsidies and reduce the deficit. Generally, eliminating taxes and subsidies has larger welfare effects beyond government revenues due to the excess burden of such measures.

Box 4-1. Additional Regulatory Reforms

The Trump administration published new rules establishing two important deregulatory healthcare reforms that will generate tens of billions in benefits to Americans over the next 10 years. The deregulatory reforms expand options in health insurance markets within the existing statutory frameworks, including the ACA. These are more fully discussed in chapter 2 of this *Report* and are briefly described here.

Association health plans. Most uninsured Americans today are non-elderly, employed adults (U.S. Census Bureau 2017). Many work for small businesses or are self-employed in unincorporated businesses where the uninsured rate has historically been and remains high, double the uninsured rate of the general population (Chase and Arensmeyer 2018). The ACA subjected health coverage by small businesses to mandated coverage of essential health benefits and price controls that are not required for large businesses.

The June 21, 2018, association health plan rule expands small businesses' ability to group together to form AHPs to offer their employees more affordable health insurance. AHPs can self-insure or purchase large group insurance, free of the ACA benefit and pricing mandates, thereby lowering premiums and decreasing administrative costs through economies of scale. The AHP rule also broadens plan participation eligibility to sole proprietors without other employees. New AHPs can form by industry or geographic area (e.g., metropolitan area, state).

This rule is still too new to be sure about its impact. The CBO (2018) has projected that after the rule is fully phased in, there will be 4 million additional enrollees in AHPs, including 400,000 people who were previously uninsured. Based on the CBO's projections, we estimate that the AHP rule will cause premiums in the ACA-compliant individual market to increase by slightly more than 1 percent (see chapter 2). We estimate that taking into account both the benefits and costs, the AHP rule will yield $7.4 billion in net benefits in 2021, plus an additional reduction in excess burden worth $3.7 billion.

Short-term, limited-duration insurance. In late 2016, shortly before leaving office, the Obama Administration issued a rule shortened the allowed total duration of short-term, limited-duration insurance contracts from 12 to 3 months, thereby limiting the appeal and utility of these STLDI plans. The 2016 rule was not required by the ACA or other laws. The Trump Administration's August 3, 2018, STLDI rule extends the allowed term length of initial STLDI contracts from 3 to 12 months and allows for the renewal of the initial insurance contract for up to 36 months, which is the same as the maximum coverage term required under COBRA continuation coverage (U.S. Congress 1985). (The 1985 Consolidated Omnibus Budget Reconciliation Act, COBRA, provides for the continuation of employer health coverage that would be otherwise canceled due to job separation or other qualifying events.)

Because STLDI plans are not considered to be individual health insurance coverage under the Health Insurance Portability and Accountability

Act and the Public Health Service Act, STLDI coverage is exempt from all ACA restrictions on insurance plan design and pricing. This allows STLDI plans to offer a form of alternative coverage for those who do not choose ACA-compliant individual coverage. The STLDI rule requires that STLDI policies must provide a notice to consumers that these plans may differ from ACA-compliant plans in the individual market and, among other differences, may have limits on preexisting conditions and health benefits, and have annual or lifetime limits.

The STLDI rule is also too new to be sure of its impact. The CBO (2018) has projected that the STLDI regulatory reform will result in an additional 2 million consumers in STLDI plans by 2023. Based on CBO projections, we estimate that the STLDI rule will increase gross premiums in the ACA-compliant individual market by slightly more than 1 percent in the same time frame (see chapter 2). Taking into account both benefits and costs, we estimate that the rule will yield benefits worth $7.3 billion in 2021, plus an additional reduction in excess burden worth $3.7 billion.

Improving Competition to Lower Prescription Drug Prices

High pharmaceutical drug prices are a major concern of many Americans and the Trump Administration. Part of the problem results from the U.S. system of patent law, in which, in exchange for innovation, inventors are granted exclusive rights to market and distribute their inventions—in this case, drugs—for a period of time during which they can collect monopoly profits. But high prices also stem from Federal statutes and the regulations of the Food and Drug Administration (FDA), which are intended to guarantee safety and efficacy, but which create barriers to market entry and hinder price competition. Under the current regulatory regime, researching, developing and gaining the FDA approval needed to bring a new drug to market can take about a decade and cost an estimated $2.6 billion (DiMasi, Grabowski, and Hansen 2016).

The evidence suggests that patients' improved health and savings resulting from faster FDA regulatory processes and earlier access to drugs exceed potential associated safety risks (Philipson and Sun 2008; Philipson et al. 2008). The approval and entry of new generic drugs into the market to compete with brand name drugs lowers drug prices. Similarly, the approval and entry of new branded drugs creates competition with other drugs in the same therapeutic class and enhances patients' and their physicians' choices of treatment options.

Under the Trump Administration, the FDA has launched a series of reforms to facilitate new pharmaceutical drug entry while ensuring the efficacy and safety of the drug supply. These reforms are already helping consumers by speeding up generic drug approvals, resulting in savings from new generic entrants totaling $26 billion over the first year and a half of the Administration

Price inflation for prescription drugs has slowed. Figure 4-7 shows that the price of drugs relative to other goods decreased during the Trump Administration compared with the trend of the previous Administration (dotted line). After 20 months of zero or slightly negative relative inflation, as of August 2018 the relative price of prescription drugs was lower than it was in December 2016. In addition, due to the way price inflation for drugs is measured, the actual reduction in inflation after January 2017 may be larger.[25] As of August 2018, the slower price inflation for prescription drugs under President Trump implies annual savings of $20.1 billion.[26] Even if the relative price inflation of prescription drugs were to return to the higher trend that prevailed before this Administration, the 2017–18 level effect would yield savings of $170 to $191 billion over 10 years.[27] Data from the Bureau of Labor Statistics through the end of 2018 show that, for the first time in 46 years, the Consumer Price Index for prescription drugs fell in nominal terms—and even more in real terms—during a calendar year.[28]

This section first discusses how the approval and market entry of new drugs leads to price competition and lower prices. Then, it outlines the Administration's FDA reforms to safely speed drug approvals. It subsequently outlines our estimates of the value generated by faster generic drug market entry. Finally, it discusses the value of the increased entry of new, innovative drugs.

Lowering Prices through Competition

Brand name drugs can command high prices because the drugmaker's exclusive sales right confers market power over prices. Once the brand name drug's patent expires, however, generic versions of the drug can enter the market, and the resulting competition drives down market prices and leads to substantial savings for patients and the healthcare system. Roughly 9 out of every 10 prescriptions in the United States are for generic drugs; but because they are so much cheaper than their brand name counterparts, they constitute only about

---

[25] Two factors contribute to this. First, the Bureau of Labor Statistics has a six-month lag for incorporating generics, so any generic entry since March 2018 is not included. Second, in 2016 the bureau changed its index from geometric to Laspeyres, and the latter has higher inflation.

[26] This was calculated by multiplying actual nominal personal consumption expenditures on prescription drugs (at a seasonally adjusted annual rate) in August 2018 by the percentage difference between the actual three-month, centered moving average relative price ratio in August 2018 and that projected by the linear trend estimated over January 2013 through December 2016.

[27] This is dependent on a real discount rate between 0.9 and 3.2 percent. The lower bound is implied by the rate on 20-year Treasury Inflation-Protected Securities and the upper bound by Shiller's cyclically adjusted earnings-to-price ratio for the Standard & Poor's 500, respectively.

[28] The Consumer Price Index for prescription drugs is the primary series used by the Bureau of Economic Analysis to construct the Personal Consumption Expenditures price index for prescription drugs that appears in figure 4-7.

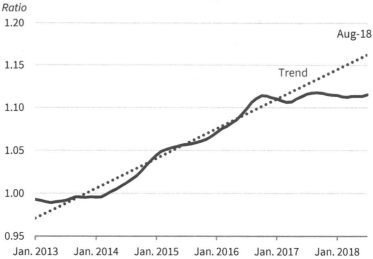

Figure 4-7. Price of Prescription Drugs Relative to PCE, 2013–18

Ratio

Aug-18

Trend

Sources: Bureau of Economic Analysis, CEA calculations.
Note: PCE = Personal Consumption Expenditures Price Index. The relative price ratio of prescription drugs is computed as the index for prescription drug prices relative to the index of overall consumption prices, as measured in the National Income and Product Accounts for the PCE. Data represent a centered 3-month centered moving average. The trend is calculated from 2013 to 2017.

23 percent of prescription drug spending (AAM 2018), reflecting the enormous savings made available to consumers.

Generic drugs. Substantial evidence shows that pharmaceutical drug prices fall dramatically when a generic drug enters the market, offering great savings to consumers (Aitken et al. 2013; Berndt, McGuire, and Newhouse 2011; Caves et al. 1991). Prices continue to decline substantially as the number of generic competitors increases. One analysis of the effect of generic entry on drug prices in the 1980s found that generic drug prices were 70 percent of brand name drug prices after the first generic entrant, 50 percent of the brand name price when four generic drugs were on the market, and 30 percent of the brand name price with 12 generic drugs (Frank and Salkever 1997). A more recent analysis using data from 2005 to 2009 found price reductions following a similar pattern (Berndt and Aitken 2011). Other analyses have confirmed this general finding. The estimates shown in figure 4-8 illustrate prices declining substantially as the number of generic market competitors increases. (For further discussion, see HHS 2010.) The brand name drug market share, in addition to prices, falls dramatically with generic competition.

Brand name drugs. Market entry of new branded drugs can also reduce the prices of other branded drugs through increased price competition. In many cases, a particular condition is treatable with several different brand

Figure 4-8. Generic Drug Price Relative to Brand Name Price, 1999–2004

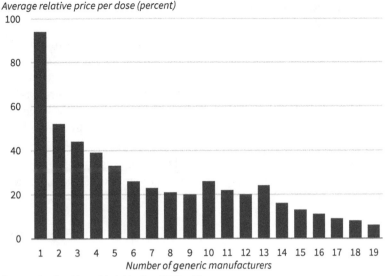

Average relative price per dose (percent)

Number of generic manufacturers

Sources: Food and Drug Administration; IMS Health.

name drugs, which are partial but not perfect substitutes for one another, and are known as a therapeutic class or category (FDA 2018c). Some of these drugs will have similar pharmacologic modes of actions. Others will have different mechanisms of action but will also be effective for the same condition. When the market evolves from a monopoly with one unique brand name product to a new stage of therapeutic competition, or oligopoly, market pricing will improve with one or more brand name competitors. Though these brand name products are not perfect substitutes for one another the way generics are, the evidence suggests that therapeutic competition between brand name drugs affects innovative drugmakers' returns at least as much as competition from generic entry (Lichtenberg and Philipson 2002). New drugs often enter the market at lower prices than the dominant existing drug in a particular therapeutic class, putting pressure on the dominant drug to lower prices to maintain market share (DeMasi 2000; Lee 2004).

Although the literature is limited on the systematic effect that therapeutic competition has on prices, there are numerous therapeutic classes in which new brand name drugs have led to vigorous price competition. A recent notable example was the introduction of new, highly effective treatments for the liver infection hepatitis C. A major breakthrough brand name drug was approved for sale in the United States in 2013. Unlike previously available therapies, it essentially offered a cure for many hepatitis C patients, albeit at an $84,000 price for a course of treatment. Within a few years, competing drugs from multiple companies came to market and drove down prices (Toich 2017).[29] The most recently approved drug covers all six genotypes of the hepatitis C virus, which not all previous drugs did; has a shorter course of treatment; and had a list price of $26,400 for a course of treatment (Andrews 2017), less than the discounted prices of the earlier drugs. It quickly outpaced other hepatitis C drugs and has captured a 50 percent market share (Pagliarulo 2018).

Another example of price competition within a therapeutic class is the case of the cholesterol-lowering drugs known as statins. The first statin was introduced in 1987. Since then, multiple new statins with higher potency and fewer side effects have come to market. Each new introduction has led to price competition with new drugs, which are often priced at a discount relative to the old ones (Alpert 2004). Prices have tumbled as these drugs have gone off patent and cheaper generic competition has entered the market (Aitken, Berndt, and Cutler 2008).

The Administration's Efforts to Enhance Generic and Innovator Competition

The Administration's deregulatory agenda includes streamlining the FDA's review process to facilitate price competition by reducing market entry barriers while securing a supply of safe and effective drugs. This includes prioritizing the approval of more generic drugs (FDA 2018b). In August 2017, the President signed into law the Food and Drug Administration Reauthorization Act, a five-year reauthorization of the Generic Drug User Fee Amendments, which empower the FDA to collect user fees for generic drug applications and to process applications in a timely manner. Last year, the FDA announced the Drug Competition Action Plan to expand access to safe and effective generic drugs. This plan's efforts focus on three key priorities to encourage generic drug competition: (1) preventing branded companies from keeping generics out of the market, (2) mitigating scientific and regulatory obstacles to approval, and (3) streamlining the generic review process. The FDA has already released guidance for companies and FDA staff members that outlines specific steps to reduce the number of review cycles and shorten the approval process.

These reforms have successfully increased the number of generics approved and have slowed drug price growth. In fiscal year (FY) 2018, the FDA approved a record 971 generic drug approvals and tentative approvals—exceeding the 937 in FY 2017 and the 835 in FY 2016 (FDA 2016, 2017, 2018a). The FDA approves generics based on a determination that they are bioequivalent to an approved innovator drug for which exclusive sales rights have expired. Generic drug entry is quicker to respond to regulatory changes than brand name drug entry, which involves a longer process for review and development. Figure 4-9 shows the 12-month moving average number of generic drug final and tentative approvals starting in January 2013. The dotted blue

---

[29] For a brief discussion of recent price competition in this market, see Walker (2018).

Figure 4-9. New Generic Drug Applications Approved, 2013–18

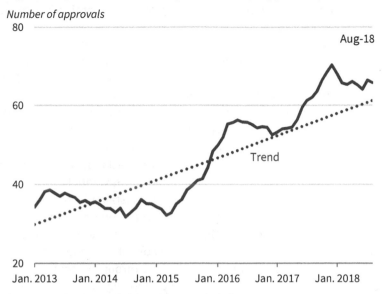

Sources: Food and Drug Administration; CEA calculations.
Note: The data include final generic drug approvals, and represent a 12-month moving average. Data preceding October 2013 are a truncated moving average, with data beginning in October 2012. The trend is calculated from 2013 to 2017.

line represents an estimated time trend from January 2013 through December 2016 projected through August 2018, the most recent observation available. Since December 2016, the number of generic drug approvals has outpaced the trend. We found that 17 percent more generic drugs have been approved each month (a monthly average of 81), during the first 20 months of the Trump Administration than were approved during the previous 20-month period (a monthly average of 69). This increase in approvals occurred despite the fact that the number of brand name drug patent expirations—necessary precursors for generic entry—declined during this period.

The FDA's 2018 Strategic Policy Roadmap addresses the entire spectrum of FDA-regulated pharmaceutical products—from small molecules to complex products and biologics—given each of their critical roles in advancing the health of patients (FDA 2018b). The roadmap includes the launch of the Medical Innovation Access Plan, Drug Competition Action Plan, Biosimilars Action Plan, and Advanced Manufacturing Strategy Roadmap. These plans are designed to:

1. Modernize the FDA's programs and increase administrative efficiencies for reviewing applications for brand name and generic products.
2. Provide product- and technology-specific guidance to increase regulatory and scientific clarity for sponsors to ensure efficient product development programs.

3. Reduce anticompetitive behavior by firms attempting to game FDA regulations or statutory authorities to delay competition from generic or biosimilar products.

The increase in new drug approvals has been as impressive as the improvement in generics. In the first 20 months of the Trump Administration, there were 11 drug approvals per month, on average, compared with 8.5 drug approvals per month during the preceding 20 month period.

A new, brand name drug can be marketed only after its New Drug Application (NDA) has been approved; for biologic drug products, the corresponding approval is for a Biologic License Application (BLA). Figure 4-10 shows the number of approved NDAs and BLAs since January 2013, reported as a 12-month moving average to smooth intermonth volatility. Notably, the 12-month average line shows a substantial and sustained rise in approvals starting in about January 2017. These new approvals reflect the emergence of many valuable new drug therapies that will add to competitive market pressures on prices for existing drugs and bring new benefits to patients.

During the sample period from January 2013 through December 2016, we estimated a linear time trend for the 12-month, moving-average sum of NDAs and BLAs approved. We then projected this trend through December 2017, the most recent observation available. As reported in figure 4-10, after falling below the trend in 2016, in 2017 actual applications approved climbed above the trend, and by the end of 2017 were 15 percent above the trend projection.[30] It is noteworthy that the approval rate began to rise rapidly a few months into the Trump Administration.

Although the FDA approves a wide array of biological products and new drugs, only some are novel, innovative products that are being introduced into clinical practice for the first time. Novel drugs can be classified as new molecular entities (NMEs), as an active molecule with no prior FDA approval, or as novel biologics. These new entities are the most meaningful NDAs and BLAs approved because they provide previously unavailable options to patients seeking therapies. Approvals of new molecular entities and novel biologics, meanwhile, more than doubled in the years 2017–18, relative to 2015–16. In 2015 and 2016, NMEs and novel biologics approvals averaged just 1.8 per month. From January 2017 through October 2018, approvals averaged 4.1 per month, with 9 approved in August 2018 alone. Given the lengthy clinical development process for new drugs, these trends do not solely reflect the actions of the Administration, but they are nevertheless influenced by this Administration's emphasis on accelerating the NDA and BLA processes.

---

[30] To test whether this outperformance of the trend was statistically significant, we regressed NDAs and BLAs approved on a linear time trend fully interacted with a post–December 2016 binary variable. The estimated coefficient on the interaction term was positive and significant at the 0.01 level, meaning that we can reject the null hypothesis of no trend break with 99 percent confidence.

Figure 4-10. New Drug Applications and Biologics License Applications Approved, 2013–17

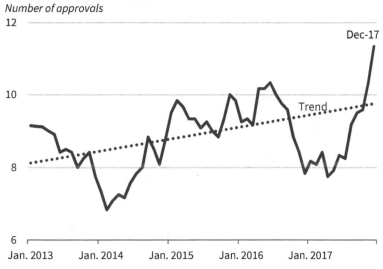

Sources: Food and Drug Administration, CEA calculations.
Note: The data represent a 12-month moving average, and data preceding July 2013 are a truncated moving average, with data beginning in July 2012. The trend is calculated from 2013 to 2017.

Estimated Reductions in Pharmaceutical Drug Costs from Generic Drug Entry

The effects of increased competition through patent expirations and generic drug entry reflect not just a fall in market prices but also a drop in overall quantity consumed, because brand name drug manufacturers often stop advertising their product, which reduces overall demand for the chemical entity (Lakdawalla and Philipson 2012). Therefore, the change in consumer welfare resulting from a patent expiration does not just involve a movement downward along a demand curve, but also an inward shift in the demand curve. The analysis that follows represents a lower bound on the value of generic entry focusing on savings alone.

We estimated the savings made available to consumers from generic drugs entering the market from January 2017 through June 2018 (CEA 2018a). The analysis represents an update of a similar analysis published by the FDA (Conrad et al. 2018). We found that generic drug approvals generated savings of about $26 billion through July 2018.[31]

---

[31] The data on generic drug approvals represent the period from January 2017 through June 2018; these are the most recent approvals data available. Estimates of savings from this set of generic entrants represent sales through July 2018, based on the most recent available sales data.

Figure 4-11. Price Decline Due to Generic Drug Entry

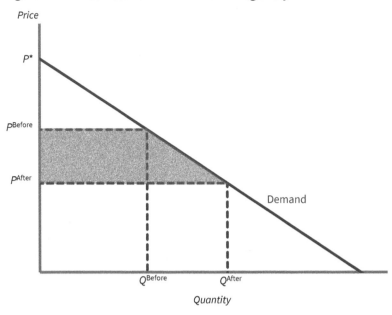

The baseline price before an entry (P^{Before}) used in this analysis is determined for each compound by aggregating sales across all drug products with the same active ingredient and dosage form for up to six months before the 2017 approval of abbreviated new drug applications, and dividing by the quantity of all drug products with the same active ingredient and dosage form that were sold (Q^{Before}). In some cases, a generic entrant is the first to compete with its brand name counterpart; in others, a generic entrant follows one or more other generic entrants. Determination of baseline prices addresses this as follows: When a brand name drug is facing its first generic entrant, the baseline price is determined using solely the brand name drug's sales; when a brand name drug already faces one or more generic competitors, the baseline price reflects both brand name and generic sales, weighted accordingly. The market price following entry of the generic drug (P^{After}) is estimated by dividing the aggregate sales volume in the market by the aggregate quantity sold, per month. Monthly savings from generic entry are then estimated for the period as

$$Monthly\ Savings = (P^{Before} - P^{After}) * Q^{Before}$$

Total savings are the sum of all monthly savings estimates.

Figure 4-11 shows the consumer benefit from the lower prices enabled by generic entry. Note that the savings estimate does not reflect the full trapezoid shown in figure 4-11. This is because the onset of generic competition, as mentioned above, is often accompanied by a cessation of marketing by the innovator drugmaker, which causes the demand curve to shift inward. We therefore limit the savings estimated to the preentry quantities observed.

We estimate that the total savings from the generic drugs that entered the market from January 2017 through June 2018 was $26 billion, in January 2018 dollars. We expect consumers to benefit further from lower drug prices in the years to come as more generic drugs are approved for sale and price competition becomes even more robust.

Estimates of the Value of Price Reductions from New Drugs

For new, innovator pharmaceutical drugs, high initial market prices give a misleading picture that overstates price growth. This is because before a new drug enters the market, it is unavailable at any price, making such a drug equivalent to one with a price so high that there is no demand for it. Economists generally interpret innovations as price reductions from the price at which the product would not sell at all due to its observed price when marketed. For instance, before the development of drugs to treat HIV in the mid-1990s, the price of a longer life for an HIV-positive individual was inaccessibly high—it could not be bought at any price anywhere in the world. But once new HIV drugs were approved, the price of a longer and healthier life for HIV-positive individuals decreased dramatically, falling from prohibitively expensive to the finite market price of the new, brand name, patented drugs. Prices fell further when these brand name drugs faced therapeutic competitors and further still when the brand name drugs lost their sales exclusivity and faced generic competition. Using the appropriate empirical methodology to measure such price declines for new drugs marketed since January 2017, we find that they have generated annualized gains to consumers of $43 billion in 2018, though lower-bound estimates of the price elasticity of demand for brand name drugs suggest that the gains could be much larger.

This way of conceptualizing the initial price change of a newly approved innovation is illustrated in figure 4-12. The price, P^*, is the prohibitively high price at which there is zero demand for the drug because it is too expensive. However, if no one is buying the drug, this is equivalent to its not yet having been discovered; in both cases, no one uses it. An innovation can be interpreted as simply reducing the price from this high level to the price at which it is marketed, P^{Brand} in the figure, resulting in quantity Q^{Brand} of drugs being bought. Therefore, the value of the new innovation to patients is simply the consumer surplus generated when the price is lowered from P^* to P^{Brand}, indicated by the shaded area in figure 4-12.

We used two methods to calculate this consumer surplus. The first applied empirical estimates of the producer surplus (profits) as a share of the social surplus arising from new NDA and BLA drugs approved since January 2017. Grabowski and others (2012), Goldman and others (2010), Jena and Philipson (2008), and Philipson and Jena (2006) estimated that the producer

Figure 4-12. Price Reductions from Brand Name Entry

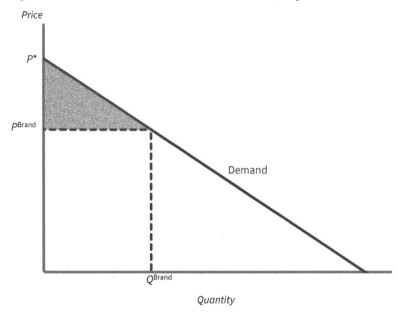

surplus is generally between 5 and 25 percent of the social surplus, with Jena and Philipson (2008) observing a median level of 15 percent, which implies that the consumer surplus is about 5.7 times the producer surplus. We applied these estimates to 2018 revenue data for the new NDAs and BLAs that were approved by netting out the variable costs of production from sales. These costs were assumed to be 16 percent of sales for brand name drugs, based on estimated differences in drug prices before and after patent expiration (Caves et al. 1991; Grabowski and Vernon 1992; Berndt and Aitken 2011; CEA 2018a).

The second approach used price and quantity data along with empirical estimates of the price elasticity of demand for pharmaceutical drug products to generate a demand schedule and to calculate the consumer surplus that arises from lowering the price from P^* to P^{Brand}, as shown in figure 4-12—in other words, calculating the shaded area of the figure as the integral of the demand curve above P^{Brand} from $Q = 0$ to $Q = Q^{Brand}$. Across 150 common drugs, Einav, Finkelstein, and Polyakova (2018) estimated an average elasticity of demand of −0.24; and across 100 common therapeutic classes, they estimated an average elasticity of −0.15. Goldman and others (2006, 2010), meanwhile, estimated elasticities of between −0.01 and −0.21.

For price and quantity in both methods, we used IQVIA National Sales Perspectives data on pharmacy and hospital acquisition costs, based on invoice prices, for new molecule entities and novel biologics approved from January 2017 through July 2018. We then averaged the estimated consumer surplus gain—calculated, first, assuming the median estimate of the producer appropriation from Jena and Philipson (2008); and, second, assuming the mean elasticity of demand for common therapeutic classes of –0.15 from Einav, Finkelstein, and Polyakova (2018).[32] Averaging the results of the two approaches indicates that the price reductions induced by the new drugs approved after January 2017 increased the total consumer surplus in 2018 by $43 billion.

Conclusion

The U.S. economy generally relies on free markets to maximize benefits for U.S. citizens. The hallmarks of any free market are consumer choice and competition. Although some have claimed that healthcare is an exceptional case that cannot be produced and allocated through the market, we argue that these claims are exaggerated and that the costs of market failure are often lower than the costs of government failure. Deviations from perfect market conditions are present in healthcare and many other markets, but promoting choice and competition is the appropriate way to maximize efficiency and consumer welfare.

The recent push in Congress to enact a highly restrictive "Medicare for All" proposal would have the opposite effect—it would decrease competition and choice. The CEA's analysis finds that, if enacted, this legislation would reduce longevity and health in the United States, decrease long-run global health by reducing medical innovation, and adversely affect the U.S. economy through the tax burden involved.

The Trump Administration has instead concentrated on deregulatory reforms that will increase choice and competition in the health insurance markets and pharmaceutical drug markets. Bringing the ACA's individual mandate penalty down to zero will allow consumers to choose how much health insurance they desire. Expanding the availability of association health plans and the duration and renewability of short-term, limited-duration health plans will increase consumers' options and spur competition. Finally, the FDA's initiatives to speed drug approvals have already had tangible benefits in record numbers of drug approvals and increased pharmaceutical competition. All these reforms are expected to bring down prices, encourage continuing innovation, and maximize consumer welfare.

---

[32] Because the Goldman et al. (2006) upper-bound estimated elasticity of –0.01 generates implausibly large consumer surplus gains when applied to all newly approved drugs, for the second method we assume an upper bound of –0.15.

Chapter 5

Unleashing the Power of American Energy

Taking advantage of America's abundant energy resources is a key tenet of the Trump Administration's plan to increase long-term economic growth and national security. This is best achieved by recognizing how prices and technological change underpin growth in the production of renewable and nonrenewable energy sources. By promoting domestic energy production and expanding U.S. energy exports, the Administration seeks to improve the relationship the U.S. economy has historically had with global energy markets.

Since the President took office, the U.S. fossil fuels sector has set production records, led by all time highs in both oil and natural gas. The energy content of fossil fuel production is at this apex thanks to petroleum's high energy content. The surge in petroleum production is a surprise, and is attributable to a confluence of technological improvements and relatively high prices. Natural gas production has also continued to increase, following a long-running trend. Coal production stabilized in 2017 and 2018, after a period of contraction in 2015 and 2016.

Increased production allows the United States to alter historic trade patterns by decreasing its net imports. The U.S. is now a net exporter of natural gas for the first time in 60 years, and petroleum exports are increasing at a pace such that the United States is projected to be a net exporter of energy by 2020. Reducing its net import position for energy products helps the United States by making its economy less sensitive to the price swings that have disrupted it in the past. Greater economic resilience at home is coupled with greater diplomatic influence and flexibility abroad as U.S. prominence in global energy markets grows.

Technological and regulatory changes are forcing the U.S. energy system to further adapt. This is especially true for the electricity sector, which is adapting to the changing slate of generation assets and to economic pressures from restructured wholesale markets. Recognizing and embracing the innovations that have helped spur these changes in the U.S. energy system, and ensuring that distorting policies do not interfere, can help all Americans and people around the world—which is why the Administration is focusing on policies supporting these priorities.

L everaging American energy abundance is a central tenet of the President's economic vision. This is best achieved by recognizing how prices and technological change underpin growth in the production of renewable and nonrenewable energy sources. In 2018, this sector of the economy yielded historic results. U.S. fossil fuels production is booming, led by all-time highs in oil and natural gas. This increase in production has helped support economic growth and allowed the United States to change historic trade patterns. Yet technological and regulatory changes are forcing the energy system to further adapt. Recognizing and embracing the innovations that have helped spur these changes in the U.S. energy system, and ensuring that distorting policies do not interfere, can help all Americans and people around the world. The Administration focuses on policies supporting these priorities.

Although proposals for a policy of energy independence have a history in the United States dating back to at least 1973, the Trump Administration's energy policy goes further by emphasizing two elements. The first is to maximize the value of U.S. production at market-determined prices. Fossil fuels, which provide 80 percent of the Nation's energy needs, loom large in this regard. Energy is useful insofar as it can ultimately provide the power, light, and work that are important economic inputs for the production of goods and services that benefit Americans. These inputs can be generated in a number of ways. For example, electricity can provide light, and electricity can be generated from a variety of sources—by burning fossil fuels like coal and natural gas, or by using renewable methods like wind and solar generation, or other means like nuclear generation.

The United States also has extensive energy resources—fossil fuel reserves; renewable resources like hydroelectric, solar, and wind; and perhaps most valuable of all, world-class engineering and research complexes that constantly innovate and improve the efficiency of both the U.S. and global energy systems. The Administration's policy of fostering maximum production embraces all these sources, with their diverse characteristics and economic applications.

The various sectors of the U.S. economy rely on different forms and sources of energy; for example, in 2017, the U.S. economy relied on petroleum for 92 percent of its transportation needs, using 72 percent of all petroleum consumed domestically. Other countries around the world satisfy their energy needs with different mixes than the United States. Because countries have different endowments of energy resources, and different energy policies, the varying demands and supplies of energy provide the opportunity for trade in power and fuels. The importance of energy trade is underscored by the prominence of a single commodity—crude oil—which in recent years has accounted for an average of over 6 percent of global trade value (United Nations 2018).

The United States can use its increased energy production to take a greater role in global energy markets, particularly those for fossil fuels. Reducing its net import position for energy products helps the United States by making its economy less sensitive to the price swings that have disrupted it in the past. Greater economic resilience at home is coupled with greater diplomatic influence and flexibility abroad as the United States' prominence in global energy markets grows. Finally, more global competition in energy supply may moderate global prices and price volatility.

This chapter outlines the key economic contours of the Trump Administration's energy agenda. The first section documents and contextualizes recent developments in U.S. fossil fuels production. The second section considers the United States' ability to engage with global energy markets through increased trade. And the third section examines specific policy issues that remain and pose challenges for the future.

U.S. Fuel Production Reached Record Levels in 2018

The United States is fortunate to have many useful energy resources—oil, natural gas, coal, solar, wind, geothermal, and more. American success in promoting fuels production is broad-based, as overall fossil fuel production has increased. In 2018, U.S. fossil fuel production set an all-time record for total energy content, as shown in figure 5-1. This record continues the recent trend—which was only interrupted by a dip in 2016, when lower prices failed to support oil and natural gas production enough to offset falling coal production. Since then, the growth in petroleum production has more than made up for lower coal production, relying on the greater energy density of crude oil to make up the difference.

Figure 5-1. Energy Content of U.S. Fossil Fuels Production, 1980–2018

British thermal units (quadrillions)

Sources: Energy Information Administration; CEA calculations.
Note: Total fossil fuels defined as quadrillion Btu-equivalents of combined crude oil, natural gas, gas plant liquids, and coal production. Data represent a 3-month moving average.

U.S. Oil Production Is At an All-Time High

Reports of the demise of U.S. oil production (Bentley 2002; Hirsch, Bezdek, and Wendling 2005; EIA 2006) appear to have been premature. Thanks to a confluence of technological proficiency in available geology and world price patterns, in 2018 U.S. oil production reached an all-time high. In November 2017, U.S. oil production surpassed a monthly production record set in 1970, with oil production reaching a monthly average of 10.1 million barrels per day (MMbpd). This trend continued into 2018, as the monthly average production for the year's first three quarters was 10.7 MMbpd. Resurgent U.S. production relies on unconventional resources once deemed too diffuse and costly to exploit. However, advanced seismography, hydraulic fracturing, directional drilling, and related technologies have changed this situation by effectively lowering the cost of accessing oil and gas trapped underground. The technical innovations pioneered and perfected in the United States (Zuckerman 2014; Gold 2014) are now paying dividends in the form of increasing production. The dividends have been paid quickly, with U.S. production increasing by 6 MMbpd in eight years—the largest increase of any country in history.

Technology that was pioneered in parts of Texas and in the western States is now applied across the country, boosting production everywhere from the historically productive Permian Basin in Texas and New Mexico to new provinces like the Eagle Ford Shale in Texas and the Bakken Shale in

North Dakota and Montana. Production in Texas increased by 11.1 percent from December 2017 levels through the first half of 2018, while the monthly average production through October 2018 was 291 percent higher than annual production in the state 10 years ago (figure 5-2). This increase more than off-sets declining production in other important regions, including Alaska and the shallow-water areas of the Gulf of Mexico.

Crude oil prices in 2018 exhibit three general characteristics. First, from the perspective of U.S. producers, price levels remained higher than the previous three years, on average. Second, price volatility was modest compared with the period 2014–16.[1] Together, these high and stable prices provided a strong incentive for producers. And third, the price discount for the main landlocked U.S. benchmark, West Texas Intermediate (WTI) crude oil—relative to the nearest waterborne benchmark, Brent crude oil—has increased to the highest level since 2013. Although both grades are priced higher due to attractive refining properties, the differential between these two close substitutes indicates that the U.S. market is separated from the global market. Many market observers take this as evidence of the existence of infrastructure constraints that require U.S. production to incur somewhat higher transportation costs that erode its value at inland pricing points. McRae (2017) documents how price basis differentials stemming from pipeline bottlenecks represent a transfer from producers to refiners and shippers, but are not transmitted to consumer prices. This is consistent with earlier work by Borenstein and Kellogg (2014), who found that the marginal barrel of gasoline is priced to Brent, leaving the consumer unaffected by a Brent–WTI basis differential.

In addition to setting a domestic production record, in 2018 the United States became the world's leading producer of crude oil after years of leading the world in combined oil and natural gas production.[2] Figure 5-3 shows the recent increase that has returned the United States to global leadership after 43 years. The production comes from a different resource base than conventional deposits in Russia and Saudi Arabia, because U.S. production, and especially production growth, rely on unconventional resources that were once considered subeconomic. However, a combination of technological innovation, market incentives, and millions of private mineral owners willing to take risks with new techniques have helped the U.S. oil and gas sector launch a new era of production. U.S. production now largely comes from geological formations like low-permeability sandstones and shales that are not developed in most other countries. An added benefit is that much of the production is

---

[1] Although less volatile than the preceding years, this period's volatility remains higher than that of many historical periods and may be an important concern for producers (McNally 2017).

[2] Oil and gas producers bring a cocktail of hydrocarbons to the surface, including crude oil, lease condensate, natural gas, and natural gas liquids. The exact proportions vary across different geologies. After they are brought to the surface together, the products are separated and sold through different channels for different uses.

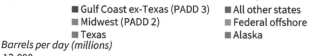

Figure 5-2. U.S. Monthly Crude Oil Production, 1981–2018

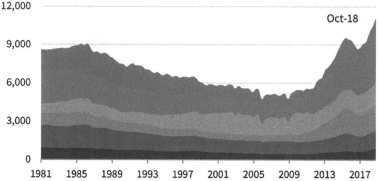

Sources: Energy Information Administration; CEA calculations.
Note: Data represent a 5-month moving average. PADD = Petroleum Administration for Defense District. PADDs were created during World War II to help organize the allocation of petroleum fuels. PADD 2 (Midwest): Illinois, Indiana, Iowa, Kansas, Kentucky, Michigan, Minnesota, Missouri, Nebraska, North Dakota, Ohio, Oklahoma, South Dakota, Tennessee, and Wisconsin. PADD 3 (Gulf Coast): Alabama, Arkansas, Louisiana, Mississippi, and New Mexico.

Figure 5-3. Crude Oil Production in the United States, Russia, and Saudi Arabia, 2008–18

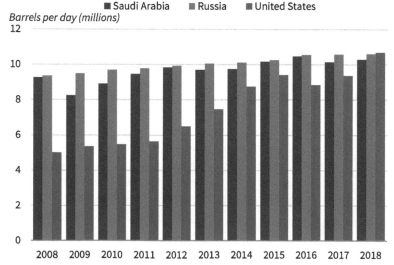

Sources: Energy Information Administration; CEA calculations.
Note: 2018 production levels are taken from EIA's 2018 *Short Term Energy Outlook* projections.

lighter and lower-sulfur grades of crude oil that command a price premium and give refiners considerable flexibility in processing because they are less costly to refine than heavier grades. The economic implications of the technological innovations that have facilitated these changes have been a long time coming (CEA 2006, 2012, 2013, 2015, 2016a, 2017). So why was 2018 the year to break production records?

In the not-too-distant past, it seemed that increased U.S. production required high prices, further reducing U.S. influence in the global market-place. Technological innovations have increased both economically feasible and technically recoverable reserves. Innovations in directional drilling and hydraulic fracturing helped lower the breakeven costs of shale oil, while improved deepwater extraction efficiency has increased interest in offshore drilling as well. The assumption was that all these methods required fairly high breakeven prices. The threat posed by unconventional U.S. production to other global producers compelled the Organization of the Petroleum Exporting Countries (OPEC) to allow prices to fall in late 2014, in an effort to protect global market share and long-run revenues. This strategy of defending market share against new entrants is historically well-known to OPEC members, and it may or may not deliver higher revenues (Adelman 1996). Although the subsequent price drop was traumatic for U.S. producers, the ultimate result was that the marginal cost of unconventional production fell, making U.S. oil more competitive in the global marketplace (Kleinberg et al. 2016). The combination of relatively high and stable prices, accumulated cost-reducing technological improvements, and the massive endowment of unconventional resources has allowed production to expand rapidly.

Some observers have taken America's world-leading production and decreased net imports as evidence that the United States has greater influence in the global oil market, but the empirical evidence suggests more work is needed to achieve this goal.[3] The responsiveness of onshore oil production to price shocks remains limited inside the continental United States. Estimates by Newell and Prest (2017) indicate that although the response of U.S. supply to price changes is larger than before the dawn of shale oil, the U.S. remains slower to react than a traditional "swing producer" (i.e., a producer that can bring additional capacity online quickly in response to demand), such as Saudi Arabia. Newell and Prest (2017) also find that the U.S. response takes several months to come online, which is substantially less timely than the 30 to 90 days associated with typical swing production. So while the United States now enjoys more production and more responsive production than it has historically done, it has not yet reached a point that would provide it with the market power associated with being a global swing producer. The United States'

---

[3] During the week ending November 30, 2018, the United States had negative net imports of petroleum for the first time since at least 1973 (data from the U.S. Energy Information Administration).

lack of spare capacity implies that other countries, notably the members of OPEC, hold the key to modulating prices by being able and willing to adjust production.

As OPEC settled into a regime of production cuts that helped support prices in 2017 and 2018, geopolitical uncertainty in key oil-producing countries also boosted prices and helped bolster U.S. production (see box 5-1). Compared with the production levels of OPEC members in 2016, supply reductions in Venezuela and other countries subtracted 492,000 barrels per day on average from OPEC's production during the period between January 2017 and August 2018. Cuts by Venezuela accounted for 75.2 percent of gross output reductions by OPEC's producers between January 2017 and August 2018.

The unexpected resurgence of U.S. production over the past decade provides evidence that is hard to square with central predictions of popular models of resource scarcity. A prominent example is the "peak oil" literature, which recognizes the physical limit on the endowment of oil to predict a date of maximum extraction rate, after which production monotonically declines.[4] Growing reliance on petroleum as a fuel has been matched by episodic concerns about its continued availability. A monotonic production decline is viewed as problematic for an economy that previously had consumed increasing amounts of oil.

The paper by Hubbert (1956) was the original technical contribution to the peak oil literature, which later blossomed into a broader following (Deffeyes 2001, 2006). Hubbert's central insight was that there is a finite amount of oil to be found, and the pace of discoveries could not accelerate indefinitely, as it had for the preceding decades. Hubbert established an initial estimate for total U.S. oil reserves of 200 billion to 250 billion barrels. Conditional on U.S. oil reserves of 200 billion barrels and the historical trajectory of discoveries and extraction, Hubbert predicted peak production in 1970, with a subsequent decline. This forecast was remarkably accurate for the lower 48 States, through about 2010; production peaked in 1970, and appeared to enter a steady decline in the following years (figure 5-4). Even when considering the massive discovery in Alaska, and the effect that Alaskan oil had on aggregate U.S. production, Hubbert's simple model predicted a peak that was only off by a couple of years and seemed to encapsulate the inherent limit to oil production.

However, Hubbert's model ignored the role of prices in promoting exploration and production, and of technological innovation in expanding proven reserves. Higher prices and technological improvements allowed access to offshore and unconventional reserves, leading to an unpredicted peak increase

---

[4] Highlighting the economic significance of physical limits follows a long tradition dating back to at least 1798, when Thomas Malthus published "An Essay on the Principle of Population," which expressed the fear that growth in population would outpace growth in food production. As the Industrial Revolution made coal an essential economic input, William Jevons (1865) translated this same argument to a nonrenewable resource, which was the first "peak fossil fuel" argument.

Box 5-1. OPEC's Oil Production Cuts

OPEC has 13 member states located in the Middle East, Africa, and South America. As of October 2018, OPEC producers enjoyed a 39 percent share of the global petroleum market, down from a post-2000 peak of 44 percent in September 2008 (OPEC 2018b; EIA 2018i). However, they collectively control 74 percent of world oil reserves, and most of the lowest extraction cost reserves (EIA 2018b). Since its formation in 1960, OPEC has alternated between strategies of maximizing market share and maintaining high prices. The oil price collapse in 2014 is attributed to OPEC protecting its market share at the expense of prices. Since then, OPEC has changed strategies and cut production to enjoy the resulting higher prices.

(In 2018, OPEC had 14 oil-producing members, along with the Republic of Congo. The Qatari state petroleum company announced on December 2, 2018, that it was leaving OPEC, effective January 1, 2019. Qatar is a substantial natural gas producer, but it only accounted for 1.9 percent of OPEC's oil production—less than 1 percent of global production.)

Through late 2015 and much of 2016, OPEC members discussed a targeted cut to help support prices. These discussions also expanded to include key non-OPEC producers, including Russia. The OPEC meeting on November 30, 2016, announced a target reduction of 1.2 MMbpd for the 12 cooperating members of OPEC—Libya and Nigeria are exempt—effective January 1, 2017,

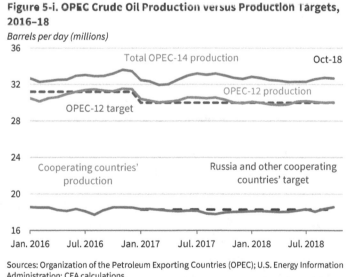

Figure 5-i. OPEC Crude Oil Production versus Production Targets, 2016–18

Barrels per day (millions)

Sources: Organization of the Petroleum Exporting Countries (OPEC); U.S. Energy Information Administration; CEA calculations.
Note: The OPEC-12 are the 14 OPEC member states, except for Libya and Nigeria, which are exempt from production cuts. The "other cooperating countries" are Russia, Mexico, and Kazakhstan, which, along with several other smaller producers, collaborate with OPEC's production schedule.

bringing its allocated production to 29.8 MMbpd and its ceiling for the OPEC-14 to 32.5 MMbpd. Subsequent OPEC meetings in May and November 2017 extended these cuts in allocations through the whole of 2018, in addition to allowing for the accession of Equatorial Guinea into OPEC with an allocation of 178,000 barrels per day (OPEC 2018a).

Cooperation by several other countries—notably Russia, Mexico, and Kazakhstan—has helped leverage the cuts by including more production share in the group agreeing to cuts. Adding the production of these cooperating countries to the OPEC-12, the global market share of the countries cooperating with OPEC's cuts increased to 68 percent of crude production in 2017. Compared with average production in 2016, the OPEC-12 and its collaborators have cut production by 1.33 MMbpd, or about 1.8 percent of global production.

According to data from the U.S. Energy Information Administration (EIA) on secondary reporting of OPEC's oil production, the target of 29.982 MMbpd for the OPEC-12 was met for only 1 of 12 months in 2017, with the largest monthly overage being 0.59 MMbpd (1.9 percent over target production). During the first six months of 2018, the OPEC-12 came in below the target by an average of 0.2 percent each month, or 57,000 barrels per day (EIA 2018i). See figure 5-i.

in domestic production. This experience contrasts sharply with forecasts influenced by peak oil theory, especially those that were ascendant 15 years ago, most of which expected peak oil extraction by 2010 (Laherrère 1999; Campbell 2003; Skrebowski 2004; Bakhtiari 2004). The prediction of decreasing U.S. oil production has been proved wrong by increased domestic production in 9 of the past 10 years (BP 2018), shattering Hubbert's (1956) original prediction shown in figure 5-4. Though there is a finite quantity of oil resources that can be discovered and extracted, ignoring the incentive for exploration and innovation created by high prices, and the impact that successful innovations have had on expanding the economic reserve base and reducing production costs, the physical limits do not circumscribe economic potential, as some analysts have hypothesized.

Although the physical endowment of oil is smaller than it once was, some context is useful. In 1956, as Hubbert was making his original forecast, U.S. proven reserves of crude oil were 30 billion barrels. At the end of 2017 proven reserves were 39.2 billion barrels. From 1957 to 2017, total U.S. crude oil production was 167.0 billion barrels. In addition to the 55.2 billion barrels extracted before 1957, Hubbert's estimate of the size of reserves was not unreasonable. However, what it did not anticipate was that today different kinds of resources would be considered reserves (known resources that can be profitably extracted with current technology at current prices). This

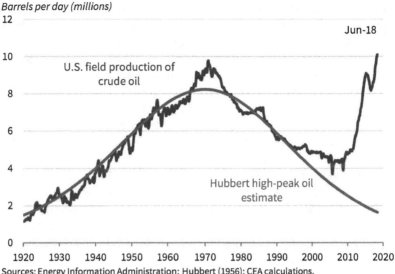

Figure 5-4. U.S. Lower-48 Production versus Hubbert's 1956 Peak Oil Prediction, 1920–2018

Barrels per day (millions)

Jun-18

U.S. field production of crude oil

Hubbert high-peak oil estimate

Sources: Energy Information Administration; Hubbert (1956); CEA calculations.
Note: Data represent a 3-month moving average. The Hubbert (1956) estimate was constructed using a stepwise logit function.

observation is not new to the economics literature (Boyce 2013), but the recent empirical record suggests that peak oil models will need to consider prices and technology to be reliable in the future. Geologists—like Hubbert—woke up every morning and looked for oil; but they expected the pace of discoveries to eventually slow down, and then production would have to decline.[5] The policy environment had no bearing; nor did prices or technology.

The point of Hubbert's paper was to emphasize the need for future energy transitions; he expected nuclear power to be more widely used. Nuclear power has its own inherent trade-offs, some of which are discussed below. Recent experience in the United States underscores the imprudence of relying upon geological forecasts alone. The incentives of prices and the role of technological innovation—which is funded by the price incentive in a market economy like the United States—are critical for understanding the production of even a nonrenewable natural resource like petroleum.

The Natural Gas Revolution Rolls On

Before technology helped U.S. oil production reach record highs, natural gas was the focus, and the "natural gas revolution" changed the national energy landscape (Deutch 2011). Hydraulic fracturing receives much of the credit. This

---

[5] Hubbert's earliest paper, describing single-peaked growth with a decline to zero, came in a 1934 publication for the Technocracy, a social and political movement of the 1930s that advocated replacing the price system with management by technocrats (Inman 2016).

technique was originally developed in 1948 to improve flow from oil wells, and it evolved in the 1990s toward greater volumes of water and sand injected to fracture rocks saturated with natural gas. This breakthrough depended on a fundamentally sound understanding of the relevant geophysics, the basis of which was pioneered in 1956 by none other than the same Hubbert of peak oil fame. Production of natural gas in the United States has continued to grow to record levels, reducing reliance on imports and expanding exports globally. For the 9th time in the past 11 years, in 2017 the United States withdrew a record amount of natural gas. Gross natural gas withdrawals in the United States have increased by more than 50 percent over the past 10 years, rising to 3,267 billion cubic feet (Bcf) in October 2018. This growth has relied on technological advances, including hydraulic fracturing and directional drilling, that have made the development of shale gas resources economic. The Appalachian, Permian, and Haynesville basins have led U.S. production growth.

The growth of U.S. natural gas production, led by shale and other unconventional resources, has been driven by the rise in nonassociated gas production. Nonassociated gas is produced from reservoirs where the gas is not found with substantial amounts of crude oil, whereas associated gas is jointly produced with crude oil. Nonassociated gas production in the United States grew by 29 percent between 2007 and 2017. The rise in nonassociated gas production has been centered in the Appalachian Basin, which stretches across New York, Pennsylvania, Ohio, and West Virginia to include the Marcellus and Utica shale plays, where total gas production grew from 1.3 Bcf per day (Bcfd) in January of 2007 to 31.5 Bcfd in January of 2019 (EIA 2018f). Unlike the other states, New York has effectively banned development of its shale resources (see box 5-2).

Associated gas production is rising again with shale oil production. This has created an infrastructure challenge, given that two types of infrastructure are needed—for oil and for natural gas. Oil has more transportation substitutes than natural gas, which depends on specific investments in pipeline capacity to move efficiently. In comparison, oil can move by rail or even truck where necessary, until pipeline capacity catches up with production (Covert and Kellogg 2017). As a result, the flaring of associated natural gas has increased. Firms that are unwilling to wait to extract oil have a choice between completing natural gas pipeline projects and seeking accommodation from regulators to allow more flaring. In the short run, the latter might be less expensive.

Total natural gas proven reserves (wet after lease separation) increased by over 87 percent between 2007 and 2017. In 2017, total proven natural gas (wet after lease separation) reserves stood at 464,292 Bcf, which corresponds to over 17 times the total U.S. consumption in the same year. The reserves are there; the technology is there. Two factors limit production. The first is finding uses for more gas at current prices; the second is building out infrastructure to move gas from where it is produced to where it is consumed. Continued

Box 5-2. The Important Economic Effects of State Regulation on Energy Production

Differences in States' regulation of hydraulic fracturing ("fracking") have important economic effects. Nowhere is the contrast as stark as between Pennsylvania and New York State, which have taken divergent regulatory tacks—Pennsylvania has been accommodating and thus has seen widespread development of its underlying shale gas resources, but more restrictive New York has elected to effectively prevent development. Pennsylvania's natural gas production expanded over 30 times between 2006 and 2017, and went from making up under 1 percent to constituting 20 percent of U.S. dry gas production. In contrast, New York placed a de facto moratorium on hydraulic fracturing in 2008 that ossified into an outright ban in 2014. In light of this regulatory ban, New York received far less investment, and its natural gas production fell by 80 percent from 2006 to 2017.

Counties along the New York–Pennsylvania border that are otherwise similar provide an ideal laboratory for understanding some effects of regulation. Boslett, Guilfoos, and Lang (2015) examined the effects of the New York moratorium, and found that among those counties most likely to experience shale gas development, residential property values declined by 23.1 percent due to the shale gas moratorium. This result is also true for rural land values; Weber and Hitaj (2015) found a 44.2 percent greater appreciation in Pennsylvania's border counties relative to New York's border counties. Cosgrove and others (2015) used a differences-in-differences approach to examine the effects of increased shale gas production between 2001 and 2013, finding that after 2008 Pennsylvania counties experienced significant increases in both industry employment and wages compared with New York counties. Komarek (2016) used New York's border counties to compare with counties in the Marcellus region that were developed, and found that developed counties had a 2.8 percent increase in employment, a 6.6 percent increase in earnings, and a 3.3 percent increase in earnings per worker.

export growth is one method by which to capitalize on vast proven natural gas reserves; but as figure 5-5 shows, current exports are quite small relative to annual production. Infrastructure investments require an expectation of production and sales over a sufficiently long time horizon to amortize the fixed costs.

U.S. consumption of natural gas by consumers has increased alongside production, thanks to low and stable prices. For 7 of the last 11 years, the United States has recorded record natural gas consumption. This increase is led by electricity generation, on pace for a 10 percent increase over the previous peak in 2016. Although natural gas consumption has increased substantially for electric power consumers and natural gas vehicles, the main

Figure 5-5. U.S. Natural Gas Trade and Withdrawals, 1940–2018

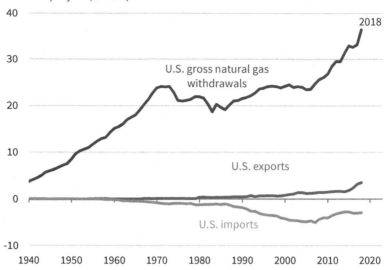

Cubic feet per year (trillions)

Source: Energy Information Administration.
Note: Trade data preceding 1973 are derived from EIA's tracking of international deliveries and receipts. Annual data for 2018 were reported as monthly data through October at a seasonally adjusted annual rate.

sources of natural gas demand are electric power generation, industrial uses, and residential uses. The shift toward using natural gas for electricity generation is a global trend—2016 and 2017 were the first two years on record in which natural gas–fired electricity generation made up a greater share than coal-fired generation in countries belonging to the Organization for Economic Cooperation and Development (OECD) (BP 2018). Electricity generation is an important component of creating enough demand to capitalize on American abundance and supporting production.[6]

The dramatic rise in unconventional natural gas production since 2007 has enabled the United States to become a net exporter, starting in 2017, for the first time since 1957. In total, U.S. exports of natural gas increased by 341.5 percent between January 2007 and October 2018 (figure 5-6). As a net exporter of natural gas, the United States occupies a strategic position to provide this resource, both to its Western Hemisphere neighbors and to its allies and trading partners around the world. Natural gas exports by pipeline to its neighbors make up the largest share of U.S. exports, with pipeline exports to Canada and Mexico accounting for 21.4 and 49.2 percent, respectively, of total U.S. natural

---

[6] An alternative interpretation is that the lower energy density of natural gas frees up other, higher-density fuels for export. Substituting an inferior product for local consumption to capture a premium in export markets is recognized in economics as the "shipping the good apples out" principle (Alchian and Allen 1964; Hummels and Skiba 2004).

Figure 5-6. U.S. Monthly Trade in Natural Gas, 2001–18

■ LNG imports
■ U.S. pipeline imports
■ U.S. pipeline exports to Canada
■ U.S. pipeline exports to Mexico
■ LNG exports

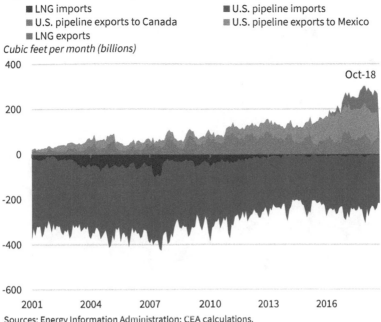

Cubic feet per month (billions)

Sources: Energy Information Administration; CEA calculations.
Note: LNG = liquefied natural gas.

gas exports in October 2018. Total U.S. natural gas imports have fallen by 44.9 percent since January 2007; Canadian pipeline imports make up 97.2 percent of total imports.

Coal Production Is Recovering after the 2015–16 Slump

U.S. coal production has recovered after facing difficult market conditions between 2012 and 2016. After averaging roughly 1.1 billion short tons of production annually from 2000 to 2009, coal production and related employment began to slip in mid-2011. By 2016, production had dropped to 728 million short tons, 65.2 percent of the average level between 2001 and 2010 (EIA 2018c). However, production rebounded in 2017, rising 6.3 percent from the preceding year to 774 million short tons. This trend continued through the first half of 2018, as production remained 10.3 percent higher than its secular low in the first half of 2016. Increased production required a small boost in coal mining employment, which has grown by 2,900 since the President's election in 2016. This increase has been helped by the production increase in relatively labor-intensive eastern regions. Different grades and characteristics of coal make these mines competitive despite requiring much more labor per unit of output.

Higher exports are a welcome fillip to an industry that has been battered by declining demand for domestic steam coal used to fire electric generation

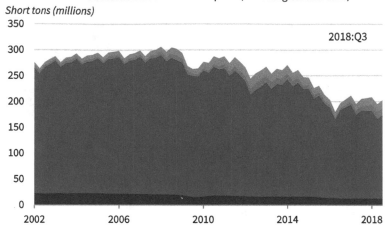

Figure 5-7. U.S. Quarterly Coal Disposition, 2002–18

- Coke exports
- Metallurgical coal exports
- Steam coal exports
- Consumption for electricity generation (steam)
- Domestic industrial consumption (metallurgical and coke)

Short tons (millions)

2018:Q3

Sources: Energy Information Administration; CEA calculations.

that stems from low natural gas prices (figure 5-7). The portfolio of electric generation technologies has expanded with greater penetration of renewables like solar and wind, and inexpensive natural gas has expanded its market share at the expense of coal. Coal producers have also been affected by increased costs from new regulatory requirements; for example, coal plant retirements in 2015 and 2016 were affected by the Mercury and Air Toxics Standards (known as MATS), which made a shutdown an attractive alternative to compliance for many plants, even those receiving a one-year waiver. Although the past two years show that these trends have slowed and coal production has stabilized at a new, lower level, a reversal of the trends that return coal to the dominant position it enjoyed for decades appears improbable. The private market is showing signs of trouble as insurers and underwriters are shying away from coal projects.

The U.S. coal industry has evolved over the decades toward western and surface production. Underground and surface operations west of the Mississippi River have shifted from under 10 percent of total production 50 years ago to well over half of all production in 2018 (EIA 2012, 2018c). Western coal production has focused on steam coal. Part of the change was influenced by Federal environmental policy, which led companies to switch inputs to low-sulfur western coal rather than reducing output or changing technology (Carlson et al. 2000). This substitution was costly, however, and railroads

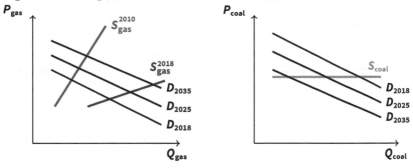

Figure 5-8. Changes in AEO Natural Gas Forecast, 2010 versus 2018

Sources: Energy Information Administration; CEA calculations.
Note: Shifts reflect differences in forecasts from 2010 and 2018 issues of the *Annual Energy Outlook* (EIA 2010, 2018e).

managed to capture some of the surplus (Busse and Keohane 2007; Gerking and Hamilton 2008). Productivity gains help account for the relatively modest employment gains; high levels of productivity in the West North Central Region spanning Kansas, Missouri, and North Dakota have led to moderate gains in employment over time, while the Mountain Region's nationwide eminence in productivity has allowed it to sustain employment levels roughly equal to those during the early 2000s (EIA 2018c; MSHA 2018).

The contrast between the outlook for natural gas and coal is captured in figure 5-8. The EIA's (2018b) *Annual Energy Outlook* shows a substantial revision between the 2010 and 2018 forecasts for natural gas, consistent with an anticipated shift of the supply curve out and down, implying more and cheaper natural gas. This is shown in the left panel of figure 5-8 with a shift in the supply curve from red to blue. Over time, the demand for natural gas shifts out to accommodate growth in energy demand. Hausman and Kellogg (2015) derived the welfare implications of contemporaneous supply and demand shocks. In contrast, a sector without technological change like coal does not get a supply shift, and even faces the prospect of declining demand because cheaper natural gas is an attractive substitute.

U.S. Fuels in the Global Marketplace

Trade is crucial for energy markets. Fuel commodities constituted more than a 9 percent share of global trade in 2017, on a value basis (United Nations 2018). The supply shift that the United States' oil and natural gas producers have experienced thanks to technology, along with its world-leading coal reserves, put it in an excellent position to trade energy products. The gains from trade are especially large in primary commodities like fossil fuels (Fally and Sayre 2018), for which the United States has a comparative advantage (CEA 2018).

U.S. Oil Exports Are At an Unprecedented High

The unexpected increase in domestic oil and natural gas production has bought the United States a new degree of leeway in energy markets, especially for transportation fuels that are particularly reliant on petroleum. Domestic production offsets the demand for imported petroleum, which has contributed to rebalancing in the global market. U.S. net imports of crude oil and petroleum products averaged 2.7 MMbpd in 2018, down from the average of 12.5 MMbpd in 2005.

World production of crude oil and other petroleum liquids continued to grow through 2018 and is expected to average over 100 MMbpd (EIA 2018i). The change in the U.S. net import position for crude oil in 2018 year was about 0.74 MMbpd, equal to about half of OPEC's estimated spare production capacity in 2018 (EIA 2018i; BP 2018). This shift also significantly affects the U.S. international position in the market for crude oil and petroleum products. The U.S. petroleum trade balance was -$199 billion after seasonal adjustment in 2017, which is less than half of the −$495 billion (inflated to $2017) 10 years earlier, and is down over $300 billion from the all-time low in 2005 (U.S. Census Bureau 2018). Although the overall trade balance deteriorated over the concurrent period, increased production has undoubtedly served as a boon to the American position internationally as well as a buffer for American consumers' sensitivity to oil prices.

Petroleum exports. The United States has witnessed a renaissance in exports of crude oil since December 2015, thanks to the lifting of a 40-year ban on crude oil exports. Through September 2018, U.S. exports of crude oil were more than triple the annual levels in 2016, the first full year of exports after the lifting of the export ban. In May 2018, exports of crude topped 2.0 MMbpd for the first time in U.S. history (figure 5-9). Melek and Ojeda (2017) found that the ban was binding during the period 2013–15, but that when general equilibrium effects are taken into account, the macroeconomic effects of removal are negligible because of adjustments in the types of crude oil refined in the United States. This suggests that crude oil exports alone do not increase U.S. GDP because crude oil and refined product prices adjust.

However, in trade that does boost GDP, the United States imports a large volume of oil and capitalizes on the large and complex refining sector to produce refined products that are exported. Crude oil and refined petroleum product exports rose by 17.5 percent in the first 10 months of 2018 from the average level in 2017, driven by increased exports to Latin American nations (figure 5-10). The silver lining is the nondurable manufacturing jobs that are supported by imported oil. There is room for further gains in this direction. Despite increasing oil-refining capacity, U.S. consumption of petroleum exceeds domestic refining capacity.

Figure 5-9. U.S. Crude Oil and Finished Product Exports, 2000–2018

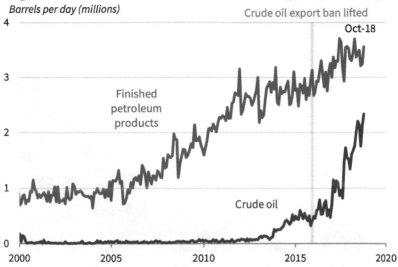

Barrels per day (millions)

Sources: Energy Information Administration; U.S. 114th Congress.
Note: H.R. 2029 repealed Section 103 of the Energy Policy and Conservation Act (42 U.S.C 6212) on December 18, 2015, which lifted the ban on U.S. exports of crude oil starting in 1977, with certain exceptions granted by the Commerce Department.

Macroeconomic effects. Abundant crude oil has other important spill-overs, notably to the macroeconomy. Trends in crude oil exports and shrinking net imports have implications for the economy's responsiveness to oil price shocks. The petroleum share of the U.S. trade balance is at historic lows; the petroleum share of the deficit was 15.8 percent in 2018, down 44.3 percentage points from secular highs of over 60 percent in 2009. The petroleum trade balance has narrowed steadily since its all-time high of $44.3 billion in November 2005 (figure 5-11). Because petroleum prices are determined in a global market and are volatile, reducing net imports of a product with inelastic demand allows domestic producers to capture windfall gains from higher prices that otherwise would be transferred to foreign producers.

Oil price spikes have historically been correlated with negative growth effects for oil-importing economies (Hamilton 1996). Exogenous oil price shocks have significant contractionary effects on GDP growth for the United States and also for most other developed economies (Jiménez-Rodríguez and Sánchez 2004). A large body of literature finds that oil price volatility imposes substantial costs on the economy, affecting consumers directly and creating uncertainty that disrupts business investment (Jaffe and Soligo 2002; Parry and Darmstadter 2003; Kilian 2008; Baumeister and Gertsman 2013; Brown and Huntington 2015). Separating the role of oil price shocks in measuring effects on real GDP growth has traditionally been a difficult empirical task. Efforts

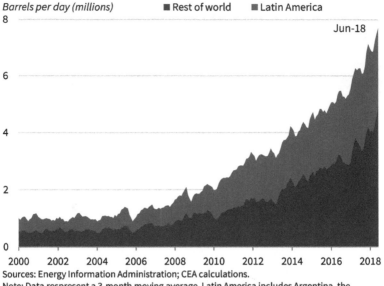

Figure 5-10. U.S. Crude and Petroleum Product Exports, 2000–2018

Barrels per day (millions) ■ Rest of world ■ Latin America

Jun-18

Sources: Energy Information Administration; CEA calculations.
Note: Data respresent a 3-month moving average. Latin America includes Argentina, the Bahamas, Brazil, Chile, Colombia, Costa Rica, Ecuador, El Salvador, Guatemala, Honduras, Jamaica, Mexico, Nicaragua, Paraguay, Saint Lucia, and Venezuela.

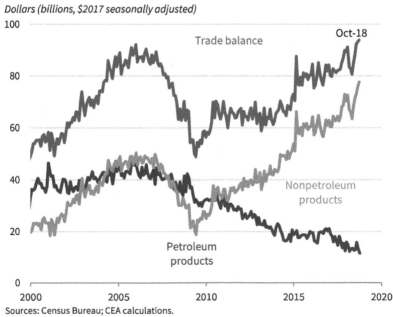

Figure 5-11. U.S. Petroleum Trade Balance, 2000–2018

Dollars (billions, $2017 seasonally adjusted)

Trade balance

Oct-18

Nonpetroleum products

Petroleum products

Sources: Census Bureau; CEA calculations.

to tease out the effects of oil price changes are impaired by the endogenous effects of monetary tightening and other countercyclical policies aimed at correcting these trends (Hoover and Perez 1994; Barsky and Kilian 2002).

As the United States continues to expand its position as an exporter in global oil markets, it better insulates itself from the adverse welfare and GDP consequences of high oil prices and price spikes. Although the United States remains a net importer of petroleum products, its smaller net import share leaves it with less exposure to oil price shocks. For example, between 2008 and 2009 the average landed cost of imported crude oil decreased from $93.33 to $60.23 per barrel, contributing to a $136 billion lower oil import bill. Because of lower imports, a similar price difference during the first three quarters of 2018 would have only saved $72 billion. In a stunning reversal, if the United States becomes an annual net exporter, it may view supply restrictions elsewhere in the world as an opportunity rather than a threat. The speed with which this transition has taken place is unprecedented.

A second effect of the changing U.S. net petroleum position is that it may increase protection from the business cycle that is exacerbated by high oil prices. Kilian and Vigfusson (2017) observe that in the period since 1974, U.S. economic recessions have been universally preceded by increases in the price of oil. However, as the authors note, increases in real oil prices do not always predict an economic contraction in a subsequent period. One metric for defining sustained increases in the price of oil is the cumulative net oil price increase over three years (Hamilton 2003). Figure 5-12 displays the apparent correlation between persistent, upward pressure on the price of oil and recessions between 1974 and 2018.

After 60 Years, the U.S. Is Again a Net Exporter of Natural Gas

Domestic production, proven reserves, and export capacity have all increased for U.S. natural gas. The supply shock for gas has created a question of where gas should flow to balance the market. Domestic consumption has increased, led by electricity generation. Petrochemical investments are up, contributing to a strong domestic chemical manufacturing base with ethane crackers along the Gulf Coast and in Pennsylvania. That leaves two main options for outlets: domestic transportation, and foreign markets.

With greater export capacity, natural gas will play an important role as a strategic resource provided by the United States to countries around the world, in addition to the trade balance in goods. The implications of exporting U.S.-produced natural gas include higher prices in the United States and exposure to global natural gas market dynamics. Policy has the ability to affect either side of the trade-off between exports and domestic supply. The Administration has promoted increased export capacity, streamlining the process for approval of export facilities, and enabling a more active role in global natural gas markets. At this point, private final investment decisions are needed for fully permitted

Figure 5-12. Real U.S. Refiners' Acquisition Costs and Recessions, 1974–2018

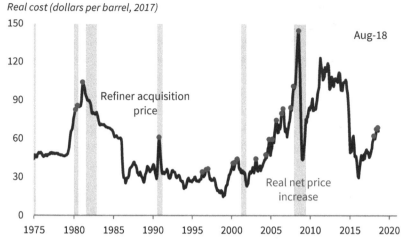

Real cost (dollars per barrel, 2017)

Sources: Kilian and Vigfusson (2017); Energy Information Administration; Bureau of Labor Statistics; National Bureau of Economic Reserach; CEA calculations.
Note: Real oil price is defined as the monthly average refiner acquisition cost for crude oil deflated using the CPI-U. The 3-year net oil increase measure is denoted as the end of a period in which the value of the real price of oil is greater than the price in the preceding 36-month period. Shading denotes a recession.

additional export terminals. As shown below, increasing export capacity offers opportunity, but the competitive global liquefied natural gas (LNG) market must be considered before making large fixed investments.

Natural gas is less fungible than petroleum, limiting trade to transportation by pipeline, or at much higher cost by chilling until it liquefies (at –260°F), which reduces its volume by 99.8 percent and allows long-distance bulk transporting by specialized tankers. In 2017, the average price of LNG was over two times the benchmark U.S. price at Henry Hub in Louisiana. However, the costs associated with cooling for transportation, plus the costs of transportation and regasifying at the destination, in addition to covering the fixed costs of specialized liquefaction and regasification trains, accumulate and reduce the economic value of expanded LNG shipments (CEA 2006).

Domestic production of natural gas has increased almost 40 percent over the last decade, and the EIA estimates that production increased by a further 10.6 percent in 2018 (EIA 2018i). The estimated increase in production from 2017 to 2018 was the largest year-over-year growth on record. The growth of LNG exports helped the United States become a net exporter of natural gas in 2017, for the first time since 1957. The 2017 surplus was also driven by a capacity expansion of 3.1 billion Bcfd (39.9 percent) into Mexico (EIA 2018j). Pipeline exports are almost always cheaper, thanks to inherently lower transportation costs. Increasing export volumes by either transportation mode helps support higher prices for U.S. producers.

The majority of U.S. natural gas exports are by pipeline to Mexico and Canada. Delivering natural gas beyond U.S. land neighbors and U.S. domestic markets that are inaccessible by pipeline, however, requires exporting by sea after the natural gas has been liquefied. LNG has grown to be 28.6 percent of total U.S. natural gas exports by volume. The capacities for both LNG exports and pipeline exports are projected to grow over the coming two years. Currently, just three facilities in the United States have a combined capacity for LNG exports of 3.8 Bcfd. However, four additional LNG export facilities currently under construction will add 8.1 Bcfd of capacity, and a further four facilities that are approved but not yet under construction will potentially add a 6.8 Bcfd of LNG export capacity (EIA 2018h).

Although less flexible than the expansion of LNG capacity, construction of more gas pipelines into Mexico could provide additional competitively-priced avenues for increasing U.S. gas exports. Capacity for planned pipelines from the United States to Mexico is projected to grow by nearly 5.6 Bcfd from 2018 through 2020. Because the centers of Mexican demand are not located near the border, complementary infrastructure investment on the Mexican side of the border is needed. In 2018, Mexico added 2.7 Bcfd, with an additional 6.9 Bcfd under construction to move imports from south and west Texas further south to population centers (Wyeno 2018).

Liquefied natural gas. Not so long ago, the United States was considered to be a critical *import* market for LNG. Investments in domestic regasification terminals to handle these imports were seen as critical for the country's energy future. Forecasts less than 10 years old projected that the United States would run a net deficit in LNG trade through the extent of their 20-plus-year horizons. These predictions were so bleak on the export front that in the 2010 edition of the *Annual Energy Outlook* (EIA 2010), the United States was forecast to import 1.38 trillion cubic feet of liquefied natural gas in 2017 and export none. The ex post scenario instead saw the U.S. run a surplus of over 600 billion cubic feet of natural gas in 2017, with exports almost 10 times the magnitude of imports.

Liquefaction of natural gas is the most economical way to export natural gas to other markets that are inaccessible by pipeline, and thus the expansion of these LNG facilities has opened previously inaccessible foreign markets for deliveries of U.S. natural gas. LNG can be sent in bulk shipments using specialized tankers, or in smaller, containerized units. In spite of these developments, the U.S. still imports LNG, especially in the Northeast and noncontiguous states and territories, where pipeline constraints are the relevant impediment to domestic shipment. Although U.S. natural gas can be exported, it cannot currently be moved between U.S. points because there are no cabotage-certified LNG tankers. New tankers would need to be built to allow this trade; none have been built in the United States since 1980.

U.S. LNG export capacity is largely clustered on the Gulf Coast. Cheniere Energy opened the first export facility, and now has three liquefaction trains in operation in Sabine Pass, Louisiana. This initial investment is the first of several liquefaction trains under construction that are expected to come online in the next two years. The second U.S. LNG export terminal to open was Cove Point in Maryland, which came fully online in March 2018. Cove Point is located to take advantage of natural gas from the Appalachian Basin. After Cove Point opened, U.S. LNG export capacity at this point was 3.82 Bcfd, or about 4.8 percent of contemporary U.S. production (FERC 2018). A third export facility in Corpus Christi loaded its first precommercial cargoes in November 2018, and expects to begin commercial shipments in 2019. Three additional LNG export terminals are currently under construction: one more in Texas, one in Georgia, and one more in Louisiana. Upon completion of all three terminals, total U.S. LNG export capacity is expected to reach almost 10 Bcfd. Beyond these projects, 7.6 Bcfd in other projects are fully permitted but not under construction for lack of a final investment decision. Figure 5-13 shows how additional export capacity could increase the value of LNG exports given current price forecasts.

U.S. LNG exports can be expected to be particularly competitive in markets with high natural gas demand and a limited access to local or pipeline-sourced supply. China and Japan are the world's two largest importers of LNG, and are likely to be attractive future markets in which to increase the U.S. share of LNG deliveries. Driven by antipollution government policies, Japan and China together imported an average of 16 Bcfd in 2017, nearly four times current U.S. export capacity. Many countries can supply LNG, and China has chosen to impose tariffs on U.S. LNG imports in retaliation for U.S. tariffs on imports from China. Growth in the global LNG market overwhelms this effect, because U.S. cargoes can be delivered around the world and do not rely on particular partners.

European markets appear promising but may prove more difficult to penetrate for U.S. imports. European countries import most of their natural gas supply by pipeline from the Middle East and Russia, limiting demand for the more expensive U.S. LNG exports. Pipeline transportation remains less costly than LNG for international shipments departing from the United States (figure 5-14). LNG accounted for only 12.4 percent of European gas demand in 2017, while pipeline imports supplied 79.6 percent of Europe's consumption (BP 2018). Although the EU had 21 Bcfd of regasification capacity in 2017, LNG imports totaled only 5.6 Bcfd on average (European Commission 2018). This spare capacity provides insurance against supply interruptions from Russian gas, but the higher cost of delivered LNG makes it less attractive for long-term commercial contracts.

Additional barriers to expansion of U.S. LNG exports may stem from the industry's focus on long-term contracts, which traditionally have had destination clauses that limit the flexibility of trade to price signals. Long-term

Figure 5-13. Historic and Projected LNG Export Revenue, 2015–25

Export revenue (millions of dollars)

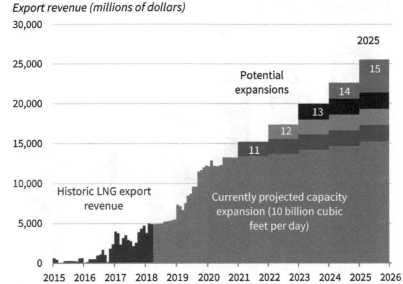

Sources: Energy Information Administration; New York Mercantile Exchange; CEA calculations.
Note: Monthly export revenue is presented at an annualized rate in nominal terms.
LNG = liquefied natural gas.

contracts reassure financiers providing capital for expensive investments in capacity. In such LNG contract structures, uncertainty over future prices and political or economic developments in the receiving country may weigh on U.S. LNG exports and investment abroad (Zhuravleva 2009). These uncertainty factors may be particularly relevant in Eastern European countries, which generally have weak and volatile economic, regulatory, and political conditions. In addition to long-term contracts, spot trading is needed for the market to recognize arbitrage gains; facilities that are locked into long-term contracts cannot capitalize on "cargoes of opportunity," such as particularly high prices in distant markets. One contractual solution to the paradox of needing both long-term and spot trades is allowing brokers to bridge the gap by paying projects for capacity and marketing LNG where it is most profitable.

Coal Exports

One reason for greater coal demand has been overseas demand; U.S. coal exports rose by 60.9 percent in 2017. This aided both the steam and metallurgical coal sectors. Exports to Europe increased by 44.5 percent, while exports to Asia increased 109.0 percent. Asian markets, especially India and South Korea, were leading purchasers of steam coal, while European countries, led by

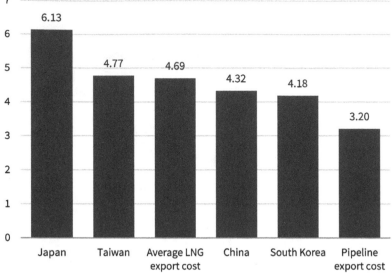

Figure 5-14. Export Prices for U.S. LNG by Destination, 2017

Dollars per thousand cubic feet

Source: Energy Information Administration.
Note: LNG = liquefied natural gas.

Ukraine and the Netherlands, purchased a plurality of U.S. metallurgical coal exports (EIA 2018c).

The coal industry has seen a minor reversal of downward trends starting in the fourth quarter of 2016. The United States exported nearly 87.2 million short tons of coal in the first three quarters of 2018, up 18.4 million short tons (27 percent) from 2017 (figure 5-15). This boom in exports was primarily driven by exports of steam coal, which grew by 44 percent in the first three quarters of 2018 over 2017 levels. U.S. coal production continued to exceed domestic consumption through 2018, allowing for renewed opportunities to further expand demand through exports; U.S. production accounted for slightly less than 10 percent of global consumption in 2017 (BP 2018).

The fuel costs of using coal to generate electricity remain among the lowest of any technology. However, thanks to the technology's higher fixed costs and inherent inflexibilities, coal-fired generation has lost market share to natural gas generation (Fell and Kaffine 2018). However, coal remains the main fuel by which many countries provide electricity to their citizens (Wolak 2017). Coal-fired generation made up 46.3 percent of electricity in non-OECD countries in 2017 and was just surpassed by natural gas in OECD countries to become the second-most-widely-used source of fuel for electric generation, after natural gas (BP 2018). The increased demand for electricity in developing regions helped bolster coal prices in 2017, leading to higher U.S. exports. Price

Figure 5-15. U.S. Quarterly Coal Exports, 2007–18

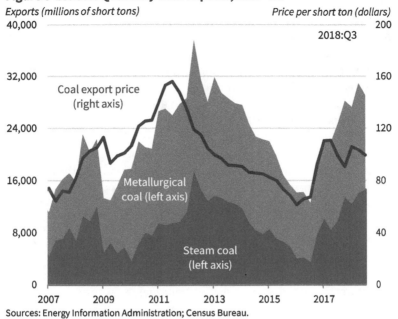

Exports (millions of short tons)   *Price per short ton (dollars)*

Sources: Energy Information Administration; Census Bureau.

increases were especially pronounced in Europe and Japan, where benchmark coal prices rose by 40.6 and 34.0 percent, respectively (BP 2018). Figure 5-15 documents the dynamic response of U.S. coal exports vis-à-vis export prices, and how rising prices in 2017 contributed to export growth.

Wolak (2017) examines the potential impact on the world coal market of increasing coal export capacity from the West Coast. Due to transportation cost differentials, the net effect is to increase U.S. exports to the Pacific Basin and to reduce Chinese domestic production. Increased Chinese access to cleaner-burning U.S. coal would drive up U.S. domestic coal prices and accelerate the switch to natural gas–fired generation in the United States. Projects expanding the Pacific Northwest's' export capacity have been proposed in Washington State, although local pressure over environmental concerns has slowed progress.

Energy policy has important implications for trade policy. Greater self-reliance reduces import dependence, while growing exports strengthen links to other countries. Increased leverage might seem like an unambiguous asset, but greater trade linkages also create potential vulnerabilities as trading partners recognize that U.S. interests may be sensitive to changes in trade flows.

Strategic Value

Energy trade can offer a strategic advantage to the United States. LNG exports to Europe provide an example of the strategic value of energy exports. In 2014, Lithuania received 97 percent of its natural gas from Russia. But Lithuania has begun diversifying its energy supply, building an LNG import terminal in 2014. Afterward, Russia's share dropped to 53 percent in 2017. Although the economic value of LNG exports to Lithuania is small, the strategic value of providing allies with alternative energy supplies is relatively large, if difficult to quantify. If the United States is the source of LNG shipments, this policy provides a double dividend of strategic and trade benefits.

The EU natural gas market also provides an example of the limitations of U.S. energy diplomacy. The EU has only reduced Russia's share from 31 percent of imports in 2014 to 29 percent in 2018 (through August). The United States only provided 0.2 percent of the EU's LNG imports in 2018.

Not all fuel transactions are dominated by strategic concerns. Venezuela exported 48 percent of its crude oil to the United States in 1999, when Hugo Chávez became president; but the amount dropped to 32 percent in 2017. Oil exports represented 90 percent of Venezuela's exports in 2017, so the Venezuelan government has a strong incentive not to disrupt this trade. The U.S. refining sector has invested in processing Venezuelan crude oil that it can buy competitively on the market. Although strategic considerations alone might suggest that the United States should substitute away from Venezuelan supplies, the advantageous economics of supply mean that the oil still flows.

Because of its prominence, oil trade is a geopolitical pressure point. In 2018, the United States sanctioned oil exports from Iran, returning to a regime that was in place before the 2015 Joint Comprehensive Plan of Action. The stated goal of U.S. sanctions is to deprive the Iranian regime of oil revenue. In anticipation of implementation on November 5, 2018, global oil prices rose through October 2018. Iran exported 2.18 MMbpd in 2017. Before the November deadline, Iranian oil exports for October 2018 were already down 30 percent from their 2017 level, to 1.78 MMbpd (figure 5-16).

In an effort to minimize harm to U.S. allies importing oil from Iran, the United States granted six-month waivers exempting certain volumes from the sanctions. Eight such waivers were granted, to China, India, Japan, Turkey, Italy, Greece, Taiwan, and South Korea.

Spare production capacity, especially among OPEC members, has been vital in stabilizing global oil markets in response to unexpected shocks, due to factors ranging from natural disasters to geopolitical conflicts (Pierru, Smith, and Zamrik 2018). Spare production capacity can be brought online within 30 days and sustained for at least 90 days. Spare capacity among OPEC producers is projected by the EIA to be slightly over 1 MMbpd through 2019 (figure 5-17). spare production capacity growth has been limited in recent years as Saudi

Figure 5-16. Iranian Crude Oil Exports, 2016–18

Barrels per day (thousands)

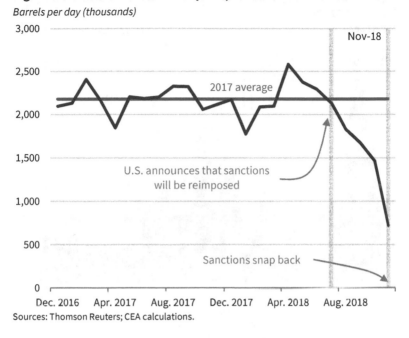

Sources: Thomson Reuters; CEA calculations.

Arabia has reached capacity. Removing Iranian crude oil from the global market places additional pressure on suppliers and transfers spare capacity to Iran. Future supply interruptions may require cooperation in using spare capacity to avoid price spikes.

Energy exports also create a vulnerability as other countries recognize that they can retaliate against U.S. exports. When China wanted to retaliate against the U.S. Section 301 tariffs, it imposed tariffs on LNG. In 2018, the United States exported 103 Bcf of LNG to China, or about 15 percent of all U.S. LNG exports. Following imposition of retaliatory tariffs, U.S. LNG exports to China dropped to zero. This reflects the near-perfect substitutability of commodity products like LNG and even crude oil. U.S. exports will not be shut out of the global marketplace, but the destination could be affected by foreign trade policy, much as U.S. agriculture has been targeted in the past.

Energy Policy

Despite the promising indications from booming fossil fuel production, and the success in improving the U.S. fossil fuels trade balance, a number of energy policy issues remain salient. In a market economy like the United States, with a competitive energy sector, opportunities to increase access to production are limited, except for perhaps on Federal land and minerals. This section discusses a number of issues facing the electricity generation sector, which are

Figure 5-17. OPEC Spare Production Capacity and Crude Oil Prices, 2001–20

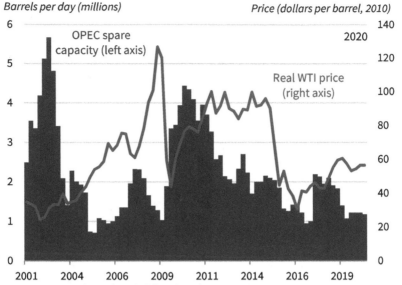

Barrels per day (millions)   *Price (dollars per barrel, 2010)*

Sources: Energy Information Administration; Thompson Reuters.
Note: OPEC = Organization of the Petroleum Exporting Countries. WTI = West Texas Intermediate crude oil. Real WTI price is calculated using the GDP price deflator.

also important for fuels production because of the large share of fuels that are destined for electric generation units—for example, 91 percent of U.S. coal is ultimately consumed by electric power generation. The electricity sector affects many important issues, including renewable and nuclear electric generation. A third issue is the general relationship of regulation to the energy sector, which has been a particular focus of deregulatory actions. Global environmental issues are an important issue facing the United States and other countries, so the discussion concludes with an assessment of U.S. energy intensity and carbon dioxide (CO_2) emissions. International environmental policy potentially affects many linked markets, as impending maritime fuel regulations illustrate.

Increasing Access to Production

Unlike the government of any other country in the world, the U. S. Federal government directly controls only a minority of the country's produced resources, because mineral ownership is largely in private hands. Although this unusual allocation has received credit for helping spur the technological revolution in oil and gas drilling (Hefner 2014), it limits the ability of the Federal government to simply "turn up the tap" on production.

A second channel for affecting production levels is through regulation. States, not the Federal government, are the primary regulators of oil and gas extraction activity. Technological change poses a challenge for regulators (Fitzgerald 2018). Only when an interstate or Federal issue is involved does the Federal government have a role (see box 5-3). Although the Obama Administration sought a more expansive Federal regulatory role, the Trump Administration has worked to reduce unnecessary Federal regulations.

Electricity Generation

Electric power is the single largest energy sector in the United States.[7] Two major economic forces have affected the sector: changing the traditional regulatory model that provided electricity through a vertically integrated industry and moving toward a more market-based system; and technological change and its attendant price effects, which have shifted the underlying economics of alternative generation technologies.

Market design has been a central concern for electricity markets, smoothing the transition from regulated vertically integrated utilities to increasing degrees of wholesale and retail competition. Fabrizio, Rose, and Wolfram (2007) documented the efficiency gains resulting from restructured electricity markets, in which firms are exposed to more market forces rather than protected under regulation. The transition has not been seamless, as Borenstein, Bushnell, and Wolak (2002) document in the case of California. The potential for market power is one of the primary motivations for utility regulation and is a key factor that should be considered in any restructuring. Market incumbents accustomed to capturing inframarginal rents may be disrupted by restructuring, or may find new opportunities.

Regional transmission organizations and independent system operators coordinate generation and transmission to ultimately satisfy the demands of electric consumers, using a variety of more and less market-oriented structures. The Federal Energy Regulatory Commission (FERC) oversees these grid operators, and has considerable discretion in approving rate requests and operational plans. FERC could take a more interventionist role in addressing issues arising from the electricity grid; as an independent regulatory body it has substantial discretion. Although the regulatory structures are similar, the different physical characteristics of electricity as compared with natural gas help explain the slower buildout of electricity transmission infrastructure (Adamson 2018).

Because electric generation units are long-lived investments with long payback periods, disruptive changes can lead to a premature retirement of units. As a policy issue, this problems stems from concern about the resiliency of the grid to severe weather events, cyber threats, and other sources of interruption to fuel deliveries and ultimately electricity. There is some evidence that fuel supply deficiencies lead to electricity outages. In 2017, the EIA reported

---

[7] This includes utility-scale electric generation and combined heat and power plants.

Box 5-3. The Federal Role in Promoting Domestic Fuels Production: The Case of Alaska

The 1968 discovery of the 25 billion barrel Prudhoe Bay oil field on Alaska's North Slope remains one of the largest single discoveries in U.S. history. At its 1988 production peak, Alaska was the top-producing U.S. State, with total crude oil production of 2 MMbpd, representing nearly 25 percent of U.S. production. Since 1988, Alaskan production has declined, and by 2017 it was less than a quarter of its peak production (485,000 barrels per day) and 5.3 percent of total U.S. crude oil. Two aspects of the rise and fall in Alaskan oil production relate to Federal policy. First, infrastructure is a critical element in order to realize the value of large and remote energy reserves like Prudhoe Bay, and Federal cooperation was needed. Second, in states with large shares of Federal land ownership, access to federally owned lands and minerals can play a critical role in promoting domestic production.

Prudhoe Bay, which is on the Alaskan northern plain alongside the Arctic Ocean, is the most remote and inhospitable oil and gas operating environment in the United States (figure 5-ii). It is distant from national and global consumers. Marketing the crude oil required constructing a 4-foot diameter pipeline 800 miles across the state. The construction of the Trans-Alaska Pipeline System (TAPS) required Congressional approval; legislation was signed into law in 1973 with the first crude oil flowing from Prudhoe Bay through the pipeline in 1977 (AOGHS 2018). Today, 97 percent of Alaska's total oil production comes from the North Slope region and flows through TAPS, and thence by tanker to other destinations. Normal geophysical decline on the North Slope, however, threatens the continued operation of TAPS. As throughput falls to 500,000 barrels per day—a fraction of the historic peak of 2 MMbpd—corrosion, ice formation, wax deposition, water dropout, and geo-technical concerns threaten operations. Throughput below 350,000 barrels per day is projected to severely reduce the reliability of pipeline operations (EIA 2018a; Alyeska Pipeline Service Company 2011).

Land and mineral ownership play an important role in production declines. Although 61.3 percent of Alaska's land is administered by the Federal government (Argueta, Hanson, and Vincent 2017), the Prudhoe Bay discovery occurred on land owned by the State of Alaska. As the wells in Prudhoe Bay and nearby fields have matured, exploration has stretched along the coastal plain. The State land where Prudhoe Bay is situated is bordered on either side by federally administered land. To the east is the Arctic National Wildlife Refuge (ANWR) and to the west is the National Petroleum Reserve–Alaska (NPR-A) (figure 5-ii). The NPR-A is 22.1 million acres and currently has limited exploration and production activity. A 2017 study by the U.S. Geological Survey (USGS 2017b) estimated total undiscovered technically recoverable reserves in the NPR-A to be 8.73 billion barrels of oil and 24.55 trillion cubic feet of natural gas. This was a major upward revision from the previous 2010

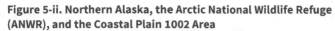

Figure 5-ii. Northern Alaska, the Arctic National Wildlife Refuge (ANWR), and the Coastal Plain 1002 Area

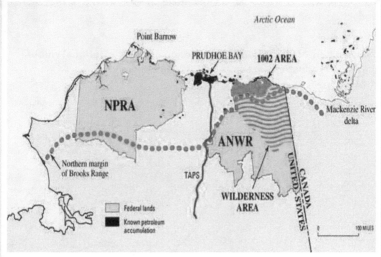

Sources: U.S. Geological Survey; Energy Information Administration.

USGS estimate of less than 1 billion barrels, and was informed in part thanks to increased exploration activity and the beginning phases of production in 2015 through 2017 (USGS 2010). The ANWR is a large tract of protected land, though only 8 percent of the refuge is of interest for oil and gas activity. This area on the coastal plain, known as the "1002 area," covers 1.5 million acres of the 19.64 million acre reserve. As a previously protected area, only one exploratory well has been drilled in the 1002 area, which was completed in 1986 (EIA 2018a). Despite a lack of exploration and its small size relative to the NPR-A, the most recent USGS assessment of the 1002 area published in 1998 estimated mean technically recoverable reserves of 7.7 billion barrels (USGS 1998).

Federal policy in 2018 prioritized expanded production on federally administered lands on Alaska's North Slope, and 2018 was a year of breakthrough success in this long-running effort (Hahn and Passell 2010). In December 2017, the Bureau of Land Management offered the largest ever lease sale in the NPR-A, with 900 tracts that cover a total of 10.3 million acres available for bid. Previously, there were 189 authorized leases covering 1.3 million acres. The President later signed a law (as part of the Tax Cuts and Jobs Act) requiring that a competitive leasing program be established for oil and gas exploration and production in the 1002 area of ANWR. The EIA has estimated that crude oil production from the 1002 area would begin in 2031, peaking in 2041 at 880,000 barrels per day, with cumulative production in the mean case at 3.4 billion barrels between 2031 and 2050. Under the EIA's ANWR high resource case, total crude oil production could greatly increase and approach the 1988 peak (figure 5-iii). Policy to expand production on other federally administered lands, including the NPR-A, could further increase production forecasts.

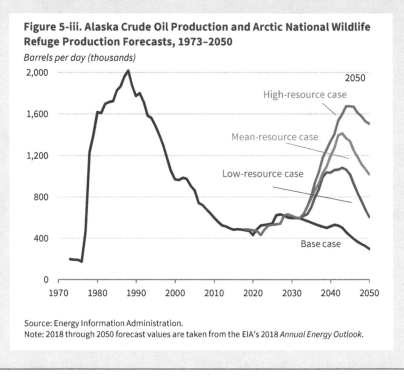

Figure 5-iii. Alaska Crude Oil Production and Arctic National Wildlife Refuge Production Forecasts, 1973–2050

Source: Energy Information Administration.
Note: 2018 through 2050 forecast values are taken from the EIA's 2018 *Annual Energy Outlook*.

94 major disturbances or unusual occurrences in the electricity supply system affecting a total of 17.1 gigawatts of capacity (EIA 2018e). Fuel supply deficiency accounted for 6 percent of these events and 1.2 percent of the total lost capacity (EIA 2018g). The low incidence and relatively small impact are testaments to the overall reliability of the national grid. However, more focused studies in particular regions have found evidence of substantial vulnerabilities (NEISO 2018; Balash et al. 2018; PJM Interconnection 2017).

In 2018, utility-scale electricity generation was dominated by roughly equal amounts of natural gas and coal, at about 30 percent of the total, followed by nuclear (20 percent), and renewables including hydroelectric (17 percent) (EIA 2018g). This is a substantial change in the generation mix from the preceding decade. Between 2000 and 2009, coal on average made up 49 percent of electricity generated, while natural gas made up 19 percent and all renewable energy accounted for less than 8 percent (EIA 2018g).

One challenge to the traditional system is the emergence of utility-scale renewable generation that operates at or near zero marginal cost. These sources are generally nondispatchable so that they enter the generation mix first, at zero cost. Renewable sources are intermittent, so the generation can fluctuate for uncontrollable reasons: such as variation in wind speeds for wind farms or in cloud cover for solar generation. The reliability of the grid therefore depends on the ability of other generation units to smooth out intermittency, or to "firm" the renewable generation into a reliable stream of power. Nuclear and large-scale coal generation units are not well suited to provide this firming service, which sometimes attracts a price premium. Natural gas–fired units, particularly open-cycle turbines, are particularly well suited for the task. The interaction of renewable capacity and natural gas generation that can firm renewables has been causally linked to reduction in coal-fired generation (Fell and Kaffine 2018).

Operating costs are separable into fuel costs and operations and maintenance costs that are incurred to keep a plant available. Some plants have higher costs than others; from an economic perspective, operating the lowest-cost plants provides the greatest value, all else being equal. The competitiveness of natural gas and renewable generation, especially in restructured electric markets, indicates the importance of low operating costs.

Nuclear plants have the lowest mean total operating costs for any generation technology except for hydroelectric. It is worth noting that the existing nuclear reactors have been online for decades, and the substantial fixed costs required to build units have already been amortized. The recent experience with cost overruns for new-build nuclear units underscores the importance of fixed costs to the bottom line of plant operators. The revenues required to earn an economic profit may be higher than the figures listed here due to sunk costs, though these are likely to vary on a plant (or even unit) basis.

Mean operating costs vary across types of generation units. If prices move in lockstep with the varying costs, margins remain the same. However, in part because of varying market structures and generation portfolios, regional wholesale and retail prices vary. In conjunction with cost differences, price variation leads to differences in operating margins.

Generation costs and operation and maintenance costs are not the only relevant costs. Different generation technologies create varying amounts of emissions and waste. Coal generation emits relatively more air pollutants than other fossil fuels, and creates a second by-product in the form of ash that requires special handling for disposal. In contrast, nuclear generation is emission-free, though it raises its own particular long-lived issue in the form of nuclear waste, which also requires special disposal. Natural gas falls somewhere in-between, with lesser amounts of harmful (and greenhouse) emissions than coal. A program accounting for the economic value of emissions could provide a boost to nuclear generation, depending on the value of emissions.

For example, in selected markets, nuclear units may be eligible for zero emission credits that supplement revenue from wholesale electricity sales.

Market design and efforts to dictate the dispatch order of plants must be carefully considered to avoid unintended consequences. Holding constant the stock of generation units, the likely effect of dispatching high-cost units more frequently is to reduce the cost of the marginal megawatt and reduce the market-clearing wholesale price in competitive generation markets. This means that the cost of keeping high-cost units running can be underestimated, because the gap between market-determined prices and operating costs will widen as a result of the policy. Using two-part tariffs or other mechanisms to address these concerns may provide workable solutions and regional flexibility to accommodate different grid characteristics.

The strategic need for an electricity generation reserve to promote the grid's resilience is a challenge that is analogous to many other economic problems. The entire portfolio of generation assets in the United States could be eligible to be part of a reserve, with different strategic weights placed on various types of generation—for example, nuclear or coal-fired generation might provide greater resilience benefits and therefore be preferentially selected into the reserve. Generation assets in regions of the country that are more susceptible to natural disasters or other exogenous interruptions might be more valuable to include in the reserve. Focusing the strategic needs into unit- or plant-specific weights can be accommodated in a voluntary reserve system, much like conservation programs that elicit landowner participation while minimizing public expenditures. A similar mechanism could be used to provide the strategic benefits of a generation reserve while minimizing the downstream costs to electricity consumers. In addition to minimizing the cost, such a program would retain private initiative to opt into the reserve, with the lowest qualified bids selected, rather than relying on the judgment of bureaucrats to select the most preferred units.

Renewables. Renewable generation technologies like wind and solar have marginal costs that are very close to zero. The fuel costs are zero—at least when the wind is blowing or the sun is shining. However, building windmills and solar farms requires substantial capital expenditures, and the relatively high fixed costs may not outweigh the low marginal costs that come with generation. Recognizing this difference, Federal policymakers have worked to provide incentives to increase installations of renewable generation capacity and penetration of these technologies into the generation mix. The Business Investment Tax Credit (ITC) and the Production Tax Credit (PTC) are the main Federal subsidies targeting renewable electric generation.[8]

---

[8] Renewables are targeted by a wide variety of State programs, including Renewable Portfolio Standards and build requirements such as those promulgated in December 2018 by the California Building Standards Commission, which will require new homes to have solar panels.

The ITC was established in 2005 and recently extended through 2022 under the 2018 Bipartisan Budget Act. The ITC provides accelerated depreciation schedules for renewable energy investments by providing an initial 30 percent depreciation rate in the year the infrastructure is installed, with the accelerated depreciation rate falling incrementally to 10 percent in the years after 2022. This effectively front-loads the depreciation of investments in renewable energy infrastructure for tax purposes and lowers the cost of capital. All else being equal, this reduces the private fixed costs of investing in renewable generation. Once renewable capacity is installed, the low marginal costs are relatively easy to cover.

The PTC, established in 1992 and most recently renewed in 2018 (H.R. 1892, Sec. 40409), and operates a bit differently. Rather than trying to reduce the fixed costs associated with construction and installation, the PTC provides an inflation-adjusted, per-megawatt-hour (MWh) tax credit for the generation of renewable energy (wind, solar, closed biomass, and geothermal systems). For qualifying renewable generation infrastructure (facilities not claiming the ITC) constructed before 2018, the PTC provides a payment during a facility's first 10 years of service. Only new wind facilities qualify for the PTC since January 1, 2018; in 2020, the PTC is slated to be phased out entirely.

Because of the inflation adjustment, the nominal value of the PTC has grown over time. For facilities beginning construction in 2017, the PTC was $23 per MWh. Qualified wind-based generation was given a three-year phasedown period, where the generation credit is reduced by 20, 40, and finally 60 percent for facilities commencing construction in 2017, 2018, and 2019, respectively.

The EIA (2018b) presents amortized values of Federal renewable energy subsidies in its annual projections of levelized costs of electricity for new generation resources. The EIA's most recent report values the amortized tax credit for solar PV at $12.50 ($2017) per MWh for generation resources entering into service in 2022. This is smaller than the contemporary $23.33 subsidy per MWh provided by the PTC for wind facilities commencing construction before 2017, but larger than its current value of $9.48 per MWh for facilities being constructed starting in 2019 (figure 5-18).

Thanks to very low marginal costs, the increased penetration of renewable generation technologies has helped lower consumer costs at the margin (Cullen 2013; Kaffine, McBee, and Lieskovsky 2013; Novan 2015). However, the displacement of existing nonrenewable generation resources is an important policy question. Bushnell and Novan (2018) focus on western electricity markets and find that the short-term response to additional renewable generation has helped lower average prices. However, the dispatch of intermittent renewable sources creates both higher and lower prices during the day, the net effect of which is to undermine the economic viability of existing baseload generators. A redesigning and rethinking of wholesale markets may be needed to accommodate low-cost renewables without sacrificing existing capability.

Figure 5-18. CEA Estimates of Federal Electricity Generation Subsidies by Fuel Type for Fiscal Year 2016

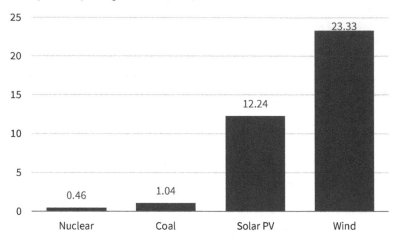

Subsidy (dollars per megawatt-hour, 2016)

Sources: Energy Information Administration; Internal Revenue Service; CEA calculations.
Note: PV = photovoltaic. Subsidy levels from the Investment Tax Credit for solar generation were unavailable for 2016. Estimates are from the EIA's 2018 *Annual Energy Outlook* for new generation deflated to 2016. These estimates may understate the level of subsidy in 2016 due to the falling price of solar photovoltaic technology over time.

Nuclear power. Since the days of Hubbert, nuclear power has enjoyed the status of a forward-looking technology. Today, the United States' 99 licensed light-water commercial reactors have an uncertain outlook. Of these reactors, 98 generated some electric power in the fourth quarter of 2018 (Nuclear Regulatory Commission 2018).[9] Between 2007 and 2018, 6 utility-scale nuclear power plants ceased operations. This represented a net decrease of slightly under 600 megawatts, or 0.6 percent of nuclear generation capacity. Between 2019 and 2022, 10 more nuclear generating facilities are scheduled to be shuttered, with a net loss of 9.47 gigawatts, or 9.5 percent of 2017's year-end capacity. Two new units are scheduled to come online in 2021, adding 2.2 gigawatts of new capacity. Of the 10 plants scheduled to close, 7 are permitted by the Nuclear Regulatory Commission to operate longer—an average of 14 years.

Deregulatory actions have increased efficiency and safety across a diverse mix of generation (Davis and Wolfram 2012; Hausman 2014). However, new concerns have been raised among government agencies over the resilience on the U.S. grid to disruption from natural or intentional causes. The vulnerability of nondispatchable generation, and also dispatchable generation with limited

---

[9] The Oyster Creek Nuclear Generation Station in Forked River, New Jersey, was shut down in September 2018, but retains an active operating license with the Nuclear Regulatory Commission.

onsite fuel storage, have been cited as potential reliability concerns for the American power system.

During the Trump Administration, FERC and the Northeastern independent system operators have borne increased scrutiny related to the resilience of the electricity infrastructure, including nuclear facilities. Nuclear power is a reliable source of generation, but reliability itself does not translate into resilience in the event of a disruption. Though reliability is measured by the ability to deliver the quantity and quality of power that consumers demand, resilience is the ability of the system to recover from an adverse shock like a weather event or an attack. The transmission and distribution systems of wires are one of the most vulnerable parts of the electric grid, as the experience of Puerto Rico since Hurricane Maria illustrates.

Finding the optimal balance between lowest-cost marginal generation and more resilient baseload coverage is not a novel challenge faced by governing bodies and operators in regions with restructured wholesale markets. Efforts to identify the correct levels of emergency generation, peak capacity, and excess capacity have led regulatory agencies to implement a diverse set of systems to ensure that the grid can handle seasonal or unexpected shocks to demand.

The constant baseload output associated with nuclear generation has limited its flexibility in restructured and more competitive markets. Because nuclear generators are price takers, and thus must accept the market rate for the electricity they generate rather than face the relatively large costs of a stepdown or shutdown, nuclear plants face continuing exposure to volatility in electricity prices (Davis and Hausman 2016). This situation has become especially pressing in the wake of falling natural gas prices and the implementation of more efficient combined cycle technology over time, as the availability of natural gas generation pushes down wholesale electric prices at the margin (Linn, Muehlenbachs, and Wang 2014). Jenkins (2018) tested alternative explanations for lower prices received by nuclear generators and found that cheap natural gas had the largest effect by far, though renewable penetration and stagnating electricity demand had statistically significant effects.

Lower wholesale electric costs caused by falling gas prices have undercut margins in nuclear plant revenues that may otherwise have been realized by nuclear operators over the past five years due to falling costs (figure 5-19). The Nuclear Energy Institute (NEI 2018) estimates that the real costs of nuclear generation have fallen by $7.85 per MWh (19 percent) over the past five years. Some of this reduction may be due to market forces pressuring closure of noneconomic plants; however, this decrease in real costs has outpaced the rate at which real retail electricity prices have fallen over the same period. The NEI estimates that the majority of these savings to have come from the lower costs of capital, which fell by 40.8 percent between 2012 and 2017, to $6.64 per MWh of generation.

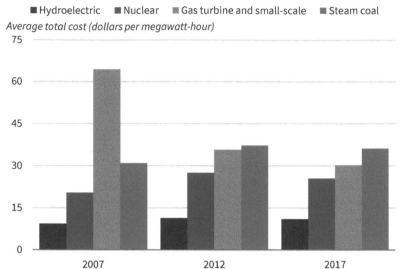

Figure 5-19. Average Total Cost for Investor-Owned Utilities by Fuel Type, 2007–17

■ Hydroelectric   ■ Nuclear   ■ Gas turbine and small-scale   ■ Steam coal

Average total cost (dollars per megawatt-hour)

Source: Energy Information Administration.
Notes: Average expenses are weighted by net generation. The gas turbine and small-scale category includes gas turbine, internal combustion, photovoltaic, and wind plant generation. Hydroelectric consists of both conventional and pumped storage technologies.

The United States' nuclear reactors are aging, and construction of new ones has been very slow. Since 2000, only 1.2 gigawatts of nuclear generation capacity have been added, out of a total of 494 gigawatts of new capacity (EIA 2018d).[10] Two nuclear units are currently under construction, but the financial struggles of these plants underscore the challenges for the civil nuclear sector. In 2013, Georgia Power—a subsidiary of Southern Company—began construction of two 1.1 gigawatt Westinghouse AP1000 reactors at its Vogtle site. Funding for these new units at the Vogtle plant is backed by two unconditional loan guarantees from the U.S. Department of Energy totaling $8.3 billion. Construction of the units is behind schedule and over budget. Moreover, construction of two similar reactors at the Summer site in South Carolina was abandoned in 2017 because of escalating costs.

Construction of the new units slowed when the designer of the reactors, Westinghouse Nuclear, filed for bankruptcy in March 2017. Although some work has continued at Vogtle, the Summer project has been abandoned.[11] The cost of the units has climbed with the delays; because these are the only new

---

[10] This long-delayed project was initiated in 1973. The reactor was finished in 2015, and was put into service in 2016.

[11] The outlook is somewhat improved after the first AP1000 reactor went into commercial operation at the Sanmen facility in China in September 2018 (IAEA 2018), demonstrating that the new reactor design is feasible.

reactors being built in the United States, the realized costs are important for setting expectations for other licensed units that have not yet begun construction. As of November 2018, the costs of completing both new reactors at Vogtle were at least $8.0 billion, with construction to hopefully be completed by the end of 2022. Such high fixed costs render nuclear uncompetitive without additional sources of revenue. The cost overruns to date on the Summer and Vogtle plants alone add $3.97 per MWh to the levelized costs of electricity from these plants, even under lifetime dispatch factors above 80 percent. The EIA currently projects levelized costs of $92.60 per MWh, leaving little headroom for these plants between costs and wholesale prices, even without including cost overruns.

Deregulation

A priority of the Trump Administration has been to reduce unnecessary Federal regulatory burdens. Executive Order 13783 was issued to promote energy independence and economic growth by developing energy resources and reviewing agency actions and regulations (82 *FR* 16093). Since the beginning of the Administration, over 300 regulatory actions have been taken, many of them reducing regulatory burdens or exempting certain activities and affecting energy production or consumption. A total of 65 regulatory actions affecting the energy sector were completed through the end of fiscal year 2018, with projected present value savings of over $5 billion. Two examples relevant to the energy sector are the Waste Prevention rule for oil and gas production and the Stream Protection Rule, which had an outsized impact on coal operations.

In September 2018, the Bureau of Land Management (BLM) rescinded certain requirements of a 2016 rule pertaining to the waste prevention and management of oil and gas resources produced on Federal lands. The new rule reestablished long-standing requirements and eliminated duplicative requirements for oil and gas drilling and extraction operations on Federal and tribal lands. With respect to the flaring of associated natural gas from oil wells, the BLM will defer to State or tribal regulations in determining if flaring will be royalty-free. In many cases, this will mean waiving the obligation to pay Federal royalties on flared gas.

In February 2017, Congress passed and President Trump signed a resolution pursuant to the Congressional Review Act repealing the Stream Protection Rule (81 *FR* 93066–445), which had taken effect on January 19, 2017. The repeal is estimated to generate an annualized $80 million in cost savings for the surface and underground coal mining industries.

Another completed action was the 2017 repeal of the Federal coal leasing program moratorium. Because western coal resources make up 55.5 percent of national production and about 80 percent of western production is from federally owned minerals (GAO 2013; CEA 2016b), the rules for the leasing and production of these minerals can affect the amount of resource that is commercially available (EIA 2018c). Passed in January of 2016, the moratorium was drafted in tandem with the BLM's 2016 order to study how to modernize Federal coal leasing. Auctions were suspended until the analysis was completed, which was expected to be in 2019. The repeal meant that the Federal leasing program for coal reverted to the preexisting rules, although the leasing rules have undergone subsequent changes under the Trump Administration (82 *FR* 36934). This action is estimated to have made available for extraction an additional 17 billion short tons of federally owned coal reserves in the Powder River Basin alone (USGS 2017a; BLM 2017).

The Federal government also auctions leases for oil and gas development, both for onshore minerals and in offshore areas. Onshore lease sales in 2018 were another tale of booms and busts. Although a September 11, 2018, auction in Nevada garnered zero bids, one week earlier, a sale of 142 parcels in New Mexico brought in a stupendous $972 million in revenue. Bullish expectations for growth in the Permian Basin's outlook and pipeline capacity continue to drive increased interest in expanding production. Year-to-date sales in 2018 were over twice the previous record level, and nearly three times those made in 2017 (ONRR 2018).

Two of the most economically significant deregulatory actions for energy have been proposed but not finalized. Repeal of the Clean Power Plan (CPP) and the Waters of the United States (WOTUS) rule are under way. Both these regulations were subject to legal challenges and stays that delayed implementation. Given the pending rulemakings, the expected level of future regulation has been dramatically reduced.

The Obama Administration passed the CPP in October 2015, with the goal of reducing CO_2 emissions from existing electric utility generating units.[12] The U.S. Environmental Protection Agency (EPA) codified final emission guidelines establishing State-specific CO_2 emission performance rates and implementation schedules for generating units. In February 2016, the CPP was enjoined by the U.S. Supreme Court at the request of West Virginia and 26 other states, which argued that the rule exceeded the EPA's authority. A repeal of the CPP was first proposed in October 2017 by the Trump Administration following pushback from State governments and industry proponents concerned about costs to consumers and outsized effects on coal-fired generation. The EPA proposed the Affordable Clean Energy rule in August 2018 as a replacement for the CPP. The final regulatory impact analysis is complete, but the rule has yet to be finalized.

The Obama Administration passed WOTUS in 2015, which expanded the interpretation of "navigable waters" under the Clean Water Act; this term was interpreted to include tributaries and bodies of water adjacent to Federal

---

[12] The Carbon Pollution Emission Guidelines for Existing Stationary Sources: Electric Generating Units (commonly referred to as the Clean Power Plan, CPP) can be found at 40 *CFR* part 60 subpart UUUU, as promulgated October 23, 2015.

Figure 5-20. Energy Intensity of GDP, 1980–2015

Energy intensity (MBtu per dollar of GDP, 2010)

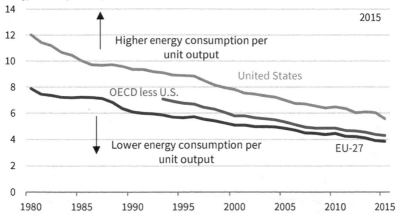

Source: Energy Information Administration; CEA calculations.
Note: Thousands of British thermal units (MBtu) per 2010 dollars of GDP at purchasing power parity of dollar-denominated expenditures. The Organization for Economic Cooperation and Development includes Australia, Austria, Belgium, Canada, Chile, the Czech Republic, Denmark, Estonia, Finland, France, Germany, Greece, Hungary, Iceland, Ireland, Israel, Italy, Japan, South Korea, Latvia, Lithuania, Luxembourg, Mexico, the Netherlands, New Zealand, Norway, Poland, Portugal, Slovakia, Slovenia, Spain, Sweden, Switzerland, Turkey, the United Kingdom, and the United States.

waters, including wetlands, ponds, and lakes, which critics argued was jurisdictional overreach. A proposal to formally rescind the WOTUS rule was issued in July 2017, and several public meetings on a new rule proposal took place during the fall of 2017. The executive order urges regulators to interpret "navigable waters" in a manner consistent with Supreme Court Justice Antonin Scalia's 2006 opinion in *Rapanos v. United States*; Scalia argued that "navigable waters" should only include navigable waters "in fact."

Environmental Implications

Energy inputs are essential to economic performance, but emissions are an increasing concern as the realities of climate change are confronted around the world. Compared with some others, the American economy has a relatively high energy intensity—meaning that more energy is used per $1 in output in the United States than in other countries. In 2015, U.S. energy intensity (measured as 1,000 British thermal units per $1 in output at purchasing power parity) was 5.56, less than half the same measure in 1980 (figure 5-20). However, the U.S. measure is 30 percent higher than the OECD ex-U.S. average and over 44 percent higher than the average of the 27 EU member countries (EIA 2018i). This relatively high dependence on energy for output helps explain why the United States has the largest negative growth effects associated with increasing oil

Figure 5-21. Annual World Carbon Dioxide Emissions, 1990–2017

CO$_2$ emissions index (1990 = 100)

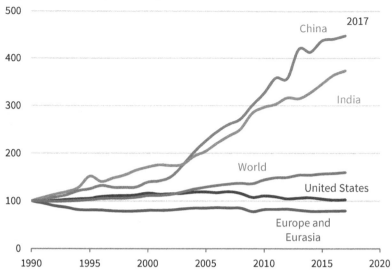

Source: Department of Energy; Energy Information Administration; United Nations Framework Convention on Climate Change; CEA calculations.
Note: CO$_2$ = carbon dioxide. Emissions levels are indexed to 1990 country-level CO$_2$ emissions. Levels for 2015–17 are estimates from the EIA's 2018 *International Energy Outlook*.

prices in the Group of Seven (Jiménez-Rodríguez and Sánchez 2004). The continental geography of the United States may be a factor by requiring more energy in the transportation sector, which is heavily dependent on petroleum. However, over time, the energy intensity of U.S. GDP has declined as energy users have sought to be more efficient, and the decreased net petroleum import position is likely to reduce the harm from future crude oil price shocks.

A second relevant measure of energy use is the total level of emissions. The United States has remained below the average global growth rate for global CO$_2$ emissions since the multilateral ratification of the United Nations Framework Convention on Climate Change (UNFCCC) in 1992. Although the United States was among one of the eventual 84 signatories to the extension of the original 1992 UNFCCC, it never ratified the 1997 Kyoto Protocol, which was the first international agreement with binding emission abatement commitments. Under this agreement, the United States would have been obligated to reduce emissions of a number of greenhouse gases by 7 percent below the

1990 level, and to achieve this reduction for an average of the years 2008–12 (figure 5-21).[13]

One concern at the time was that other countries would not be bound by similar standards. U.S. gross CO_2 emissions are estimated to have grown at an average annual rate of 0.09 percent during the period between 1990 and 2017, while emissions in China and India are estimated to have grown at average rates more than 50 times as fast (5.7 and 5.0 percent a year, respectively) (EIA 2017). The European countries and Japan committed to, respectively, 8 and 6 percent emission reductions under Kyoto, but both failed to meet these goals. Emissions during the period 2008–12 eclipsed the 1990 reduction benchmarks by 11.1 percent for the EU and 8.8 percent for Japan (EIA 2018i); see box 5-4.

Although the U.S. Congress did not ratify the Kyoto Protocol, U.S. emissions markedly broke their trend after the agreement took effect in 2005. Although U.S. emissions grew by 18.8 percent between 1990 and 2004, emissions in 2016 were down 12.8 percent from 2004 levels. This inflection in U.S. emission trends was concurrent with a similar pattern in the European nations, which shrank their emissions by 16.7 percent between 2004 and 2016 after they grew by over 20 percent in the period 1990–2004.

Many factors affect emissions. Although technological change has been an important driver for the United States, other countries have adopted a policy-based approach. For example, the EU Emissions Trading System has helped participating countries reduce their CO_2 emissions by 16.7 percent starting in 2004, the year before the policy took effect, until 2016. The U.S. reduction of 12.8 percent during the same period was largely achieved without a Federal policy intervention.

Other types of emissions reveal a similar story: emissions of six air pollutants (carbon monoxide, particulate matter, sulfur dioxide, nitrous oxides, and volatile organic compounds) have all declined since 1990. Shapiro and Walker (2018) statistically decompose the declining emissions intensity of U.S. manufacturing, and find support for increasing regulatory stringency rather than compositional shifts in manufacturing (see boxes 5-4 and 5-5).

---

[13] Gaseous emissions into the atmosphere can cause greenhouse effects by directly absorbing radiation, or by affecting radiative forcing and cloud formation. The Intergovernmental Panel on Climate Change (IPCC) developed the Global Warming Potential (GWP) measurement to compare relative ability for anthropogenic emissions to trap heat. The GWP measures the equivalent amount of CO_2 emissions that would be required to create an equal amount of radiative forcing caused by the emission of 1 ton of a given gas over a 100-year horizon. The IPCC's accounting lists these GWPs for inventoried emissions: methane (CH_4) = 25, nitrous oxide (N_2O) = 298, hydrofluorocarbons (HFCs) = 124 to 14,800, perfluorocarbons (PFCs) = 7,390 to 12,200, sulfur hexafluoride (SF_6) = 22,800, and nitrogen trifluoride (NF_3) = 17,200.

Box 5-4. Long-Term Improvements in Environmental Quality

By many measurements, air and water quality in the United States has improved dramatically in the last 30 years and additional gains continue to be seen. Since 1990, concentrations of sulfur dioxide in the air have fallen by 88 percent, nitrogen dioxide by 56 percent, lead particulates by 80 percent, and carbon monoxide by 77 percent (EPA 2018a, 2018c). Less sulfur and nitrogen in the air has meant less acid rain and healthier lakes, while lower levels of lead and carbon monoxide protect citizens from respiratory illness (Sullivan et al. 2018). Water quality has also improved markedly in other dimensions, with streams and lakes having more dissolved oxygen and less bacteria (Keiser and Shapiro 2018).

The improvements stem from various sources, including innovations in the private sector and government policies. An illustrative example is the decline in sulfur dioxide emissions (see figure 5-iv, left axis). The most recent declines have come as abundant natural gas, made available through hydraulic fracturing and horizontal drilling, has encouraged the retirement of coal-fired electricity generation, as described in the section of the text on coal production. The electricity generation sector accounted for more than 70 percent of the total decline in sulfur dioxide emissions from 1990 to 2017 (the last year of available data), with large reductions since the mid-2000s,

Figure 5-iv. Sulfur Dioxide Emissions and Rainwater Acidity, 1990–2017

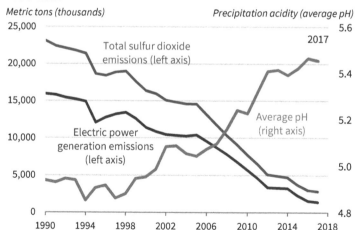

Sources: Environmental Protection Agency; National Atmospheric Deposition Program; CEA calculations.
Note: Average national rainwater pH is calculated as the precipitation-weighted negative logarithm of the concentration of hydrogen ions in rainwater accross 157 measurement sites in the United States.

when natural gas production began expanding. The more recent reductions in emissions build on early reductions that occurred following the 1990 Clean Air Act Amendments and an associated Federal cap-and-trade program implemented in 1995.

Less sulfur dioxide in the air has also improved water quality. When sulfur dioxide interacts with water and oxygen, it creates sulfuric acid and leads to acid rain, which makes streams and lakes more acidic and less hospitable to fish and other aquatic life. Data on the chemical properties of precipitation across the U.S. show that acidity has declined since 1990, with large improvements in the last decade. Data collected by the National Atmospheric Deposition Program (NADP 2018) from 157 measurement sites show that the acidity of rainwater fell by 40.3 percent from 1990 to 2017.

Box 5-5. International Environmental Standards and Liquid Fuels Markets: IMO 2020

Under a 2016 agreement by the International Maritime Organization (IMO), an 86 percent reduction in the sulfur content in marine bunker fuel used by 94,000 ocean-going vessels will be imposed on January 1, 2020. Sulfur emissions have been regulated in the United States, primarily in the electricity generation and transportation sectors, due to sulfur dioxide's adverse effects on public health (Burtraw and Szambelan 2009). Within 200 miles of U.S. coastlines, in waters known as Emission Control Areas (ECAs), ships must already limit the sulfur content of fuel burned to 0.1 percent (see figure 5-v). Similar ECAs exist in coastal waters off Canada and Northern Europe. Although the United States already adheres to a stricter sulfur standard, the IMO's decision to limit sulfur content in marine fuels to 0.5 percent in the open seas could have consequences for global fuel prices and shipping costs (IEA 2018).

Ships can pursue various strategies in order to comply with the new regulation, including refitting to LNG-fueled engines, the installation of scrubbers to remove sulfur from exhaust, and switching to lower-sulfur fuels. Given the high capital costs and supply constraints associated with refitting or installing scrubbers, initially, the majority of ships will likely comply by switching to a fuel compliant with the 0.5 percent sulfur limit—predominantly either distillate fuels (marine gas oil, MGO) or a lower-sulfur-content residual fuels (ultra-low or very-low-sulfur fuel oil, ULSFO and VLSFO). It is possible that some vessels will not comply initially, and the penalties are unclear at this point. The percentage of noncomplying ships will affect the amount of total high-sulfur fuel oil that will be displaced by MGO or ULSFO.

Global bunker fuel demand is estimated currently to be 4–5 MMbpd. HSFO and MGO constitute most bunker fuel demand, with HSFO consumption estimated to be roughly 3–3.25 MMbpd and MGO consumption estimated to

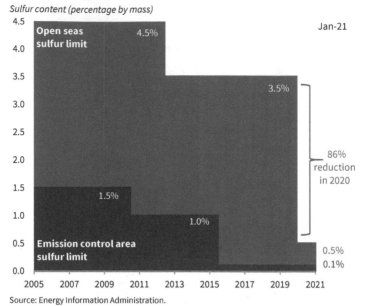

Figure 5-v. Global Marine Fuel Sulfur Limits, 2005–21

Sulfur content (percentage by mass)

Open seas sulfur limit: 4.5%, 3.5%

86% reduction in 2020

Jan-21

Emission control area sulfur limit: 1.5%, 1.0%, 0.5%, 0.1%

Source: Energy Information Administration.

be 0.8–1.25 MMbpd. LNG and LSFO (including VLSFO and ULSFO) currently constitute trivial portions of bunker fuel consumption. Though global bunker fuel represents about 5 percent of total oil demand, fuel switching by ships in 2020 may cause significant disruptions in specific product markets, with consequent price movements for all users of fuel.

Demand shifts to compliant fuels in January 2020 will be met by increasing refinery runs of MGO and ULSFO. Total desulfurization capacity by the global refining fleet is estimated to be 67 MMbpd. IMO 2020 will strain refiners because 1.5–2 MMbpd of HSFO will be displaced. As a result, the IEA (2018) estimates that existing ULSFO capacity will be able to cover only 0.6 MMbpd, or 30–40 percent, of initial HSFO displacement. Consequently, 60–70 percent of initial HSFO displacement will be filled by MGO for total bunker fuel demand to remain unchanged between 2019 and 2020, requiring greater diesel throughput by refiners. The IEA estimates that diesel capacity will increase by 1.0–1.5 MMbpd by 2020, though only 0.6–1.1 MMbpd of this additional capacity will go toward marine bunker fuel versus other diesel consumers. Under the IEA's estimates of refining capacity and supply of MGO and ULSFO, this would leave a shortfall in compliant fuel to fill HSFO displacement ranging from 0.2 MMbpd (under a high-end estimate of additional diesel and ULSFO capacity) to 0.6 MMbpd (under a low-end estimate of additional diesel and ULSFO capacity) (IEA 2018). The shortfall will likely trigger higher prices, though estimates of price shocks to fuels including diesel, gasoline, and jet fuel vary substantially.

To meet increasing MGO and ULSFO demand in the long run, refineries will need to increase their desulfurization capacity. Meeting MGO demand will require reconfiguration to optimize distillate product capacity. Meeting ULSFO demand will require upgrading to include the addition of cokers, hydrocracker, hydrotreater, and sulfur reduction units (Imsirovic and Prior 2018). Although the United States—followed by the Middle East, Russia, and China—is projected to provide most of the incremental diesel production in 2020, ULSFO production will be driven by complex refiners. A total of 8 of the 12 most complex refiners globally, as measured by the Nelson Index, are in the United States (Bahndari et al. 2018). The U.S. refining industry is well positioned to benefit from increased global demand for both MGO and ULSFO in 2020. However, U.S. fuel consumers may pay higher prices in the medium term as a result.

Conclusion

America's energy sector has bright prospects thanks to technological change and abundant resources that are already delivering record-breaking production. Improving technology has helped U.S. fossil fuel production, led by oil and natural gas, to defy projections and reach an all-time high in 2018. Investments in technology have relied on an appetite for risk-taking on the part of extraction firms and mineral owners. Successful innovation has expanded the U.S. resource base and now offers the prospect of decades of continued production. Lower expectations of the regulatory burden for extraction activities have also helped stimulate production, though the empirical magnitude of this effect has not been estimated. Domestic production will help provide energy resources to the U.S. economy that should bolster growth.

The United States' production has expanded so much that both domestic consumption and exports have increased. Natural gas consumption continues to hit all-time highs, and is increasingly penetrating electric power generation. This penetration has disrupted legacy baseload generation, including nuclear and coal. As grid operators wrestle with how to increase resilience and ensure continued reliability, the future balance between the legacy baseload and newer generators like natural gas and renewables will be struck, and this balance may differ regionally.

Expanded production also yields a dividend in America's foreign trade and its interactions with partners and allies. Growing exports of crude oil, refined petroleum products, natural gas, and coal are all evidence of greater linkages. For the first time since 1957, the United States is a net exporter of natural gas. The shrinking level of U.S. net imports of petroleum provides indirect benefits through macroeconomic channels by reducing sensitivity to oil price shocks. If the United States becomes an annual net exporter of petroleum, higher oil prices would, on average, help the U.S. economy. In this case, the net gains for producers, and to their private partners that own mineral deposits, would outweigh the higher costs for consumers. Such a change would have a number of important policy implications.

Policies focused on reducing regulatory hurdles and eliminating distorting subsidies and preferences will provide the greatest gains in cost-effectiveness and efficiency. This is especially true in electricity markets, where a dramatic increase in renewable generation capacity has threatened traditional generation assets. The restructuring of electricity markets is a deregulatory action if carried out effectively; future restructuring will need to account for renewables and to be more responsive to consumer demand, given that dynamic pricing and other strategies offer substantial efficiency gains.

Chapter 6

Ensuring a Balanced Financial Regulatory Landscape

Although it has been more than a decade since the financial crisis of 2008, its consequences continue to be felt. It revealed the financial sector's vulnerability to instability. And it also exposed shortcomings in the government's support for financial institutions that exacerbated the crisis. This experience vividly demonstrated the enormous consequences that can result from systemic financial crises if they are not properly addressed, and it revealed the need for measured reforms that could strengthen the financial system without imposing regulatory burdens that do little to enhance financial stability.

Unfortunately, the reforms spelled out in the 2010 Dodd-Frank Wall Street Reform and Consumer Protection Act fell far short of these standards. In a rush to respond forcefully to the financial crisis, the Dodd-Frank Act became law in 2010 without there having been sufficient study of the factors that led to the crisis, nor of the costs and benefits of its provisions. Too many of Dodd-Frank's provisions were redundant, unnecessarily complex, and overreaching in their application. As we argue in this chapter, the results of this flawed approach to regulatory reform were an increase in the regulatory burden and heightened uncertainty. We believe this situation exacerbated the slowest pace of economic growth in any U.S. expansion since 1950.

From its start, the Trump Administration has maintained a focus on creating and implementing a more measured approach to financial regulation that can preserve stability while addressing the shortcomings of the Dodd-Frank Act. Two weeks after taking office, President Trump issued an Executive Order outlining seven "Core Principles for Regulating the United States Financial

System." This Executive Order also directed the U.S. Department of the Treasury to determine the extent to which current laws, regulations, and other policies promote—or inhibit conformance to—these Core Principles. Thus far, the Treasury has released four reports on the state of regulation that have resulted in more than 300 specific policy recommendations. In addition, the Treasury has released reports dealing with the operation of the Financial Stability Oversight Council and the Orderly Liquidation Authority, the resolution facility created by the Dodd Frank Act.

Action has quickly followed. On May 24, 2018, the President signed into law one of the single most important pieces of deregulation of his Administration to date: the Economic Growth, Regulatory Relief, and Consumer Protection Act, also known as S.2155. As this chapter explains, this law reduces the regulatory burden in a number of ways, but without affecting the safety and soundness of the financial system.

This chapter begins with a summary of some of the events that led up to, and marked the culmination of, the financial crisis of 2008. These events epitomize some of the policies that needed to be addressed in the wake of the crisis. The second section describes the 2010 Dodd-Frank Act and how it fell short in a number of ways in restoring the full capacity of the U.S. financial industry. The third section outlines this Administration's approach to financial reform, which directly addresses the problem of systemic risk without undermining the banking industry's ability to support the economy and contribute to the prosperity of the American people.

The Causes and Consequences of the 2008 Systemic Crisis

The sequence of events that led up to the 2008 financial crisis and accounts of how the crisis unfolded have been explored in great detail elsewhere (e.g., Financial Crisis Inquiry Commission 2011; FDIC 2017). Although many policies and practices exacerbated the crisis—government policies that focused on increasing homeownership at any cost, credit-rating agencies falling asleep at the switch, weak underwriting standards, risky mortgage structures, and a misplaced faith that the housing market would always go up, to name a few—this chapter focuses on examples of crucial regulatory failures that led to the crisis.

Reinhart and Rogoff (2009) define a systemic banking crisis as the result of either (1) bank runs that lead to bank failures, or (2) the failure of one or more important institutions that results in a string of additional failures. Systemic financial crises have been shown to render a nation's banking system unable to carry out its fundamental role in the economy (Reinhart and Rogoff 2009). Because banks are critically important agents of the monetary system, systemic crises can have very large, adverse effects on real economic activity—and real people. In recent decades, banking activities have increasingly migrated to nonbank financial institutions, such as money market funds, hedge funds, and a variety of other investment vehicles. To the extent that these nonbank institutions fund themselves with short-term liabilities, they are also subject to runs that threaten the financial system's stability.

The Boom/Bust Cycle in Residential Real Estate

As we discuss later in this chapter, the historic rise in U.S. home prices between the mid-1990s and the mid-2000s and the historic decline in home prices that ensued constituted a sequence of events that resulted in the financial crisis of 2008. But these were by no means exogenous events that arose outside the financial system. Instead, the rise in home prices was fueled by an ample supply of mortgage credit at favorable rates and, starting in 2004, an unprecedented relaxation of mortgage lending standards.

While home prices were rising, virtually every group involved in the financial system was reaping short-term benefits. Mortgage lenders originated large volumes of loans. Homeowners saw increases in the value of their homes. Home builders saw record sales. Homebuyers were able to obtain credit on relaxed terms, with a minimum of due diligence. Housing investors were able to finance multiple homes at once, and mortgage investors earned high yields in what was otherwise a low-yield environment. This self-reinforcing cycle of optimism only lasted as long as home prices continued to rise. At the national level, home prices more than doubled between 1996 and 2006. In a number of large coastal markets, home prices increased even faster during this period, growing by an average of 207 percent among the six coastal cities included in the S&P CoreLogic Case-Shiller 10-City Composite Home Price Index (figures 6-1 and 6-2).

During 2003, U.S. first-lien mortgage originations totaled $3.7 trillion, of which the vast majority ($3.3 trillion) were prime mortgages, government mortgages, or jumbo mortgages.[1] These totals remain all-time highs for mortgage originations in these categories. Mortgage refinancings hit $2.8 trillion in 2003, or 76 percent of total mortgage originations, both of which were also historic highs. But as mortgage interest rates rose in 2004, originations of prime mortgages fell by more than half. In that same year, the mortgage lending

---

[1] Jumbo mortgages are those that are generally made to prime borrowers, but exceed the conforming size limit of the government-sponsored enterprises and must be privately financed.

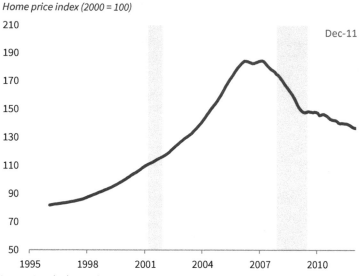

Figure 6-1. S&P CoreLogic Case-Shiller Home Price Index, National Value, 1996–2011

Home price index (2000 = 100)

Dec-11

Source: Standard & Poor's.
Note: Shading denotes a recession.

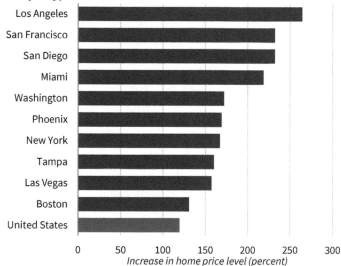

Figure 6-2. Increase in S&P CoreLogic Case-Shiller Home Price Index by City, 1996–2006

Increase in home price level (percent)

Sources: Standard & Poor's; CEA calculations.
Note: Data represent the increase in home prices between December 1996 and December 2006.

business abruptly shifted to riskier subprime and Alt-A mortgages. Between 2004 and 2006, more than $2.7 trillion in subprime and Alt-A mortgages were originated—three times the dollar amount originated in the previous three years. Many of these would eventually be backed by the U.S. government and by taxpayers, who were often on the hook for losses in these portfolios (see box 6-1).

When credit standards were lowered, the market became hotter, and home prices rose even faster. Home prices had been growing faster than disposable personal incomes since 1999, but they accelerated to double digits in 2004 and peaked at an annual rate of more than 14 percent in 2005. Despite the risks inherent in subprime, Alt-A, and nontraditional mortgage loans, these mortgages performed very well as long as home prices continued to rise. In 2006, subprime mortgages past due by 90 days or more made up just 3.1 percent of total balances.

Average U.S. home prices peaked in February 2007. During the next five years, they would decline, on net, by 26 percent. Price declines were even more pronounced in cities where nontraditional "affordability" loans had increased the most, again, some of which were on the books of the government-sponsored enterprises (Fannie Mae and Freddie Mac), and where home prices had risen the fastest before 2007. To compete for its lost "market share," the Federal Housing Administration of the U.S. Department of Housing and Urban Development lowered its down payment requirements and relaxed its underwriting standards. Just as all parties involved appeared to prosper in the self-reinforcing cycle of the housing boom, virtually all parties, including taxpayers, would be adversely affected by the self-reinforcing housing bust that started in 2007.

By one measure, the total value of U.S. home equity declined by more than half between 2006 and 2009, trimming total household net worth by $6.3 trillion. Because subprime borrowers could not repay when their loans reset, and could not qualify to refinance when the value of their home declined, subprime mortgage performance declined sharply. By 2009, subprime mortgages past due by 90 days or more quadrupled, to 13.6 percent. The annual number of mortgage foreclosures nearly tripled, on average, from 831,000 between 2004 and 2006 to 2.4 million between 2008 and 2011. Though not all these foreclosure proceedings would result in the repossession of a home, those that did introduced deadweight costs of up to 20 percent of the value of the property (Capone 1996). Forced sale of repossessed properties played a substantial role in the self-reinforcing cycle that was driving home prices downward (figures 6-3 and 6-4).

The ultimate losses to the holders of mortgage credit have been somewhat difficult to estimate. These losses accrued to federally insured banks, to thrifts and credit unions, to the government-sponsored enterprises (GSEs)—including Fannie Mae and Freddie Mac—and to holders of private mortgage-backed

Box 6-1. Defining Subprime, Alt-A, and Nontraditional Mortgages

Subprime, Alt-A, and nontraditional mortgages were categories of high-risk loans that included terms or underwriting standards that made them much riskier than prime loans. Subprime mortgages were made to households with limited or impaired credit histories. Most of them came with a relatively affordable "introductory rate" for the first two or three years and imposed heavy penalties on borrowers who chose to refinance during that introductory period. After this introductory period, the interest rate was reset to a much higher level, which the borrower could avoid only with a refinancing and by paying additional fees.

"Alt-A" was the label given to a class of mortgage loans that were generally made to households with stronger credit histories. But they often eased underwriting standards, including the requirement for borrowers to document their incomes. Of the Alt-A mortgages originated in 2006, 83 percent required little or no documentation of borrower income. Nontraditional mortgages were a large subset of Alt-A loans that allowed borrowers to defer repayment of principal through interest-only, payment option, and negative-amortization structures.

Both before and after the housing crisis, subprime, Alt-A and nontraditional mortgage loans were considered too risky to make. This judgment was validated by the exceptionally high default rate they incurred during the

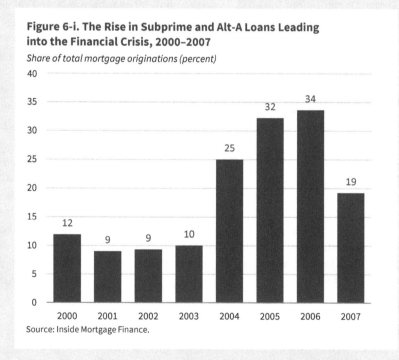

Figure 6-i. The Rise in Subprime and Alt-A Loans Leading into the Financial Crisis, 2000–2007

Share of total mortgage originations (percent)

Source: Inside Mortgage Finance.

housing crisis. Among subprime loans made in 2007, 36.6 percent defaulted within 24 months. For Alt-A loans, cumulative defaults for that vintage were 25.1 percent, while for prime loans the default rate was 6.7 percent. Figure 6-i shows the rise in these types of mortgages in the years leading up to the financial crisis.

securities (MBSs), which largely backed subprime and nontraditional mortgages. It was the private MBSs and the derivatives based on their value, which had been distributed to institutions and investors around the world, that made the toll of mortgage losses especially difficult to estimate. Nonetheless, the total losses on U.S. mortgages and mortgage-related instruments during the crisis have been projected to range into the hundreds of billions of dollars.[2]

Implicit Government Support That Undermined Market Discipline

Mortgage finance had evolved a great deal in the half century leading up to the crisis. As recently as 1975, depository institutions (banks and savings institutions) held 74 percent of total mortgage debt outstanding. It was in the 1970s that the GSEs began to build a substantial market share in financing mortgage credit. Their share of mortgage loans outstanding hit 10 percent in 1974, 30 percent in 1985, and more than 50 percent in every year between 1994 and 2003.

The growing presence of the GSEs in the mortgage market arose in part from the financial and technological innovations that favored their wholesale approach. A provision of the Tax Reform Act of 1986 defined the real estate mortgage investment conduit as a tax-preferred vehicle for funding mortgages in securitized pools, funded by a wide range of investors. The resulting division of mortgage origination, funding, and servicing has been called the "unbundling" of mortgage finance. But their ultimate competitive advantage came from their close relationship with the Federal government. The GSEs are exempt from State and local taxes and from Federal regulations on the issuance and holdings of securities. Investors perceive an implicit Federal guarantee on the MBSs they issued, and their securities have exemptions or are given another type of special status under a number of Federal regulations. These implicit guarantees and exemptions resulted in a subsidy that totaled about 40 basis points in the precrisis period, and benefited both mortgage borrowers and GSE shareholders (Ligon and Beach 2013).[3]

---

[2] For example, see reports by the Financial Crisis Inquiry Commission (FCIC 2011, xvi) and the International Monetary Fund (IMF 2008, 50).

[3] A Heritage Foundation study cites research by Passmore, Sherlund, and Burgess (2005) and other sources.

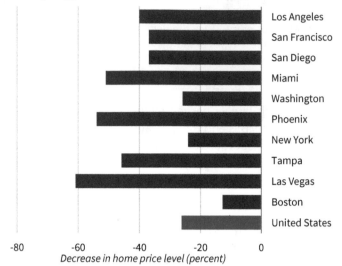

Figure 6-3. Decrease in S&P CoreLogic Case-Shiller Home Price Index by City, 2006–11

Decrease in home price level (percent)

Sources: Standard & Poor's; CEA calculations.
Note: Data represent the decrease in home prices between December 2006 and December 2011.

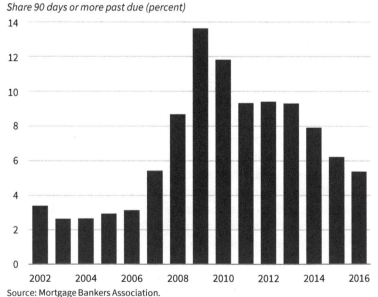

Figure 6-4. Percentage of U.S. Conventional Subprime Mortgages 90 Days or More Past Due, 2002–16

Share 90 days or more past due (percent)

Source: Mortgage Bankers Association.

Because of the implicit guarantee, the GSEs were able to operate with higher leverage than other financial institutions while still maintaining confidence in the strength of their MBS guarantee. Studies find that in 2007, they operated with leverage that was significantly greater than their commercial bank competitors (Baily, Litan, and Johnson 2008). These factors provided an implicit subsidy to the GSEs that enabled them to grow and that may have encouraged them to take on more risk. Besides expanding their securitization businesses, the GSEs also took advantage of their implicit guarantee and low capital requirements to issue subsidized debt to fund investments in mortgage loans that they retained on their balance sheets. Their combined debt obligations totaled $2.9 trillion at the end of 2007. According to a 2010 report by the International Monetary Fund, "[GSEs] were pivotal in developing key markets for securitized credit and hedging instruments, but their implicit guarantee and social policy mandates [exacerbated] a softening in credit discipline and a buildup of systemic risk" (IMF 2010, 10).

Wallison (2011) cites the expansion of the GSEs' affordable housing goals in the late 1990s and early 2000s as one factor that led the GSEs to lower their lending standards. He also maintains that though it was difficult to estimate year-by-year GSE purchases of subprime and Alt-A loans, they made up 37 percent of loans held or securitized by the GSEs as of June 2008.[4] However, other data and research suggest that private MBSs had a large role in financing the increase in subprime and Alt-A lending starting in 2004 (Belsky and Richardson 2010). Originations of subprime and Alt-A mortgages during their peak years of 2004–6 totaled $2.7 trillion. In those same years, issuance of private MBSs backed by subprime and Alt-A loans totaled $2.1 trillion, accounting for 78 percent of originations in dollar terms (figure 6-5).

The sources of risk introduced through private MBS mortgage conduits were similar to the sources of risk for the GSEs. They operated with high rates of leverage, which in this case was the small share of the mortgage pools that were backed by the subordinate tranches that were in a first-loss position. In addition, their portfolios were characterized by imperfect information that created moral hazard, or the incentive to take on risk at the expense of their investors. This imperfect information was in part the product of the overoptimistic credit ratings that were applied to private MBSs by credit-rating agencies. For example, of all the private MBSs rated by Moody's in 2006 as investment grade (Baa or higher), 76 percent would ultimately be downgraded to junk status. The MBS downgrades by Standard and Poor's (S&P) and Fitch were of similar magnitude (FCIC 2011).

Another factor that amplified the risks were the many structured investment vehicles (SIVs) that held private MBSs and funded them with short-term, wholesale, market-based instruments. Gary Gorton (2007) is generally credited

---

[4] Wallison (2011) cites work by Pinto (2010) that estimates the GSEs' total exposure to subprime and Alt-A loans.

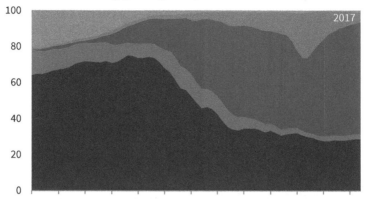

Figure 6-5. Share of U.S. Home Mortgage Debt Held by Financial Sectors, 1955–2017

■ Insurance companies, pensions etc.   ■ Private ABS and finance companies

■ GSEs and GSE pools   ■ Other

■ Depository institutions

Share of U.S. home mortgage debt (percent)

Sources: Federal Reserve Bank of Saint Louis; CEA calculations.
Note: GSEs = government-sponsored enterprises. ABS = asset-backed security.

with identifying the role of the SIVs in financing subprime mortgages, their funding strategies, and how they exacerbated the financial crisis. Brunnermeier and others (2009) also examined the relationship between asset funding and systemic risk, with a focus on how financial regulations have historically failed to distinguish between short-term and long-term funding sources.

With this portfolio structure, the SIVs performed the functions of maturity transformation and credit enhancement that are traditionally carried out by banks. As with banks, this transformation created value and returns, but also proved to be subject to runs during a period of financial distress. During the precrisis years, the SIVs had substantial exposures (about 25 percent) to private MBSs, and an even larger exposure (more than 40 percent) to other financial institutions (FCIC 2011). They held stable valuations and were able to obtain funding through the financial markets as long as home prices continued to rise. These stable valuations were suddenly cast into doubt in the summer of 2007, when home prices began to fall and the subprime and nontraditional mortgages that backed the private MBSs began to default in large numbers. It was then that investors in the repurchase agreements (repos) and commercial paper that funded SIVs became much more reluctant to continue doing so. They required vastly higher "haircuts" on their collateral, or simply stopped investing in SIVs altogether. When investors' confidence collapsed, the large banks and investment companies that had created the SIVs faced significant liquidity demands themselves, having provided credit and liquidity lines to the SIVs. Though they were not legally obligated to do so, these sponsors frequently stood behind the SIVs they had sponsored, because they were also heavily dependent on repo financing (figure 6-6).

The rise of off-balance-sheet financing of subprime and nontraditional mortgages was a leap into the dark for financial markets. Trillions of dollars in credit were indirectly provided to U.S. homebuyers by investors from around the world. When home prices were rising, and when mortgage defaults were low, this private nonbank financing arrangement was thought by many to distribute U.S. mortgage risk in an optimal way. However, when home prices began to decline, it quickly became clear that the private MBSs that were financing subprime and nontraditional mortgage loans were much riskier than anticipated. Moreover, because private MBSs had come to play a substantial role as collateral for short-term borrowing, their downgrades created a major disruption in the overnight lending market. The "run on repo" that resulted was reminiscent of the destructive bank runs that had been associated with previous systemic crises in the United States and around the world.

An Ineffective and Uncoordinated Regulatory Response

Regulatory arbitrage that moved risky mortgage lending away from regulated depository institutions and toward private and governments-sponsored conduits played a role in undermining market discipline. But financial regulators also failed to detect and respond to emerging risks in the mortgage markets.

At the end of 2007, regulated depository institutions still held $3.1 trillion in mortgage loans. Regulatory authority over mortgage lending by banks and thrifts was divided between four Federal regulators and 50 State regulators. This divided authority tended to undermine these regulators' ability to prevent or respond to the emerging crisis. For example, State measures intended to reduce predatory mortgage lending during the precrisis years were overridden by the Office of Thrift Supervision and the Office of the Comptroller of the Currency (OCC), which successfully claimed that their authority preempted that of the State regulators.

Even before Dodd-Frank imposed a flurry of new postcrisis regulations, regulators already had a number of authorities that could have addressed emerging risks in mortgage lending before the crisis. The 1968 Truth in Lending Act gave the Federal Reserve the authority to establish rules governing mortgage lending that would apply to any type of lender. Although the Fed did implement this authority in its 1969 Regulation Z, the rule's enforcement was left to a multiplicity of Federal and State regulators (FCIC 2011). The 1994 Home Ownership and Equity Protection Act gave the Federal Reserve additional powers to regulate abusive and predatory lending practices that especially affected low-income borrowers. This was perhaps the farthest-reaching Federal authority to address emerging risks in mortgage lending. However, this power was

Figure 6-6. Gross Repurchase Agreement Funding to Banks and Broker-Dealers, 1990–2010

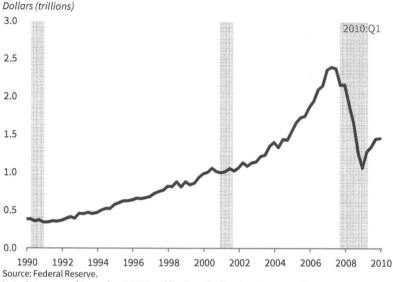

Dollars (trillions)

Source: Federal Reserve.
Note: Data are as of December 9, 2010, publication. Shading denotes a recession.

not exercised until 2008, when the housing crisis was already well under way (Lincoln 2008).

Regulatory capital standards that were in place before the crisis proved to be insufficient to preserve the financial viability of a number of large, complex banks during the crisis. Moreover, the risk-weighting approach of these capital standards actually created incentives to take on more risk. The Basel I standards put in place in 1992 turned out to promote bank holdings of MBSs as opposed to holding whole mortgage loans. Under these standards, pass-through MBSs issued by the GSEs were given a low 20 percent risk weight. A 2001 amendment tied these risk weightings in part to agency credit ratings, which also generally resulted in a low risk weight for GSE obligations. These low risk weights permitted the holders of GSE bonds to hold less capital than if they had actually held the underlying mortgage loans, which had risk weights of 50 to 100 percent. Moreover, the GSEs' 20 percent MBS risk weight also applied to private MBSs after 2001, provided that they received high ratings from the credit-rating agencies. As discussed above, the structured approach to funding private MBSs generally enabled their senior tranches to receive a AAA rating, qualifying them for the 20 percent risk weight.

Wallison (2011) estimates that this disparity in risk weighting resulted in a reduction in risk-based capital requirements from 4 percent for banks holding whole mortgages to just 1.6 percent for banks holding MBSs. Although holding securities as opposed to loans could enhance the liquidity of bank portfolios, their liquidity ultimately depends on the quality of these securities. As discussed above, it was the sudden illiquidity of private MBSs and the externalities this introduced in the financial markets that exacerbated the financial crisis.

Like the vast majority of their private sector counterparts, most regulatory economists also did not realize the risks that were building in housing markets and mortgage finance until it was too late. One factor may have been the sudden change in mortgage lending practices that occurred in 2004. Introducing large volumes of high-risk mortgages accelerated the rate of increase in home prices, making the housing market an apparent source of strength in the economy. But to the extent that the price increases were the product of risky mortgage lending, they could not be sustained. When home prices leveled off, and then began to fall in 2006, defaults and foreclosures rose sharply. The resulting instability in the housing and mortgage markets would eventually snowball into what became a systemic financial crisis.

The Consequences of the Financial Crisis

The financial crisis of 2008 was an explosion of the risks that had been building in mortgage finance and the financial system as a whole. Rescues of large banks and nonbank financial companies during previous crises had helped to create the perception that the largest banking organizations would be deemed "Too Big to Fail," and that their investors would be protected from loss in a crisis. These expectations were shattered on September 15, 2008, when Lehman Brothers, a $639 billion investment bank, did not receive such assistance and was forced to declare Chapter 11 bankruptcy. Lehman Brothers' bankruptcy meant that many of its counterparties around the world would not be made whole, and would find their claims tied up for years, leading to large losses.

Fannie Mae and Freddie Mac were placed in a government conservatorship on September 6, 2008. In combination, Freddie and Fannie held or guaranteed $5.2 trillion in mortgage debt, or about 45 percent of U.S. households' total mortgage obligations. The GSEs continue to operate in conservatorship more than 10 years after the crisis.

At the height of the crisis, three extraordinary programs of government support were implemented to restore liquidity to financial markets, solidify the capital base and the banking system's funding, and enable financial institutions and markets to make credit available to finance an economic recovery. First, the Federal Reserve expanded greatly on its traditional lender-of-last-resort function by introducing a series of special liquidity facilities that made loans available for longer terms, to a wider range of institutions, and on a wider range of collateral than it had ever done through the discount window. Second, Congress initially authorized the sum of $700 billion for the Troubled Assets Relief Program—known as TARP—to assist financial institutions in dealing with the large volumes of impaired assets on their balance sheets. And third, in

Figure 6-7. National and Long-Term Unemployment Rate, 2000–2018

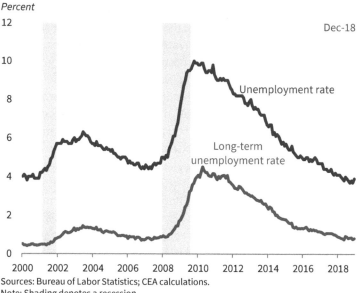

Percent

Sources: Bureau of Labor Statistics; CEA calculations.
Note: Shading denotes a recession.

October 2008 the FDIC instituted its Temporary Liquidity Guarantee Program to help stabilize the banking industry's funding base.

These three assistance programs represented an unprecedented expansion of government support for the banking system. In total, the financial commitments behind these programs has been estimated at about $14 trillion, although the programs' net cost was a small fraction of this amount. The programs can be described as successful in addressing the immediate dangers posed by the crisis. But over the longer term, they set new precedents for government support that undermine market discipline in banking. Moreover, they violate the principle that financial institutions themselves—and not taxpayers—should be responsible for their losses.

The shockwaves of the 2008 financial crisis caused enormous harm to real economic activity. From peak to trough, real GDP fell by more than 4 percent, making this the deepest U.S. recession since the 1930s. In the six months after September 2008, the industrial production index for durable materials fell by 21 percent—its largest decline in more than 50 years. The monthly unemployment rate peaked near 10 percent in October 2009, the highest rate since June 1983. Around the time of the crisis, the United States experienced the longest stretch of unemployment above 8 percent, over three years, since the Great Depression. From peak to trough, nearly 8.7 million nonfarm workers lost their jobs (figure 6-7).

The net economic effects of the crisis have generally been expressed as the shortfall between potential U.S. GDP and actual GDP in the wake of the crisis. Studies that have projected the long-term effect of the crisis on GDP generally arrive at estimates of forgone economic activity that exceed $10 trillion (GAO 2013; Luttrell, Atkinson, and Rosenblum 2013). The enormous scale of these effects have become an important consideration in evaluating the impact of the Dodd-Frank Act, which was passed as a response to the crisis.

The Consequences of the Dodd-Frank Act

After the 2008 financial crisis, there was a push to reform the regulation of the U.S. financial system. The large economic dislocations resulting from the crisis were still obvious, as were the potential benefits of policies that could reduce the likelihood and cost of a future systemic crisis. However, in the rush to implement reforms, the costs and benefits of various regulatory reforms were not properly analyzed and weighed. In 2009, the Financial Crisis Inquiry Commission (FCIC) was created to examine the causes of the crisis. Its final report was released in January 2011—six months *after* sweeping reforms were made under the Dodd-Frank Act. The failure to construct an appropriate framework for considering costs and benefits *before* passing legislation led to reforms that were often overreaching, misguided, and inefficient. This failure to analyze—fully and properly—the likely effects of new regulatory policies made the costs of the crisis greater than they needed to be. Researchers have found evidence of a number of regulatory problems that have emerged in the postcrisis period, including regulatory arbitrage, rising compliance costs, and financial market illiquidity.[5]

Addressing Systemic Risk

The Dodd-Frank Act aimed to address key factors that had undermined market discipline and helped trigger the systemic crisis. It created new processes in an attempt to identify and respond to emerging threats to financial stability. Title I of the act created the Financial Stability Oversight Council, chaired by the Secretary of the Treasury and including as members the heads of eight financial regulatory agencies, an independent insurance expert, and five nonvoting members. The council was given detailed criteria for determining whether a company will be subject to Federal Reserve supervision and the application of enhanced prudential standards. Separately, Dodd-Frank also imposed enhanced prudential standards on all bank holding companies with assets of $50 billion or more.

Title I of Dodd-Frank also required every banking company with at least $50 billion in assets and every designated nonbank financial company to hold

---

[5] See Choi, Holcomb, and Morgan (2018); Peirce, Robinson, and Stratmann (2014); and Roberts, Sarkar, and Shachar (2018).

more capital and liquidity to ensure their safety and soundness, and to file an annual resolution plan that could be used as a guide for their rapid and orderly resolution through bankruptcy (figures 6-8 and 6-9).

Title II of Dodd-Frank established an orderly liquidation process to quickly and efficiently liquidate or otherwise resolve a large, complex financial institution that is close to failing. It established a two-part test, under which the Secretary of the Treasury establishes that the institution is in default or is in danger of default, and then evaluates the systemic risk that would be involved with such a default. Title II requires that bankruptcy first be considered as a means to resolve the failed institution. If bankruptcy is deemed unable to bring about an orderly resolution, Title II provides the FDIC with receivership powers that apply to bank holding companies or nonbank financial companies. It establishes a fixed order of claims that helps to ensure that the executives, directors, and shareholders of the institution stand last in line to receive payment.

The overarching goal of the Dodd-Frank reforms—which sought to end Too Big to Fail, strengthen capital and liquidity requirements, and restore market discipline—was to prevent a future bailout by U.S. taxpayers. However, the generally one-size-fits-all approach that Dodd-Frank took in pursuing these goals turned out to be unnecessarily costly and, in some cases, counterproductive. Moreover, an overreliance on regulatory discipline as opposed to market discipline has turned out to rely too much on the judgment of bank regulators, which are not infallible (Viscusi and Gayer 2016).

Dodd-Frank's Ill-Considered Approach

The economist Paul Romer once said that a crisis is a terrible thing to waste, and the Obama Administration paraphrased him in the wake of the 2008 financial crisis, placing government deeply into the markets, especially the financial ones. The complex series of events that led to the crisis called for careful study before reforms were rushed out the door. Legislation passed in May 2009 created the FCIC to examine the causes of the crisis. The FCIC's report and conclusions, released in January 2011, did not receive bipartisan support, but they did provide first-hand accounts of a wide range of bankers, regulators, and analysts that could have been considered as reforms were being planned.

Unfortunately, Congress passed, and President Obama signed, the Dodd-Frank Act even before the FCIC released its report. Congress rushed out this 849-page piece of legislation, which mandated 390 new rules and regulations. Dodd-Frank would stand out from previous financial legislation in the degree to which it mandates how American businesses can and cannot conduct the financial transactions that are vital to both their well-being and that of the U.S. economy.

Even in the dense world of Federal regulation, Dodd-Frank stands out in its size, complexity, and redundancy. It addressed regulatory policy at a

Figure 6-8. Tier 1 Capital Ratios of U.S. G-SIBs, 2001–18

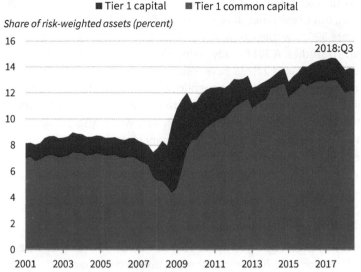

■ Tier 1 capital   ■ Tier 1 common capital

Share of risk-weighted assets (percent)

Source: Federal Reserve Bank of New York.
Note: U.S. G-SIBs = global systemically important banks; these are banks with assets of more than $500 billion.

Figure 6-9. Liquid Assets of U.S. G-SIBs, 2000–18

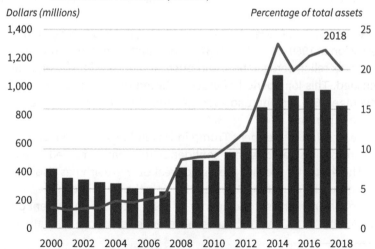

▬ Cash and U.S. Treasuries as a percentage of total assets (right axis)
━ Cash and U.S. Treasuries (left axis)

Dollars (millions)   *Percentage of total assets*

Sources: Federal Deposit Insurance Corporation; CEA calculations.
Note: U.S. G-SIBs = global systemically important banks; these banks have assets of more than $500 billion.

number of agencies; created a new regulatory body, the Consumer Financial Protection Bureau (CFPB); and merged another agency, the Office of Thrift Supervision, out of existence. It required the Federal financial regulatory agencies to create 390 new rules, of which 280 have been finalized, and to complete more than 70 studies. A 2017 study, using data from RegData 3.0, showed that Dodd-Frank had placed 27,278 new restrictions on the U.S. financial industry and the economy as a whole (McLaughlin, Francis, and Sherouse 2017).[6]

The Trump Administration has made it a priority to address the regulatory overreach created by the Dodd-Frank Act, while also striving to ensure the safety and soundness of the Nation's financial system. The discussion here addresses the consequences of some of Dodd-Frank's most important regulatory reforms and how they have in many cases failed to resolve the issues that led to the financial crisis.

Dodd-Frank's Consequences

Although it has been eight and a half years since Dodd-Frank was signed into law, it still has not been fully implemented, due in large part to its complexity. However, the initial results of this partisan legislation are not encouraging.

Until a recent uptick in growth, the postcrisis economic recovery has been atypically weak. The economic expansion began in July 2009, and at the end of 2018 it had concluded its 114th month, making it the second-longest expansion in U.S. history. Until 2017, it was also among the most tepid expansions on record. Real economic growth averaged 2.2 percent between the middle of 2009 (the start of the expansion) and the end of 2016. This marked the slowest growth in any expansion since the National Income and Product Accounts were introduced in 1947.

Before 2007, the severest downturn during this era had been the double-dip recession of 1980–81 and 1981–82. A combination of a pro-growth agenda—including tax relief, deregulation, and price stability—led the Reagan Recovery that ensued. This long period of growth started off with two years of growth that averaged 6.7 percent, and average annual growth of 4.3 percent during the entire expansion.

The election of President Trump in November 2016 produced an immediate increase in small business confidence that has remained in place ever since.[7] The 4-quarter moving average of real GDP growth has risen for 9 consecutive quarters, exceeding 3 percent for only the fifth time in the 37 quarters of the expansion. In the second quarter of 2018, after the enactment of the Tax Cuts and Jobs Act (TCJA), real economic growth rose to an annualized rate of

---

[6]RegData 3.0 measures the number of regulatory restrictions in a textual analysis that identifies words and phrases that have been added to the *Federal Register* that are generally associated with a required or prohibited activity.

[7] Further discussion of the effect of the 2016 election on business confidence and the effect of the 2017 Tax Cuts and Jobs Act on economic activity can be found in chapter 1 of this *Report*.

more than 4 percent for the first time in four years. The recovery of business confidence, hiring, and investment spending since 2016 suggests that we will see higher potential growth in the years ahead.

The slow pace of growth in the first eight years of the expansion was, at least in part, attributable to the persistent effects of the severe 2007–9 recession. But the regulatory requirements imposed during this period, including those mandated by the 2010 Dodd-Frank Act, were also responsible for holding back the pace of the economic recovery.[8] A 2015 study projected that Dodd-Frank's requirements and the compliance costs it continues to introduce will result in a reduction of about $895 billion in GDP between 2016 and 2025 (Holtz-Eakin 2015).

Although the financial crisis had lingering effects throughout the economy long after the recession officially ended, additional public policy choices also played a role in slower growth than would have typically been expected after such a deep recession. Some of these policies reduced labor force participation, labor productivity, and capital investment, and thus were factors in the subpar macro performance through 2016 (figure 6-10).

Dodd-Frank was especially a factor in discouraging small business lending and mortgage lending, and in promoting consolidation among small and midsized banks (Peirce, Robinson, and Stratmann 2014). The importance of small businesses to the U.S. economy goes well beyond the roughly two-thirds of new jobs they typically create. Small businesses have traditionally been a source of strength for their communities and a source of innovation where new and different ideas can be pursued. They rely heavily for funding on community banks, which have a local focus that helps them meet the credit needs of small businesses.

Small businesses were hit especially hard by the recession, and they recovered slowly during the early years of the expansion. Since mid-2010, small loans to farms and businesses held by FDIC-insured institutions have declined by 2 percent, while total farm and business loans have increased by more than 50 percent. The monthly *Small Business Economic Trends* report, which is published by the National Federation of Independent Business, recorded some of its lowest annual values on record for small-business optimism during the early stages of the recovery. The federation's optimism index would rise above its long-term average only once over 116 months, ending in November 2016. Small business optimism has remained above the historical average in every month since then.

Mortgage lending has also been slow to recover since the crisis. The annual volume of purchase mortgage originations in 2017 remained below that of the peak years 2003–6. The level of mortgage debt outstanding in the third quarter of 2018 also remained lower that of the peak level reached in 2008.

---

[8] Chapter 2 of this *Report* includes an extensive discussion of the effects of regulation on economic activity.

Figure 6-10. Average Economic Growth By Expansion Period, 1983–2018

Compound annual growth rate

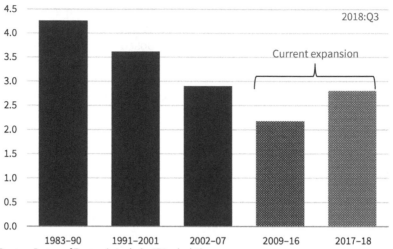

Sources: Bureau of Economic Analysis; CEA calculations.
Note: Change in real GDP is calculated from the peak to trough of expansion periods.

Moreover, mortgage finance has become increasingly dominated by the GSEs—including Fannie Mae, Freddie Mac, and Ginnie Mae—in spite of their role in the crisis. These entities have accounted for funding 81 percent of the net increase in mortgage lending over the past two years. The increasing dominance of the GSEs can be attributed in no small part to the higher requirements placed on portfolio mortgage lending and private mortgage securitization. As mandated by Dodd-Frank, the 2014 interagency Risk Retention Rule requires private issuers of MBSs to retain at least 5 percent of the credit risk in the mortgage pool, unless the loan meets the definition of a Qualified Residential Mortgage that makes it a low-risk loan. Fannie Mae and Freddie Mac are not subject to this rule while operating in conservatorship or receivership with capital support from the Federal government.

Another area of concern about Dodd-Frank is the overall increase in compliance cost it imposes, particularly on small and midsized banks. The hundreds of regulations required under Dodd-Frank, and the thousands of pages of detailed requirements included with each regulation, have raised concerns about what has come to be called "regulatory burden" (Hoskins and Labonte 2015). This burden refers not only to the marginal cost imposed by new rules but also to the cumulative increase in the number and scope of

Box 6-2. Measuring the Regulatory Burden on the Financial Sector

Banking is one of the most regulated U.S. industries. McLaughlin and Sherouse (2016) ranked U.S. industries in terms of the regulatory restrictions they face. They found that though the median industry faced 1,130 regulatory restrictions, depository and nondepository credit intermediation both faced over 16,000 restrictions. The only industries facing more restrictions were petroleum and coal production, electric power generation, and motor vehicle manufacturing.

As with total noninterest expenses, there are economies of scale in regulatory compliance. For example, Dahl and others (2018) found that mean total compliance costs were about 10 percent of total noninterest expenses in 2017 for banks with less than $100 million in assets, compared with 5 percent for banks with assets between $1 billion and $10 billion.

Regulation may also impose a wide range of indirect costs on banks and their customers that exceed the paperwork costs associated with compliance. These include the opportunity costs of loans not made and products not offered, along with effects on deposit rates offered and loan rates charged by regulated banks. Such costs not only hurt the bottom line of the bank but can also reduce the welfare of bank customers and economic activity generally.

Through the fourth quarter of 2018, community banks held just 16 percent of the total loans of FDIC-insured institutions, but they held 42 percent of the industry's small loans to farms and businesses. Recent research finds that by raising fixed regulatory compliance costs, the Dodd-Frank Act disproportionately raised the average cost of loan origination by small banks and reduced their share of small commercial and industrial loans (Bordo and Duca 2018). They further observe a relative tightening of bank credit standards on commercial and industrial loans to small versus large firms in response to Dodd-Frank.

regulations imposed on banks over time.[9] They consist of both the overhead costs of complying with a regulation and the opportunity costs of restrictions on bank activities. These costs raise concerns about their effect on both bank performance and the cost and availability of credit (see box 6-2).

---

[9] In the FDIC's 2012 "Community Banking Study," community bankers reported that "no one regulation or practice had a significant effect on their institution." Instead, they cited "the cumulative effects of all the regulatory requirements that have built up over time." They also explained that the increases in the regulatory cost over the previous five years could be attributed to the time spent by both regulatory specialists and employees that typically carry out other responsibilities (FDIC 2012, appendix B).

A More Measured Approach to Financial Regulation

Since its first days in office, the Trump Administration has been working to correct the regulatory overreach introduced by the Dodd-Frank Act and to restore the ability of the financial system to support growth in the economy and our Nation's standard of living.

Core Principles for Regulating the U.S. Financial System

Seven Core Principles for financial regulation were outlined in Executive Order 13772, issued in February 2017. These principles reflect a commitment to taking measures that will:

1. Empower Americans to make independent financial decisions and informed choices in the marketplace, save for retirement, and build individual wealth.
2. Prevent taxpayer-funded bailouts.
3. Foster economic growth and vibrant financial markets through more rigorous regulatory impact analysis that addresses systemic risk and market failures, such as moral hazard and information asymmetry.
4. Enable American companies to be competitive with foreign firms in domestic and foreign markets.
5. Advance American interests in international financial regulatory negotiations and meetings.
6. Make regulation efficient, effective, and appropriately tailored.
7. Restore public accountability within Federal financial regulatory agencies and rationalize the Federal financial regulatory framework.

These Core Principles are designed to promote the ability of financial institutions to do their job of providing credit and other financial services to the U.S. economy. Under Dodd-Frank, banks have been regulated like public utilities, where government oversight boards dictate the manner in which business should be conducted. The Administration's approach is consistent with a greater reliance on market discipline and somewhat less reliance on regulatory discipline. The leaders of financial regulatory agencies that have been appointed by the Administration understand and endorse this concept. And this will make it possible for them to pursue a more coordinated and measured approach to reform that will not undermine financial stability but will make regulation simpler and less costly to implement.

Recommendations for Meeting the Core Principles

During the past two years, the U.S. Department of the Treasury has issued four reports that made detailed recommendations consistent with the Administration's Core Principles. These four reports have focused, in order, on (1) banks and credit unions; (2) capital markets; (3) asset management and insurance; and (4) nonbank financials, financial technology (known as fintech), and innovation.

With regard to depository institutions, the Treasury has recommended a series of changes designed to simplify regulations and reduce their implementation costs, while maintaining high standards of safety and soundness and ensuring the accountability of the financial system to the American public. These recommendations are summarized and discussed in the next paragraphs. A number of these recommendations were implemented in the Economic Growth, Regulatory Relief, and Consumer Protection Act of 2018, which is generally referred to as S.2155. These cases are noted in the next paragraphs, and the overall effects of S.2155 are summarized later in the chapter.[10]

Improving regulatory efficiency and effectiveness. To address the U.S. regulatory structure, consideration should be given to changes in the regulatory structure that reduce fragmentation, overlap, and duplication among Federal financial regulators. This could include consolidating regulators with similar missions, as well as more clearly defining regulatory mandates. At a minimum, steps should be taken to increase the coordination of supervision and examination activities.

The experience of the financial crisis points to the need for improved coordination among the financial regulators. While risks were rapidly building in subprime and Alt-A lending, the need to coordinate across several regulatory agencies made it more difficult to respond in a timely way. Interagency guidance issued in 2006 and 2007 on commercial real estate lending and mortgage lending did little to discourage the riskiest nonbank lenders, but it did lead to industry concerns that regulators were placing strict caps on making loans in those categories.

To improve the regulatory engagement model, sound governance of financial institutions, where policies are developed and their implementation is monitored, is essential. Hopt (2013) emphasizes the need to clearly separate the management and control functions, and to assign committees to carry out specific governance responsibilities. The failure of board governance and oversight of their banking organizations was found to be a major impediment to risk management and a factor exacerbating the financial crisis. A successful governance model requires both highly qualified board members and a commitment to procedures that promote discipline and accountability across the organization.

The approach currently taken by regulators may not be promoting effective governance. Prescriptive regulations may tend to blur the division of responsibilities between the board and management and impose a

---

[10] These recommendations are paraphrased in the next subsections from the U.S. Department of the Treasury's report *A Financial System That Creates Economic Opportunities: Banks and Credit Unions* (U.S. Department of the Treasury 2017).

one-size-fits-all approach that unnecessarily restricts banking activities and the services they provide to their customers. This is particularly problematic for midsized and community financial institutions, which have less formal governance structures. It would be helpful to clearly define the board's role and responsibilities for regulatory oversight and governance, and to do so more consistently across regulatory jurisdictions. More transparency and consistency across the agencies could help to assure all regulated banks that they are being treated fairly.

Encouraging more constructive engagement between bank regulators, board members, and managers would help to ensure that the bank itself can more effectively meet the needs of its customers while managing the risks it faces. This requires that the board be held to the highest standards when implementing regulatory compliance procedures, and that the board—not the regulator—hold management to the same standards. A step forward in improving the governance of large banks was the Federal Reserve's August 2017 proposal, now out for comment, to create a governance-rating system for banks with assets greater than $50 billion.

It is also important to enhance the use of regulatory cost-benefit analysis. As concerns about regulatory burden have increased in the postcrisis period, cost-benefit analysis has taken on a more prominent role in financial regulation. There are requirements for cost-benefit analysis in rulemaking that apply to most Federal agencies. These requirements have been outlined in Executive Order 12866 (1993), and in the subsequent Office of Management and Budget (OMB) "Circular A-4" (2003). These directives call for an analysis of proposed rules that addresses (1) the policy objectives of the proposed rule; (2) the rule's expected effects, including costs and benefits for the parties directly involved as well as externalities that are created for other stakeholders; and (3) an analysis of regulatory alternatives.

The independent financial regulatory agencies have long been exempt from oversight by OMB in most aspects of regulatory analysis. At the same time, these agencies have increasingly adopted a cost-benefit approach to rulemaking, and have devoted more resources to regulatory analysis in recent years. This analysis has been largely based on the main requirements outlined by OMB's directives.

Financial regulators are also subject to a number of legislative mandates that serve to make the regulatory process more transparent and better informed. For example, the Administrative Procedure Act established general requirements for a notice-and-comment process that keeps the industry and the public informed about proposed rules and solicits their comments, which often provides valuable information that can inform the rulemaking process. The Regulatory Flexibility Act—known as RegFlex—requires agencies to consider the impact of regulations on small entities. If a rulemaking is expected to have a "significant economic impact on a substantial number of small entities," the agency is required to assess that impact.[11]

There is an active debate as to whether cost-benefit analysis can be a reliable guide to regulatory policy in banking and finance. Some question whether it is possible to reliably project, much less quantify, the costs and the benefits of bank regulations (Coates 2015). Given the discussion above of imperfect information and market failures in banking, it is clear that important outcomes in banking and finance depend heavily on intangible factors such as public confidence and market liquidity. Requiring strict quantification of costs and benefits in financial regulation is viewed by some as being both unrealistic and an excessive restriction on the ability of independent regulators to apply their judgment in addressing emerging risks. Others, including Sunstein (2015), contend that a useful cost-benefit analysis can still be performed, even when there are serious gaps in the available information on costs and benefits.

These two schools of thought might not be as far apart as they initially seem. The experience of the financial crisis, and the regulatory burdens that were imposed after the crisis, both point to rather obvious conclusions about the relative costs and benefits of regulations that apply to various types of institutions.

One conclusion is that regulation is relatively more burdensome for small and midsized banks than for large banks. Research has repeatedly shown that regulatory compliance costs are subject to economies of scale, as are other types of nonregulatory overhead expenses. Regulation also imposes external costs on the customers of small and midsized banks, which disproportionally include small businesses. The value of small businesses in creating new jobs and new businesses is widely recognized, and has been a motivating force behind calls for applying cost-benefit analysis to bank regulations.

Another fairly obvious conclusion from the financial crisis is that the benefits of safety and soundness regulations are exponentially higher when applied to systemically important institutions than when they are applied to small and midsized institutions. As the experience of the crisis clearly showed, the negative externalities associated with the failures of systemically important institutions included severe distress in global financial markets and enormous losses in U.S. economic activity. The magnitude and the incidence of these negative externalities largely determine the benefits of regulations that reduce the probability of failure (box 6-3).

The framework for cost-benefit analysis by financial regulators could be improved. They should be encouraged to adopt uniform and consistent methods to analyze costs and benefits, and to ensure that their cost-benefit analyses exhibit as much analytical rigor as possible. The standards of transparency and public accountability will be served by conducting rigorous cost-benefit

---

[11] This requirement was established under the Regulatory Flexibility Act, Public Law 96-354, 94 Stat. 1164 (5 U.S.C. § 601).

analyses and making better use of notices of proposed rulemakings to solicit public comment that is helpful in evaluating a rule's possible effects. This type of public analysis will be particularly helpful for proposed regulations that are "economically significant," as defined in Executive Order 12866.

Aligning the financial system to support the U.S. economy. With the goal of ensuring access to credit, the 2017 Treasury report on banks and credit unions identified a series of regulatory factors that may be unnecessarily limiting access to credit for consumers and businesses (U.S. Department of the Treasury 2017). Addressing these constraints on credit availability will be necessary to enable the U.S. economy to operate at its full potential. Regulatory constraints also should not be allowed to unduly restrict banks' ability to meet their customers' needs in a rapidly changing financial marketplace. The U.S. has been—and should continue to be—a global leader in introducing innovative new financial products. The regulatory environment should support this innovation while ensuring that it does not compromise the financial system's stability or fail to protect the interests of consumers.

Among the most important elements in achieving this balance are the requirements for capital and liquidity. Adequate capitalization of bank balance sheets helps to ensure that banks face market discipline that reduces their incentives to take excessive risks. At the same time, higher capital standards can limit the ability of banks to add new loans to their balance sheets. Achieving this balance is important to promoting stability while ensuring that the availability of credit is not impaired.

With regard to engaging and leading the global marketplace, the competitiveness of American financial institutions in global markets is another area that was addressed in the 2017 Treasury report. It recommended active participation by U.S. regulators in global forums, and emphasized the need for coordination among U.S. regulatory agencies. Banking is very much a global marketplace. Not only do the largest U.S. banks have interests abroad, but foreign banks have continued to play a larger role in U.S. financial markets. Coordination between regulatory jurisdictions around the world has improved since the financial crisis. On net, these trends should be seen as positive developments over the long term. The U.S. regulatory agencies should engage their counterparts overseas in ways that serve the interests of U.S. financial institutions, the U.S. economy, and the American people.

The Treasury made several recommendations addressing bank capital standards. More study is needed of the somewhat complex capital and liquidity requirements that have been placed on U.S. global systemically important banks (G-SIBs). If not properly calibrated, these regulations could place U.S. banks at a competitive disadvantage without contributing to financial stability and safe and sound banking. Additional research should explore several aspects of G-SIB regulation, including "the U.S. G-SIB surcharge, the mandatory minimum debt ratio included in the Federal Reserve's total loss

Box 6-3. Evaluating the Costs and Benefits of Bank Regulations

An example of the trade-off between benefits and costs as applied to large banks can be seen in the FDIC's 2016 final Rule on Recordkeeping for Timely Deposit Insurance Determination. This rule addresses a particular problem that the FDIC has faced in closing failed institutions in a timely and efficient manner due to the difficulty in identifying related deposit accounts from large bank systems. The problem arises in part from complex coverage rules spelled out in statutes, along with the sometimes disconnected information systems that large banks have accumulated over the years through acquisitions. The rule requires banking organizations with more than 2 million deposit accounts to improve their data systems to facilitate the calculation of the deposit insurance coverage for each account.

When the final rule was adopted, the FDIC estimated that it would apply to apply to 38 institutions, each with 2 million or more deposit accounts. Taken together, these institutions hold more than $10 trillion in total assets and manage over 400 million deposit accounts. Some, but not all, of these institutions could be considered systemically important. But the FDIC's experience in resolving institutions with so many accounts shows that it is doubtful that they could be promptly resolved unless their data systems met the standards of the rule. The result could be a significant delay in the full availability of funds to bank depositors, which threatens to reduce the confidence of other large institutions that their funds would be promptly available in a time of distress.

The benefit of the rule is measured in terms of the assurance that depositors would have prompt access to their funds as well as the confidence of depositors in other large institutions. The accuracy of any estimate of the dollar value of these benefits is doubtful at best. However, as the experience of the recent financial crisis has shown, maintaining confidence in the financial system offers potentially large benefits to the public.

The costs of complying with the rule are not negligible. Based on a consultant's estimate that is documented in the rule's preamble, the initial and ongoing costs of implementation will likely be about $386 million. This figure represents 0.25 percent of the pretax income of these banks in 2015. Another way to place these costs in context is that they represent 93 cents for every one of the 416 million accounts these institutions manage. Equally important are the potential opportunity costs that may be imposed on banks that are subject to the rule. For example, banks may shy away from the 2 million account threshold to avoid incurring the cost of implementing this rule. Though these opportunity costs are more difficult to quantify than compliance costs, these negative external effects should be taken into account when considering the potential effects of such a rule.

The decision as to whether the rule's benefits outweighed its costs was made on the basis of this information and the judgment of the FDIC's Board of Directors. Whether it is worth 25 basis points of pretax earnings for one year, and the opportunity costs of forgone business opportunities, to enhance the stability of the financial system is ultimately a judgment call. What is important is that this judgment be informed with good information where available, and not clouded by estimates whose accuracy may be vastly overstated.

absorbing capacity . . . and minimum debt rule, and the calibration of the [enhanced supplementary leverage ratio]" applied to each banking company (U.S. Department of the Treasury 2017, 16).

The Treasury report continued to be supportive of the ongoing Basel Committee process. The goals of establishing international bank capital standards are to strengthen the capital standards that apply to G-SIBs in general, and level the competitive playing field by establishing a floor for global risk-based capital standards. The complexity of capital rules for G-SIBs remains a challenge in achieving these goals.

U.S. bank regulators will need to carefully consider the implications of any changes in the Basel III standardized approach to account for credit risk. It is important to evaluate both the possible impact on systemic risk and the effect on credit availability. Making these evaluations public as capital rules are introduced will be helpful to inform this debate as to the proper balance inherent in capital regulation.

Reducing the regulatory burden and unnecessary complexity through "tailoring." Allowing community banks and credit unions to thrive is a key aspect of the 2017 Treasury report's recommendations. Previous discussions of economies of scale in regulatory compliance and the widespread diseconomies associated with the potential failure of a systemically important institution inescapably lead to the conclusion that most community banks and credit unions are overregulated. These institutions have a role in the U.S. economy that is more important, in relative terms, than the share of industry assets they hold. For example, in 2014 there were 646 U.S. counties in which the only banking office was one operated by a community bank (Breitenstein and McGee 2015). Yet these smaller institutions pose virtually no systemic risk that would justify burdensome regulation. Moreover, they are diverse in terms of their business models and customer bases, and can benefit from less rigid regulatory requirements. These considerations have led to calls for "tailoring" regulatory requirements in banking to better meet the needs and challenges that pertain to individual institutions.

A 2017 report by the Congressional Research Service (Perkins 2017) defines tailoring as a departure from current threshold-based (typically asset-based) standards for regulation, to new standards that would (1) raise or lower the current threshold; (2) abandon numerical thresholds altogether; or (3) use alternative methods to tailor regulation based on bank activities, capital levels, or greater regulator discretion. Introducing regulatory thresholds of this type can potentially distort the decisions made by regulated banks as they seek to maneuver around regulatory requirements. Accordingly, the more financial regulation can be tailored to match the business model and complexity of individual institutions, the more efficient the regulatory system will be in preserving safety and soundness, promoting innovation, and minimizing regulatory burden.

Examples thus far of tailoring regulation have included the expansion of size-based exemptions from a number of regulatory requirements. For example, the Economic Growth, Regulatory Relief, and Consumer Protection Act of 2018, or S.2155, simplified the capital standards applied to banks with assets less than $10 billion and exempted them from the U.S. Basel III risk-based capital system. It also raised the Small Bank Holding Company Policy Statement asset threshold from $1 billion to $3 billion. Requirements for data reporting are being relaxed for banks with up to $5 billion in assets, and the frequency of on-site examinations are being relaxed for banks with assets of less than $3 billion. And the threshold for exemption from the CFPB's ability-to-repay / qualified mortgage rule was raised from $2 billion to $10 billion.

Based in part on a Treasury recommendation, the National Credit Union Administration has raised the threshold for stress-testing requirements for federally insured credit unions from $10 billion to $15 billion in assets. The National Credit Union Administration has also raised the asset size threshold for applying a risk-weighted capital framework from $100 million to $500 million. These steps promote greater equality with bank capital requirements that apply to commercial banks of a similar size and complexity.

Refining capital, liquidity, and leverage standards. Improving, and appropriately tailoring, the regulatory standards for capital, leverage, and liquidity remain an essential element of postcrisis regulatory reforms. The 2017 Treasury report made a number of recommendations aimed at both decreasing the burden of statutory stress-testing and improving its effectiveness by tailoring the stress-testing requirements to the size and complexity of banks. The May 2018 enactment of S.2155 implemented many of these recommendations.

Section 165 of Dodd-Frank required the Federal Reserve to establish enhanced prudential standards for certain bank holding companies and foreign banking organizations and for nonbank financial companies that have been designated by the Financial Stability Oversight Council as systemically important financial institutions (SIFIs). These standards included enhanced requirements for:

1. Risk-based and leverage capital and liquidity.
2. The submission of periodic resolution plans.
3. Limits on single-counterparty credit exposures.
4. Periodic stress tests to evaluate capital adequacy.

5. A debt-to-equity limit to be applied to companies that the Financial Stability Oversight Council determined pose a grave threat to financial stability.

Section 165 also authorized the Federal Reserve to "establish additional prudential standards, including three enumerated standards—a contingent capital requirement, enhanced public disclosures, and short-term debt limits—and other prudential standards" that the Federal Reserve determined to be appropriate (Federal Reserve Board of Governors 2018, 595).

The 2017 Treasury report contained a number of recommendations to better tailor the requirements placed on midsized and regional banks—those with total assets between $10 billion and $250 billion—to the actual risk that they pose to financial stability. For the company-led annual Dodd-Frank Act Stress Test (DFAST), the report recommended raising the dollar threshold above the $10 billion level to reduce the regulatory burden placed on banks that are, in fact, not systemically important. This recommendation was largely implemented with the May 2018 passage of S.2155. Under S.2155, institutions with total assets below $100 billion are exempt from DFAST, while banks with assets between $100 billion and $250 billion are only subject to DFAST at the discretion of the Federal Reserve. This approach gives regulators the flexibility to tailor the stress-testing requirement to each bank's business model, balance sheet, and organizational complexity. It not only reduces the compliance burden of banks that are not systemically important but also relieves them from assessments related to enhanced regulation.

The Treasury report also recommended adjusting the thresholds applied under the Comprehensive Capital Analysis and Review (CCAR), and to adjust the review to a two-year cycle. Given that stress-testing results are forecast over a nine-quarter cycle, extending the CCAR review cycle to two years should not compromise the review's quality. These changes, however, are covered by separate legal authorities and will need to be implemented over time on an interagency basis.

Another important element of the 2017 Treasury report's recommendations was a proposed "off-ramp" exemption from compliance with DFAST, CCAR, and certain other prudential standards for any bank that elects to maintain a sufficiently high level of capital. Providing this choice of a simplified capital standard over a more complex standard will help to ensure that the institution is subject to capital requirements that are appropriate to its particular situation, thereby helping to minimize the regulatory cost of compliance. This, too, has largely been implemented through the Economic Growth, Regulatory Relief, and Consumer Protection Act.

In addition, the Treasury recommended that the Federal Reserve subject its stress-testing and capital planning review frameworks to public notice and comment. This type of transparency will help to inform market participants about the nature of this analysis and enable them to make more informed decisions about the institutions that are subject to these reviews. In February 2019, the Federal Reserve finalized its implementation of enhanced disclosure of the models used in its supervisory stress test (see box 6-4).

The 2017 Treasury report also made specific recommendations related to a number of other important Dodd-Frank standards—including those related to liquidity and funding for SIFIs, the resolution plans filed by SIFIs under Title I of Dodd-Frank, the Supplementary Leverage Ratio, the enhanced Supplementary Leverage Ratio that forms part of bank capital requirements, and the Volcker Rule's limitations on proprietary trading. In each of these areas, what was originally a well-motivated attempt to address areas of risk-taking that preceded the banking crisis turned out to be an overprescribed fix that unnecessarily raised the costs of regulatory compliance. The recommendations of the 2017 Treasury report include narrowing the application of the liquidity coverage ratio and recalibrating how the Net Stable Funding Ratio and Fundamental Review of the Trading Book interact with the liquidity coverage ratio and other relevant regulations. In addition, the report showed how the requirement for resolution plans to be filed by SIFIs under Title I of Dodd-Frank could be relaxed without abandoning an important element of lowering the potential for systemic risk. This measured tailoring of regulatory requirements to match the risks that are being addressed is a fundamental element of the regulatory reform efforts that have been, and continue to be, pursued by the Administration.

Regulatory reforms enacted thus far. Having established this agenda for reform with the Economic Growth, Regulatory Relief, and the Consumer Protection Act of 2018, the Administration is concentrating on implementing it. The most prominent accomplishment to date in implementing the Administration's agenda was the May 2018 passage of the Economic Growth, Regulatory Relief, and Consumer Protection Act (hereafter, the act), also referred to as S.2155. Unlike the Dodd-Frank Act, S.2155 garnered significant bipartisan support, receiving a 67–31 vote in the U.S. Senate and a 258–159 vote in the U.S. House of Representatives before being signed into law by the President.

The act exemplifies the shift away from the insufficiently tailored regulation found in portions of Dodd-Frank and to a more right-sized approach. These changes directly address some of the shortcomings of the Dodd-Frank Act described earlier in this chapter, and does so in four main areas, Titles I though IV of the act.

Title I provides relief to portfolio mortgage lenders who originate and hold residential mortgage loans on their balance sheet. Its expected effect will be to loosen unnecessary regulatory constraints on the availability of mortgage credit to U.S. households. Dodd-Frank had created a potential liability for banks that originated loans that later defaulted, unless those loans met the terms of the "qualified mortgage," a definition established in 2013 by the CFPB.

Box 6-4. Restoring Market Discipline in Banking

Market discipline can be promoted by equity capital requirements and practices for failed bank resolution that help to ensure that the owners of the bank are first in line to absorb losses if the bank should fail. It has proven to be a highly effective, and sometimes disruptive, means to limit risk-taking among financial institutions. Market discipline is the antithesis of moral hazard, where the costs of risk-taking are imposed on parties other than the owners of the bank. At the same time, a sudden collapse in the confidence of bank depositors and bondholders can exert enough market discipline to force the failure of the bank.

There are two basic approaches to enhancing the market discipline that discourage banks from taking on excessive risk: a minimum capital requirement, and a framework to resolve failed banks in an orderly fashion.

Minimum capital requirements represent a commitment, in advance, of private capital to absorb losses incurred by the bank. As such, this capital helps to limit moral hazard. The more capital the bank holds, the greater the share of failure cost that will be absorbed by the bank's owners before losses are imposed on other stakeholders. Other things being equal, this alignment of incentives to take risks will limit the subsidization of risk-taking bank owners and will result in a level of risk-taking that is closer to the socially optimal level. Undercapitalized banks have been cited as factors exacerbating both the savings-and-loan crisis of the late 1980s and the financial crisis of 2008 (FDIC 1997, 2017).

An orderly resolution process to resolve failed banks is another essential element of market discipline. An orderly bank resolution will impose losses on equity claims first, and then on unsecured debt, before imposing losses on uninsured depositors and the FDIC's Deposit Insurance Fund. This process helps to ensure that the equity holders that control the bank are in a first-loss position, even if their equity cannot completely cover the losses generated by the failure. An orderly resolution process for failed banks is essential for long-term financial stability. Since 1989, more than 2,000 FDIC-insured institutions have failed and have been resolved, with no losses to insured depositors.

During the recent crisis, we saw instances in which the FDIC chose *not* to impose losses on the equity and debt holders of very large and complex failing banks, and instead provided them with open bank assistance. These exceptions from normal procedures were based on concerns that imposing losses on uninsured creditors would transmit these losses to other banks and financial companies and worsen the systemic crisis. In the short run, this expansion of government support clearly helped to maintain the stability of the financial system. Over the long term, these actions could be expected to undermine market discipline, subsidize growth and risk-taking, and create competitive inequities between large and small banks. These considerations underlie the provisions of Section 1106 of the Dodd-Frank Act, which effectively ended the FDIC's authority to provide open bank assistance, even in a crisis situation.

> To summarize, a regulatory approach based on market discipline must (1) create strong capital standards that limit moral hazard, and (2) enhance the ability to properly impose market discipline in the event of a failure. Historical experience shows that the ability to maintain market discipline according to these principles has been inversely related to the size and complexity of the institutions to which they are applied.

The potential liability for defaulted loans under the "ability-to-repay" provision of Dodd-Frank was thought to impose market discipline on the mortgage lending process. But it also applied to mortgage loans held on the bank balance sheet, which already faced market discipline to the extent that private capital stood first in line to cover any losses from the loan.

Title I simply extends the presumption of ability-to-repay compliance to *all* mortgages originated and held by banks and credit unions with assets under $10 billion, which will be presumed to meet the definition of a qualified mortgage. Title I also provides an exemption for depository institutions that make few mortgage loans from reporting requirements under the Home Mortgage Disclosure Act. Title I of the act defers to the judgment of the managers of small and midsized banks about the quality of the mortgages they make and hold on their own balance sheets, and steps back from having regulators make this judgment for them.

Title II's provisions are aimed at reducing the regulatory burden placed on community banks without undermining the market discipline they face. Title II exempts banks with under $10 billion in assets from the Volcker Rule, which prohibits proprietary trading by banks. This exemption reflects the fact that very few small and midsized banks engage in proprietary trading. Title II also established the new Community Bank Leverage Ratio. Banks with limited amounts of certain assets and off-balance-sheet exposures will be able to choose this relatively simple measure of capitalization and be exempted from the more complicated Basel risk-based capital standards. In its November 9, 2018, proposal to implement the Community Bank Leverage Ratio, the FDIC proposed setting the standard at 9 percent of tangible equity to total assets. An estimated 80 percent of community banks would be eligible to adopt this simplified capital standard.

The provisions of Title II are designed to simplify and streamline the regulatory standards that apply to community banks. Their relatively simple business models do not require complex regulatory approaches. And the economies of scale they face in the cost of regulatory compliance make it imperative that the standards applied to them are simple and straightforward (box 6-5).

Title III of the Economic Growth, Regulatory Relief, and Consumer Protection Act addresses a number of issues related to consumer protection.

One of these is the need to give consumers more control over their own credit reports, which are a valuable reputational asset for all Americans. Title III requires the credit reporting agencies to provide updated fraud alerts to consumers for at least a year following a security incident, and gives consumers a right to place security freezes on their credit reports for free to prevent them from being inappropriately downgraded. Credit-reporting agencies will be required to omit certain medical debts from the credit reports of U.S. veterans.

These requirements recognize the importance of the consumer financial information on which we all rely to gain access to credit. Although these provisions do not directly affect the safety and soundness of regulated banks, they do recognize the priority of fairness in handling this valuable and sensitive information.

Title IV of the act addresses what was probably the biggest cost-benefit miscalculation made in the Dodd-Frank Act. Dodd-Frank required that all banking organizations with assets of $50 billion or more be subject to enhanced prudential standards. This approach relies too heavily on asset size as a measure of systemic importance. A better measure of the systemic importance of a particular bank is the FDIC's ability to resolve the institution successfully without creating financial instability. In cases where an institution is deemed resolvable, subjecting it to heightened regulatory requirements imposes high regulatory costs but gives very little benefit in terms of preserving financial stability.

The designation carries with it a number of regulatory requirements designed to introduce regulatory discipline as well as market discipline to designated institutions. To the extent that the institution is already resolvable, there would appear to be little benefit to the designation. In a case like this, the considerable regulatory costs imposed on SIFIs are for naught.

Under Title IV, banks with $250 billion or more in assets continue to be subject to the heightened regulatory standards already imposed by Dodd-Frank. Banks with between $100 billion and $250 billion in assets are statutorily required to be subject only to the Dodd-Frank Act's supervisory stress tests, while the Federal Reserve has the ability to impose other regulatory requirements as appropriate. Banks with assets between $50 billion and $100 billion will no longer be subject to the heightened regulatory requirements under Dodd-Frank.

The regulatory relief provided to midsized and regional banks will be an important step toward enhancing the banking system's ability to meet the credit needs of the U.S. economy. At the end of 2018, there were 32 banks with between $50 billion and $250 billion in total assets. Together, they hold 22 percent of the banking industry's assets. But few or none of them can truly be deemed to pose a systemic risk. As a result, the benefits of subjecting them to heightened prudential requirements, in which they are likely to fall far short of the costs they incur by being regulated in this manner, are questionable.

Box 6-5. Factors Driving the Long-Term Consolidation in Banking

The number of federally insured banks and savings institutions declined from 18,033 at the end of 1985 to 5,406 at the end of 2018, a total decline of 70 percent. This consolidation has been characterized by two main features. First, there has been a dramatic decline in the number of very small institutions, those with assets less than $100 million. In 1985, there were 13,631 institutions with assets less than $100 million, making up 76 percent of federally insured banks and thrifts. By 2018, this number had declined to just 1,278, making up just 24 percent of all banks and thrifts. Some 98 percent of the net decline in federally insured institutions over this period took place among banks with less than $100 million in assets.

This decline of the smallest banks can be attributed in large part to economies of scale in banking. A rough measure of economies of scale is the difference in total noninterest expenses as a percentage of average assets for banks in different size categories. FDIC-insured community banks reported a noninterest expense ratio of 2.75 percent in 2018, compared with 2.59 percent for the larger noncommunity banks. This 16-basis-point difference in overhead expenses translates into expenses that were $3.5 billion higher than they would have been at the ratio reported by noncommunity banks. This figure represents more than 13 percent of community bank net income in 2018.

Hughes and others (2018) compare average operating costs and costs associated with overhead, reporting and compliance, and telecommunica-

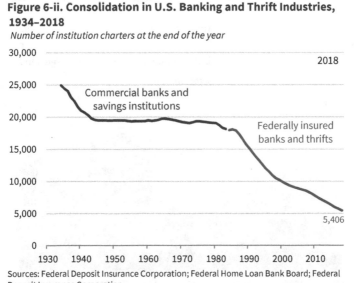

Figure 6-ii. Consolidation in U.S. Banking and Thrift Industries, 1934–2018

Number of institution charters at the end of the year

Sources: Federal Deposit Insurance Corporation; Federal Home Loan Bank Board; Federal Deposit Insurance Corporation.
Note: Data for commercial banks and savings institutions are from historical sources. Data for federally insured banks and thrifts are from call reports and thrift financial reports.

tions across three asset size categories. They show that large community banks and midsized banks both have efficiency advantages over small community banks. Looking back to the mid-1980s, we see that total noninterest expenses as a percentage of average assets have diverged from what was rough parity in the late 1990s to an advantage of up to 100 basis points for the largest banks by 2017. Larger banks may benefit from economies of scale in absorbing the costs of technology and regulatory compliance, both of which have become more important over time.

The second main feature of banking industry consolidation since the mid-1980s has been the emergence of a few very large institutions that have absorbed large shares of industry assets. The share of industry assets held by the four largest banking organizations rose from 11 percent in 1985 to 40 percent at the end of 2018. Here, too, economies of scale have played an important role. The ratio of noninterest expenses to total assets for banks larger than $250 billion in total assets fell by more than 100 basis points between 2000 and 2018.

Consolidation since 1985 has come about through failures (2,619 between the end of 1985 and the end of 2018), intercompany mergers (8,722 since 1985), and intracompany consolidation of charters (5,123 since 1985). Most of the failures took place during two crisis periods, first in the 1980s and early 1990s, and then following the financial crisis of 2008. Voluntary

Figure 6-iii. Share of Industry Assets Held by U.S. Banking Organizations That Became the Four Largest by 2008, 1985–2018

■ Percent held by charters ultimately acquired by the four largest banking organizations

■ Percent held by banking organizations that became the four largest in 2008

Share of industry assets at the end of the quarter

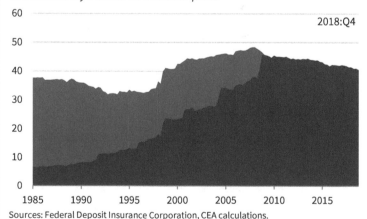

Sources: Federal Deposit Insurance Corporation, CEA calculations.

mergers and charter consolidations during this period were spurred not only by the prospect of economies of scale but also by the decline in regulatory restrictions on branching and interstate banking. Geographic deregulation facilitated the formation of larger, more efficient banks. Though this promoted greater efficiency and opportunities for diversification, it also helped create large, complex banks that have benefited from the perceived implicit government support of systemically important banks (figures 6-ii and 6-iii).

There are a number of pending regulatory proposals to implement the provisions of S.2155. Taken together, Titles I though IV of the act represent a new approach to regulating financial institutions that reflect the Core Principles delineated at the outset of this Administration. They will relieve community and regional banks from excessive and costly regulatory requirements that should really only apply to SIFIs. Moreover, they preserve the elements of regulatory reform that were designed to contain the systemic risks that led to the financial crisis of 2008. But they take an approach that appropriately tailors regulatory requirements according to the activities and structure of the bank, and the level of risk that it poses to financial stability.

Signing the bipartisan S.2155 bill into law is the most visible reform yet put into place by President Trump. This act is expected to have a range of long-term benefits for financial institutions, the economy, and the public. It levels the competitive playing field between the smaller community banks and credit unions and the larger, more complex financial institutions. It recognizes the vital importance of small and midsized banks, as well as the high costs and negligible benefits of subjecting them to regulatory requirements better suited for the largest financial institutions. S.2155 is expected to reduce regulatory burdens and help to expand the credit made available to small businesses that are the lifeblood of local communities across the nation.

Additional steps taken to address regulatory concerns. As important as S.2155 is in scaling back costly and unnecessary regulations, a number of other, less well-known measures have been adopted that also represent progress in implementing the Administration's agenda.

Addressing the CFPB's arbitration rule was one crucial step. In July 2017, the CFPB released a rule intended to ban certain financial companies from using mandatory arbitration clauses in consumer contracts, and to permit consumers to participate in class action lawsuits. But the new rule was later reconsidered after it was shown to adversely increase the cost of credit for consumers. In November 2017, the rule was nullified under the Congressional Review Act after a joint resolution to do so was signed into law by President Trump.

Another priority is reform of the Community Reinvestment Act (CRA). In 1977, the CRA was enacted to encourage banks to meet the credit needs of all segments of their communities, including low- and moderate-income households. In response to growing feedback—including from the Department of the Treasury—that the CRA requires modernizing (especially with the rise in online banking), in August 2018 the OCC published its Advanced Notice of Proposed Rulemaking to seek input on the best ways to update the regulatory framework that supports the CRA. To improve credit availability in the areas most in need, the OCC is soliciting input on topics such as how to improve the current approach to performance evaluations, expand the activities that qualify for CRA, and better define communities.

The data collection rule under the Home Mortgage Disclosure Act also needs improvement. In 2015, the CFPB had issued an update to the 1975 Home Mortgage Disclosure Act, which expanded data disclosure requirements for lending institutions. The new rule, which was set to go into effect January 1, 2018, was delayed pending a review of and improvements to the CFPB's data security systems. The CFPB, with interagency assistance, concluded that its "security posture is well-organized and maintained," and it has recently sought comments from relevant parties as it considers whether changes to its data governance and data collections programs would be appropriate. It seeks to balance the protection of privacy without hindering its ability to accomplish its objectives and statutory mandate.

Another needed initiative is updating the commercial real estate appraisal rule. In a coordinated effort between the OCC, the Federal Reserve, and the FDIC, effective in April 2018, the threshold for commercial real estate appraisals was raised from $250,000 to $500,000. The rule amends Title XI of the Financial Institutions Reform, Recovery, and Enforcement Act of 1989, partly in response to concerns among relevant stakeholders that the prior threshold level did not reflect the appreciation of commercial real estate in the 24 years since the threshold was initially set. The three agencies determined that the increased appraisal level would materially reduce regulatory burden and the amount of transactions requiring an appraisal, while not sacrificing the safety and soundness of financial institutions.

The regulatory capital rule for small banks, with respect to transitions, is another improvement. The OCC, the Federal Reserve, and the FDIC adopted a final "Transitions Rule" that extends the 2017 regulatory capital treatment for certain items for smaller banks. The relief provided under this rule specifically applies to banking organizations that are not subject to the capital rules' advanced approaches, which tend to be smaller banks. This rule went into effect on January 1, 2018.

And finally, the regulatory capital rule for small banks, with respect to simplifications, is being considered. The "Simplification Rule"—which was proposed by the OCC, the Federal Reserve, and the FDIC in October 2017—would aim to simplify compliance with certain aspects of the capital rule, particularly for smaller banks.

Conclusion

This chapter has chronicled the financial crisis of 10 years ago—its causes, its costs, and its consequences. The financial crisis of 2008 was the most severe systemic financial event in the U.S. since at least the 1930s. It was a self-reinforcing crisis that arose within the financial industry itself but soon spread to the wider economy. The crisis exposed weaknesses in institutional and regulatory structures that were in dire need of reform. Before it was over, the Federal government was required to provide assistance to financial institutions that was unprecedented in its scale and its scope.

Notwithstanding this extraordinary support, the crisis took a heavy toll on U.S. economic activity that affected the vast majority of Americans. The declines in manufacturing, construction, employment, and overall economic activity that came after the crisis were historically large and long lasting. These economic effects underscored the need for an appropriate regulatory response that would enhance the stability of financial markets and institutions, and would protect the American people from the consequences of enduring a future crisis.

The Financial Crisis Inquiry Commission was organized in 2009 to examine the causes of the crisis and inform the regulatory reforms that were sure to follow. The FCIC released a 662-page report in January 2011 documenting the various factors that exacerbated the financial crisis. This report did not receive bipartisan support. But it did provide first-hand accounts of a wide range of bankers, regulators, and analysts that could have been considered as reforms were being planned. Yet even before this report was published, Congress passed the 2010 Dodd-Frank Act—a sweeping overhaul of financial regulation that did not result in a rapid economic recovery and that has had a number of unintended consequences.

The Dodd-Frank Act has proven to be a misguided approach to regulatory reform. It called for almost 400 new rules, not all of which have been implemented. The act placed unnecessary burdens on banks and their customers through its frequent overreach and its prescriptive approach to regulation. There is a growing body of evidence that Dodd-Frank's one-size-fits-all approach has been very costly for community banks and for the small businesses that depend on them for credit. Studies confirm the economies of scale that are associated with regulatory compliance, and support the notion that postcrisis regulatory changes have had a disproportionate effect on small and midsized banks. This regulatory approach has had substantial economic consequences. The average pace of economic growth in the first eight years of the expansion, through 2016, was the slowest of any U.S. expansion since 1950.

Dodd-Frank was especially problematic in discouraging small business lending and in promoting consolidation among small and midsized banks. Although community banks had little to do with the onset of the financial crisis, their numbers have fallen by more than 2,400, or one-third, since 2008. FDIC data show that community banks are vitally important to communities that are not served by larger institutions. They also make small business loans in proportions that are almost three times higher than their share of total industry loans. Similarly, the importance of small businesses for the U.S. economy goes well beyond the roughly two-thirds of new jobs they typically create. Small businesses have traditionally been a source of strength for their communities and a source of innovation where new and different ideas can be pursued. They spark innovation. And they rely heavily for funding on community banks, which have a local focus that helps them meet their credit needs.

From its first days, the Trump Administration outlined a more informed approach to financial regulation that will make the Nation's financial system more efficient and more effective. Seven Core Principles for financial regulation were outlined at the outset of the Administration, calling for an end to taxpayer bailouts, a more accountable regulatory framework, more and better analysis before imposing new regulations, a leveling of the competitive playing field between U.S. and foreign banks, and other steps to enable Americans to make their own informed financial decisions in a stable financial system. From the start, it was emphasized that well-reasoned financial reforms would be essential to bring the pace of the United States' economic growth and its standard of living up to their true potential.

During the past two years, the Department of the Treasury has issued four reports that made detailed recommendations consistent with the Administration's Core Principles. With regard to depository institutions, the Treasury has recommended a series of changes designed to simplify regulations and reduce their implementation costs, while maintaining high standards of safety and soundness and ensuring the accountability of the financial system to the American public. These recommendations have been discussed at length in this chapter.

A number of these recommendations were implemented in the Economic Growth, Regulatory Relief, and Consumer Protection Act of 2018, which was enacted in May 2018 and is generally referred to as S.2155. The act addresses some of the most important shortcomings associated with Dodd-Frank, and does so in a way that does not undermine the safety and soundness of the banking industry. It provides regulatory relief to small banks by recognizing their judgment in terms of the mortgage loans they hold, simplifying their capital requirements, and giving them a presumption of compliance with regard to proprietary trading, which few of them do in the first place.

Most importantly, S.2155 scales back the heightened regulatory standards that were applied to midsized banks—those with assets between $50 billion and $250 billion—that were treated as systemically important banks under Dodd-Frank. As a result, more than 30 midsized and regional banks that hold 22 percent of industry assets can get relief from unnecessary regulatory standards that would otherwise limit their ability to grow, prosper, and serve their customers. This change is an example of how a one-size-fits-all approach is giving way to "tailored" regulatory standards that are matched to the actual level of risk imposed by each institution.

The Administration's agenda is ambitious, and its accomplishments thus far are many. This effort is part of the Administration's overall push, along with other forms of deregulation (see chapter 2) and tax reform (see chapter 1) to reverse the historically slow economic growth of the immediate postcrisis period, and to enhance the performance of the economy so it can reach its true potential. The election of President Trump in November 2016 produced an immediate increase in small business confidence that has remained in place ever since. The pace of economic activity has quickened during the Administration's first two years. After the enactment of the Tax Cuts and Jobs Act, real economic growth rose to an annualized rate of more than 4 percent for the first time in four years. The recovery in business confidence, hiring, and investment spending since 2016 suggests that we will see higher potential growth in the years ahead.

Most important, these commonsense adjustments to the financial regulatory framework signal an end to the war on Wall Street that took place in the immediate aftermath of the 2008 financial crisis. The implicit support for the largest banks and the government-sponsored enterprises has been rolled back by the reforms enacted thus far. The diverse U.S. financial system will continue to include elements that meet the needs of corporations, of Main Street, and of everyone and everything in between. A smoothly functioning and prosperous financial industry has long been one of the pillars that has supported the development of the U.S. economy into the largest and most stable in the world. The sensible financial reforms being pursued by the Trump Administration suggest that this institutional strength is back, and will endure in the decades to come.

Chapter 7

Adapting to Technological Change with Artificial Intelligence while Mitigating Cyber Threats

Although technological change has always had significant effects on economic activity, artificial intelligence (AI) and high-speed automation are among its most important recent manifestations. The expansion of computing power and availability of big data have fueled remarkable advances in computer science, enabling technology to perform tasks that traditionally required humans and significant amounts of time. However, along with these advances' prospects for encouraging continued productivity growth, they also threaten to significantly disrupt the labor market, particularly among people whose work involves routine and manual tasks. Astute policymaking will play an integral role in leveraging technology as an asset for the country, while mitigating potential disruptions.

The first section of this chapter briefly defines AI and corresponding advances in computer science. AI's most distinctive feature is that it can be used to manage a wide range of highly complex tasks with little required supervision, relative to conventional technology. This general applicability broadens the types of tasks where AI could plausibly be a substitute for human labor, underscoring both the economic promise of AI and its potential risks.

The second section places AI within the broader historical context of technological change and highlights the CEA's predictions for its short-, medium-, and long-run effects on productivity and wages. Although we may experience a span of years where AI substitutes for human-based labor for many tasks, AI, like much technological change, will ultimately benefit labor through greater productivity and real wage growth.

The third section explores AI's heterogeneous effects and automation across industries and the skill distribution. Using autonomous vehicles as a case study, we show that one of the key factors for understanding the impact of technological change on employment is the price elasticity of demand. AI is expected to have a positive net effect on industrial employment, though there could be subsector-specific price declines based on changing consumer demand.

The fourth section pivots to the possible risks of technological advances. Building on findings in the 2018 *Economic Report of the President* on the cost of cybersecurity breaches, we analyze how measurement problems related to these breaches make it difficult to estimate their costs. We present new data from 2018 on the pervasiveness of cybersecurity vulnerabilities and the paucity of firms' responses to them across *Fortune* 500 companies.

The fifth and final section highlights the role of policy and the considerable strides that have been taken by the Trump Administration during the past two years. The Administration will continue to embrace technological change, while maximizing its promise and minimizing its risk.

Recent years have seen enormous advances in computer science, leading to skyrocketing hardware and software capabilities. The refinement of computers continues to advance at a rapid rate. The computational power that took up enormous refrigerated rooms a few decades ago has been miniaturized to a fraction of its former size. Moreover, computer scientists and engineers have made remarkable discoveries in artificial intelligence (AI) and automation. These advances have complemented years of rapid growth in computer processing power, along with the explosive growth in the availability of digitized data. According to two prominent scholars, "the key building blocks are already in place for digital technologies to be as important and transformational to society and the economy as the steam engine" (Brynjolfsson and McAfee 2014, 9).

In last year's *Report*, we highlighted one aspect of the rapid diffusion of computer technology: the increasing exposure of the economy to malicious cyber activity—for example, cybercrime. We found that cybercrime had expanded so much that in 2016 alone that it caused up to $109 billion in harm to the economy. Yet computers have, of course, created many more benefits than costs, and their rapid evolution promises to fundamentally transform the economy in the decade ahead. In 2016, President Obama's Council of Economic Advisers published a sweeping report outlining the likely economic impact and policy challenges of accelerating technological change. One metric of how rapidly the sector is advancing is that already, in 2018 and 2019, enough change has occurred so an update of the previous reports is essential for meeting the challenges of the next decade and beyond. We look ahead in wonder at the possibilities of advanced thinking machines, but also worry that automation will proceed at such a rapid pace that many workers in today's economy will suddenly find themselves superfluous or disconnected from competitive job opportunities. We also consider the additional cybersecurity risks posed by the increased reliance on information technology.

In this chapter, we dig deeper than we did a year ago into the promise and risks of the ongoing computer science revolution. We begin by reviewing the latest developments in AI and automation, discussing their likely economic effects. The central theme of the first section of this chapter is that a narrow, static focus on possible job losses paints a misleading picture of AI's likely effects on the Nation's economic well-being. With technological advances, specific types of legacy positions are usually eliminated, though new jobs and evolving work roles are created—increasing real wages, national income, and prosperity over time. Automation can complement labor, adding to its value; and even when it substitutes for labor in certain areas, it can lead to higher employment in other types of work and raise overall economic welfare. This will likely be what happens as AI transforms more and more aspects of the economy, though new challenges will arise about cybersecurity. In the years to come, AI appears poised to automate tasks that had long been assumed to be out of reach. Thus, we also analyze the important role of reskilling, apprenticeship initiatives, and future hiring processes to help mitigate the potentially disruptive employment effects of technological change and automation throughout the skill distribution.

One key question for economists today is whether—in addition to improving traditional productive processes—AI will alter processes whereby creative new ideas are generated and implemented. In other words, is AI simply the next phase in automation, or is it a real break from the past with unique implications? We explore both possibilities, but conclude that AI is likely to have major effects on the value of different skill sets and the rate at which they appreciate and depreciate. In particular, in the long run, aggregate wages will be higher because of these new advances.

We then turn to an update of our previous research on the economic vulnerabilities associated with the diffusion of technology and mobile computing capabilities into virtually every corner of our lives. Technology is leading to new and constantly evolving complex security challenges because individuals, firms, and governments are already reliant on interconnected and interdependent technology. Whereas past conflicts unfolded on land, sea, and air, future conflicts and criminal activity will increasingly take place in cyberspace. Drawing on new data, we document that cyber vulnerabilities are quite prevalent—even in *Fortune* 500 companies with significant resources at their disposal. Although these new data do not allow us to update our 2018 estimate of the economic costs of malicious cyber activity, the latest data suggest that our previous estimate might have been too low, given the underreporting of cybercrime. We conclude by discussing the initiatives that are being implemented by the Trump Administration and the policy challenges that lawmakers will likely face in the years ahead.

What Is Artificial Intelligence?

Although there is no universal definition of artificial intelligence (AI),[1] the Future of Artificial Intelligence Act of 2017 (H.R. 4625), for example, defines AI as "any artificial system that performs tasks under varying and unpredictable circumstances, without significant human oversight, or that can learn from their experience and improve their performance. . . . They may solve tasks requiring human-like perception, cognition, planning, learning, communication, or physical action."[2] These intelligent systems generally use machine learning to form predictions and adaptively make adjustments based on new information in their environment (Russell and Norvig 2010). Because AI has such a wide array of applications across sectors and disciplines, it is viewed as a general purpose technology and important source of economic growth (Agrawal, Gans, and Goldfarb 2018). Automation technologies usually focus on automating a specific process, or multiple commonly understood processes, to reduce labor intensity, which differs greatly from highly complex, human-like decision logic, which has already been observed in the emerging embodiments of AI.

Although the general concepts and algorithms within AI are decades old, AI has emerged as an especially powerful and widely applied tool for

---

[1] A recent study by Deloitte (2017) contains survey results that point out ambiguity in how many top executives and everyday citizens define AI.

[2] Similarly, in the National Defense Authorization Act for Fiscal Year 2019, "the term 'artificial intelligence' includes the following: (1) Any artificial system that performs tasks under varying and unpredictable circumstances without significant human oversight, or that can learn from experience and improve performance when exposed to data sets. (2) An artificial system developed in computer software, physical hardware, or other context that solves tasks requiring human-like perception, cognition, planning, learning, communication, or physical action. (3) An artificial system designed to think or act like a human, including cognitive architectures and neural networks. (4) A set of techniques, including machine learning, that is designed to approximate a cognitive task. (5) An artificial system designed to act rationally, including an intelligent software agent or embodied robot that achieves goals using perception, planning, reasoning, learning, communicating, decision making, and acting."

Figure 7-1. Error Rate of Image Classification by Artificial Intelligence and Humans, 2010–17

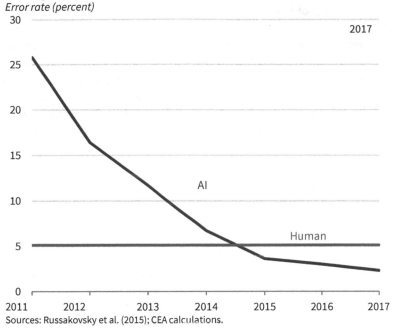

Error rate (percent)

Sources: Russakovsky et al. (2015); CEA calculations.

performing not only existing tasks much more efficiently but also new tasks that were traditionally viewed as infeasible. To give just one example, research-ers have created AI algorithms capable of classifying images even more reliably than humans can do under certain conditions, and at a much faster rate and scale than ever before (figure 7-1)—although these algorithms can still be tricked by savvy programmers (CSAIL 2017). More examples abound in other areas, ranging from natural language processing to theorem proving (Artificial Intelligence Index 2017). Other types of computer science and AI advances include solutions to automate high-skill human cognitive tasks, such as automated reasoning and intelligent decision support systems (Arai et al. 2014; Davenport and England 2015; Kerber, Lange, and Rowat 2016; Mulligan, Davenport, and England 2018).

The convergence of two factors have made these remarkable advances possible. First, accumulated decades of sustained growth in technology have led to an explosion in computing power. As Gordon Moore (1965) first observed, computing power historically doubles every 18 months. These advances have led to an increase in transistor density, which, combined with the declining cost of manufacturing integrated circuits, have led to a staggering increase in computing power (Brynjolfsson and McAfee 2014).[3] Moreover, lower manufacturing costs for hardware have been complemented by annual price declines in cloud computing of 17 percent between 2009 and 2016 (Byrne, Corrado, and Sichel 2018).

Second, the colossal increase in data availability has complemented the surge in computing power, allowing researchers to develop and test AI algorithms on much larger data sets.[4] The emergence of big data has been driven by "digitization," which means the ability to take different types of information and media, ranging from text to video, and convert them into streams of ones and zeros—"the native language of computers and their kin" (Brynjolfsson and McAfee 2014, 37). Researchers have also found creative ways to convert different types of digital media into comprehensive sets of numeric quantities, which often involve "feature engineering," or optimizing the permutations of data inputs, to produce reliable predictions (Arel, Rose, and Karnowski 2010).

Machine Learning

Machine learning (ML) is integral to the design and implementation of AI (Russel and Norvig 2010). Unlike computers, which tend to execute a set of prespecified rules, AI is defined by the ability to learn and adapt to its environment.[5] There are three main types of ML algorithms—supervised, unsupervised, and reinforcement learning—which we summarize in the next paragraphs (Hastie, Tibshirani, and Friedman 2009).

First, supervised learning algorithms take a set of descriptive variables that are matched with a corresponding label ("outcome variable") and "learns" the relationship between the two. For example, to predict college attainment, a researcher could use data on whether the individual has a college degree, together with a set of individual characteristics, such as parental education and gender, to estimate classification models. Supervised learning algorithms take a subset of the sample and search for the parameters that best fit the data based on a prespecified objective function.

Second, unsupervised learning algorithms, in contrast to supervised ones, take a set of feature variables as inputs and detect patterns in the data. Though these algorithms have not been as prolifically applied as supervised

---

[3] An integral part of the efficiency gains among producers of computer equipment is the rapid decline in effective prices of semiconductors due to advances in chip technology (Triplett 1996). These empirical patterns have also continued during the past decade. For example, Byrne, Oliner, and Sichel (2017) find that semiconductor prices fell by 42 percent, relative to the meager 6 percent decline in the producer price index between 2004 and 2009.

[4] Computer scientists often refer to the process of developing and testing AI algorithms as "training." The process refers to estimating model parameters on a subsample, subsequently using the estimated parameters to predict out-of-sample. The quality of the out-of-sample prediction is used to, sometimes iteratively, tune model parameters.

[5] Russell and Norvig (2010, 43) remark that algorithms in deterministic settings are not a form of AI because they are executing a set of preprogrammed tasks.

learning algorithms, they are often used to simplify otherwise computationally demanding problems by reducing the number of variables that need to be kept track of, sometimes referred to as "dimensionality reduction" (Bonhomme, Lamadon, and Manresa 2017).

Third, reinforcement learning algorithms have been among the most influential class of algorithms in the emerging set of AI and big data applications. Unlike supervised and unsupervised algorithms, reinforcement learning algorithms do not require complete representation of input/output pairs, but rather only require an objective function. This function specifies how the intelligent system responds to its environment under arbitrary degrees of stochasticity (i.e., the extent to which it involves a random variable). Consider the game of chess, which contains millions of potential moves. Though individuals face cognitive limitations that preclude internal simulation of thousands, and potentially millions, of scenarios simultaneously, "deep learning" reinforcement learning algorithms have largely overcome these limitations. For example, Google's new AI algorithm, AlphaZero, defeated the world's best chess engine, Stockfish. Unlike Deep Blue—the IBM supercomputer that defeated Garry Kasparov, the world's leading chess champion in 1997—AlphaZero trained itself to play like a human, but at an unprecedented scale and aptitude (Gibbs 2017).

One way a reader can picture this evolution of computing power is by considering the computer modeling of sports outcomes. It is now common for commentators at sporting events to announce midgame the probability, given the current score, that the team that is currently ahead in the score will indeed win the game. At one point during the 2017 American football championship game Super Bowl LI, the New England Patriots had a mere 0.3 percent chance of victory (ESPN Analytics 2018). This probability was calculated based on data from previous games and an analysis of the percentage of times that a team went on to win after trailing by a certain margin deep into the third quarter. Algorithms used by various networks and media platforms allow for these odds to be constructed from historical performance data of past teams that have been in similar situations.

Moreover, as with other games, like chess, estimating probabilities of winning can grow in complexity because of real-time interactions between the players, as well as the astronomical number of possible outcomes that can be reached, even without repetitive actions between the start and end of a game. In a game with finite outcomes, given an enormously powerful computer and a set of initial conditions describing the configuration of pieces on the board, a program could explore all possible moves and responses from that state and "solve" the game. The optimal computer would then, for a given player, recommend a move from that initial state associated with the highest probability of victory for that player.

However, because there are infinite possible future states associated with almost every state of the world in a chess match, software must discover the types of moves that tend to lead to victory because exploring all future paths and developing a discrete solution is impossible for a problem with infinite outcomes. A computer equipped with AI, however, allows for a combination of human rationality with computing probabilities of victory. This provides improved predictions that can lead the AI algorithm to "play" the game, rather than attempting to solve it.

Applications of AI Technology

Today, facial recognition is possible because data (e.g., images) can be not only digitized but also collected and analyzed at scale. Suppose our AI machine, in addition to assessing the remaining possible outcomes, could also discern the identities of the players themselves and use this information to further revise its predictions based on knowledge about the two players. For instance, the probabilities of victory associated with an advantageous position would need to be updated if player 1 was an amateur and player 2 was a professional. However, if player 1's position was so advantageous that the odds of victory were 99.7 percent, even someone as talented as the professional could lose if forced to start from a severely disadvantaged position. In addition to assessing situations from a static perspective, an AI algorithm that can discern the identity of the player through facial recognition can choose strategies that are tailored to the player's weaknesses.

Another example of how AI can complement society and human tasks is through its effects on the delivery and production of educational services. One of the primary types of AI educational applications are personalized learning algorithms that allow instructors to tailor information to the unique ways that individuals learn. For example, Georgia State University sends customized text messages to students during the college enrollment process, which Page and Gehlbach (2017) find is associated with a 3.3-percentage-point increase in the probability that individuals will enroll on time.

Similarly, Arizona State University uses adaptive and hybrid learning platforms that enable teachers to offer more targeted learning experiences (Bailey et al. 2018). These platforms provide instructors with real-time intelligence to assess how well their students understand each concept, allowing instructors to pivot, when needed, to improve the learning experience. In sum, economists find significant returns on student outcomes from these "edtech" programs (Escueta et al. 2017). Given that at least 54 percent of all employees will require significant reskilling and/or upskilling by 2022 (World Economic Forum 2018), educational institutions will need to become increasingly adaptive, finding ways to integrate technology to simultaneously reduce costs, improve quality, and raise agility.

AI systems have mastered tasks that have traditionally been performed by humans. One way of measuring the breadth of these AI-based applications is to examine the clusters of emerging research content. Using the universe of Scopus and Elsevier articles, Elsevier (2018, 34) identified seven clusters of AI capabilities, including "machine learning and probabilistic reasoning, neural networks, computer vision, natural language processing and knowledge representation, search and optimization, fuzzy systems, and planning and decisionmaking." Moreover, using the subset of papers that have been uploaded to the research platform arXiv, Elsevier (2018) finds that articles about core AI categories that are posted on arXiv have increased by 37.4 percent in the past five years.

These sustained research efforts will continue to expand AI's capabilities. Indeed, Brynjolfsson and McAfee (2014, 52) remark that "we're going to see artificial intelligence do more and more, and as this happens costs will go down, outcomes will improve, and our lives will get better." Already, AI is being applied in four main areas of the marketplace, according to Lee and Triolo (2017): (1) the Internet (e.g., online marketplaces); (2) business (e.g., data-driven decisionmaking); (3) perception (e.g., facial and voice recognition); and (4) autonomous systems (e.g., vehicles and drones). Take, for instance, the domain of perception AI. One discovery helps individuals who have historically been visually impaired to use a device with digital sensors that can survey the physical environment and create sound waves through the bones of the head. The technology clips onto eyeglasses, and after being oriented toward text within the user's vision and signaled to read the source by the wearer, the device reads and verbalizes the text (Brynjolfsson and McAfee 2014). Similarly, Brynjolfsson and McElheran (2016) also illustrate how manufacturing establishments using data to influence their decisionmaking exhibit greater productivity than their counterparts. Companies in the digital economy will increasingly compete based on their ability to use data efficiently and strategically.

Technological Progress and the Demand for Labor

This section explores the interaction between technological progress and the demand for labor. First, it gives a brief history of technological change and work. Then it describes the effects of technological progress on investment and wages. Finally, it considers how specialization and comparative advantage affect trade between people and machines.

A Brief History of Technological Change and Work

Do technological advances reduce employment? That is not a new question—concern about job losses caused by automation dates back at least two centuries. During the early 19th century, English artisans (Luddites) in the rapidly changing textile industry famously attempted to destroy the mills and automated machine looms that they believed threatened their livelihoods. Despite the opposition of the Luddites to automation, the next two centuries witnessed a transition to mechanization of much of the physical labor performed by workers (Galor and Weil 2000). The agriculture sector provides a notable example. Tractors replaced horsepower and manual labor in 19th-century plowing work, and labor-intensive manual tasks were mechanized (Rasmussen 1982). Similar examples abound among many types of skilled artisanal work after the introduction of machine tools, as well as the transformation of manufacturing after advances such as steam power and electricity.

Automation's effects on labor are no longer confined to manufacturing and agriculture (Brynjolfsson and McAfee 2014; Autor 2015; Polson and Scott 2018). Computers and constantly evolving software have eliminated the need for many of the administrative and clerical tasks that had long been performed by white-collar workers in commercial business. Indeed, before the word "computer" referred to a microprocessor on a desk, it was a job title for a person who laboriously performed simple arithmetic or more complex mathematical calculations. Today, an accountant or financial specialist can do in seconds what would have once taken hours or days of painstaking computation by a team of educated people. An online tax preparation system can do much of what a professional certified public accountant might have done, while being faster and more accurate. White-collar work environments are likely to undergo further disruptive changes as AI technologies continue expanding into logistics and inventory management, financial services, complex language translation, the writing of business reports, and even legal services. Even medical diagnoses are likely to involve AI technologies in the foreseeable future.

Economists and policymakers have long studied the question of job displacement caused by technological advancement. In just one example, in 1964 Congress authorized the National Commission on Technology, Automation, and Economic Progress to study the effects of technological advancement, particularly in relation to unemployment. The commission's 1966 report included the finding that "technology eliminates jobs, not work" (Bowen 1966, 9). In a more contemporary discussion, David Autor (2015, 5) noted that "journalists and even expert commentators tend to overstate the extent of machine substitution for human labor and ignore the strong complementarities between automation and labor that increase productivity, raise earnings, and augment demand for labor." Though the introduction of new technologies can create job displacement, examining technological change from a historical perspective shows that these transformations do not lead to permanently lower employment, but rather an increase in demand for new tasks (Mokyr, Vickers, and Ziebarth 2015).

Effects of Technological Progress on Investment and Wages

Capital investments, such as in machines and software, embody AI, which Brynjolfsson, Rock, and Syverson (2017) call a general purpose technology. New investments that embody AI are expected to be more like ("closer substitutes for") labor than traditional capital investments were. Here, we begin by relating capital to labor and productivity and explain why labor is expected to receive most of the net benefits from AI in the long run. In particular, we argue that, though AI is expected to increase real wages on average, the economy has three phases of adjustment where the wage effects are different. In the anticipation phase, real wages are somewhat elevated as businesses begin to switch to activities that are intensive in cognitive tasks, but still do not have machines to adequately perform those tasks. Then, AI arrives and can fill many of the positions, temporarily depressing real wages during the implementation phase as workers compete with the new machines. In the long run, business formation catches up with the new technology and real wages are higher.

Growth in labor productivity can come from changes in three distinct factors: a rise in the quality of labor, which can occur with greater education, training, or skill attainment; a rise in capital, which occurs when firms invest in productive inputs, such as machines, factories, or computers; or a rise in what economists call total factor productivity (TFP), which pertains to other determinants of productivity, ranging from regulatory frictions to unmeasured quality improvements (Solow 1957).

TFP growth often increases real wages and the return to capital in the short run because it makes the factors more productive.[6] A greater return to capital also stimulates additional investment leading to business creation and growth. As a result of the additional capital, real wages rise and, because new capital competes with old capital, the return to capital declines. Indeed, a century or more of economic growth has increased real wages by more than a factor of five (Fisk 2001; Zwart, van Leeuwen, and van Leeuwen-Li 2014), while the return to capital has been almost constant over time (Caselli and Feyrer 2007; Mulligan and Threinen 2011). Nearly all the long-run benefits of TFP go to labor by reducing the effective prices of goods and services or by raising total compensation (Caselli and Feyrer 2007; CEA 2018c).

Although real wages trend up and the return to capital does not, as discussed above, labor's share of gross domestic product (GDP) can be constant, rising, or falling, depending on the type of technological change and the degree to which the new investment substitutes for labor in the production process. In other words, some types of TFP growth may reduce labor's share of GDP in the long run even while the entire benefit from TFP growth goes to workers in the form of higher real wages. For example, Karabarbounis and Neiman (2014)

---

[6] Our discussion of wages in the text that follows views it as representing all compensation from work, including fringe benefits.

show that the decline in the relative price of investment goods (e.g., due to the expansion of information technology and computers) helps to account for the decline in the labor share.

Although the TFP growth occurring during most of the 20th century did not reduce labor's share of national income (Kaldor 1961), AI might reduce it in the long run to the degree that it is more substitutable for labor than 20th-century capital investments were. The transition to a labor-substitutable AI is illustrated in figure 7-2 from the perspective of the capital market. Because a downward-sloping capital demand curve shows the relationship between the amount of capital and its marginal contribution to output, the area under the curve up to the equilibrium amount of capital is equal to the total amount of output. This output is divided between capital and labor, with capital's income equal to the rectangular area, which has dimensions equal to the amount of capital and the rental rate per unit of capital. In the figure, the triangular area above the rectangle is the output not paid to capital, which is labor income.

The arrival of AI makes new capital investments more productive, which is why the capital demand curve is shifted up by the discovery. Initially, AI investments earn returns greater than the normal capital return, as at the point b in figure 7-2, which stimulates more investment. The additional investment begins to drive down the return to capital, but more slowly than investment did in earlier eras, because the new investment does not compete as directly with existing capital, which is why the new demand curve is flatter than the old one. In the long run, the return to capital falls back to normal, the economy is at point c in figure 7-2, and labor income has increased by the amount of the shaded area L.[7] Labor's share is lower in the long run than it was before AI arrived, as shown in the diagram by the fact that the rectangular increment to capital income is disproportionate to L. Ironically, the addition to capital income is a symptom of more investment and real wage growth due to the assumption that AI investments are more substitutable for labor than older types of capital.

In the short run, after the arrival of AI, new investment that is a good substitute for labor reduces real wages to the extent that human workers compete with AI for jobs and the additional business formation is not yet complete. This phase resembles the commonly expressed concern that workers would be harmed by AI. In terms of figure 7-2 the capital rental rate r at point b is temporarily elevated, at the expense of labor income. However, it is important to also consider the phase *before* AI arrives. Here, real wages are elevated by the anticipation of AI because businesses are formed with the expectation that they will eventually have both human and machine labor, but in the meantime will need to perform their operations entirely with human labor.

---

[7] In the limit in which AI is a perfect substitute for human workers, the area L is zero. The subsection of this chapter titled "Trade between People and Machines" explains why the perfect-substitution case is ruled out by market forces.

Figure 7-2. The Effect of AI on the Amount of Capital and the Distribution of Factor Incomes

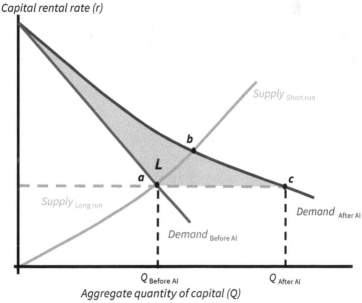

Capital rental rate (r)

Aggregate quantity of capital (Q)

Source: Adapted from Jaffe et al. (2019).

This stylized discussion highlights the situation that though AI can depress real wages for a period if it is a good substitute for labor, ultimately AI will raise real wages above what they were before AI because of the investment and increased productivity that it stimulates. These conclusions are consistent with not only theoretical models of economics featuring AI in general equilibrium (Aghion, Jones, and Jones 2017) but also with evidence on how the introduction of robots raised labor productivity across 17 countries between 1993 and 2007 (Graetz and Michaels 2018). Moreover, taking the information technology (IT) revolution as an analogue, Autor, Katz, and Krueger (1998) show that the introduction of computers led to strong and persistent growth for skilled workers, which accounts for the increased demand (and subsequent expansion of supply) for workers who have gone to college.

In summary, even though AI is expected to temporarily decrease real wages, in the long run it will increase real wages, on average, because of the investment it stimulates. The next section highlights the role of comparative advantage behind the reallocation of tasks across and within sectors of the labor market (Acemoglu and Autor 2011), explaining how firms will apply AI in ways that are complementary to labor and therefore have a more positive effect on real wages, and a less negative effect on labor's share of GDP than shown in figure 7-2.

Trade between People and Machines

When and how much is AI likely to substitute for human tasks? The principle of comparative advantage tells us that human workers can benefit from being in the same market with machines, even if these machines excel at many traditionally human tasks. The benefit comes from workers' specialization in the tasks humans can do better than machines, or at least the tasks where humans are at the smallest disadvantage (Autor 2015). Specialization allows the machines to be used on their best tasks without wasting resources on tasks that people can do at a lower opportunity cost. To put it another way, even if it were technologically possible to let machines do all tasks, and do them better than humans do, an owner of the machines would sacrifice profits by deploying them without regard for specialization.

Consider the operation of a store that requires cashier tasks, communication with suppliers, the delivery of products, and arranging displays. The AI machines perform the arrangement tasks 10 times better (in terms of speed and accuracy) than humans, and perform the other tasks 20 times better. Given comparative advantage, and assuming that the machines are cheap enough to justify using them for any task, profit-maximizing deployment will have workers performing the arrangement tasks, thereby freeing up machines to do the other tasks where they are especially productive. The theory of comparative advantage means that humans inevitably have a comparative role to play, even if they do not have an absolute advantage in every task.

Moreover, the choice of which machines to deploy is not merely determined by what is technically possible with engineering and computer science.[8] Robocop, *Star Wars'* C-3PO, and other near-human machines are great entertainment, but in many situations they would be poor investments precisely because of their close similarities to humans.[9] Because machines and AI are ultimately another form of capital, designing machines to complement, rather than substitute for, humans will be more profitable. In other words, the potential for specialization implies that producers will look for ways to magnify differences with people. For example, Abel and others (2017) explain how providing algorithms with expert (human) advice—part of a broader class of "Human-in-the-Loop Reinforcement Learning"—can improve various aspects of learning and prediction.

---

[8] Consider the analogous case of agricultural tobacco production. Though some countries, like Brazil, display very labor-intensive tobacco production (Varga and Bonato 2007), U.S. production of tobacco is highly mechanized (Sykes 2008). For a similar illustration from cotton production, see FAO (2015). In this sense, the mere presence of capital does not guarantee its use; the opportunity cost of labor in an economy will drive the division of labor and degree of specialization. Lagakos and Waugh (2013) formalize these insights within a general equilibrium Roy model with agriculture and nonagriculture sectors.

[9] Research in human–machine interaction finds situations in which people can more easily and intuitively work with robotic partners when the robots look and behave in ways similar to humans. In these cases, people can project human expectations of how robots should act, and thus do not need to be trained (or study user manuals) in order to figure out how to work with the robot.

The purposeful acquisition of comparative advantage has long been observed in human labor markets (Becker and Murphy 1992). Consider an electrician and a carpenter who work together to build a high-quality house. Their comparative advantage is obvious at the time that they are building the house, but neither of them was born with his or her specialized skills. They both chose to specialize knowing directly—or perhaps indirectly, through market prices—that they would be a more valued member of a construction team if they could excel at carpentry, or excel at electrical work, rather than having mediocre skills at both types of tasks. Robotics research already suggests that productivity is enhanced when machines specialize (Nitschke, Schut, and Eiben 2012). Also see, for example, box 7-1, which describes the Defense Advanced Research Projects Agency's (DARPA's) initiatives regarding "partnering with machines." In light of these examples of complementarity between AI and humans, the entertainment industry's anthropomorphic portrayal of robotics and artificial intelligence is somewhat misleading about how much these types of investments will substitute for human workers.

The concern, of course, is that the price associated with human tasks will decline to a point where humans are driven out of the workforce and are not incentivized to work. For example, some manufacturers might find that production is cheaper with complete automation, rather than by retaining a mix of some human employees and AI. However, specialization and trade also occur at the market level. A robot-intensive business may engage in one phase of production, selling its output to a person-intensive business at a later phase of production. In this sense, even if certain tasks traditionally performed by humans are instead now done by machines, humans will nonetheless hold a comparative advantage for other tasks and thus will continue to play a role in production processes.

Although there are some concerns about complete automation of human activities (Frey and Osborne 2017), the emerging empirical evidence suggests that the main effects of AI and automation are on the composition of tasks within a job, rather than on occupations in general. For example, Brynjolfsson, Rock, and Mitchell (2018) introduce an index of suitability for machine learning (SML), and they find that, though most occupations have at least some tasks that are SML, few (if any) have tasks that are all SML. Similarly, Nedelkoska and Quintini (2018) use data on skills across occupations and 32 countries, and they find that, though 14 percent of jobs are likely to be automated by over 70 percent, 26 percent of jobs face a change of automation of 30 percent or less. The key observation is that, as automation progresses, workers will increasingly be drawn to the jobs and tasks that are more difficult to automate. Astute policymaking will nonetheless play a role in promoting workforce development, particularly for less educated workers—through, for example, the Pledge to America's Workers, which we discuss later in the chapter.

Box 7-1. DARPA: Strategic Investments in Artificial Intelligence and Cybersecurity

The Defense Advanced Research Projects Agency (DARPA) is focused on a future where AI is a complement to humans in the production of goods, services, and ideas—that is, where humans can safely "partner with machines" more as colleagues, rather than as tools (DARPA 2018a). To facilitate this vision, DARPA is actively funding the development and application of a so-called third wave of AI technologies that would result in intelligent machines capable of reasoning in context. In particular, DARPA announced a $2 billion, multiyear investment in new and existing programs in September 2018. These investment areas include "security clearance vetting or accrediting software systems for operational deployment; improving the robustness and reliability of AI systems; enhancing the security and resiliency of machine learning and AI technologies; reducing power, data, and performance inefficiencies; and pioneering the next generation of AI algorithms and applications, such as 'explainability' and commonsense reasoning" (DARPA 2018a).

DARPA has already piloted a number of successful programs, including the Cyber Grand Challenge in 2016—a competition that showcased the state of the art in Cyber Reasoning Systems (DARPA 2018b). Competing systems played an "attack-defend" style of "Capture the Flag," where contestants were tasked with developing AI algorithms to "autonomously identify and patch vulnerabilities in their own software while simultaneously attacking the other teams' weaknesses" (Hoadley and Lucas 2018).

Although conventional cybersecurity programs may take up to several months to find and patch problems, the competing and largely rules-based algorithms found the bugs in seconds. According to DARPA (2016), "the need for automated, scalable, machine-speed vulnerability detection and patching is large and growing fast as more and more systems . . . get connected to and become dependent upon the Internet." The major innovation in the Cyber Grand Challenge was the demonstration that AI can play both an offensive and defensive role. DARPA continues to build out these human-machine cyber detection capabilities for pinpointing and addressing vulnerabilities through its Computers and Humans Exploring Software Security program, known as CHESS. The activities funded by CHESS involve helping computers and humans work collaboratively through tasks, such as finding zero-day vulnerabilities at scale and speed.

The Uneven Effects of Technological Change

This section delineates the uneven effects of technological change. It first considers these changes' differential effects by occupation and skill. Then it explores the scale and factor-substitution effects of an industry's technological progress and how they moderate the effect on labor. Finally, the section asks when we will see the effects of AI on the economy.

Differential Effects by Occupation and Skill

Many types of technological change affect workers and industries in heterogeneous ways. For example, the widespread adoption of computers and information technology during the past several decades has enormously increased productivity for certain types of workers, but has brought comparatively little or no productivity enhancement for others (Acemoglu et al. 2014). Because earnings are determined by workers' productivity, such changes in technology are expected to have varying effects on workers with different sets of skills, such as workers with or without a college or graduate education (Katz and Murphy 1992).

Economists have concluded that "skill-biased technical change" can account for most of the observed rise in earnings disparities between some higher-skilled workers (whose productivity was greatly enhanced by technology, like computers) and some lower-skilled workers (who were less affected), which was amplified during the IT revolution (Autor, Katz, and Krueger 1998; Autor, Levy, and Murnane 2003). This disparity is in part explained by the complementarity between capital and certain types of skills (Krusell et al. 2000). In the context of AI and automation, the complementary relationship means that there is processing power that mainly benefits workers who use computer technology. In this sense, the more rapid increase in earnings among college-educated workers, despite the corresponding rise in the supply of these workers, represents a skills premium for individuals who can leverage technology to augment their productivity (Juhn, Murphy, and Pierce 1993).

The Scale and Factor–Substitution Effects of an Industry's Technological Progress

Technological progress allows an industry to produce the same output with fewer inputs (e.g., workers). At first glance, we might therefore expect workers to leave the industry and find work elsewhere. One could point to the example of changes in agriculture in the 20th century, when the agricultural employment share dropped from 41 to 2 percent between 1900 and 2000 (Autor 2015), at the same time that agricultural TFP rapidly increased (Herrendorf, Rogerson, and Valentinyi 2014). See box 7-2 for an example of technological change in the agricultural sector that has fueled productivity.

Box 7-2. Technological Change in Agriculture and Rural America

Agriculture has been one of the sectors experiencing rapid technological change, including the computer science revolution. For example, output per hour in the agricultural sector grew annually by 4.3 percent between 1948 and 2011, whereas it grew annually by 2.4 percent in manufacturing (Wang et al. 2015).

For example, precision agriculture—which refers to a broad class of AI applications allowing for precise control over agricultural inputs based on detailed, site-specific data—has allowed farmers to improve the productivity of soil by better understanding the characteristics that are most conducive to growth within a specific geographic area; see figure 7-i for evidence on its incidence across peanut and soybean farming. Moreover, these systems contain sensors that allow farmers to monitor crop yields and self-guided tractors and variable rate planters that vary their seeding and fertilizer rates based on fertility and past yield data. In brief, these technologies have allowed corn and soybean farmers, among others, to produce more at lower costs (Schimmelpfennig 2016).

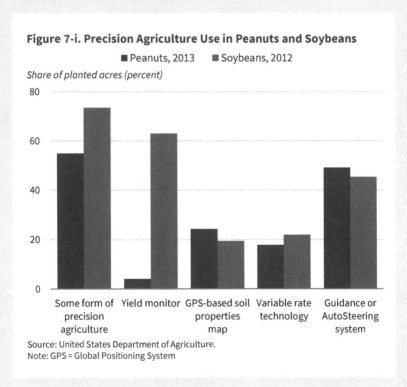

Figure 7-i. Precision Agriculture Use in Peanuts and Soybeans

■ Peanuts, 2013   ■ Soybeans, 2012

Share of planted acres (percent)

Source: United States Department of Agriculture.
Note: GPS = Global Positioning System

AI is also used in animal agriculture. For example, over 35,000 robotic milking systems are in operation globally on dairy farms. According to Salfer and others (2017), farms using robotic milking systems are much more productive, selling 43 percent more milk per hired worker and 9 percent more milk per cow. Moreover, rather than displacing humans, the introduction of automation in dairy farms has allowed labor and management to reallocate their time toward maintaining animal health, analyzing records, and managing reproduction and nutrition on the farms. For example, John Deere runs a two-year associate degree program to help its employees not only stay current on the latest farming machine tools but also acquire new skills in data science (Burkner et al. 2017).

However, rural Americans have not always seen the gains of technological progress (Forman, Goldfarb, and Greenstein 2012). Motivated by these disparities, President Trump signed Executive Order 13821 in January 2018 (White House 2018c), expanding and streamlining access to broadband in rural America. Given the importance of high-speed Internet access for data science capabilities, connectivity in rural America is essential for its economic competitiveness. Moreover, the Trump Administration is committed to investing in and promoting workforce development through, for example, the Pledge to America's Workers, which we discuss in below in this chapter's main text.

However, as an industry's productivity advances, it is producing each unit of output at a lower cost and thereby selling at lower prices. Consumers of this output respond by purchasing more, which is a force toward more industry employment known as the "scale effect" on labor demand. The productivity revolution in agriculture did result in more production and higher sales of food. However, because consumers' demand for agricultural output is price inelastic—consumers spend less of their budget on agriculture when it becomes cheaper—the "factor-substitution effect" dominated the scale effect on the demand for agricultural labor.[10]

If demand for a good is price elastic—meaning that consumers spend more of their budget on the good when prices fall—then cost-reducing technology might raise that sector's shares of employment and GDP. Consider the recent history of taxi dispatchers, who take calls from individuals desiring a ride and direct a driver to the pickup point. About a decade ago, companies discovered how to use a smartphone to perform the tasks of the dispatcher, and these companies famously distributed such an app to millions of smartphone users. The result was a dramatic increase in the number of people working in the transportation industry, broadly understood to include drivers for Uber,

---

[10] The decomposition of labor demand into scale and factor-substitution effects is usually attributed to Alfred Marshall (1890) and John Hicks (1932).

Lyft, and other ride-sharing platforms. By observing what happened to overall employment in the industry (which provides rides for passengers, and which now includes ride sharing in addition to traditional taxis), we can see that it had price-elastic demand. The cost reductions associated with the new technology increased the number of rides even more than it increased the number of humans giving rides.

Although there is some difficulty in measuring participants in the sharing economy in ways that are directly comparable with traditional taxi employment, there is emerging evidence of its expansion. For example, JPMorgan Chase (2018) found that the share of families generating earnings on transportation platforms over the course of a year increased to 2.4 percent of the labor force in March 2018 after the inception of ride sharing in about 2010 (figure 7-3).[11] A large part of the increase came from the introduction of 460,000 driver-partners in just three years under the Uber platform alone (Hall and Krueger 2018). Increasing empirical evidence suggests that these ride-sharing applications not only have provided significant flexibility for drivers (Chen et al., forthcoming; Koustas 2019) but also have generated social welfare benefits for those who are not platform participants (Cohen et al. 2016; Makridis and Paik 2018).

These ride-sharing applications are an early, pre–autonomous vehicle (AV) manifestation of transportation as a service. Whereas transportation has traditionally been about assets (i.e., vehicle ownership), it may increasingly move toward services as more AVs enter the market. For example, even though PricewaterhouseCoopers (PwC) estimates that the transportation sector may require 138 million fewer cars in Europe and the U.S. by 2030 (PwC 2018a), it also estimates that the market for shared, on-demand vehicles may grow to $1.4 trillion by 2030, in comparison with $87 billion in 2017 (PwC 2018b). Though predicting the growth in the AV market is outside the scope of this Report, the emerging patterns in ride sharing and AVs are illustrative examples of the impact of technological change.

When Will We See the Effects of AI on the Economy?

Some economists have noted a puzzling productivity paradox with the historical and ongoing patterns described above. Although most researchers agree that the recent advances in AI and automation promise production possibilities that are even greater than the initial emergence of the digital

---

[11] The National Academies (2017) also cite estimates pointing toward growth from 10 to 16 percent in alternative work arrangements between 2005 and 2015. According to Katz and Krueger (2018), who did a survey in November 2015, 0.5 percent of workers report working through an online intermediary. Though there is debate about the measurement of alternative work arrangements, a recent assessment by Katz and Krueger (2019) concludes that, despite the only modest increase in these arrangements obtained from the 2005 and 2017 Contingent Work Surveys in the Current Population Survey, this survey's data are likely underestimates.

Figure 7-3. Share of Respondents Reporting Income from Ride-Sharing Platforms in the Past Year, 2013–18

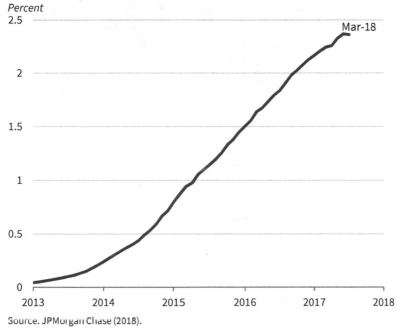

Percent

Source. JPMorgan Chase (2018).

economy (Brynjolfsson and McAfee 2014), the growth of labor productivity, at least in the way it has traditionally been measured, has been surprisingly sluggish.[12] For example, in contrast to the 2.8 percent annual growth in aggregate labor productivity seen in the United States between 1995 and 2004, its annual growth between 2005 and 2015 was only 1.3 percent (Syverson 2017). This pattern is consistent with growth across other economies; Syverson (2017) found the annual growth rate in labor productivity was 2.3 percent between 1995 and 2004 in 29 sampled countries, but fell to 1.1 percent between 2005 and 2015.

If technological change and the adoption of AI have been especially rapid during the past decade, what can account for the slower growth of labor productivity? One possibility is that the productivity effects of technology may have been oversold (Gordon 2000) and the period of rapid growth of the Information Age was a temporary aberration in a long-run trend toward slower technology-related productivity growth (Gordon 2018). However, Oliner and Sichel (2000) show, using a multisector neoclassical growth model with both IT and non-IT capital, that the increase in IT and corresponding efficiency gains account for two-thirds of the increase in labor productivity for the nonfarm

---

[12]As the Nobel laureate Robert Solow famously said, "You can see the computer age everywhere but in the productivity statistics."

business sector over the 1990s.[13] Moreover, Byrne, Oliner, and Sichel (2013) apply the same framework and fit more recent data between 2004 and 2012, suggesting that there is no inconsistency with theory. Jorgensen and Stiroh (2000) also obtain slightly lower contributions to growth from computer hardware because they use a broader definition of output. Yet another related explanation is that the expansion of credit in the early 2000s led to a misallocation of investment into less productive sectors, creating a drag on growth (Borio et al. 2016). However, productivity has recently ticked up (e.g., see chapter 10 of this *Report*). Therefore, secular stagnation and the misallocation of investment do not appear to be viable explanations.

Another possibility is that our official estimates of growth and productivity fail to capture many of the recent gains from technological advancement. Many of today's new technologies involve little or no direct cost to consumers, but give them great utility. These developments include, for example, Internet social networks, information search capabilities, and downloadable media. A quick Internet search today can yield information that, a few generations ago, would have required a team of individuals searching a university library—such benefits are not captured in our measurement of GDP. Though these benefits are clearly important factors behind consumer welfare (Brynjolfsson, Eggers, and Gannamaneni 2018), mismeasurement between 2005 and 2015 would need to be unrealistically high to account for the sluggish GDP growth, relative to the overall trend (Syverson 2017).

Perhaps the strongest argument for why productivity statistics in recent history have not shown the expected benefits from the new technologies is that, for practical reasons, there have so far simply been lags between productivity and the widespread implementation of AI and ML. The theoretical genesis of this argument is an insight from Paul David (1990). Much as the dynamo and the computer were fundamental components of a broader technological infrastructure, AI is a similar general purpose technology. Although these discoveries often have immediate effects on productivity, their full impact is not realized until all the complementary investments are made, thereby creating a lag with investment. Brynjolfsson, Rock, and Syverson (2017) apply this logic to AI, reconciling the productivity paradox. Under their preferred interpretation of the data, we are simply awaiting the results of a necessary trial-and-error process and the productivity benefits will eventually be realized.

---

[13] An integral part of the efficiency gains among producers of computer equipment is the rapid decline in effective prices of semiconductors due to advances in chip technology (Triplett 1996). Byrne, Oliner, and Sichel (2017) find that semiconductor prices measured with a hedonic index fell at an estimated annual rate of 42 percent between 2009 and 2013, much faster than the 6 percent decline experienced by the microprocessor producer price index series that provides a broader measure that subsumes semiconductors.

Cybersecurity Risks of Increased Reliance on Computer Technology

Although technological advances and the emergence of AI have the potential to raise productivity and economic growth, the widespread reliance on technology also exposes the economy to new threats of malicious cyber activity. Cyber threat actors may be nation-states, cyber terrorists, organized criminal groups, "hacktivists" (individuals or collectives that aim to advance their social agenda through cyber interference), or simply disgruntled individuals. These threats transcend the typical boundaries of conflict, which have been analyzed through the lens of land, sea, and air. However, the emergence of the "Internet of Things" implies that anything connected to the Internet is vulnerable to malicious cyber intrusions, introducing threat vectors throughout the Internet ecosystem (Hoffman 2009).

Malicious cyber activity imposes costs on the U.S. economy through the theft of intellectual property and personally identifiable information, denial-of-service attacks, data and equipment destruction, and ransomware attacks. The CEA estimated this cost to be as high as $109 billion in 2016 (CEA 2018b). Most innovations, however, lead to little-understood risks, whether for new drugs or computer technologies. This section describes our current assessment of the scope of cyber vulnerabilities, how they vary by industry, and the factors that may exacerbate failures to adopt cybersecurity best practices.

Assessing the Scope of the Cyber Threat

The 2018 *Economic Report of the President* (CEA 2018b) estimated the 2016 costs of malicious cyber activity by adding up the costs experienced by the private sector, the public sector, and private individuals. It estimated the costs to the private sector using event-study methodology, whereby it quantified the loss of firm value as a result of an adverse cyber event. It estimated the costs to the corporate sector using event-study methodology, whereby it quantified the loss of firm value as a result of an adverse cyber event. The estimate further took into account the spillover effect of these costs to economically linked firms. On the basis of a sample of cyber incidents occurring between January 2000 and January 2017, the *Report* estimated that the total economic cost for 2016 ranged between $57 and $109 billion.

Although these event studies provide an important starting point for evaluating the costs of cybersecurity incidents, they presuppose that the timing of the event was reliably recorded and that investors knew the distribution of new risks induced by the event. However, to give just one example, when the largest recorded data breach, according to the Privacy Rights Clearinghouse, occurred in late 2013, it was not reported until September 2016 (Lee 2016). Delays between the time when an incident takes place and the time it is reported are a function of not only a firm's ability to identify the incident but also of varying State laws that mandate disclosure (Bisogni 2016).[14] The affected firm's own estimate of the damage caused by the 2013 breach has been updated and increased on several occasions, illustrating how difficult it can be to accurately calculate the cost. Moreover, data on the number of records or systems that have been breached often contain significant measurement error and sampling variability.

In addition to reporting discrepancies across States, there are also discrepancies across sectors. Makridis and Dean (2018) study sector discrepancies using data from the Privacy Rights Clearinghouse and the Department of Health and Human Services to investigate the relationship between recorded breaches and firm outcomes. Though they find some evidence of a negative association between productivity and record breaches in the Health and Human Services data, where healthcare companies face greater disclosure requirements, they do not find such evidence in the data from the Privacy Rights Clearinghouse covering all sectors. Publicly traded companies, based on requirements from the Securities and Exchange Commission (SEC 2011), must provide timely and ongoing information in the periodic reports of material cybersecurity risks and incidents that trigger disclosure obligations. Beyond the Federal securities laws, other reporting standards in specific sectors, like the Health Insurance Portability and Accountability Act, may result in disclosures of other data breaches that are not material.

Since 2009, the National Cybersecurity and Communications Integration Center (NCCIC) of the Department of Homeland Security (DHS) has served as the Nation's flagship cyber defense, incident response, and operational integration center. The NCCIC serves as the national hub for cyber and communication information, technical expertise, and operational integration, operating a 24/7 watch floor tasked with providing situational awareness, analysis, and incident response capabilities to the Federal government; private sector stakeholders; and State, Local, Tribal, and Territorial Partners. Through this process, DHS has been collecting robust data on the types of incidents that are having an impact on the Nation. Furthermore, the Federal Bureau of Investigation (FBI) also maintains CyWatch, a 24/7 command center for cyber intrusion prevention and response operations based on consensual monitoring and third parties that report to the FBI. CyWatch monitors must notify companies whose network security has been breached (34 U.S.C. § 20141 creates an obligation for Federal law enforcement agencies to notify victims of a crime). After notification, CyWatch shares information with its partner law enforcement agencies—including the Department of Defense, DHS, and National Security

---

[14] Using data from the Privacy Rights Clearinghouse, Bisogni, Asghari, and Van Eeten (2017) estimate that adoption of the "inform credit agency" and the "notification publication by informed attorneys general" State provisions would increase the number of publicly reported cybersecurity breaches by at least 46 percent.

Figure 7-4. Cybersecurity Breaches That Were Made Public, 2005–18

Number of breaches

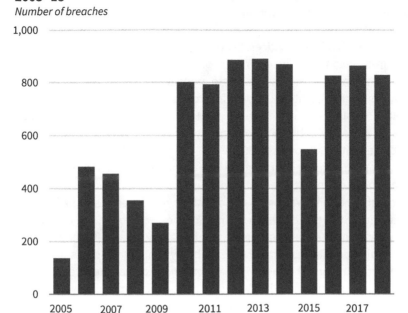

Sources: Privacy Rights Clearinghouse; CEA calculations.

Agency—to improve preparedness and attribution behind attacks and guide appropriate responses.[15]

Despite the serious limitations associated with data from the Privacy Rights Clearinghouse, they nonetheless provide a time series proxy for the increased frequency of data breaches since 2005; see figure 7-4. Although there is an upward trend in cyber breaches between 2005 and 2018, these data largely understate the number of data breaches (Bisogni, Asghari, and Van Eeten 2017; ITRC 2019). The Internet Crime Complaint Center, a partnership between the FBI and National White Collar Crime Center, gives victims of cybercrime an accessible reporting mechanism for alerting the authorities about suspected criminal or civil violations. Although not directly comparable, the 2017 "Internet Crime Report" announced a total of 301,580 complaints of cyber breaches in 2017. Even though these complaints represent a broader range of potential Internet crimes, the number far exceeds the 863 publicly reported incidents.

Recommending possible solutions for these cyber vulnerabilities requires an accurate understanding of their sources. We suggest that there are at least

---

[15] Though exact attribution in cyberspace is possible, it requires not only technical expertise but also leadership and information sharing and coordinating across the layers of an organization (Rid and Buchanan 2015).

two underlying drivers behind the above-mentioned empirical regularities. First, organizations could lack informational awareness. Much like the quantitative management science literature on the adoption of best practices in business (Bloom et al. 2013), many organizations might simply not be aware of basic cyber hygiene practices. Second, the executives of organizations could suffer from incomplete incentives to promote cybersecurity practices. If, for example, financial metrics are easier to measure, relative to cybersecurity, then managers might allocate too little effort to cybersecurity due to a "multitasking problem" (Holmstrom and Milgrom 1991). Particularly because cybersecurity breaches generate network externalities, the private sector could underinvest in cybersecurity (Gordon et al. 2015).

Our preceding evidence on the lack of many basic cybersecurity practices among the most profitable companies in the U.S. economy suggests that a lack of information awareness and a lack of resources are unlikely to be the primary culprits behind existing vulnerabilities. Moreover, the "Cybersecurity Framework" of the National Institute of Standards and Technology's (NIST 2014), which details best practices, is publicly available and has been disseminated through many channels. These facts suggest that the alternative culprit could be incomplete incentives arising from agency problems within organizations that lead managers to overlook cyber hygiene.

Information sharing and dissemination of best practices must remain a priority, particularly for small businesses that are more likely to lack the resources or infrastructure to search out and implement best practices. In particular, information needs to be publicly available, transparent, and shared to disseminate best practices and call attention to dangerous practices. For example, Gal-Or and Ghose (2005) show that industry-based information sharing and analysis centers can lead to improvements in social welfare, but the degree of competition in the marketplace is an important moderating factor that determines whether a firm participates. In particular, unless firms in an industry understand the downside associated with their vulnerability to cyberattacks, they may not realize the gains that can come from collaboration through information sharing.

Many security operations companies also provide a source of market discipline by promoting transparency and information vis-à-vis cyber vulnerabilities (such organizations that raise firms' awareness of cybersecurity flaws are often referred to as "white hat hackers"). Conversely, a survey by Malwarebytes (2018) suggests that roughly 1 in 10 U.S. security professionals admit to considering participating in "black hat hacker" activity, which involves exploiting discovered cybersecurity vulnerabilities for financial gain. Roughly 50 percent of security professionals say they have known or know someone involved in black hat hacking activities.

Potential Vulnerabilities by Industry

The prevalence of cyber threats suggests that firms are relatively unprepared to protect themselves. Indeed, according to Hiscox (2018a), in 2017 nearly three-quarters of organizations based in the United Kingdom, the United States, Germany, Spain, and the Netherlands failed basic cyber readiness tests. Even though the United States ranks higher than most countries in cyber readiness (Makridis and Smeets 2018), its preparedness is still poor enough to concern policymakers studying the impact of cyber insecurity on the U.S. economy.

To better understand these cybersecurity risks at a more granular level, Rapid7, an Internet security firm whose business model involves collecting publicly observable data on cybersecurity practices of any firm with an Internet presence, shared its 2018 data for *Fortune* 500 companies with the CEA. Using public data and a proprietary methodology, Rapid7 matches uniquely identified Internet protocol addresses of Internet-connected devices to a specific firm. Though the security scan is voluntary, only 4 percent of *Fortune* 500 firms opt out. These data show that the majority of *Fortune* 500 companies are vulnerable to cyberattacks, and thus fail to take even the most basic security measures. And though there are many metrics for gauging vulnerabilities, we focus here on an important and transparent metric: whether email has been configured for protection against spam.

Motivated by the frequency of phishing email attacks, which are the most common method used by malicious cyber actors to penetrate network security, configuring a secure email network is one of the first lines of defense. One metric for email security is whether the organization has adopted the Domain-Based Message Authentication, Reporting & Conformance (DMARC) protocol. Although it is not a panacea for all types of phishing attacks, DMARC allows senders and receivers to authenticate whether a message is legitimately from a sender. Adopting DMARC for email makes it easier for organizations to not only identify spam and phishing messages, but also to keep them out of employees' inboxes, thereby reducing the probability that an employee accidentally clicks on a link. Moreover, properly configured DMARC records are able to actively quarantine or reject emails that are a threat to safety by allowing the message's sender to signal to the recipient that the message is protected by a Sender Policy Framework and/or as DomainKeys Identified Mail. We note, however, that DMARC is only one metric out of many and that having it does not guarantee cyber safety.

Figure 7-5 reports the percentage of all *Fortune* 500 firms without a DMARC email configuration, together with value added, across industrial sectors. This figure illustrates significant exposure across industries, ranging from 40 percent of firms in business services to 93 percent of those in chemicals that are not implementing DMARC protocol. Moreover, although we do not interpret the relationship between value added and a lack of DMARC as causal, the data suggest that a 10-percentage-point increase in share of firms without DMARC in a sector is associated with $345 billion less in value added in that sector (in 2017 dollars). This suggests that greater adoption of DMARC could avoid breaches and phishing scams.

Given that the combined market value of the *Fortune* 500 firms is over $21 trillion, these results suggest that much of this value may be exposed to cyber thefts of intellectual property, various destructive and ransomware attacks, and the destruction of reputational capital. Moreover, as outlined in the 2018 *Economic Report of the President*, an attack on entities—especially large, publicly traded *Fortune* 500 firms that are part of the Nation's critical infrastructure—could have effects throughout the U.S. economy, affecting other firms in the supply chain and individual customers. Given the limited preparedness among *Fortune* 500 companies—manifested by not only the failure to adopt DMARC, but also a range of other cyber vulnerabilities detailed by Rapid7 (2018)—an additional concern is that smaller firms may have even less robust cybersecurity measures in place (Hiscox 2018b).

The Federal government continues to modernize its cyber practices. OMB and DHS worked together to transform the Trusted Internet Connection (TIC) policies and processes so that Federal departments and agencies can take advantage of common and advanced cloud computing capabilities to meet their requirements. AI is not specifically identified in the policy updates, but departments and agencies are now able to use outside expertise in the cloud, which can include using AI and other methods, while continuously meeting appropriate cybersecurity and privacy controls. In alignment with the action steps identified in the *Report to the President on Federal IT Modernization* (American Technology Council 2017), those cooperating in the interagency effort continue to identify if there are any real or perceived policy limitations, by working through cases of real-world use that support their current and future needs. This continuous approach is instrumental for realizing the value of AI and other methods that best meet national needs.

The Federal government is more prepared than the private sector to protect against phishing attacks, which are a primary method for hackers to gain access to enterprises, due to the 2017 Binding Operational Directive 18-01, which introduced requirements for agencies to enhance email and web security. Using data from the 2018 Federal "Cyber Exposure Scorecard," figure 7-6 plots the number of government agencies with various email configurations. In the figure, "fully rejects" means that an organization has properly configured its email, whereas "no rejections" means that it is vulnerable to an attack. Government agencies' use of the DMARC email configuration is 47.9 percent, which is better than the average of 26 percent in the private sector. Moreover, of the 1,018 Federal second-level "dot-gov" domains, 86 percent have a valid DMARC record with a policy of "reject." Though adoption of DMARC is only one of many indicators of cyber hygiene, and was linked to the implementation

Figure 7-5. Industries That Are Most Lacking the DMARC Protocol Among *Fortune* 500 Companies by Value Added, 2017

Value added by industry (billions, 2017)

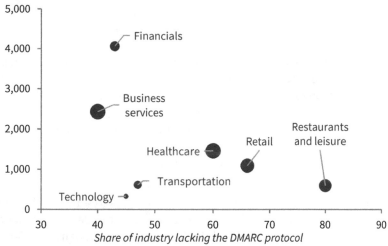

Share of industry lacking the DMARC protocol

Sources: Rapid7; Bureau of Labor Statistics; Bureau of Economic Analysis; CEA calculations.
Note: DMARC = Domain-Based Message Authentication, Reporting & Conformance, which is an email validation system designed to detect and prevent the use of forged sender addresses for phishing and email-based malware. Points are scaled by industry employment in 2017, and only the top 10 sectors (ranked by employment) are plotted.

Figure 7-6. DMARC Protocol Use Across Government Agencies, 2018

Number of agencies

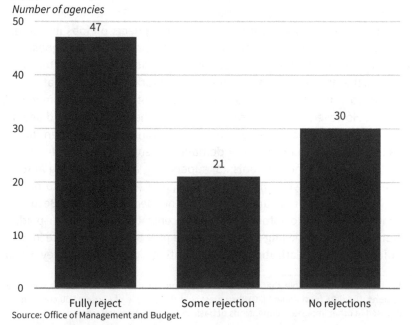

Source: Office of Management and Budget.

of Binding Operational Directive 18-01 across Federal agencies, these results nonetheless suggest that Federal cyber best practices could set an example for the private sector.[16]

The Role of Policy

This section discusses the longer-run policy implications of both AI advancement and cybersecurity issues, and details the Trump Administration's current policies in these areas. The discussion highlights the Administration's priorities for AI readiness and implementation, reskilling, and cybersecurity initiatives to contend with the changing nature of work and emerging technological threats.

Policy Considerations as AI Advances: Preparing for a Reskilling Challenge

As discussed in earlier in this chapter, economists agree that technological change resulting from AI will affect the structure of the demand for labor in the years to come (Brynjolfsson and McAfee 2014; Agrawal, Gans, and Goldfarb 2018). One potential challenge that policymakers could face as AI advances is an increase in the number of workers who need new skills to find work in a changed labor market. Reskilling efforts, both for workers whose jobs have been displaced by technology and for those who need new skills to operate new technologies, could become more urgent as the demand for labor enters a new phase of its decades-long evolution. For example, the World Economic Forum (2018) found in a sample of firms that at least 54 percent of all employees will require significant reskilling and/or upskilling by 2022.

In 2016, the Obama Administration's Council of Economic Advisers examined the economics of AI, including its possible effects on jobs in the future, predicting that "2.2 to 3.1 million existing part- and full-time U.S. jobs may be threatened or substantially altered," by AI. In addition, it predicted roughly 364,000 self-employed "drivers" (ride-sharing workers) would be at risk from a shift toward use of autonomous vehicles as of May 2015 estimates (CEA 2016, 15). However, they also concluded that other workers could see a rise in productivity and increasing demand for certain skills. They identified four areas that could see a rise in labor demand: (1) engaging with AI to complete tasks, (2) developing new AI tools, (3) supervising and maintaining AI tools to ensure they are achieving the desired aims, and (4) responding to paradigm shifts where entirely new approaches are needed (CEA 2016). Because the jobs most vulnerable to automation are concentrated among lower-paid, less-educated workers, reskilling programs could play an important role in helping avert further wage polarization and reallocating skills to where they are most

---

[16] Although it is also possible that the Federal government does not perform as well in other dimensions, the data from Rapid7 (2018) suggest that the sample of *Fortune* 500 companies also are exposed in other important dimensions of basic cybersecurity practices.

needed. The CEA (2016) made three primary recommendations: (1) investing and developing AI for its many benefits in both the public and private sectors, (2) educating and training workers so they are prepared for the jobs of the future, and (3) helping workers transition across jobs to ensure shared gains from technological change.

More recently, in discussing how automation may interact with the economy and workforce, the CEA (2018a) has referred to an observation made in a report by the National Academies (2017, 140), that continued advance of information technology implies "workers will require skills that increasingly emphasize creativity, adaptability, and interpersonal skills over routine information processing and manual tasks." This report also reiterates findings by the Organization for Economic Cooperation and Development (OECD 2018), among others, that workers who have not obtained a college degree are most at risk for displacement by automation. Similarly, motivated by the declining college and cognitive skills premium—as documented by Beaudry, Green, and Sand (2016); Valletta (2016); and Gallipoli and Makridis (2018)—individuals in occupations that involve greater IT-based tasks have continued experiencing rising wage premiums. All these pieces of empirical evidence point to the need for digital skills in the emerging labor market.

Policymakers may also address the concern that job losses from automation could disproportionately affect those who are least able to afford the tuition costs of reskilling programs up front, and those who are least likely to be able to sustain a forfeiture of labor income for the duration of the reskilling period. Gallipoli and Makridis (2018) find that individuals in jobs that tend to require more routine and manual skills are especially exposed to the growing demand for IT-based tasks. Another factor to consider in future policymaking is the unpredictable nature of disruption on the workforce. In determining federally funded programs to address displaced workers, the CEA (2018a, 21) cautions against programs targeting specific industries, instead suggesting that "keeping programs as flexible as possible reduces the need for continual re-optimization and increases the return on Federal dollars spent."

In addition to studying reskilling challenges, the Trump Administration has also established the President's National Council of the American Worker to develop and implement a strategy aimed at expanding educational attainment, training, and nontraditional degree programs that will prepare workers for the emergence of automation and AI (White House 2018a). Chapter 3 of this *Report* discusses the reskilling challenge in detail, including the job openings rates by industry.

The opportunity for reskilling is perhaps greatest in the field of cybersecurity, where there is a shortage of skilled workers (Burning Glass 2018). Figure 7-7, for example, uses 2018 data from CyberSeek (2018)—a partnership between Burning Glass Technologies, the Computing Technology Industry Association, and the National Initiative for Cybersecurity Education—to

Figure 7-7. Supply-and-Demand Ratio for Cybersecurity Jobs, 2018

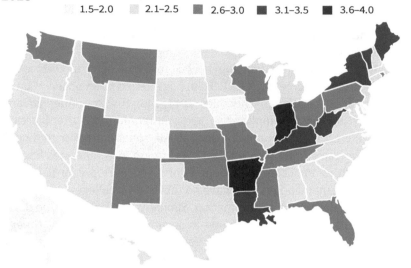

| | 1.5–2.0 | | 2.1–2.5 | | 2.6–3.0 | | 3.1–3.5 | | 3.6–4.0 |

Source: CyberSeek (2018).

characterize the ratio of supply and demand for cybersecurity workers across locations (e.g., States). Although no State has a ratio less than 1, the vast cross-sectional heterogeneity highlights how different State labor markets face very different intensities of shortage (e.g., the District of Columbia has a value of 1.4, vs. Kentucky, which has a value of 3.2). To put these numbers in perspective, a value of 2 means that half of a State's existing cybersecurity workforce would need to change jobs every year to meet new postings, underscoring the amount of turnover that would be required to meet the skills gap.

The Administration's Policies to Promote Cybersecurity

It is essential that the Federal government and the private sector promote cyber best practices and cyber hygiene. For example, as discussed above, many Federal agencies have properly configured their email systems with DMARC. DHS's National Cybersecurity Assessments and Technical Services team determined that 71 of the 96 Federal agencies surveyed have cybersecurity programs that are either at risk or at high risk, for at least four reasons, according to OMB (2018a); in the next paragraph, we summarize these factors from the "Federal Cybersecurity Risk Determination Report and Action Plan" (White House 2018a).

Government agencies, along with the private sector, are not always aware of the situational context and/or the resources that exist to tackle the current threat environment. For example, 38 percent of the Federal cyber incidents that were reported in 2018 did not specifically identify an attack vector. Organizations continue to adopt best practices, but there can be challenges with implementation. For example, only 49 percent of agencies have the ability to detect white-list software running on their systems.[17] Moreover, the lack of network visibility means that agencies may be unable to detect data exfiltration. For example, only 27 percent of agencies report that they have the ability to detect and investigate attempts to access large volumes of data. Finally, the lack of organizational and managerial policies surrounding the ownership of cybersecurity risk results in chief information officers or chief information security officers who lack the authority to make the relevant organization-wide decisions, but are nonetheless charged with the responsibility of maintaining network security. For example, only 16 percent of agencies achieved the government-wide target for encrypting inactive data.

These challenges are only going to grow, given the proliferation of data and increasing use of machine learning. Countries and malicious actors may turn toward counter-AI operations that attempt to alter and/or manipulate data (Weinbaum and Shanahan 2018). Individuals throughout the Federal civilian government, Department of Defense, intelligence community, and private sector will need to evolve to meet the expectations with identifying, protecting, detecting, responding, and recovering from threats in a timely manner. The Trump Administration—particularly through OMB, in partnership with the Department of Homeland Security, NIST, and the General Services Administration—is working to actively address these shortcomings. For example, the update to the TIC initiative is only one component of a broader effort by the Federal Chief Information Security Officer Council to obtain and test use-cases, particularly from the private sector (OMB 2018c). Moreover, as discussed in box 7-1, DARPA is developing new AI capabilities that help national security personnel more rapidly and reliably identify and address cybersecurity threats.

The Administration's Policies to Maintain American Leadership in Artificial Intelligence

The Trump Administration's AI agenda prioritizes advancing U.S. leadership in AI as well as helping the Nation's workforce adapt to the changes that are coming. As evidenced in the Administration's 2017 and 2018 budget priorities memoranda and highlighted at the White House AI summit in May 2018, the Administration continues to prioritize research-and-development funding for AI research and computing infrastructure, machine learning, and autonomous systems (OSTP 2018). To complement these active financial investments, the Administration also chartered the Select Committee on Artificial Intelligence under the National Science and Technology Council. This committee advises the White House on interagency research-and-development priorities, to foster

---

[17] An application white list refers to a set of applications that are authorized to be present according to a well-defined benchmark (Sedgewick, Souppaya, and Scarfone 2015).

collaboration between the private sector and academia, to identify opportunities to leverage Federal data and computational resources, and to improve the efficiency of government planning and coordination. The recent Executive Order on "Maintaining American Leadership in Artificial Intelligence" has formalized these commitments by calling for increased prioritization of investments, engaging in development of standards, and training and workforce development initiatives (White House 2019).

Second, the Administration has implemented policies that are conducive to more rapid economic growth and innovation by removing regulatory barriers, including those on the deployment of AI-powered technologies. In September 2017, the Department of Transportation released an update of the 2016 Federal Automated Vehicles Policy, providing nonregulatory guidance for AV developers, which was later further updated in October 2018 to provide a framework and multimodal approach to the safe integration of AVs into the surface transportation system. Similarly, the Administration is developing new rules in compliance with the Space Policy Directive–2 to streamline the licensing process for commercial space enterprises (White House 2018d). The Administration is also taking steps internationally to ensure that there is a level playing field for AI technologies. For example, at the World Trade Organization, and in trade agreements like the United States–Mexico–Canada Agreement, the Administration is protecting U.S. intellectual property and limiting the ability of foreign governments to require disclosure of proprietary computer source code and algorithms. These actions will better protect the competitiveness of our digital suppliers, and promoting access to government-generated public data, to enhance innovative use in commercial applications and services (USTR 2018).

Third, the Administration has begun integrating advances in AI and related technologies to improve the delivery of government services to the American people. The President's Management Agenda calls for the use of automation software to improve the efficiency of government services and maximize the applications of Federal data to help evaluate and modify Federal programs (OMB 2018b). In addition, in April 2017, the Department of Energy (DOE) and the Department of Veterans Affairs launched the Million Veteran Program Computational Health Analytics for Medical Precision to Improve Outcomes Now—known as CHAMPION—which uses high-performance computing infrastructure in the DOE National Laboratories to analyze large quantities of data and make recommendations that focus on suicide prevention and enhanced predictions and diagnoses of diseases (DOE 2017).

Recognizing that AI holds promise not only for greater economic opportunity but also for national security aims, the Trump Administration has directed considerable resources and leadership into targeted strategic investments, particularly at the nexus of AI and cybersecurity. One example, as discussed in box 7-1, is the Defense Advanced Research Projects Agency (DARPA 2018c), which is actively investing in a "third wave" of AI technologies to make AI more transparent and accessible for deployment across both the public and private sectors. In particular, these initiatives focus on identifying ways for humans to use AI as tools for more effectively completing their tasks and maintaining network security.

To complement these broad-based research-and-development funding priorities, the Administration signed a memorandum directing, "Secretary of Education DeVos to place high quality STEM [science, technology, engineering, and mathematics] education, particularly Computer Science, at the forefront of the Department of Education's priorities" (White House 2017b). The Department of Education is working to devote over $200 million a year in grant funds toward these STEM and computer science activities, in addition to exploring other administrative actions that will advance computer science in K–12 and postsecondary institutions. Moreover, box 7-3 describes the emerging National Cyber Education Program, which is a prime example of an initiative focused on increasing the supply of STEM talent, specifically for the cybersecurity field.

The Administration's Implementation of the National Cyber Strategy

In addition to the National Security Strategy (White House 2017a), the Administration has also developed the comprehensive 2018 National Cyber Strategy, the first of its kind in over 15 years, to address the cybersecurity challenges of the coming decades (White House 2018b). This strategy's fourfold overarching goals mirror the pillars of the 2017 National Security Strategy; we paraphrase and synthesize these four objectives here, together with their priority areas.

The first objective is protecting the American people, the Homeland, and the American way of life. To do this, the Administration is securing Federal networks and information, securing critical infrastructure, and combating cybercrime and improving incident reporting. Three priorities associated with this objective involve improving risk management and incident reporting practices, modernizing Federal technology and security systems, and streamlining processes and roles and responsibilities.

The second objective is promoting American prosperity. To accomplish this, the Administration is fostering a vibrant and resilient digital economy, encouraging and protecting U.S. ingenuity, and developing a superior cybersecurity workforce. The priorities associated with this objective include promoting an agile and next-generation digital infrastructure, protecting intellectual property, and creating a pipeline and incentive structure that cultivate highly skilled cybersecurity and technology workers.

The third objective is to preserve peace through strength. To do this, the Administration is enhancing cyber stability through norms of responsible

Box 7-3. Educating the Cyber Workforce of Tomorrow

One of the most commonly cited workforce challenges within both the public and private sectors is the shortage of skilled workers. According to recent estimates from International Information System Security Certification Consortium—known as ISC²—there is a shortage of 2.9 million cybersecurity employees globally (ISC² 2018). Moreover, numerous survey results suggest that organizations are increasingly more likely to report a shortage of cyber-security skills (Oltsik 2018; Burning Glass 2018).

Although there is debate about the its magnitude, there is a general recognition that more workers are needed to fill the increasing demand for cybersecurity skills, particularly as the paths by which hackers can gain access to computers and network servers expand in the growing digital economy. A national program that could help cultivate a new generation of cyber professionals prepared to meet the needs of the government, the defense community, and the private sector constitutes an Administration priority for both national security and the economy.

One example of a long-run and scalable solution is the National Cyber Education Program, which is a joint public–private initiative supported by the Trump Administration that seeks to inspire and educate children in elementary through high school about potential career paths and tools for careers in cybersecurity. This program is a multipart, public–private education initiative within the NIST Framework and with themes from the National Integrated Cyber Education Research Center at its core and strong support and leadership from a large educational services firm that serves 30 million K–12 students and 3 million teachers through its online education platform. This initiative includes these features:

1. Core curricular cyber content for grades K–12.
2. Virtual professional development for improving skills among STEM and cybersecurity educators to deliver content effectively and across disciplines.
3. Transformative learning tools and curricula for students to promote both technical content and real-world applications.
4. A career portal for connecting students with cybersecurity opportunities in government and the private sector, as well as regional conferences that provide access to counselors, educators, and industry professionals.
5. Tools for cybersecurity industry partners to engage their local communities, particularly schools, through volunteerism and mentorship.

The National Cyber Education Program has an estimated total budget of $20 to $25 million, which will be provided by a combination of committed private sponsors.

behavior and attributing and deterring unacceptable behavior in cyberspace. A priority related to this objective is countering malign cyber influence with information operations and better intelligence.

The fourth objective is to advance American influence. To accomplish this, the Administration is promoting an open, interoperable, reliable, and secure Internet and building international cyber capacity. Two priorities related to this objective include developing partnerships across the public and private sectors to promote innovation and cutting-edge technologies and promoting free and secure markets worldwide. As discussed in box 7-3, the National Cyber Education Program is an example of a public–private initiative that empowers teachers with the resources to improve learning outcomes and career pathways for students, particular for the emerging cyber workforce.

The Trump Administration is advancing these four objectives through a combination of short- and long-run efforts. In the long run, U.S. policymakers seek to prioritize an active and prepared pipeline of technology workers with mastery of information security practices. In the short run, the United States will continue strengthening network security, especially in critical infrastructure sectors. OMB issued a memorandum in May 2018 detailing the risk assessment process, which builds upon the Federal Information Security Modernization Act of 2014 Chief Information Officer metrics from 2017 and the Inspectors General metrics from 2016 (OMB 2018a). These metrics are based on the NIST Framework for Improving Critical Infrastructure Cybersecurity (NIST 2014), which provides best practices to which both public and private organizations can adhere, and aims to create predictability and encourage the adoption of best practices throughout government. Although no system in today's geopolitical environment is completely secure, these actions are setting the groundwork for a safe and secure digital infrastructure; see box 7-4 for a discussion of how Estonia became one of the world's leading countries in digital infrastructure.

Further Artificial Intelligence and Future of Work Policy Considerations

Motivated by the increasingly rapid pace of technological change and its implications for individuals, there are several lines of inquiry about the role of government.[18] First, some have suggested, as part of the social safety net, the

---

[18] We do not, however, discuss in depth the concerns about AI reaching a point of singularity, or general intelligence, whereby algorithms can create new ideas on their own without human assistance. Though the concept of singularity and the prospect of accelerated knowledge creation could lead to a large gain in productivity (Nordhaus 2015), an alternative scenario is one where algorithms would begin to dictate decisionmaking over human judgment. These discussions are beyond the scope of this chapter and the bulk of ongoing policy deliberations.

Box 7-4. Estonia: A Case Study of Modern Cybersecurity Practices

Although residents of Estonia rarely had access to electronic devices or the Internet a few decades ago, it has become an economic success story and digital leader in its region. Between 1995 and 2017, its real GDP grew by 141.5 percent (vs. 69.8 percent in the United States). According to the Estonian government, 99 percent of public services were available online as of 2017. Estonia does not use a centralized or master database, but rather X-Road—a software platform that allows links among its public and private e-service databases. According to the Estonian government, X-Road saves over 800 years of working time every year, reducing bureaucracy and raising efficiency (Vainsalu 2017).

Though Estonia "was, effectively, a disconnected society" in the early 2000s, moving toward a digital economy through the introduction of its X-road infrastructure has allowed the country to raise productivity and become more secure (Vassil 2015). Consider, for instance, queries involving vehicle registration data. Typically, this search would require three police officers working for about 20 minutes; but the X-Road software platform eases the retrieval of information, so a single officer can complete the search within a few seconds (Vassil 2015). All of Estonia's government services, ranging from collecting taxes to health records for personalized medical services, are made secure and readily accessible with the proper authentication credentials. These technological strides are arguably a major factor behind Estonia's emergence as one of the top countries for doing business, ranking as the most competitive tax system in the OECD, according to the Tax Foundation (2014), and as the seventh-most-free economy in the world, according to the Heritage Foundation (2018).

Interestingly, the number of queries through X-Road has grown exponentially, which is remarkable because similar digital services, such as data repositories and services, tend to grow linearly (Vassil 2015). An integral part of Estonia's success through X-Road has been its data security and privacy features. For example, citizens may use digital signatures, secured with a 2,048-bit encryption, to perform daily tasks such as banking and notarizing documents. Public safety has improved because the presence of digital identification cards has shortened response times to 10 seconds or less for 93 percent of emergency calls (Estonia 2018). In fact, as of 2018, the only legal transactions that one could not make online were marriage, divorces, and real estate. The core of these online activities is a 2000 digital signature law that created a framework for digital contracting.

Of course, the transition to a digital economy has come with increased targeting from other state and nonstate actors. Healthcare, energy, and the public sector face continuous cyberattacks, primarily from malware infections or outdated software. Perhaps Estonia's largest attack was in 2007; it involved distributed denial-of-service attacks that disabled computer networks, halting communication between the country's two largest banks and causing reverberations for political parties. After the attack, Estonia established the NATO Cooperative Cyber Defense Center of Excellence in its capital, Tallin, in addition to founding the Cyber Defense League, which works to counter cyberattacks (Czosseck, Ottis, and Talihärm 2011). These increased security precautions and this institutional infrastructure have helped thwart attacks, including a large attempted attack on the country's digital identification cards, raising public confidence. The system is highly secure because access to databases via X-Road is gated via a secure identification card using two-factor authentication and end-to-end encryption (Estonia 2018).

Estonia has continued to prioritize improving its digital economy, in addition to developing a broader global network in partnership with other countries; see, for example, Estonia's "Digital Agenda 2020," which details plans to improve the well-being of its people and public administration through digitization (Estonia 2018).

provision of a universal basic income, which would help individuals potentially suffering from job displacement. Proponents argue, for example, that the scale of technological change is unlike anything developed countries have experienced in the past and, therefore, social safety nets must evolve to adapt to the new risks. However, a universal basic income would not only discourage work, especially in light of the existing social safety net (e.g., unemployment insurance and food stamps), but would also undermine the intrinsic value that work plays in creating meaning and purpose in peoples' lives (Opportunity America 2018).

Second, given the wide array of applications of AI for national security and warfare, there is an ongoing debate about whether AI should be regulated to prevent an "AI arms race" among countries (Taddeo 2018; Horowitz 2018). Particularly because AI is a general purpose technology (Agrawal, Gans, and Goldfarb 2018), the dual uses of AI developments mean that they will diffuse rapidly upon entering the private sector. One primary fear, for example, is that AI algorithms could make decisions about troop and/or drone deployments, which would put human lives at risk without the traditional human decision-making process. Much like the concerns about autonomous vehicles and passenger safety, some policymakers and researchers are calling for greater guidance on regulating AI when lives are at stake.

Third, although machine learning algorithms have been remarkably successful at predicting individual outcomes using increasingly accessible and granular data, many researchers and policymakers have voiced concern about the potential for these algorithms to propagate bias and discrimination (Kleinberg, Mullainathan, and Raghavan 2018). If the data on which algorithms are trained exhibit certain biases, then AI could propagate these biases on a wider and more subtle scale. Though these concerns are valid, the implications for regulation are ambiguous. In particular, Kleinberg, Mullainathan, and Raghavan (2018) outline three conditions that are required for algorithmic fairness at the heart of these debates about algorithmic classification—showing that, except in special cases, no method can satisfy all three conditions simultaneously. In this sense, though concerns about algorithmic fairness ought to continue being voiced, policymakers should approach with caution when formulating policy to avoid simply reacting to the latest fad or worry.

Fourth, some are concerned that the emergence of big data and AI will pose a threat to competition because larger companies will be better equipped to train models on larger data (Seamans 2017; Bessen 2018). For example, companies with access to more data might be able to reduce business uncertainty by incorporating more information into their forecasts, thereby obtaining lower costs of capital (Begenau, Farboodi, and Veldkamp 2018). However, a countervailing force is the impact of AI on the cost of entry and creative destruction. For instance, the discovery and application of cloud computing allow firms to rent computer power and/or data storage. Aside from the 25 to 50 percent direct cost savings observed in government (West 2010), the indirect effects on entry costs and competition, particularly in concentrated markets, may be larger (Colciago and Etro 2013). Nonetheless, regulation and competition policy around big data and AI will remain an active ongoing debate.

Despite these general categories of concerns, caution is especially important when considering prospective regulation. For example, according to Stanford University's One Hundred Year Study of Artificial Intelligence, "The Study Panel's consensus is that attempts to regulate 'AI' in general would be misguided, because there is no clear definition of AI (it isn't any one thing), and the risks and considerations are very different in different domains" (Stanford University 2016). Moreover, because AI is an inherently global technology, regulation in one country could put companies that are competing in an international marketplace due to cross-country linkages at a significant disadvantage.

Conclusion

Recent advances in computer science and artificial intelligence technology are revolutionizing the U.S. economy. In many fields, tasks that traditionally required humans can now easily be performed by AI algorithms. Although these discoveries have the potential to "be as important and transformational to society and the economy as the steam engine," according to Brynjolfsson and McAfee (2014, 9), they are also creating known and unknown dependencies and challenges, such as accelerated polarization in the labor market and increased exposure to cybersecurity threats.

This chapter has defined and reviewed recent developments in AI and automation. Unlike traditional forms of information technology (e.g., computers) that require humans to provide instructions and programmatic commands, intelligent systems are defined by their applicability to a wide range of tasks that need little supervision. For example, Google's new AI algorithm, AlphaZero, successfully trained itself how to play and subsequently defeat the world's best chess engine, Stockfish. Similarly, DARPA has also created tools capable of reliably and rapidly identifying cybersecurity vulnerabilities. Apart from these gaming and national security applications, AI is also frequently applied in the private sector—through, for example, data-driven decisionmaking business analytics and precision agriculture.

Drawing on historical examples, we have demonstrated the potential effects of AI technology on the U.S. labor market. Although advances in AI, and the introduction of technology more broadly, will inevitably change the composition of tasks and jobs by making some tasks typically performed by humans obsolete, we have shown in the text above that humans will continue to have an important economic function because of their comparative advantage over AI in other tasks, even if they do not hold an absolute advantage. This means that companies and entrepreneurs will find it more profitable to design technology capital that complements human capabilities. However, to alleviate the potentially adverse effects of AI on individuals and jobs that are more exposed to disruption, the Trump Administration has responded proactively by supporting and funding reskilling and apprenticeship initiatives in areas where humans retain a comparative advantage. For example, the Pledge to America's Workers, an initiative from the National Council for the American Worker, already has over 6.5 million pledges toward reskilling workers.

In addition, we have applied economic theory to analyze the wage patterns among industries that are adopting AI technology. In the initial anticipation phase, firms know that they will be more productive, but, because they currently lack the AI capital, raise real wages. However, in the arrival phase, which is typically the primary focus among the popular press, the introduction of AI substitutes for labor as workers compete with machines, thereby depressing real wages. But as business formation catches up with the new technology, real wages ultimately rise to levels above what they were before AI.

We have also explored ongoing cybersecurity vulnerabilities, along with future threats, as dependence on technology increases. The CEA (2018b) estimated the cost of attacks on these vulnerabilities to be $109 billion in 2016. Drawing on new data from Rapid7 across industries, we find that cybersecurity vulnerabilities are more pronounced than previously thought, even among well-established *Fortune* 500 firms. The prevalence of these vulnerabilities, coupled with the underreporting of public cybersecurity breaches, suggests that traditional measures of the cost of malicious cyberattacks may be greater than previously anticipated. We have discussed potential causes behind the failure to adopt cybersecurity best practices in the private sector, along with the policy implications, including tools already being used by the Federal government to prevent malicious cyberattacks and phishing attempts.

We conclude by highlighting the Trump Administration's current policy initiatives to tackle the risks posed by continued technological change in the labor market and new cybersecurity threats. The 2018 National Council for the American Worker, for example, has introduced initiatives to promote reskilling and apprenticeships to help workers transition into new and emerging jobs. For example, the Pledge to America's Workers already has over 6.5 million commitments to these aims by companies. In a similar vein, the 2018 National Cyber Strategy lays out a comprehensive framework for engaging and dealing with cybersecurity threats. For example, the "Federal Cybersecurity Risk Determination Report and Action Plan" (White House 2018a) establishes a detailed risk assessment process based on best practices from the NIST Framework to create predictability and the adoption of best practices throughout the Federal government. Moreover, by modernizing educational curricula and equipping teachers with new multimedia content and tools, the emerging National Cyber Education Partnership will help address the cybersecurity skills gap that currently threatens U.S. economic and national security.

The expansion of artificial intelligence and automation is already having profound effects on the U.S. economy and geopolitical landscape. Although we are only beginning to see their manifestations, and thus the full scale of potential threats and benefits cannot be entirely quantified, these changes pose both new challenges and opportunities. The Trump Administration is committed to policymaking that leverages technological change as an asset rather than a liability, to advancing economic gains for American workers, and to promoting best practices for our digital infrastructure so that America can remain the most prosperous and competitive country during the emerging technological transformation.

Chapter 8

Markets versus Socialism

When the Council of Economic Advisers was founded in 1946, our Nation was at a crucial crossroads. There was bipartisan concern that the transition away from a war economy would lead to another depression, and there was much public debate over the best policies to ensure prosperity. As detailed in the first CEA *Annual Report to the President*, there were two distinct schools of thought that Congress implicitly charged the CEA's members to evaluate. One held "that 'individual free enterprise' could, through automatic processes of the market, effect the transition to full-scale peacetime business and (even with recurrent depressions) the highest practicable level of prosperity thereafter." The other school held "that the economic activities of individuals and groups need, under modern industrial conditions, more rather than less supplementation and systemizing (though perhaps less direct regulation) by central government." The three members of the first CEA contrasted the "Roman" view that economic prosperity can be handed down by a powerful central government with the "Spartan" view that much of American history at times "carried a cult of individual self-reliance to the point of brutality." The report warned against "100 percenters" of both views, as each misunderstood the role of government in fostering prosperity, and it advised that "the great body of American thinking on economic matters runs toward a more balanced middle view."

The focus of that first report reminds us that there was a time in American history when grand debates over the merits of competing economic systems were front and center, and the terms of the debates and characteristics of the competing views were widely known. It is clear that such a time may be returning. Detailed policy proposals from self-declared "socialists" are gaining support in Congress and are receiving significant public attention. Yet it is much less clear today than it was in 1946 exactly what a typical voter has in mind when he or she thinks of "socialism," or whether those who today describe themselves as socialists would be considered "100 percenters" by the first CEA.

There is undoubtedly ample confusion concerning the meaning of the word "socialist," but economists generally agree about how to define socialism, and they have devoted enormous time and resources to studying its costs and benefits. With an eye on this broad body of literature, this chapter discusses socialism's historic visions and intents, its economic features, its impact on economic performance, and its relationship with recent policy proposals in the United States.

Inevitably, this chapter uses evidence to weigh in on the relative empirical merits of capitalism and socialism, a topic that can be quite divisive. In his land-mark book *Capitalism, Socialism and Democracy*, Joseph Schumpeter (1942, 145) predicted that socialism would become the only respectable ideology of the two, in part because the scholarship regarding both would be dominated by university professors. At the American university, he warned, capitalism "stands its trial before judges who have the sentence of death in their pockets. . . . Well, here we have numbers; a well-defined group situation of proletarian hue; and a group interest in shaping a group attitude that will much more realistically account for hostility to the capitalist order than could the theory."

As documented in this chapter, the scholarship has not become as one-sided as Schumpeter envisioned. The chapter first briefly reviews the historical and modern socialist interpretations of market economies and the challenges socialist policy proposals face in terms of distorting incentives. Thereafter, we review the evidence from the highly socialist countries showing that they experienced sharp declines in output, especially in the industries that were taken over by the state. We review the experiences of economies with less extreme socialism and show that they also generate less output, although the shortfall is not as drastic as with the highly socialist countries. Finally, we assess the economic impact of the current American proposal for socialized medicine,

"Medicare for All," and we find that the taxes needed to finance it would reduce the size of the U.S. economy.

T o economists, socialism is not a zero-one designation. Whether a country or industry is socialist is a question of the degree to which (1) the means of production, distribution, and exchange are owned or regulated by the state; and (2) the state uses its control to distribute the country's economic output without regard for final consumers' willingness to pay or exchange (i.e., giving resources away "for free").[1] As explained below, this definition conforms with both statements and policy proposals from leading socialists, ranging from Karl Marx to Vladimir Lenin to Mao Zedong to modern self-described socialists.[2]

In modern models of capitalist economies, there is, of course, an ample role for government. In particular, there are public goods and goods with externalities that will be inefficiently supplied by the free market. Public goods are undersupplied in a completely free market because there is a free-rider problem. For example, if national defense, a public good enjoyed by the whole country, were sold at local supermarkets, few would contribute because they would feel their individual purchase would not matter and they would prefer others to contribute while still being defended. Consequently, the market would not provide sufficient defense. However, socialist regimes go well beyond government intervention into markets with public goods or externalities.

This chapter is an empirical analysis of socialism that takes as its benchmark current U.S. public policies. This benchmark has the advantage of being measureable, but it necessarily differs from theoretical concepts of "capitalism" or "free markets" because the U.S. government may not limit its activity to theoretically defined public goods. Relative to the U.S. benchmark, we find that socialist public policies, though ostensibly well-intentioned, have clear

---

[1] Criterion 1 is from the *Oxford English Dictionary*, which defines socialism as public policy based on "a political and economic theory of social organization which advocates that the means of production, distribution, and exchange should be owned or regulated by the community as a whole." Criterion 2 further focuses the discussion to rule out state ownership or regulation for other purposes, such as fighting a war. See Sunstein (2019); and see Samuelson and Nordhaus (1989, 833), who describe "democratic socialist governments [that] expanded the welfare state, nationalized industries, and planned the economy."

[2] For classical socialists, "communism" is a purely theoretical concept that has never yet been put into practice, which is why the second "S" in USSR stands for "Socialist." Communism is, in their view, a social arrangement where there is neither a state nor private property; the abolition of property is not sufficient for communism. As Lenin explained, "The goal of socialism is communism." The supposed purpose of the "Great Leap Forward" was for China to transition from socialism to communism before the USSR did (Dikötter 2010). The classical definition therefore stands in contrast to vernacular usage of communism to refer to historical instances of socialism where the degree of state control was the highest, such as the USSR, Cuba, North Korea, or Maoist China. This chapter therefore avoids the term "communism."

opportunity costs that are directly related to the degree to which they tax and regulate.

We begin our investigation by looking closely at the most extreme socialist cases, which are Maoist China, the USSR under Lenin and Stalin, Castro's Cuba, and other primarily agricultural countries (Pipes 2003). Referring to these same countries, Janos Kornai (1992, xxi) explained that the "development and the break-up and decline of the socialist system amount to the most important political and economic phenomena of the twentieth century. At the height of this system's power and extent, a third of humanity lived under it." Not long ago, distinguished economists in the U.S. and Europe offered favorable assessments of highly socialist economies, and many contemporary commentators appear to have forgotten or overlooked this record. Moreover, as one analyzes the impact of moving away from a purely socialist model, as many modern proposals envision, it may be helpful to understand the history of extreme examples.

Socialists in the highly socialist countries accused the agriculture sector of being unfair and unproductive (equivalently, food was too expensive in terms of the labor required to produce it) because farmers, who had been working on their land for generations, were too unsophisticated and because the market failed to achieve economies of scale. Government takeovers of agriculture, which forcibly converted private farms into state-owned farms directed by government employees and party apparatchiks, were advertised as the way for socialist countries to produce more food with fewer workers so resources could be shifted into other industries.

In practice, however, socialist takeovers of agriculture delivered the opposite of what was promised.[3] Food production plummeted, and tens of millions of people died from starvation in the USSR, China, and other agricultural economies where the state took command. Planning the nonagricultural parts of those economies also proved impossible.

Present-day socialists do not want the dictatorship or state brutality that often coincided with the most extreme cases of socialism. However, peaceful democratic implementation of socialist policies does not eliminate the fundamental incentive and information problems created by high tax rates, large state organizations, and the centralized control of resources. Venezuela is a modern industrialized country that elected Hugo Chávez as its leader to implement socialist policies, and the result was less output in oil and other industries that were nationalized. In other words, the lessons from socialized agriculture carry over to government takeovers of oil, health insurance, and other modern industries: They produce less rather than more, even in today's information age, where central planning is possibly easier.

---

[3] Many socialist scholars concur on this point (Nolan 1988, 6; Roemer 1995, 23–24; Nove 2010).

Proponents of socialism acknowledge that the experiences of the USSR and other highly socialist countries are not worth repeating, but they continue to advocate increased taxation and state control. Such policies would also have negative output effects, albeit of a lesser magnitude, as are seen in cross-country studies of the effect of greater economic freedom on real gross domestic product (GDP). A broad body of academic literature quantifies the extent of economic freedom in several dimensions, including taxation and spending, the extent of state-owned enterprises, economic regulation, and other factors. This literature finds a strong association between greater economic freedom and better economic performance, suggesting that replacing U.S. policies with highly socialist policies, such as Venezuela's, would reduce real GDP more than 40 percent in the long run, or about $24,000 a year for the average person.

Participants in the American policy discourse sometimes cite the Nordic countries as socialist success stories. However, in many respects, the Nordic countries' policies now differ significantly from policies that economists view as characteristic of socialism. Indeed, Nordic representatives have vehemently objected to the characterization that they are socialist (Rasmussen 2015). Nordic healthcare is not free, but rather requires substantial cost sharing. As compared with the U.S. rates at present, including implicit taxes, marginal labor income tax rates in the Nordic countries today are only somewhat greater. Nordic taxation overall is greater and is surprisingly less progressive than U.S. taxes. The Nordic countries also tax capital income less and regulate product markets less than the United States does, but they regulate labor markets more. Living standards in the Nordic countries, as measured by per capita GDP and consumption, are at least 15 percent lower than those in the United States.

With an eye toward the inaccurate description of Nordic practices, some in the U.S. have proposed nationalizing payments for healthcare—which makes up more than a sixth of the U.S. economy—through the recent "Medicare for All" proposal. This proposal would create a monopoly government health insurer to provide healthcare for "free" (i.e., without cost sharing) and to centrally set all prices paid to suppliers, such as doctors and hospitals. We find that if this policy were financed through higher taxes, GDP would fall by 9 percent, or about $7,000 per person in 2022. As shown in chapter 4 of this *Report*, evidence on the productivity and effectiveness of single-payer systems suggests that "Medicare for All" would reduce longevity and health, particularly among seniors, even though it would only slightly increase the fraction of the population with health insurance.[4]

To the extent that policy proposals mimic the 100 percent experience, the burden is on advocates to explain how their latest policy agenda would

---

[4] This *Report* refers to the specific "Medicare for All" bills in Congress (S. 1804; H.R. 676). The economic effects of other healthcare reform proposals, or aspirations, are not necessarily the same even if they share the same name.

overcome the undeniable problems observed when socialist policies were tried in the past. As the sociology professor Paul Starr (2016) put it, "Much of [modern American socialists'] platform ignores the economic realities that European socialists long ago accepted."[5] Marx's 200th birthday is a good time to gather and review the overwhelming evidence.[6]

The "Economics of Socialism" section of this chapter begins by briefly reviewing the historical and modern socialist interpretations of market economies and some of the challenges with socialist policy proposals. The subsequent section reviews the evidence from the highly socialist countries, by which we mean countries that were implementing the most state control of production and incomes. Highly socialist countries experienced sharp declines in output, especially in the industries that were taken over by the state. Economies with less extreme forms of socialism also generate less output, although the shortfall is not as drastic as with the highly socialist countries, as shown in the section titled "Socialism and Living Standards in a Broad Cross Section of Countries." A section on the Nordic-countries provides a more detailed examination of them. The final section assesses the economic impact of the headline American proposal, "Medicare for All."[7]

The Economics of Socialism

Historically, philosophers and even some well-regarded economists have offered socialist theories of the causes of income and wealth inequality, and they have advocated for state solutions that are commonly echoed by modern socialists. They both argue that there is "exploitation" in the market sector and there are virtually unlimited economies of scale in the public sector. Profits are undeserved and unnecessarily add to the costs of goods and services. The solutions include single-payer systems, prohibitions of for-profit business, state-determined prices to replace the "anarchy of the market," high tax rates ("from each according to his ability"), and public policies that hand out much of the Nation's goods and services free of charge ("to each according to his needs") (Gregory 2004; Marx 1875).

The Socialist Economic Narrative: Exploitation Corrected by Central Planning

When Marx was writing over 150 years ago, obviously exploitive practices were still familiar. The modern socialist view is that exploitation remains real but is somewhat hidden in the market for labor (Gurley 1976a). Much inequality

---

[5] See also Boettke (1990).

[6] See also Acemoglu and Robinson (2015), who review Marx's key predictions about trends for wages and profits and find them to be falsified by the evidence.

[7] The CEA previously released research on topics covered in this chapter. The text that follows builds on *The Opportunity Costs of Socialism* (CEA 2018a), a research paper produced by the CEA.

arises, it is said, because market activity is a zero-sum game, with owners and workers paid according to the power they possess (or lack), rather than their marginal products. From the workers' perspective, profits are an unwarranted cost in the production process and are reflected in an unnecessarily low level of wages. The contest over the fraction of output paid in wages, known among socialists as the "class struggle," can take place in the political arena, in the private sector with union activity and the like, or violently with riots or revolution (Przeworksi and Sprague 1986).

As Karl Marx put it, "Modern bourgeois private property is the final and most complete expression of the system of producing and appropriating products, that is based on class antagonisms, on the exploitation of the many by the few" (Marx and Engels 1848, 24). The Chinese leader Mao Zedong, who cited Marxism as the model for his country, described "the ruthless economic exploitation and political oppression of the peasants by the landlord class" (Cotterell 2011, chap. 6). The Democratic Socialists of America, and elected officials who are affiliated with and endorsed by them, today express similar concerns that workers are harmed when the profit motive is allowed to be an important part of the economic system.[8]

The French economist Thomas Piketty, whose 2014 book *Capital in the 21st Century* recalls Marx's *Das Kapital*, asserts that inequality today is "terrifying" and that public policy can and must reduce it; wealth holders must be heavily taxed.[9] Piketty (2014) concludes that the Soviet approach and other attempts to "abolish private ownership" should at least be admired for being "more logically consistent."

Historical and contemporary socialists argue that heavy taxation need not reduce national output because a public enterprise uses its efficiency and bargaining power to achieve better outcomes. Mao touted the "superiority of large cooperatives." He decreed that the Chinese government would be the single payer for grain, prohibiting farmers from selling their grain to any other person or business (Dikötter 2010).[10] In describing China, the British economists Joan Robinson and Solomon Adler (1958, 3) celebrated that "the agricultural producers' cooperatives have finally put an end to the minute fragmentation of the land." Lenin stressed transforming "agriculture from small, backward, individual farming to large-scale, advanced, collective agriculture, to joint cultivation of the land." Proponents of socialism in America today

---

[8] See Stone and Gong (2018) and Day (2018a). See also Bernhardt et al. (2008), Sanders (2018), and Section 103 of the House "Medicare for All" bill (H.R. 676), which prohibits health providers from participating unless they are a public or not-for-profit institution.

[9] Piketty (2014, 572) writes that "the right solution is a progressive annual tax on capital," and that "the primary purpose of the capital tax is not to finance the social state but to regulate capitalism" (p. 518).

[10] Lenin (1918) also enforced a grain monopoly in the USSR.

argue that the Federal government can run healthcare more efficiently than many competing private enterprises.[11]

State ownership of the means of production is an often-repeated Marxist proposal for ending worker exploitation by leveraging scale economies. This aspect of socialism is less visible in modern American socialism, because in most instances, socialists would allow individuals to be the legal owners of capital and their own labor.[12] However, the economic significance of ownership is control over the use of an asset and of the income it generates, rather than the legal title by itself. In other words, the economic value of ownership is sharply diminished if the legal owner has little control and little of the income.[13] Full ownership in the economic sense is rejected by socialists; they maintain that private owners left to themselves would not achieve full economies of scale and would continue exploiting workers. Public monopolies, "public options," profit prohibitions, and the regulatory apparatus allow the socialist state to control asset use, and high tax rates allow the state to determine how much income everyone receives, without necessarily abolishing ownership in the narrow legal sense.

Historical socialists—such as Lenin, Mao, and Castro—ran their countries without democracy and civil liberties. Modern democratic socialists are different in these important ways. Nevertheless, even when socialist policies are peacefully implemented under the auspices of democracy, economics has much to say about their effects.

The Role of Incentives in Raising and Spending Money

Any productive economic system needs incentives: means of motivating effort, useful application of knowledge, and the creation and maintenance of productive assets. The higher an economy's tax rates, the more its industries are monopolized by a public enterprise, and the more its goods and services are distributed free of charge, then the more disincentives reduce the value created in the economy.

Mancur Olson's famous 1965 book *The Logic of Collective Action* showed how large groups have trouble achieving common goals without individual incentives. As an important example, Olson disputed Marx's claim that business

---

[11] The CEA notes that it is directed by the 1946 Employment Act to "formulate and recommend national economic policy to promote employment, production, and purchasing power under free competitive enterprise" (sec. 4a).

[12] Even the USSR and other highly socialist countries had elements of private property (Dolot 2011, 134; see also Pryor 1992, chap. 4). The CEA also notes that American socialists may not only intend to prohibit private health insurance but also, for example, intend to nationalize energy companies (Day 2018b).

[13] Epstein (1985) and Fischel (1995). See also Samuelson and Nordhaus (1989, 837), who define a socialist economy as one "in which the major economic decisions are made administratively, without profits as a central motive force for production," and Roemer (1994), who defines socialism independent of legal property rights.

Figure 8-1. Four Ways to Spend Money

		On whom money is spent	
		The purchaser	Someone else
Whose money is spent	The purchaser's	Economize and seek highest value	Economize, but don't seek highest value
	Someone else's	Don't economize, but seek highest value	Don't economize and don't seek highest value

owners were working together to reduce wages, even though Olson acknowledged that business owners would have greater profits if wages were lower. The paradox, Olson said, is that the market wage is the result of a great many employers' individual actions. Any specific employer decides the wage and working conditions to offer based on its own profits, without valuing the effects of its decision on the profits of competing employers. The result of competition among employers is that wages are in line with worker productivity, even though wages below that would enhance the profits of employers as a group.

The kinds of free-rider problems analyzed by Olson are also a challenge for socialist planning, because the persons deciding on resource allocations—that is, how much to spend on a product and how that product should be manufactured and delivered to the final consumer—are different from those providing the resources and different from the final consumer who is ultimately using them. As the Nobel Prize–winning economist Milton Friedman demonstrated with his illustration of "four ways to spend money" (see figure 8-1), consumers in the market system spend their own money, and are therefore more careful how much to spend and on what the money is spent (Friedman and Friedman 1980). To the extent that they also use what they purchased—the upper left corner in figure 8-1—they are also more discerning, so that the items purchased are of good value. They will gather and consider information that helps compare the values of different options.

The upper right hand corner of figure 8-1 gives the case of spending one's own money on someone else, which introduces inefficiencies because the recipient may place a lower value on the spending. The inefficiency of the lower left corner is exemplified by the larger spending that takes place when spending on oneself using other people's money, as with fully reimbursed corporate travel or entertainment. The lower right category is the one applicable to government employees who spend tax revenue on government program beneficiaries; not only is there a tendency to overspend using other people's money, but that spending may have little value from the perspective of program beneficiaries.[14]

Many presentations of socialist policy options, even those by expert economists, ignore the distinction between individual and group action stressed by Olson. The "Medicare for All" bills currently in Congress, for example, supposedly just swap household expenditures on health insurance that occur under a private system for household expenditures on taxes earmarked for the public program.[15] But this swap fundamentally changes the types of healthcare that are ultimately received by consumers, the size of the healthcare budget, and the size of the overall economy. In a private system, a consumer has some control over his or her spending on health insurance—by, for example, selecting a plan with different benefits, or switching to a more efficient provider. Insurers in a private system must be responsive to consumer demands if they want to attract and retain customers and thus stay in business.[16] Individuals also have little reason to economize on anything that they can obtain without payment (Arrow 1963; Pauly 1968).

In a socialist system, the state decides the amount to be spent, how it is spent, and when and where the services are received by the consumer. A consumer who is unhappy with the state's choices has little recourse, especially if private businesses are prohibited from competing with the state (as they are under "Medicare for All"). It may be argued that "giant" private corporations also limit consumer choice, but this comparison ignores how corporations are subject to competition. For example, a consumer can purchase goods from Walmart rather than Amazon, not to mention a whole host of other retailers. Amazon is legally permitted to entice Walmart customers, and vice versa, with low prices, better products, free shipping, and so on. Whereas retail customers are not forced to open their wallets, giant state enterprises are guaranteed revenue through taxation and are often legally protected from competition.[17] Those who maintain that Amazon and Walmart are too large might note that

---

[14] The gap between program spending and value to beneficiaries has been measured by Gallen (2015), Finkelstein and McKnight (2008), and Olsen (2008), among others.

[15] Cooper (2018) refers to it as the "taxes-for-premiums swap." Krugman (2017) writes that "most people would gain more from the elimination of insurance premiums than they would lose from the tax hike" without mentioning any of the economic problems with spending someone else's money on someone else. As Von Mises (1990, chap. 1) observed long ago, advocates of socialist policies "invariably explain how . . . roast pigeons will in some way fly into the mouths of the comrades, but they omit to show how this miracle is to take place."

[16] See also Shleifer (1998).

[17] Interestingly, socialist policies could simultaneously reduce the size of private enterprises with antitrust and other policies and enlarge government enterprises with legal protections from competition.

the single-payer revenues proposed in "Medicare for All" will be about eight times the revenue for either of these corporations.[18]

Another problem with the socialist system is that "other people's money" starts to disappear when the "other people" realize that they have little incentive to earn and innovate because what they receive has little to do with how much they make.[19] An important reason that people work and put forth effort is to obtain goods and services that they want. Under socialism, the things they want may be unavailable because the market no longer exists, or are made available without the need for working.

Noneconomists sometimes claim that high taxes do not prevent anyone from working, as long as the tax rate is less than 100 percent, because everyone strives to have more income rather than less. This "income maximization" hypothesis is contradicted by the most basic labor market observations, not to mention decades of research.[20] Earning additional income requires sacrifices (a loss of free time, relocating to an area with better-paying jobs, training, taking an inconvenient schedule, etc.), and people evaluate whether the net income earned is enough to justify the sacrifices. Socialism's high tax rates fundamentally tilt this trade-off in favor of less income.

The Economic Consequences of "Free" Goods and Services

Because market prices reveal economically important information about costs and consumer wants, regulations and spending programs that distribute goods or services at below-market prices, such as those that are "free," have a number of unintended consequences (Hayek 1945). Fewer goods and services will be produced, and what is produced may be misallocated to consumers with comparatively little need. We explain in this section why the very idea that a single-payer government program will use its market power to obtain lower prices is an acknowledgment that the program will be purchasing less quantity or quality.

On the demand side of a market, people vary in their willingness to pay for the product or service, and their willingness varies over time. The market system allocates the available goods to consumers who are willing to pay more than the market price, while those not willing to pay the price go without. Willingness to pay is related to income, but it is also related to "need," at least as consumers perceive need. Consumers are, for example, willing to pay more for food when they are hungry and to buy health insurance when they are

---

[18] Chapter 4 of this *Report* estimates that "Medicare for All" would be financed with about $2.4 trillion in 2022. In 2017, Walmart's U.S. revenues were about $0.3 trillion, while Amazon's U.S. revenues were less than $0.2 trillion. The final section of this chapter also explains why "Medicare for All" would sharply reduce consumer spending, which suggests that 2017 revenues would be an optimistic projection for what retail corporations would earn with "Medicare for All" in place.

[19] For an analysis of the private sector's innovation advantage, see Winston (2010).

[20] E.g., Prescott (2004), Rogerson (2006), Chetty et al. (2011) and Mulligan (2012).

older. In this way, the market has a tendency to allocate goods and services when and to whom they are needed.

If the government decrees that a product shall be free, then something other than a willingness to pay the market price will determine who receives the available supply. It may be a willingness to wait in line, or political connections, or membership in a privileged demographic group, or a government eligibility formula (Shleifer and Vishny 1992; Barzel 1997; Glaeser and Luttmer 2003). By comparison with the market, giving a product away for free may sometimes have the effect of taking the good away from consumers when they need it most and transferring it to consumers when they need it least. As we show in chapter 4 of this *Report*, single-payer healthcare programs tend to reallocate healthcare from the old to the young. Centrally planned agricultural systems have, in effect, taken food products away from starving people in rural areas and transferred the products to urban consumers or sold them on the international market.

Prices that are below their competitive levels also affect supply. Although a single government payer has market power that it can use to reduce the incomes of suppliers, the price reduction is accomplished by reducing the quantity or quality of what it purchases in order to squeeze its suppliers.[21] This may be one reason why single-payer healthcare systems have longer appointment waiting times than in the U.S. system (see chapter 4 of this *Report*), and why "free" Nordic colleges yield lower financial returns than higher education in the United States, even though the Nordic returns include no tuition expense (see the Nordic section below).

Von Mises (1920) and Hayek (1945) emphasized the value of market prices for coordinating and executing decisions in complex economies and went so far as to assert that central planning is impossible because it eschews markets. Perhaps contrary to their expectations, centrally planned economies did survive for decades, although these economies performed poorly and survived so long only because of their deviations from the socialist program (Gregory 2004, 5–6).

Socialism's Track Record

Socialism is a continuum. No country has zero state ownership, zero regulation, and zero taxes. Even the most highly socialist countries have retained elements of private property, with consumers sometimes spending their own money on themselves (Pryor 1992). This chapter therefore begins with the

---

[21] This effect is the monopsony mirror image of monopoly pricing. Sellers with market power typically exercise it by constraining the quantity or quality of what they produce and thereby squeeze the buyers in the market (Williamson 1968; Farrell and Shapiro 1990; Whinston 2006). Buyers with market power typically exercise it by constraining the quantity or quality of what they purchase.

historically common highly socialist regimes, by which we mean countries that implemented the most state control of production and incomes for at least a decade.[22] Highly socialist policies continue "to have considerable emotional appeal throughout the world to those who believe that it offers economic progress and fairness, free of chaotic market forces" (Gregory 2004, x). Of more than a dozen countries meeting these criteria, this section emphasizes Maoist China, Castro's Cuba, and the USSR under Lenin and Stalin, which are the subject of much scholarship, and Venezuela, which has been unusual as an industrialized economy with elements of democracy that nonetheless pursued highly socialist policies.[23]

Many of the highly socialist economies were agricultural, with state and collective farming systems implemented by socialist governments to achieve purported economies of scale and, pursuant to socialist ideology, to punish private landowners. Agricultural output dropped sharply when socialism was implemented, causing food shortages. Between China and the USSR, tens of millions of people starved. It took quite some time for sympathetic scholars outside the socialist countries to acknowledge that large, state-owned farms were less productive than small private ones.

The economic failures of highly socialist policies have been described at length by both survivors and scholars who have reviewed the evidence in state archives. Not only did highly socialist countries discourage the supply of effort and capital with poor incentives, but they also allocated these resources perversely because central planning made production decisions react to output and input prices in the opposite direction from those of a market economy.

Although agriculture is not a large part of the U.S. economy, present-day socialists echo the historical socialists by arguing that healthcare, education, and other sectors are unfair and unproductive, and they promise that large state organizations will deliver fairness and economies of scale. It is therefore worth acknowledging that socialist takeovers of agriculture have delivered the opposite of what was promised.

Present-day socialists do not want the dictatorship or state brutality that often coincided with the most extreme cases of socialism, and they do not propose to nationalize agriculture. However, the peaceful democratic implementation of socialist policies does not eliminate the fundamental incentive and information problems created by high tax rates, large state organizations, and the centralized control of resources. As we report at the end of this section,

---

[22] The highly socialist countries are sometimes called "communist" or "centrally planned" although, as noted above, communism has a different meaning in the theory of socialism. We presume that, in contrast to the Nordic countries, central government spending far exceeds private spending in highly socialist countries—although, with pervasive state ownership and centralized control, it is difficult to construct accurate measures of the components of spending that would be comparable between highly socialist countries and the rest of the world.

[23] Also recall, from the "Economics of Socialism" section above, the parallels between modern socialist rhetoric and the statements attributed to Mao, Castro, and Lenin.

Venezuela is a modern industrialized country that elected Hugo Chávez as its leader to implement socialist policies, and the result was less output in oil and other industries that were nationalized.[24]

When evaluating the misalignment between the promises of highly socialist regimes to eliminate the misery and exploitation of the poor and the actual effects of their policies, it is instructive to look at a major guide that economists use to determine value: the revealed preference of the population—in other words, people voting with their feet. The implementation of highly socialist policies, such as in Venezuela, has been associated with high emigration rates. Perhaps more telling is that historically socialist regimes—such as the USSR, China, North Korea, and Cuba—have forcibly prevented people from leaving.

State and Collective Farming

State and collective farming (hereafter, "state farming") is a historically common practice in highly socialist countries.[25] The state acquires private farmland, and often much livestock, by force. The land is organized in large parcels, typically about one per village, as compared with the multitude of parcels in a typical village before collectivization. Villagers are required to work on the land, with the output belonging to the state. Decisions are made by government employees and party apparatchiks, who may have had little or no experience or specialized knowledge in comparison with the original landowners (Pryor 1992). These decisions include devising and implementing complex systems of production targets and quality requirements (Nolan 1988).

The socialist narrative emphasizes exploitation and class struggle, which in an agricultural economy refers to the power dynamic that determines the division of agricultural income between landlords and farm workers. State farms purport to end the exploitation by eliminating the landlords, known as kulaks in the USSR.[26] Another advantage of state farms, from the socialist perspective, was economies of scale (Pryor 1992). In principle, the knowledge and

---

[24] See also the sections of this chapter on socialism in the Nordic countries and on "Medicare for All," and chapter 4 of this *Report*, which include analyses of single-payer healthcare. Further evidence about the effects of socialism on nonagricultural industries are reported by Conquest (2005), Gregory (2004), Horowitz and Suchlicki (2003), and Kornai (1992). Johnson and Brooks (1983, 9) describe how the "Soviet rural road system can only be described as a disgrace, the result of decades of socialist neglect."

[25] Among the highly socialist countries, state or collective farms were formed, e.g., in the USSR; elsewhere in the Soviet Bloc; and in Vietnam, North Korea, China, Cuba, South Yemen, Congo, Ethiopia, Cambodia, and Laos (Pryor 1992, chap. 4). In principle, participation in collective farms was voluntary, and operations were collectively managed by villagers, whereas state farms were owned and managed by government with the farm workers as government employees. In practice, even the collective farms may come "under the control of the Communist Party and the government," as they did in the USSR (Dolot 2011, chap. 2). See also Johnson and Brooks (1983, 4–5), Conquest (1986, 171), and Pryor (1992, 12–14).

[26] With landlords resisting the seizure of their property, the state often imprisoned or murdered landlords (Conquest 1986; Rummel 2011).

techniques of the best farmer could be applied to all the land rather than the comparatively small plot that the best farmer owned.[27] Capital may be easier to obtain for a larger organization. Writing about the USSR in 1929, Joseph Stalin stressed transforming "agriculture from small, backward, individual farming to large-scale, advanced, collective agriculture, to joint cultivation of the land." Writing about China in 1958, the British economist Joan Robinson asserted that "the minute fragmentation of the land" that prevailed before collective farming was a major source of inefficiency. The family itself was sometimes criticized as operating on too small a scale; in China, household utensils were confiscated and villagers were assigned to communal kitchens for eating and food preparation (Jisheng 2012).[28]

Eyewitnesses tell a different story concerning the operation of state farms, and central planning more generally. In Cuba and the USSR, for example, the managers of state farms were chosen from the ranks of the Communist Party, rather than because of management skill or agricultural knowledge (Dolot 2011).[29] "The state monopoly stifled incentives for increasing production," describes a Chinese eyewitness (Jisheng 2012, 174–77). Production units sometimes had an incentive to produce less and to hoard inputs, in order to obtain more favorable allocations the next year (Gregory 1990).

Unintended Consequences

State farms reduced agricultural productivity rather than increasing it. The unwarranted faith in state farms had a doubly negative effect on agricultural output. Not only was less produced per worker, but workers were removed from agriculture, on the mistaken understanding that farming was becoming more productive (Conquest 1986) and would produce surpluses that would finance the growth of industry (Gregory 2004). For China and the USSR, both the lack of food and reliance on central planning, rather than market mechanisms, resulted in millions of deaths by starvation.

Statistics from highly socialist regimes are informative, but necessarily imprecise. Gregory (1990), Kornai (1992), and others explain how officials in these regimes deceive their superiors and the public. Refugees from the regimes may be free to talk after their escape, but they may not constitute a

---

[27] The CEA is not aware of socialist explanations of why the best farmer owned comparatively little land or did not contribute his or her talents to a larger but purely voluntary collective. A neoclassical explanation might involve credit constraints and the like, or simply that it would not be efficient for the best farmer to control more land than he or she chose to purchase in the marketplace (i.e., the market reflects genuine limitations on scale economies; see also Conquest 1986).

[28] See also Lenin (1951).

[29] See also O'Connor's (1968, 205) description of Cuban state farms with "[inefficiencies] arising from overcentralized decisionmaking, together with a shortage of qualified personnel which was aggravated by a tendency to place politically reliable people in top administrative posts even when they lacked technical skills."

random sample of the populations they left and may have imperfect memories. Readers are advised that the estimates in this section are necessarily inexact.

In Cuba, the disincentives inherent in the socialist system sharply reduced agricultural production. As O'Connor (1968, 206–7), explains, "Because wage rates bore little or no relationship to labor productivity and [state farm] income, there were few incentives for workers to engage wholeheartedly in a collective effort." Table 8-1 shows the change in agricultural production in Cuba spanning the agrarian reform period of 1959–63, when about 70 percent of farmland was nationalized (Zimbalist and Eckstein 1987). Production of livestock fell between 14 percent (fish) and 84 percent (pork). Among the major crops, production fell between 5 percent (rice) and 75 percent (malanga). The biggest crop, sugar, fell 35 percent. There was not a major Cuban famine, however, because of Soviet assistance and emigration.[30]

The CEA also notes that, though Cuba had a gross national income similar to that of Puerto Rico before the Cuban Revolution in the late 1950s, by 2000 the Cuban gross national income had fallen almost two-thirds relative to Puerto Rico's.[31]

In the USSR, the collectivization of agriculture occurred with the First Five-Year Plan, from 1928 to 1932. Horses were important for doing farm work, but their numbers fell by 47 percent, in part because nobody had much incentive to care for them when they became collective property (Conquest 1986). In the Central Asian parts of the USSR, the number of cattle fell more than 75 percent, and the number of sheep more than 90 percent (Conquest 1986). Looking at official Soviet data for about 1970, Johnson and Brooks (1983) concluded that the entire program of socialist policies—"excessive centralization of the planning, control, and management of agriculture, inappropriate price policies, and defective incentive systems for farm managers and workers and for enterprises that supply inputs to agriculture"—was reducing Soviet agricultural productivity about 50 percent.[32]

A famine ensued in 1932 and 1933, and about 6 million people died from starvation (Courtois et al. 1999).[33] The death rates were high in Ukraine, a nor-

---

[30] On Soviet economic aid to Cuba, see Walters (1966).

[31] This is per Collins, Bosworth, and Soto-Class (2006) and the Barro-Lee data set, using GDP for Cuba in 1950. The result is more extreme if the comparison is based on GDP, because people and businesses outside Puerto Rico have substantial claims on the production occurring there.

[32] This is likely an underestimate because, as Johnson and Brooks acknowledge, their research project was made possible through cooperation with the Soviet government.

[33] Conquest (1986, 301) cites 7 million.

Table 8-1. Agricultural Production in Cuba After the Nationalization of Farms

Livestock	Change from 1957–58 to 1963–64 (percent)	Crop	Change from 1957–58 to 1963–64 (percent)
Beef	−45	Sugar	−35
Pork	−84	Corn	−39
Poultry	−36	Rice	−5
Fish	−14	Malanga	−75
Eggs	−40	Yucca	−56
Milk	−39	Potatoes	−50

Source: Salazar-Carrillo and Nodarse-Leon (2015).

mally fertile region from which the Soviet planners had been exporting food.[34] Figure 8-2 shows the time series for Ukrainian deaths by sex, along with births. This time series also appears to show that millions more people were not born because of the famine.

Mao's government implemented the so-called Great Leap Forward for China from 1958 to 1962, including a policy of mass collectivization of agriculture that provided "no wages or cash rewards for effort" on farms.[35] The per capita output of grain fell 21 percent from 1957 to 1962; for aquatic products, the drop was 31 percent; and for cotton, edible oil, and meat, it was about 55 percent (Lin 1992; Nolan 1988).[36] During the Great Chinese Famine from 1959 to 1961, an estimated 45 million people died (Dikötter 2010). Figure 8-3 shows the time series for deaths and births, which form a pattern similar to Ukraine's, except that the absolute number of deaths was an order of magnitude greater.

Failed agricultural policies are not the only way that civilians died at the hands of their highly socialist state. Rummel (1994), Courtois and others (1999), Pipes (2003), and Holmes (2009) document noncombatant deaths in the Soviet Bloc, Yugoslavia, Cuba, China, Cambodia, Vietnam, Laos, North Korea, and Ethiopia. These deaths exclude deaths in military combat but include deaths in purges, massacres, concentration camps, forced migration, and both escape attempts and famines. The death rate in famines was particularly high in North Korea, where about 600,000 people died from starvation in the late 1990s out

---

[34] In fact, the USSR as a whole was exporting grain at that time (Dalrymple 1964, 271; Courtois et al. 1999, 167). Note that there were also starvation deaths elsewhere in the USSR (Conquest 1986). In contrast to the famines associated with highly socialist regimes, Ó Gráda (2000) and Goodspeed (2016, 2017) find that one important margin of adjustment during the Irish Famine of 1845–51 was substantially increased net imports of relatively cheap corn and other grains, and similarly dramatically increased exports of higher-value agricultural output such as eggs, dairy products, and cattle.

[35] See Meng, Qian, and Yared (2015, 1572), summarizing Walker (1965).

[36] For aggregate productivity time series, see Cheremukhin et al. (2015).

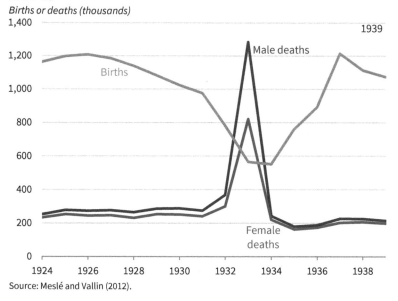

Figure 8-2. Annual Trend of Births and Deaths in Ukraine, by Gender, 1924–39

Births or deaths (thousands)

Source: Meslé and Vallin (2012).

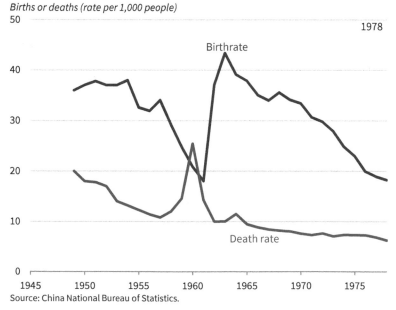

Figure 8-3. Birthrates and Death Rates in China, 1949–78

Births or deaths (rate per 1,000 people)

Source: China National Bureau of Statistics.

of a population of about 22 million (Goodkind, West, and Johnson 2011).[37] Cambodia's Communist period was especially violent.

The total noncombatant civilian deaths in the highly socialist countries were a combination of the effects of government takeovers of important industries and brutal political systems. Modern American socialists are against state brutality. But it is a mistake to ignore the highly socialist tragedies altogether, because it was high taxes, large state organizations, and centralized control that delivered the opposite of what was promised and forced consumers to endure intolerably small supplies of food and other consumer goods. In other words, the low output of state farms and centralized planning were results of economic failures that cannot be rectified with more peaceful implementation. Venezuela, discussed below, is a case in point.

Though the nationalization of agriculture depressed output, the privatization of the same land brought it surging back. Johan Norberg explains how, when Chinese villagers began to (secretly) privatize their land, the "farmers did not start the workday when the village whistle blew any longer—they went out much earlier and worked much harder. . . . Grain output in 1979 was six times higher than the year before."[38]

Although socialist policies are ostensibly implemented to reduce poverty and inequality, it was the end of highly socialist policies in China that brought these results on a worldwide scale. China's major reforms began in 1978, which is about the time that the poverty rate in China, and therefore world poverty rates and world inequality, began a remarkable decline (Sala-i-Martin 2006).[39] Policy changes in India also coincided with reduced poverty in that country, although it is debated whether the early Indian policies were socialist (Basu 2008). The end of socialism in the USSR increased poverty there, but this was not enough to offset, by worldwide measures, the progress elsewhere in the world (Pinkovskiy and Sala-i-Martin 2009).

Lessons Learned

Before the First Five-Year Plan, the USSR's economists had observed the productivity losses that came with attempts to collectivize farming. Conquest (1986, 108) describes how they "still defended small scale agriculture in 1929—but soon had to repudiate that position." The political leadership then prohibited the types of economic analysis that might show the opportunity costs of state farms (Conquest 1986).

---

[37] The CEA did not find comparable data on deaths for highly socialist regimes in Afghanistan, Angola, Benin, Congo, Mozambique, Somalia, and South Yemen. Such data may be lacking because their implementations may have been comparably peaceful from a civilian perspective. Of course, state brutality is not limited to highly-socialist countries.

[38] See Norberg (2016, chap. 1), citing Zhou (1996).

[39] See also the official rural poverty measure (State Council of the People's Republic of China 2016), which fell from 98 percent in 1978 to 6 percent in 2015.

Although the eyewitnesses saw in real time the economic problems with large state organizations, some distinguished economists outside the socialist countries dismissed evidence that might suggest socialism to be a failure in the USSR or China. For instance, Paul Samuelson (1976), the first American to win the Nobel Prize in economics, expressed surprise that the Soviet collective farms were not more productive than private land allotments. As recently as 1989, Samuelson and William Nordhaus (1989, 837) were still writing that "the Soviet economy is proof that, contrary to what many skeptics had earlier believed, a socialist command economy can function and even thrive." John Gurley (1969), one of the 11 economists during the history of the *American Economic Review* who have served as its managing editor, wrote that "the basic overriding economic fact about China is that for twenty years it has fed, clothed, and housed everyone, has kept them healthy and has educated most. Millions have not starved."[40] As recently as 1984, John Kenneth Galbraith asserted that "the Russian system succeeds because, in contrast with the Western industrial economies, it makes full use of its manpower."[41]

The infamous journalist Walter Duranty privately estimated that 7 million people died from the Soviet famine, but instead he published Soviet-censored descriptions in the *New York Times* during those years.[42] Meanwhile, the highly socialist governments themselves eventually acknowledged the value of private enterprises. As a means of increasing national output, Cuba, China, the USSR, and other highly socialist countries eventually permitted private enterprises both in and outside the agriculture sector to coexist with state-owned enterprises.[43]

Central Planning in Practice

The Soviet leadership promised that "scientific planning" would replace the "chaos of the market," whereas in practice central planning proved primitive, unreliable, and incapable of adjusting to change (Lazarev and Gregory 2003). Centralized deliveries were notoriously unreliable; managers relied on informal markets to exchange materials outside the official plan. Adding to managerial

---

[40] Gurley republished these ideas later (e.g., Gurley 1976b, 13). Today, it must be acknowledged that the Great Chinese Famine was in the middle of Gurley's "twenty years" period, when everyone in China was supposedly fed.

[41] According to Schumpeter (1943, chap. XIII), these attitudes are to be expected. He says that intellectuals benefit from criticizing the social system in which they live, and that it is the abundance of the market system that allows intellectuals to be a large share of the population.

[42] He won a 1932 Pulitzer Prize for some of his publications about the USSR (Conquest 1986, 320). Though he personally visited the famine regions in 1933, his *New York Times* publications that year denied that there was a famine, and mocked a journalist who reported otherwise (Conquest 1986, 319; Applebaum 2017). Conquest explains how Duranty was further honored in New York City for telling "people what they wished to hear." The *New York Times* "publicly acknowledg[ed] his failures" in the 1980s (*New York Times* Company 2003).

[43] See Johnson and Brooks (1983, 5–6), Zimbalist and Eckstein (1987, 13), Pipes (2003, 871), and Dikötter (2010, xxii).

confusion and uncertainty was the fact that plans were constantly being changed based on interventions by ministry and party officials (Gregory 2004). Consumer goods were allocated based on coupon rationing or standing in line; illegal markets also proved to be more reliable for obtaining consumer goods.

Ludwig Von Mises (1990) and F. A. Hayek (1945) warned that planning an economy without prices, profit motives, and incentives is impossible. Managers in planned economies were government employees who lack incentives and even guidance to run their factories. On a more practical level, planning complexity meant that only a few commodities could be planned from the center, and then only in the form of crude aggregates like square meters of cloth or tons of steel (Zaleski 1980).

The first two five-year plans were grossly underfulfilled (Zaleski 1980). Soviet plan fulfillment improved over time, but this was not a sign of "better" planning. Rather, Soviet planners institutionalized "planning from the achieved level," which meant that the current operational plan was almost entirely last year's plan plus marginal adjustments (Birman 1978). Planning from the achieved level froze Soviet resource allocation in place and, curiously, created opposition to technological change as a disruptive threat to the plan.

Central planning ultimately proved to be a rather complex—and unplanned—mixture of political intervention, petty tutelage, and illegal markets (Zaleski 1980, 486; Lazarev and Gregory 2003; Gregory 2004, 189).

The Case of Venezuela Today: An Industrialized Country with Socialist Policies

Venezuela is not an agricultural economy, but in pursuing socialist policies, it nationalized important parts of its economy, implemented effectively high marginal tax rates, and centrally controlled prices of consumer and other goods. As with the other highly socialist countries, its state-owned enterprises have proven to be unproductive. Millions of people have already fled the country.

The economies of the highly socialist countries described above are agricultural and labor intensive. An oil-rich country such as Venezuela that managed its oil assets well and paid cash royalties to its citizens independent of how much they earn could in principle be providing income for its citizens with zero marginal tax rates.[44] The economy could also be unregulated and without state-owned enterprises (with oil assets rented to private businesses to operate), and therefore not be socialist in any aspect of the definition introduced in the "Economics of Socialism" section above. However, this is not the path taken by Venezuela over the past 20 years, when it nationalized most oil assets and many other businesses, implemented effectively high marginal tax rates, and centrally controlled prices of consumer and other goods.

[44] For example, the oil-rich State of Alaska has no sales or state income taxes. Oil-rich Norway, conversely, has marginal tax rates that are similar to those of the other Nordic countries.

In 1999, "Hugo Chávez convinced the people of Venezuela they were being robbed by the greedy oil companies, dramatically raised taxes and royalties on new and existing projects. . . . The state-owned oil entity no longer possessed the know-how to develop its resources and production began declining" (*Oil Sands Magazine* 2016). Oil revenues were spent on generous social programs rather than on investing in the country's oil production capacity or cutting taxes (*Economist* 2017; Monaldi 2018).[45] As shown in figure 8-4, Venezuela's oil production has been declining, while production in Canada, which has petroleum resources similar to Venezuela's, has been increasing.[46]

Venezuela nationalized several other businesses, ranging from cell phones to medicines. According to Transparency International (2017, 52), "From 2001 to 2017, the Venezuelan state went from owning 74 public enterprises to 526, four times more than Brazil (130) and ten times more than Argentina," and by 2016 state enterprise employment reached 6 percent of the entire workforce.

Earning and spending are heavily taxed in Venezuela. The top rate on personal income is 34 percent, plus 11 percent for payroll. The value-added tax rate is 16 percent. Inflation is a tax implicitly paid while a worker or consumer holds currency; even during normal times, inflation was 2 percent a month. Import restrictions are relevant because, in a well-functioning economy based on natural resources, many consumer goods would be imported. Currency transactions, and international financial transactions generally, are tightly controlled, which means that an importer would in effect pay a tax when obtaining the foreign currency required to purchase foreign goods. As of 2012, the import tariff rate was 12.1 percent on nonagricultural goods. Imports are also at risk of theft by the border patrol. If we take the foreign exchange and import theft rates to each be 10 percent, this puts the overall tax rate on earning for the purpose of obtaining consumption goods at over 60 percent (this applies a 48 percent import share to consumption).

The Venezuelan economy does not benefit from price signals in the way that less-regulated economies do. High inflation, which is expected to reach 1 million percent a year in 2018, makes it difficult to discern relative prices (Fischer, Hall, and Taylor 1981). Even without inflation, many prices are not determined by the market. In Venezuela, the 2011 Law of Fair Costs and Prices gives the Superintendency of Fair Costs and Prices (known as SUNDECOP) "broad authority to regulate the prices of almost all goods and services sold to the public," deciding "whether prices are 'fair' and to identify businesses that make 'excessive profits through speculation'" (USTR 2013). "Basic goods like

---

[45] Under Hugo Chávez, the Venezuelan government "constructed a free healthcare program for people living in poor and marginalized areas," largely by importing about 31,000 medical personnel from Cuba (Brading 2013, chap. 4; Westhoff et al. 2010; Wilson 2015).

[46] The success of Canada's oil industry over the same time frame is one reason why the CEA believes that the economic disaster in Venezuela cannot be blamed on world oil markets.

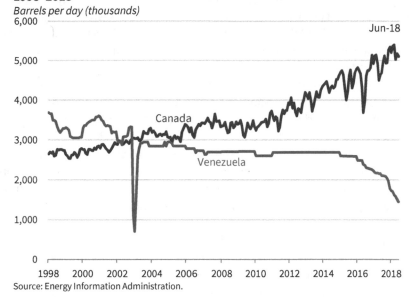

Figure 8-4. Total Production of Petroleum and Other Liquid Fuels, 1998–2018

Barrels per day (thousands)

Source: Energy Information Administration.

flour and aspirin had fixed prices and were so cheap that companies had no incentive to make them" (Kurmanaev 2018).

Emigration has proven to be an important way in which Venezuelan policies have reduced the supply of goods and services. Talented workers have emigrated from the oil industry and from medical practices (Dube 2017). Overall, about 2 million people have emigrated from the country in recent years (Alhadeff 2018).

Economic Freedom and Living Standards in a Broad Cross Section of Countries

Of course, not all countries have pushed socialist policies to the extremes discussed in the previous section. To the extent that socialist policies would involve lesser increases in tax rates, the extensive literature on the effects of taxation could be used to assess some of the consequences of more moderate socialism, which is an approach pursued in the "Medicare for All" section of this chapter.[47] But the tax literature does not address state-owned enterprises and centralized price setting, or how these practices interact with high tax rates.

An extensive economic growth literature is helpful in this regard because it documents a relationship between real GDP and the degree of socialism, measured in a large sample of countries as the opposite of economic freedom.

---

[47] An extensive review is provided by the CEA (2018b, chap. 1).

The studies suggest that moving U.S. policies to highly socialist policies would reduce real GDP at least 40 percent in the long run. Alternatively, adopting a 1975 Nordic level of socialism, which is about halfway toward our highly socialist benchmark of 2014 Venezuela, would reduce real GDP by at least 19 percent in the long run.[48] These effects are similar to those obtained with alternative methods in the final two sections of this chapter.

The growth studies mainly rely on the Fraser Institute, which in 1996, in conjunction with 10 other economic institutes, published the book *Economic Freedom of the World 1975–1995*. Fraser has subsequently provided annual updates of its Economic Freedom of the World (EFW) Index, which measures the degree to which the policies and institutions of countries are supportive of economic freedom. Forty-two indicators are used to construct a summary index for each country and year that ranges between 1 for the least free and 10 for the most free. The indicators are aggregated to five main categories, which are then given equal weight in the overall index. The first category is the size of the government in terms of spending, taxation, and the size of government-controlled enterprises. The second is the legal system and property rights in terms of the protection of persons having such rights. The third category is referred to as "sound money," which measures policies related to inflation. The fourth is free international trade, which means that citizens are free to trade with other countries. And the fifth category is limited regulation, which addresses the freedom to exchange and trade domestically. Note that each category is an indicator of economic freedom, rather than political freedom or civil liberties.

Of particular interest in this chapter are the recent EFW Index values for the U.S. (8.0), the Nordic countries (averaging 7.5), and Venezuela (2.9).[49] Venezuela in 2016 was one of the least free in the entire country panel.[50] Also of interest is the Nordic average in 1975 (5.5), which was about when socialism peaked in those countries. In other words, the Nordic countries were once about halfway between where the U.S. and Venezuela have been recently, but now have economic freedoms that are much closer to those of the U.S.

The EFW Index is related to our discussion of more socialist policies that involve increased public financing, public production, and regulations that

---

[48] In 2017, 19 and 40 percent of annual U.S. per capita GDP were, respectively, about $11,000 and $24,000.

[49] The year 2016 is the most recent one with comprehensive coverage. Alesina and Angeletos (2005) explain why fundamentally similar countries can nonetheless take quite different approaches to socialism and, conversely, that small political changes could result in a dramatic increase in a country's socialism.

[50] We also note that the highly socialist countries tend to be excluded from the data, in part because it is difficult to construct accurate measures of the components of spending that would be comparable between highly socialist countries and the rest of the world. Among the countries with EFW indices, the Marxist governments of 1990 Nicaragua and 1980 Congo have EFW values below 3.5, although so too do a few repressive anti-Marxist governments.

replace each citizen's ability to spend his or her own money on himself or herself with the government's spending other people's money on others. As reviewed by Hall and Lawson (2014), the EFW Index has been cited and utilized in hundreds of academic articles. Their review discusses 402 articles, of which 198 used the EFW Index as an independent variable in an empirical study. They report that over two-thirds of these studies found economic freedom to correspond to improved types of economic performance, such as faster growth, better living standards, and more happiness, as well as other measures.

In particular, a large subliterature focuses on the correlation between the EFW Index and economic investment and growth, as reviewed by De Haan, Lundström, and Sturm (2006). One major study—by Gwartney, Holcombe, and Lawson (2006)—found that a 1-unit increase in the EFW Index from 1980 to 2000 was associated with a 2.6-percentage-point increase in private investment as a share of GDP, and thereby with a 1.2-percentage-point increase in annualized economic growth over 20 years.[51] This suggests that going from the U.S. EFW level to Venezuela's would reduce GDP by about two-thirds after 20 years.[52] Going back to 1975, Nordic values of the EFW Index would reduce GDP more than 40 percent.

Another study, by Easton and Walker (1997), found effects that are smaller although still economically significant. They estimate the elasticity of the steady state level of GDP per worker with respect to the EFW Index as 0.61, so that going to Venezuela's EFW would reduce real GDP per worker by about 40 percent in the long run.[53] With the 1975 Nordic value of EFW, long-run GDP per worker would be reduced at least 19 percent. To the extent that socialism reduces the fraction of the population that works, the reductions in GDP per capita are even greater.

This evidence is suggestive as to the opportunity costs of socialism, but of course cross-country correlations are not necessarily causal. Moreover, the EFW Index is not exactly the inverse of socialism, and the various ingredients of the index can be difficult to measure. This evidence therefore needs to be

---

[51] The other independent variables in the model are tropical location, coastal population, and human capital growth.

[52] The CEA notes that, at very low levels of economic freedom and therefore tax rates near 100 percent, it is difficult to predict GDP. The effects of, say, a 95 percent tax rate should be quite different from the effects of a 90 percent tax rate, because in the latter case workers keep twice as much as they do in the former. As noted above, the data for the least-free countries are often lacking or are of especially poor quality.

[53] The other independent variables in the model are a transformation of the population growth rate, the physical investment rate, and schooling. Also recall this chapter's estimates of the output effects of highly socialist policies: reductions of at least two-thirds (all of Cuba, as of the 21st century), about half (Soviet agriculture, c. 1970), and about three-fourths (Venezuelan oil production). Also of interest is the comparison of North Korea with South Korea; highly socialist North Korea appears to have about a 90 percent shortfall in GDP per capita (Rice et al. 2018). The CEA therefore refers to the output effect of highly socialist policies as "at least 40 percent" (negative).

considered together with the case studies in the high-socialism and Nordic sections as well as the tax-impact analysis in the "Medicare for All" section.

The Nordic Countries' Policies and Incomes Compared with Those of the United States

The Nordic countries include Denmark, Finland, Iceland, Norway, and Sweden. This section looks at these countries in more detail because they are often singled out as supposedly having socialist policies and admirable economic outcomes. Combining state, local, and central governments, public spending is about half of GDP in the Nordic countries, as compared with 38 percent of GDP in the United States (OECD 2018b). However, the Nordic countries today are hardly socialist, because they have internationally low corporate taxes, have low regulation of business, allow the private sector to participate in the provision of primary and secondary schooling, link full social benefits to having a work history, and require cost sharing for healthcare at the time of service.[54] Though these countries have universal-coverage health insurance, they do not impose a single payer on the entire nation, despite being more homogeneous countries than the United States (Anell, Glenngård, and Merkur 2012; Vuorenkoski, Mladovsky, and Mossialos 2008; Olejaz et al. 2012; Ringard et al. 2013; Sigurgeirsdóttir, Waagfjörð, and Maresso 2014).[55]

We find that today, the Nordic countries' marginal tax rates on labor income are not in fact far above those in the U.S., once implicit employment and income taxes are considered. The Nordic countries' living standards are still at least 15 percent lower than those of the U.S., in large part because people work less. The private and social returns to a college education are higher in the U.S., even though college education is at least as common here. These results are consistent with the basic economic idea that redistribution and single-payer systems have significant costs in terms of reducing national incomes.

The Nordic countries themselves recognized the economic harm of high tax rates vis-à-vis creating and retaining businesses and motivating work effort, which is why their marginal tax rates on personal and corporate income have fallen 20 or 30 points, or more, from their peaks in the 1970s and 1980s (Stenkula, Johansson, and Du Rietz 2014).

Measuring Tax Policies in the Nordic Countries

The Nordic countries are reputed to have taxes that are higher but "fairer" than those in the United States. However, the Nordic-country average tax rate on capital income is lower than in the United States, even since the Tax Cuts and

---

[54] Also see the "Medicare for All" section of this chapter.
[55] The exception is Iceland, which is a nation of less than 350,000 people and therefore smaller than even the least-populous U.S. State, Wyoming.

Jobs Act lowered the top U.S. statutory corporate tax rate by 13 percentage points.[56] Nordic taxes on labor are only somewhat higher than in the United States, especially once implicit taxes are acknowledged.

A key difference between Nordic and U.S. taxation is that the former is broader based and the latter is considerably more progressive. With lower thresholds for their income tax brackets, the Nordic economies apply their highest marginal tax rate to taxpayers earning only a marginally above-average income, meaning that low- and middle-income tax filers face substantially higher average rates in the Nordic countries than in the United States. Moreover, the Nordic countries rely more heavily on value-added, or consumption, taxes, which are not progressive. The higher tax revenue share of GDP in the Nordic economies is thus predominantly accounted for by a broader base, rather than by "taxing the rich." As shown below, Senator Bernie Sanders is currently proposing tax rates that are above the Nordic-country average in six of seven tax categories, with the exception being sales / value-added taxes.[57]

As shown in table 8-2, the corporate income tax rate in the Nordic countries ranges from 20 to 23 percent, which was about half the U.S. Federal and State statutory rate until 2018. Other tax rates vary significantly among the Nordic countries. The top personal rate on dividend income is 29 percent in the U.S., compared with 22 percent in Iceland, 29 percent in Finland, 30 percent in Sweden, 31 percent in Norway, and 42 percent in Denmark. Sweden and Norway have no estate tax, while the top estate tax rates range from 10 to 19 percent in the other three Nordic countries, as compared with 43 percent in the U.S.[58]

Senator Sanders has made specific proposals for the taxation of capital in the United States. He voted against cutting the corporate income tax, which in 2016 had the Organization for Economic Cooperation and Development's (OECD's) highest combined statutory rate of about 39 percent for Federal and State taxes combined, and he now supports repealing the cut (Bollier 2018). This rate is well above where the U.S. and the Nordic countries are now. The senator has proposed a 68 percent rate on dividends and capital gains, which is more than double, or about 39 points above, where the U.S. is now.[59] He has

---

[56] Low corporate tax rates raise wages by encouraging capital accumulation.

[57] Senator Sanders, who is the leading socialist in Federal politics today, proposes to repeal the Tax Cuts and Jobs Act, which reduced the combined Federal-State statutory corporate rate by 13 percentage points (Bollier 2018). The other rate proposals are reported on Senator Sander's website (http://sanders.senate.gov) and by Cole and Greenberg (2016).

[58] All the countries have a zero rate for comparatively small estates. U.S. rates include the population-weighted average of State estate and inheritance tax rates.

[59] The 68 percent rate includes 3.9 percentage points for State and local taxes (Potosky 2016), the top Sanders bracket inclusive of 2.2 percentage points for his additional personal income surtax (54.2), and Sanders's 10 percent Affordable Care Act tax on investment income. See also Sammartino et al. (2016). The 68 percent does not include any phase-out of the rebate of Senator Sanders's proposed carbon tax.

Table 8-2. Tax Policies in the United States and the Nordic Countries, 2015–18

	Tax Rate						Nordic average minus U.S.	Senator Sanders's proposal minus U.S.
	Denmark	Finland	Iceland	Norway	Sweden	U.S.		
Taxes on capital								
Statutory corporate income tax rate								
	22	20	20	23	22	26	–4	13
Top personal rate on dividend income								
	42	29	22	31	30	29	1	39
Top personal rate on capital gains								
	42	33	20	27	30	29	1	39
Top estate or inheritance tax rate								
	15	19	10	0	0	43	–35	24
Taxes on labor or consumption								
Payroll tax rate (on a base of employer cost)								
	0	26	6	19	29	14	2	7
Top individual income tax rate								
	56	49	44	39	60	46	3	12
Sales or value-added tax								
	25	24	24	25	25	6	19	–
Excise and nonrecurrent tax								
	4	4	3	3	2	1	2	1
Progressivity of household taxes (mid-2000s)								
	1.02	1.20	0.90	0.95	1.00	1.35	–0.34	–

Sources: Organization for Economic Cooperation and Development (OECD); PricewaterhouseCoopers; Tax Foundation; Tax Policy Center; CEA calculations.

Note: The OECD progressivity measure is the top decile's tax share divided by its income share, and would be 1 for a proportional income tax. Corporate, dividend, and sales tax rates are for 2018. All other rates are for 2015–17. Excise and nonrecurrent tax rates are calculated as the ratio of revenues to GDP and include taxes on emissions and environmental discharges.

also proposed adding 24 points to the top estate tax rate, even though the U.S. rate is already well above Nordic rates.

The Nordic countries are similar to the U.S. in terms of their payroll tax rates (combined for employer and employee) and the top personal income tax rate.[60] Even excluding implicit taxes, the overall top marginal tax rate on personal income in the United States in 2017, 46.3 percent (as calculated by the OECD), was only 3 percentage points below the Nordic average of about

[60] Some of the Nordic countries have privatized much of their old-age social security programs (Turner 2005).

50 percent.[61] Senator Sanders also proposes increasing both payroll and personal income tax rates above the Nordic average, especially as regards the top personal rate.

None of the entries in table 8-2 incorporate implicit taxes, which refer to the loss or gain of transfer income that occurs when a household works or earns more. In the Nordic countries, implicit tax rates can be negative because working or earning more entitles a person to additional transfer income that helps offset some of the extra payroll, income, or sales tax that he or she will pay. In other words, a Nordic citizen with a history of working or earning more will receive a *greater* benefit when he or she has earned more in the past. For example, work is required in order to be eligible for full paid family leave, unemployment, or retirement benefits.[62] As a result, the disincentive to work in a Nordic country may be somewhat less than what is shown in table 8-2.

In the U.S., working and earning does cause a program beneficiary to lose benefits, which is not the case for Nordic-country health and other benefits. In other words, U.S. programs tend to have positive implicit taxes on work because the people who work and earn more are paid fewer benefits.[63] Table 8-2 shows a gap between Nordic and U.S. marginal tax rates on labor income, but the true gap would likely be smaller if implicit taxes were fully considered.

Margaret Thatcher (1976) observed that "socialism started by saying it was going to tax the rich, very rapidly it was taxing the middle income groups. Now, it's taxing people quite highly with incomes way below." Obtaining large amounts of tax revenue ultimately involves resorting to high tax rates on the poor and middle class because these groups in the aggregate generate much of the Nation's income—what economists call "widening the tax base" (Becker and Mulligan 2003). Another way that the Nordic countries broadly levy high rates is with a value-added tax (VAT), which is essentially a national sales tax. Regardless of whether they are rich, poor, or in between, Nordic consumers are required to pay an additional VAT of 24 or 25 percent on their purchases,

---

[61] The Tax Cuts and Jobs Act temporarily reduces the Federal rate, and therefore the combined State-Federal rate, by less than 3 points.

[62] See Anderson et al. (2007), Rogerson (2007), and Kleven (2014), who describes "the strong subsidization of goods that are complementary to working." See also Gruber and Wise (1999) on retirement benefits. U.S. unemployment and retirement benefits can be tied to work history, too (Feldstein and Samwick 1992), but by comparison with the Nordic countries, these negative implicit taxes are smaller because the full benefit amounts are smaller. U.S. welfare programs have sometimes required work from able-bodied adults (Mulligan 2012; chapter 9 of this *Report*). The CEA also notes that Senator Sanders proposes to increase implicit marginal income tax rates by phasing out the rebate of a proposed carbon tax (Mermin, Burman, and Sammartino 2016). The collection of such a tax also shares some economic features with sales taxes.

[63] Health premium tax credits and Medicaid eligibility are two important examples in the health area (Mulligan 2015). Food stamps and public housing are two more U.S. assistance programs that have positive implicit tax rates on employment and income.

on top of all the other taxes that they pay.[64] By comparison, in the U.S. sales are taxed by States rather than the Federal government, but no State has a rate much above 10 percent, and the national average sales tax rate is about 6 percent. Excise taxes and nonrecurrent taxes—which include carbon taxes and sales taxes on specific products such as gasoline, tobacco products, alcoholic beverages, and automobiles—are also higher in the Nordic countries (see the second-to-last row of table 8-2).

Even without the VAT, the high Nordic rates apply to everyone, not just high-income households. The OECD prepares a measure of progressivity that is the share of nationwide household taxes paid by the top 10 percent of citizens (ranked by their income), expressed as a ratio of the share of national aggregate income.[65] The ratio would be 1 if the household taxes were a fixed proportion of income. A regressive tax would have a ratio less than 1; a progressive tax would have a ratio greater than 1. As shown in table 8-2's last row, four of the Nordic countries have essentially proportional household taxes.[66] The average progressivity of all five countries is 1.01, which is 0.34 *less* progressive than in the U.S.

Another indication of the progressivity of U.S. income taxation relative to the Nordic countries is the threshold, expressed as a multiple of the average wage, at which the top marginal income tax rate comes into effect.[67] As shown in figure 8-5, in the United States, the top marginal rate only applies to income above 8 times the average wage. In contrast, on average, in the Nordic countries the top marginal income tax rate applies to income that is only 1.5 times the average wage. Indeed, in Denmark, earnings that are just 1.3 times the average are already subject to the top tax rate. To put this in perspective, if the U.S. tax code were as flat as that of Denmark, a filer earning just $70,000 a year (about in the middle of the household income distribution) would already face the top marginal personal income tax rate of 46.3 percent, whereas the U.S. code allows a filer to earn as much as 6 times that, or $423,904, before paying the top rate.

Lower personal income tax progressivity in the Nordic countries, combined with lower taxation on capital and, on average, only modestly higher marginal personal income tax rates on the right tail of the income distribution, means that a core feature of the Nordic tax model is higher tax rates on average and near-average income workers and their families. That is, contrary to the assertions of American proponents of Nordic-style democratic socialism,

---

[64] The sales price of retail items is usually quoted inclusive of the VAT. Note that a sales tax rate cannot be added to income tax rates to get a meaningful overall rate because the sales tax is levied on a smaller base. For example, a 25 percent sales tax is like a 20 percent income tax.

[65] The OECD (2018c) refers to income and payroll—the employee part only—taxes as "household taxes."

[66] Household taxes, which include personal income taxes, can be essentially proportional even while personal income tax rates rise with income because payroll tax rates fall with income and/or high-income taxpayers have disproportionate deductions from income for tax purposes.

[67] The term "average" refers to the mean.

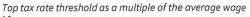

Figure 8-5. The Progressivity of Personal Income Tax Structures in the Nordic Countries and the United States, 2017

Top tax rate threshold as a multiple of the average wage

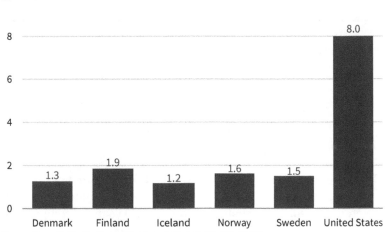

Source: Organization for Economic Cooperation and Development.
Note: If the U.S. threshold as a multiple of the average wage were lowered to Denmark's, the top marginal tax rate would apply to filers earning only $68,802.

the Nordic model of taxation does not heavily rely on punitive rates on high-income households but rather on imposing high rates on households in the middle of the income distribution. This is illustrated in table 8-3, which reports that even after accounting for transfers, a one-income couple earning the average wage, with two children, faces an all-in average personal income tax rate of 22 percent in the Nordic countries (counting government transfers as a negative tax), as compared with a rate of 14.2 percent in the United States. This comparison for the various family types suggests that American families earning the average wage would be taxed $2,000 to $5,000 more a year net of transfers if the United States had current Nordic policies.

Measuring Regulation in the Nordic Countries

According to the Fraser Institute's Economic Freedom of the World Index, the Nordic economies—and particularly Denmark and Sweden—are above the OECD mean with respect to regulatory freedom, while the Heritage Foundation ranks all the Nordic economies higher than the United States for business freedom (Gwartney, Lawson, and Hall 2017; Miller, Kim, and Roberts 2018). OECD data show that the Nordic countries have less regulation in their product markets and more regulation in their labor markets in comparison with the United States. The Nordic countries are fairly similar to the average OECD member country on the regulation measures.

Table 8-3. All-In Average Personal Income Tax Rate, Less Transfers, at the Average Wage, 2017

Country	Single individual with two children, less transfers (percent)	One-income-earner couple with two children, less transfers (percent)
Denmark	16.5	25.3
Finland	21.8	24.7
Iceland	24.8	18.6
Norway	19.4	22.5
Sweden	18.8	18.8
United States	17.1	14.2

Source: Organization for Economic Cooperation and Development.

The top rows of table 8-4 show how the OECD ranks all five Nordic countries as having less product market regulation than the United States, largely due to Nordic deregulation actions over the past 20 years. In comparison with the Nordic countries, the study finds the United States to be especially high on price controls and command-and-control regulation of business operations.[68] As shown in chapter 2 of this *Report*, the Trump Administration has taken steps to reduce the costs of Federal regulations and to prevent the regulatory state from growing as it had in the past.

Unlike the United States, the Nordic countries do not have minimum wage laws, although the vast majority of jobs have wages limited by collective bargaining agreements. The Nordic countries have more employment protection legislation, which can make labor markets more rigid, although the Nordic economies obtain labor market flexibility with intensive use of temporary employees.[69]

Income and Work Comparisons with the United States.

The average real GDP per capita in the United States is about 20 percent above the averages in Denmark, Finland, Iceland, and Sweden. The comparison with Norway is also similar, if we adjust for Norway's large oil income. Indeed,

---

[68] See also McCloskey (2016, 24) and the regulation components of the Fraser Economic Freedom of the World Index. The OECD product market survey was limited to the State of New York, and therefore may not be representative of the rest of the country. The data show the U.S. suffering from relatively high regulatory protection of incumbents due to exemptions from antitrust laws for publicly controlled firms (OECD 2018c). In addition, the OECD notes that U.S. product market regulation is more restrictive than other OECD economies due to the prevalence of State-level ownership of certain enterprises, particularly in the energy and transportation sectors. To the extent that the Nordic countries have lower product market regulation, this may somewhat offset their higher marginal tax rates on labor income (Fang and Rogerson 2011).

[69] U.S. temporary employment is about 2 percent of overall employment (per the Saint Louis Federal Reserve Bank's series TEMPHELPS and PAYEMS), whereas it ranges from 9 to 17 percent in the Nordic countries (Svalund 2013).

Table 8-4. Regulation Policies in the United States and the Nordic Countries, 2013

| | Regulation index | | | | | | | |
| | | | | | | Nordic | OECD | |
Regulation policy	Denmark	Finland	Iceland	Norway	Sweden	average	average	U.S.
Product markets	1.2	1.3	1.5	1.5	1.5	1.4	1.7	1.6
Public ownership	2.8	3	2.6	3.3	3.4	3	2.7	3
Price controls	0.6	0.9	1.4	0.7	0.4	0.8	1.4	2.6
Command-and-control regulation	1.4	1.7	1.3	1.2	1.6	1.5	1.9	2.2
Employment protection	2.1	2.4	2	2.2	2.5	2.3	2.0	0.5
Addendum: Temporary employment as percent of total	10	13	9	7	13	10	–	2

Sources: Organization for Economic Cooperation and Development; European Commission.

Note: The index is a measure of regulatory strictness. OECD product market measures for the U.S. refer only to New York State . Each table entry is a regulation index, and a higher value indicates more regulation.

Alaska and North Dakota—U.S. States that, like Norway, have high energy production per person—enjoy per capita GDP that is 15 and 4 percent higher, respectively, than Norway's.

Adults in Denmark and Norway work about 20 percent less, and in Sweden and Finland about 10 percent less, than American adults do, while work hours are similar in Iceland and the United States. Arguably, the citizens of these countries are partly "compensated" for lower incomes in terms of having additional free time, but note that all the countries have significant taxes on labor so that the national value of free time is less than the private value.[70]

To begin understanding the financial consequences of living in a Nordic country rather than the U.S., consider the cost of owning and operating a Honda Civic sedan, which is one of the more popular personal vehicles in the U.S. We take the case of a standard four-door Civic, which is available in all the Nordic countries (see figure 8-6). The car's base price in the U.S. is $20,568 (including a 5.75 percent average vehicle sales tax), as compared with $39,617 in Denmark (including the VAT and vehicle taxes). Fuel taxes, which are higher in the Nordic countries than in the U.S., also add to the cost of ownership in the Nordic countries. In Denmark, for example, personal vehicles are excise taxed at 85 percent of the sticker price for the first $30,000, and an additional

---

[70] In other words, labor taxes have a deadweight cost that is revealed in part as additional free time (Feldstein 1999).

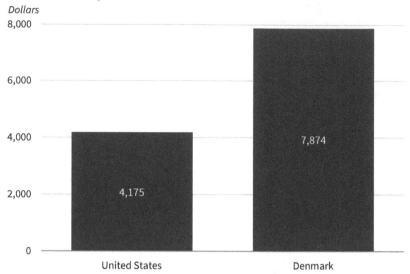

Figure 8-6. Average Annual Cost of a Honda Civic in the United States versus Denmark, 2018

Dollars

Sources: Honda Motor Company; *Wall Street Journal*; Bloomberg; CEA calculations.
Note: Estimates are based on the base price of a four-door Honda Civic sedan.

150 percent tax is added for more than $30,000. As a result, owning and operating the automobile costs Danish consumers substantially more than it costs American consumers. In the U.S., the average annual cost of owning a Honda Civic, accounting for the purchase price and fuel costs, is $4,175. The average consumer in Denmark, for example, must pay $7,874 each year to afford a Civic. The greater ownership costs in the Nordic countries reflect a combination of higher retail prices (including the VAT), higher fuel costs, and other combinations of registration and owner taxes.

Figure 8-7 extends the automobile results to all goods and services in the economy by using real income and production statistics. The blue bars show real GDP per capita in the home country relative to the average for the entire U.S.[71] Four of the bars are negative, meaning that those countries have less GDP per capita. Despite being an oil-rich country, Norway's average GDP per capita is only somewhat above the U.S. average, and is 13 percent below the average GDP per capita in the oil-rich State of Alaska (not shown in the figure).

Furthermore, it has been noted that the true U.S./Nordic output gap is likely even greater because the U.S. has more nonmarket household production, such as at-home child care or home schooling, than the Nordic countries do. Nordic countries tend to do more of their child care in the marketplace

---

[71] Note that GDP includes both private and public sectors and therefore resources received by households from the public sector. The U.S./Nordic gap for disposable income would be even more dramatic.

Figure 8-7. Real Income and GDP per Capita of People of Nordic Ancestry, by Place of Residence, 2015

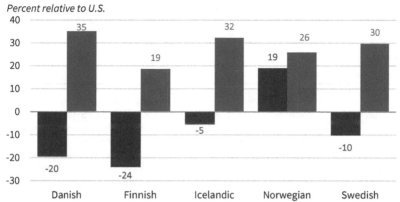

■ Living in home country (real GDP per capita)

■ Living in the United States (real income per capita)

Sources: Census Bureau; Organization for Economic Cooperation and Development; CEA calculations.

Note: International comparisons are for real GDP on a purchasing-power basis.

because child care is a government job. As Sherwin Rosen (1997, 82) described Sweden, "a large fraction of women work in the public sector to take care of the children of other women who work in the public sector to care for the parents of the women who are looking after their children. If Swedish women take care of each other's parents in exchange for taking care of each other's children, how much additional real output comes of it?"

Figure 8-7's red bars show the per capita income of people with Nordic ancestry living in the U.S., and who therefore are not subject to Nordic tax rates and regulations.[72] They have incomes of about 30 percent more than the average American and, based also on the red bars, about 50 percent more income than the average in their home country. This suggests that the incomes of Nordic people are not lower because, apart from public policy, low incomes are somehow cultural.

However, the difference between the incomes of Nordic people in the U.S. and Nordic people living in the Nordic countries is too large to be entirely due to policy differences between the two sets of countries. One contributing factor may be that ancestry is self-reported and that, holding actual ancestry constant, the propensity to identify with Nordic ancestry may be correlated with income. Another factor may be that there was positive self-selection bias among Nordic emigrants to the United States. That is, those who emigrated

---

[72] Most of them were born in the U.S. See also Sanandaji (2015, 2016).

Table 8-5. Actual Individual Consumption per Head at Current Prices and Purchasing Power Parity, 2016

Country	Consumption (United States = 100)
Denmark	69
Finland	70
Iceland	69
Norway	82
Sweden	68
United States	100

Source: Organization for Economic Cooperation and Development (OECD).
Note: Actual individual consumption (AIC) consists of the consumption goods and services acquired by individual households. According to the OECD, AIC is the sum of three components: (1) "The value of households' expenditures on consumption goods or services including expenditures on nonmarket goods or services sold at prices that are not economically significant"; (2) "The value of the expenditures incurred by government units on individual consumption goods or services provided to households as social transfers in kind"; and (3) "The value of the expenditures incurred by NPISHs [nonprofit institutions serving households] on individual consumption goods or services provided to households as social transfers in kind."

from the Nordic countries to the United States would be earning more than the home country average if they and their families had not emigrated.[73]

Another indicator of differences in material well-being in the Nordic economies and the United States is average individual consumption per head.[74] Table 8-5 reports average individual consumption per head at current prices and exchange rates, adjusted for purchasing power parity, with the United States indexed to 100. In 2016, the most recent year for which data are available, average individual consumption per head was 31 percent lower in Denmark than in the United States, and 32 percent lower in Sweden than in the United States. The only Nordic economy in which average consumption is within 20 percent of the U.S. level is Norway, where average consumption per head is 82 percent of the U.S. level.

Though the Nordic economies exhibit lower output and consumption per capita, they also exhibit lower levels of relative income inequality as conventionally measured. Table 8-6 reports Gini coefficients, a standard way of measuring inequality, for disposable income after taxes and transfers in the Nordic economies and the United States in 2015. On average, the U.S. Gini coefficient is about 0.1 percentage point higher than the Nordic economies',

---

[73] However, recent research suggests the sign of selection bias for Nordic emigrants is ambiguous. Specifically, Abramitzky, Boustan, and Eriksson (2012) study Norwegian emigration to the United States during the "Age of Mass Migration," from 1850 to 1913, exploiting within-household variation in emigration status to compare outcomes for Norwegian brothers who emigrated versus those who did not. They find negative selection bias among migrants from urban areas, and mixed results for those from rural areas. These results are also consistent with those of Borjas (1987, 1991).
[74] Economists often prefer consumption to income as a measurement of living standards because it is less sensitive to transitory shocks. Also see chapter 9 of this *Report*.

Table 8-6. Relative Income Inequality, 2015

Country	Gini coefficient	Palma ratio
Denmark	0.26	1.7
Finland	0.26	1.7
Iceland	0.25	1.7
Norway	0.26	1.7
Sweden	0.27	1.7
United States	0.39	2.3

Source: Organization for Economic Cooperation and Development.

Note: Data for Iceland are for 2014. Gini coefficient values are based on disposable income, post taxes and transfers. Palma ratio values are based on the P90/P50 disposable income decile ratio.

indicating higher relative income inequality. The Palma ratio—the ratio of disposable income at the 90th percentile to disposable income at the 50th percentile—is also higher in the United States than in the Nordic countries, as reported in table 8-6.

However, by some measures, even low-income American households have better living standards than the average person living in a Nordic country. Using 1999 data, Fredrik Bergström and Robert Gidehag (2004) found that all the States of the United States had a smaller percentage of households with incomes below $25,000 than Sweden did. As a country, the percentage was less than 30 for the United States, as compared with more than 40 for Sweden. Robert Rector and Kirk Johnson (2004) reviewed evidence from a sample of 15 European countries and found that homes were smaller for the *average* in all three of the sample's Nordic countries (Denmark, Finland, and Sweden) than they were for *poor* households in the United States. Conversely, though the OECD Gini database shows median incomes to be greater in the United States than in Denmark, Finland, Iceland, and Sweden, it shows the opposite at the 10th percentile of the income distribution.[75]

Returns to "Free" Higher Education in the Nordic Countries

An OECD (2018a) study of education systems reports that college tuitions are zero in Denmark, Finland, and Norway.[76] Given that modern American socialists advocate free college tuition and stipends paid for by the Federal government (i.e., taxpayers), it is worth looking at the Nordic experience in this area to see whether, consistent with the economics of socialism, offering college for free (to the student) affects its quality.[77]

---

[75] More work is needed to properly account for in-kind transfers and other government programs. For an analysis of the U.S. data, see chapter 9 of this *Report*.

[76] No data were reported for Iceland or Sweden.

[77] See the College for All Act of 2017, introduced in the U.S. Senate as S. 806.

The same OECD study estimates that, though many American students pay tuition, Americans are somewhat more likely to attain tertiary (post–high school) education on average.[78] In comparison with the tertiary schooling returns in the Nordic countries, American college graduates earn their tuition investment back with interest, and also a lot more. To put it another way, the rates of return to a college education in the Nordic countries are low, and propensities to invest in it are not high, despite the fact that such an investment requires no tuition payments out of pocket.

Figure 8-8's bars, measured in U.S. dollars adjusted for purchasing power parity, show the OECD's estimates of the possibly negative net present financial value of a college education in the four countries, for men, discounted with an 8 percent interest rate.[79] The OECD's estimates of the financial payoff to a U.S. college education are far greater, despite the fact that tuition payments count as negatives in the calculations.

The calculations are comparing two lifetime cash-flow profiles: (1) beginning work after high school and getting the earnings (after taxes) associated with that level of education; and (2) earning nothing during the college years, and paying tuition (if any), but then earning (after taxes) associated with a college education. Note that high school profile 1 has positive cash flows during the college ages, whereas college profile 2 has negative or zero cash flows according to the amount of tuition. A positive value means that investing the positive college age cash flows from the high school profile 1 at 8 percent yields less than the borrowing to pay tuition if any and then enjoying the extra earnings associated with college. A negative value, as for Norway, means that a student who could invest his or her high school earnings at 8 percent a year (real) would be financially ahead by working rather than going to college. The U.S. value of $108,700 means that the present value (discounted at 8 percent) of the college profile 2 exceeds the present value of the high school profile 1 by $108,700.[80]

Taxes and tuition subsidies are among the reasons that the financial value of a college education varies across countries. Their effects on the results can be removed by looking at earnings before taxes and by including public tuition subsidies as a cost. Even from this social (private plus public) perspective, the U.S. financial return is more than double the Nordic returns.[81] This

---

[78] Also note that the Nordic governments also pay living stipends to college students.

[79] The country pattern is similar with the lesser discount rates also shown by the OECD, and similar for women (although female returns are not shown with the 8 percent rate). Among the various discount rates used by the OECD (2018a), the CEA uses the one closest to the net marginal product of physical capital.

[80] The net present value is even greater if smaller discount rates are used (OECD 2018a, 109).

[81] The data provided by OECD (2018a) only permit adding private and social returns when both are discounted at 2 percent per year.

Figure 8-8. Net Lifetime Private Financial Returns from Attaining Tertiary Education, 2017

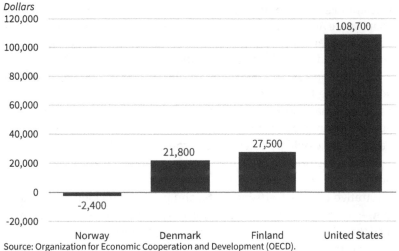

Source: Organization for Economic Cooperation and Development (OECD).
Note: Data are equivalent dollars converted using purchasing power parity for GDP, and are discounted at an 8 percent annual rate. The OECD publishes all the parameters used in the CEA's analysis for males, but not for females.

is consistent with the economic hypothesis advanced in the "Economics of Socialism" section above that making a good "free" reduces its quality.[82]

Socialized Medicine: The Case of "Medicare for All"

Over the next few decades, the health sector is projected to grow to a fourth or even a third of the U.S. economy (CMS 2018a), which demonstrates the great importance of health to Americans and why the Trump Administration is pursuing market reforms to reduce prices and enhance quality. At the same time, a free, single-payer healthcare system continues to be the cornerstone of current socialist policy proposals in the United States. The Senate and House "Medicare for All" (M4A) plans, sponsored or cosponsored by 141 members of the 115th Congress, are designed to use the scale economies of a public

---

[82] On the returns to postsecondary education in Norway, see Kirkeboen, Leuven, and Mogstad (2016); and on the effects of free college in England on education expenditures per student, see Murphy, Scott-Clayton, and Wyness (2017). Note that the returns pattern in figure 8-8 cannot be explained by a higher propensity to attain college in the Nordic countries because the tertiary education attainment rates among persons age 25–54 range from 31 to 35 percent in the Nordic countries, whereas the U.S. rate is 36 percent (OECD 2018a, table A1.1); these percentages do not include short-cycle tertiary degrees, although the conclusions would be similar if they were included. In the United Kingdom, the free college program was ended because it was reducing quality.

monopoly to sharply cut costs (S. 1804; H.R. 676).[83] These plans make it unlawful for a private business to sell health insurance, or for a private employer to
offer health insurance to its employees. Although, at the time of passing the
Affordable Care Act, it was promised that consumers could keep their doctor or
their plan, M4A takes the opposite approach: All private health insurance plans
will be prohibited after a four-year transition period (box 8-1).[84]

This section relates "Medicare for All" to the economic issues raised
above. According to the Senate and House bills, M4A would be a Federal program having a nationwide monopoly on health insurance. The price paid to
the government monopoly, the analogue to revenue received by private health
insurance plans, would be determined through tax policy.

Echoing historic claims about state-run enterprises, it is claimed that
the government monopoly would be more productive by avoiding "waste" on
administrative costs, advertising costs, and profits and would use its bargaining power to obtain better deals from healthcare providers. It is routinely
claimed that single-payer programs are more efficient.[85]

Socialized medicine is an important example of the issues raised by
Milton Freidman's four spending categories portrayed in figure 8-1 above. It
has individuals (government employees) spending other people's money (tax
revenue) on other people than themselves (program participants). The quality
or productivity of health insurance would be determined through centrally
planned rules and regulations. As opposed to a market with competition, if a
patient did not like the tax charged or the quality of the care provided by the
government monopoly, he or she would have no recourse. In addition, price
competition in healthcare itself, as opposed to health insurance, would be
eliminated because all the prices paid to providers and suppliers of healthcare
would be set centrally by the single payer. Chapter 4 of this *Report* shows how in
fact single-payer healthcare systems have delivered lower quality healthcare in
terms of wait times, patient survival rates, and rates of healthcare innovation.

A smaller economy is another adverse effect, due to M4A's disincentives
to work and earn. If financed solely through higher taxes, we find that the program would reduce long-run GDP by 9 percent and household incomes after
taxes and health expenditures by 19 percent.

"Medicare for All" from an International Perspective

"Medicare for All" bears little resemblance to the U.S. Federal program long
known as Medicare. M4A so completely eliminates private insurance, profit

---

[83] See also Sanders (2017).

[84] This also echoes back to the socialization of agriculture. For example, the Chinese Communist
Party's collectivization agenda was initially discouraged by the "deep attachment" of the peasants
to their land (Walker 1965, 4).

[85] See Kliff (2014), Frank (2017), and Konrad (2017). See also Weisbart (2012). The China scholar
Peter Nolan (1988, 4) warns that "none [of socialism's errors] has been so important as the
misplaced belief in the virtues of large-scale . . . units of production."

Box 8-1. What Is "Medicare for All"?

"Medicare for All" (M4A) bills introduced in the U.S. Senate and House of Representatives propose a "free," single-payer, universal coverage healthcare system" (S. 1804; H.R. 676). All private health insurance plans, including those now serving more than 150 million Americans who have employer-provided insurance and more than 40 million Medicare enrollees, would be prohibited after a four-year transition period.

As a "free" program, all financing would come from Federal revenues rather than premiums from members or cost sharing at the time of service.

As a single-payer system, the proposal makes it unlawful for a private business to sell health insurance, or for a private employer to offer health insurance to its employees, where health insurance refers to any insurance that covers "medically necessary or appropriate" hospital services, ambulatory patient services, primary and preventive services, prescription drugs, medical devices, biological products, mental health services, substance abuse treatment, laboratory/diagnostic services, reproductive care, maternity care, newborn care, pediatrics, oral health services, audiology services, vision services, or short-term rehabilitative and habilitative services and devices (sections 107 and 201 of the "Medicare for All" Act of 2017 and section 104 of the House bill). The House bill (section 102) goes further with dietary and nutritional therapies, long term care, palliative care, chiropractic services, and podiatric care all prohibited from coverage by private or employer plans.

As a universal coverage system, all U.S. residents would be automatically enrolled.

It has been noted that M4A does not turn health providers into government employees (although section 103 of the House bill requires all participating providers to surrender their for-profit status). Nevertheless, because the bill makes private health insurance unlawful, health providers have no choice but to receive their income and instructions from the nationwide health insurance monopoly (the Federal government) or from the relatively few people who want to purchase their services without insurance.

"Medicare for All" bears little resemblance to the U.S. Federal program long known as Medicare. M4A so completely eliminates private insurance, profit motives, and consumer choice and incentives that programs like it are unusual elsewhere in the world. The current Medicare program is neither a single-payer system nor a public provider of healthcare because healthcare providers under the program are often for-profit institutions and are receiving much of their reimbursement from private, for-profit insurers, among others.

motives, and consumer choice and consumer incentives that programs like it are unusual elsewhere in the world. The economics of socialism section of this chapter helps explain this state of affairs; health system performance has been shown to be poor without making important uses of the price system, profit motives, and competition among private businesses.

According to the Senate and House bills, M4A is a universal coverage program, a single-payer system, and a "free" healthcare system. These are three distinct policy stances, and the latter two are what set it apart from the current Medicare program and from most government healthcare systems in other nations. Universal coverage programs automatically cover all citizens, but they do so in a variety of ways in terms of numbers of payers and patient cost sharing at the point of use. A single-payer system has a single monopoly payer of healthcare providers. Because one or more private businesses might take an interest in selling health insurance or providing it to their employees, a truly single-payer system is an unlikely market outcome unless the government explicitly prohibits private health insurance, as the Senate and House M4A bills do.[86] A free healthcare system does not, aside from the normal tax obligations, charge patients for health insurance premiums or at the point of use.

The current Medicare program is not a single-payer system because health providers under the program are receiving much of their reimbursement from private, for-profit insurers, among others. Using documents provided on the website of the Centers for Medicare & Medicaid Services, the CEA counted more than 1,000 private Medicare plans coming from hundreds of parent companies.[87] Moreover, Medicare covers services from, among others, for-profit healthcare providers. The current Medicare program is not free healthcare either; beneficiaries must pay both premiums and, at the point of use, cost sharing. According to the economics of socialism cited in the first section of this chapter, "Medicare for All" would have little similarity to the current Medicare program because M4A would be "free"; would prohibit all payers other than the Federal government; and, according to the House bill, would prohibit the profit motive among both healthcare providers and health insurers.[88]

Universal coverage systems are common internationally, but they are different from free health care and from single-payer systems. All the Nordic countries' health systems have user fees or out-of-pocket payments, whose share of overall health spending is similar to what it is currently the case in the United States—although Denmark is the Nordic outlier, in that its patient cost sharing is essentially limited to prescription drugs.[89] The Nordic systems

---

[86] The term "single payer" is sometimes used more broadly to refer to a health insurance market that has many payers but with just one of them making most of the payments. This *Report* uses "single payer" to refer to one, rather than many.

[87] This combines Medicare Part C and Part D.

[88] Moreover, even if M4A made no changes to Medicare operations, it still would have the problem of taking a program that functions well for about a sixth of the population and making it work on a vastly larger scale. The problem of scale is examined more closely at the end of this chapter.

[89] See Rice et al. (2018); Globerman (2016); Anell, Glenngård, and Merkur (2012); Olejaz et al. (2012); Ringard et al. (2013); Sigurgeirsdóttir, Waagfjörð, and Maresso (2014); and Vuorenkoski, Mladovsky, and Mossialos (2008).

are sometimes described as single payer, but in reality these systems are geographically decentralized and have elements of private insurance. Private and for-profit health providers and health insurers exist in these countries and are accounting for a growing share of the market. Private health insurance is important in a number of other universal-coverage countries, such as Switzerland, where all residents are required to purchase health insurance.[90]

Effects on Overall Economic Activity

Here, we use an extension of the neoclassical growth model to estimate (1) the tax rate increase required to finance M4A entirely with taxes on labor income, and (2) the long-run equilibrium GDP associated with the higher tax rate.[91] The model is extended to have three goods and calibrated to fit the GDP, private health spending, and all other spending in the baseline situation of no M4A. The baseline economy has a 48 percent average marginal tax rate on labor income, which reflects the combination of various payroll, income, and sales taxes that are currently in place in the U.S., including implicit taxes on employment and income. Private health spending is assumed to be exempt from labor income taxation, which is an approximation of the current situation in which employer-sponsored insurance premiums are exempt.

This model is then used to simulate the effect of raising the tax rate across the board enough so that government revenue is sufficient to pay for all healthcare (as noted in chapter 4 of this *Report*, about $18,000 in additional taxation per household in 2022) without cutting any other government programs.[92] Although a significant amount of tax revenue and a significant reduction in disposable income are obtained by broadening the tax base (private health spending may be legally deductible under M4A, but its amount is assumed to be zero), the rate must still increase by 14 percentage points across

---

[90] See Sturny (2017). The Netherlands achieves universal coverage by mandating the purchase of health insurance from private insurers (Wammes et al. 2017). Private health insurance is also required in Japan (Matsuda 2017).

[91] The long-run GDP effects would be of greater magnitude if partially financed with capital-income taxes.

[92] Note that the $18,000 exceeds what households would be paying privately under the current system. Even if those two amounts were equal, swapping household expenditures on private health insurance for household expenditures on taxes earmarked for the public program fundamentally changes the types of healthcare that are ultimately received by consumers and the size of the overall economy.

the board in order for the Federal government to have enough revenue to pay for the Nation's health expenditures.[93]

As a measure of the average incentive to work, the average after-tax share kept by households at the margin is reduced by 27 percent due to the higher tax rate. National income and GDP are thereby reduced by 9 percent in the long run, as illustrated in table 8-7, where national income falls from 100 to 91.0.[94] In 2022, for example, 9 percent of GDP is expected to be about $7,000 per person, or $17,000 per household. Although private health expenditures are eliminated, the amount of income that the private sector has after taxes and health expenditures still falls by 19 percent (about $17,000 per household in 2022), because the tax rate is higher and M4A removes a major tax exclusion. In other words, M4A is not just a swap of taxes for private health spending. Moving health spending onto the Federal budget reduces private sector economic activity so much that households are spending 19 percent less on nonhealth items than they would be without M4A. From a national perspective, healthcare is much more expensive with M4A than it is without it, not only because households need to pay for healthcare through taxes but also because the economy is smaller.

The Mercatus Center at George Mason University calculated the cost of M4A from a Federal accounting perspective as $32 trillion over 10 years (Blahous 2018). This is its version of the CEA's 11.3 addition (34 percent increase, or about $18,000 per household in 2022) to the tax payments shown in table 8-7's second row. Proponents of M4A point out that there is a benefit helping to offset the $32 trillion, which is true but incomplete. In the CEA's framework, the offsetting benefit is the reduction in private health spending of 9.5, shown in table 8-7's third row measured on a scale with baseline national income equal to 100. But the economics of socialism point to additional effects, one of which is also shown in table 8-7's first row: There is less national income and therefore substantially less to spend on nonhealth goods and services.[95] The national income opportunity cost is similar in magnitude to, *but not included in*, Mercatus's Federal accounting cost estimate or the CEA's

---

[93] A more detailed macroeconomic model could recognize that (1) the health insurance tax exclusion is in effect a negative tax on employment because it is tied to employment; (2) the Affordable Care Act is a positive tax on employment (Mulligan 2015); and (3) government health spending is of a different quality than private spending. Both aspects 1 and 2 are eliminated by M4A. In order to be conservative about the economic harm of M4A, the model used in this chapter assumes that M4A financing includes substantial broadening of the tax base. Without base broadening, it is unclear whether the economy would be capable of generating the tax revenue needed by M4A.

[94] As a comparison with the 9 percent, consider this chapter's cross-country finding that changing the U.S. policies to those of the Nordic countries when they were at peak socialism would reduce long-run GDP by at least 19 percent. In other words, the 9 percent effect of M4A is about half the effect of peak Nordic socialism.

[95] The other cost is the loss of quality of the health spending when it is shifted from private to public, as discussed above in the main text.

Table 8-7. National Accounts with and without "Medicare for All," 2022

National Accounts	Without "Medicare for All" (index)	With "Medicare for All" (index)	Impact (percent)
National income	100	91	–9
Taxes	33.0	44.3	34
Private health spending	9.5	0.0	–100
Taxes and health spending	42.5	44.3	4
National income less taxes and less private health spending	*57.5*	*46.7*	*–19*
Disposable national income	67.0	46.7	–30

Sources: Bureau of Economic Analysis; CEA calculations.
Note: "Medicare for All" is financed entirely with taxes. The index equals 100 for national income without "Medicare for All."

tax increase estimate. The Mercatus study did not consider any reduction in national income, which we estimate to be about $20 trillion over 10 years as a result of M4A.[96]

Conclusion

This chapter has examined socialism's historic and current visions and intents, its economic features, its impact on economic performance, and its relationship with recent policy proposals in the United States. A large body of evidence shows how high tax rates, state monopolies, and centralized control disincentivize effort and innovation and substantially reduce the quantity and quality of a nation's output. This evidence includes before/after estimates of the consequences of nationalizing agriculture, and later privatizing it; analysis of highly socialist policies; before/after estimates of the effects of a government takeover of the oil industry; cross-country relationships between economic freedom, GDP per worker, and other macroeconomic variables; comparisons of the rates of return between "free" and tuition-paid colleges; comparisons of conditional mortality between the U.S. and single-payer countries (see chapter 4 of this *Report*); and application of a broad body of economic literature on the effects of raising tax rates.

The China scholar Peter Nolan (1988, 4) once advocated socialism—until he observed the results. He explains that "errors of all kinds have been made in the socialist countries' rural policies, but . . . none has been so important as the misplaced belief in the virtues of large-scale . . . units of production." He adds that "stimulating the productive forces, and, consequently, the possibilities for

---

[96] The loss of national income is not fully a cost because of the offsetting savings on using less labor and capital in the economy. At the same time, the factor savings are not a full offset because factor incomes are subject to large tax rates, thereby generating a large gap between the social and private values of factor supplies.

human self-fulfillment, in a poor peasant economy (indeed, in any economy) requires harnessing . . . market competition."

The CEA does not expect that socialist policies would cause food shortages in the United States, because modern socialists are not proposing to nationalize food production. The historical evidence suggests that the proposed socialist program for the U.S. would make shortages, or otherwise degrade quality, of whatever product or service is put under a public monopoly. The pace of innovation would slow, and living standards generally would be lower. These are the opportunity costs of socialism from a modern American perspective.

Chapter 9

Reducing Poverty and Increasing Self-Sufficiency in America

Despite strong economic growth and a tight labor market, millions of nondisabled, working-age Americans remain on the sidelines of the labor market, struggling to make ends meet. President Lyndon B. Johnson—facing a similar situation in the 1960s—declared a War on Poverty. In this chapter, we show that though President Johnson's War on Poverty is largely over and has been a success based on 1963 standards of material hardship, it was not won by helping low-income Americans become self-sufficient, as President Johnson envisioned. We then describe how to wage a new war on poverty based on contemporary standards of material hardship but with a renewed focus on work, and how the Trump Administration's actions have already made important initial progress along these lines. Bringing workers off the sidelines in this way will not only help maintain the current pace of strong economic growth, but just as important, will also ensure that all nondisabled, working-age Americans can share in the dignity of work.

In the chapter's first section, we show that President Johnson's War on Poverty, based on 1963 standards of material hardship, is largely over and has been a success. Limitations in both the Official Poverty Measure (OPM) and the Supplemental Poverty Measure (SPM) that the Census Bureau produces each year make them incapable of fully capturing this success. When we use a new, Full-Income Poverty Measure (FPM) that is anchored to 1963 standards—and which thus includes the full impact of government taxes and transfers (both cash and in-kind, including the market value of health insurance); which better accounts for inflation, by using the Personal Consumption Expenditures

Price Index; and which uses the household instead of the family as the sharing unit—we find that the poverty rate declined from 19.5 percent in 1963 to 2.3 percent in 2017. This is far more than the decline from 19.5 to 12.3 percent that the OPM reports for the same period. Of course, the FPM would count a larger share of Americans as poor if it increased the standards of material hardship to reflect economic growth since 1963. However, the task of establishing these new poverty thresholds is the responsibility of elected policymakers rather than researchers.

In the second section, we show that, contrary to President Johnson's vision, it was substantial increases in the availability and generosity of government transfers to households in the bottom part of the income distribution rather than increases in their self-sufficiency that lifted nondisabled, working-age people out of poverty. The proportion of nondisabled, working-age adults (age 18–64) living in a household that receives welfare benefits (AFDC/TANF, food stamps / SNAP, housing assistance, and Medicaid) increased from 4.0 percent in 1967 to 27.6 percent in 2017, whereas growth in their work rates began to reverse after 2000. This decline in self-sufficiency has resulted in the situation today where millions of nondisabled, working-age adults receive these welfare benefits while not working.

In the third section, we argue that a new war on poverty should focus on reducing material hardship (based on modern standards that are explicitly determined by policymakers) through work for nondisabled, working-age people whenever possible. We discuss how the highly successful welfare reforms during the 1990s that required, supported, and rewarded work can serve as a model for current efforts. The Trump Administration has taken important actions along these lines—strengthening work requirements in noncash welfare programs; increasing child care assistance for low-income families; and increasing the reward for full-time, full-year work as part of the Tax Cuts and Jobs Act of 2017 by increasing the Child Tax Credit. Additional progress could be achieved by further expanding work requirements in noncash welfare programs such as food stamps / SNAP and Medicaid, including to nondisabled, working-age adults with children.

U nder the Trump Administration, strong economic growth and a tight labor market have brought millions of Americans off the sidelines and into the workforce. Nonetheless, millions of Americans remain out of the labor force, and many of them rely on welfare programs and struggle to make ends meet. Alleviating material hardship among low-income Americans is essential; but in the long run, it is important to achieve this goal through work and increased earnings. Bringing more nondisabled, working-age (18–64 years) welfare recipients off the sidelines will not only help maintain the country's pace of strong economic growth but also ensure that all Americans can share in the dignity of work.

In the early 1960s, the United States faced a similar situation. The country was experiencing strong economic growth. But as President Lyndon B. Johnson recognized, not all Americans were participating in the growing economy, and many people faced severe material hardship. In response, President Johnson declared a War on Poverty in 1964. In a March 16, 1964, address to Congress, he stated (Johnson 1965, 376):

> I have called for a national war on poverty. Our objective: total victory. There are millions of Americans—one fifth of our people—who have not shared in the abundance which has been granted to most of us, and on whom the gates of opportunity have been closed.

In the first section of the chapter, we show that President Johnson's War on Poverty, based on 1963 standards of material hardship, is largely over and has been a success. When we use the new, Full-Income Poverty Measure (FPM) anchored in 1963—which includes the full impact of government taxes and transfers (both cash and in-kind, including the market value of health insurance); which better accounts for inflation, by using the Personal Consumption (PCE) Price Index; and which uses the household instead of the family as the sharing unit—we find that the poverty rate declined from 19.5 percent in 1963 to 2.3 percent in 2017. This is far more than the decline from 19.5 to 12.3 percent the Official Poverty Measure (OPM) reports over the same period. Even the 17.1-percentage-point reduction we find based on the FPM likely understates the actual reduction in poverty. The FPM is based on the Current Population Survey–Annual Social and Economic Supplement (CPS-ASEC), the same survey used by the Census Bureau to determine the OPM. Meyer, Mok, and Sullivan (2015) show that this survey substantially underreports government transfers and that this underreporting has increased over time, which would tend to artificially dampen the reduction of poverty under the FPM. Of course, more

Americans would today be counted as poor if standards of material hardship were updated to reflect the decades of economic growth since 1963, in which the entire income distribution shifted far to the right. However, the task of defining poverty thresholds is the responsibility of policymakers rather than researchers.

Although President Johnson's War on Poverty has largely been won, based on the FPM, victory was not achieved by making more Americans self-sufficient, as he envisioned (Johnson 1965, 376):

> The War on Poverty is not a struggle simply to support people, to make them dependent on the generosity of others. It is a struggle to give people a chance. It is an effort to allow them to develop and use their capacities, as we have been allowed to develop and use ours, so that they can share, as others share, in the promise of this Nation.

In the second section, we show that contrary to President Johnson's vision, it was substantial increases in the availability and generosity of government transfers to the bottom part of the income distribution rather than increases in work that lifted nondisabled, working-age people out of poverty. We show that the share of nondisabled, working-age adults living in a household that receives welfare benefits—Medicaid, food stamps / the Supplemental Nutrition Assistance Program (SNAP), housing assistance, or Aid to Families with Dependent Children (AFDC) / Temporary Assistance for Needy Families (TANF)—increased from 4.0 percent in 1967 to 27.6 percent in 2017, while growth in their work rates has reversed since 2000. This decline in self-sufficiency has culminated in a situation where large numbers of nondisabled, working-age adults receive welfare benefits while not working. We find that in December 2013, the majority of adults receiving SNAP and Medicaid, the two largest welfare programs in the United States, were nondisabled and of working age. However, a majority of these nondisabled, working-age adults receiving benefits from these programs in December 2013 did not work during that month. Unless welfare programs are improved to more effectively promote work, many of these nondisabled, working-age adults will be unable to share in the dignity of consistent work and of achieving their own success.

A new war on poverty should focus on reducing material hardship (based on modern standards determined by policymakers) through work and increased earnings, as President Trump said in his State of the Union Address on January 30, 2018:

> We can lift our citizens from welfare to work, from dependence to independence, and from poverty to prosperity.

In the third section, we discuss how welfare reform during the 1990s serves as a model for success, and how this model has been reflected in the

Trump Administration's actions to promote work among nondisabled, working-age welfare recipients. Welfare reform in the 1990s (1) required work, by expanding work requirements in the cash-based TANF program; (2) supported work, by consolidating and improving child care programs; and (3) rewarded work, through expansion of the Earned Income Tax Credit (EITC). We show how these efforts successfully boosted work for the groups of nondisabled, working-age welfare recipients who were most affected, and led to improvements in child outcomes. However, using the Survey of Income and Program Participation (SIPP), we estimate that, as of December 2013, there were over 16 times more nondisabled, working-age adults receiving assistance from non-cash welfare programs than TANF cash assistance. Given that these noncash welfare programs generally lack strong work requirements, further efforts to promote work are needed.

The Trump Administration has taken important actions that are aligned with the successful welfare reform model. President Trump signed Executive Order 13828, directing agencies to strengthen and expand work requirements under existing laws whenever possible. The Centers for Medicare & Medicaid Services (CMS) has granted waivers to several States to implement community engagement requirements among certain nondisabled, working-age adults who receive Medicaid coverage. In addition, the U.S. Department of Agriculture (USDA) has proposed a new rule that would limit the use of waivers for existing work requirements among childless adults receiving SNAP benefits.

The President also increased work supports by signing into law a bill that substantially increases child care assistance available for low-income families. Furthermore, the Administration substantially bolstered the reward for full-time, full-year work as part of the Tax Cuts and Jobs Act of 2017 by increasing both the Child Tax Credit (CTC) and the refundable component of the CTC for those with earnings but no Federal income tax liability.

Additional progress could be achieved by further expanding work requirements in noncash welfare programs—including to nondisabled, working-age adults with children—as described in the recent Council of Economic Advisers report *Expanding Work Requirements in Non-Cash Welfare Programs* (CEA 2018). These efforts will help ensure that progress in reducing poverty based on modern standards will increasingly be achieved by assisting nondisabled, working-age adults secure and maintain employment.

The timing for these reforms is ideal in the light of the Nation's current strong economic growth and a tight labor market. The unemployment rate was 3.9 percent in December 2018, and the strong economy has helped reduce the SNAP caseload by 4.7 million people (through October 2018) since President Trump was elected (USDA 2018d), a decline of more than 10 percent. At the same time, indicators of material hardship have declined. For example, the share of Americans experiencing food insecurity sometime during the year declined from 12.3 percent in 2016 to 11.8 percent in 2017, and has fallen by

3.1 percentage points since 2011 (Coleman-Jensen et al. 2018). Work-focused welfare reforms can ensure further progress, so that as many nondisabled, working-age Americans as possible can share in the benefits of a growing economy, escape material hardship, and enjoy the dignity of work.[1]

The Success of the War on Poverty

> I have called for a national war on poverty. Our objective: total victory. There
> are millions of Americans—one-fifth of our people—who have not shared
> in the abundance which has been granted to most of us, and on whom the
> gates of opportunity have been closed.
>
> —President Lyndon B. Johnson, March 16, 1964, in an address to Congress
> (Johnson 1965, 376)

In 1964, President Lyndon B. Johnson declared a War on Poverty. As part of this war, he advanced major new Federal programs that provided assistance to low-income Americans and were intended to reduce the poverty rate below the 19.5 percent rate recorded in 1963. This section assesses the progress that has been made in President Johnson's War on Poverty based on those 1963 standards. (For an in-depth analysis of the creation of the Full-Income Poverty Measure—and its value in measuring the success of President's Johnson War on Poverty—see Burkhauser et al. 2019, from which this section is adapted.)

We begin by discussing the basic elements of any poverty measure. We then demonstrate why current poverty measures—including the Official Poverty Measure and the Supplemental Poverty Measure (SPM), each published annually by the Census Bureau—are incapable of assessing progress on the War on Poverty that President Johnson declared. Specifically, existing poverty measures fail to satisfy these three necessary conditions for assessing progress:

1. Define poverty based on the 1963 standards.
2. Properly adjust for inflation over time.
3. Capture the posttax value of all sources of income, including access to health insurance.

Next, we describe the Full-Income Poverty Measure, which satisfies each of these three conditions, as developed by Burkhauser and others (2019). When anchoring the FPM to the official poverty rate of 19.5 percent in 1963, we find that the poverty rate fell to 2.3 percent in 2017. This is far more than the decline from 19.5 to 12.3 percent that the OPM reports over this period. However, even

---

[1] The CEA previously released research on topics covered in this chapter. The text that follows builds on the following research paper produced by the CEA: "Expanding Work Requirements in Non-Cash Welfare Programs" (CEA 2018). In addition, the first section of this chapter is adapted from the paper by Burkhauser et al. (2019)..

the 2.3 percent poverty rate in 2017 under the FPM likely understates progress in reducing poverty because of the substantial and increasing extent of under-reporting of transfer income in the CPS-ASEC (Meyer, Mok, and Sullivan 2015).

The Elements of a Poverty Measure

The "unit of analysis" in all official poverty studies is the individual. However, because most individuals live in families or households, official poverty studies collect information on the resources of all members of the person's "sharing unit" and assume that this sharing unit's members share these resources equally. Effectively, this means that the poverty status of each member of the sharing unit is the same. The poverty threshold will depend on the number of persons in the sharing unit; and, for the most part, official poverty studies assume that economies of scale lead to poverty thresholds that increase less than proportionately as additional persons are included. The appropriate economies of scale to assume in determining thresholds as well as what constitutes a sharing unit are subjects of debate. However, there is far more debate about the sources of income (or consumption) that should be considered as resources when determining the thresholds, the share of the population that should fall below the initial thresholds, and how these thresholds should vary over time. Any changes to the way resources are measured, however, should also be incorporated when setting the poverty thresholds so that the share of people living in poverty in the anchor year is the same as that found by the poverty measure with which it is being compared. Failing to do so can lead to an inaccurate picture of poverty trends across measures.

In the next paragraphs, we briefly summarize the key elements of the major poverty measures used in the United States. (For a more detailed discussion of poverty measure fundamentals, as well as how the concepts behind them differ in the United States and the European Union, see Besharov and Couch 2009; Burkhauser 2009; and Besharov and Couch 2012. For a discussion of the Council of Economic Advisers' role in establishing the elements of President Johnson's War on Poverty, see Lampman 1971.)

Defining resources. Resources can be defined on the basis of consumption or income. A conceptual advantage of consumption-based poverty measures is that the consumption of goods and services, not the money that allows access to them, is what satisfies our desires. Individuals with little or no income in a given year could nonetheless have assets from which to draw to purchase consumption goods. Income-based poverty measures would misidentify such people as poor. Furthermore, as a practical matter, consumption-based measures may suffer less from an underreporting of resources (Meyer and Sullivan 2012a). Meyer and Sullivan (2003) show that differences in income and spending can be substantial, especially for families with low reported incomes. Despite the advantages of consumption-based poverty measures, income-based measures are more common, which in part reflects the relatively greater ease in collecting income data and thus the greater availability of published data on income that can be used to track poverty trends (Burkhauser 2009).

Among income-based poverty measures, various sources of income are used. For example, the OPM includes wage, salary, self-employment, property, and other private sources of cash income, as well as government cash social insurance transfers like Social Security (including Old-Age, Survivors, and Disability Insurance benefits) and cash welfare transfers like TANF. Other measures, like the SPM, also include the value of some noncash government transfers, such as SNAP benefits and housing assistance, and focus on disposable income by subtracting income and payroll taxes paid and adding tax credits received.

However, even these additions fall short of fully incorporating all the available income sources. The importance of including the market value of health insurance (calculated as the average cost for an employer or government of providing health insurance based on an individual's State of residence and risk class) is demonstrated in studies of income distribution trends by Burkhauser, Larrimore, and Simon (2012, 2013); Armour, Burkhauser, and Larrimore (2013); and Larrimore, Burkhauser, and Armour (2015). Beginning in 2013, the Congressional Budget Office (CBO 2013) adopted the same definition of the value of health insurance in its reports on trends in the distribution of income and Federal taxes. Poverty measures that entirely exclude the value of health insurance as a source of income effectively place a zero value on such insurance and hence do not capture all the resources people receive that can help lift them above poverty thresholds.

Kaestner and Lubotsky (2016, 73) review the literature on the inclusion of the value of health insurance in measures of income inequality and confirm its importance: "While there is some debate about how to value Medicare and Medicaid benefits for the purpose of assessing how those programs influence inequality, our estimates and those in Burkhauser et al. (2013) indicate that measured inequality is about 25 to 30 percent smaller if the average cost of these programs are added to recipients' incomes." However, primarily on the basis of a working version of a paper by Finkelstein, Hendren, and Luttmer (forthcoming)—which finds that the availability of uncompensated care reduces the value of formal health insurance to some low-income individuals—Kaestner and Lubotsky (2016) consider the alternative approach of valuing health insurance at a positive amount but less than its full market value. They show that doing so will result in a smaller effect on inequality. Burkhauser, Larrimore, and Lyons (2017) also report their results' sensitivity to values based on the findings of Finkelstein, Hendren, and Luttmer (forthcoming).

Sharing units and economies of scale. A poverty measure must also define the unit that shares these resources. Although the OPM uses the family as the sharing unit (all members of a household who are related by blood or marriage), the household is more common in survey-based analyses of income trends. The increase in the share of adults unrelated by blood or marriage who are nonetheless living in a household together and are sharing household resources is one of the major arguments for the use of the household rather than the family as the sharing unit.

There are also differences in the equivalence scales that researchers use. Burkhauser, Smeeding, and Merz (1996) show that using a scale based on the square root of the number of members in the sharing unit approximates the OPM poverty thresholds. Importantly, they also show that though the choice of scale will have substantial effects on the characteristics of the kind of sharing units that they classify as consisting of people who are living in poverty (e.g., larger sharing units headed by a working-age person with children vs. older persons without children), this choice has little effect on trends in overall poverty rates in a country. For examples of the use of the square root of the number of members of the sharing unit to determine equivalence scales, see Gottschalk and Smeeding (1997); Canberra Group (2011); and Forster and d'Ercole (2012).

Absolute versus relative standards. Once poverty thresholds are set, a decision must be made with respect to how they are updated over time. This is the case regardless of how the original thresholds were established to identify the share of the population that is poor. Thresholds under relative poverty measures change each year relative to how living standards change for the rest of the population. For example, the European Union not only set the original poverty thresholds for each of its member countries at 60 percent of the median income of that country, it then increased the country's poverty thresholds each year based on increases in the country's median income (technically, the European Union calls this the "at-risk-of-poverty" threshold). Doing so maintains the same relative distance between poverty thresholds and median income over time. The Organization for Economic Cooperation and Development uses a similar method, setting its original country thresholds at 50 percent of median income and increasing country poverty thresholds each year by increases in the country's median income. Importantly, the decision on where in the income distribution to set the original poverty thresholds and the justification for doing so are independent of how these thresholds change over time.

Although a relative poverty measure can be informative about the material hardship of individuals at the lower end of the distribution relative to those in the middle, it is not a good measure of changes in their absolute material hardship over time. For example, if the real income available to everyone in the country doubled, a relative poverty measure would show no change in the poverty rate despite substantial increases in the real income of the poor. Likewise, if real median income fell by a greater percentage than did the income of those in the bottom part of the distribution, the share of the population living in poverty would fall. In contrast to relative poverty measures, absolute measures update thresholds over time based only on inflation, ensuring that changes in the poverty rate only occur when real income for those at the lower end of the resource distribution increases or decreases. Again, the decision to use an absolute standard for changing thresholds over time is independent of how one chooses the original thresholds.

Where to set the initial poverty thresholds and whether to use a relative or absolute poverty standard to adjust them each year are important policy decisions. These decisions will not only determine the initial share of the population that is living in poverty when "a war on poverty" is declared, but also how the future success of that war will be determined. Success based on an absolute measure is determined by improvements according to a constant level of material hardship, whereas success based on a relative measure is determined by larger improvements by the poor than for the country as a whole—or, in other words, by continually surpassing a shifting goalpost in real terms.

In his War on Poverty, President Johnson chose a set of poverty thresholds such that about one-fifth of the U.S. population was poor, and he made a policy decision that reducing the share of poor Americans was an important priority for American policy. On the basis of advice from the CEA and others, these thresholds, which were set in nominal dollars, were adjusted each year to hold them constant in real terms over time, reflecting an absolute measure of poverty (see box 9-1). President Johnson left it for future policymakers to decide if and when these real poverty thresholds should increase rather than be tied to increases in the real income of the rest of the population.

Because both the initial level of the poverty thresholds and the way they increase each year are value judgments, policymakers should ultimately make these critical policy decisions because they are the elected representatives of the people. The role of policy advisers and of the general academic community is to provide policymakers with the best information to make these value judgments. This information includes the most accurate way to measure the initial set of resources reflected in poverty thresholds, the unit of analysis, the sharing unit, and the equivalence scale. For absolute standards, it includes the proper measure of inflation; and for relative standards, it includes the implications of tying poverty thresholds to different points in the income distribution.

Although the choice of an absolute or a relative poverty standard for changing thresholds over time remains controversial (and should remain the decision of policymakers), what should not be controversial is the method used to determine the success or failure of President Johnson's War on Poverty. To assess the success or failure of this War on Poverty, it is important to anchor technically superior alternative measures of poverty to the original 19.5 percent share of Americans based on the OPM in 1963, whose poverty the President was committed to reducing. Then, the nominal dollar values of these thresholds must be adjusted each year by the most appropriate measure of inflation in order to hold them constant in real terms. Doing so accurately establishes the terms of engagement for the War on Poverty and will produce

Box 9-1. The CEA's Role at the Beginning of the War on Poverty

On January 8, 1964, President Johnson declared a War on Poverty in his State of the Union Address to Congress. Less than two weeks later, on January 20, 1964, the White House published its annual *Economic Report of the President*, by the Council of Economic Advisers, featuring a chapter titled "The Problem of Poverty in America." This chapter helped define the terms of engagement for President Johnson's War on Poverty with respect to its initial poverty thresholds and how they would change over time.

The CEA set a poverty threshold of $3,000 per family (regardless of family size) and a poverty threshold of $1,500 for all single individuals, so that about 20 percent of Americans would have incomes below these thresholds in 1962. This is a poverty rate roughly equal to the 19.5 percent poverty rate, later determined using the OPM for 1963, that we use in this chapter as the baseline for assessing progress. (Note also that using the square root of the number of members in the sharing unit to determine equivalent income for each member of a four person family whose total family income was $3,000 would make each member of that family as well off as a single person with $1,500 in income. The FPM uses this equivalence scale.) In a March 1964 address to Congress, President Johnson also referred to the 20 percent baseline, stating: "There are millions of Americans—one-fifth of our people—who have not shared in the abundance which has been granted to most of us, and on whom the gates of opportunity have been closed" (Johnson 1965, 376). In another speech in February 1964, President Johnson explicitly linked his 20 percent baseline to the CEA's thresholds, referencing the "20 percent that earns less than $3,000 per year" (Johnson 1965, 287).

The CEA focused on an absolute standard for how these thresholds would change over time. This is the case, because in their calculations (CEA 1964, 59), showing how the poverty rate had declined from 32 percent of families in 1947 to 20 percent of families in 1962, they maintained the same real thresholds in each year by adjusting their dollar value only for inflation.

In addition, the CEA noted that though its income definition included only "money income," a full-income definition that also included noncash sources would have been desirable, stating that "if it were possible to obtain estimates of total income—including nonmoney elements—for various types of families, those data would be preferable for the analysis which follows" (CEA 1964, 58).

As the CEA's chairman, Walter Heller was the preeminent advocate for a major antipoverty initiative under President John F. Kennedy. On the day after President Kennedy's assassination, Heller proposed this antipoverty initiative to President Johnson, and, according to an oral history of this period, "Lyndon Johnson instantly embraced the proposal and within weeks declared 'unconditional war on poverty'" (Gillette 2010, 2). In addition, the CEA led an interagency taskforce beginning in 1963 that focused on defining and alleviating poverty. Robert Lampman, the CEA's Senior Staff Economist at the time, and later the primary author of the poverty chapter in the 1964 *Economic Report of the President*, was described as the "intellectual architect of the War on Poverty" by former CEA Member James Tobin in Lampman's *New York Times* obituary (Passell 1997).

Lampman later wrote in his seminal 1971 book on the origins and nature of poverty, *Ends and Means of Reducing Income Poverty*: "While income poverty is a relative matter, I do not think we should engage in frequent changes of the poverty line, other than to adjust for price changes. As I see it, the elimination of income poverty is usefully thought of as a one-time operation in pursuit of a goal unique to this generation. That goal should be achieved before 1980, at which time the next generation will have set new economic and social goals, perhaps including a new distributional goal for themselves" (Lampman 1971, 53). This view is consistent with using an absolute poverty measure to assess progress in President Johnson's War on Poverty, based on poverty standards set at the time.

the most accurate measure of its success in reducing poverty as the President defined it.

The Inability of Existing Poverty Measures to Assess the War on Poverty

To answer the question "What progress has been made in President Johnson's War on Poverty?" a poverty measure must satisfy three basic conditions:

1. *The poverty measure should set poverty thresholds such that the poverty rate was 19.5 percent in 1963.* President Johnson declared the War on Poverty in 1964 with the goal of reducing the poverty rate below a baseline of about 20 percent. The President referred to this baseline when stating in 1964 that "one-fifth of our people" are living in poverty. The CEA (1964) also estimated a poverty rate of about 20 percent in 1962. The poverty rate calculated later under the OPM in 1963 was 19.5 percent. A poverty measure that sets thresholds such that the poverty rate was higher or lower than about 20 percent in 1963 is inconsistent with the value judgments made by policymakers with respect to the share of Americans facing material hardship at the time.

2. *The poverty measure should be based on an absolute standard and should properly adjust for inflation over time.* The outcome of President Johnson's War on Poverty should be decided based on standards at the time he declared it, not based on shifting goalposts as the economy grows. Moreover, his objective of "total victory"—as well as the activities of his economic advisers at the time and the reflections of Robert Lampman (1971), as discussed in box 9-1—suggests that he

was focused on alleviating poverty based on an absolute measure of hardship over time rather than a relative one.

3. *The posttax value of all resources available to a person should be included.* President Johnson's War on Poverty focused on new Federal programs that would provide assistance to low-income Americans, including the Food Stamp Act of 1964, which expanded and made permanent the existing pilot food stamp program; and the Social Security Amendments of 1965, which created Medicaid and Medicare. Later reforms directed a large amount of assistance to those living in poverty, including the EITC (enacted in 1975) and the CTC (enacted in 1997). Thus, it is important to use a posttax measure of income that incorporates the value of noncash benefits.

No existing poverty measure from the Census Bureau or academic researchers satisfies all these criteria. The OPM by definition meets the first criterion, in that the poverty rate under the OPM was 19.5 percent in 1963; but it does not fully satisfy the second or third criteria. The SPM meets none of these criteria fully. An academic research measure, the absolute SPM (Wimer et al. 2016), also meets none of these criteria fully. A consumption-based poverty measure (CPM)—developed by Bruce Meyer and James Sullivan (2003, 2012a, 2012b, 2017a, 2018)—may satisfy the second criterion but not the first or third ones. We next summarize these existing poverty measures and explain how each one fails to fully satisfy these criteria. Table 9-1 compares the basic elements of these existing poverty measures with the elements of the FPM discussed later in the chapter.

The Official Poverty Measure. The OPM was developed in response to President Johnson's War on Poverty and was similar in design to the one developed by the CEA. Mollie Orshansky (1965), a statistician and economist at the Social Security Administration, developed a poverty measure with a threshold that varied based on family size; but its threshold value for a family of four turned out to be very close to the $3,000 level proposed by the CEA, and the 19.5 percent poverty population that the OPM captured in 1963 was very similar to the roughly one-fifth of Americans whom the CEA and President Johnson had targeted as poor at the outset of the War on Poverty in 1964. Orshansky set a family's poverty threshold as three times the budget needed to afford a low-cost food plan, as determined by the USDA, given that food expenses typically represented about one-third of total family expenditures at the time.

In 1968, the Census Bureau published estimates of trends for poverty based on Orshansky's poverty measure, updating poverty thresholds each year based on changes in the USDA food plan cost estimates (U.S. Census Bureau 1968). Then, in 1969, the Census Bureau released its first official poverty estimates in which poverty thresholds were adjusted annually based on inflation using the Consumer Price Index produced by the Bureau of Labor Statistics (BLS), which at the time was the measure that is now referred to as

Table 9-1. Basic Elements of Poverty Measures

Element	Official Poverty Measure	Supplemental Poverty Measure	Absolute Supplemental Poverty Measure	Consumption-Based Poverty Measure	Full-Income Poverty Measure
Source	Census Bureau	Census Bureau	Wimer et al. (2016)	Meyer and Sullivan (2012b)	Burkhauser et al. (2019)
How thresholds are updated	CPI-U	Quasi-relative*	CPI-U-RS	Meyer-Sullivan Adjusted CPI-U-RS	PCE
Spending excluded	NA	NA	NA	None, with exceptions**	NA
Income excluded	In-kind transfers, tax credits, health insurance, capital gains	Health insurance, capital gains	Health insurance, capital gains	NA	Capital gains
Deduct income and payroll taxes from income	No	Yes	Yes	NA	Yes
Expenses deducted	No	Health, childcare, work expenses	Health, childcare, work expenses	NA	No
Regional cost of living adjustment	No	Yes	No	No	No
Sharing unit	Family	Family, unmarried partners & their children, unrelated children under 15	Family, unmarried partners & their children, unrelated children under 15	Household members who share resources and expenses	Household
Sharing unit size adjustment	Based on cost of food plan for family of given size	1 or 2 adults, no children: $A^{0.5}$ 1 adult, with children: $[A+0.8+0.5(C-1)]^{0.7}$ All others: $[A+0.5C]^{0.7}$ where A is number of adults, C is number of children			$N^{0.5}$ where N is number of people

Sources: Census Bureau; Wimer et al. (2016); Meyer and Sullivan (2012b); Meyer and Sullivan (2018); Burkhauser et al. (2019).

Note: CPI-U = Consumer Price Index for All Urban Consumers; RS = Research Series. See Burkhauser et al. (2019) for further details.

*Equal to 5-year average of spending on necessities by moderate income households multiplied by 1.2.

**Except spending on home and vehicle purchases (replaced by flow value of ownership), health, and education

the Consumer Price Index for Urban Wage Earners and Clerical Workers (CPI-W), as directed by the then–Bureau of the Budget (U.S. Census Bureau 1969; HHS 2000). Later, in May 1978, the Office of Management and Budget issued the directive defining poverty for statistical purposes. Also, it was in 1978 when the BLS also started publishing the Consumer Price Index for All Urban Consumers (CPI-U).

The OPM is based on pretax, postcash transfer income, excluding important in-kind benefits—such as food stamps (or SNAP); Medicaid and rental housing assistance; and tax credits that were implemented later, including the EITC, the CTC, and the Additional CTC (ACTC), which is the refundable portion of the CTC. These sources of income were either relatively minor or were nonexistent when the OPM was first implemented; thus, they were not initially important to capture in the data used to estimate poverty rates.

However, it is widely recognized that the rising importance of these sources of income renders the OPM incapable of assessing progress in the War on Poverty. The final report of the most influential external panel of experts on the effectiveness of the OPM as a measure of trends for poverty found that "the current U.S. measure of poverty is demonstrably flawed judged by today's knowledge; it needs to be replaced" (Citro and Michael 1995, xvii). More recently, on the 50th anniversary of the War on Poverty, the 2014 *Economic Report of the President*, in a chapter on progress in poverty reduction, stated that "the official poverty measure (OPM) has several flaws that distort our understanding of both the level of poverty and how it has changed over time" (CEA 2014, 224). Both these sources considered the OPM's inability to capture the growth of in-kind transfers as a major flaw.

Because in-kind programs have grown dramatically since the War on Poverty began—and when the CTC and EITC did not exist—the downward trend in poverty when omitting them is flatter than it would otherwise be. Figure 9-1 shows the percentage of the population enrolled in the three main noncash welfare programs between 1963 and 2017, based on administrative records. The share of the population receiving Medicaid increased from 0.0 (before the program's inception in 1965) to 22.2 percent; the share receiving SNAP increased from 0.2 percent (in 1964, when the program had not yet been implemented nationally) to 13.0 percent; and the share of households receiving rental housing assistance increased from 0.9 to 3.5 percent, excluding those benefiting from the Low-Income Housing Tax Credit. In 2016, the U.S. spent $673 billion on these three noncash welfare programs alone (CEA 2018). By not including them as resources going to family members, the OPM will in effect put a zero value on all these program benefits and miss their importance in reducing material hardship to the degree that they are taken up by the bottom part of the income distribution (and reflecting them in setting the poverty thresholds, to the extent that they existed in 1963).

The OPM also does not account for other in-kind programs—like the Special Supplemental Nutrition Program for Women, Infants, and Children; the school meal programs; the Low-Income Home Energy Assistance Program; and child care subsidies. In addition, in tax year 2016 the U.S. spent $67 billion on

Figure 9-1. Percentage of the Population Enrolled in Noncash Welfare Programs, 1963–2017

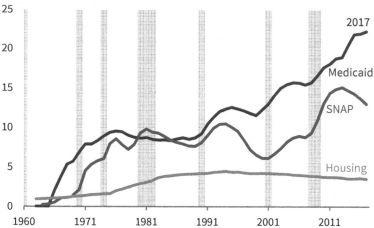

Share of population (percent)

Sources: Truffer et al. (2012, 2016); CMS (2018a); USDA (2018c); Collinson et al. (2016); HUD (2018); National Bureau of Economic Research; CEA calculations.

Note: For rental housing assistance, shares are the number of assisted households divided by the total number of U.S. households, because the CEA is unaware of administrative data tracking individual recipients of housing assistance throughout this entire period. Shading denotes a recession for at least four months of a given year.

the EITC and $27 billion on the ACTC, which are mainly targeted to families with children that have low to moderate earnings, and which did not exist in 1963 at the outset of the War on Poverty (IRS 2016). The OPM, by looking at pretax income rather than posttax income, will miss the value of these tax changes to the after-tax resources of families.

Another criticism of the OPM that prevents it from tracking changes in absolute standards of economic hardship since the War on Poverty began is that it adjusts thresholds each year using the BLS's CPI-U, which has historically overstated inflation (Boskin et al. 1996). The BLS has improved the CPI-U over time by accounting for how consumers respond to increasing prices by substituting to different goods, but historical CPI-U index values have not been changed to reflect this form of substitution. Although the BLS has created the CPI-U Research-Series (CPI-U-RS) to make these adjustments since 1978, it did not do so in earlier years. In addition, the CPI-U-RS does not account for the ability of consumers to substitute between broader categories of products when prices increase, which leads it to overstate inflation even during years when it is available. Another BLS measure, called the Chained CPI-U (C-CPI-U), accounts for this form of substitution across broader product categories, but it has only been available since 2000.[2]

Although the CPI-U, CPI-U-RS, and C-CPI-U are unable to hold real poverty thresholds constant throughout the 1963–2017 period, an alternative inflation measure produced by the Bureau of Economic Analysis, called the Personal Consumption Expenditures (PCE) Price Index, can better do so. The PCE Price Index accounts for consumer substitution and is available through-out the period we consider. It is the measure emphasized by the Federal Reserve Board, and it is the inflation measure used by the CBO in its reports on the distribution of household income over time. (For a fuller discussion of why the PCE Price Index is a preferred inflation index, see Winship 2016.)

As alternatives to the official government inflation measures noted above, researchers have created measures that attempt to correct for substitu-tion bias and also bias from the failure to account for the introduction of new or higher-quality goods. Meyer and Sullivan (2012b) have created an alternate series that shows slower inflation than the PCE Price Index. Their series, which we refer to as the Meyer-Sullivan adjusted CPI-U-RS, adjusts for biases in the CPI-U-RS based on estimates from the Boskin Commission (Boskin et al. 1996)—a panel of experts convened by the Senate Finance Committee to better measure inflation rates—as well as follow-up work by Hausman (2003), Berndt (2006), and Gordon (2006).

Figure 9-2 shows the importance of using the different inflation measures outlined above in determining how much the nominal dollar value of poverty thresholds must increase each year to hold their real dollar values at 1963 levels. Compared with 1963 thresholds, in 2017 the CPI-U would generate a threshold that is 8.0 times as high in nominal dollars to hold the real value of the thresholds constant. To the degree that this is an overstatement of infla-tion, it will effectively raise the real level of these poverty thresholds and exag-gerate the share of people living in poverty in 2017 relative to 1963. In contrast, all the other measures of inflation shown result in smaller changes in nominal thresholds. The CPI-U-RS is 7.1 times as high relative to 1963, the C-CPI-U is 6.7 times as high, the PCE Price Index is 6.2 times as high, and the Meyer-Sullivan adjusted CPI-U-RS is 4.5 times as high. Using the PCE Price Index would generate nominal thresholds in 2017 that are 78 percent (6.2/8.0) as high as thresholds using the CPI-U, which is used in the OPM. Using the Meyer-Sullivan adjusted CPI-U-RS would generate thresholds that are 56 percent (4.5/8.0) as high.

The Supplemental Poverty Measure. The SPM is a more recent poverty measure published by the Census Bureau alongside the OPM; but like the OPM,

---

[2] Because the Chained CPI and CPI-U-RS were not available in 1963, for the period 1963–78, we use CPI-U inflation growth for all three series; and from 1978 to 2000, we use CPI-U-RS inflation growth for both the Chained CPI and CPI-U-RS. This likely increases the observed inflation growth in each series relative to a scenario in which the adjustments were available for the entire period.

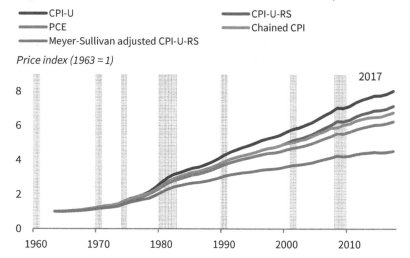

Figure 9-2. Price Indices of Various Inflation Measures, 1963–2017

CPI-U
CPI-U-RS
PCE
Chained CPI
Meyer-Sullivan adjusted CPI-U-RS

Price index (1963 = 1)

2017

Sources: Meyer and Sullivan (2012b, 2018); Bureau of Labor Statistics; Bureau of Economic
Analysis; National Bureau of Economic Research; CEA calculations.
Note: CPI-U = Consumer Price Index for all Urban Consumers. CPI-U-RS = CPI-U Research Series.
PCE = Personal Consumption Expenditures Price Index. The Meyer-Sullivan adjusted CPI-U-RS is
calculated by subtracting 0.8 percentage points from the growth rate in the CPI-U-RS for 1978–
2017, and subtracting 1.1 percentage points from the growth rate for 1963–1977. Shading denotes
a recession for at least four months of a given year.

its characteristics do not allow it to assess progress in President Johnson's War
on Poverty. Building on concepts outlined in 1995 in a Congressionally commissioned National Academy of Sciences committee report titled *Measuring
Poverty: A New Approach*, the SPM represents a fundamental shift away from an
absolute poverty standard and toward a relative one for purposes of changing
the thresholds over time (Citro and Michael 1995). A key feature of the SPM is
the adoption of so-called quasi-relative thresholds, which are based on expenditures by moderate-income households (those at the 30th to 36th percentiles
of the expenditure distribution) on basic necessities, including housing, food,
clothing, and utilities. Spending on these necessities is then multiplied by 1.2
to generate poverty thresholds that reflect expenditures on necessities not
reflected in these categories.

Of course, like the original OPM, the initial SPM thresholds are arbitrary.
However, the OPM thresholds are politically relevant for establishing public
policy goals because they produce a poverty rate (19.5 percent in 1963) that is
consistent with President Johnson's declaration of the War on Poverty, when
he stated that one-fifth of Americans were living in poverty. Unless the SPM
thresholds were set so that in 1963 the poverty rate under the SPM was similarly 19.5 percent, the SPM would redefine the original standards determined
by policymakers at the beginning of the War on Poverty. In addition, these

1963 SPM thresholds would need to be updated each year based on inflation to hold them constant in real terms over time. Instead, the SPM thresholds are not anchored to the scientifically arbitrary but politically relevant 19.5 percent poverty rate in 1963, and they are updated over time based on a quasi-relative method. Because real expenditures by moderate-income households have in fact increased since 1963, the SPM thresholds have increased in real terms, redefining the poverty standards set by President Johnson at the beginning of the War on Poverty.

Nonetheless, from a conceptual perspective, the SPM greatly improves on the OPM by including more sources of income. The SPM includes noncash transfers such as SNAP and housing benefits, although it excludes the market value of health insurance. The CEA (2014, 227) notes that the SPM "does not provide an accurate picture of the benefits of health care," because while the SPM includes resources freed up from reduced out-of-pocket expenses as people obtain insurance, it excludes the value of healthcare that people receive; and as a result, "the measured trend in SPM poverty may understate progress in decreasing economic hardship since the War on Poverty began by ignoring these benefits of increased access to insurance." The SPM is also a posttax measure of income, and so it includes the EITC and CTC, while subtracting taxes paid. The SPM also makes several other adjustments to income by deducting child care and out of pocket medical expenses, and its thresholds can vary across geographical areas based on housing costs and differences in expenses.

Although deducting expenses provides a measure of the resources left available for other types of consumption, doing so can also lead to perverse results. For example, the Affordable Care Act increased the number of people covered by health insurance, and it heavily subsidized this coverage for lower-income families. However, in many cases those who use medical services must pay some out-of-pocket expenses, and the SPM would subtract these expenses from income but not count the value of the subsidized insurance in its measure of poverty. In fact, Meyer and Sullivan (2012a) find that the deduction of out-of-pocket medical expenses leads the SPM to include as poor more people with higher levels of consumption, higher levels of educational attainment, larger homes, and higher likelihoods of health insurance coverage, relative to the OPM. In addition, the need to make geographical adjustments for the cost of living are less compelling when people have freedom of movement to other areas in the country with different costs of living (Burkhauser 2009). The fact that, over time, they do not move may be explained by the fact that higher costs of living generally reflect an area's higher levels of amenities.

Though the Census Bureau has estimated poverty rates under the SPM only for 2009 and later, Fox and others (2015) create an SPM with poverty rates for each year between 1967 and 2012. However, the SPM is not comparable to the OPM, for two key conceptual reasons. First, it is not anchored to the OPM in 1963. Second, it does not maintain an absolute standard because thresholds are adjusted each year based on changed spending by moderate-income households.

The absolute SPM. Wimer and others (2016) created a variation of the SPM, which they called an "anchored SPM." Despite its name, the anchored SPM cannot be compared with the OPM because it is not actually anchored to the OPM in 1963 or any other year. Rather, it is anchored to itself in a given year. That is, the initial SPM thresholds are arbitrarily defined in a given year based on expenditures by moderate-income households in that period, and then thresholds are updated each year before or after, based on inflation. Hence, like any vessel not anchored to its mooring—in this case, President Johnson's initial 19.5 percent share of the population living in poverty 1963—it will drift out to sea. Though it is not anchored to the OPM, this alternative version of the SPM is (at least conceptually) an absolute poverty measure because its thresholds are updated each year based on inflation. Thus, we refer to it as the "absolute SPM" to distinguish it from poverty measures that are in fact anchored to the OPM. And though the absolute SPM is conceptually an absolute poverty measure, it uses the CPI-U-RS to adjust thresholds each year. Because the CPI-U-RS tends to overstate inflation, declines in poverty under the absolute SPM over time will be shallower than trends based on a less biased measure of inflation. In addition, the absolute SPM omits the market value of health insurance as a source of income.

The consumption-based poverty measure. A final poverty measure is the CPM, which was developed by Bruce Meyer and James Sullivan in a series of academic papers (Meyer and Sullivan 2003, 2012a, 2012b, 2017a, 2018). They base their CPM on how much households spend rather than on their income in a given year. As noted above, consumption-based measures have a conceptual advantage over income-based measures in that households with low incomes but high capacities to consume in a given year (e.g., because they have higher asset levels or higher capacities to borrow) are not counted as poor. In addition, a practical advantage of consumption-based measures is that they are not affected by the increasing underreporting of income, and especially of welfare benefits in the CPS-ASEC, although they are still subject to biases in reporting of spending patterns.

Although the CPM deviates from the OPM by incorporating a broader set of resources available for consumption, it is, like the OPM (and unlike the SPM), an absolute poverty measure. The CPM holds the real dollar value of its thresholds constant over time based on the Meyer-Sullivan adjusted CPI-U-RS as its measure of inflation. Moreover, unlike both the SPM and the absolute SPM, the CPM is anchored to the OPM. However, the underlying consumption data from the Consumer Expenditure Survey are unavailable in 1963 and are available only intermittently before 1980, so the earliest year in which Meyer and Sullivan anchor the CPM to the OPM is 1980. As a result, the CPM is unable to directly assess progress in President Johnson's War on Poverty. Another issue with the CPM is that it does not include the market value of health insurance and thus does not capture all the power of the government's in-kind transfers to increase the resources going to the bottom part of the distribution measured by income or consumption.[3]

Figure 9-3 shows each of the poverty measures we discuss above—the OPM, SPM, absolute SPM, and CPM. The OPM fell from 19.5 percent in 1963 to 12.3 percent in 2017 based on historical poverty rates produced by the Census Bureau. The SPM was first available in 1967, based on the analysis of Fox and others (2015). It fell from 18.6 percent in 1967 to 13.9 percent in 2017. The absolute SPM in 1967 used the 1967 SPM thresholds, and it updates these annually based on inflation, using the CPI-U-RS (Wimer et al. 2016). It fell from 18.6 percent in 1967 to 10.7 percent in 2015, the latest year available (for details of calculating various anchored SPM poverty trends, see Burkhauser et al. 2019). However, note that in 1967, the absolute SPM was 4.4 percentage points higher than the poverty rate under the OPM, and it undoubtedly would have been considerably lower in 2015 if it had been anchored to the OPM in 1967 or 1963.

Unlike the absolute SPM, the CPM was anchored to the OPM in 1980— CPM thresholds are defined such that the poverty rate under the CPM was equal to the poverty rate under the OPM in 1980. The CPM fell from 30.2 percent in 1961 to 2.8 percent in 2017. That is, in 1961 the CPM began at a poverty rate 8.3 percentage points higher than the OPM—and thus was likely also exceeding the OPM poverty rate in 1963. The CPM also omits the market value of health insurance—which was expanded substantially after Medicaid and Medicare were enacted in 1965. Yet it still reaches a poverty rate of under 3 percent by 2017. If it had been possible to do so, anchoring the CPM to the OPM in 1963 and including the market value of health insurance almost surely would have led to an even lower poverty rate in 2017. The trend in the CPM strongly suggests that President Johnson's War on Poverty, based on 1963 standards, is largely over and has been a success.

Given the steep downward trend in the CPM, it is noteworthy that the absolute SPM does not follow the same trend. The poverty rates under the absolute SPM (13.6 percent) and the CPM (13.0 percent) were relatively similar as of 1980, but then the CPM fell by 9.6 percentage points by 2015, while the absolute SPM fell by only 2.9 percentage points. This was despite the fact that both the absolute SPM and CPM are intended to only increase the nominal value of their thresholds by the inflation rate to hold them constant in real

---

[3] Meyer and Sullivan (2012b) show poverty rates under a consumption-based poverty measure that includes a value of health insurance. However, as described by Meyer and Sullivan (2013), the market value of health insurance is included only for families when the market value is equal to at most one-third of total expenditures. For other families, health insurance is valued at one-third of total expenditures, which can be much less than the market value for families with low expenditures.

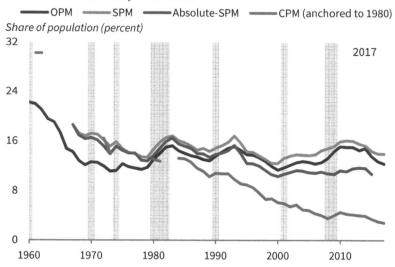

Figure 9-3. Percentage of the Population Living in Poverty, Based on Various Measures, 1960–2017

OPM ━━━ SPM ━━━ Absolute-SPM ━━━ CPM (anchored to 1980)

Share of population (percent)

2017

Sources: Fox et al. (2015); Wimer et al. (2017); Meyer and Sullivan (2018); Burkhauser et al. (2019); Census Bureau; National Bureau of Economic Research; CEA calculations.
Note: OPM = Official Poverty Measure. SPM = Supplemental Poverty Measure. CPM = Consumption-based Poverty Measure. Absolute-SPM applies the cost of living adjustment (see Burkhauser et al. 2019). Shading denotes a recession for at least four months of a given year.

terms (absolute standard) and both include a broad set of resources excluding the market value of health insurance. One possible reason for this difference is the fact that the CPM uses a consumption-based measure instead of an income-based measure and thus is less subject to increasing underreporting of welfare benefits over time. However, another key difference driving this result is the use of the Meyer-Sullivan CPI-U-RS inflation adjustment for the CPM versus the use by Wimer and others (2016) of the unadjusted CPI-U-RS for their absolute SPM.

The Full–Income Poverty Measure

None of the existing poverty measures discussed above are capable of measuring the full extent of progress in President Johnson's War on Poverty. Therefore, we use a poverty measure developed by Burkhauser and others (2019), called the Full-Income Poverty Measure, that allows us to do so—although even this trend will likely understate progress due to increasing underreporting of transfer income in the CPS-ASEC (Meyer, Mok, and Sullivan 2015). The FPM uses an absolute poverty standard to adjust thresholds each year, and it is anchored to the OPM in 1963. That is, its poverty thresholds are scaled such that the proportion of people living in poverty in 1963 is equal to 19.5 percent, which was the poverty rate under the OPM in 1963. Its poverty thresholds are updated over time using the PCE Price Index, the measure of inflation that Burkhauser and others (2019) prefer.

The FPM's sharing unit is the household; this is broader than the sharing unit used by the OPM, and closer but not identical to the sharing unit used by the CPM and SPM, which do not necessarily include all household members in the sharing unit. Using the household as the sharing unit reflects the increasing prevalence of cohabitation in the United States, and thus the sharing of resources across families within the same household, and is standard practice in studies of income distributions (Canberra Group 2011; Fry and Cohn 2011). Its poverty thresholds are adjusted proportionally based on the square root of the number of people in the household. For example, relative to the poverty threshold for a one-person household, the poverty threshold for a two-person household is 1.44 times as high, the threshold for a three-person household is 1.73 times as high, and the threshold for a four-person household is twice as high.

The FPM estimates the share of people living in poverty using a post-tax (comprehensive or full), posttransfer definition of income that Elwell and Burkhauser (2018) developed back to 1959 and that was also developed by others back to 1979—most recently, by Burkhauser, Larrimore, and Lyons (2017). It subtracts Federal income and payroll taxes but adds tax credits, including the EITC and CTC, as well as cash transfers. In addition, it includes the market value of noncash transfers, including SNAP; subsidized school lunches; rental housing assistance; and public health insurance (Medicare and Medicaid). The market value of public health insurance is calculated based on the cost of its provision to different risk classes of individuals based on their age, disability status, and State of residence (for additional details, see Elwell and Burkhauser 2018). The market value of employer-provided health insurance is included as well. This method of valuing health insurance for determining income has been used since 2013 by the CBO in its reports on the distribution of income.[4]

Although the FPM includes a comprehensive set of income sources, it will nonetheless understate income due to underreporting of transfers in the survey data it uses, which are from the CPS-ASEC (see box 9-2). Meyer, Mok, and Sullivan (2015) show that respondents to the CPS-ASEC and other major surveys underreport transfers, and that this underreporting has increased over time. For example, in the average year between 2000 and 2012, CPS-ASEC

---

[4] For discussions of the importance of using the market value of health insurance in measures of income that are used to capture the real costs of government programs, see Burkhauser, Larrimore, and Simon (2012, 2013); Armour, Burkhauser, and Larrimore (2013); Larrimore, Burkhauser, and Armour (2015); and Burkhauser, Larrimore, and Lyons (2017). These researchers argue that it is more reasonable to do so in such cases than for behavioral analysis where the value that beneficiaries put on this in-kind transfer is the primary reason for its inclusion or for studies of the incidence of a tax change to determine its ultimate distributional consequences. For studies that focus on the value beneficiaries place on government health insurance, see Gallen (2015); and Finkelstein, Hendren, and Luttmer (forthcoming).

Box 9-2. Obtaining Better Evidence through Better Data

Research that evaluates social and economic trends and the effects of government policies on them is useful for designing effective policy. Understanding how people's circumstances vary over time and from place to place can help ensure that policies properly target problems. And understanding the impact that policies have on different types of people across an array of outcomes can help ensure that policies have their intended effects while minimizing unintended ones.

Such research is only as good as the underlying data. For example, surveys are a valuable tool for assessing trends and conducting policy evaluation. Surveys can be designed to capture consistent information on a nationally representative sample of people over time. However, surveys also have important limitations, including sampling and nonsampling errors. Some common nonsampling errors are caused by randomly selected survey respondents who do not submit responses (i.e., nonresponse errors) and also by respondents who misreport (response errors). Administrative records are one means of improving the quality of survey data. See Burkhauser and others (2018) for a recent example of the use of individual tax record data to capture the income of top income groups reported in survey data whose credibility depends on the underreporting of top income in the survey data being caused by response errors rather than nonresponse errors.

Recent efforts have made important strides in advancing the capability of research to inform policy development through improvements in data quality. In January 2019, President Trump signed into law the "Foundations for Evidence-Based Policymaking Act of 2018." This law builds the capacity of Federal agencies to evaluate policy, makes data more accessible and shareable across agencies, and provides for strong protection of confidential data. It builds on the September 2017 final report of the bipartisan U.S. Commission on Evidence-Based Policymaking, which outlined ways to better leverage and combine government data to improve the quality of this evidence for public policy making, while at the same time improving the privacy protection of individuals (Abraham and Haskins 2017). The emerging work by Bruce Meyer, James Sullivan, and other researchers, in their creation of the "Comprehensive Income Dataset" (Meyer and Sullivan 2017b), provides an example of the potential benefits of improvements in data quality along these lines in the United States. This data set may help overcome many of the issues related to relying on surveys alone to measure income because it will directly link the rich, self-reported information that individuals provide in survey data to the generally more accurate information on their earnings and transfer program receipt from administrative data. This data set may improve our understanding of the distribution of a comprehensive measure of income and poverty, as well as provide new insights into which Americans fall through the cracks of the social safety net.

respondents reported 42 percent fewer dollars in SNAP benefits than they actually received according to administrative data. This underreporting has tended to increase by about 0.6 percentage point each year. Meyer, Mittag, and Goerge (2018) link individual survey data to individual-level administrative data in Illinois and Maryland, and find that half of true SNAP recipients in these two states do not report SNAP receipt in the CPS-ASEC. In addition to transfers, Larrimore and Splinter (2019) find that employer-provided health insurance is also underreported in the CPS-ASEC. However, households that receive employer-provided health insurance but fail to report it are unlikely to fall below the poverty threshold when accounting for other sources of income, and thus this will have less effect in overstating poverty. Burtless and Pulliam (2018) note that underreporting of money income may be emerging since 2003 as well.

Figure 9-4 shows the poverty rate under the FPM between 1963 and 2017, in comparison with the poverty rate under the OPM. The poverty rate under the FPM fell from 19.5 percent in 1963 to 2.3 percent in 2017. In fact, the rate under the FPM fell to 4.2 percent by 1978, suggesting dramatic progress in the War on Poverty in its first 15 years, along the lines that the 1964 *Economic Report of the President* envisioned and that Robert Lampman expected as late as 1971 (see box 9-1). However, the FPM then rose rapidly to 6.4 percent by 1983, in large part because of the double-dip recession between 1980 and 1982 and the failure of transfer program benefits to keep up with the double-digit inflation during much of this period. However, the poverty rate then fell almost continuously until 2001, when it reached 2.6 percent. The poverty rate under the FPM never again exceeded 2.8 percent, even during the Great Recession, and it fell to 2.3 percent in 2017.

We next illustrate the characteristics of the FPM that drive the dramatic reduction in poverty relative to the OPM. Figure 9-5 shows the OPM modified only based on the equivalence scale change as a baseline, which has little effect on the poverty trend. For example, in 2017 the poverty rate under the OPM was 12.3 percent, compared with 12.5 percent under the OPM with the adjusted equivalence scale (for further details, see Burkhauser et al. 2019). Relative to this baseline of the OPM with an adjusted equivalence scale, figure 9-5 shows how other iterative changes made under the FPM affect the poverty rate trend. Note that all iterations of this crosswalk from the OPM are anchored so as to match the 19.5 percent share of the population that President Johnson's War on Poverty determined were poor in 1963. Using the household instead of the family as the sharing unit reduces the poverty rate 54 years later, in 2017, to 10.7 percent—lower than the 12.5 percent using the OPM with the adjusted equivalence scale. Using a posttax measure of income reduces the 2017 poverty rate further, to 8.8 percent. Incorporating the market value of noncash transfers except for health insurance reduces the poverty rate to 6.9 percent. Incorporating the market value of health insurance reduces the poverty rate to

Figure 9-4. Percentage of the Population Living in Poverty, Based on the Official Poverty Measure (OPM) and the Full-Income Poverty Measure (FPM), 1963–2017

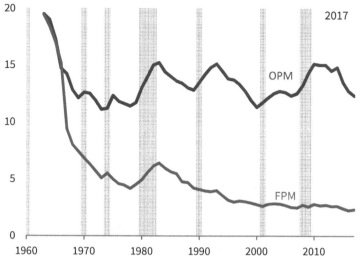

Share of population (percent)

Sources: Burkhauser et al. (2019); Census Bureau; National Bureau of Economic Research; CEA calculations.

Note: Shading denotes a recession for at least four months of a given year.

3.4 percent. Moving from the CPI-U to the CPI-U-RS reduces the poverty rate to 2.8 percent. Using the PCE Price Index reduces the poverty rate to 2.3 percent, the estimate under the preferred FPM specification of Burkhauser and others (2019). If we were instead to use Meyer-Sullivan's adjusted CPI-U-RS, the poverty rate under the FPM falls to 1.6 percent in 2017. Though the order in which one adds these FPM elements will affect the difference they make in reducing the poverty rate, it is clear that the sharing unit used, the use of a posttax measure of income, the inclusion of noncash transfers (except health insurance), the inclusion of the market value of health insurance, and the measure of inflation used are all important drivers of the poverty trend under the FPM.[5] The inclusion of the market value of health insurance is especially important.

Note that the debate over the importance of including the market value of health insurance was a topic of disagreement among members of the original National Academy of Sciences Panel in 1995 and the research papers that informed their deliberations. Blinder (1985), one of the researchers whose work is discussed in the panel's report, showed that excluding the value of government- and employer-subsidized health insurance distorts who will be included in the poverty population. In his dissent from the panel's recommendations,

---

[5] Burkhauser et al. (2019) provide additional analysis of the sensitivity of assumptions in the FPM and the sources of differences in its trends from those of the absolute SPM and CPM.

Figure 9-5. Percentage of the Population Living in Poverty, Crosswalk from the Official Poverty Measure (OPM) to the Full-Income Poverty Measure (FPM), 1963–2017

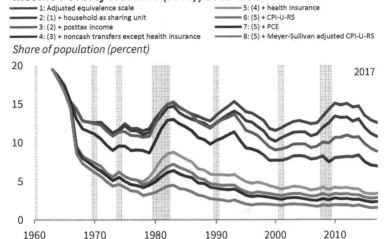

- 1: Adjusted equivalence scale
- 2: (1) + household as sharing unit
- 3: (2) + posttax income
- 4: (3) + noncash transfers except health insurance
- 5: (4) + health insurance
- 6: (5) + CPI-U-RS
- 7: (5) + PCE
- 8: (5) + Meyer-Sullivan adjusted CPI-U-RS

Share of population (percent)

Sources: Burkhauser et al. (2019); National Bureau of Economic Research; CEA calculations.
Note: CPI-U-RS = Consumer Price Index for All Urban Consumers, Research Series. PCE = Personal Consumption Expenditures Price Index. The Meyer-Sullivan adjusted CPI-U-RS is calculated by subtracting 0.8 percentage points from the growth rate in the CPI-U-RS for 1978–2017, and subtracting 1.1 percentage points from the growth rate for 1963–77. Shading denotes a recession for at least four months of a given year.

panel member John Cogan strongly argued against subtracting out-of-pocket expenditures from income rather than including medical care as a necessity like food and shelter in both the thresholds and as a resource. In addition, he stated that "much of the impetus for changing the way in which resources are counted comes from the fact that the current method ignores the value of billions of dollars in noncash benefits for food, housing and medical care that are spent on low-income families" (quoted by Citro and Michael 1995, 389).

Using the FPM—which is anchored to the population initially determined to be living in poverty in 1963, adjusts its nominal thresholds each year to hold these living standards constant in real terms, and uses a full measure of posttax, posttransfer real income—we show that President Johnson's War on Poverty is largely over and has been a success. Though this conclusion stands in stark contrast to conventional wisdom (and according to poverty rates based on the OPM or SPM), it should not be surprising.

Figure 9-6 shows the distribution of full household, size-adjusted income (i.e., the PCE Price Index's inflation-adjusted disposable income, including cash and in-kind transfers, plus health insurance) across all Americans in 1963 and in 2017. The entire distribution has moved far to the right (exhibiting first-order stochastic dominance), reflecting substantial real income gains (including transfers) throughout the income distribution over the past five decades.

Figure 9-6. Individual-Level, Posttax, Posttransfer Household Size–Adjusted Income Distribution, Including In-Kind Transfers and Market Value of Health Insurance, Using PCE Inflation

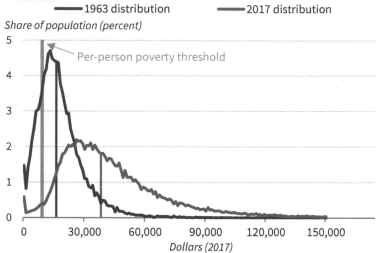

Sources: Burkhauser et al. (2019); National Bureau of Economic Research; CEA calculations.
Note: PCE = Personal Consumption Expenditures Price Index. The poverty threshold, $9,019 in 2017 dollars, is calculated such that in 1963, 19.5 percent of individuals have a household size–adjusted income that falls below it. The red and blue vertical lines represent the median income level for a given year.

Median (full) income more than doubled (from $16,143 in 1963 to $38,484 in 2017). In 2017, only 2.3 percent of people remained below the real poverty threshold (as reported previously under the FPM in figures 9-4 and 9-5), compared with 19.5 percent in 1963. President Johnson's War on Poverty is largely over and has been a success. Nonetheless, continuing to increase the resources of people at the lower end of the income distribution is an important goal, and it is appropriate for policymakers to consider raising the poverty thresholds to better reflect today's standard of living.

However, from a policy perspective, the measure that policy advisers create to determine a policy's success must accurately measure the goals that policymakers set. The SPM, for example, is a case of policy advisers fundamentally changing the goals of policymakers by shifting from an absolute to a quasi-relative measure of poverty. Doing so in this automatic way takes the task of adjusting the absolute poverty thresholds of President Johnson out of the hands of policymakers. In addition, doing so means that the SPM does not accurately assess progress over the past 55 years in solving the problem of poverty as envisioned by President Johnson. In 1995, Cogan made some of these same fundamental points in his dissenting statement to the National Academy of Sciences Panel:

I dissent because the report's recommendations—to choose three particular commodities upon which to base the calculation of poverty and to exclude other commodities; to establish a normative range of values within which the poverty line should fall; to increase the poverty line over time to account for perceived improvements in the standard of living; and to exclude medical expenses from family resources—are the outcome of highly subjective judgements. These are judgements that do not result from scientific inquiry and, therefore, in my opinion, are improperly placed in this report (quoted by Citro and Michael 1995, 390).

Cogan's criticism of the conclusion of the majority of this distinguished panel of academics is valid in the sense that any initial choice of poverty thresholds is normatively rather than scientifically based. The same is the case for the decision to change these thresholds using an absolute or relative standard. Because both the initial level of the poverty thresholds and the way they increase each year are value judgments, policymakers should ultimately make these critical policy decisions because they are the elected representatives of the people.

Robert Lampman—as noted above, the "intellectual architect of the War on Poverty"—made a similar argument in his seminal 1971 book: "The elimination of income poverty is usefully thought of as a one-time operation in pursuit of a goal unique to this generation." And once this goal has been achieved, "the next generation will have set new economic and social goals, perhaps including a new distributional goal for themselves" (Lampman 1971, 53).

To better inform the policymakers who make these value judgments, the National Academy of Sciences Panel should have anchored its proposed poverty measure alternatives to the original 19.5 percent of Americans that President Johnson had determined to be poor in 1963. It could have then shown how their more sophisticated measures of poverty would have more accurately measured poverty trends over time, updated only with inflation each year and then using a relative standard.[6] Doing so would have first established if President Johnson's War on Poverty had been won based on his terms of engagement. Having done so, they could then have proposed changing the poverty thresholds for a new war on poverty based on modern standards for their generation. The Full-Income Poverty Measure fills this gap and shows that President Johnson's War on Poverty is largely over and has been a success, suggesting that policymakers should consider setting new, higher poverty standards than those defined by President Johnson over 50 years ago.

---

[6] The quasi-relative poverty measure developed by the panel could have, for example, adjusted the definition of "moderate-income" households based on a different point in the expenditure distribution, or it could have changed the multiplier applied to their purchases of basic goods, such that the poverty rate in 1963 under the new measure was equal to 19.5 percent.

The Failure to Promote Self-Sufficiency

> The war on poverty is not a struggle simply to support people, to make
> them dependent on the generosity of others. It is a struggle to give people a
> chance. It is an effort to allow them to develop and use their capacities, as
> we have been allowed to develop and use ours, so that they can share, as
> others share, in the promise of this nation.
>
> —President Lyndon B. Johnson, March 16, 1964, in an address to Congress
> (Johnson 1965, 376)

Although poverty, when more accurately measured, has fallen dramatically
since 1963, success has been achieved more by increases in transfers going
to the bottom part of the income distribution, rather than by helping all
nondisabled, working-age Americans become self-sufficient (i.e., working and
not relying on welfare programs). In this section, we first document the rise in
the reliance on key welfare programs—Medicaid; food stamps / SNAP, housing
assistance; and AFDC/TANF—by nondisabled, working-age adults; and at the
same time, a reversal of growth in their work rates after 2000. This decline in
self-sufficiency has resulted in a situation where large numbers of nondisabled,
working-age adults receive these welfare benefits while not working.

In December 2013, the majority of adults covered by Medicaid insurance
and receiving SNAP benefits, the two largest U.S. welfare programs, were
nondisabled and of working age. However, a majority of these nondisabled,
working-age adults receiving benefits from these programs in December 2013
did not work during that month. And this lack of work among these individuals
is not short-lived. In any given month during a two-year window centering on
December 2013 (January 2013 through December 2014), between 48 and 56
percent of December 2013 SNAP recipients did not work.

Trends in Self-Sufficiency

In our trends measuring changes in self-sufficiency, we focus only on those
people society generally expects to work or be preparing for work as a condition of receiving welfare—nondisabled, working-age adults—although we note
that in practice, programs generally exempt certain nondisabled, working-age
adults from work requirements. Before welfare reform in the 1990s, nondisabled, working-age mothers who received welfare were not in general expected
to work. The AFDC program provided cash assistance to families with children
without time limits or strong work requirements. This reflected the societal
expectations of a previous era, when women were not expected to work in the
formal sector. However, the dramatic rise in labor force participation among
women, especially married mothers, led to calls for a welfare system that also
required, supported, and rewarded work for single mothers. This eventually

resulted in the Federal overhaul of the AFDC program in 1996, creating the TANF program, which required States to impose time limits and work requirements on assistance for nondisabled, working-age parents. However, as we will see these work orientated TANF welfare reforms did not extend to the three other major welfare programs we will discuss in this section.

Adults are considered to be disabled, according to our definition, if they report receiving public disability benefits, and are of working age if they are age 18–64. As we will show, the vast majority of adults who fit this nondisabled, working-age definition (about three-fourths) are working in the labor market in a given month.

Figure 9-7 shows the percentage of nondisabled, working-age adults living in a household in which at least one member received welfare benefits during some point in the year, for 1967 through 2017. Due to increased under-reporting of benefits in the CPS-ASEC, these trends likely understate the rise in household welfare receipt (Meyer, Mok, and Sullivan 2015). Between 1967 (before all States and counties had implemented Medicaid and SNAP) and 2017, the proportion of nondisabled, working-age adults living in a household in which at least one member received Medicaid, food stamps/SNAP, housing assistance or AFDC/TANF increased from 4.0 to at least 27.6 percent. Much of this growth occurred between 2007 and 2017, when the rate increased by 10.1 percentage points. This was driven by increased demand for Medicaid and SNAP programs; and perhaps more important, increased program generosity during the Great Recession and its aftermath (for an analysis of how program generosity changed and of its implications for reduced employment during this time, see Mulligan 2012). In terms of specific programs, Medicaid insurance coverage in one's household has increased the most among nondisabled, working-age adults, growing from 3.6 to 25.6 percent between 1967 and 2017, followed by food stamps / SNAP receipt, which increased from 0.5 to 7.7 percent. The receipt of housing assistance increased less drastically from 0.4 to 1.9 percent. AFDC/TANF receipt decreased from 3.6 to 1.1 percent between 1967 and 2017, reflecting welfare reform in the 1990s that replaced the former AFDC program with one that provided temporary benefits but focused on moving its beneficiaries into employment.

The growth in welfare receipt shown in figure 9-7 is partly a function of the expansion of these programs in covering new groups of people. Though such policy changes tend to reduce self-sufficiency, they do not necessarily reflect changed behavior by newly eligible nondisabled, working-age adults. Figure 9-8 shows how the work behavior of nondisabled, working-age adults has changed over a similar period. In fact, between 1968 and 2000, the share of nondisabled, working-age adults who work in a given month increased from 65.7 percent to 78.1 percent. As shown in figure 9-8, the growth in work is completely due to the rise among nondisabled, working-age females, whose work rate increased from 46.2 to 72.2 percent over this period. The rise of

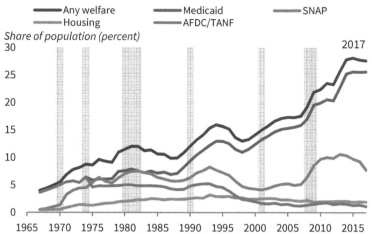

Figure 9-7. Percentage of Nondisabled, Working-Age Adults Living in a Household that Receives Assistance During the Year, 1967–2017

Any welfare ▬▬ Medicaid ▬▬ SNAP
Housing ▬▬ AFDC/TANF

Share of population (percent)

Sources: Current Population Survey; National Bureau of Economic Research; CEA calculations.
Note: Working-age adult refers to individuals age 18-64. Disabled refers to all adult individuals who receive disability benefits (Supplemental Security Income or Social Security Disability Insurance). Welfare recipients are identified based on receipt of Medicaid, SNAP/food stamps, rental housing assistance or AFDC/TANF at any time during the full calendar year by anyone in the household. Shading denotes a recession for at least four months of a given year.

nondisabled, working-age females in the workforce reflects changing societal expectations as married mothers moved into the workforce, as well as welfare reform during the 1990s, which later incentivized single mothers to move into the workforce. Meanwhile, work rates for nondisabled, working-age males fell from 86.8 percent in 1968 to 84.1 percent in 2000, a trend reflective of various potential forces such as expanded welfare programs and rising incarceration (see Eberstadt 2016). Since 2000, the positive work trend for nondisabled, working-age females has reversed, and the decline in work among nondisabled, working-age males has continued. Overall, the work rate among all nondisabled, working-age adults fell by 2.0 percentage points between 2000 and 2017, from 78.1 to 76.0 percent. The reversal of the increase in work rates among nondisabled, working-age females and the steady decline in work rates among nondisabled, working-age males over the past five decades, in combination with dramatic increases in household reliance on welfare programs, amount to a general decline in self-sufficiency among nondisabled, working-age adults in the United States.

Figure 9-8. Percentage of Nondisabled, Working-Age Adults Employed, by Gender, 1968–2017

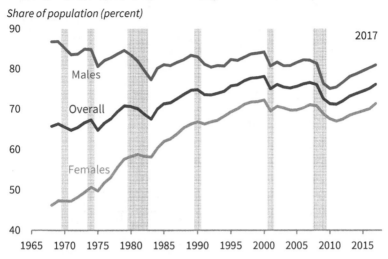

Share of population (percent)

Sources: Current Population Survey; National Bureau of Economic Research; CEA calculations.
Note: Working-age adult refers to individuals age 18-64. Disabled refers to all adult individuals who receive disability benefits (Supplemental Security Income or Social Security Disability Insurance) during the previous year. Employment is based on work during March of each year. Shading denotes a recession for at least four months of a given year.

Work among Nondisabled, Working–Age Recipients of Key Welfare Programs

As shown above, an increasing number of nondisabled, working-age adults are receiving assistance from major welfare programs. In table 9-2, using the SIPP for December 2013, we estimate the number of nondisabled, working-age adults who themselves received benefits (rather than living in a household in which one individual received benefits) from each of these four major welfare programs—Medicaid, SNAP, housing assistance, and TANF.[7] There were 17.2 million nondisabled, working-age adults receiving Medicaid, 18.4 million receiving SNAP, 4.0 million receiving housing assistance, and 1.1 million receiving TANF.[8] These nondisabled, working-age adults respectively represented 61, 67, 59, and 92 percent of all adults in each program.

Although the majority of adults in each of these major welfare programs are nondisabled and of working age, many do not work while receiving benefits.

---

[7] Although these data are somewhat dated, the SIPP allows us to observe welfare receipt and employment status in the same month. Using December 2013 as our reference month allows us to examine work status of welfare recipients in a two-year period beginning with January 2013 and ending in December 2014, the latest available month of SIPP data.

[8] These estimates adjust for underreporting of welfare benefits relative to administrative data caseloads by assuming that each type of individual listed in table 9-2 is equally likely to fail to report benefits, and using administrative data on total caseloads to scale these estimates up.

Table 9-2. Number of People by Welfare Receipt, Age and Disability Status, December 2013

Category	Children (millions)	Disabled or aged adults (millions)	Nondisabled, working-age adults (millions)	Total (millions)	Adult recipients who are non-disabled and of working age (percent)
Medicaid	31.8	10.8	17.2	59.8	61.5
SNAP	19.8	8.9	18.4	47.1	67.4
Housing assistance	3.3	2.8	4.0	10.1	58.6
TANF	2.7	0.1	1.1	3.9	92.2
Overall population	73.5	56.6	181.8	311.9	76.2

Sources: Survey of Income and Program Participation, 2014 Wave 1; HHS (2014); HUD (2018); Truffer at al. (2016); USDA (2018a); CEA calculations.

Note: For each program, receipt was identified based on December 2013. "Children" refers to all individuals under the age of 18. "Working-age adult" refers to individuals age 18–64. "Aged" refers to all individuals age 65 and over. "Disabled" refers to all adult individuals who receive disability benefits (Supplemental Security Income, Social Security Disability Insurance, or Veterans disability benefits). To estimate the number of recipients in each category for each program, the share of program recipients identified using the SIPP (as of December 2013) was multiplied by the December 2013 administrative caseload for SNAP and TANF, the number of 2013 full-year equivalent recipients for Medicaid, and the number of 2013 rental housing assistance recipients (due to lack of monthly administrative data).

Table 9-3 shows that among nondisabled, working-age adults in each program in December 2013, 53 percent of the 17.2 million receiving Medicaid did not work; 54 percent of the 18.4 million receiving SNAP did not work; 45 percent of the 4.0 million receiving housing assistance did not work; and 71 percent of the 1.1 million receiving TANF did not work. The especially high nonwork rate among TANF recipients is in part a result of work-oriented reforms that have pushed many off the rolls and into the workforce, leaving behind a relatively small number who are less likely to work. AFDC enrollment peaked at 14.2 million total recipients in 1994, compared with 3.9 million total TANF recipients in December 2013, and so the number of nondisabled, working-age recipients presumably fell dramatically as well. In addition, many TANF recipients may comply with work requirements by engaging in training or other work-related activities not reported as formal employment.

The work rates of nondisabled, working-age adults receiving welfare stand in stark contrast to the overall population. In December 2013, just 26 percent of all nondisabled, working-age adults did not work. In addition, 53 percent of all nondisabled, working-age adults worked at least 40 hours a week, compared with between 9 and 28 percent working at least 40 hours a week among those receiving benefits from each program.

Table 9-3. Percentage of Nondisabled, Working-Age Adults Working Various Weekly Average Hours by Welfare Receipt, December 2013

	Number (millions)	Weekly hours of work (percentage of row group)				
		0	1 to 19	20 to 29	30 to 39	40+
Medicaid	17.2	53.1	7.1	8.6	9.1	22.1
SNAP	18.4	53.5	6.7	9.7	10.8	19.3
Housing	4.0	45.3	6.8	9.3	10.9	27.6
TANF	1.1	70.8	5.6	6.2	8.1	9.4
Overall population	181.8	26.3	5.1	6.0	9.8	52.8

Sources: Survey of Income and Program Participation, 2014 wave 1; HHS (2014); HUD (2018); Truffer at al. (2016); USDA (2018a); CEA calculations.

Note: For each program, receipt was identified based on December 2013. Adults refer to all individuals age 18 or over. Working-age refers to individuals age 18–64. Disabled refers to all adult individuals who receive disability benefits (Supplemental Security Income, Social Security Disability Insurance, or veterans disability benefits). To estimate the number of nondisabled working-age recipients, the share of program recipients identified using the SIPP (as of December 2013) was multiplied by the December 2013 administrative caseload for SNAP and TANF, the number of 2013 full-year equivalent recipients for Medicaid, and the number of 2013 rental housing assistance recipients (due to a lack of monthly administrative data).

Altogether, table 9-3 shows that in a one-month snapshot of individuals receiving welfare benefits, a large share do not work and the vast majority do not work full-time. Others have noted that work behavior during a given month of benefit receipt does not necessarily reflect work behavior over longer time horizons. Hartley and others (2018) focus on adults age 18 to 59 who receive disability benefits and do not have a dependent child under 6, and Bauer, Schanzenbach and Shambaugh (2018) focus on a similar group of individuals except that they also exclude students. Each of these groups is narrower than our group of nondisabled, working-age adults. Using simulated data based on the CPS-ASEC, Hartley and others (2018) find that among their specified group of adults who received SNAP at any time during a given year, about 67 percent worked at some point during that same year (based on data from 2011 through 2015). Using the SIPP, Bauer, Schanzenbach, and Shambaugh (2018) find that among their specified group of adults who received SNAP at any time between January 2013 and December 2014, 70 percent worked in at least one month during this two-year period.

However, these analyses are not informative about how much the people included in table 9-3 work over an extended time frame. Instead, they focus on a different sample of people—those who receive SNAP at *any* time during a one or two-year period. A limitation of this approach is that an individual who receives SNAP for 1 month during the year is treated no differently from an individual who receives SNAP in all 12 months of a one-year period. This is the case even though the individual receiving SNAP during all 12 months is dependent on the program for 12 times as long and would cost the program 12 times as much holding monthly benefit levels constant. As an extreme example, looking at the lifetime work behavior of people who ever received SNAP at some point during their lifetime would provide little information about the work behavior of the SNAP caseload at a point in time. The snapshots of work behavior we provide in table 9-3 implicitly weight each welfare recipient based on months of welfare receipt—because, for example, an individual receiving SNAP in all 12 months of the year is 12 times as likely to be included in the population as an individual receiving SNAP in only one month during the year.

In figure 9-9, we extend our analysis of the population of welfare recipients in December 2013 and show how their work behavior varies over a two-year period, between January 2013 and December 2014. This answers the question, for example: Of those people receiving welfare in December 2013, how many were working 10 months before this time (in February 2013) or 10 months in the future (in October 2014)? Rather than looking at how many of these December 2013 welfare recipients worked at all during this two-year period, we estimate how many worked in each of the 24 months. If December 2013 welfare recipients were mostly working in every month of this 24-month period except for December 2013, then the snapshot we provide in table 9-3 would not be reflective of a major work problem among welfare recipients. In such a case, welfare receipt may reflect short-term assistance for short-lived bouts of joblessness. However, if December 2013 welfare recipients were not only working at low rates in December 2013 but also working at low rates in January 2013 and December 2014 and the months in between, then this work problem is a longer-lasting one among this population.

In figure 9-9, we consider the same 18.4 million nondisabled, working-age adults who received SNAP in December 2013, but we look at their work behavior in every month between January 2013 and December 2014. In December 2013, 54 percent of the 18.4 million individuals did not work, replicating the snapshot in table 9-3. According to figure 9-9, a similar share of these same people failed to work in each month during the two-year window. For example, of the 18.4 million nondisabled, working-age adults who received SNAP in December 2013, 56 percent did not work in January 2013 (among those in this group who were also nondisabled and of working age in January 2013). From January 2013 to December 2014, between 48 and 56 percent of December 2013 nondisabled, working-age SNAP recipients did not work any hours in a given month. The shares of those working for other ranges of hours are also relatively constant across months in this 24-month period.[9]

---

[9] The break in work rates between December 2013 and January 2014 is likely a result of the way the SIPP is administered. Respondents were surveyed in 2014 about their activity between January 2013 and December 2013, and then again in 2015 about their activity between January 2014 and December 2014. Respondents likely have better recall about their most recent month of employment. Also, the lower work rate in January 2013 than in December 2014 likely reflects the improving economy during this period.

Figure 9-9. Hours Worked among December 2013 Nondisabled, Working-Age SNAP Recipients, January 2013 to December 2014

Share of people (percent)

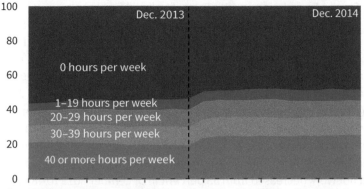

Sources: Survey of Income and Program Participation, 2014 waves 1 and 2; CEA calculations.
Note: Data represent the weekly work hours distribution of December 2013 nondisabled, working-age SNAP recipients. The December 2013 nondisabled, working-age SNAP recipients are excluded during months in which they are not nondisabled or not of working age. Working-age adults refer to individuals age 18–64. Disabled refers to all individuals who receive disability benefits (Supplemental Security Income, Social Security Disability Insurance, or veterans' disability benefits). Hours of work are based on each individual's reported average hours of work per week during each month.

Of course, figure 9-9 does not indicate whether certain December 2013 nondisabled, working-age SNAP recipients work throughout the two-year period while others never do, or if individuals switch back and forth from work to nonwork. Based on the SIPP, 31 percent of December 2013 nondisabled, working-age SNAP recipients—who were nondisabled and working-age in every month between January 2013 and December 2014—never worked throughout the 24-month period, and 52 percent worked in 12 months or less.

Overall, figure 9-9 shows that the snapshot of work behavior among SNAP recipients given in table 9-3 is representative of the same population's work behavior in other months within a two-year window. In addition, close to one-third work in none of the months during a 24-month window and over half work in 12 months or less (among those who are nondisabled and working-age throughout the entire 24-month window). Thus, the lack of work is an important and sustained problem for nondisabled, working-age welfare recipients. Policies that encourage and require work—or preparation for work—could help address it.

As discussed above, we use SIPP data rather than more recent CPS data because CPS data do not allow us to identify those who are working and receiving welfare in a given month. However, using the more precise but less recent SIPP data raises two important caveats to our results pertaining to December 2013 welfare recipients for those interested in what is happening now. First, Medicaid eligibility was expanded in 27 States in 2014 to all adults with household incomes below 138 percent of the poverty line, and an additional 5 States expanded Medicaid eligibility between 2015 and the end of 2018 (Kaiser Family Foundation 2018). Thus, Medicaid is likely to both currently cover a larger number of nondisabled, working-age adults; and the proportion who work may have changed. To address potential effects of this policy reform, we use the most recent available wave of the 2014 SIPP that allows us to document Medicaid receipt and work behavior as of December 2014, after 27 out of 33 States that expanded Medicaid eligibility by the end of 2018 had already done so. We estimate that the number of nondisabled, working-age adults who receive Medicaid increased from 17.2 million (61 percent of all adult recipients) in December 2013 to 22.1 million (66 percent of all adult recipients) in December 2014. The share of nondisabled, working-age Medicaid recipients who did not work decreased from 53 percent in December 2013 to 48 percent in December 2014. Thus, policy changes to the Medicaid program do not change our basic conclusion that in any given month, the large majority of adult Medicaid recipients are nondisabled and of working age, and that about half do not work during that month. In addition, though the share of nondisabled, working-age adults who do not work modestly decreased, the absolute number who do not work increased.

A second caveat of our December 2013 results is that the labor market has continued to improve since then, with the national unemployment rate falling from 6.7 percent in December 2013 to 3.9 percent in December 2018. This is likely to have brought some nondisabled, working-age adults off the welfare rolls and increased the work rates of continued recipients. To address such changes brought about by the improving economy, we use the USDA's SNAP Quality Control survey, which asks a nationally representative sample of SNAP recipients during a specific month of SNAP receipt whether they were working in that month, in addition to their age and disability status. On the basis of the USDA data, the share of SNAP adult recipients in a given month who were nondisabled and of working age fell from 74.2 percent in 2013 to 70.6 percent in 2017. In addition, the portion of these nondisabled, working-age adults who do not work in a given month fell from 65.7 percent in 2013 to 62.5 percent in 2017. Although an improving economy has reduced the share of SNAP recipients who are nondisabled and of working age, and the share of them who do not work, the majority of nondisabled, working-age SNAP recipients in a given month continue not to work. Ultimately, the general patterns of welfare receipt and work behavior we identify in our December 2013 results appear to hold based on data that are more recent as well.

A New War on Poverty

> We can lift our citizens from welfare to work, from dependence to independence, and from poverty to prosperity.
>
> —President Donald J. Trump, January 30, 2018, in his State of the Union Address to Congress

When more accurately measured, substantial progress has been made in reducing material hardship since President Johnson declared his War on Poverty in 1964. However, this success has generally been achieved more by transferring resources to low-income, nondisabled, working-age Americans than by assisting them in becoming self-sufficient. In doing so, our past policies have failed to afford all nondisabled, working-age Americans the opportunity to share in the dignity of work and of earning their own success. Going forward, continuing to focus on reducing poverty—based on modern standards of material hardship—is an important goal, but for nondisabled, working-age adults it is important to do so through work and increased earnings. On April 10, 2018, President Trump signed Executive Order 13828, "Reducing Poverty in America by Promoting Opportunity and Economic Mobility." The order's first "Principle of Economic Mobility" is to "improve employment outcomes and economic independence (including by strengthening work requirements for work-capable people and introducing new work requirements when legally permissible)." Other Principles of Economic Mobility focus on the importance of social networks, overcoming barriers to work, maintaining accountability and flexibility, and targeting assistance to those who need it most. The vision outlined in this Executive Order, in combination with other Trump Administration actions, can help bring about a new war on poverty that more effectively promotes work as the best route out of poverty for nondisabled, working-age adults based on modern standards of material hardship.

This section describes how this new war on poverty can be won, using as a model welfare reform in the 1990s that required, supported, and rewarded work. We document how these efforts successfully boosted work for single mothers with children. Then we discuss reforms of noncash welfare programs, showing how we can use lessons learned from that experience in the 1990s to benefit different groups of nondisabled, working-age adults—and their children—who receive assistance from major noncash welfare programs which, for the most part, do not currently reflect strong work expectations. The Trump Administration has already taken a number of important actions that better promote work among nondisabled, working-age welfare recipients, while other actions—such as continued expansion of work requirements in noncash welfare programs—could bring about further progress.

The timing for these reforms is ideal in light of the current strong period of economic growth and tight labor market. The unemployment rate was 3.9 percent in December 2018, and the strong economy has helped reduce the SNAP caseload by 4.7 million people (through October 2018) since President Trump was elected in November 2016, a decline of more than 10 percent (USDA 2018d). At the same time, indicators of material hardship have declined. For example, the share of Americans experiencing food insecurity sometime during the year declined from 12.3 percent in 2016 to 11.8 percent in 2017, and has fallen by 3.1 percentage points since 2011 (Coleman-Jensen et al. 2018). Work-oriented welfare reforms can ensure further progress, so that as many Americans as possible can partake in the benefits of a growing economy, alleviating material hardship and offering them the dignity of work.

The Success of Welfare Reform

Before welfare reform in the 1990s, nondisabled, working-age adults who received welfare were not in general expected to work. The Aid to Families with Dependent Children (AFDC) program provided cash assistance to families with children without time limits or strong requirements. Those families with sufficiently low incomes received monthly cash benefits determined by States and funded in combination by the Federal and State governments. The reward for work for the mostly single mothers who qualified could be quite low, reflecting a high phase-out rate of AFDC and other welfare benefits, in addition to taxes paid on work. This structure reflected societal expectations of a previous era in which women were not expected to work in the formal sector. However, the dramatic rise in labor force participation among women, especially married mothers, led to calls for a welfare system that required, supported and rewarded work for single mothers as well. States began experimenting with reforms to the AFDC program that reduced phase-out rates for benefits, allowing mothers to keep more of their earnings when joining the workforce. States also experimented with work requirements and time limits for mothers, as well as providing training and work supports when necessary. The large tide of State experimentation with welfare reform led to the Federal overhaul of the AFDC program in 1996, creating the TANF program, which required States to impose time limits and work requirements on assistance for nondisabled, working-age parents, but gave States substantial flexibility in deciding how to do so.[10]

In addition to efforts to require work, new efforts were made to support and reward work by compensating for work-related costs, lost welfare benefits, and increased taxes as work effort increases. The Child Care and Development Block Grant (CCDBG) was created in 1990 and, as part of welfare reform, child care subsidies tied to the AFDC program were consolidated, devolved in large part to the States, and expanded (Long et al. 1998). In addition, the relatively

---

[10] For a detailed account of welfare reform during this period, see Haskins (2007).

small Federal EITC was expanded several times in the early 1990s. The expansions were largest for parents with children, and especially for those with two or more children. The EITC expansions provided the largest work incentives for single mothers who did not have a spouse already bringing in earnings that would have placed the family in the phase-out or ineligible region of the benefit schedule.

Figure 9-10 reflects the success of these reforms in the 1990s. Though TANF was not made effective until 1997, the diamonds in the figure indicate the number of States (and the District of Columbia) that had implemented major reforms of their AFDC program through waivers (ranging from zero in 1985 to 51 in 1997 and later). For the groups of nondisabled, working-age adults most affected by welfare reform, employment rates grew in conjunction with reforms of AFDC and EITC expansions. Single mothers made up the group most heavily affected by welfare reforms. The share of single mothers with a youngest child under 6 who worked in the month of March increased by 18 percentage points between 1990 and 2000, from 49 to 66 percent. Work rates for single mothers with a youngest child between 6 and 17 years increased by 8 percentage points, from 71 to 79 percent, between 1990 and 2000.

Welfare reforms were less likely to incentivize married women to enter the workforce. Married women only rarely received AFDC benefits, and they were less likely to benefit from the EITC by entering the workforce. Thus, the welfare reforms of the 1990s should not have increased their work participation as much as the reforms did for single mothers. Indeed, work rates for married women with a youngest child under age 6, and those age 6–17, each increased by between 4 and 5 percentage points over this period. Finally, women without children were unaffected by welfare reforms, except for a small expansion of the EITC for childless adults. Consistent with the lack of significant policy reforms affecting them, single and married women (age 18–64) without children saw employment gains of zero and 5 percentage points, respectively, during this decade.

A number of studies have attempted to parse out which elements of welfare reform and a concurrent strong economy produced the employment gains shown in figure 9-10. They generally find that the strong economy, expanded EITC, and reform of the AFDC program through State experimentation and the conversion into TANF were the most important factors (e.g., Meyer and Rosenbaum 2001; Grogger 2003; Fang and Keane 2004). Though instructive, quantifying the precise roles of all the various components of welfare reform is difficult. Many changes were enacted simultaneously with potentially interacting effects; it is difficult to accurately and consistently categorize specific AFDC/TANF reforms and their effective dates; and it is difficult if not impossible to measure changes in attitudes by welfare caseworkers and the broader societal messages received by welfare recipients. Still, the evidence is clear that welfare reforms that incentivize work—at least when pursued as a combination of work

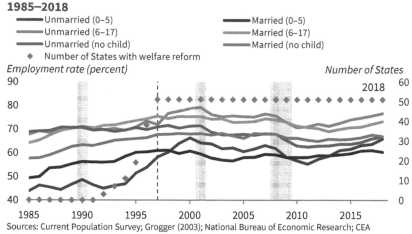

Figure 9-10. Female Employment, by Marital Status and Youngest Child's Age, and Number of States with Welfare Reform, 1985–2018

Sources: Current Population Survey; Grogger (2003); National Bureau of Economic Research; CEA calculations.
Note: The universe is all females age 18–64. The ages of the youngest children are shown in parentheses. The number of States with welfare reform refers to any Statewide reform to the State's AFDC program, as categorized by Grogger (2003), including the District of Columbia. Employment is based on work during March of each year. Shading denotes a recession for at least four months of a given year.

requirements, supports, and rewards—can substantially boost employment and reduce welfare dependency.

Lessons from Welfare Reform for Work Requirements in Noncash Programs

Welfare reform was a success in reorienting the primary cash assistance program for nondisabled, working-age adults around work. However, noncash welfare programs have not undergone the same transformation. As seen in figure 9-7, the share of nondisabled, working-age adults living in a household in which one member receives Medicaid increased from 12.4 percent in 2000 to 25.6 in 2017, and for SNAP it increased from 4.3 to 7.7 over the same period. These noncash programs have come to serve a much larger number of non-disabled, working-age adults than TANF cash-based assistance. In December 2013, there were 1.1 million nondisabled, working-age adults receiving TANF cash assistance, compared with 17.2 million receiving Medicaid, 18.4 million receiving SNAP, and 4.0 million receiving housing assistance (table 9-4). Thus, there were at least 16 times more nondisabled, working-age adults receiving noncash assistance (from Medicaid, SNAP, or housing assistance programs) than TANF cash assistance in December 2013. Table 9-4 also shows which types of nondisabled, working-age adults receive benefits from each of these programs. Adults with children in the household make up the large majority of nondisabled, working-age adults in each program, and adults with children under age 6 make up the majority of those with children. Out of the 17.2 million nondisabled, working-age adults on Medicaid in December 2013, 5.1 million had no children, 5.2 million had a youngest child age 6 to 17, and 6.9 million had a child under age 6 in the household. Of the 18.4 million nondisabled, working-age adults receiving SNAP in December 2013, 6.0 million had no children in the household, 5.1 million had a youngest child age 6–17, and 7.4 million had a child under age 6. Housing assistance follows a similar pattern for its much lower 4.0 million total nondisabled, working-age adults.

The large number of nondisabled, working-age adults receiving benefits from Medicaid, SNAP, and housing assistance shown in table 9-4 largely avoid facing work requirements in these noncash programs, especially compared with the extensive TANF work requirements. The work requirements in each program are summarized in the next paragraphs.

Temporary Assistance for Needy Families. TANF has strong work require-ments that cover a large share of its relatively small population of nondisabled, working-age cash recipients. Although specific provisions vary across States, all nondisabled, working-age adults are potentially subject to work require-ments, generally with the exception of single parents with infants. For example, only California and Vermont exempt single parents with children under age 2 from work requirements, 23 States only exempt single parents with children under age 1, 11 States only exempt single parents with a child between the ages of 1 month and 11 months, and 9 States have no such exemption (Urban Institute 2018). Single parents with a child under age 6 are required to work or engage in work activities for at least 20 hours a week, assuming that child care (not necessarily subsidized) is available. Single parents with no child under age 6 must work at least 30 hours a week. Two-parent families must work a combined 35 hours a week, and those with federally subsidized child care must work a combined 55 hours a week. States retain significant discretion in defin-ing the sanctions for violating requirements and determining which recipients to exempt based on hardship or other factors. States must meet the Federal Work Participation Rate, which requires a portion of the caseload to partici-pate in work or allowable work activities for the federally mandated minimum number of hours (the statute requires a 50 percent work participation rate for overall caseloads and a 90 percent rate for two-parent caseloads, but various credits allow States to lower these targets).

Medicaid. The three major noncash welfare programs have much weaker work requirements that cover smaller shares of their nondisabled, working-age recipients. Medicaid insurance, which covered over 15 times as many nondisabled, working-age adults as TANF in 2013 (table 9-4), does not in general impose any work requirements, in accordance with Title XIX of the Social Security Act. The Trump Administration has, however, supported recent

Table 9-4. Number of Nondisabled, Working–Age Adults by Welfare Program Receipt, by Category, December 2013

Category	Medicaid (millions)	SNAP (millions)	Housing (millions)	TANF (millions)
No child, age 18–49	3.5	3.6	1.2	0.1
No child, age 50–64	1.6	2.3	0.5	0.1
Youngest child age 6–17	5.2	5.1	1.0	0.4
Youngest child age 0–5	6.9	7.4	1.2	0.5
Total	17.2	18.4	4.0	1.1

Sources: Survey of Income and Program Participation, 2014 wave 1; HHS (2014); HUD (2018); Truffer at al. (2016); USDA (2018a); CEA calculations.

Note: For each program, receipt was identified based on December 2013. Only nondisabled, working-age adults were included. Working age refers to individuals age 18–64. Disabled refers to all adult individuals who receive disability benefits (Supplemental Security Income, Social Security Disability Insurance, or Veterans disability benefits). No child, age 18–49 (no child, age 50–64) refers to nondisabled, working-age adults between the ages of 18 and 49 (50–64) who have no children in the household. Youngest child age 6–17 (youngest child age 0–5) refers to nondisabled, working-age adults who have a youngest child age 6–17 (0–5) in the household. To estimate the number of recipients in each category for each program, the share of program recipients identified using the SIPP (as of December 2013) was multiplied by the December 2013 administrative caseload for SNAP and TANF, the number of 2013 full-year-equivalent recipients of Medicaid, and the number of 2013 rental housing assistance recipients (due to a lack of monthly administrative data).

State-level efforts to expand community engagement incentives in their Medicaid programs, which are discussed in detail in box 9-3.

Supplemental Nutrition Assistance Program. SNAP, which served over 17 times as many nondisabled, working-age adults as TANF in 2013 (table 9-4), does have Federal prescriptions for work requirements, albeit ones that cover a smaller share of nondisabled, working-age recipients than TANF requirements. Nondisabled adults age 18–49 with no dependents under age 18 face the strictest work requirements. They may receive SNAP benefits for only three months every three years unless they meet the work test—80 hours of work (or work activities) each month. However, States can obtain waivers from this requirement based on poor economic conditions. States make extensive use of these waivers to avoid work requirements for SNAP recipients, even when job market conditions are favorable (see box 9-4). A recently proposed rule from the U.S. Department of Agriculture would address this problem and ensure that waivers are obtained only in areas where it is truly difficult to find jobs. Other SNAP recipients face less strict work requirements. Nondisabled SNAP recipients age 16–59 face a general requirement that they must accept suitable jobs available to them. SNAP recipients age 60 and over and recipients with dependent children under age 6 are completely exempt from work requirements. Though States may choose to impose stronger work requirements than those mandated by Federal law, few have chosen to do so.

Housing assistance. Housing assistance programs (including Section 8 housing vouchers, Section 8 project-based assistance, and public

Box 9-3. Medicaid Community Engagement Demonstration Projects

In response to State interest, on January 11, 2018, the CMS (2018b) announced that it would consider approving demonstration projects by States that proposed to implement community engagement requirements for nonpregnant, nondisabled, working-age adults. A total of 15 States have applied to implement demonstration projects through Section 1115 waivers (Kaiser Family Foundation 2018). The CMS intends to evaluate whether incentivizing work and other forms of community engagement in these States improves health outcomes and facilitates upward mobility out of poverty and toward independence, and whether such incentives help to ensure the long-term fiscal sustainability of the Medicaid program. States can design their own community engagement requirement definitions, which can include activities such as paid employment, job training, community service, education, and drug treatment.

Figure 9-i shows the 15 States that have submitted applications to the CMS in order to implement community engagement requirements in their Medicaid programs (Kaiser Family Foundation 2018). Among these, 10 States (Arizona, Alabama, Kansas, Maine, Michigan, Mississippi, North Carolina, Ohio, South Dakota, and Utah) have waivers pending approval; 4 States (Indiana, Kentucky, Wisconsin, and New Hampshire) had their waivers approved but have not yet implemented their projects; and 1 State (Arkansas) has already begun implementing its project.

Arkansas was the first State to implement its demonstration project, with its waiver granted in March 2018 and community engagement requirements going into effect in June 2018. The State currently requires that certain adults receiving health coverage under Arkansas Works—the program serving the State's new Medicaid expansion population—work, volunteer, or participate in other work-related activities for at least 80 hours a month in order to retain eligibility for health insurance coverage under the program. Failure to comply (either through self-reporting or automatic reporting of work status through other means) for three months during a year results in a termination of coverage until the beginning of the following year. Only adults age 30–49 were subject to requirements as of October 2018. Adults age 19–29 are subject to requirements as of January 2019 (Rudowitz, Musumeci, and Hall 2018).

Only a small fraction of Arkansas Medicaid recipients are covered by these community engagement requirements, and the large majority of those covered comply with the requirements in a given month. As of October 1, 2018, there were just over 915,000 Medicaid recipients in Arkansas. Just over 496,000 of those recipients were adults, of whom about 253,000 had coverage through Arkansas Works (Arkansas Department of Human Services 2018b). Among the 253,000 Arkansas Works enrollees, just over 69,000 were covered by community engagement requirements in October 2018. About 57,000 (82 percent) complied with the requirement in October (mostly through an exemption from the need to report work hours), while the remaining 12,000 (18 percent) did not. Of those who did not comply in October, 3,815 recipients lost Medicaid coverage due to three months of noncompliance with the community engagement requirement (Arkansas Department of Human Services 2018a).

A total of 16,932 Arkansas Works recipients have had their coverage terminated during the demonstration project due to three months of noncompliance with the work requirement in 2018 (Rudowitz, Musumeci, and Hall 2018). These recipients were allowed to reenroll beginning in January 2019. Further evidence from Arkansas and other States will help determine whether community engagement requirements are effective in improving overall health and upward mobility toward independence.

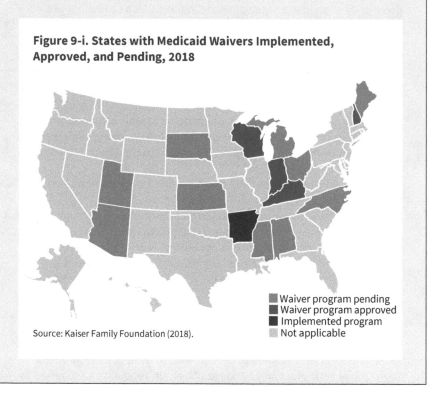

Figure 9-i. States with Medicaid Waivers Implemented, Approved, and Pending, 2018

Waiver program pending
Waiver program approved
Implemented program
Not applicable

Source: Kaiser Family Foundation (2018).

housing)—which served more than three times as many nondisabled, working-age adults as TANF in 2013 (table 9-4)—generally lack strong work requirements. Though a requirement exists in the public housing program for nondisabled, working-age adults who are not working or enrolled in a self-sufficiency program to participate in 8 hours per month of community engagement or other activities, it is not necessarily enforced (HUD 2015). Under the Moving to Work demonstration program, authorized public housing authorities may

Box 9-4. Addressing Problems with SNAP Work Requirement Waivers

The 1996 Personal Responsibility and Work Opportunity Reconciliation Act (PRWORA) implemented significant work requirements in SNAP for some nondisabled, working-age adults. Specifically, so-called able-bodied adults without dependents (ABAWDs) who are age 18–49 could receive SNAP benefits for only 3 months in a 36-month period unless they worked for at least 80 hours each month or participated in a job program. These work requirements can be waved, however, in places with poor macroeconomic conditions when it is difficult to find work. According to section 6(o) of the Food and Nutrition Act of 2008, the USDA Secretary is required to waive work requirements for ABAWDs if (1) the unemployment rate in an area is 10 percent or higher, or (2) if there are not sufficient jobs in an area. The "lack of sufficient jobs" criterion has been interpreted in current regulations to be satisfied by several possible conditions, including an area average unemployment rate that is 20 percent higher than the national unemployment rate for a recent 24-month period. Regulations also give States substantial flexibility in defining an area where requirements can be waived. For example, a State can apply for a Statewide waiver or for waivers that cover any set of contiguous counties (or other jurisdictions).

Although waivers were intended to exempt ABAWDs from work requirements when finding a job was especially difficult, they have frequently been used to waive requirements even in areas with ample job opportunities. In December 2018, the U.S. unemployment rate was 3.9 percent. The criterion that work requirements can be waived when the area's unemployment rate is 20 percent higher than the national unemployment rate allows areas with an unemployment rate of 4.9 percent to qualify (assuming a 20 percent higher unemployment rate than the national rate over a 24-month period). A 4.9 percent unemployment rate is near the natural rate of unemployment—currently about 4.6 percent—which reflects normal churn in the labor market rather than insufficient jobs for those who want them.

Another issue with waivers is that States have wide discretion in combining counties, cities, and other types of jurisdictions into an "area" that, in the aggregate, can satisfy the relevant conditions and gain eligibility for a waiver. States can strategically form these areas to maximize the number of ABAWDs that are covered by a waiver. For example, they can combine low-unemployment counties with high-unemployment counties so that, in combination, the area narrowly exceeds the threshold for a sufficiently high unemployment rate relative to the national average. States can then pair remaining high-unemployment counties with other low-unemployment counties in a similar fashion to exempt as many ABAWDs as possible. States can form an unlimited number of such areas as long as the counties or other jurisdictions within any combined area are contiguous to at least one other jurisdiction in the area.

As a result of these waiver criteria, many ABAWDs are exempted from work requirements even when they live in areas with low unemployment rates. As of the fourth quarter of fiscal year 2018, despite a national unemployment rate of 3.8 percent, seven regions received exemptions for their entire State, district, or territory, and 29 States received exemptions for a part of their State (see figure 9-ii). Nevada, for instance, had a statewide exemption despite an unemployment rate of 4.4 percent in December 2018 (USDA 2018b). California had a full-State waiver beginning in fiscal year 2009 that continued through the third quarter of fiscal year 2018. Starting in September 2018, California excluded 3 of its 58 counties so that the remaining 55 counties would have a sufficiently high unemployment rate to retain eligibility for a waiver (USDA 2018a). California did so by grouping together 55 counties with a combined average unemployment rate of 5.9 percent over the 24-month period between April 2015 and March 2017, exactly 20 percent higher than the 4.95 percent national unemployment rate during the same period. Other States have also sought to waive work requirements in the midst of strong labor markets. During the first quarter of 2016, when the national unemployment rate was under 5 percent, 32 States and territories had a full-State waiver (including California, Florida, New York, Pennsylvania, Illinois, and Georgia), and 12 had a partial-State waiver (USDA 2016). Only 9 States (Delaware, Iowa, Indiana,

Figure 9-ii. States Waiving SNAP Time Limit for Able-Bodied Adults (18–49) Without Dependents, Fourth Quarter of Fiscal Year 2018

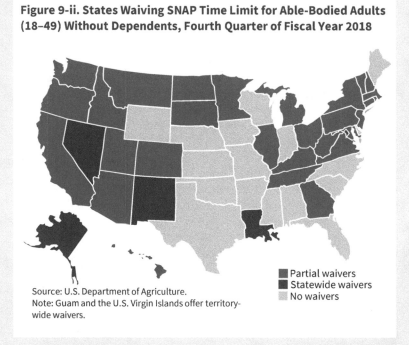

Partial waivers
Statewide waivers
No waivers

Source: U.S. Department of Agriculture.
Note: Guam and the U.S. Virgin Islands offer territory-wide waivers.

experiment with stronger work requirements. However, out of close to 3,000 public housing authorities across the United States, only 39 authorities, or about 1 percent, are designated as Moving to Work agencies, and of these, just 9 had implemented work requirements for some portion of recipients as of 2015 (Levy, Edmonds, and Simington 2018). Thus, strong work requirements are not common in housing assistance programs.

Evidence supporting the expansion of work requirements. As described in detail In the 2018 CEA report *Expanding Work Requirements in Non-Cash Welfare Programs* (CEA 2018), continued efforts to expand work requirements in noncash programs similar to those in TANF would likely boost the work effort among the much greater number of nondisabled, working-age recipients currently receiving assistance from noncash programs. There are two sets of evidence for such an effect. First, welfare programs that lack work requirements tend to reduce employment. Imposing work requirements in these programs should therefore increase employment, because the only way for nonexempt recipients to avoid losing benefits is to work. Second, experiments in the 1990s that applied work requirements to States' AFDC programs generally increased work effort, supporting evidence from statistical studies showing that these interventions tended to increase employment.

A number of studies, based on randomized experiments or quasi-experimental designs, provide empirical support for noncash welfare programs discouraging work. Hoynes and Schanzenbach (2012) utilized the staggered, county-wide rollout of the food stamp program in the 1960s and 1970s to estimate that food stamp receipt reduced hours worked among female heads of households by over 50 percent and reduced employment by up to 27 percentage points among recipients in general. More recently, East (2018) found that after welfare reform in 1996, the receipt of food stamps by unmarried, noncitizen immigrant women reduced their hours worked by 51 percent and their employment by 43 percent. Recent studies find significant employment effects of Medicaid on work rates among childless adults: Garthwaite, Gross, and Notowidigo (2014) find that *losing* Medicaid coverage *increases* employment by 63 percentage points; and Dague, DeLeire, and Leininger (2017) find that gaining Medicaid coverage reduces employment by 5 percentage points for this population. Meanwhile, Dave and others (2015) find that Medicaid receipt substantially reduces employment among pregnant women. However, other studies find weaker or no effects of Medicaid on employment. For example, Baicker and others (2014) find that employment only fell by a statistically insignificant 1.6 percentage points based on a randomized controlled trial in Oregon. Regarding housing assistance, Jacob and Ludwig (2012) evaluated the impact of receipt of a Section 8 housing voucher on adult employment, utilizing a random lottery in Chicago to allocate vouchers. They found that labor force participation fell by 6 percent and earnings fell by 10 percent as a result of receiving these vouchers. Two randomized, controlled trials funded by the U.S. Department of Housing and Urban Development provide additional evidence that housing vouchers reduce employment in the short run among both TANF recipients and homeless families (Mills et al. 2006; Gubits et al. 2015, 2016). Taken as a whole, the empirical evidence suggests that noncash welfare programs reduce work—and thus expanding work requirements in these programs should tend to increase work. This would especially be true if work requirements were applied to all major noncash welfare programs, given that many nondisabled, working-age recipients receive benefits from multiple programs that can in the aggregate result in strong work disincentives.

Experience from 1990s-era welfare reforms, which transformed AFDC into TANF, can also inform how expanded work requirements in noncash programs would affect work. Before the 1996 passage of PRWORA, States conducted experiments with a number of specific changes to their cash welfare programs. Bloom and Michalopoulos (2001) analyzed the results of 29 randomized controlled trials conducted in the 1980s and 1990s on the effects of various welfare reforms. The 20 experiments that included work requirements overwhelmingly showed that work requirements increased employment and earnings while reducing welfare spending. Hamilton and others (2001) found that employment-focused programs that prioritized employment over education had larger effects. The results of these experiments complement statistical studies showing that employment among single mothers, who were most directly affected by welfare reform, saw the largest increases in employment during this reform's early years. Though a number of factors can explain these trends, including the growing generosity of the EITC and the growing economy, the preponderance of the research suggests that reforms to the AFDC program, including time limits and work requirements, played an important role as well (for a review of this literature, see Ziliak 2016).

Complementing Work Requirements with Work Supports and Rewards

Although solely expanding work requirements in noncash welfare programs would bring more nondisabled, working-age recipients into the workforce, complementary policies that support and reward work can promote work even further. The success of work requirements in increasing work effort among welfare recipients in the 1990s was supported in part by improvements made to child care assistance programs. In 1990, the Child Care and Development Block Grant program was created to provide Federal funds to States for child care, complementing the child care assistance that was being newly provided in the former AFDC program. In 1996, PRWORA consolidated these separate child care programs into one mandatory child care block grant and reauthorized CCDBG; together, these were referred to as the Child Care and Development Fund, which provided funding to States—through the mandatory child care block grant and the discretionary CCDBG—to help low-income families access child care, with minimal Federal rules and broad flexibility for States.

Supporting work. Although the improvement of child care programs targeted to low-income families supported an increase in work, it was not the major factor in employment gains during the 1990s. Meyer and Rosenbaum (2001) find that the expansion of Federal child care assistance played only a minor role in encouraging work among single mothers between 1984 and 1996. More recent evidence on the impact of child care provision on work among single mothers similarly suggests that the effects may be modest (Fitzpatrick 2010; Morrissey 2017). In addition, lower-income mothers commonly use informal types of child care that do not require direct payment, or work nonstandard hours during which formal child care is unavailable (Rachidi 2016).

Although child care subsidies alone may be insufficient to promote work among recipients of noncash welfare programs, they can nonetheless play a complimentary role in encouraging work. As discussed in chapter 3 of this *Report*, child care costs can make up a substantial share of wages for many parents of young children. This is particularly true for the large share of nondisabled adults receiving noncash welfare benefits who have children under the age of 6, because child care costs can make up an especially large share of wages for these workers with low wages. Based on 2017 State-level data from ChildCare Aware, the combined hourly child care cost for two children (one infant and one four-year-old) exceeded the minimum wage in 38 States. These child care costs can thus substantially reduce the reward for work for those with low wages, and potentially eliminate the reward for work altogether for those with multiple children requiring care. Work requirements may be insufficient in this context for stimulating parents to seek employment.

The Trump Administration has mitigated these work disincentives by substantially bolstering child care programs for low-income families. In 2018, the CCDBG was increased by $2.4 billion, and this increase was sustained in 2019. The Child Care and Development Fund, which includes CCDBG and other funds, distributed a total of $8.1 billion to States to offer child care subsidies to low-income families who require child care in order to work, go to school, or enroll in training programs. In addition, Federal child care assistance is offered through TANF, Head Start, and other programs.

In addition to these direct forms of child care assistance, both SNAP and housing assistance programs already provide significant potential child care assistance that is automatically available to all families that are induced to work via any future expanded work requirements in these programs. This is because both programs allow recipients to deduct child care expenses from their income when determining benefit levels. For every $1 spent on child care, a child care expense deduction provides families with a child care subsidy (in the form of food or housing benefits) equal to the rate at which benefits phase out with income, as long as their income does not exceed its eligibility limits. The phasing-out rate ranges from $0.24 to $0.36 per $1 in income for SNAP, and is about $0.30 for the rental housing assistance programs. For families enrolled in both SNAP and a housing program, the deduction can be taken for both programs, creating a combined subsidy of about $0.54 to $0.66 for every $1 spent on child care. Of course, one limitation of these child care subsidies is that they cannot exceed the total benefit received, and families are still subject to gross income tests, which can be important given that families may deduct housing and medical expenses in SNAP as well.

Rewarding work. In addition to child care policies that support work, rewarding work via the EITC was a central component of efforts in the 1990s to make work pay, and has been highly successful in increasing work and reducing welfare receipt among single mothers (Eissa and Liebman 1996; Ellwood 2000; Meyer and Rosenbaum 2001; Grogger 2003). The EITC was established under the Tax Reduction Act of 1975, and it was made permanent in 1978. The maximum EITC benefit remained small until several expansions during the late 1980s and early 1990s. In 2018, the maximum annual credit was $6,431 for a family with three or more children, $5,716 for a family with two children, $3,461 for a family with one child, and $519 for a family without children. About half the States supplement these Federal credits with their own State EITC. The EITC incentivizes work because it is available only to tax units with earnings. Starting with the first $1 earned, the Federal EITC increases by between $0.34 and $0.45 for families with children, and by $0.0765 for those without children. EITC benefits are phased in with each $1 in earnings until reaching a plateau, and eventually the EITC is phased out as earnings increase further. For an unmarried adult with two children, the EITC is phased in until earnings reach $14,290, and is phased out starting when earnings reach $18,660, with the EITC fully phased out at earnings of $45,802. As shown in figure 9-11, the EITC is

Figure 9-11. Earned Income Tax Credit Schedule, by Number of Children and Filing Type, Tax Year 2018

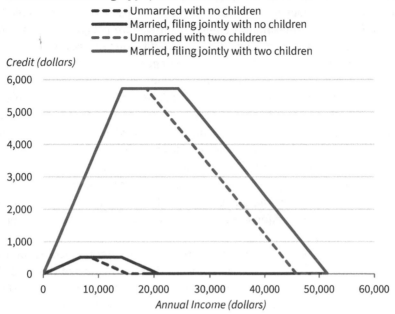

Source: Internal Revenue Service.

phased out at a somewhat higher level of earnings for married couples, reflecting the fact that both parents may earn income.

Despite the success of the EITC in encouraging work among single mothers during welfare reform, there are limitations on the effectiveness of further expansions for families. The current maximum EITC is already high for families with children, which means that the benefits must be phased out over a substantial range of income. This can result in high implicit tax rates for single mothers moving from part-time to full-time work, and can discourage work by second earners in married couples (see CEA 2018). Chetty, Friedman, and Saez (2013) find evidence of decreased work effort in the phase-out region of the EITC, and Eissa and Hoynes (2004) find that second earners in married couples work less in the phase-out region as well. Though the overall employment effect of the EITC is still likely positive, further expansions of the EITC could exacerbate these issues.

The EITC for childless adults is much less generous, with a maximum benefit of just over $500, so modest expansions would not have the same effect on implicit tax rates faced by families with children whose higher EITC benefits must be phased out over a larger range of earnings. However, the ability of EITC expansions to promote work by focusing on childless adults may nonetheless be limited. First, as seen in table 9-4, the majority of nondisabled, working-age adults receiving benefits from Medicaid, SNAP, and housing assistance programs have children, so EITC expansions for those without children would affect a smaller segment of the welfare caseload. Second, childless adults receive lower maximum benefits from welfare programs due to their smaller family sizes, and as a result, their benefits fully phase out sooner and so their implicit tax on work is lower. This suggests that additional incentives to join the workforce may have less of an impact. In fact, a recent randomized controlled trial that provided an expanded EITC-type benefit of up to an extra $2,000 annually to low-income childless adults found a relatively modest 1.9-percentage-point effect on work participation (Miller et al. 2018). Third, childless adults in general have high employment rates, and so most of the cost of an expanded EITC for childless adults would go toward those who are already working, leading some to reduce their number of hours worked. Thus, an expanded EITC for childless adults may ultimately not be a cost-effective way to increase the workforce participation of nondisabled adults receiving noncash welfare benefits.

However, the CTC is not restricted to low- or-moderate income families, and thus it avoids some of the issues with further expansions of the EITC. The CTC was first established in 1997 and was then expanded in 2001. Like the EITC, the CTC is only provided to families with earnings, although the CTC requires the presence of children under 17 (who have Social Security numbers). Through 2017, the maximum CTC was $1,000 per child, with no limit on the number of children a family could claim. As long as a family's Federal income tax liability exceeded the number of dependent children multiplied by $1,000, it received this full amount—for example, a family with two children that had a tax liability of at least $2,000 received a $2,000 credit. The CTC also had a refundable portion—the Additional Child Tax Credit—that provided a refundable credit worth up to 15 percent of earned income above $3,000, up to a maximum of $1,000 per dependent. Unlike the EITC, the CTC did not phase out until much higher levels of earnings. In 2017, it first began to phase out at $75,000 of income for unmarried filers and at $110,000 for joint filers.

The 2017 Tax Cuts and Jobs Act (TCJA) substantially expanded the CTC. Relative to 2017, the TCJA (1) doubles the per-child, nonrefundable credit from $1,000 to $2,000; (2) increases the maximum refundable portion from $1,000 to $1,400 per dependent; (3) phases in the refundable portion beginning at $2,500 instead of $3,000 of earned income; and (4) increases the income level at which the CTC begins to phase out to $200,000 (from $75,000) for unmarried filers and $400,000 (from $110,000) for joint filers. Figure 9-12 illustrates how these changes affect the combined ACTC and CTC for a single parent with two children. For any given level of earnings above $2,500, the reward for work from the combined credit is higher. For example, in 2018 a single mother with two children who earns between $3,000 and $16,000 a year would receive $75 more under the TCJA than under the previous law. If she earns $20,000 a year (or 40

Figure 9-12. Child Tax Credit for a Family With Two Children, Unmarried and Married Parents, Under the the Previous Law and Tax Cuts and Jobs Act (TCJA), 2018

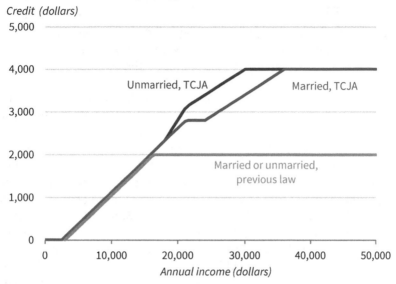

Sources: Internal Revenue Service; Open Source Policy Center (n.d.); CEA calculations.
Note: The combination of the Child Tax Credit and the Additional Child Tax Credit is shown.

hours per week for 50 weeks, earning $10 per hour), she would receive $825 more. At $25,000 in earnings, she would receive $1,500 more. With earnings of $30,000 or more, she would receive an additional $2,000 (until entering the phase-out range). Although other tax provisions also changed under the TCJA, the overall reward for work is higher than under the previous law. For example, a single mother with two children and $20,000 ($25,000) in earnings received $601 ($1,078) more in 2018 than in 2017 (Open Source Policy Center n.d.).

The expanded CTC under the TCJA substantially increases the reward for full-time, full-year work for nondisabled, working-age adults on noncash welfare programs without exacerbating strong work disincentives for unmarried part-time workers and second earners in the vast majority of families. Part-time work at low wages by unmarried adults receives only a small additional reward, although the EITC already provides substantial benefits in these cases. In addition, the greater reward for work from the expanded CTC would complement expanded work requirements in noncash welfare programs. Mead (2014) argues that the success of the EITC expansions in the 1990s was due to work requirements that ensured people initially entered the workforce and then received higher EITC benefits that rewarded work and hence ensured that they remained there. Similarly, the expanded CTC under the TCJA could most effectively draw more nondisabled, working-age adults on noncash welfare programs into full-time, full-year work to the extent that work requirements in these programs are also further expanded.

Benefits for Children

In addition to encouraging work among nondisabled, working-age welfare recipients, requiring, supporting, and rewarding work may benefit children living in families with parents who are subject to these reforms. Evidence from randomized controlled trials on welfare reforms in the 1990s suggests that when programs required work but offered no additional financial incentives, children's academic achievement was unaffected, but when work requirements were paired with additional financial incentives, children's outcomes improved (Morris et al. 2001; Duncan, Morris, and Rodrigues 2011). Meanwhile, research shows that tax credits that link benefits to work significantly improve child outcomes. The EITC leads to improved test scores, educational attainment, adult employment, and infant health (Dahl and Lochner 2012, 2017; Chetty et al. 2011; Hoynes, Miller, and Simon 2015; Manoli and Turner 2018; Michelmore and Bastian 2018). In an extensive review of the literature on the EITC, Nichols and Rothstein (2016, 187) note that "there is robust evidence of quite large effects of the EITC on children's academic achievement," compared with the "relatively small estimates of effects of family income on student outcomes that come from non-EITC settings." In explaining why the EITC may lead to larger improvements in child outcomes than those due to housing assistance, Jacob, Kapustin, and Ludwig (2015) suggest one reason for the discrepancy could be that the EITC simultaneously provides income and encourages adult employment, potentially exposing children to higher-quality child care environments at early ages.

Consistent with these positive effects on childhood outcomes, welfare reform during the 1990s tended to increase resources available for consumption among affected families. Meyer and Sullivan (2008) find that after welfare reform, consumption increased (or at least did not decrease) among single-mother families across the distribution, even for those in the bottom decile of consumption. Moreover, Meyer and Sullivan (2004) find that consumption by single mothers appears to have increased more than consumption by single women without children and married women with children, groups that were less affected by welfare reform. This suggests that welfare reform served to reduce material hardship, or at least did not increase it. These reductions in material hardship have persisted, with Meyer and Sullivan (2012b) estimating that consumption-based poverty rates among single-parent families fell from 28 percent in 1990 to 23 percent in 1995 to 15 percent in 2000, and down to 9 percent in 2010.

The actions taken by the Trump Administration that promote work among low-income Americans could thus both increase work among nondisabled, working-age adults and improve child outcomes. Expanding work requirements for childless adults, increasing child care assistance for low-income families, and increasing tax-based rewards for work among adults with children, in combination with strong economic growth, are already bringing more nondisabled, working-age adults into the workforce and, at the same time, reducing reliance on welfare programs. Further progress could be achieved by expanding work requirements in noncash welfare programs to additional groups of nondisabled, working-age adults, including those with children who make up the majority of these recipients, as described in the report *Expanding Work Requirements in Non-Cash Welfare Programs* (CEA 2018). These efforts will help ensure that progress in reducing poverty based on modern standards of material hardship will increasingly be achieved by helping nondisabled, working-age adults increase their earnings through work.

Conclusion

President Lyndon B. Johnson declared a War on Poverty in 1963. Based on 1963 standards of material hardship, his War on Poverty is largely over and has been a success. Limitations in both the OPM and the SPM that the Census Bureau produces each year make them incapable of fully capturing this success. When we use a new FPM that is anchored to 1963 standards—and that thus includes the full impact of government taxes and transfers (both cash and in-kind, including the market value of health insurance); that better accounts for inflation, by using the Personal Consumption Expenditures Price Index; and that uses the household instead of the family as the sharing unit—we find that the poverty rate declined from 19.5 percent in 1963 to 2.3 percent in 2017. This is far more than the decline from 19.5 to 12.3 percent that the OPM reports for the same period. Of course, the FPM would count a larger share of Americans as poor if it increased the standards of material hardship to reflect economic growth since 1963. However, the task of establishing these new poverty thresholds is the responsibility of elected policymakers rather than researchers.

Although the War on Poverty was successful in reducing material hardship, it did not do so through increases in self-sufficiency, as President Johnson envisioned. Rather, it was substantial increases in the availability and generosity of government transfers to households in the bottom part of the income distribution that lifted nondisabled, working-age people out of poverty. The proportion of nondisabled, working-age adults (age 18–64) living in a household that receives welfare benefits (AFDC/TANF, food stamps / SNAP, housing assistance, and Medicaid) increased from 4.0 percent in 1967 to 27.6 percent in 2017, whereas growth in their work rates began to reverse after 2000. This decline in self-sufficiency has resulted in the situation today where millions of nondisabled, working-age adults receive these welfare benefits while not working.

A new war on poverty should focus on reducing material hardship (based on modern standards that are explicitly determined by policymakers) through work for nondisabled, working-age people whenever possible. The highly successful welfare reforms during the 1990s that required, supported, and rewarded work can serve as a model for current efforts. The Trump Administration has taken important actions along these lines—strengthening work requirements in noncash welfare programs; increasing child care assistance for low-income families; and increasing the reward for full-time, full-year work as part of the Tax Cuts and Jobs Act of 2017 by increasing the Child Tax Credit. Additional progress could be achieved by further expanding work requirements in noncash welfare programs, such as food stamps / SNAP and Medicaid, including for nondisabled, working-age adults with children.

Chapter 10

The Year in Review and the Years Ahead

Economic growth increased again during 2018. After growing by about 2.0 percent during the four quarters of both 2015 and 2016, economic growth increased to 2.5 percent during 2017, and then picked up again—to 3.2 percent, at a compound annual rate—during the first three quarters of 2018, compared with the Administration's forecast of 3.1 percent for the four quarters of 2018. On the demand side, much of the faster growth during these past two years was accounted for by investment and (to a lesser extent) by net exports offsetting slightly slower growth in residential investment and State and local government. Consumer spending growth edged slightly lower, from 2.7 percent in 2017 to 2.6 percent through 2018:Q3 at an annual rate. On the supply side, the rise in growth (during the first three quarters of 2018, relative to average growth after the 2007:Q4 business cycle peak) was accounted for by slightly higher growth in real output per hour, a stabilization of the labor force participation rate after a protracted period of decline, a lengthening of the workweek, and further increases in the employment share of the labor force, more than offsetting a decline in population growth. By the fourth quarter, the unemployment rate had fallen to 3.8 percent, the lowest quarterly rate since 1969. Nominal average hourly earnings increased by 3.4 percent during the 12 months of 2018, up from a 2.7 percent year-earlier rate and 2.1 percent average annual rate during the business cycle expansion from 2009:Q3 through 2016:Q4.

The 3.2 percent annualized growth in real gross domestic product (GDP) during the first three quarters of 2018 exceeded consensus expectations for the second year in a row. Blue Chip Economic Indicators' December 2017 survey forecasted growth of only 2.4 percent during the four quarters of 2018. The unemployment rate fell another –0.3 percentage point, to 3.8 percent (fourth quarter to fourth quarter). Over the course of 2018, the economy added 2.7 million nonfarm jobs, averaging 223,000 per month, with sizable job gains in most of the major sectors. It is unusual for jobs to increase at this rate nine years into an economic expansion. Labor productivity growth in the nonfarm business sector rose from a pre–Tax Cuts and Jobs Act (TCJA) expansion average of 1.1 percent to 1.8 percent at an annual rate during the first three quarters of 2018. In addition, although the labor force participation rate has risen slightly overall, and among prime-age workers specifically, long-term trends in overall participation due to the aging Baby Boom generation will require fresh policy actions to offset (such as those discussed in chapter 3 of this *Report*).

In this chapter, we also report on the Administration's progress in 2018 toward achieving the five pillars of U.S. trade policy, as enumerated by the Office of the U.S. Trade Representative (USTR 2018a) in its 2018 *Annual Report*: supporting our national security, strengthening the U.S. economy, negotiating better trade deals, aggressively enforcing U.S. trade laws, and reforming the multilateral trading system.

Acknowledging both upside and downside risks, the Trump Administration's policy-inclusive forecast (which assumes full implementation of the Administration's economic agenda) is for real GDP to grow at an average annual rate of 3.0 percent during the 11 years between 2018 and 2029. As noted in the 2018 *Economic Report of the President* and in chapter 1 of this *Report*, we expect growth to moderate slightly after 2020, as the capital-to-output ratio approaches its new, post-TCJA steady state, and as the effects of the TCJA's personal income tax provisions on the rate of growth dissipate—leaving a permanent, positive, level effect. This moderation will be partially offset, however, by the supply-side effects of the assumed enactment of new deregulatory actions and infrastructure investment. With growth moderating in the latter half of the budget window, from 3.2 percent in 2019 to 2.8 percent in 2029, the

Administration expects unemployment to rise to a natural rate of 4.2 percent, which will also maintain price stability.

G rowth during both 2017 and 2018 surpassed expectations, as shown in figure 10-1. In January 2017, the Blue Chip consensus forecast for fourth quarter–to–fourth quarter growth of real GDP was 2.3 percent in both 2017 and 2018, while the Congressional Budget Office (CBO) projected growth of 2.3 and 1.9 percent, respectively. Actual real GDP growth during 2017 and annualized growth during the first three quarters of 2018 was 2.5 and 3.2 percent, respectively.

Consider the expenditure-side components of real GDP in turn: During the first three quarters of 2018, real consumer spending grew at a 2.6 percent annual rate, similar to the 2.7 percent pace during 2017. Real disposable personal income grew at a 2.8 percent annual rate, and the saving rate was roughly flat from 2017:Q1 to 2018:Q3. Business fixed investment grew 7.5 percent at an annual rate through 2018:Q3, up from 6.3 percent during 2017, and up from only 1.8 percent during 2016. Private nonresidential fixed investment contributed almost one-third of GDP growth, rising from a pre-TCJA expansion average of 0.6 percentage point to 1.0 percentage point. Residential investment fell 2.8 percent at an annual rate during the first three quarters of 2018, retracing some of the year-earlier gain. Inventory investment added 0.5 percentage point to average growth during the first three quarters of 2018, and accounted for much of the quarterly fluctuations in GDP, with a large 2018:Q3 contribution, which was partially offset by negative contributions in 2018:Q2. Government purchases added 0.4 percentage point to overall GDP growth during the first three quarters of 2018, with nearly half of this accounted for by State and local purchases and half by defense purchases. Exports contributed 0.3 percentage point to real GDP growth during the first three quarters of 2018, a notable increase from the average contribution of –0.1 percentage point in the years 2015–16.

Over the course of 2018, the U.S. economy added 2.7 million nonfarm jobs, averaging 223,000 per month, up from 179,000 per month during 2017. By 2018:Q4, the unemployment rate had fallen to 3.8 percent, the lowest quarterly rate since 1969, and down 0.3 percentage point since 2017:Q4. The unemployment rate for African Americans was down 1.3 percentage points during the 24 months through December 2018, to 6.6 percent. The 2018 yearly average unemployment rate of 6.5 percent for African Americans was the lowest rate recorded in a series that began in 1972.

The annual average labor force participation rate has ticked up under President Trump to 62.9 percent from 62.8 percent in 2016—an improvement in contrast to a general pattern of decline since 2007. The influences responsible

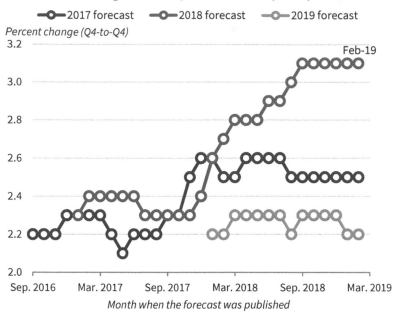

Figure 10-1. Evolution of Blue Chip Consensus Forecasts for Real GDP Growth during the Four Quarters of 2017, 2018, and 2019

—○— 2017 forecast   —○— 2018 forecast   —○— 2019 forecast

Percent change (Q4-to-Q4)

Source: Blue Chip Economic Indicators.

for the past decline in the participation rate include the retirement of Baby Boom generation cohorts, an atypically slow recovery from the 2007–9 recession, and government policies that discouraged participation (see chapter 3 of this *Report* and Mulligan 2012). The stabilization of the participation rate during the years 2016–18, with a modest uptick toward the end of 2018, reflects a tightening labor market that is bringing people off the sidelines and offsets the continued transition into retirement of peak Baby Boom cohorts. Administration policies to promote labor market reskilling, as well as marginal personal income tax rate reductions under the TCJA, have likely complemented the tightening labor market to promote higher participation.

Most of the key inflation measures increased slightly during 2018, from below the Federal Reserve's target of 2.0 percent—as measured by the Personal Consumption Expenditures (PCE) Price Index—to rates roughly in line with this target. The PCE and core PCE (excluding volatile food and energy) price indices rose by 1.8 and 1.9 percent over the 12 months ending in November 2018, up from 1.8 and 1.6 percent during 2017, respectively. As measured instead by the core Consumer Price Index (CPI), inflation increased to 2.2 percent during the 12 months of 2018 from a year-earlier rate of 1.8 percent. Market-based measures of inflation expectations show that inflation is expected to remain at roughly its current pace.

The small uptick in inflation during the past year is notable because it was accompanied by low and declining unemployment. Factors that have kept inflation low include low import prices and confidence in the Federal Reserve's ability to hit its target. Real average hourly earnings of nonfarm private sector employees rose by 1.4 percent during the 12 months through December, deflating by the CPI inflation measure, as nominal wage growth continued to exceed the subdued pace of price inflation, which was more than double the 0.6 percent real wage gain during 2016 and 2017. When measuring inflation using the PCE Price Index, real average hourly earnings rose slightly faster (by 1.5 percent) during the 12 months through November 2018.

Challenges in the labor market remain for 2019 and the longer term, including increased opioid dependence, the improving but still low rate of labor productivity and real wage growth, and downward pressure on the labor force participation rate from demographic shifts (see chapter 3). However, these challenges may be confronted with good policymaking regarding tax reform, work requirements, expanding labor market opportunities, and deregulation. Capital deepening, a key driver of labor productivity, has improved during the past year in response to the last year's tax bill, the TCJA. Meanwhile, though demographics are a principal determinant of long-run trends in labor force participation, much can be done to support rising participation for specific age groups. Policy has reduced participation in the past, and many of these changes are reversible. For example, as demonstrated in chapters 3 and 9 of this *Report*, policies designed to mitigate the demand-side effects of rising unemployment during the Great Recession and other structural factors—such as geographic immobility—have had persistently negative effects on the labor supply of both prime-age and young adults. Recent policy proposals, such as proposed work requirements for some public benefits, can help reverse these negative effects.

Assuming full implementation of the President's economic agenda, the Administration projects real GDP to grow by 3.2 percent during the four quarters of 2019, and by 2.8 percent in the long term. After a further near-term decline, the long-term unemployment rate is projected to gradually rise to a natural rate of 4.2 percent, while inflation, as measured by the chained price index for GDP, is expected to remain stable at its current rate of about 2.0 percent. Yields on 10-year Treasury notes are expected to rise from the projected yield of 2.9 percent in 2018 to historically more normal levels of 3.7 or 3.8 percent during the decade of the 2020s.

Output

Real GDP grew by 3.2 percent at a compound annual rate through the first three quarters of 2018, a pace that, if sustained through the end of the year, would mark the fastest four-quarter growth in any calendar year since 2004. Real gross domestic output—an average of GDP and gross domestic income—grew at a similar 3.2 percent annual rate during the first three quarters of 2018, up from 2.4 percent during the four quarters of 2017. Most of the growth during the first three quarters of 2018 can be attributed to strong increases in consumer spending, business fixed investment, and government spending. These were somewhat offset by declines in residential investment and net exports.

Consumer Spending

Consumer spending was the major demand-side contributor to real GDP growth during 2018, not because it grew especially rapidly, but because it constitutes 69 percent of real GDP. Real consumer spending grew at roughly the same rate (2.6 percent, at an annual rate) as disposable income (2.8 percent), so the personal saving rate changed little (on net) from 2017:Q4 to 2018:Q3 (figure 10-2).

One noteworthy development in 2018 was the huge upward revision in the saving rate. In July 2018, the Commerce Department's revision of the National Income and Product Accounts showed that the previously released 2017 saving rate almost doubled, from 3.4 percent to 6.7 percent (also shown in figure 10-2). Small revisions extend back historically, but revisions of 0.5 percentage point or more affected data from 1976 forward, and upward saving rate revisions of about 1.50 percentage points affected data from 2012 to 2016. For the period 2007–17, large upward revisions to proprietors' income were "almost entirely attributable to revised estimates of the misreporting of nonfarm proprietors' income, based on IRS data, which exceed $100 billion for 2012–14" (BEA 2018, 26). For 2017, the huge upward revision of 3.3 percentage points resulted from both proprietors' income and new administrative data for wages and salaries collected through the unemployment insurance tax system. The prerevision saving rate data might have been viewed as worrisome because it suggested that the saving rate was falling to such a low level that it constrained the growth of consumer spending. The large upward revision dispelled that view.

Real consumer spending grew at a pace similar to that of real income during 2018, so that the saving rate was little changed during the four quarters of the year. The real wages and salaries component of income tends to track real spending well, as was the case in 2017 and 2018. During the first three quarters of 2018, for example, real wage and salary income grew by 2.3 percent at a compound annual rate, while real consumer spending grew by 2.6 percent. In addition to income, consumer spending was supported by strong consumer sentiment, a declining ratio of debt service payments to disposable personal income through 2018:Q3, improving access to credit, and continued gains in wealth.

During the first three quarters of 2018, growth was strong for real household purchases of goods, which grew at a 3.0 percent annualized rate, while

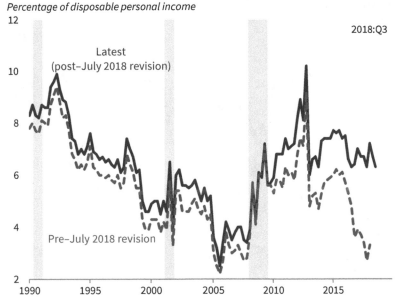

Figure 10-2. Personal Saving Rate, 1990–2018

Percentage of disposable personal income

Latest
(post–July 2018 revision)

2018:Q3

Pre–July 2018 revision

Source: Bureau of Economic Analysis.
Note: Data for the pre–July 2018 revision are through 2018:Q1. Shading denotes a recession.

service purchases grew moderately, by 2.4 percent. Consumer sentiment increased in 2018 (figure 10-3). During 2018, the two major indices of consumer sentiment reached their highest quarterly averages since 2000. The Conference Board Index increased faster during 2018, partly because it includes a question on employment expectations, while the University of Michigan's overall Consumer Sentiment Index does not.

Household wealth peaked at a value equivalent to 7.0 years of income in 2018:Q3, the highest household wealth-to-income ratio since records began in 1947. However, a nearly 15 percent drop in the stock market during 2018:Q4 lowers our end-of-year wealth-to-income ratio estimate below year-earlier levels. Despite a net decline during the past four quarters, the wealth-to-income ratio is predicted to remain high from a historical perspective (figure 10-4).

Consumer spending tends to move up and down in parallel with wealth, as seen in the positively correlated co-movement of wealth and consumption in figure 10-4. And so one might have expected the increases in the consumption rate during 2016 and 2017 to be in parallel with the rising wealth-to-income ratio. In contrast, the consumption rate remained roughly flat from 2016 through 2018:Q3. It could be argued, therefore, that the predicted 2018:Q4 level of wealth (despite the projected declines during that quarter) could have supported a higher level of consumer spending relative to income (or equivalently, a lower saving rate) than observed during 2018. Or viewed

Figure 10-3. Consumer Sentiment, 1980–2018

Index (1985 = 100)

Consumer Sentiment Index, University of Michigan

2018:Q4

Consumer Confidence Index, Conference Board

Sources: University of Michigan; Conference Board; CEA calculations.
Note: Shading denotes a recession.

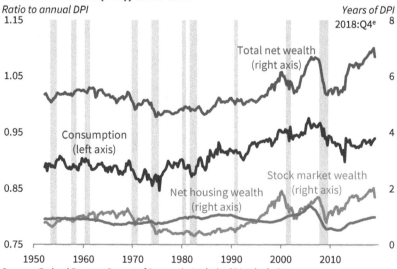

Figure 10-4. Consumption and Wealth Relative to Disposable Personal Income (DPI), 1952–2018

Ratio to annual DPI   *Years of DPI*

2018:Q4e

Total net wealth (right axis)

Consumption (left axis)

Stock market wealth (right axis)

Net housing wealth (right axis)

Sources: Federal Reserve; Bureau of Economic Analysis; CEA calculations.
Note: Shading denotes a recession. The CEA estimated the 2018:Q4 data from the latest daily or monthly data.

another way, the historically high level of the wealth-to-income ratio (seen in figure 10-4) can be expected to buffer whatever negative effects might ensue from the predicted 2018:Q4 decline in wealth, so that it would have only a small negative effect on consumer spending this year.

For a discussion of investment in 2018, see chapter 1 of this *Report*, "Evaluating the Effects of the Tax Cuts and Jobs Act."

Government Purchases

Real government purchases—Federal, State, and local consumption, plus gross investment—contributed 0.4 percentage point to real GDP growth through the third quarter of 2018, up from 0.2 and 0.0 percentage point in 2016 and 2017, respectively (figure 10-5). Real Federal purchases increased by 3.3 percent through 2018:Q3 at an annual rate, up from 1.3 percent growth during 2017. Defense purchases—defense consumption and gross investment—which grew by 4.6 percent during the same period, accounted for nearly all of the faster growth of real Federal purchases. The growth of defense purchases partially offset several years of declining real defense capital stock. State and local government purchases—consumption plus gross investment—contributed 0.2 percentage point to real GDP growth during the first three quarters of 2018, growing 1.6 percent over this time frame, after falling 0.5 percent during 2017.

State and local purchases as a share of nominal GDP fell from their historical peak of 13.0 percent in 2009 to 10.8 percent in 2017 and 2018, as State and local governments curtailed spending in the face of budget pressures. Even so, State and local government purchases as a share of nominal GDP have exceeded the Federal share since 1984 (figure 10-5). State and local governments employ about 13 percent of nonfarm workers and added 105,000 jobs during 2018.

Net Exports

Real U.S. exports of goods and services rose by 2.5 percent at an annual rate during the first three quarters of 2018, a strong growth rate but down from 4.7 percent in 2017—the largest four-quarter rate of growth since 2013. Exports contributed 0.3 percentage point at an annual rate to real GDP growth during the three quarters through 2018:Q3 (figure 10-6). The pickup of U.S. export growth during 2017 and the slower growth in 2018 reflected the pattern of growth among our trading partners, with relatively synchronized global growth in 2017 succeeded by evident decoupling in 2018, when U.S. growth increased while foreign growth slowed. Meanwhile, real U.S. imports increased by 3.8 percent at an annual rate during the first three quarters of 2018, faster than exports.

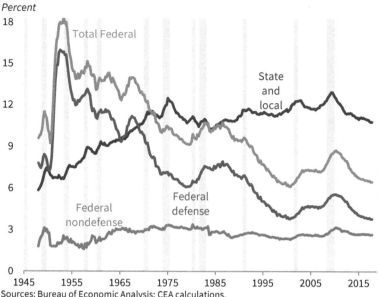

Figure 10-5. Government Purchases as a Share of Nominal GDP, 1948–2018

Percent

Sources: Bureau of Economic Analysis; CEA calculations.
Note: Shading denotes a recession.

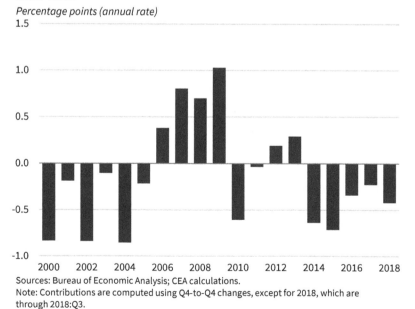

Figure 10-6. Contribution of Net Exports to U.S. Real GDP Growth, 2000–2018

Percentage points (annual rate)

Sources: Bureau of Economic Analysis; CEA calculations.
Note: Contributions are computed using Q4-to-Q4 changes, except for 2018, which are through 2018:Q3.

The Trade Year in Review

This section reviews trade activities in 2018. First, it looks at U.S. trade policy during the year. Second, it discusses two global safeguards imposed to temporarily protect domestic industries from imports. Third, it examines major trade actions aimed at reducing imports of steel and aluminum to address the national security issues resulting from such imports. Fourth, it considers the year's largest trade action: the imposition of import tariffs on $250 billion in goods from China. Fifth, it explains how the United States successfully updated its trade agreement with South Korea and modernized its agreement with Mexico and Canada. And sixth, it presents a case study of how the U.S. decided to withdraw from the Universal Postal Union, reflecting the Administration's vision of how to best advance our Nation's interests.

U.S. Trade Policy in 2018

After decades of underperforming trade deals that put American families and businesses at a disadvantage, President Trump has been clear that he intends to pursue free, fair, and reciprocal trade for the United States and its workers. In 2018, the Trump Administration made strides toward realizing his vision for the future of American and global trading relations—a vision in which he stands up for American workers and actively responds to economic competitors that do not adhere to international trading norms.

The Administration's trade policy rests on five pillars, as enumerated by the Office of the U.S. Trade Representative (USTR 2018a) in its 2018 *Annual Report*: supporting our national security, strengthening the U.S. economy, negotiating better trade deals, aggressively enforcing U.S. trade laws, and reforming the multilateral trading system.

Table 10-1 provides a timeline of major events for the primary trade policy actions in 2018 that are discussed in this section. In keeping with the pillars laid out by USTR, it is worth noting that an economic lens is not well suited to analyze all active trade policy issues. For example, reform of the World Trade Organization is a priority for the United States. However, the issues there center on transparency, the vitality of the negotiating and monitoring functions, judicial overreach, enforcement, publication, compliance, the willingness of countries to engage in negotiations, and issues of legal interpretation. The CEA (2018a) has catalogued some of these structural topics; they are not raised again here.

The changes in the global trading system during the past generation have triggered a reconsideration of policies in the United States and around the world. As a measure of the growing importance of trade, the value of imports plus exports as a share of U.S. GDP tripled from 1960 to 2017. Economic forces have changed historical production patterns and factor allocations. The CEA (2018a) presents a comprehensive review of the benefits of increased trade and the costs that arise as a result, particularly the distributional consequences. These effects have triggered a political response that has fueled resolve to address the underlying shifts. Fortunately, addressing the issues and pressures facing the global trading system could deliver large and lasting economic net benefits.

The Organization for Economic Cooperation and Development (OECD 2018) has highlighted the gains from reduced global barriers to trade. Reducing trade barriers in each sector to the lowest levels currently observed in any economy belonging to the Group of Twenty would expand global trade by 3 percent. President Trump's goal of zero tariffs, zero nontariff barriers, and zero subsidies promises to deliver these and greater gains to American consumers and workers, and to other countries around the world.

In 2018, the Trump Administration took three principal tariff actions that are designed to protect American workers, firms, and national security. (These three actions are explained in detail in the next subsections.) In addition to working with our trading partners to eliminate unfair trading practices, the President elected to use tariffs to protect U.S. workers, businesses, and national security. The tariffs implemented in 2018 raised the U.S. average applied tariff by 1.1 percentage points, from 1.5 percent in January 2018 to 2.6 percent in November 2018.

Tariffs provide benefits as well as costs. The Federal government benefited from $14.4 billion in revenue collected in 2018 from newly imposed tariffs. Revenue was historically a major impetus for tariff policy, though it has not been one for more than a century (Irwin 2017). In addition to this revenue, domestic producers also stand to benefit from price increases supported by tariff protections. Offsetting these benefits are the costs paid by consumers in the form of higher prices and reduced consumption. Foreign exporters also bear some of tariffs' economic incidence, although the extent varies across products. The foreign incidence is smallest for substitutable products such as commodities.

Concurrent with higher tariffs, the United States has successfully updated its trade agreements with key trade partners in record time, signing a revised U.S.–South Korea Free Trade Agreement in September and a new United States–Mexico–Canada Agreement in November. These agreements include new, enforceable rules that promote free, fair, and reciprocal trade. The many dimensions that modern trade agreements address make the quick timetable of these agreements all the more impressive. The expected long-term gains are substantial for Americans from new trade patterns that are not bedeviled by current problems like weak intellectual property laws and enforcement, losses in manufacturing capacity, and barriers to expanded exports. In addition, the USTR has notified Congress of its intent to enter into negotiations with the European Union and Japan. And the USTR has also notified Congress that it intends to begin negotiations with the United Kingdom as soon as it is willing to do so after Brexit resolves issues surrounding future trading relationships.

In the remainder of this section, the United States' 2018 trade policy actions are introduced sequentially. First, its three tariff actions are discussed. Understanding the differences between these trade actions and how they interacted with one another is key to understanding trade policy in 2018 and for years to come as the Administration's agenda progresses.

Section 201: Solar Cells and Large Residential Washing Machines

The first major actions in 2018 were two global safeguards imposed to temporarily protect domestic industries from imports. These actions proceeded contemporaneously at the request of U.S. firms that petitioned for relief from import competition in 2017, with the result that a combination of tariffs and quotas was imposed in late January. Global safeguard investigations are conducted by the U.S. International Trade Commission (USITC) under several different legal authorities. The 2018 safeguards invoked Section 201 of the Trade Act of 1974—a provision that had not been used since 2001, when the USITC conducted an investigation into imports of steel products that resulted in the imposition of tariff remedies. In both the solar cells and large residential washing machine cases, previous antidumping and countervailing duties had not been effective, in part because foreign producers shifted production to countries not subject to duties.

In 2017, the USITC completed two investigations. First, in November, an investigation determined that imported crystalline silicon photovoltaic (CSPV) cells and modules were a substantial cause of serious injury to the domestic industry.[1] Then, in December, an investigation determined that the imports of large residential washing machines were a substantial cause of serious injury to the domestic industry. The recommendations of the USITC commissioners were submitted to the President, who, under the statute, has substantial discretion in deciding on the ultimate remedy. On January 23, 2018, the President decided that tariff rate quotas (TRQs) would go into effect 15 days later, on February 7 (83 *FR* 3541, 83 *FR* 3553).[2] The TRQs apply to imports of these goods

---

[1] The investigation included assemblies of cells. A photovoltaic module consists of several photovoltaic cells that are connected together. Similarly, a photovoltaic module is an intermediate input used in the construction of a photovoltaic array, which is the complete power-generating unit. The CSPV is not the only solar technology, but is the most common, and most photovoltaic cells are manufactured using mono- or polycrystalline silicon. A recent report by the CEA (2018a) included a more detailed history of the solar safeguards dispute, investigation, and remedy.

[2] TRQs combine features of both a tariff and a quota. In a TRQ, a lower or zero tariff rate applies to imports of the good until some quota quantity is reached, after which point imports face a different, higher tariff rate.

from all countries and last for four years for CSPV cells and modules and three years for washers.[3]

The purpose of the global safeguard is to provide sufficient temporary relief from import competition in order to allow domestic firms to compete on a level playing field. During previous Administrations, tax incentives were offered to developers of renewable electric generation. But the Trump Administration has worked to eliminate these preferences to provide all sources of energy with the same advantage. Demand for CSPV products has historically been quite sensitive to these tax policies, which are now lower with the expiration of the production tax credit. As a result, after a substantial surge in late 2017, CSPV imports fell, and prices also fell, by 13 percent from January through December 2018. The petitioning firm, Suniva, is currently in bankruptcy, while the petition supporter, SolarWorld, was acquired in April 2018 by a competitor, SunPower.

After the Section 201 action, 31 percent fewer foreign washers were imported between February and November 2018 compared with the same period in 2017; industrial production of major electrical household appliances increased by 2 percent between December 2017 and 2018; and the CPI for washers and laundry equipment increased by 12 percent year-over-year in December. Industrial production also includes dryers, which are commonly purchased along with washers. The quota for washers was filled on October 22, meaning that the higher out-of-quota rate applied to imports until the quota reset in February 2019.

No official retaliatory tariffs were announced in response to these Section 201 actions, but China did launch a countervailing duty investigation of U.S. sorghum exports three days before both of the U.S. safeguards went into effect. This echoes events in September 2009, when China launched an investigation into U.S. exports of chicken the day after a U.S. safeguard tariff was applied to Chinese tires by the Obama Administration. In April 2018, China imposed anti-dumping and countervailing duties of 179 percent on imports of U.S. sorghum (valued at $72 million in May 2017), but China removed and reimbursed these duties on May 18, 15 days after a U.S. trade delegation met in Beijing and after significant domestic criticism from Chinese sorghum purchasers. Nonetheless, while China purchased 79 percent of U.S. sorghum exports in the 2016 marketing year (from September 2016 through August 2017), U.S. sorghum exports to China in the 2017 marketing year were down 11 percent, and U.S. exporters directed shipments to other markets.

---

[3] In 2018, CSPV module imports from all countries faced a tariff of 30 percent, while cell imports from all countries faced an in-quota rate of zero and an out-of-quota rate of 30 percent. Washing machines and parts faced in-quota rate of 20 percent, and an out-of-quota rate of 50 percent. In both cases, the restrictions gradually loosen over the duration of the remedy. The washer safeguard applied to all residential washers, not just the large residential washers with a capacity larger than 10 kilograms described in the original petition.

Section 232: Steel and Aluminum

The second major trade actions of 2018 were aimed at reducing imports of steel and aluminum in order to address the threatened impairment of the United States' national security caused by such imports. Although the investigations of primary aluminum and steel were separate actions, they followed similar and contemporaneous tracks, and both resulted in the application of tariffs beginning in March 2018. These actions were taken based on the President's authority under Section 232 of the Trade Expansion Act of 1962.

In April 2017, the Department of Commerce initiated investigations into whether imports of steel and primary aluminum threatened to impair U.S. national security. In January 2018, Commerce reported to the President that current levels of both steel and primary aluminum imports threaten to impair U.S. national security. In light of this finding, President Trump imposed import tariffs of 10 percent on a wide range of aluminum products and also a 25 percent tariff on steel and an array of steel products, which became effective March 23.

The March 23 tariffs did not apply to a number of countries—including major importers and exporters of steel and aluminum, like Canada and the members of the European Union—as the United States entertained country-specific alternative arrangements. In May 2018, the United States negotiated alternative means to address the threatened impairment to national security caused by imports of steel from Argentina, Brazil, and South Korea, including the imposition of quantitative restrictions on imports of steel from these countries. Argentina and Brazil were able to reach a similar agreement on quantitative restrictions for aluminum, though South Korea remained subject to the aluminum tariff. Australia reached an agreement to avoid both the tariff and quota on steel and aluminum. In total, the quotas represented 17 percent of U.S. steel and 3 percent of U.S. aluminum imports in 2017. Canada, Mexico, and the EU did not reach a similar agreement, and on June 1, a 25 and 10 percent tariff was imposed on steel and aluminum imports, respectively. The tariff on Japan went into effect March 23 at the same rates. Concurrently, the United States and South Korea agreed to an alternative means to address the threat to national security posed by steel imports from South Korea. As part of the Section 232 agreement, imports of steel from South Korea became subject to a quantitative restriction equivalent to 70 percent of U.S. steel imports from South Korea based on an annual average across 2015 and 2017.

The President also determined that the Section 232 actions should have an exclusion process to allow domestic firms to import specific products not available in the United States without paying a tariff. Other domestic producers are able to file objections to exclusion requests claiming that domestic supplies are indeed available. This mechanism provides a means for steel users

Table 10-1. Timeline of Trade Events

	2017	2018											
		Jan.	Feb.	Mar.	Apr.	May	June	July	Aug.	Sep.	Oct.	Nov.	Dec.
Section 201	Suniva files solar petition (May 17, 2017)	Presidential Proclamations for solar and washer TRQs under Section 201 (Jan. 23, 2018)	Solar and washer tariffs go into effect (Feb. 7, 2018)		Sorghum AD/CVD duties imposed by China (Apr. 4, 2018)	Sorghum AD/CVD duties removed by China (May 18, 2018)					Washer quota filled, now subject to 50 percent tariff (Oct. 22, 2018)		
	Whirlpool files washer petition (June 5, 2017)		Sorghum AD/CVD investigation by China begins (Feb. 4, 2018)										
Section 232	Department of Commerce initiates steel investigations under Section 232 (Apr. 19, 2017)	Department of Commerce submits steel report (Jan. 11, 2018)		Steel tariffs go into effect, with exemptions (Mar. 23, 2018)	Retaliation by China (Apr. 2, 2018)		Exemptions are replaced with quotas (June 1, 2018)	Retaliation by Canada (July 1, 2018)	Rate increases for steel from Turkey (Aug. 13, 2018)				
	Commerce initiates aluminum investigation under Section 232 (Apr. 26, 2017)	Department of Commerce submits aluminum report (Jan. 17, 2018)		Aluminum tariffs go into effect, with exemptions (Mar. 23, 2018)			Exemptions are replaced with quotas (June 1, 2018)		Retaliation by Russia (Aug. 6, 2018)				
							Retaliation by Mexico (June 5, 2018)		Additional retaliation by Turkey				
							Retaliation by Turkey (June 21, 2018)						
							Retaliation by EU						

	2017	Jan.	Feb.	Mar.	Apr.	May	June	July	Aug.	Sep.	Oct.	Nov.	Dec.
2018													
Section 301	USTR initiates Section 301 investigation (Aug. 18, 2017)			USTR releases Section 301 Report (Mar. 22, 2018)				Tranche 1 on $34 billion (July 6, 2018)	Tranche 2 on $16 billion (Aug. 23, 2018)	Tranche 3 on $200 billion (Sep. 24, 2018)			President Trump announces agreement to delay increases of tariffs on Tranche 3 (Dec. 1, 2018)
								Retaliation 1 on $34 billion (July 5, 2018)	Retaliation 2 on $16 billion (Aug. 23, 2018)	Retaliation 3 on $60 billion (Sep. 24, 2018)			
FTAs	USTR informs Korea of intention to re-negotiate KORUS (July 12, 2017)			Re-negotiated KORUS agreement reached in principle (Mar. 28, 2018)						Re-negotiated KORUS agreement signed (Sep. 24, 2018)			
	President Trump informs Congress of intention to re-negotiate NAFTA (May 18, 2017)								U.S. reaches deal in principle with Mexico (Aug. 27, 2018)	U.S. reaches deal in principle with Canada (Sep. 30, 2018)		USMCA agreement signed (Nov. 30, 2018)	

Sources: Council of Economic Advisers using information from the White House, *Federal Register*, Office of the U.S. Trade Representative, U.S. Customs and Border Protection, U.S. Department of Commerce, and the World Trade Organization.

that cannot source steel or aluminum domestically to acquire inputs without paying tariffs.

Since the tariffs went into effect, imports have decreased while production has increased for steel and aluminum. Domestic primary aluminum production increased by 10 percent from March to December 2018, while employment in alumina and aluminum production rose by 100 jobs over the same period. From April to November 2018, aluminum imports were 15 percent lower than in the same period one year earlier (before the imposition of tariffs). U.S. Midwest aluminum prices fell 6.6 percent between when the tariff actions went in force (March 22) and December 31 2018. In the steel industry, production increased by 6 percent from March to December 2018, with iron and steel mills and ferroalloy production employment increasing by 6,200 over the same period. From April to November 2018, steel imports were 11 percent lower than in the same period one year earlier. From March to December 2018, the producer price index of iron and steel rose 7.5 percent.

In response to U.S. actions under Section 232, Canada, China, the EU, Mexico, Russia, and Turkey imposed retaliatory tariffs on a total of $30 billion of U.S. 2017 exports.[4] These retaliations were symmetric, insofar as they were import tariffs against U.S. exports, but they targeted a wide array of products beyond steel and aluminum. However, these retaliatory tariffs are being challenged by the United States at the World Trade Organization.

Section 301: China

The United States' largest trade action of 2018 was its imposition of import tariffs on $250 billion worth of goods from China in three tranches (2017 import value). The tariffs follow a thorough process initiated by the Trump Administration in August 2017, when the USTR opened an investigation into Chinese policies and practices regarding technology and intellectual property under Section 301 of the Trade Act of 1974. The USTR (2018b) issued a report in March 2018 that detailed a variety of unfair Chinese policies and practices: (1) forced technology transfer from U.S. inventors and companies; (2) nonmarket-based terms for technology licenses; (3) Chinese state-directed and -facilitated acquisition of strategic U.S. assets; and (4) cyber-enabled intrusions into U.S. commercial networks to steal trade secrets for commercial gain.

Initial negotiations to address China's policies and practices failed to yield satisfactory outcomes, resulting in the United States imposing additional tariffs on $50 billion worth of Chinese imports. The first Section 301 action applied an additional 25 percent ad valorem tariffs to Chinese imports worth $34 billion in 2017 import value and took effect on July 6. A second tranche

---

[4] In addition, India announced retaliatory tariffs , but has repeatedly delayed numerous implementation dates. Japan has notified the World Trade Organization of its intent to impose retaliatory tariffs but has not produced a list of goods or announced an expected date.

consisted of an additional 25 percent tariffs on a further $16 billion in 2017 imports from China, taking effect on August 23.

Rather than changing its practices, China announced retaliatory tariffs on U.S. goods. The first and second tranches were met with symmetric responses against $34 and $16 billion worth of 2017 U.S. exports, respectively. Notably, the first tranche of retaliation included a 25 percent tariff on $14 billion worth of U.S. soybean exports—the Chinese market represented over 57 percent of total U.S. soybean exports in 2017. Soybeans were the largest single product among dozens of agricultural exports targeted (see box 10-1).

The United States subsequently took supplemental tariff action under the authority of Section 301. A third tranche, of an additional 10 percent ad valorem tariffs applied to $200 billion in 2017 import value, took effect on September 24.[5] When the third tranche was announced, China was unable to retaliate symmetrically on a quantitative basis with import tariffs because China's imports from the U.S. were less than $200 billion. However, China targeted $53 billion in 2017 U.S. exports with a range of tariff rates up to 25 percent. After the three tranches of tariffs and retaliation, $27 billion worth of 2017 U.S. exports to China remain unaffected, while $262 billion worth of 2017 imports to the United States have not been targeted with Section 301 tariffs.

---

[5] In December 2018, given ongoing negotiations with China, the Administration announced a delay in the implementation date for the increase in tariffs on the third tranche of goods, which was due to take place on January 1, 2019.

On December 1, 2018, China and the United States agreed to a 90-day period during which to negotiate structural changes with respect to forced technology transfer, intellectual property protection, and other issues. During this time, the United States agreed to delay increasing its tariffs on $200 billion worth of Chinese imports from 10 to 25 percent, as had been scheduled to occur on January 1, 2019, until March 1, 2019.

Trade Agreements

In 2018, the United States successfully updated its trade agreement with South Korea and modernized its trade agreement with Mexico and Canada. The Administration also formally announced its intention to enter into negotiations for a trade agreement with the EU and Japan, and its wish to initiate negotiations with the United Kingdom as soon as it is ready to do so after it leaves the EU.

North America. Canada and Mexico are key U.S. trading partners—in the four quarters ending in 2018:Q3, a total of 24.9 percent of U.S. two-way trade in goods and services was with Canada or Mexico. Canada and Mexico are even more dependent on North American trade, with 71.9 and 65.1 percent of their total trade in the region, respectively. Since 1994, the North American Free Trade Agreement (NAFTA) has governed trading relationships in the region. Although some contend that NAFTA delivered broad net benefits to the U.S. economy (Caliendo and Parro 2015), the benefits were not evenly dispersed, and the costs of adjustment fell disproportionately on certain workers—such as those in the Upper Midwest with less educational attainment (Hakobyan and McLaren 2016). President Trump informed Congress in May 2017 of his intention to renegotiate NAFTA.

On November 30, 2018, President Trump signed the United States–Mexico–Canada Agreement (USMCA), thereby fulfilling his promise to the American people to renegotiate NAFTA. Once passed by Congress, USMCA will modernize the rules of trade and create a gold standard for modern provisions, such as digital trade, intellectual property rights, state-owned enterprises, and advanced customs procedures. In addition, USMCA will rebalance the terms of trade between all three countries to ensure that American workers and businesses across all sectors of the economy—manufacturing, services, and agriculture—receive benefits. The centerpiece of USMCA is a revision of the automotive rules of origin provisions that dictate when motor vehicles will be allowed to cross borders tariff free (see box 10-2).[6]

USMCA also makes substantial improvements in many other areas, including in labor and environmental protections, new disciplines on digital trade, and expanded dairy market access. With respect to labor, USMCA

---

[6] For a recent study of the impact of rules of origin on trade within NAFTA, see Conconi et al. (2018). Rules of origin led to a substantial reduction in the amount of intermediate goods imported by Mexico from nonparty countries.

commits Mexico to adopt legislation recognizing the right of workers to engage in collective bargaining; and unlike NAFTA, the provisions in both labor and environment chapters are enforceable and subject to trade sanctions. USMCA increases Canadian import quotas for U.S. dairy products and also eliminates Canadian milk-pricing rules that limited opportunities for U.S. producers (see box 10-3).

South Korea. The U.S.–South Korea Free Trade Agreement (KORUS) is a bilateral agreement that entered into force in March 2012. At the President's direction, the USTR informed South Korea of its intention to amend the KORUS Agreement on July 12, 2017. On March 28, the United States and South Korea reached an agreement in principle on KORUS amendments.

On September 24, the United States and South Korea signed a revised KORUS Agreement. Among other improvements, these revisions sought to achieve a level playing field for automobile trade. One issue of improvement was regulatory harmonization; the two countries have different safety standards, and thus an automobile deemed safe and legal to sell in one country may not be accepted in the other. The amended KORUS gave each automaker exporting from the United States an additional annual quota of 25,000 vehicles (doubling the total to 50,000 units a year) that are recognized as meeting South Korean safety standards as long as they meet U.S. standards. This improvement provides greater certainty for U.S.-based auto exporters to Korea to further increase sales and exports. The quota is also high enough to accommodate all vehicles exported to South Korea in 2017. The update also delayed

Box 10-3. USMCA and Canadian Dairy

Canada has a dairy supply management program that includes milk quotas and price supports for Canadian dairy farmers. A major achievement of USMCA is that it gives U.S. dairy producers an exclusive quota of 50,000 metric tons for fluid milk by the sixth year of the agreement, with a farmgate value of nearly $20 million. Under the current system, the U.S. producers must compete with producers from many other countries. USMCA also includes greater access for value-added products like cheese, cream, powdered dairy products, and yogurt.

A second major breakthrough was Canada's agreement to eliminate milk price classes 6 and 7, which allowed marketing of surplus skimmed milk and milk protein products. Before the creation of class 7 in 2017, the value of annual U.S. exports to Canada of powdered milk components was over $100 million. USMCA restores the Canadian export market for these powdered milk products and helps reduce low-priced Canadian surplus products from competing with U.S. dairy products in the global marketplace. The increased access for U.S. dairy products to the Canadian market plus the elimination of Canadian milk price classes 6 and 7 could increase the value of annual exports of U.S. dairy products to Canada by over $328 million by year six of the agreement.

the date on which Korean light trucks would enter the U.S. duty free, pushing it back from 2021 to 2041. U.S. tariffs were to begin to fall starting in 2019, reaching duty free in 2021.

New agreements. Building on these successes, the Trump Administration is seeking more new trade agreements that will help American workers and U.S. commerce. On October 16, 2018, the Administration notified Congress of its intent to enter into free trade agreement negotiations with Japan and the EU, and with the U.K. These agreements could benefit the United States through reducing trade barriers in several areas, including agriculture, manufacturing, and services.

For example, in agriculture, Japan imposes a variable system of tariffs on pork imports, with rates as high as $2.18 per pound; for beef, Japanese tariffs range from 38.5 to 50 percent. A number of international competitors, such as Australia, face much lower Japanese tariffs, so a free trade agreement with Japan could level the playing field for U.S. exporters. For the EU, there are a number of nontariff barriers that impede trade. Beyond agriculture, other tariffs and nontariff barriers stand in the way of U.S. goods and services exports to Japan. For the U.S., a number of nontariff barriers impede trade. Arita, Mitchell, and Beckman (2015) estimate that removing even a subset of agricultural barriers could increase U.S. exports to the EU by $4.1 billion, compared with the 2011 baseline. Negotiations with the EU will also focus on making rules for standards and product testing fairer and reciprocal. Finally, depending on the terms of Brexit, negotiations with the U.K. could also further open that market to American goods and services.

Case Study: The Universal Postal Union

The United States had been a member of the Universal Postal Union (UPU) since its founding in 1874; but in October 2018, the U.S. submitted notice of its intention to withdraw from the organization.[7] This action reflects the Administration's priority of achieving a U.S. role in the international postal system consistent with the vision articulated in the August 23, 2018, Presidential Memorandum, a vision that would advance the interests of the U.S. alongside those of a number of other countries.

The historic nature of the set of reforms to the international postal system to be undertaken by the U.S. in 2019 reflects the historic nature of the changes in the economics of the international postal system that have occurred in recent years. These reforms are poised to occur through steps taken by the U.S. upon its exit from the UPU in October 2019. In the event that the UPU passes reforms that fully reflect the principles of the Presidential Memorandum before then, however, the U.S. could achieve its objectives without withdrawing. The U.S. therefore stands poised to adopt a remuneration system for items likely to contain goods that consist of nondiscriminatory "self-declared" rates that do not favor foreign mailers over domestic mailers or postal operators over non-postal operators. The only question is the compatibility of this achievement with U.S. membership in the UPU.

The United States' commitment to ensuring the provision of the benefits that the UPU originally intended to deliver at the time of its founding in 1874 has not changed. However, developments in the state of technology and the global economy have, in recent years, upended the economics of the international postal system. These changes have resulted in the UPU's "terminal dues" remuneration system imposing net costs on the national economies of certain member countries, including the United States. Although the costs imposed by the UPU's remuneration system for items likely to contain goods have in recent years increased for the U.S., the costs of exiting the UPU have decreased. As a result, the costs of U.S. membership in the UPU relative to its benefits has trended upward. In the spirit of the Nobel Prize–winning economist Milton Friedman's admonition against the evaluation of "policies and programs by their intentions rather than results," the Administration's approach to the U.S. role in the international postal system reflects its prioritization of the results that the international postal system delivers.

The emergence of substitutes for some of the services provided by the UPU has lowered the cost of U.S. withdrawal from the organization. Technological

---

[7] This subsection was first published by the Council of Economic Advisers in January 2019.

change has created these substitutes. For example, the very first article of the Treaty of Bern that is the UPU's foundation underscores the goal of creating of "a single postal territory for the reciprocal exchange of correspondence between their post-offices." One plausible substitute for this function, email, is estimated to generate over $8,000 in value per year for the median consumer and is available to anyone with access to the Internet at a typical marginal cost of zero (Brynjolfsson, Eggers, and Gannameneni 2018). A single substitute for the exchange of correspondence, then, appears to generate annual economic value for today's median consumer in excess of the entirety of real U.S. GDP per capita in 1874 (Bolt et al. 2018). Analysis of the international postal sector corroborates a direct link between global decline in volumes of letters since 1990 and the rise of technology like email (Copenhagen Economics 2017). Due to technology, then, the "exchange of correspondence" across international borders could occur for the roughly 90 percent of American adults who use the Internet without access to the UPU's single postal network (Anderson, Perrin, and Jiang 2018). This decreases the cost of a prospective exit from the UPU relative to a world where services like email could not substitute for international mail's role in facilitating the exchange of correspondence.

Although the costs of an exit from the UPU have decreased, the costs attributable to its remuneration system for items likely to contain goods have not. The UPU's existing "terminal dues" remuneration system determines the rates (i.e., prices) that one country's designated postal operator receives from a foreign postal operator for completing the delivery of mail originating in the foreign country. But these prices do not, under the status quo, need to have any relationship to either the cost that the designated postal operator incurs for completing the delivery or to the prices that it would charge a domestic mailer (i.e., customer of the postal service) for completing similar services. This creates conditions ripe for prices deviating from what they would be in the world of "unrestricted and undistorted competition in the provision of international postal services" envisioned in the August 23 Presidential Memorandum. Under the status quo, for instance, foreign mailers can pay prices that are a fraction of those offered to U.S. producers for delivering the same goods between the same two places by the U.S. Postal Service (Fountain and Malone 2018; Navarro 2018).

Instead, the scope of the economic costs that the terminal dues remuneration system could impose has increased due to the increase in volumes of goods transiting the international postal stream in recent years (Copenhagen Economics 2017). With the introduction of goods into the international postal stream, distortions in the pricing of international postal services created by the UPU's remuneration system can impose costs on producers and consumers that do not transact directly with any postal operator. These distortions in the pricing of international postal services for items likely to contain goods would be expected, like any set of price distortions, to lead to the types of misallocations of the factors of production that lower standards of living in both developed and developing countries (e.g., Jones 2013; Restuccia and Rogerson 2017). If, by contrast, the international mail were to consist exclusively of letters (i.e., correspondence), these distortions of prices within the postal sector would affect only the postal operators and mailers of letters directly involved in postal transactions.

The rise of e-commerce allows these price distortions within the postal sector to impose burdens on actors throughout the global economy. According to one survey of e-commerce consumers in 31 countries, 84 percent of cross-border goods purchased online are of the type that would be subject to the terminal dues system if delivered by a designated postal operator (International Postal Corporation 2018). Any economics textbook would lead to the conclusion that these distortions in the price of shipping, in a competitive e-commerce market, induce additional distortions in underlying economic activity. First, these differences in consumer prices could influence and distort outcomes within the e-commerce sector, in which the sensitivity of consumer demand to price differences can exceed its sensitivity during bricks-and-mortar shopping (e.g., Ellison and Ellison 2009).

Second, any distortions in the prices of e-commerce goods could induce substitution toward online and away from offline retail vendors. New evidence that consumers have rates of substitution between online and offline vendors comparable to their rates of substitution between offline vendors underscores the plausibility of distortions accruing through this channel (Dolfen et al. 2018). And at least some offline establishments appear to generate positive local externalities or spillovers in terms of employment and output (e.g., Shoag and Veuger 2018), a condition that would both enlarge the magnitude of the aggregate costs that could be imposed by online/offline substitution and broaden the scope of who bears these costs to include workers and producers even in the nontradable sector. Complementing this retail-specific evidence, Barrot and others (2017) demonstrate that the differences in the local exposure to the general import competition generated by differences in shipping costs can affect local employment, local output, and even household finances.[8]

A paucity of data on the value of goods transiting the international postal system prevents estimating the aggregate macroeconomic burden imposed by the price distortions that result from the terminal dues system for items likely to contain goods. Nonetheless, in the case of the United States, the economics of the current U.S. role in the existing terminal dues system permits the inference that these distortions exist, and that the incidence of the burden they

---

[8] However, the official trade data from the U.S. Census Bureau that inform the approach of Barrot et al. (2017) would not capture information about any goods that enter the U.S. through the international postal system. Barrot et al. (2018) detail the methodology for constructing the data used by Barrot et al. (2017), including the role of official trade statistics from the U.S. Census Bureau.

impose could fall on a variety of actors in the tradable and even nontradable sectors. Given the upward trend over time in the share of e-commerce items in the international postal system, in the absence of a change to the remuneration system, these economic costs of the distortions it imposes would only increase (Copenhagen Economics 2017).

This Administration's approach to the reform of the terminal dues system, though consistent with the spirit of U.S. concerns about the UPU's relationship to "marketplace competition in international mail" expressed as early as the Reagan Administration, reflects the novelty of these developments in the international postal sector's role in economic activity (Reagan 1986). The Administration's attempts at terminal dues reform in 2018 amounted to a strategy of voice in the canonical "exit, voice, or loyalty" economics framework articulated by Hirschman (1970) for rational approaches for the redress of grievances from within an organization. But sufficient progress toward the realization of the vision laid out in the Presidential Memorandum has yet to materialize, and, per Hirschman (1970), voice and exit can be substitutes as well as complements. If negotiations continue to fail to yield sufficient progress, the U.S. stands poised to continue on its path toward an exit from the UPU rather than continue its strategy of voice from within.

The vision articulated in the August 23 Presidential Memorandum looks toward the international postal system's future rather than its past. In 1874, the UPU's founders spoke of an international organization that would facilitate correspondence around the world. But since 1990, the volume of letters transiting the international postal system has trended downward, while the volume of items containing goods has trended upward (Copenhagen Economics 2017). Developing countries, in particular, seem to substitute electronic correspondence for letters (Copenhagen Economics 2017).

Given these changes in the international postal stream and its underlying economics, realizing the vision of "undistorted and unrestricted competition" articulated in the Presidential Memorandum would deliver benefits to both developing and developed countries, a reality reflected in the unanimous endorsement of the concerns voiced by the U.S. by the 28 members of the Postal Union of the Americas, Spain, and Portugal (2018). Other countries, including China and the Netherlands, seem to favor the UPU, embracing a remuneration system for items likely to contain goods that dates to an era when the international mail comprised many fewer goods and many more letters. To minimize the distortions created by postal remuneration policy given the underlying economics of the postal sector, the U.S. intends to adopt a system of self-declared and nondiscriminatory rates of remuneration for items likely to contain goods. The U.S. would welcome the opportunity to realize this forward-looking vision for its role in the international postal system as a member of the international postal union that it helped to found.

Policy Developments

Principal developments in the realm of economic policy pertain to fiscal policy and monetary matters. This section considers each in turn, with regulatory policy addressed in chapters 2, 5, and 6 of this *Report*, on, respectively, deregulation, energy, and banking.

Fiscal Policy

The most important fiscal policy actions during fiscal year 2018 were the Tax Cuts and Jobs Act (signed on December 22, 2017) and the Bipartisan Budget Act of 2018 (BBA; signed on February 9, 2018). The tax cut, together with the relaxing of the budget caps from the Budget Control Act of 2011, resulted in an increase in the Federal deficit in 2018. For a discussion of the TCJA, see chapter 1 of this *Report*.

For nearly the first six months of the fiscal year (October 1, 2017–March 23, 2018), Congress funded the Federal government through a string of five short-term continuing resolutions (CRs), funding the various budget accounts at the level of the preceding fiscal year. The last of these CRs, on February 9, 2018, was accompanied by the BBA. This final CR provided funding through March 23, 2018, when Congress passed the Consolidated Appropriations Act of 2018, which settled the remaining budget issues for 2018.

The legislation that enacted the first CR of the 2018 fiscal year also suspended the debt ceiling from October 1 through December 8 (when the limit was increased and reset at the debt level on that day), after which the Treasury resorted to extraordinary measures to keep the government functioning. On February 9, as part of the BBA, the debt limit was lifted again for the period through March 1, 2019.

The Bipartisan Budget Act of 2018, which was signed into law by President Trump on February 9, 2018, raised the statutory discretionary spending limits imposed by the Budget Control Act of 2011 (BCA) for two years at the beginning of the budget window, offsetting this by extending the mandatory budget sequester by two years later in the budget window (from 2025 to 2027). For fiscal year (FY) 2018, the BBA increased the defense limit by $80 billion (to $629 billion) and the nondefense limit by $63 billion (to $579 billion). For FY 2019, it increased the defense limit by $85 billion (to $647 billion) and the nondefense limit by $68 billion (to $597 billion). The national defense discretionary spending budgets for FY 2018 and FY 2019 also include $71 billion and $69 billion, respectively, in supplemental funding for Overseas Contingency Operations. The budget caps do not apply to spending designated for these operations or emergency purposes. The BBA also:

1. Included a continuing resolution to fund the government through March 23, 2018, because most appropriations to government agencies and programs were set to expire February 8, 2018.

2. Suspended the debt ceiling until March 1, 2019.
3. Granted $90 billion in disaster relief funding for areas affected by hurricanes and wildfires.

The BBA is the third in a series of discretionary spending cap increases made to the BCA, including the Bipartisan Budget Act of 2013 and the Bipartisan Budget Act of 2015. The BCA, the Federal statute that the BBA amended, imposed annual statutory discretionary limits on both military and nondefense spending. It also required annual reductions to the initial discretionary spending limits and created automatic mandatory spending reductions (known as "sequestration"), which would be triggered by the absence of a deficit reduction agreement. In the wake of the BBA, these sequester rules are scheduled to be reinstated in FY 2020.

On October 1, 2018, the beginning of FY 2019, the President signed spending bills for the Departments of Defense, Labor, Education, and Health and Human Services, while the rest of the government was funded through more continuing resolutions through December 21, 2018. When the CR was not renewed, a shutdown of these unfunded Federal departments and agencies began on December 22, 2018, and continued through January 25, 2019, when Congress and the President agreed to another three-week continuing resolution.

During the shutdown's five weeks, the CBO (2019) estimated that an average of roughly 300,000 nonessential Federal employees were furloughed, while essential employees worked—temporarily—without pay. Although legislation to eventually pay the furloughed Federal workers was passed and signed, those paychecks were not delivered until the shutdown was over. The cost to the Federal government for work that was paid for but not performed was about $94 million per day of the shutdown. The National Income and Product Accounts treat work that is paid for but not performed as a component of nominal GDP but not real GDP.

An unknown number of Federal contractors were also furloughed. After factoring in the work missed by Federal contractors, the CBO (2019) estimates that real GDP growth was reduced by, respectively, 0.2 and 0.4 percentage point at an annual rate in 2018:Q4 and 2019:Q1. A rebound in growth in 2019:Q2 returns the level of real GDP to its previous path, although much of the output lost during the shutdown will not be recovered. As a result of the partial government shutdown, real fourth-quarter over fourth-quarter GDP growth is expected to be slightly lower in 2018, and slightly higher in 2019, relative to the nonshutdown counterfactual.

Monetary Policy

Before the year began, the Federal Open Market Committee (FOMC) expected to continue gradually raising the Federal funds rate during 2018, with the caveat that the precise path of rate hikes would depend on the economy's course, especially employment and inflation. In its December 2017 forecast, the median FOMC participant expected *three* 25-basis-point rate hikes during 2018, which would have elevated the Federal funds rate from the 1.25–1.50 percent range at the end of 2017 to the 2.00–2.25 range at the end of 2018 (FOMC 2017b). Against the backdrop of stronger growth and a lower unemployment rate than expected, the FOMC raised rates *four* times, to the 2.25–2.50 percent range. Along the way, the FOMC noted that the inflation rate, which began the year below its 2 percent target, had moved up; and by May 2018, the FOMC began noting that core and overall inflation had "moved close to 2 percent" (FOMC 2018a).

In its final meeting of 2018, the FOMC signaled that some further rate hikes would likely be appropriate to meet its objectives, with the median FOMC participant expecting the Federal funds rate to reach 2.9 percent (i.e., two further rate hikes) by the end of 2019 (FOMC 2018b).[9]

Another dimension of monetary policy during 2018 was the reduction of the Federal Reserve's holdings of Treasury and agency mortgage-backed securities. The Federal Reserve's total holdings of Treasury securities and agency mortgage-backed securities peaked at $4.24 trillion during the period of quantitative easing (2009–14; see figure 10-7). By acquiring these assets (and taking them off the market), the Federal Reserve raised the price (and lowered interest rates) at these longer maturities. During the interval when these holdings were at or close to their peak (2014–17), it is estimated that they reduced the yields on 10-year Treasury securities by more than a full percentage point.

In June 2017, the FOMC announced a plan to reduce these holdings by allowing them to mature without replacement (FOMC 2017b). According to this plan, initially up to $10 billion per month would be allowed to roll off the balance sheet, and this upper limit would increase—in steps of $10 billion per month—every three months until it would reach $30 billion per month for Treasury securities and $20 billion per month for agency mortgage-backed securities. The plan was initiated in October 2017, with $10 billion per month in securities allowed to mature without replacement. Following the June 2017 plan, this cap on maturation without replacement was increased by further increments of $10 billion per month four times during 2018, until it reached its intended plateau of $50 billion per month in October 2018. By December 2018, these holdings of Treasury and agency securities had fallen to $3.88 trillion.

---

[9] "The Committee judges that some further gradual increases in the target range for the Federal funds rate will be consistent with sustained expansion of economic activity, strong labor market conditions, and inflation near the Committee's symmetric 2 percent objective over the medium term" (Federal Reserve 2016).

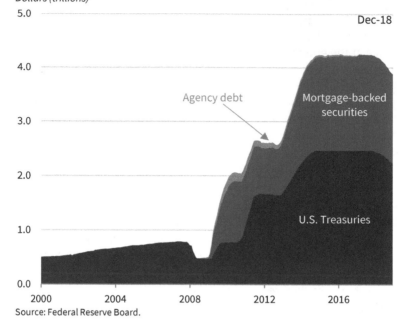

Figure 10-7. The Federal Reserve's Total Assets, 2000–2018

Dollars (trillions)

Dec-18

Agency debt

Mortgage-backed securities

U.S. Treasuries

Source: Federal Reserve Board.

With this pace of asset reduction operating in the background, the FOMC regards changes in the Federal funds rate as its active tool for adjusting the stance of monetary policy.[10]

Productivity

During the postwar period, from 1947:Q1 through 2007:Q4, real output per hour of all persons in the nonfarm business sector grew at a compound annual rate of 2.3 percent. During the current business cycle through 2017:Q4, real output per hour grew at a compound annual rate of just 1.2 percent, or just 1.1 percent since the start of the expansion in 2009:Q3. During the first three quarters of 2018, growth in real output per hour rose to 1.8 percent at a compound annual rate.

As discussed in chapters 1 and 8 of the 2018 *Economic Report of the President*, contributing to this slowdown in labor productivity growth was a declining contribution of capital intensity. Whereas, during the postwar period through 2007, the average contribution of capital intensity to labor productivity growth averaged 0.9 percentage point, during the current cycle through

---

[10] From Jerome Powell's press conference on December 19, 2018: "So, we thought carefully about this on how to normalize policy and came to the view that we would effectively have the balance sheet runoff on automatic pilot and use monetary policy, rate policy, to adjust to incoming data" (Federal Reserve 2018c).

2017:Q4, the contribution declined to just 0.5 percentage point (to 0.0 percentage point during the eight full years after the start of the recovery). In 2014 and 2015, the five-year average contribution of capital deepening to labor productivity growth actually turned negative for the first time in measured history. The 2018 *Economic Report* demonstrated that this was due in large part to an internationally uncompetitive corporate tax rate that deterred domestic capital formation. By lowering the cost of capital, the TCJA was intended to raise demand for capital services, and thus capital's contribution to labor productivity growth. The CEA therefore anticipates that as the economy approaches a higher target capital-to-output ratio in response to the TCJA, the contribution of capital deepening to labor productivity growth will increase.

Inflation

Most measures of wage and price inflation increased during 2018, with the increase from a too-low level to ones roughly compatible with the Federal Reserve's target of 2 percent inflation for the PCE Chain-Type Price Index. (For a discussion of wage inflation, see chapter 3 of this *Report* and CEA 2018b.)

The PCE Price Index increased by 1.8 percent during the 12 months through November 2018 (as shown in figure 10-8). This growth rate was slightly elevated by a 3.9 percent increase in energy prices. Core PCE inflation—which removes volatile components like food and energy prices—was 1.9 percent during the 12 months through November 2018, up from 1.6 percent during 2017. Therefore, relative to the Federal Reserve's target, inflation has increased from a too-low pace to a pace roughly in line with that target. A market-based measure of inflation expectations (the expected five-year CPI inflation rate five years from now) shows that inflation is expected to remain near its current pace of 2.2 percent.

The moderate rate of consumer price inflation during 2018 is close to year-earlier expectations. For example, the December 2017 Blue Chip consensus forecast for CPI inflation was 2.1 percent over the four quarters of 2018 (virtually matching the 2.0 percent realized value at a compound annual rate through 2018:Q3). Though the unemployment rate averaging 3.9 percent in 2018 was a 49-year low, the unemployment rate is just one factor affecting the path of inflation. An important factor holding down inflation has been international competition in the form of low import prices relative to U.S. prices. Nonpetroleum import prices have generally fallen during the past five years relative to U.S. prices.

Financial Markets

During 2018, most U.S. equity indices reached all-time highs in September before falling toward the year end; the yield curve flattened, in part due to

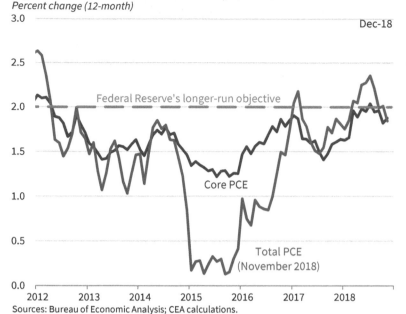

Figure 10-8. Consumer Price Inflation, 2012–18
Percent change (12-month)

Dec-18

Federal Reserve's longer-run objective

Core PCE

Total PCE
(November 2018)

Sources: Bureau of Economic Analysis; CEA calculations.
Note: PCE = Personal Consumption Expenditures Price Index.

asymmetric monetary policy normalization across advanced economies; and credit default spreads rose. Oil prices increased in the first half of the year, but fell substantially in the second half and ended with the December prices of Brent Crude Oil at $57.39 per barrel, down $6.65 from 12 months earlier. In a response to low oil prices, the Organization of the Petroleum Exporting Countries agreed in December—together with Russia—to slice production by 1.2 million barrels per day, with the cuts coming from Saudi Arabia and Russia. The perceived volatility of the financial markets—as measured by the Chicago Board Options Exchange's Market Volatility Index (VIX), which translates prices for stock options into a measure of volatility—more than doubled from December 2017 to December 2018, though for 2018 as a whole, the VIX remained below its long-run postwar average.

Equity Markets

U.S. equity markets fluctuated during 2018, peaking around September before falling in December. From the end of 2017 through its September 2018 peak, the Standard & Poor's 500 index rose 9.6 percent, but subsequent declines cumulated to a net loss of 6.2 percent by year-end 2018. The VIX, which uses the prices of options to uncover investors' expectations of volatility for the S&P 500, more than doubled, from 10.3 on average in December 2017 to 25.0 on average in December 2018 (figure 10-9), to a year-end value of 25.42. This is elevated compared with an average of 17.37 during the current expansion

Figure 10-9. The CBOE's Market Volatility Index, 2018

Percent

Sources: Bloomberg; CEA calculations.
Note: CBOE = Chicago Board Options Exchange.

(VIX levels below 15 are generally considered low), but below levels observed in 2010, 2011, and 2015.

Cryptocurrencies, in particular bitcoin, experienced massive declines in 2018. The price for bitcoin reached an all-time high of nearly $18,700 toward the end of 2017. In 2018, the price plummeted by 74.3 percent to $3,674. Bitcoin experienced numerous blows in 2018 that caused its price to tumble. First, security concerns, regulatory challenges, and a lack of mainstream institutional adoption are key reasons why bitcoin has fallen out of favor with investors. For example, the Securities and Exchange Commission announced in December that it plans to postpone its decision on whether to approve a proposed bitcoin exchange-traded fund until next year (SEC 2018b). Bitcoin competitors—such as Ether, Litecoin, and XRP—have experienced similar declines.

Interest Rates and Credit Spreads

During 2018, short-term yields on Treasury bills and notes (those with a maturity of two years or less) mostly edged higher, following the lead of the Federal Reserve, which raised the Federal funds rate four times, for a cumulative hike of 100 basis points, during the course of the year to the 2.25–2.50 percent range. Similarly, the yield on 10-year Treasury notes increased 28 basis points, to 2.68 percent, during the 12 months of the year, with most of this increase in January

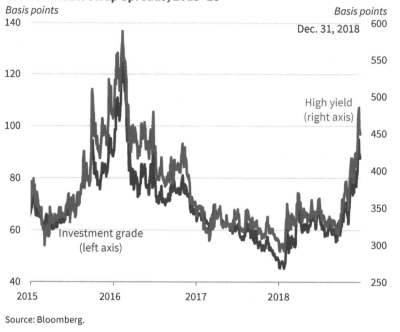

Figure 10-10. North American Investment Grade and High-Yield Credit Defualt Swap Spreads, 2015–18

Basis points

Dec. 31, 2018

High yield (right axis)

Investment grade (left axis)

Source: Bloomberg.

and February 2018. For the first time since 2014, the 10-year yield exceeded 3 percent in October and November 2018 before falling to 2.68 percent during the last week of December.

Market participants' perceptions of bond default risk, which are gauged by credit default swap (CDS) spreads, rose sharply during the year. Credit default swaps pay their purchasers in the event of a default, and are essentially insurance policies on the bond to which they are attached. The increase in this measure of perceived risk was similar to the perceptions of equity-market risk (as indicated by the VIX, discussed above). An aggregate of North American investment-grade CDS spreads rose 38.7 basis points over the year, to their highest levels in more than two years (figure 10-10). Moreover, CDS spreads on high-yield bonds rose 142.8 basis points, also to their highest levels in more than two years.

Meanwhile, consensus forecasts of long-run U.S. interest rates remained unchanged. The long-term forecast for the 10-year Treasury yield by the Blue Chip panel of professional forecasters remained unchanged at 3.7 percent from March to October 2018. Similarly, the market-implied expectation for the 10-year Treasury yield (10 years from now) edged up, from 2.99 percent on the last trading day in December 2017 to 3.28 percent in December 2018, with most of the increase early in 2018.

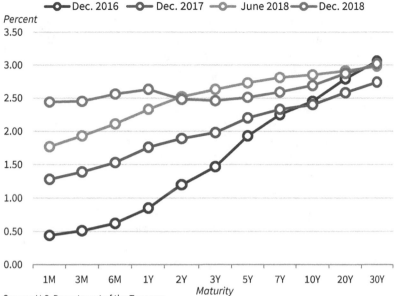

Figure 10-11. U.S. Treasuries' Yield Curve, 2016–18

—○— Dec. 2016   —○— Dec. 2017   —○— June 2018   —○— Dec. 2018

Source: U.S. Department of the Treasury.
Note: December dates represent the last trading day of each respective year. For maturity, M = month and Y = year.

The yield curve for U.S. Treasury notes flattened noticeably during the 12 months of 2018, as yields on short-term debt increased faster than yields on long-term debt (figure 10-11). Normally, yields on longer-term debt are higher because investors' money is locked up over a longer period and thus require more compensation. The 10-year U.S. Treasury yield ended the year at 2.69 percent, 29 basis points above its level at the end of 2017. The spread between 10-year and 2-year Treasury notes narrowed to 19.6 basis points by December 2018. The December figure is below the average of 95 basis points and is at the 19th percentile relative to the 1978–2018 historical distribution.

The yield-curve spread is considered a leading indicator, but two qualifications should be considered. First, at the 19th percentile, it is low but not extremely low. Second, Federal Reserve holdings of long-term debt remain considerable because of asset purchases during the period of quantitative easing. Third, earlier normalization of monetary policy—particularly unconventional monetary policy—in the United States relative to Europe and Japan, combined with high substitutability of advanced-economy sovereign debt, likely placed continued downward pressure on the longer end of the U.S. yield curve through the international portfolio balance channel.

The mortgage rate for 30-year fixed rate contracts was up 68 basis points during 2018, finishing at 4.60 percent. Mortgage rates generally move in parallel with the 10-year Treasury yield, which has increased by 297 basis points over the same time frame. Toward the end of 2018, the 30-year fixed mortgage rate fell along with other interest rates.

Market measures of risk perception increased during 2018. Borrowing costs for BBB-rated companies increased faster than 10-year U.S. Treasury yields in 2018, with the BBB spread over 10-year U.S. Treasuries increasing from 60 basis points at the end of 2017 to 186 basis points at the end of December 2018, roughly matching its average postrecession spread of 185 basis points. Widening corporate credit spreads relative to Treasury notes, consistent with rising CDS spreads for corporate debt over the year, indicate that markets perceived a higher probability of corporate debt defaults at the end of 2018 than at the start of the year. With CDS and BBB spreads rising, corporate bond issuance has tapered from its robust pace in 2017; in 2018, corporate bond issuers issued $1.4 trillion in debt, down from $1.7 trillion in 2017.[11] This decline may in part have been in response to the new cap (established by the TCJA) on interest deductibility, which limits the deduction to no more than 30 percent of earnings before interest, taxes, depreciation, and amortization—commonly called EBITDA—and thereby incentivizes the substitution of equity for debt.

The Global Macroeconomic Situation

Exports are a key contributor to economic growth in the United States, nearly doubling as a share of GDP over the past three decades. As figure 10-12 shows, U.S. export growth tends to rise and fall with foreign GDP.[12] This section provides an overview of the macroeconomic situation among the United States' major trading partners. It also discusses several major ongoing global trends that affect the demand for U.S. products, including (1) the global slump in productivity growth; (2) the puzzlingly low wage growth in the advanced economies, despite strengthening labor markets; and (3) the increasing pockets of financial vulnerability across certain emerging market and developing economies.

Developments in 2018

In contrast to the United States, where real GDP growth exceeded forecasts by the OECD and the International Monetary Fund, growth rates edged lower in the rest of the world in 2018, as can be seen in figure 10-12. Real GDP among major U.S. trading partners grew by 1.9 percent during the four quarters through 2018:Q3, down from 2.4 percent during the year-earlier period, but similar to the 2.0 percent average annual rate of growth during the five

---

[11] This measure was provided by the Securities Industry and Financial Markets Association, and it includes all nonconvertible corporate debt, medium-term notes, and Yankee bonds, but excludes all issues with maturities of one year or less and certificates of deposit.

[12] The CEA calculates trade-weighted global growth as a weighted average of real GDP growth for 25 foreign economies and the euro zone, using these economies' share of U.S. goods exports as weights.

Figure 10-12. Foreign Real GDP and U.S. Real Export Growth, 2000–2018

Percent change (four-quarter)

Trade-weighted foreign real GDP growth

2018:Q3

U.S. real export growth

Sources: Bureau of Economic Analysis; national sources; Haver Analytics; CEA calculations.
Note: Data are through 2018:Q3, because 2018:Q4 data are not yet available for all countries.

preceding years. As estimated by the OECD and the IMF, growth slowed in 2018 in the euro area, China, Japan, and Canada (as shown in the year-over-year growth figures in table 10-2). Growth is expected to slow further in 2019, in the euro area and China.

In part, these slowdowns reflect macroeconomic policies that are becoming less accommodative, particularly through monetary policy normalization, and the continuation of headwinds from trade uncertainty and tighter financial conditions. Upside risks include the harnessing of underutilized capacity in many regions including the European periphery and the BRICS economies—Brazil, Russia, India, China, and South Africa—as well as a global reduction in barriers to trade due to the Administration's trade negotiations. Downside risks include an elevation of global trade barriers, including as might happen from a disorderly exit of the U.K. from the European Union, additional financial market pressures in emerging market economies, persisting financial vulnerabilities from high debt levels abroad, and political uncertainty, particularly in Europe. Fortunately, inflationary pressures remain mild, particularly in light of recent declines in energy prices, and risks of higher or lower inflation appear symmetric.

Labor market conditions are still improving, with the OECD-wide unemployment rate at 5.3 percent in December, only 0.1 percentage point above the

Table 10-2. Year-over-Year Real GDP Growth for Selected Areas and Countries, 2017–19

Share of U.S. trade (2017)	Euro area			China			Japan			Canada			Mexico		
	15.9			13.5			5.4			12.9			11.8		
	2017	2018	2019	2017	2018	2019	2017	2018	2019	2017	2018	2019	2017	2018	2019
IMF	2.4	1.8	1.6	6.9	6.6	6.2	1.9	0.9	1.1	3.0	2.1	1.9	2.1	2.1	2.1
OECD	2.5	1.9	1.8	6.9	6.6	6.3	1.7	0.9	1.0	3.0	2.1	2.2	2.3	2.2	2.5

Sources: Bureau of Economic Analysis; International Monetary Fund (IMF); Organization for Economic Cooperation and Development (OECD).

Note: IMF forecasts are from January 2019, and OECD forecasts are from November 2018.

series low. Business survey data also point to slower growth in the near term in both the advanced and emerging-market economies.

Real GDP growth has been weaker than expected in other advanced economies, especially in Europe, in part reflecting the disruption of production in Germany resulting from new vehicle emission standards and heightened political uncertainty, and Japan, where several natural disasters adversely affected domestic demand and airport traffic in the third quarter of 2018. GDP growth also slowed in China in the fourth quarter, reflecting ongoing deleveraging efforts and softer industrial production, as well as in India.

The euro area. During the four quarters through 2018:Q4, real GDP in the euro area grew by 1.2 percent, a substantial slowing from the 2.7 percent pace during the year-earlier period. Growth in the euro area has been driven by fixed investment, which grew at a 3.2 percent annual rate during the first three quarters of 2018 (detailed 2018:Q4 data were not available at the time of writing).

Recently, the European Central Bank (ECB 2018a) announced that it intends to wind down its monetary stimulus. This past June marked four years since the ECB became the first major central bank to cut one of its benchmark interest rates below zero, and now the ECB is ending its asset purchase program, which has increased its balance sheet by €2.5 trillion. The ECB continued purchasing assets at the rate of €30 billion a month until the end of September 2018. Then, its Governing Council reduced asset purchases to €15 billion per month through December, after which the asset purchase program ended. The ECB (2018b) also announced in December that it will sustain its record-low interest rates until at least the end of the summer of 2019. The deposit rate (for commercial bank reserves held at the central bank) remains at minus 0.40 percent; the main refinancing rate (the interest rate banks pay when borrowing money from the ECB) remains at 0.00 percent; the marginal lending facility rate remains at 0.25 percent. The ECB recently stated that its Governing Council "intends to continue reinvesting, in full, the principal payments from maturing securities purchased under the Asset Purchase Program for an extended period of time past the date when it starts raising the key ECB interest rates, and in any case for as long as necessary to maintain favorable liquidity conditions and an ample degree of monetary accommodation" (ECB 2018b).

After the phasing out of its asset purchases, the ECB will continue holding these assets on its balance sheet, which will reduce euro area interest rates and will assist euro area countries with particularly high public debt burdens to borrow at record low interest rates. That said, phasing out of new purchases implies that the ECB is gaining confidence that the recovery in the euro area will continue to be robust. Signs from Italy and Spain, however, suggest political instability and a Euroskeptic coalition in Italy could bring debt problems.

The overall CPI in the euro area rose by 1.6 percent during the 12 months of 2018, up from the 1.4 percent pace during the year-earlier period, and still below the 2.0 percent cap established by the ECB. Core CPI inflation—which excludes food, energy, alcohol, and tobacco—was 1.0 percent over the same interval, up slightly from a 0.9 percent increase during the year-earlier period.

The dollar value of exports from the 19 EU member countries that use the euro has been slowing. In the 12 months through December, the dollar value of nominal exports of goods from the euro area decreased by 4.0 percent, a deceleration from the 20.6 percent increase during the year-earlier period. The dollar value of nominal imports of goods also decreased (0.2 percent in the 12 months through December), also decelerating from a 22.2 percent increase during the year-earlier.

Japan. During the four quarters through 2018:Q4, Japan's economy was virtually stationary, with real GDP remaining essentially unchanged, down from the 2.4 percent pace during the year-earlier period, and well below the 1.1 percent average annual pace during the preceding seven years.

The long-term growth of Japan's real GDP has been low, handicapped by an aging and declining population, making negative growth more likely. The prime-age (25–54 years) population has fallen at a 0.5 percent annual rate during the past decade. Exports have contributed to Japan's slowdown. During the 12 months of 2018, the dollar value of nominal exports of goods from Japan decreased by 1.7 percent, down from the 15.1 percent increase during the year-earlier period.

The labor market in Japan continues to remain tight. Japan's unemployment rate fell by 0.3 percentage point during the 12 months of 2018 to 2.4 percent in December, the lowest since 1992. Moreover, the ratio of job openings to job applicants averaged 1.61 during 2018, the highest since 1973. When this ratio exceeds 1, it indicates a tight labor market, but Japan has yet to see a sustained increase in nominal wages. Despite the low unemployment rate, consumer prices in Japan rose only 0.2 percent during the 12 months through December, down from the 1.0 percent pace one year earlier. Core inflation,

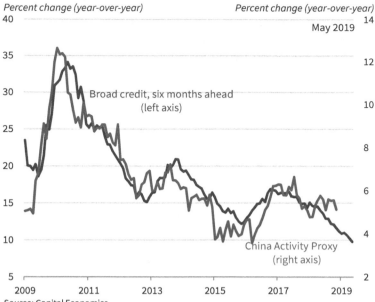

Figure 10-13. China's Broad Credit and Activity Proxy, 2009–19

Percent change (year-over-year)   *Percent change (year-over-year)*

Broad credit, six months ahead
(left axis)

May 2019

China Activity Proxy
(right axis)

Source: Capital Economics.
Note: Capital Economics' China Activity Proxy aggregates (1) tonnage of inland freight shipping; (2) electricity output; (3) floor space under construction; (4) passengers traveling by rail, road, water, and air; and (5) cargo volumes and seaports. Data for the China Activity Proxy are through November 2018.

which excludes fresh food and energy, was 0.3 percent during the 12 months of 2018, unchanged from the year-earlier increase.

Except for the effects of a consumption tax increase in 2014, Japan has experienced low or negative inflation for most of the past 25 years. These low or negative inflation rates have been a chronic problem and present several macroeconomic obstacles. Negative inflation dampens consumer spending and limits monetary policy because it is difficult for the central bank to lower interest rates much below zero. Another issue in Japan remains the country's demographics. Japan has the oldest population in the world, and it is destined to get older. In 2018, individuals age 65 and older accounted for 28.0 percent of Japan's population.

The Bank of Japan has continuously reaffirmed its decision to maintain "extremely low" interest rates, against the tide of other major central banks that are scaling back monetary stimuli. The bank confirmed a negative interest rate of –0.1 percent over the short term. The bank also stated its plans to continue purchases of 10-year Japanese Government Bonds so that yields will float at about zero percent (Bank of Japan 2018). The Bank of Japan released its Tankan survey of manufacturers in December for 2018:Q4, showing a drop of 6 points from 2017:Q4 to a still-strong 19 points, indicating that the percentage of manufacturers showing growth exceeded those that showed declines by 19 points.

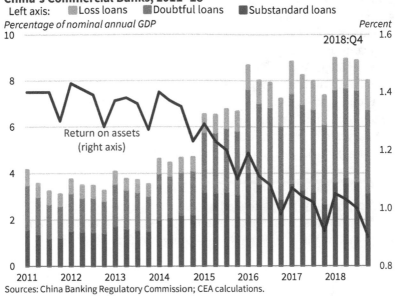

Figure 10-14. Nonperforming Loans and Return on Assets for China's Commercial Banks, 2011–18

Left axis: ▨ Loss loans ▨ Doubtful loans ■ Substandard loans

Percentage of nominal annual GDP   *Percent*

Return on assets (right axis)

2018:Q4

Sources: China Banking Regulatory Commission; CEA calculations.

Figure 10-15. Emerging Market Credit to Nonfinancial Corporations, 2008–18

Percentage of nominal GDP

2018:Q2

China

Emerging market economies

Emerging markets, excluding China

Sources: Bank for International Settlements; national sources; CEA calculations.
Note: Emerging market economies include Argentina, Brazil, Chile, China (including Hong Kong), Hungary, India, Indonesia, Malaysia, Mexico, Poland, Russia, South Africa, South Korea, Thailand, and Turkey.

China. China's official statistics show a slowdown of real GDP to 6.4 percent during the four quarters of 2018, from 6.7 percent during 2017. These official growth rates have been remarkably stable, with every four-quarter growth rate during the past five years in the interval between 6.4 and 7.6 percent. In contrast, an alternate measure of China's economic activity (Capital Economics' China Activity Proxy) shows growth during 2018 at about 5.4 percent, similar to 2017, but down noticeably from rates during the two preceding years. Broad credit growth (which generally foreshadows the China Activity Proxy by six months) has also been decreasing (figure 10-13).

As a share of nominal GDP, China's nonperforming loans have risen in each of the past six years, to an 8.7 percent average during 2018, while the return on total loans has fallen (figure 10-14). In addition, excessive credit may be restraining China's economic growth. The total credit available to nonfinancial corporations has plateaued at about 150 percent of annual GDP (figure 10-15), far in excess of that in other emerging market economies, and well in excess of the roughly 70 percent for the United States.

The Outlook

In accordance with the Employment Act of 1946, an essential component of this annual report is to set forth "current and foreseeable trends in the levels of employment, production, and purchasing power," and a program for carrying out the objective of "creating and maintaining . . . conditions under which there will be afforded useful employment opportunities, including self-employment, for those able, willing, and seeking to work, and to promote maximum employment, production, and purchasing power." Since 1996, execution of this mandate has involved providing an 11-year economic forecast that assumes full enactment and implementation of the Administration's economic agenda.

To better distinguish the effects of legislatively contingent policy objectives from current law projections, we decompose this forecast into a current-law baseline and intermediate and top lines that reflect the estimated growth effects discussed in this *Report* and the 2018 *Economic Report of the President*. To construct our current law baseline, we treat the Tax Cuts and Jobs Act as an unanticipated shock arriving in the fourth quarter of 2017. Adapting the approach of Fernald and others (2017), we then decompose pre-2017:Q4 growth rates into trend, cyclical, and higher-frequency components using Okun's law and a partial linear regression model with a frequency filter to estimate the long-run growth rate.

We then estimate an unrestricted vector autoregressive model on detrended growth rates through 2017:Q3 of real GDP, the unemployment gap, the labor force participation rate, real personal consumption expenditures, and the yield spread of 10-year over 3-month Treasuries. We determine optimal lag length by satisfaction of the Akaike and Hannan-Quinn information criteria. Postestimation and vector autoregressive forecasting, we then add the estimated long-run trend, plus the TCJA's estimated effects. As reported in the 2018 *Economic Report of the President*, these estimated effects reflect the economic effects of the individual and corporate tax cuts, as well as the impact on net exports of reduced profit shifting, for which we assume adjustment lags.

We then construct an intermediate forecast by adding to the current-law baseline the estimated effects of the Administration's infrastructure plan, as reported in the 2018 *Economic Report of the President*, and making the TCJA's individual provisions permanent. Finally, we construct our top-line, full, policy-inclusive forecast by adding to the intermediate forecast the effects of the Administration's labor market and deregulatory agendas, as respectively discussed in chapters 3 and 2 of this *Report*. The top-line forecast constitutes the Administration's official, "Troika" forecast by the Council of Economic Advisers, Office of Management and Budget, and Department of the Treasury.

GDP Growth during the Next Three Years

As illustrated in figure 10-16 and reported in the third column ("Real GDP") of table 10-3, the Administration anticipates economic growth to remain at or above 3.0 percent through 2023, assuming full implementation of the economic agenda detailed in this *Report* and its predecessor. We expect near-term growth to be supported by the continuing effects of the TCJA, discussed in chapter 1, as well as new measures to promote increased labor force participation and deregulatory actions, discussed in chapters 3 and 2, and an infrastructure program, discussed in chapter 4 of the 2018 *Economic Report of the President*, which we assume will commence in 2019 with observable effects on output beginning in 2020.

The Administration also expects the labor market to continue to exhibit strength in the near term, with the civilian unemployment rate remaining below 4.0 percent through 2022, as reported in the sixth column, "Unemployment rate," of table 10-3. Despite low unemployment, inflation is expected to remain low and close to the Federal Reserve's 2.0 percent target for the PCE Price Index. The Administration therefore expects inflation beyond 2018 to remain stable at 2.0 percent through 2021, as shown in the fourth column ("GDP price index") of table 10-3.

GDP Growth over the Longer Term

As discussed in the 2018 *Economic Report of the President* and in chapter 1 of this *Report*, over the longer term, the Administration's current-law baseline forecast is for output growth to moderate as the capital-to-output ratio asymptotically approaches a higher steady-state level in response to business tax reform, and as the near-term effects of the TCJA's individual provisions on the rate of growth dissipate into a permanent level effect. As reflected by our intermediate forecast, we expect the latter moderation to be partially offset in

Table 10-3. The Administration's Economic Forecast, 2017–29

| Year | Percent change (Q4-to-Q4) | | | | | Level (calendar year) | | |
	Nominal GDP	Real GDP (chain-type)	GDP price index (chain-type)	Consumer Price Index	Unemployment rate (percent)	Interest rate, 91-day Treasury bills (percent)	Interest rate, 10-year Treasury notes (percent)
2017 (actual)	4.5	2.5	2.0	2.1	4.4	0.9	2.3
2018	5.3	3.1	2.1	2.3	3.9	1.9	2.9
2019	5.3	3.2	2.0	2.2	3.6	2.7	3.4
2020	5.2	3.1	2.0	2.3	3.6	3.1	3.6
2021	5.1	3.0	2.0	2.3	3.7	3.2	3.8
2022	5.1	3.0	2.0	2.3	3.9	3.2	3.8
2023	5.1	3.0	2.0	2.3	4.0	3.1	3.7
2024	5.1	3.0	2.0	2.3	4.1	3.0	3.7
2025	5.0	2.9	2.0	2.3	4.2	3.0	3.7
2026	4.9	2.8	2.0	2.3	4.2	3.0	3.7
2027	4.9	2.8	2.0	2.3	4.2	3.0	3.7
2028	4.9	2.8	2.0	2.3	4.2	3.0	3.7
2029	4.9	2.8	2.0	2.3	4.2	3.0	3.7

Sources: Bureau of Economic Analysis; Bureau of Labor Statistics; Department of the Treasury; Office of Management and Budget; CEA calculations.
Note: This forecast was based on data available as of November 1, 2018. The interest rate on 91-day Treasury bills is measured on a secondary-market discount basis.

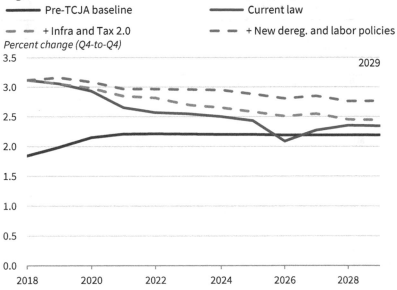

Figure 10-16. Forecast for Growth Rate of Real GDP, 2018-29

Sources: Bureau of Economic Analysis; Bureau of Labor Statistics; Department of the Treasury; Office of Management and Budget; CEA calculations.
Note: This forecast was based on data available as of November 1, 2018.

2026 and 2027 by making permanent the TCJA's individual provisions, which are currently legislated to expire on December 31, 2025. Also reflected in our intermediate forecast is the effect of the Administration's plan for raising investment in public infrastructure—estimates of which were reported in the 2018 *Economic Report*—which, as noted above, we assume commencing in 2019 with observable effects on output beginning in 2020.

The Administration's full policy-inclusive forecast is reported as the top line of figure 10-16. In addition to successful implementation of the President's infrastructure plan and extension of the TCJA's individual provisions, this forecast assumes full achievement of the Administration's agenda with respect to deregulation, as reported in chapter 2, and labor market policies designed to incentivize higher labor force participation, reported in chapter 3. Though we anticipate growth moderating toward the end of the budget window, to 2.8 percent, on average between 2018 and 2029 the policy-inclusive forecast is for output to grow at an annual rate of 3.0 percent. Relative to the current-law baseline, we estimate that full policy implementation would cumulatively raise the level of output by 4.4 percent over the budget window. Reflecting moderating growth in the latter half of the budget window, the Administration expects unemployment to converge to a natural rate of 4.2 percent, consistent with the Federal Open Market Committee's December 2018 "Summary of Economic Projections," which reports a range of participant estimates from 4.0 to 4.6

Table 10-4. Supply-Side Components of Actual and Potential Real Output Growth, 1953–2029

	Component	Growth rate (p.p.)	
		1953:Q2–2018:Q3	2018–2029
1	Civilian noninstitutional population age 16+	1.4	0.9
2	Labor force participation rate	0.1	−0.2
3	Employed share of the labor force	0.0	0.0
4	Ratio of nonfarm business employment to household employment	0.0	0.0
5	Average weekly hours (nonfarm business)	−0.2	0.1
6	Output per hour (productivity, nonfarm business)	2.0	2.6
7	Ratio of real GDO to nonfarm business output	−0.3	−0.5
8	Sum: Actual real GDO[a]	3.0	3.0
	Memo:		
9	Potential real GDO	3.0	3.0
10	Output per worker differential: GDO vs. nonfarm	−0.3	−0.4

[a] Real GDO and real nonfarm business output are measured as the average of income- and product-side measures.

Sources: Bureau of Labor Statistics; Bureau of Economic Analysis; Department of the Treasury; Office of Management and Budget; CEA calculations.

Note: GDO = gross domestic output, which is the average of GDP and gross domestic income. All contributions are in percentage points (p.p.) at an annual rate, with the forecast finalized to November 1, 2018. The total may not add up, due to rounding. The period 1953:Q2 was a business cycle peak; 2018:Q3 is the latest quarter with available data. Population, labor force, and household employment have been adjusted for discontinuities in the population series.

percent, with a median estimate of 4.4 percent (Federal Reserve 2018a). The unemployment rate rising to 4.2 percent is also expected to maintain a rate of inflation at 2.0 percent, as measured by the GDP chained price index (see the fourth column of table 10-3).

As shown in table 10-4, the Administration anticipates that the primary contributor to increased growth through 2029 will be higher output per hour worked. As discussed in chapter 1, despite a modest rise in 2017, U.S. labor productivity growth was disappointing in recent years before the TCJA, owing to a lack of capital deepening. By substantially raising the target capital stock and attracting increased net capital inflows, including investment both by foreign firms and overseas affiliates of U.S. multinational enterprises, we expect enactment of business tax reform to considerably increase capital per worker, and thus labor productivity. Already during the first three quarters of 2018, labor productivity growth in the business sector doubled relative to its pre-TCJA, postrecession average—from 1.0 to 2.0 percent at a compound annual rate. Labor productivity growth in the nonfarm business sector similarly rose, from a 2009:Q3–2017:Q4 average of 1.1 percent to 1.8 percent at a compound annual rate during the first three quarters of 2018. If fully implemented, we also expect the labor market policies articulated in chapters 3 and 9 to partially offset the effects of demographic-related trends in labor force participation, as reflected in line 2 of table 10-4.

Upside and Downside Forecast Risks

As noted in the 2018 *Economic Report of the President*, upside risks to the forecast include higher net capital inflows due to international capital mobility exceeding estimates, which would attenuate the potential crowding out of private fixed investment in response to business tax reform and public infrastructure investment. Second, academic studies demonstrating that individual marginal income tax rates may have differential effects across the age distribution suggest that estimated trends in labor force participation may overstate the growth-detracting effect of demography. Third, insofar as growth estimates presented in this *Report* and its predecessor have been derived from standard neoclassical growth models, they may omit the positive externalities and spillover effects captured by endogenous growth models such as that of Ehrlich, Li, and Liu (2017). Tax reform that incentivizes investment in human capital, regulatory reform that eliminates prohibitive barriers to entry for more innovative and entrepreneurial firms, and health investments and labor market policies that facilitate human capital accumulation may, therefore, yield higher growth dividends than are estimated here.

Because the Administration's forecast is policy-inclusive, a key downside risk is the political contingency of full implementation of the President's economic agenda, particularly in light of the inherent unpredictability of the legislative process. In addition, by definition the policy-inclusive forecast assumes that the Administration's policies will be implemented and remain in place throughout the forecast window. In scenarios where future administrations or Congress partially or fully reverse the TCJA, or otherwise raise taxes, or significantly expand the Federal regulatory state, economic growth would be lower or even negative. Chapter 8 of this *Report*, for example, calculates that the "Medicare for All" bills currently in Congress would reduce real GDP by about 9 percent in the long run if financed by taxes on labor income.

In addition, recent proposals to introduce a top marginal income tax rate of 70 percent on personal income over $10 million would, if enacted, result in lower output and Federal government tax revenue. Using open source software available from the Open Source Policy Center, the CEA estimates that though such a proposal would generate, on a static basis, $210 billion over 10 years, dynamic estimates indicate a net revenue loss. Specifically, assuming an income elasticity of taxable income of –0.135 and a substitution elasticity of taxable income of 0.43 (from Gruber and Saez 2002), and an elasticity of long-term capital gains of –0.79 (from Dowd, McClelland, and Muthitacharoen 2012), the cumulative 10-year change in personal income tax revenue is -$54 billion. Including the effect on payroll tax revenue, the combined cumulative effect is –$66 billion. Assuming an elasticity of GDP with respect to 1 minus the average marginal tax rate of 0.36 (from Barro and Redlick 2011), GDP would decline by 0.2 percent in year one. Because this decline constitutes a permanent level effect, cumulatively over 10 years, nominal economic output would be $531 billion smaller, relative to the CBO's January 2019 10-year GDP projections.

Cyberattacks and cyber thefts constitute additional downside risks that we have attempted to quantify in chapter 7 of this *Report*. A slowing global economy—as projected by the IMF (2019) and OECD (2018)—also poses a near-term downside risk, as more synchronized growth observed in 2017 was succeeded by evident decoupling in 2018. In particular, the deceleration of economic activity and sentiment in China and parts of Europe, along with high public debt levels in several advanced and emerging economies and high corporate debt levels in the United States, may generate economic headwinds.

Conclusion

For the second consecutive year, the U.S. economy outperformed expectations by a substantial margin. In October 2017, the Congressional Budget Office projected that during the four quarters of 2018, real GDP would grow by 2.0 percent, the unemployment rate would decline by 0.1 percentage point to 4.2 percent, and employment growth would average 107,000 jobs per month. In actuality, real GDP grew by 3.2 percent at a compound annual rate through 2018:Q3—virtually in line with the Administration's own forecast for an unprecedented second successive year—the unemployment rate declined by 0.3 percentage point from 2017:Q4 to a 49-year low of 3.8 percent in 2018:Q4, and employment growth averaged 223,000 jobs per month during 2018.

As the chapters that constitute this *Report* demonstrate, 2017 and 2018 were not merely continuations of trends already under way during the postrecession expansion, but rather constituted a distinct break from the previous pace of economic and employment growth after the start of the current expansion in 2009:Q3. In particular, the effects on business expansion and domestic capital formation of deregulatory actions and business tax reform have been substantial. In addition, labor market policies and reductions in effective marginal personal income tax rates have helped to attenuate previous downward trends in labor force participation. Looking ahead, this *Report* recommends further implementation of policies to expand the supply-side potential of the U.S. economy to sustain growth in the years to come.

References

Chapter 1

Abel, A. 1983. "Optimal Investment under Uncertainty." *American Economic Review* 73, no. 1: 228–33.

Alstadsaeter, A., M. Jacob, and R. Michaely. 2017. "Do Dividend Taxes Affect Corporate Investment?" *Journal of Public Economics* 151: 74–83.

Arulampalam, W., M. Devereux, and G. Maffini. 2012. "The Direct Incidence of Corporate Income Tax on Wages." *European Economic Review* 56, no. 6: 1038–54.

Asness, C., T. Hazelkorn, and S. Richardson. 2018. "Buyback Derangement Syndrome." *Journal of Portfolio Management* 44, no. 5: 50–57.

Auerbach, A. 1979. "Wealth Maximization and the Cost of Capital." *Quarterly Journal of Economics* 93, no. 3: 433–46.

Auerbach, A., and K. Hassett. 1992. "Tax Policy and Business Fixed Investment In the United States." *Journal of Public Economics* 47, no. 2: 141–70.

———. 2002. "On the Marginal Source of Investment Funds." *Journal of Public Economics* 87, no. 1: 205–32.

Averett, S., H. Peters, and D. Waldman. 1997. "Tax Credits, Labor Supply, and Child Care." *Review of Economics and Statistics* 79, no. 1: 125–35.

Bar-Ilan, A., and W. Strange. 1996. "Investment Lags." *American Economic Review* 86, no. 3: 610–22.

Barro, R., and J. Furman. 2018. "Macroeconomic Effects of the 2017 Tax Reform." *Brookings Papers on Economic Activity*, Spring, 257–345.

Barro, R., and C. Redlick. 2011. "Macroeconomic Effects from Government Purchases and Taxes." *Quarterly Journal of Economics* 126, no.1: 51–102.

Barth, E., A. Bryson, J. Davis, and R. Freeman. 2016. "It's Where You Work: Increases in Earnings Dispersion across Establishments and Individuals in the U.S." *Journal of Labor Economics* 34, no. S2 (part 2): S67–S97.

BEA (Bureau of Economic Analysis). 2018. "U.S. Direct Investment Abroad (USDIA)." https://www.bea.gov/index.php/help/glossary/us-direct-investment-abroad-usdia.

Bilicka, K., and M. Devereux. 2012. *CBT Corporate Tax Ranking 2012*. Oxford: Oxford University Centre for Business Taxation.

Blanchard, O., and R. Perotti. 2002. "An Empirical Characterization of the Dynamic Effects of Changes in Government Spending and Taxes on Output." *Quarterly Journal of Economics* 117, no. 4: 1329–68.

Blau, D., and P. Robins. 1989. "Fertility, Employment, and Child-Care Costs." *Demography* 26, no. 2: 287–99.

Blouin, J., and L. Krull. 2009. "Bringing It Home: A Study of the Incentives Surrounding the Repatriation of Foreign Earnings under the American Jobs Creation Act of 2004." *Journal of Accounting Research* 47, no. 4: 1027–59.

Bradford, D. 1981. "The Incidence and Allocation Effects of a Tax on Corporate Distributions." *Journal of Public Economics* 15, no.1: 1–22.

Brav, A., J. Graham, C. Harvey, and R. Michaely. 2005. "Payout Policy in the 21st Century." *Journal of Financial Economics* 77, no. 3: 483–527.

Brennan, M., and A. Thakor. 1990. "Shareholder Preferences and Dividend Policy." *Journal of Finance* 45, no. 4: 993–1018.

Business Roundtable. 2018. "Business Roundtable CEO Economic Outlook Index Reaches Highest Level in Survey's 15-Year History." https://www.businessroundtable.org/about-us/ceo-economic-outlook-index/ceo-survey-q1-2018.

Caballero, R. 1991. "On the Sign of the Investment Uncertainty Relationship." *American Economic Review* 81, no. 1: 279–88.

Caballero, R., E. Engel, and J. Haltiwanger. 1995. "Plant-Level Adjustment and Aggregate Investment Dynamics." *Brookings Papers on Economic Activity* 26, no. 2: 1–54.

Caldara, D., and C. Kamps. 2017. "The Analytics of SVARs: A Unified Framework to Measure Fiscal Multipliers." *Review of Economic Studies* 84, no. 3: 1015–40.

Card, D., A. Cardoso, J. Heining, and P. Kline. 2018. "Firms and Labor Market Inequality: Evidence and Some Theory." *Journal of Labor Economics* 36, no. S1: S13–S70.

CEA (Council of Economic Advisers). 2017a. "Corporate Tax Reform and Wages: Theory and Evidence." https://www.whitehouse.gov/sites/whitehouse.gov/files/documents/Tax%20Reform%20and%20Wages.pdf.

———. 2017b. "Evaluating the Anticipated Effects of Changes to the Mortgage Interest Deduction." https://www.whitehouse.gov/sites/whitehouse.gov/files/images/Effects%20of%20Changes%20to%20the%20Mortgage%20Interest%20Deduction%20FINAL.pdf.

———. 2018. "Taxes and Growth." In *Economic Report of the President*. Washington: U.S. Government Publishing Office.

Chetty, R., and E. Saez. 2005. "Dividend Taxes and Corporate Behavior: Evidence from the 2003 Dividend Tax Cut." *Quarterly Journal of Economics* 120, no. 3: 791–833.

Clausing, K. 2018. "Profit Shifting Before and After the Tax Cuts and Jobs Act." Unpublished paper. https://papers.ssrn.com/sol3/papers.cfm?abstract_id=3274827.

Cochrane, J. 2018. "Stock Buybacks Are Proof of Tax Reform's Success." *Wall Street Journal*, March 5. https://www.wsj.com/articles/stock-buybacks-are-proof-of-tax-reforms-success-1520292384.

Cummins, J., and K. Hassett. 1992. "The Effects of Taxation on Investment: New Evidence from Firm Level Panel Data." *National Tax Journal* 45, no. 3: 243–51.

Cummins, J., K. Hassett, and R. Hubbard. 1996. "Tax Reforms and Investment: A Cross-Country Comparison." *Journal of Public Economics* 62, nos. 1–2: 237–73.

Cummins, J., K. Hassett, R. Hubbard, and R. Hall. 1994. "A Reconsideration of Investment Behavior Using Tax Reforms as Natural Experiments." *Brookings Papers on Economic Activity* 25, no. 2: 1–74.

Cummins, J., K. Hassett, and S. Oliner. 2006. "Investment Behavior, Observable Expectations, and Internal Funds." *American Economic Review* 96, no. 3: 796–810.

De Long, J., and L. Summers. 1992. "Macroeconomic Policy and Long-Run Growth." Paper presented at Symposium on Policies for Long-Run Growth, sponsored by Federal Reserve Bank of Kansas City, Jackson Hole, WY, August 27–29. https://www.kansascityfed.org/publicat/sympos/1992/s92long.pdf.

Desai, M., C. Foley, and J. Hines. 2016. "Trade Credit and Taxes." *Review of Economics and Statistics* 98, no. 1: 132–39.

Desai, M., and A. Goolsbee. 2004. "Investment, Overhang, and Tax Policy." *Brookings Papers on Economic Activity*, no. 2: 285–355.

Devereux, M., R. Griffith, and A. Klemm. 2002. "Corporate Income Tax: Reforms and Competition." *Economic Policy* 17, no. 35: 451–95.

Dharmapala, D., C. Foley, and K. Forbes. 2011. "Watch What I Do, Not What I Say: The Unintended Consequences of the Homeland Investment Act." *Journal of Finance* 66, no. 3: 753–87.

Dittmar, A. 2000. "Why Do Firms Repurchase Stock?" *Journal of Business* 73, no. 3: 331–55.

Dittmar, A., and J. Mahrt-Smith. 2007. "Corporate Governance and the Value of Cash Holdings." *Journal of Financial Economics* 83, no. 3: 599–634.

Djankov, S., T. Ganser, C. McLiesh, R. Ramalho, and A. Shleifer. 2010. "The Effect of Corporate Taxes on Investment and Entrepreneurship." *American Economic Journal: Macroeconomics* 2, no. 3: 31–64.

Dwenger, N. 2014. "User Cost of Capital Revisited." *Economica* 81, no. 321: 161–86.

Dyreng, S., and R. Hills. 2018. "Foreign Earnings Repatriations and Domestic Employment." Working paper, Duke University. http://tax.unc.edu/wp-content/uploads/2018/04/Foreign-Earnings-Repatriations-and-Domestic-Employment.pdf.

Eisner, R., and M. Nadiri. 1968. "Investment Behavior and Neo-classical Theory." *Review of Economics and Statistics* 50, no.3: 369–82.

Faulkender, M., and M. Petersen. 2012. "Investment and Capital Constraints: Repatriations under the American Jobs Creation Act." *Review of Financial Studies* 25, no. 11: 3351–88.

Favero, C., and F. Giavazzi. 2012. "Measuring Tax Multipliers: The Narrative Method in Fiscal VARs." *American Economic Journal: Economic Policy* 4, no. 2: 69–94.

Feldman, R. 2002. "Mortgage Rates, Homeownership Rates, and Government-Sponsored Enterprises." *Federal Reserve Bank of Minneapolis: The Region* 16: 5–23.

Fernald, J., R. Hall, J. Stock, and M. Watson. 2017. "The Disappointing Recovery of Output after 2009." Working paper, Brookings Institution. https://www.brookings.edu/wp-content/uploads/2017/08/fernaldtextsp17bpea.pdf.

Fried, J., and C. Wang. 2018. "Are Buybacks Really Shortchanging Investment?" *Harvard Business Review*, March–April, 88–95.

Gale W., H. Gelfond, A. Krupkin, M. Mazur, and E. Toder. 2018. "Effects of the Tax Cuts and Jobs Act: A Preliminary Analysis." Working paper, Tax Policy Center, Urban Institute, and Brookings Institution. https://www.brookings.edu/wp-content/uploads/2018/06/ES_20180608_tcja_summary_paper_final.pdf.

Gale, W., and J. Scholz. 1994. *Intergenerational Transfers and the Accumulation of Wealth*. NBER Working Paper 1827. Cambridge, MA: National Bureau of Economic Research.

Giroud, X., and J. Rauh. 2018. *State Taxation and the Reallocation of Business Activity: Evidence from Establishment-Level Data*. NBER Working Paper 21534. Cambridge, MA: National Bureau of Economic Research.

Goolsbee, A. 1998. "Investment Tax Incentives, Prices, and the Supply of Capital Goods." *Quarterly Journal of Economics* 113, no.1: 121–48.

———. 2000. "The Importance of Measurement Error in the Cost of Capital." *National Tax Journal* 53, no. 2: 215–28.

———. 2004. "Taxes and the Quality of Capital." *Journal of Public Economics* 88, nos. 3–4: 519–43.

Graham, J., M. Hanlon, and T. Shevlin. 2010. "Barriers to Mobility: The Lockout Effect of U.S. Taxation of Worldwide Corporate Profits." *National Tax Journal* 63, no. 4: 1111–44.

Grullon, G., and R. Michaely. 2004. "The Information Content of Share Repurchase Programs." *Journal of Finance* 59, no. 2: 651–80.

Guay, W., and J. Harford. 2000. "The Cash-Flow Permanence and Information Content of Dividend Increases Versus Repurchases." *Journal of Financial Economics* 57, no. 3: 385–415.

Guvenen, F., R. Mataloni, D. Rassier, and K. Ruhl. 2017. *Offshore Profit Shifting and Domestic Productivity Measurement*. NBER Working Paper 23324. Cambridge, MA: National Bureau of Economic Research.

Haan, P., and K. Wrohlich. 2011. "Can Child Care Policy Encourage Employment and Fertility? Evidence from a Structural Model." *Labour Economics* 18, no. 4: 498–512.

Hall, R., and D. Jorgenson. 1967. "Tax Policy and Investment Behavior." *American Economic Review* 57: 391–414.

Hanlon, M., J. Hoopes, and J. Slemrod. 2018. *Tax Reform Made Me Do It!* NBER Working Paper 23324. Cambridge, MA: National Bureau of Economic Research.

Hartman, R. 1972. "The Effects of Price and Cost Uncertainty on Investment." *Journal of Economic Theory* 5, no. 2: 258–66.

Herrick, A. 2018. "Estimates of TCJA Repatriation of Foreign Earnings on Investment and GDP." Issues paper for Penn-Wharton Budget Model. http://budgetmodel. wharton.upenn.edu/issues/2018/8/29/ estimates-of-tcja-repatriation-of-foreign-earnings-on-investment-and-gdp.

Hines, J. 2010. "Treasure Islands." *Journal of Economic Perspectives* 4, no. 24: 103-1–25.

Hines, J., and E. Rice. 1994. "Fiscal Paradise: Foreign Tax Havens and American Business." *Quarterly Journal of Economics* 109, no. 1: 149–82.

Jagannathan, M., C. Stephens, and M. Weisbach. 2000. "Financial Flexibility and the Choice Between Dividends and Stock Repurchases." *Journal of Financial Economics* 57, no. 3: 355–84.

JCT (Joint Committee on Taxation). 2017. "Macroeconomic Analysis of the Conference Agreement for H.R. 1, The 'Tax Cuts and Jobs Act.'" https://www.jct.gov/ publications.html?func=startdown&id=5055.

Jensen, M. 1986. "Agency Costs of Free Cash Flow, Corporate Finance, and Takeovers." *American Economic Review* 76, no. 2: 323–29.

Jorgenson, D. 1963. "Capital Theory and Investment Behavior." *American Economic Review* 53, no. 2: 247–59.

Keane, M., and R. Rogerson. 2012. "Micro and Macro Labor Supply Elasticities: A Reassessment of Conventional Wisdom." *Journal of Economic Literature* 50, no. 2: 464–79.

———. 2015. "Reconciling Micro and Macro Labor Supply Elasticities: A Structural Perspective." *Annual Review of Economics* 7: 89–117.

King, M. 1977. *Public Policy and the Corporation*. London: Chapman & Hall.

Kotlikoff, L., and L. Summers. 1981. "The Role of Intergenerational Transfers in Aggregate Capital Accumulation." *Journal of Political Economy* 89, no. 4: 706–32.

———. 1988. "The Contribution of Intergenerational Transfers to Total Wealth: A Reply." *Journal of Economic Perspectives* 2, no. 2: 41–81.

Krueger, A., and L. Summers. 1986. *Reflections on the Inter-Industry Wage Structure*. NBER Working Paper 1968. Cambridge, MA: National Bureau of Economic Research

———. 1988. "Efficiency Wages and the Inter-industry Wage Structure." *Econometrica* 56, no. 2: 259–93.

Lieberknecht, P., and V. Wieland. 2018. "On the Macroeconomic and Fiscal Effects of the Tax Cuts and Jobs Act." Paper presented at Second Research Conference of Macroeconomic Modelling and Model Comparison Network, Stanford University, Stanford, CA, June 7–8.

Mertens, K. 2018. *The Near Term Growth Impact of the Tax Cuts and Jobs Act*. Research Department Working Paper 1803. Dallas: Federal Reserve Bank of Dallas.

Mertens, K., and J. Montiel Olea. 2018. "Marginal Tax Rates and Income: New Time Series Evidence." *Quarterly Journal of Economics* 133, no. 4: 1803–84.

Mertens, K., and M. Ravn. 2012. "Empirical Evidence on the Aggregate Effects of Anticipated and Unanticipated U.S. Tax Policy Shocks." *American Economic Journal: Economic Policy* 4, no. 2: 145–81.

———. 2013. "The Dynamic Effects of Personal and Corporate Income Tax Changes in the United States." *American Economic Review* 103, no. 4: 1212–47.

———. 2014. "A Reconciliation of SVAR and Narrative Estimates of Tax Multipliers." *Journal of Monetary Economics* 68:1–19.

NAR (National Association of Realtors). 2017. "NAR Statement on Tax Reform." https://www.nar.realtor/nar-statement-on-tax-reform.

National Association of Business Economists. 2018. "Sales Strong, with Costs and Wages Rising in Second Quarter of 2018; NABE Panel Expects Additional Investment and Job Gains." https://nabe.com/NABE/Surveys/Business_Conditions_Surveys/July_2018_Business_Conditions_Survey_Summary.aspx.

Passmore, W., S. Sherlund, and G. Burgess. 2005. "The Effect of Housing Government-Sponsored Enterprises on Mortgage Rates." *Real Estate Economics* 33, no. 3: 427–63. http://citeseerx.ist.psu.edu/viewdoc/download?doi=10.1.1.454.9940&rep=rep1&type=pdf.

Phillips, R., M. Gardner, A. Robins, and M. Surka. 2017. "Offshore Shell Games 2017: The Use of Offshore Tax Havens by *Fortune* 500 Companies." https://uspirg.org/sites/pirg/files/reports/USP%20ShellGames%20Oct17%201.2.pdf.

Pomerleau, K. 2018. "A Hybrid Approach: The Treatment of Foreign Profits under the Tax Cuts and Jobs Act." Tax Foundation. https://taxfoundation.org/treatment-foreign-profits-tax-cuts-jobs-act/.

Poterba, J. 1997. *The Estate Tax and After-Tax Investment Returns.* NBER Working Paper 6337. Cambridge, MA: National Bureau of Economic Research,

Poterba, J., and T. Sinai. 2008. "Tax Expenditures for Owner-Occupied Housing: Deductions for Property Taxes and Mortgage Interest and the Exclusion of Imputed Rental Income." *American Economic Review: Papers and Proceedings* 98, no. 2: 84–89.

PwC (PricewaterhouseCoopers). 2017. "Impact of Tax Reform Options on Owner-Occupied Housing, Prepared for the National Association of Realtors." https://narfocus.com/billdatabase/clientfiles/172/21/2888.pdf.

Redmiles, M. 2008. "The One-Time Received Dividend Deduction." *Statistics of Income Bulletin*, Spring, 102–14.

Romer, C., and D. Romer. 2010. "The Macroeconomic Effects of Tax Changes: Estimates Based on a New Measure of Fiscal Shocks." *American Economic Review* 100, no. 3: 763–801.

Singh, K., and A. Mathur. 2018. *The Impact of GILTI and FDII on the Investment Location Choice of U.S. Multinationals.* Working Paper 2018-05. Washington, DC: American Enterprise Institute.

Smolyansky, M., G. Suarez, and A. Tabova. 2018. *U.S. Corporations' Repatriation of Offshore Profits*. FEDS Note. Washington: Board of Governors of the Federal Reserve System.

Song, J., D. Price, F. Guvenen, N. Bloom, and T. Wachter. 2019. "Firming Up Inequality." *Quarterly Journal of Economics* 134, no. 1: 1–50.

Whittington, L. 1992. "Taxes and the Family: The Impact of the Tax Exemption for Dependents on Marital Fertility." *Demography* 29, no.2: 215–26.

Williamson, J., and S. Bawa. 2018. *Estimated Effects of the Tax Cuts and Jobs Act on Farms and Farm Households*. Economic Research Report 252. U.S. Department of Agriculture, Economic Research Service. Washington: U.S. Government Publishing Office.

Yagan, D. 2015. "Capital Tax Reform and the Real Economy: The Effects of the 2003 Dividend Tax Cut." *American Economic Review* 105, no. 12: 3531–63.

Zion, D., R. Gomatam, and R. Graziano. 2015. "Parking A-Lot Overseas." Credit Suisse Securities Research & Analytics. https://research-doc.credit-suisse.com/docVi ew?language=ENG&format=PDF&source_id=em&document_id=1045617491& serialid=jHde13PmaivwZHRANjglDIKxoEiA4WVARdLQREk1A7g%3d.

Zucman, G., T. Torslov, and L. Wier. 2018. *The Missing Profits of Nations*. NBER Working Paper 24701. Cambridge, MA: National Bureau of Economic Research.

Zwick, E., and J. Mahon. 2017. "Tax Policy and Heterogenous Investment Behavior." *American Economic Review* 107, no. 1: 217–48.

Chapter 2

Aldy, J. 2014. "Learning from Experience: An Assessment of the Retrospective Reviews of Agency Rules and the Evidence for Improving the Design and Implementation of Regulatory Policy." http://nrs.harvard.edu/urn-3:HUL. InstRepos:23936082.

Allcott, H., and M. Greenstone. 2012. "Is There an Energy Efficiency Gap?" *Journal of Economic Perspectives* 26, no. 1: 3–28.

Allcott, H., and C. Knittel. 2019. "Are Consumers Poorly Informed about Fuel Economy? Evidence from Two Experiments." *American Economic Journal: Economic Policy* 11, no. 1: 1–37.

Allcott, H., and D. Taubinsky. 2015. "Evaluating Behaviorally Motivated Policy: Experimental Evidence from the Lightbulb Market." *American Economic Review* 105, no. 8: 2501–38.

Allcott, H., and N. Wozny. 2014. "Gasoline Prices, Fuel Economy, and the Energy Paradox." *Review of Economics and Statistics* 96, no. 5: 779–95.

Ashley, E., C. Nardinelli, and R. Lavaty. 2015. "Estimating the Benefits of Public Health Policies That Reduce Harmful Consumption." *Health Economics* 24: 617–24.

Auerbach, A., and J. Hines Jr. 2002. "Taxation and Economic Efficiency." *Handbook of Public Economics* 3: 1347–21.

Avalere. 2018. "Association Health Plans: Projecting the Impact of the Proposed Rule." Prepared for America's Health Insurance Plans.

Ballard, C., and D. Fullerton. 1992. "Distortionary Taxes and the Provision of Public Goods." *Journal of Economic Perspectives* 6, no. 3: 117–31.

Barkume, A. 2010. "The Structure of Labor Costs with Overtime Work in U.S. Jobs." *Industrial and Labor Relations Review* 64, no. 1: 128–42.

Bauer, D. 2015. "The Misclassification of Independent Contractors: The Fifty-Four-Billion-Dollar Problem." *Rutgers Journal of Law and Public Policy* 12, no. 2: 138–78.

Becker, G., and K. Murphy. 1992. "The Division of Labor, Coordination Costs, and Knowledge." *Quarterly Journal of Economics* 107, no. 4: 1137–60.

Becker, G., K. Murphy, and M. Grossman. 2006. "The Market for Illegal Goods: The Case of Drugs." *Journal of Political Economy* 114, no. 1: 38–60.

Belfield, C., A. Bowden, and V. Rodriguez. 2018. "Evaluating Regulatory Impact Assessments in Education Policy." *American Journal of Evaluation*, 1–19.

BLS (Bureau of Labor Statistics). 2018a. "Independent Contractors Made Up 6.9 Percent of Employment in May 2017." https://www.bls.gov/opub/ted/2018/independent-contractors-made-up-6-point-9-percent-of-employment-in-may-2017.htm.

———. 2018b. "Multifactor Productivity." https://www.bls.gov/mfp/home.htm.

Blumberg, L., M. Buettgens, and R. Wang. 2018. *Updated Estimates of the Potential Impact of Short-Term, Limited Duration Policies*. Washington: Urban Institute.

Borenstein, S., and N. Rose. 2014. "How Airline Markets Work . . . or Do They? Regulatory Reform in the Airline Industry." In *Economic Regulation and Its Reform*, edited by N. Rose. Chicago: University of Chicago Press.

Breyer, S. 1993. *Breaking the Vicious Circle: Toward Effective Risk Regulation*. Cambridge, MA: Harvard University Press.

British Columbia. 2017. "Achieving a Modern Regulatory Environment: B.C.'s Regulatory Reform Initiative." Government of British Columbia. https://www2.gov.bc.ca/assets/gov/government/about-the-bc-government/regulatory-reform/pdfs/5330_regreform_ar_2017_web.pdf.

Broughel, J. 2015. "What the United States Can Learn from the European Commission's Better Regulation Initiative." *European Journal of Risk Regulation* 3: 380–81.

Busse, M., C. Knittel, and F. Zettelmeyer. 2013. "Are Consumers Myopic? Evidence from New and Used Car Purchases." *American Economic Review* 103, no. 1: 220–56.

Carey, M. 2016. "Methods of Estimating the Total Cost of Federal Regulations." https://crsreports.congress.gov/product/pdf/R/R44348.

Caves, R. 1962. *Air Transport and Its Regulators: An Industry Study*. Cambridge, MA: Harvard University Press.

CBO (Congressional Budget Office). 2017. "Federal Subsidies for Health Insurance Coverage for People Under Age 65: 2017 to 2027." https://www.cbo.gov/

system/files/115th-congress-2017-2018/reports/53826-healthinsurancecoverage.pdf.

———. 2018. "Federal Subsidies for Health Insurance Coverage for People Under Age 65: 2018 to 2028." https://www.cbo.gov/system/files/115th-congress-2017-2018/reports/53826-healthinsurancecoverage.pdf.

CCIIO (Center for Consumer Information and Insurance Oversight). 2011. "Essential Health Benefits Bulletin." https://www.cms.gov/CCIIO/Resources/Files/Downloads/essential_health_benefits_bulletin.pdf.

CEA (Council of Economic Advisers). 1970. *Economic Report of the President*. Washington: U.S. Government Printing Office.

———. 1980. *Economic Report of the President*. Washington: U.S. Government Printing Office.

———. 2018. *Economic Report of the President*. Washington: U.S. Government Publishing Office.

———. 2019. "Deregulating Health Insurance Markets: Value to Market Participants." https://www.whitehouse.gov/wp-content/uploads/2019/02/Deregulating-Health-Insurance-Markets-FINAL.pdf.

Cetin, T., and E. Deakin. 2017. "Regulation of Taxis and the Rise of Ridesharing." *Transport Policy*, September, 1–10.

Chetty, R. 2015. "Behavioral Economics and Public Policy: A Pragmatic Perspective." *American Economic Review* 105, no. 5: 1–33.

CMS (Centers for Medicare & Medicaid Services). 2018. "Estimated Financial Effects of the Short-Term, Limited-Duration Policy Proposed Rule." https://www.cms.gov/Research-Statistics-Data-and-Systems/Research/ActuarialStudies/Downloads/STLD20180406.pdf.

Coase, R., 1960. "The Problem of Social Cost." *Journal of Law and Economics* 3: 1–44.

Coglianese, C. 2018. "Improving Regulatory Analysis at Independent Agencies." *American University Law Review* 67: 733–67.

Cohen, P., R. Hahn, J. Hall, S. Levitt, and R. Metcalfe. 2016. *Using Big Data to Estimate Consumer Surplus: The Case of Uber*. NBER Working Paper 22627. Cambridge, MA: National Bureau of Economic Research.

Crafts, N. 2006. "Regulation and Productivity Performance." *Oxford Review of Economic Policy* 22, no. 2: 186–202.

Crain, W., and N. Crain. 2014. *The Cost of Federal Regulation to the U.S. Economy, Manufacturing, and Small Businesses*. Report for the National Association of Manufacturers. https://www.nam.org/Data-and-Reports/Cost-of-Federal-Regulations/Federal-Regulation-Full-Study.pdf.

Crews, C. 2018. "Ten Thousand Commandments: An Annual Snapshot of the Federal Regulatory State." Competitive Enterprise Institute.

Dafny, L., K. Ho, and M. Varela. 2013. "Let Them Have Choice: Gains from Shifting Away from Employer-Sponsored Health Insurance and Toward an Individual Exchange." *American Economic Journal: Economic Policy* 5, no. 1: 32–58.

DeMenno, M. 2017. "Technocracy, Democracy, and Public Policy: An Evaluation of Public Participation in Retrospective Regulatory Review." *Regulation and Governance*, October.

Demski, J. 2008. *Managerial Uses of Accounting Information*. New York: Springer.

DOT (U.S. Department of Transportation). 2018. "Preparing for the Future of Transportation." https://www.transportation.gov/sites/dot.gov/files/docs/policy-initiatives/automated-vehicles/320711/preparing-future-transportation-automated-vehicle-30.pdf.

Dougan, W., and J. Snyder. 1993. "Are Rents Fully Dissipated?" *Public Choice* 77, no. 4: 793–813.

Douglas, G., and J. Miller. 1974. *Economic Regulation of Domestic Air Transport: Theory and Policy*. Washington: Brookings Institution.

Dudley, S., and B. Mannix. 2018. "Improving Regulatory Benefit-Cost Analysis." *Journal of Law & Politics* 34, no. 1: 1–20.

Eisenback, J. 2010. "The Role of Independent Contractors in the U.S. Economy." Navigant Economics.

Elejalde-Ruiz, A. 2016. "Is McDonald's Responsible for Franchise Workers? Labor Law Hearing Set to Begin." *Chicago Tribune*, March 9.

Farrell, J., and C. Shapiro. 1990. "Horizontal Mergers: An Equilibrium Analysis." *American Economic Review* 80, no. 1: 107–26.

FDA (U.S. Food and Drug Administration). 2014. "Food Labeling: Nutrition of Standard Menu Items in Restaurants and Similar Retail Food Establishments." https://www.fda.gov/downloads/AboutFDA/ReportsManualsForms/Reports/EconomicAnalyses/UCM426165.pdf.

Feldstein, M. 1999. "Tax Avoidance and the Deadweight Loss of the Income Tax." *Review of Economics and Statistics* 81, no. 4: 674--680.

Fisher, I. 1930. *The Theory of Interest: As Determined by Impatience to Spend Income and Opportunity to Invest It*. Pacifica, CA: Kelley.

Fraas, A., and R. Morgenstern. 2014. "Identifying the Analytical Implications of Alternative Regulatory Philosophies." *Journal of Benefit-Cost Analysis* 5, no. 1: 137–71.

FRED. 2018. "Professional and Business Services: Temporary Help Services." FRED Economic Data, Federal Reserve Bank of Saint Louis. https://fred.stlouisfed.org/series/temphelpn.

Friedman, M. 1953. "The Effects of Full Employment Policy on Economic Stability: A Formal Analysis." In *Essays in Positive Economics*, edited by M. Friedman. Chicago: University of Chicago Press.

Furchtgott-Roth, D. 2018. "Executive Branch Overreach in Labor Regulation." Manhattan Institute, New York.

GAO (U.S. Government Accountability Office). 2007. "Reexamining Regulations: Opportunities Exist to Improve Effectiveness and Transparency of Retrospective Reviews." https://www.gao.gov/new.items/d07791.pdf.

———. 2014. "Reexamining Regulations: Agencies Often Made Regulatory Changes, but Could Strengthen Linkages to Performance Goals." https://www.gao.gov/products/GAO-14-268.

Garvey, T. 2017. "A Brief Overview of Rulemaking and Judicial Review." https://fas.org/sgp/crs/misc/R41546.pdf.

Gayer, T., and W. Viscusi. 2013. "Overriding Consumer Preferences with Energy Regulations." *Journal of Regulatory Economics* 43, no. 3: 248–64.

———. 2016. "Determining the Proper Scope of Climate Change Policy Benefits in U.S. Regulatory Analyses: Domestic verses Global Approaches." *Review of Environmental Economics and Policy* 10: 245–63.

Gayer, T., R. Litan, and P. Wallach. 2017. "Evaluating the Trump Administration's Regulatory Reform Program." Brookings Institution. https://www.brookings.edu/research/evaluating-the-trump-administrations-regulatory-reform-program/.

Gitis, B. 2017. "The NLRB's New Joint Employer Standard, Unions, and the Franchise Business Model." American Action Forum. https://www.americanactionforum.org/wp-content/uploads/2017/04/Joint-Employer-and-Franchises.pdf.

Glaeser, E. 2006. "Paternalism and Psychology." *University of Chicago Law Review* 73: 133–56.

Goulder, L., and R. Williams III. 2003. "The Substantial Bias from Ignoring General Equilibrium Effects in Estimating Excess Burden, and a Practical Solution." *Journal of Political Economy* 111, no. 4: 898–927.

Government of Canada. 2015. "Annual Report on the Application of the One-for-One Rule: 2014-15." https://www.canada.ca/en/treasury-board-secretariat/services/federal-regulatory-management/annual-report-application-one-for-one-rule-2014-2015.html.

Gray, W. 1987. "The Cost of Regulation: OSHA, EPA and the Productivity Slowdown." *American Economic Review* 77, no. 5: 998–1006.

Greenhouse, S. 2014. "McDonald's Ruling Could Open Door for Unions." *New York Times* July 30.

Hahn, R., and P. Dudley. 2007. "How Well Does the U.S. Government Do Benefit-Cost Analysis?" *Review of Environmental Economics and Policy* 1, no. 2: 192–211.

Hahn, R., and P. Tetlock. 2008. "Has Economic Analysis Improved Regulatory Decisions?" *Journal of Economic Perspectives* 22, no. 1: 67–84.

Hansen, L., and T. Sargent. 2008. *Robustness.* Princeton, N.J.: Princeton University Press.

Harberger, A. 1954. "Monopoly and Resource Allocation." *American Economic Review* 44, no. 2: 77–87.

———. 1964. "Taxation, Resource Allocation, and Welfare." In *The Role of Direct and Indirect Taxes in the Federal Reserve System: A Conference Report of the NBER and the Brookings Institution*, edited by National Bureau of Economic Research. Princeton, NJ: Princeton University Press.

Harrington, W., R. Morgenstern, and P. Nelson. 2000. "On the Accuracy of Regulatory Cost Estimates." *Journal of Policy Analysis and Management* 19, no. 2: 297–322.

Haveman, R., and B. Weisbrod. 1975. "Defining Benefits of Public Programs: Some Guidance for Policy Analysts." *Policy Analysis* 1, no. 1: 169–96.

Hayek, F. 1945. "The Use of Knowledge in Society." *American Economic Review* 35, no. 4: 519–30.

Hazilla, M., and R. Kopp. 1990. "Social Cost of Environmental Quality Regulations: A General Equilibrium Analysis." *Journal of Political Economy* 98, no. 4: 853–73.

Hendrikse, G., and T. Jiang. 2007. "Plural Form in Franchising: An Incomplete Contracting Approach." In *Economics and Management Networks: Franchising, Strategic Alliances, and Cooperatives*, edited by G. Cliquet et al. Heidelberg: Physica-Verlag.

Institute of Medicine. 2009. *Secondhand Smoke Exposure and Cardiovascular Effects: Making Sense of the Evidence*. Report from Institute of Medicine and Committee on Secondhand Smoke Exposure and Acute Coronary Events. Washington: National Academies Press.

Joskow, P., and N. Rose. 1989. "The Effects of Economic Regulation." *Handbook of Industrial Organization* 2: 1450–98.

Kahn, A. 1979. "Applications of Economics to an Imperfect World." *American Economic Review* 69, no. 2: 1–13.

———. 1988. "I Would Do It Again." *Regulation*, no. 2: 22–28.

Karaca-Mandic, P., J. Abraham, and C. Phelps. 2011. "How Do Health Insurance Loading Fees Vary by Group Size? Implications for Healthcare Reform." *International Journal of Healthcare Finance and Economics* 11: 181–207.

Krueger, A., and O. Ashenfelter. 2018. *Theory and Evidence on Employer Collusion in the Franchise Sector*. NBER Working Paper 24831. Cambridge, MA: National Bureau of Economic Research.

Levy, H., E. Norton, and J. Smith. 2018. "Tobacco Regulation and Cost-Benefit Analysis." *American Journal of Health Economics* 4, no. 1: 1–25.

Luna, N. 2018. "McDonald's and NLRB Reach Settlement in Joint-Employer Case." *Nation's Restaurant News*, March 19.

Madrian, B., and D. Shea. 2001. "The Power of Suggestion: Inertia in 401(k) Participation and Savings Behavior." *Quarterly Journal of Economics* 116, no. 4: 1149–87.

Malone, T., and J. Lusk. 2016. "Brewing Up Entrepreneurship: Government Intervention in Beer." *Journal of Entrepreneurship and Public Policy* 5, no. 3: 325–42.

Morgenstern, R. 2018. "Retrospective Analysis of U.S. Federal Environmental Regulation." *Journal of Benefit-Cost Analysis* 9, no. 2: 285–304.

Morrison, R. 2013. "Lester Jones on Beer Taxes." Tax Policy Podcast, Tax Foundation.

Morse, A. 2016. *The Business Impact Target: Cutting the Cost of Regulation*. London: National Audit Office.

Mulligan, C. 2015a. "Misallocations, Substitution, and the Robustness of Activist Public Policy." Manuscript, University of Chicago, January.

———. 2015b. *Side Effects and Complications: The Economic Consequences of Health Care Reform*. Chicago: University of Chicago Press.

Mulligan, C., and K. Tsui. 2016. *The Upside-Down Economics of Regulated and Otherwise Rigid Prices*. NBER Working Paper 22305. Cambridge, MA: National Bureau of Economic Research.

Murray, B., A. Keeler, and W. Thurman. 2005. "Tax Interaction Effects, Environmental Regulation, and 'Rule of Thumb' Adjustments to Social Cost." *Environmental and Resource Economics* 30: 73–92.

NFIB (National Federation of Independent Business). 2001. "The National Small Business Poll."

NHTSA (National Highway Traffic Safety Administration) and EPA (U.S. Environmental Protection Agency). 2018. "The Safer Affordable Fuel-Efficient (SAFE) Vehicles Rule for Model Year 2021–2026 Passenger Cars and Light Trucks." https://www.nhtsa.gov/sites/nhtsa.dot.gov/files/documents/ld-cafe-co2-nhtsa-2127-al76-epa-pria-180823.pdf.

Niskanen, W. 1971. *Bureaucracy and Representative Government*. Chicago: Aldine-Atherton.

NLRB (National Labor Relations Board). 2014. "NLRB Office of the General Counsel Authorizes Complaints Against McDonald's Franchisees and Determines McDonald's, USA, LLC Is a Joint Employer." https://www.nlrb.gov/news-outreach/news-story/nlrb-office-general-counsel-authorizes-complaints-against-mcdonalds.

Norton, S. 2004. "Towards a More General Theory of Franchise Governance." In *Economics and Management of Franchising Networks*, edited by J. Windsperger, G. Cliquet, G. Hendrikse, and M. Tuunanen. Heidelberg: Springer.

OECD (Organization for Economic Cooperation and Development). 2018. "Table I.7: Top Statutory Personal Tax Rate and Top Marginal Tax Rates for Employees." https://stats.oecd.org/index.aspx?DataSetCode=TABLE_I7.

OMB (Office of Management and Budget). 1997. "1997 Report to Congress on the Benefits and Costs of Federal Regulations." https://obamawhitehouse.archives.gov/omb/inforeg_chap2#t1.

———. 2000. "Report to Congress on the Benefits and Costs of Federal Regulations." https://www.whitehouse.gov/sites/whitehouse.gov/files/omb/assets/OMB/inforeg/2000fedreg-report.pdf.

———. 2002. "Stimulating Smarter Regulation: 2002 Report to Congress on the Costs and Benefits of Federal Regulations and Unfunded Mandates on State, Local, and Tribal Entities." https://www.whitehouse.gov/sites/whitehouse.gov/files/omb/assets/OMB/inforeg/2002_report_to_congress.pdf.

———. 2003. "Circular A-4: Regulatory Impact Analysis—A Primer." https://obamawhitehouse.archives.gov/omb/circulars_a004_a-4/.

———. 2005. "Validating Regulatory Analysis: 2005 Report to Congress on the Benefits and Costs of Federal Regulations and Unfunded Mandates on State, Local, and Tribal Entities." https://www.whitehouse.gov/sites/whitehouse.gov/files/omb/assets/OMB/inforeg/2005_cb/final_2005_cb_report.pdf.

———. 2006. "2006 Report to Congress on the Costs and Benefits of Federal Regulations and Unfunded Mandates on State, Local, and Tribal Entities." https://www.whitehouse.gov/sites/whitehouse.gov/files/omb/assets/OMB/inforeg/2006_cb/2006_cb_final_report.pdf.

———. 2013. "2013 Report to Congress on the Benefits and Costs of Federal Regulations and Unfunded Mandates on State, Local, and Tribal Entities." https://www.whitehouse.gov/sites/whitehouse.gov/files/omb/inforeg/inforeg/2013_cb/2013_cost_benefit_report-updated.pdf.

———. 2017a. "Regulatory Reform: Two-for-One Status Report and Regulatory Cost Caps." https://www.reginfo.gov/public/pdf/eo13771/FINAL_TOPLINE_All_20171207.pdf

———. 2017b. "2017 Draft Report to Congress on the Benefits and Costs of Federal Regulations and Agency Compliance with the Unfunded Mandates Reform Act." https://www.whitehouse.gov/wpcontent/uploads/2017/12/draft_2017_cost_benefit_report.pdf.

———. 2018. "Regulatory Reform under Executive Order 13771: Final Accounting for Fiscal Year 2018." https://www.reginfo.gov/public/pdf/eo13771/EO_13771_Final_Accounting_for_Fiscal_Year_2018.pdf.

Phillips, M. 2014. "Amicus Brief of the General Counsel." Case 32-RC-109684, National Labor Relations Board.

Pizer, W., M. Alder, J. Aldy, D. Anthoff, M. Cropper, et al. 2014. "Using and Improving the Social Cost of Carbon." *Science* 346, no. 6214: 1189–90.

Pollitz, K., M. Long, A. Semanskee, and R. Kamal. 2018. *Understanding Short-Term Limited Duration Health Insurance*. San Francisco: Kaiser Family Foundation. http://files.kff.org/attachment/Issue-Brief-Understanding-Short-Term-Limited-Duration-Health-Insurance.

Potter, R. 2017. "Why Trump Can't Undo the Regulatory State So Easily." Brookings Institution.

Rao, P., S. Nowak, and C. Eibner. 2018. "What Is the Impact on Enrollment and Premiums If the Duration of Short-Term Health Insurance Plans Is Increased?" Commonwealth Fund. https://www.commonwealthfund.org/publications/fund-reports/2018/jun/what-impact-enrollment-and-premiums-if-duration-short-term.

Raso, C. 2017. "Assessing Regulatory Retrospective Review under the Obama Administration." Brookings Institution. https://www.brookings.edu/research/assessing-regulatory-retrospective-review-under-the-obama-administration/.

Renda, A. 2017. "One Step Forward, Two Steps Back? The New U.S. Regulatory Budgeting Rules in Light of the International Experience." *Journal of Benefit-Cost Analysis* 8, no. 3: 291–304.

Romer, D. 2011. *Advanced Macroeconomics*. New York: McGraw-Hill.

Rose, N. 2012. "After Airline Deregulation and Alfred E. Kahn." *American Economic Review* 102, no. 3: 376–80.

Rosen, J. 2016. "Putting Regulators on a Budget." https://www.nationalaffairs.com/publications/detail/putting-regulators-on-a-budget.

Rosen, J., and B. Callanan. 2014. "The Regulatory Budget Revisited." *Administrative Law Review* 66, no. 4: 835–60.

Saez, E., J. Slemrod, and S. Giertz. 2012. "The Elasticity of Taxable Income with Respect to Marginal Tax Rates: A Critical Review." *Journal of Economic Literature* 50: 3–50.

Sallee, J., S. West, and W. Fan. 2016. "Do Consumers Recognize the Value of Fuel Economy? Evidence from Used Car Prices and Gasoline Price Fluctuations." *Journal of Public Economics* 135: 61–73.

Stigler, G. 1971. "The Theory of Economic Regulation." *Bell Journal of Economics and Management* Science 2, no. 1: 3–21.

Sunstein, C. 2014. "Opening Keynote Address: The Regulatory Lookback." *Boston University Law Review* 94: 579–602.

———. 2018. *The Cost-Benefit Revolution*. Cambridge, MA: MIT Press.

Thaler, R., and C. Sunstein. 2009. *Nudge: Improving Decisions about Health, Wealth, and Happiness*. New York: Penguin Books.

Tirole, J. 1988. *The Theory of Industrial Organization*. Cambridge, MA: MIT Press.

Trejo, S. 1991. "The Effects of Overtime Pay Regulation on Worker Compensation." *American Economic Review* 81, no. 4: 719–40.

Tullock, G. 1967. "The Welfare Costs of Tariffs, Monopolies and Theft." *Western Economic Journal* 5: 224–32.

U.S. Chamber of Commerce Foundation. 2014a. "Food Truck Nation: U.S. Chamber of Commerce Foundation Food Truck Index." https://www.foodtrucknation.us/wp-content/themes/food-truck-nation/Food-Truck-Nation-Full-Report.pdf.

———. 2014b. "Regulatory Climate Index 2014." https://www.uschamberfoundation.org/sites/default/files/CityReg%20Report_0.pdf.

U.S. Congress. 1985. "H.R. 3128 Consolidated Omnibus Budget Reconciliation Act of 1985." https://www.congress.gov/bill/99th-congress/house-bill/3128.

Weber, C. 2014. "Toward Obtaining a Consistent Estimate of the Elasticity of Taxable Income Using Difference-in-Differences." *Journal of Public Economics* 117: 90–103.

Whinston, M. 2006. *Lectures on Antitrust Economics*. Cambridge, MA: MIT Press.

White House. 1981. "Executive Order 12291 on Federal Regulation." https://www.archives.gov/federal-register/codification/executive-order/12291.html.

———. 2018. "Memorandum of Agreement: Review of Tax Regulations under Executive Order 12866." https://www.whitehouse.gov/wp-content/uploads/2018/04/OIRA-TreasuryMOA_4.11.18.pdf.

Williamson, O. 1968. "Economies as an Antitrust Defense: The Welfare Tradeoffs." *American Economic Review* 58, no. 1: 18–36.

World Bank. 2018. "Doing Business: Rankings & Ease of Doing Business Score— Economy Rankings." www.doingbusiness.org/en/rankings.

Zerbe, R., Jr., and H. McCurdy. 1999. "The Failure of Market Failure." *Journal of Policy Analysis and Management* 18, no. 4: 558–78.

Chapter 3

Akerlof, G. 1970. "The Market for Lemons: Quality Uncertainty and the Market Mechanism." *Quarterly Journal of Economics* 84, no. 3: 488–500.

Aliprantis, D., and M. Schweitzer. 2018. "Opioids and the Labor Market." Federal Reserve Bank of Cleveland. https://www.clevelandfed.org/newsroom-and-events/publications/working-papers/2018-working-papers/wp-1807-opioids-and-the-labor-market.aspx.

Ashenfelter, O., H. Farber, and M. Ransom. 2010. "Labor Market Monopsony." *Journal of Labor Economics* 28, no. 2: 203–10.

Baker, M., J. Gruber, and K. Milligan. 2008. "Universal Child Care, Maternal Labor Supply, and Family Well-Being." *Journal of Political Economy* 116, no. 4: 709–45.

Baughman, R., and S. Dickert-Conlin. 2009. "The Earned Income Tax Credit and Fertility." *Journal of Population Economics* 22, no. 3: 537–63.

Bernstein, J., and K. Hassett. 2015. "Unlocking Private Capital to Facilitate Economic Growth in Distressed Areas." Economic Innovation Group. https://eig.org/wp-content/uploads/2015/04/Unlocking-Private-Capital-to-Facilitate-Growth.pdf.

Bertrand, M., and S. Mullainathan. 2004. "Are Emily and Greg More Employable Than Lakisha and Jamal? A Field Experiment on Labor Market Discrimination." *American Economic Review* 94, no. 4: 991–1013.

Bhuller, M., G. Dahl, K. Løken, and M. Mogstad. 2018. "Incarceration, Recidivism, and Employment." University of California, San Diego. https://econweb.ucsd.edu/~gdahl/papers/incarceration-recidivism-employment.pdf.

Bivens, J., L. Mishel, and J. Schmitt. 2018. "It's Not Just Monopoly and Monopsony: How Market Power Has Affected American Wages." Economic Policy Institute Research Report. https://www.epi.org/publication/its-not-just-monopoly-and-monopsony-how-market-power-has-affected-american-wages.

Blau, D. 2007. "Unintended Consequences of Child Care Regulations." *Labour Economics* 14, no. 3: 513–38.

BLS (U.S. Bureau of Labor Statistics). 2018. "Overview of BLS Statistics on Pay and Benefits." https://www.bls.gov/bls/wages.htm.

Borio, C., E. Kharroubi, C. Upper, and F. Zampolli. 2015. "Labour Reallocation and Productivity Dynamics: Financial Causes, Real Consequences." Working Paper

534. Bank for International Settlements. https://www.bis.org/publ/work534.pdf.

Bound, J., and R. Freeman. 1992. "What Went Wrong? The Erosion of Relative Earnings and Employment among Young Black Men in the 1980s." *Quarterly Journal of Economics* 107, no. 7: 201–32.

Brill, M., C. Holman, C. Morris, R. Raichoudhary, and N. Yosif. 2017. "Understanding the Labor Productivity and Compensation Gap." *Beyond the Numbers: Productivity* (Bureau of Labor Statistics) 6, no. 6. https://www.bls.gov/opub/btn/volume-6/understanding-the-labor-productivity-and-compensation-gap.htm.

Burns, C., and J. Macdonald. 2017. "America's Diverse Family Farms, 2018 Edition." U.S. Department of Agriculture. https://www.ers.usda.gov/webdocs/publications/81408/eib-164.pdf?v=0.

Busso, M., J. Gregory, and P. Kline. 2013. "Assessing the Incidence and Efficiency of a Prominent-Place-Based Policy." *American Economic Review* 103, no. 2: 897–947.

Card, D., J. Kluve, and A. Weber. 2010. "Active Labour Market Policy Evaluations: A Meta-analysis." *Economic Journal* 120, no. 548: F452–77.

Care. 2018. "This Is How Much Child Care Costs in 2018." https://www.care.com/c/stories/2423/how-much-does-child-care-cost.

Carpenter, D., L. Knepper, A. Erickson, and J. Ross. 2012. "License to Work: A National Study of Burdens from Occupational Licensing." https://www.ij.org/images/pdf_folder/economic_liberty/occupational_licensing/licensetowork.pdf.

Carson, E. 2018. "Prisoners in 2016." Bureau of Justice Statistics, Bulletin NCJ251149. https://www.bjs.gov/content/pub/pdf/p16.pdf.

CBO (U.S. Congressional Budget Office). 2018. "The Budget and Economic Outlook: 2018 to 2028."

CEA (Council of Economic Advisers). 2017. "The Underestimated Cost of the Opioid Crisis." https://www.whitehouse.gov/sites/whitehouse.gov/files/images/The%20Underestimated%20Cost%20of%20the%20Opioid%20Crisis.pdf.

———. 2018a. "Addressing America's Reskilling Challenge." https://www.whitehouse.gov/wp-content/uploads/2018/07/Addressing-Americas-Reskilling-Challenge.pdf.

———.2018b. *Economic Report of the President*. Washington: U.S. Government Publishing Office. https://www.whitehouse.gov/wp-content/uploads/2018/02/ERP_2018_Final-FINAL.pdf.

———. 2018c. "How Much are Workers Getting Paid? A Primer on Wage Measurement." https://www.whitehouse.gov/wp-content/uploads/2018/09/How-Much-Are-Workers-Getting-Paid-A-Primer-on-Wage-Measurement-Sept-2018.pdf.

———. 2018d. "Military Spouses in the Labor Market." https://www.whitehouse.gov/wp-content/uploads/2018/05/Military-Spouses-in-the-Labor-Market.pdf.

———.2018e. "Returns on Investments in Recidivism-Reducing Programs." https://www.whitehouse.gov/wp-content/uploads/2018/05/Returns-on-Investments-in-Recidivism-Reducing-Programs.pdf.

CEA, Department of the Treasury, and Department of Labor. 2015. "Occupational Licensing: A Framework for Policymakers." https://obamawhitehouse.archives.gov/sites/default/files/docs/licensing_report_final_nonembargo.pdf.

Charles, K., E. Hurst, and M. Schwartz. 2018. *The Transformation of Manufacturing and the Decline in U.S. Employment*. NBER Working Paper 24468. Cambridge, MA: National Bureau of Economic Research. http://www.nber.org/papers/w24468.pdf.

ChildCare Aware of America. 2018. "The U.S. and the High Cost of Childcare: A Review of Prices and Proposed Solutions for a Broken System." http://usa.childcareaware.org/advocacy-public-policy/resources/research/costofcare.

Couch, K., and R. Fairlie. 2010. "Last Hired, First Fired? Black-White Unemployment and the Business Cycle." *Demography* 47, no. 1: 227–47.

Crump, R., G. Goda, and K. Mumford. 2011. "Fertility and the Personal Exemption: Comment." *American Economic Review* 101, no. 4: 1616–28.

Currie, J., J. Jin, and M. Schnell. 2018. *U.S. Employment and Opioids: Is There a Connection?* NBER Working Paper 24440. Cambridge, MA: National Bureau of Economic Research. https://www.nber.org/papers/w24440.pdf.

Currie, J., and V. Hotz. 2004. "Accidents Will Happen? Unintentional Childhood Injuries and the Effects of Child Care Regulations." *Journal of Health Economics* 23, no. 1: 25–59.

Daly, M., and B. Hobijn. 2017. "Composition and Aggregate Real Wage Growth." *American Economic Review* 107, no. 5: 349–52.

Darity, W., Jr., and P. Mason. 1998. "Evidence on Discrimination in Employment: Codes of Color, Codes of Gender." *Journal of Economic Perspectives* 12, no. 2: 63–90.

Decker, P., and W. Corson. 1995. "International Trade and Worker Displacement: Evaluation of the Trade Adjustment Assistance Program." *Industrial and Labor Relations Review* 48, no. 4: 758–74.

Department of the Treasury and DOD (Department of Defense). 2012. "Supporting Our Military Families: Best Practices for Streamlining Occupational Licensing across State Lines." https://www.treasury.gov/connect/blog/Pages/Supporting-Our-Military-Families.aspx.

Desai, M., C. Foley, and J. Hines Jr. 2007. "Labor and Capital Shares of the Corporate Tax Burden: International Evidence." http://www.people.hbs.edu/ffoley/labcapshr.pdf.

DOD (U.S. Department of Defense). 2016. "2016 Demographics: Profile of the Military Community." http://download.militaryonesource.mil/12038/MOS/Reports/2016-Demographics-Report.pdf.

Economic Innovation Group. 2018. "Opportunity Zones: The Map Comes into Focus." https://eig.org/news/opportunity-zones-map-comes-focus.

Elsby, M., B. Hobijn, and A. Sahin. 2010. "The Labor Market in the Great Recession." Brookings Institution. https://www.brookings.edu/wp-content/uploads/2016/07/2010a_bpea_eslby.pdf.

Federal Reserve Bank of Atlanta. 2018. "Wage Growth Tracker." https://www.frbatlanta.org/chcs/wage-growth-tracker.aspx.

Federal Reserve Board of Governors. 2000. "Monetary Policy Report to the Congress Pursuant to the Full Employment and Balanced Growth Act of 1978." https://www.federalreserve.gov/boarddocs/hh/2000/February/FullReport.pdf.

———. 2018a. "Report on the Economic Well-Being of U.S. Households in 2017." https://www.federalreserve.gov/consumerscommunities/shed.htm.

———. 2018b. "Survey of Household Economics and Decisionmaking." https://www.federalreserve.gov/consumerscommunities/shed.htm.

Felix, A. 2007. "Passing the Burden: Corporate Tax Incidence in Open Economies." Federal Reserve Bank of Kansas City. https://www.kansascityfed.org/Publicat/RegionalRWP/RRWP07-01.pdf.

———. 2009. "Do State Corporate Income Taxes Reduce Wages?" Federal Reserve Bank of Kansas City. https://www.kansascityfed.org/PUBLICAT/ECONREV/PDF/09q2felix.pdf.

Fernald, J. 2015. "Productivity and Potential Output Before, During, and After the Great Recession." *NBER Macroeconomics* 2014, no. 29: 1–51.

Fiore, A., L. Niehem, J. Hurst, J. Son, A. Sadachar, D. Russell, D. Swenson, and C. Seeger. 2015. "Will They Stay or Will They Go? Community Features Important in Migration Decisions of Recent University Graduates." *Economic Development Quarterly* 29, no. 1: 23–37.

Flood, S., M. King, R. Rodgers, S. Ruggles, and R. Warren. 2018. "Integrated Public Use Microdata Series, Current Population Survey: Version 6.0." https://doi.org/10.18128/DO30.V6.0.

Freedman, M. 2012. "Teaching New Markets Old Tricks: The Effects of Subsidized Investment on Low-Income Neighborhoods." *Journal of Public Economics* 2012, no. 96: 1000–1014.

Gelfond, H., and L. Looney. 2018. "Learning from Opportunity Zones: How to Improve Place-Based Policies." Brookings Institution. https://www.brookings.edu/wp-content/uploads/2018/10/Looney_Opportunity-Zones_final.pdf.

Ghertner, R., and L. Groves. 2018."The Opioid Crisis and Economic Opportunity: Geographic and Economic Trends." https://aspe.hhs.gov/system/files/pdf/259261/ASPEEconomicOpportunityOpioidCrisis.pdf.

Gittleman, M., M. Klee, and M. Kleiner. 2018. "Analyzing the Labor Market Outcomes of Occupational Licensing." *Industrial Relations* 57, no. 1: 57–100.

Gittleman, M., and M. Kleiner. 2016. "Wage Effects of Unionization and Occupational Licensing Coverage in the United States." *Industrial and Labor Relations Review* 69, no. 1: 142–72.

Goetz, S., M. Partridge, and H. Stephens. 2018. "The Economic Status of Rural America in the President Trump Era and Beyond." *Applied Economic Perspectives and Policy* 40, no. 1: 97–118.

Goetz, S., and A. Rupasingha. 2009. "Determinants of Growth in Non-Farm Proprietor Densities in the U.S., 1990–2000." *Small Business Economics* 32, no. 4: 425–38.

Gorry, D., and D. Thomas. 2017. "Regulation and the Cost of Childcare." *Journal of Applied Economics* 49, no. 41: 4138–47.

Gramlich, J. 2018. "The Gap Between the Number of Blacks and Whites in Prisons is Shrinking." Pew Research Center. http://www.pewresearch.org/fact-tank/2018/01/12/shrinking-gap-between-number-of-blacks-and-whites-in-prison.

Gurley-Calvez, T., T. Gilbert, K. Harper, D. Marples, and K. Daly. 2009. "Do Tax Incentives Affect Investment? An Analysis of the New Markets Tax Credit." *Public Finance Review* 37, no. 4: 371–98.

Harger, K., and A. Ross. 2016. "Do Capital Tax Incentives Attract New Businesses? Evidence across Industries from the New Markets Tax Credit." *Journal of Regional Science* 56, no. 5: 733–53.

Harris, M., L. Kessler, M. Murray, and M. Glenn. 2018. "Prescription Opioids and Labor Market Pains: The Effect of Schedule II Opioids on Labor Force Participation and Unemployment." http://cber.haslam.utk.edu/staff/harris/Opioids_HKMG.pdf.

Hashimoto, M. 1982. "Minimum Wage Effects on Training on the Job." *American Economic Review* 72, no. 5: 1070–87.

Hassett, K., and A. Mathur. 2006. "Taxes and Wages." American Enterprise Institute. http://pcsi.pa.go.kr/files/20060706_TaxesandWages.pdf.

Havnes, T., and M. Mogstad. 2011. "No Child Left Behind: Subsidized Child Care and Children's Long-Run Outcomes." *American Economic Journal: Economic Policy* 3, no. 2: 97–129.

Hellerstein, J., D. Neumark, and K. Troske. 1999. "Wages, Productivity, and Worker Characteristics: Evidence from Plant-Level Production Functions and Wage Equations." *Journal of Labor Economics* 17, no. 3: 409–46.

Herbst, C. 2017. "Universal Child Care, Maternal Employment, and Children's Long-Run Outcomes: Evidence from the U.S. Lanham Act of 1940." *Journal of Labor Economics* 35, no. 2: 519–64.

Herbst, C., and E. Tekin. 2016. "The Impact of Child-Care Subsidies on Child Development: Evidence from Geographic Variation in the Distance to Social Service Agencies" *Journal of Policy Analysis and Management* 35, no. 1: 94–116.

HHS (Department of Health and Human Services). 2014. "Research Brief #1: Trends in Child Care Center Licensing Regulations and Policies for 2014." Administration for Children and Families, Office of Child Care. https://www.naralicensing.org/assets/docs/ChildCareLicensingStudies/2014CCStudy/center_licensing_trends_brief_2014.pdf.

——— 2015. "Prices Charged in Early Care and Education: Initial Findings from the National Survey of Early Care and Education." https://www.acf.hhs.gov/sites/default/files/opre/es_price_of_care_toopre_041715_2.pdf.

Holzer, H., P. Offner, and E. Sorensen. 2005. "Declining Employment among Young Black Less-Educated Men: The Role of Incarceration and Child Support." *Journal of Policy Analysis and Management* 24, no. 2: 329–50.

Hotz, V., and M. Xiao. 2011. "The Impact of Regulations on the Supply and Quality of Care in Child Care Markets." *American Economic Review* 101, no. 5: 1775–805.

Ilg, R., and S. Haugen. 2000. "Earnings and Employment Trends in the 1990s." *Monthly Labor Review* 123, no. 3: 21–33.

IRS (Internal Revenue Service). 2018. "Internal Revenue Bulletin: 2018–10." https://www.irs.gov/irb/2018-10_IRB#RP-2018-18.

Johnson, J., and M. Kleiner. 2017. "Is Occupational Licensing a Barrier to Interstate Migration" Federal Reserve Bank of Minneapolis. https://www.minneapolisfed.org/research/sr/sr561.pdf.

Juhn, C., and S. Potter. 2006. "Changes in Labor Force Participation in the United States." *Journal of Economic Perspectives* 20, no. 3: 27–46.

Kaplan, G., and S. Schulhofer-Wohl. 2017. "Understanding the Long-Run Decline in Interstate Migration." *International Economic Review* 58, no. 1: 57–94.

Kaye, S. 2010. "The Impact of the 2007–09 Recession on Workers with Disabilities." *Monthly Labor Review* 2010, no. 10: 19–30. https://www.bls.gov/opub/mlr/2010/10/art2full.pdf.

Kim, Y., and P. Orazem. 2016. "Broadband Internet and New Firm Location Decisions in Rural Areas." *American Journal of Agricultural Economics* 99, no. 1: 285–302.

Kleiner, M. 2000. "Occupational Licensing." *Journal of Economic Perspectives* 14, no. 4: 189–202.

Kleiner, M., and A. Krueger. 2010. "The Prevalence and Effects of Occupational Licensing." *British Journal of Industrial Relations* 48, no. 4: 676–87.

Kleiner, M., A. Krueger, and A. Mas. 2011. "A Proposal to Encourage States to Rationalize Occupational Licensing Practices." Brookings Institution. http://www.hhh.umn.edu/file/9441/download.

Kluve, J. 2010. "The Effectiveness of European Active Labor Market Programs." *Labour Economics* 17, no. 6: 904–18.

Knop, B., and A. Mohanty. 2018. "Child Care Costs in the Redesigned Survey of Income and Program Participation (SIPP): A Comparison to the Current Population Survey Annual Social and Economic Supplement (CPS ASEC)." Census Bureau Working Paper 2018–21. https://www.census.gov/library/working-papers/2018/demo/SEHSD-WP2018-21.html.

Krueger, A. 2017. "Where Have All the Workers Gone? An Inquiry into the Decline of the U.S. Labor Force Participation Rate." Brookings Institution. https://www.brookings.edu/wp-content/uploads/2017/09/1_krueger.pdf.

Laird, J., and T. Nielsen. 2016. "The Effects of Physician Prescribing Behaviors on Prescription Drug Use and Labor Supply: Evidence from Movers in Denmark." Harvard University. https://scholar.harvard.edu/files/lairdja/files/Laird_JMP_1.pdf.

LaLumia, S., J. Sallee, and N. Turner. 2015. "New Evidence on Taxes and the Timing of Birth." *American Economic Journal: Economic Policy* 7, no. 2: 258–93.

Leduc, S., and D. Wilson. 2017. "Has the Wage Phillips Curve Gone Dormant?" Federal Reserve Bank of San Francisco. https://www.frbsf.org/economic-research/publications/economic-letter/2017/october/has-wage-phillips-curve-gone-dormant.

Lefebvre, P., and P. Merrigan. 2008. "Child-Care Policy and the Labor Supply of Mothers with Young Children: A Natural Experiment from Canada." *Journal of Labor Economics* 26, no. 3: 519–48.

Lefebvre, P., P. Merrigan., and M. Verstraete. 2009. "Dynamic Labour Supply Effects of Childcare Subsidies: Evidence from a Canadian Natural Experiment on Low-Fee Universal Child Care. *Labour Economics* 16, no. 5: 490–502.

Lerman, R. 2014. "Do Firms Benefit from Apprenticeship?" IZA World of Labor. https://wol.iza.org/articles/do-firms-benefit-from-apprenticeship-investments/long.

Manyika, J., S. Lund, M. Chui, J. Bughin, J. Woetzel, P. Batra, R. Ko, and S. Sanghvi. 2017. "Jobs Lost, Jobs Gained: Workforce Transitions in a Time of Automation." McKinsey Global Institute. https://www.mckinsey.com/featured-insights/future-of-organizations-and-work/jobs-lost-jobs-gained-what-the-future-of-work-will-mean-for-jobs-skills-and-wages.

McClelland, R., and S. Mok. 2012. "A Review of Recent Research on Labor Supply Elasticities." Congressional Budget Office Working Paper 2012–12. https://www.cbo.gov/sites/default/files/cbofiles/attachments/10-25-2012-Recent_Research_on_Labor_Supply_Elasticities.pdf.

Meyer, B. 2002. "Labor Supply at the Extensive and Intensive Margins: The EITC, Welfare, and Hours Worked." *American Economic Review* 92, no. 2: 373–79.

Milligan, K. 2005. "Subsidizing the Stork: New Evidence on Tax Incentives and Fertility." *Review of Economics and Statistics* 87, no. 3: 539–55.

Molloy, R., C. Smith, and A. Wozniak. 2011. "Internal Migration in the United States." *Journal of Economic Perspectives* 25, no. 3: 173–96.

———. 2017. "Job Changing and the Decline in Long Distance Migration in the United States." *Demography* 54, no. 2: 631–53.

Morrissey, T. 2017. "Child Care and Parent Labor Force Participation: A Review of the Research Literature." *Review of Economics of the Household* 15, no. 1: 1–24.

Moss, P., and C. Tilly. 1996. "Soft Skills and Race: An Investigation of Black Men's Employment Problems." *Work and Occupations* 23, no. 23: 252–76.

Muehlemann, S., P. Ryan, and S. Wolter. 2013. "Monopsony Power, Pay Structure, and Training." *ILR Review* 66, no. 5: 1097–114.

National Center on Early Childhood Quality Assurance. 2015. "Increasing Quality in Early Care and Education Programs: Effects on Expenses and Revenues." https://childcareta.acf.hhs.gov/sites/default/files/public/pcqc_increase_quality_final.pdf.

NBER (National Bureau of Economic Research). 2010. "U.S. Business Cycle Expansions and Contractions." https://www.nber.org/cycles.html.

Neal, D., and A. Rick. 2014. *The Prison Boom and the Lack of Black Progress after Smith and Welch*. NBER Working Paper 20283. Cambridge, MA: National Bureau of Economic Research. https://www.nber.org/papers/w20283.

Neal, D., and W. Johnson. 1996. "The Role of Premarket Factors in Black-White Wage Differences." *Journal of Political Economy* 104, no. 5: 869–95.

Neumark, D., and J. Kolko. 2010. "Do Enterprise Zones Create Jobs? Evidence from California's Enterprise Zone Program." *Journal of Urban Economics* 2010, no. 68: 1–19.

Neumark, D., and D. Rothstein. 2005. *Do School-to-Work Programs Help the "Forgotten Half?"* NBER Working Paper 11636. Cambridge, MA: National Bureau of Economic Research. https://www.nber.org/papers/w11636.

Neumark, D., and W. Wascher. 2003. "Minimum Wages and Skill Acquisition: Another Look at Schooling Effects." *Economics of Education Review* 22, no. 1: 1–10.

NFIB (National Federation of Independent Business). 2018a. "October 2018 Report: Small Business Optimism Index." http://www.nfib.com/surveys/small-business-economic-trends/.

———. 2018b. "Small Business Introduction to the Tax Cuts and Jobs Act: Part 1." https://www.nfib.com/assets/TCJA-Survey.pdf.

NIH (National Institutes of Health). 2018. "Overdose Death Rates." https://www.drugabuse.gov/related-topics/trends-statistics/overdose-death-rates.

Nollenberger, N., and N. Rodríguez-Planas. 2015. "Full-Time Universal Childcare in a Context of Low Maternal Employment: Quasi-Experimental Evidence from Spain." *Labour Economics* 2015, no. 36: 124–36.

North Carolina State Board of Dental Examiners v. Federal Trade Commission. 2015. https://www.supremecourt.gov/opinions/14pdf/13-534_19m2.pdf.

OECD (Organization for Economic Cooperation and Development). 2013. "Time for the U.S. to Reskill? What the Survey of Adult Skills Says." https://www.oecd-ilibrary.org/education/time-for-the-u-s-to-reskill_9789264204904-en.

———. 2018a. "OECD Economic Survey of the United States 2018." http://www.oecd.org/eco/surveys/economic-survey-united-states.htm.

———. 2018b. "Putting a Face Behind the Jobs at Risk of Automation." http://www.oecd.org/employment/Automation-policy-brief-2018.pdf.

Oreopoulos, P., M. Page, and A. Stevens. 2008. "The Intergenerational Effect of Worker Displacement." *Journal of Labor Economics* 26, no. 3: 455–83.

Ozimek, A. 2017. "There Is No U.S. Wage Growth Mystery." Moody's Analytics. https://www.economy.com/dismal/analysis/datapoints/296127/There-Is-No-US-Wage-GrowthMystery.

Pager, D., B. Western, and N. Sugie. 2009. "Sequencing Disadvantage: Barriers to Employment Facing Young Black and White Men with Criminal Records." *Annals of the American Academy of Political and Social Science* 623, no. 1: 195–213.

PwC (PricewaterhouseCoopers). 2018. "Will Robots Really Steal Our Jobs? An International Analysis of the Potential Long-Term Impact of Automation." https://www.pwc.com/hu/hu/kiadvanyok/assets/pdf/impact_of_automation_on_jobs.pdf.

Reichert, C., J. Cromartie, and R. Arthun. 2014. "Impacts of Return Migration on Rural U.S. Communities." *Rural Sociology Journal* 79, no. 2: 200–226.

Rinz, K. 2018. "Labor Market Concentration, Earnings Inequality, and Earnings Mobility." Census Bureau Working Paper 2018–10. https://www.census.gov/content/dam/Census/library/working-papers/2018/adrm/carra-wp-2018-10.pdf.

Rupasingha, A., and S. Goetz. 2013. "Self-Employment and Local Economic Performance: Evidence from U.S. Counties." *Papers in Regional Science* 92, no. 1: 141–62.

Schochet, P., R. D'Amico, J. Berk, S. Dolfin, and N. Wozny. 2012. "Estimated Impacts for Participants in the Trade Adjustment Assistance (TAA) Program Under the 2002 Amendments." U.S. Department of Labor. http://wdr.doleta.gov/research/FullText_Documents/ETAOP%5F2013%5F10%5FParticipant%5FImpact%5FReport%2Epdf.

Sentencing Project. 2018. "Trends in U.S. Corrections." https://www.sentencingproject.org/wp-content/uploads/2016/01/Trends-in-US-Corrections.pdf.

Shapiro, C. 1986. "Investment, Moral Hazard, and Occupational Licensing." *Review of Economic Studies* 53, no. 5: 843–62.

Shulman, S. 1987. "Discrimination, Human Capital, and Black-White Unemployment: Evidence from Cities." *Journal of Human Resources* 22, no. 3: 361–76.

Stevens, A., and J. Schaller. 2010. "Short-Run Effects of Parental Job Loss on Children's Academic Achievement." *Economic of Education Review* 30, no. 2: 289–99.

Task Force on Apprenticeship Expansion. 2018. "Final Report to the President of the United States." https://www.dol.gov/apprenticeship/docs/task-force-apprenticeship-expansion-report.pdf.

Tsvetkova, A., M. Partridge, and M. Betz. 2017. "Entrepreneurial and Employment Responses to Economic Conditions across the Rural-Urban Continuum." *Annals of the American Academy of Political and Social Science* 672, no. 1: 83–102.

Twomey, J., and J. Monks. 2011. "Monopsony and Salary Suppression: The Case of Major League Soccer in the United States." *American Economist* 56, no. 1: 20–8.

Urban Institute. 2012. "Net Income Change Calculator." http://nicc.urban.org/netincomecalculator.

USDA (U.S. Department of Agriculture). 2017a. "Manufacturing Is Relatively More Important to the Rural Economy than the Urban Economy." https://www.usda.gov/media/blog/2017/09/12/manufacturing-relatively-more-important-rural-economy-urban-economy.

———2017b. "Report to the President of the United States from the Task Force on Agriculture and Rural Prosperity." https://www.usda.gov/sites/default/files/documents/rural-prosperity-report.pdf.

———. 2017c. "Rural Employment and Unemployment." https://www.ers.usda.gov/topics/rural-economy-population/employment-education/rural-employment-and-unemployment.

———.2017d. "Rural Manufacturing at a Glance." https://www.ers.usda.gov/webdocs/publications/84758/eib-177.pdf?v=0.

———. 2017e. "Urban Areas Offer Higher Earnings for Workers with More Education." https://www.ers.usda.gov/amber-waves/2017/july/urban-areas-offer-higher-earnings-for-workers-with-more-education.

———. 2018a. "Ag and Food Sectors and the Economy." https://www.ers.usda.gov/data-products/ag-and-food-statistics-charting-the-essentials/ag-and-food-sectors-and-the-economy.

———. 2018b. "Farming and Farm Income." https://www.ers.usda.gov/data-products/ag-and-food-statistics-charting-the-essentials/farming-and-farm-income.

———. 2018c. "Rural Education." https://www.ers.usda.gov/topics/rural-economy-population/employment-education/rural-education.

Webber, D. 2015. "Firm Market Power and the Earnings Distribution." *Labour Economics* 2015, no. 35: 123–34.

Weller, C. 2011. "The Black and White Labor Gap in America." Center for American Progress. https://www.americanprogress.org/issues/economy/reports/2011/07/25/9992/the-black-and-white-labor-gap-in-america.

Western, B., and B. Pettit. 2000. "Incarceration and Racial Inequality in Men's Employment." *Industrial and Labor Relations Review* 54, no. 1: 3–16.

———. 2005. "Black-White Wage Inequality, Employment Rates, and Incarceration." *American Journal of Sociology* 111, no. 2: 553–78.

White House. 2017. "Presidential Executive Order on Promoting Agriculture and Rural Prosperity in America." https://www.whitehouse.gov/presidential-actions/presidential-executive-order-promoting-agriculture-rural-prosperity-america.

———. 2018a. "Federal Interagency Council on Crime Prevention and Improving Reentry." https://www.whitehouse.gov/presidential-actions/federal-interagency-council-crime-prevention-improving-reentry.

———. 2018b. "The Opioid Crisis." https://www.whitehouse.gov/opioids.

———. 2018c. "Presidential Executive Order on Streamlining and Expediting Requests to Locate Broadband Facilities in Rural America." https://www.whitehouse.

gov/presidential-actions/
presidential-executive-order-streamlining-expediting-requests-locate-
broadband-facilities-rural-america.

Wilmoth, D. 2017. "The Retreat of the Rural Entrepreneur." U.S. Small Business Administration. https://www.sba.gov/sites/default/files/advocacy/Retreat-Rural-Entrepreneur.pdf.

Wilson, V. 2015. "Black Unemployment Is Significantly Higher Than White Unemployment, Regardless of Educational Attainment." Economic Policy Institute. https://www.epi.org/publication/
black-unemployment-educational-attainment.

Yellen, J. 2016. "Current Conditions and the Outlook for the U.S. Economy." Board of Governors of the Federal Reserve System. https://www.federalreserve.gov/
newsevents/speech/yellen20160606a.htm.

Chapter 4

AAM (Association for Accessible Medicines). 2018. "Generic Drug Access & Savings in the U.S.: Access in Jeopardy." https://accessiblemeds.org/sites/default/
files/2018_aam_generic_drug_access_and_savings_report.pdf.

Acemoglu, D., and J. Linn. 2004. "Market Size in Innovation: Theory and Evidence from the Pharmaceutical Industry." *Quarterly Journal of Economics* 119, no. 3: 1049–90.

Aitken, M., E. Berndt, B. Bosworth, I. Cockburn, R. Frank, M. Kleinrock, and B. Shapiro. 2013. *The Regulation of Prescription Drug Competition and Market Responses: Patterns in Prices and Sales Following Loss of Exclusivity.* NBER Working Paper 19487. Cambridge, MA: National Bureau of Economic Research.

Aitken, M., E. Berndt, and D. Cutler. 2008. "Prescription Drug Spending Trends in the United States: Looking Beyond the Turning Point." *Health Affairs* 28, no. 1: 151–60.

Alpert, B. 2004. "Drug War." *Barrons*, June 14. https://www.barrons.com/articles/
SB108690508847334356.

Andrews, M. 2017. "FDA's Approval of a Cheaper Drug for Hepatitis C Will Likely Expand Treatment." NPR, October 4. http://www.npr.org/sections/health-shots/2017/10/04/555156577/
fdas-approval-of-a-cheaper-drug-for-hepatitis-c-will-likely-expand-treatment.

Arrow, K. 1963. "Uncertainty and the Welfare Economics of Medical Care." *American Economic Review* 53, no. 5: 941–73.

Berndt, E., and M. Aitken. 2011. "Brand Loyalty, Generic Entry and Price Competition in Pharmaceuticals in the Quarter Century after the 1984 Waxman-Hatch Legislation." *International Journal of the Economics of Business* 18, no. 2: 177–201.

Berndt, E., T. McGuire, and J. Newhouse. 2011. "A Primer on the Economics of Prescription Pharmaceutical Pricing in Health Insurance Markets." *Forum for Health Economics & Policy* 14, no. 2.

Blahous, C. 2018a. "The Costs of a National Single-Payer Healthcare System." Mercatus Working Paper. Arlington, VA: Mercatus Center at George Mason University.

———. 2018b. "How Much Would Medicare for All Cut Doctor and Hospital Reimbursements?" https://economics21.org/m4a-reimbursements-blahous.

Blume-Kohout, M., and N. Sood. 2013. "Market Size and Innovation: Effects of Medicare Part D on Pharmaceutical Research and Development." *Journal of Public Economics* 97: 327–36.

Boardman, A., and A. Vining. 1989. "Ownership and Performance in Competitive Environments: A Comparison of the Performance of Private, Mixed, and State-Owned Enterprises." *Journal of Law & Economics* 32, no. 1: 1–33.

Book, R. 2009. "Medicare Administrative Costs Are Higher, Not Lower, Than for Private Insurance." Heritage Foundation. https://www.heritage.org/node/14322/print-display.

Brook, R., E. Keeler, K. Lohr, J. Newhouse, J. Ware, W. Rogers, A. Davies, et al. 2006. "The Health Insurance Experiment: A Classic RAND Study Speaks to the Current Health Care Reform Debate." RAND Health. https://www.rand.org/pubs/research_briefs/RB9174.html.

Busch, F., and P. Houchens. 2018. "The Individual Mandate Repeal: Will It Matter?" Milliman. http://www.milliman.com/insight/2018/The-individual-mandate-repeal-Will-it-matter/.

Buttorff, C., T. Ruder, and M. Bauman. 2017. "Multiple Chronic Conditions in the United States." RAND Corporation. https://www.rand.org/pubs/tools/TL221.html.

Candon, M., S. Zuckerman, D. Wissoker, B. Saloner, G. Kenney, K. Rhodes, and D. Polsky. 2017. "Declining Medicaid Fees and Primary Care Appointment Availability for New Medicaid Patients." *Journal of the American Medical Association* 178, no. 1: 145–46.

Caves, R., M. Whinston, M. Hurwitz, and A. Pakes. 1991. "Patent Expiration, Entry, and Competition in the U.S. Pharmaceutical Industry." *Brookings Papers on Economic Activity: Microeconomics*, no. 1: 1–66. https://www.brookings.edu/wp-content/uploads/1991/01/1991_bpeamicro_caves.pdf.

CBO (U.S. Congressional Budget Office). 2009. "Cost Estimate of Senate Amendment, Patient Protection and Affordable Care Act, to H.R. 3590." https://www.cbo.gov/sites/default/files/111th-congress-2009-2010/costestimate/41423-hr-3590-senate.pdf.

———. 2015. "Budgetary and Economic Effects of Repealing the Affordable Care Act." https://www.cbo.gov/sites/default/files/114th-congress-2015-2016/reports/50252effectsofacarepeal.pdf.

———. 2016. "Private Health Insurance Premiums and Federal Policy." https://www.cbo.gov/sites/default/files/114th-congress-2015-2016/reports/51130-Health_Insurance_Premiums.pdf

———. 2017. "Repealing the Individual Health Insurance Mandate: An Updated Estimate." https://www.cbo.gov/system/files/115th-congress-2017-2018/reports/53300-individualmandate.pdf.

———. 2018. "Federal Subsidies for Health Insurance Coverage for Consumers Under Age 65: 2018 to 2028." https://www.cbo.gov/publication/53826.

CEA (Council of Economic Advisers). 2017. "Understanding Recent Developments in the Individual Health Insurance Market." Council of Economic Advisers Issue Brief. https://obamawhitehouse.archives.gov/sites/default/files/page/files/201701_individual_health_insurance_market_cea_issue_brief.pdf.

———. 2018a. The Administration's FDA Reforms and Reduced Biopharmaceutical Drug Prices. Washington: White House. https://www.whitehouse.gov/wp-content/uploads/2018/10/The-Administrations-FDA-Reforms-and-Reduced-Biopharmaceutical-Drug-Prices.pdf.

———. 2018b. *Economic Report of the President.* Washington: U.S. Government Publishing Office.

———. 2018c. *The Opportunity Costs of Socialism.* Washington: White House. https://www.whitehouse.gov/wp-content/uploads/2018/10/The-Opportunity-Costs-of-Socialism.pdf.

———. 2019. *Deregulating Health Insurance Markets: Value to Market Participants.* Washington: White House. https://www.whitehouse.gov/wp-content/uploads/2019/02/Deregulating-Health-Insurance-Markets-FINAL.pdf.

Chandra, A., A. Finkelstein, A. Sacarny, and C. Syverson. 2016a. "Healthcare Exceptionalism? Productivity and Allocation in the U.S. Healthcare Sector." *American Economic Review* 106, no. 8: 2110–44.

———. 2016b. "Productivity Dispersion in Medicine and Manufacturing." *American Economic Review* 106, no. 5: 99–103.

Chase, D., and J. Arensmeyer. 2018. "The Affordable Care Act's Impact on Small Business." Commonwealth Fund. https://www.commonwealthfund.org/publications/issue-briefs/2018/oct/affordable-care-act-impact-small-business.

Chernew, M., Z. Cooper, E. Larsen-Hallock, and F. Morton. 2018. *Are Health Care Services Shoppable? Evidence from the Consumption of Lower-Limb MRI Scans.* NBER Working Paper 24869. Cambridge, MA: National Bureau of Economic Research.

CIHI (Canadian Institute for Health Information). 2018. "How Canada Compares: Results from the Commonwealth Fund's 2017 International Health Policy Survey of Seniors." https://www.cihi.ca/sites/default/files/document/commonwealth-survey-2017-chartbook-en-rev2-web.pptx.

CMS (Centers for Medicare & Medicaid Services). 2017. "2017 Actuarial Report on the Financial Outlook for Medicaid." https://www.cms.gov/Research-Statistics-Data-and-Systems/Research/ActuarialStudies/Downloads/MedicaidReport2017.pdf.

———. 2018. "Projected Medicare Expenditures under an Illustrative Scenario with Alternative Payment Updates to Medicare Providers." https://www.cms.gov/Research-Statistics-Data-and-Systems/Statistics-Trends-and-Reports/ReportsTrustFunds/Downloads/2018TRAlternativeScenario.pdf

Collins, S., and M. Gunja. 2018 "Premium Tax Credits Are the Individual Market's Stabilizing Force." Commonwealth Fund. https://www.commonwealthfund.org/blog/2018/premium-tax-credits-are-individual-markets-stabilizing-force.

Conrad, R., W. Liu, Z. Tillman, A. So, A. Schick, C. Nardinelli, and R. Lutter. 2018. "Estimating Cost Savings from Generic Drug Approvals in 2017." U.S. Food and Drug Administration. https://www.fda.gov/downloads/Drugs/ResourcesForYou/Consumers/BuyingUsingMedicineSafely/GenericDrugs/UCM609808.pdf.

Cullis, J., P. Jones, and C. Propper. 2000. "Waiting Lists and Medical Treatment: Analysis and Policies." In *Handbook of Health Economics*, vol. 1, edited by A. Culyer and J. Newhouse. Amsterdam: Elsevier.

Cutler, D. 2004. *Your Money or Your Life: Strong Medicine for America's Health Care System*. New York: Oxford University Press.

Cutler, D., and M. McClellan. 2001. "Is Technological Change in Medicine Worth it?" *Health Affairs* 25, no. 5: 11-29.

DeMasi, J. 2000. "Price Trends for Prescription Pharmaceuticals: 1995–1999." Background report prepared for Conference on Pharmaceutical Pricing Practices, Utilization, and Costs, sponsored by U.S. Department of Health and Human Services, Washington, August 8.

Desai, S., L. Hatfield., A. Hicks., M. Chernew, and A. Mehrotra. 2016. "Association between Availability of a Price Transparency Tool and Outpatient Spending." *Journal of the American Medical Association* 315, no. 17: 1874–81.

DiMasi, J., H. Grabowski, and R. Hansen. 2016. "Innovation in the Pharmaceutical Industry: New Estimates of R&D Costs." *Journal of Health Economics* 47: 20–33.

Durlauf, S., and B. Lawrence. 2008. *The New Palgrave Dictionary of Economics*. New York: Palgrave Macmillan.

Eibner, C., and S. Nowak. 2018. "The Effect of Eliminating the Individual Mandate Penalty and the Role of Behavioral Factors." Commonwealth Fund. http://www.commonwealthfund.org/publications/fund-reports/2018/jul/eliminatingindividual-mandate-penalty-behavioral-factors.

Einav, L., A. Finkelstein, and M. Polyakova. 2018. "Private Provision of Social Insurance: Drug-Specific Price Elasticities and Cost Sharing in Medicare Part D." *American Economic Journal: Economic Policy* 10, no. 3: 122–53.

Faber, M., M. Bosch, H. Wollersheim, S. Leatherman, and R. Grol. 2009. "Public Reporting in Health Care: How Do Consumers Use Quality-of-Care Information? A Systematic Review." *Medical Care* 47, no.1: 1-8.

Farmer, C., S. Hosek, and D. Adamson. 2016. "Balancing Demand and Supply for Veterans' Health Care: A Summary of Three RAND Assessments Conducted under the Veterans Choice Act." Rand Health. https://www.rand.org/content/dam/rand/pubs/research_reports/RR1100/RR1165z4/RAND_RR1165z4.pdf.

FDA (U.S. Food and Drug Administration). 2016. "Activities Report of the Generic Drugs Program (FY 2016) Monthly Performance."

———. 2017. "Activities Report of the Generic Drugs Program (FY 2017) Monthly Performance." https://www.fda.gov/Drugs/DevelopmentApprovalProcess/HowDrugsareDevelopedandApproved/ApprovalApplications/AbbreviatedNewDrugApplicationANDAGenerics/ucm584749.htm.

———. 2018a. "Activities Report of the Generic Drugs Program (FY 2018) Monthly Performance." https://www.fda.gov/drugs/developmentapprovalprocess/howdrugsaredevelopedandapproved/approvalapplications/abbreviatednewdrugapplicationandagenerics/ucm375079.htm.

———. 2018b. "Healthy Innovation, Safer Families: FDA's 2018 Strategic Policy Roadmap—Summary of Strategic Policy Areas." https://www.fda.gov/downloads/AboutFDA/ReportsManualsForms/Reports/UCM592001.pdf.

———. 2018c. "USP Therapeutic Categories Model Guidelines." https://www.fda.gov/RegulatoryInformation/LawsEnforcedbyFDA/SignificantAmendmentstotheFDCAct/FoodandDrugAdministrationAmendmentsActof2007/FDAAAImplementationChart/ucm232402.htm.

Feldstein, M. 1999. "Tax Avoidance and the Deadweight Loss of the Income Tax." *Review of Economic and Statistics* 81, no. 4: 674–80.

Finkelstein, A. 2004. "Static and Dynamic Effects of Health Policy: Evidence from the Vaccine Industry." *Quarterly Journal of Economics* 119, no. 2: 527–64.

Finkelstein, A., N. Hendren, and E. Luttmer. 2015. *The Value of Medicaid: Interpreting Results from the Oregon Health Insurance Experiment.* NBER Working Paper 21308. Cambridge, MA: National Bureau of Economic Research.

Finkelstein, A., N. Mahoney, and M. Notowidigdo. 2017. "What Does (Formal) Health Insurance Do, and for Whom?" Working paper, University of Chicago. http://faculty.chicagobooth.edu/neale.mahoney/research/papers/Finkelstein_Mahoney_Noto_AR_2017.pdf.

Frakt, A. 2016. "Price Transparency Is Nice. Just Don't Expect It to Cut Health Costs." *New York Times*, December 19. https://www.nytimes.com/2016/12/19/upshot/price-transparency-is-nice-just-dont-expect-it-to-cut-health-costs.html?module=inline.

Frank, R., and D. Salkever. 1997. "Generic Entry and the Price of Pharmaceuticals." *Journal of Economics and Management Strategy* 6, no. 1: 75–90.

Frost, A., and D. Newman. 2016. "Spending on Shoppable Services in Health Care." Health Cost Institute. https://www.healthcostinstitute.org/images/easyblog_articles/110/Shoppable-Services-IB-3.2.16_0.pdf.

Gaes, G. 2008. "Cost, Performance Studies Look at Prison Privatization." *National Institute of Justice Journal* 259: 32–36.

Gallen, T. 2015. "Using Participant Behavior to Measure the Value of Social Programs: The Case of Medicaid." PhD diss., University of Chicago.

Gallen, T., and C. Mulligan. 2018. "Wedges, Labor Market Behavior, and Health Insurance Coverage under the Affordable Care Act." *National Tax Journal* 71, no. 1: 75–120.

GAO (U.S. Government Accountability Office). 2018. "Veterans Choice Program." https://www.gao.gov/assets/700/692271.pdf.

Garthwaite, C., T. Gross, and M. Notowidigdo. 2018. "Hospitals as Insurers of Last Resort." *American Economic Journal: Applied Economics* 10, no. 1: 1-39.

Ghanta, P. 2013. "List of Countries with Universal Healthcare." https://truecostblog.com/2009/08/09/countries-with-universal-healthcare-by-date/.

Goldman, D., A. Jena, D. Lakdawalla, J. Malin, J. Malkin, and E. Sun. 2010. "The Value of Specialty Oncology Drugs." *Health Services Research* 45, no. 1: 115–32.

Goldman, D., G. Joyce, G. Lawless, W. Crown, and V. Willey. 2006. "Benefit Design and Specialty Drug Use." *Health Affairs* 25, no. 5: 1319–31.

Goulder, L., and R. Williams III. 2003. "The Substantial Bias from Ignoring General Equilibrium Effects in Estimating Excess Burden, and a Practical Solution." *Journal of Political Economy* 111, no. 4898–927. Chicago: University of Chicago Press.

Grabowski, D., D. Lakdawalla, D. Goldman, M. Eber, L. Liu, T. Abdelgawad, A. Kuznik, M. Chernew, and T. Philipson. 2012. "The Large Social Value Resulting from Use of Statins Warrants Steps to Improve Adherence and Broaden Treatment." *Health Affairs* 31, no. 10: 2276–85.

Grabowski, H., and J. Vernon. 1992. "Brand Loyalty, Entry and Price Competition in Pharmaceuticals after the 1984 Drug Act." *Journal of Law and Economics* 35: 331–50.

Gruber, J. 2010. *Health Care Reform Is a "Three-Legged Stool": The Costs of Partially Repealing the Affordable Care Act*. Washington: Center for American Progress.

HHS (U.S. Department of Health and Human Services). 2010. "Expanding the Use of Generic Drugs." Issue Brief, Office of the Assistant Secretary for Planning and Evaluation. https://aspe.hhs.gov/system/files/pdf/76151/ib.pdf.

———. 2018. *Reforming America's Healthcare System Through Choice and Competition*. Published jointly with the Department of the Treasury and the Department of Labor. https://www.hhs.gov/sites/default/files/Reforming-Americas-Healthcare-System-Through-Choice-and-Competition.pdf.

Himmelstein, D. 2014. "A Comparison of Hospital Administrative Costs in Eight Nations: U.S. Costs Exceed All Others by Far." Commonwealth Fund. https://www.commonwealthfund.org/publications/journalarticle/2014/sep/comparison-hospital-administrative-costs-eight-nations-us.

Ho, J., and S. Preston. 2010. "U.S. Mortality in an International Context: Age Variations." *Population and Development Review* 36, no. 4: 749–73.

Hoxby, C. 2014. "Covering the Costs." In *What Lies Ahead for America's Children and Their Schools*, edited by E. Finn and R. Sousa. Stanford, CA: Hoover Institution Press.

Jena, A., and T. Philipson. 2008. "Cost-Effectiveness Analysis and Innovation." *Journal of Health Economics* 27, no. 5: 1224–36.

Kaiser Family Foundation. 2017a. "Health Insurance Coverage of the Total Population." https://www.kff.org/other/state-indicator/total-population/?currentTimefram e=0&sortModel=%7B%22colId%22:%22Location%22,%22sort%22:%22asc%2 2%7D.

———. 2017b. "Medicare Advantage 2017 Spotlight: Enrollment Market Update." https://www.kff.org/medicare/issue-brief/ medicare-advantage-2017-spotlight-enrollment-market-update/

———. 2018. "Data Note: Changes in Enrollment in the Individual Health Insurance Market." https://www.kff.org/health-reform/issue-brief/ data-note-changes-in-enrollment-in-the-individual-health-insurance- market/.

Kessler, G. 2017. "Medicare, Private Insurance and Administrative Costs: A Democratic Talking Point." *Washington Post*, September 19. https://www.washingtonpost. com/news/fact-checker/wp/2017/09/19/medicare-private-insurance-and- administrative-costs-a-democratic-talking-point/?utm_term=.b96f58ff9cc7.

Ketchum, J., C. Lucarelli, and C. Powers. 2015. "Paying Attention or Paying Too Much in Medicare Part D." *American Economic Review* 105, no. 1: 204–33.

Kless, S., C. Wolfe, and C. Curtis. 2017. "Brief Summaries of Medicare & Medicaid." U.S. Department of Health and Human Services. https://www.cms.gov/Research- Statistics-Data-and-Systems/Statistics-Trends-and-Reports/ MedicareProgramRatesStats/Downloads/MedicareMedicaidSummaries2017. pdf.

Lakdawalla, D., D. Goldman, P. Michaud, N. Sood, R. Lempert, Z. Cong, H. de Vries, and I. Gutierrez. 2009. "U.S. Pharmaceutical Policy in a Global Marketplace." *Health Affairs* 28, no. 1: w138–w150.

Lakdawalla, D., and T. Philipson. 2012. "Does Intellectual Property Restrict Output? An Analysis of Pharmaceutical Markets." *Journal of Law and Economics* 55, no. 1: 151–87.

Lee, T. 2004. "'Me Too' Products: Friend or Foe?" *New England Journal of Medicine* 350: 211–12.

Leland, H. 1979. "Quacks, Lemons, and Licensing: A Theory of Minimum Quality Standards." *Journal of Political Economy* 87, no. 6: 1328–46.

Lichtenberg, F., and T. Philipson. 2002. "The Dual Role of Intellectual Property Regulations: Within- and Between-Patent Competition in the U.S. Pharmaceuticals Industry." *Journal of Law and Economics* 45, no. S2: 643–72.

Mossialos, E., M. Wenzl, R. Osborn, and C. Anderson. 2017. "International Profiles of Health Care Systems." Commonwealth Fund. https://www.

commonwealthfund.org/publications/fund-reports/2017/may/
international-profiles-health-care-systems.

Mulligan, C. 2015. *Side Effects and Complications: The Economic Consequences of Health Care Reform*. Chicago: University of Chicago Press.

Mulligan, C., and T. Philipson. 2000. *Merit Motives and Government Intervention: Public Finance in Reverse*. NBER Working Paper 7698. Cambridge, MA: National Bureau of Economic Research.

———. 2004. "Insurance Market Participation under Symmetric Information." Paper presented at American Economic Association Meetings.

Mulligan, C., and K. Tsui. 2016. *The Upside-Down Economics of Regulated and Otherwise Rigid Prices*. NBER Working Paper 22305. Cambridge, MA: National Bureau of Economic Research.

Murrin, S. 2018. "Medicaid Fraud Control Units Fiscal Year 2017 Annual Report." Office of Inspector General, U.S. Department of Health and Human Services.

Newhouse, J. 1993. *Free for All? Lessons from the RAND Health Insurance Experiment*. Cambridge, MA: Harvard University Press.

Nyman, J. 2004. "Is 'Moral Hazard' Inefficient? The Policy Implications of a New Theory." *Health Affairs* 23, no. 5: 194–99.

Pagliarulo, N. 2018. "AbbVie Surprised Investors with Its Hepatitis C Success. Will It Last?" AbbVie, Biopharmadive. https://www.biopharmadive.com/news/abbvies-surprised-investors-mavyret-hepatitis-c-success-will-it-last/529158/.

Pauly, M. 1968. "The Economics of Moral Hazard: Comment." *American Economic Review* 58, no. 3: 531–37.

Pauly, M., A. Leive, and S. Harrington. 2018. "Losses (and Gains) from Health Reform for Non-Medicaid Uninsured." *Journal of Risk and Insurance*, July. https://doi.org/10.1111/jori.12255.

Philipson, T. 2013. "What's Wrong with Private Insurance?" *Forbes*, October 20. https://www.forbes.com/sites/tomasphilipson/2013/10/20/whats-wrong-with-private-insurance/.

Philipson, T., E. Berndt, A. Gottschalk, and E. Sun. 2008. "Cost-Benefit Analysis of the FDA: The Case of the Prescription Drug User Fee Acts." *Journal of Public Economics* 92, nos. 5–6: 1306–25.

Phillipson, T., M. Eber, D. Lakdawalla, M. Corral, R. Conti, and D. Goldman. 2012. "An Analysis of Whether Higher Healthcare Spending in the United States versus Europe Is "Worth it" in the Case of Cancer." *Health Affairs* 31, no. 4: 670–81.

Philipson, T., and A. Jena. 2006. "Who Benefits from New Medical Technologies? Estimates of Consumer and Producer Surpluses for HIV/AIDS Drugs." *Forum for Health Economics & Policy*, (De Gruyter) 9, no. 2: 1–33.

Philipson, T., and E. Sun. 2008. "Is the Food and Drug Administration Safe and Effective?" *Journal of Economic Perspectives* 22, no. 1: 85–102.

Reinhardt, U. 2010. "Health Care, Uncertainty and Morality." *New York Times*, Economix Blog, August 13. https://economix.blogs.nytimes.com/2010/08/13/health-care-uncertainty-and-morality/?mtrref=the60sat50.blogspot.com.

Ringel, J., S. Hosek, B. Vollaard, and S. Mahnovski. 2002. *The Elasticity of Demand for Health Care: A Review of the Literature and Its Application to the Military Health System*. Santa Monica, CA: RAND Corporation. https://www.rand.org/pubs/monograph_reports/MR1355.html.

Robinson, C., T. Brown, and C. Whaley. 2017. "Reference Pricing Changes 'Choice Architecture' of Healthcare for Consumers." *Health Affairs* 36, no. 3: 524–30.

Sacks, D. 2018. "The Health Insurance Marketplaces." *Journal of American Medical Association* 320, no. 6: 549–50.

Saez, E., J. Slemrod, and S. Giertz. 2012. "The Elasticity of Taxable Income with Respect to Marginal Tax Rates: A Critical Review." *Journal of Economic Literature* 50: 3–50.

Sood, N., E. Sun, L. Daugherty, and A. Ghosh. 2008. "How Much Is Too Much? An Analysis of Health Plan Profits and Administrative Costs in California." California HealthCare Foundation. https://www.chcf.org/wp-content/uploads/2017/12/PDF HowMuchIsTooMuchPlanProfits.pdf.

Stigler, G. 1971. "The Theory of Economic Regulation." *Bell Journal of Economics and Management Science* 2, no. 1: 3–21.

Toich, L. 2017. "Will Hepatitis C Virus Medication Costs Drop in the Years Ahead?" *Pharmacy Times*, February 8. http://www.pharmacytimes.com/resource-centers/hepatitisc/will-hepatitis-c-virus-medicaton-costs-drop-in-the-years-ahead.

U.S. Census Bureau. 2017. "Selected Characteristics of the Uninsured in the United States." https://factfinder.census.gov/faces/tableservices/jsf/pages/productview.xhtml?src=bkmk.

U.S. Congress. 1985. "H.R.3128 Consolidated Omnibus Budget Reconciliation Act of 1985." https://www.congress.gov/bill/99th-congress/house-bill/3128.

Walker, J. 2018. "Gilead to Slice List Prices of Liver Drugs." *Wall Street Journal*, September 24. https://www.wsj.com/articles/gilead-to-slice-list-prices-of-liver-drugs-1537818060.

Weber, C. 2014. "Towards Obtaining a Consistent Estimate of the Elasticity of Taxable Income Using Difference-in-Differences." *Journal of Public Economics* 117: 90–103.

Weiner, J., R. Rosenquist, and E. Hartman. 2018. "State Efforts to Close the Health Coverage Gap." https://ldi.upenn.edu/brief/state-efforts-close-health-coverage-gap.

Weisbart, E. 2012. "A Single-Payer System Would Reduce U.S. Health Care Costs." *Virtual Monitor* 14, no. 11: 897–903.

White, C., and M. Eguchi. 2014. "Reference Pricing: A Small Piece of the Health Care Price and Quality Puzzle." NIHCR Research Brief 18, National Institute for

Health Care Reform. https://nihcr.org/analysis/improving-care-delivery/
prevention-improving-health/reference-pricing2/#ib4.

Woodman, J. 2015. *Patients Beyond Borders: Everybody's Guide to Affordable, World-Class Medical Travel*. Chapel Hill, NC: Healthy Travel Media.

Woolhandler, S., T. Campbell, and D. Himmelstein. 2003. "Costs of Health Care Administration in the United States and Canada." *New England Journal of Medicine* 349, no. 8: 768–75.

Yin, W. 2008. "Market Incentives and Pharmaceutical Innovation." *Journal of Health Economics* 27, no. 4: 1060–77.

Zeckhauser, R. 1970. "Medical Insurance: A Case Study of the Trade-Off Between Risk Spreading and Appropriate Incentives." *Journal of Economic Theory* 2, no. 1: 10–26.

Zerbe, R., and H. McCurdy. 1999. "The Failure of Market Failure." *Journal of Policy Analysis and Management* 18, no. 4: 558–78.

Chapter 5

Adamson, S. 2018. "Comparing Interstate Regulation and Investment in U.S. Gas and Electric Transmission." *Economics of Energy and Environmental Policy* 7, no. 1: 7–24.

Adelman, M. 1996. *Genie Out of the Bottle: World Oil Markets since 1970*. Cambridge, MA: MIT Press.

Alchian, A., and W. Allen. 1964. *University Economics*. Belmont, CA: Wadsworth.

Alyeska Pipeline Service Company. 2011. "Low Flow Impact Study." https://www.alyeska-pipe.com/assets/uploads/pagestructure/TAPS_Operations_LowFlow/editor_uploads/LoFIS_Summary_Report_P6%2027_FullReport.pdf.

AOGHS (American Oil & Gas Historical Society). 2018. "Trans-Alaska Pipeline History." https://aoghs.org/transportation/trans-alaska-pipeline/

Argueta, C., L. Hanson, and C. Vincent. 2017. "Federal Land Ownership: Overview and Data." Congressional Research Service. https://fas.org/sgp/crs/misc/R42346.pdf

Bahndari, N., N. Mehta, V. Joshi, P. Creuset, and T. Chen. 2018. "The IMO 2020: Global Shipping's Blue Sky Moment." Goldman Sachs Equity Research, May 30. http://www.weltinnenpolitik.net/wp-content/uploads/2018/06/IMO-2020-Global-Shipping-Blue-Sky-Moment.pdf.

Bakhtiari, A. 2004. "World Oil Production Capacity Model Suggests Output Peak by 2006–07." *Oil & Gas Journal*, April 26, 18–19.

Balash, P., K. Kern, J. Brewer, J. Adder, C. Nichols, G. Pickpaugh, and E. Shuster. 2018. "Reliability, Resilience and the Oncoming Wave of Retiring Baseload Units." *DOE National Energy Technology Laboratory* 1, March 13. https://www.districtenergy.org/HigherLogic/System/DownloadDocumentFile.ashx?DocumentFileKey=246e582e-81b7-cc50-c9c5-50031845aca0&forceDialog=0.

Barsky, R., and L. Kilian. 2002. "Do We Really Know That Oil Caused the Great Stagflation? A Monetary Alternative." *NBER Macroeconomics Annual* 16: 137–83.

Baumeister, C., and G. Peersman. 2013. "Time-Varying Effects of Oil Supply Shocks on the U.S. Economy." *American Economic Review: Macroeconomics* 5, no. 4: 1–28.

Bentley, R. 2002. "Global Oil & Gas Depletion: An Overview." *Energy Policy* 30: 189–205. http://www.oilcrisis.com/bentley/depletionoverview.pdf.

BLM (Bureau of Land Management). 2017. "Federal Coal Program Programmatic Environmental Impact Statement (PEIS): Scoping Report Appendices." U.S. Department of the Interior. https://www.eenews.net/assets/2017/01/11/document_gw_03.pdf.

Borenstein, S., J. Bushnell, and F. Wolak. 2002. "Measuring Market Inefficiencies in California's Restructured Wholesale Electricity Market." *American Economic Review* 92, no. 5: 1376–1405.

Borenstein, S., and R. Kellogg. 2014. "The Incidence of an Oil Glut: Who Benefits from Cheap Crude Oil in the Midwest?" *Energy Journal* 35, no. 1: 15–33.

Boslett, A., T. Guilfoos, and C. Lang. 2015. "Valuation of Expectations: A Hedonic Study of Shale Gas Development and New York's Moratorium." *Journal of Environmental Economics and Management* 77: 14–30.

Boyce, J. 2013. "Prediction and Inference in the Hubbert-Deffeyes Peak Oil Model." *Energy Journal* 34, no. 2: 91–144.

BP. 2018. *BP Statistical Review of World Energy.* London: BP. https://www.bp.com/content/dam/bp/business-sites/en/global/corporate/pdfs/energy-economics/statistical-review/bp-stats-review-2018-full-report.pdf.

Brown, S., and H. Huntington. 2015. "Evaluating U.S. Oil Security and Import Reliance." *Energy Policy* 79: 5–22.

Burtraw, D., and S. Szambelan. 2009. "U.S. Emissions Trading Markets for SO_2 and NO_x." RFF Discussion Paper 09-40. Resources for the Future, Washington.

Bushnell, J., and K. Novan. 2018. *Setting with the Sun: The Impacts of Renewable Energy on Wholesale Power Markets.* NBER Working Paper 24980. Cambridge, MA: National Bureau of Economic Research.

Busse, M., and N. Keohane. 2007. "Market Effects of Environmental Regulation: Coal, Railroads, and the 1990 Clean Air Act." *RAND Journal of Economics* 38, no. 4: 1159–79.

Campbell, C. 2003. "Industry Urged to Watch for Regular Oil Production Peaks, Depletion Signals." *Oil & Gas Journal*, July 14, 38–47.

Carlson, C., D. Burtraw, M. Cropper, and K. Palmer. 2000. "Sulfur Dioxide Control by Electric Utilities: What Are the Gains from Trade?" *Journal of Political Economy* 108, no. 6: 1292–1326.

CEA (Council of Economic Advisers). 2006. *Economic Report of the President.* Washington: U.S. Government Publishing Office.

———. 2012. *Economic Report of the President*. Washington: U.S. Government Publishing Office.

———. 2013. *Economic Report of the President*. Washington: U.S. Government Publishing Office.

———. 2015. *Economic Report of the President*. Washington: U.S. Government Publishing Office.

———. 2016a. *Economic Report of the President*. Washington: U.S. Government Publishing Office.

———. 2016b. "The Economics of Mineral Leasing on Federal Lands: Ensuring a Fair Return to Taxpayers." https://obamawhitehouse.archives.gov/sites/default/files/page/files/20160622_cea_coal_leasing.pdf.

———. 2017. *Economic Report of the President*. Washington: U.S. Government Publishing Office.

Cosgrove, B., D. LaFave, S. Dissanayake, and M. Donihue. 2015. "The Economic Impact of Shale Gas Development: A Natural Experiment along the New York/Pennsylvania Border." *Agricultural and Resource Economics Review* 44, no. 2: 20–39.

Covert, T., and R. Kellogg. 2017. *Crude by Rail, Option Value, and Pipeline Investment*. NBER Working Paper 23855. Cambridge, MA: National Bureau of Economic Research.

Cullen, J., 2013. "Measuring the Environmental Benefits of Wind-Generated Electricity." *American Economic Journal: Economic Policy* 5, no. 4: 107–33.

Davis, L., and C. Hausman. 2016. "Market Impacts of a Nuclear Power Plant Closure." *American Economic Journal: Applied Economics* 8, no. 2: 92–122.

Davis, L., and C. Wolfram. 2012. "Deregulation, Consolidation, and Efficiency: Evidence from U.S. Nuclear Power." *American Economic Journal: Applied Economics* 4, no. 4: 194–225.

Deffeyes, K. 2001. *Hubbert's Peak: The Impending World Oil Shortage*. Princeton, NJ: Princeton University Press.

———. 2006. *Beyond Oil: The View from Hubbert's Peak*. New York: Hill & Wang.

Deutch, J. 2011. "The Good News About Gas: The Natural Gas Revolution and Its Consequences." *Foreign Affairs* 90, no. 1: 82–93.

EIA (U.S. Energy Information Administration). 2006. *Annual Energy Outlook 2006 with Projections to 2030*. https://www.eia.gov/outlooks/archive/aeo06/aeoref_tab.html.

———. 2010. *Annual Energy Outlook 2010 with Projections to 2030*. https://www.eia.gov/outlooks/archive/aeo10/aeoref_tab.html.

———. 2012. *Annual Energy Review 2011*. https://www.eia.gov/totalenergy/data/annual/showtext.php?t=ptb0702.

———. 2017. *International Energy Outlook 2017*. https://www.eia.gov/outlooks/aeo/data/ browser/#/?id=10-IEO2017.

———. 2018a. "Analysis of Projected Crude Oil Production in the Arctic National Wildlife Refuge." https://www.eia.gov/outlooks/aeo/pdf/ANWR.pdf.

———. 2018b. *Annual Energy Outlook 2018.* https://www.eia.gov/outlooks/aeo/.

———. 2018c. "Coal Data Browser." https://www.eia.gov/coal/data/browser/.

———. 2018d. "Electric Power Annual." https://www.eia.gov/electricity/annual/.

———. 2018e. "Electric Power Monthly: Table B.2, Major Disturbances and Unusual Occurrences, 2017." https://www.eia.gov/electricity/monthly/epm_table_grapher.php?t=epmt_b_2.

———. 2018f. "Nonassociated Natural Gas Proved Reserves, Wet After Lease Separation." https://www.eia.gov/dnav/ng/NG_ENR_NANG_A_EPG0_R40_BCF_A.htm/.

———. 2018g. "November 2018 Monthly Energy Review." https://www.eia.gov/totalenergy/data/monthly/index.php.

———. 2018h. "Pipeline Projects." https://www.eia.gov/naturalgas/pipelines/EIA-NaturalGasPipelineProjects.xlsx.

———. 2018i. "Short-Term Energy Outlook Data Browser." https://www.eia.gov/outlooks/steo/data/browser/.

———. 2018j. "U.S. State-to-State Capacity." https://www.eia.gov/naturalgas/pipelines/EIA-StatetoStateCapacity.xlsx.

EPA (Environmental Protection Agency). 2018a. "Air Pollutant Emissions Trends Data: Average Annual Emissions: Criteria Pollutants National Tier 1 for 1970–2017." March 27, 2018. https://www.epa.gov/air-emissions-inventories/air-pollutant-emissions-trends-data.

———. 2018b. "Inventory of U.S. Greenhouse Gas Emissions and Sinks: 1990–2016." EPA 430-R-18-003. https://www.epa.gov/ghgemissions/inventory-us-greenhouse-gas-emissions-and-sinks-1990-2016.

———. 2018c. "Our Nation's Air 2018." https://gispub.epa.gov/air/trendsreport/2018/#highlights.

European Commission. 2018. "Liquefied Natural Gas." https://ec.europa.eu/energy/en/topics/oil-gas-and-coal/liquefied-natural-gas-lng.

Fabrizio, K., N. Rose, and C. Wolfram. 2007. "Do Markets Reduce Costs? Assessing the Impact of Regulatory Restructuring on U.S. Electric Generation Efficiency." *American Economic Review* 97, no. 4: 1250–77.

Fally, T., and J. Sayre. 2018. *Commodity Trade Matters.* NBER Working Paper 24965. Cambridge, MA: National Bureau of Economic Research. https://ideas.repec.org/p/nbr/nberwo/24965.html.

Fell, H., and D. Kaffine. 2018. "The Fall of Coal: Joint Impacts of Fuel Prices and Renewables on Generation and Emissions." *American Economic Journal: Economic Policy* 10, no. 2: 90–116.

FERC (Federal Energy Regulatory Commission). 2018. "North American LNG Import/Export Terminals—Approved." https://www.ferc.gov/industries/gas/indus-act/lng/lng-approved.pdf.

Fitzgerald, T. 2018. "Regulatory Obsolescence through Technological Changes in Oil and Gas Extraction." *William & Mary Environmental Law & Policy Review* 43, no. 1.

GAO (U.S. Government Accountability Office). 2013. *Coal Leasing: BLM Could Enhance Appraisal Process, More Explicitly Consider Coal Exports, and Provide More Public Information*. GAO Publication 14-140. Washington: U.S. Government Publishing Office.

Gerking, S., and S. Hamilton. 2008. "What Explains the Increased Utilization of Powder River Basin Coal in Electric Power Generation?" *American Journal of Agricultural Economics* 90, no. 4: 933–50.

Gold, R. 2014. *The Boom: How Fracking Ignited the American Energy Revolution and Changed the World*. New York: Simon & Schuster.

Hahn, R., and P. Passell. 2010. "The Economics of Allowing More U.S. Oil Drilling. *Energy Economics* 32, no. 3: 638–50.

Hamilton, J. 1996. "This Is What Happened to the Oil Price–Macroeconomy Relationship." *Journal of Monetary Economics* 38, no. 2: 215–20.

———. 2003. "What Is an Oil Shock?" *Journal of Econometrics* 113: 363–98.

Hausman, C. 2014. "Corporate Incentives and Nuclear Safety." *American Economic Journal: Economic Policy* 6, no. 3: 178–206.

Hausman, C., and R. Kellogg. 2015. "Welfare and Distributional Implications of Shale Gas." *Brookings Papers on Economic Activity*, Spring, 71–125.

Hefner, R., III. 2014. "The United States of Gas: Why the Shale Revolution Could Have Happened Only in America." *Foreign Affairs* 93, no. 3: 9–14.

Hirsch, R., R. Bezdek, and R. Wendling. 2005. "Peaking of World Oil Production: Impacts, Mitigation, and Risk Management." Office of Science and Technical Information, U.S. Department of Energy, NETL-IR-2005-093. https://www.osti.gov/servlets/purl/939271.

Hoover, K., and S. Perez. 1994. "Post Hoc Ergo Propter Once More: An Evaluation of 'Does Monetary Policy Matter?' in the Spirit of James Tobin." *Journal of Monetary Economics* 34: 47–73.

Hubbert, M. 1956. "Nuclear Energy and the Fossil Fuels." Paper presented at Spring Meeting of Southern District of American Petroleum Institute, San Antonio, March 7–9. http://www.hubbertpeak.com/hubbert/1956/1956.pdf.

———. 1962. "Energy Resources: A Report to the Committee on Natural Resources of the National Academy of Sciences, National Research Council." https://www.nap.edu/read/18451/chapter/3.

Hummels, D., and A. Skiba. 2004. "Shipping the Good Apples Out? An Empirical Confirmation of the Alchian-Allen Conjecture." *Journal of Political Economy* 112, no. 6: 1384–1402.

IAEA (International Atomic Energy Agency). 2018. "SANMEN-1." IAEA Power Reactor Information System. https://pris.iaea.org/PRIS/CountryStatistics/ReactorDetails.aspx?current=879.

IEA (International Energy Agency). 2018. "Oil 2018: Analysis and Forecasts to 2023." https://www.iea.org/oilmarketreport/.

Imsirovic, A., and B. Pryor. 2018. "IMO 20202 and the Brent-Dubai Spread." Oxford Institute for Energy Studies. https://www.oxfordenergy.org/publications/imo-2020-brent-dubai-spread/.

Inman, M. 2016. *The Oracle of Oil: A Maverick Geologist's Quest for a Sustainable Future*. New York: W. W. Norton.

Jaffe, A., and R. Soligo. 2002. "The Role of Inventories in Oil Market Stability." *Quarterly Review of Economics and Finance* 42, no. 2: 401–15.

Jenkins, J. 2018. "What's Killing Nuclear Power in U.S. Electricity Markets? Drivers of Wholesale Price Declines at Nuclear Generators in the PJM Interconnection." CEEPR Working Paper 2018-001, Massachusetts Institute of Technology.

Jevons, W. 1865. *The Coal Question: An Inquiry Concerning the Progress of the Nation, and the Probable Exhaustion of the Coal-Mines*. London: Macmillan.

Jiménez-Rodríguez, R., and M. Sánchez. 2004. *Oil Price Shocks and Real GDP Growth: Empirical Evidence for Some OECD Countries*. ECB Working Paper 362. Frankfurt: European Central Bank.

Kaffine, D., B. McBee, and J. Lieskovsky. 2013. "Emissions Savings from Wind Power Generation in Texas. *Energy Journal* 34, no. 1: 155–75.

Keiser, D., and J. Shapiro. 2018. "Consequences of the Clean Water Act and the Demand for Water Quality." *Quarterly Journal of Economics* 134, no. 1: 345–96.

Kilian, L. 2008. "Exogenous Oil Supply Shocks: How Big Are They and How Much Do They Matter for the U.S. Economy?" *Review of Economics and Statistics* 90, no. 2: 216–40.

Kilian, L., and R. Vigfusson. 2017. "The Role of Oil Price Shocks in Causing U.S. Recessions." *Journal of Money, Credit and Banking* 49: 1747–76.

Kleinberg, R., S. Paltsev, C. Ebinger, D. Hobbs, and T. Boersma. 2016. "Tight Oil Development Economics: Benchmarks, Breakeven Points, and Inelasticities." CEEPR Working Paper 2016-12, Massachusetts Institute of Technology.

Komarek, T. 2016. "Labor Market Dynamics and the Unconventional Natural Gas Boom: Evidence from the Marcellus Region." *Resource and Energy Economics* 45: 1–17.

Laherrère, J. 1999. "World Oil Supply: What Goes Up Must Come Down, but When Will It Peak?" *Oil & Gas Journal*, February 1. https://www.ogj.com/articles/print/volume-97/issue-5/in-this-issue/general-interest/world-oil-supply-what-goes-up-must-come-down-but-when-will-it-peak.html.

Linn, J., L. Muehlenbachs, and Y. Wang. 2014. "How Do Natural Gas Prices Affect Electricity Consumers and the Environment?" Resources for the Future Discussion Paper 14-19. http://www.rff.org/files/sharepoint/WorkImages/Download/RFF-DP-14-19.pdf.

Malthus, T. 1798. "An Essay on the Principle of Population as It Affects the Future Improvement of Society." http://www.esp.org/books/malthus/population/malthus.pdf.

McNally, R. 2017. *Crude Volatility: The History and the Future of Boom-Bust Oil Prices*. New York: Columbia University Press.

McRae, S. 2017. *Crude Oil Price Differentials and Pipeline Infrastructure*. NBER Working Paper 24170. Cambridge, MA: National Bureau of Economic Research.

Melek, N., and E. Ojeda. 2017. "Lifting the US Crude Oil Export Ban: Prospects for Increasing Oil Market Efficiency." *Economic Review–Federal Reserve Bank of Kansas*, second quarter. https://www.kansascityfed.org/~/media/files/publicat/econrev/econrevarchive/2017/2q17cakirmelekojeda.pdf.

MSHA (Mine Safety and Health Administration). 2018. "Quarterly Mine Employment and Coal Production Report." U.S. Department of Labor, Form 7000-2. https://www.govinfo.gov/content/pkg/CFR-2018-title30-vol1/pdf/CFR-2018-title30-vol1.pdf.

NADP (National Atmospheric Deposition Program). 2018. "National Trends Network (NTN): Precipitation-Weighted Mean (PWM) Concentrations." http://nadp.slh.wisc.edu/data/ntn/ntnAllsites.aspx.

NEI (Nuclear Energy Institute). 2018. "Nuclear Costs in Context." https://www.nei.org/CorporateSite/media/filefolder/resources/reports-and-briefs/nuclear-costs-context-201810.pdf.

NEISO (New England Independent System Operator). 2018. "Operational Fuel-Security Analysis." January 17. https://www.iso-ne.com/static-assets/documents/2018/01/20180117_operational_fuel-security_analysis.pdf.

Newell, R., and B. Prest. 2017. *The Unconventional Oil Supply Boom: Aggregate Price Response from Microdata*. NBER Working Paper 23973. Cambridge, MA: National Bureau of Economic Research. https://www.nber.org/papers/w23973.

Novan, K. 2015. "Valuing the Wind: Renewable Energy Policies and Air Pollution Avoided." *American Economic Journal: Economic Policy* 7, no. 3: 291–326.

Nuclear Regulatory Commission. 2018. "Power Reactor Status Reports for 2018." https://www.nrc.gov/reading-rm/doc-collections/event-status/reactor-status/2018/.

ONRR (Office of Natural Resources Revenue). 2018. "Oil and Gas Lease Sale Data CY 1988-2018." U.S. Bureau of Land Management.

OPEC (Organization of the Petroleum Exporting Countries). 2018a. "Annual Statistical Bulletin." https://www.opec.org/opec_web/en/publications/202.htm.

———. 2018b. "Monthly Oil Market Report." https://www.opec.org/opec_web/en/publications/338.htm.

Parry, I., and J. Darmstadter. 2003. *The Costs of U.S. Oil Dependency*. Washington: Resources for the Future.

Pierru, A., J. Smith, and T. Zamrik. 2018. "OPEC's Impact on Oil Price Volatility: The Role of Spare Capacity." *Energy Journal* 39, no. 2: 103–22.

PJM Interconnection. 2017. "PJM's Evolving Resource Mix and System Reliability." https://www.pjm.com/~/media/library/reports-notices/special-reports/20170330-pjms-evolving-resource-mix-and-system-reliability.ashx.

Shapiro, J., and R. Walker. 2018. "Why Is Pollution from U.S. Manufacturing Declining? The Roles of Environmental Regulation, Productivity, and Trade." *American Economic Review* 108, no. 12: 3814–54.

Skrebowski, C. 2004. "Oil Field Mega Projects—2004." *Petroleum Review* 68, no 684: 18–20.

Sullivan, T., C. Driscoll, C. Beier, D. Burtraw, I. Fernandez, J. Galloway, D. Gay, C. Goodale, G. Likens, G. Lovett, and S. Watmough. 2018. "Air Pollution Success Stories in the United States: The Value of Long-Term Observations." *Environmental Science and Policy* 84: 65–73.

United Nations. 2018. "UN Comtrade Database." Department of Economic and Social Affairs, Statistics Division, Trade Statistics Branch. https://comtrade.un.org/data/.

U.S. Census Bureau. 2018. "USA Trade Online." https://usatrade.census.gov/.

USGS (U.S. Geological Survey). 1998. "The Oil and Gas Resource Potential of the Arctic National Wildlife Refuge 1002 Area, Alaska." https://pubs.usgs.gov/of/1998/ofr-98-0034/ANWR1002.pdf.

———. 2010. "2010 Updated Assessment of Undiscovered Oil and Gas Resources of the National Petroleum Reserve in Alaska (NPRA)." https://pubs.usgs.gov/fs/2010/3102/

———. 2017a. "Assessing U.S. Coal Resources and Reserves." *Fact Sheet 2017-3067.* https://pubs.er.usgs.gov/publication/fs20173067.

———. 2017b. "Assessment of Undiscovered Oil and Gas Resources in the Cretaceous Nanushuk and Torok Formations, Alaska North Slope, and Summary of Resource Potential of the National Petroleum Reserve in Alaska." https://pubs.usgs.gov/fs/2017/3088/fs20173088.pdf.

Weber, J. 2012. "The Effects of a Natural Gas Boom on Employment and Income in Colorado, Texas, and Wyoming." *Energy Economics* 34, no. 5: 1580–88. https://doi.org/10.1016/j.eneco.2011.11.013.

Weber, J., and C. Hitaj. 2015. "What Can We Learn About Shale Gas Development from Land Values? Opportunities, Challenges, and Evidence from Texas and Pennsylvania." *Agricultural and Resource Economics Review* 44, no. 2: 40–58.

Wolak, F. 2017. "Assessing the Impact of the Diffusion of Shale Oil and Gas Technology on the Global Coal Market." Unpublished paper, Stanford University.

Wyeno, R. 2018. "Natural Gas Infrastructure in Mexico." *S&P Global: Platts*, November 8–9.

Zhuravleva, P. 2010. "Analysis of LNG Arbitrage Examines Main Barriers to Developing Market." *LNG Journal.*

Zuckerman, G. 2014. *The Frackers: The Outrageous Inside Story of the New Billionaire Wildcatters*. New York: Penguin.

Chapter 6

Angell, C., and N. Williams. 2005. "FYI Revisited: U.S. Home Prices—Does Bust Always Follow Boom?" *FYI: An Update on Emerging Issues in Banking* (Federal Deposit Insurance Corporation), May 2. http://www.fdic.gov/bank/analytical/fyi/050205fyi.pdf.

Baily, M., R. Litan, and M. Johnson. 2008. "The Origins of the Financial Crisis." Working paper, Brookings Fixing Finance Series. https://www.brookings.edu/wp-content/uploads/2016/06/11_origins_crisis_baily_litan.pdf.

Belsky, E., and N. Richardson. 2010. "Understanding the Boom and Bust in Nonprime Mortgage Lending." Joint Center for Housing Studies at Harvard University. http://www.jchs.harvard.edu/sites/default/files/ubb10-1.pdf.

Bordo, M., and J. Duca. 2018. *The Impact of the Dodd-Frank Act on Small Business*. NBER Working Paper 24501. Cambridge, MA: National Bureau of Economic Research.

Breitenstein, E., and J. McGee. 2015. "Brick-and-Mortar Banking Remains Prevalent in an Increasingly Virtual World." *FDIC Quarterly* 9, no. 1. https://www.fdic.gov/bank/analytical/quarterly/2015-vol9-1/fdic-4q2014-v9n1-brickandmortar.pdf.

Brunnermeier, M., A. Crockett, C. Goodhart, A. Persaud, and H. Shin. 2009. *The Fundamental Principles of Financial Regulation*. Geneva Report on the World Economy. Princeton, NJ: Princeton University. https://www.princeton.edu/~markus/research/papers/Geneva11.pdf.

Capone, C. 1996. *Providing Alternatives to Mortgage Foreclosure: A Report to Congress*. U.S. Department of Housing and Urban Development. Washington: U.S. Government Printing Office. https://www.huduser.gov/portal/Publications/pdf/alt.pdf.

Choi D., M. Holcomb, and D. Morgan. 2018. "Bank Leverage Limits and Regulatory Arbitrage: New Evidence on a Recurring Question." *Federal Reserve Bank of New York Staff Reports*, no. 856.

Coates, J. 2015. "Cost-Benefit Analysis of Financial Regulation: Case Studies and Implications." *Yale Law Journal* 124, no. 4: 882–1345.

Dahl, D., J. Fuchs, A. Meyer, and M. Neely. 2018. "Compliance Costs, Economies of Scale and Compliance Performance." Federal Reserve Bank of Saint Louis, Division of Bank Supervision. https://www.communitybanking.org/~/media/files/compliance%20costs%20economies%20of%20scale%20and%20compliance%20performance.pdf.

FCIC (Financial Crisis Inquiry Commission). 2011. *The Financial Crisis Inquiry Report*. Washington: U.S. Government Publishing Office. https://www.gpo.gov/fdsys/pkg/GPO-FCIC/pdf/GPO-FCIC.pdf.

FDIC (Federal Deposit Insurance Corporation). 1997. *History of the Eighties, Volume I: An Examination of the Banking Crises of the 1980s and Early 1990s.* Washington: FDIC.

———. 2008. "JPMorgan Chase Acquires Banking Operations of Washington Mutual." Press release. https://www.fdic.gov/news/news/press/2008/pr08085.html.

———. 2012. "Community Banking Study." https://www.fdic.gov/regulations/resources/cbi/report/cbi-full.pdf.

———. 2017. *Crisis and Response: An FDIC History, 2008–13.* Washington: FDIC.

———. 2018. "Quarterly Bank Profile, Fourth Quarter 2018." https://www.fdic.gov/bank/analytical/qbp/2018dec/qbp.pdf.

Federal Reserve Board of Governors. 2018. "Report to Congress on Implementation of Enhanced Prudential Standards." https://www.federalreserve.gov/publications/files/report-to-congress-on-eps-implementation-201801.pdf.

FFIEC (Federal Financial Institutions Examination Council). 1996. "Uniform Financial Institutions Rating System." *Federal Register* 61, no. 245: 67021–29.

GAO (U.S. Government Accountability Office). 2013. "Financial Regulatory Reform: Financial Crisis Losses and Potential Impacts of the Dodd-Frank Act." Report to Congressional Requesters GAO-13-180. https://www.gao.gov/assets/660/651322.pdf.

Gorton, G. 2007. *The Panic of 2007.* NBER Working Paper 14358. Cambridge, MA: National Bureau of Economic Research.

Holtz-Eakin, D. 2015. "The Growth Consequences of Dodd-Frank." American Action Forum. https://www.americanactionforum.org/research/the-growth-consequences-of-dodd-frank/.

Hopt, K. 2013. "Corporate Governance of Banks and Other Financial Institutions after the Financial Crisis." *Journal of Corporate Law Studies* 13, part 2: 219–53.

Hoskins, S., and M. Labonte. 2015. "An Analysis of the Regulatory Burden on Small Banks." Congressional Research Service. https://fas.org/sgp/crs/misc/R43999.pdf.

Hughes, J., J. Jagtiani, L. Mester, and C. Moon. 2018. "Does Scale Matter in Community Bank Performance? Evidence Obtained by Applying Several New Measures of Performance." Working paper, Federal Reserve Bank of Philadelphia. https://www.philadelphiafed.org/-/media/research-and-data/publications/working-papers/2018/wp18-11.pdf.

IMF (International Monetary Fund). 2008. *Global Financial Stability Report: Containing Systemic Risks and Restoring Financial Soundness.* Washington: IMF. http://www.imf.org/External/Pubs/FT/GFSR/2008/01/pdf/text.pdf.

———. 2010. *Financial System Stability Assessment.* Washington: IMF. https://www.imf.org/external/pubs/ft/scr/2010/cr10247.pdf.

Ligon, J., and W. Beach. 2013. *The Housing Market Without Fannie Mae and Freddie Mac: Economic Effects of Eliminating Government-Sponsored Enterprises in Housing.* Washington: Heritage Foundation. https://www.heritage.org/housing/report/

housing-market-without-fannie-mae-and-freddie-mac-economic-effects-eliminating.

Lincoln, T. 2008. "Regulators' Failure to Heed Warnings Allowed Subprime Mortgage Lending to Spin of Control." Public Citizen. https://www.citizen.org/sites/default/files/chapter-one-regulators-failure-to-heed-warnings.pdf.

Luttrell, D., T. Atkinson, and H. Rosenblum. 2013. "Assessing the Costs and Consequences of the 2007–09 Financial Crisis and Its Aftermath." *Federal Reserve Bank of Dallas Economic Letter* 8, no. 7: 1–4.

McLaughlin, P., D. Francis, and O. Sherouse. 2017. "Dodd-Frank Is One of the Biggest Regulatory Events Ever." Mercatus Center at George Mason University. https://www.mercatus.org/publications/dodd-frank-one-biggest-regulatory-events-ever.

McLaughlin, P., and O. Sherouse. 2016. "The McLaughlin-Sherouse List: The 10 Most-Regulated Industries of 2014." Mercatus Center at George Mason University. https://www.mercatus.org/publication/mclaughlin-sherouse-list-10-most-regulated-industries-2014.

Passmore, W., S. Sherlund, and G. Burgess. 2005. "The Effect of Housing Government-Sponsored Enterprises on Mortgage Rates." *Real Estate Economics* 33, no. 3: 427–63.

Peirce, H., I. Robinson, and T. Stratmann. 2014. *How Are Small Banks Faring Under Dodd-Frank?* Working Paper 14-5. Arlington, VA: Mercatus Center at George Mason University.

Perkins, D. 2017. "Tailoring Bank Regulations: Differences in Bank Size, Activities, and Capital Levels." Congressional Research Service. https://fas.org/sgp/crs/misc/R45051.pdf.

Pinto, E. 2010. "Triggers of the Financial Crisis." American Enterprise Institute. http://www.aei.org/paper/100174.

Reinhart, C., and K. Rogoff. 2009. *This Time Is Different: Eight Centuries of Financial Folly.* Princeton, NJ: Princeton University Press.

Roberts, D., A. Sarkar, and O. Shachar. 2018. "Bank Liquidity Provision and Basel Liquidity Regulations." *Federal Reserve Bank of New York Staff Reports*, no. 852.

Sunstein, C. 2015. "Financial Regulation and Cost-Benefit Analysis." *Yale Law Journal Forum* 124, no. 4: 882–1345.

U.S. Department of the Treasury. 2017. *A Financial System That Creates Economic Opportunities: Banks and Credit Unions.* Washington: U.S. Government Publishing Office. https://www.treasury.gov/press-center/press-releases/Documents/A%20Financial%20System.pdf.

Viscusi, W., and T. Gayer. 2016. "Behavioral Public Choice: The Behavioral Paradox of Government Policy." *Harvard Journal of Law & Public Policy* 38, no. 3: 973–1007.

Wallison, P. 2011. "Financial Crisis Inquiry Commission Report, Dissenting Statement." American Enterprise Institute. http://fcic-static.law.stanford.edu/cdn_media/ fcic-reports/fcic_final_report_wallison_dissent.pdf.

Chapter 7

Abel, D., J. Salvatier, A. Stuhlmuller, and O. Evans. 2017. "Agent-Agnostic Human-in-the-Loop Reinforcement Learning." Cornell University. https://arxiv.org/ abs/1701.04079.

Acemoglu, D., and D. Autor. 2011. "Skills, Tasks, and Technologies: Implications for Employment and Earnings." In *Handbook of Labor Economics, Volume 4, Part B*, edited by O. Ashenfelter and D. Card. Amsterdam: Elsevier.

Acemoglu, D., D. Dorn, G. Hanson, and B. Price. 2014. "Return of the Solow Paradox? IT, Productivity, and Employment in U.S. Manufacturing." *American Economic Review* 104, no. 5: 394–99.

Acemoglu, D., and P. Restrepo. 2018. "The Race between Man and Machine: Implications of Technology for Growth, Factor Shares, and Employment." *American Economic Review* 108, no. 6: 1488–1542.

Aghion, P., B. Jones, and C. Jones. 2017. *Artificial Intelligence and Economic Growth*. NBER Working Paper 23928. Cambridge, MA: National Bureau of Economic Research.

Agrawal, A., J. Gans, and A. Goldfarb. 2018. "Economic Policy for Artificial Intelligence." *Innovation Policy and the Economy* 19: 139–59.

American Technology Council. 2017. *Report to the President on Federal IT Modernization*. https://itmodernization.cio.gov/assets/report/Report%20 to%20the%20President%20on%20IT%20Modernization%20-%20Final.pdf.

Arai, N., T. Matsuzaki, H. Iwane, and H. Anai. 2014. "Mathematics by Machine." In *ISSAC '14: Proceedings of the 39th International Symposium on Symbolic and Algebraic Computation.* New York: ACM.

Arel, I., D. Rose, and T. Karnowski. 2010. "Deep Machine Learning: A New Frontier in Artificial Intelligence." *IEEE Computational Intelligence Magazine* 5, no. 4: 13–18.

Artificial Intelligence Index. 2017. *Artificial Intelligence Index: 2017 Annual Report*. http:// cdn.aiindex.org/2017-report.pdf.

Autor, D. 2015. "Why Are There Still So Many Jobs? The History and Future of Workplace Automation." *Journal of Economic Perspectives* 29, no. 3: 3–30.

Autor, D., L. Katz, and A. Krueger. 1998. "Computing Inequality: Have Computers Changed the Labor Market?" *Quarterly Journal of Economics* 113, no. 4: 1169–1213.

Autor, D., F. Levy, and R. Murnane. 2003. "The Skill Content of Recent Technological Change: An Empirical Exploration." *Quarterly Journal of Economics* 118, no. 4: 1279–1333.

Bailey, A., N. Vaduganathan, T. Henry, R. Laverdiere, and L. Pugliese. 2018. "Making Digital Learning Work: Success Strategies from Six Leading Universities and Community Colleges." Boston Consulting Group and Arizona State University. https://edplus.asu.edu/sites/default/files/BCG-Making-Digital-Learning-Work-Apr-2018%20.pdf.

Beaudry, P., D. Green, and B. Sand. 2016. "The Great Reversal in the Demand for Skill and Cognitive Tasks." *Journal of Labor Economics* 34, no. 1: S199–S247.

Becker, G., and K. Murphy. 1992. "The Division of Labor, Coordination Costs, and Knowledge." *Quarterly Journal of Economics* 107, no. 4: 1137–60.

Begenau, J., M. Farboodi, and L. Veldkamp. 2018. "Big Data in Finance and the Growth of Large Firms." *Journal of Monetary Economics* 97: 71–87.

Bessen, J. 2018. "The Policy Challenge of Artificial Intelligence." *CPI Antitrust Chronicle*, June. https://www.competitionpolicyinternational.com/wp-content/uploads/2018/06/CPI-Bessen.pdf.

Bisogni, F. 2016. "Proving Limits of State Data Breach Notification Laws: Is a Federal Law the Most Adequate Solution? *Journal of Information Policy* 6: 154–205.

Bisogni, F., H. Asghari, and M. Van Eeten. 2017. "Estimating the Size of the Iceberg from Its Tip: An Investigation into Unreported Data Breach Notifications." Paper prepared for Workshop on the Economics of Information Security. https://weis2017.econinfosec.org/wp-content/uploads/sites/3/2017/05/WEIS_2017_paper_54.pdf.

Bloom, N., B. Eifert, A. Mahajan, D. McKenzie, and J. Roberts. 2013. "Does Management Matter? Evidence from India." *Quarterly Journal of Economics* 128, no. 1: 1–51.

Bonhomme, S., T. Lamadon, and E Manresa. 2017. "Discretizing Unobserved Heterogeneity." Working paper. http://www.lamadon.com/paper/BonhommeLamadonManresa2017.pdf.

Borio, C., E. Kharroubi, C. Upper, and F. Zampini. 2016. "Labour Reallocation and Productivity Dynamics: Financial Causes, Real Consequences." Working paper, Bank for International Settlements. https://www.bis.org/publ/work534.pdf.

Bowe, H. 1966. *Report of the National Commission on Technology, Automation, and Economic Progress, Volume 1.* Washington: U.S. Government Printing Office.

Bresnahan, T., E. Brynjolfsson, and L. Hitt. 2002. "Information Technology, Workplace Organization, and the Demand for Skilled Labor: Firm-Level Evidence." *Quarterly Journal of Economics* 117, no. 1: 339–76.

Brynjolfsson E., F. Eggers, and A. Gannamaneni. 2018. *Using Massive Online Choice Experiments to Measure Changes in Well-Being.* NBER Working Paper 24514. Cambridge, MA: National Bureau of Economic Research.

Brynjolfsson, E., and A. McAfee. 2014. *The Second Machine Age: Work, Progress, and Prosperity in a Time of Brilliant Technologies.* New York: W. W. Norton.

Brynjolfsson, E., and K. McElheran. 2016. "Data in Action: Data-Driven Decision Making in U.S. Manufacturing." Working paper, U.S. Census Bureau. https://www2.census.gov/ces/wp/2016/CES-WP-16-06.pdf.

Brynjolfsson, E., and T. Mitchell. 2017. "What Can Machine Learning Do? Workforce Implications." *Science* 358, no. 6370: 1530–34.

Brynjolfsson, E., D. Rock, and T. Mitchell. 2018. "What Can Machines Learn and What Does It Mean for Occupations and the Economy?" *American Economic Review, Papers & Proceedings* 108: 43–47.

Brynjolfsson, E., D. Rock, and C. Syverson. 2017. *Artificial Intelligence and the Modern Productivity Paradox: A Clash of Expectations and Statistics*. NBER Working Paper 24001. Cambridge, MA: National Bureau of Economic Research.

Burkner, H., A. Bhattacharya, T. Lewis, and V. Rastogi. 2017. "How Business Leaders Can Rebuild Trust and Renew the Social Contract." Boston Consulting Group. https://www.bcg.com/en-us/publications/2017/globalization-leadership-talent-business-leaders-rebuild-trust-renew-social-contract.aspx.

Burning Glass. 2018. "How Big Is the Skills Gap?" Blog, Burning Glass Technologies. https://www.burning-glass.com/blog/how-big-is-the-skills-gap/.

Byrne, D., C. Corrado, and D. Sichel. 2018. *The Rise of Cloud Computing: Minding Your P's, Q's, and K's*. NBER Working Paper 25188. Cambridge, MA: National Bureau of Economic Research.

Byrne, D., S. Oliner, and D. Sichel. 2013. "Is the Information Technology Revolution Over?" *International Productivity Monitor* 25: 20–36.

———. 2017. "How Fast Are Semiconductor Prices Falling?" Working paper, Board of Governors of the Federal Reserve System.

Caselli, F., and J. Feyrer. 2007. "The Marginal Product of Capital." *Quarterly Journal of Economics* 122, no. 2: 535–68.

Cashell, B., W. Jackson, M. Jickling, and B. Webel. 2004. "The Economic Impact of Cyber-Attacks." Congressional Research Service Report for Congress. https://fas.org/sgp/crs/misc/RL32331.pdf.

CEA (Council of Economic Advisers). 2015. "Productivity Growth in the Advanced Economies: The Past, the Present, and Lessons for the Future." https://obamawhitehouse.archives.gov/sites/default/files/docs/20150709_productivity_advanced_economies_piie.pdf.

———. 2016. "Artificial Intelligence, Automation, and the Economy." https://obamawhitehouse.archives.gov/sites/whitehouse.gov/files/documents/Artificial-Intelligence-Automation-Economy.pdf.

———. 2018a. *Addressing America's Reskilling Challenge*. Washington: White House.

———. 2018b. *Economic Report of the President*. Washington: U.S. Government Publishing Office.

———. 2018c. *How Much Are Workers Getting Paid? A Primer on Wage Measurement*. Washington: White House.

Chen, M., J. Chevalier, P. Rossi, and E. Oehlsen. Forthcoming. "The Value of Flexible Work: Evidence from Uber Drivers." *Journal of Political Economy*.

Cohen, P., R. Hahn, J. Hall, S. Levitt, and R. Metcalfe. 2016. *Using Big Data to Estimate Consumer Surplus: The Case of Uber*. NBER Working Paper 22627. Cambridge, MA: National Bureau of Economic Research.

Colciago, A., and F. Etro. 2013. "Cloud Computing, Structural Change, and Job Creation." In *Broadband in Latin America: Beyond Connectivity*, edited by V. Jordan, H. Galperin, and W. Peres. Santiago: United Nations Economic Commission for Latin America and the Caribbean.

Comin, D., D. Lashkari, and M. Mestieri. 2017. "Structural Change with Long-Run Income and Price Effects." Working paper. https://www.dartmouth.edu/~dcomin/Publications_files/CLM_rev_10_2017.pdf.

Cramer, J., and A. Krueger. 2016. "Disruptive Change in the Taxi Business: The Case of Uber." *American Economic Review* 106, no. 5: 177–82.

CSAIL (Computer Science & Artificial Intelligence Lab). 2017. "Fooling Google's Image-Recognition AI 1000x Faster." Massachusetts Institute of Technology. https://www.csail.mit.edu/news/fooling-googles-image-recognition-ai-1000x-faster.

Cukier, K., and V. Mayer-Schoenberger. 2013. "The Rise of Big Data: How It's Changing the Way We Think About the World." *Foreign Affairs* 92, no. 3: 28–40.

Culkin, R., and S. Das. 2017. "Machine Learning in Finance: The Case of Deep Learning for Option Pricing." Working paper, Santa Clara University. https://srdas.github.io/Papers/BlackScholesNN.pdf.

CyberSeek. 2018. "Cybersecurity Supply/Demand Heat Map." https://www.cyberseek.org/heatmap.html.

Czosseck, C., R. Ottis, and A. Talihärm. 2011. "Estonia after the 2007 Cyber Attacks: Legal, Strategic, and Organisational Changes in Cybersecurity." *International Journal of Cyber Warfare and Terrorism* 1: 24–34. https://ccdcoe.org/articles/2011/czosseck_ottis_taliharm_estonia_after_the_2007_cyber_attacks.pdf.

DARPA (Defense Advanced Research Projects Agency). 2016. "'Mayhem' Declared Preliminary Winner of Historic Cyber Grand Challenge." *DARPA News and Events*, August 4. https://www.darpa.mil/news-events/2016-08-04.

———. 2018a. "AI Next Campaign." https://www.darpa.mil/work-with-us/ai-next-campaign.

———. 2018b. "Computers and Humans Exploring Software Security (CHESS)." https://www.darpa.mil/program/computers-and-humans-exploring-software-security.

———. 2018c. "DARPA Announces $2 Billion Campaign to Develop Next Wave of AI Technologies." https://www.darpa.mil/news-events/2018-09-07

Davenport, J., and M. England. 2015. "Recent Advances in Real Geometric Reasoning." In *Automated Deduction in Geometry*, edited by F. Botana and P. Quaresma. Berlin: Springer-Verlag.

David, P. 1990. "The Dynamo and the Computer: An Historical Perspective on the Modern Productivity Paradox." *American Economic Review* 80, no. 2: 355–61.

Deloitte. 2017. "Bullish on the Business Value of Cognitive: Leaders in Cognitive and AI Weigh In on What's Working and What's Next." *The 2017 Deloitte State of Cognitive Survey*. https://www2.deloitte.com/content/dam/Deloitte/us/Documents/deloitte-analytics/us-da-2017-deloitte-state-of-cognitive-survey.pdf.

de Zwart, P., B. van Leeuwen, and J. van Leeuwen-Li. 2014. "Real Wages since 1820." In *How Was Life? Global Well-Being since 1820*, edited by J. van Zanden et al. Paris: OECD Publishing.

DOE (U.S. Department of Energy). 2017. "DOE and VA Team Up to Improve Healthcare for Veterans." https://www.energy.gov/articles/doe-and-va-team-improve-healthcare-veterans.

Einav, L., and J. Levin. 2014. "Economics in the Age of Big Data." *Science* 346, no. 6210.

Elsevier. 2018. *Artificial Intelligence: How Knowledge Is Created, Transferred, and Used—Trends in China, Europe, and the United States*. Amsterdam: Elsevier Artificial Intelligence Resource Center. https://p.widencdn.net/jj2lej/ACAD-RL-AS-RE-ai-report-WEB.

Escueta, M., V, Quan, A. Nickow, and P. Oreopoulos. 2017. *Education Technology: An Evidence-Based Review*. NBER Working Paper 23744. Cambridge, MA: National Bureau of Economic Research.

ESPN Analytics. 2018. "Charting the Patriots' Incredible Super Bowl LI Comeback." http://www.espn.com/blog/statsinfo/post/_/id/128369/the-2016-nfl-playoffs-viewed-through-win-probability.

Estonia. 2018. "E-Estonia: Public Safety." https://e-estonia.com/#.

Estonia Ministry of Economic Affairs and Communications. 2018. "Digital Agenda 2020 for Estonia." https://www.mkm.ee/sites/default/files/digital_agenda_2020_estonia_engf.pdf.

FAO (Food and Agriculture Organization of the United Nations). 2015. "Measuring Sustainability in Cotton Farming Systems: Towards a Guidance Framework." http://www.fao.org/3/a-i4170e.pdf.

FBI (U.S. Federal Bureau of Investigation). 2016. "Incidents Identified by Sector, Activity, and Actor Type."

Feldman, R., S. Govindaraj, J. Livnat, and B. Segal. 2010. "Management's Tone Change, Post Earnings Announcement Drift and Accruals." *Review of Accounting Studies* 15: 915–53.

Fisk, D. 2001. "American Labor in the 20th Century." *Compensation and Working Conditions* (Bureau of Labor Statistics), Fall. https://www.bls.gov/opub/mlr/cwc/american-labor-in-the-20th-century.pdf.

Forman, C., A. Goldfarb, and S. Greenstein. 2012. "The Internet and Local Wages: A Puzzle." *American Economic Review* 102, no. 1: 556–75.

Frey, C., and M. Osborne. 2017. "The Future of Employment: How Susceptible Are Jobs to Computerisation?" *Technological Forecasting and Social Change* 114: 254–80.

Gallipoli, G., and C. Makridis. 2018. "Structural Transformation and the Rise of Information Technology." *Journal of Monetary Economics* 97: 91–110.

Gal-Or, E., and A. Ghose. 2005. "The Economic Incentives for Sharing Security Information." *Information Systems Research* 16, no. 2: 186–208.

Galor, O., and D. Weil. 2000. "Population, Technology, and Growth: From Malthusian Stagnation to the Demographic Transition and Beyond." *American Economic Review* 90, no. 4: 806–28.

Gibbs, S. 2017. "AlphaZero AI Beats Champion in Chess Program After Teaching Itself in Four Hours." *The Guardian*, December 7. https://www.theguardian.com/technology/2017/dec/07/alphazero-google-deepmind-ai-beats-champion-program-teaching-itself-to-play-four-hours.

Goldfarb, A., and C. Tucker. Forthcoming. "Digital Economics." *Journal of Economic Literature*.

Gordon, L., M. Loeb, W. Lucyshyn, and L. Zhou. 2015. "Increasing Cybersecurity Investments in Private Firms." *Journal of Cybersecurity* 1, no. 1: 3–17.

Gordon, R. 2000. "Does the 'New Economy' Measure Up to the Great Inventions of the Past?" *Journal of Economic Perspectives* 14, no. 4: 49–74.

———. 2018. *Why Has Economic Growth Slowed When Innovation Appears to Be Accelerating?* NBER Working Paper 24554. Cambridge, MA: National Bureau of Economic Research.

Graetz, G., and G. Michaels. 2018. "Robots at Work." *Review of Economics and Statistics* 100, no. 5: 753–68.

Hall, J., and A. Krueger. 2018. "An Analysis of the Labor Market for Uber's Driver-Partners in the United States." *ILR Review* 71, no. 3: 705–32.

Hall, R., and C. JonesI. 2007. "The Value of Life and the Rise in Health Spending." *Quarterly Journal of Economics* 122, no. 1: 39–72.

Hansen, G., and E. Prescott. 2002. "Malthus to Solow." *American Economic Review* 92, no. 4: 1205–17.

Hastie, T., R. Tibshirani, and J. Friedman. 2009. *The Elements of Statistical Learning: Data Mining, Inference, and Prediction, 2nd Edition*. New York: Springer.

Heritage Foundation. 2018. "2018 Index of Economic Freedom." https://www.heritage.org/international-economies/commentary/2018-index-economic-freedom.

Herrendorf, B., C. Herrington, and A. Valentinyi. 2015. "Sectoral Technology and Structural Transformation." *American Economic Journal: Macroeconomics* 7, no. 4: 104–33.

Herrendorf, B., R. Rogerson, and A. Valentinyi. 2014. "Growth and Structural Transformation." In *Handbook of Economic Growth, Volume 2B*, edited by P. Aghion and S. Durlauf. Amsterdam: Elsevier.

Hicks, J. 1932. *The Theory of Wages*. 2nd ed. London: Macmillan.

Hiscox. 2018a. "2018 Hiscox Cyber Readiness Report." https://www.hiscox.com/sites/default/files/content/2018-Hiscox-Cyber-Readiness-Report.pdf.

———. 2018b. "2018 Hiscox Small Business Cyber Risk Report." https://www.hiscox. com/documents/2018-Hiscox-Small-Business-Cyber-Risk-Report.pdf.

Hoadley, D., and N. Lucas. 2018. "Artificial Intelligence and National Security." Congressional Research Service. https://fas.org/sgp/crs/natsec/R45178.pdf.

Hoffman, F. 2009. "Hybrid Warfare and Challenges." *Small Wars Journal* 52: 34–39.

Holmstrom, B., and P. Milgrom. 1991. "Multitask Principal–Agent Analyses: Incentive Contracts, Asset Ownership, and Job Design." *Journal of Law, Economics, & Organization* 7: 24–52.

Horowitz, M. 2018. "The Algorithms of August." *Foreign Policy*, September 12. https:// foreignpolicy.com/2018/09/12/ will-the-united-states-lose-the-artificial-intelligence-arms-race/.

ISC^2 (International Information System Security Certification Consortium). 2018. "Cybersecurity Professionals Focus on Developing New Skills as Workforce Gap Widens." https://www.isc2.org/-/media/ISC2/Research/2018-ISC2-Cybersecurity-Workforce-Study.ashx?la=en&hash=4E09681D0FB51698D9BA6 BF13EEABFA48BD17DB0.

ITRC (Identity Theft Resource Center). 2019. "ITRC Multi-Year Data Breach Chart Jan. 1, 2005–Dec. 31, 2018." https://www.idtheftcenter.org/wp-content/ uploads/2019/02/Multi-Year-Chart.pdf.

Jaffe, S., R. Minton, C. Mulligan, and K. Murphy. 2019. *Chicago Price Theory*. Princeton, NJ: Princeton University Press. Forthcoming.

Jha, S., and E. Topol. 2016. "Adapting to Artificial Intelligence: Radiologists and Pathologists as Information Specialists." *Journal of the American Medical Association* 316, no. 22: 2353–54.

Jones, C. 2016. "The Facts of Economic Growth." In *Handbook of Macroeconomics, Volume 2A*, edited by J. Taylor and H. Uhlig. Amsterdam: Elsevier.

Jorgensen, D. 2005. "Accounting for Growth in the Information Age." In *Handbook of Economic Growth, Volume 1A*, edited by P. Aghion and S. Durlauf. Amsterdam: Elsevier.

Jorgensen, D., and K. Stiroh. 2000. "U.S. Economic Growth in the New Millennium." *Brookings Papers on Economic Activity*, no. 1: 125–211.

Jorgenson, D., K. Stiroh, R. Gordon, and D. Sichel. 2000. "Raising the Speed Limit: U.S. Economic Growth in the Information Age." *Brookings Papers on Economic Activity*, no. 1: 125–235.

JPMorgan Chase. 2018. "The Online Platform Economy in 2018: Drivers, Workers, Sellers, and Lessors." https://www.jpmorganchase.com/corporate/institute/ report-ope-2018.htm.

Juhn, C., K. Murphy, and B. Pierce. 1993. "Wage Inequality and the Rise in Returns to Skill." *Journal of Political Economy* 101, no. 3: 410–42.

Kaldor, N. 1961. "Capital Accumulation and Economic Growth." In *The Theory of Capital*, edited by D. Hague. Proceedings of a conference held by International Economic Association. London: Palgrave Macmillan.

Karabarbounis, L., and B. Neiman. 2014. "The Global Decline of the Labor Share." *Quarterly Journal of Economics* 129, no. 1: 61–103.

Katz, L., and A. Krueger. 2018. "The Rise and Nature of Alternative Work Arrangements in the United States, 1995–2015." *Industrial and Labor Relations Review*, in press.

———. 2019. *Understanding Trends in Alternative Work Arrangements in the United States.* NBER Working Paper 25425. Cambridge, MA: National Bureau of Economic Research.

Katz, L., and K. Murphy. 1992. "Changes in Relative Wages, 1963–1987: Supply and Demand Factors." *Quarterly Journal of Economics* 107, no. 1: 35–78.

Kerber, M., C. Lange, and C. Rowat. 2016. "An Introduction to Mechanized Reasoning." *Journal of Mathematical Economics* 66: 26–39.

Kleinberg, J., J. Ludwig, S. Mullainathan, and A. Rambachan. 2018. "Algorithmic Fairness." *American Economic Review, Papers & Proceedings* 108: 22–27.

Kleinberg, J., S. Mullainathan, and M. Raghavan. 2018. "Inherent Trade-Offs in the Fair Determination of Risk Scores." Working paper, ArXiv. https://arxiv.org/pdf/1609.05807.pdf.

Kott, A., and C. Arnold. 2013. "The Promises and Challenges of Continuous Monitoring and Risk Scoring." *IEEE Security & Privacy* 11, no. 1: 90–93.

Koustas, D. 2019. "What Do Big Data Tell Us About Why People Take Gig Economy Jobs?" *American Economic Review, Papers & Proceedings* 109, forthcoming.

Koza, J., F. Bennett, D. Andre, and M. Keane. 1996. "Automated Design of Both the Topology and Sizing of Analog Electrical Circuits Using Genetic Programming." In *Artificial Intelligence in Design '96*, edited by J. Gero and F. Sudweeks. Dordrecht: Springer.

Krusell, P., L. Ohanian, J. Rios-Rull, and G. Violante. 2000. "Capital–Skill Complementarity and Inequality: A Macroeconomic Analysis." *Econometrica* 68, no. 5: 1029–53.

Lagakos, D., and M. Waugh. 2013. "Selection, Agriculture, and Cross-Country Productivity Differences." *American Economic Review* 103, no. 2: 948–80.

Lee, K., and P. Triolo. 2017. "China's Artificial Intelligence Revolution: Understanding Beijing's Structural Advantages." Eurasia Group. https://www.eurasiagroup.net/files/upload/China_Embraces_AI.pdf.

Lee, W. 2016. "2013 Yahoo Breach: Over 1 Billion Accounts Had Data Stolen." Government Technology. http://www.govtech.com/security/2013-Yahoo-Breach-Over-1-Billion-Accounts-Had-Data-Stolen.html.

Makridis, C., and B. Dean. 2018. "Measuring the Economic Effects of Data Breaches on Firm Outcomes: Challenges and Opportunities." *Journal of Economic and Social Measurement* 43, nos. 1–2: 59–83.

Makridis, C., and Y. Paik. 2018. "Valuing the Welfare Gains of Uber." Unpublished paper. https://papers.ssrn.com/sol3/papers.cfm?abstract_id=3299228.

Makridis, C., and M. Smeets. 2018. "Determinants of Cyber Readiness." *Journal of Cyber Policy*, forthcoming. https://papers.ssrn.com/sol3/papers.cfm?abstract_id=3216231.

Malwarebytes. 2018. "White Hat, Black Hat and the Emergence of the Gray Hat: The True Cost of Cybercrime." https://go.malwarebytes.com/OstermanCostofCybercrimeQ3FY19_GLOBAL_Press.html.

Marshall, A. 1890. *Principles of Economics*. 1st ed. London: Macmillan.

Mokyr, J., C. Vickers, and N. Ziebarth. 2015. "The History of Technological Anxiety and the Future of Economic Growth: Is This Time Different?" *Journal of Economic Perspectives* 29, no. 3: 31–50.

Moore, G. 1965. "Cramming More Components onto Integrated Circuits," *Electronics*, April 19, 114–17.

Mulligan, C., J. Davenport, and M. England. 2018. "TheoryGuru: A Mathematica Package to Apply Quantifier Elimination Technology to Economics." In *Mathematical Software: ICMS 2018*, edited by J. Davenport et al. New York: Springer International.

Mulligan, C., and L. Threinen. 2011. *The Marginal Products of Residential and Non-Residential Capital through 2009*. NBER Working Paper 15897. Cambridge, MA: National Bureau of Economic Research.

National Academies. 2017. *Information Technology and the U.S. Workforce: Where Are We and Where Do We Go from Here?* Report of National Academies of Sciences, Engineering, and Medicine, Committee on Information Technology, Automation, and the U.S. Workforce. Washington: National Academies Press.

Naylor, C. 2018. "On the Prospects for a (Deep) Learning Health Care System." *Journal of the American Medical Association*, August 30. http://www.fsk.it/attach/Content/News/6636/o/jama_naylor_2018.pdf.

Nedelkoska, L., and G. Quintini. 2018. *Automation, Skills Use, and Training*. OECD Social, Employment, and Migration Working Paper 202. Paris: OECD Publishing. http://dx.doi.org/10.1787/2e2f4eea-en.

Ngai, L., and C. Pissarides. 2007. "Structural Change in a Multisector Model of Growth." *American Economic Review* 97, no. 1: 429–43.

NIST (National Institute of Standards and Technology). 2014. "Framework for Improving Critical Infrastructure Cybersecurity, Version 1.0, February 12." https://www.nist.gov/sites/default/files/documents/cyberframework/cybersecurity-framework-021214.pdf.

Nitschke, G., M. Schut, and A. Eiben. 2012. "Evolving Behavioral Specialization in Robot Teams to Solve a Collective Construction Task." *Swarm and Evolutionary Computation* 2: 25–38.

Nordhaus, W. 2015. *Are We Approaching an Economic Singularity? Information Technology and the Future of Economic Growth*. NBER Working Paper 21547. Cambridge, MA: National Bureau of Economic Research. https://ideas.repec.org/p/nbr/nberwo/21547.html.

Oliner, S., and D. Sichel. 2000. "The Resurgence of Growth in the Late 1990s: Is the Information Technology the Story?" *Journal of Economic Perspectives* 14, no. 4: 3–22.

Oltsik, J. 2018. "Research Suggests Cybersecurity Skills Shortage is Getting Worse." CSO Online. https://www.csoonline.com/article/3247708/security/research-suggests-cybersecurity-skills-shortage-is-getting-worse.html.

OMB (Office of Management and Budget). 2007. "M-08-05: Memorandum for the Heads of Executive Departments and Agencies." https://georgewbush-whitehouse.archives.gov/omb/memoranda/fy2008/m08-05.pdf.

———. 2018a. "Federal Cybersecurity Risk Determination Report and Action Plan." https://www.whitehouse.gov/wp-content/uploads/2018/05/Cybersecurity-Risk-Determination-Report-FINAL_May-2018-Release.pdf.

———. 2018b. "President's Management Agenda." https://www.whitehouse.gov/wp-content/uploads/2018/03/Presidents-Management-Agenda.pdf.

———. 2018c. "Update to the Trusted Internet Connections (TIC) Initiative." https://policy.cio.gov/tic-draft/.

Opportunity America. 2018. "Work, Skills, Community: Restoring Opportunity for the Working Class." Report of study group convened by Opportunity America, cosponsored by American Enterprise Institute and Brookings Institution. https://www.aei.org/wp-content/uploads/2018/11/Work-Skills-Community-FINAL-PDF.pdf.

OSTP (Office of Science and Technology Policy). "Summary of the 2018 White House Summit on Artificial Intelligence for American Industry." https://www.whitehouse.gov/wp-content/uploads/2018/05/Summary-Report-of-White-House-AI-Summit.pdf.

Page, L., and H. Gehlbach. 2017. "How an Artificially Intelligent Virtual Assistant Helps Students Navigate the Road to College." *AERA Open* 3, no. 4: 1–12.

Polson, N., and J. Scott. 2018. AIQ: How Artificial Intelligence Works and How We Can Harness Its Power for a Better World. London: Transworld.

PwC (PricewaterhouseCoopers). 2018a. "Five Trends Transforming the Automotive Industry." https://www.pwc.at/de/publikationen/branchen-und-wirtschaftsstudien/eascy-five-trends-transforming-the-automotive-industry_2018.pdf. Accessed January 2, 2019.

———. 2018b. "The 2018 Strategy & Digital Auto Report." https://www.strategyand.pwc.com/media/file/Digital-Auto-Report-2018.pdf. Accessed January 2, 2019.

Rapid7. 2018. "Industry Cyber-Exposure Report: *Fortune* 500." https://www.rapid7.com/info/industry-cyber-exposure-report-fortune-500/.

Rasmussen, W. 1982. "The Mechanization of Agriculture." *Scientific American* 247, no. 3: 76–89.

Rid, T., and B. Buchanan. 2015. "Attributing Cyber Attacks." *Journal of Strategic Studies* 38, nos. 1–2: 4–37.

Rognlie, M. 2015. "Deciphering the Fall and Rise in the Net Capital Share: Accumulation or Scarcity?" *Brookings Papers on Economic Activity* 46, no. 1: 1–69.

Romer, D. 2011. *Advanced Macroeconomics*. New York: McGraw-Hill Education.

Russakovsky, O., J. Deng, H. Su, J. Krause, S. Satheesh, S. Ma, Z. Huang, A. Karpathy, A. Khosla, M. Bernstein, A. Berg, and L. Fei-Fei. 2015. "ImageNet Large Scale Visual Recognition Challenge." *International Journal of Computer Vision* 115, no. 3: 211–52.

Russell, S., and P. Norvig. 2010. Artificial Intelligence: A Modern Approach, 3rd Edition. London: Pearson.

Salfer, J., M. Endres, W. Lazarus, K. Minegishi, and B. Berning. 2017. "Dairy Robotic Milking Systems: What Are the Economics?" Extension. https://articles. extension.org/pages/73995/ dairy-robotic-milking-systems-what-are-the-economics.

Schimmelpfennig, D. 2016. *Farm Profits and Adoption of Precision Agriculture*. USDA Economic Research Service Report 217. Washington: U.S. Government Publishing Office. https://www.ers.usda.gov/webdocs/publications/80326/ err-217.pdf?v=0.

Seamans, R. 2017. "Artificial Intelligence and Big Data: Good For Innovation?" *Forbes*, September 7. https://www.forbes.com/sites/washingtonbytes/2017/09/07/ artificial-intelligence-and-big-data-good-for-innovation/#29576acf4ddb.

SEC (U.S. Securities and Exchange Commission). 2011. "CF Disclosure Guidance: Topic No. 2." https://www.sec.gov/divisions/corpfin/guidance/cfguidance-topic2. htm.

———. 2018. "Statement on Commission Statement and Guidance on Public Company Cybersecurity Disclosures." https://www.sec.gov/news/public-statement/ statement-stein-2018-02-21.

Sedgewick, A., M. Souppaya, and K. Scarfone. 2015. *Guide to Application Whitelisting*. NIST Special Publication 800-167. https://nvlpubs.nist.gov/nistpubs/ specialpublications/nist.sp.800-167.pdf.

Shapiro, C., and H. Varian. 1998. *Information Rules: A Strategic Guide to the Network Economy*. Boston: Harvard Business Press.

Solow, R. 1957. "Technical Change and the Aggregate Production Function." *Review of Economics and Statistics* 39, no. 3: 312–20.

Stanford University. 2016. "Policy and Legal Considerations." In *Report on One Hundred Year Study of Artificial Intelligence*. https://ai100.stanford.edu/2016-report/ section-iii-prospects-and-recommendations-public-policy/ai-policy-now- and-future/policy.

Stiroh, K. 2002. "Information Technology and the U.S. Productivity Revival: What Do the Industry Data Say?" *American Economic Review* 92, no. 5: 1559–76.

Sykes, L. 2008. "Mechanization and Labor Reduction: A History of U.S. Flue-Cured Tobacco Production, 1950 to 2008." *Tobacco Science*, Fall, 1–83. https://www. tobaccoscienceonline.org/doi/full/10.3381/sp1.

Syverson, C. 2017. "Challenges to Mismeasurement Explanations for the U.S. Productivity Slowdown." *Journal of Economic Perspectives* 31, no. 2: 165–86.

Taddeo, M. 2018. "Regulate Artificial Intelligence to Avert Cyber Race." *Nature*, April 16. https://www.nature.com/articles/d41586-018-04602-6.

Tax Foundation. 2014. "Estonia Has the Most Competitive Tax System in the OECD." https://taxfoundation.org/estonia-has-most-competitive-tax-system-oecd/.

Triplett, J. 1996. "High-Tech Industry Productivity and Hedonic Price Indices." In *OECD Proceedings: Industry Productivity, International Comparison, and Measurement Issues.* Paris: OECD Publishing.

U.S. Bureau of Labor Statistics. 2019. "Current Employment Statistics, Establishment Survey." Retrieved from FRED, Federal Reserve Bank of Saint. Louis. https://fred.stlouisfed.org/series/CES4300000001.

USTR (Office of the U.S. Trade Representative). 2018. "United States–Mexico–Canada Trade Fact Sheet: Modernizing NAFTA into a 21st Century Trade Agreement." https://ustr.gov/about-us/policy-offices/press-office/fact-sheets/2018/october/united-states%E2%80%93mexico%E2%80%93canada-trade-fa-1.

Vainsalu, H. 2017. "How Do Estonians Save Annually 820 Years of Work Without Much Effort?" https://e-estonia.com/how-save-annually-820-years-of-work/.

Valletta, R. 2016. "Recent Flattening in the Higher Education Wage Premium: Polarization, Skill Downgrading, or Both?" In *Education, Skills, and Technical Change: Implications for Future U.S. Growth*, edited by C. Hulten and V. Ramey. Chicago: University of Chicago Press for National Bureau of Economic Research.

Vargas, M., and A. Bonato. 2007. "Tobacco Growing, Family Farmers, and Diversification Strategies in Brazil: Current Prospects and Future Potential for Alternative Crops." Study Commissioned by Ministry of Agrarian Development of Brazil and conduced as a technical document for Second Section of Conference of Parties to the WHO Framework Convention on Tobacco Control. https://www.who.int/tobacco/framework/cop/events/2007/brazil_study.pdf.

Varian, H. 2018. *Artificial Intelligence, Economics, and Industrial Organization.* NBER Working Paper 24839. Cambridge, MA: National Bureau of Economic Research.

Vassil, K. 2015. "Estonian e-Government Ecosystem: Foundation, Applications, Outcomes." Background Paper for *World Development Report 2016: Digital Dividends.* http://pubdocs.worldbank.org/en/165711456838073531/WDR16-BP-Estonian-eGov-ecosystem-Vassil.pdf.

Wang, S., P. Heisey, D. Schimmelpfennig, and E. Ball. 2015. *Agricultural Productivity Growth in the United States: Measurement, Trends, and Drivers.* Economic Research Report 189. U.S. Department of Agriculture, Economic Research Service. Washington: U.S. Government Publishing Office.

Weinbaum, C., and J. Shanahan. 2018. "Intelligence in a Data-Driven Age." *Joint Force Quarterly* 90: 4–9.

West, D. 2010. "Saving Money Through Cloud Computing." Brooking Institution. https://www.brookings.edu/research/saving-money-through-cloud-computing/.

White House. 2017a. *National Security Strategy*. https://www.whitehouse.gov/wp-content/uploads/2017/12/NSS-Final-12-18-2017-0905.pdf.

———. 2017b. "President Trump Signs Memorandum for STEM Education Funding." https://www.whitehouse.gov/articles/president-trump-signs-memorandum-stem-education-funding/.

———. 2018a. "Executive Order Establishing the President's National Council for the American Worker." https://www.whitehouse.gov/presidential-actions/executive-order-establishing-presidents-national-council-american-worker/.

———. 2018b. *National Cyber Strategy of the United States of America*. https://www.whitehouse.gov/wp-content/uploads/2018/09/National-Cyber-Strategy.pdf.

———. 2018c. "Presidential Executive Order on Streamlining and Expediting Requests to Locate Broadband Facilities in Rural America." https://www.whitehouse.gov/presidential-actions/presidential-executive-order-streamlining-expediting-requests-locate-broadband-facilities-rural-america/.

———. 2018d. "Space Policy Directive-2, Streamlining Regulations on Commercial Use of Space." https://www.whitehouse.gov/presidential-actions/space-policy-directive-2-streamlining-regulations-commercial-use-space/.

———. 2019. "Executive Order on Maintaining American Leadership in Artificial Intelligence." https://www.whitehouse.gov/presidential-actions/executive-order-maintaining-american-leadership-artificial-intelligence/.

World Economic Forum. 2018. *The Future of Jobs Report, 2018*. Centre for the New Economy and Society. Geneva: World Economic Forum. http://www3.weforum.org/docs/WEF_Future_of_Jobs_2018.pdf.

Zeira, J. 1998. "Workers, Machines, and Economic Growth." *Quarterly Journal of Economics* 113, no. 4: 1091–1117.

Chapter 8

Abramitzky, R., L. Boustan, and K. Eriksson. 2012. "Europe's Tired, Poor, Huddled Masses: Self-Selection and Economic Outcomes in the Age of Mass Migration." *American Economic Review* 102, no. 5: 1832–56.

Acemoglu, D., and J. Robinson. 2015. "The Rise and Decline of General Laws of Capitalism." *Journal of Economic Perspectives* 29, no. 1: 3–28.

Alesina, A., and G. Angeletos. 2005. "Fairness and Redistribution." *American Economic Review* 95, no. 4: 960–80.

Alhadeff, S. 2018. *Venezuela Emigration, Explained*. Washington: Woodrow Wilson International Center for Scholars.

Andersen, T., B. Holmström, S. Honkapohja, S. Korkman, H. Söderström, and J. Vartiainen. 2007. "The Nordic Model: Embracing Globalization and Sharing Risks." *ETLA B*, Research Institute of the Finnish Economy, no. 232.

Anell, A., A. Glenngård, and S. Merkur. 2012. "Sweden: Health System Review." *Health Systems in Transition* 14, no. 5: 1–159.

Applebaum, A. 2017. "How Stalin Hid Ukraine's Famine from the World." *The Atlantic*, October. https://www.theatlantic.com/international/archive/2017/10/red-famine-anne-applebaum-ukraine-soviet-union/542610/.

Barzel, Y. 1997. *Economic Analysis of Property Rights*. Cambridge: Cambridge University Press.

Basu, K. 2008. "The Enigma of India's Arrival: A Review of Arvind Virmani's *Propelling India: From Socialist Stagnation to Global Power*." *Journal of Economic Literature* 46, no. 2: 396–406.

BEA (U.S. Bureau of Economic Analysis). 2018a. "Table 1.12: National Income by Type of Income." https://apps.bea.gov/iTable/iTable.cfm?reqid=19&step=2#reqid=19&step=2&isuri=1&1921=survey.

———. 2018b. "Table 3.1: Government Current Receipts and Expenditures." https://apps.bea.gov/iTable/iTable.cfm?reqid=19&step=2#reqid=19&step=2&isuri=1&1921=survey.

Becker, G., and C. Mulligan. 2003. "Deadweight Costs and the Size of Government." *Journal of Law and Economics* 46, no. 2: 293–340.

Becker, G., K. Murphy, and M. Grossman. 2006. "The Market for Illegal Goods: The Case of Drugs." *Journal of Political Economy* 114, no. 1: 38–60.

Bergström, F., and R. Gidehag. 2004. *EU versus USA*. Stockholm: Timbro.

Bernhardt, A., H. Boushey, L. Dresser, and C. Tilly. 2008. *The Gloves-Off Economy: Workplace Standards at the Bottom of America's Labor Market*. Ithaca, NY: Cornell University Press.

Birman, I. 1978. "From the Achieved Level." *Soviet Studies* 30, no. 2: 153–72.

Blahous, C. 2018. *The Costs of a National Single-Payer Healthcare System*. Mercatus Working Paper. Arlington, VA: Mercatus Center at George Mason University.

Boettke, P. 1990. *The Political Economy of Soviet Socialism: The Formative Years, 1918–1928*. New York: Springer.

Bollier, J. 2018. "Bernie Sanders Returns Saturday to Green Bay on Repeal the Trump Tax Tour." *Green Bay Press Gazette*, February 12. https://www.greenbaypressgazette.com/story/news/2018/02/12/bernie-sanders-returns-saturday-green-bay-repeal-trump-tax-tour/359545002/.

Borjas, G. 1987. "Self-Selection and the Earnings of Immigrants." *American Economic Review* 77, no. 4: 531–53.

———. 1991. "Immigration and Self-Selection." In *Immigration, Trade, and the Labor Market*, edited by J. Abowd and R. Freeman. Chicago: University of Chicago Press.

Brading, R. 2013. *Populism in Venezuela*. New York: Routledge.

Buera, F., A. Monge-Naranjo, and G. Primiceri. 2011. "Learning the Wealth of Nations." *Econometrica* 79, no. 1: 1–45.

Casey, N. 2018. "Venezuela Inflation Could Reach One Million Percent by Year's End." *New York Times*, July 23. https://www.nytimes.com/2018/07/23/world/americas/venezuela-inflation-crisis.html.

CEA (Council of Economic Advisers). 2018a. *The Opportunity Costs of Socialism*. Washington: White House. https://www.whitehouse.gov/briefings-statements/cea-report-opportunity-costs-socialism/.

———. 2018b. *Economic Report of the President*. Washington: U.S. Government Publishing Office.

Cheremukhin, A., M. Golosov, S. Guriev, and A. Tsyvinski. 2015. *The Economy of the People's Republic of China from 1953*. NBER Working Paper 21397. Cambridge, MA: National Bureau of Economic Research.

Chetty, R., A. Guren, D. Manoli, and A. Weber. 2011. "Are Micro and Macro Labor Supply Elasticities Consistent? A Review of Evidence on the Intensive and Extensive Margins." *American Economic Review* 101, no. 3: 471–75.

Cole, A., and S. Greenberg. 2016. "Details and Analysis of Senator Bernie Sanders's Tax Plan." Tax Foundation. https://taxfoundation.org/details-and-analysis-senator-bernie-sanders-s-tax-plan/.

Collins, S., B. Bosworth, and M. Soto-Class. 2006. *The Economy of Puerto Rico*. Washington: Brookings Institution Press.

Conquest, R. 1986. *The Harvest of Sorrow: Soviet Collectivization and the Terror-Famine*. New York: Oxford University Press.

———. 2005. *The Dragons of Expectation: Reality and Delusion in the Course of History*. New York: W. W. Norton.

Cooper, R. 2018. "How to Pay for Medicare-for-All." *The Week*, August 31. http://theweek.com/articles/792893/how-pay-medicareforall.

Cotterell, A. 2011. *China: A History*. New York: Random House.

Courtois, S., N. Werth, J. Panne, A. Paczkowski, K. Bartosek, J. Margolin. 1999. *The Black Book of Communism*. Cambridge, MA: Harvard University Press.

Dalrymple, D. 1964. "The Soviet Famine of 1932–1934." *Soviet Studies* 15, no. 3: 250–84.

Day, M. 2018a. "An Interview with Julia Salazar." *Jacobin*, July 6. https://www.jacobinmag.com/2018/07/julia-salazar-interview-socialist-new-york-senate.

———. 2018b. "Democratic Socialism, Explained by a Democratic Socialist." *Vox*, August 1. https://www.vox.com/first-person/2018/8/1/17637028/bernie-sanders-alexandria-ocasio-cortez-cynthia-nixon-democratic-socialism-jacobin-dsa.

Deere, C., M. Meurs, and N. Pérez. 1992. "Toward a Periodization of the Cuban Collectivization Process: Changing Incentives and Peasant Response." *Cuban Studies* 22: 115–49.

De Haan, J., S. Lundström, and J. Sturm. 2006. "Market-Oriented Institutions and Policies and Economic Growth: A Critical Survey." *Journal of Economic Surveys* 20, no. 2: 157–91.

Dikötter, F. 2010. *Mao's Great Famine: The History of China's Most Devastating Catastrophe, 1958–62*. London: Bloomsbury.

Dolot, M. 2011. *Execution by Hunger: The Hidden Holocaust*. New York: W. W. Norton.

Dube, R. 2017. "Doctors Flee Desperate Venezuela to Work in Safer Places." *Wall Street Journal*, June 12. https://www.wsj.com/articles/doctors-flee-desperate-venezuela-to-work-in-safer-places-1497303556.

Easton, S., and M. Walker. 1997. "Income, Growth, and Economic Freedom." *American Economic Review* 87, no. 2: 328–32.

Economist. 2017. "How Chávez and Maduro Have Impoverished Venezuela." April 6. https://www.economist.com/finance-and-economics/2017/04/06/how-chavez-and-maduro-have-impoverished-venezuela.

Epstein, R. 1985. *Takings: Private Property and the Power of Eminent Domain*. Cambridge, MA: Harvard University Press.

European Commission. 2017. "Eurostat: Temporary Employees as Percentage of the Total Number of Employees." https://ec.europa.eu/eurostat/web/products-datasets/-/tesem110.

Fang, L., and R. Rogerson. 2011. "Product Market Regulation and Market Work: A Benchmark Analysis." *American Economic Journal: Macroeconomics* 3, no. 2: 163–88.

Farrell, J., and C. Shapiro. 1990. "Horizontal Mergers: An Equilibrium Analysis." *American Economic Review* 80, no. 1: 107–26.

Feldstein, M. 1999. "Tax Avoidance and the Deadweight Loss of the Income Tax." *Review of Economic and Statistics* 81, no. 4: 674–80.

Feldstein, M., and A. Samwick. 1992. *Social Security Rules and Marginal Tax Rates*. NBER Working Paper 3962. Cambridge, MA: National Bureau of Economic Research.

Finkelstein, A., and R. McKnight. 2008. "What Did Medicare Do? The Initial Impact of Medicare on Mortality and Out-of-Pocket Medical Spending." *Journal of Public Economics* 92, no. 7: 1644–68.

Finn, E., Jr., and R. Sousa. 2014. *What Lies Ahead for America's Children and Their Schools*. Stanford, CA: Hoover Institution Press.

Fischel, W. 1995. *Regulatory Takings: Law, Economics, and Politics*. Cambridge, MA: Harvard University Press.

Fischer, S., R. Hall, and J. Taylor. 1981. "Relative Shocks, Relative Price Variability, and Inflation." *Brookings Papers on Economic Activity*, no. 2: 381–441.

Frank, R. 2017. "Why Single-Payer Health Care Saves Money." *New York Times*, July 7. https://www.nytimes.com/2017/07/07/upshot/why-single-payer-health-care-saves-money.html.

Fraser Institute. 1996. *Economic Freedom of the World 1975–1995*. Vancouver: Fraser Institute. https://www.fraserinstitute.org/sites/default/files/EconomicFreedomoftheWorld1975-1995.pdf.

Friedman, M., and R. Friedman. 1980. *Free to Choose: A Personal Statement*. New York: Harcourt.

Galbraith, J. 1984. "A Visit to Russia." *New Yorker*, September 3. https://www.newyorker.com/magazine/1984/09/03/a-visit-to-russia.

Gallen, T. 2015. "Using Participant Behavior to Measure the Value of Social Programs: The Case of Medicaid." PhD diss., University of Chicago.

Ghanta, P. 2013. "List of Countries with Universal Healthcare." True Cost Blog. https://truecostblog.com/2009/08/09/countries-with-universal-healthcare-by-date/.

Glaeser, E., and E. Luttmer. 2003. "The Misallocation of Housing under Rent Control." *American Economic Review* 93, no. 4: 1027–46.

Globerman, S. 2016. *Select Cost Sharing in Universal Health Care Countries*. Vancouver: Fraser Institute. https://www.fraserinstitute.org/sites/default/files/select-cost-sharing-in-universal-health-care-countries.pdf.

Goodkind, D., L. West, and P. Johnson. 2011. "A Reassessment of Mortality in North Korea, 1993–2008." Paper presented at Annual Meeting of the Population Association of America, Washington, March 31–April 2.

Goodspeed, T. 2016. "Microcredit and Adjustment to Environmental Shock: Evidence from the Great Famine in Ireland." *Journal of Development Economics* 121: 258–77.

———. 2017. *Famine and Finance: Credit and the Great Famine of Ireland*. London: Palgrave Macmillan.

Gregory, P. 1990. "The Stalinist Command Economy." *Annals of the American Academy of Political and Social Science* 507, no. 1: 18–25.

———. 2004. *The Political Economy of Stalinism: Evidence from the Soviet Secret Archives*. Cambridge: Cambridge University Press.

Grosse-Tebbe, S., and J. Figueras. 2004. *Snapshots of Health Systems* Copenhagen: World Health Organization.

Gruber, J., and D. Wise. 1999. *Social Security and Retirement Around the World*. Chicago: University of Chicago Press.

Gurley, J. 1969. "Capitalist and Maoist Economic Development." In *America's Asia*, edited by E. Friedman and M. Selden. New York: Random House.

———. 1976a. *Challengers to Capitalism: Marx, Lenin, and Mao*. San Francisco: San Francisco Book Company.

———. 1976b. *China's Economy and the Maoist Strategy*. New York: Monthly Review Press.

Gwartney, J., R. Holcombe, and R. Lawson. 2006. "Institutions and the Impact of Investment on Growth." *Kyklos* 59, no. 2: 255–73.

Gwartney, J., R. Lawson, and J. Hall. 2017. *Economic Freedom of the World: 2017 Report*. Vancouver: Fraser Institute. https://www.fraserinstitute.org/sites/default/files/economic-freedom-of-the-world-2017.pdf.

Hall, J., and A. Lawson. 2014. "Economic Freedom of the World: An Accounting of the Literature." *Contemporary Economic Policy* 32, no. 1: 1–19.

Hayek, F. 1945. "The Use of Knowledge in Society." *American Economic Review* 35, no. 4: 519–30.

Henry J. Kaiser Family Foundation. 2016. "Medicare Beneficiaries as a Percent of Total Population." https://www.kff.org/medicare/state-indicator/medicare-beneficiaries-as-of-total-pop/?currentTimeframe=0&sortModel=%7B%22coll d%22:%22Location%22,%22sort%22:%22asc%22%7D.

Hodge, S. 2011. "No Country Leans on Upper-Income Households as Much as U.S." Tax Foundation. https://taxfoundation.org/no-country-leans-upper-income-households-much-us/.

Holmes, L. 2009. *Communism: A Very Short Introduction*. Oxford: Oxford University Press.

Jisheng, Y. 2012. *Tombstone: The Great Chinese Famine, 1958–1962*. New York: Farrar, Straus & Giroux.

Johnson, D., and K. Brooks. 1983. *Prospects for Soviet Agriculture in the 1980s*. Bloomington: Indiana University Press.

Kirkeboen, L., E. Leuven, and M. Mogstad. 2016. "Field of Study, Earnings, and Self-Selection." *Quarterly Journal of Economics* 131, no. 3: 1057–111.

Kleven, H. 2014. "How Can Scandinavians Tax So Much?" *Journal of Economic Perspectives* 28, no. 4: 77–98.

Kliff, S. 2014. "How Vermont's Single-Payer Health Care Dream Fell Apart." *Vox*, December 22. https://www.vox.com/2014/12/22/7427117/single-payer-vermont-shumlin.

Konrad, W. 2017. "How Exactly Would Single-Payer Health Care Work?" CBS News. https://www.cbsnews.com/news/is-single-payer-health-insurance-realistic/.

Kornai, J. 1992. *The Socialist System: The Political Economy of Communism*. Oxford: Oxford University Press.

Krugman, P. 2017. "Three Legs Good, No Legs Bad." *New York Times*, July 10. https://www.nytimes.com/2017/07/10/opinion/obamacare-repeal.html.

Kurmanaev, A. 2018. "The Tragedy of Venezuela." *Wall Street Journal*, May 24. https://www.wsj.com/articles/the-tragedy-of-venezuela-1527177202.

Lazarev, V., and P. Gregory. 2003. "Commissars and Cars: A Case Study in the Political Economy of Dictatorship." *Journal of Comparative Economics* 31, no. 1: 1–19.

Lenin, V. 1918. "Organisation of Food Detachments." https://www.marxists.org/archive/lenin/works/1918/jun/27.htm.

———. 1951. "Woman in Society." In *The Woman Question: Selections from the Writings of Marx, Engels, Lenin, and Stalin*. New York: International Publishers.

Lin, J. 1992. "Rural Reforms and Agricultural Growth in China." *American Economic Review* 82, no. 1: 34–51.

Marx, K. 1867. *Das Kapital, Volume I*. English edition of 1887.

———. 1875. *Critique of the Gotha Programme*. Online edition. https://www.marxists.org/archive/marx/works/1875/gotha/.

Marx, K., and F. Engels. 1848. *Communist Manifesto*. Online edition. https://www.marxists.org/archive/marx/works/download/pdf/Manifesto.pdf.

Matsuda, R. 2017. "The Japanese Health Care System." International Health Care System Profiles. http://international.commonwealthfund.org.

McCloskey, D. 2016. *Bourgeois Equality: How Ideas, Not Capital or Institutions, Enriched the World*. Chicago: University of Chicago Press.

McKenzie, B. 2018. "Increase in the Venezuelan VAT General Rate from 12% to 16%." https://www.lexology.com/library/detail. aspx?g=39ab8f59-1767-4d80-a55c-495276006fa3.

Meng, X., N. Qian, and P. Yared. 2015. "The Institutional Causes of China's Great Famine, 1959–1961." *Review of Economic Studies* 82, no. 4: 1568–611.

Mermin, G., L. Burman, and F. Sammartino. 2016. "An Analysis of Senator Bernie Sanders's Tax Proposals." Tax Policy Center.

Meslé, F., and J. Vallin. 2012. *Mortality and Causes of Death in 20th-Century Ukraine*. New York: Springer Science & Business Media.

Miller, T., A. Kim, and J. Roberts. 2018. "2018 Index of Economic Freedom." Heritage Foundation. https://www.heritage.org/index/pdf/2018/book/index_2018.pdf.

Monaldi, F. 2018. "The Death Spiral of Venezuela's Oil Sector and What Can Be Done About It." *Forbes*, January 24. https://www.forbes.com/sites/ thebakersinstitute/2018/01/24/ the-death-spiral-of-venezuelas-oil-sector-what-if-anything-can-be-done-about-it/#524226ea7e60.

Mulligan, C. 2012. *The Redistribution Recession: How Labor Market Distortions Contracted the Economy*. New York: Oxford University Press.

———. 2015. *Side Effects: The Economic Consequences of Healthcare Reform*. Chicago: University of Chicago Press.

Mulligan, C., and K. Tsui. 2016. *The Upside-Down Economics of Regulated and Otherwise Rigid Prices*. NBER Working Paper 22305. Cambridge, MA: National Bureau of Economic Research.

Neal, D. 1997. "The Effect of Catholic Secondary Schooling on Educational Attainment." *Journal of Labor Economics* 15, no. 1: 98–123.

———. 1998. "What Have We Learned about the Benefits of Private Schooling?" *Federal Reserve Bank of New York Economic Policy Review*, March. https://pdfs. semanticscholar.org/7b95/7d60c0c988e1d32fe364acc36cb337b1623d.pdf.

New York Times Company. 2003. "*New York Times* Statement about 1932 Pulitzer Prize Awarded to Walter Duranty." *New York Times* website, https://www.nytco. com/ new-york-times-statement-about-1932-pulitzer-prize-awarded-to-walter-duranty/.

Nolan, P. 1988. *The Political Economy of Collective Farms: An Analysis of China's Post-Mao Rural Reforms*. Cambridge: Polity Press.

Norberg, J. 2016. *Progress: Ten Reasons to Look Forward to the Future*. London: Oneworld.

Nove, A. 2010. *The Economics of Feasible Socialism*. New York: Routledge.

O'Connor, J. 1968. "Agrarian Reforms in Cuba, 1959–63." *Science & Society* 32, no. 2: 169–217.

OECD (Organization for Economic Cooperation and Development). 2018a. *Education at a Glance 2018.* Paris: OECD Publishing.

———. 2018b. "General Government Spending (Indicator)." https://www.oecd-ilibrary.org/governance/general-government-spending/indicator/english_a31cbf4d-en.

———. 2018c. "Table I.7: Top Statutory Personal Tax Rate and Top Marginal Tax Rates for Employees." https://stats.oecd.org/index.aspx?DataSetCode=TABLE_I7.

Ó Gráda, C. 2000. *Black '47 and Beyond: The Great Irish Famine in History, Economy, and Memory.* Princeton, NJ: Princeton University Press.

Oil Sands Magazine. 2016. "Why Venezuela Is Alberta's Biggest Competitor." February 15. https://www.oilsandsmagazine.com/news/2016/2/15/why-venezuela-is-albertas-biggest-competitor.

Olejaz, M., A. Nielsen, A. Rudkjøbing, H. Birk, A. Krasnik, and C. Hernández-Quevedo. 2012. "Denmark: Health System Review." *Health Systems in Transition* 14, no. 2.

Olsen, E. 2008. "Getting More from Low-Income Housing Assistance." Brookings Institution. https://www.brookings.edu/research/getting-more-from-low-income-housing-assistance/.

Olson, M. 1965. *The Logic of Collective Action: Public Goods and the Theory of Groups.* Cambridge, MA: Harvard University Press.

Pauly, M. 1968. "The Economics of Moral Hazard: Comment." *American Economic Review* 58: 531–37.

Piketty, T. 2014. *Capital in the 21st Century.* Cambridge, MA: Harvard University Press.

Pinkovskiy, M., and X. Sala-i-Martin. 2009. *Parametric Estimations of the World Distribution of Income.* NBER Working Paper 15433. Cambridge, MA: National Bureau of Economic Research.

Pipes, R. 2003. *Communism: A History.* New York: Modern Library.

Potosky, Emily. 2016. "How High Are Capital Gains Taxes in Your State?" Tax Foundation, July 25. https://taxfoundation.org/how-high-are-capital-gains-taxes-your-state.

Prescott, E. 2004. "Why Do Americans Work So Much More Than Europeans?" *Federal Reserve Bank of Minneapolis Quarterly Review* 28, no. 1: 2–15.

Pryor, F. 1992. *The Red and the Green: The Rise and Fall of Collectivized Agriculture in Marxist Regimes.* Princeton, NJ: Princeton University Press.

Przeworski, A., and J. Sprague. 1986. *Paper Stones: A History of Electoral Socialism.* Chicago: University of Chicago Press.

PwC (PricewaterhouseCoopers). 2018a. "Value-Added Tax (VAT) Rates." http://taxsummaries.pwc.com/ID/Value-added-tax-(VAT)-rates.

———. 2018b. "Venezuela: Overview." http://taxsummaries.pwc.com/ID/Venezuela-Overview.

Rasmussen, L. 2015. "Nordic Solutions and Challenges: A Danish Perspective." Institute of Politics of Harvard Kennedy School, Cambridge, MA. YouTube. https://www.youtube.com/watch?v=MgrJnXZ_WGo.

Rector, R., and K. Johnson. 2004. *Understanding Poverty in America*. Washington: Heritage Foundation.

Rice, T., W. Quentin, A. Anell, A. Barnes, P. Rosenau, L. Unruh, and E. Van Ginneken. 2018. "Revisiting Out-of-Pocket Requirements: Trends in Spending, Financial Access Barriers, and Policy in Ten High-Income Countries." *BMC Health Services Research* 18, no. 1: 371.

Ringard, A., A. Sagan, I. Saunes, and A. Lindahl. 2013. "Norway: Health System Review." *Health Systems in Transition* 15, no. 8.

Robinson, J., and S. Adler. 1958. *China: An Economic Perspective*. Washington: Fabian Society.

Roemer, J. 1994. *A Future for Socialism*. Cambridge, MA: Harvard University Press.

———. 1995. "A Future for Socialism." *Theoria: A Journal of Social and Political Theory* 85: 17–46.

Rogerson, R. 2006. "Understanding Differences in Hours Worked." *Review of Economic Dynamics*, no. 3: 365–409.

———. 2007. "Taxation and Market Work: Is Scandinavia an Outlier?" *Economic Theory* 32, no. 1: 59–85.

Rosen, S. 1997. "Public Employment, Taxes, and the Welfare State in Sweden." In *The Welfare State in Transition: Reforming the Swedish Model*, edited by R. Freeman, R. Topel, and B. Swedenborg. Chicago: University of Chicago Press.

Rummel, R. 1994. *Death by Government*. New Brunswick, NJ: Transaction.

———. 2011. *China's Bloody Century: Genocide and Mass Murder since 1900*. New York: Transaction.

Sala-i-Martin, X. 2006. "The World Distribution of Income: Falling Poverty and . . . Convergence, Period." *Quarterly Journal of Economics* 121, no. 2: 351–97.

Salazar-Carrillo, J., and A. Nodarse-Leon. 2015. *Cuba: From Economic Take-Off to Collapse under Castro*. New York: Transactions.

Sammartino, F., L. Burman, J. Nunns, J. Rosenberg, and J. Rohaly. 2016. "An Analysis of Senator Bernie Sanders's Tax Proposals." Tax Policy Center, March 4. https://www.taxpolicycenter.org/sites/default/files/alfresco/publication-pdfs/2000639-an-analysis-of-senator-bernie-sanderss-tax-proposals.pdf.

Samuelson, P. 1976. *Economics, 10th Edition*. New York: McGraw-Hill.

Samuelson, P., and W. Nordhaus. 1989. *Economics, 13th Edition*. New York: McGraw-Hill.

Sanandaji, N. 2015. *Scandinavian Unexceptionalism*. London: Institute of Economic Affairs.

———. 2016. *Debunking Utopia: Exposing the Myth of Nordic Socialism*. Washington: WND Books.

Sanders, B. 2017. "Options to Finance Medicare for All." https://www.sanders.senate.gov/download/options-to-finance-medicare-for-all?inline=file.

———. 2018. "Disneyland Workers Face Ruthless Exploitation: Their Fight Is Our Fight." *The Guardian*, June 7.

Schumpeter, J. 1942. *Capitalism, Socialism, and Democracy*. New York: Harper Brothers.

Shleifer, A. 1998. "State versus Private Ownership." *Journal of Economic Perspectives* 12, no. 4: 133–50.

Shleifer, A., and R. Vishny. 1992. "Pervasive Shortages Under Socialism." *RAND Journal of Economics* 23, no. 2: 237–46.

Sigurgeirsdóttir, S., J. Waagfjörð, and A. Maresso. 2014. "Iceland: Health System Review." *Health Systems in Transition* 16, no. 6.

Starr, P. 2016. "Why Democrats Should Beware Sanders' Socialism." *Politico*, February 22. https://www.politico.com/magazine/story/2016/02/bernie-sanders-2016-socialism-213667.

State Council of the People's Republic of China. 2016. "China's Progress in Poverty Reduction and Human Rights." http://english.gov.cn/policies/latest_releases/2016/10/17/content_281475468533275.htm.

Stenkula, M., D. Johansson, and G. Du Rietz. 2014. "Marginal Taxation on Labour Income in Sweden from 1862 to 2010." *Scandinavian Economic History Review* 62, no. 2: 163–87.

Sturny, Isabell. 2017. "The Swiss Health Care System." International Health Care System Profiles. http://international.commonwealthfund.org.

Sunstein, C. 2019. "Trump Is Right to Warn Democrats about 'Socialism.'" Bloomberg Opinion, February 7.

Svalund, J. 2013. "Labor Market Institutions, Mobility, and Dualization in the Nordic Countries." *Nordic Journal of Working Life Studies* 3, no. 1: 123–44.

Thatcher, M. 1976. "Interview for Thames TV *This Week*." https://www.margaretthatcher.org/document/102953.

Transparency International. 2017. "The Bolivarian Project Enlarged the Platform of State-Owned Enterprises to Increase Economic, Political and Social Control." https://transparencia.org.ve/project/the-bolivarian-project-enlarged-the-platform-of-state-owned-enterprises-to-increase-economic-political-and-social-control/.

Turner, J. 2005. *Social Security Privatization Around the World*. Washington: AARP Public Policy Institute.

U.S. Energy Information Administration. 2018. "International Energy Statistics." https://www.eia.gov/beta/international/data/browser/#/?pa=0000000000000000000000000000000vg&f=M&c=0000010000000000000000000000000000000000000002&ct=0&tl_id=5-M&vs=INTL.53-1-CAN-TBPD.M~~INTL.53-1-VEN-TBPD.M&vo=0&v=T&start=199401&end=201806.

USTR (Office of the U.S. Trade Representative). 2013. "Venezuela." http://www.sice.oas.org/ctyindex/USA/USTR_Reports/2013/NTE/2013%20NTE%20Venezuela%20Final.pdf.

Vallin, J., F. Meslé, S. Adamets, and S. Pyrozkov. 2012. "The Crisis of the 1930s." In *Mortality and Causes of Death in 20th-Century Ukraine*, edited by F. Meslé and J. Vallin. New York: Springer.

Von Mises, L. 1990. *Economic Calculation in the Socialist Commonwealth.* Translated from the German by S. Alder. Auburn, AL: Ludwig Von Mises Institute. (Orig. pub. 1920.)

Vuorenkoski, L., P. Mladovsky, and E. Mossialos. 2008. "Finland: Health System Review." *Health Systems in Transition* 10, no. 4.

Walker, K. 1965. *Planning in Chinese Agriculture: Socialisation and the Private Sector, 1956–1962.* New York: Psychology Press.

Walters, R. 1966. "Soviet Economic Aid to Cuba: 1959–64." *International Affairs* 42, no. 1: 74–86.

Wammes, J., et al. 2017. "The Dutch Health Care System." International Health Care System Profiles. http://international.commonwealthfund.org.

Weisbart, E. 2012. "A Single-Payer System Would Reduce U.S. Health Care Costs." *Virtual Monitor* 14, no. 11: 897–903.

Westhoff, W., R. Rodriguez, C. Cousins, and R. McDermott. 2010. "Cuban Healthcare Providers in Venezuela: A Case Study." *Public Health* 124, no. 9: 519–24.

Whinston, M. 2006. *Lectures on Antitrust Economics.* Cambridge, MA: MIT Press.

Williamson, O. 1968. "Economies as an Antitrust Defense: The Welfare Trade-Offs." *American Economic Review* 58, no. 1: 18–36.

Wilson, P. 2015. "The Collapse of Chávezcare." *Foreign Policy*, April 27. https://foreignpolicy.com/2015/04/27/chavez-maduro-healthcare-venezuela-cuba/.

Winston, C. 2010. *Last Exit: Privatization and Deregulation of the U.S. Transportation System.* Washington: Brookings Institution Press.

Woodman, J. 2015. *Patients Beyond Borders: Everybody's Guide to Affordable, World-Class Medical Travel.* Chapel Hill, NC: Healthy Travel Media.

Yin, W. 2008. "Market Incentives and Pharmaceutical Innovation." *Journal of Health Economics* 27, no. 4: 1060–77.

Zaleski, E. 1980. *Stalinist Planning for Economic Growth, 1933–1952.* Chapel Hill: University of North Carolina Press.

Zhou, K. 1996. *How the Farmers Changed China: The Power of the People.* Boulder, CO: Westview Press.

Zimbalist, A., and S. Eckstein. 1987. "Patterns of Cuban Development: The First Twenty-Five Years." *World Development* 15, no. 1: 5–22.

Chapter 9

Abraham, K., and R. Haskins. 2017. *The Promise of Evidence-Based Policymaking: Report of the Commission on Evidence-Based Policymaking*. Washington: Commission on Evidence-Based Policymaking. https://www.cep.gov/report/cep-final-report.pdf.

Arkansas Department of Human Services. 2018a. "Arkansas Works Program: October 2018 Report."

———. 2018b. "Monthly Enrollment and Expenditures Report: Calendar Year 2018."

Armour, P., R. Burkhauser, and J. Larrimore. 2013. "Deconstructing Income and Income Inequality Measures: A Crosswalk from Market Income to Comprehensive Income." *American Economic Review: Papers and Proceedings* 103, no. 3: 173–77.

Baicker, K., A. Finkelstein, J. Song, and S. Taubman. 2014. "The Impact of Medicaid on Labor Market Activity and Program Participation: Evidence from the Oregon Health Insurance Experiment." *American Economic Review* 104, no. 5: 322–28.

Bauer, L., D. Schanzenbach, and J. Shambaugh. 2018. "Work Requirements and Safety Net Programs." Hamilton Project, October.

Berndt, E. 2006. "The Boskin Commission Report After a Decade: After-life or Requiem?" *International Productivity Monitor, Centre for the Study of Living Standards* 12: 61–73.

Besharov, D., and K. Couch. 2009. "European Measures of Income, Poverty, and Social Exclusion: Recent Developments and Lessons for U.S. Poverty Measurement." *Journal of Policy Analysis and Management* 28, no. 4: 713–15.

———. 2012. Counting the Poor: New Thinking About European Poverty Measures and Lessons for the United States. New York: Oxford University Press.

Blinder, A. 1985. "Comment: Measuring Income—What Kind Should Be In?" In *Proceedings of the Bureau of the Census Conference on the Measurement of Noncash Benefits*. Washington: U.S. Department of Commerce.

Bloom, D., and C. Michalopoulos. 2001. *How Welfare and Work Policies Affect Employment and Income: A Synthesis of Research*. New York: Manpower Demonstration Research Corporation.

Boskin, M., E. Dulberger, R. Gordon, Z. Griliches, and D. Jorgenson. 1996. "Toward a More Accurate Measure of the Cost of Living: Final Report to the Senate Finance Committee from the Advisory Commission to Study the Consumer Price Index."

Burkhauser, R. 2009. "Deconstructing European Poverty Measures: What Relative and Absolute Scales Measure." *Journal of Policy Analysis and Management* 28, no. 4: 715–24.

Burkhauser, R., K. Corinth, J. Elwell, and J. Larrimore. 2019. "Evaluating the Success of President Johnson's War on Poverty: Revisiting the Historical Record Using a Full Income Poverty Measure." Working paper.

Burkhauser, R., N. Hérault, S. Jenkins, and R. Wilkins. 2018. "Top Incomes and Inequality in the U.K.: Reconciling Estimates from Household Survey and Tax Return Data." *Oxford Economic Papers* 70, no. 2: 301–26.

Burkhauser, R., J. Larrimore, and S. Lyons. 2017. "Measuring Health Insurance Benefits: The Case of People with Disabilities." *Contemporary Economic Policy* 35, no. 3: 439–56.

Burkhauser, R., J. Larrimore, and K. Simon. 2012. "A 'Second Opinion' on the Economic Health of the American Middle Class." *National Tax Journal* 65, no. 1: 7–32.

———. 2013. "Measuring the Impact of Valuing Health Insurance on Levels and Trends in Inequality and How the Affordable Care Act of 2010 Could Affect Them." *Contemporary Economic Policy* 31, no. 4: 779–94.

Burkhauser, R., T. Smeeding, and J. Merz. 1996. "Relative Inequality and Poverty in Germany and the United States Using Alternative Equivalence Scales." *Review of Income and Wealth* 42, no. 4: 381–400.

Burtless, G., and C. Pulliam. 2018. "Income Data from the Census May Not Tell Full Story on Middle-Class Trends." Brookings Institution, September 17.

Canberra Group. 2011. *Handbook on Household Income Statistics*, 2nd ed. Geneva: United Nations Economic Commission for Europe.

CBO (Congressional Budget Office). 2013. "The Distribution of Household Income and Federal Taxes, 2010." https://www.cbo.gov/sites/default/files/113th-congress-2013-2014/reports/44604-averagetaxrates.pdf.

CEA (Council of Economic Advisers). 1964. "The Problem of Poverty in America." In *Economic Report of the President*. Washington: U.S. Government Printing Office.

———. 2014. "The War on Poverty 50 Years Later: A Progress Report." In *Economic Report of the President*. Washington: U.S. Government Publishing Office.

———. 2018. *Expanding Work Requirements in Non-Cash Welfare Programs*. Washington: White House. https://www.whitehouse.gov/wp-content/uploads/2018/07/Expanding-Work-Requirements-in-Non-Cash-Welfare-Programs.pdf.

Chetty, R., J. Friedman, and J. Rockoff. 2011. "New Evidence on the Long-Term Impacts of Tax Credits." *Proceedings: Annual Conference on Taxation and Minutes of the Annual Meeting of the National Tax Association* 104: 116–24.

Chetty, R., J. Friedman, and E. Saez. 2013. "Using Differences in Knowledge across Neighborhoods to Uncover the Impacts of the EITC on Earnings." *American Economic Review* 103, no. 7: 2683–2721.

ChildCare Aware of America. 2018. "The U.S. and the High Cost of Childcare: A Review of Prices and Proposed Solutions for a Broken System." http://usa.childcareaware.org/advocacy-public-policy/resources/research/costofcare/.

Citro, C., and R. Michael. 1995. *Measuring Poverty: A New Approach*. Report for National Research Council. Washington: National Academies Press.

CMS (Centers for Medicare & Medicaid Services). 2018a. "CMS Fast Facts." Available at https://www.cms.gov/Research-Statistics-Data-and-Systems/Statistics-Trends-and-Reports/CMS-Fast-Facts/index.html

———. 2018b. "Re: Opportunities to Promote Work and Community Engagement among Medicaid Beneficiaries." SMD 18-002. U.S. Department of Health and Human Services.

Coleman-Jensen, A., M. Rabbitt, C. Gregory, and A. Singh. 2018. "Household Food Security in the United States in 2017." Report ER-256. U.S. Department of Agriculture, Economic Research Service.

Collinson, R., I. Ellen, and J. Ludwig. 2016. "Low-Income Housing Policy." In *Economics of Means-Tested Transfer Programs in the United States, Volume 2*, edited by R. Moffitt. Chicago: University of Chicago Press for National Bureau of Economic Research.

Dague, L., T. DeLeire, and L. Leininger. 2017. "The Effect of Public Insurance Coverage for Childless Adults on Labor Supply." *American Economic Journal: Economic Policy* 9, no. 2: 124–54.

Dahl, G., and L. Lochner. 2012. "The Impact of Family Income on Child Achievement: Evidence from the Earned Income Tax Credit." *American Economic Review* 102, no. 5: 1927–56.

———. 2017. "The Impact of Family Income on Child Achievement: Evidence from the Earned Income Tax Credit: Reply." *American Economic Review* 107, no. 2: 629–31.

Dave, D., S. Decker, R. Kaestner, and K. Simon. 2015. "The Effect of Medicaid Expansions in the Late 1980s and Early 1990s on the Labor Supply of Pregnant Women." *American Journal of Health Economics* 1, no. 2: 165–93.

Duncan, G., P. Morris, and C. Rodrigues. 2011. "Does Money Really Matter? Estimating Impacts of Family Income on Young Children's Achievement with Data from Random-Assignment Experiments." Developmental Psychology 47, no. 5: 1263–79.

East, C. 2018. "Immigrants' Labor Supply Response to Food Stamp Access." *Labour Economics* 51: 202–26.

Eberstadt, N. 2016. *Men Without Work: America's Invisible Crisis*. West Conshohocken, PA: Templeton Press.

Eissa, N., and H. Hoynes. 2004. "Taxes and the Labor Market Participation of Married Couples: The Earned Income Tax Credit." *Journal of Public Economics* 88: 1931–58.

Eissa, N., and J. Liebman. 1996. "Labor Supply Response to the Earned Income Tax Credit." *Quarterly Journal of Economics* 111, no. 2: 605–37.

Ellwood, D. 2000. "The Impact of the Earned Income Tax Credit and Social Policy Reforms on Work, Marriage, and Living Arrangements." *National Tax Journal* 53, no. 4: 1063–1105.

Elwell, J., and R. Burkhauser. 2018. "Income Growth and Its Distribution from Eisenhower to Obama: The Growing Importance of In-Kind Transfers." Working paper.

Fang, H., and M. Keane. 2004. "Assessing the Impact of Welfare Reform on Single Mothers." *Brookings Papers on Economic Activity*, no. 1: 1–116.

Finkelstein, A., N. Hendren, and E. Luttmer. Forthcoming. "The Value of Medicaid: Interpreting Results from the Oregon Health Insurance Experiment." *Journal of Political Economy*, November, 1–78.

Fitzpatrick, M. 2010. "Preschoolers Enrolled and Mothers at Work? The Effects of Universal Prekindergarten." *Journal of Labor Economics* 28, no. 1: 51–85.

Flood, S., M. King, R. Rodgers, S. Ruggles, and R. Warren. 2018. "Integrated Public Use Microdata Series, Current Population Survey: Version 6.0." Current Population Survey. https://cps.ipums.org/cps.

Forster, M., and M. D'Ercole. 2012. "The OECD Approach to Measuring Income Distribution and Poverty." In *Counting the Poor: New Thinking About European Poverty Measures and Lessons for the United States*, edited by D. Besharov and K. Couch. New York: Oxford University Press.

Fox, L., C. Wimer, I. Garfinkel, N. Kaushal, and J. Waldfogel. 2015. "Waging War on Poverty: Poverty Trends Using a Historical Supplemental Poverty Measure." *Journal of Policy Analysis and Management* 34, no. 3: 567–92.

Fry, R., and D. Cohn. 2011. "Living Together: The Economics of Cohabitation." Pew Research Center, Washington.

Gallen, T. 2015. "Using Participant Behavior to Measure the Value of Social Programs: The Case of Medicaid." *Proceedings: Annual Conference on Taxation and Minutes of the Annual Meeting of the National Tax Association* 108: 1–54.

Garthwaite, C., T. Gross, and M. Notowidigdo. 2014. "Public Health Insurance, Labor Supply, and Employment Lock." *Quarterly Journal of Economics* 129, no. 2: 653–96.

Gillette, M. 2010. *Launching the War on Poverty: An Oral History*. New York: Oxford University Press.

Gordon, R. 2006. *The Boskin Commission Report: A Retrospective One Decade Later*. NBER Working Paper 12311. Cambridge, MA: National Bureau of Economic Research.

Gottschalk, P., and T. Smeeding. 1997. "Cross-National Comparisons of Earnings and Income Inequality." *Journal of Economic Literature* 35, no. 2: 633–87.

Grogger, J. 2003. "The Effects of Time Limits, the EITC, and Other Policy Changes on Welfare Use, Work, and Income Among Female-Headed Families." *Review of Economics and Statistics* 85, no. 2: 394–408.

Gubits, D., M. Shinn, S. Bell, M. Wood, S. Dastrup, C. Solari, S. Brown, L. Dunton, W. Lin, D. McInnis, J. Rodriguez, G. Savidge, and B. Spellman. 2015. "Family Options Study: Short-Term Impacts of Housing and Services Interventions for Homeless Families." U.S. Department of Housing and Urban Development, Office of Policy Development and Research.

Gubits, D., M. Shinn, M. Wood, S. Bell, S. Dastrup, C. Solari, S. Brown, D. McInnis, T. McCall, and U. Kattel. 2016. "Family Options Study: 3-Year Impacts of Housing and Services Interventions for Homeless Families." U.S. Department of Housing and Urban Development, Office of Policy Development and Research.

Hamilton, G., S. Freedman, L. Gennetian, C. Michalopoulos, J. Walter, D. Adams-Ciardullo, A. Gassman-Pines, S. McGroder, M. Zaslow, J. Brooks, S. Ahluwalia, E. Small, and B. Ricchetti. 2001. "National Evaluation of Welfare-to-Work Strategies: How Effective Are Different Welfare-to-Work Approaches? Five-Year Adult and Child Impacts for Eleven Programs." U.S. Department of Health and Human Services and U.S. Department of Education.

Hartley, R., S. Collyer, J. Waldfogel, and C. Wimer. 2018. "Recent Trends in Food Stamp Usage and Implications for Increased Work Requirements." *Poverty and Social Policy Briefs* 2, no. 5: 1–7.

Haskins, R. 2007. *Work over Welfare: The Inside Story of the 1996 Welfare Reform Law.* Washington: Brookings Institution Press.

Hausman, J. 2003. "Sources of Bias and Solutions to Bias in the Consumer Price Index." *Journal of Economic Perspectives* 17, no. 1: 23–44.

HHS (U.S. Department of Health and Human Services). 2000. "Reasons for Measuring Poverty in the United States in the Context of Public Policy: A Historical Review, 1916–1995."

———. 2014. "TANF & SSP: Total Number of Recipients: Fiscal and Calendar Year 2013 Average Monthly Number Families: October 2012 through December 2013." Office of Family Assistance. Administration for Children and Families.

Hoynes, H., D. Miller, and D. Simon. 2015. "Income, the Earned Income Tax Credit, and Infant Health." *American Economic Journal: Economic Policy* 7, no. 1: 172–211.

Hoynes, H., and D. Schanzenbach. 2012. "Work Incentives and the Food Stamp Program." *Journal of Public Economics* 96, nos. 1–2: 151–62.

HUD (U. S. Department of Housing and Urban Development). 2015. "Monitoring of the Community Service and Self-Sufficiency Requirement." Office of Public and Indian Housing. Audit Report 2015-KC-001. https://www.hudoig.gov/sites/default/files/documents/2015-KC-0001.pdf.

———. 2018. "Assisted Housing: National and Local: Picture of Subsidized Households." https://www.huduser.gov/portal/datasets/assthsg.html#2009-2017_query.

IRS (Internal Revenue Service). 2016. "Statistics of Income, 2016: Individual Income Tax Returns." https://www.irs.gov/pub/irs-pdf/p1304.pdf.

Jacob, B., M. Kapustin, and J. Ludwig. 2015. "The Impact of Housing Assistance on Child Outcomes: Evidence from a Randomized Housing Lottery." *Quarterly Journal of Economics* 130, no. 1: 465–506.

Jacob, B., and J. Ludwig. 2012. "The Effects of Housing Assistance on Labor Supply: Evidence from a Voucher Lottery." *American Economic Review* 102, no. 1: 272–304.

Johnson, L. 1965. Public Papers of the Presidents of the United States: Lyndon B. Johnson: Containing the Public Messages, Speeches, and Statements of the President 1963–64 (in Two Books). Washington: U.S. Government Printing Office.

Kaestner, R., and D. Lubotsky. 2016. "Health Insurance and Income Inequality." *Journal of Economic Perspectives* 30, no. 2: 53–78.

Kaiser Family Foundation. 2018. "Medicaid Waiver Tracker: Approved and Pending Section 1115 Waivers by State." December 7. https://www.kff.org/medicaid/issue-brief/medicaid-waiver-tracker-approved-and-pending-section-1115-waivers-by-state/.

Lampman, R. 1971. *Ends and Means of Reducing Income Poverty*. Institute for Research on Poverty Monograph Series. Chicago: Markham.

Larrimore, J., R. Burkhauser, and P. Armour. 2015. "Accounting for Income Changes over the Great Recession Relative to Previous Recessions: The Impact of Taxes and Transfers." *National Tax Journal* 68, no. 2: 218–318.

Larrimore, J., and D. Splinter. 2019. "How Much Does Health Insurance Cost? Comparison of Premiums in Administrative and Survey Data." *Economics Letters* 174: 132–35.

Levy, D., L. Edmonds, and J. Simington. 2018. "Work Requirements in Public Housing Authorities: Experiences to Date and Knowledge Gaps." January. Urban Institute, Washington.

Long, S., G. Kirby, R. Kurka, and S. Boots. 1998. *Child Care Assistance Under Welfare Reform: Early Responses by the States*. Assessing the New Federalism, Occasional Paper 15. Washington: Urban Institute.

Manoli, D., and N. Turner. 2018. "Cash-on-Hand and College Enrollment: Evidence from Population Tax Data and the Earned Income Tax Credit." *American Economic Journal: Economic Policy* 10, no. 2: 242–71.

Mead, L. 2014. "Overselling the Earned Income Tax Credit." *National Affairs*, Fall.

Meyer, B., and D. Rosenbaum. 2001. "Welfare, the Earned Income Tax Credit, and the Labor Supply of Single Mothers." *Quarterly Journal of Economics* 116, no. 3: 1063–1114.

Meyer, B., and J. Sullivan. 2003. "Measuring the Well-Being of the Poor Using Income and Consumption." *Journal of Human Services* 38: 1180–1220.

———. 2004. "The Effects of Welfare and Tax Reform: The Material Well-Being of Single Mothers in the 1980s and 1990s." *Journal of Public Economics* 88: 1387–1420.

———. 2008. "Changes in the Consumption, Income, and Well-Being of Single-Mother-Headed Families." *American Economic Review* 98, no. 5: 2221–41.

———. 2012a. "Identifying the Disadvantaged: Official Poverty, Consumption Poverty, and the New Supplemental Poverty Measure." *Journal of Economic Perspectives*, Summer, 111–36.

———. 2012b. "Winning the War: Poverty from the Great Society to the Great Recession." *Brookings Papers on Economic Activity*, Fall, 133–83.

———. 2013. *Winning the War: Poverty from the Great Society to the Great Recession*. NBER Working Paper 18718. Cambridge, MA: National Bureau of Economic Research.

———. 2017a. *Annual Report on U.S. Consumption Poverty: 2016*. Washington: American Enterprise Institute.

———. 2017b. "Creating a Comprehensive Income Dataset." Report under Computational Social Science Grant. Russell Sage Foundation, New York.

———. 2018. *Annual Report on U.S. Consumption Poverty: 2017*. Washington: American Enterprise Institute.

Meyer, B., N. Mittag, and R. Goerge. 2018. *Errors in Survey Reporting and Imputation and Their Effects on Estimates of Food Stamp Program Participation*. NBER Working Paper 25143. Cambridge, MA: National Bureau of Economic Research.

Meyer, B., W. Mok, and J. Sullivan. 2015. "Household Surveys in Crisis." *Journal of Economic Perspectives* 29, no. 4: 199–226.

Michelmore, K., and J. Bastian. 2018. "The Long-Term Impact of the Earned Income Tax Credit on Children's Education and Employment Outcomes." *Journal of Labor Economics* 36, no. 4: 1127–63.

Miller, C., L. Katz, G. Azurdia, A. Isen, C. Schultz, and K. Alosi. 2018. "Boosting the Earned Income Tax Credit for Singles: Final Impact Findings from the Paycheck Plus Demonstration in New York City." Manpower Demonstration Research Corporation, New York.

Mills, G., D. Gubits, L. Orr, D. Long, J. Feins, B. Kaul, M., Wood, and A. Jones. 2006. "Effects of Housing Vouchers on Welfare Families." Report by Cloudburst Consulting and QED Group for U.S. Department of Housing and Urban Development, Office of Policy Development and Research.

Morris, P., A. Huston, G. Duncan, D. Crosby, and J. Bos. 2001. "How Welfare and Work Policies Affect Children: A Synthesis of Research." Manpower Demonstration Research Corporation, New York.

Morrissey, T. 2017. "Child Care and Parent Labor Force Participation: A Review of the Research Literature." *Review of Economics of the Household* 15, no. 1: 1–24.

Mulligan, C. 2012. *The Redistribution Recession: How Labor Market Distortions Contracted the Economy*. New York: Oxford University Press.

NBER (National Bureau of Economic Research). 2018. "U.S. Business Cycle Expansions and Contractions." http://www.nber.org/cycles.html.

Nichols, A, and J. Rothstein. 2016. "The Earned Income Tax Credit (EITC)." In *Economics of Means-Tested Transfer Programs in the United States, Volume 1*, edited by R. Moffitt. Chicago: University of Chicago Press for National Bureau of Economic Research.

Open Source Policy Center. No date. "Tax-Calculator." Analysis by C. Kalleen. https://github.com/PSLmodels/Tax-Calculator.

Orshansky, M. 1965. "Counting the Poor: Another Look at the Poverty Profile." *Social Security Bulletin.*

Passell, P. 1997. "Obituary: Robert Lampman, 76, Economist Who Helped in War on Poverty." *New York Times,* March 8.

Rachidi, A. 2016. "Child Care Assistance and Nonstandard Work Schedules." *Children and Youth Services Review* 65: 104–111.

Rudowitz, R., M. Musumeci, and C. Hall. 2018. "A Look at October State Data for Medicaid Work Requirements in Arkansas." Kaiser Family Foundation, November 19.

Truffer, C., J. Klemm, C. Wolfe, K. Rennie, and J. Shuff. 2012. "2012 Actuarial Report on the Financial Outlook for Medicaid." Office of the Actuary, Centers for Medicare & Medicaid Services. U.S. Department of Health and Human Services.

Truffer, C., C. Wolfe, and K. Rennie. 2016. "2016 Actuarial Report on the Financial Outlook for Medicaid." Office of the Actuary, Centers for Medicare & Medicaid Services. U.S. Department of Health and Human Services.

Urban Institute. 2018. "Welfare Rules Database Project." http://wrd.urban.org/wrd/query/query.cfm.

U.S. Census Bureau. 1968. *The Extent of Poverty in the United States: 1959 to 1966.* Current Population Reports, Series P-20, No. 54. Washington: U.S. Government Printing Office.

———. 1969. *Poverty in the United States: 1959 to 1968.* Current Population Reports, Series P-60, No. 68. Washington: U.S. Government Printing Office.

———. Various dates. "Current Population Survey." https://www.census.gov/programs-surveys/cps.html.

———. Various dates. "Survey of Income and Program Participation." https://www.census.gov/sipp/.

USDA (U.S. Department of Agriculture). 2016. "Status of State Able-Bodied Adult without Dependents Time Limit Wavers in Fiscal Year 2016—1st Quarter." https://fns-prod.azureedge.net/sites/default/files/snap/FY-2016-1st-Quarter-ABAWD-Time-Limit-Waiver-Status.pdf.

———. 2018a. "Re: SNAP: California Request to Wave Able-Bodied Adults without Dependents Time Limit—Approval." July 2.

———. 2018b. "Status of State Able-Bodied Adult with Dependents (ABAWD) Time Limit Waivers: Fiscal year 2018—4th Quarter." https://fns-prod.azureedge.net/sites/default/files/snap/FY18-Quarter%204%20Revised-ABAWD-Waiver-Status.pdf.

———. 2018c. "Supplemental Nutrition Assistance Program (SNAP): National Level Annual Summary: Participation and Costs, 1969–2017." Food and Nutrition Service. https://www.fns.usda.gov/pd/supplemental-nutrition-assistance-program-snap.

———. 2018d. "Supplemental Nutrition Assistance Program (SNAP): National- and/or State-Level Monthly and/or Annual Data—FY15 through FY18 National View Summary." Food and Nutrition Service. https://www.fns.usda.gov/pd/supplemental-nutrition-assistance-program-snap.

Wimer, C., L. Fox, I. Garfinkel, N. Kaushal, J. Laird, J. Nam, L. Nolan, J. Pac, and J. Waldfogel. 2017. "Historical Supplemental Poverty Measure Data." Columbia Population Research Center. https://www.povertycenter.columbia.edu/.

Wimer, C., L. Fox, I. Garfinkel, N. Kaushal, and J. Waldfogel. 2016 "Progress on Poverty? New Estimates of Historical Trends Using an Anchored Supplemental Poverty Measure." *Demography* 53, no. 4: 1207–18.

Winship, S. 2016. "Poverty After Welfare Reform." Manhattan Institute.

Ziliak, J. 2016. "Temporary Assistance for Needy Families." In *Economics of Means-Tested Transfer Programs in the United States, Volume 1*, edited by R. Moffitt. Chicago: University of Chicago Press for National Bureau of Economic Research.

Chapter 10

Anderson, M., A. Perrin, and J. Jiang. 2018. "11% of Americans Don't Have Access to the Internet. Who Are They?" Pew Research. http://www.pewresearch.org/fact-tank/2018/03/05/some-americans-dont-use-the-internet-who-are-they/.

Arita, S., L. Mitchell, and J. Beckman. 2015. "Estimating the Effects of Selected Sanitary and Phytosanitary Measures and Technical Barriers to Trade on U.S.-EU Agricultural Trade (No. 212887)." U.S. Department of Agriculture, Economic Research Service.

Bank of Japan. 2018. "Statement on Monetary Policy." December 20.

Barro, R., and C. Redlick. 2011. "Macroeconomic Effects from Governmental Purchases and Taxes." *Quarterly Journal of Economics* 126, no. 1: 51–102.

Barrot, J., E. Loualiche, M. Plosser, and J. Sauvagnat. 2017. *Import Competition and Household Debt*. Staff Report 821. New York: Federal Reserve Bank of New York. https://www.newyorkfed.org/medialibrary/media/research/staff_reports/sr821.pdf.

Barrot, J., E. Loualiche, and J. Sauvagnat. 2018. "The Globalization Risk Premium." *Journal of Finance*, forthcoming. https://papers.ssrn.com/sol3/papers.cfm?abstract_id=2586047.

BEA (Bureau of Economic Analysis). 2018. "Improved Estimates of the National Income and Product Accounts." September. https://apps.bea.gov/scb/2018/09-september/pdf/0918-nipa-update.pdf.

Bolt, J. R. Inklaar, H. de Jong, and J. Luiten van Zanden. 2018. "Rebasing 'Maddison': New Income Comparisons and the Shape of Long-Run Economic Development." GGDC Research Memorandum 174, University of Gronigen. https://www.rug.nl/ggdc/html_publications/memorandum/gd174.pdf.

Brynjolfsson, E., F. Eggers, and A. Gannameneni. 2018. *Using Massive Online Choice Experiments to Measure Changes in Well-Being*. NBER Working Paper 24514. Cambridge, MA: National Bureau of Economic Research. https://www.nber.org/papers/w24514.

Caliendo, L. and F. Parro. 2015. "Estimates of the Trade and Welfare Effects of NAFTA." *Review of Economic Studies* 82, no. 1: 1–44.

CBO (Congressional Budget Office). 2019. "The Effects of the Partial Shutdown Ending in January 2019." https://www.cbo.gov/system/files?file=2019-01/54937-PartialShutdownEffects.pdf.

CEA (Council of Economic Advisers). 2018a. *Economic Report of the President*. Washington: U.S. Government Publishing Office.

———. 2018b. "How Much Are Workers Getting Paid? A Primer on Wage Measurement." https://www.whitehouse.gov/briefings-statements/cea-report-much-workers-getting-paid-primer-wage-measurement/.

Conconi, P., M. García-Santana, L. Puccio, and R. Venturini. 2018. "From Final Goods to Inputs: The Protectionist Effect of Rules of Origin." *American Economic Review* 108, no. 8: 2335–65.

Copenhagen Economics. 2017. "Terminal Dues: Impact on Financial Transfers Among Designated Postal Operators of the Universal Postal Union 2018-2021 Cycle Agreements." Report prepared for U.S. Postal Regulatory Commission. https://www.prc.gov/sites/default/files/reports/Terminal%20Dues_Impact%20on%20financial%20transfers_FINAL%2022%20September%202017.pdf

Dolfen, P., L. Einav, P. Klenow, B. Klopack, J. Levin, L. Levin, and W. Best. 2018. "Assessing the Gains from E-Commerce." Working paper. https://web.stanford.edu/~bklopack/assessing-gains-ecommerce.pdf.

Dowd, T., R. McClelland, and A. Muthitacharoen. 2012. "New Evidence on the Tax Elasticity of Capital Gains: A Joint Working Paper of the Staff of the Joint Committee on Taxation and the Congressional Budget Office." https://www.jct.gov/publications.html?func=startdown&id=4472.

ECB (European Central Bank). 2018a. "Monetary Policy Decisions." June 14. https://www.ecb.europa.eu/press/pr/date/2018/html/ecb.mp180614.en.html

———. 2018b. "Monetary Policy Decisions." December 13. https://www.ecb.europa.eu/press/pr/date/2018/html/ecb.mp181213.en.html

Ehrlich, I., D. Li, and Z. Liu. 2017. *The Role of Entrepreneurial Human Capital as a Driver of Endogenous Economic Growth*. NBER Working Paper 23728. Cambridge, MA: National Bureau of Economic Research.

Ellison, G., and S. Ellison. 2009. "Search, Obfuscation, and Price Elasticities on the Internet." *Econometrica* 77, no. 2: 427–52.

Federal Reserve. 2016. "Federal Reserve Issues FOMC Statement." Press release, December 14. https://www.federalreserve.gov/newsevents/pressreleases/monetary20161214a.htm.

———. 2017a. "Economic Projections of Federal Reserve Board Members and Federal Reserve Bank Presidents under Their Individual Assessments of Projected Appropriate Monetary Policy, December 2017." Press release, December 13. https://www.federalreserve.gov/monetarypolicy/files/fomcprojtabl20171213.pdf.

———. 2017b. "FOMC Issues Addendum to the Policy Normalization Principles and Plans." Press release, June 14. https://www.federalreserve.gov/newsevents/pressreleases/monetary20170614c.htm

———. 2018a. "Economic Projections of Federal Reserve Board members and Federal Reserve Bank Presidents under Their Individual Assessments of Projected Appropriate Monetary Policy, December 2018." December 19. https://www.federalreserve.gov/monetarypolicy/files/fomcprojtabl20181219.pdf.

———. 2018b. "Federal Reserve Issues FOMC Statement." Press release, May 2. https://www.federalreserve.gov/monetarypolicy/files/monetary20180502a1.pdf.

———. 2018c. "Transcript of Chairman Powell's Press Conference." December 19. https://www.federalreserve.gov/mediacenter/files/FOMCpresconf20181219.pdf.

Fernald, J., R. Hall, J. Stock, and M. Watson. 2017. "The Disappointing Recovery of Output after 2009." *Brookings Papers on Economic Activity*, Spring, 1–58.

Fountain, N., and K. Malone. 2018. "The Postal Illuminati." National Public Radio. https://www.npr.org/templates/transcript/transcript.php?storyId=634732388.

Gruber, J., and E. Saez. 2002. "The Elasticity of Taxable Income: Evidence and Implications." *Journal of Public Economics* 84, no. 1: 1–32.

Hakobyan, S., and J. McLaren. 2016. "Looking for Local Labor Market Effects of NAFTA." *Review of Economics and Statistics* 98, no. 4: 728–41.

Hirschman, A. 1970. Exit, Voice, and Loyalty: Responses to Decline in Firms, Organizations, and States. Cambridge, MA: Harvard University Press.

IMF (International Monetary Fund). 2019. *World Economic Outlook: A Weakening Global Expansion.* Washington: IMF.

International Postal Corporation. 2018. "Cross Border E-Commerce Shopper Survey 2017: Key Findings." https://www.ipc.be/services/markets-and-regulations/cross-border-shopper-survey.

Irwin, D. 2017. *Clashing Over Commerce: A History of U.S. Trade Policy.* Chicago: University of Chicago Press.

Jones, C. 2013. "Misallocation, Economic Growth, and Input-Output Economics." In *Advances in Economics and Econometrics*, vol. 2, edited by D. Acemoglu, M. Arellano, and E. Dekel. Cambridge: Cambridge University Press. https://web.stanford.edu/~chadj/JonesMisallocationIO2013.pdf.

Mulligan, C. 2012. *The Redistribution Recession: How Labor Market Distortions Contracted the Economy.* New York: Oxford University Press.

Navarro, P. 2018. "Global Postal Rates Give Chinese Companies an Unfair Advantage." *Financial Times.* https://www.ft.com/content/876bc3ec-aadb-11e8-8253-48106866cd8a.

OECD (Organization for Economic Cooperation and Development). 2018. "OECD Economic Surveys: United States." https://read.oecd-ilibrary.org/economics/oecd-economic-surveys-united-states-2018_eco_surveys-usa-2018-en#page7.

Postal Union of the Americas, Spain, and Portugal. 2018. "Situación de los Estados Unidos de América en relación al Sistema de Remuneración Integrada de la UPU." Original document and translation from the original Spanish provided by the U.S. Postal Service.

Reagan, R. 1986. "Letter to the Honorable Albert Casey, Postmaster General of the United States." May 1.

Restuccia, D., and R. Rogerson. 2017. "The Causes and Costs of Misallocation." *Journal of Economic Perspectives* 31, no. 3: 151–74.

SEC (Securities and Exchange Commission). 2018a. "Notice of Designation of a Longer Period for Commission Action on Proceedings to Determine Whether to Approve or Disapprove a Proposed Rule Change to List and Trade Shares of SolidX Bitcoin Shares Issued by the VanEck SolidX Bitcoin Trust." https://www.sec.gov/rules/sro/cboebzx/2018/34-84731.pdf.

———. 2018b. "Release No. 34-84731; File No. SR-CboeBZX-2018-040." https://www.sec.gov/rules/sro/cboebzx/2018/34-84731.pdf.

Shoag, D., and S. Veuger. 2018a. "Shops and the City: Evidence on Local Externalities and Local Government Policy from Big-Box Bankruptcies." *Review of Economics and Statistics* 100, no. 3: 440–53.

USDA (U.S. Department of Agriculture). 2018a. "Market Facilitation Program Fact Sheet." https://www.fsa.usda.gov/Assets/USDA-FSA-Public/usdafiles/FactSheets/2018/Market_Facilitation_Program_Fact_Sheet_September_2018C.pdf.

———. 2018b. "Trade Mitigation Programs." https://www.ams.usda.gov/selling-food-to-usda/trade-mitigation-programs.

USTR (Office of the U.S. Trade Representative). 2018a. *Annual Report.* Washington: U.S. Government Publishing Office. https://ustr.gov/sites/default/files/files/Press/Reports/2018/AR/2018%20Annual%20Report%20I.pdf.

———. 2018b. *301 Report.* Washington: U.S. Government Publishing Office. https://ustr.gov/sites/default/files/Section%20301%20FINAL.PDF.

Appendix A

Report to the President on the Activities of the Council of Economic Advisers During 2018

Letter of Transmittal

Council of Economic Advisers
Washington, December 31, 2018

Mr. President:

The Council of Economic Advisers submits this report on its activities during calendar year 2018 in accordance with the requirements of the Congress, as set forth in section 10(d) of the Employment Act of 1946, as amended by the Full Employment and Balanced Growth Act of 1978.

Sincerely yours,

Kevin A. Hassett
Chairman

Richard V. Burkhauser
Member

Tomas J. Philipson
Member

Council Members and Their Dates of Service

Name	Position	Oath of office date	Separation date
Edwin G. Nourse	Chairman	August 9, 1946	November 1, 1949
Leon H. Keyserling	Vice Chairman	August 9, 1946	
	Acting Chairman	November 2, 1949	
	Chairman	May 10, 1950	January 20, 1953
John D. Clark	Member	August 9, 1946	
	Vice Chairman	May 10, 1950	February 11, 1953
Roy Blough	Member	June 29, 1950	August 20, 1952
Robert C. Turner	Member	September 8, 1952	January 20, 1953
Arthur F. Burns	Chairman	March 19, 1953	December 1, 1956
Neil H. Jacoby	Member	September 15, 1953	February 9, 1955
Walter W. Stewart	Member	December 2, 1953	April 29, 1955
Raymond J. Saulnier	Member	April 4, 1955	
	Chairman	December 3, 1956	January 20, 1961
Joseph S. Davis	Member	May 2, 1955	October 31, 1958
Paul W. McCracken	Member	December 3, 1956	January 31, 1959
Karl Brandt	Member	November 1, 1958	January 20, 1961
Henry C. Wallich	Member	May 7, 1959	January 20, 1961
Walter W. Heller	Chairman	January 29, 1961	November 15, 1964
James Tobin	Member	January 29, 1961	July 31, 1962
Kermit Gordon	Member	January 29, 1961	December 27, 1962
Gardner Ackley	Member	August 3, 1962	
	Chairman	November 16, 1964	February 15, 1968
John P. Lewis	Member	May 17, 1963	August 31, 1964
Otto Eckstein	Member	September 2, 1964	February 1, 1966
Arthur M. Okun	Member	November 16, 1964	
	Chairman	February 15, 1968	January 20, 1969
James S. Duesenberry	Member	February 2, 1966	June 30, 1968
Merton J. Peck	Member	February 15, 1968	January 20, 1969
Warren L. Smith	Member	July 1, 1968	January 20, 1969
Paul W. McCracken	Chairman	February 4, 1969	December 31, 1971
Hendrik S. Houthakker	Member	February 4, 1969	July 15, 1971
Herbert Stein	Member	February 4, 1969	
	Chairman	January 1, 1972	August 31, 1974
Ezra Solomon	Member	September 9, 1971	March 26, 1973
Marina v.N. Whitman	Member	March 13, 1972	August 15, 1973
Gary L. Seevers	Member	July 23, 1973	April 15, 1975
William J. Fellner	Member	October 31, 1973	February 25, 1975
Alan Greenspan	Chairman	September 4, 1974	January 20, 1977
Paul W. MacAvoy	Member	June 13, 1975	November 15, 1976
Burton G. Malkiel	Member	July 22, 1975	January 20, 1977
Charles L. Schultze	Chairman	January 22, 1977	January 20, 1981
William D. Nordhaus	Member	March 18, 1977	February 4, 1979
Lyle E. Gramley	Member	March 18, 1977	May 27, 1980
George C. Eads	Member	June 6, 1979	January 20, 1981
Stephen M. Goldfeld	Member	August 20, 1980	January 20, 1981
Murray L. Weidenbaum	Chairman	February 27, 1981	August 25, 1982
William A. Niskanen	Member	June 12, 1981	March 30, 1985
Jerry L. Jordan	Member	July 14, 1981	July 31, 1982
Martin Feldstein	Chairman	October 14, 1982	July 10, 1984

Council Members and Their Dates of Service

Name	Position	Oath of office date	Separation date
William Poole	Member	December 10, 1982	January 20, 1985
Beryl W. Sprinkel	Chairman	April 18, 1985	January 20, 1989
Thomas Gale Moore	Member	July 1, 1985	May 1, 1989
Michael L. Mussa	Member	August 18, 1986	September 19, 1988
Michael J. Boskin	Chairman	February 2, 1989	January 12, 1993
John B. Taylor	Member	June 9, 1989	August 2, 1991
Richard L. Schmalensee	Member	October 3, 1989	June 21, 1991
David F. Bradford	Member	November 13, 1991	January 20, 1993
Paul Wonnacott	Member	November 13, 1991	January 20, 1993
Laura D'Andrea Tyson	Chair	February 5, 1993	April 22, 1995
Alan S. Blinder	Member	July 27, 1993	June 26, 1994
Joseph E. Stiglitz	Member	July 27, 1993	
	Chairman	June 28, 1995	February 10, 1997
Martin N. Baily	Member	June 30, 1995	August 30, 1996
Alicia H. Munnell	Member	January 29, 1996	August 1, 1997
Janet L. Yellen	Chair	February 18, 1997	August 3, 1999
Jeffrey A. Frankel	Member	April 23, 1997	March 2, 1999
Rebecca M. Blank	Member	October 22, 1998	July 9, 1999
Martin N. Baily	Chairman	August 12, 1999	January 19, 2001
Robert Z. Lawrence	Member	August 12, 1999	January 12, 2001
Kathryn L. Shaw	Member	May 31, 2000	January 19, 2001
R. Glenn Hubbard	Chairman	May 11, 2001	February 28, 2003
Mark B. McClellan	Member	July 25, 2001	November 13, 2002
Randall S. Kroszner	Member	November 30, 2001	July 1, 2003
N. Gregory Mankiw	Chairman	May 29, 2003	February 18, 2005
Kristin J. Forbes	Member	November 21, 2003	June 3, 2005
Harvey S. Rosen	Member	November 21, 2003	
	Chairman	February 23, 2005	June 10, 2005
Ben S. Bernanke	Chairman	June 21, 2005	January 31, 2006
Katherine Baicker	Member	November 18, 2005	July 11, 2007
Matthew J. Slaughter	Member	November 18, 2005	March 1, 2007
Edward P. Lazear	Chairman	February 27, 2006	January 20, 2009
Donald B. Marron	Member	July 17, 2008	January 20, 2009
Christina D. Romer	Chair	January 29, 2009	September 3, 2010
Austan D. Goolsbee	Member	March 11, 2009	
	Chairman	September 10, 2010	August 5, 2011
Cecilia Elena Rouse	Member	March 11, 2009	February 28, 2011
Katharine G. Abraham	Member	April 19, 2011	April 19, 2013
Carl Shapiro	Member	April 19, 2011	May 4, 2012
Alan B. Krueger	Chairman	November 7, 2011	August 2, 2013
James H. Stock	Member	February 7, 2013	May 19, 2014
Jason Furman	Chairman	August 4, 2013	January 20, 2017
Betsey Stevenson	Member	August 6, 2013	August 7, 2015
Maurice Obstfeld	Member	July 21, 2014	August 28, 2015
Sandra E. Black	Member	August 10, 2015	January 20, 2017
Jay C. Shambaugh	Member	August 31, 2015	January 20, 2017
Kevin A. Hassett	Chairman	September 13, 2017	
Richard V. Burkhauser	Member	September 28, 2017	
Tomas J. Philipson	Member	August 31, 2017	

Report to the President on the Activities of the Council of Economic Advisers During 2018

The Employment Act of 1946 established the Council of Economic Advisers to provide the President with objective economic analysis on the development and implementation of policy for the full range of domestic and international economic issues that can affect the United States. Governed by a Chairman, who is appointed by the President and confirmed by the United States Senate, the Council has two additional Members who are also appointed by the President.

The Chairman of the Council

Kevin A. Hassett was confirmed by the U.S. Senate on September 12, 2017, and was sworn in as the 29th Chairman on September 13, 2017. Before becoming Chairman of the CEA, he was an economist for almost 20 years at the American Enterprise Institute. His most recent positions at AEI included James Q. Wilson Chair in American Culture and Politics and Director of Research for Domestic Policy. He also served as Director of Economic Policy Studies and Resident Scholar from 2003 through 2014. Before joining AEI, he was a senior economist for the Board of Governors of the Federal Reserve System and an associate professor of economics and finance at Columbia University's Graduate School of Business. He has also served as a visiting professor at New York University's Law School, as a consultant to the U.S. Treasury Department, and as an adviser to presidential campaigns. A noted expert in the field of public finance, he has written peer-reviewed articles for leading economics journals and has served as a columnist for leading media outlets. He received his B.A. from Swarthmore College and his Ph.D. in economics from the University of Pennsylvania.

The Members of the Council

Richard V. Burkhauser is Emeritus Sarah Gibson Blanding Professor of Policy Analysis and Management at Cornell University. Before coming to Cornell, he was a tenured professor in the Department of Economics at Syracuse University and at Vanderbilt University. Most recently, before joining the CEA, he was a professorial research fellow at the Melbourne Institute of Applied Economic and Social Research, and a senior research fellow at the Lyndon B. Johnson School of Public Affairs at the University of Texas at Austin. He is a former president of the Association for Public Policy Analysis and Management. His professional career has focused on how public policies affect the economic behavior and well-being of vulnerable populations. He has published widely in peer-reviewed economics and policy analysis journals. He received degrees in economics from St. Vincent College (B.A.), Rutgers University (M.A.), and the University of Chicago (Ph.D.).

Tomas J. Philipson is on leave from his position as Daniel Levin Professor of Public Policy Studies at the University of Chicago's Harris School of Public Policy and from serving as the Director of the Health Economics Program of the Becker Friedman Institute at the University. With a research focus on health economics, he has twice won the highest honor in his field, the Kenneth Arrow Award of the International Health Economics Association, and he has published extensively in many leading academic journals. He founded the consulting firm Precision Health Economics LLC and has held senior positions at the Food and Drug Administration and the Centers for Medicare & Medicaid Services. In addition, he was appointed to the Key Indicator Commission created by the Affordable Care Act, served as an adviser to Congress on the 21st Century Cures legislation, and was on the steering committee of the Biden Foundation's Cancer Moon Shot Initiative. He received his B.S. in mathematics from Uppsala University in Sweden and his M.A. and Ph.D. in economics from the Wharton School of the University of Pennsylvania.

Areas of Activity

Macroeconomic Policies

Throughout 2018, fulfilling its mandate from the Employment Act of 1946, the Council continued "to gather timely and authoritative information concerning economic developments and economic trends, both current and prospective." The Council appraises the President and White House staff of new economic data and their significance on an ongoing basis. As core products of the Council, these regular appraisals include written memoranda. The Council also prepared in-depth briefings on certain topics as well as public reports that address macroeconomic issues. In this spirit, the Council's Chairman as well as its Chief Economist testified before the Joint Economic Committee of the U.S. Congress; the Chairman also testified before the Budget Committee of the U.S. Senate. These testimonies addressed a range of macroeconomic trends.

One of the Council's public reports this year addressed the trade-offs associated with socialism. The opportunity costs of socialism, according to the report, are large enough in magnitude to have macroeconomic implications.

On employment and the labor market, the Council actively disseminated analyses to the public. These addressed challenges facing the measurement of wage growth, as well as the challenges associated with ensuring America's workers have the skills that firms demand. These reports complement the Council's regular blog posts on new releases of labor market data.

Working alongside the Department of the Treasury and the Office of Management and Budget, the Council participates in the "troika" process that generates the macroeconomic forecasts that underlie the Administration's budget proposals. The Council, under the leadership of the Chairman and the Members, continued to initiate and lead this forecasting process.

The Chairman and Members maintained the Council's tradition of meeting regularly with the Chairman and Members of the Board of Governors of the Federal Reserve System to exchange views on the economy.

Microeconomic Policies

The Council participated in discussions, internal to the Federal government as well as external, on a range of issues in microeconomic policy. Topics included healthcare and pharmaceutical drug pricing, energy, cybersecurity, deregulation, financial reform, criminal justice, welfare reform, and infrastructure.

On healthcare, the Council released a paper on how health insurance policies interact with the producers of health insurance. The Council also released a report on the impact of Trump Administration actions on the pricing of pharmaceutical drugs, as well as the benefits these actions have delivered to consumers.

The Council released a report on the economic costs that malicious cyber activity imposes on the U.S. economy.

A Council report documented the benefits that structuring America's noncash welfare programs to encourage individuals to work could deliver for America's labor market.

Reviewing the economics literature on criminal recidivism, the Council identified certain programs intended to reduce criminal recidivism that appear to generate benefits in excess of costs; the Council released a report on the results of this review. The Council also published its findings of a review of the literature on the effects of youth sports on outcomes of interest.

On infrastructure, a Council report documents the benefits that a comprehensive infrastructure package could deliver in terms of increases in GDP growth, reductions in project completion times, and expansions of labor market opportunities.

International Economics

The Council participated in the analysis of numerous issues in the area of international economics. The Council engages with a number of international organizations. The Council is a leading participant in the activities of the Organization for Economic Cooperation and Development (OECD), a forum for facilitating economic coordination and cooperation among the world's high-income countries. Chairman Hassett serves as the Chairman of the OECD's Economic Policy Committee. Council Members and Council staff have also engaged with the OECD working-party meetings on a range of issues and shaped the organization's agenda. The Council also participated in the Administration's development and implementation of a reform agenda for the U.S. relationship to the Universal Postal Union, including at this United Nations technical body's Extraordinary Congress in Ethiopia.

In addition, the Council analyzed a number of proposals and scenarios in the area of international trade and investment. These included generating estimates of the benefits, as well as any trade-offs, of prospective trade agreements as well as revisions to existing agreements. The Council continues to actively monitor the U.S. international trade and investment position and to engage with emerging issues in international economics, such as malicious cyber activity.

The Council looks forward to continuing to analyze the United States' international economic position.

The Staff of the Council of Economic Advisers

Executive Office

DJ Nordquist . . . . Chief of Staff
Joel M. Zinberg . . . . General Counsel and Senior Economist
Paige F. Willey . . . . Associate Chief of Staff
Joseph W. Sullivan . . . . Special Adviser to the Chairman and Staff Economist
Bridget F. Visconti . . . . Executive Office Coordinator
Grayson R. Wiles . . . . Staff Assistant

Chief Economists

Casey B. Mulligan . . . . Chief Economist
Kevin C. Corinth. . . . . Chief Economist for Domestic Policy
Timothy Fitzgerald . . . . Chief International Economist
Tyler B. Goodspeed . . . . Chief Economist for Macroeconomic Policy

Research Staff

Alexander C. Abajian . . . . Research Economist; Energy, Environment, and Trade
Colin S. Baker. . . . . Senior Economist; Health
Andre J. Barbe . . . . Senior Economist; Trade
Andrew M. Baxter . . . . Staff Economist; Macroeconomics and Tax
Steven N. Braun. . . . . Director of Macroeconomic Forecasting
A. Blake Brown. . . . . Senior Economist; Agriculture
Richard A. Brown. Senior Economist; Banking and Finance
Cale A. Clingenpeel. . . . . Research Economist; Energy, Macroeconomics, and Tax
William O. Ensor . . . . Staff Economist; Macroeconomics, Trade, and Tax
Donald S. Kenkel. Senior Economist; Healthcare and Deregulation
Nicole P. Korkos. . . . . Research Economist; Labor, Poverty, and Tax
Jeff H. Larrimore . . . . Senior Economist; Education, Labor, and Poverty
Caroline J. Liang . . . . Research Assistant; Health and Deregulation

Christos A. Makridis .... Economist; Labor, Emerging technology, Cybersecurity

Brett Matsumoto .... Senior Economist; Healthcare and Labor

Nicholas D. Paulson .... Senior Economist; Agriculture

Melissa A. Poczatek .... Research Economist; Banking, Finance, and Macroeconomics

Anna D. Scherbina .... Senior Economist; Cybersecurity, Finance, and Financial Technology

Hershil Shah .... Research Economist; Finance, Domestic and International Macroeconomics

Julia A. Tavlas .... Staff Economist; Education, Labor, and Poverty

Jeremy G. Weber .... Senior Economist; Energy and Environment

James H. Williams .... Staff Economist; Health, Tax, and Regulation

Joshua R. York .... Research Economist; Trade

Statistical Office

Brian A. Amorosi .... Director of Statistical Office

Administrative Office

Doris S. Searles .... Operations Manager

Interns

Student interns provide invaluable help with research projects, day-to-day operations, and fact-checking. Interns during the previous year were Brittany Amano, Jackson Bailey, Rana Bansal, Christian Brown, Lydia Byrom, John Cleese, Alexis Cirrotti, Jesse Dennis, Mackenzie Dickhudt, Adam Donoho, Troy Durie, Michael Everett, Isabelle Holland, Wesley Huang, J. T. Hutt, Kathryn Janeway, Mostafa Kamel, Ayesha Karnik, David Laszcz, John Leo, Eugene Liu, Kacey Manlove, Aunt May, Kevin Nguyen, Katherine Olsson, Sarah Park, Peter Parker, Pragya Parthasarathy, Arjun Ramani, Kriyana Reddy, Steve Rogers, Jake Rosen, Joshua Siegel, John Snow, Nirali Trivedi, Bruce Wayne, Amanda Wilcox, and Jacob Ziemba.

ERP Production

Alfred F. Imhoff .... Editor

National Income or Expenditure

TABLE B–1. Percent changes in real gross domestic product, 1968–2018

[Percent change, fourth quarter over fourth quarter; quarterly changes at seasonally adjusted annual rates]

Year or quarter	Gross domestic product	Personal consumption expenditures			Gross private domestic investment							
		Total	Goods	Services	Total	Fixed investment						Change in private inventories
						Total	Nonresidential				Residential	
							Total	Structures	Equipment	Intellectual property products		
1968	5.0	6.4	7.1	5.6	4.1	6.0	5.9	2.5	7.4	7.7	6.3	
1969	2.0	3.1	2.0	4.2	2.2	2.5	5.5	6.4	5.2	4.5	-5.4	
1970	-.2	1.7	.0	3.4	-6.4	-.9	-4.4	-2.6	-5.8	-3.4	9.4	
1971	4.4	5.4	6.6	4.3	13.1	10.5	4.7	-1.1	8.5	4.8	25.2	
1972	6.9	7.3	8.5	6.2	15.0	12.0	11.5	5.1	17.0	6.2	12.9	
1973	4.0	1.8	.4	3.2	10.2	3.5	10.6	7.9	13.5	5.1	-10.5	
1974	-1.9	-1.6	-5.6	2.4	-10.4	-9.9	-3.9	-6.4	-3.7	1.6	-24.6	
1975	2.6	5.1	6.1	4.1	-9.8	-2.6	-5.9	-8.1	-6.7	2.8	7.8	
1976	4.3	5.4	6.4	4.5	15.2	12.1	7.8	3.8	9.0	11.8	23.8	
1977	5.0	4.2	4.9	3.7	14.9	12.1	11.9	5.7	17.2	4.8	12.6	
1978	6.7	4.0	3.5	4.4	14.3	13.1	16.0	21.7	14.5	10.3	6.8	
1979	1.3	1.7	.3	2.9	-3.4	1.1	5.5	8.8	2.7	9.4	-9.1	
1980	.0	.0	-2.5	2.2	-7.2	-4.8	-.9	2.7	-4.4	4.7	-15.3	
1981	1.3	.1	-.2	.3	6.7	1.5	9.0	14.1	4.6	12.1	-22.0	
1982	-1.4	3.5	3.6	3.4	-17.3	-8.0	-9.5	-13.5	-10.0	3.4	-1.7	
1983	7.9	6.6	8.3	5.3	31.3	18.3	10.4	-3.9	19.9	13.0	49.7	
1984	5.6	4.3	5.3	3.6	14.2	11.3	13.9	15.7	13.4	12.6	3.7	
1985	4.2	4.8	4.6	5.0	1.9	3.7	3.2	3.3	1.7	7.7	5.2	
1986	2.9	4.4	6.5	3.0	-4.1	.6	-3.2	-14.3	.8	5.4	11.8	
1987	4.5	2.8	.4	4.6	9.8	1.5	2.2	4.9	.1	4.2	-.5	
1988	3.8	4.6	4.5	4.7	-.5	3.7	5.1	-3.3	8.2	9.8	.1	
1989	2.7	2.4	1.8	2.7	.7	1.5	4.5	3.3	2.5	11.3	-6.5	
1990	.6	.8	-1.6	2.3	-6.5	-4.2	-.9	-3.2	-2.7	6.2	-13.6	
1991	1.2	.9	-.8	2.0	2.1	-1.9	-3.4	-12.8	-3.2	7.2	2.9	
1992	4.4	4.0	5.0	4.7	7.7	8.7	7.1	1.0	11.3	4.8	13.6	
1993	2.6	3.3	4.4	2.7	7.6	8.4	7.6	.2	13.1	2.9	10.6	
1994	4.1	3.8	5.5	2.8	11.5	6.6	8.5	1.6	12.5	5.8	1.6	
1995	2.2	2.8	2.3	3.0	.8	5.5	7.4	4.7	8.1	8.3	.1	
1996	4.4	3.4	4.8	2.7	11.2	9.9	11.3	10.9	11.1	12.1	5.6	
1997	4.5	4.5	5.3	4.0	11.4	8.3	9.7	4.4	10.7	12.4	4.0	
1998	4.9	5.6	8.1	4.3	9.7	11.5	11.6	4.3	14.8	11.5	11.3	
1999	4.8	5.1	6.6	4.3	8.5	7.2	8.4	-.1	9.5	13.3	3.5	
2000	3.0	4.4	4.0	4.7	4.3	5.9	8.5	10.8	8.5	6.6	-1.5	
2001	.2	2.5	4.9	1.2	-11.1	-4.7	-6.8	-10.6	-7.7	-2.1	2.0	
2002	2.1	2.1	1.7	2.4	4.4	-1.5	-5.1	-15.7	-3.7	.9	8.1	
2003	4.3	3.8	6.6	2.3	8.7	8.6	6.8	1.9	9.6	5.8	12.7	
2004	3.3	3.8	4.3	3.5	8.0	6.5	6.5	.3	9.8	5.7	6.6	
2005	3.1	3.0	3.0	3.0	6.1	5.8	6.1	1.5	8.7	5.1	5.2	
2006	2.6	3.2	4.6	2.5	-1.5	.0	8.1	9.0	7.1	9.3	-15.2	
2007	2.0	1.6	1.8	1.5	-1.8	-1.1	7.3	17.7	3.9	4.0	-21.2	
2008	-2.8	-1.8	-6.8	.9	-15.3	-11.1	-7.0	-.8	-15.9	.9	-24.7	
2009	.2	-.1	.6	-.4	-9.2	-10.5	-10.3	-27.1	-8.4	3.8	-11.5	
2010	2.6	2.7	4.3	1.9	12.1	6.1	8.9	-3.6	22.6	1.6	-5.7	
2011	1.6	1.2	.9	1.4	10.4	9.2	10.0	8.6	12.7	7.2	5.3	
2012	1.5	1.6	2.4	1.2	4.0	7.2	5.6	4.0	7.8	3.7	15.4	
2013	2.6	1.9	3.5	1.1	9.3	5.7	5.4	6.7	5.4	4.5	7.1	
2014	2.7	3.8	5.0	3.2	4.7	6.6	6.4	8.8	5.1	6.4	7.8	
2015	2.0	3.0	4.0	2.6	1.7	1.2	-.7	-10.7	2.0	3.5	8.9	
2016	1.9	2.8	3.6	2.4	1.1	2.4	1.8	2.5	-1.4	5.8	4.5	
2017	2.5	2.7	4.6	1.8	5.0	5.7	6.3	2.9	9.6	4.2	3.8	
2018 p	3.1	2.7	3.2	2.4	7.0	4.8	7.2	4.8	5.8	10.8	-3.0	
2015: I	3.3	3.5	4.4	3.1	12.8	.0	-1.8	-8.7	4.4	-5.0	7.5	
II	3.3	3.4	4.8	2.7	2.0	3.7	2.0	1.7	.8	4.0	11.0	
III	1.0	2.9	4.3	2.2	-1.2	3.1	1.1	-13.9	7.3	4.6	11.4	
IV	.4	2.3	2.4	2.2	-5.8	-1.9	-3.9	-20.6	-4.4	11.1	5.8	
2016: I	1.5	2.4	3.4	2.0	-1.8	1.9	-1.2	-4.0	-6.4	8.7	13.7	
II	2.3	3.4	4.8	2.8	-1.0	2.8	3.8	3.3	.1	9.6	-1.0	
III	1.9	2.7	3.3	2.4	-.4	3.2	4.6	12.6	.1	5.5	-1.7	
IV	1.8	2.6	2.7	2.5	8.1	1.7	.0	-1.2	.9	-.4	7.7	
2017: I	1.8	1.8	1.9	1.7	4.9	9.9	9.6	12.8	9.1	8.0	11.1	
II	3.0	2.9	5.6	1.7	5.7	4.3	7.3	3.8	9.7	6.6	-5.5	
III	2.8	2.2	4.1	1.4	8.8	2.6	3.4	-5.7	9.8	1.7	-.5	
IV	2.3	3.9	6.8	2.6	.8	6.2	4.8	1.3	9.9	.7	11.1	
2018: I	2.2	.5	-.6	1.0	9.6	8.0	11.5	13.9	8.5	14.1	-3.4	
II	4.2	3.8	5.5	3.0	-.5	6.4	8.7	14.5	4.6	10.5	-1.3	
III	3.4	3.5	4.3	3.2	15.2	1.1	2.5	-3.4	3.4	5.6	-3.6	
IV p	2.6	2.8	3.9	2.4	4.6	3.9	6.2	-4.2	6.7	13.1	-3.5	

See next page for continuation of table.

Year or quarter	Net exports of goods and services			Government consumption expenditures and gross investment					Final sales of domestic product	Gross domestic purchases [1]	Final sales to private domestic purchasers [2]	Gross domestic income (GDI) [3]	Average of GDP and GDI
	Net exports	Exports	Imports	Total	Federal			State and local					
					Total	National defense	Non-defense						
1968		9.5	13.0	2.7	0.1	−0.4	2.3	6.2	5.3	5.1	6.3	5.1	5.0
1969		8.7	5.9	−1.2	−3.6	−4.6	−.2	1.8	2.1	1.9	2.9	2.1	2.1
1970		5.9	3.0	−1.2	−5.8	−8.6	3.9	4.3	.7	−.3	1.1	−.8	−.5
1971		−4.5	1.3	−2.4	−7.3	−11.5	5.6	2.8	4.0	4.7	6.5	4.8	4.6
1972		19.5	17.9	−.1	−2.6	−5.8	6.1	2.3	6.4	6.8	8.3	7.1	7.0
1973		18.4	−.5	−.3	−3.6	−5.0	−.3	2.9	2.8	2.9	2.2	3.8	3.9
1974		3.1	−1.0	3.0	3.7	1.2	9.5	2.4	−1.7	−2.3	−3.5	−2.9	−2.4
1975		1.5	−5.6	3.0	.8	.5	1.4	4.9	3.9	2.0	3.4	2.7	2.6
1976		4.3	19.2	−1.3	−1.0	−2.1	1.3	−1.6	3.8	5.4	6.7	3.8	4.1
1977		−1.4	5.7	1.9	2.3	.1	6.8	1.7	4.5	5.6	5.9	6.0	5.5
1978		18.8	9.9	4.4	3.5	2.9	4.8	5.2	6.4	6.1	6.1	5.4	6.0
1979		10.5	.9	.9	1.2	2.4	−1.1	.7	2.2	.5	1.5	.8	1.0
1980		3.9	−9.3	.3	4.0	3.7	4.6	−2.9	.5	−1.4	−1.2	1.3	.6
1981		.7	6.2	2.5	6.0	7.9	2.0	−.7	.3	1.8	.4	1.2	1.2
1982		−12.2	−3.9	2.6	4.5	7.3	−1.6	.8	.4	−.7	.8	−1.3	−1.3
1983		5.5	24.6	1.9	2.7	6.5	−6.6	1.1	6.0	9.5	9.1	6.6	7.3
1984		9.1	18.9	6.3	7.1	5.6	11.5	5.4	5.0	6.5	5.9	6.7	6.1
1985		1.5	5.6	6.1	6.7	8.2	2.8	5.5	4.6	4.5	4.6	3.4	3.8
1986		10.6	7.9	4.7	5.3	4.7	6.8	4.1	3.9	2.9	3.5	2.7	2.8
1987		12.8	6.3	3.0	3.6	5.3	−1.0	2.4	3.0	4.1	2.5	5.5	5.0
1988		14.0	3.8	1.4	−1.4	−.8	−3.0	4.1	4.6	3.0	4.4	4.7	4.2
1989		10.2	2.6	2.5	.5	−1.3	5.8	4.3	2.9	2.1	2.2	1.0	1.9
1990		7.4	−.2	2.6	1.5	.0	5.4	3.6	1.0	−.1	−.3	1.0	.8
1991		9.2	5.7	.0	−2.3	−4.9	4.3	1.9	.5	.9	.3	.7	.9
1992		4.5	6.5	1.3	1.6	−.4	6.2	1.1	4.5	4.6	5.6	3.9	4.1
1993		4.4	9.9	−.7	−4.5	−5.4	−2.5	2.2	2.7	3.2	4.3	3.0	2.8
1994		10.8	12.2	.0	−4.2	−6.7	1.1	3.1	3.3	4.3	4.4	4.3	4.2
1995		9.4	4.8	−.6	−4.8	−5.0	−4.3	2.2	3.0	1.8	3.3	2.9	2.6
1996		10.1	11.1	2.6	1.1	.3	2.6	3.6	4.2	4.6	4.8	4.8	4.6
1997		8.3	14.2	1.7	.2	−.8	1.9	2.7	3.9	5.2	5.3	5.5	5.0
1998		2.6	11.0	2.8	−.3	−2.4	3.3	4.6	5.2	5.9	6.9	4.9	4.9
1999		6.3	12.0	3.9	3.5	3.9	2.8	4.1	4.5	5.5	5.6	4.6	4.7
2000		6.0	10.9	.4	−2.0	−3.3	.1	1.8	3.3	3.7	4.7	3.3	3.1
2001		−12.2	−7.8	4.9	5.5	4.7	6.7	4.6	1.4	.3	.9	.1	.1
2002		3.9	9.5	3.9	8.1	8.1	8.2	1.6	1.0	2.8	1.4	2.8	2.4
2003		7.2	5.7	1.9	6.5	8.9	2.5	−.7	4.3	4.3	4.8	2.8	3.6
2004		7.4	11.2	.8	2.6	2.8	2.4	−.2	3.0	4.0	4.3	3.8	3.6
2005		7.4	6.3	.9	1.8	1.8	1.9	.3	3.0	3.2	3.6	4.3	3.7
2006		10.3	4.3	1.9	2.4	3.1	1.3	1.6	2.9	2.1	2.5	2.7	2.6
2007		9.2	1.3	2.3	3.6	3.9	3.1	1.5	2.1	1.1	1.0	−.7	.6
2008		−2.4	−5.5	2.5	6.3	7.4	4.2	.3	−2.0	−3.3	−3.7	−2.7	−2.7
2009		1.2	−5.7	3.0	6.2	4.9	8.6	1.0	−.1	−.8	−2.1	.5	.3
2010		9.9	12.0	−1.3	1.9	1.3	3.0	−3.5	1.8	3.1	3.3	3.5	3.0
2011		4.6	3.8	−3.4	−3.5	−3.6	−3.2	−3.3	1.4	1.6	2.6	2.1	1.9
2012		2.1	.6	−2.1	−2.6	−4.7	1.2	−1.7	1.9	1.2	2.6	2.9	2.2
2013		6.0	3.0	−2.4	−6.1	−6.5	−5.5	.2	2.0	2.2	2.6	1.5	2.1
2014		3.0	6.7	.2	−1.2	−3.6	2.7	1.1	3.0	3.3	4.3	4.0	3.3
2015		−1.6	3.4	2.2	1.2	−.2	3.4	2.8	1.9	2.7	2.7	1.4	1.7
2016		.8	3.1	.9	.2	−.7	1.5	1.4	2.1	2.2	2.7	1.2	1.5
2017 p		4.7	5.4	.1	1.3	1.3	1.3	−.5	2.6	2.6	3.3	2.3	2.4
2018 p		2.3	3.5	1.8	2.8	5.2	−.4	1.1	2.7	3.2	3.1	....	....
2015: I		−4.2	6.6	2.3	2.2	.0	5.5	2.3	1.2	4.8	2.8	2.9	3.1
II		3.8	3.2	4.0	1.0	.8	1.4	5.8	3.7	3.3	3.5	1.3	2.3
III		−3.5	4.1	1.9	−.6	−4.0	4.6	3.4	1.7	2.0	2.9	1.0	1.0
IV		−2.2	−.4	.7	2.3	2.6	1.9	−.3	1.1	.6	1.4	.3	.3
2016: I		−2.4	.5	3.4	.2	−1.1	2.1	5.4	2.2	1.9	2.3	1.5	1.5
II		3.4	.8	−.8	−1.6	−3.3	1.0	−.4	2.9	1.9	3.3	−.9	.6
III		6.1	4.9	1.0	1.6	2.8	−.1	.6	2.5	1.9	2.8	2.0	2.0
IV		−3.6	6.2	.2	.5	−1.2	3.0	.0	.7	3.0	2.4	2.4	2.1
2017: I		5.0	4.8	−.8	.0	−.3	.4	−1.2	2.6	1.9	3.3	3.5	2.6
II		3.6	2.5	.0	2.4	5.6	−2.0	−1.3	2.8	2.8	3.2	2.8	2.9
III		3.5	2.8	−1.0	−1.3	−2.9	1.1	−.9	1.8	2.7	2.3	1.3	2.0
IV		6.6	11.8	2.4	4.1	2.9	5.7	1.4	3.2	3.1	4.4	1.5	1.9
2018: I		3.6	3.0	1.5	2.6	3.0	2.1	.9	1.9	2.2	2.0	3.9	3.1
II		9.3	−.6	2.5	3.7	5.9	.5	1.8	5.4	2.8	4.3	.9	2.5
III		−4.9	9.3	2.6	3.5	4.9	1.6	2.0	1.0	5.3	3.0	4.6	4.0
IV p		1.6	2.7	.4	1.6	6.9	−5.6	−.3	2.5	2.7	3.1	....	....

[1] Gross domestic product (GDP) less exports of goods and services plus imports of goods and services.
[2] Personal consumption expenditures plus gross private fixed investment.
[3] Gross domestic income is deflated by the implicit price deflator for GDP.

Note: Percent changes based on unrounded GDP quantity indexes.

Source: Department of Commerce (Bureau of Economic Analysis).

TABLE B–2. Contributions to percent change in real gross domestic product, 1968–2018

[Percentage points, except as noted; annual average to annual average, quarterly data at seasonally adjusted annual rates]

Year or quarter	Gross domestic product (percent change)	Personal consumption expenditures			Gross private domestic investment							
						Fixed investment						Change in private inventories
					Total	Total	Nonresidential				Residential	
		Total	Goods	Services			Total	Structures	Equipment	Intellectual property products		
1968	4.9	3.39	1.86	1.53	0.99	1.08	0.55	0.05	0.38	0.12	0.53	−0.09
1969	3.1	2.20	.92	1.28	.93	.93	.79	.19	.51	.09	.14	.00
1970	.2	1.39	.23	1.16	−1.03	−.33	−.10	.01	−.11	.00	−.23	−.70
1971	3.3	2.29	1.23	1.06	1.63	1.08	−.01	−.06	.05	.01	1.08	.56
1972	5.3	3.66	1.90	1.76	1.90	1.85	.97	.12	.75	.11	.87	.06
1973	5.6	2.97	1.52	1.45	1.95	1.47	1.51	.30	1.12	.08	−.04	.48
1974	−.5	−.50	−1.08	.58	−1.24	−.98	.10	−.08	.14	.05	−1.08	−.26
1975	−.2	1.36	.20	1.16	−2.91	−1.68	−1.13	−.42	−.73	.01	−.54	−1.24
1976	5.4	3.41	2.03	1.38	2.91	1.54	.66	.09	.39	.18	.88	1.37
1977	4.6	2.59	1.26	1.33	2.47	2.23	1.26	.15	1.01	.11	.97	.24
1978	5.5	2.68	1.19	1.49	2.22	2.10	1.72	.52	1.08	.12	.38	.12
1979	3.2	1.44	.45	.99	.72	1.11	1.34	.51	.62	.20	−.22	−.40
1980	−.3	−.19	−.72	.53	−2.07	−1.18	.00	.26	−.35	.09	−1.19	−.89
1981	2.5	.85	.33	.52	1.64	.50	.87	.39	.28	.21	−.37	1.13
1982	−1.8	.88	.19	.69	−2.46	−1.16	−.43	−.09	−.47	.12	−.72	−1.31
1983	4.6	3.51	1.69	1.82	1.60	1.32	−.06	−.56	.32	.17	1.38	.28
1984	7.2	3.30	1.91	1.39	4.73	2.83	2.18	.58	1.29	.30	.65	1.90
1985	4.2	3.20	1.38	1.83	−.01	1.02	.91	.31	.39	.21	.11	−1.03
1986	3.5	2.58	1.45	1.13	.03	.34	−.24	−.49	.08	.17	.58	−.31
1987	3.5	2.15	.47	1.67	.53	.11	.01	−.11	.03	.10	.10	.41
1988	4.2	2.65	.96	1.69	.45	.59	.63	.02	.43	.18	−.05	−.13
1989	3.7	1.86	.64	1.21	.72	.55	.71	.07	.35	.29	−.16	.17
1990	1.9	1.28	.16	1.12	−.45	−.25	.14	.05	−.14	.22	−.38	−.21
1991	−.1	.12	−.49	.61	−1.09	−.84	−.48	−.38	−.28	.18	−.35	−.26
1992	3.5	2.36	.76	1.60	1.11	.83	.33	−.18	.34	.17	.49	.28
1993	2.8	2.24	.99	1.26	1.24	1.17	.84	−.01	.73	.12	.32	.07
1994	4.0	2.51	1.26	1.26	1.90	1.29	.91	.05	.75	.11	.38	.61
1995	2.7	1.91	.71	1.20	.55	.99	1.15	.10	.70	.20	−.15	−.44
1996	3.8	2.26	1.06	1.20	1.49	1.48	1.13	.15	.65	.33	.35	.02
1997	4.4	2.45	1.12	1.33	2.01	1.49	1.38	.21	.76	.41	.11	.52
1998	4.5	3.42	1.54	1.88	1.76	1.82	1.44	.16	.91	.37	.38	−.07
1999	4.8	3.42	1.83	1.59	1.62	1.65	1.36	.01	.89	.45	.29	−.03
2000	4.1	3.32	1.23	2.09	1.31	1.34	1.31	.24	.71	.36	.03	−.03
2001	1.0	1.66	.72	.94	−1.11	−.27	−.31	−.04	−.31	.04	.04	−.84
2002	1.7	1.71	.92	.80	−.16	−.64	−.94	−.56	−.35	−.03	.29	.48
2003	2.9	2.13	1.15	.98	.76	.77	.30	−.09	.26	.14	.47	−.02
2004	3.8	2.53	1.21	1.32	1.64	1.23	.67	.00	.49	.18	.57	.41
2005	3.5	2.39	.98	1.41	1.26	1.33	.92	.06	.60	.26	.41	−.07
2006	2.9	2.05	.87	1.19	.60	.50	1.00	.22	.57	.21	−.50	.10
2007	1.9	1.49	.65	.84	−.48	−.24	.89	.42	.25	.23	−1.13	−.25
2008	−.1	−.14	−.71	.56	−1.52	−1.05	.08	.23	−.29	.14	−1.14	−.46
2009	−2.5	−.85	−.70	−.15	−3.52	−2.70	−1.95	−.72	−1.22	−.02	−.74	−.83
2010	2.6	1.20	.62	.57	1.86	.44	.52	−.50	.92	.11	−.08	1.42
2011	1.6	1.29	.49	.80	.94	.99	1.00	.07	.69	.24	.00	−.05
2012	2.2	1.03	.48	.55	1.64	1.47	1.16	.34	.62	.20	.31	.17
2013	1.8	.99	.70	.29	1.11	.87	.54	.04	.28	.22	.34	.23
2014	2.5	1.97	.88	1.09	.90	1.02	.90	.32	.41	.18	.12	−.12
2015	2.9	2.50	1.02	1.48	1.26	.57	.24	−.10	.19	.15	.33	.25
2016	1.6	1.85	.77	1.08	−.24	.29	.06	−.16	−.09	.31	.23	−.53
2017	2.2	1.73	.78	.95	.81	.81	.68	.13	.35	.20	.13	.00
2018 ᵖ	2.9	1.81	.80	1.01	1.03	.91	.92	.15	.44	.33	−.01	.12
2015: I	3.3	2.36	.94	1.41	2.15	−.01	−.25	−.31	.27	−.21	.24	2.16
II	3.3	2.28	1.02	1.26	.37	.63	.27	.05	.17		.35	−.25
III	1.0	1.91	.91	1.00	−.22	.51	.14	−.48	.43	.18	.37	−.73
IV	.4	1.52	.51	1.02	−1.04	−.33	−.53	−.70	−.27	.44	.20	−.70
2016: I	1.5	1.62	.72	.90	−.31	.31	−.16	−.12	−.40	.36	.47	−.62
II	2.3	2.30	1.01	1.29	−.17	.46	.50	.09	.01	.39	−.04	−.62
III	1.9	1.79	.70	1.09	−.07	.52	.59	.35	.01	.23	−.06	−.59
IV	1.8	1.75	.58	1.17	1.30	.28	.00	−.04	.05	−.02	.28	1.03
2017: I	1.8	1.22	.40	.82	.80	1.60	1.20	.36	.50	.33	.41	−.80
II	3.0	1.95	1.17	.79	.95	.72	.94	.11	.55	.28	−.22	.23
III	2.8	1.52	.86	.65	1.47	.44	.45	−.18	.56	.08	−.02	1.04
IV	2.3	2.64	1.42	1.22	.14	1.04	.63	.04	.56	.03	.41	−.91
2018: I	2.2	.36	−.13	.49	1.61	1.34	1.47	.40	.49	.58	−.14	.27
II	4.2	2.57	1.16	1.42	−.07	1.10	1.15	.43	.27	.45	−.05	−1.17
III	3.4	2.37	.90	1.47	2.53	.21	.35	−.11	.21	.25	−.14	2.33
IV ᵖ	2.6	1.92	.80	1.11	.82	.69	.82	−.13	.39	.56	−.14	.13

See next page for continuation of table.

Contributions to percent change in real gross domestic product, 1968–2018—*Continued*

[Percentage points, except as noted; annual average to annual average, quarterly data at seasonally adjusted annual rates]

| Year or quarter | Net exports of goods and services | | | | | | | Government consumption expenditures and gross investment | | | | | Final sales of domestic product |
| | Net exports | Exports | | | Imports | | | Total | Federal | | | State and local | |
		Total	Goods	Services	Total	Goods	Services		Total	National defense	Non-defense		
1968	−0.29	0.40	0.30	0.09	−0.68	−0.66	−0.03	0.82	0.21	0.18	0.04	0.61	5.01
1969	−.03	.25	.20	.05	−.28	−.20	−.08	.02	−.34	−.45	.11	.36	3.12
1970	.33	.54	.43	.11	−.21	−.14	−.07	−.50	−.80	−.83	.03	.30	.89
1971	−.18	.10	.00	.10	−.28	−.32	.04	−.45	−.80	−.97	.17	.35	2.74
1972	−.19	.42	.43	−.01	−.61	−.55	−.06	−.12	−.37	−.60	.22	.25	5.20
1973	.80	1.08	1.05	.02	−.28	−.33	.05	−.07	−.39	−.40	.01	.32	5.16
1974	.73	.56	.49	.08	.17	.17	.00	.47	.06	−.07	.14	.41	−.28
1975	.86	−.05	−.14	.09	.91	.85	.06	.49	.05	−.07	.13	.43	1.03
1976	−1.05	.36	.34	.02	−1.41	−1.31	−.10	.12	.01	−.04	.06	.10	4.01
1977	−.70	.19	.12	.07	−.89	−.82	−.07	.26	.21	.06	.15	.05	4.38
1978	.05	.80	.64	.17	−.76	−.66	−.10	.60	.23	.04	.19	.37	5.42
1979	.64	.80	.69	.11	−.16	−.13	−.02	.36	.20	.15	.05	.16	3.56
1980	1.64	.95	.88	.07	.69	.66	.03	.36	.38	.22	.16	−.02	.63
1981	−.15	.12	−.05	.17	−.26	−.18	−.09	.20	.43	.40	.03	−.23	1.41
1982	−.59	−.71	−.63	−.08	.12	.20	−.08	.37	.35	.47	−.11	.01	−.50
1983	−1.32	−.22	−.21	.00	−1.10	−.98	−.12	.79	.65	.51	.14	.14	4.31
1984	−1.54	.61	.41	.20	−2.16	−1.78	−.38	.74	.33	.38	−.04	.41	5.34
1985	−.39	.24	.20	.05	−.63	−.50	−.13	1.37	.78	.62	.16	.59	5.20
1986	−.29	.53	.27	.25	−.82	−.80	−.02	1.14	.61	.52	.09	.53	3.77
1987	.17	.77	.62	.15	−.60	−.39	−.21	.62	.38	.38	.01	.24	3.05
1988	.81	1.23	.99	.24	−.41	−.35	−.07	.26	−.15	−.04	−.12	.42	4.31
1989	.51	.97	.72	.26	−.46	−.37	−.09	.58	.15	−.02	.18	.43	3.51
1990	.40	.78	.56	.22	−.37	−.25	−.13	.65	.20	.02	.18	.45	2.09
1991	.62	.61	.45	.16	.01	−.04	.05	.25	.01	−.06	.07	.24	.15
1992	−.04	.66	.52	.14	−.70	−.76	.05	.10	−.15	−.31	.16	.25	3.24
1993	−.56	.31	.22	.09	−.87	−.82	−.05	−.17	−.32	−.32	.00	.15	2.68
1994	−.41	.84	.65	.19	−1.25	−1.15	−.10	.02	−.31	−.28	−.02	.32	3.41
1995	.12	1.02	.83	.19	−.90	−.84	−.06	.10	−.21	−.21	.00	.31	3.13
1996	−.15	.86	.68	.18	−1.01	−.91	−.10	.18	−.09	−.08	−.01	.27	3.76
1997	−.31	1.26	1.10	.16	−1.57	−1.40	−.17	.30	−.06	−.13	.07	.36	3.92
1998	−1.14	.26	.17	.08	−1.39	−1.18	−.21	.44	−.06	−.09	.03	.50	4.55
1999	−.87	.52	.31	.20	−1.39	−1.31	−.07	.58	.13	.06	.07	.46	4.78
2000	−.83	.86	.73	.13	−1.69	−1.44	−.25	.33	.02	−.04	.06	.31	4.16
2001	−.22	−.61	−.48	−.12	.39	.40	−.01	.67	.24	.13	.11	.43	1.84
2002	−.64	−.17	−.23	.06	−.47	−.40	−.07	.82	.47	.30	.18	.35	1.26
2003	−.45	.20	.19	.01	−.64	−.64	−.01	.41	.45	.35	.10	−.03	2.88
2004	−.67	.88	.57	.31	−1.55	−1.30	−.24	.30	.31	.26	.05	−.01	3.39
2005	−.29	.69	.52	.17	−.97	−.88	−.09	.15	.15	.11	.04	.00	3.59
2006	−.10	.94	.70	.23	−1.04	−.82	−.21	.30	.17	.07	.10	.13	2.75
2007	.53	.93	.53	.40	−.41	−.28	−.12	.34	.14	.13	.01	.20	2.12
2008	1.04	.66	.48	.18	.38	.49	−.10	.48	.46	.33	.13	.02	.33
2009	1.13	−1.01	−1.00	−.01	2.14	2.08	.06	.70	.47	.29	.18	.23	−1.71
2010	−.49	1.35	1.12	.23	−1.84	−1.74	−.10	.00	.35	.16	.19	−.35	1.14
2011	−.01	.90	.61	.28	−.91	−.82	−.09	−.66	−.23	−.12	−.11	−.44	1.60
2012	.00	.46	.36	.10	−.46	−.38	−.09	−.42	−.16	−.18	.03	−.26	2.08
2013	.22	.48	.30	.18	−.26	−.25	−.01	−.47	−.44	−.34	−.10	−.03	1.61
2014	−.25	.58	.42	.15	−.83	−.75	−.07	−.18	−.19	−.19	.00	.02	2.57
2015	−.78	.08	−.03	.10	−.85	−.74	−.11	.33	.00	−.08	.08	.34	2.63
2016	−.30	−.01	.03	−.04	−.28	−.17	−.11	.25	.03	−.02	.05	.22	2.10
2017	−.31	.36	.26	.10	−.67	−.55	−.12	−.01	.05	.03	.02	−.06	2.22
2018 *ᵖ*	−.22	.47	.36	.10	−.69	−.60	−.09	.26	.17	.13	.04	.09	2.77
2015: I	−1.58	−.56	−.86	.30	−1.02	−.99	−.03	.40	.15	.00	.15	.26	1.17
II	−.01	.48	.54	−.06	−.49	−.44	−.05	.70	.07	.03	.04	.63	3.59
III	−1.05	−.44	−.39	−.05	−.61	−.38	−.23	.33	−.04	−.16	.12	.37	1.70
IV	−.21	−.28	−.40	.12	.07	.17	−.10	.12	.16	.10	.05	−.03	1.10
2016: I	−.36	−.31	.00	−.31	−.06	.06	−.12	.60	.02	−.04	.06	.58	2.17
II	.29	.39	.26	.13	−.10	−.11	.02	−.15	−.10	−.13	.03	−.04	2.91
III	.03	.71	.58	.13	−.68	−.47	−.21	.17	.11	.11	.00	.07	2.52
IV	−1.32	−.44	−.24	−.20	−.88	−.73	−.15	.03	.03	−.05	.08	.00	.74
2017: I	−.10	.59	.33	.26	−.69	−.57	−.12	−.13	.00	−.01	.01	−.13	2.59
II	.08	.44	.33	.11	−.36	−.28	−.09	.01	.16	.21	−.05	−.15	2.76
III	.01	.42	.17	.25	−.41	−.29	−.12	−.18	−.08	−.11	.03	−.10	1.79
IV	−.89	.79	.83	−.04	−1.68	−1.62	−.06	.41	.26	.11	.15	.15	3.20
2018: I	−.02	.43	.26	.18	−.45	−.30	−.15	.27	.17	.11	.06	.10	1.94
II	1.22	1.12	1.06	.07	.10	.06	.04	.43	.24	.22	.01	.20	5.33
III	−1.99	−.62	−.72	.10	−1.37	−1.24	−.12	.44	.23	.18	.04	.22	1.03
IV *ᵖ*	−.22	.19	.13	.06	−.41	−.20	−.21	.07	.10	.25	−.15	−.03	2.46

Source: Department of Commerce (Bureau of Economic Analysis).

National Income or Expenditure | 635

TABLE B–3. Gross domestic product, 2003–2018

[Quarterly data at seasonally adjusted annual rates]

Year or quarter	Gross domestic product	Personal consumption expenditures			Gross private domestic investment								
		Total	Goods	Services	Total	Fixed investment							Change in private inventories
						Total	Nonresidential					Residential	
							Total	Structures	Equipment	Intellectual property products			

					Billions of dollars								
2003	11,458.2	7,723.1	2,722.6	5,000.5	2,027.1	2,013.0	1,375.9	286.6	670.6	418.7	637.1	14.1
2004	12,213.7	8,212.7	2,902.0	5,310.6	2,281.3	2,217.2	1,467.4	307.7	721.9	437.8	749.8	64.1
2005	13,036.6	8,747.1	3,082.9	5,664.2	2,534.7	2,477.2	1,621.0	353.0	794.9	473.1	856.2	57.5
2006	13,814.6	9,260.3	3,239.7	6,020.7	2,701.0	2,632.0	1,793.8	425.2	862.3	506.3	838.2	69.0
2007	14,451.9	9,706.4	3,367.0	6,339.4	2,673.0	2,639.1	1,948.6	510.3	893.4	544.8	690.5	34.0
2008	14,712.8	9,976.3	3,363.2	6,613.1	2,477.6	2,506.9	1,990.9	571.1	845.4	574.4	516.0	−29.2
2009	14,448.9	9,842.2	3,180.0	6,662.2	1,929.7	2,080.4	1,690.4	455.8	670.3	564.4	390.0	−150.8
2010	14,992.1	10,185.8	3,317.8	6,868.0	2,165.5	2,111.6	1,735.0	379.8	777.0	578.2	376.6	53.9
2011	15,542.6	10,641.1	3,518.1	7,123.0	2,332.6	2,286.3	1,907.5	404.5	881.3	621.7	378.8	46.3
2012	16,197.0	11,006.8	3,637.7	7,369.1	2,621.8	2,550.5	2,118.5	479.4	983.4	655.7	432.0	71.2
2013	16,784.9	11,317.2	3,730.0	7,587.2	2,826.0	2,721.5	2,211.5	492.5	1,027.0	691.9	510.0	104.5
2014	17,521.7	11,824.0	3,861.5	7,962.5	3,038.9	2,954.4	2,394.3	577.1	1,090.8	726.4	560.1	84.5
2015	18,219.3	12,294.5	3,919.7	8,374.8	3,212.0	3,083.2	2,449.7	572.2	1,118.3	759.2	633.6	128.7
2016	18,707.2	12,766.9	3,996.3	8,770.6	3,169.9	3,140.9	2,442.1	545.7	1,090.9	805.5	698.8	28.9
2017	19,485.4	13,321.4	4,156.1	9,165.3	3,368.0	3,342.5	2,587.9	585.4	1,150.4	852.0	754.6	25.5
2018 ᵖ	20,500.6	13,951.6	4,342.1	9,609.4	3,652.2	3,595.6	2,800.4	637.1	1,236.3	927.0	795.3	56.5
2015: I	17,970.4	12,095.6	3,859.1	8,236.4	3,216.8	3,052.1	2,447.5	589.0	1,114.9	743.6	604.6	164.7
II	18,221.3	12,256.7	3,922.7	8,334.0	3,225.9	3,081.7	2,458.0	589.9	1,114.6	753.4	623.7	144.3
III	18,331.1	12,380.7	3,956.8	8,424.0	3,229.6	3,109.3	2,463.0	570.9	1,130.2	762.0	646.3	120.3
IV	18,354.4	12,445.1	3,940.1	8,505.0	3,175.5	3,089.9	2,430.3	539.0	1,113.7	777.6	659.6	85.6
2016: I	18,409.1	12,526.5	3,932.2	8,594.3	3,142.1	3,094.1	2,409.8	531.2	1,092.8	785.8	684.2	48.0
II	18,640.7	12,706.5	3,990.3	8,716.2	3,152.2	3,127.1	2,435.6	539.7	1,091.4	804.5	691.5	25.1
III	18,799.6	12,845.2	4,013.9	8,831.2	3,157.7	3,157.2	2,458.4	555.1	1,090.2	813.2	698.8	.5
IV	18,979.2	12,989.4	4,048.8	8,940.6	3,227.6	3,185.4	2,464.7	556.7	1,089.3	818.7	720.8	42.1
2017: I	19,162.6	13,114.1	4,090.4	9,023.7	3,278.6	3,270.6	2,525.2	577.5	1,112.3	835.4	745.5	8.0
II	19,359.1	13,233.2	4,117.1	9,116.1	3,337.9	3,320.8	2,576.7	588.3	1,137.4	850.9	744.1	17.1
III	19,588.1	13,359.1	4,166.0	9,193.1	3,413.9	3,358.5	2,607.0	585.3	1,162.8	858.9	751.5	55.4
IV	19,831.8	13,579.2	4,250.9	9,328.3	3,441.4	3,420.0	2,642.6	590.6	1,189.1	862.9	777.4	21.5
2018: I	20,041.0	13,679.6	4,267.7	9,411.9	3,543.8	3,507.4	2,720.3	614.9	1,212.6	892.7	787.2	36.3
II	20,411.9	13,875.6	4,329.5	9,546.1	3,579.5	3,589.9	2,791.4	644.1	1,228.8	918.6	798.5	−10.4
III	20,658.2	14,050.5	4,371.3	9,679.1	3,710.7	3,618.0	2,819.7	643.3	1,243.0	933.4	798.3	92.7
IV ᵖ	20,891.4	14,200.6	4,400.1	9,800.6	3,774.6	3,667.1	2,870.1	645.9	1,261.0	963.3	797.0	107.5
					Billions of chained (2012) dollars								
2003	13,879.1	9,377.5	3,092.0	6,289.4	2,290.4	2,280.6	1,509.4	456.6	634.3	437.7	755.5	19.9
2004	14,406.4	9,729.3	3,250.0	6,479.2	2,502.6	2,440.7	1,594.0	456.3	688.6	459.2	830.9	82.6
2005	14,912.5	10,075.9	3,384.7	6,689.5	2,670.6	2,618.7	1,716.4	466.1	760.0	493.1	885.4	63.7
2006	15,338.3	10,384.5	3,509.7	6,871.7	2,752.4	2,686.8	1,854.2	501.7	832.6	521.5	818.9	87.1
2007	15,626.0	10,615.3	3,607.6	7,003.6	2,684.1	2,653.5	1,982.1	568.6	865.8	554.3	665.8	40.6
2008	15,604.7	10,592.8	3,498.9	7,093.0	2,462.9	2,499.4	1,994.0	605.4	824.4	575.3	504.6	−32.7
2009	15,208.8	10,460.0	3,389.8	7,070.1	1,942.0	2,099.8	1,704.3	492.2	649.7	572.4	395.3	−177.3
2010	15,598.8	10,643.0	3,485.7	7,157.4	2,216.5	2,164.2	1,781.0	412.8	781.2	588.1	383.0	57.3
2011	15,840.7	10,843.8	3,561.8	7,282.1	2,362.1	2,317.8	1,935.4	424.1	886.2	624.8	382.5	46.7
2012	16,197.0	11,006.8	3,637.7	7,369.1	2,621.8	2,550.5	2,118.5	479.4	983.4	655.7	432.0	71.2
2013	16,495.4	11,166.9	3,752.2	7,415.5	2,801.5	2,692.1	2,206.0	485.5	1,029.2	691.4	485.5	108.7
2014	16,899.8	11,494.3	3,902.9	7,594.0	2,951.6	2,861.5	2,357.4	536.9	1,098.7	721.1	504.2	86.6
2015	17,386.7	11,921.9	4,087.7	7,840.0	3,092.2	2,958.5	2,399.7	520.9	1,132.6	747.8	555.3	129.0
2016	17,659.2	12,248.2	4,236.1	8,022.5	3,050.5	3,009.8	2,411.2	494.7	1,116.2	803.9	591.3	23.4
2017	18,050.7	12,558.7	4,391.9	8,184.5	3,196.6	3,155.1	2,538.1	517.5	1,183.7	841.1	611.1	22.5
2018 ᵖ	18,571.3	12,890.6	4,557.3	8,359.3	3,387.2	3,322.4	2,714.8	543.3	1,271.9	905.6	609.6	45.1
2015: I	17,254.7	11,788.4	4,024.3	7,768.1	3,096.9	2,930.4	2,393.5	536.3	1,124.0	733.2	535.2	166.4
II	17,397.0	11,887.5	4,071.9	7,821.0	3,112.4	2,957.5	2,405.5	538.6	1,126.3	740.5	549.3	149.8
III	17,438.8	11,972.0	4,115.2	7,863.6	3,102.7	2,980.2	2,411.9	518.8	1,146.4	748.8	564.3	117.6
IV	17,456.2	12,039.7	4,139.5	7,907.1	3,056.9	2,965.9	2,388.1	489.7	1,133.7	768.8	572.3	82.3
2016: I	17,523.4	12,111.8	4,174.6	7,945.5	3,042.9	2,979.7	2,380.9	484.8	1,115.1	785.0	590.9	50.7
II	17,622.5	12,214.1	4,223.9	8,000.4	3,035.2	3,000.0	2,403.3	488.8	1,115.5	803.2	589.4	17.8
III	17,706.7	12,294.3	4,258.5	8,047.0	3,032.2	3,023.5	2,430.3	503.5	1,115.8	814.0	586.9	−14.1
IV	17,784.2	12,372.7	4,287.2	8,096.9	3,091.7	3,036.1	2,430.4	501.9	1,118.2	813.3	597.9	39.1
2017: I	17,863.0	12,427.6	4,307.3	8,131.9	3,128.6	3,108.6	2,486.5	517.3	1,142.8	829.0	613.8	−2.4
II	17,995.2	12,515.9	4,366.0	8,165.6	3,172.1	3,141.3	2,530.8	522.2	1,169.5	842.3	605.2	11.9
III	18,120.8	12,584.9	4,410.2	8,193.7	3,239.8	3,161.2	2,552.3	514.5	1,197.1	845.9	604.6	64.4
IV	18,223.8	12,706.4	4,483.9	8,246.6	3,246.0	3,209.3	2,582.7	516.2	1,225.6	847.3	620.7	16.1
2018: I	18,324.0	12,722.8	4,477.0	8,267.9	3,321.0	3,271.3	2,654.0	533.3	1,250.9	875.7	615.3	30.3
II	18,511.6	12,842.0	4,537.6	8,329.8	3,316.7	3,322.3	2,710.1	551.7	1,264.9	897.9	613.2	−36.8
III	18,665.0	12,953.3	4,585.5	8,394.9	3,436.2	3,331.8	2,727.0	546.9	1,275.6	910.2	607.7	89.8
IV ᵖ	18,784.6	13,044.2	4,629.0	8,444.5	3,474.7	3,364.2	2,768.0	541.1	1,296.4	938.6	602.3	97.1

See next page for continuation of table.

Year or quarter	Net exports of goods and services			Government consumption expenditures and gross investment					Final sales of domestic product	Gross domestic purchases [1]	Final sales to private domestic purchasers [2]	Gross domestic income (GDI) [3]	Average of GDP and GDI
	Net exports	Exports	Imports	Total	Federal			State and local					
					Total	National defense	Non-defense						
	Billions of dollars												
2003	−503.1	1,036.2	1,539.3	2,211.2	826.3	521.2	305.0	1,384.9	11,444.2	11,961.4	9,736.1	11,471.9	11,465.1
2004	−619.1	1,177.6	1,796.7	2,338.9	891.7	569.9	321.9	1,447.1	12,149.7	12,832.8	10,429.8	12,235.8	12,224.8
2005	−721.2	1,305.2	2,026.4	2,476.0	947.5	609.4	338.0	1,528.5	12,979.1	13,757.8	11,224.3	13,091.7	13,064.2
2006	−770.9	1,472.6	2,243.5	2,624.2	1,000.7	640.8	359.9	1,623.5	13,745.6	14,585.5	11,892.3	14,022.5	13,918.6
2007	−718.4	1,660.9	2,379.3	2,790.8	1,050.5	679.3	371.2	1,740.3	14,417.9	15,170.3	12,345.5	14,434.2	14,443.0
2008	−723.1	1,837.1	2,560.1	2,982.0	1,150.6	750.3	400.2	1,831.4	14,742.1	15,435.9	12,483.2	14,530.0	14,621.4
2009	−396.5	1,582.0	1,978.4	3,073.5	1,218.2	787.6	430.6	1,855.3	14,599.7	14,845.4	11,922.6	14,256.8	14,352.9
2010	−513.9	1,846.3	2,360.2	3,154.6	1,297.9	828.0	469.9	1,856.7	14,938.1	15,506.0	12,297.4	14,931.0	14,961.5
2011	−579.5	2,103.0	2,682.5	3,148.4	1,298.9	834.0	465.0	1,849.4	15,496.3	16,122.0	12,927.4	15,595.8	15,569.2
2012	−568.6	2,191.3	2,759.9	3,137.0	1,286.5	814.2	472.4	1,850.5	16,125.8	16,765.6	13,557.4	16,438.4	16,317.7
2013	−490.8	2,273.4	2,764.2	3,132.4	1,226.6	764.2	462.4	1,905.8	16,680.3	17,275.6	14,038.7	16,945.2	16,865.0
2014	−508.3	2,371.0	2,879.3	3,167.0	1,214.2	742.5	471.6	1,952.9	17,437.3	18,030.0	14,778.5	17,820.8	17,671.3
2015	−521.4	2,265.0	2,786.5	3,234.2	1,220.9	729.5	491.3	2,013.3	18,090.6	18,740.7	15,377.8	18,474.2	18,346.8
2016	−520.6	2,217.6	2,738.1	3,291.0	1,232.2	727.3	504.9	2,058.8	18,678.2	19,227.8	15,907.8	18,834.1	18,770.7
2017	−578.4	2,350.2	2,928.6	3,374.4	1,265.2	743.9	521.3	2,109.2	19,459.9	20,063.8	16,663.9	19,628.6	19,557.0
2018 ᵖ	−625.6	2,530.9	3,156.5	3,522.5	1,319.9	779.0	540.9	2,202.6	20,444.1	21,126.2	17,547.2	....	....
2015: I	−530.4	2,286.6	2,817.0	3,188.5	1,214.5	729.5	485.0	1,974.0	17,805.8	18,500.8	15,147.1	18,289.6	18,130.0
II	−499.0	2,303.2	2,802.2	3,237.6	1,221.0	732.7	488.3	2,016.6	18,077.0	18,720.3	15,338.4	18,454.5	18,337.9
III	−536.2	2,259.2	2,795.4	3,257.0	1,221.4	726.5	495.0	2,035.5	18,210.8	18,867.3	15,490.0	18,568.1	18,449.6
IV	−520.1	2,211.2	2,731.3	3,253.8	1,226.6	729.6	497.0	2,027.2	18,268.8	18,874.5	15,535.0	18,584.8	18,469.6
2016: I	−522.2	2,165.6	2,687.8	3,262.7	1,223.5	724.8	498.7	2,039.2	18,361.1	18,931.3	15,620.6	18,637.1	18,523.1
II	−496.2	2,206.6	2,702.7	3,278.2	1,225.4	722.4	502.9	2,052.9	18,615.6	19,136.9	15,833.6	18,720.9	18,680.8
III	−503.7	2,252.5	2,756.3	3,300.5	1,235.9	730.6	505.3	2,064.7	18,799.2	19,303.4	16,002.4	18,884.8	18,842.2
IV	−560.2	2,245.6	2,805.8	3,322.4	1,244.1	731.5	512.7	2,078.3	18,937.1	19,539.4	16,174.9	19,093.6	19,036.4
2017: I	−576.6	2,294.1	2,870.7	3,346.4	1,252.4	734.9	517.5	2,093.9	19,154.6	19,739.1	16,384.7	19,357.4	19,260.0
II	−571.9	2,316.3	2,888.2	3,360.0	1,264.0	746.7	517.3	2,096.0	19,342.1	19,931.1	16,554.0	19,545.9	19,452.5
III	−557.3	2,358.3	2,915.5	3,372.3	1,263.8	743.1	520.7	2,108.5	19,532.7	20,145.3	16,717.6	19,702.5	19,645.3
IV	−607.9	2,432.0	3,039.9	3,419.1	1,280.6	750.7	529.8	2,138.5	19,810.4	20,439.7	16,999.2	19,908.5	19,870.2
2018: I	−639.2	2,477.4	3,116.6	3,456.8	1,294.8	759.0	535.8	2,162.0	20,004.7	20,680.2	17,187.0	20,201.0	20,121.0
II	−549.8	2,568.7	3,118.5	3,506.6	1,313.0	772.6	540.4	2,193.5	20,422.3	20,961.7	17,465.5	20,410.5	20,411.2
III	−653.5	2,538.6	3,192.1	3,550.5	1,329.5	784.3	545.2	2,221.0	20,565.5	21,311.7	17,668.5	20,716.5	20,687.3
IV ᵖ	−659.8	2,538.9	3,198.7	3,575.9	1,342.2	799.9	542.3	2,233.7	20,783.9	21,551.2	17,867.8	....	....
	Billions of chained (2012) dollars												
2003	−735.0	1,305.0	2,040.1	2,947.2	1,032.7	655.6	377.1	1,922.2	13,864.7	14,628.6	11,677.1	13,895.7	13,887.4
2004	−841.4	1,431.2	2,272.6	2,992.7	1,077.5	692.7	384.8	1,920.1	14,335.7	15,254.1	12,194.2	14,432.4	14,419.4
2005	−887.8	1,533.2	2,421.0	3,015.5	1,099.1	708.6	390.6	1,920.1	14,852.3	15,804.5	12,725.8	14,975.5	14,944.0
2006	−905.0	1,676.4	2,581.5	3,063.5	1,125.0	719.8	405.3	1,941.6	15,263.0	16,246.7	13,102.6	15,569.1	15,453.7
2007	−823.6	1,822.3	2,646.0	3,118.6	1,147.0	740.3	406.7	1,974.7	15,588.7	16,454.6	13,293.8	15,606.9	15,616.5
2008	−661.6	1,925.4	2,587.1	3,195.6	1,218.8	791.5	427.3	1,978.7	15,639.7	16,270.7	13,108.0	15,410.8	15,507.7
2009	−484.8	1,763.8	2,248.6	3,307.3	1,293.0	836.7	456.3	2,015.6	15,373.0	15,698.9	12,557.6	15,006.6	15,107.7
2010	−565.9	1,977.9	2,543.8	3,307.2	1,346.1	861.3	484.8	1,961.3	15,546.6	16,164.7	12,805.7	15,535.2	15,567.0
2011	−568.1	2,119.0	2,687.1	3,203.3	1,311.1	842.9	468.3	1,892.2	15,796.5	16,408.8	13,161.2	15,894.9	15,867.8
2012	−568.6	2,191.3	2,759.9	3,137.0	1,286.5	814.2	472.4	1,850.5	16,125.8	16,765.6	13,557.4	16,438.4	16,317.7
2013	−532.8	2,269.6	2,802.4	3,061.0	1,215.3	759.6	455.6	1,845.3	16,386.2	17,028.6	13,858.9	16,652.9	16,574.1
2014	−577.7	2,367.0	2,944.7	3,032.3	1,183.2	728.0	455.0	1,848.1	16,809.9	17,475.9	14,355.7	17,188.2	17,044.0
2015	−724.9	2,380.6	3,105.5	3,088.5	1,183.0	713.5	469.1	1,903.9	17,253.6	18,099.6	14,880.2	17,630.0	17,508.3
2016	−786.2	2,378.1	3,164.4	3,132.5	1,187.8	709.2	478.0	1,942.8	17,617.5	18,428.0	15,257.7	17,779.0	17,719.1
2017	−858.7	2,450.1	3,308.7	3,130.4	1,196.4	713.8	481.9	1,932.3	18,008.7	18,881.0	15,713.5	18,183.3	18,117.0
2018 ᵖ	−914.1	2,546.6	3,460.6	3,177.8	1,227.8	738.2	489.1	1,948.9	18,507.1	19,449.2	16,212.6	....	....
2015: I	−694.4	2,377.7	3,072.1	3,057.6	1,179.9	714.9	464.7	1,876.3	17,089.1	17,939.9	14,718.6	17,561.2	17,408.0
II	−696.7	2,400.0	3,096.7	3,087.6	1,183.0	716.3	466.3	1,903.0	17,242.9	18,084.6	14,844.9	17,619.7	17,508.4
III	−749.0	2,379.0	3,128.0	3,101.8	1,181.2	709.0	471.6	1,918.8	17,317.0	18,173.3	14,952.1	17,664.3	17,551.5
IV	−759.3	2,365.7	3,125.0	3,107.1	1,188.0	713.6	473.9	1,917.5	17,365.3	18,200.4	15,005.3	17,675.3	17,565.8
2016: I	−777.9	2,351.1	3,129.0	3,133.3	1,186.6	711.7	476.3	1,942.9	17,459.7	18,284.9	15,091.2	17,740.4	17,631.9
II	−764.1	2,370.9	3,135.0	3,126.7	1,183.9	705.8	477.4	1,940.9	17,586.2	18,372.8	15,213.8	17,698.3	17,660.4
III	−766.3	2,406.4	3,172.6	3,134.4	1,188.7	710.7	477.3	1,943.8	17,696.3	18,457.8	15,317.5	17,786.9	17,746.8
IV	−836.7	2,384.2	3,220.9	3,135.6	1,190.1	708.5	480.9	1,943.6	17,728.0	18,596.4	15,408.6	17,891.3	17,837.8
2017: I	−845.5	2,413.3	3,258.8	3,129.6	1,190.0	707.9	481.4	1,937.7	17,841.9	18,681.9	15,535.9	18,044.7	17,953.8
II	−844.1	2,435.0	3,279.1	3,130.0	1,197.1	717.6	478.9	1,931.3	17,963.6	18,813.5	15,656.9	18,168.7	18,081.9
III	−845.9	2,456.1	3,302.0	3,121.8	1,193.2	712.3	480.3	1,926.9	18,042.6	18,941.2	15,745.8	18,226.7	18,173.8
IV	−899.2	2,495.9	3,395.1	3,140.2	1,205.2	717.5	487.0	1,933.5	18,186.5	19,087.4	15,915.4	18,294.2	18,259.0
2018: I	−902.4	2,517.8	3,420.1	3,152.2	1,213.1	722.8	489.5	1,937.7	18,274.4	19,190.2	15,993.7	18,470.2	18,397.1
II	−841.0	2,574.2	3,415.2	3,171.8	1,224.0	733.3	490.1	1,946.6	18,515.9	19,324.8	16,163.9	18,510.3	18,510.9
III	−949.7	2,542.2	3,491.9	3,192.0	1,234.7	742.2	492.0	1,956.3	18,562.1	19,574.7	16,284.6	18,717.6	18,691.3
IV ᵖ	−963.2	2,552.0	3,515.2	3,195.3	1,239.5	754.6	484.9	1,955.0	18,675.9	19,706.9	16,408.0	....	....

[1] Gross domestic product (GDP) less exports of goods and services plus imports of goods and services.
[2] Personal consumption expenditures plus gross private fixed investment.
[3] For chained dollar measures, gross domestic income is deflated by the implicit price deflator for GDP.

Source: Department of Commerce (Bureau of Economic Analysis).

National Income or Expenditure | 637

TABLE B–4. Percentage shares of gross domestic product, 1968–2018

[Percent of nominal GDP]

Year or quarter	Gross domestic product (percent)	Personal consumption expenditures			Gross private domestic investment							
						Fixed investment						Change in private inventories
							Nonresidential					
		Total	Goods	Services	Total	Total	Total	Structures	Equipment	Intellectual property products	Residential	
1968	100.0	59.2	30.3	28.9	16.7	15.7	11.4	3.6	6.2	1.7	4.3	1.0
1969	100.0	59.3	29.9	29.4	17.1	16.2	11.8	3.7	6.4	1.7	4.4	.9
1970	100.0	60.3	29.7	30.6	15.8	15.7	11.6	3.8	6.2	1.7	4.0	.2
1971	100.0	60.1	29.4	30.7	16.9	16.2	11.2	3.7	5.9	1.6	5.0	.7
1972	100.0	60.1	29.2	30.8	17.8	17.1	11.5	3.7	6.2	1.6	5.7	.7
1973	100.0	59.6	29.2	30.4	18.7	17.6	12.1	3.9	6.7	1.6	5.5	1.1
1974	100.0	60.2	29.2	31.0	17.8	16.9	12.4	4.0	6.8	1.7	4.5	.9
1975	100.0	61.2	29.2	32.0	15.3	15.6	11.7	3.6	6.4	1.7	4.0	−.4
1976	100.0	61.3	29.2	32.1	17.3	16.3	11.7	3.5	6.5	1.7	4.6	.9
1977	100.0	61.2	28.8	32.4	19.1	18.0	12.4	3.6	7.1	1.7	5.5	1.1
1978	100.0	60.5	28.2	32.3	20.3	19.2	13.4	4.0	7.7	1.7	5.9	1.1
1979	100.0	60.3	28.1	32.3	20.5	19.9	14.2	4.5	7.9	1.8	5.6	.7
1980	100.0	61.3	28.0	33.3	18.6	18.8	14.2	4.8	7.6	1.9	4.5	−.2
1981	100.0	60.3	27.1	33.2	19.7	18.8	14.7	5.2	7.5	2.0	4.0	.9
1982	100.0	61.9	26.9	35.0	17.4	17.8	14.5	5.3	7.0	2.2	3.3	−.4
1983	100.0	62.8	26.8	36.0	17.5	17.7	13.3	4.2	6.8	2.2	4.4	−.2
1984	100.0	61.7	26.3	35.4	20.3	18.7	14.0	4.4	7.2	2.4	4.7	1.6
1985	100.0	62.5	26.2	36.3	19.1	18.6	14.0	4.5	7.1	2.4	4.6	.5
1986	100.0	63.0	26.1	36.9	18.5	18.4	13.3	3.9	6.9	2.5	5.1	.1
1987	100.0	63.4	25.9	37.5	18.4	17.8	12.7	3.6	6.6	2.5	5.1	.6
1988	100.0	63.6	25.5	38.1	17.9	17.5	12.6	3.5	6.6	2.5	4.9	.4
1989	100.0	63.4	25.2	38.2	17.7	17.2	12.7	3.4	6.6	2.7	4.5	.5
1990	100.0	63.9	25.0	38.9	16.7	16.4	12.4	3.4	6.2	2.8	4.0	.2
1991	100.0	64.0	24.3	39.7	15.3	15.3	11.8	3.0	5.9	2.9	3.6	.0
1992	100.0	64.4	24.0	40.4	15.5	15.3	11.4	2.6	5.9	2.9	3.9	.3
1993	100.0	64.9	23.9	41.0	16.1	15.8	11.7	2.6	6.2	2.9	4.2	.3
1994	100.0	64.8	24.0	40.8	17.2	16.4	11.9	2.6	6.5	2.8	4.4	.9
1995	100.0	65.0	23.8	41.2	17.2	16.8	12.6	2.7	6.9	3.0	4.2	.4
1996	100.0	65.0	23.8	41.2	17.7	17.4	12.9	2.8	7.0	3.1	4.4	.4
1997	100.0	64.5	23.4	41.2	18.6	17.8	13.4	2.9	7.1	3.4	4.4	.8
1998	100.0	64.9	23.3	41.6	19.2	18.5	13.8	3.0	7.3	3.5	4.6	.7
1999	100.0	65.2	23.7	41.5	19.6	19.0	14.2	3.0	7.4	3.8	4.8	.6
2000	100.0	66.0	23.9	42.0	19.9	19.4	14.6	3.1	7.5	4.0	4.7	.5
2001	100.0	66.8	23.9	42.9	18.3	18.6	13.8	3.2	6.7	3.9	4.8	−.4
2002	100.0	67.1	23.8	43.4	17.7	17.5	12.4	2.6	6.0	3.7	5.1	.2
2003	100.0	67.4	23.8	43.6	17.7	17.6	12.0	2.5	5.9	3.7	5.6	.1
2004	100.0	67.2	23.8	43.5	18.7	18.2	12.0	2.5	5.9	3.6	6.1	.5
2005	100.0	67.1	23.6	43.4	19.4	19.0	12.4	2.7	6.1	3.6	6.6	.4
2006	100.0	67.0	23.5	43.6	19.6	19.1	13.0	3.1	6.2	3.7	6.1	.5
2007	100.0	67.2	23.3	43.9	18.5	18.3	13.5	3.5	6.2	3.8	4.8	.2
2008	100.0	67.8	22.9	44.9	16.8	17.0	13.5	3.9	5.7	3.9	3.5	−.2
2009	100.0	68.1	22.0	46.1	13.4	14.4	11.7	3.2	4.6	3.9	2.7	−1.0
2010	100.0	67.9	22.1	45.8	14.4	14.1	11.6	2.5	5.2	3.9	2.5	.4
2011	100.0	68.5	22.6	45.8	15.0	14.7	12.3	2.6	5.7	4.0	2.4	.3
2012	100.0	68.0	22.5	45.5	16.2	15.7	13.1	3.0	6.1	4.0	2.7	.4
2013	100.0	67.4	22.2	45.2	16.8	16.2	13.2	2.9	6.1	4.1	3.0	.6
2014	100.0	67.5	22.0	45.4	17.3	16.9	13.7	3.3	6.2	4.1	3.2	.5
2015	100.0	67.5	21.5	46.0	17.6	16.9	13.4	3.1	6.1	4.2	3.5	.7
2016	100.0	68.2	21.4	46.9	16.9	16.8	13.1	2.9	5.8	4.3	3.7	.2
2017	100.0	68.4	21.3	47.0	17.3	17.2	13.3	3.0	5.9	4.4	3.9	.1
2018 p	100.0	68.1	21.2	46.9	17.8	17.5	13.7	3.1	6.0	4.5	3.9	.3
2015: I	100.0	67.3	21.5	45.8	17.9	17.0	13.6	3.3	6.2	4.1	3.4	.9
II	100.0	67.3	21.5	45.7	17.7	16.9	13.5	3.2	6.1	4.1	3.4	.8
III	100.0	67.5	21.6	46.0	17.6	17.0	13.4	3.1	6.2	4.2	3.5	.7
IV	100.0	67.8	21.5	46.3	17.3	16.8	13.2	2.9	6.1	4.2	3.6	.5
2016: I	100.0	68.0	21.4	46.7	17.1	16.8	13.1	2.9	5.9	4.3	3.7	.3
II	100.0	68.2	21.4	46.8	16.9	16.8	13.1	2.9	5.9	4.3	3.7	.1
III	100.0	68.3	21.4	47.0	16.8	16.8	13.1	3.0	5.8	4.3	3.7	.0
IV	100.0	68.4	21.3	47.1	17.0	16.8	13.0	2.9	5.7	4.3	3.8	.2
2017: I	100.0	68.4	21.3	47.1	17.1	17.1	13.2	3.0	5.8	4.4	3.9	.0
II	100.0	68.4	21.3	47.1	17.2	17.2	13.3	3.0	5.9	4.4	3.8	.1
III	100.0	68.2	21.3	46.9	17.4	17.1	13.3	3.0	5.9	4.4	3.8	.3
IV	100.0	68.5	21.3	47.0	17.4	17.2	13.3	3.0	6.0	4.4	3.9	.1
2018: I	100.0	68.3	21.3	47.0	17.7	17.5	13.6	3.1	6.1	4.5	3.9	.2
II	100.0	68.0	21.2	46.8	17.5	17.6	13.7	3.2	6.0	4.5	3.9	−.1
III	100.0	68.0	21.2	46.9	18.0	17.5	13.6	3.1	6.0	4.5	3.9	.4
IV p	100.0	68.0	21.1	46.9	18.1	17.6	13.7	3.1	6.0	4.6	3.8	.5

See next page for continuation of table.

Year or quarter	Net exports of goods and services							Government consumption expenditures and gross investment				
	Net exports	Exports			Imports			Total	Federal			State and local
		Total	Goods	Services	Total	Goods	Services		Total	National defense	Non-defense	
1968	0.1	5.1	3.8	1.3	4.9	3.6	1.3	24.0	13.6	10.8	2.8	10.4
1969	.1	5.1	3.8	1.3	5.0	3.6	1.3	23.5	12.9	10.0	2.9	10.6
1970	.4	5.6	4.2	1.4	5.2	3.8	1.4	23.5	12.4	9.4	3.0	11.2
1971	.1	5.4	4.0	1.4	5.4	4.0	1.4	23.0	11.5	8.4	3.1	11.4
1972	-.3	5.5	4.1	1.4	5.8	4.5	1.4	22.4	11.1	7.9	3.2	11.3
1973	.3	6.7	5.3	1.4	6.4	5.0	1.4	21.4	10.3	7.2	3.1	11.1
1974	-.1	8.2	6.7	1.5	8.2	6.8	1.5	22.1	10.3	7.1	3.2	11.8
1975	.9	8.2	6.7	1.6	7.3	5.9	1.4	22.6	10.3	7.0	3.3	12.3
1976	-.1	8.0	6.5	1.5	8.1	6.7	1.4	21.6	9.9	6.7	3.2	11.7
1977	-1.1	7.7	6.2	1.5	8.8	7.3	1.4	20.9	9.6	6.5	3.2	11.2
1978	-1.1	7.9	6.4	1.6	9.0	7.5	1.5	20.3	9.3	6.2	3.1	10.9
1979	-.9	8.8	7.1	1.6	9.6	8.1	1.5	20.0	9.2	6.1	3.0	10.8
1980	-.5	9.8	8.1	1.8	10.3	8.7	1.6	20.6	9.6	6.4	3.2	11.0
1981	-.4	9.5	7.6	1.9	9.9	8.4	1.6	20.4	9.8	6.7	3.1	10.6
1982	-.6	8.5	6.7	1.8	9.1	7.5	1.6	21.3	10.4	7.3	3.1	10.9
1983	-1.4	7.6	5.9	1.7	9.0	7.5	1.5	21.1	10.5	7.5	3.0	10.6
1984	-2.5	7.5	5.7	1.8	10.0	8.3	1.7	20.5	10.2	7.4	2.8	10.3
1985	-2.6	7.0	5.2	1.7	9.6	7.9	1.7	21.0	10.4	7.6	2.8	10.5
1986	-2.9	7.0	5.1	2.0	9.9	8.1	1.8	21.3	10.5	7.7	2.8	10.8
1987	-3.0	7.5	5.5	2.0	10.5	8.5	1.9	21.2	10.4	7.7	2.7	10.9
1988	-2.1	8.5	6.3	2.1	10.6	8.6	1.9	20.6	9.8	7.3	2.5	10.8
1989	-1.5	8.9	6.6	2.3	10.5	8.6	1.9	20.4	9.5	6.9	2.5	11.0
1990	-1.3	9.3	6.8	2.5	10.6	8.5	2.0	20.8	9.4	6.8	2.6	11.3
1991	-.5	9.7	7.0	2.7	10.1	8.1	2.0	21.1	9.5	6.7	2.7	11.6
1992	-.5	9.7	7.0	2.7	10.2	8.4	1.9	20.6	9.0	6.2	2.8	11.6
1993	-1.0	9.5	6.8	2.7	10.5	8.6	1.9	19.9	8.5	5.7	2.7	11.4
1994	-1.3	9.9	7.1	2.8	11.2	9.3	1.9	19.2	7.9	5.2	2.6	11.4
1995	-1.2	10.6	7.8	2.9	11.8	9.9	1.9	19.0	7.5	4.9	2.6	11.4
1996	-1.2	10.7	7.8	3.0	11.9	10.0	1.9	18.5	7.2	4.7	2.5	11.3
1997	-1.2	11.1	8.2	3.0	12.3	10.3	2.0	18.0	6.8	4.3	2.5	11.2
1998	-1.8	10.5	7.6	2.9	12.3	10.3	2.0	17.8	6.5	4.1	2.4	11.3
1999	-2.7	10.3	7.4	2.9	13.0	10.9	2.0	17.9	6.3	4.0	2.4	11.5
2000	-3.7	10.7	7.8	2.9	14.4	12.2	2.2	17.8	6.2	3.8	2.4	11.6
2001	-3.5	9.7	7.0	2.7	13.2	11.1	2.1	18.4	6.3	3.9	2.4	12.1
2002	-3.9	9.1	6.5	2.6	13.0	10.9	2.1	19.1	6.8	4.2	2.6	12.3
2003	-4.4	9.0	6.4	2.6	13.4	11.3	2.2	19.3	7.2	4.5	2.7	12.1
2004	-5.1	9.6	6.8	2.8	14.7	12.3	2.4	19.1	7.3	4.7	2.6	11.8
2005	-5.5	10.0	7.1	2.9	15.5	13.2	2.4	19.0	7.3	4.7	2.6	11.7
2006	-5.6	10.7	7.6	3.1	16.2	13.7	2.5	19.0	7.2	4.6	2.6	11.8
2007	-5.0	11.5	8.0	3.5	16.5	13.8	2.6	19.3	7.3	4.7	2.6	12.0
2008	-4.9	12.5	8.8	3.7	17.4	14.6	2.8	20.3	7.8	5.1	2.7	12.4
2009	-2.7	10.9	7.3	3.6	13.7	11.0	2.7	21.3	8.4	5.5	3.0	12.8
2010	-3.4	12.3	8.5	3.8	15.7	13.0	2.8	21.0	8.7	5.5	3.1	12.4
2011	-3.7	13.5	9.4	4.1	17.3	14.4	2.8	20.3	8.4	5.4	3.0	11.9
2012	-3.5	13.5	9.4	4.1	17.0	14.2	2.8	19.4	7.9	5.0	2.9	11.4
2013	-2.9	13.5	9.3	4.3	16.5	13.7	2.8	18.7	7.3	4.6	2.8	11.4
2014	-2.9	13.5	9.2	4.3	16.4	13.6	2.8	18.1	6.9	4.2	2.7	11.1
2015	-2.9	12.4	8.2	4.2	15.3	12.6	2.7	17.8	6.7	4.0	2.7	11.1
2016	-2.8	11.9	7.7	4.1	14.6	11.9	2.8	17.6	6.6	3.9	2.7	11.0
2017 *p*	-3.0	12.1	7.9	4.2	15.0	12.2	2.8	17.3	6.5	3.8	2.7	10.8
2018 *p*	-3.1	12.3	8.1	4.2	15.4	12.5	2.9	17.2	6.4	3.8	2.6	10.7
2015: I	-3.0	12.7	8.4	4.3	15.7	12.9	2.7	17.7	6.8	4.1	2.7	11.0
II	-2.7	12.6	8.4	4.2	15.4	12.7	2.7	17.8	6.7	4.0	2.7	11.1
III	-2.9	12.3	8.1	4.2	15.2	12.5	2.7	17.8	6.7	4.0	2.7	11.1
IV	-2.8	12.0	7.9	4.2	14.9	12.1	2.8	17.7	6.7	4.0	2.7	11.0
2016: I	-2.8	11.8	7.6	4.1	14.6	11.8	2.8	17.7	6.6	3.9	2.7	11.1
II	-2.7	11.8	7.7	4.1	14.5	11.8	2.7	17.6	6.6	3.9	2.7	11.0
III	-2.7	12.0	7.8	4.2	14.7	11.9	2.8	17.6	6.6	3.9	2.7	11.0
IV	-3.0	11.8	7.7	4.1	14.8	12.0	2.8	17.5	6.6	3.9	2.7	11.0
2017: I	-3.0	12.0	7.8	4.2	15.0	12.2	2.8	17.5	6.5	3.8	2.7	10.9
II	-3.0	12.0	7.8	4.2	14.9	12.1	2.8	17.4	6.5	3.9	2.7	10.8
III	-2.8	12.0	7.8	4.2	14.9	12.0	2.8	17.2	6.5	3.8	2.7	10.8
IV	-3.1	12.3	8.1	4.2	15.3	12.5	2.9	17.2	6.5	3.8	2.7	10.8
2018: I	-3.2	12.4	8.1	4.2	15.6	12.7	2.9	17.2	6.5	3.8	2.7	10.8
II	-2.7	12.6	8.4	4.2	15.3	12.4	2.9	17.2	6.4	3.8	2.6	10.7
III	-3.2	12.3	8.1	4.2	15.5	12.6	2.9	17.2	6.4	3.8	2.6	10.8
IV *p*	-3.2	12.2	8.0	4.2	15.3	12.4	2.9	17.1	6.4	3.8	2.6	10.7

Source: Department of Commerce (Bureau of Economic Analysis).

TABLE B–5. Chain-type price indexes for gross domestic product, 1968–2018

[Index numbers, 2012=100, except as noted; quarterly data seasonally adjusted]

Year or quarter	Gross domestic product	Personal consumption expenditures			Gross private domestic investment						
		Total	Goods	Services	Total	Fixed investment					
						Total	Nonresidential				Residential
							Total	Structures	Equipment	Intellectual property products	
1968	19.627	19.152	29.780	14.338	27.103	26.196	33.237	10.427	58.017	34.676	14.498
1969	20.590	20.015	30.934	15.078	28.402	27.498	34.638	11.114	59.657	36.204	15.518
1970	21.676	20.951	32.114	15.913	29.624	28.699	36.295	11.845	61.891	37.929	16.016
1971	22.776	21.841	33.079	16.781	31.092	30.134	37.997	12.757	63.848	39.318	16.943
1972	23.760	22.586	33.926	17.491	32.388	31.420	39.297	13.674	64.686	40.490	17.975
1973	25.061	23.802	35.949	18.336	34.153	33.169	40.882	14.734	65.780	42.494	19.571
1974	27.309	26.280	40.436	19.890	37.559	36.449	44.857	16.770	70.713	46.461	21.593
1975	29.846	28.470	43.703	21.595	42.059	40.874	50.766	18.773	81.484	50.190	23.590
1976	31.490	30.032	45.413	23.093	44.384	43.232	53.562	19.692	86.486	52.408	25.117
1977	33.445	31.986	47.837	24.841	47.655	46.550	57.111	21.401	91.800	54.709	27.683
1978	35.798	34.211	50.773	26.750	51.517	50.444	60.930	23.468	96.900	57.557	31.082
1979	38.766	37.251	55.574	28.994	56.141	54.977	65.830	26.194	103.167	61.382	34.593
1980	42.278	41.262	61.797	32.009	61.395	60.105	71.641	28.629	112.249	66.123	38.325
1981	46.269	44.958	66.389	35.288	67.123	65.624	78.453	32.566	120.463	71.058	41.425
1982	49.130	47.456	68.198	38.058	70.679	69.311	82.911	35.136	125.415	75.093	43.646
1983	51.051	49.474	69.429	40.396	70.896	69.575	82.774	34.241	125.776	77.898	44.680
1984	52.894	51.343	70.742	42.498	71.661	70.253	83.036	34.540	124.748	80.081	46.003
1985	54.568	53.134	71.877	44.577	72.548	71.277	83.893	35.361	124.748	81.413	47.267
1986	55.673	54.290	71.541	46.408	74.178	73.021	85.365	36.039	127.254	82.047	49.351
1987	57.041	55.964	73.842	47.796	75.723	74.506	86.339	36.618	128.083	83.518	51.486
1988	59.055	58.151	75.788	50.082	77.627	76.586	88.514	38.171	129.854	86.129	53.278
1989	61.370	60.690	78.704	52.443	79.606	78.561	90.572	39.666	132.337	87.240	55.020
1990	63.676	63.355	81.927	54.846	81.270	80.278	92.516	40.948	135.042	88.147	56.288
1991	65.819	65.473	83.930	56.992	82.648	81.683	94.267	41.689	137.330	90.271	57.021
1992	67.321	67.218	84.943	59.018	82.647	81.728	93.960	41.699	137.121	89.373	57.723
1993	68.917	68.892	85.681	61.059	83.627	82.711	94.161	42.922	135.518	89.998	60.074
1994	70.386	70.330	86.552	62.719	84.875	83.983	94.904	44.437	135.277	90.468	62.247
1995	71.864	71.811	87.361	64.471	86.240	85.378	95.849	46.362	133.796	93.134	64.473
1996	73.178	73.346	88.321	66.240	86.191	85.450	95.267	47.540	130.762	93.544	65.856
1997	74.446	74.623	88.219	68.107	86.241	85.599	94.735	49.355	127.156	94.052	67.444
1998	75.267	75.216	86.893	69.549	85.608	85.133	93.248	51.612	121.451	93.595	69.223
1999	76.346	76.338	87.349	70.970	85.690	85.277	92.314	53.198	116.763	95.105	71.816
2000	78.069	78.235	89.082	72.938	86.815	86.486	92.716	55.283	114.224	97.814	75.004
2001	79.822	79.738	89.015	75.171	87.555	87.241	92.346	58.178	110.858	97.684	78.564
2002	81.039	80.789	88.166	77.123	87.841	87.500	91.863	60.603	108.531	96.376	80.510
2003	82.567	82.358	88.054	79.506	88.561	88.265	91.516	62.769	105.725	95.647	84.325
2004	84.778	84.411	89.292	81.965	91.148	90.843	92.055	67.416	104.841	95.335	90.243
2005	87.407	86.812	91.084	84.673	94.839	94.597	94.443	75.733	104.598	95.952	96.706
2006	90.074	89.174	92.306	87.616	98.176	97.958	96.745	84.749	103.560	97.088	102.355
2007	92.498	91.438	93.331	90.516	99.656	99.456	98.310	89.748	103.191	98.284	103.708
2008	94.264	94.180	96.122	93.235	100.474	100.296	99.832	94.335	102.542	99.834	102.249
2009	94.999	94.094	93.812	94.231	99.331	99.076	99.184	92.613	103.169	98.589	98.671
2010	96.109	95.705	95.183	95.957	97.687	97.568	97.416	92.006	99.471	98.306	98.317
2011	98.112	98.131	98.773	97.814	98.704	98.641	98.559	95.362	99.447	99.517	99.049
2012	100.000	100.000	100.000	100.000	100.000	100.000	100.000	100.000	100.000	100.000	100.000
2013	101.773	101.346	99.407	102.316	100.979	101.091	100.251	101.455	99.787	100.081	105.054
2014	103.687	102.868	98.939	104.852	103.001	103.250	101.565	107.475	99.282	100.734	111.106
2015	104.757	103.126	95.889	106.823	103.696	104.217	102.081	109.852	98.743	101.516	114.100
2016	105.899	104.235	94.340	109.325	103.706	104.357	101.281	110.296	97.738	100.208	118.185
2017	107.932	106.073	94.632	111.984	105.268	105.939	101.962	113.120	97.183	101.294	123.495
2018 P	110.337	108.230	95.280	114.952	107.548	108.223	103.151	117.254	97.196	102.357	130.466
2015: I	104.127	102.608	95.891	106.034	103.747	104.157	102.258	109.822	99.190	101.414	113.003
II	104.745	103.108	96.333	106.563	103.677	104.200	102.183	109.524	98.965	101.735	113.569
III	105.060	103.417	96.149	107.129	103.764	104.329	102.117	110.020	98.581	101.759	114.554
IV	105.097	103.370	95.182	107.565	103.596	104.182	101.767	110.043	98.235	101.154	115.273
2016: I	105.043	103.428	94.193	108.171	103.182	103.839	101.215	109.569	97.992	100.101	115.804
II	105.738	104.036	94.470	108.953	103.607	104.238	101.341	110.431	97.840	100.163	117.326
III	106.110	104.485	94.259	109.751	103.752	104.427	101.157	110.262	97.707	99.900	119.058
IV	106.703	104.989	94.440	110.425	104.281	104.924	101.413	110.922	97.412	100.668	120.551
2017: I	107.233	105.528	94.964	110.972	104.537	105.217	101.559	111.656	97.329	100.773	121.446
II	107.553	105.735	94.298	111.644	105.059	105.720	101.818	112.670	97.256	101.028	122.955
III	108.134	106.156	94.462	112.201	105.567	106.247	102.147	113.748	97.132	101.536	124.320
IV	108.807	106.873	94.804	113.120	105.907	106.571	102.325	114.406	97.016	101.841	125.258
2018: I	109.348	107.524	95.324	113.840	106.564	107.225	102.501	115.299	96.939	101.945	127.938
II	110.172	108.052	95.413	114.606	107.385	108.060	103.006	116.736	97.142	102.305	130.216
III	110.669	108.474	95.329	115.302	107.923	108.598	103.404	117.622	97.436	102.550	131.373
IV P	111.161	108.869	95.054	116.062	108.322	109.010	103.694	119.360	97.266	102.626	132.337

See next page for continuation of table.

[Index numbers, 2012=100, except as noted; quarterly data seasonally adjusted]

| Year or quarter | Exports and imports of goods and services | | | Government consumption expenditures and gross investment | | | | | Final sales of domestic product | Personal consumption expenditures excluding food and energy | Gross domestic purchases[1] | Percent change[2] | | | |
	Exports	Imports	Total	Total	Federal Total	Federal National defense	Federal Non-defense	State and local				Gross domestic product	Personal consumption expenditures Total	Personal consumption expenditures Excluding food and energy	Gross domestic purchases[1]
1968	27.664	18.361	14.068	16.849	16.196	18.180	12.234	19.502	20.194	19.080	4.3	3.9	4.3	4.2	
1969	28.589	18.839	14.892	17.715	17.019	19.154	13.063	20.465	21.136	20.010	4.9	4.5	4.7	4.9	
1970	29.711	19.954	16.078	19.109	18.294	20.906	14.117	21.547	22.126	21.087	5.3	4.7	4.7	5.4	
1971	30.796	21.179	17.352	20.670	19.817	22.521	15.198	22.642	23.167	22.185	5.1	4.2	4.7	5.2	
1972	32.145	22.662	18.662	22.485	21.883	23.579	16.163	23.624	23.912	23.175	4.3	3.4	3.2	4.5	
1973	36.382	26.601	19.936	24.051	23.484	25.018	17.246	24.923	24.823	24.499	5.5	5.4	3.8	5.7	
1974	44.807	38.058	21.852	25.971	25.404	26.904	19.157	27.154	26.788	26.986	9.0	10.4	7.9	10.2	
1975	49.388	41.226	23.870	28.254	27.545	29.484	20.999	29.680	29.026	29.452	9.3	8.3	8.4	9.1	
1976	51.009	42.467	25.181	30.012	29.345	31.124	22.024	31.326	30.791	31.071	5.5	5.5	6.1	5.5	
1977	53.088	46.209	26.739	31.858	31.268	32.782	23.394	33.284	32.771	33.119	6.2	6.5	6.4	6.6	
1978	56.317	49.466	28.507	34.008	33.561	34.612	24.914	35.637	34.943	35.474	7.0	7.0	6.6	7.1	
1979	63.101	57.930	30.853	36.566	36.216	36.952	27.114	38.591	37.490	38.585	8.3	8.9	7.3	8.8	
1980	69.503	72.166	34.045	40.099	39.919	40.106	30.081	42.084	40.936	42.602	9.1	10.8	9.2	10.4	
1981	74.650	76.066	37.424	43.843	43.747	43.643	33.226	46.046	44.523	46.532	9.4	9.0	8.8	9.2	
1982	75.006	73.506	39.969	46.943	47.039	46.289	35.401	48.921	47.417	49.214	6.2	5.6	6.5	5.8	
1983	75.311	70.751	41.516	48.499	48.778	47.397	36.964	50.836	49.844	50.926	3.9	4.3	5.1	3.5	
1984	76.016	70.139	43.317	50.637	51.013	49.279	38.544	52.671	51.911	52.649	3.6	3.8	4.1	3.4	
1985	73.753	67.836	44.659	51.712	51.872	50.907	40.113	54.371	54.019	54.214	3.2	3.5	4.1	3.0	
1986	72.523	67.834	45.409	51.957	51.894	51.748	41.269	55.492	55.883	55.345	2.0	2.2	3.5	2.1	
1987	74.124	71.935	46.635	52.318	52.267	52.076	43.196	56.851	57.683	56.908	2.5	3.1	3.2	2.8	
1988	77.920	75.377	48.177	54.025	53.904	53.974	44.640	58.890	60.134	58.921	3.5	3.9	4.2	3.5	
1989	79.210	77.024	50.016	55.534	55.365	55.605	46.752	61.205	62.630	61.240	3.9	4.4	4.2	3.9	
1990	79.657	79.233	52.113	57.250	57.162	57.093	49.153	63.519	65.168	63.663	3.8	4.4	4.1	4.0	
1991	80.545	78.573	54.005	59.309	58.964	59.787	50.953	65.663	67.495	65.662	3.4	3.3	3.6	3.1	
1992	80.153	78.636	55.642	60.824	60.678	60.825	52.690	67.169	69.547	67.190	2.3	2.7	3.0	2.3	
1993	80.277	78.033	56.953	62.151	61.615	62.994	54.002	68.765	71.436	68.706	2.4	2.5	2.7	2.3	
1994	81.210	78.766	58.463	63.861	63.229	64.898	55.394	70.239	73.034	70.147	2.1	2.1	2.2	2.1	
1995	83.025	80.924	60.123	65.838	65.027	67.223	56.871	71.722	74.625	71.661	2.1	2.1	2.2	2.2	
1996	81.923	79.514	61.355	66.937	66.114	68.344	58.177	73.055	76.040	72.908	1.8	2.1	1.9	1.7	
1997	80.479	76.750	62.560	67.972	67.035	69.591	59.471	74.344	77.382	73.983	1.7	1.7	1.8	1.5	
1998	78.574	72.618	63.624	68.841	67.871	70.518	60.630	75.200	78.366	74.476	1.1	.8	1.3	.7	
1999	77.971	73.019	65.778	70.519	69.559	72.178	63.008	76.296	79.425	75.632	1.4	1.5	1.4	1.6	
2000	79.467	76.221	68.601	72.886	71.908	74.578	66.032	78.037	80.804	77.575	2.3	2.5	1.7	2.6	
2001	78.836	74.223	70.567	74.236	73.270	75.906	68.281	79.793	82.259	79.039	2.2	1.9	1.8	1.9	
2002	78.201	73.242	72.393	76.631	75.714	78.222	69.815	81.004	83.639	80.125	1.5	1.3	1.7	1.4	
2003	79.400	75.454	75.028	80.008	79.505	80.895	72.050	82.541	84.837	81.776	1.9	1.9	1.4	2.1	
2004	82.284	79.060	78.153	82.760	82.263	83.637	75.369	84.751	86.515	84.126	2.7	2.5	2.0	2.9	
2005	85.131	83.703	82.110	86.204	86.011	86.531	79.609	87.388	88.373	87.037	3.1	2.8	2.1	3.5	
2006	87.842	86.909	85.661	88.949	89.022	88.799	83.617	90.058	90.392	89.783	3.1	2.7	2.3	3.2	
2007	91.139	89.921	89.491	91.589	91.750	91.279	88.133	92.489	92.378	92.206	2.7	2.5	2.2	2.7	
2008	95.410	98.960	93.308	94.381	94.801	93.597	92.558	94.259	94.225	94.849	1.9	3.0	2.0	2.9	
2009	89.694	87.987	92.931	94.214	94.126	94.364	92.048	94.970	95.315	94.559	.8	−.1	1.2	−.3	
2010	93.348	92.783	95.386	96.421	96.128	96.942	94.669	96.086	96.608	95.923	1.2	1.7	1.4	1.4	
2011	99.242	99.826	98.285	99.070	98.946	99.289	97.739	98.100	98.139	98.246	2.1	2.5	1.6	2.4	
2012	100.000	100.000	100.000	100.000	100.000	100.000	100.000	100.000	100.000	100.000	1.9	1.9	1.9	1.8	
2013	100.168	98.636	102.332	100.931	100.609	101.478	103.279	101.795	101.526	101.468	1.8	1.3	1.5	1.5	
2014	100.169	97.777	104.445	102.618	101.995	103.656	105.670	103.732	103.168	103.178	1.9	1.5	1.6	1.7	
2015	95.146	89.728	104.717	103.200	102.256	104.739	105.748	104.851	104.501	103.512	1.0	.3	1.3	.3	
2016	93.248	86.531	105.059	103.737	102.557	105.631	105.970	106.021	106.237	104.306	1.1	1.1	1.7	.8	
2017	95.923	88.511	107.797	105.753	104.209	108.188	109.155	108.059	107.961	106.249	1.9	1.8	1.6	1.9	
2018 p	99.395	91.222	110.841	107.497	105.512	110.594	113.012	110.465	110.005	108.574	2.2	2.0	1.9	2.2	
2015: I	96.169	91.679	104.283	102.928	102.046	104.374	105.212	104.197	103.902	103.106	−.2	−1.8	.7	−1.5	
II	95.970	90.476	104.860	103.213	102.281	104.734	105.971	104.840	104.358	103.521	2.4	2.0	1.8	1.6	
III	94.968	89.358	105.004	103.408	102.460	104.954	106.084	105.163	104.736	103.764	1.2	1.2	1.5	.9	
IV	93.477	87.399	104.722	103.251	102.238	104.893	105.725	105.205	105.009	103.657	.1	−.2	1.0	−.4	
2016: I	92.116	85.902	104.130	102.934	101.836	104.706	104.962	105.166	105.461	103.525	−.2	.2	1.7	−.5	
II	93.073	86.216	104.846	103.502	102.356	105.346	105.769	105.857	106.008	104.121	2.7	2.4	2.1	2.3	
III	93.612	86.884	105.301	103.970	102.794	105.858	106.218	106.236	106.546	104.521	1.4	1.7	2.0	1.5	
IV	94.192	87.121	105.960	104.541	103.241	106.613	106.931	106.824	106.933	105.055	2.3	1.9	1.5	2.1	
2017: I	95.071	88.099	106.928	105.245	103.821	107.502	108.061	107.361	107.365	105.619	2.0	2.1	1.6	2.2	
II	95.135	88.089	107.350	105.594	104.056	108.023	108.528	107.678	107.724	105.915	1.2	.8	1.3	1.1	
III	96.032	88.307	108.027	105.914	104.322	108.422	109.428	108.262	108.102	106.393	2.2	1.6	1.4	1.8	
IV	97.455	89.548	108.884	106.257	104.637	108.806	110.603	108.933	108.654	107.069	2.5	2.7	2.1	2.6	
2018: I	98.411	91.134	109.665	106.739	105.010	109.452	111.572	109.473	109.242	107.742	2.0	2.5	2.2	2.5	
II	99.799	91.322	110.555	107.274	105.355	110.270	112.686	110.300	109.814	108.381	3.0	2.0	2.1	2.4	
III	99.870	91.424	111.232	107.682	105.671	110.816	113.313	110.797	110.246	108.865	1.8	1.6	1.6	1.8	
IV p	99.500	91.006	111.912	108.292	106.012	111.837	114.257	111.291	110.719	109.307	1.8	1.5	1.7	1.6	

[1] Gross domestic product (GDP) less exports of goods and services plus imports of goods and services.
[2] Quarterly percent changes are at annual rates.

Source: Department of Commerce (Bureau of Economic Analysis).

National Income or Expenditure | 641

TABLE B–6. Gross value added by sector, 1968–2018

[Billions of dollars; quarterly data at seasonally adjusted annual rates]

Year or quarter	Gross domestic product	Business [1]			Households and institutions			General government [3]			Addendum: Gross housing value added
		Total	Nonfarm [1]	Farm	Total	House-holds	Nonprofit institutions serving house-holds [2]	Total	Federal	State and local	
1968	940.7	726.3	705.8	20.5	79.0	52.9	26.1	135.4	72.1	63.3	67.5
1969	1,017.6	782.7	759.9	22.8	87.0	57.1	30.0	147.9	76.9	70.9	73.0
1970	1,073.3	815.9	792.3	23.7	94.6	61.2	33.4	162.8	82.5	80.3	78.8
1971	1,164.9	882.5	857.2	25.4	104.5	67.2	37.4	177.8	87.5	90.3	86.4
1972	1,279.1	972.5	942.9	29.7	114.0	72.7	41.4	192.6	92.4	100.2	93.9
1973	1,425.4	1,094.0	1,047.2	46.8	124.6	78.5	46.1	206.8	96.4	110.4	101.4
1974	1,545.2	1,182.8	1,138.5	44.2	137.2	85.5	51.7	225.3	102.5	122.8	110.4
1975	1,684.9	1,284.8	1,239.2	45.6	151.6	93.7	58.0	248.4	110.5	138.0	121.3
1976	1,873.4	1,443.3	1,400.2	43.0	164.9	101.7	63.2	265.3	117.3	148.0	130.9
1977	2,081.8	1,616.2	1,572.7	43.5	179.9	110.7	69.2	285.7	125.2	160.6	144.2
1978	2,351.6	1,838.2	1,787.5	50.7	202.1	124.8	77.3	311.3	135.8	175.5	160.2
1979	2,627.3	2,062.8	2,002.7	60.1	226.3	139.5	86.9	338.2	145.4	192.8	177.7
1980	2,857.3	2,225.8	2,174.4	51.4	258.2	158.8	99.3	373.4	159.8	213.5	204.0
1981	3,207.0	2,502.0	2,437.0	65.0	291.6	179.2	112.4	413.5	178.3	235.2	231.6
1982	3,343.8	2,568.6	2,508.2	60.4	323.8	198.2	125.6	451.4	195.7	255.6	258.6
1983	3,634.0	2,801.9	2,757.0	44.9	352.5	213.6	138.9	479.7	207.1	272.6	280.6
1984	4,037.6	3,136.7	3,072.6	64.2	383.8	230.9	152.8	517.1	225.3	291.9	303.1
1985	4,339.0	3,369.6	3,305.9	63.7	411.8	248.2	163.6	557.5	240.0	317.6	333.8
1986	4,579.6	3,539.3	3,479.4	59.9	447.0	268.4	178.6	593.3	250.6	342.7	364.5
1987	4,855.2	3,735.2	3,673.2	62.0	489.5	289.8	199.7	630.4	261.0	369.4	392.1
1988	5,236.4	4,019.3	3,957.9	61.4	539.8	316.4	223.4	677.4	278.5	398.8	424.2
1989	5,641.6	4,326.7	4,252.8	73.9	586.0	341.4	244.6	728.8	292.8	436.1	452.7
1990	5,963.1	4,542.0	4,464.2	77.8	636.3	367.6	268.8	784.9	306.7	478.2	487.0
1991	6,158.1	4,645.0	4,574.7	70.4	677.3	386.6	290.7	835.8	323.5	512.2	515.3
1992	6,520.3	4,920.2	4,840.4	79.9	720.3	407.1	313.2	879.8	329.6	550.2	545.2
1993	6,858.6	5,177.4	5,106.2	71.3	772.8	437.6	335.1	908.3	331.5	576.9	578.4
1994	7,287.2	5,523.7	5,440.1	83.6	824.7	472.7	352.0	938.8	332.6	606.2	619.6
1995	7,639.7	5,795.1	5,726.7	68.4	877.8	506.9	370.9	966.9	333.0	633.9	662.6
1996	8,073.1	6,159.5	6,066.9	92.6	923.2	534.6	388.7	990.3	331.8	658.6	695.0
1997	8,577.6	6,578.8	6,490.6	88.1	975.9	565.7	410.2	1,022.9	333.5	689.3	731.9
1998	9,062.8	6,959.2	6,880.2	79.0	1,040.6	601.6	439.0	1,063.0	336.8	726.2	774.8
1999	9,630.7	7,400.1	7,329.2	70.9	1,112.4	645.2	467.3	1,118.1	345.0	773.1	826.2
2000	10,252.3	7,876.1	7,800.1	76.0	1,191.9	693.5	498.5	1,184.3	360.3	824.0	881.7
2001	10,581.8	8,062.0	7,983.9	78.1	1,267.2	744.7	522.6	1,252.6	370.3	882.3	943.5
2002	10,936.4	8,264.4	8,190.4	74.0	1,343.6	780.7	562.9	1,328.4	397.8	930.6	985.1
2003	11,458.2	8,642.4	8,551.3	91.1	1,411.0	816.6	594.4	1,404.8	434.7	970.1	1,016.4
2004	12,213.7	9,240.6	9,121.2	119.4	1,494.5	868.4	626.1	1,478.7	459.4	1,019.3	1,075.2
2005	13,036.6	9,898.0	9,793.5	104.5	1,583.3	933.4	649.8	1,555.4	488.4	1,067.0	1,151.9
2006	13,814.6	10,509.1	10,412.8	96.3	1,673.6	991.2	682.4	1,631.9	509.9	1,122.1	1,224.2
2007	14,451.9	10,994.6	10,878.9	115.7	1,730.3	1,016.9	713.4	1,726.9	535.7	1,191.2	1,273.4
2008	14,712.8	11,054.9	10,935.4	119.5	1,836.8	1,075.2	761.6	1,821.2	569.1	1,252.1	1,349.5
2009	14,448.9	10,669.9	10,566.8	103.1	1,895.5	1,097.0	798.5	1,883.5	603.0	1,280.5	1,393.8
2010	14,992.1	11,140.5	11,022.8	117.6	1,905.5	1,091.0	814.5	1,946.1	640.0	1,306.1	1,400.2
2011	15,542.6	11,612.9	11,460.7	152.2	1,956.8	1,108.0	848.8	1,972.9	659.8	1,313.1	1,445.7
2012	16,197.0	12,189.5	12,040.5	148.9	2,018.4	1,128.0	890.3	1,989.1	663.7	1,325.5	1,478.5
2013	16,784.9	12,670.5	12,485.9	184.6	2,075.0	1,157.0	918.0	2,039.3	658.4	1,380.9	1,511.2
2014	17,521.7	13,274.1	13,106.1	167.9	2,159.4	1,204.0	955.4	2,088.3	667.1	1,421.2	1,592.4
2015	18,219.3	13,821.1	13,674.7	146.4	2,256.1	1,251.5	1,004.6	2,142.1	674.6	1,467.5	1,690.5
2016	18,707.2	14,172.9	14,043.4	129.5	2,350.3	1,304.4	1,045.9	2,184.1	685.5	1,498.5	1,771.8
2017	19,485.4	14,792.2	14,659.4	132.8	2,447.7	1,364.6	1,083.1	2,245.4	700.3	1,545.1	1,847.6
2018 ᵖ	20,500.6	15,645.8	15,519.1	126.7	2,556.1	1,433.7	1,122.4	2,298.7	710.4	1,588.3	1,941.0
2015: I	17,970.4	13,630.5	13,486.8	143.7	2,215.5	1,230.4	985.0	2,124.5	672.0	1,452.4	1,652.2
II	18,221.3	13,841.2	13,696.0	145.2	2,242.0	1,243.0	999.0	2,138.1	673.2	1,464.9	1,677.6
III	18,331.1	13,911.2	13,759.9	151.3	2,270.6	1,258.9	1,011.6	2,149.3	675.9	1,473.5	1,704.7
IV	18,354.4	13,901.6	13,756.4	145.2	2,296.4	1,273.5	1,022.8	2,156.4	677.4	1,479.1	1,727.6
2016: I	18,409.1	13,930.4	13,797.5	132.9	2,315.9	1,285.0	1,030.9	2,162.8	679.1	1,483.7	1,745.1
II	18,640.7	14,126.1	13,991.7	134.4	2,338.8	1,299.2	1,039.6	2,175.8	683.2	1,492.6	1,765.0
III	18,799.6	14,248.2	14,119.2	129.0	2,359.8	1,309.5	1,050.2	2,191.7	687.7	1,504.0	1,779.6
IV	18,979.2	14,386.8	14,265.4	121.5	2,386.6	1,323.8	1,062.8	2,205.9	692.1	1,513.7	1,797.6
2017: I	19,162.6	14,517.4	14,380.4	137.0	2,419.6	1,345.1	1,074.5	2,225.6	697.2	1,528.3	1,821.7
II	19,359.1	14,680.5	14,544.4	136.1	2,439.8	1,358.5	1,081.3	2,238.8	699.2	1,539.6	1,838.3
III	19,588.1	14,878.5	14,749.1	129.4	2,456.4	1,371.8	1,084.6	2,253.2	701.8	1,551.4	1,856.6
IV	19,831.7	15,092.6	14,963.9	128.8	2,475.2	1,382.9	1,092.3	2,264.0	702.9	1,561.1	1,873.9
2018: I	20,041.0	15,256.0	15,127.4	128.6	2,511.1	1,406.0	1,105.1	2,274.0	704.7	1,569.2	1,903.0
II	20,411.9	15,582.2	15,449.6	132.5	2,541.1	1,424.6	1,116.5	2,288.7	708.1	1,580.6	1,928.6
III	20,658.2	15,776.2	15,655.5	120.7	2,572.7	1,443.3	1,129.5	2,309.2	712.6	1,596.6	1,954.3
IV ᵖ	20,891.4	15,968.8	15,843.8	125.0	2,599.6	1,460.9	1,138.7	2,322.9	716.2	1,606.7	1,978.0

[1] Gross domestic business value added equals gross domestic product excluding gross value added of households and institutions and of general government. Nonfarm value added equals gross domestic business value added excluding gross farm value added.
[2] Equals compensation of employees of nonprofit institutions, the rental value of nonresidential fixed assets owned and used by nonprofit institutions serving households, and rental income of persons for tenant-occupied housing owned by nonprofit institutions.
[3] Equals compensation of general government employees plus general government consumption of fixed capital.

Source: Department of Commerce (Bureau of Economic Analysis).

TABLE B-7. Real gross value added by sector, 1968–2018

[Billions of chained (2012) dollars; quarterly data at seasonally adjusted annual rates]

Year or quarter	Gross domestic product	Business [1] Total	Nonfarm [1]	Farm	Households and institutions Total	House-holds	Nonprofit institutions serving house-holds [2]	General government [3] Total	Federal	State and local	Addendum: Gross housing value added
1968	4,792.3	3,174.9	3,135.9	43.6	622.1	365.4	254.6	1,189.3	537.8	615.7	459.5
1969	4,942.1	3,272.7	3,232.1	45.1	648.6	379.9	267.1	1,221.2	543.2	643.9	480.4
1970	4,951.3	3,271.3	3,227.9	46.4	660.5	388.7	269.5	1,226.5	525.5	672.7	496.4
1971	5,114.3	3,394.9	3,348.6	48.8	690.6	408.3	279.5	1,228.7	506.6	700.2	520.8
1972	5,383.3	3,616.6	3,574.1	48.8	717.9	425.2	289.6	1,226.9	487.2	724.6	545.5
1973	5,687.2	3,867.8	3,833.7	48.2	741.9	438.8	300.0	1,232.9	473.6	750.1	562.9
1974	5,656.5	3,808.8	3,776.2	47.2	772.2	458.4	310.3	1,257.1	473.8	777.4	590.5
1975	5,644.8	3,772.6	3,714.5	56.1	799.1	471.5	324.2	1,276.0	472.1	801.0	609.4
1976	5,949.0	4,027.5	3,980.8	53.4	809.4	477.7	328.4	1,286.8	473.3	811.7	615.4
1977	6,224.1	4,258.1	4,209.4	56.2	815.8	477.6	335.3	1,300.3	475.2	824.3	624.3
1978	6,568.6	4,529.7	4,490.5	54.1	846.3	500.5	342.1	1,325.1	481.5	843.7	646.7
1979	6,776.6	4,690.6	4,642.4	59.2	869.8	510.8	355.7	1,339.9	482.5	859.1	659.2
1980	6,759.2	4,648.3	4,602.9	57.6	896.0	525.3	367.4	1,359.9	490.3	871.1	682.5
1981	6,930.7	4,783.9	4,707.8	76.0	913.2	531.0	379.3	1,369.5	498.5	871.0	695.9
1982	6,805.8	4,646.5	4,563.8	79.7	940.9	538.3	401.1	1,385.7	507.7	876.9	712.1
1983	7,117.7	4,892.8	4,846.6	55.1	979.7	559.3	419.0	1,397.7	520.6	873.5	739.6
1984	7,632.8	5,326.8	5,256.6	73.5	1,002.2	569.8	431.3	1,418.3	534.1	879.0	753.8
1985	7,951.1	5,575.2	5,488.1	87.1	1,019.6	582.8	435.3	1,461.1	551.1	904.3	785.0
1986	8,226.4	5,777.7	5,695.7	83.3	1,051.5	594.4	456.5	1,500.5	564.4	930.7	806.3
1987	8,511.0	5,985.1	5,902.7	84.1	1,090.9	609.5	481.9	1,537.5	582.2	949.1	825.1
1988	8,866.5	6,241.4	6,171.6	74.8	1,146.9	634.8	513.6	1,580.7	593.4	981.6	852.3
1989	9,192.1	6,480.4	6,398.4	85.0	1,193.5	654.5	541.3	1,619.4	602.4	1,011.9	870.1
1990	9,365.5	6,584.1	6,494.1	91.7	1,231.8	667.2	568.3	1,659.8	612.9	1,042.2	887.5
1991	9,355.4	6,544.0	6,453.2	92.3	1,257.0	677.5	583.9	1,676.7	616.4	1,055.9	905.7
1992	9,684.9	6,821.1	6,715.4	106.6	1,288.8	692.8	600.7	1,683.9	606.3	1,073.9	927.7
1993	9,951.5	7,015.7	6,922.7	94.4	1,355.2	726.4	634.0	1,687.9	596.3	1,088.7	961.0
1994	10,352.4	7,354.0	7,241.3	114.3	1,400.9	763.3	641.4	1,689.5	579.7	1,107.7	1,002.0
1995	10,630.3	7,580.0	7,490.0	91.0	1,442.7	789.7	656.3	1,691.9	561.2	1,129.6	1,037.8
1996	11,031.4	7,931.9	7,827.1	105.3	1,471.4	805.9	669.0	1,695.2	547.8	1,147.1	1,055.7
1997	11,521.9	8,348.3	8,230.6	118.1	1,516.7	828.7	691.7	1,708.1	538.8	1,169.7	1,081.1
1998	12,038.3	8,781.0	8,666.5	114.0	1,567.5	850.2	722.2	1,726.8	533.1	1,194.6	1,106.4
1999	12,610.5	9,277.8	9,159.7	116.8	1,610.7	883.9	730.3	1,742.1	528.9	1,214.4	1,144.2
2000	13,131.0	9,728.6	9,593.7	138.2	1,640.6	923.9	717.8	1,770.3	531.7	1,240.0	1,184.9
2001	13,262.1	9,796.7	9,668.7	128.1	1,676.7	953.7	723.3	1,801.4	533.2	1,269.6	1,218.3
2002	13,493.1	9,968.0	9,835.5	133.5	1,702.5	960.1	743.4	1,835.6	542.6	1,294.4	1,221.4
2003	13,879.1	10,295.0	10,153.1	145.1	1,735.0	984.3	751.3	1,858.5	557.0	1,302.8	1,234.6
2004	14,406.4	10,736.4	10,581.6	159.8	1,803.1	1,024.9	778.7	1,871.5	565.1	1,307.5	1,278.2
2005	14,912.5	11,157.9	10,995.0	168.8	1,867.3	1,078.1	788.9	1,888.4	572.3	1,317.0	1,339.1
2006	15,338.3	11,533.3	11,370.8	165.5	1,898.7	1,107.0	790.9	1,903.9	576.7	1,328.3	1,376.2
2007	15,626.0	11,795.2	11,646.9	144.6	1,896.1	1,096.5	799.2	1,930.9	584.6	1,347.3	1,380.2
2008	15,604.7	11,679.1	11,527.7	148.5	1,953.1	1,131.2	821.4	1,970.9	606.3	1,365.3	1,424.7
2009	15,208.8	11,245.6	11,079.9	170.7	1,956.2	1,122.8	833.1	2,006.7	636.6	1,370.5	1,432.1
2010	15,598.8	11,607.3	11,443.9	165.1	1,975.0	1,126.3	848.6	2,016.3	658.0	1,358.5	1,449.0
2011	15,840.7	11,830.4	11,673.0	157.5	2,003.1	1,129.9	873.1	2,007.2	664.3	1,343.0	1,476.5
2012	16,197.0	12,189.5	12,040.5	148.9	2,018.4	1,128.0	890.3	1,989.1	663.7	1,325.5	1,478.5
2013	16,495.4	12,487.3	12,307.3	179.8	2,032.8	1,135.7	897.1	1,975.7	652.0	1,323.7	1,481.2
2014	16,899.8	12,868.0	12,687.1	180.3	2,061.8	1,158.1	903.7	1,971.9	647.0	1,324.7	1,525.8
2015	17,386.7	13,318.6	13,126.3	193.1	2,096.4	1,173.3	923.1	1,976.0	642.5	1,332.9	1,574.7
2016	17,659.2	13,539.5	13,339.4	203.3	2,130.9	1,190.6	940.2	1,993.7	645.3	1,347.8	1,602.7
2017	18,050.7	13,893.7	13,699.9	190.2	2,160.6	1,209.3	951.3	2,004.1	646.1	1,357.3	1,619.3
2018 P	18,571.3	14,374.0	14,183.1	181.8	2,199.5	1,231.8	967.7	2,010.0	648.8	1,360.5	1,647.4
2015: I	17,254.7	13,206.2	13,016.0	190.8	2,079.8	1,165.3	914.6	1,972.4	643.5	1,328.6	1,556.3
II	17,397.0	13,338.6	13,148.5	189.8	2,089.1	1,168.6	920.5	1,974.2	642.4	1,331.3	1,568.0
III	17,438.8	13,363.7	13,169.3	195.7	2,102.5	1,176.1	926.4	1,977.2	641.9	1,334.8	1,581.8
IV	17,456.2	13,366.1	13,171.5	196.1	2,114.3	1,183.2	931.1	1,980.0	642.4	1,337.1	1,592.9
2016: I	17,523.4	13,419.4	13,222.3	199.5	2,121.8	1,186.8	934.9	1,986.4	644.4	1,341.4	1,598.3
II	17,622.5	13,506.0	13,304.6	205.7	2,130.1	1,191.0	939.0	1,991.1	645.1	1,345.4	1,603.7
III	17,706.7	13,579.9	13,376.7	208.2	2,133.7	1,191.2	942.5	1,998.2	646.0	1,351.6	1,603.8
IV	17,784.2	13,652.8	13,454.1	199.7	2,137.9	1,193.5	944.3	1,999.2	645.6	1,352.9	1,605.0
2017: I	17,863.0	13,715.7	13,518.4	196.8	2,151.4	1,204.2	947.3	2,001.7	646.1	1,355.0	1,614.3
II	17,995.2	13,840.9	13,645.7	192.8	2,158.7	1,209.2	949.4	2,002.7	645.2	1,356.7	1,618.3
III	18,120.8	13,959.2	13,767.0	187.3	2,164.6	1,211.5	953.1	2,005.4	646.1	1,358.6	1,621.1
IV	18,223.8	14,058.9	13,868.4	183.7	2,167.8	1,212.3	955.5	2,006.6	646.9	1,359.0	1,623.5
2018: I	18,324.0	14,145.0	13,957.5	178.3	2,183.8	1,222.2	961.6	2,005.2	647.0	1,357.5	1,635.3
II	18,511.6	14,320.6	14,129.0	183.5	2,194.8	1,228.5	966.2	2,008.0	648.3	1,358.9	1,643.5
III	18,665.0	14,458.8	14,268.0	181.0	2,205.0	1,234.9	970.1	2,014.0	650.8	1,362.6	1,651.4
IV P	18,784.6	14,571.5	14,377.9	184.5	2,214.4	1,241.5	972.9	2,012.8	649.0	1,363.0	1,659.4

[1] Gross domestic business value added equals gross domestic product excluding gross value added of households and institutions and of general government. Nonfarm value added equals gross domestic business value added excluding gross farm value added.
[2] Equals compensation of employees of nonprofit institutions, the rental value of nonresidential fixed assets owned and used by nonprofit institutions serving households, and rental income of persons for tenant-occupied housing owned by nonprofit institutions.
[3] Equals compensation of general government employees plus general government consumption of fixed capital.

Source: Department of Commerce (Bureau of Economic Analysis).

Table B–8. Gross domestic product (GDP) by industry, value added, in current dollars and as a percentage of GDP, 1997–2017

[Billions of dollars; except as noted]

Year	Gross domestic product	Total private industries	Agriculture, forestry, fishing, and hunting	Mining	Construction	Manufacturing			Utilities	Wholesale trade	Retail trade
						Total manufacturing	Durable goods	Non-durable goods			
					Value added						
1997	8,577.6	7,432.0	108.6	95.1	339.6	1,382.9	823.8	559.1	171.5	527.5	579.9
1998	9,062.8	7,871.5	99.8	81.7	379.8	1,430.6	850.7	579.9	163.7	563.7	626.9
1999	9,630.7	8,378.3	92.6	84.5	417.6	1,488.9	874.9	614.1	179.9	584.0	652.6
2000	10,252.3	8,929.3	98.3	110.6	461.3	1,550.2	924.8	625.4	180.1	622.6	685.5
2001	10,581.8	9,188.9	99.8	123.9	486.5	1,473.8	833.4	640.5	181.3	613.8	709.5
2002	10,936.4	9,462.0	95.6	112.4	493.6	1,468.5	832.8	635.7	177.6	613.1	732.6
2003	11,458.2	9,905.9	114.0	139.0	525.2	1,524.2	863.2	661.0	184.0	641.4	769.6
2004	12,213.7	10,582.5	142.9	166.5	584.6	1,608.1	905.1	703.0	199.2	697.1	795.6
2005	13,036.6	11,326.4	128.3	225.7	651.8	1,693.4	956.8	736.6	198.1	754.9	840.8
2006	13,814.6	12,022.6	125.1	273.3	697.1	1,793.8	1,004.4	789.4	226.8	811.5	869.9
2007	14,451.9	12,564.8	144.1	314.0	715.3	1,844.7	1,030.6	814.1	231.9	857.8	869.2
2008	14,712.8	12,731.2	147.2	392.2	648.9	1,800.8	999.7	801.1	241.7	884.3	848.7
2009	14,448.9	12,403.9	130.0	275.8	565.6	1,702.1	881.0	821.2	258.2	834.2	827.6
2010	14,992.1	12,884.1	146.3	305.8	525.1	1,797.0	964.3	832.7	278.8	888.9	851.5
2011	15,542.6	13,405.5	180.9	356.3	524.4	1,867.6	1,015.2	852.4	287.5	934.9	871.9
2012	16,197.0	14,037.5	179.6	358.8	553.4	1,927.1	1,061.7	865.3	279.7	997.4	908.4
2013	16,784.9	14,572.3	215.6	386.5	587.6	1,991.9	1,102.0	889.9	286.3	1,040.1	949.5
2014	17,521.7	15,250.0	200.8	413.0	636.4	2,047.4	1,130.7	916.6	298.2	1,088.2	973.8
2015	18,219.3	15,878.8	181.2	257.9	694.9	2,123.0	1,182.7	940.3	299.0	1,141.7	1,021.4
2016	18,707.2	16,319.4	164.9	216.2	745.5	2,085.2	1,182.0	903.1	302.7	1,136.6	1,052.0
2017	19,485.4	17,031.7	169.2	268.6	781.4	2,179.6	1,226.6	953.0	307.5	1,174.1	1,087.1
	Percent				Industry value added as a percentage of GDP (percent)						
1997	100.0	86.6	1.3	1.1	4.0	16.1	9.6	6.5	2.0	6.2	6.8
1998	100.0	86.9	1.1	.9	4.2	15.8	9.4	6.4	1.8	6.2	6.9
1999	100.0	87.0	1.0	.9	4.3	15.5	9.1	6.4	1.9	6.1	6.8
2000	100.0	87.1	1.0	1.1	4.5	15.1	9.0	6.1	1.8	6.1	6.7
2001	100.0	86.8	.9	1.2	4.6	13.9	7.9	6.1	1.7	5.8	6.7
2002	100.0	86.5	.9	1.0	4.5	13.4	7.6	5.8	1.6	5.6	6.7
2003	100.0	86.5	1.0	1.2	4.6	13.3	7.5	5.8	1.6	5.6	6.7
2004	100.0	86.6	1.2	1.4	4.8	13.2	7.4	5.8	1.6	5.7	6.5
2005	100.0	86.9	1.0	1.7	5.0	13.0	7.3	5.7	1.5	5.8	6.4
2006	100.0	87.0	.9	2.0	5.0	13.0	7.3	5.7	1.6	5.9	6.3
2007	100.0	86.9	1.0	2.2	4.9	12.8	7.1	5.6	1.6	5.9	6.0
2008	100.0	86.5	1.0	2.7	4.4	12.2	6.8	5.4	1.6	6.0	5.8
2009	100.0	85.8	.9	1.9	3.9	11.8	6.1	5.7	1.8	5.8	5.7
2010	100.0	85.9	1.0	2.0	3.5	12.0	6.4	5.6	1.9	5.9	5.7
2011	100.0	86.2	1.2	2.3	3.4	12.0	6.5	5.5	1.8	6.0	5.6
2012	100.0	86.7	1.1	2.2	3.4	11.9	6.6	5.3	1.7	6.2	5.6
2013	100.0	86.8	1.3	2.3	3.5	11.9	6.6	5.3	1.7	6.2	5.7
2014	100.0	87.0	1.1	2.4	3.6	11.7	6.5	5.2	1.7	6.2	5.6
2015	100.0	87.2	1.0	1.4	3.8	11.7	6.5	5.2	1.6	6.3	5.6
2016	100.0	87.2	.9	1.2	4.0	11.1	6.3	4.8	1.6	6.1	5.6
2017	100.0	87.4	.9	1.4	4.0	11.2	6.3	4.9	1.6	6.0	5.6

[1] Consists of agriculture, forestry, fishing, and hunting; mining; construction; and manufacturing.

[2] Consists of utilities; wholesale trade; retail trade; transportation and warehousing; information; finance, insurance, real estate, rental, and leasing; professional and business services; educational services, health care, and social assistance; arts, entertainment, recreation, accommodation, and food services; and other services, except government.

Note: Data shown in Tables B–8 and B–9 are consistent with the 2018 annual revision of the industry accounts released in July 2018. For details see *Survey of Current Business*, December 2018.

See next page for continuation of table.

TABLE B-8. Gross domestic product (GDP) by industry, value added, in current dollars and as a percentage of GDP, 1997–2017—*Continued*

[Billions of dollars; except as noted]

Year	Transportation and warehousing	Information	Finance, insurance, real estate, rental, and leasing	Professional and business services	Educational services, health care, and social assistance	Arts, entertainment, recreation, accommodation, and food services	Other services, except government	Government	Private goods-producing industries [1]	Private services-producing industries [2]
					Value added					
1997	257.3	394.1	1,612.4	840.6	590.6	301.8	230.3	1,145.6	1,926.1	5,505.9
1998	280.0	434.6	1,710.1	914.0	615.8	322.1	248.7	1,191.3	1,991.8	5,879.7
1999	290.0	485.0	1,837.1	997.2	653.9	354.1	260.8	1,252.3	2,083.7	6,294.6
2000	307.8	471.3	1,974.7	1,105.1	695.4	386.5	279.7	1,323.0	2,220.4	6,708.9
2001	308.1	502.4	2,128.1	1,155.5	749.9	390.7	265.6	1,392.9	2,184.1	7,004.8
2002	305.7	550.6	2,217.0	1,189.9	807.0	413.5	284.9	1,474.4	2,170.1	7,291.9
2003	321.4	564.9	2,295.9	1,247.4	862.8	432.1	283.8	1,552.3	2,302.4	7,603.5
2004	352.1	620.4	2,389.1	1,341.0	927.3	461.2	297.3	1,631.3	2,502.2	8,080.3
2005	375.8	642.3	2,606.2	1,446.4	970.5	481.2	310.7	1,710.3	2,699.3	8,627.1
2006	410.4	652.0	2,743.9	1,546.6	1,035.4	511.5	325.0	1,792.0	2,889.4	9,133.2
2007	413.9	706.9	2,848.3	1,666.7	1,087.9	533.5	330.5	1,887.1	3,018.1	9,546.7
2008	426.8	743.0	2,762.7	1,777.1	1,184.8	542.7	330.3	1,981.6	2,989.1	9,742.1
2009	404.6	721.9	2,867.7	1,688.7	1,267.5	533.3	326.5	2,045.1	2,673.6	9,730.3
2010	433.0	753.3	2,943.0	1,766.8	1,310.7	555.8	328.0	2,108.0	2,774.3	10,109.8
2011	451.4	759.8	3,045.3	1,856.7	1,354.7	580.9	333.1	2,137.1	2,929.3	10,476.3
2012	472.0	759.0	3,261.0	1,964.7	1,407.4	621.4	348.0	2,159.5	3,018.8	11,018.7
2013	491.1	828.9	3,322.8	2,017.3	1,447.2	651.3	356.3	2,212.5	3,181.6	11,390.8
2014	521.9	840.6	3,552.9	2,117.9	1,492.6	690.1	376.3	2,271.7	3,297.6	11,952.4
2015	563.4	915.0	3,754.6	2,233.3	1,563.5	737.3	392.5	2,340.5	3,257.0	12,621.8
2016	577.4	998.1	3,929.8	2,299.0	1,639.4	770.8	401.8	2,387.8	3,211.8	13,107.6
2017	608.7	1,050.8	4,057.1	2,426.3	1,700.3	804.7	416.1	2,453.7	3,398.9	13,632.8
					Industry value added as a percentage of GDP (percent)					
1997	3.0	4.6	18.8	9.8	6.9	3.5	2.7	13.4	22.5	64.2
1998	3.1	4.8	18.9	10.1	6.8	3.6	2.7	13.1	22.0	64.9
1999	3.0	5.0	19.1	10.4	6.8	3.7	2.7	13.0	21.6	65.4
2000	3.0	4.6	19.3	10.8	6.8	3.8	2.7	12.9	21.7	65.4
2001	2.9	4.7	20.1	10.9	7.1	3.7	2.5	13.2	20.6	66.2
2002	2.8	5.0	20.3	10.9	7.4	3.8	2.6	13.5	19.8	66.7
2003	2.8	4.9	20.0	10.9	7.5	3.8	2.5	13.5	20.1	66.4
2004	2.9	5.1	19.6	11.0	7.6	3.8	2.4	13.4	20.5	66.2
2005	2.9	4.9	20.0	11.1	7.4	3.7	2.4	13.1	20.7	66.2
2006	3.0	4.7	19.9	11.2	7.5	3.7	2.4	13.0	20.9	66.1
2007	2.9	4.9	19.7	11.5	7.5	3.7	2.3	13.1	20.9	66.1
2008	2.9	5.0	18.8	12.1	8.1	3.7	2.2	13.5	20.3	66.2
2009	2.8	5.0	19.8	11.7	8.8	3.7	2.3	14.2	18.5	67.3
2010	2.9	5.0	19.6	11.8	8.7	3.7	2.2	14.1	18.5	67.4
2011	2.9	4.9	19.6	11.9	8.7	3.7	2.1	13.7	18.8	67.4
2012	2.9	4.7	20.1	12.1	8.7	3.8	2.1	13.3	18.6	68.0
2013	2.9	4.9	19.8	12.0	8.6	3.9	2.1	13.2	19.0	67.9
2014	3.0	4.8	20.3	12.1	8.5	3.9	2.1	13.0	18.8	68.2
2015	3.1	5.0	20.6	12.3	8.6	4.0	2.2	12.8	17.9	69.3
2016	3.1	5.3	21.0	12.3	8.8	4.1	2.1	12.8	17.2	70.1
2017	3.1	5.4	20.8	12.5	8.7	4.1	2.1	12.6	17.4	70.0

Note (cont'd): Value added is the contribution of each private industry and of government to GDP. Value added is equal to an industry's gross output minus its intermediate inputs. Current-dollar value added is calculated as the sum of distributions by an industry to its labor and capital, which are derived from the components of gross domestic income.

Value added industry data shown in Tables B–8 and B–9 are based on the 2012 North American Industry Classification System (NAICS).

Source: Department of Commerce (Bureau of Economic Analysis).

National Income or Expenditure | 645

TABLE B–9. Real gross domestic product by industry, value added, and percent changes, 1997–2017

Year	Gross domestic product	Total private industries	Agriculture, forestry, fishing, and hunting	Mining	Construction	Manufacturing			Utilities	Whole-sale trade	Retail trade
						Total manufacturing	Durable goods	Non-durable goods			
					Chain-type quantity indexes for value added (2012=100)						
1997	71.136	70.417	78.122	73.569	124.924	73.952	54.862	108.774	82.684	68.023	76.897
1998	74.324	73.791	76.225	76.540	130.646	76.995	59.373	106.919	78.993	74.707	84.286
1999	77.857	77.614	78.531	74.233	136.033	81.273	63.518	110.673	92.023	77.183	87.388
2000	81.070	81.097	90.102	65.831	141.541	87.116	70.928	111.745	93.244	81.126	90.310
2001	81.880	81.675	86.959	76.178	138.629	83.415	66.355	110.500	77.009	82.663	93.582
2002	83.306	83.128	90.001	78.193	134.131	84.146	67.757	109.712	79.706	83.546	97.689
2003	85.689	85.527	96.987	69.241	136.316	88.809	72.791	113.126	77.930	88.159	102.703
2004	88.945	89.042	104.744	69.643	141.182	95.078	78.019	120.927	82.678	91.924	104.467
2005	92.070	92.473	109.218	70.809	141.809	97.970	83.413	118.785	78.378	96.071	107.851
2006	94.698	95.475	111.013	81.679	138.846	103.527	89.812	122.532	83.261	98.749	108.686
2007	96.475	97.063	98.327	87.975	134.563	106.948	93.989	124.516	84.935	102.073	105.144
2008	96.343	96.460	100.402	85.158	121.446	104.777	94.526	118.051	89.475	101.967	101.290
2009	93.899	93.523	111.362	97.660	104.296	95.141	80.927	114.724	84.828	89.701	97.020
2010	96.306	95.938	107.954	86.193	98.928	100.289	91.144	112.361	95.043	95.040	99.094
2011	97.800	97.577	103.799	89.398	97.334	100.663	97.290	104.898	98.680	96.794	99.277
2012	100.000	100.000	100.000	100.000	100.000	100.000	100.000	100.000	100.000	100.000	100.000
2013	101.842	101.886	116.603	103.938	102.485	103.068	102.463	103.817	98.916	102.293	103.112
2014	104.339	104.590	117.229	114.270	103.855	104.088	103.295	105.073	94.753	106.377	104.687
2015	107.345	107.855	125.070	123.838	108.210	104.653	104.609	104.698	94.206	110.669	108.159
2016	109.027	109.617	130.438	117.925	111.839	103.426	104.104	102.550	98.932	109.418	112.306
2017	111.445	111.973	124.175	119.653	112.716	105.952	107.384	104.120	97.916	111.767	116.797
					Percent change from year earlier						
1997											
1998	4.5	4.8	−2.4	4.0	4.6	4.1	8.2	−1.7	−4.5	9.8	9.6
1999	4.8	5.2	3.0	−3.0	4.1	5.6	7.0	3.5	16.5	3.3	3.7
2000	4.1	4.5	14.7	−11.3	4.0	7.2	11.7	1.0	1.3	5.1	3.3
2001	1.0	.7	−3.5	15.7	−2.1	−4.2	−6.4	−1.1	−17.4	1.9	3.6
2002	1.7	1.8	3.5	2.6	−3.2	.9	2.1	−.7	3.5	1.1	4.4
2003	2.9	2.9	7.8	−11.4	1.6	5.5	7.4	3.1	−2.2	5.5	5.1
2004	3.8	4.1	8.0	.6	3.6	7.1	7.2	6.9	6.1	4.3	1.7
2005	3.5	3.9	4.3	1.7	.4	3.0	6.9	−1.8	−5.2	4.5	3.2
2006	2.9	3.2	1.6	15.4	−2.1	5.7	7.7	3.2	6.2	2.8	.8
2007	1.9	1.7	−11.4	7.7	−3.1	3.3	4.7	1.6	2.0	3.4	−3.3
2008	−.1	−.6	2.1	−3.2	−9.7	−2.0	.6	−5.2	5.3	−.1	−3.7
2009	−2.5	−3.0	10.9	14.7	−14.1	−9.2	−14.4	−2.8	−5.2	−12.0	−4.2
2010	2.6	2.6	−3.1	−11.7	−5.1	5.4	12.6	−2.1	12.0	6.0	2.1
2011	1.6	1.7	−3.8	3.7	−1.6	.4	6.7	−6.6	3.8	1.8	.2
2012	2.2	2.5	−3.7	11.9	2.7	−.7	2.8	−4.7	1.3	3.3	.7
2013	1.8	1.9	16.6	3.9	2.5	3.1	2.5	3.8	−1.1	2.3	3.1
2014	2.5	2.7	.5	9.9	1.3	1.0	.8	1.2	−4.2	4.0	1.5
2015	2.9	3.1	6.7	8.4	4.2	.5	1.3	−.4	−.6	4.0	3.3
2016	1.6	1.6	4.3	−4.8	3.4	−1.2	−.5	−2.1	5.0	−1.1	3.8
2017	2.2	2.1	−4.8	1.5	.8	2.4	3.2	1.5	−1.0	2.1	4.0

[1] Consists of agriculture, forestry, fishing, and hunting; mining; construction; and manufacturing.
[2] Consists of utilities; wholesale trade; retail trade; transportation and warehousing; information; finance, insurance, real estate, rental, and leasing; professional and business services; educational services; health care, and social assistance; arts, entertainment, recreation, accommodation, and food services; and other services, except government.

See next page for continuation of table.

Year		Private industries—Continued								
	Transportation and warehousing	Information	Finance, insurance, real estate, rental, and leasing	Professional and business services	Educational services, health care, and social assistance	Arts, entertainment, recreation, accommodation, and food services	Other services, except government	Government	Private goods-producing industries[1]	Private services-producing industries[2]
	Chain-type quantity indexes for value added (2012=100)									
1997	85.155	45.779	64.494	63.672	65.203	78.811	115.601	87.669	81.548	67.403
1998	89.482	50.548	67.298	66.614	65.487	80.968	120.416	88.689	84.672	70.856
1999	90.225	56.651	71.498	69.758	67.685	85.402	121.187	89.756	88.733	74.618
2000	90.015	55.600	75.255	73.866	70.186	90.569	123.985	91.578	94.034	77.602
2001	83.969	58.897	79.439	75.941	71.869	87.406	111.728	92.511	91.428	79.044
2002	80.939	64.594	80.102	76.841	74.748	89.727	114.785	94.159	91.560	80.849
2003	83.784	66.612	81.058	79.221	77.673	92.055	111.552	95.294	94.958	82.982
2004	90.758	74.307	82.263	81.173	81.384	96.188	113.022	96.155	100.536	85.949
2005	95.120	79.284	87.902	84.782	82.907	96.474	113.811	97.036	102.929	89.658
2006	100.720	82.056	90.292	87.152	86.241	99.144	114.372	97.580	107.432	92.253
2007	99.935	90.123	91.815	90.025	86.891	98.599	111.727	98.528	108.998	93.847
2008	99.042	95.903	88.295	94.309	92.433	96.435	107.629	100.447	104.880	94.207
2009	93.111	93.560	92.578	88.315	95.708	90.853	101.336	100.560	97.869	92.358
2010	97.611	98.866	93.968	91.987	96.712	94.349	99.397	101.063	98.681	95.192
2011	99.380	100.275	95.903	95.662	98.366	97.660	98.508	100.747	98.817	97.237
2012	100.000	100.000	100.000	100.000	100.000	100.000	100.000	100.000	100.000	100.000
2013	101.455	109.095	99.099	101.293	101.289	102.128	99.257	99.297	103.878	101.342
2014	104.199	111.375	102.078	105.774	103.124	105.419	101.973	99.052	106.056	104.189
2015	106.843	123.989	104.466	109.026	106.384	107.750	102.775	99.071	108.647	107.629
2016	108.108	137.040	105.620	111.004	108.985	108.347	102.076	100.074	108.464	109.881
2017	112.458	146.805	105.698	115.681	110.820	110.329	102.591	100.803	110.208	112.390
	Percent change from year earlier									
1997	....	....	....	....	....	....	....	....	....	....
1998	5.1	10.4	4.3	4.6	0.4	2.7	4.2	1.2	3.8	5.1
1999	.8	12.1	6.2	4.7	3.4	5.5	.6	1.2	4.8	5.3
2000	−.2	−1.9	5.3	5.9	3.7	6.1	2.3	2.0	6.0	4.0
2001	−6.7	5.9	5.6	2.8	2.4	−3.5	−9.9	1.0	−2.8	1.9
2002	−3.6	9.7	.8	1.2	4.0	2.7	2.7	1.8	.1	2.3
2003	3.5	3.1	1.2	3.1	3.9	2.6	−2.8	1.2	3.7	2.6
2004	8.3	11.6	1.5	2.5	4.8	4.5	1.3	.9	5.9	3.6
2005	4.8	6.7	6.9	4.4	1.9	.3	.7	.9	2.4	4.3
2006	5.9	3.5	2.7	2.8	4.0	2.8	.5	.6	4.4	2.9
2007	−.8	9.8	1.7	3.3	.8	−.5	−2.3	1.0	1.5	1.7
2008	−.9	6.4	−3.8	4.8	6.4	−2.2	−3.7	1.9	−3.8	.4
2009	−6.0	−2.4	4.9	−6.4	3.5	−5.8	−5.8	.1	−6.7	−2.0
2010	4.8	5.7	1.5	4.2	1.0	3.8	−1.9	.5	.8	3.1
2011	1.8	1.4	2.1	4.0	1.7	3.5	−.9	−.3	.1	2.1
2012	.6	−.3	4.3	4.5	1.7	2.4	1.5	−.7	1.2	2.8
2013	1.5	9.1	−.9	1.3	1.3	2.1	−.7	−.7	3.9	1.3
2014	2.7	2.1	3.0	4.4	1.8	3.2	2.7	−.2	2.1	2.8
2015	2.5	11.3	2.3	3.1	3.2	2.2	.8	.0	2.4	3.3
2016	1.2	10.5	1.1	1.8	2.4	.6	−.7	1.0	−.2	2.1
2017	4.0	7.1	.1	4.2	1.7	1.8	.5	.7	1.6	2.3

Note: Data are based on the 2012 North American Industry Classification System (NAICS).
See Note, Table B–8.

Source: Department of Commerce (Bureau of Economic Analysis).

TABLE B–10. Personal consumption expenditures, 1968–2018

[Billions of dollars; quarterly data at seasonally adjusted annual rates]

Year or quarter	Personal consumption expenditures	Goods — Total	Durable — Total[1]	Durable — Motor vehicles and parts	Nondurable — Total[1]	Nondurable — Food and beverages purchased for off-premises consumption	Nondurable — Gasoline and other energy goods	Services — Total	Household consumption expenditures — Total[1]	Household consumption expenditures — Housing and utilities	Household consumption expenditures — Health care	Household consumption expenditures — Financial services and insurance	Addendum: Personal consumption expenditures excluding food and energy[2]
1968	556.9	284.6	84.8	35.4	199.8	88.8	23.2	272.2	263.4	92.7	36.6	25.2	431.8
1969	603.6	304.7	90.5	37.4	214.2	95.4	25.0	299.0	289.5	101.0	42.1	27.7	469.3
1970	646.7	318.8	90.0	34.5	228.8	103.5	26.3	327.9	317.5	109.4	47.7	30.1	501.7
1971	699.9	342.1	102.4	43.2	239.7	107.1	27.6	357.8	346.1	120.0	53.7	33.1	548.5
1972	768.2	373.8	116.4	49.4	257.4	114.5	29.4	394.3	381.5	131.2	59.8	37.1	605.8
1973	849.6	416.6	130.5	54.4	286.1	126.7	34.3	432.9	419.2	143.5	67.2	39.9	668.5
1974	930.2	451.5	130.2	48.2	321.4	143.0	43.8	478.6	463.1	158.6	76.1	44.1	719.7
1975	1,030.5	491.3	142.2	52.6	349.2	156.6	48.0	539.2	522.2	176.5	89.0	51.8	797.3
1976	1,147.5	546.3	168.6	68.2	377.7	167.3	53.0	601.4	582.4	194.7	101.8	56.8	894.7
1977	1,274.0	600.4	192.0	79.8	408.4	179.8	57.8	673.6	653.0	217.8	115.7	65.1	998.6
1978	1,422.3	663.6	213.3	89.2	450.2	196.1	61.5	758.7	735.7	244.3	131.2	76.7	1,122.4
1979	1,585.4	737.9	226.3	90.2	511.6	218.4	80.4	847.5	821.4	273.4	148.8	83.6	1,239.7
1980	1,750.7	799.8	226.4	84.4	573.4	239.2	101.9	950.9	920.8	312.5	171.7	91.7	1,353.1
1981	1,934.0	869.4	243.9	93.0	625.4	255.3	113.4	1,064.6	1,030.4	352.1	201.9	98.5	1,501.5
1982	2,071.3	899.3	253.0	100.0	646.3	267.1	108.4	1,172.0	1,134.0	387.5	225.2	113.7	1,622.9
1983	2,281.6	973.8	295.0	122.9	678.8	277.0	106.5	1,307.8	1,267.1	421.2	253.1	141.0	1,817.2
1984	2,492.3	1,063.7	342.2	147.2	721.5	291.1	108.2	1,428.6	1,383.3	457.5	276.5	150.8	2,008.1
1985	2,712.8	1,137.6	380.4	170.1	757.2	303.0	110.5	1,575.2	1,527.3	500.6	302.2	178.2	2,210.3
1986	2,886.3	1,195.6	421.4	187.5	774.2	316.4	91.2	1,690.7	1,638.0	537.0	330.2	187.7	2,391.3
1987	3,076.3	1,256.3	442.0	188.2	814.3	324.3	96.4	1,820.0	1,764.3	571.6	366.0	189.5	2,566.6
1988	3,330.0	1,337.3	475.1	202.2	862.3	342.8	99.9	1,992.7	1,929.4	614.4	410.1	202.9	2,793.1
1989	3,576.8	1,423.8	494.3	207.8	929.5	365.4	110.4	2,153.0	2,084.9	655.2	451.2	222.3	3,002.1
1990	3,809.0	1,491.3	497.1	205.1	994.2	391.2	124.2	2,317.7	2,241.8	696.5	506.2	230.8	3,194.9
1991	3,943.4	1,497.4	477.2	185.7	1,020.3	403.0	121.1	2,446.0	2,365.9	735.2	555.8	250.1	3,314.4
1992	4,197.6	1,563.3	508.1	204.8	1,055.2	404.5	125.0	2,634.3	2,546.4	771.1	612.8	277.0	3,561.7
1993	4,452.0	1,642.3	551.5	224.7	1,090.8	413.5	126.9	2,809.6	2,719.6	814.9	648.8	314.0	3,796.6
1994	4,721.0	1,746.6	607.2	249.8	1,139.4	432.1	129.2	2,974.4	2,876.6	863.3	680.5	327.9	4,042.5
1995	4,962.6	1,815.5	635.7	255.7	1,179.8	443.7	133.4	3,147.1	3,044.7	913.7	719.9	347.0	4,267.2
1996	5,244.6	1,917.7	676.3	273.5	1,241.4	461.9	144.7	3,326.9	3,216.9	962.4	752.1	372.1	4,513.0
1997	5,536.8	2,006.5	715.5	293.1	1,291.0	474.8	147.7	3,530.3	3,424.7	1,009.8	790.9	408.9	4,787.8
1998	5,877.2	2,108.4	779.3	320.2	1,329.1	487.4	132.4	3,768.8	3,645.0	1,065.5	832.0	446.1	5,132.4
1999	6,279.1	2,287.1	855.6	350.7	1,431.5	515.5	146.5	3,992.0	3,853.8	1,123.1	863.6	486.4	5,491.2
2000	6,762.1	2,453.2	912.6	363.2	1,540.6	540.6	184.5	4,309.0	4,150.9	1,198.6	918.4	543.0	5,899.4
2001	7,065.6	2,525.6	941.5	383.3	1,584.1	564.0	178.0	4,540.0	4,361.0	1,287.5	996.6	525.7	6,174.0
2002	7,342.7	2,598.8	985.4	401.3	1,613.4	575.1	167.9	4,743.9	4,545.5	1,333.6	1,082.9	534.7	6,454.1
2003	7,723.1	2,722.6	1,017.8	401.5	1,704.8	599.6	196.4	5,000.5	4,795.0	1,394.1	1,154.0	560.3	6,766.8
2004	8,212.7	2,902.0	1,080.6	409.3	1,821.4	632.6	232.7	5,310.6	5,104.3	1,469.1	1,238.9	605.5	7,179.2
2005	8,747.1	3,082.9	1,128.6	410.0	1,954.3	668.2	283.8	5,664.2	5,453.9	1,583.6	1,320.5	659.0	7,605.3
2006	9,260.3	3,239.7	1,158.3	394.9	2,081.3	700.3	319.7	6,020.7	5,781.5	1,682.4	1,391.9	695.0	8,039.7
2007	9,706.4	3,367.0	1,188.0	400.6	2,179.0	737.3	345.5	6,339.4	6,090.6	1,758.2	1,478.2	737.2	8,413.4
2008	9,976.3	3,363.2	1,098.8	343.3	2,264.5	769.1	391.1	6,613.1	6,325.8	1,835.4	1,555.3	756.6	8,592.6
2009	9,842.2	3,180.0	1,012.1	318.6	2,167.9	772.9	287.0	6,662.2	6,373.0	1,877.7	1,632.7	711.3	8,567.0
2010	10,185.8	3,317.8	1,049.0	344.5	2,268.9	786.9	336.7	6,868.0	6,573.6	1,903.9	1,699.6	754.4	8,840.8
2011	10,641.1	3,518.1	1,093.5	365.2	2,424.6	819.5	413.8	7,123.0	6,811.1	1,955.9	1,757.1	797.9	9,188.9
2012	11,006.8	3,637.7	1,144.2	396.6	2,493.5	846.2	421.9	7,369.1	7,027.5	1,996.3	1,821.3	820.1	9,531.1
2013	11,317.2	3,730.0	1,189.4	417.5	2,540.6	864.0	418.2	7,587.2	7,234.6	2,055.3	1,858.2	858.4	9,815.1
2014	11,824.0	3,861.5	1,242.4	442.3	2,619.2	897.6	403.3	7,962.5	7,596.3	2,154.5	1,938.3	908.7	10,290.9
2015	12,294.5	3,919.7	1,306.6	473.9	2,613.1	921.0	309.2	8,374.8	8,007.8	2,257.9	2,062.5	963.1	10,838.6
2016	12,766.9	3,996.3	1,346.6	483.7	2,649.7	944.2	274.9	8,770.6	8,378.4	2,353.0	2,171.6	989.1	11,326.9
2017	13,321.4	4,156.1	1,406.5	498.2	2,749.6	965.8	307.0	9,165.3	8,761.9	2,447.8	2,271.2	1,060.4	11,822.1
2018 *p*	13,951.6	4,342.1	1,461.5	506.8	2,880.7	1,001.3	346.7	9,609.4	9,170.4	2,559.8	2,375.5	1,124.0	12,366.8
2015: I	12,095.6	3,859.1	1,281.4	463.5	2,577.7	917.3	303.5	8,236.4	7,877.7	2,231.0	2,024.6	947.3	10,633.3
II	12,256.7	3,922.7	1,308.3	480.2	2,614.4	916.6	323.0	8,334.0	7,974.0	2,243.7	2,049.5	966.2	10,792.6
III	12,380.7	3,956.8	1,317.2	479.1	2,639.5	923.8	322.1	8,424.0	8,054.2	2,272.2	2,078.4	968.5	10,910.5
IV	12,445.1	3,940.1	1,319.3	472.7	2,620.8	926.5	288.1	8,505.0	8,125.2	2,284.6	2,097.5	970.3	11,018.2
2016: I	12,526.5	3,932.2	1,323.7	471.3	2,608.5	934.4	260.0	8,594.3	8,212.4	2,306.2	2,123.3	969.1	11,121.0
II	12,706.5	3,990.3	1,336.3	474.9	2,654.0	946.7	275.3	8,716.2	8,332.9	2,341.1	2,170.0	978.1	11,264.4
III	12,845.2	4,013.9	1,357.7	489.6	2,656.3	946.5	273.0	8,831.2	8,430.0	2,375.1	2,171.9	1,000.0	11,394.8
IV	12,989.4	4,048.8	1,368.7	499.0	2,680.1	949.3	291.3	8,940.6	8,538.2	2,389.4	2,221.1	1,009.4	11,527.3
2017: I	13,114.1	4,090.4	1,375.6	489.1	2,714.8	953.2	307.1	9,023.7	8,620.5	2,402.4	2,238.2	1,029.3	11,640.8
II	13,233.2	4,117.1	1,393.4	489.7	2,723.7	959.5	292.6	9,116.1	8,710.4	2,438.2	2,248.7	1,050.8	11,751.7
III	13,359.1	4,166.0	1,411.2	497.7	2,754.8	967.9	301.0	9,193.1	8,791.9	2,458.2	2,284.6	1,066.9	11,863.9
IV	13,579.2	4,250.9	1,445.7	516.4	2,805.2	982.6	327.3	9,328.3	8,924.9	2,492.6	2,313.2	1,094.4	12,031.8
2018: I	13,679.6	4,267.7	1,434.5	498.5	2,833.2	988.3	340.6	9,411.9	8,992.5	2,515.6	2,331.0	1,102.5	12,116.5
II	13,875.6	4,329.5	1,458.7	504.6	2,870.8	998.0	347.0	9,546.1	9,111.8	2,548.5	2,357.8	1,114.4	12,291.7
III	14,050.5	4,371.3	1,468.5	506.2	2,902.8	1,007.4	352.0	9,679.1	9,232.8	2,571.2	2,392.6	1,128.8	12,457.0
IV *p*	14,200.6	4,400.1	1,484.2	517.9	2,915.9	1,011.4	347.2	9,800.6	9,344.6	2,604.0	2,420.7	1,150.3	12,601.9

[1] Includes other items not shown separately.
[2] Food consists of food and beverages purchased for off-premises consumption; food services, which include purchased meals and beverages, are not classified as food.

Source: Department of Commerce (Bureau of Economic Analysis).

TABLE B–11. Real personal consumption expenditures, 2002–2018

[Billions of chained (2012) dollars; quarterly data at seasonally adjusted annual rates]

Year or quarter	Personal consumption expenditures	Goods						Services					Addendum: Personal consumption expenditures excluding food and energy [2]
		Total	Durable		Nondurable			Total	Household consumption expenditures				
			Total [1]	Motor vehicles and parts	Total [1]	Food and beverages purchased for off-premises consumption	Gasoline and other energy goods		Total [1]	Housing and utilities	Health care	Financial services and insurance	
2002	9,088.7	2,947.6	820.2	416.9	2,157.5	744.5	455.2	6,151.1	5,966.4	1,707.6	1,440.7	700.3	7,716.7
2003	9,377.5	3,092.0	879.3	429.2	2,233.6	761.8	455.6	6,289.4	6,087.7	1,730.5	1,479.3	704.3	7,976.2
2004	9,729.3	3,250.0	952.1	441.1	2,306.5	779.5	459.4	6,479.2	6,275.1	1,773.8	1,531.2	728.5	8,298.2
2005	10,075.9	3,384.7	1,004.9	435.1	2,383.4	809.2	457.4	6,689.5	6,487.6	1,846.6	1,581.9	767.9	8,605.9
2006	10,384.5	3,509.7	1,049.3	419.0	2,461.6	834.0	456.3	6,871.7	6,640.7	1,882.5	1,618.2	785.8	8,894.3
2007	10,615.3	3,607.6	1,099.7	427.3	2,503.4	845.2	455.4	7,003.6	6,765.7	1,900.7	1,657.2	808.3	9,107.6
2008	10,592.8	3,498.9	1,036.4	373.1	2,463.9	831.0	437.5	7,093.0	6,815.4	1,921.2	1,697.9	825.0	9,119.2
2009	10,460.0	3,389.8	973.0	346.7	2,423.1	825.3	440.1	7,070.1	6,781.3	1,943.1	1,735.1	809.5	8,988.1
2010	10,643.0	3,485.7	1,027.3	360.0	2,461.3	837.7	437.9	7,157.4	6,859.0	1,966.8	1,761.7	810.5	9,151.3
2011	10,843.8	3,561.8	1,079.7	370.1	2,482.9	839.0	427.8	7,282.1	6,969.3	1,993.0	1,788.7	831.4	9,363.2
2012	11,006.8	3,637.7	1,144.2	396.6	2,493.5	846.2	421.9	7,369.1	7,027.5	1,996.3	1,821.3	820.1	9,531.1
2013	11,166.9	3,752.2	1,214.1	415.3	2,538.5	855.5	429.7	7,415.5	7,069.8	2,006.4	1,832.6	815.2	9,667.6
2014	11,494.3	3,902.9	1,301.0	439.8	2,603.7	872.1	430.1	7,594.0	7,247.9	2,044.4	1,890.4	819.2	9,974.9
2015	11,921.9	4,087.7	1,399.4	471.4	2,691.7	884.9	449.9	7,840.0	7,506.1	2,089.4	2,000.1	841.9	10,371.8
2016	12,248.2	4,236.1	1,476.8	486.5	2,763.9	916.8	452.0	8,022.5	7,677.3	2,116.6	2,081.7	827.4	10,661.9
2017	12,558.7	4,391.9	1,577.9	507.2	2,822.0	938.9	446.5	8,184.5	7,842.2	2,129.9	2,145.8	848.4	10,950.3
2018 p	12,890.6	4,557.3	1,667.4	518.3	2,901.0	968.4	444.0	8,359.3	7,992.4	2,160.2	2,203.2	856.3	11,241.8
2015: I	11,788.4	4,024.3	1,365.0	461.9	2,662.3	881.6	447.6	7,768.1	7,438.5	2,083.3	1,972.1	839.3	10,234.5
II	11,887.5	4,071.9	1,396.0	476.6	2,679.4	883.1	448.0	7,821.0	7,493.1	2,083.8	1,990.0	846.2	10,342.3
III	11,972.0	4,115.2	1,413.2	475.8	2,705.5	886.0	453.2	7,863.6	7,528.6	2,095.8	2,011.2	841.1	10,417.5
IV	12,039.7	4,139.5	1,423.5	471.2	2,719.7	888.8	450.9	7,907.1	7,564.3	2,094.6	2,026.9	841.1	10,493.0
2016: I	12,111.8	4,174.6	1,434.9	470.9	2,743.4	900.8	461.5	7,945.5	7,604.1	2,101.7	2,048.1	830.1	10,545.5
II	12,214.1	4,223.9	1,457.9	477.0	2,770.0	917.0	452.2	8,000.4	7,661.4	2,116.5	2,085.6	822.7	10,626.4
III	12,294.3	4,258.5	1,494.3	493.2	2,769.2	921.9	449.1	8,047.0	7,694.9	2,127.5	2,077.0	828.8	10,695.2
IV	12,372.7	4,287.2	1,520.2	504.9	2,773.2	927.4	445.1	8,096.9	7,748.8	2,120.5	2,116.2	827.9	10,780.4
2017: I	12,427.6	4,307.3	1,527.2	494.3	2,786.3	930.2	442.8	8,131.9	7,786.8	2,114.8	2,127.3	842.7	10,842.6
II	12,515.9	4,366.0	1,559.2	498.0	2,813.9	932.3	450.6	8,165.6	7,821.9	2,130.0	2,129.2	844.7	10,909.5
III	12,584.9	4,410.2	1,588.6	508.4	2,829.9	939.7	447.1	8,193.7	7,855.0	2,131.6	2,156.8	851.0	10,975.1
IV	12,706.4	4,483.9	1,636.6	528.3	2,857.7	953.5	445.4	8,246.6	7,904.9	2,143.2	2,169.7	855.1	11,073.9
2018: I	12,722.8	4,477.0	1,628.2	510.7	2,858.6	958.6	441.9	8,267.9	7,915.2	2,146.0	2,177.3	852.7	11,091.8
II	12,842.0	4,537.6	1,662.3	518.6	2,886.7	965.2	446.6	8,329.8	7,963.5	2,158.1	2,188.9	852.2	11,193.5
III	12,953.3	4,585.5	1,677.4	516.2	2,919.2	973.3	442.8	8,394.9	8,022.7	2,163.7	2,214.3	855.3	11,299.7
IV p	13,044.2	4,629.0	1,701.6	527.7	2,939.7	976.5	444.8	8,444.5	8,068.2	2,172.9	2,232.1	864.9	11,382.2

[1] Includes other items not shown separately.
[2] Food consists of food and beverages purchased for off-premises consumption; food services, which include purchased meals and beverages, are not classified as food.

Source: Department of Commerce (Bureau of Economic Analysis).

National Income or Expenditure | 649

TABLE B–12. Private fixed investment by type, 1968–2018

[Billions of dollars; quarterly data at seasonally adjusted annual rates]

Year or quarter	Private fixed investment	Nonresidential											Residential		
		Total nonresidential	Structures	Equipment						Intellectual property products			Total residential¹	Structures	
				Total¹	Information processing equipment			Industrial equipment	Transportation equipment	Total¹	Software	Research and development²		Total¹	Single family
					Total	Computers and peripheral equipment	Other								
1968	147.9	107.7	33.6	58.5	10.6	1.9	8.7	17.3	17.6	15.6	1.3	9.9	40.2	39.3	19.5
1969	164.4	120.0	37.7	65.2	12.8	2.4	10.4	19.1	18.9	17.2	1.8	11.0	44.4	43.4	19.7
1970	168.0	124.6	40.3	66.4	14.3	2.7	11.6	20.3	16.2	17.9	2.3	11.5	43.4	42.3	17.5
1971	188.6	130.4	42.7	69.1	14.9	2.8	12.2	19.5	18.4	18.7	2.4	11.9	58.2	56.9	25.8
1972	219.0	146.6	47.2	78.9	16.7	3.5	13.2	21.4	21.8	20.6	2.8	12.9	72.4	70.9	32.8
1973	251.0	172.7	55.0	95.1	19.9	3.5	16.3	26.0	26.6	22.7	3.2	14.6	78.3	76.6	35.2
1974	260.5	191.1	61.2	104.3	23.1	3.9	19.2	30.7	26.3	25.5	3.9	16.4	69.5	67.6	29.7
1975	263.5	196.8	61.4	107.6	23.8	3.6	20.2	31.3	25.2	27.8	4.8	17.5	66.7	64.8	29.6
1976	306.1	219.3	65.9	121.2	27.5	4.4	23.1	34.1	30.0	32.2	5.2	19.6	86.8	84.6	43.9
1977	374.3	259.1	74.6	148.7	33.7	5.7	28.0	39.4	39.3	35.8	5.5	21.8	115.2	112.8	62.2
1978	452.6	314.6	93.6	180.6	42.3	7.6	34.8	47.7	47.3	40.4	6.3	24.9	138.0	135.3	72.8
1979	521.7	373.8	117.7	208.1	50.3	10.2	40.2	56.2	53.6	48.1	8.1	29.1	147.8	144.7	72.3
1980	536.4	406.9	136.2	216.4	58.9	12.5	46.4	60.7	48.4	54.4	9.8	34.2	128.5	126.1	52.9
1981	601.4	472.9	167.3	240.9	69.6	17.1	52.5	65.5	50.6	64.8	11.8	39.7	128.5	124.9	52.0
1982	595.9	485.1	177.6	234.9	74.2	18.9	55.3	62.7	46.8	72.7	14.0	44.8	110.8	107.2	41.5
1983	643.3	482.2	154.3	246.5	83.7	23.9	59.8	58.9	53.5	81.3	16.4	49.6	161.1	156.9	72.5
1984	754.7	564.3	177.4	291.9	101.2	31.6	69.6	68.1	64.4	95.0	20.4	56.9	190.4	185.6	86.4
1985	807.8	607.8	194.5	307.9	106.6	33.7	72.9	72.5	69.0	105.3	23.8	63.0	200.1	195.0	87.4
1986	842.6	607.8	176.5	317.7	111.1	33.4	77.7	75.4	70.5	113.5	25.6	66.5	234.8	229.3	104.1
1987	865.0	615.2	174.2	320.9	112.2	35.8	76.4	76.7	68.1	120.1	29.0	69.2	249.8	244.0	117.2
1988	918.5	662.3	182.8	346.8	120.8	38.0	82.8	84.2	72.9	132.7	33.3	76.4	256.2	250.1	120.1
1989	972.0	716.0	193.7	372.2	130.7	43.1	87.6	93.3	67.9	150.1	40.6	84.1	256.0	249.9	120.9
1990	978.9	739.2	202.9	371.9	129.6	38.6	90.9	92.1	70.0	164.4	45.4	91.5	239.7	233.7	112.9
1991	944.7	723.6	183.6	360.8	129.2	37.7	91.5	89.3	71.5	179.1	48.7	101.0	221.2	215.4	99.4
1992	996.7	741.9	172.6	381.7	142.1	44.0	98.1	93.0	74.7	187.7	51.1	105.4	254.7	248.8	122.0
1993	1,086.0	799.2	177.2	425.1	153.3	47.9	105.4	102.2	89.4	196.9	57.2	106.3	286.8	280.7	140.1
1994	1,192.7	868.9	186.8	476.4	167.0	52.4	114.6	113.0	107.7	205.7	60.4	109.2	323.8	317.6	162.3
1995	1,286.3	962.2	207.3	528.1	188.4	66.1	122.3	129.0	116.1	226.8	65.5	121.2	324.1	317.7	153.5
1996	1,401.3	1,043.2	224.6	565.3	204.7	72.8	131.9	136.5	123.2	253.3	74.5	134.5	358.1	351.7	170.8
1997	1,524.7	1,149.1	250.3	610.9	222.8	81.4	141.4	140.4	135.5	288.0	93.8	148.1	375.6	369.3	175.2
1998	1,673.0	1,254.1	276.0	660.0	240.1	87.9	152.2	147.4	147.1	318.1	109.2	160.6	418.8	412.1	199.4
1999	1,826.2	1,364.5	285.7	713.6	259.8	97.2	162.5	149.1	174.4	365.1	136.6	177.5	461.8	454.5	223.8
2000	1,983.9	1,498.4	321.0	766.1	293.8	103.2	190.6	162.9	170.8	411.3	156.8	199.0	485.4	477.7	236.8
2001	1,973.1	1,460.1	333.5	711.5	265.9	87.6	178.4	151.9	154.2	415.0	157.7	207.7	513.1	505.2	249.1
2002	1,910.4	1,352.8	287.0	659.6	236.7	79.7	157.0	141.7	141.6	406.2	152.5	196.1	557.6	549.6	265.9
2003	2,013.0	1,375.9	286.6	670.6	242.7	79.9	162.8	143.4	134.1	418.7	155.0	201.0	637.1	628.8	310.6
2004	2,217.2	1,467.4	307.7	721.9	255.8	84.2	171.6	144.2	159.2	437.8	166.3	207.4	749.8	740.8	377.6
2005	2,477.2	1,621.0	353.0	794.9	267.0	84.2	182.8	162.4	179.6	473.1	178.6	224.7	856.2	846.6	433.5
2006	2,632.0	1,793.8	425.2	862.3	288.5	92.6	195.9	181.6	194.3	506.3	189.5	245.6	838.2	828.1	416.0
2007	2,639.1	1,948.6	510.3	893.4	310.9	95.4	215.5	194.1	188.8	544.8	206.4	268.0	690.5	680.6	305.2
2008	2,506.9	1,990.9	571.1	845.4	306.3	93.9	212.4	194.3	148.7	574.4	223.8	284.2	516.0	506.4	185.8
2009	2,080.4	1,690.4	455.8	670.3	275.6	88.9	186.7	153.7	74.9	564.4	226.0	274.6	390.0	381.2	105.3
2010	2,111.6	1,735.0	379.8	777.0	307.5	99.6	207.9	155.2	135.8	578.2	226.4	282.4	376.6	367.4	112.6
2011	2,286.3	1,907.5	404.5	881.3	313.3	95.6	217.7	191.5	177.8	621.7	249.8	303.4	378.8	369.1	108.2
2012	2,550.5	2,118.5	479.4	983.4	331.2	103.5	227.7	211.2	215.3	655.7	272.1	313.4	432.0	421.5	132.0
2013	2,721.5	2,211.5	492.5	1,027.0	341.7	102.1	239.6	209.3	242.5	691.9	283.7	337.9	510.0	499.0	170.8
2014	2,954.4	2,394.3	577.1	1,090.8	345.7	101.6	244.1	218.9	272.2	726.4	297.5	357.6	560.1	548.8	193.6
2015	3,083.2	2,449.7	572.2	1,118.3	353.2	101.4	251.8	218.6	304.9	759.2	307.3	374.8	633.6	621.9	221.1
2016	3,140.9	2,442.1	545.7	1,090.9	354.3	99.3	255.0	215.0	290.5	805.5	327.5	398.8	698.8	686.7	242.5
2017	3,342.5	2,587.9	585.4	1,150.4	381.9	109.2	272.7	231.3	284.3	852.0	352.9	417.9	754.6	742.2	270.2
2018 ᵖ	3,595.6	2,820.4	637.1	1,236.3	409.6	118.1	291.5	248.4	304.9	927.0	385.1	457.7	795.3	782.4	285.0
2015: I	3,052.1	2,447.5	589.0	1,114.9	347.5	100.6	246.9	218.4	299.0	743.6	304.5	364.1	604.6	593.1	213.6
II	3,081.7	2,458.0	589.9	1,114.6	350.1	101.7	248.4	220.5	301.9	753.4	305.7	370.9	623.7	612.0	215.5
III	3,109.3	2,463.0	570.9	1,130.2	357.8	103.5	254.3	217.4	315.4	762.0	307.2	376.9	646.3	634.5	224.6
IV	3,089.9	2,430.3	539.0	1,113.7	357.4	99.8	257.5	218.0	303.3	777.6	311.7	387.4	659.6	647.8	230.8
2016: I	3,094.1	2,409.8	531.2	1,092.8	349.0	99.1	249.9	212.2	298.8	785.8	319.0	388.1	684.2	672.2	240.4
II	3,127.1	2,435.6	539.7	1,091.4	353.1	99.8	253.2	214.2	295.2	804.5	325.5	400.1	691.5	679.4	241.2
III	3,157.2	2,458.4	555.1	1,090.2	356.3	98.2	258.2	215.3	287.5	813.2	330.0	403.7	698.8	686.6	238.1
IV	3,185.4	2,464.7	556.7	1,089.3	358.8	100.1	258.6	218.1	280.5	818.7	335.4	403.2	720.8	708.6	250.2
2017: I	3,270.6	2,525.2	577.5	1,112.3	368.5	103.2	265.4	222.1	282.4	835.4	342.7	412.1	745.5	733.1	259.6
II	3,320.8	2,576.7	588.3	1,137.4	379.0	110.1	268.8	230.1	279.4	850.9	353.5	416.5	744.1	731.8	267.7
III	3,358.5	2,607.0	585.3	1,162.8	385.5	113.9	272.6	234.6	285.0	858.9	359.7	417.8	751.5	739.1	273.6
IV	3,420.0	2,642.6	590.6	1,189.1	393.7	109.7	284.0	238.5	290.4	862.9	355.9	425.0	777.4	764.7	279.8
2018: I	3,507.4	2,720.3	614.9	1,212.6	401.9	116.9	285.0	243.9	300.7	892.7	370.3	439.7	787.2	774.6	287.1
II	3,589.9	2,791.4	644.1	1,228.8	410.2	121.0	289.1	243.4	303.5	918.6	381.6	453.1	798.5	785.6	288.5
III	3,618.0	2,819.7	643.3	1,243.0	415.8	120.3	295.5	250.2	302.9	933.4	389.0	459.7	798.3	785.3	286.1
IV ᵖ	3,667.1	2,870.1	645.9	1,261.0	410.6	114.1	296.5	256.0	312.6	963.3	399.6	478.4	797.0	784.0	278.5

[1] Includes other items not shown separately.
[2] Research and development investment includes expenditures for software.

Source: Department of Commerce (Bureau of Economic Analysis).

TABLE B–13. Real private fixed investment by type, 2002–2018

[Billions of chained (2012) dollars; quarterly data at seasonally adjusted annual rates]

Year or quarter	Private fixed investment	Nonresidential											Residential		
		Total nonresidential	Structures	Equipment						Intellectual property products			Structures		
				Total [2]	Information processing equipment			Industrial equipment	Transportation equipment	Total [2]	Software	Research and development [3]	Total residential [2]	Total [2]	Single family
					Total	Computers and peripheral equipment [1]	Other								
2002	2,183.4	1,472.7	473.5	607.8	133.3	35.9	98.3	181.4	162.4	421.5	125.5	244.1	692.6	685.1	327.1
2003	2,280.6	1,509.4	456.6	634.3	150.4	40.2	111.1	182.2	150.3	437.7	133.5	246.1	755.5	747.7	362.0
2004	2,440.7	1,594.0	456.3	688.6	169.4	45.7	124.7	178.8	171.2	459.2	149.3	248.1	830.9	822.1	405.4
2005	2,618.7	1,716.4	466.1	760.0	187.6	51.8	136.5	194.2	192.1	493.1	163.4	261.6	885.4	876.3	432.8
2006	2,686.8	1,854.2	501.7	832.6	217.0	64.7	152.4	210.6	206.4	521.5	173.5	279.6	818.9	809.5	390.4
2007	2,653.5	1,982.1	568.6	865.8	247.2	73.9	173.3	217.3	197.7	554.3	191.1	296.1	665.8	656.6	283.5
2008	2,499.4	1,994.2	605.4	824.4	260.6	79.7	180.9	208.3	155.0	575.3	206.7	304.8	504.6	495.7	178.1
2009	2,099.8	1,704.3	492.2	649.7	247.5	81.1	165.5	162.7	72.5	572.4	212.9	297.4	395.3	386.9	105.3
2010	2,164.2	1,781.0	412.8	781.2	289.1	94.1	195.1	162.5	141.5	588.1	220.9	298.5	383.0	373.8	114.3
2011	2,317.8	1,935.4	424.1	886.2	303.2	93.9	209.3	194.9	181.8	624.8	245.2	311.0	382.5	372.4	109.1
2012	2,550.5	2,118.5	479.4	983.4	331.2	103.5	227.7	211.2	215.3	655.7	272.1	313.4	432.0	421.5	132.0
2013	2,692.1	2,206.0	485.5	1,029.2	351.8	103.0	248.8	208.4	238.5	691.4	287.2	333.8	485.5	474.1	161.8
2014	2,861.5	2,357.4	536.9	1,098.7	368.6	102.6	266.4	216.6	264.4	721.1	305.3	345.3	504.2	491.8	171.9
2015	2,958.5	2,399.7	520.9	1,132.6	393.5	103.5	291.0	217.0	291.4	747.8	319.9	352.8	553.3	541.9	191.5
2016	3,009.8	2,411.2	494.7	1,116.2	410.9	103.0	309.7	214.4	274.3	803.9	345.9	382.0	591.3	576.8	201.1
2017	3,155.1	2,538.1	517.5	1,183.7	459.8	113.8	348.4	228.6	264.2	841.1	379.3	386.8	611.1	595.7	214.8
2018 p	3,322.4	2,714.8	543.3	1,271.9	503.6	122.8	383.8	240.9	282.6	905.6	419.4	411.1	609.6	594.3	217.6
2015: I	2,930.4	2,393.5	536.3	1,124.0	380.1	101.8	279.1	216.3	286.7	733.2	315.5	344.4	535.2	522.2	185.7
II	2,957.5	2,405.5	538.6	1,126.3	386.7	103.6	283.9	218.7	288.9	740.5	318.8	347.3	549.3	536.0	187.6
III	2,980.2	2,411.9	518.8	1,146.4	401.1	105.9	296.1	215.8	301.0	748.8	319.8	353.1	564.3	550.8	194.6
IV	2,965.9	2,388.1	489.7	1,133.7	406.0	102.6	305.0	217.2	289.0	768.8	325.7	366.5	572.3	558.6	198.4
2016: I	2,979.7	2,380.9	484.8	1,115.1	399.6	102.3	298.8	211.8	284.0	785.0	334.4	374.6	590.9	576.7	204.7
II	3,000.0	2,403.3	488.8	1,115.5	405.9	103.2	304.3	213.9	279.8	803.2	343.0	384.8	589.4	575.1	202.1
III	3,023.5	2,430.3	503.5	1,115.8	415.1	101.8	315.6	214.6	270.5	814.0	349.8	387.7	586.9	572.4	195.7
IV	3,036.1	2,430.4	501.9	1,118.2	423.0	104.8	320.3	217.5	262.9	813.3	356.2	380.7	597.9	583.2	202.1
2017: I	3,108.6	2,486.5	517.3	1,142.8	439.7	107.7	334.5	220.6	262.0	829.0	366.2	386.7	613.8	598.7	208.5
II	3,141.3	2,530.8	522.2	1,169.5	455.2	114.8	342.2	227.7	259.0	842.3	377.7	389.5	605.2	590.0	213.1
III	3,161.2	2,552.3	514.5	1,197.1	466.8	118.7	349.7	231.6	264.7	845.9	387.9	384.0	604.5	589.2	216.6
IV	3,209.3	2,582.7	516.2	1,225.6	477.5	113.9	367.1	234.6	270.9	847.3	385.3	386.8	620.7	605.0	220.9
2018: I	3,271.1	2,654.0	533.3	1,250.9	490.5	121.3	371.7	238.5	280.3	875.7	402.1	398.8	615.3	599.7	223.1
II	3,322.3	2,710.1	551.7	1,264.9	502.9	125.7	379.3	236.6	281.3	897.9	414.2	408.6	613.2	597.8	220.6
III	3,331.8	2,727.0	546.9	1,275.6	511.8	125.0	389.7	242.0	278.8	910.2	423.3	411.8	607.7	592.4	217.5
IV p	3,364.2	2,768.0	541.1	1,296.4	509.2	119.1	394.5	246.8	289.9	938.6	437.9	425.0	602.3	587.2	209.3

[1] Because computers exhibit rapid changes in prices relative to other prices in the economy, the chained-dollar estimates should not be used to measure the component's relative importance or its contribution to the growth rate of more aggregate series. The quantity index for computers can be used to accurately measure the real growth rate of this series. For information on this component, see Survey of Current Business Table 5.3.1 (for growth rates), Table 5.3.2 (for contributions), and Table 5.3.3 (for quantity indexes).

[2] Includes other items not shown separately.

[3] Research and development investment includes expenditures for software.

Source: Department of Commerce (Bureau of Economic Analysis).

National Income or Expenditure | 651

TABLE B–14. Foreign transactions in the national income and product accounts, 1968–2018

[Billions of dollars; quarterly data at seasonally adjusted annual rates]

Year or quarter	Current receipts from rest of the world					Current payments to rest of the world										Balance on current account, NIPA[2]
	Total	Exports of goods and services			Income receipts	Total	Imports of goods and services			Income payments	Current taxes and transfer payments to rest of the world (net)				
		Total	Goods[1]	Services[1]			Total	Goods[1]	Services[1]		Total	From persons (net)	From government (net)	From business (net)	
1968	58.0	47.9	35.7	12.2	10.1	56.5	46.6	33.9	12.6	4.0	5.9	1.0	4.6	0.3	1.5
1969	63.7	51.9	38.7	13.2	11.8	62.1	50.5	36.8	13.7	5.7	5.9	1.1	4.5	.3	1.6
1970	72.5	59.7	45.0	14.7	12.8	68.8	55.8	40.9	14.9	6.4	6.6	1.3	4.9	.4	3.7
1971	77.0	63.0	46.2	16.8	14.0	76.7	62.3	46.6	15.8	6.4	7.9	1.4	6.1	.4	.3
1972	87.1	70.8	52.6	18.3	16.3	91.2	74.2	56.9	17.3	7.7	9.2	1.4	7.4	.5	–4.0
1973	118.8	95.3	75.8	19.5	23.5	109.9	91.2	71.8	19.3	10.9	7.9	1.6	5.6	.7	8.9
1974	156.5	126.7	103.5	23.2	29.8	150.5	127.5	104.5	22.9	14.3	8.7	1.4	6.4	1.0	6.0
1975	166.7	138.7	112.5	26.2	28.0	146.9	122.7	99.0	23.7	15.0	9.1	1.3	7.1	.7	19.8
1976	181.9	149.5	121.5	28.0	32.4	174.8	151.1	124.6	26.5	15.5	8.1	1.4	5.7	1.1	7.1
1977	196.5	159.3	128.4	30.9	37.2	207.5	182.4	152.6	29.8	16.9	8.1	1.4	5.3	1.4	–10.9
1978	233.1	186.9	149.9	37.0	46.3	245.8	212.3	177.4	34.8	24.7	8.8	1.6	5.9	1.4	–12.6
1979	298.5	230.1	187.3	42.9	68.3	299.6	252.7	212.8	39.9	36.4	10.6	1.7	6.8	2.0	–1.2
1980	359.9	280.8	230.4	50.3	79.1	351.4	293.8	248.6	45.3	44.9	12.6	2.0	8.3	2.4	8.5
1981	397.3	305.2	245.2	60.0	92.0	393.9	317.8	267.8	49.9	59.1	17.0	5.6	8.3	3.2	3.4
1982	384.2	283.2	222.6	60.7	101.0	387.5	303.2	250.5	52.6	64.5	19.8	6.3	9.7	3.4	–3.3
1983	378.9	277.0	214.0	62.9	101.9	413.9	328.6	272.7	56.0	64.8	20.5	7.0	10.1	3.4	–35.1
1984	424.2	302.4	231.3	71.1	121.9	514.3	405.1	336.3	68.8	85.6	23.6	7.9	12.2	3.5	–90.1
1985	415.9	303.2	227.5	75.7	112.7	530.2	417.2	343.3	73.9	87.3	25.7	8.3	14.4	2.9	–114.3
1986	432.3	321.0	231.4	89.6	111.3	575.0	452.9	370.0	82.9	94.4	27.8	9.1	15.4	3.2	–142.7
1987	487.2	363.9	265.6	98.4	123.3	641.3	508.7	414.8	93.9	105.8	26.8	10.0	13.4	3.4	–154.1
1988	596.7	444.6	332.1	112.5	152.1	712.4	554.0	452.1	101.9	129.5	29.0	10.8	13.7	4.5	–115.7
1989	682.0	504.3	374.8	129.5	177.7	774.3	591.0	484.8	106.2	152.9	30.4	11.4	14.2	4.6	–92.4
1990	740.7	551.9	403.3	148.6	188.8	815.6	629.7	508.1	121.7	154.2	31.7	12.2	14.7	4.8	–74.9
1991	763.3	594.9	430.1	164.8	168.4	755.4	673.5	500.7	122.8	136.8	–4.9	14.1	–24.0	5.0	7.9
1992	785.1	633.1	455.3	177.7	152.1	830.7	667.8	544.9	122.9	121.0	41.9	14.5	22.0	5.4	–45.6
1993	810.4	654.8	467.7	187.1	155.6	889.8	720.0	592.8	127.2	124.4	45.4	17.1	22.9	5.4	–79.4
1994	905.5	720.9	518.4	202.6	184.5	1,021.1	813.4	676.8	136.6	161.6	46.1	18.9	21.1	6.0	–115.6
1995	1,042.6	812.8	592.4	220.4	229.8	1,148.5	902.6	757.4	145.1	201.9	44.1	20.3	15.6	8.2	–105.9
1996	1,114.0	867.6	628.8	238.8	246.4	1,229.0	964.0	807.4	156.5	215.5	49.5	22.6	20.0	6.9	–115.0
1997	1,233.9	953.8	699.9	253.9	280.1	1,364.0	1,055.8	885.7	170.1	256.8	51.4	25.7	16.7	9.1	–130.1
1998	1,239.8	953.0	692.6	260.4	286.8	1,445.1	1,115.7	930.8	184.9	269.4	60.0	29.7	17.4	13.0	–205.3
1999	1,350.9	992.8	711.7	281.1	320.2	1,629.3	1,248.6	1,051.2	197.4	294.7	86.0	58.4	27.3	.3	–278.4
2000	1,518.0	1,096.3	795.9	300.3	380.6	1,914.4	1,471.3	1,250.1	221.2	345.6	97.6	61.9	31.0	4.7	–396.4
2001	1,394.1	1,024.6	741.2	283.4	324.1	1,777.0	1,392.6	1,173.8	218.8	275.3	109.1	71.7	27.7	9.7	–383.0
2002	1,370.4	998.7	709.0	289.7	314.8	1,813.6	1,424.1	1,194.4	229.8	269.6	119.9	82.1	33.0	4.8	–443.2
2003	1,456.1	1,036.2	737.1	299.1	353.8	1,969.4	1,539.3	1,291.3	248.0	295.4	134.6	89.4	38.7	6.5	–513.2
2004	1,689.3	1,177.6	830.0	347.7	446.9	2,314.5	1,796.7	1,507.3	289.4	368.8	149.0	85.4	41.4	22.2	–625.2
2005	1,941.5	1,305.2	921.9	383.3	566.0	2,678.8	2,026.4	1,715.5	311.0	488.1	164.3	90.6	52.1	21.7	–737.3
2006	2,259.9	1,472.6	1,044.9	427.7	712.0	3,061.7	2,243.5	1,895.7	347.8	661.5	156.7	95.0	47.4	14.2	–801.9
2007	2,603.0	1,660.9	1,161.3	499.6	866.6	3,313.7	2,379.3	1,999.7	379.6	757.6	176.9	105.5	55.6	15.7	–710.8
2008	2,775.8	1,837.1	1,292.5	544.5	848.8	3,458.9	2,560.1	2,144.3	415.9	694.2	204.6	129.5	60.5	14.6	–683.2
2009	2,321.5	1,582.0	1,058.4	523.6	647.8	2,693.6	1,978.4	1,585.4	393.1	505.8	209.3	133.2	68.7	7.4	–372.1
2010	2,657.2	1,846.3	1,272.4	573.8	715.2	3,093.9	2,360.2	1,944.8	415.4	519.5	214.2	141.9	70.0	2.4	–436.7
2011	2,996.3	2,103.0	1,462.3	640.7	789.2	3,461.8	2,682.5	2,240.5	441.9	552.8	226.6	157.8	74.6	–5.9	–465.6
2012	3,104.3	2,191.3	1,521.6	669.7	799.7	3,552.4	2,759.9	2,301.4	458.5	567.4	225.2	151.8	73.2	.2	–448.1
2013	3,228.0	2,273.4	1,559.2	714.2	823.4	3,596.5	2,764.2	2,296.4	467.8	592.7	239.6	167.7	72.7	–.8	–368.5
2014	3,371.0	2,371.0	1,614.9	756.1	854.2	3,746.6	2,879.3	2,391.5	487.8	612.5	254.8	177.6	72.3	4.9	–375.6
2015	3,240.1	2,265.0	1,494.4	770.7	839.3	3,664.2	2,786.5	2,287.3	499.1	613.1	264.7	181.2	73.1	10.4	–424.1
2016	3,219.6	2,217.6	1,442.7	774.9	859.1	3,665.4	2,738.1	2,221.0	517.2	643.8	283.5	188.7	75.6	19.2	–445.8
2017	3,466.5	2,350.2	1,535.9	814.3	957.1	3,939.0	2,928.6	2,378.5	550.0	713.4	297.0	201.1	74.3	21.6	–472.5
2018 p		2,530.9	1,666.7	864.2			3,156.5	2,568.8	587.7		296.0	199.0	80.0	16.9	
2015: I	3,257.8	2,286.6	1,515.3	771.3	835.7	3,684.8	2,817.0	2,324.3	492.7	603.4	264.4	179.2	78.4	6.8	–427.0
II	3,300.0	2,303.2	1,531.6	771.6	854.8	3,694.3	2,802.2	2,306.6	495.6	635.5	256.6	180.4	67.9	8.3	–394.3
III	3,244.0	2,259.2	1,489.7	769.5	853.9	3,701.9	2,795.4	2,292.1	503.3	635.3	271.3	181.4	76.6	13.2	–457.9
IV	3,158.8	2,211.2	1,440.9	770.3	812.8	3,575.8	2,731.3	2,226.4	505.0	578.0	266.5	183.8	69.4	13.3	–417.0
2016: I	3,132.5	2,165.6	1,402.3	763.3	828.7	3,595.2	2,687.8	2,177.7	510.2	624.6	282.8	185.2	82.0	15.6	–462.7
II	3,209.0	2,206.6	1,434.1	772.5	860.7	3,623.2	2,702.7	2,191.7	511.0	648.2	272.3	187.1	70.1	15.1	–414.2
III	3,248.9	2,252.5	1,469.4	783.2	854.5	3,697.8	2,756.3	2,236.1	520.2	656.6	284.9	189.6	76.5	18.8	–448.9
IV	3,288.1	2,245.6	1,464.9	780.7	892.6	3,745.6	2,805.8	2,278.4	527.3	645.8	294.0	192.9	73.8	27.3	–457.5
2017: I	3,361.4	2,294.1	1,497.3	796.9	899.3	3,823.7	2,870.7	2,336.1	534.6	666.6	286.4	195.1	74.5	16.8	–462.3
II	3,388.6	2,316.3	1,510.8	805.4	924.9	3,896.2	2,888.2	2,344.6	543.6	708.7	299.3	198.7	71.7	28.9	–507.6
III	3,512.0	2,358.3	1,536.7	821.6	979.6	3,947.2	2,915.5	2,358.9	556.7	724.6	307.0	212.2	70.3	24.6	–435.2
IV	3,603.8	2,432.0	1,598.8	833.2	1,024.5	4,088.7	3,039.9	2,474.6	565.3	753.7	295.1	198.5	80.5	16.0	–484.9
2018: I	3,687.2	2,477.4	1,628.1	849.3	1,063.2	4,201.1	3,116.6	2,537.1	579.4	794.4	290.1	199.4	71.6	19.1	–513.9
II	3,806.5	2,568.7	1,706.4	862.4	1,078.6	4,230.3	3,118.5	2,536.5	582.0	811.6	300.2	200.6	86.3	13.3	–423.8
III	3,774.7	2,538.6	1,668.6	870.0	1,071.5	4,302.4	3,192.1	2,602.4	589.7	816.5	293.8	198.1	77.0	18.7	–527.6
IV p		2,538.9	1,663.7	875.2			3,198.7	2,599.0	599.8		299.8	198.1	85.1	16.6	

[1] Certain goods, primarily military equipment purchased and sold by the Federal Government, are included in services. Beginning with 1986, repairs and alterations of equipment were reclassified from goods to services.
[2] National income and product accounts (NIPA).

Source: Department of Commerce (Bureau of Economic Analysis).

TABLE B–15. Real exports and imports of goods and services, 2002–2018

[Billions of chained (2012) dollars; quarterly data at seasonally adjusted annual rates]

Year or quarter	Exports of goods and services						Imports of goods and services					
	Total	Goods [1]				Services [1]	Total	Goods [1]				Services [1]
		Total	Durable goods	Non-durable goods	Non-agricultural goods			Total	Durable goods	Non-durable goods	Non-petroleum goods	
2002	1,277.1	900.6	524.7	388.8	797.3	376.5	1,944.4	1,634.0	785.6	896.4	1,207.4	309.4
2003	1,305.0	927.1	542.4	396.4	821.8	377.8	2,040.1	1,729.0	831.2	948.7	1,276.4	310.5
2004	1,431.2	1,008.3	604.0	410.3	904.9	422.8	2,272.6	1,926.8	951.0	1,012.5	1,430.8	345.2
2005	1,533.2	1,085.4	663.4	423.3	975.8	447.6	2,421.0	2,062.3	1,036.9	1,053.0	1,543.4	358.6
2006	1,676.4	1,193.0	739.4	451.5	1,073.6	483.3	2,581.5	2,190.9	1,135.6	1,069.5	1,664.8	390.2
2007	1,822.3	1,276.1	796.6	475.7	1,148.3	546.0	2,646.0	2,236.0	1,168.3	1,078.9	1,714.6	409.2
2008	1,925.4	1,350.4	835.0	512.7	1,215.0	574.7	2,587.1	2,160.8	1,130.6	1,040.7	1,657.1	425.2
2009	1,763.8	1,190.3	694.5	499.9	1,060.0	572.9	2,248.6	1,830.1	902.3	948.3	1,375.9	415.9
2010	1,977.9	1,368.7	818.1	551.7	1,223.8	609.2	2,543.8	2,112.7	1,115.6	1,001.5	1,636.1	430.8
2011	2,119.0	1,465.3	893.7	571.6	1,321.6	653.8	2,687.1	2,242.5	1,227.0	1,016.2	1,769.8	444.6
2012	2,191.3	1,521.6	937.7	583.9	1,376.4	669.7	2,759.9	2,301.4	1,326.4	975.0	1,867.1	458.5
2013	2,269.6	1,570.0	960.1	609.9	1,422.9	699.5	2,802.4	2,341.9	1,385.9	956.1	1,932.5	460.6
2014	2,367.0	1,642.4	1,001.1	641.4	1,484.0	724.7	2,944.7	2,472.7	1,508.8	964.3	2,076.6	472.7
2015	2,380.6	1,637.2	979.6	659.5	1,475.8	742.2	3,105.5	2,615.2	1,610.3	1,004.4	2,209.0	491.8
2016	2,378.1	1,642.7	966.4	681.9	1,473.7	735.3	3,164.4	2,651.4	1,631.8	1,019.3	2,232.1	512.5
2017	2,450.1	1,697.3	988.5	716.8	1,525.1	753.4	3,308.7	2,773.5	1,747.5	1,018.9	2,344.6	534.9
2018 [p]	2,546.6	1,777.3	1,021.5	765.9	1,593.3	772.1	3,460.6	2,909.8	1,837.5	1,063.7	2,479.1	552.0
2015: I	2,377.7	1,632.2	983.5	649.7	1,471.0	744.0	3,072.1	2,590.3	1,592.7	998.0	2,185.9	483.7
II	2,400.0	1,658.3	989.2	671.6	1,490.7	741.5	3,096.7	2,612.9	1,603.5	1,009.9	2,208.2	486.0
III	2,379.0	1,639.1	979.3	661.8	1,479.0	739.1	3,128.0	2,633.0	1,623.5	1,008.6	2,224.2	496.4
IV	2,365.7	1,619.2	966.4	654.8	1,462.6	744.2	3,125.0	2,624.5	1,621.5	1,001.2	2,218.0	501.1
2016: I	2,351.1	1,619.9	958.2	665.9	1,465.8	730.4	3,129.0	2,622.0	1,607.9	1,015.2	2,209.4	506.5
II	2,370.9	1,634.2	963.6	675.6	1,477.0	736.0	3,135.0	2,629.3	1,608.9	1,022.1	2,213.4	505.6
III	2,406.4	1,664.9	969.3	703.7	1,474.3	741.7	3,172.6	2,656.4	1,640.6	1,014.2	2,232.9	515.3
IV	2,384.2	1,651.9	974.4	682.5	1,477.9	732.9	3,220.9	2,697.6	1,669.6	1,025.6	2,272.5	522.5
2017: I	2,413.3	1,669.0	969.6	707.9	1,497.7	744.5	3,258.8	2,729.9	1,700.8	1,024.8	2,294.2	528.3
II	2,435.0	1,686.2	975.9	719.6	1,510.4	749.3	3,279.1	2,745.8	1,727.4	1,011.9	2,317.6	532.4
III	2,456.1	1,694.8	995.5	705.6	1,519.2	760.8	3,302.0	2,762.6	1,749.5	1,004.7	2,340.0	538.1
IV	2,495.9	1,739.2	1,013.0	734.3	1,573.0	756.7	3,395.1	2,855.6	1,812.2	1,034.2	2,426.5	540.8
2018: I	2,517.8	1,753.0	1,031.1	728.4	1,581.5	766.9	3,420.1	2,872.7	1,818.1	1,045.8	2,449.8	548.1
II	2,574.2	1,809.2	1,029.6	791.4	1,607.9	769.8	3,415.2	2,870.0	1,799.9	1,062.4	2,437.7	546.1
III	2,542.2	1,769.8	1,008.8	772.3	1,577.8	774.5	3,491.9	2,942.2	1,863.2	1,070.1	2,501.3	551.9
IV [p]	2,552.0	1,777.0	1,016.3	771.6	1,606.0	777.2	3,515.2	2,954.2	1,868.9	1,076.5	2,527.4	561.9

[1] Certain goods, primarily military equipment purchased and sold by the Federal Government, are included in services. Repairs and alterations of equipment are also included in services.

Source: Department of Commerce (Bureau of Economic Analysis).

National Income or Expenditure | 653

TABLE B–16. Sources of personal income, 1968–2018

[Billions of dollars; quarterly data at seasonally adjusted annual rates]

Year or quarter	Personal income	Compensation of employees — Total	Wages and salaries — Total	Wages and salaries — Private industries	Wages and salaries — Government	Supplements to wages and salaries — Total	Employer contributions for employee pension and insurance funds	Employer contributions for government social insurance	Proprietors' income with inventory valuation and capital consumption adjustments — Total	Farm	Nonfarm	Rental income of persons with capital consumption adjustment
1968	730.9	530.8	472.0	375.3	96.7	58.8	38.8	20.0	73.8	11.7	62.2	20.1
1969	800.3	584.5	518.3	412.7	105.6	66.1	43.4	22.8	77.0	12.8	64.2	20.3
1970	865.0	623.3	551.6	434.3	117.2	71.8	47.9	23.8	77.8	12.9	64.9	20.7
1971	932.8	665.0	584.5	457.8	126.8	80.4	54.0	26.4	83.9	13.4	70.5	21.8
1972	1,024.5	731.3	638.8	500.9	137.9	92.5	61.4	31.2	95.1	17.0	78.1	22.7
1973	1,140.8	812.7	708.8	560.0	148.8	103.9	64.1	39.8	112.5	29.1	83.4	23.1
1974	1,251.8	887.7	772.3	611.8	160.5	115.4	70.7	44.7	112.2	23.5	88.7	23.2
1975	1,369.4	947.2	814.8	638.6	176.2	132.4	85.7	46.7	118.2	22.0	96.2	22.3
1976	1,502.6	1,048.3	899.7	710.8	188.9	148.6	94.2	54.4	131.0	17.2	113.8	20.3
1977	1,659.2	1,165.8	994.2	791.6	202.6	171.7	110.6	61.1	144.5	16.0	128.5	15.9
1978	1,863.7	1,316.8	1,120.6	900.6	220.0	196.2	124.7	71.5	166.0	19.9	146.1	16.5
1979	2,082.7	1,477.2	1,253.3	1,016.2	237.1	223.9	141.3	82.6	179.4	22.2	157.3	16.1
1980	2,323.6	1,622.2	1,373.4	1,112.0	261.5	248.8	159.9	88.9	171.6	11.7	159.9	19.0
1981	2,605.1	1,792.5	1,511.4	1,225.5	285.8	281.2	177.5	103.6	179.7	19.0	160.7	23.8
1982	2,791.6	1,893.0	1,587.5	1,280.0	307.5	305.5	195.7	109.8	171.2	13.3	157.9	23.8
1983	2,981.1	2,012.5	1,677.5	1,352.7	324.8	335.0	215.1	119.9	186.3	6.2	180.1	24.4
1984	3,292.7	2,215.9	1,844.9	1,496.8	348.1	371.0	231.9	139.0	228.2	20.9	207.3	24.7
1985	3,524.9	2,387.3	1,982.6	1,608.7	373.9	404.8	257.0	147.7	241.1	21.0	220.1	26.2
1986	3,733.1	2,542.1	2,102.3	1,705.1	397.2	439.7	281.9	157.9	256.5	22.8	233.7	18.3
1987	3,961.6	2,722.4	2,258.3	1,833.2	423.1	466.1	299.9	166.3	286.5	28.9	257.6	16.6
1988	4,283.4	2,948.0	2,439.8	1,987.7	452.0	508.2	323.6	184.6	325.5	26.8	298.7	22.5
1989	4,625.6	3,139.6	2,583.1	2,101.9	481.1	556.6	362.9	193.7	341.1	33.0	308.1	21.5
1990	4,913.8	3,340.4	2,741.2	2,222.2	519.0	599.2	392.7	206.5	353.2	32.2	321.0	28.2
1991	5,084.9	3,450.5	2,814.5	2,265.7	548.8	636.0	420.9	215.1	354.2	26.8	327.4	38.6
1992	5,420.9	3,668.2	2,965.5	2,393.5	572.0	702.7	474.3	228.4	400.2	34.8	365.4	60.6
1993	5,657.9	3,817.3	3,079.3	2,490.3	589.0	737.9	498.3	239.7	428.0	31.4	396.6	90.1
1994	5,947.1	4,006.2	3,236.6	2,627.1	609.5	769.6	515.5	254.1	456.6	34.7	422.0	113.7
1995	6,291.4	4,198.1	3,418.0	2,789.0	629.0	780.1	515.9	264.1	481.2	22.0	459.2	124.9
1996	6,678.5	4,416.9	3,616.5	2,968.4	648.1	800.5	525.7	274.8	543.8	37.3	506.4	142.5
1997	7,092.5	4,708.8	3,876.8	3,205.0	671.9	832.0	542.4	289.6	584.0	32.4	551.6	147.1
1998	7,606.7	5,071.1	4,181.6	3,480.3	701.3	889.5	582.3	307.2	640.2	28.5	611.7	165.2
1999	8,001.9	5,402.8	4,458.0	3,724.2	733.8	944.8	621.4	323.3	696.4	28.1	668.3	178.5
2000	8,652.6	5,848.1	4,825.9	4,046.1	779.8	1,022.2	677.0	345.2	753.9	31.5	722.4	183.5
2001	9,005.6	6,039.1	4,954.4	4,132.4	822.0	1,084.7	726.7	358.0	831.0	32.1	798.9	202.4
2002	9,159.0	6,135.6	4,996.3	4,123.4	872.9	1,139.3	773.2	366.0	869.8	19.9	849.8	211.1
2003	9,487.5	6,354.1	5,138.7	4,224.8	914.0	1,215.3	832.8	382.5	896.9	36.5	860.4	231.5
2004	10,035.1	6,720.1	5,421.6	4,469.2	952.3	1,298.5	889.7	408.8	962.0	51.5	910.5	248.9
2005	10,598.2	7,066.6	5,691.9	4,700.6	991.3	1,374.7	946.7	428.1	978.0	46.8	931.2	232.0
2006	11,381.7	7,479.9	6,057.0	5,022.4	1,034.5	1,422.9	975.6	447.3	1,049.6	33.1	1,016.6	202.3
2007	12,007.8	7,878.9	6,396.8	5,308.2	1,088.5	1,482.1	1,020.4	461.7	994.0	40.3	953.8	184.4
2008	12,442.2	8,057.0	6,534.2	5,390.4	1,143.9	1,522.7	1,051.3	471.4	960.9	40.2	920.7	256.7
2009	12,059.1	7,758.5	6,248.6	5,073.4	1,175.2	1,509.9	1,051.8	458.1	938.5	28.1	910.5	327.3
2010	12,551.6	7,924.9	6,372.1	5,180.9	1,191.2	1,552.9	1,083.9	469.0	1,108.7	39.0	1,069.7	394.2
2011	13,326.8	8,225.9	6,625.9	5,431.1	1,194.9	1,600.0	1,107.3	492.7	1,229.3	64.9	1,164.4	478.6
2012	14,010.1	8,566.7	6,927.5	5,729.2	1,198.3	1,639.2	1,125.9	513.3	1,347.3	60.9	1,286.4	518.0
2013	14,181.1	8,834.2	7,113.2	5,905.2	1,208.0	1,721.0	1,194.7	526.3	1,403.6	88.3	1,315.3	557.0
2014	14,991.8	9,248.1	7,473.2	6,236.3	1,236.9	1,774.8	1,228.1	546.7	1,447.6	70.1	1,377.5	608.4
2015	15,719.5	9,696.8	7,854.4	6,578.7	1,275.8	1,842.4	1,272.8	569.7	1,421.9	56.4	1,365.5	651.8
2016	16,125.1	9,956.2	8,080.7	6,773.0	1,307.7	1,875.6	1,294.2	581.4	1,419.3	37.5	1,381.8	694.8
2017 ᴾ	16,830.9	10,407.2	8,453.8	7,108.1	1,345.7	1,953.4	1,348.1	605.3	1,500.9	38.9	1,462.0	730.2
2018 ᴾ	17,581.4	10,855.7	8,834.7	7,456.2	1,378.6	2,021.0	1,389.8	631.2	1,579.8	37.5	1,542.2	760.0
2015: I	15,471.3	9,554.1	7,734.5	6,471.0	1,263.4	1,819.6	1,258.7	560.9	1,431.0	54.5	1,376.5	631.1
II	15,681.7	9,665.8	7,827.1	6,554.0	1,273.1	1,838.7	1,270.9	567.8	1,410.4	55.8	1,354.6	647.2
III	15,842.9	9,752.5	7,900.7	6,620.4	1,280.3	1,851.8	1,278.9	572.9	1,429.5	60.2	1,369.3	659.2
IV	15,882.1	9,814.9	7,955.4	6,669.2	1,286.2	1,859.6	1,282.5	577.0	1,416.5	55.0	1,361.4	669.7
2016: I	15,946.5	9,839.5	7,981.5	6,688.1	1,293.4	1,858.0	1,283.3	574.7	1,415.2	40.9	1,374.4	685.2
II	16,031.6	9,890.2	8,025.0	6,723.5	1,301.6	1,865.2	1,287.5	577.7	1,404.6	41.2	1,363.4	694.0
III	16,170.6	9,986.1	8,106.7	6,792.8	1,313.9	1,879.4	1,296.4	583.1	1,418.8	36.7	1,382.0	696.3
IV	16,351.8	10,109.3	8,209.6	6,887.6	1,321.9	1,899.7	1,309.8	589.9	1,438.6	31.0	1,407.6	703.8
2017: I	16,604.4	10,249.2	8,325.0	6,991.3	1,333.7	1,924.2	1,327.4	596.8	1,475.1	42.3	1,432.9	719.0
II	16,721.2	10,339.9	8,395.7	7,054.3	1,341.4	1,944.2	1,342.7	601.5	1,495.0	41.5	1,453.5	724.4
III	16,895.1	10,471.2	8,506.6	7,156.3	1,350.2	1,964.6	1,355.7	608.8	1,507.5	36.4	1,471.1	732.0
IV	17,103.1	10,568.6	8,588.1	7,230.4	1,357.7	1,980.5	1,366.4	614.0	1,526.1	35.4	1,490.6	745.3
2018: I	17,319.2	10,710.1	8,710.6	7,347.5	1,363.1	1,999.4	1,376.3	623.2	1,549.9	35.2	1,514.7	749.3
II	17,466.7	10,782.9	8,770.8	7,399.6	1,371.2	2,012.0	1,385.0	627.1	1,568.5	37.0	1,531.5	754.2
III	17,657.3	10,907.9	8,879.2	7,493.6	1,385.6	2,028.7	1,394.6	634.1	1,580.0	27.9	1,552.0	767.4
IV ᴾ	17,882.4	11,022.1	8,978.3	7,584.0	1,394.3	2,043.8	1,403.3	640.5	1,620.7	50.0	1,570.7	769.0

See next page for continuation of table.

[Billions of dollars; quarterly data at seasonally adjusted annual rates]

Year or quarter	Personal income receipts on assets			Personal current transfer receipts								Less: Contributions for government social insurance, domestic
					Government social benefits to persons						Other current transfer receipts, from business (net)	
	Total	Personal interest income	Personal dividend income	Total	Total [1]	Social security [2]	Medicare [3]	Medicaid	Unemployment insurance	Other		
1968	88.8	65.3	23.5	56.1	53.3	24.6	5.9	4.0	2.2	10.8	2.8	38.7
1969	100.3	76.1	24.2	62.3	59.0	26.4	6.7	4.6	2.3	12.4	3.3	44.1
1970	114.9	90.6	24.3	74.7	71.7	31.4	7.3	5.5	4.2	16.0	2.9	46.4
1971	125.1	100.1	25.0	88.1	85.4	36.6	8.0	6.7	6.2	19.4	2.7	51.2
1972	136.6	109.8	26.8	97.9	94.8	40.9	8.8	8.2	6.0	21.4	3.1	59.2
1973	155.4	125.5	29.9	112.6	108.6	50.7	10.2	9.6	4.6	23.3	3.9	75.5
1974	180.6	147.4	33.2	133.3	128.6	57.6	12.7	11.2	7.0	28.4	4.7	85.2
1975	201.0	168.0	32.9	170.0	163.1	65.9	15.6	13.9	18.1	35.7	6.8	89.3
1976	220.0	181.0	39.0	184.3	177.6	74.5	18.8	15.5	16.4	38.7	6.7	101.3
1977	251.6	206.9	44.7	194.6	189.5	83.2	22.1	16.7	13.1	40.9	5.1	113.1
1978	285.8	235.1	50.7	209.9	203.4	91.4	25.5	18.6	9.4	44.9	6.5	131.3
1979	327.1	269.7	57.4	235.6	227.3	102.6	29.9	21.1	9.7	49.9	8.2	152.7
1980	396.9	332.9	64.0	280.1	271.5	118.6	36.2	23.9	16.1	62.1	8.6	166.2
1981	485.8	412.2	73.6	319.0	307.8	138.6	43.5	27.7	15.9	66.3	11.2	195.7
1982	557.0	479.5	77.6	355.5	343.1	153.7	50.9	30.2	25.2	66.8	12.4	208.9
1983	599.5	516.3	83.3	384.3	370.5	164.4	57.8	33.9	26.4	71.5	13.8	226.0
1984	680.8	590.1	90.6	400.6	380.9	173.0	64.7	36.6	16.0	74.3	19.7	257.5
1985	726.3	628.9	97.4	425.4	403.1	183.3	69.7	39.7	15.9	78.0	22.3	281.4
1986	768.2	662.1	106.0	451.6	428.6	193.6	75.3	43.6	16.5	83.0	22.9	303.4
1987	791.1	679.0	112.2	468.1	447.9	201.0	81.6	47.8	14.6	86.4	20.2	323.1
1988	851.4	721.7	129.7	497.5	476.9	213.9	86.3	53.0	13.3	93.6	20.6	361.5
1989	964.3	806.5	157.8	544.2	521.1	227.4	98.2	60.8	14.4	103.1	23.2	385.2
1990	1,005.3	836.5	168.8	596.9	574.7	244.1	107.6	73.1	18.2	113.9	22.2	410.1
1991	1,003.7	823.5	180.2	668.1	650.5	264.2	117.5	96.9	26.8	127.0	17.6	430.2
1992	998.8	809.8	189.1	748.0	731.8	281.8	132.6	116.2	39.6	142.9	16.3	455.0
1993	1,007.0	802.3	204.7	793.0	778.9	297.9	146.8	130.1	34.8	150.0	14.1	477.4
1994	1,049.8	814.6	235.2	829.0	815.7	312.2	164.4	139.4	23.9	156.1	13.3	508.2
1995	1,136.6	878.6	258.0	883.5	864.7	327.7	181.2	149.6	21.7	164.0	18.7	532.8
1996	1,201.2	899.0	302.2	929.2	906.3	342.0	194.9	158.2	22.3	167.6	22.9	555.1
1997	1,285.0	947.1	337.9	954.9	935.4	356.6	206.9	163.1	20.1	166.4	19.4	587.2
1998	1,370.9	1,015.5	355.4	983.9	957.9	369.2	205.6	170.2	19.7	170.0	26.0	624.7
1999	1,359.3	1,012.7	346.6	1,026.2	992.2	379.9	208.7	184.6	20.5	174.4	34.0	661.3
2000	1,485.7	1,102.2	383.5	1,087.3	1,044.9	401.4	219.1	199.5	20.7	179.1	42.4	705.8
2001	1,473.7	1,104.3	369.3	1,192.6	1,145.8	425.1	242.6	227.3	31.9	192.4	46.8	733.2
2002	1,408.9	1,010.1	398.8	1,285.2	1,251.0	446.9	259.7	250.0	53.5	211.3	34.2	751.5
2003	1,437.2	1,005.0	432.1	1,347.3	1,321.0	463.5	276.7	264.5	53.2	231.2	26.3	779.3
2004	1,512.1	950.4	561.7	1,421.2	1,404.5	485.5	304.4	289.8	36.4	254.3	16.8	829.2
2005	1,678.2	1,100.4	577.8	1,516.7	1,490.9	512.7	332.1	304.4	31.8	273.5	25.8	873.3
2006	1,958.6	1,235.8	722.8	1,613.8	1,593.0	544.1	399.1	299.1	30.4	281.5	20.8	922.5
2007	2,183.8	1,368.6	815.3	1,728.1	1,697.3	575.7	428.2	324.2	32.7	294.9	30.8	961.4
2008	2,200.9	1,396.3	804.6	1,955.1	1,919.3	605.5	461.6	338.3	51.1	417.7	35.8	988.4
2009	1,852.2	1,299.3	553.0	2,146.7	2,107.7	664.5	493.0	369.6	131.2	398.0	39.0	964.3
2010	1,782.3	1,238.5	543.9	2,325.2	2,281.4	690.2	513.4	396.9	138.9	484.2	43.7	983.7
2011	1,950.9	1,269.4	681.5	2,358.7	2,310.1	713.3	535.6	406.0	107.2	484.8	48.5	916.7
2012	2,165.6	1,330.5	835.1	2,363.0	2,322.6	762.1	554.7	417.5	83.6	434.4	40.4	950.5
2013	2,066.3	1,273.0	793.3	2,424.3	2,385.9	799.0	572.8	440.0	62.5	432.5	38.4	1,104.3
2014	2,301.2	1,347.8	953.4	2,540.3	2,497.2	834.6	598.6	490.9	35.5	453.9	43.1	1,153.8
2015	2,471.3	1,438.1	1,033.3	2,683.0	2,632.5	871.8	634.0	536.0	32.2	468.8	50.6	1,205.3
2016	2,516.6	1,440.9	1,075.7	2,778.1	2,717.4	896.5	662.2	562.7	31.7	471.6	60.7	1,239.9
2017	2,631.6	1,523.0	1,108.6	2,859.7	2,804.0	926.1	695.3	577.4	29.1	477.6	55.7	1,298.6
2018 *p*	2,766.1	1,614.4	1,151.7	2,980.9	2,920.2	974.9	734.5	601.4	25.5	474.7	60.7	1,361.1
2015: I	2,399.8	1,354.6	1,045.3	2,643.1	2,596.4	861.8	621.5	523.7	32.8	468.4	46.7	1,187.8
II	2,479.1	1,457.2	1,021.9	2,680.6	2,631.7	869.5	630.6	538.0	31.9	472.6	48.9	1,201.4
III	2,517.1	1,492.3	1,024.7	2,696.5	2,644.8	874.3	638.5	540.5	32.1	469.1	51.6	1,211.8
IV	2,489.3	1,448.1	1,041.2	2,712.0	2,656.9	881.6	645.3	541.7	31.9	464.9	55.1	1,220.2
2016: I	2,485.9	1,430.9	1,055.1	2,746.6	2,687.4	886.4	651.3	550.2	32.4	475.3	59.2	1,225.9
II	2,505.5	1,434.9	1,070.6	2,769.8	2,708.3	894.0	657.9	558.6	32.0	473.4	61.4	1,232.4
III	2,524.5	1,439.8	1,084.6	2,788.5	2,726.8	899.5	665.5	566.5	31.6	470.6	61.8	1,243.6
IV	2,550.4	1,458.1	1,092.3	2,807.3	2,747.1	906.0	673.9	575.8	30.7	467.0	60.3	1,257.6
2017: I	2,607.4	1,523.9	1,083.5	2,834.2	2,777.4	916.2	683.1	573.6	30.4	479.1	56.9	1,280.5
II	2,610.9	1,490.9	1,120.0	2,841.6	2,786.6	922.8	691.7	569.3	29.0	476.4	55.0	1,290.6
III	2,615.1	1,500.1	1,115.1	2,875.3	2,820.5	929.8	699.6	583.6	28.8	478.9	54.8	1,306.0
IV	2,692.9	1,577.2	1,115.7	2,887.6	2,831.5	935.5	706.6	583.2	28.0	476.1	56.1	1,317.3
2018: I	2,719.5	1,597.6	1,121.9	2,933.9	2,875.7	960.8	713.7	590.3	27.6	477.8	58.2	1,343.6
II	2,747.8	1,606.5	1,141.2	2,965.8	2,905.4	969.1	724.5	602.6	25.5	475.8	60.4	1,352.4
III	2,772.2	1,616.2	1,156.0	2,997.2	2,935.6	977.8	739.9	607.8	24.7	474.5	61.6	1,367.4
IV *p*	2,825.0	1,637.2	1,187.8	3,026.7	2,964.1	991.8	759.8	604.7	24.1	470.5	62.6	1,381.1

[1] Includes Veterans' benefits, not shown seperately.
[2] Includes old-age, survivors, and disability insurance benefits that are distributed from the federal old-age and survivors insurance trust fund and the disability insurance trust fund.
[3] Includes hospital and supplementary medical insurance benefits that are distributed from the federal hospital insurance trust fund and the supplementary medical insurance trust fund.

Source: Department of Commerce (Bureau of Economic Analysis).

National Income or Expenditure | 655

TABLE B-17. Disposition of personal income, 1968–2018

[Billions of dollars, except as noted; quarterly data at seasonally adjusted annual rates]

| Year or quarter | Personal income | Less: Personal current taxes | Equals: Disposable personal income | Less: Personal outlays | | | | Equals: Personal saving | Percent of disposable personal income [2] | | |
| | | | | Total | Personal consumption expenditures | Personal interest payments [1] | Personal current transfer payments | | Personal outlays | | Personal saving |
									Total	Personal consumption expenditures	
1968	730.9	87.0	643.9	571.0	556.9	12.1	2.0	72.9	88.7	86.5	11.3
1969	800.3	104.5	695.8	619.8	603.6	13.9	2.2	76.1	89.1	86.7	10.9
1970	865.0	103.1	762.0	664.4	646.7	15.1	2.6	97.6	87.2	84.9	12.8
1971	932.8	101.7	831.1	719.2	699.9	16.4	2.8	111.9	86.5	84.2	13.5
1972	1,024.5	123.6	900.8	789.3	768.2	18.0	3.2	111.5	87.6	85.3	12.4
1973	1,140.8	132.4	1,008.4	872.6	849.6	19.6	3.4	135.8	86.5	84.3	13.5
1974	1,251.8	151.0	1,100.8	954.5	930.2	20.9	3.4	146.3	86.7	84.5	13.3
1975	1,369.4	147.6	1,221.8	1,057.8	1,030.5	23.4	3.8	164.0	86.6	84.3	13.4
1976	1,502.6	172.7	1,330.0	1,175.6	1,147.7	23.5	4.4	154.4	88.4	86.3	11.6
1977	1,659.2	197.9	1,461.4	1,305.4	1,274.0	26.6	4.8	155.9	89.3	87.2	10.7
1978	1,863.7	229.6	1,634.1	1,459.0	1,422.3	31.3	5.4	175.1	89.3	87.0	10.7
1979	2,082.7	268.9	1,813.8	1,627.0	1,585.4	35.5	6.0	186.8	89.7	87.4	10.3
1980	2,323.6	299.5	2,024.1	1,800.1	1,750.7	42.5	6.9	224.1	88.9	86.5	11.1
1981	2,605.1	345.8	2,259.3	1,993.9	1,934.0	48.4	11.5	265.5	88.3	85.6	11.8
1982	2,791.6	354.7	2,436.9	2,143.5	2,071.3	58.5	13.8	293.3	88.0	85.0	12.0
1983	2,981.1	352.9	2,628.2	2,364.2	2,281.6	67.4	15.1	264.0	90.0	86.8	10.0
1984	3,292.7	377.9	2,914.8	2,584.5	2,492.3	75.0	17.1	330.3	88.7	85.5	11.3
1985	3,524.9	417.8	3,107.1	2,822.1	2,712.8	90.6	18.8	284.9	90.8	87.3	9.2
1986	3,733.1	437.8	3,295.3	3,004.7	2,886.3	97.3	21.1	290.6	91.2	87.6	8.8
1987	3,961.6	489.6	3,472.0	3,196.6	3,076.3	97.1	23.2	275.4	92.1	88.6	7.9
1988	4,283.4	505.9	3,777.5	3,457.0	3,330.0	101.3	25.6	320.5	91.5	88.2	8.5
1989	4,625.6	567.7	4,057.8	3,717.9	3,576.8	113.1	28.0	340.0	91.6	88.1	8.4
1990	4,913.8	594.7	4,319.1	3,958.0	3,809.0	118.4	30.6	361.1	91.6	88.2	8.4
1991	5,084.9	588.9	4,496.0	4,100.0	3,943.4	119.9	36.7	396.0	91.2	87.7	8.8
1992	5,420.9	612.8	4,808.1	4,354.2	4,197.6	116.1	40.5	453.9	90.6	87.3	9.4
1993	5,657.9	648.8	5,009.2	4,611.5	4,452.0	113.9	45.6	397.7	92.1	88.9	7.9
1994	5,947.1	693.1	5,254.0	4,890.6	4,721.0	119.9	49.8	363.4	93.1	89.9	6.9
1995	6,291.4	748.4	5,543.0	5,155.9	4,962.6	140.4	52.9	387.1	93.0	89.5	7.0
1996	6,678.5	837.1	5,841.4	5,459.2	5,244.6	157.0	57.6	382.3	93.5	89.8	6.5
1997	7,092.5	931.8	6,160.7	5,770.4	5,536.8	169.7	63.9	390.3	93.7	89.9	6.3
1998	7,606.7	1,032.4	6,574.2	6,127.7	5,877.2	180.9	69.5	446.5	93.2	89.4	6.8
1999	8,001.9	1,111.9	6,890.0	6,540.6	6,279.1	187.5	74.1	349.4	94.9	91.1	5.1
2000	8,652.6	1,236.3	7,416.3	7,058.0	6,762.1	214.8	81.0	358.3	95.2	91.2	4.8
2001	9,005.6	1,239.0	7,766.6	7,374.9	7,065.6	220.0	89.3	391.6	95.0	91.0	5.0
2002	9,159.0	1,052.2	8,106.8	7,633.1	7,342.7	195.7	94.7	473.7	94.2	90.6	5.8
2003	9,487.5	1,003.5	8,484.0	8,012.5	7,723.1	190.9	98.5	471.5	94.4	91.0	5.6
2004	10,035.1	1,048.7	8,986.4	8,522.6	8,212.7	202.2	107.7	463.8	94.8	91.4	5.2
2005	10,598.2	1,212.4	9,385.8	9,089.1	8,747.1	230.5	111.5	296.7	96.8	93.2	3.2
2006	11,381.7	1,356.8	10,024.9	9,639.3	9,260.3	258.4	120.5	385.6	96.2	92.4	3.8
2007	12,007.8	1,492.2	10,515.6	10,123.9	9,706.4	284.6	132.9	391.6	96.3	92.3	3.7
2008	12,442.2	1,507.2	10,935.0	10,390.1	9,976.3	268.8	144.9	544.9	95.0	91.2	5.0
2009	12,059.1	1,152.0	10,907.1	10,240.6	9,842.2	254.0	144.3	666.5	93.9	90.2	6.1
2010	12,551.6	1,237.3	11,314.3	10,573.5	10,185.8	242.8	144.8	740.9	93.5	90.0	6.5
2011	13,326.8	1,453.2	11,873.6	11,023.7	10,641.1	232.1	150.6	849.8	92.8	89.6	7.2
2012	14,010.1	1,508.9	12,501.2	11,393.6	11,006.8	232.4	154.4	1,107.6	91.1	88.0	8.9
2013	14,181.1	1,675.8	12,505.3	11,703.9	11,317.2	229.5	157.2	801.4	93.6	90.5	6.4
2014	14,991.8	1,785.4	13,206.4	12,236.1	11,824.0	241.6	170.4	970.3	92.7	89.5	7.3
2015	15,719.5	1,935.2	13,784.3	12,740.1	12,294.5	260.9	184.7	1,044.2	92.4	89.2	7.6
2016	16,125.1	1,954.3	14,170.9	13,222.7	12,766.9	269.2	186.5	948.2	93.3	90.1	6.7
2017	16,830.9	2,034.6	14,796.3	13,809.5	13,321.4	293.9	194.2	986.8	93.3	90.0	6.7
2018 p	17,581.4	2,050.4	15,531.0	14,487.6	13,951.6	334.0	202.1	1,043.4	93.3	89.8	6.7
2015: I	15,471.3	1,900.1	13,571.2	12,529.3	12,095.6	252.7	181.1	1,041.9	92.3	89.1	7.7
II	15,681.7	1,940.0	13,741.7	12,700.1	12,256.7	259.1	184.3	1,041.6	92.4	89.2	7.6
III	15,842.9	1,943.7	13,899.3	12,830.8	12,380.7	263.8	186.2	1,068.5	92.3	89.1	7.7
IV	15,882.1	1,957.1	13,925.0	12,900.3	12,445.1	268.0	187.2	1,024.7	92.6	89.4	7.4
2016: I	15,946.5	1,919.9	14,026.7	12,979.1	12,526.5	263.4	189.1	1,047.6	92.5	89.3	7.5
II	16,031.6	1,944.2	14,087.4	13,155.8	12,706.5	267.1	182.1	931.6	93.4	90.2	6.6
III	16,170.6	1,968.7	14,202.0	13,302.2	12,845.2	270.7	186.4	899.7	93.7	90.4	6.3
IV	16,351.8	1,984.3	14,367.5	13,453.6	12,989.4	275.7	188.5	913.9	93.6	90.4	6.4
2017: I	16,604.4	2,004.9	14,599.6	13,584.7	13,114.1	280.6	190.0	1,014.9	93.0	89.8	7.0
II	16,721.2	2,014.2	14,707.0	13,716.7	13,233.2	288.7	194.9	990.2	93.3	90.0	6.7
III	16,895.1	2,048.5	14,846.6	13,853.3	13,359.1	300.0	194.1	993.4	93.3	90.0	6.7
IV	17,103.1	2,070.9	15,032.2	14,083.3	13,579.2	306.1	197.9	948.9	93.7	90.3	6.3
2018: I	17,319.2	2,030.0	15,289.2	14,194.8	13,679.6	314.9	200.3	1,094.3	92.8	89.5	7.2
II	17,466.7	2,035.3	15,431.4	14,403.8	13,875.6	326.4	201.7	1,027.7	93.3	89.9	6.7
III	17,657.3	2,064.9	15,592.4	14,596.3	14,050.5	340.2	205.6	996.0	93.6	90.1	6.4
IV p	17,882.4	2,071.3	15,811.1	14,755.6	14,200.6	354.4	200.6	1,055.5	93.3	89.8	6.7

[1] Consists of nonmortgage interest paid by households.
[2] Percents based on data in millions of dollars.

Source: Department of Commerce (Bureau of Economic Analysis).

[Quarterly data at seasonally adjusted annual rates, except as noted]

Year or quarter	Disposable personal income				Personal consumption expenditures				Gross domestic product per capita (dollars)		Population (thousands)[1]
	Total (billions of dollars)		Per capita (dollars)		Total (billions of dollars)		Per capita (dollars)				
	Current dollars	Chained (2012) dollars	Current dollars	Chained (2012) dollars	Current dollars	Chained (2012) dollars	Current dollars	Chained (2012) dollars	Current dollars	Chained (2012) dollars	
1968	643.9	3,362.1	3,208	16,748	556.9	2,907.5	2,774	14,483	4,686	23,873	200,745
1969	695.8	3,476.5	3,432	17,148	603.6	3,015.9	2,977	14,876	5,019	24,377	202,736
1970	762.0	3,637.0	3,715	17,734	646.7	3,086.9	3,153	15,051	5,233	24,142	205,089
1971	831.1	3,805.2	4,002	18,321	699.9	3,204.8	3,370	15,430	5,609	24,625	207,692
1972	900.8	3,988.4	4,291	18,999	768.2	3,401.0	3,659	16,201	6,093	25,644	209,924
1973	1,008.4	4,236.5	4,758	19,989	849.6	3,569.4	4,009	16,841	6,725	26,834	211,939
1974	1,100.8	4,188.7	5,146	19,583	930.2	3,539.5	4,349	16,547	7,224	26,445	213,898
1975	1,221.8	4,291.4	5,657	19,869	1,030.5	3,619.7	4,771	16,759	7,801	26,136	215,981
1976	1,330.0	4,428.5	6,098	20,306	1,147.7	3,821.5	5,262	17,523	8,590	27,278	218,086
1977	1,461.4	4,568.8	6,634	20,740	1,274.0	3,983.0	5,783	18,081	9,450	28,254	220,289
1978	1,634.1	4,776.4	7,340	21,455	1,422.3	4,157.3	6,388	18,674	10,563	29,505	222,629
1979	1,813.8	4,869.1	8,057	21,630	1,585.4	4,256.1	7,043	18,907	11,672	30,104	225,106
1980	2,024.1	4,905.6	8,888	21,542	1,750.7	4,242.8	7,688	18,631	12,547	29,681	227,726
1981	2,259.3	5,025.4	9,823	21,849	1,934.0	4,301.6	8,408	18,702	13,943	30,132	230,008
1982	2,436.9	5,135.0	10,494	22,113	2,071.3	4,364.6	8,919	18,795	14,399	29,308	232,218
1983	2,628.2	5,312.2	11,216	22,669	2,281.6	4,611.7	9,737	19,680	15,508	30,374	234,333
1984	2,914.8	5,677.1	12,330	24,016	2,492.3	4,854.3	10,543	20,535	17,080	32,289	236,394
1985	3,107.1	5,847.6	13,027	24,518	2,712.8	5,105.6	11,374	21,407	18,192	33,337	238,506
1986	3,295.3	6,069.8	13,691	25,219	2,886.3	5,316.4	11,992	22,089	19,028	34,179	240,683
1987	3,472.0	6,204.1	14,297	25,548	3,076.3	5,496.9	12,668	22,636	19,993	35,047	242,843
1988	3,777.5	6,496.0	15,414	26,508	3,330.0	5,726.5	13,589	23,368	21,368	36,181	245,061
1989	4,057.8	6,686.2	16,403	27,027	3,576.8	5,893.5	14,458	23,823	22,805	37,157	247,387
1990	4,319.1	6,817.4	17,264	27,250	3,809.0	6,012.2	15,225	24,031	23,835	37,435	250,181
1991	4,496.0	6,867.0	17,734	27,086	3,943.4	6,023.0	15,554	23,757	24,290	36,900	253,530
1992	4,808.1	7,152.9	18,714	27,841	4,197.6	6,244.7	16,338	24,306	25,379	37,696	256,922
1993	5,009.2	7,271.1	19,245	27,935	4,452.0	6,462.2	17,104	24,828	26,350	38,234	260,282
1994	5,254.0	7,470.6	19,943	28,356	4,721.0	6,712.6	17,919	25,479	27,660	39,295	263,455
1995	5,543.0	7,718.9	20,792	28,954	4,962.6	6,910.7	18,615	25,923	28,658	39,875	266,588
1996	5,841.4	7,964.2	21,658	29,528	5,244.6	7,150.5	19,445	26,511	29,932	40,900	269,714
1997	6,160.7	8,255.8	22,570	30,246	5,536.8	7,419.7	20,284	27,183	31,424	42,211	272,958
1998	6,574.2	8,740.4	23,806	31,651	5,877.2	7,813.8	21,283	28,295	32,818	43,593	276,154
1999	6,890.0	9,025.6	24,666	32,312	6,279.1	8,225.4	22,479	29,447	34,478	45,146	279,328
2000	7,416.3	9,479.5	26,262	33,568	6,762.1	8,643.4	23,945	30,607	36,305	46,498	282,398
2001	7,766.6	9,740.1	27,230	34,149	7,065.6	8,861.1	24,772	31,067	37,100	46,497	285,225
2002	8,106.8	10,034.5	28,153	34,848	7,342.7	9,088.7	25,499	31,563	37,980	46,858	287,955
2003	8,484.0	10,301.4	29,192	35,446	7,723.1	9,377.5	26,574	32,267	39,426	47,756	290,626
2004	8,986.4	10,645.9	30,643	36,302	8,212.7	9,729.3	28,004	33,176	41,648	49,125	293,262
2005	9,385.8	10,811.6	31,710	36,527	8,747.1	10,075.9	29,552	34,041	44,044	50,381	295,993
2006	10,024.9	11,241.9	33,549	37,621	9,260.3	10,384.5	30,990	34,752	46,231	51,330	298,818
2007	10,515.6	11,500.3	34,855	38,119	9,706.4	10,615.3	32,173	35,186	47,902	51,794	301,696
2008	10,935.0	11,610.8	35,906	38,125	9,976.3	10,592.8	32,758	34,783	48,311	51,240	304,543
2009	10,907.1	11,591.7	35,500	37,728	9,842.2	10,460.0	32,034	34,045	47,028	49,501	307,240
2010	11,314.3	11,822.1	36,524	38,163	10,185.8	10,643.0	32,881	34,357	48,396	50,354	309,780
2011	11,873.6	12,099.8	38,052	38,777	10,641.1	10,843.8	34,102	34,752	49,811	50,766	312,033
2012	12,501.2	12,501.2	39,780	39,780	11,006.8	11,006.8	35,025	35,025	51,541	51,541	314,255
2013	12,505.3	12,339.1	39,521	38,996	11,317.2	11,166.9	35,766	35,291	53,046	52,131	316,421
2014	13,206.4	12,838.1	41,436	40,281	11,824.0	11,494.3	37,099	36,064	54,976	53,025	318,717
2015	13,784.3	13,366.5	42,938	41,637	12,294.5	11,921.9	38,298	37,137	56,753	54,160	321,026
2016	14,170.9	13,595.2	43,830	42,049	12,766.9	12,248.2	39,487	37,883	57,860	54,619	323,317
2017	14,796.3	13,949.2	45,470	42,866	13,321.4	12,558.7	40,937	38,593	59,880	55,471	325,410
2018 [p]	15,531.0	14,349.9	47,432	43,825	13,951.6	12,890.6	42,609	39,368	62,610	56,717	327,436
2015: I	13,571.2	13,226.6	42,389	41,313	12,095.6	11,788.4	37,780	36,821	56,130	53,895	320,157
II	13,741.7	13,327.8	42,852	41,561	12,256.7	11,887.5	38,221	37,069	56,820	54,250	320,683
III	13,899.3	13,440.4	43,257	41,829	12,380.7	11,972.0	38,531	37,259	57,050	54,273	321,315
IV	13,925.0	13,471.4	43,253	41,843	12,445.1	12,039.7	38,656	37,346	57,010	54,221	321,947
2016: I	14,026.7	13,562.3	43,497	42,057	12,526.5	12,111.8	38,845	37,559	57,087	54,340	322,476
II	14,087.4	13,541.5	43,614	41,924	12,706.5	12,214.1	39,339	37,815	57,712	54,559	322,998
III	14,202.0	13,592.9	43,887	42,005	12,845.2	12,294.3	39,694	37,992	58,094	54,717	323,606
IV	14,367.5	13,685.4	44,318	42,214	12,989.4	12,372.7	40,068	38,165	58,544	54,858	324,187
2017: I	14,599.6	13,835.3	44,970	42,616	13,114.1	12,427.6	40,395	38,280	59,026	55,023	324,648
II	14,707.0	13,909.8	45,237	42,785	13,233.2	12,515.9	40,704	38,498	59,547	55,352	325,107
III	14,846.6	13,986.2	45,588	42,946	13,359.1	12,584.9	41,021	38,643	60,148	55,642	325,667
IV	15,032.2	14,065.9	46,080	43,118	13,579.2	12,706.4	41,626	38,951	60,793	55,864	326,218
2018: I	15,289.2	14,219.8	46,803	43,530	13,679.6	12,722.8	41,876	38,947	61,350	56,093	326,670
II	15,431.4	14,282.0	47,171	43,657	13,875.6	12,842.0	42,415	39,256	62,395	56,586	327,138
III	15,592.4	14,374.8	47,582	43,866	14,050.5	12,953.3	42,876	39,528	63,040	56,958	327,697
IV [p]	15,811.1	14,523.6	48,170	44,247	14,200.6	13,044.2	43,263	39,740	63,647	57,229	328,237

[1] Population of the United States including Armed Forces overseas. Annual data are averages of quarterly data. Quarterly data are averages for the period.

Source: Department of Commerce (Bureau of Economic Analysis and Bureau of the Census).

National Income or Expenditure | 657

Table B-19. Gross saving and investment, 1968–2018

[Billions of dollars, except as noted; quarterly data at seasonally adjusted annual rates]

Year or quarter	Gross saving										
	Total gross saving	Net saving							Consumption of fixed capital		
		Total net saving	Net private saving			Net government saving			Total	Private	Government
			Total	Personal saving	Undistributed corporate profits[1]	Total	Federal	State and local			
1968	214.6	101.2	111.5	72.9	38.6	−10.3	−13.8	3.5	113.4	80.6	32.8
1969	233.1	108.2	110.3	76.1	34.2	−2.0	−5.1	3.1	124.9	89.4	35.5
1970	228.2	91.4	124.8	97.6	27.2	−33.4	−34.8	1.4	136.8	98.3	38.6
1971	246.1	97.2	149.4	111.9	37.5	−52.2	−50.9	−1.3	148.9	107.6	41.3
1972	277.6	116.6	159.6	111.5	48.0	−42.9	−49.0	6.1	161.0	117.5	43.5
1973	335.3	156.6	189.3	135.8	53.5	−32.7	−38.3	5.6	178.7	131.5	47.2
1974	349.2	142.3	186.0	146.3	39.7	−43.7	−41.3	−2.3	206.9	153.2	53.7
1975	348.1	109.6	218.3	164.0	54.3	−108.7	−97.9	−10.7	238.5	178.8	59.7
1976	399.3	139.1	224.4	154.4	70.0	−85.3	−80.9	−4.4	260.2	196.5	63.7
1977	459.4	169.6	242.5	155.9	86.6	−72.9	−73.4	.5	289.8	221.1	68.7
1978	548.0	220.8	278.0	175.1	102.9	−57.2	−62.0	4.9	327.2	252.1	75.1
1979	613.5	239.6	288.2	186.8	101.4	−48.6	−47.4	−1.2	373.9	290.7	83.1
1980	630.1	201.7	296.4	224.1	72.3	−94.7	−88.8	−5.9	428.4	335.0	93.5
1981	743.9	256.6	354.9	265.5	89.4	−98.2	−88.1	−10.2	487.2	381.9	105.3
1982	725.8	188.9	379.0	293.3	85.6	−190.1	−167.4	−22.8	537.0	420.4	116.6
1983	716.7	154.1	379.7	264.0	115.7	−225.6	−207.2	−18.4	562.6	438.8	123.8
1984	881.6	283.2	479.9	330.3	149.5	−196.7	−196.5	−.2	598.4	463.5	134.9
1985	881.0	240.8	442.5	284.9	157.5	−201.7	−199.2	−2.4	640.1	496.4	143.7
1986	864.5	179.2	399.1	290.6	108.5	−219.9	−215.9	−4.0	685.3	531.6	153.7
1987	948.9	218.5	398.6	275.4	123.2	−180.1	−165.7	−14.4	730.4	566.3	164.1
1988	1,076.6	292.1	463.4	320.5	142.9	−171.3	−160.0	−11.3	784.5	607.9	176.6
1989	1,109.8	271.5	450.2	340.0	110.3	−178.7	−159.4	−19.3	838.3	649.6	188.6
1990	1,113.4	224.8	464.4	361.1	103.2	−239.5	−203.3	−36.2	888.5	688.4	200.1
1991	1,153.4	221.0	529.5	396.0	133.5	−308.5	−248.4	−60.1	932.4	721.5	210.9
1992	1,147.6	187.4	592.8	453.9	139.0	−405.5	−334.5	−71.0	960.2	742.9	217.4
1993	1,163.4	159.9	545.9	397.7	148.2	−386.0	−313.5	−72.5	1,003.5	778.2	225.3
1994	1,295.1	239.5	559.0	363.4	195.7	−319.6	−255.6	−63.9	1,055.6	822.5	233.1
1995	1,426.3	303.9	616.5	387.1	229.4	−312.5	−242.1	−70.4	1,122.4	880.7	241.7
1996	1,578.9	403.6	636.8	382.3	254.5	−233.2	−179.4	−53.8	1,175.3	929.1	246.2
1997	1,780.5	541.2	675.1	390.3	284.9	−133.9	−92.0	−42.0	1,239.3	987.8	251.6
1998	1,930.6	620.8	649.5	446.5	203.0	−28.7	1.4	−30.1	1,309.7	1,052.2	257.6
1999	2,010.3	611.4	583.4	349.4	234.1	28.0	66.9	−38.9	1,398.9	1,132.2	266.7
2000	2,127.3	616.1	501.2	358.3	142.9	114.8	155.5	−40.6	1,511.2	1,231.5	279.7
2001	2,076.9	477.4	582.4	391.6	190.8	−105.0	14.0	−119.0	1,599.5	1,311.7	287.8
2002	2,003.6	345.6	799.9	473.7	326.2	−454.4	−271.5	−182.9	1,658.0	1,361.8	296.2
2003	1,991.7	272.6	858.0	471.5	386.5	−585.4	−404.1	−181.3	1,719.1	1,411.9	307.1
2004	2,164.3	342.5	892.4	463.8	428.6	−549.9	−400.9	−149.0	1,821.8	1,497.1	324.7
2005	2,365.8	394.8	803.5	296.7	506.8	−408.7	−305.9	−102.8	1,971.0	1,622.6	348.4
2006	2,657.9	533.8	846.4	385.6	460.8	−312.6	−227.6	−85.0	2,124.1	1,751.8	372.3
2007	2,536.6	283.8	679.2	391.6	287.6	−395.4	−266.1	−129.3	2,252.8	1,852.5	400.3
2008	2,241.2	−117.7	734.3	544.9	189.4	−852.0	−631.1	−220.9	2,358.8	1,931.8	427.0
2009	2,008.3	−363.2	1,227.1	666.5	560.6	−1,590.3	−1,248.9	−341.3	2,371.5	1,928.7	442.8
2010	2,312.2	−78.7	1,553.9	740.9	813.0	−1,632.6	−1,325.1	−307.5	2,390.9	1,933.8	457.2
2011	2,556.9	82.4	1,599.4	849.8	749.6	−1,517.1	−1,242.0	−275.1	2,474.5	1,997.3	477.2
2012	3,036.0	460.0	1,821.5	1,107.6	713.9	−1,361.4	−1,078.6	−282.8	2,576.0	2,082.4	493.6
2013	3,218.2	537.0	1,440.3	801.4	638.9	−903.3	−637.9	−265.4	2,681.2	2,176.6	504.6
2014	3,564.2	747.2	1,585.7	970.3	615.4	−838.5	−601.8	−236.7	2,817.0	2,300.6	516.3
2015	3,664.4	746.9	1,539.4	1,044.2	495.2	−792.5	−568.9	−223.6	2,917.5	2,395.3	522.2
2016	3,482.5	492.0	1,402.9	948.2	454.7	−910.9	−665.1	−245.8	2,990.5	2,463.5	527.0
2017	3,681.8	565.6	1,520.1	986.8	533.3	−954.5	−695.4	−259.1	3,116.2	2,574.6	541.5
2018 ᵖ	....	....	....	1,043.4		....	....	....	3,274.0	2,712.7	561.3
2015: I	3,715.1	828.7	1,610.2	1,041.9	568.2	−781.5	−551.6	−229.8	2,886.4	2,366.0	520.4
II	3,691.7	784.1	1,593.4	1,041.6	551.7	−809.3	−571.6	−237.7	2,907.6	2,385.9	521.8
III	3,639.7	708.8	1,576.2	1,068.5	507.7	−867.4	−611.0	−256.4	2,930.9	2,407.4	523.5
IV	3,610.9	665.9	1,377.7	1,024.7	353.0	−711.8	−541.3	−170.5	2,945.0	2,421.8	523.2
2016: I	3,543.8	590.2	1,478.2	1,047.6	430.6	−888.0	−638.0	−250.0	2,953.5	2,431.4	522.2
II	3,448.4	468.9	1,382.9	931.6	451.3	−914.0	−668.8	−245.2	2,979.6	2,453.5	526.1
III	3,421.0	419.6	1,335.0	899.7	435.3	−915.4	−674.9	−240.5	3,001.5	2,473.5	527.9
IV	3,516.6	489.2	1,415.4	913.9	501.5	−926.3	−678.6	−247.7	3,027.5	2,495.7	531.8
2017: I	3,648.2	583.3	1,505.0	1,014.9	490.2	−921.8	−655.9	−265.8	3,064.9	2,529.3	535.7
II	3,659.3	558.3	1,490.6	990.2	500.4	−932.4	−661.5	−270.9	3,101.1	2,561.9	539.2
III	3,733.3	598.6	1,513.8	993.4	520.5	−915.3	−660.5	−254.7	3,134.8	2,590.9	543.8
IV	3,686.3	522.4	1,570.9	948.9	622.0	−1,048.5	−803.6	−244.9	3,163.9	2,616.4	547.5
2018: I	3,849.6	646.2	1,846.4	1,094.3	752.1	−1,200.2	−969.9	−230.4	3,203.4	2,651.1	552.3
II	3,829.9	576.1	1,812.2	1,027.7	784.5	−1,236.1	−993.7	−242.4	3,253.8	2,694.5	559.3
III	3,927.9	630.2	1,822.3	996.0	826.2	−1,192.1	−960.6	−231.5	3,297.7	2,733.4	564.3
IV ᵖ	....	....	....	1,055.5		....	....	....	3,341.1	2,771.9	569.2

[1] With inventory valuation and capital consumption adjustments.

See next page for continuation of table.

[Billions of dollars, except as noted; quarterly data at seasonally adjusted annual rates]

Year or quarter	Gross domestic investment, capital account transactions, and net lending, NIPA [2]							Addenda:						
	Gross domestic investment				Capital account transactions (net) [3]	Net lending or net borrowing (–), NIPA [2,4]	Statistical discrepancy	Gross private saving	Gross government saving			Net domestic investment	Gross saving as a percent of gross national income	Net saving as a percent of gross national income
	Total	Total	Gross private domestic investment	Gross government investment					Total	Federal	State and local			
1968	217.7	216.2	156.9	59.2		1.5	3.1	192.1	22.5	10.4	12.1	102.8	22.7	10.7
1969	234.7	233.1	173.6	59.5	0.0	1.6	1.6	199.7	33.4	20.7	12.8	108.2	22.8	10.6
1970	233.6	229.8	170.0	59.8	.0	3.7	5.3	223.0	5.2	–7.2	12.4	93.0	21.2	8.5
1971	255.6	255.3	196.8	58.5	.0	.3	9.5	257.0	–10.9	–21.8	10.9	106.4	21.2	8.4
1972	284.8	288.8	228.1	60.7	.0	–4.1	7.2	277.1	0.6	–18.8	19.4	127.8	21.7	9.1
1973	341.4	332.6	266.9	65.6	.0	8.8	6.1	320.8	14.5	–6.0	20.4	153.9	23.4	10.9
1974	356.6	350.7	274.5	76.2	.0	5.9	7.4	339.1	10.1	–6.0	16.0	143.8	22.5	9.2
1975	361.5	341.7	257.3	84.4	.1	19.8	13.3	397.1	–48.9	–59.2	10.3	103.1	20.7	6.5
1976	420.0	412.9	323.2	89.6	.1	7.0	20.7	420.9	–21.6	–39.2	17.6	152.6	21.4	7.4
1977	478.9	489.8	396.6	93.2	.1	–11.0	19.4	463.6	–4.2	–28.2	24.0	199.9	22.1	8.1
1978	571.3	583.9	478.4	105.6	.1	–12.7	23.3	530.1	17.9	–12.4	30.3	256.7	23.3	9.4
1979	658.6	659.8	539.7	120.1	.1	–1.3	45.1	579.0	34.6	7.2	27.3	285.9	23.5	9.2
1980	674.6	666.0	530.1	135.9	.1	8.4	44.4	631.4	–1.2	–28.4	27.1	237.6	22.1	7.1
1981	781.9	778.6	631.2	147.3	.1	3.3	38.1	736.8	7.1	–20.6	27.6	291.3	23.2	8.0
1982	734.7	738.0	581.0	156.9	.1	–3.4	8.8	799.4	–73.5	–92.0	18.4	201.0	21.5	5.6
1983	773.6	808.7	637.5	171.2	.1	–35.2	57.0	818.5	–101.8	–126.1	24.3	246.1	19.8	4.3
1984	923.2	1,013.3	820.1	193.2	.1	–90.2	41.6	943.4	–61.8	–105.9	44.1	414.9	21.9	7.0
1985	935.2	1,049.5	829.7	219.9	.1	–114.5	54.3	938.9	–57.9	–102.3	44.4	409.4	20.4	5.6
1986	944.6	1,087.2	849.1	238.1	.1	–142.8	80.1	930.7	–66.2	–112.4	46.2	401.9	19.1	4.0
1987	992.7	1,146.8	892.2	254.6	.1	–154.2	43.8	964.9	–16.0	–55.6	39.6	416.4	19.7	4.5
1988	1,079.6	1,195.4	937.0	258.4	.1	–115.9	3.0	1,071.3	5.3	–41.0	46.4	410.9	20.5	5.6
1989	1,177.8	1,270.1	999.7	270.4	.3	–92.7	68.0	1,099.9	9.9	–32.5	42.4	431.9	19.8	4.9
1990	1,208.9	1,283.8	993.4	290.4	7.4	–82.3	95.5	1,152.8	–39.4	–69.8	30.4	395.3	18.9	3.8
1991	1,246.3	1,238.4	944.3	294.1	5.3	2.6	93.0	1,250.9	–97.6	–108.3	10.8	306.0	18.9	3.6
1992	1,263.6	1,309.1	1,013.0	296.1	–1.3	–44.3	115.9	1,335.7	–188.1	–191.2	3.1	348.9	17.8	2.9
1993	1,319.3	1,398.7	1,106.8	291.9	.9	–80.2	156.0	1,324.1	–160.7	–166.5	5.8	395.2	17.3	2.4
1994	1,435.1	1,550.7	1,256.5	294.2	1.3	–116.9	140.0	1,381.6	–86.4	–105.3	18.8	495.0	18.1	3.3
1995	1,519.3	1,625.2	1,317.5	307.7	.4	–106.3	93.0	1,497.2	–70.9	–88.6	17.7	502.8	18.8	4.0
1996	1,637.0	1,752.0	1,432.1	320.0	.2	–115.2	58.1	1,565.9	13.0	–25.7	38.7	576.7	19.6	5.0
1997	1,792.1	1,922.2	1,595.6	326.6	.5	–130.6	11.6	1,662.9	117.6	62.3	55.3	682.9	20.7	6.3
1998	1,875.3	2,080.7	1,736.7	344.0	.2	–205.6	–55.2	1,701.7	228.9	156.8	72.1	770.9	21.1	6.8
1999	1,977.2	2,255.5	1,887.1	368.5	4.5	–282.8	–33.2	1,715.6	294.7	225.0	69.7	856.6	20.7	6.3
2000	2,030.8	2,427.3	2,038.4	388.9	.3	–396.8	–96.5	1,732.7	394.6	318.6	76.0	916.0	20.5	5.9
2001	1,963.8	2,346.7	1,934.8	411.9	–12.9	–370.0	–113.1	1,894.1	182.8	178.5	4.4	747.2	19.3	4.4
2002	1,930.9	2,374.1	1,930.4	443.7	.5	–443.7	–72.7	2,161.7	–158.2	–104.7	–53.5	716.1	18.1	3.1
2003	1,978.1	2,491.3	2,027.1	464.2	2.1	–515.3	–13.7	2,270.0	–278.2	–231.8	–46.4	772.2	17.3	2.4
2004	2,142.2	2,767.5	2,281.3	486.2	–2.8	–622.4	–22.1	2,389.5	–225.2	–220.4	–4.8	945.6	17.6	2.8
2005	2,310.7	3,048.0	2,534.7	513.3	–12.9	–724.5	–55.1	2,426.1	–60.3	–115.4	55.1	1,077.0	18.0	3.0
2006	2,450.0	3,251.8	2,701.0	550.9	2.1	–803.9	–207.9	2,598.2	59.7	–26.3	86.0	1,127.7	18.9	3.8
2007	2,554.3	3,265.0	2,673.0	592.0	–.1	–710.7	17.7	2,531.7	4.9	–53.3	58.2	1,012.2	17.4	2.0
2008	2,424.0	3,107.2	2,477.6	629.6	–5.4	–677.8	182.9	2,666.2	–425.0	–405.3	–19.7	748.4	15.3	–.8
2009	2,200.5	2,572.6	1,929.7	642.9	.6	–372.7	192.2	3,155.8	–1,147.5	–1,015.3	–132.2	201.1	13.9	–2.5
2010	2,373.3	2,810.0	2,165.5	644.5	.7	–437.4	61.0	3,487.6	–1,175.4	–1,081.3	–94.1	419.1	15.3	–.5
2011	2,503.6	2,969.2	2,332.6	636.6	1.6	–467.2	–53.2	3,596.8	–1,039.9	–987.0	–52.9	494.7	16.1	.5
2012	2,794.7	3,242.8	2,621.8	621.0	–6.5	–441.6	–241.3	3,903.8	–867.8	–817.0	–50.8	666.8	18.2	2.8
2013	3,057.9	3,426.4	2,826.0	600.4	.8	–369.4	–160.3	3,616.9	–398.7	–372.0	–26.6	745.2	18.7	3.1
2014	3,265.2	3,640.8	3,038.9	601.8	.4	–376.0	–299.0	3,886.3	–322.2	–331.8	9.6	823.8	19.7	4.1
2015	3,409.4	3,833.5	3,212.0	621.5	.4	–424.5	–254.9	3,934.6	–270.3	–298.0	27.7	916.0	19.6	4.0
2016	3,355.5	3,801.4	3,169.9	631.5	.5	–446.3	–126.9	3,866.4	–383.9	–394.4	10.5	810.9	18.3	2.6
2017 ᵖ	3,538.6	4,011.2	3,368.0	643.2	3.7	–476.2	–143.2	4,094.7	–412.9	–419.4	6.5	895.0	18.5	2.8
2018 ᵖ	....	4,330.8	3,652.2	678.7	....							1,056.8	....	....
2015: I	3,396.0	3,822.9	3,216.8	606.1	.4	–427.4	–319.2	3,976.2	–261.0	–280.3	19.2	936.5	20.1	4.5
II	3,458.5	3,852.8	3,225.9	626.9	.4	–394.7	–233.2	3,979.2	–287.5	–300.8	13.3	945.2	19.8	4.2
III	3,402.7	3,860.6	3,229.6	631.0	.4	–458.3	–237.0	3,983.7	–344.0	–339.9	–4.1	929.7	19.4	3.8
IV	3,380.5	3,797.5	3,175.5	622.0	.4	–417.4	–230.4	3,799.5	–188.6	–271.0	82.4	852.5	19.2	3.5
2016: I	3,315.8	3,778.5	3,142.1	636.4	.6	–463.3	–228.0	3,909.6	–365.8	–368.9	3.1	825.0	18.8	3.1
II	3,368.2	3,782.4	3,152.2	630.2	.4	–414.6	–80.2	3,836.4	–387.9	–398.9	10.9	802.8	18.2	2.5
III	3,335.9	3,784.8	3,157.7	627.1	.4	–449.3	–85.2	3,808.6	–387.5	–404.1	16.6	783.3	17.9	2.2
IV	3,402.3	3,859.8	3,227.6	632.2	.4	–457.9	–114.3	3,911.1	–394.5	–405.9	11.4	832.4	18.2	2.5
2017: I	3,453.4	3,915.7	3,278.6	637.1	.4	–462.8	–194.9	4,034.3	–386.1	–382.0	–4.1	850.7	18.6	3.0
II	3,472.6	3,980.2	3,337.9	642.3	.4	–508.0	–186.8	4,052.5	–393.2	–386.5	–6.7	879.1	18.5	2.8
III	3,618.9	4,054.1	3,413.9	640.2	13.2	–448.4	–114.4	4,104.8	–371.4	–383.8	12.4	919.3	18.7	3.0
IV	3,609.7	4,094.6	3,441.4	653.2	.6	–485.5	–76.6	4,187.3	–501.0	–525.3	24.3	930.7	18.3	2.6
2018: I	3,689.7	4,203.6	3,543.8	659.8	.4	–514.3	–159.9	4,497.5	–647.9	–690.0	42.1	1,000.2	18.8	3.2
II	3,831.3	4,255.1	3,579.5	675.6	.4	–424.2	1.4	4,506.7	–676.8	–711.7	34.9	1,001.3	18.5	2.8
III	3,869.6	4,397.2	3,710.7	686.5	–1.8	–525.8	–58.3	4,555.6	–627.8	–676.3	48.6	1,099.5	18.7	3.0
IV ᵖ	....	4,467.4	3,774.6	692.8								1,126.3	....	

[2] National income and product accounts (NIPA).
[3] Consists of capital transfers and the acquisition and disposal of nonproduced nonfinancial assets.
[4] Prior to 1982, equals the balance on current account, NIPA.

Source: Department of Commerce (Bureau of Economic Analysis).

TABLE B–20. Median money income (in 2017 dollars) and poverty status of families and people, by race, 2009-2017

Race, Hispanic origin, and year	Families[1] Number (mil-lions)	Median money income (in 2017 dol-lars)[3]	Below poverty level[2] Total Number (mil-lions)	Total Percent	Female householder, no husband present Number (mil-lions)	Female householder Percent	People below poverty level[2] Number (mil-lions)	Percent	Median money income (in 2017 dollars) of people 15 years old and over with income[3] Males All people	Males Year-round full-time workers	Females All people	Females Year-round full-time workers
TOTAL (all races)[4]												
2009	78.9	$68,819	8.8	11.1	4.4	29.9	43.6	14.3	$36,860	$56,308	$24,002	$42,644
2010[5]	79.6	67,869	9.4	11.8	4.8	31.7	46.3	15.1	36,286	56,506	23,408	43,310
2011	80.5	66,601	9.5	11.8	4.9	31.2	46.2	15.0	36,030	54,959	23,049	42,255
2012	80.9	66,575	9.5	11.8	4.8	30.9	46.5	15.0	36,265	54,212	23,018	42,806
2013[6]	81.2	67,262	9.1	11.2	4.6	30.6	45.3	14.5	37,131	53,695	23,255	42,790
2013[7]	82.3	69,007	9.6	11.7	5.2	32.2	46.3	14.8	37,555	54,195	23,321	42,897
2014	81.7	69,062	9.5	11.6	4.8	30.6	46.7	14.8	37,626	53,332	23,051	42,285
2015	82.2	73,149	8.6	10.4	4.4	28.2	43.1	13.5	38,426	54,059	24,593	43,202
2016	82.9	74,271	8.1	9.8	4.1	26.6	40.6	12.7	39,705	54,623	25,427	44,128
2017	83.1	75,938	7.8	9.3	4.0	25.7	39.7	12.3	40,396	55,834	25,486	44,379
WHITE, non-Hispanic[8]												
2009	54.5	77,126	3.8	7.0	1.7	23.3	18.5	9.4	42,130	82,204	25,127	57,103
2010[5]	53.8	77,634	3.9	7.2	1.7	24.1	19.3	9.9	41,862	81,951	24,467	56,971
2011	54.2	76,273	4.0	7.3	1.8	23.4	19.2	9.8	41,668	82,392	24,277	57,425
2012	54.0	76,455	3.8	7.1	1.7	23.4	18.9	9.7	41,449	81,863	24,497	57,260
2013[6]	53.8	76,547	3.7	6.9	1.6	22.6	18.8	9.6	42,289	80,951	25,064	57,140
2013[7]	54.7	78,663	4.0	7.3	1.9	25.8	19.6	10.0	43,063	83,317	25,015	59,203
2014	53.8	79,453	3.9	7.3	1.7	23.7	19.7	10.1	42,570	82,265	24,880	57,789
2015	53.8	83,320	3.5	6.4	1.6	21.7	17.8	9.1	43,671	84,075	26,518	59,766
2016	54.1	83,834	3.4	6.3	1.6	21.1	17.3	8.8	44,333	86,000	27,065	62,785
2017	53.9	85,852	3.2	6.0	1.4	19.8	17.0	8.7	45,836	87,487	27,116	63,152
BLACK[8]												
2009	9.4	43,990	2.1	22.7	1.5	36.7	9.9	25.8	27,187	45,081	22,299	37,108
2010[5]	9.6	43,485	2.3	24.1	1.7	38.7	10.7	27.4	26,248	42,504	22,135	38,357
2011	9.7	44,232	2.3	24.2	1.7	39.0	10.9	27.6	25,641	43,990	21,578	38,389
2012	9.8	43,338	2.3	23.7	1.6	37.8	10.9	27.2	26,658	42,588	21,415	37,503
2013[6]	9.9	43,834	2.3	22.8	1.6	38.5	11.0	27.2	26,198	43,879	21,127	37,292
2013[7]	9.9	44,153	2.2	22.4	1.7	36.7	10.2	25.2	26,477	42,621	22,206	36,512
2014	9.9	44,724	2.3	22.9	1.6	37.2	10.8	26.2	27,538	42,798	21,730	36,617
2015	9.8	47,369	2.1	21.1	1.5	33.9	10.0	24.1	28,354	43,157	22,363	38,397
2016	10.0	50,427	1.9	19.0	1.3	31.6	9.2	22.0	30,275	42,884	23,326	38,140
2017	10.0	50,597	1.8	18.2	1.3	30.8	9.0	21.2	30,112	43,699	23,639	37,550
ASIAN[8]												
2009	3.6	85,929	.3	9.4	.1	16.9	1.7	12.5	42,754	61,191	27,880	51,112
2010[5]	3.9	84,748	.4	9.3	.1	21.1	1.9	12.2	40,362	59,158	26,549	47,232
2011	4.2	79,732	.4	9.7	.1	19.1	2.0	12.3	39,687	61,477	24,073	45,233
2012	4.1	83,286	.4	9.4	.1	19.2	1.9	11.7	43,028	64,448	24,960	49,600
2013[6]	4.4	80,524	.4	8.7	.1	14.9	1.8	10.5	42,322	63,403	26,182	47,511
2013[7]	4.4	87,265	.4	10.2	.1	25.7	2.3	13.1	45,100	64,525	27,239	49,770
2014	4.5	85,749	.4	8.9	.1	18.9	2.1	12.0	42,392	62,498	26,317	50,316
2015	4.7	93,998	.4	8.0	.1	16.2	2.1	11.4	45,221	66,985	27,452	51,856
2016	4.7	95,509	.3	7.2	.1	19.4	1.9	10.1	47,592	68,680	27,347	52,486
2017	4.9	92,784	.4	7.8	.1	15.5	2.0	10.0	48,842	70,817	28,260	52,227
HISPANIC (any race)[8]												
2009	10.4	45,503	2.4	22.7	1.1	38.8	12.4	25.3	25,490	36,235	18,565	31,935
2010[5]	11.3	44,280	2.7	24.3	1.3	42.6	13.5	26.5	25,261	35,878	18,356	32,783
2011	11.6	43,758	2.7	22.9	1.3	41.2	13.2	25.3	25,921	35,049	18,382	32,880
2012	12.0	43,602	2.8	23.5	1.3	40.7	13.6	25.6	26,304	34,780	17,890	31,563
2013[6]	12.1	44,552	2.6	21.6	1.3	40.4	12.7	23.5	26,784	34,729	18,721	32,463
2013[7]	12.4	43,150	2.9	23.1	1.4	40.5	13.4	24.7	25,508	34,114	17,868	32,854
2014	12.5	46,759	2.7	21.5	1.3	37.9	13.1	23.6	27,648	36,394	18,226	31,953
2015	12.8	48,969	2.5	19.6	1.2	35.5	12.1	21.4	29,085	37,221	19,561	32,755
2016	13.0	52,204	2.3	17.3	1.1	32.7	11.1	19.4	31,168	39,004	20,334	32,726
2017	13.2	53,614	2.2	16.3	1.1	32.7	10.8	18.3	30,691	39,901	20,312	32,439

[1] The term "family" refers to a group of two or more persons related by birth, marriage, or adoption and residing together. Every family must include a reference person.

[2] Poverty thresholds are updated each year to reflect changes in the consumer price index for all urban consumers (CPI-U).

[3] Adjusted by consumer price index research series (CPI-U-RS).

[4] Data for American Indians and Alaska natives, native Hawaiians and other Pacific Islanders, and those reporting two or more races are included in the total but not shown separately.

[5] Reflects implementation of Census 2010-based population controls comparable to succeeding years.

[6] The 2014 Current Population Survey (CPS) Annual Social and Economic Supplement (ASEC) included redesigned income questions, which were implemented to a subsample of the 98,000 addresses using a probability split panel design. These 2013 data are based on the 2014 ASEC sample of 68,000 addresses that received income questions similar to those used in the 2013 ASEC and are consistent with data in earlier years.

[7] These 2013 data are based on the 2014 ASEC sample of 30,000 addresses that received redesigned income questions and are consistent with data in later years.

[8] The CPS allows respondents to choose more than one race. Data shown are for "white alone, non-Hispanic," "black alone," and "Asian alone" race categories. ("Black" is also "black or African American.") Family race and Hispanic origin are based on the reference person.

Note: For details see *Income and Poverty in the United States* in publication Series P–60 on the CPS ASEC.

Source: Department of Commerce (Bureau of the Census).

TABLE B–21. Real farm income, 1954–2018
[Billions of chained (2018) dollars]

Year	Income of farm operators from farming [1]						Production expenses	Net farm income
	Gross farm income							
	Total	Value of agricultural sector production				Direct Federal Government payments		
		Total	Crops [2,3]	Animals and animal products [3]	Farm-related income [4]			
1954	258.9	256.9	109.2	134.0	13.7	1.9	165.2	93.7
1955	250.0	248.3	106.5	127.9	13.9	1.7	165.6	84.4
1956	245.2	241.2	104.2	123.4	13.5	4.0	164.0	81.3
1957	242.7	235.6	95.3	126.7	13.6	7.1	165.4	77.3
1958	265.6	258.2	102.3	141.7	14.2	7.4	175.8	89.8
1959	255.0	250.4	99.4	135.8	15.2	4.6	182.9	72.1
1960	256.2	251.5	104.0	131.9	15.5	4.7	181.7	74.4
1961	266.4	256.5	103.9	136.6	16.1	9.8	187.8	78.5
1962	274.8	263.5	108.1	139.0	16.3	11.3	196.5	78.3
1963	278.3	267.4	115.1	135.3	17.0	10.9	202.7	75.5
1964	267.4	253.6	106.6	129.4	17.6	13.8	201.1	66.3
1965	288.9	273.6	118.1	137.7	17.8	15.3	208.9	80.1
1966	304.7	284.9	110.6	156.1	18.2	19.8	220.4	84.3
1967	296.4	278.3	112.8	146.6	19.0	18.1	224.0	72.4
1968	291.8	272.3	106.5	146.9	18.9	19.5	222.4	69.3
1969	302.6	282.2	105.6	157.3	19.3	20.4	225.9	76.7
1970	299.7	280.8	104.6	156.8	19.4	18.9	226.5	73.2
1971	301.2	286.0	113.6	152.6	19.8	15.2	228.4	72.8
1972	330.7	312.3	120.6	171.6	20.1	18.4	240.3	90.4
1973	435.9	424.4	189.7	213.1	21.6	11.5	284.5	151.4
1974	397.4	395.2	198.8	173.2	23.2	2.1	287.1	110.3
1975	372.1	369.1	186.5	159.1	23.5	3.0	277.7	94.4
1976	361.0	358.4	169.6	163.5	25.2	2.6	290.2	70.8
1977	359.2	353.2	168.9	156.3	28.0	6.0	293.5	65.7
1978	396.3	387.0	174.7	181.6	30.7	9.3	318.6	77.7
1979	429.4	425.5	189.9	202.8	32.7	3.9	351.3	78.1
1980	390.0	386.6	168.1	183.7	34.8	3.4	347.8	42.2
1981	397.0	392.4	188.4	168.1	36.0	4.6	332.9	64.2
1982	369.0	361.2	161.4	158.5	41.2	7.9	315.4	53.6
1983	332.9	312.8	123.0	151.5	38.2	20.1	302.0	30.9
1984	350.8	333.2	162.3	150.4	20.4	17.6	296.5	54.2
1985	326.0	310.4	149.1	139.6	21.7	15.6	268.3	57.7
1986	309.7	286.3	125.6	140.4	20.3	23.4	248.0	61.7
1987	326.1	293.7	124.9	146.7	22.2	32.4	252.5	73.6
1988	332.8	305.7	129.5	147.1	29.1	27.1	258.6	74.1
1989	344.8	325.2	146.7	150.2	28.4	19.6	261.2	83.7
1990	343.1	327.0	144.3	156.2	26.5	16.1	262.8	80.2
1991	322.3	308.5	136.2	146.4	25.8	13.8	254.8	67.5
1992	329.0	314.0	146.1	143.0	24.9	15.0	246.7	82.3
1993	328.6	307.1	132.5	147.4	27.2	21.5	253.7	74.9
1994	339.1	326.8	157.7	140.8	28.3	12.4	256.6	82.5
1995	324.0	312.9	147.4	134.9	30.6	11.2	262.9	61.1
1996	355.9	344.8	174.6	138.9	31.3	11.1	267.0	89.0
1997	353.1	342.0	166.9	142.9	32.2	11.1	277.0	76.1
1998	341.3	323.2	149.8	138.2	35.1	18.2	272.2	69.1
1999	339.9	308.8	134.2	137.7	36.8	31.1	270.9	69.0
2000	341.9	309.1	134.3	140.2	34.5	32.9	270.2	71.7
2001	345.8	314.7	131.5	147.2	36.1	31.0	269.8	75.9
2002	314.3	297.3	133.4	127.4	36.5	16.9	260.9	53.4
2003	346.1	324.0	145.3	140.5	38.3	22.1	264.5	81.6
2004	384.2	367.3	163.0	161.9	42.3	16.9	270.3	113.9
2005	377.2	346.4	144.5	159.9	42.0	30.8	277.7	99.5
2006	355.8	336.5	145.6	146.3	44.6	19.4	285.4	70.4
2007	405.5	391.3	180.4	165.3	45.5	14.2	321.9	83.6
2008	427.1	412.8	203.6	163.3	45.8	14.3	335.7	91.4
2009	391.4	377.2	191.4	139.1	46.7	14.2	319.0	72.3
2010	409.7	395.5	193.2	161.2	41.1	14.2	321.1	88.6
2011	473.3	461.6	224.4	184.3	52.8	11.7	345.4	127.9
2012	496.8	485.1	235.2	186.8	63.1	11.7	390.3	106.5
2013	525.1	513.1	253.6	196.4	63.1	11.9	390.8	134.3
2014	514.6	504.2	219.5	228.4	56.3	10.4	416.2	98.5
2015	464.4	453.0	194.0	204.7	54.3	11.4	379.0	85.5
2016	429.5	415.9	196.7	172.7	46.5	13.5	365.3	64.2
2017	439.7	427.9	194.2	181.5	52.2	11.8	362.5	77.1
2018 p	435.4	421.8	191.2	176.8	53.8	13.6	369.1	66.3

[1] The GDP chain-type price index is used to convert the current-dollar statistics to 2018=100 equivalents.
[2] Crop receipts include proceeds received from commodities placed under Commodity Credit Corporation loans.
[3] The value of production equates to the sum of cash receipts, home consumption, and the value of the change in inventories.
[4] Includes income from forest products sold, the gross imputed rental value of farm dwellings, machine hire and custom work, and other sources of farm income such as commodity insurance indemnities.

Note: Data for 2018 are forecasts.

Source: Department of Agriculture (Economic Research Service).

Labor Market Indicators

Table B–22. Civilian labor force, 1929–2018

[Monthly data seasonally adjusted, except as noted]

Year or month	Civilian noninstitutional population [1]	Civilian labor force					Not in labor force	Civilian labor force participation rate [2]	Civilian employment/ population ratio [3]	Unemployment rate, civilian workers [4]
		Total	Employment			Unemployment				
			Total	Agricultural	Nonagricultural					
	Thousands of persons 14 years of age and over								Percent	
1929	....	49,180	47,630	10,450	37,180	1,550	....	....	....	3.2
1930	....	49,820	45,480	10,340	35,140	4,340	....	....	....	8.7
1931	....	50,420	42,400	10,290	32,110	8,020	....	....	....	15.9
1932	....	51,000	38,940	10,170	28,770	12,060	....	....	....	23.6
1933	....	51,590	38,760	10,090	28,670	12,830	....	....	....	24.9
1934	....	52,230	40,890	9,900	30,990	11,340	....	....	....	21.7
1935	....	52,870	42,260	10,110	32,150	10,610	....	....	....	20.1
1936	....	53,440	44,410	10,000	34,410	9,030	....	....	....	16.9
1937	....	54,000	46,300	9,820	36,480	7,700	....	....	....	14.3
1938	....	54,610	44,220	9,690	34,530	10,390	....	....	....	19.0
1939	....	55,230	45,750	9,610	36,140	9,480	....	....	....	17.2
1940	99,840	55,640	47,520	9,540	37,980	8,120	44,200	55.7	47.6	14.6
1941	99,900	55,910	50,350	9,100	41,250	5,560	43,990	56.0	50.4	9.9
1942	98,640	56,410	53,750	9,250	44,500	2,660	42,230	57.2	54.5	4.7
1943	94,640	55,540	54,470	9,080	45,390	1,070	39,100	58.7	57.6	1.9
1944	93,220	54,630	53,960	8,950	45,010	670	38,590	58.6	57.9	1.2
1945	94,090	53,860	52,820	8,580	44,240	1,040	40,230	57.2	56.1	1.9
1946	103,070	57,520	55,250	8,320	46,930	2,270	45,550	55.8	53.6	3.9
1947	106,018	60,168	57,812	8,256	49,557	2,356	45,850	56.8	54.5	3.9
	Thousands of persons 16 years of age and over									
1947	101,827	59,350	57,038	7,890	49,148	2,311	42,477	58.3	56.0	3.9
1948	103,068	60,621	58,343	7,629	50,714	2,276	42,447	58.8	56.6	3.8
1949	103,994	61,286	57,651	7,658	49,993	3,637	42,708	58.9	55.4	5.9
1950	104,995	62,208	58,918	7,160	51,758	3,288	42,787	59.2	56.1	5.3
1951	104,621	62,017	59,961	6,726	53,235	2,055	42,604	59.2	57.3	3.3
1952	105,231	62,138	60,250	6,500	53,749	1,883	43,093	59.0	57.3	3.0
1953	107,056	63,015	61,179	6,260	54,919	1,834	44,041	58.9	57.1	2.9
1954	108,321	63,643	60,109	6,205	53,904	3,532	44,678	58.8	55.5	5.5
1955	109,683	65,023	62,170	6,450	55,722	2,852	44,660	59.3	56.7	4.4
1956	110,954	66,552	63,799	6,283	57,514	2,750	44,402	60.0	57.5	4.1
1957	112,265	66,929	64,071	5,947	58,123	2,859	45,336	59.6	57.1	4.3
1958	113,727	67,639	63,036	5,586	57,450	4,602	46,088	59.5	55.4	6.8
1959	115,329	68,369	64,630	5,565	59,065	3,740	46,960	59.3	56.0	5.5
1960	117,245	69,628	65,778	5,458	60,318	3,852	47,617	59.4	56.1	5.5
1961	118,771	70,459	65,746	5,200	60,546	4,714	48,312	59.3	55.4	6.7
1962	120,153	70,614	66,702	4,944	61,759	3,911	49,539	58.8	55.5	5.5
1963	122,416	71,833	67,762	4,687	63,076	4,070	50,583	58.7	55.4	5.7
1964	124,485	73,091	69,305	4,523	64,782	3,786	51,394	58.7	55.7	5.2
1965	126,513	74,455	71,088	4,361	66,726	3,366	52,058	58.9	56.2	4.5
1966	128,058	75,770	72,895	3,979	68,915	2,875	52,288	59.2	56.9	3.8
1967	129,874	77,347	74,372	3,844	70,527	2,975	52,527	59.6	57.3	3.8
1968	132,028	78,737	75,920	3,817	72,103	2,817	53,291	59.6	57.5	3.6
1969	134,335	80,734	77,902	3,606	74,296	2,832	53,602	60.1	58.0	3.5
1970	137,085	82,771	78,678	3,463	75,215	4,093	54,315	60.4	57.4	4.9
1971	140,216	84,382	79,367	3,394	75,972	5,016	55,834	60.2	56.6	5.9
1972	144,126	87,034	82,153	3,484	78,669	4,882	57,091	60.4	57.0	5.6
1973	147,096	89,429	85,064	3,470	81,594	4,365	57,667	60.8	57.8	4.9
1974	150,120	91,949	86,794	3,515	83,279	5,156	58,171	61.3	57.8	5.6
1975	153,153	93,775	85,846	3,408	82,438	7,929	59,377	61.2	56.1	8.5
1976	156,150	96,158	88,752	3,331	85,421	7,406	59,991	61.6	56.8	7.7
1977	159,033	99,009	92,017	3,283	88,734	6,991	60,025	62.3	57.9	7.1
1978	161,910	102,251	96,048	3,387	92,661	6,202	59,659	63.2	59.3	6.1
1979	164,863	104,962	98,824	3,347	95,477	6,137	59,900	63.7	59.9	5.8
1980	167,745	106,940	99,303	3,364	95,938	7,637	60,806	63.8	59.2	7.1
1981	170,130	108,670	100,397	3,368	97,030	8,273	61,460	63.9	59.0	7.6
1982	172,271	110,204	99,526	3,401	96,125	10,678	62,067	64.0	57.8	9.7
1983	174,215	111,550	100,834	3,383	97,450	10,717	62,665	64.0	57.9	9.6
1984	176,383	113,544	105,005	3,321	101,685	8,539	62,839	64.4	59.5	7.5
1985	178,206	115,461	107,150	3,179	103,971	8,312	62,744	64.8	60.1	7.2
1986	180,587	117,834	109,597	3,163	106,434	8,237	62,752	65.3	60.7	7.0
1987	182,753	119,865	112,440	3,208	109,232	7,425	62,888	65.6	61.5	6.2
1988	184,613	121,669	114,968	3,169	111,800	6,701	62,944	65.9	62.3	5.5
1989	186,393	123,869	117,342	3,199	114,142	6,528	62,523	66.5	63.0	5.3

[1] Not seasonally adjusted.
[2] Civilian labor force as percent of civilian noninstitutional population.
[3] Civilian employment as percent of civilian noninstitutional population.
[4] Unemployed as percent of civilian labor force.

See next page for continuation of table.

[Monthly data seasonally adjusted, except as noted]

Year or month	Civilian noninstitutional population [1]	Civilian labor force					Not in labor force	Civilian labor force participation rate [2]	Civilian employment/ population ratio [3]	Unemployment rate, civilian workers [4]
		Total	Employment			Unemployment				
			Total	Agricultural	Nonagricultural					
	Thousands of persons 16 years of age and over							Percent		
1990	189,164	125,840	118,793	3,223	115,570	7,047	63,324	66.5	62.8	5.6
1991	190,925	126,346	117,718	3,269	114,449	8,628	64,578	66.2	61.7	6.8
1992	192,805	128,105	118,492	3,247	115,245	9,613	64,700	66.4	61.5	7.5
1993	194,838	129,200	120,259	3,115	117,144	8,940	65,638	66.3	61.7	6.9
1994	196,814	131,056	123,060	3,409	119,651	7,996	65,758	66.6	62.5	6.1
1995	198,584	132,304	124,900	3,440	121,460	7,404	66,280	66.6	62.9	5.6
1996	200,591	133,943	126,708	3,443	123,264	7,236	66,647	66.8	63.2	5.4
1997	203,133	136,297	129,558	3,399	126,159	6,739	66,837	67.1	63.8	4.9
1998	205,220	137,673	131,463	3,378	128,085	6,210	67,547	67.1	64.1	4.5
1999	207,753	139,368	133,488	3,281	130,207	5,880	68,385	67.1	64.3	4.2
2000 [5]	212,577	142,583	136,891	2,464	134,427	5,692	69,994	67.1	64.4	4.0
2001	215,092	143,734	136,933	2,299	134,635	6,801	71,359	66.8	63.7	4.7
2002	217,570	144,863	136,485	2,311	134,174	8,378	72,707	66.6	62.7	5.8
2003	221,168	146,510	137,736	2,275	135,461	8,774	74,658	66.2	62.3	6.0
2004	223,357	147,401	139,252	2,232	137,020	8,149	75,956	66.0	62.3	5.5
2005	226,082	149,320	141,730	2,197	139,532	7,591	76,762	66.0	62.7	5.1
2006	228,815	151,428	144,427	2,206	142,221	7,001	77,387	66.2	63.1	4.6
2007	231,867	153,124	146,047	2,095	143,952	7,078	78,743	66.0	63.0	4.6
2008	233,788	154,287	145,362	2,168	143,194	8,924	79,501	66.0	62.2	5.8
2009	235,801	154,142	139,877	2,103	137,775	14,265	81,659	65.4	59.3	9.3
2010	237,830	153,889	139,064	2,206	136,858	14,825	83,941	64.7	58.5	9.6
2011	239,618	153,617	139,869	2,254	137,615	13,747	86,001	64.1	58.4	8.9
2012	243,284	154,975	142,469	2,186	140,283	12,506	88,310	63.7	58.6	8.1
2013	245,679	155,389	143,929	2,130	141,799	11,460	90,290	63.2	58.6	7.4
2014	247,947	155,922	146,305	2,237	144,068	9,617	92,025	62.9	59.0	6.2
2015	250,801	157,130	148,834	2,422	146,411	8,296	93,671	62.7	59.3	5.3
2016	253,538	159,187	151,436	2,460	148,976	7,751	94,351	62.8	59.7	4.9
2017	255,079	160,320	153,337	2,454	150,883	6,982	94,759	62.9	60.1	4.4
2018	257,791	162,075	155,761	2,425	153,336	6,314	95,716	62.9	60.4	3.9
2016: Jan	252,397	158,371	150,622	2,390	148,160	7,749	94,026	62.7	59.7	4.9
Feb	252,577	158,705	150,934	2,454	148,444	7,771	93,872	62.8	59.8	4.9
Mar	252,768	159,079	151,146	2,555	148,375	7,932	93,689	62.9	59.8	5.0
Apr	252,969	158,891	150,963	2,572	148,377	7,928	94,077	62.8	59.7	5.0
May	253,174	158,700	151,074	2,556	148,511	7,626	94,475	62.7	59.7	4.8
June	253,397	158,899	151,104	2,514	148,673	7,795	94,498	62.7	59.6	4.9
July	253,620	159,150	151,450	2,423	149,006	7,700	94,470	62.8	59.7	4.8
Aug	253,854	159,582	151,766	2,564	149,285	7,817	94,272	62.9	59.8	4.9
Sept	254,091	159,810	151,877	2,432	149,514	7,933	94,281	62.9	59.8	5.0
Oct	254,321	159,768	151,949	2,330	149,610	7,819	94,553	62.8	59.7	4.9
Nov	254,540	159,629	152,150	2,394	149,839	7,480	94,911	62.7	59.8	4.7
Dec	254,742	159,779	152,276	2,323	149,947	7,503	94,963	62.7	59.8	4.7
2017: Jan	254,082	159,693	152,128	2,411	149,709	7,565	94,389	62.9	59.9	4.7
Feb	254,246	159,854	152,417	2,437	149,939	7,437	94,392	62.9	59.9	4.7
Mar	254,414	160,036	152,958	2,503	150,260	7,078	94,378	62.9	60.1	4.4
Apr	254,588	160,169	153,150	2,682	150,432	7,019	94,419	62.9	60.2	4.4
May	254,767	159,910	152,920	2,501	150,397	6,991	94,857	62.8	60.0	4.4
June	254,957	160,124	153,176	2,466	150,816	6,948	94,833	62.8	60.1	4.3
July	255,151	160,383	153,456	2,349	151,073	6,927	94,769	62.9	60.1	4.3
Aug	255,357	160,706	153,591	2,378	151,312	7,115	94,651	62.9	60.1	4.4
Sept	255,562	161,190	154,399	2,286	152,143	6,791	94,372	63.1	60.4	4.2
Oct	255,766	160,436	153,847	2,487	151,353	6,588	95,330	62.7	60.2	4.1
Nov	255,949	160,626	153,945	2,461	151,562	6,682	95,323	62.8	60.1	4.2
Dec	256,109	160,636	154,065	2,512	151,628	6,572	95,473	62.7	60.2	4.1
2018: Jan	256,780	161,123	154,482	2,480	152,030	6,641	95,657	62.7	60.2	4.1
Feb	256,934	161,900	155,213	2,450	152,695	6,687	95,033	63.0	60.4	4.1
Mar	257,097	161,646	155,160	2,331	152,664	6,486	95,451	62.9	60.4	4.0
Apr	257,272	161,551	155,216	2,312	152,860	6,335	95,721	62.8	60.3	3.9
May	257,454	161,667	155,539	2,353	153,127	6,128	95,787	62.8	60.4	3.8
June	257,642	162,129	155,592	2,363	153,267	6,537	95,513	62.9	60.4	4.0
July	257,843	162,209	155,964	2,493	153,425	6,245	95,633	62.9	60.5	3.9
Aug	258,066	161,802	155,604	2,346	153,376	6,197	96,264	62.7	60.3	3.8
Sept	258,290	162,055	156,069	2,478	153,634	5,986	96,235	62.7	60.4	3.7
Oct	258,514	162,694	156,582	2,418	154,135	6,112	95,821	62.9	60.6	3.8
Nov	258,708	162,821	156,803	2,556	154,297	6,018	95,886	62.9	60.6	3.7
Dec	258,888	163,240	156,945	2,522	154,520	6,294	95,649	63.1	60.6	3.9

[5] Beginning in 2000, data for agricultural employment are for agricultural and related industries; data for this series and for nonagricultural employment are not strictly comparable with data for earlier years. Because of independent seasonal adjustment for these two series, monthly data will not add to total civilian employment.

Note: Labor force data in Tables B-22 through B-28 are based on household interviews and usually relate to the calendar week that includes the 12th of the month. Historical comparability is affected by revisions to population controls, changes in occupational and industry classification, and other changes to the survey. In recent years, updated population controls have been introduced annually with the release of January data, so data are not strictly comparable with earlier periods. Particularly notable changes were introduced for data in the years 1953, 1960, 1962, 1972, 1973, 1978, 1980, 1990, 1994, 1997, 1998, 2000, 2003, 2008 and 2012. For definitions of terms, area samples used, historical comparability of the data, comparability with other series, etc., see *Employment and Earnings* or concepts and methodology of the CPS at http://www.bls.gov/cps/documentation.htm#concepts.

Source: Department of Labor (Bureau of Labor Statistics).

[Thousands of persons 16 years of age and over, except as noted; monthly data seasonally adjusted]

Year or month	All civilian workers	Men 20 years and over	Women 20 years and over	Both sexes 16–19	White Total	White Men 20 years and over	White Women 20 years and over	Black or African American Total	Black or African American Men 20 years and over	Black or African American Women 20 years and over	Asian Total	Hispanic or Latino Total	Hispanic or Latino Men 20 years and over	Hispanic or Latino Women 20 years and over
1975	85,846	48,018	30,726	7,104	76,411	43,192	26,731	7,894	3,998	3,388	....	3,663	2,117	1,224
1976	88,752	49,190	32,226	7,336	78,853	44,171	27,958	8,227	4,120	3,599	....	3,720	2,109	1,288
1977	92,017	50,555	33,775	7,688	81,700	45,326	29,306	8,540	4,273	3,758	....	4,079	2,335	1,370
1978	96,048	52,143	35,836	8,070	84,936	46,594	30,975	9,102	4,483	4,047	....	4,527	2,568	1,537
1979	98,824	53,308	37,434	8,083	87,259	47,546	32,357	9,359	4,606	4,174	....	4,785	2,701	1,638
1980	99,303	53,101	38,492	7,710	87,715	47,419	33,275	9,313	4,498	4,267	....	5,527	3,142	1,886
1981	100,397	53,582	39,590	7,225	88,709	47,846	34,275	9,355	4,520	4,329	....	5,813	3,325	2,029
1982	99,526	52,891	40,086	6,549	87,903	47,209	34,710	9,189	4,414	4,347	....	5,805	3,354	2,040
1983	100,834	53,487	41,004	6,342	88,893	47,618	35,476	9,375	4,531	4,428	....	6,072	3,523	2,127
1984	105,005	55,769	42,793	6,444	92,120	49,461	36,823	10,119	4,871	4,773	....	6,651	3,825	2,357
1985	107,150	56,562	44,154	6,434	93,736	50,061	37,907	10,501	4,992	4,977	....	6,888	3,994	2,456
1986	109,597	57,569	45,556	6,472	95,660	50,818	39,050	10,814	5,150	5,128	....	7,219	4,174	2,615
1987	112,440	58,726	47,074	6,640	97,789	51,649	40,242	11,309	5,357	5,365	....	7,790	4,444	2,872
1988	114,968	59,781	48,383	6,805	99,812	52,466	41,316	11,658	5,509	5,548	....	8,250	4,680	3,047
1989	117,342	60,837	49,745	6,759	101,584	53,292	42,346	11,953	5,602	5,727	....	8,573	4,853	3,172
1990	118,793	61,678	50,535	6,581	102,261	53,685	42,796	12,175	5,692	5,884	....	9,845	5,609	3,567
1991	117,718	61,178	50,634	5,906	101,182	53,103	42,862	12,074	5,706	5,874	....	9,828	5,623	3,603
1992	118,492	61,496	51,328	5,669	101,669	53,357	43,327	12,151	5,681	5,978	....	10,027	5,757	3,693
1993	120,259	62,355	52,099	5,805	103,045	54,021	43,910	12,382	5,793	6,095	....	10,361	5,992	3,800
1994	123,060	63,294	53,606	6,161	105,190	54,676	45,116	12,835	5,964	6,320	....	10,788	6,189	3,989
1995	124,900	64,085	54,396	6,419	106,490	55,254	45,643	13,279	6,137	6,556	....	11,127	6,367	4,116
1996	126,708	64,897	55,311	6,500	107,808	55,977	46,164	13,542	6,167	6,762	....	11,642	6,655	4,341
1997	129,558	66,284	56,613	6,661	109,856	56,986	47,063	13,969	6,325	7,013	....	12,726	7,307	4,705
1998	131,463	67,135	57,278	7,051	110,931	57,500	47,342	14,556	6,530	7,290	....	13,291	7,570	4,928
1999	133,488	67,761	58,555	7,172	112,235	57,934	48,098	15,058	6,702	7,663	....	13,720	7,576	5,290
2000	136,891	69,634	60,067	7,189	114,424	59,119	49,145	15,156	6,741	7,703	6,043	15,735	8,859	5,903
2001	136,933	69,776	60,417	6,740	114,430	59,245	49,369	15,006	6,627	7,741	6,180	16,190	9,100	6,121
2002	136,485	69,734	60,420	6,332	114,013	59,124	49,448	14,872	6,657	7,610	6,215	16,590	9,341	6,367
2003	137,736	70,415	61,402	5,919	114,235	59,348	49,823	14,739	6,586	7,638	6,756	17,372	10,063	6,541
2004	139,252	71,572	61,773	5,907	115,239	60,159	50,040	14,909	6,681	7,707	5,994	17,930	10,395	6,752
2005	141,730	73,050	62,702	5,978	116,949	61,255	50,589	15,313	6,901	7,876	6,244	18,632	10,872	6,913
2006	144,427	74,431	63,834	6,162	118,833	62,259	51,359	15,765	7,079	8,068	6,522	19,613	11,391	7,321
2007	146,047	75,337	64,799	5,911	119,792	62,806	51,996	16,051	7,245	8,240	6,839	20,382	11,827	7,662
2008	145,362	74,750	65,039	5,573	119,126	62,304	52,124	15,953	7,151	8,260	6,917	20,346	11,769	7,707
2009	139,877	71,341	63,699	4,837	114,996	59,626	51,231	15,025	6,628	7,956	6,635	19,647	11,256	7,649
2010	139,064	71,230	63,456	4,378	114,168	59,438	50,997	15,010	6,680	7,944	6,705	19,906	11,438	7,788
2011	139,869	72,182	63,360	4,327	114,690	60,118	50,881	15,051	6,765	7,906	6,867	20,269	11,685	7,918
2012	142,469	73,403	64,640	4,426	114,769	60,193	50,911	15,856	7,104	8,313	7,705	21,878	12,212	8,858
2013	143,929	74,176	65,295	4,458	115,379	60,511	51,198	16,151	7,304	8,408	8,136	22,514	12,638	9,056
2014	146,305	75,471	66,287	4,548	116,788	61,289	51,798	16,732	7,613	8,663	8,325	23,492	13,202	9,431
2015	148,834	76,776	67,323	4,734	117,944	61,959	52,161	17,472	7,938	9,032	8,706	24,400	13,624	9,853
2016	151,436	78,084	68,387	4,965	119,313	62,575	52,771	17,982	8,228	9,219	9,213	25,249	14,055	10,217
2017	153,337	78,919	69,344	5,074	120,176	63,009	53,179	18,587	8,500	9,514	9,448	25,938	14,355	10,543
2018	155,761	80,211	70,424	5,126	121,461	63,719	53,682	19,091	8,745	9,751	9,832	27,012	14,873	11,045
2017: Jan	152,128	78,440	68,633	5,055	119,328	62,673	52,708	18,446	8,430	9,455	9,289	25,450	14,179	10,341
Feb	152,417	78,439	68,971	5,007	119,595	62,749	52,952	18,392	8,370	9,450	9,382	25,722	14,239	10,485
Mar	152,958	78,472	69,343	5,143	120,110	62,753	53,269	18,399	8,384	9,487	9,312	25,983	14,286	10,612
Apr	153,150	78,807	69,239	5,104	120,115	63,007	53,076	18,530	8,499	9,479	9,443	25,799	14,275	10,479
May	152,920	78,748	69,134	5,037	119,876	62,938	52,959	18,548	8,463	9,499	9,473	25,824	14,298	10,453
June	153,176	78,755	69,250	5,171	120,130	62,901	53,122	18,549	8,500	9,436	9,438	25,941	14,393	10,444
July	153,456	78,863	69,529	5,065	120,234	62,948	53,353	18,618	8,516	9,504	9,420	26,048	14,404	10,582
Aug	153,591	78,972	69,508	5,111	120,356	63,069	53,299	18,551	8,479	9,482	9,482	25,963	14,318	10,596
Sept	154,399	79,453	69,694	5,252	120,870	63,235	53,574	18,818	8,666	9,537	9,630	26,239	14,525	10,641
Oct	153,847	79,278	69,545	5,025	120,426	63,213	53,257	18,641	8,536	9,547	9,564	26,027	14,412	10,602
Nov	153,945	79,344	69,670	4,931	120,522	63,289	53,333	18,714	8,554	9,616	9,394	26,115	14,415	10,687
Dec	154,065	79,493	69,587	4,985	120,585	63,370	53,231	18,827	8,598	9,672	9,547	26,140	14,522	10,584
2018: Jan	154,482	79,719	69,620	5,143	120,899	63,502	53,272	18,696	8,572	9,549	9,587	26,434	14,660	10,736
Feb	155,213	80,186	69,849	5,178	121,241	63,651	53,456	19,118	8,889	9,642	9,630	26,656	14,724	10,821
Mar	155,160	80,091	69,946	5,123	121,180	63,698	53,381	19,063	8,752	9,718	9,786	26,528	14,694	10,695
Apr	155,216	80,108	70,033	5,074	121,228	63,724	53,451	18,911	8,674	9,716	9,760	26,865	14,891	10,869
May	155,539	80,299	70,161	5,079	121,298	63,738	53,496	19,096	8,790	9,755	9,727	26,834	14,843	10,930
June	155,592	80,006	70,455	5,131	121,357	63,680	53,635	19,057	8,580	9,834	9,825	27,077	14,952	11,072
July	155,964	80,217	70,622	5,125	121,507	63,681	53,764	19,151	8,756	9,793	9,842	27,223	15,006	11,137
Aug	155,604	80,149	70,563	4,892	121,074	63,513	53,616	19,108	8,828	9,769	9,951	26,935	14,852	11,025
Sept	156,069	80,251	70,710	5,108	121,507	63,664	53,792	19,265	8,800	9,874	9,943	27,102	14,832	11,188
Oct	156,582	80,388	70,935	5,258	121,923	63,785	54,062	19,290	8,814	9,825	9,956	27,266	14,854	11,266
Nov	156,803	80,633	70,949	5,221	122,036	63,960	54,023	19,232	8,771	9,789	10,050	27,524	15,063	11,308
Dec	156,945	80,501	71,218	5,226	122,318	64,046	54,226	19,107	8,709	9,749	9,929	27,701	15,107	11,487

[1] Beginning in 2003, persons who selected this race group only. Persons whose ethnicity is identified as Hispanic or Latino may be of any race. Prior to 2003, persons who selected more than one race were included in the group they identified as the main race. Data for "black or African American" were for "black" prior to 2003. See *Employment and Earnings* or concepts and methodology of the Current Population Survey (CPS) at http://www.bls.gov/cps/documentation.htm#concepts for details.

Note: Detail will not sum to total because data for all race groups are not shown here.
See footnote 5 and Note, Table B–22.

Source: Department of Labor (Bureau of Labor Statistics).

Year or month	All civilian workers	By sex and age Men 20 years and over	Women 20 years and over	Both sexes 16–19	White Total	Men 20 years and over	Women 20 years and over	Black or African American Total	Men 20 years and over	Women 20 years and over	Asian Total	Hispanic or Latino ethnicity[1] Total	Men 20 years and over	Women 20 years and over
1975	7,929	3,476	2,684	1,767	6,421	2,841	2,166	1,369	571	469	....	508	225	160
1976	7,406	3,098	2,588	1,719	5,914	2,504	2,045	1,334	528	477	....	485	217	166
1977	6,991	2,794	2,535	1,663	5,441	2,211	1,946	1,393	512	528	....	456	195	153
1978	6,202	2,328	2,292	1,583	4,698	1,797	1,713	1,330	462	510	....	452	175	168
1979	6,137	2,308	2,276	1,555	4,664	1,773	1,699	1,319	473	513	....	434	168	160
1980	7,637	3,353	2,615	1,669	5,884	2,629	1,964	1,553	636	574	....	620	284	190
1981	8,273	3,615	2,895	1,763	6,343	2,825	2,143	1,731	703	671	....	678	321	212
1982	10,678	5,089	3,613	1,977	8,241	3,991	2,715	2,142	954	793	....	929	461	293
1983	10,717	5,257	3,632	1,829	8,128	4,098	2,643	2,272	1,002	878	....	961	491	302
1984	8,539	3,932	3,107	1,499	6,372	2,992	2,264	1,914	815	747	....	800	393	258
1985	8,312	3,715	3,129	1,468	6,191	2,834	2,283	1,864	757	750	....	811	401	269
1986	8,237	3,751	3,032	1,454	6,140	2,857	2,213	1,840	765	728	....	857	438	278
1987	7,425	3,369	2,709	1,347	5,501	2,584	1,922	1,684	666	706	....	751	374	241
1988	6,701	2,987	2,487	1,226	4,944	2,268	1,766	1,547	617	642	....	732	351	234
1989	6,528	2,867	2,467	1,194	4,770	2,149	1,758	1,544	619	625	....	750	342	276
1990	7,047	3,239	2,596	1,212	5,186	2,431	1,852	1,565	664	633	....	876	425	289
1991	8,628	4,195	3,074	1,359	6,560	3,284	2,248	1,723	745	698	....	1,092	575	339
1992	9,613	4,717	3,469	1,427	7,169	3,620	2,512	2,011	886	800	....	1,311	675	418
1993	8,940	4,287	3,288	1,365	6,655	3,263	2,400	1,844	801	729	....	1,248	629	418
1994	7,996	3,627	3,049	1,320	5,892	2,735	2,197	1,666	682	685	....	1,187	558	431
1995	7,404	3,239	2,819	1,346	5,459	2,465	2,042	1,538	593	620	....	1,140	530	404
1996	7,236	3,146	2,783	1,306	5,300	2,363	1,998	1,592	639	643	....	1,132	495	438
1997	6,739	2,882	2,585	1,271	4,836	2,140	1,784	1,560	585	673	....	1,069	471	401
1998	6,210	2,580	2,424	1,205	4,484	1,920	1,688	1,426	524	622	....	1,026	436	376
1999	5,880	2,433	2,285	1,162	4,273	1,813	1,616	1,309	480	561	....	945	374	376
2000	5,692	2,376	2,235	1,081	4,121	1,731	1,595	1,241	499	512	227	954	388	371
2001	6,801	3,040	2,599	1,162	4,969	2,275	1,849	1,416	573	582	288	1,138	495	436
2002	8,378	3,896	3,228	1,253	6,137	2,943	2,269	1,693	695	738	389	1,353	636	496
2003	8,774	4,209	3,314	1,251	6,311	3,125	2,276	1,787	760	772	366	1,441	693	555
2004	8,149	3,791	3,150	1,208	5,847	2,785	2,172	1,729	733	755	277	1,342	635	504
2005	7,591	3,392	3,013	1,186	5,350	2,450	2,054	1,700	699	734	259	1,191	536	464
2006	7,001	3,131	2,751	1,119	5,002	2,281	1,927	1,549	640	656	205	1,081	497	414
2007	7,078	3,259	2,718	1,101	5,143	2,408	1,930	1,445	622	588	229	1,220	576	446
2008	8,924	4,297	3,342	1,285	6,509	3,179	2,384	1,788	811	732	285	1,678	860	567
2009	14,265	7,555	5,157	1,552	10,648	5,746	3,745	2,606	1,286	1,032	522	2,706	1,474	911
2010	14,825	7,763	5,534	1,528	10,916	5,828	3,960	2,852	1,396	1,165	543	2,843	1,519	1,001
2011	13,747	6,898	5,450	1,400	9,889	5,046	3,818	2,831	1,360	1,204	518	2,629	1,345	984
2012	12,506	5,984	5,125	1,397	8,915	4,347	3,564	2,544	1,152	1,119	483	2,514	1,195	995
2013	11,460	5,568	4,565	1,327	8,033	3,994	3,102	2,429	1,082	1,069	448	2,257	1,090	855
2014	9,617	4,585	3,926	1,106	6,540	3,141	2,623	2,141	973	943	436	1,878	864	764
2015	8,296	3,959	3,371	966	5,662	2,751	2,249	1,846	835	811	347	1,726	820	686
2016	7,751	3,675	3,151	925	5,345	2,594	2,100	1,655	737	724	349	1,548	720	627
2017	6,982	3,287	2,868	827	4,765	2,288	1,923	1,501	663	657	333	1,401	632	585
2018	6,314	2,976	2,578	759	4,354	2,094	1,743	1,322	582	573	304	1,323	591	547
2017: Jan	7,565	3,565	3,128	872	5,298	2,552	2,158	1,530	669	661	361	1,579	706	692
Feb	7,437	3,516	3,060	861	5,021	2,431	2,017	1,602	718	702	338	1,504	676	620
Mar	7,078	3,435	2,829	814	4,864	2,356	1,949	1,579	769	642	316	1,375	643	528
Apr	7,019	3,176	2,956	887	4,794	2,218	1,965	1,599	665	725	312	1,389	617	594
May	6,991	3,213	2,952	825	4,683	2,260	1,927	1,541	613	722	362	1,397	629	598
June	6,948	3,258	2,888	803	4,698	2,304	1,887	1,413	564	690	347	1,329	569	578
July	6,927	3,264	2,888	775	4,610	2,246	1,896	1,484	651	649	371	1,429	680	595
Aug	7,115	3,417	2,872	826	4,796	2,310	1,950	1,529	719	631	393	1,409	716	519
Sept	6,791	3,186	2,818	787	4,675	2,218	1,917	1,432	630	623	357	1,404	607	615
Oct	6,588	3,123	2,658	806	4,408	2,122	1,728	1,469	665	651	297	1,329	577	548
Nov	6,682	3,103	2,657	922	4,618	2,155	1,790	1,480	677	613	292	1,310	580	545
Dec	6,572	3,101	2,686	785	4,642	2,190	1,900	1,354	595	590	241	1,359	581	591
2018: Jan	6,641	3,196	2,618	827	4,419	2,201	1,638	1,554	697	674	301	1,397	667	521
Feb	6,687	3,072	2,746	870	4,621	2,236	1,798	1,399	559	621	294	1,366	591	595
Mar	6,486	3,059	2,634	793	4,461	2,179	1,791	1,389	565	600	311	1,412	674	553
Apr	6,335	3,055	2,525	755	4,447	2,195	1,742	1,321	593	528	279	1,354	626	541
May	6,128	2,958	2,429	741	4,392	2,106	1,756	1,198	590	481	214	1,373	596	589
June	6,537	3,097	2,701	740	4,408	2,142	1,804	1,314	587	571	322	1,292	595	560
July	6,245	2,801	2,673	771	4,209	1,933	1,774	1,345	569	631	314	1,279	508	552
Aug	6,197	2,895	2,590	712	4,272	2,014	1,757	1,276	565	587	309	1,317	574	582
Sept	5,986	2,853	2,398	735	4,110	1,996	1,586	1,239	549	548	360	1,287	592	501
Oct	6,112	2,889	2,507	715	4,177	1,986	1,716	1,274	586	501	324	1,248	594	501
Nov	6,018	2,775	2,529	714	4,299	2,000	1,796	1,219	539	515	284	1,296	533	550
Dec	6,294	2,999	2,550	745	4,362	2,064	1,769	1,353	575	611	334	1,261	544	515

[1] See footnote 1 and Note, Table B–23.

Note: See footnote 5 and Note, Table B–22.

Source: Department of Labor (Bureau of Labor Statistics).

TABLE B–25. Civilian labor force participation rate, 1975–2018
[Percent [1]; monthly data seasonally adjusted]

Year or month	All civilian workers	Men 20 years and over	Men 20–24 years	Men 25–54 years	Men 55 years and over	Women 20 years and over	Women 20–24 years	Women 25–54 years	Women 55 years and over	Both sexes 16–19 years	White	Black or African American	Asian	Hispanic or Latino ethnicity
1975	61.2	80.3	84.5	94.4	49.4	46.0	64.1	55.1	23.1	54.0	61.5	58.8	....	60.8
1976	61.6	79.8	85.2	94.2	47.8	47.0	65.0	56.8	23.0	54.5	61.8	59.0	....	60.8
1977	62.3	79.7	85.6	94.2	47.4	48.1	66.5	58.5	22.9	56.0	62.5	59.8	....	61.6
1978	63.2	79.8	85.9	94.3	47.2	49.6	68.3	60.6	23.1	57.8	63.3	61.5	....	62.9
1979	63.7	79.8	86.4	94.4	46.6	50.6	69.0	62.3	23.2	57.9	63.9	61.4	....	63.6
1980	63.8	79.4	85.9	94.2	45.6	51.3	68.9	64.0	22.8	56.7	64.1	61.0	....	64.0
1981	63.9	79.0	85.5	94.1	44.5	52.1	69.6	65.3	22.7	55.4	64.3	60.8	....	64.1
1982	64.0	78.7	84.9	94.0	43.8	52.7	69.8	66.3	22.7	54.1	64.3	61.0	....	63.6
1983	64.0	78.5	84.8	93.8	43.0	53.1	69.9	67.1	22.4	53.5	64.3	61.5	....	63.8
1984	64.4	78.3	85.0	93.9	41.8	53.7	70.4	68.2	22.2	53.9	64.6	62.2	....	64.9
1985	64.8	78.1	85.0	93.9	41.0	54.7	71.8	69.6	22.0	54.5	65.0	62.9	....	64.6
1986	65.3	78.1	85.8	93.8	40.4	55.5	72.4	70.8	22.1	54.7	65.5	63.3	....	65.4
1987	65.6	78.0	85.2	93.7	40.4	56.2	73.0	71.9	22.0	54.7	65.8	63.8	....	66.4
1988	65.9	77.9	85.0	93.6	39.9	56.8	72.7	72.7	22.3	55.3	66.2	63.8	....	67.4
1989	66.5	78.1	85.3	93.7	39.6	57.7	72.4	73.6	23.0	55.9	66.7	64.2	....	67.6
1990	66.5	78.2	84.4	93.4	39.4	58.0	71.3	74.0	22.9	53.7	66.9	64.0	....	67.4
1991	66.2	77.7	83.5	93.1	38.5	57.9	70.1	74.1	22.6	51.6	66.6	63.3	....	66.5
1992	66.4	77.7	83.3	93.0	38.4	58.5	70.9	74.6	22.8	51.3	66.8	63.9	....	66.8
1993	66.3	77.3	83.2	92.6	37.7	58.5	70.9	74.6	22.8	51.5	66.8	63.2	....	66.2
1994	66.6	76.8	83.1	91.7	37.8	59.3	71.0	75.3	24.0	52.7	67.1	63.4	....	66.1
1995	66.6	76.7	83.1	91.6	37.9	59.4	70.3	75.6	23.9	53.5	67.1	63.7	....	65.8
1996	66.8	76.8	82.5	91.8	38.3	59.9	71.3	76.1	23.9	52.3	67.2	64.1	....	66.5
1997	67.1	77.0	82.5	91.8	38.9	60.5	72.7	76.7	24.6	51.6	67.5	64.7	....	67.9
1998	67.1	76.8	82.0	91.8	39.1	60.4	73.0	76.5	25.0	52.8	67.3	65.6	....	67.9
1999	67.1	76.7	81.9	91.7	39.6	60.7	73.2	76.8	25.6	52.0	67.3	65.8	....	67.7
2000	67.1	76.7	82.6	91.6	40.1	60.6	73.1	76.7	26.1	52.0	67.3	65.8	67.2	69.7
2001	66.8	76.5	81.6	91.3	40.9	60.6	72.7	76.4	27.0	49.6	67.0	65.3	67.2	69.5
2002	66.6	76.3	80.7	91.0	42.0	60.5	72.1	75.9	28.5	47.4	66.8	64.8	67.2	69.1
2003	66.2	75.9	80.0	90.6	42.6	60.6	70.8	75.6	30.0	44.5	66.5	64.3	66.4	68.3
2004	66.0	75.8	79.6	90.5	43.2	60.3	70.5	75.3	30.5	43.9	66.3	63.8	65.9	68.6
2005	66.0	75.8	79.1	90.5	44.2	60.4	70.1	75.3	31.4	43.7	66.3	64.2	66.1	68.0
2006	66.2	75.9	79.6	90.6	44.9	60.5	69.5	75.5	32.3	43.7	66.5	64.1	66.2	68.7
2007	66.0	75.9	78.7	90.9	45.2	60.6	70.1	75.4	33.2	41.3	66.4	63.7	66.5	68.8
2008	66.0	75.7	78.7	90.5	46.0	60.9	70.0	75.8	33.9	40.2	66.3	63.7	67.0	68.5
2009	65.4	74.8	76.2	89.7	46.3	60.8	69.6	75.6	34.7	37.5	65.8	62.4	66.0	68.0
2010	64.7	74.1	74.5	89.3	46.4	60.3	68.3	75.2	35.1	34.9	65.1	62.2	64.7	67.5
2011	64.1	73.4	74.7	88.7	46.3	59.8	67.8	74.7	35.1	34.1	64.5	61.4	64.6	66.5
2012	63.7	73.0	74.5	88.7	46.8	59.3	67.4	74.5	35.1	34.3	64.0	61.5	63.9	66.4
2013	63.2	72.5	73.9	88.4	46.5	58.8	67.5	73.9	35.1	34.5	63.5	61.2	64.6	66.0
2014	62.9	71.9	73.9	88.2	45.9	58.5	67.7	73.9	34.9	34.0	63.1	61.2	63.6	66.1
2015	62.7	71.7	73.0	88.3	45.9	58.2	68.3	73.7	34.7	34.3	62.8	61.5	62.8	65.9
2016	62.8	71.7	73.0	88.5	46.2	58.3	68.0	74.3	34.7	35.2	62.9	61.6	63.2	65.8
2017	62.9	71.6	74.1	88.6	46.1	58.5	68.5	75.0	34.7	35.2	62.8	62.3	63.6	66.1
2018	62.9	71.6	73.2	89.0	46.2	58.5	69.0	75.3	34.7	35.1	62.8	62.3	63.5	66.3
2017: Jan	62.9	71.7	74.2	88.8	45.9	58.3	67.9	74.5	34.9	35.4	62.8	62.3	63.7	66.0
Feb	62.9	71.7	73.8	88.6	46.0	58.5	69.5	74.8	34.7	35.1	62.8	62.3	63.8	66.4
Mar	62.9	71.6	73.5	88.5	46.2	58.6	69.3	74.9	34.9	35.6	62.9	62.2	63.0	66.6
Apr	62.9	71.6	74.0	88.5	46.1	58.6	69.0	75.1	34.6	35.8	62.9	62.6	63.4	66.1
May	62.8	71.5	74.2	88.4	45.9	58.4	67.6	74.9	34.8	35.0	62.7	62.4	63.7	66.0
June	62.8	71.5	73.6	88.5	46.0	58.4	67.4	75.0	34.8	35.7	62.8	61.9	63.7	66.0
July	62.9	71.5	74.5	88.6	45.9	58.6	68.6	75.1	34.9	34.8	62.7	62.3	64.0	66.4
Aug	62.9	71.7	74.6	88.5	46.2	58.5	69.1	75.0	34.8	35.4	62.9	62.2	64.4	66.0
Sept	63.1	71.8	74.9	88.6	46.4	58.6	69.2	75.2	34.8	36.0	63.0	62.6	64.5	66.5
Oct	62.7	71.6	74.3	88.6	46.1	58.3	69.3	74.9	34.5	34.8	62.6	62.1	63.8	65.7
Nov	62.8	71.6	74.1	88.6	46.2	58.3	67.8	75.2	34.5	34.9	62.8	62.3	63.0	65.7
Dec	62.7	71.6	73.3	89.0	45.9	58.3	67.6	75.0	34.6	34.4	62.8	62.2	62.7	65.7
2018: Jan	62.7	71.7	74.7	89.0	45.8	58.1	68.8	74.9	34.1	35.6	62.7	62.2	62.9	65.9
Feb	63.0	71.9	74.8	89.3	46.1	58.4	68.4	75.2	34.5	36.0	63.0	62.9	62.8	66.2
Mar	62.9	71.8	75.5	89.2	45.9	58.3	68.9	75.1	34.6	35.3	62.9	62.7	63.2	65.9
Apr	62.8	71.7	73.9	89.2	46.0	58.2	68.7	74.9	34.7	34.8	62.9	61.9	63.0	66.4
May	62.8	71.8	73.4	89.0	46.4	58.2	69.0	74.8	34.7	34.7	62.8	62.1	62.6	66.2
June	62.9	71.6	73.4	88.9	46.1	58.6	69.2	75.4	34.9	35.0	62.8	62.2	63.7	66.5
July	62.9	71.4	72.4	88.8	46.3	58.7	70.3	75.5	34.7	35.2	62.8	62.5	63.8	66.6
Aug	62.7	71.4	71.1	88.8	46.3	58.5	68.7	75.4	34.9	33.4	62.6	62.1	63.8	65.9
Sept	62.7	71.4	72.8	88.7	46.1	58.4	69.1	75.2	35.0	34.9	62.7	62.4	64.3	66.1
Oct	62.9	71.5	72.1	89.0	46.1	58.7	68.6	75.8	34.9	35.6	62.9	62.5	64.1	66.2
Nov	62.9	71.5	72.1	89.0	46.3	58.6	68.8	75.6	35.0	35.4	63.0	62.1	64.2	66.8
Dec	63.1	71.5	72.1	89.0	46.4	58.8	69.2	75.9	35.1	35.6	63.1	62.1	63.6	67.0

[1] Civilian labor force as percent of civilian noninstitutional population in group specified.
[2] See footnote 1, Table B–23.

Note: Data relate to persons 16 years of age and over, except as noted.
See footnote 5 and Note, Table B–22.

Source: Department of Labor (Bureau of Labor Statistics).

TABLE B–26. Civilian employment/population ratio, 1975–2018

[Percent [1]; monthly data seasonally adjusted]

Year or month	All civilian workers	Men 20 years and over	Men 20–24 years	Men 25–54 years	Men 55 years and over	Women 20 years and over	Women 20–24 years	Women 25–54 years	Women 55 years and over	Both sexes 16–19 years	White	Black or African American	Asian	Hispanic or Latino ethnicity
1975	56.1	74.8	72.4	89.0	47.0	42.3	56.0	51.0	21.9	43.3	56.7	50.1		53.4
1976	56.8	75.1	74.9	89.5	45.7	43.5	57.3	52.9	21.9	44.2	57.5	50.8		53.8
1977	57.9	75.6	76.3	90.1	45.5	44.8	59.0	54.8	21.9	46.1	58.6	51.4		55.4
1978	59.3	76.4	78.0	91.0	45.7	46.6	61.4	57.3	22.3	48.3	60.0	53.6		57.2
1979	59.9	76.5	78.9	91.1	45.2	47.7	62.4	59.0	22.5	48.5	60.6	53.8		58.3
1980	59.2	74.6	75.1	89.4	44.1	48.1	61.8	60.1	22.1	46.6	60.0	52.3		57.6
1981	59.0	74.0	74.2	89.0	42.9	48.6	61.8	61.2	21.9	44.6	60.0	51.3		57.4
1982	57.8	71.8	71.0	86.5	41.6	48.4	60.6	61.2	21.6	41.5	58.8	49.4		54.9
1983	57.9	71.4	71.3	86.1	40.6	48.8	60.9	62.0	21.4	41.5	58.9	49.5		55.1
1984	59.5	73.2	74.9	88.4	39.8	50.1	62.7	63.9	21.3	43.7	60.5	52.3		57.9
1985	60.1	73.3	75.3	88.7	39.3	51.0	64.1	65.3	21.1	44.4	61.0	53.4		57.8
1986	60.7	73.3	76.3	88.5	38.8	52.0	64.9	66.6	21.3	44.6	61.5	54.1		58.5
1987	61.5	73.8	76.8	89.0	39.0	53.1	66.1	68.2	21.3	45.5	62.3	55.6		60.5
1988	62.3	74.2	77.5	89.5	38.6	54.0	66.6	69.3	21.7	46.8	63.1	56.3		61.9
1989	63.0	74.5	77.8	89.9	38.3	54.9	66.4	70.4	22.4	47.5	63.8	56.9		62.2
1990	62.8	74.3	76.7	89.1	38.0	55.2	65.2	70.6	22.2	45.3	63.7	56.7		61.9
1991	61.7	72.7	73.8	87.5	36.8	54.6	63.2	70.1	21.9	42.0	62.6	55.4		59.8
1992	61.5	72.1	73.1	86.8	36.4	54.8	63.6	70.1	21.8	41.0	62.4	54.9		59.1
1993	61.7	72.3	73.8	87.0	35.9	55.0	64.0	70.4	22.0	41.7	62.7	55.0		59.1
1994	62.5	72.6	74.6	87.2	36.2	56.2	64.5	71.5	23.1	43.4	63.5	56.1		59.5
1995	62.9	73.0	75.4	87.6	36.5	56.5	64.0	72.2	23.0	44.2	63.8	57.1		59.7
1996	63.2	73.2	74.7	87.9	37.0	57.0	64.9	72.8	23.1	43.5	64.1	57.4		60.6
1997	63.8	73.7	75.2	88.4	37.7	57.8	66.8	73.5	23.8	43.4	64.6	58.2		62.6
1998	64.1	73.9	75.4	88.8	38.0	58.0	67.3	73.6	24.4	45.1	64.7	59.7		63.1
1999	64.3	74.0	75.6	89.0	38.5	58.5	68.0	74.1	24.9	44.7	64.8	60.6		63.4
2000	64.4	74.2	76.6	89.0	39.1	58.4	67.9	74.2	25.5	45.2	64.9	60.9	64.8	65.7
2001	63.7	73.3	74.2	87.9	39.6	58.1	67.3	73.4	26.3	42.3	64.2	59.7	64.2	64.9
2002	62.7	72.3	72.5	86.6	40.3	57.5	65.6	72.3	27.5	39.6	63.4	58.1	63.2	63.9
2003	62.3	71.7	71.5	85.9	40.7	57.5	64.2	72.0	28.9	36.8	63.0	57.4	62.4	63.1
2004	62.3	71.9	71.6	86.3	41.5	57.4	64.3	71.8	29.4	36.4	63.1	57.2	63.0	63.8
2005	62.7	72.4	71.5	86.9	42.7	57.6	64.5	72.0	30.4	36.5	63.4	57.7	63.4	64.0
2006	63.1	72.9	72.7	87.3	43.5	58.0	64.2	72.5	31.4	36.9	63.8	58.4	64.3	65.2
2007	63.0	72.8	71.7	87.5	43.7	58.2	65.0	72.5	32.2	34.8	63.6	58.4	64.3	64.9
2008	62.2	71.6	69.7	86.0	44.2	57.9	63.8	72.3	32.7	32.6	62.8	57.3	64.3	63.3
2009	59.3	67.6	63.3	81.5	43.0	56.2	61.1	70.2	32.6	28.4	60.2	53.2	61.2	59.7
2010	58.5	66.8	61.3	81.0	42.8	55.5	59.4	69.3	32.9	25.9	59.4	52.3	59.9	59.0
2011	58.4	67.0	63.0	81.4	43.1	55.0	58.7	69.0	32.9	25.8	59.4	51.7	60.0	58.9
2012	58.6	67.5	63.8	82.5	43.8	55.0	59.2	69.2	33.1	26.1	59.4	53.0	60.1	59.5
2013	58.6	67.4	63.5	82.8	43.8	54.9	59.8	69.3	33.3	26.6	59.4	53.2	61.2	60.0
2014	59.0	67.8	64.9	83.6	43.9	55.2	60.9	70.0	33.4	27.3	59.7	54.3	60.4	61.2
2015	59.3	68.1	65.1	84.4	44.1	55.4	62.5	70.3	33.5	28.5	59.9	55.7	60.4	61.6
2016	59.7	68.5	66.2	85.0	44.4	55.7	63.0	71.1	33.5	29.7	60.2	56.4	60.9	62.0
2017	60.1	68.8	67.9	85.4	44.6	56.1	64.2	72.1	33.6	30.3	60.4	57.6	61.5	62.7
2018	60.4	69.0	66.6	86.2	44.7	56.4	64.7	72.8	33.7	30.6	60.7	58.3	61.6	63.2
2017: Jan	59.9	68.6	67.5	85.3	44.4	55.8	63.2	71.4	33.6	30.2	60.1	57.5	61.3	62.2
Feb	59.9	68.6	66.9	85.1	44.5	56.0	65.0	71.7	33.5	29.9	60.2	57.3	61.6	62.7
Mar	60.1	68.6	67.2	85.1	44.6	56.3	65.0	72.0	33.8	30.7	60.5	57.3	60.9	63.2
Apr	60.2	68.8	67.8	85.4	44.7	56.2	64.7	72.0	33.5	30.5	60.5	57.6	61.4	62.7
May	60.0	68.7	68.3	85.2	44.5	56.0	64.0	71.8	33.6	30.1	60.3	57.6	61.4	62.6
June	60.1	68.6	67.5	85.3	44.6	56.1	63.1	72.1	33.7	30.9	60.4	57.6	61.4	62.8
July	60.1	68.7	68.5	85.2	44.6	56.3	64.0	72.3	33.7	30.2	60.4	57.7	61.6	62.9
Aug	60.1	68.7	68.8	85.0	44.7	56.2	64.6	72.1	33.7	30.5	60.5	57.4	61.8	62.6
Sept	60.4	69.1	68.4	85.6	45.0	56.3	64.8	72.4	33.6	31.3	60.7	58.2	62.2	63.1
Oct	60.2	68.9	68.3	85.7	44.5	56.1	65.0	72.2	33.5	30.0	60.4	57.6	61.8	62.5
Nov	60.1	68.9	67.8	85.7	44.7	56.2	63.8	72.5	33.5	29.4	60.4	57.8	61.1	62.5
Dec	60.2	68.9	67.5	86.1	44.4	56.1	63.4	72.3	33.5	29.7	60.5	58.0	61.2	62.5
2018: Jan	60.2	68.9	68.7	86.0	44.3	56.0	64.3	72.2	33.3	30.6	60.5	57.4	60.9	62.6
Feb	60.4	69.3	69.2	86.4	44.5	56.1	64.3	72.4	33.5	30.9	60.7	58.6	61.0	63.0
Mar	60.4	69.1	69.9	86.2	44.4	56.2	64.9	72.4	33.5	30.5	60.6	58.4	61.2	62.5
Apr	60.3	69.1	68.2	86.2	44.6	56.2	64.8	72.3	33.7	30.3	60.6	57.9	61.3	63.2
May	60.4	69.2	67.6	86.3	45.0	56.3	64.7	72.4	33.7	30.3	60.6	58.4	61.3	63.0
June	60.4	68.9	67.4	86.1	44.6	56.5	64.6	72.8	33.8	30.6	60.6	58.2	61.7	63.4
July	60.5	69.0	67.1	86.2	44.9	56.6	65.9	72.9	33.7	30.6	60.7	58.4	61.8	63.7
Aug	60.3	68.9	65.7	86.0	44.9	56.5	64.6	72.9	33.8	29.2	60.4	58.2	61.8	62.8
Sept	60.4	68.9	67.4	85.9	44.8	56.5	64.8	72.9	34.0	30.5	60.6	58.6	62.1	63.1
Oct	60.6	69.0	66.7	86.2	44.9	56.7	64.4	73.4	33.8	31.4	60.8	58.7	62.1	63.3
Nov	60.6	69.1	66.8	86.4	44.9	56.6	64.8	73.1	34.0	31.1	60.8	58.4	62.4	63.8
Dec	60.6	69.0	66.4	86.1	45.0	56.8	64.7	73.4	34.1	31.2	60.9	58.0	61.5	64.1

[1] Civilian employment as percent of civilian noninstitutional population in group specified.
[2] See footnote 1, Table B–23.

Note: Data relate to persons 16 years of age and over, except as noted.
See footnote 5 and Note, Table B–22.

Source: Department of Labor (Bureau of Labor Statistics).

TABLE B–27. Civilian unemployment rate, 1975–2018

[Percent [1]; monthly data seasonally adjusted]

Year or month	All civilian workers	By sex and age			By race or ethnicity [2]				U-6 measure of labor under-utiliza-tion [3]	By educational attainment (25 years & over)			
		Men 20 years and over	Women 20 years and over	Both sexes 16–19	White	Black or African American	Asian	Hispanic or Latino ethnicity		Less than a high school diploma	High school graduates, no college	Some college or associate degree	Bachelor's degree and higher [4]
1975	8.5	6.8	8.0	19.9	7.8	14.8	....	12.2	....	....	....	....	....
1976	7.7	5.9	7.4	19.0	7.0	14.0	....	11.5	....	....	....	....	....
1977	7.1	5.2	7.0	17.8	6.2	14.0	....	10.1	....	....	....	....	....
1978	6.1	4.3	6.0	16.4	5.2	12.8	....	9.1	....	....	....	....	....
1979	5.8	4.2	5.7	16.1	5.1	12.3	....	8.3	....	....	....	....	....
1980	7.1	5.9	6.4	17.8	6.3	14.3	....	10.1	....	....	....	....	....
1981	7.6	6.3	6.8	19.6	6.7	15.6	....	10.4	....	....	....	....	....
1982	9.7	8.8	8.3	23.2	8.6	18.9	....	13.8	....	....	....	....	....
1983	9.6	8.9	8.1	22.4	8.4	19.5	....	13.7	....	....	....	....	....
1984	7.5	6.6	6.8	18.9	6.5	15.9	....	10.7	....	....	....	....	....
1985	7.2	6.2	6.6	18.6	6.2	15.1	....	10.5	....	....	....	....	....
1986	7.0	6.1	6.2	18.3	6.0	14.5	....	10.6	....	....	....	....	....
1987	6.2	5.4	5.4	16.9	5.3	13.0	....	8.8	....	....	....	....	....
1988	5.5	4.8	4.9	15.3	4.7	11.7	....	8.2	....	....	....	....	....
1989	5.3	4.5	4.7	15.0	4.5	11.4	....	8.0	....	....	....	....	....
1990	5.6	5.0	4.9	15.5	4.8	11.4	....	8.2	....	....	....	....	....
1991	6.8	6.4	5.7	18.7	6.1	12.5	....	10.0	....	....	....	....	....
1992	7.5	7.1	6.3	20.1	6.6	14.2	....	11.6	....	11.5	6.8	5.6	3.2
1993	6.9	6.4	5.9	19.0	6.1	13.0	....	10.8	....	10.8	6.3	5.2	2.9
1994	6.1	5.4	5.4	17.6	5.3	11.5	....	9.9	10.9	9.8	5.4	4.5	2.6
1995	5.6	4.8	4.9	17.3	4.9	10.4	....	9.3	10.1	9.0	4.8	4.0	2.4
1996	5.4	4.6	4.8	16.7	4.7	10.5	....	8.9	9.7	8.7	4.7	3.7	2.2
1997	4.9	4.2	4.4	16.0	4.2	10.0	....	7.7	8.9	8.1	4.3	3.3	2.0
1998	4.5	3.7	4.1	14.6	3.9	8.9	....	7.2	8.0	7.1	4.0	3.0	1.8
1999	4.2	3.5	3.8	13.9	3.7	8.0	....	6.4	7.4	6.7	3.5	2.8	1.8
2000	4.0	3.3	3.6	13.1	3.5	7.6	3.6	5.7	7.0	6.3	3.4	2.7	1.7
2001	4.7	4.2	4.1	14.7	4.2	8.6	4.5	6.6	8.1	7.2	4.2	3.3	2.3
2002	5.8	5.3	5.1	16.5	5.1	10.2	5.9	7.5	9.6	8.4	5.3	4.5	2.9
2003	6.0	5.6	5.1	17.5	5.2	10.8	6.0	7.7	10.1	8.8	5.5	4.8	3.1
2004	5.5	5.0	4.9	17.0	4.8	10.4	4.4	7.0	9.6	8.5	5.0	4.2	2.7
2005	5.1	4.4	4.6	16.6	4.4	10.0	4.0	6.0	8.9	7.6	4.7	3.9	2.3
2006	4.6	4.0	4.1	15.4	4.0	8.9	3.0	5.2	8.2	6.8	4.3	3.6	2.0
2007	4.6	4.1	4.0	15.7	4.1	8.3	3.2	5.6	8.3	7.1	4.4	3.6	2.0
2008	5.8	5.4	4.9	18.7	5.2	10.1	4.0	7.6	10.5	9.0	5.7	4.6	2.6
2009	9.3	9.6	7.5	24.3	8.5	14.8	7.3	12.1	16.2	14.6	9.7	8.0	4.6
2010	9.6	9.8	8.0	25.9	8.7	16.0	7.5	12.5	16.7	14.9	10.3	8.4	4.7
2011	8.9	8.7	7.9	24.4	7.9	15.8	7.0	11.5	15.9	14.1	9.4	8.0	4.3
2012	8.1	7.5	7.3	24.0	7.2	13.8	5.9	10.3	14.7	12.4	8.3	7.1	4.0
2013	7.4	7.0	6.5	22.9	6.5	13.1	5.2	9.1	13.8	11.0	7.5	6.4	3.7
2014	6.2	5.7	5.6	19.6	5.3	11.3	5.0	7.4	12.0	9.0	6.0	5.4	3.2
2015	5.3	4.9	4.8	16.9	4.6	9.6	3.8	6.6	10.4	8.0	5.4	4.5	2.6
2016	4.9	4.5	4.4	15.7	4.3	8.4	3.6	5.8	9.6	7.4	5.2	4.1	2.5
2017	4.4	4.0	4.0	14.0	3.8	7.5	3.4	5.1	8.5	6.5	4.6	3.8	2.3
2018	3.9	3.6	3.5	12.9	3.5	6.5	3.0	4.7	7.7	5.6	4.1	3.3	2.1
2017: Jan	4.7	4.3	4.4	14.7	4.3	7.7	3.7	5.8	9.3	7.4	5.2	3.8	2.5
Feb	4.7	4.3	4.2	14.7	4.0	8.0	3.5	5.5	9.1	7.6	4.9	4.0	2.4
Mar	4.4	4.2	3.9	13.7	3.9	7.9	3.3	5.0	8.7	6.6	4.9	3.7	2.4
Apr	4.4	3.9	4.1	14.8	3.8	7.9	3.2	5.1	8.6	6.4	4.6	3.7	2.4
May	4.4	3.9	4.1	14.1	3.8	7.7	3.7	5.1	8.5	6.3	4.7	4.0	2.3
June	4.3	4.0	4.0	13.4	3.8	7.1	3.6	4.9	8.5	6.5	4.6	3.8	2.3
July	4.3	4.0	4.0	13.3	3.7	7.4	3.8	5.2	8.5	7.0	4.5	3.8	2.3
Aug	4.4	4.1	4.0	13.9	3.8	7.6	4.0	5.1	8.6	6.1	5.0	3.7	2.4
Sept	4.2	3.9	3.9	13.0	3.7	7.1	3.6	5.1	8.3	6.7	4.4	3.6	2.3
Oct	4.1	3.8	3.7	13.8	3.5	7.3	3.0	4.9	8.0	6.0	4.3	3.7	2.1
Nov	4.2	3.8	3.7	15.8	3.7	7.3	3.0	4.8	8.0	5.2	4.4	3.6	2.1
Dec	4.1	3.8	3.7	13.6	3.7	6.7	2.5	4.9	8.1	6.3	4.2	3.6	2.1
2018: Jan	4.1	3.9	3.6	13.9	3.5	7.7	3.0	5.0	8.2	5.5	4.4	3.4	2.2
Feb	4.1	3.7	3.8	14.4	3.7	6.8	3.0	4.9	8.2	5.6	4.4	3.5	2.2
Mar	4.0	3.7	3.6	13.4	3.6	6.8	3.1	5.1	7.9	5.6	4.3	3.5	2.2
Apr	3.9	3.7	3.5	13.0	3.5	6.5	2.8	4.8	7.8	5.8	4.3	3.4	2.1
May	3.8	3.6	3.3	12.7	3.5	5.9	2.2	4.9	7.7	5.5	3.9	3.2	2.0
June	4.0	3.7	3.7	12.6	3.5	6.5	3.2	4.6	7.8	5.6	4.1	3.3	2.3
July	3.9	3.4	3.6	13.1	3.3	6.6	3.1	4.5	7.5	5.0	4.0	3.2	2.2
Aug	3.8	3.5	3.5	12.7	3.4	6.3	3.0	4.7	7.4	5.7	3.9	3.5	2.0
Sept	3.7	3.4	3.3	12.6	3.3	6.0	3.5	4.5	7.5	5.6	3.7	3.2	2.0
Oct	3.8	3.5	3.4	12.0	3.3	6.2	3.1	4.4	7.5	5.9	4.0	3.0	2.0
Nov	3.7	3.3	3.4	12.0	3.4	6.0	2.7	4.5	7.6	5.6	3.5	3.1	2.2
Dec	3.9	3.6	3.5	12.5	3.4	6.6	3.3	4.4	7.6	5.8	3.8	3.3	2.1

[1] Unemployed as percent of civilian labor force in group specified.
[2] See footnote 1, Table B–23.
[3] Total unemployed, plus all persons marginally attached to the labor force, plus total employed part time for economic reasons, as a percent of the civilian labor force plus all persons marginally attached to the labor force.
[4] Includes persons with bachelor's, master's, professional, and doctoral degrees.

Note: Data relate to persons 16 years of age and over, except as noted.
See Note, Table B–22.

Source: Department of Labor (Bureau of Labor Statistics).

TABLE B-28. Unemployment by duration and reason, 1975-2018

[Thousands of persons, except as noted; monthly data seasonally adjusted [1]]

Year or month	Un-employ-ment	Duration of unemployment						Reason for unemployment					
		Less than 5 weeks	5-14 weeks	15-26 weeks	27 weeks and over	Average (mean) duration (weeks)[2]	Median duration (weeks)	Job losers[3]			Job leavers	Re-entrants	New entrants
								Total	On layoff	Other			
1975	7,929	2,940	2,484	1,303	1,203	14.2	8.4	4,386	1,671	2,714	827	1,892	823
1976	7,406	2,844	2,196	1,018	1,348	15.8	8.2	3,679	1,050	2,628	903	1,928	895
1977	6,991	2,919	2,132	913	1,028	14.3	7.0	3,166	865	2,300	909	1,963	953
1978	6,202	2,865	1,923	766	648	11.9	5.9	2,585	712	1,873	874	1,857	885
1979	6,137	2,950	1,946	706	535	10.8	5.4	2,635	851	1,784	880	1,806	817
1980	7,637	3,295	2,470	1,052	820	11.9	6.5	3,947	1,488	2,459	891	1,927	872
1981	8,273	3,449	2,539	1,122	1,162	13.7	6.9	4,267	1,430	2,837	923	2,102	981
1982	10,678	3,883	3,311	1,708	1,776	15.6	8.7	6,268	2,127	4,141	840	2,384	1,185
1983	10,717	3,570	2,937	1,652	2,559	20.0	10.1	6,258	1,780	4,478	830	2,412	1,216
1984	8,539	3,350	2,451	1,104	1,634	18.2	7.9	4,421	1,171	3,250	823	2,184	1,110
1985	8,312	3,498	2,509	1,025	1,280	15.6	6.8	4,139	1,157	2,982	877	2,256	1,039
1986	8,237	3,448	2,557	1,045	1,187	15.0	6.9	4,033	1,090	2,943	1,015	2,160	1,029
1987	7,425	3,246	2,196	943	1,040	14.5	6.5	3,566	943	2,623	965	1,974	920
1988	6,701	3,084	2,007	801	809	13.5	5.9	3,092	851	2,241	983	1,809	816
1989	6,528	3,174	1,978	730	646	11.9	4.8	2,983	850	2,133	1,024	1,843	677
1990	7,047	3,265	2,257	822	703	12.0	5.3	3,387	1,028	2,359	1,041	1,930	688
1991	8,628	3,480	2,791	1,246	1,111	13.7	6.8	4,694	1,292	3,402	1,004	2,139	792
1992	9,613	3,376	2,830	1,453	1,954	17.7	8.7	5,389	1,260	4,129	1,002	2,285	937
1993	8,940	3,262	2,584	1,297	1,798	18.0	8.3	4,848	1,115	3,733	976	2,198	919
1994	7,996	2,728	2,408	1,237	1,623	18.8	9.2	3,815	977	2,838	791	2,786	604
1995	7,404	2,700	2,342	1,085	1,278	16.6	8.3	3,476	1,030	2,446	824	2,525	579
1996	7,236	2,633	2,287	1,053	1,262	16.7	8.3	3,370	1,021	2,349	774	2,512	580
1997	6,739	2,538	2,138	995	1,067	15.8	8.0	3,037	931	2,106	795	2,338	569
1998	6,210	2,622	1,950	763	875	14.5	6.7	2,822	866	1,957	734	2,132	520
1999	5,880	2,568	1,832	755	725	13.4	6.4	2,622	848	1,774	783	2,005	469
2000	5,692	2,558	1,815	669	649	12.6	5.9	2,517	852	1,664	780	1,961	434
2001	6,801	2,853	2,196	951	801	13.1	6.8	3,476	1,067	2,409	835	2,031	459
2002	8,378	2,893	2,580	1,369	1,535	16.6	9.1	4,607	1,124	3,483	866	2,368	536
2003	8,774	2,785	2,612	1,442	1,936	19.2	10.1	4,838	1,121	3,717	818	2,477	641
2004	8,149	2,696	2,382	1,293	1,779	19.6	9.8	4,197	998	3,199	858	2,408	686
2005	7,591	2,667	2,304	1,130	1,490	18.4	8.9	3,667	933	2,734	872	2,386	666
2006	7,001	2,614	2,121	1,031	1,235	16.8	8.3	3,321	921	2,400	827	2,237	616
2007	7,078	2,542	2,232	1,061	1,243	16.8	8.5	3,515	976	2,539	793	2,142	627
2008	8,924	2,932	2,804	1,427	1,761	17.9	9.4	4,789	1,176	3,614	896	2,472	766
2009	14,265	3,165	3,828	2,775	4,496	24.4	15.1	9,160	1,630	7,530	882	3,187	1,035
2010	14,825	2,771	3,267	2,371	6,415	33.0	21.4	9,250	1,431	7,819	889	3,466	1,220
2011	13,747	2,677	2,993	2,061	6,016	39.3	21.4	8,106	1,230	6,876	956	3,401	1,284
2012	12,506	2,644	2,866	1,859	5,136	39.4	19.3	6,877	1,183	5,694	967	3,345	1,316
2013	11,460	2,584	2,759	1,807	4,310	36.5	17.0	6,073	1,136	4,937	932	3,207	1,247
2014	9,617	2,471	2,432	1,497	3,218	33.7	14.0	4,878	1,007	3,871	824	2,829	1,086
2015	8,296	2,399	2,302	1,267	2,328	29.2	11.6	4,063	974	3,089	819	2,535	879
2016	7,751	2,362	2,226	1,158	2,005	27.5	10.6	3,740	966	2,774	858	2,330	823
2017	6,982	2,270	2,008	1,017	1,687	25.0	10.0	3,434	956	2,479	778	2,079	690
2018	6,314	2,170	1,876	917	1,350	22.7	9.3	2,990	852	2,138	794	1,928	602
2017: Jan	7,565	2,427	2,076	1,186	1,834	25.0	10.2	3,650	1,043	2,607	873	2,158	786
Feb	7,437	2,507	2,128	1,049	1,772	25.3	10.1	3,651	970	2,682	813	2,210	750
Mar	7,078	2,272	2,047	1,091	1,677	25.4	10.5	3,501	959	2,541	785	2,061	796
Apr	7,019	2,332	2,076	1,067	1,650	24.4	10.1	3,538	953	2,584	779	2,022	703
May	6,991	2,159	1,935	1,113	1,680	25.0	10.6	3,428	872	2,556	782	2,103	674
June	6,948	2,269	1,943	934	1,708	25.1	10.1	3,422	879	2,544	809	2,038	682
July	6,927	2,181	2,020	1,001	1,739	24.9	10.1	3,329	1,009	2,320	744	2,096	696
Aug	7,115	2,202	2,028	1,065	1,722	24.3	10.4	3,519	1,017	2,502	785	2,148	653
Sept	6,791	2,256	1,931	964	1,720	26.4	10.2	3,356	909	2,446	748	2,073	663
Oct	6,588	2,162	1,957	866	1,628	25.5	9.7	3,236	872	2,365	746	1,998	622
Nov	6,682	2,248	1,919	970	1,597	25.1	9.7	3,175	928	2,248	751	2,035	708
Dec	6,572	2,230	1,984	892	1,511	23.8	8.9	3,249	923	2,326	726	1,985	568
2018: Jan	6,641	2,271	1,927	959	1,428	23.9	9.4	3,243	908	2,335	724	1,959	638
Feb	6,687	2,458	1,900	933	1,403	22.9	9.3	3,227	871	2,356	784	1,954	703
Mar	6,486	2,266	1,976	900	1,337	24.2	9.2	3,107	865	2,242	860	1,966	615
Apr	6,335	2,121	1,975	1,018	1,311	23.0	9.8	2,965	865	2,100	812	2,001	615
May	6,128	2,019	1,906	967	1,197	21.3	9.3	2,882	829	2,054	844	1,868	569
June	6,537	2,218	1,865	862	1,467	21.2	9.0	3,055	901	2,154	801	2,078	579
July	6,245	2,092	1,818	959	1,418	23.1	9.6	2,996	879	2,117	835	1,804	592
Aug	6,197	2,199	1,722	927	1,320	22.6	9.2	2,868	855	2,013	866	1,864	586
Sept	5,986	2,065	1,751	861	1,379	24.1	9.3	2,796	812	1,984	739	1,889	588
Oct	6,112	2,062	1,845	859	1,370	22.4	9.4	2,858	793	2,066	731	1,914	605
Nov	6,018	2,128	1,842	865	1,259	21.7	9.0	2,842	804	2,038	697	1,880	577
Dec	6,294	2,126	2,027	897	1,306	21.8	9.1	2,903	762	2,141	839	1,958	588

[1] Because of independent seasonal adjustment of the various series, detail will not sum to totals.
[2] Beginning with 2011, includes unemployment durations of up to 5 years; prior data are for up to 2 years.
[3] Beginning with 1994, job losers and persons who completed temporary jobs.

Note: Data relate to persons 16 years of age and over.
See Note, Table B-22.

Source: Department of Labor (Bureau of Labor Statistics).

Table B–29. Employees on nonagricultural payrolls, by major industry, 1975–2018

[Thousands of jobs; monthly data seasonally adjusted]

Year or month	Total nonagricultural employment	Private industries									
		Total private	Goods-producing industries						Private service-providing industries		
			Total	Mining and logging	Construction	Manufacturing			Total	Trade, transportation, and utilities [1]	
						Total	Durable goods	Nondurable goods		Total	Retail trade
1975	77,069	62,250	21,318	802	3,608	16,909	10,266	6,643	40,932	15,583	8,604
1976	79,502	64,501	22,025	832	3,662	17,531	10,640	6,891	42,476	16,105	8,970
1977	82,593	67,334	22,972	865	3,940	18,167	11,132	7,035	44,362	16,741	9,363
1978	86,826	71,014	24,156	902	4,322	18,932	11,770	7,162	46,858	17,633	9,882
1979	89,933	73,865	24,997	1,008	4,562	19,426	12,220	7,206	48,869	18,276	10,185
1980	90,533	74,158	24,263	1,077	4,454	18,733	11,679	7,054	49,895	18,387	10,249
1981	91,297	75,117	24,118	1,180	4,304	18,634	11,611	7,023	50,999	18,577	10,369
1982	89,689	73,706	22,550	1,163	4,024	17,363	10,610	6,753	51,156	18,430	10,377
1983	90,295	74,284	22,110	997	4,065	17,048	10,326	6,722	52,174	18,642	10,640
1984	94,548	78,389	23,435	1,014	4,501	17,920	11,050	6,870	54,954	19,624	11,227
1985	97,532	81,000	23,585	974	4,793	17,819	11,034	6,784	57,415	20,350	11,738
1986	99,500	82,661	23,318	829	4,937	17,552	10,795	6,757	59,343	20,765	12,082
1987	102,116	84,960	23,470	771	5,090	17,609	10,767	6,842	61,490	21,271	12,422
1988	105,378	87,838	23,909	770	5,233	17,906	10,969	6,938	63,929	21,942	12,812
1989	108,051	90,124	24,045	750	5,309	17,985	11,004	6,981	66,079	22,477	13,112
1990	109,527	91,112	23,723	765	5,263	17,695	10,737	6,958	67,389	22,634	13,186
1991	108,427	89,881	22,588	739	4,780	17,068	10,220	6,848	67,293	22,249	12,900
1992	108,802	90,015	22,095	689	4,608	16,799	9,946	6,853	67,921	22,094	12,831
1993	110,935	91,946	22,219	666	4,779	16,774	9,901	6,872	69,727	22,347	13,024
1994	114,399	95,124	22,774	659	5,095	17,020	10,132	6,889	72,350	23,096	13,494
1995	117,407	97,975	23,156	641	5,274	17,241	10,373	6,868	74,819	23,800	13,900
1996	119,836	100,297	23,409	637	5,536	17,237	10,486	6,751	76,888	24,205	14,146
1997	122,951	103,287	23,886	654	5,813	17,419	10,705	6,714	79,401	24,665	14,393
1998	126,157	106,248	24,354	645	6,149	17,560	10,911	6,649	81,894	25,150	14,613
1999	129,240	108,933	24,465	598	6,545	17,322	10,831	6,491	84,468	25,734	14,974
2000	132,024	111,235	24,649	599	6,787	17,263	10,877	6,386	86,585	26,187	15,284
2001	132,087	110,969	23,873	606	6,826	16,441	10,336	6,105	87,096	25,945	15,242
2002	130,649	109,136	22,557	583	6,716	15,259	9,485	5,774	86,579	25,458	15,029
2003	130,347	108,764	21,816	572	6,735	14,509	8,964	5,546	86,948	25,245	14,922
2004	131,787	110,166	21,882	591	6,976	14,315	8,925	5,390	88,284	25,487	15,063
2005	134,051	112,247	22,190	628	7,336	14,227	8,956	5,271	90,057	25,910	15,285
2006	136,453	114,479	22,530	684	7,691	14,155	8,981	5,174	91,949	26,223	15,359
2007	137,999	115,781	22,233	724	7,630	13,879	8,808	5,071	93,548	26,573	15,526
2008	137,241	114,732	21,335	767	7,162	13,406	8,463	4,943	93,398	26,236	15,289
2009	131,313	108,758	18,558	694	6,016	11,847	7,284	4,564	90,201	24,850	14,528
2010	130,362	107,871	17,751	705	5,518	11,528	7,064	4,464	90,121	24,581	14,446
2011	131,932	109,845	18,047	788	5,533	11,726	7,273	4,453	91,798	25,008	14,674
2012	134,175	112,255	18,420	848	5,646	11,927	7,470	4,457	93,835	25,416	14,847
2013	136,381	114,529	18,738	863	5,856	12,020	7,548	4,472	95,791	25,801	15,085
2014	138,958	117,076	19,226	891	6,151	12,185	7,674	4,512	97,850	26,321	15,363
2015	141,843	119,814	19,610	813	6,461	12,336	7,765	4,571	100,204	26,824	15,611
2016	144,352	122,128	19,750	668	6,728	12,354	7,714	4,640	102,379	27,195	15,832
2017	146,624	124,275	20,084	676	6,969	12,439	7,741	4,699	104,191	27,409	15,846
2018 p	149,073	126,622	20,709	732	7,289	12,688	7,945	4,743	105,913	27,659	15,832
2017: Jan	145,695	123,385	19,874	649	6,857	12,368	7,701	4,667	103,511	27,404	15,941
Feb	145,836	123,516	19,931	655	6,890	12,386	7,701	4,685	103,585	27,371	15,888
Mar	145,963	123,634	19,959	660	6,904	12,395	7,704	4,691	103,675	27,353	15,862
Apr	146,176	123,844	19,993	669	6,921	12,403	7,706	4,697	103,851	27,360	15,849
May	146,304	123,971	20,008	674	6,929	12,405	7,714	4,691	103,963	27,353	15,822
June	146,533	124,177	20,054	678	6,956	12,420	7,726	4,694	104,123	27,374	15,821
July	146,737	124,369	20,054	679	6,958	12,417	7,718	4,699	104,315	27,376	15,814
Aug	146,924	124,563	20,132	685	6,988	12,459	7,751	4,708	104,431	27,385	15,811
Sept	146,942	124,579	20,158	687	7,004	12,467	7,759	4,708	104,421	27,422	15,811
Oct	147,202	124,828	20,200	687	7,026	12,487	7,773	4,714	104,628	27,448	15,813
Nov	147,422	125,040	20,269	692	7,060	12,517	7,797	4,720	104,771	27,482	15,828
Dec	147,596	125,207	20,330	692	7,093	12,545	7,821	4,724	104,877	27,484	15,807
2018: Jan	147,767	125,393	20,386	699	7,126	12,561	7,838	4,723	105,007	27,502	15,809
Feb	148,097	125,697	20,497	706	7,199	12,592	7,865	4,727	105,200	27,560	15,833
Mar	148,279	125,870	20,527	714	7,201	12,612	7,886	4,726	105,343	27,591	15,834
Apr	148,475	126,054	20,587	723	7,230	12,634	7,903	4,731	105,467	27,589	15,838
May	148,745	126,318	20,650	728	7,267	12,655	7,917	4,738	105,668	27,630	15,856
June	149,007	126,554	20,706	735	7,284	12,687	7,944	4,743	105,848	27,622	15,822
July	149,185	126,727	20,744	734	7,303	12,707	7,961	4,746	105,983	27,643	15,824
Aug	149,467	126,973	20,794	742	7,337	12,715	7,973	4,742	106,179	27,693	15,830
Sept	149,575	127,081	20,832	745	7,354	12,733	7,987	4,746	106,249	27,692	15,804
Oct	149,852	127,366	20,892	751	7,379	12,762	8,006	4,756	106,474	27,715	15,794
Nov	150,048	127,566	20,921	748	7,384	12,789	8,022	4,767	106,645	27,783	15,827
Dec p	150,270	127,772	20,974	753	7,412	12,809	8,039	4,770	106,798	27,776	15,815

[1] Includes wholesale trade, transportation and warehousing, and utilities, not shown separately.

Note: Data in Tables B–29 and B–30 are based on reports from employing establishments and relate to full- and part-time wage and salary workers in nonagricultural establishments who received pay for any part of the pay period that includes the 12th of the month. Not comparable with labor force data (Tables B–22 through B–28), which include proprietors, self-employed persons, unpaid family workers, and private household workers; which count persons as

See next page for continuation of table.

[Thousands of jobs; monthly data seasonally adjusted]

Year or month	Private industries—Continued						Government			
	Private service-providing industries—Continued									
	Information	Financial activities	Profes- sional and business services	Education and health services	Leisure and hospitality	Other services	Total	Federal	State	Local
1975	2,061	4,047	6,056	5,497	5,544	2,144	14,820	2,882	3,179	8,758
1976	2,111	4,155	6,310	5,756	5,794	2,244	15,001	2,863	3,273	8,865
1977	2,185	4,348	6,611	6,052	6,065	2,359	15,258	2,859	3,377	9,023
1978	2,287	4,599	6,997	6,427	6,411	2,505	15,812	2,893	3,474	9,446
1979	2,375	4,843	7,339	6,768	6,631	2,637	16,068	2,894	3,541	9,633
1980	2,361	5,025	7,571	7,077	6,721	2,755	16,375	3,000	3,610	9,765
1981	2,382	5,163	7,809	7,364	6,840	2,865	16,180	2,922	3,640	9,619
1982	2,317	5,209	7,875	7,526	6,874	2,924	15,982	2,884	3,640	9,458
1983	2,253	5,334	8,065	7,781	7,078	3,021	16,011	2,915	3,662	9,434
1984	2,398	5,553	8,493	8,211	7,489	3,186	16,159	2,943	3,734	9,482
1985	2,437	5,815	8,900	8,679	7,869	3,366	16,533	3,014	3,832	9,687
1986	2,445	6,128	9,241	9,086	8,156	3,523	16,838	3,044	3,893	9,901
1987	2,507	6,385	9,639	9,543	8,446	3,699	17,156	3,089	3,967	10,100
1988	2,585	6,500	10,121	10,096	8,778	3,907	17,540	3,124	4,076	10,339
1989	2,622	6,562	10,588	10,652	9,062	4,116	17,927	3,136	4,182	10,609
1990	2,688	6,614	10,881	11,024	9,288	4,261	18,415	3,196	4,305	10,914
1991	2,677	6,561	10,746	11,556	9,256	4,249	18,545	3,110	4,355	11,081
1992	2,641	6,559	11,001	11,948	9,437	4,240	18,787	3,111	4,408	11,267
1993	2,668	6,742	11,527	12,362	9,732	4,350	18,989	3,063	4,488	11,438
1994	2,738	6,910	12,207	12,872	10,100	4,428	19,275	3,018	4,576	11,682
1995	2,843	6,866	12,878	13,360	10,501	4,572	19,432	2,949	4,635	11,849
1996	2,940	7,018	13,497	13,761	10,777	4,690	19,539	2,877	4,606	12,056
1997	3,084	7,255	14,371	14,185	11,018	4,825	19,664	2,806	4,582	12,276
1998	3,218	7,565	15,183	14,570	11,232	4,976	19,909	2,772	4,612	12,525
1999	3,419	7,753	15,994	14,939	11,543	5,087	20,307	2,769	4,709	12,829
2000	3,630	7,783	16,704	15,252	11,862	5,168	20,790	2,865	4,786	13,139
2001	3,629	7,900	16,514	15,814	12,036	5,258	21,118	2,764	4,905	13,449
2002	3,395	7,956	16,016	16,398	11,986	5,372	21,513	2,766	5,029	13,718
2003	3,188	8,078	16,029	16,835	12,173	5,401	21,583	2,761	5,002	13,820
2004	3,118	8,105	16,440	17,230	12,493	5,409	21,621	2,730	4,982	13,909
2005	3,061	8,197	17,003	17,676	12,816	5,395	21,804	2,732	5,032	14,041
2006	3,038	8,367	17,619	18,154	13,110	5,438	21,974	2,732	5,075	14,167
2007	3,032	8,348	17,998	18,676	13,427	5,494	22,218	2,734	5,122	14,362
2008	2,984	8,206	17,792	19,228	13,436	5,515	22,509	2,762	5,177	14,571
2009	2,804	7,838	16,634	19,630	13,077	5,367	22,555	2,832	5,169	14,554
2010	2,707	7,695	16,783	19,975	13,049	5,331	22,490	2,977	5,137	14,376
2011	2,674	7,697	17,389	20,318	13,353	5,360	22,086	2,859	5,078	14,150
2012	2,676	7,784	17,992	20,769	13,768	5,430	21,920	2,820	5,055	14,045
2013	2,706	7,886	18,575	21,086	14,254	5,483	21,853	2,769	5,046	14,037
2014	2,726	7,977	19,124	21,439	14,696	5,567	21,882	2,733	5,050	14,098
2015	2,750	8,123	19,695	22,029	15,160	5,622	22,029	2,757	5,077	14,195
2016	2,794	8,287	20,114	22,639	15,660	5,691	22,224	2,795	5,110	14,319
2017 ᵖ	2,814	8,451	20,508	23,188	16,051	5,770	22,350	2,805	5,165	14,379
2018 ᵖ	2,828	8,569	20,999	23,667	16,347	5,845	22,450	2,796	5,176	14,477
2017: Jan	2,817	8,399	20,336	22,942	15,884	5,729	22,310	2,810	5,150	14,350
Feb	2,812	8,397	20,340	23,005	15,920	5,740	22,320	2,812	5,164	14,344
Mar	2,811	8,408	20,373	23,046	15,939	5,745	22,329	2,810	5,167	14,352
Apr	2,804	8,426	20,403	23,098	16,010	5,750	22,332	2,800	5,167	14,365
May	2,804	8,432	20,454	23,130	16,029	5,761	22,333	2,810	5,170	14,353
June	2,809	8,447	20,491	23,170	16,061	5,771	22,356	2,807	5,170	14,379
July	2,810	8,460	20,537	23,238	16,118	5,776	22,368	2,807	5,174	14,387
Aug	2,818	8,473	20,573	23,278	16,123	5,781	22,361	2,802	5,168	14,391
Sept	2,814	8,480	20,586	23,298	16,043	5,778	22,363	2,801	5,161	14,401
Oct	2,814	8,485	20,627	23,317	16,145	5,792	22,374	2,804	5,160	14,410
Nov	2,815	8,493	20,662	23,355	16,163	5,801	22,382	2,797	5,166	14,419
Dec	2,821	8,500	20,693	23,380	16,195	5,804	22,389	2,795	5,164	14,430
2018: Jan	2,812	8,502	20,730	23,445	16,208	5,808	22,374	2,795	5,147	14,432
Feb	2,812	8,528	20,774	23,481	16,233	5,812	22,400	2,792	5,155	14,453
Mar	2,824	8,537	20,816	23,518	16,244	5,813	22,409	2,792	5,160	14,457
Apr	2,829	8,541	20,878	23,542	16,262	5,826	22,421	2,793	5,169	14,459
May	2,831	8,556	20,929	23,581	16,300	5,841	22,427	2,793	5,168	14,466
June	2,831	8,567	20,980	23,646	16,343	5,859	22,453	2,795	5,178	14,480
July	2,832	8,572	21,017	23,694	16,378	5,847	22,458	2,796	5,179	14,483
Aug	2,826	8,583	21,075	23,754	16,395	5,853	22,494	2,796	5,190	14,508
Sept	2,822	8,597	21,128	23,779	16,371	5,860	22,494	2,797	5,204	14,493
Oct	2,832	8,611	21,183	23,816	16,450	5,867	22,486	2,798	5,197	14,491
Nov	2,829	8,614	21,217	23,845	16,489	5,868	22,482	2,804	5,180	14,498
Dec ᵖ	2,825	8,618	21,246	23,912	16,544	5,877	22,498	2,799	5,188	14,511

Note (cont'd): employed when they are not at work because of industrial disputes, bad weather, etc., even if they are not paid for the time off; which are based on a sample of the working-age population; and which count persons only once—as employed, unemployed, or not in the labor force. In the data shown here, persons who work at more than one job are counted each time they appear on a payroll.

Establishment data for employment, hours, and earnings are classified based on the 2017 North American Industry Classification System (NAICS). For further description and details see *Employment and Earnings*.

Source: Department of Labor (Bureau of Labor Statistics).

TABLE B–30. Hours and earnings in private nonagricultural industries, 1975–2018

[Monthly data seasonally adjusted]

Year or month	All employees							Production and nonsupervisory employees [1]						
	Average weekly hours	Average hourly earnings		Average weekly earnings				Average weekly hours	Average hourly earnings		Average weekly earnings			
				Level		Percent change from year earlier					Level		Percent change from year earlier	
		Current dollars	1982–84 dollars [2]	Current dollars	1982–84 dollars [2]	Current dollars	1982–84 dollars [2]		Current dollars	1982–84 dollars [3]	Current dollars	1982–84 dollars [3]	Current dollars	1982–84 dollars [3]
1975	....	....	....	....	....	....	....	36.0	$4.74	$8.76	$170.45	$315.06	5.4	-3.4
1976	....	....	....	....	....	....	....	36.0	5.06	8.85	182.36	318.81	7.0	1.2
1977	....	....	....	....	....	....	....	35.9	5.44	8.93	195.34	320.76	7.1	.6
1978	....	....	....	....	....	....	....	35.8	5.88	8.96	210.17	320.38	7.6	-.1
1979	....	....	....	....	....	....	....	35.6	6.34	8.67	225.46	308.43	7.3	-3.7
1980	....	....	....	....	....	....	....	35.2	6.84	8.25	240.83	290.51	6.8	-5.8
1981	....	....	....	....	....	....	....	35.2	7.43	8.13	261.29	285.88	8.5	-1.6
1982	....	....	....	....	....	....	....	34.7	7.86	8.11	272.98	281.71	4.5	-1.5
1983	....	....	....	....	....	....	....	34.9	8.20	8.22	286.34	286.91	4.9	1.8
1984	....	....	....	....	....	....	....	35.1	8.49	8.22	298.08	288.56	4.1	.6
1985	....	....	....	....	....	....	....	34.9	8.73	8.17	304.37	284.72	2.1	-1.3
1986	....	....	....	....	....	....	....	34.7	8.92	8.21	309.69	285.17	1.7	.2
1987	....	....	....	....	....	....	....	34.7	9.14	8.12	317.33	282.07	2.5	-1.1
1988	....	....	....	....	....	....	....	34.6	9.44	8.07	326.50	279.06	2.9	-1.1
1989	....	....	....	....	....	....	....	34.5	9.81	8.00	338.42	276.04	3.7	-1.1
1990	....	....	....	....	....	....	....	34.3	10.20	7.91	349.63	271.03	3.3	-1.8
1991	....	....	....	....	....	....	....	34.1	10.51	7.83	358.46	266.91	2.5	-1.5
1992	....	....	....	....	....	....	....	34.2	10.77	7.79	368.20	266.43	2.7	-.2
1993	....	....	....	....	....	....	....	34.3	11.05	7.78	378.89	266.64	2.9	.1
1994	....	....	....	....	....	....	....	34.5	11.34	7.79	391.17	268.66	3.2	.8
1995	....	....	....	....	....	....	....	34.3	11.65	7.78	400.04	267.05	2.3	-.6
1996	....	....	....	....	....	....	....	34.3	12.04	7.81	413.25	268.17	3.3	.4
1997	....	....	....	....	....	....	....	34.5	12.51	7.94	431.86	274.02	4.5	2.2
1998	....	....	....	....	....	....	....	34.5	13.01	8.15	448.59	280.90	3.9	2.5
1999	....	....	....	....	....	....	....	34.3	13.49	8.27	463.15	283.79	3.2	1.0
2000	....	....	....	....	....	....	....	34.3	14.02	8.30	480.99	284.78	3.9	.3
2001	....	....	....	....	....	....	....	33.9	14.54	8.38	493.61	284.50	2.6	-.1
2002	....	....	....	....	....	....	....	33.9	14.96	8.50	506.54	287.97	2.6	1.2
2003	....	....	....	....	....	....	....	33.7	15.37	8.55	517.76	287.96	2.2	.0
2004	....	....	....	....	....	....	....	33.7	15.68	8.50	528.84	286.63	2.1	-.5
2005	....	....	....	....	....	....	....	33.8	16.12	8.44	544.02	284.83	2.9	-.6
2006	....	....	....	....	....	....	....	33.9	16.75	8.50	567.09	287.72	4.2	1.0
2007	34.4	$20.92	$10.09	$719.85	$347.18			33.8	17.42	8.59	589.18	290.57	3.9	1.0
2008	34.3	21.56	10.01	739.02	343.25	2.7	-1.1	33.6	18.06	8.56	607.42	287.80	3.1	-1.0
2009	33.8	22.17	10.33	749.98	349.58	1.5	1.8	33.1	18.61	8.88	615.96	293.83	1.4	2.1
2010	34.1	22.56	10.35	769.63	352.95	2.6	1.0	33.4	19.05	8.90	636.19	297.33	3.3	1.2
2011	34.3	23.03	10.24	790.85	351.58	2.8	-.4	33.6	19.44	8.77	652.89	294.66	2.6	-.9
2012	34.5	23.49	10.23	809.57	352.61	2.4	.3	33.7	19.74	8.73	665.65	294.24	2.0	-.1
2013	34.4	23.96	10.29	825.02	354.15	1.9	.4	33.7	20.13	8.78	677.70	295.52	1.8	.4
2014	34.5	24.47	10.34	844.91	356.90	2.4	.8	33.7	20.61	8.85	694.85	298.51	2.5	1.0
2015	34.5	25.02	10.56	864.21	364.62	2.3	2.2	33.7	21.03	9.07	708.90	305.81	2.0	2.4
2016	34.4	25.64	10.68	881.20	367.16	2.0	.7	33.6	21.54	9.20	723.31	309.01	2.0	1.0
2017	34.4	26.33	10.74	906.30	369.74	2.8	.7	33.7	22.06	9.23	742.62	310.65	2.7	.5
2018 p	34.5	27.11	10.80	936.29	372.86	3.3	.8	33.8	22.71	9.26	767.05	312.90	3.3	.7
2017: Jan	34.4	25.98	10.66	893.71	366.61	1.8	-.7	33.6	21.82	9.17	733.15	308.21	2.1	-.4
Feb	34.3	26.08	10.69	894.54	366.67	2.4	-.3	33.6	21.86	9.19	734.50	308.63	2.3	-.5
Mar	34.3	26.11	10.71	895.57	367.41	2.3	-.1	33.5	21.89	9.21	733.32	308.49	2.0	-.4
Apr	34.4	26.17	10.72	900.25	368.88	2.5	.3	33.7	21.94	9.22	739.38	310.74	2.5	.4
May	34.4	26.22	10.75	901.97	369.72	2.5	.7	33.6	21.98	9.24	738.53	310.63	2.3	.5
June	34.4	26.28	10.79	904.03	370.23	2.5	.8	33.7	22.03	9.26	742.41	311.98	2.6	1.1
July	34.4	26.36	10.79	906.78	371.04	2.6	.8	33.7	22.08	9.27	744.10	312.48	2.6	.9
Aug	34.4	26.39	10.76	907.82	370.09	2.9	.9	33.6	22.11	9.24	742.90	310.63	2.3	.4
Sept	34.3	26.51	10.76	909.29	369.00	2.5	.3	33.6	22.19	9.23	745.58	310.11	2.6	.3
Oct	34.4	26.47	10.73	910.57	369.27	2.3	.3	33.7	22.18	9.22	747.47	310.83	2.5	.4
Nov	34.5	26.55	10.73	915.98	370.34	3.1	.9	33.7	22.24	9.21	749.49	310.48	2.7	.3
Dec	34.5	26.64	10.75	919.08	370.74	3.0	.9	33.8	22.31	9.22	754.08	311.61	3.4	1.2
2018: Jan	34.4	26.71	10.73	918.82	369.18	2.8	.7	33.6	22.36	9.20	751.30	309.16	2.5	.3
Feb	34.5	26.75	10.73	922.88	370.09	3.2	.9	33.8	22.40	9.20	757.12	310.89	3.1	.7
Mar	34.5	26.84	10.76	925.98	371.14	3.4	1.0	33.7	22.49	9.23	757.91	311.19	3.4	.9
Apr	34.5	26.90	10.76	928.05	371.29	3.1	.7	33.8	22.55	9.24	762.19	312.38	3.1	.5
May	34.5	26.99	10.77	931.16	371.50	3.2	.5	33.8	22.62	9.24	764.56	312.45	3.5	.6
June	34.5	27.05	10.77	933.23	371.61	3.2	.4	33.8	22.67	9.24	766.25	312.44	3.2	.1
July	34.5	27.11	10.78	935.30	371.75	3.1	.2	33.8	22.71	9.24	767.60	312.45	3.2	.0
Aug	34.5	27.23	10.81	939.44	372.97	3.5	.8	33.8	22.80	9.27	770.64	313.24	3.7	.8
Sept	34.5	27.30	10.83	941.85	373.74	3.6	1.3	33.7	22.86	9.29	770.38	313.13	3.3	1.0
Oct	34.5	27.35	10.82	943.58	373.26	3.6	1.1	33.7	22.90	9.27	771.73	312.56	3.2	.6
Nov	34.4	27.43	10.85	943.59	373.31	3.0	.8	33.7	22.99	9.32	774.76	314.08	3.4	1.2
Dec p	34.5	27.53	10.89	949.79	375.82	3.3	1.4	33.7	23.09	9.37	778.13	315.86	3.2	1.4

[1] Production employees in goods-producing industries and nonsupervisory employees in service-providing industries. These groups account for four-fifths of the total employment on private nonfarm payrolls.
[2] Current dollars divided by the consumer price index for all urban consumers (CPI-U) on a 1982–84=100 base.
[3] Current dollars divided by the consumer price index for urban wage earners and clerical workers (CPI-W) on a 1982–84=100 base.

Note: See Note, Table B–29.

Source: Department of Labor (Bureau of Labor Statistics).

Year and month	Total private			Goods-producing			Service-providing [1]			Manufacturing		
	Total compensation	Wages and salaries	Benefits [2]	Total compensation	Wages and salaries	Benefits [2]	Total compensation	Wages and salaries	Benefits [2]	Total compensation	Wages and salaries	Benefits [2]
Indexes on NAICS basis, December 2005=100; not seasonally adjusted												
December:												
2001 [3]	87.3	89.9	81.3	86.0	90.0	78.5	87.8	89.8	82.4	85.5	90.2	77.2
2002	90.0	92.2	84.7	89.0	92.6	82.3	90.4	92.1	85.8	88.7	92.8	81.3
2003	93.6	95.1	90.2	92.6	94.9	88.2	94.0	95.2	91.0	92.4	95.1	87.3
2004	97.2	97.6	96.2	96.9	97.2	96.3	97.3	97.7	96.1	96.9	97.4	96.0
2005	100.0	100.0	100.0	100.0	100.0	100.0	100.0	100.0	100.0	100.0	100.0	100.0
2006	103.2	103.2	103.1	102.5	102.9	101.7	103.4	103.3	103.7	101.8	102.3	100.8
2007	106.3	106.6	105.6	105.0	106.0	103.2	106.7	106.8	106.6	103.8	104.9	101.7
2008	108.9	109.4	107.7	107.5	109.0	104.7	109.4	109.6	108.9	105.9	107.7	102.5
2009	110.2	110.8	108.7	108.6	110.0	105.8	110.8	111.1	109.9	107.0	108.9	103.6
2010	112.5	112.8	111.9	111.1	111.6	110.1	113.0	113.1	112.6	110.0	110.7	108.8
2011	115.0	114.6	115.9	113.8	113.5	114.4	115.3	114.9	116.4	113.1	112.7	113.9
2012	117.1	116.6	118.2	115.6	115.4	116.0	117.6	117.0	119.1	114.9	114.8	115.0
2013	119.4	119.0	120.5	117.7	117.6	118.0	120.0	119.4	121.5	117.0	117.2	116.6
2014	122.2	121.6	123.5	120.3	120.1	120.7	122.8	122.1	124.6	119.8	119.8	119.8
2015	124.5	124.2	125.1	123.2	123.2	123.1	124.9	124.5	125.9	122.8	123.0	122.5
2016	127.2	127.1	127.3	125.8	126.2	124.9	127.7	127.4	128.3	125.5	126.2	124.3
2017	130.5	130.6	130.2	128.9	129.3	128.0	131.0	131.0	131.2	128.9	129.3	128.0
2018	134.4	134.7	133.6	131.9	133.0	129.6	135.2	135.2	135.1	131.6	132.9	129.1
2018: Mar	131.9	132.0	131.6	129.9	130.4	129.0	132.6	132.5	132.7	130.0	130.4	129.1
June	132.9	132.9	132.9	130.9	131.4	129.8	133.5	133.3	134.1	130.8	131.3	129.8
Sept	133.8	134.0	133.2	131.2	132.2	129.3	134.6	134.5	134.6	130.9	132.0	128.9
Dec	134.4	134.7	133.6	131.9	133.0	129.6	135.2	135.2	135.1	131.6	132.9	129.1
Indexes on NAICS basis, December 2005=100; seasonally adjusted												
2017: Mar	128.3	128.3	128.3	126.6	127.1	125.4	128.8	128.6	129.5	126.3	127.1	125.0
June	129.0	129.0	129.1	127.2	127.8	126.0	129.6	129.4	130.3	127.0	127.8	125.6
Sept	130.0	130.0	130.0	128.3	128.7	127.5	130.5	130.3	131.0	128.3	128.7	127.7
Dec	130.6	130.7	130.5	128.9	129.4	128.0	131.2	131.1	131.5	129.0	129.5	128.1
2018: Mar	131.9	132.0	131.6	130.0	130.5	129.0	132.5	132.5	132.6	129.9	130.4	129.1
June	132.7	132.8	132.7	130.8	131.4	129.7	133.4	133.2	133.9	130.7	131.2	129.7
Sept	133.7	133.9	133.2	131.1	132.1	129.2	134.5	134.5	134.6	130.9	132.0	128.8
Dec	134.5	134.8	133.9	131.9	133.1	129.5	135.3	135.3	135.4	131.7	133.1	129.2
Percent change from 12 months earlier, not seasonally adjusted												
December:												
2001 [3]	4.1	3.8	5.2	3.6	3.6	3.7	4.4	3.8	5.6	3.4	3.6	3.5
2002	3.1	2.6	4.2	3.5	2.9	4.8	3.0	2.6	4.1	3.7	2.9	5.3
2003	4.0	3.1	6.5	4.0	2.5	7.2	4.0	3.4	6.1	4.2	2.5	7.4
2004	3.8	2.6	6.7	4.6	2.4	9.2	3.5	2.6	5.6	4.9	2.4	10.0
2005	2.9	2.5	4.0	3.2	2.9	3.8	2.8	2.4	4.1	3.2	2.7	4.2
2006	3.2	3.2	3.1	2.5	2.9	1.7	3.4	3.3	3.7	1.8	2.3	.8
2007	3.0	3.3	2.4	2.4	3.0	1.5	3.2	3.4	2.8	2.0	2.5	.9
2008	2.4	2.6	2.0	2.4	2.8	1.5	2.5	2.6	2.2	2.0	2.7	.8
2009	1.2	1.3	.9	1.0	.9	1.1	1.3	1.4	.9	1.0	1.1	1.1
2010	2.1	1.8	2.9	2.3	1.5	4.1	2.0	1.8	2.5	2.8	1.7	5.0
2011	2.2	1.6	3.6	2.4	1.7	3.9	2.0	1.6	3.4	2.8	1.8	4.7
2012	1.8	1.7	2.0	1.6	1.7	1.4	2.0	1.8	2.3	1.6	1.9	1.0
2013	2.0	2.1	1.9	1.8	1.9	1.7	2.0	2.1	2.0	1.8	2.1	1.4
2014	2.3	2.2	2.5	2.2	2.1	2.3	2.3	2.3	2.6	2.4	2.2	2.7
2015	1.9	2.1	1.3	2.4	2.6	2.0	1.7	2.0	1.0	2.5	2.7	2.3
2016	2.2	2.3	1.8	2.1	2.4	1.5	2.2	2.3	1.9	2.2	2.6	1.5
2017	2.6	2.8	2.3	2.5	2.5	2.5	2.6	2.8	2.3	2.7	2.5	3.0
2018	3.0	3.1	2.6	2.3	2.9	1.3	3.2	3.2	3.0	2.1	2.8	.9
2018: Mar	2.8	2.9	2.5	2.7	2.6	2.9	2.9	3.0	2.4	2.8	2.6	3.3
June	2.9	2.9	2.8	2.8	2.7	2.9	2.9	2.9	2.8	2.9	2.7	3.3
Sept	2.9	3.1	2.5	2.2	2.6	1.3	3.1	3.1	2.7	1.9	2.6	.9
Dec	3.0	3.1	2.6	2.3	2.9	1.3	3.2	3.2	3.0	2.1	2.8	.9
Percent change from 3 months earlier, seasonally adjusted												
2017: Mar	0.8	0.9	0.6	0.6	0.7	0.4	0.8	0.8	0.7	0.5	0.6	0.5
June	.5	.5	.6	.5	.6	.5	.6	.6	.6	.6	.6	.5
Sept	.8	.8	.7	.9	.7	1.2	.7	.7	.5	1.0	.7	1.7
Dec	.5	.5	.4	.5	.5	.4	.5	.6	.4	.5	.6	.3
2018: Mar	1.0	1.0	.8	.9	.9	.8	1.0	1.1	.8	.7	.7	.8
June	.6	.6	.8	.6	.7	.5	.7	.5	1.0	.6	.6	.5
Sept	.8	.8	.4	.2	.5	-.4	.8	1.0	.5	.2	.6	-.7
Dec	.6	.7	.5	.6	.8	.2	.6	.6	.6	.6	.8	.3

[1] On Standard Industrial Classification (SIC) basis, data are for service-producing industries.
[2] Employer costs for employee benefits.
[3] Data on North American Industry Classification System (NAICS) basis available beginning with 2001; not strictly comparable with earlier data on SIC basis.

Note: Changes effective with the release of March 2006 data (in April 2006) include changing industry classification to NAICS from SIC and rebasing data to December 2005=100. Historical SIC data are available through December 2005.
Data exclude farm and household workers.

Source: Department of Labor (Bureau of Labor Statistics).

TABLE B–32. Productivity and related data, business and nonfarm business sectors, 1970–2018

[Index numbers, 2012=100; quarterly data seasonally adjusted]

Year or quarter	Labor productivity (output per hour) Business sector	Labor productivity (output per hour) Nonfarm business sector	Output [1] Business sector	Output [1] Nonfarm business sector	Hours of all persons [2] Business sector	Hours of all persons [2] Nonfarm business sector	Compensation per hour [3] Business sector	Compensation per hour [3] Nonfarm business sector	Real compensation per hour [4] Business sector	Real compensation per hour [4] Nonfarm business sector	Unit labor costs Business sector	Unit labor costs Nonfarm business sector	Implicit price deflator [5] Business sector	Implicit price deflator [5] Nonfarm business sector
1970	42.3	43.6	26.8	26.8	63.5	61.5	12.1	12.2	65.3	66.0	28.6	28.0	24.9	24.5
1971	44.0	45.3	27.9	27.8	63.3	61.4	12.8	13.0	66.3	67.1	29.1	28.6	26.0	25.6
1972	45.5	46.8	29.7	29.7	65.3	63.4	13.6	13.8	68.3	69.2	30.0	29.5	26.9	26.4
1973	46.8	48.3	31.7	31.8	67.8	66.0	14.7	14.9	69.4	70.1	31.4	30.8	28.3	27.3
1974	46.0	47.5	31.2	31.4	67.9	66.1	16.1	16.3	68.3	69.1	34.9	34.2	31.1	30.2
1975	47.6	48.8	31.0	30.9	65.0	63.3	17.8	18.0	69.3	70.0	37.3	36.8	34.1	33.4
1976	49.2	50.5	33.0	33.1	67.1	65.5	19.2	19.4	70.8	71.3	39.0	38.4	35.8	35.2
1977	50.1	51.3	34.9	35.0	69.7	68.1	20.7	20.9	71.8	72.5	41.4	40.8	38.0	37.4
1978	50.7	52.1	37.2	37.3	73.3	71.6	22.5	22.7	72.7	73.5	44.3	43.7	40.6	39.8
1979	50.8	52.0	38.5	38.6	75.7	74.2	24.7	24.9	72.9	73.6	48.6	47.9	44.0	43.1
1980	50.8	51.9	38.1	38.2	75.1	73.6	27.3	27.6	72.5	73.3	53.8	53.1	47.9	47.2
1981	51.9	52.8	39.2	39.1	75.6	74.1	29.9	30.3	72.6	73.4	57.6	57.4	52.3	51.8
1982	51.6	52.3	38.1	37.9	73.9	72.5	32.1	32.5	73.5	74.3	62.2	62.1	55.3	55.0
1983	53.4	54.5	40.1	40.3	75.2	73.9	33.6	33.9	73.6	74.5	62.8	62.3	57.3	56.9
1984	54.9	55.7	43.7	43.7	79.6	78.4	35.0	35.4	73.8	74.6	63.8	63.6	58.9	58.5
1985	56.2	56.6	45.7	45.6	81.4	80.5	36.8	37.1	75.0	75.6	65.6	65.5	60.4	60.2
1986	57.7	58.3	47.4	47.3	82.1	81.1	38.9	39.2	77.9	78.6	67.4	67.3	61.3	61.1
1987	58.1	58.7	49.1	49.0	84.5	83.6	40.4	40.7	78.1	78.8	69.5	69.5	62.4	62.2
1988	59.0	59.6	51.2	51.3	86.9	86.0	42.5	42.8	79.4	80.0	72.1	71.8	64.4	64.1
1989	59.6	60.2	53.2	53.1	89.1	88.3	43.8	44.1	78.4	78.9	73.4	73.3	66.8	66.5
1990	60.8	61.2	54.0	53.9	88.8	88.2	46.5	46.7	79.3	79.7	76.5	76.4	69.0	68.7
1991	61.8	62.2	53.7	53.6	86.9	86.2	48.7	48.9	80.1	80.5	78.8	78.7	71.0	70.9
1992	64.7	65.0	56.0	55.8	86.5	85.9	51.7	52.0	83.0	83.4	79.9	80.0	72.1	72.1
1993	64.7	65.0	57.6	57.5	88.9	88.4	52.4	52.6	82.1	82.4	81.0	80.9	73.8	73.8
1994	65.1	65.5	60.3	60.1	92.7	91.8	52.8	53.1	81.0	81.5	81.1	81.1	75.1	75.1
1995	65.6	66.2	62.2	62.2	94.8	94.0	54.1	54.5	81.0	81.6	82.5	82.2	76.5	76.5
1996	67.2	67.6	65.1	65.0	96.9	96.1	56.0	56.3	81.8	82.2	83.4	83.3	77.7	77.5
1997	68.6	68.9	68.5	68.4	99.8	99.2	58.3	58.5	83.2	83.6	84.9	84.9	78.8	78.9
1998	70.8	71.0	72.0	72.0	101.8	101.3	61.7	61.9	87.0	87.3	87.2	87.2	79.3	79.4
1999	73.6	73.7	76.1	76.1	103.4	103.2	64.7	64.8	89.3	89.4	87.9	87.9	79.8	80.0
2000	76.1	76.2	79.8	79.7	104.8	104.6	69.2	69.4	92.4	92.6	90.9	91.0	81.0	81.3
2001	78.3	78.3	80.4	80.3	102.7	102.6	72.4	72.4	93.9	93.9	92.5	92.5	82.3	82.6
2002	81.6	81.7	81.8	81.7	100.2	100.0	74.0	74.0	94.5	94.6	90.7	90.7	82.9	83.3
2003	84.8	84.8	84.5	84.3	99.6	99.5	76.8	76.8	95.9	95.9	90.5	90.6	83.9	84.2
2004	87.4	87.2	88.1	87.9	100.8	100.8	80.4	80.3	97.7	97.7	92.0	92.1	86.1	86.2
2005	89.3	89.1	91.5	91.3	102.5	102.5	83.3	83.2	98.0	97.9	93.2	93.4	88.7	89.1
2006	90.3	90.1	94.6	94.4	104.7	104.8	86.5	86.4	98.6	98.5	95.7	95.9	91.1	91.6
2007	91.8	91.7	96.8	96.7	105.4	105.5	90.4	90.2	100.1	99.9	98.4	98.4	93.2	93.4
2008	92.8	92.6	95.8	95.7	103.3	103.3	92.8	92.7	99.0	98.9	100.0	100.1	94.7	94.9
2009	96.1	95.9	92.3	92.0	96.0	95.9	93.6	93.6	100.2	100.2	97.4	97.5	94.9	95.4
2010	99.3	99.2	95.2	95.0	95.9	95.8	95.3	95.3	100.4	100.4	95.9	96.1	96.0	96.3
2011	99.2	99.1	97.1	96.9	97.8	97.8	97.3	97.4	99.4	99.5	98.1	98.2	98.2	98.2
2012	100.0	100.0	100.0	100.0	100.0	100.0	100.0	100.0	100.0	100.0	100.0	100.0	100.0	100.0
2013	100.9	100.5	102.4	102.2	101.5	101.7	101.5	101.3	100.0	99.8	100.6	100.8	101.5	101.5
2014	101.6	101.3	105.6	105.4	103.9	104.0	104.2	104.1	100.9	100.9	102.5	102.8	103.2	103.3
2015	102.8	102.6	109.3	109.0	106.3	106.2	107.1	107.3	103.6	103.8	104.2	104.6	103.8	104.2
2016	102.9	102.8	111.1	110.8	107.9	107.8	108.2	108.5	103.4	103.6	105.2	105.5	104.7	105.3
2017	104.1	103.9	114.0	113.8	109.5	109.5	111.9	112.1	104.6	104.8	107.5	107.9	106.5	107.0
2018 [p]	....	....	....	....	111.8	111.9	....	....	....	....	....	....	....	....
2015: I	102.4	102.3	108.3	108.1	105.8	105.6	106.2	106.4	103.4	103.7	103.6	104.0	103.2	103.6
II	103.0	102.9	109.4	109.2	106.2	106.1	107.2	107.4	103.7	103.9	104.0	104.4	103.8	104.2
III	103.2	103.0	109.6	109.4	106.2	106.2	107.7	107.9	103.8	104.0	104.3	104.7	104.1	104.5
IV	102.4	102.3	109.7	109.4	107.1	107.0	107.5	107.7	103.6	103.8	104.9	105.3	104.0	104.4
2016: I	102.5	102.3	110.1	109.8	107.4	107.3	107.5	107.7	103.6	103.8	104.9	105.2	103.8	104.4
II	102.7	102.6	110.8	110.5	107.9	107.7	107.6	107.9	103.0	103.3	104.8	105.2	104.6	105.2
III	103.1	102.9	111.4	111.1	108.1	108.0	108.2	108.5	103.1	103.4	105.0	105.4	104.9	105.6
IV	103.5	103.2	112.0	111.7	108.2	108.2	109.7	109.7	103.8	103.9	105.9	106.3	105.4	106.0
2017: I	103.5	103.4	112.5	112.3	108.7	108.6	110.8	111.0	104.1	104.3	107.0	107.4	105.8	106.4
II	103.9	103.8	113.5	113.3	109.3	109.2	111.2	111.4	104.4	104.6	107.0	107.3	106.1	106.6
III	104.6	104.3	114.5	114.3	109.5	109.6	112.7	112.8	105.3	105.3	107.7	108.1	106.6	107.1
IV	104.3	104.3	115.3	115.2	110.6	110.5	113.0	113.3	104.7	105.0	108.3	108.7	107.4	107.9
2018: I	104.5	104.3	116.0	115.9	111.1	111.1	114.2	114.3	104.9	105.1	109.3	109.6	107.9	108.4
II	105.4	105.1	117.5	117.3	111.5	111.7	114.4	114.4	104.6	104.6	108.5	108.8	108.8	109.3
III	105.9	105.7	118.6	118.5	112.0	112.1	115.2	115.3	104.9	104.9	108.8	109.1	109.1	109.7
IV [p]	....	....	....	....	112.5	112.6	....	....	....	....	....	....	....	....

[1] Output refers to real gross domestic product in the sector.
[2] Hours at work of all persons engaged in sector, including hours of employees, proprietors, and unpaid family workers. Estimates based primarily on establishment data.
[3] Wages and salaries of employees plus employers' contributions for social insurance and private benefit plans. Also includes an estimate of wages, salaries, and supplemental payments for the self-employed.
[4] Hourly compensation divided by consumer price series. The trend for 1978-2017 is based on the consumer price index research series (CPI-U-RS). The change for prior years and recent quarters is based on the consumer price index for all urban consumers (CPI-U).
[5] Current dollar output divided by the output index.

Source: Department of Labor (Bureau of Labor Statistics).

TABLE B–33. Changes in productivity and related data, business and nonfarm business sectors, 1970–2018

[Percent change from preceding period; quarterly data at seasonally adjusted annual rates]

Year or quarter	Output per hour of all persons		Output[1]		Hours of all persons[2]		Compensation per hour[3]		Real compensation per hour[4]		Unit labor costs		Implicit price deflator[5]	
	Business sector	Nonfarm business sector	Business sector	Nonfarm business sector	Business sector	Nonfarm business sector	Business sector	Nonfarm business sector	Business sector	Nonfarm business sector	Business sector	Nonfarm business sector	Business sector	Nonfarm business sector
1970	2.0	1.5	0.0	-0.1	-2.0	-1.6	7.5	7.0	1.7	1.2	5.4	5.4	4.3	4.4
1971	4.1	3.9	3.8	3.7	-.3	-.2	6.0	6.1	1.6	1.7	1.9	2.1	4.2	4.3
1972	3.3	3.4	6.5	6.7	3.1	3.2	6.3	6.4	3.0	3.1	2.9	2.9	3.4	3.1
1973	3.0	3.1	6.9	7.3	3.8	4.1	7.9	7.6	1.6	1.3	4.8	4.4	5.2	3.5
1974	-1.7	-1.6	-1.5	-1.5	.2	.1	9.3	9.5	-1.5	-1.4	11.2	11.3	9.8	10.4
1975	3.5	2.7	-1.0	-1.6	-4.3	-4.3	10.7	10.5	1.4	1.3	6.9	7.6	9.7	10.7
1976	3.3	3.5	6.8	7.2	3.3	3.6	8.0	7.8	2.1	1.9	4.5	4.1	5.2	5.4
1977	1.8	1.7	5.7	5.7	3.8	3.9	8.0	8.2	1.4	1.6	6.1	6.4	5.9	6.2
1978	1.2	1.4	6.4	6.7	5.1	5.2	8.4	8.6	1.3	1.5	7.1	7.1	6.9	6.5
1979	.2	-.2	3.6	3.4	3.4	3.6	9.7	9.6	.2	.1	9.5	9.8	8.4	8.4
1980	.0	.0	-.9	-.9	-.9	-.8	10.7	10.7	-.4	-.4	10.7	10.8	8.9	9.5
1981	2.2	1.6	2.9	2.3	.7	.7	9.5	9.7	.1	.2	7.1	8.0	9.2	9.6
1982	-.6	-.9	-2.9	-3.1	-2.3	-2.2	7.3	7.2	1.2	1.1	8.0	8.2	5.7	6.2
1983	3.5	4.2	5.3	6.2	1.8	2.0	4.5	4.6	.2	.3	1.0	.4	3.6	3.5
1984	2.9	2.2	8.9	8.5	5.8	6.1	4.4	4.3	.2	.1	1.5	2.0	2.8	2.8
1985	2.3	1.7	4.7	4.4	2.3	2.6	5.1	4.9	1.6	1.4	2.7	3.1	2.6	3.1
1986	2.8	3.0	3.6	3.8	.8	.8	5.6	5.8	3.8	3.9	2.8	2.7	1.4	1.4
1987	.6	.6	3.6	3.6	3.0	3.0	3.8	3.8	.3	.4	3.2	3.2	1.9	1.9
1988	1.5	1.6	4.3	4.6	2.7	2.9	5.3	5.1	1.6	1.5	3.7	3.4	3.2	3.1
1989	1.2	.9	3.8	3.7	2.6	2.7	3.0	2.9	-1.3	-1.4	1.8	2.0	3.7	3.6
1990	2.0	1.7	1.6	1.5	-.4	-.2	6.2	6.0	1.2	1.0	4.2	4.2	3.3	3.4
1991	1.6	1.6	-.6	-.6	-2.2	-2.2	4.7	4.8	1.0	1.1	3.0	3.1	2.9	3.1
1992	4.6	4.5	4.2	4.1	-.4	-.4	6.1	6.2	3.5	3.6	1.4	1.6	1.6	1.7
1993	.1	.1	2.9	3.1	2.7	3.0	1.5	1.2	-1.0	-1.3	1.4	1.1	2.3	2.3
1994	.6	.7	4.8	4.6	4.2	3.9	.7	1.0	-1.3	-1.1	.1	.3	1.8	1.9
1995	.7	1.1	3.1	3.4	2.3	2.3	2.4	2.5	.0	.1	1.7	1.4	1.8	1.8
1996	2.5	2.1	4.6	4.5	2.1	2.3	3.6	3.5	.9	.8	1.1	1.3	1.6	1.4
1997	2.2	1.9	5.2	5.2	3.0	3.2	4.0	3.9	1.8	1.7	1.8	1.9	1.5	1.7
1998	3.1	3.1	5.2	5.3	2.0	2.2	5.9	5.8	4.5	4.4	2.7	2.6	.6	.7
1999	4.0	3.8	5.7	5.7	1.6	1.8	4.8	4.6	2.7	2.5	.8	.8	.6	.8
2000	3.5	3.3	4.9	4.7	1.4	1.4	7.0	7.0	3.4	3.5	3.4	3.6	1.5	1.6
2001	2.8	2.7	.7	.8	-2.0	-1.9	4.6	4.3	1.7	1.5	1.7	1.6	1.6	1.6
2002	4.3	4.3	1.7	1.7	-2.4	-2.5	2.2	2.3	.6	.7	-1.9	-1.9	.7	.8
2003	3.9	3.8	3.3	3.2	-.6	-.6	3.8	3.7	1.5	1.4	-.2	-.1	1.3	1.1
2004	3.0	2.9	4.3	4.2	1.2	1.3	4.6	4.5	1.9	1.8	1.6	1.6	2.5	2.3
2005	2.2	2.2	3.9	3.9	1.7	1.7	3.6	3.7	.2	.3	1.4	1.4	3.1	3.3
2006	1.1	1.1	3.4	3.4	2.2	2.3	3.9	3.9	.6	.6	2.7	2.7	2.7	2.8
2007	1.6	1.7	2.3	2.4	.6	.7	4.5	4.3	1.6	1.5	2.8	2.6	2.3	2.0
2008	1.0	1.1	-1.0	-1.0	-2.0	-2.1	2.7	2.8	-1.1	-1.0	1.6	1.7	1.5	1.6
2009	3.6	3.5	-3.7	-3.9	-7.1	-7.2	.9	.9	1.2	1.3	-2.7	-2.5	.2	.5
2010	3.3	3.4	3.2	3.3	-.1	-.1	1.8	1.9	.1	.2	-1.5	-1.5	1.2	1.0
2011	-.1	.0	1.9	2.0	2.0	2.0	2.1	2.2	-1.0	-.9	2.2	2.2	2.3	1.9
2012	.8	.9	3.0	3.1	2.2	2.3	2.8	2.7	.6	.5	2.0	1.8	1.9	1.9
2013	.9	.5	2.4	2.2	1.5	1.7	1.5	1.3	.0	-.2	.6	.8	1.5	1.5
2014	.7	.8	3.0	3.1	2.3	2.3	2.6	2.8	.9	1.1	1.9	2.0	1.7	1.8
2015	1.2	1.3	3.5	3.5	2.3	2.1	2.9	3.1	2.7	2.9	1.7	1.8	.6	.8
2016	.2	.1	1.7	1.6	1.5	1.5	1.0	1.1	-.2	-.2	.9	.9	.9	1.1
2017	1.1	1.1	2.6	2.7	1.5	1.6	3.4	3.4	1.2	1.2	2.3	2.2	1.7	1.6
2018 ᵖ	....	....	....	....	2.1	2.2								
2015: I	2.8	3.1	4.1	4.1	1.3	.9	5.1	5.5	7.8	8.2	2.2	2.3	-1.3	-.6
II	2.4	2.1	4.1	4.1	1.7	2.0	3.8	3.5	1.1	.8	1.4	1.4	2.2	2.1
III	.7	.5	.8	.6	.0	.1	2.0	1.9	.4	.3	1.3	1.4	1.3	1.2
IV	-3.0	-2.9	.1	.1	3.2	3.0	-.8	-.7	-1.0	-.8	2.2	2.3	-.3	-.2
2016: I	.2	.3	1.6	1.6	1.4	1.3	.0	.1	.1	.1	-.2	-.2	-.8	-.3
II	.7	.9	2.6	2.5	1.9	1.6	.3	.7	-2.3	-2.0	-.4	-.2	3.1	3.2
III	1.6	1.3	2.2	2.2	.6	.9	2.5	2.2	.6	.3	.9	.9	1.3	1.5
IV	1.9	1.3	2.2	2.3	.3	1.0	5.6	4.7	2.7	1.9	3.6	3.4	1.7	1.8
2017: I	-.2	.4	1.9	1.9	2.0	1.5	4.0	4.7	1.0	1.6	4.2	4.2	1.8	1.3
II	1.6	1.6	3.7	3.8	2.1	2.2	1.3	1.3	1.2	1.2	-.3	-.3	.8	.8
III	2.8	2.3	3.5	3.6	.7	1.3	5.6	5.1	3.4	2.9	2.8	2.8	2.0	2.1
IV	-1.1	-.3	2.9	3.0	4.1	3.3	1.2	1.9	-2.1	-1.3	2.4	2.3	2.9	2.9
2018: I	.6	.3	2.5	2.6	1.9	2.3	4.3	3.8	.8	.2	3.7	3.4	1.9	1.8
II	3.6	3.0	5.1	5.0	1.5	2.0	.5	.0	-1.1	-1.6	-2.9	-2.8	3.6	3.6
III	1.8	2.2	3.9	4.0	2.1	1.7	2.9	3.2	.9	1.2	1.1	.9	1.1	1.4
IV ᵖ	....	....	....	....	1.7	1.6								

[1] Output refers to real gross domestic product in the sector.
[2] Hours at work of all persons engaged in the sector. See footnote 2, Table B–32.
[3] Wages and salaries of employees plus employers' contributions for social insurance and private benefit plans. Also includes an estimate of wages, salaries, and supplemental payments for the self-employed.
[4] Hourly compensation divided by a consumer price index. See footnote 4, Table B–32.
[5] Current dollar output divided by the output index.

Note: Percent changes are calculated using index numbers to three decimal places and may differ slightly from percent changes based on indexes in Table B–32, which are rounded to one decimal place.

Source: Department of Labor (Bureau of Labor Statistics).

Production and Business Activity

TABLE B–34. Industrial production indexes, major industry divisions, 1974–2018

[2012=100, except as noted; monthly data seasonally adjusted]

Year or month	Total industrial production [1]		Manufacturing					Mining	Utilities
	Index, 2012=100	Percent change from year earlier [2]	Total [1]	Percent change from year earlier [2]	Durable	Nondurable	Other (non-NAICS) [1]		
1974	46.3	−0.3	43.8	−0.2	28.5	67.5	123.4	91.2	49.5
1975	42.2	−8.9	39.2	−10.6	24.8	62.6	117.3	89.1	50.5
1976	45.5	7.9	42.7	9.0	27.1	68.3	121.0	89.7	52.9
1977	48.9	7.6	46.4	8.6	29.8	73.0	132.6	91.8	55.1
1978	51.6	5.5	49.2	6.1	32.1	75.6	137.2	94.7	56.5
1979	53.2	3.0	50.7	3.1	33.7	76.1	140.1	97.5	57.7
1980	51.8	−2.6	48.9	−3.6	32.2	73.7	144.9	99.3	58.1
1981	52.5	1.3	49.4	1.0	32.5	74.4	148.4	101.9	58.9
1982	49.8	−5.2	46.7	−5.5	29.7	73.3	150.1	96.8	57.0
1983	51.1	2.7	48.9	4.8	31.2	76.7	154.4	91.7	57.4
1984	55.7	8.9	53.7	9.8	35.6	80.2	161.5	97.6	60.8
1985	56.4	1.2	54.6	1.6	36.4	80.7	167.9	95.7	62.3
1986	56.9	1.0	55.8	2.2	37.0	83.0	171.3	88.8	62.9
1987	59.9	5.2	59.0	5.7	39.2	87.4	181.1	89.6	65.9
1988	63.0	5.2	62.1	5.3	42.1	90.4	180.3	92.0	69.9
1989	63.6	.9	62.6	.8	42.6	90.9	177.8	91.0	72.1
1990	64.2	1.0	63.1	.8	42.7	92.4	175.7	92.2	73.5
1991	63.2	−1.5	61.9	−1.9	41.4	92.1	168.5	90.3	75.3
1992	65.1	2.9	64.2	3.7	43.6	94.5	165.1	88.6	75.3
1993	67.2	3.3	66.5	3.6	46.1	95.9	166.2	88.4	77.9
1994	70.8	5.3	70.4	5.9	50.0	99.2	164.8	90.0	79.5
1995	74.0	4.6	74.0	5.1	54.1	100.9	164.8	89.9	82.3
1996	77.4	4.5	77.6	4.9	59.1	101.2	163.2	91.5	84.6
1997	83.0	7.2	84.2	8.4	66.1	105.0	177.0	93.3	84.5
1998	87.8	5.8	89.8	6.7	73.0	106.7	187.5	91.6	86.8
1999	91.7	4.4	94.3	5.1	79.3	107.3	192.9	86.9	89.5
2000	95.2	3.9	98.2	4.1	85.0	107.8	192.4	88.8	92.0
2001	92.3	−3.1	94.6	−3.6	81.6	104.7	179.9	89.1	91.7
2002	92.6	.4	95.1	.5	81.9	106.0	173.8	84.9	94.4
2003	93.8	1.3	96.4	1.3	84.2	106.2	168.9	85.1	96.0
2004	96.4	2.7	99.4	3.1	88.2	107.8	169.7	85.0	97.4
2005	99.6	3.3	103.4	4.1	93.4	110.5	169.1	84.0	99.5
2006	101.8	2.3	106.1	2.6	97.8	111.2	167.1	86.1	99.2
2007	104.4	2.5	109.0	2.8	102.7	112.5	157.7	86.8	102.3
2008	100.8	−3.5	103.8	−4.8	99.2	105.8	143.9	88.0	101.9
2009	89.2	−11.5	89.5	−13.8	80.6	97.7	120.3	83.1	99.0
2010	94.1	5.5	94.7	5.8	89.2	99.8	111.2	87.2	102.8
2011	97.1	3.1	97.5	2.9	94.7	99.9	106.0	92.6	102.4
2012	100.0	3.0	100.0	2.6	100.0	100.0	100.0	100.0	100.0
2013	102.0	2.0	100.9	.9	102.1	100.0	95.0	106.3	102.2
2014	105.2	3.1	102.0	1.1	105.1	99.3	93.8	117.8	103.5
2015	104.1	−1.0	101.5	−.5	103.9	99.6	90.4	113.8	102.7
2016	102.1	−1.9	100.7	−.8	101.7	100.4	88.0	102.7	102.3
2017	103.7	1.6	101.9	1.2	103.3	101.8	81.9	109.3	101.0
2018 [p]	108.0	4.1	104.4	2.5	106.8	103.9	76.1	123.3	105.5
2017: Jan	102.5	−.5	101.5	.1	103.0	100.9	85.1	104.1	99.4
Feb	102.2	−.2	101.6	.7	103.0	101.2	85.5	106.4	92.2
Mar	102.7	1.2	101.1	.4	102.6	100.8	84.1	106.7	100.6
Apr	103.7	1.9	102.2	1.9	104.0	101.7	83.2	107.9	100.4
May	103.7	2.1	101.8	1.6	103.1	101.8	82.3	108.5	102.8
June	103.8	1.8	101.9	1.5	103.1	102.2	81.8	109.5	101.2
July	103.6	1.4	101.7	1.0	102.3	102.5	80.4	109.3	102.1
Aug	103.2	1.1	101.4	1.1	102.6	101.7	79.9	108.7	100.6
Sept	103.2	1.2	101.3	.7	103.5	100.4	80.4	110.1	99.8
Oct	104.8	2.7	102.6	1.8	103.9	102.8	81.7	111.6	103.0
Nov	105.3	3.4	102.9	2.1	104.2	103.1	79.9	113.9	103.3
Dec	105.8	2.9	102.8	1.7	104.3	103.1	78.3	115.1	106.6
2018: Jan	105.4	2.8	102.3	.8	104.0	102.2	78.2	113.9	108.8
Feb	105.9	3.7	103.8	2.2	105.6	103.6	79.8	117.1	98.4
Mar	106.4	3.6	103.7	2.5	105.8	103.1	80.1	118.4	102.6
Apr	107.7	3.8	104.3	2.0	106.3	103.9	79.5	119.5	108.5
May	106.8	3.0	103.3	1.4	104.7	103.6	77.6	120.7	105.7
June	107.4	3.5	104.0	2.0	106.1	103.9	74.4	122.8	104.1
July	107.9	4.1	104.4	2.7	106.0	104.8	73.7	123.8	104.2
Aug	108.8	5.5	104.9	3.4	107.5	104.4	73.8	126.5	105.4
Sept [p]	109.0	5.7	105.2	3.8	108.1	104.3	74.7	127.6	104.1
Oct [p]	109.3	4.4	105.0	2.3	108.0	104.1	75.1	127.9	107.5
Nov [p]	110.0	4.5	105.3	2.4	108.6	104.2	73.7	129.3	109.9
Dec [p]	110.1	4.1	106.1	3.2	109.9	104.7	71.6	131.2	102.4

[1] Total industry and total manufacturing series include manufacturing as defined in the North American Industry Classification System (NAICS) plus those industries—logging and newspaper, periodical, book, and directory publishing—that have traditionally been considered to be manufacturing and included in the industrial sector.

[2] Percent changes based on unrounded indexes.

Note: Data based on NAICS; see footnote 1.

Source: Board of Governors of the Federal Reserve System.

Table B-35. Capacity utilization rates, 1974–2018

[Percent [1]; monthly data seasonally adjusted]

Year or month	Total industry [2]	Manufacturing				Mining	Utilities	Stage-of-process		
		Total [2]	Durable goods	Nondurable goods	Other (non-NAICS) [2]			Crude	Primary and semi-finished	Finished
1974	85.1	84.5	84.7	84.2	82.7	91.1	86.4	91.0	87.3	80.4
1975	75.8	73.7	71.8	76.1	77.3	89.5	84.9	84.0	75.2	73.8
1976	79.8	78.3	76.4	81.2	77.6	89.6	85.4	87.0	80.1	76.9
1977	83.4	82.5	81.2	84.4	83.2	89.5	86.7	89.1	84.5	79.9
1978	85.1	84.4	83.8	85.3	85.0	89.7	86.9	88.7	86.2	82.3
1979	85.0	84.1	84.1	83.9	85.6	91.2	86.9	90.0	85.9	81.8
1980	80.8	78.7	77.6	79.7	86.7	91.3	85.3	89.4	78.7	79.4
1981	79.6	76.9	75.1	78.8	87.5	90.9	84.1	89.3	77.2	77.5
1982	73.6	70.9	66.5	76.4	87.4	84.1	79.7	82.3	70.5	73.1
1983	74.8	73.4	68.7	79.4	87.9	79.8	79.1	79.9	74.4	73.0
1984	80.4	79.3	76.9	82.1	89.4	85.8	81.6	85.8	81.1	77.2
1985	79.2	78.1	75.7	80.5	90.3	84.4	81.5	83.8	79.8	76.6
1986	78.6	78.4	75.4	81.8	88.7	77.6	80.6	79.2	79.7	77.1
1987	81.1	81.0	77.6	84.8	90.4	80.3	83.2	82.8	82.7	78.7
1988	84.3	84.0	82.0	86.2	88.6	84.1	86.5	86.3	85.8	81.7
1989	83.8	83.3	81.9	85.0	85.4	85.1	86.5	86.8	84.7	81.7
1990	82.5	81.6	79.4	84.2	83.7	86.9	86.2	87.9	82.6	80.6
1991	79.9	78.5	75.4	82.3	80.8	85.4	87.5	85.5	80.0	78.2
1992	80.5	79.5	77.0	82.7	80.0	85.3	86.0	85.9	81.4	78.1
1993	81.4	80.4	78.6	82.7	81.2	85.8	87.9	85.8	83.2	78.2
1994	83.5	82.8	81.6	84.5	81.3	86.8	88.0	87.8	86.2	79.2
1995	83.9	83.1	82.2	84.5	82.2	87.6	89.0	89.0	86.3	79.8
1996	83.3	82.1	81.5	83.1	80.6	90.5	90.4	89.1	85.5	79.3
1997	84.0	83.0	82.1	83.8	85.6	91.8	89.8	90.4	85.9	80.2
1998	82.7	81.5	80.5	82.2	86.8	89.3	92.3	87.0	84.0	80.1
1999	81.7	80.4	80.0	80.1	87.0	86.2	93.8	86.1	84.2	77.8
2000	81.4	79.6	79.4	79.0	87.2	90.5	93.9	88.5	83.8	76.7
2001	76.1	73.8	71.4	75.8	82.6	89.9	89.8	85.5	77.3	72.5
2002	74.9	73.0	69.9	76.0	81.4	86.0	87.5	83.2	77.3	70.5
2003	75.9	73.9	71.0	76.9	81.6	87.8	85.7	85.0	78.1	71.3
2004	78.1	76.4	73.9	78.8	82.5	88.2	84.6	86.5	80.1	73.3
2005	80.0	78.4	76.4	80.3	81.9	88.5	85.3	86.6	81.7	75.6
2006	80.4	78.7	77.6	79.8	79.8	90.2	84.0	88.0	81.3	76.4
2007	80.7	78.8	78.6	79.3	76.3	89.4	86.1	88.6	81.0	77.2
2008	77.8	74.6	74.7	74.3	77.2	90.0	84.4	87.5	76.7	74.1
2009	68.5	65.5	61.4	69.9	69.8	80.3	80.7	77.9	65.7	68.2
2010	73.6	70.7	68.7	73.4	66.4	83.9	83.1	83.3	71.8	71.3
2011	76.2	73.6	72.6	75.4	65.3	85.7	81.6	84.5	74.3	74.0
2012	77.2	74.9	75.4	75.4	63.0	86.9	78.5	85.4	74.7	75.4
2013	77.6	75.0	75.4	75.6	62.0	86.9	80.0	85.8	75.7	74.7
2014	79.0	75.8	76.8	75.7	63.5	90.2	80.9	88.3	76.9	75.4
2015	77.3	75.8	75.9	76.7	63.5	83.9	80.0	82.7	76.5	75.8
2016	75.3	74.6	73.8	76.4	63.5	77.6	78.8	78.5	75.4	74.1
2017	76.1	74.8	74.2	76.4	61.1	84.5	76.3	83.8	75.0	74.2
2018 P	78.0	75.7	75.8	77.1	58.6	92.0	78.0	89.9	76.3	75.1
2017: Jan	75.4	74.7	74.3	76.0	62.5	80.0	75.8	80.3	74.9	74.0
Feb	75.1	74.7	74.2	76.1	62.9	82.0	70.2	81.5	73.9	74.0
Mar	75.5	74.3	73.9	75.7	62.1	82.3	76.4	82.1	74.8	73.6
Apr	76.2	75.1	74.9	76.4	61.6	83.4	76.2	83.4	75.0	74.6
May	76.2	74.8	74.2	76.4	61.2	84.0	77.9	84.0	75.2	74.1
June	76.2	74.8	74.1	76.7	61.0	84.9	76.5	84.7	75.0	74.1
July	76.1	74.6	73.5	76.8	60.1	84.8	77.1	84.8	74.7	74.0
Aug	75.7	74.4	73.6	76.2	59.9	84.3	75.9	83.4	74.3	74.1
Sept	75.7	74.2	74.2	75.2	60.5	85.3	75.2	82.5	74.4	74.3
Oct	76.8	75.2	74.4	76.9	61.6	86.4	77.4	85.4	75.5	74.6
Nov	77.1	75.3	74.6	77.1	60.5	87.9	77.6	86.7	75.9	74.3
Dec	77.3	75.2	74.6	77.0	59.4	88.6	79.9	86.9	76.4	74.3
2018: Jan	77.0	74.7	74.3	76.3	59.5	87.4	81.5	85.3	76.3	74.2
Feb	77.2	75.7	75.4	77.2	60.8	89.5	73.6	86.9	75.5	75.2
Mar	77.5	75.6	75.5	76.8	61.2	90.1	76.6	87.9	76.1	74.6
Apr	78.2	75.9	75.7	77.3	60.9	90.5	80.9	88.3	77.3	75.1
May	77.5	75.1	74.5	77.0	59.7	90.9	78.7	89.1	76.3	73.9
June	77.8	75.5	75.4	77.1	57.3	92.0	77.3	90.1	76.1	74.6
July	78.0	75.7	75.2	77.7	56.9	92.3	77.3	90.6	75.9	75.0
Aug	78.5	76.0	76.2	77.3	57.1	93.9	78.0	91.9	76.3	75.3
Sept P	78.5	76.1	76.6	77.1	58.0	94.2	76.9	92.0	76.0	75.7
Oct P	78.6	75.9	76.4	76.9	58.4	93.9	79.3	91.5	76.5	75.5
Nov P	78.9	76.0	76.7	76.9	57.4	94.4	80.9	92.0	77.2	75.4
Dec P	78.8	76.5	77.6	77.2	56.0	95.3	75.2	92.6	76.2	76.1

[1] Output as percent of capacity.
[2] See footnote 1 and Note, Table B–34.

Source: Board of Governors of the Federal Reserve System.

New private housing units started, authorized, and completed and houses sold,
1975–2018

[Thousands; monthly data at seasonally adjusted annual rates]

Year or month	New housing units started				New housing units authorized [1]				New housing units completed	New houses sold
	Total	Type of structure			Total	Type of structure				
		1 unit	2 to 4 units [2]	5 units or more		1 unit	2 to 4 units	5 units or more		
1975	1,160.4	892.2	64.0	204.3	939.2	675.5	63.8	199.8	1,317.2	549
1976	1,537.5	1,162.4	85.8	289.2	1,296.2	893.6	93.1	309.5	1,377.2	646
1977	1,987.1	1,450.9	121.7	414.4	1,690.0	1,126.1	121.3	442.7	1,657.1	819
1978	2,020.3	1,433.3	125.1	462.0	1,800.5	1,182.6	130.6	487.3	1,867.5	817
1979	1,745.1	1,194.1	122.0	429.0	1,551.8	981.5	125.4	444.8	1,870.8	709
1980	1,292.2	852.2	109.5	330.5	1,190.6	710.4	114.5	365.7	1,501.6	545
1981	1,084.2	705.4	91.2	287.7	985.5	564.3	101.8	319.4	1,265.7	436
1982	1,062.2	662.6	80.1	319.6	1,000.5	546.4	88.3	365.8	1,005.5	412
1983	1,703.0	1,067.6	113.5	522.0	1,605.2	901.5	133.7	570.1	1,390.3	623
1984	1,749.5	1,084.2	121.4	543.9	1,681.8	922.4	142.6	616.8	1,652.2	639
1985	1,741.8	1,072.4	93.5	576.0	1,733.3	956.6	120.1	656.6	1,703.3	688
1986	1,805.4	1,179.4	84.0	542.0	1,769.4	1,077.6	108.4	583.5	1,756.4	750
1987	1,620.5	1,146.4	65.1	408.7	1,534.8	1,024.4	89.3	421.1	1,668.8	671
1988	1,488.1	1,081.3	58.7	348.0	1,455.6	993.8	75.7	386.1	1,529.8	676
1989	1,376.1	1,003.3	55.3	317.6	1,338.4	931.7	66.9	339.8	1,422.8	650
1990	1,192.7	894.8	37.6	260.4	1,110.8	793.9	54.3	262.6	1,308.0	534
1991	1,013.9	840.4	35.6	137.9	948.8	753.5	43.1	152.1	1,090.8	509
1992	1,199.7	1,029.9	30.9	139.0	1,094.9	910.7	45.8	138.4	1,157.5	610
1993	1,287.6	1,125.7	29.4	132.6	1,199.1	986.5	52.4	160.2	1,192.7	666
1994	1,457.0	1,198.4	35.2	223.5	1,371.6	1,068.5	62.2	241.0	1,346.9	670
1995	1,354.1	1,076.2	33.8	244.1	1,332.5	997.3	63.8	271.5	1,312.6	667
1996	1,476.8	1,160.9	45.3	270.8	1,425.6	1,069.5	65.8	290.3	1,412.9	757
1997	1,474.0	1,133.7	44.5	295.8	1,441.1	1,062.4	68.4	310.3	1,400.5	804
1998	1,616.9	1,271.4	42.6	302.9	1,612.3	1,187.6	69.2	355.5	1,474.2	886
1999	1,640.9	1,302.4	31.9	306.6	1,663.5	1,246.7	65.8	351.1	1,604.9	880
2000	1,568.7	1,230.9	38.7	299.1	1,592.3	1,198.1	64.9	329.3	1,573.7	877
2001	1,602.7	1,273.3	36.6	292.8	1,636.7	1,235.6	66.0	335.2	1,570.8	908
2002	1,704.9	1,358.6	38.5	307.9	1,747.7	1,332.6	73.7	341.4	1,648.4	973
2003	1,847.7	1,499.0	33.5	315.2	1,889.2	1,460.9	82.5	345.8	1,678.7	1,086
2004	1,955.8	1,610.5	42.3	303.0	2,070.1	1,613.4	90.4	366.2	1,841.9	1,203
2005	2,068.3	1,715.8	41.1	311.4	2,155.3	1,682.0	84.0	389.3	1,931.4	1,283
2006	1,800.9	1,465.4	42.7	292.8	1,838.9	1,378.2	76.6	384.1	1,979.4	1,051
2007	1,355.0	1,046.0	31.7	277.3	1,398.4	979.9	59.6	359.0	1,502.8	776
2008	905.5	622.0	17.5	266.0	905.4	575.6	34.4	295.4	1,119.7	485
2009	554.0	445.1	11.6	97.3	583.0	441.1	20.7	121.1	794.4	375
2010	586.9	471.2	11.4	104.3	604.6	447.3	22.0	135.3	651.7	323
2011	608.8	430.6	10.9	167.3	624.1	418.5	21.6	184.0	584.9	306
2012	780.6	535.3	11.4	233.9	829.7	518.7	25.9	285.1	649.2	368
2013	924.9	617.6	13.6	293.7	990.8	620.8	29.0	341.1	764.4	429
2014	1,003.3	647.9	13.7	341.7	1,052.1	640.3	29.9	382.0	883.8	437
2015	1,111.8	714.5	11.5	385.8	1,182.6	696.0	32.1	454.5	968.2	501
2016	1,173.8	781.5	11.5	380.8	1,206.6	750.8	34.8	421.1	1,059.7	561
2017	1,203.0	848.9	11.4	342.7	1,282.0	820.0	37.2	424.8	1,152.9	613
2018 P	1,246.6	872.8	14.0	359.7	1,310.7	852.7	37.6	420.4	1,191.7	....
2017: Jan	1,225	807	....	415	1,329	798	30	501	1,086	596
Feb	1,289	875	....	395	1,248	825	45	378	1,148	618
Mar	1,179	824	....	346	1,279	825	36	418	1,189	643
Apr	1,165	834	....	314	1,255	796	36	423	1,095	593
May	1,122	791	....	317	1,205	784	35	386	1,169	604
June	1,225	860	....	359	1,312	813	37	462	1,234	616
July	1,185	839	....	335	1,258	817	42	399	1,197	556
Aug	1,172	878	....	286	1,300	803	36	461	1,091	558
Sept	1,158	831	....	310	1,254	831	36	387	1,086	637
Oct	1,265	888	....	359	1,343	854	35	454	1,188	618
Nov	1,303	948	....	347	1,323	864	41	418	1,144	712
Dec	1,210	847	....	359	1,320	877	38	405	1,197	636
2018: Jan	1,334	886	....	435	1,366	870	45	451	1,218	633
Feb	1,290	900	....	372	1,323	886	46	391	1,289	663
Mar	1,327	882	....	431	1,377	851	40	486	1,229	672
Apr	1,276	898	....	357	1,364	863	41	460	1,257	633
May	1,329	938	....	379	1,301	843	34	424	1,251	653
June	1,177	851	....	316	1,292	853	36	403	1,216	612
July	1,184	861	....	317	1,303	873	28	402	1,195	606
Aug	1,280	890	....	373	1,249	827	35	387	1,230	601
Sept	1,237	879	....	349	1,270	854	40	376	1,148	613
Oct	1,209	863	....	327	1,265	847	36	382	1,111	562
Nov P	1,214	812	....	387	1,322	848	39	435	1,128	657
Dec P	1,078	758	....	302	1,326	829	37	460	1,097	....

[1] Authorized by issuance of local building permits in permit-issuing places: 20,100 places beginning with 2014; 19,300 for 2004–2013; 19,000 for 1994–2003; 17,000 for 1984–93; 16,000 for 1978–83; and 14,000 for 1975–77.
[2] Monthly data do not meet publication standards because tests for identifiable and stable seasonality do not meet reliability standards.

Note: One-unit estimates prior to 1999, for new housing units started and completed and for new houses sold, include an upward adjustment of 3.3 percent to account for structures in permit-issuing areas that did not have permit authorization.

Source: Department of Commerce (Bureau of the Census).

[Amounts in millions of dollars; monthly data seasonally adjusted]

Year or month	Total manufacturing and trade			Manufacturing			Merchant wholesalers [1]			Retail trade			Retail and food services sales
	Sales [2]	Inventories [3]	Ratio [4]	Sales [2]	Inventories [3]	Ratio [4]	Sales [2]	Inventories [3]	Ratio [4]	Sales [2,5]	Inventories [3]	Ratio [4]	
SIC: [6]													
1978	260,320	400,931	1.54	126,905	211,691	1.67	66,413	86,934	1.31	67,002	102,306	1.53	
1979	297,701	452,640	1.52	143,936	242,157	1.68	79,051	99,679	1.26	74,713	110,804	1.48	
1980	327,233	508,924	1.56	154,391	265,215	1.72	93,099	122,631	1.32	79,743	121,078	1.52	
1981	355,822	545,786	1.53	168,129	283,413	1.69	101,180	129,654	1.28	86,514	132,719	1.53	
1982	347,625	573,908	1.67	163,351	311,852	1.95	95,211	127,428	1.36	89,062	134,628	1.49	
1983	369,286	590,287	1.56	172,547	312,379	1.78	99,225	130,075	1.28	97,514	147,833	1.44	
1984	410,124	649,780	1.53	190,682	339,516	1.73	112,199	142,452	1.23	107,243	167,812	1.49	
1985	422,583	664,039	1.56	194,538	334,749	1.73	113,459	147,409	1.28	114,586	181,881	1.52	
1986	430,419	662,738	1.55	194,657	322,654	1.68	114,960	153,574	1.32	120,803	186,510	1.56	
1987	457,735	709,848	1.50	206,326	338,109	1.59	122,968	163,903	1.29	128,442	207,836	1.55	
1988	497,157	767,222	1.49	224,619	369,374	1.57	134,521	178,801	1.30	138,017	219,047	1.54	
1989	527,039	815,455	1.52	236,698	391,212	1.63	143,760	187,009	1.28	146,581	237,234	1.58	
1990	545,909	840,594	1.52	242,686	405,073	1.65	149,506	195,833	1.29	153,718	239,688	1.56	
1991	542,815	834,609	1.53	239,847	390,950	1.65	148,306	200,448	1.33	154,661	243,211	1.54	
1992	567,176	842,809	1.48	250,394	382,510	1.54	154,150	208,302	1.32	162,632	251,997	1.52	
NAICS: [6]													
1992	540,199	835,800	1.53	242,002	378,609	1.57	147,261	196,914	1.31	150,936	260,277	1.67	167,842
1993	567,195	863,125	1.50	251,708	379,806	1.50	154,018	204,842	1.30	161,469	278,477	1.68	179,425
1994	609,854	926,395	1.46	269,843	399,934	1.44	164,575	221,978	1.29	175,436	304,483	1.66	194,186
1995	654,689	985,385	1.48	289,973	424,802	1.44	179,915	238,392	1.29	184,801	322,191	1.72	204,219
1996	686,923	1,004,646	1.45	299,766	430,366	1.44	190,362	241,058	1.27	196,796	333,222	1.67	216,983
1997	723,443	1,045,495	1.42	319,558	443,227	1.37	198,154	258,454	1.26	205,731	343,814	1.64	227,178
1998	742,391	1,077,183	1.44	324,984	448,373	1.39	202,260	272,297	1.32	215,147	356,513	1.62	237,746
1999	786,178	1,137,260	1.40	335,991	463,004	1.35	216,597	290,182	1.30	233,591	384,074	1.59	257,249
2000	833,868	1,195,064	1.41	350,715	480,748	1.35	234,546	309,191	1.29	248,606	405,955	1.59	273,961
2001	818,160	1,118,552	1.42	330,875	427,353	1.38	232,096	297,536	1.32	255,189	393,663	1.58	281,576
2002	823,234	1,139,700	1.36	326,227	423,205	1.29	236,294	301,310	1.26	260,713	415,185	1.55	288,256
2003	854,700	1,147,856	1.34	334,616	408,363	1.25	248,190	308,274	1.22	271,894	431,219	1.56	301,038
2004	926,002	1,241,644	1.30	359,081	441,122	1.19	277,501	340,128	1.17	289,421	460,394	1.56	320,550
2005	1,005,821	1,314,008	1.27	395,173	474,330	1.17	303,208	367,978	1.17	307,440	471,700	1.51	340,479
2006	1,069,032	1,408,429	1.28	417,963	523,093	1.20	328,438	398,924	1.17	322,631	486,412	1.49	357,863
2007	1,128,176	1,486,746	1.28	443,288	561,789	1.22	351,956	424,379	1.17	332,932	500,578	1.49	369,978
2008	1,160,722	1,465,186	1.31	455,750	542,696	1.26	377,030	445,307	1.20	327,943	477,183	1.52	365,965
2009	988,802	1,330,869	1.38	368,648	504,298	1.39	319,115	397,383	1.29	301,039	429,188	1.47	338,706
2010	1,088,890	1,449,499	1.27	409,273	553,333	1.28	361,447	441,618	1.15	318,171	454,548	1.39	357,081
2011	1,206,660	1,564,021	1.26	457,658	605,929	1.29	407,090	487,289	1.15	341,913	470,803	1.35	383,192
2012	1,267,248	1,652,863	1.28	474,727	624,177	1.30	434,002	523,034	1.17	358,519	505,652	1.38	402,199
2013	1,303,229	1,717,465	1.29	484,145	629,893	1.30	447,546	543,932	1.19	371,538	543,640	1.41	416,814
2014	1,340,932	1,776,773	1.31	490,630	640,143	1.31	463,682	575,944	1.21	386,620	560,686	1.43	434,638
2015	1,294,787	1,806,740	1.39	459,918	635,272	1.39	441,036	583,576	1.33	393,833	587,892	1.46	445,791
2016	1,286,409	1,839,188	1.42	446,225	630,894	1.41	435,490	596,276	1.35	404,695	612,018	1.49	459,575
2017	1,356,014	1,902,544	1.38	467,076	659,189	1.37	466,127	616,821	1.29	422,811	626,534	1.47	479,196
2018 [p]	1,444,204	1,994,489	1.35	499,975	681,549	1.35	500,885	661,843	1.28	443,343	651,097	1.44	503,035
2017: Jan	1,333,366	1,842,312	1.38	459,695	632,817	1.38	456,431	594,234	1.30	417,240	615,261	1.47	473,357
Feb	1,333,242	1,846,792	1.39	459,901	633,881	1.38	458,290	596,018	1.30	415,051	616,893	1.49	471,165
Mar	1,333,933	1,851,752	1.39	460,313	634,109	1.38	457,612	597,622	1.31	416,008	620,021	1.49	472,041
Apr	1,336,631	1,848,718	1.38	459,759	635,340	1.38	457,801	595,717	1.30	419,071	617,661	1.47	475,145
May	1,335,203	1,854,654	1.39	462,459	635,407	1.37	455,105	598,107	1.31	417,639	621,140	1.49	473,752
June	1,342,005	1,863,379	1.39	462,442	636,761	1.38	459,614	601,801	1.31	419,949	624,817	1.49	476,074
July	1,345,285	1,869,267	1.39	464,204	639,738	1.38	460,512	605,894	1.32	420,569	623,635	1.48	476,685
Aug	1,356,602	1,882,004	1.39	467,460	642,665	1.37	467,917	610,597	1.30	421,225	628,742	1.49	477,452
Sept	1,376,904	1,884,562	1.37	472,250	648,947	1.37	474,091	612,650	1.29	430,563	622,965	1.45	487,096
Oct	1,385,361	1,884,375	1.36	475,599	651,201	1.37	477,567	609,856	1.28	432,195	623,318	1.44	488,900
Nov	1,403,578	1,892,739	1.35	483,203	653,855	1.35	485,814	613,960	1.26	434,561	624,924	1.44	491,795
Dec	1,414,511	1,902,544	1.35	484,979	659,189	1.36	492,439	616,821	1.25	437,093	626,534	1.43	494,578
2018: Jan	1,406,327	1,915,012	1.36	488,179	661,479	1.35	483,516	623,030	1.29	434,632	630,503	1.45	492,034
Feb	1,411,971	1,925,817	1.36	489,307	663,710	1.36	487,805	627,913	1.29	434,859	634,194	1.46	492,530
Mar	1,420,071	1,923,669	1.35	492,699	664,712	1.35	489,608	629,230	1.29	437,764	629,727	1.44	496,077
Apr	1,429,298	1,929,393	1.35	493,302	667,132	1.35	496,410	629,865	1.27	439,586	632,396	1.44	497,776
May	1,447,550	1,935,563	1.34	496,450	668,607	1.35	506,959	631,955	1.25	444,141	635,001	1.43	503,955
June	1,451,814	1,937,569	1.33	501,641	670,214	1.34	505,806	632,717	1.25	444,367	634,638	1.43	505,168
July	1,455,246	1,950,641	1.34	501,661	676,154	1.35	506,874	636,339	1.26	446,711	638,148	1.43	508,230
Aug	1,461,984	1,961,025	1.34	505,207	676,738	1.34	510,369	642,214	1.26	446,408	642,073	1.44	507,872
Sept	1,466,193	1,970,561	1.34	508,879	680,834	1.34	511,058	646,756	1.27	446,256	642,971	1.44	506,749
Oct	1,467,492	1,982,473	1.35	508,280	682,058	1.34	508,186	652,318	1.28	451,026	648,097	1.44	511,616
Nov [p]	1,459,719	1,981,834	1.36	505,772	681,661	1.35	501,933	654,714	1.30	452,014	645,459	1.43	512,200
Dec [p]	1,448,122	1,994,489	1.38	504,894	681,549	1.35	497,162	661,843	1.33	446,066	651,097	1.46	505,826

[1] Excludes manufacturers' sales branches and offices.
[2] Annual data are averages of monthly not seasonally adjusted figures.
[3] Seasonally adjusted, end of period. Inventories beginning with January 1982 for manufacturing and December 1980 for wholesale and retail trade are not comparable with earlier periods.
[4] Inventory/sales ratio. Monthly inventories are inventories at the end of the month to sales for the month. Annual data beginning with 1982 are the average of monthly ratios for the year. Annual data for 1978–81 are the ratio of December inventories to monthly average sales for the year.
[5] Food services included on Standard Industrial Classification (SIC) basis and excluded on North American Industry Classification System (NAICS) basis. See last column for retail and food services sales.
[6] Effective in 2001, data classified based on NAICS. Data on NAICS basis available beginning with 1992. Earlier data based on SIC. Data on both NAICS and SIC basis include semiconductors.

Source: Department of Commerce (Bureau of the Census).

Prices

TABLE B–38. Changes in consumer price indexes, 1975–2018

[For all urban consumers; percent change]

Year or month	All items	All items less food and energy					Food			Energy [4]		C-CPI-U [5]
		Total [1]	Shelter [2]	Medical care [3]	Apparel	New vehicles	Total [1]	At home	Away from home	Total [1,3]	Gasoline	
						December to December, NSA						
1975	6.9	6.7	7.2	9.8	2.4	7.3	6.6	6.2	7.4	11.4	11.0	
1976	4.9	6.1	4.2	10.0	4.6	4.8	.5	-.8	6.0	7.1	2.8	
1977	6.7	6.5	8.8	8.9	4.3	7.2	8.1	7.9	7.9	7.2	4.8	
1978	9.0	8.5	11.4	8.8	3.1	6.2	11.8	12.5	10.4	7.9	8.6	
1979	13.3	11.3	17.5	10.1	5.5	7.4	10.2	9.7	11.4	37.5	52.1	
1980	12.5	12.2	15.0	9.9	6.8	7.4	10.2	10.5	9.6	18.0	18.9	
1981	8.9	9.5	9.9	12.5	3.5	6.8	4.3	2.9	7.1	11.9	9.4	
1982	3.8	4.5	2.4	11.0	1.6	1.4	3.1	2.3	5.1	1.3	-6.7	
1983	3.8	4.8	4.7	6.4	2.9	3.3	2.7	1.8	4.1	-.5	-1.6	
1984	3.9	4.7	5.2	6.1	2.0	2.5	3.8	3.6	4.2	.2	-2.5	
1985	3.8	4.3	6.0	6.8	2.8	3.6	2.6	2.0	3.8	1.8	3.0	
1986	1.1	3.8	4.6	7.7	.9	5.6	3.8	3.7	4.3	-19.7	-30.7	
1987	4.4	4.2	4.8	5.8	4.8	1.8	3.5	3.5	3.7	8.2	18.6	
1988	4.4	4.7	4.5	6.9	4.7	2.2	5.2	5.6	4.4	.5	-1.8	
1989	4.6	4.4	4.9	8.5	1.0	2.4	5.6	6.2	4.6	5.1	6.5	
1990	6.1	5.2	5.2	9.6	5.1	2.0	5.3	5.8	4.5	18.1	36.8	
1991	3.1	4.4	3.9	7.9	3.4	3.2	1.9	1.3	2.9	-7.4	-16.2	
1992	2.9	3.3	2.9	6.6	1.4	2.3	1.5	1.5	1.4	2.0	2.0	
1993	2.7	3.2	3.0	5.4	.9	3.3	2.9	3.5	1.9	-1.4	-5.9	
1994	2.7	2.6	3.0	4.9	-1.6	3.3	2.9	3.5	1.9	2.2	6.4	
1995	2.5	3.0	3.5	3.9	.1	1.9	2.1	2.0	2.2	-1.3	-4.2	
1996	3.3	2.6	2.9	3.0	-.2	1.8	4.3	4.9	3.1	8.6	12.4	
1997	1.7	2.2	3.4	2.8	1.0	-.9	1.5	1.0	2.6	-3.4	-6.1	
1998	1.6	2.4	3.3	3.4	-.7	.0	2.3	2.1	2.5	-8.8	-15.4	
1999	2.7	1.9	2.5	3.7	-.5	-.3	1.9	1.7	2.3	13.4	30.1	
2000	3.4	2.6	3.4	4.2	-1.8	.0	2.8	2.9	2.4	14.2	13.9	2.6
2001	1.6	2.7	4.2	4.7	-3.2	-.1	2.8	2.6	3.0	-13.0	-24.9	1.3
2002	2.4	1.9	3.1	5.0	-1.8	-2.0	1.5	.8	2.3	10.7	24.8	2.0
2003	1.9	1.1	2.2	3.7	-2.1	-1.8	3.6	4.5	2.3	6.9	6.8	1.7
2004	3.3	2.2	2.7	4.2	-.2	.6	2.7	2.4	3.0	16.6	26.1	3.2
2005	3.4	2.2	2.6	4.3	-1.1	-.4	2.3	1.7	3.2	17.1	16.1	2.9
2006	2.5	2.6	4.2	3.6	.9	-.9	2.1	1.4	3.2	2.9	6.4	2.3
2007	4.1	2.4	3.1	5.2	-.3	-.3	4.9	5.6	4.0	17.4	29.6	3.7
2008	.1	1.8	1.9	2.6	-1.0	-3.2	5.9	6.6	5.0	-21.3	-43.1	.2
2009	2.7	1.8	.3	3.4	1.9	4.9	-.5	-2.4	1.9	18.2	53.5	2.5
2010	1.5	.8	.4	3.3	-1.1	-.2	1.5	1.7	1.3	7.7	13.8	1.3
2011	3.0	2.2	1.9	3.5	4.6	3.2	4.7	6.0	2.9	6.6	9.9	2.9
2012	1.7	1.9	2.2	3.2	1.8	1.6	1.8	1.3	2.5	.5	1.7	1.5
2013	1.5	1.7	2.5	2.0	.6	.4	1.1	.4	2.1	.5	-1.0	1.3
2014	.8	1.6	2.9	3.0	-2.0	.5	3.4	3.7	3.0	-10.6	-21.0	.5
2015	.7	2.1	3.2	2.6	-.9	.2	.8	-.4	2.6	-12.6	-19.7	.4
2016	2.1	2.2	3.6	4.1	-.1	.3	-.2	-2.0	2.3	5.4	9.1	1.8
2017	2.1	1.8	3.2	1.8	-1.6	-.5	1.6	.9	2.5	6.9	10.7	1.7
2018	1.9	2.2	3.2	2.0	-.1	-.3	1.6	.6	2.8	-.3	-2.1	1.8
						Change from year earlier, NSA						
2017: Jan	2.5	2.3	3.5	3.9	1.0	0.9	-0.2	-1.9	2.4	10.8	20.3	2.3
Feb	2.7	2.2	3.5	3.5	.4	.5	.0	-1.7	2.4	15.2	30.7	2.6
Mar	2.4	2.0	3.5	3.5	.6	.2	.5	-.9	2.4	10.9	19.9	2.1
Apr	2.2	1.9	3.5	3.0	.5	.4	.5	-.8	2.3	9.3	14.3	1.8
May	1.9	1.7	3.3	2.7	-.9	.3	.9	-.2	2.3	5.4	5.8	1.5
June	1.6	1.7	3.3	2.7	-.7	.0	.9	-.1	2.2	2.3	-.4	1.2
July	1.7	1.7	3.2	2.6	-.4	-.6	1.1	.3	2.1	3.4	3.0	1.3
Aug	1.9	1.7	3.3	1.8	-.6	-.7	1.1	.3	2.2	6.4	10.4	1.5
Sept	2.2	1.7	3.2	1.6	-.2	-1.0	1.2	.4	2.4	10.1	19.3	1.9
Oct	2.0	1.8	3.2	1.7	-.6	-1.4	1.3	.6	2.3	6.4	10.8	1.6
Nov	2.2	1.7	3.2	1.7	-1.6	-1.1	1.4	.6	2.4	9.4	16.5	1.8
Dec	2.1	1.8	3.2	1.8	-1.6	-.5	1.6	.9	2.5	6.9	10.7	1.7
2018: Jan	2.1	1.8	3.2	2.0	-.7	-1.2	1.7	1.0	2.5	5.5	8.5	1.6
Feb	2.2	1.8	3.1	1.8	.4	-1.5	1.4	.5	2.6	7.7	12.6	1.8
Mar	2.4	2.1	3.3	2.0	.3	-1.2	1.3	.4	2.5	7.0	11.1	2.0
Apr	2.5	2.1	3.4	2.2	.8	-1.6	1.4	.5	2.5	7.9	13.4	2.1
May	2.8	2.2	3.5	2.4	1.4	-1.1	1.2	.1	2.7	11.7	21.8	2.4
June	2.9	2.3	3.4	2.5	.6	-.5	1.4	.4	2.8	12.0	24.3	2.5
July	2.9	2.4	3.5	1.9	.3	.2	1.4	.4	2.8	12.1	25.4	2.7
Aug	2.7	2.2	3.4	1.5	-1.4	.3	1.4	.5	2.6	10.2	20.3	2.5
Sept	2.3	2.2	3.3	1.7	-.6	.5	1.4	.4	2.6	4.8	9.1	2.0
Oct	2.5	2.1	3.2	1.7	-.4	.5	1.4	.1	2.5	8.9	16.1	2.3
Nov	2.2	2.2	3.2	2.0	-.4	.3	1.2	.4	2.6	3.1	5.0	2.0
Dec	1.9	2.2	3.2	2.0	-.1	-.3	1.6	.6	2.8	-.3	-2.1	1.8

[1] Includes other items not shown separately.
[2] Data beginning with 1983 incorporate a rental equivalence measure for homeowners' costs.
[3] Commodities and services.
[4] Household energy--electricity, utility (piped) gas service, fuel oil, etc.--and motor fuel.
[5] Chained consumer price index (C-CPI-U) introduced in 2002. Reflects the effect of substitution that consumers make across item categories in response to changes in relative prices. Data for 2018 are subject to revision.

Source: Department of Labor (Bureau of Labor Statistics).

TABLE B–39. Price indexes for personal consumption expenditures, and percent changes, 1972–2018

[Chain-type price index numbers, 2012=100; monthly data seasonally adjusted]

Year or month	Personal consumption expenditures (PCE)						Percent change from year earlier					
	Total	Goods	Services	Food¹	Energy goods and services²	PCE less food and energy	Total	Goods	Services	Food¹	Energy goods and services²	PCE less food and energy
1972	22.586	33.926	17.491	22.371	10.716	23.912	3.4	2.6	4.2	4.8	2.6	3.2
1973	23.802	35.949	18.336	25.202	11.640	24.823	5.4	6.0	4.8	12.7	8.6	3.8
1974	26.280	40.436	19.890	29.034	15.176	26.788	10.4	12.5	8.5	15.2	30.4	7.9
1975	28.470	43.703	21.595	31.217	16.672	29.026	8.3	8.1	8.6	7.5	9.9	8.4
1976	30.032	45.413	23.093	31.798	17.791	30.791	5.5	3.9	6.9	1.9	6.7	6.1
1977	31.986	47.837	24.841	33.671	19.294	32.771	6.5	5.3	7.6	5.9	8.4	6.4
1978	34.211	50.773	26.750	36.892	20.380	34.943	7.0	6.1	7.7	9.6	5.6	6.6
1979	37.251	55.574	28.994	40.516	25.414	37.490	8.9	9.5	8.4	9.8	24.7	7.3
1980	41.262	61.797	32.009	43.922	33.203	40.936	10.8	11.2	10.4	8.4	30.6	9.2
1981	44.958	66.389	35.288	47.051	37.668	44.523	9.0	7.4	10.2	7.1	13.4	8.8
1982	47.456	68.198	38.058	48.289	38.326	47.417	5.6	2.7	7.8	2.6	1.7	6.5
1983	49.474	69.429	40.396	48.844	38.684	49.844	4.3	1.8	6.1	1.1	.9	5.1
1984	51.343	70.742	42.498	50.312	39.172	51.911	3.8	1.9	5.2	3.0	1.3	4.1
1985	53.134	71.877	44.577	50.859	39.585	54.019	3.5	1.6	4.9	1.1	1.1	4.1
1986	54.290	71.541	46.408	52.056	34.685	55.883	2.2	–.5	4.1	2.4	–12.4	3.5
1987	55.964	73.842	47.796	53.699	35.069	57.683	3.1	3.2	3.0	3.2	1.1	3.2
1988	58.151	75.788	50.082	55.300	35.337	60.134	3.9	2.6	4.8	3.0	.8	4.2
1989	60.690	78.704	52.216	58.216	37.425	62.630	4.4	3.8	4.7	5.3	5.9	4.2
1990	63.355	81.927	54.846	61.060	40.589	65.168	4.4	4.1	4.6	4.9	8.5	4.1
1991	65.473	83.930	56.992	62.977	40.769	67.495	3.3	2.4	3.9	3.1	.4	3.6
1992	67.218	84.943	59.018	63.461	40.959	69.547	2.7	1.2	3.6	.8	.5	3.0
1993	68.892	85.681	61.059	64.348	41.331	71.436	2.5	.9	3.5	1.4	.9	2.7
1994	70.330	86.552	62.719	65.426	41.493	73.234	2.1	1.0	2.7	1.7	.4	2.2
1995	71.811	87.361	64.471	66.844	41.819	74.625	2.1	.9	2.8	2.2	.8	2.2
1996	73.346	88.321	66.240	68.883	43.777	76.040	2.1	1.1	2.7	3.1	4.7	1.9
1997	74.623	88.219	68.107	70.195	44.236	77.382	1.7	–.1	2.8	1.9	1.0	1.8
1998	75.216	86.893	69.549	71.077	40.502	78.366	.8	–1.5	2.1	1.3	–8.4	1.3
1999	76.338	87.349	70.970	72.241	42.143	79.425	1.5	.5	2.0	1.6	4.1	1.4
2000	78.235	89.082	72.938	73.933	49.843	80.804	2.5	2.0	2.8	2.3	18.3	1.7
2001	79.738	89.015	75.171	76.089	51.088	82.258	1.9	–.1	3.1	2.9	2.5	1.8
2002	80.789	88.166	77.123	77.239	48.110	83.639	1.3	–1.0	2.6	1.5	–5.8	1.7
2003	82.358	88.054	79.506	78.701	54.190	84.837	1.9	–.1	3.1	1.9	12.6	1.4
2004	84.411	89.292	81.965	81.157	60.339	86.515	2.5	1.4	3.1	3.1	11.3	2.0
2005	86.812	91.084	84.673	82.575	70.752	88.373	2.8	2.0	3.3	1.7	17.3	2.1
2006	89.174	92.306	87.616	83.963	78.812	90.392	2.7	1.3	3.5	1.7	11.4	2.3
2007	91.438	93.331	90.516	87.239	83.557	92.378	2.5	1.1	3.3	3.9	6.0	2.2
2008	94.180	96.122	93.235	92.552	95.464	94.225	3.0	3.0	3.0	6.1	14.3	2.0
2009	94.094	93.812	94.231	93.651	77.393	95.315	–.1	–2.4	1.1	1.2	–18.9	1.2
2010	95.705	95.183	95.957	93.931	85.120	96.608	1.7	1.5	1.8	.3	10.0	1.4
2011	98.131	98.773	97.814	97.682	98.601	98.139	2.5	3.8	1.9	4.0	15.8	1.6
2012	100.000	100.000	100.000	100.000	100.000	100.000	1.9	1.2	2.2	2.4	1.4	1.9
2013	101.346	99.407	102.316	100.989	99.109	101.526	1.3	–.6	2.3	1.0	–.9	1.5
2014	102.868	98.939	104.852	102.925	98.259	103.168	1.5	–.5	2.5	1.9	–.9	1.6
2015	103.126	95.889	106.823	104.086	80.617	104.501	.3	–3.1	1.9	1.1	–18.0	1.3
2016	104.235	94.340	109.325	102.997	74.770	106.237	1.1	–1.6	2.3	–1.0	–7.3	1.7
2017	106.073	94.632	111.984	102.858	81.292	107.961	1.8	.3	2.4	–.1	8.7	1.6
2018 ᵖ	108.230	95.280	114.952	103.398	87.691	110.005	2.0	.7	2.7	.5	7.9	1.9
2017: Jan	105.557	95.294	110.841	102.274	83.183	107.308	2.0	.7	2.7	–1.5	12.5	1.9
Feb	105.600	94.994	111.066	102.399	81.281	107.459	2.2	1.1	2.7	–1.5	17.5	1.9
Mar	105.427	94.603	111.009	102.726	79.686	107.328	1.9	.7	2.4	–.7	12.4	1.6
Apr	105.701	94.650	111.402	102.910	80.353	107.585	1.8	.2	2.5	–.6	10.0	1.6
May	105.705	94.181	111.660	102.954	78.264	107.713	1.6	–.3	2.5	–.2	5.4	1.6
June	105.800	94.064	111.869	102.875	77.538	107.873	1.5	–.5	2.4	–.1	2.0	1.6
July	105.871	94.078	111.970	103.033	76.920	107.976	1.5	–.1	2.2	.2	3.4	1.5
Aug	106.117	94.395	112.178	102.991	79.855	108.086	1.5	.1	2.2	.3	7.0	1.4
Sept	106.480	94.913	112.456	102.976	84.154	108.246	1.8	.6	2.3	.4	11.3	1.5
Oct	106.664	94.691	112.858	103.057	82.867	108.527	1.7	.2	2.4	.5	6.8	1.6
Nov	106.900	94.874	113.124	102.996	85.801	108.627	1.9	.6	2.4	.6	10.1	1.6
Dec	107.056	94.845	113.379	103.109	85.601	108.808	1.8	.4	2.5	.9	7.4	1.6
2018: Jan	107.406	95.538	113.543	103.129	88.186	109.054	1.8	.3	2.4	.8	6.0	1.6
Feb	107.556	95.411	113.842	102.995	88.148	109.240	1.9	.4	2.5	.6	8.4	1.7
Mar	107.610	95.023	114.135	103.189	85.680	109.431	2.1	.4	2.8	.5	7.5	2.0
Apr	107.865	95.374	114.337	103.504	86.989	109.618	2.0	.8	2.6	.6	8.3	1.9
May	108.085	95.467	114.627	103.259	87.794	109.845	2.3	1.4	2.7	.3	12.2	2.0
June	108.207	95.398	114.853	103.442	87.662	109.978	2.3	1.4	2.7	.6	13.1	2.0
July	108.365	95.396	115.098	103.527	87.227	110.177	2.4	1.4	2.8	.5	13.4	2.0
Aug	108.458	95.337	115.273	103.482	88.875	110.190	2.2	1.0	2.8	.5	11.3	1.9
Sept ᵖ	108.599	95.254	115.535	103.521	88.490	110.370	2.0	.4	2.7	.5	5.2	2.0
Oct ᵖ	108.812	95.440	115.762	103.399	90.256	110.520	2.0	.8	2.6	.3	8.9	1.8
Nov ᵖ	108.866	95.080	116.042	103.595	87.740	110.715	1.8	.2	2.6	.6	2.3	1.9
Dec ᵖ	108.929	94.641	116.382	103.733	85.238	110.922	1.7	–.2	2.6	.6	–.4	1.9

¹ Food consists of food and beverages purchased for off-premises consumption; food services, which include purchased meals and beverages, are not classified as food.
² Consists of gasoline and other energy goods and of electricity and gas services.

Source: Department of Commerce (Bureau of Economic Analysis).

Money Stock, Credit, and Finance

Table B–40. Money stock and debt measures, 1980–2018

[Averages of daily figures, except debt end-of-period basis; billions of dollars, seasonally adjusted]

Year and month	M1 — Sum of currency, demand deposits, travelers checks, and other checkable deposits	M2 — M1 plus savings deposits, retail MMMF balances, and small time deposits [1]	Debt — Debt of domestic nonfinancial sectors [2]	Percent change — From year or 6 months earlier [3] M1	From year or 6 months earlier [3] M2	From previous period [4] Debt
December:						
1980	408.5	1,599.8	4,051.5	7.0	8.6	9.6
1981	436.7	1,755.5	4,464.7	6.9	9.7	10.2
1982	474.8	1,905.9	4,900.3	8.7	8.6	10.2
1983	521.4	2,123.5	5,497.7	9.8	11.4	12.1
1984	551.6	2,306.4	6,308.4	5.8	8.6	14.8
1985	619.8	2,492.1	7,341.7	12.4	8.1	16.1
1986	724.7	2,728.0	8,216.7	16.9	9.5	12.0
1987	750.2	2,826.4	8,936.1	3.5	3.6	9.0
1988	786.7	2,988.2	9,753.9	4.9	5.7	9.2
1989	792.9	3,152.5	10,501.9	.8	5.5	7.5
1990	824.7	3,271.8	11,218.1	4.0	3.8	6.6
1991	897.0	3,372.2	11,746.7	8.8	3.1	4.7
1992	1,024.9	3,424.7	12,298.0	14.3	1.6	4.7
1993	1,129.6	3,474.5	13,021.3	10.2	1.5	5.8
1994	1,150.7	3,486.4	13,701.7	1.9	.3	5.2
1995	1,127.5	3,629.5	14,386.3	−2.0	4.1	4.9
1996	1,081.3	3,810.5	15,136.4	−4.1	5.0	5.2
1997	1,072.3	4,023.0	15,975.4	−.8	5.6	5.6
1998	1,095.0	4,365.7	17,044.3	2.1	8.5	6.7
1999	1,122.2	4,628.1	18,218.2	2.5	6.0	6.7
2000	1,088.6	4,914.4	19,106.0	−3.0	6.2	4.8
2001	1,183.2	5,419.6	20,183.0	8.7	10.3	5.7
2002	1,220.2	5,757.5	21,532.8	3.1	6.2	6.7
2003	1,306.2	6,052.6	23,238.5	7.0	5.1	7.8
2004	1,376.0	6,404.3	26,149.3	5.3	5.8	9.2
2005	1,374.3	6,667.4	28,431.5	−.1	4.1	8.8
2006	1,366.4	7,056.8	30,869.7	−.6	5.8	8.5
2007	1,373.0	7,457.3	33,360.5	.5	5.7	8.1
2008	1,601.1	8,181.1	35,138.7	16.6	9.7	5.8
2009	1,691.9	8,483.4	36,109.9	5.7	3.7	3.7
2010	1,835.8	8,789.1	37,475.2	8.5	3.6	4.3
2011	2,163.5	9,650.9	38,684.4	17.9	9.8	3.6
2012	2,460.6	10,445.6	40,375.9	13.7	8.2	4.8
2013	2,664.4	11,015.7	41,795.9	8.3	5.5	3.8
2014	2,940.7	11,670.1	43,456.7	10.4	5.9	4.1
2015	3,094.9	12,335.9	45,187.1	5.2	5.7	4.4
2016	3,342.4	13,209.6	47,185.9	8.0	7.1	4.5
2017 [p]	3,612.0	13,851.9	49,131.4	8.1	4.9	4.0
2018 [p]	3,744.0	14,387.6		3.7	3.9	
2017: Jan	3,390.9	13,282.3		8.8	6.2	
Feb	3,404.7	13,340.0		5.4	5.7	
Mar	3,445.5	13,405.3	47,614.5	7.2	5.7	3.1
Apr	3,454.2	13,470.4		7.1	5.6	
May	3,517.3	13,521.3		9.7	5.2	
June	3,525.9	13,551.6	48,151.3	11.0	5.2	4.6
July	3,550.9	13,617.1		9.4	5.0	
Aug	3,580.7	13,672.0		10.3	5.0	
Sept	3,574.2	13,717.9	48,732.9	7.5	4.7	4.9
Oct	3,606.7	13,779.8		8.8	4.6	
Nov	3,630.6	13,809.9		6.4	4.3	
Dec	3,612.0	13,851.9	49,131.4	4.9	4.4	3.3
2018: Jan	3,653.2	13,867.7		5.8	3.7	
Feb	3,622.5	13,890.4		2.3	3.2	
Mar	3,656.4	13,941.1	49,904.5	4.6	3.3	6.3
Apr	3,660.3	13,974.1		3.0	2.8	
May	3,654.7	14,035.2		1.3	3.3	
June	3,655.0	14,107.5	50,772.5	2.4	3.7	5.2
July	3,676.9	14,148.5		1.3	4.0	
Aug	3,679.8	14,190.4		3.2	4.3	
Sept	3,703.5	14,224.8	51,323.8	2.6	4.1	4.4
Oct	3,718.7	14,250.9		3.2	4.0	
Nov	3,695.2	14,276.5		2.2	3.4	
Dec [p]	3,744.0	14,387.6		4.9	4.0	

[1] Money market mutual fund (MMMF). Savings deposits include money market deposit accounts.
[2] Consists of outstanding debt securities and loans of the U.S. Government, State and local governments, and private nonfinancial sectors. Quarterly data shown in last month of quarter. End-of-year data are for fourth quarter.
[3] Annual changes are from December to December; monthly changes are from six months earlier at an annual rate.
[4] Debt growth of domestic nonfinancial sectors is the seasonally adjusted borrowing flow divided by the seasonally adjusted level of debt outstanding in the previous period. Annual changes are from fourth quarter to fourth quarter; quarterly changes are from previous quarter at an annual rate.

Note: For further information on the composition of M1 and M2, see the H.6 release.
For further information on the debt of domestic nonfinancial sectors and the derivation of debt growth, see the Z.1 release.

Source: Board of Governors of the Federal Reserve System.

TABLE B–41. Consumer credit outstanding, 1970–2018

[Amount outstanding (end of month); millions of dollars, seasonally adjusted]

Year and month	Total consumer credit [1]	Revolving	Nonrevolving [2]
December:			
1970	131,551.55	4,961.46	126,590.09
1971	146,930.18	8,245.33	138,684.84
1972	166,189.10	9,379.24	156,809.86
1973	190,086.31	11,342.22	178,744.09
1974	198,917.84	13,241.26	185,676.58
1975	204,002.00	14,495.27	189,506.73
1976	225,721.59	16,489.05	209,232.54
1977	260,562.70	37,414.82	223,147.88
1978	306,100.39	45,690.95	260,409.43
1979	348,589.11	53,596.43	294,992.67
1980	351,920.05	54,970.05	296,950.00
1981	371,301.44	60,928.00	310,373.44
1982	389,848.74	66,348.30	323,500.44
1983	437,068.86	79,027.25	358,041.61
1984	517,278.98	100,385.63	416,893.35
1985	599,711.23	124,465.80	475,245.43
1986	654,750.24	141,068.15	513,682.08
1987	686,318.77	160,853.91	525,464.86
1988 [3]	731,917.76	184,593.12	547,324.64
1989	794,612.18	211,229.83	583,382.34
1990	808,230.57	238,642.62	569,587.95
1991	798,028.97	263,768.55	534,260.42
1992	806,118.69	278,449.67	527,669.02
1993	865,650.58	309,908.02	555,742.56
1994	997,301.74	365,569.56	631,732.19
1995	1,140,744.36	443,920.09	696,824.27
1996	1,253,437.09	507,516.57	745,920.52
1997	1,324,757.33	540,005.56	784,751.77
1998	1,420,996.44	581,414.78	839,581.66
1999	1,531,105.96	610,696.47	920,409.49
2000	1,716,969.72	682,646.37	1,034,323.35
2001	1,867,852.87	714,840.73	1,153,012.14
2002	1,972,112.21	750,947.45	1,221,164.76
2003	2,077,360.69	768,258.31	1,309,102.38
2004	2,192,246.17	799,552.18	1,392,693.99
2005	2,290,928.13	829,518.36	1,461,409.78
2006	2,456,715.70	923,876.78	1,532,838.92
2007	2,609,476.53	1,001,625.30	1,607,851.24
2008	2,643,788.96	1,003,997.04	1,639,791.92
2009	2,555,016.64	916,076.63	1,638,940.01
2010	2,646,811.26	839,102.67	1,807,708.59
2011	2,757,072.85	840,628.23	1,916,444.63
2012	2,918,258.06	844,250.89	2,074,007.16
2013	3,093,385.81	855,592.83	2,237,792.98
2014	3,314,567.08	889,120.64	2,425,446.44
2015	3,413,611.57	907,914.38	2,505,697.19
2016	3,647,219.54	969,424.58	2,677,794.96
2017	3,831,160.11	1,024,028.38	2,807,131.73
2018 [p]	4,010,049.02	1,044,593.92	2,965,455.10
2017: Jan	3,663,854.05	971,742.81	2,692,111.24
Feb	3,681,440.56	977,201.29	2,704,239.28
Mar	3,694,010.45	980,362.15	2,713,648.30
Apr	3,707,109.06	981,491.86	2,725,617.20
May	3,724,537.61	988,317.33	2,736,220.28
June	3,735,509.47	991,456.11	2,744,053.36
July	3,750,829.16	993,314.27	2,757,514.90
Aug	3,764,061.37	998,319.71	2,765,741.66
Sept	3,772,190.77	1,003,461.55	2,768,729.22
Oct	3,791,192.52	1,009,223.08	2,781,969.45
Nov	3,819,825.20	1,019,837.23	2,799,987.97
Dec	3,831,160.11	1,024,028.38	2,807,131.73
2018: Jan	3,843,405.57	1,025,226.37	2,818,179.20
Feb	3,854,287.30	1,025,165.54	2,829,121.77
Mar	3,862,530.43	1,023,479.35	2,839,051.07
Apr	3,863,818.50	1,014,850.26	2,848,968.24
May	3,886,264.16	1,023,482.72	2,862,781.44
June	3,890,991.65	1,022,541.51	2,868,450.14
July	3,908,515.63	1,023,163.26	2,885,352.36
Aug	3,931,952.82	1,027,566.52	2,904,386.30
Sept	3,945,210.51	1,028,049.07	2,917,161.44
Oct	3,971,086.57	1,038,026.75	2,933,059.82
Nov	3,993,495.02	1,042,858.48	2,950,636.54
Dec [p]	4,010,049.02	1,044,593.92	2,965,455.10

[1] Covers most short- and intermediate-term credit extended to individuals. Credit secured by real estate is excluded.
[2] Includes automobile loans and all other loans not included in revolving credit, such as loans for mobile homes, education, boats, trailers, or vacations. These loans may be secured or unsecured. Beginning with 1977, includes student loans extended by the Federal Government and by SLM Holding Corporation.
[3] Data newly available in January 1989 result in breaks in these series between December 1988 and subsequent months.

Source: Board of Governors of the Federal Reserve System.

Money Stock, Credit, and Finance | 683

Year	U.S. Treasury securities					Corporate bonds (Moody's)		High-grade municipal bonds (Standard & Poor's)	New-home mortgage yields[4]	Prime rate charged by banks[5]	Discount window (Federal Reserve Bank of New York)[5,6]		Federal funds rate[7]
	Bills (at auction)[1]		Constant maturities[2]			Aaa[3]	Baa				Primary credit	Adjustment credit	
	3-month	6-month	3-year	10-year	30-year								
1948	1.040	....	....	....	....	2.82	3.47	2.40	....	1.75–2.00	....	1.34	....
1949	1.102	....	....	....	....	2.66	3.42	2.21	....	2.00	....	1.50	....
1950	1.218	....	....	....	....	2.62	3.24	1.98	....	2.07	....	1.59	....
1951	1.552	....	....	....	....	2.86	3.41	2.00	....	2.56	....	1.75	....
1952	1.766	....	....	....	....	2.96	3.52	2.19	....	3.00	....	1.75	....
1953	1.931	....	2.47	2.85	....	3.20	3.74	2.72	....	3.17	....	1.99	....
1954	.953	....	1.63	2.40	....	2.90	3.51	2.37	....	3.05	....	1.60	....
1955	1.753	....	2.47	2.82	....	3.06	3.53	2.53	....	3.16	....	1.89	1.79
1956	2.658	....	3.19	3.18	....	3.36	3.88	2.93	....	3.77	....	2.77	2.73
1957	3.267	....	3.98	3.65	....	3.89	4.71	3.60	....	4.20	....	3.12	3.11
1958	1.839	....	2.84	3.32	....	3.79	4.73	3.56	....	3.83	....	2.15	1.57
1959	3.405	3.832	4.46	4.33	....	4.38	5.05	3.95	....	4.48	....	3.36	3.31
1960	2.93	3.25	3.98	4.12	....	4.41	5.19	3.73	....	4.82	....	3.53	3.21
1961	2.38	2.61	3.54	3.88	....	4.35	5.08	3.46	....	4.50	....	3.00	1.95
1962	2.78	2.91	3.47	3.95	....	4.33	5.02	3.18	....	4.50	....	3.00	2.71
1963	3.16	3.25	3.67	4.00	....	4.26	4.86	3.23	5.89	4.50	....	3.23	3.18
1964	3.56	3.69	4.03	4.19	....	4.40	4.83	3.22	5.83	4.50	....	3.55	3.50
1965	3.95	4.05	4.22	4.28	....	4.49	4.87	3.27	5.81	4.54	....	4.04	4.07
1966	4.88	5.08	5.23	4.93	....	5.13	5.67	3.82	6.25	5.63	....	4.50	5.11
1967	4.32	4.63	5.03	5.07	....	5.51	6.23	3.98	6.46	5.63	....	4.19	4.22
1968	5.34	5.47	5.68	5.64	....	6.18	6.94	4.51	6.97	6.31	....	5.17	5.66
1969	6.68	6.85	7.02	6.67	....	7.03	7.81	5.81	7.81	7.96	....	5.87	8.21
1970	6.43	6.53	7.29	7.35	....	8.04	9.11	6.51	8.45	7.91	....	5.95	7.17
1971	4.35	4.51	5.66	6.16	....	7.39	8.56	5.70	7.74	5.73	....	4.88	4.67
1972	4.07	4.47	5.72	6.21	....	7.21	8.16	5.27	7.60	5.25	....	4.50	4.44
1973	7.04	7.18	6.96	6.85	....	7.44	8.24	5.18	7.96	8.03	....	6.45	8.74
1974	7.89	7.93	7.84	7.56	....	8.57	9.50	6.09	8.92	10.81	....	7.83	10.51
1975	5.84	6.12	7.50	7.99	....	8.83	10.61	6.89	9.00	7.86	....	6.25	5.82
1976	4.99	5.27	6.77	7.61	....	8.43	9.75	6.49	9.00	6.84	....	5.50	5.05
1977	5.27	5.52	6.68	7.42	7.75	8.02	8.97	5.56	9.02	6.83	....	5.46	5.54
1978	7.22	7.58	8.29	8.41	8.49	8.73	9.49	5.90	9.56	9.06	....	7.46	7.94
1979	10.05	10.02	9.70	9.43	9.28	9.63	10.69	6.39	10.78	12.67	....	10.29	11.20
1980	11.51	11.37	11.51	11.43	11.27	11.94	13.67	8.51	12.66	15.26	....	11.77	13.35
1981	14.03	13.78	14.46	13.92	13.45	14.17	16.04	11.23	14.70	18.87	....	13.42	16.39
1982	10.69	11.08	12.93	13.01	12.76	13.79	16.11	11.57	15.14	14.85	....	11.01	12.24
1983	8.63	8.75	10.45	11.10	11.18	12.04	13.55	9.47	12.57	10.79	....	8.50	9.09
1984	9.53	9.77	11.92	12.46	12.41	12.71	14.19	10.15	12.38	12.04	....	8.80	10.23
1985	7.47	7.64	9.64	10.62	10.79	11.37	12.72	9.18	11.55	9.93	....	7.69	8.10
1986	5.98	6.03	7.06	7.67	7.78	9.02	10.39	7.38	10.17	8.33	....	6.32	6.80
1987	5.82	6.05	7.68	8.39	8.59	9.38	10.58	7.73	9.31	8.21	....	5.66	6.66
1988	6.69	6.92	8.26	8.85	8.96	9.71	10.83	7.76	9.19	9.32	....	6.20	7.57
1989	8.12	8.04	8.55	8.49	8.45	9.26	10.18	7.24	10.13	10.87	....	6.93	9.21
1990	7.51	7.47	8.26	8.55	8.61	9.32	10.36	7.25	10.05	10.01	....	6.98	8.10
1991	5.42	5.49	6.82	7.86	8.14	8.77	9.80	6.89	9.32	8.46	....	5.45	5.69
1992	3.45	3.57	5.30	7.01	7.67	8.14	8.98	6.41	8.24	6.25	....	3.25	3.52
1993	3.02	3.14	4.44	5.87	6.59	7.22	7.93	5.63	7.20	6.00	....	3.00	3.02
1994	4.29	4.66	6.27	7.09	7.37	7.96	8.62	6.19	7.49	7.15	....	3.60	4.21
1995	5.51	5.59	6.25	6.57	6.88	7.59	8.20	5.95	7.87	8.83	....	5.21	5.83
1996	5.02	5.09	5.99	6.44	6.71	7.37	8.05	5.75	7.80	8.27	....	5.02	5.30
1997	5.07	5.18	6.10	6.35	6.61	7.26	7.86	5.55	7.71	8.44	....	5.00	5.46
1998	4.81	4.85	5.14	5.26	5.58	6.53	7.22	5.12	7.07	8.35	....	4.92	5.35
1999	4.66	4.76	5.49	5.65	5.87	7.04	7.87	5.43	7.04	8.00	....	4.62	4.97
2000	5.85	5.92	6.22	6.03	5.94	7.62	8.36	5.77	7.52	9.23	....	5.73	6.24
2001	3.44	3.39	4.09	5.02	5.49	7.08	7.95	5.19	7.00	6.91	....	3.40	3.88
2002	1.62	1.69	3.10	4.61	5.43	6.49	7.80	5.05	6.43	4.67	....	1.17	1.67
2003	1.01	1.06	2.10	4.01	....	5.67	6.77	4.73	5.80	4.12	2.12	....	1.13
2004	1.38	1.57	2.78	4.27	....	5.63	6.39	4.63	5.77	4.34	2.34	....	1.35
2005	3.16	3.40	3.93	4.29	....	5.24	6.06	4.29	5.94	6.19	4.19	....	3.22
2006	4.73	4.80	4.77	4.80	4.91	5.59	6.48	4.42	6.63	7.96	5.96	....	4.97
2007	4.41	4.48	4.35	4.63	4.84	5.56	6.48	4.42	6.41	8.05	5.86	....	5.02
2008	1.48	1.71	2.24	3.66	4.28	5.63	7.45	4.80	6.05	5.09	2.39	....	1.92
2009	.16	.29	1.43	3.26	4.08	5.31	7.30	4.64	5.14	3.25	.50	....	.16
2010	.14	.20	1.11	3.22	4.25	4.94	6.04	4.16	4.80	3.25	.72	....	.18
2011	.06	.10	.75	2.78	3.91	4.64	5.66	4.29	4.56	3.25	.75	....	.10
2012	.09	.13	.38	1.80	2.92	3.67	4.94	3.14	3.69	3.25	.75	....	.14
2013	.06	.09	.54	2.35	3.45	4.24	5.10	3.96	4.00	3.25	.75	....	.11
2014	.03	.06	.90	2.54	3.34	4.16	4.85	3.78	4.22	3.25	.75	....	.09
2015	.06	.17	1.02	2.14	2.84	3.89	5.00	3.48	4.01	3.26	.76	....	.13
2016	.33	.46	1.00	1.84	2.59	3.67	4.72	3.07	3.76	3.51	1.01	....	.39
2017	.94	1.05	1.58	2.33	2.89	3.74	4.44	3.36	3.97	4.10	1.60	....	1.00
2018	1.94	2.10	2.63	2.91	3.11	3.93	4.80	3.53	4.53	4.91	2.41	....	1.83

[1] High bill rate at auction, issue date within period, bank-discount basis. On or after October 28, 1998, data are stop yields from uniform-price auctions. Before that date, they are weighted average yields from multiple-price auctions.

See next page for continuation of table.

TABLE B–42. Bond yields and interest rates, 1948–2018—*Continued*

[Percent per annum]

Year and month	U.S. Treasury securities					Corporate bonds (Moody's)		High-grade municipal bonds (Standard & Poor's) [3]	New-home mortgage yields [4]	Prime rate charged by banks [5]	Discount window (Federal Reserve Bank of New York) [5,6]		Federal funds rate [7]
	Bills (at auction) [1]		Constant maturities [2]										
	3-month	6-month	3-year	10-year	30-year	Aaa [3]	Baa				Primary credit	Adjustment credit	
											High-low	High-low	High-low
2014: Jan	0.05	0.07	0.78	2.86	3.77	4.49	5.19	4.38	4.45	3.25–3.25	0.75–0.75	....	0.07
Feb	.06	.08	.69	2.71	3.66	4.45	5.10	4.25	4.04	3.25–3.25	0.75–0.75	....	.07
Mar	.05	.08	.82	2.72	3.62	4.38	5.06	4.16	4.35	3.25–3.25	0.75–0.75	....	.08
Apr	.04	.05	.88	2.71	3.52	4.24	4.90	4.02	4.33	3.25–3.25	0.75–0.75	....	.09
May	.03	.05	.83	2.56	3.39	4.16	4.76	3.80	4.01	3.25–3.25	0.75–0.75	....	.09
June	.03	.06	.90	2.60	3.42	4.25	4.80	3.72	4.27	3.25–3.25	0.75–0.75	....	.10
July	.03	.06	.97	2.54	3.33	4.16	4.73	3.75	4.25	3.25–3.25	0.75–0.75	....	.09
Aug	.03	.05	.93	2.42	3.20	4.08	4.69	3.53	4.25	3.25–3.25	0.75–0.75	....	.09
Sept	.02	.05	1.05	2.53	3.26	4.11	4.80	3.55	4.23	3.25–3.25	0.75–0.75	....	.09
Oct	.02	.05	.88	2.30	3.04	3.92	4.69	3.35	4.23	3.25–3.25	0.75–0.75	....	.09
Nov	.02	.07	.96	2.33	3.04	3.92	4.79	3.49	4.16	3.25–3.25	0.75–0.75	....	.09
Dec	.04	.11	1.06	2.21	2.83	3.79	4.74	3.39	4.14	3.25–3.25	0.75–0.75	....	.12
2015: Jan	.03	.10	.90	1.88	2.46	3.46	4.45	3.16	4.05	3.25–3.25	0.75–0.75	....	.11
Feb	.02	.07	.99	1.98	2.57	3.61	4.51	3.26	3.91	3.25–3.25	0.75–0.75	....	.11
Mar	.02	.11	1.02	2.04	2.63	3.64	4.54	3.29	3.93	3.25–3.25	0.75–0.75	....	.11
Apr	.03	.10	.87	1.94	2.59	3.52	4.48	3.40	3.92	3.25–3.25	0.75–0.75	....	.12
May	.02	.08	.98	2.20	2.96	3.98	4.89	3.77	3.89	3.25–3.25	0.75–0.75	....	.12
June	.01	.08	1.07	2.36	3.11	4.19	5.13	3.76	3.98	3.25–3.25	0.75–0.75	....	.13
July	.03	.12	1.03	2.32	3.07	4.15	5.20	3.73	4.10	3.25–3.25	0.75–0.75	....	.13
Aug	.09	.21	1.03	2.17	2.86	4.04	5.19	3.57	4.12	3.25–3.25	0.75–0.75	....	.14
Sept	.06	.23	1.01	2.17	2.95	4.07	5.34	3.56	4.09	3.25–3.25	0.75–0.75	....	.14
Oct	.01	.10	.93	2.07	2.89	3.95	5.34	3.48	4.02	3.25–3.25	0.75–0.75	....	.12
Nov	.13	.33	1.20	2.26	3.03	4.06	5.46	3.50	4.00	3.25–3.25	0.75–0.75	....	.12
Dec	.26	.52	1.28	2.24	2.97	3.97	5.46	3.23	4.03	3.50–3.25	1.00–0.75	....	.24
2016: Jan	.25	.44	1.14	2.09	2.86	4.00	5.45	3.01	4.04	3.50–3.50	1.00–1.00	....	.34
Feb	.32	.44	.90	1.78	2.62	3.96	5.34	3.21	4.01	3.50–3.50	1.00–1.00	....	.38
Mar	.32	.48	1.04	1.89	2.68	3.82	5.13	3.28	3.92	3.50–3.50	1.00–1.00	....	.36
Apr	.23	.37	.92	1.81	2.62	3.62	4.79	3.04	3.86	3.50–3.50	1.00–1.00	....	.37
May	.27	.41	.97	1.81	2.63	3.65	4.68	2.95	3.82	3.50–3.50	1.00–1.00	....	.37
June	.29	.41	.86	1.64	2.45	3.50	4.53	2.84	3.81	3.50–3.50	1.00–1.00	....	.38
July	.31	.40	.79	1.50	2.23	3.28	4.22	2.57	3.74	3.50–3.50	1.00–1.00	....	.39
Aug	.30	.43	.85	1.56	2.26	3.32	4.24	2.77	3.68	3.50–3.50	1.00–1.00	....	.40
Sept	.32	.48	.90	1.63	2.35	3.41	4.31	2.86	3.58	3.50–3.50	1.00–1.00	....	.40
Oct	.34	.48	.99	1.76	2.50	3.51	4.38	3.13	3.57	3.50–3.50	1.00–1.00	....	.40
Nov	.44	.57	1.22	2.14	2.86	3.86	4.71	3.36	3.63	3.50–3.50	1.00–1.00	....	.41
Dec	.52	.64	1.49	2.49	3.11	4.06	4.83	3.81	3.74	3.75–3.50	1.25–1.00	....	.54
2017: Jan	.52	.61	1.48	2.43	3.02	3.92	4.66	3.68	4.06	3.75–3.75	1.25–1.25	....	.65
Feb	.53	.64	1.47	2.42	3.03	3.95	4.64	3.74	4.21	3.75–3.75	1.25–1.25	....	.66
Mar	.72	.84	1.59	2.48	3.08	4.01	4.68	3.78	4.16	4.00–3.75	1.50–1.25	....	.79
Apr	.81	.94	1.44	2.30	2.94	3.87	4.57	3.54	4.10	4.00–4.00	1.50–1.50	....	.90
May	.89	1.02	1.48	2.30	2.96	3.85	4.55	3.47	4.04	4.00–4.00	1.50–1.50	....	.91
June	.99	1.09	1.49	2.19	2.80	3.68	4.37	3.06	4.00	4.25–4.00	1.75–1.50	....	1.04
July	1.08	1.12	1.54	2.32	2.88	3.70	4.39	3.03	3.88	4.25–4.25	1.75–1.75	....	1.15
Aug	1.03	1.12	1.48	2.21	2.80	3.63	4.31	3.23	3.97	4.25–4.25	1.75–1.75	....	1.16
Sept	1.04	1.15	1.51	2.20	2.78	3.63	4.30	3.27	3.89	4.25–4.25	1.75–1.75	....	1.15
Oct	1.08	1.22	1.68	2.36	2.88	3.60	4.32	3.31	3.76	4.25–4.25	1.75–1.75	....	1.15
Nov	1.23	1.35	1.81	2.35	2.80	3.57	4.27	3.03	3.81	4.25–4.25	1.75–1.75	....	1.16
Dec	1.35	1.48	1.96	2.40	2.77	3.51	4.22	3.21	3.90	4.50–4.25	2.00–1.75	....	1.30
2018: Jan	1.43	1.59	2.15	2.58	2.88	3.55	4.26	3.29	3.94	4.50–4.50	2.00–2.00	....	1.41
Feb	1.53	1.72	2.36	2.86	3.13	3.82	4.51	3.54	4.15	4.50–4.50	2.00–2.00	....	1.42
Mar	1.70	1.87	2.42	2.84	3.09	3.87	4.64	3.58	4.33	4.75–4.50	2.25–2.00	....	1.51
Apr	1.76	1.93	2.52	2.87	3.07	3.85	4.67	3.55	4.52	4.75–4.75	2.25–2.25	....	1.69
May	1.87	2.03	2.66	2.98	3.13	4.00	4.83	3.38	4.55	4.75–4.75	2.25–2.25	....	1.70
June	1.91	2.08	2.65	2.91	3.05	3.96	4.83	3.15	4.58	5.00–4.75	2.50–2.25	....	1.82
July	1.96	2.12	2.70	2.89	3.01	3.87	4.79	3.45	4.62	5.00–5.00	2.50–2.50	....	1.91
Aug	2.03	2.18	2.71	2.89	3.04	3.88	4.77	3.58	4.57	5.00–5.00	2.50–2.50	....	1.91
Sept	2.13	2.28	2.84	3.00	3.15	3.98	4.88	3.63	4.64	5.25–5.00	2.75–2.50	....	1.95
Oct	2.24	2.39	2.94	3.15	3.34	4.14	5.07	3.88	4.67	5.25–5.25	2.75–2.75	....	2.19
Nov	2.34	2.46	2.91	3.12	3.36	4.22	5.22	3.64	4.77	5.25–5.25	2.75–2.75	....	2.20
Dec	2.38	2.49	2.67	2.83	3.10	4.02	5.13	3.69	4.84	5.50–5.25	3.00–2.75	....	2.27

[2] Yields on the more actively traded issues adjusted to constant maturities by the Department of the Treasury. The 30-year Treasury constant maturity series was discontinued on February 18, 2002, and reintroduced on February 9, 2006.
[3] Beginning with December 7, 2001, data for corporate Aaa series are industrial bonds only.
[4] Effective rate (in the primary market) on conventional mortgages, reflecting fees and charges as well as contract rate and assuming, on the average, repayment at end of 10 years. Rates beginning with January 1973 not strictly comparable with prior rates.
[5] For monthly data, high and low for the period. Prime rate for 1948 are ranges of the rate in effect during the period.
[6] Primary credit replaced adjustment credit as the Federal Reserve's principal discount window lending program effective January 9, 2003.
[7] Beginning March 1, 2016, the daily effective federal funds rate is a volume-weighted median of transaction-level data collected from depository institutions in the Report of Selected Money Market Rates (FR 2420). Between July 21, 1975 and February 29, 2016, the daily effective rate was a volume-weighted mean of rates on brokered trades. Prior to that, the daily effective rate was the rate considered most representative of the day's transactions, usually the one at which most transactions occurred.

Sources: Department of the Treasury, Board of Governors of the Federal Reserve System, Federal Housing Finance Agency, Moody's Investors Service, Bloomberg, and Standard & Poor's.

[Billions of dollars]

End of year or quarter	All proper-ties	Farm proper-ties	Nonfarm properties				Nonfarm properties by type of mortgage					
							Government underwritten				Conventional [2]	
			Total	1- to 4-family houses	Multi-family proper-ties	Com-mercial proper-ties	Total [1]	1- to 4-family houses			Total	1- to 4-family houses
								Total	FHA-insured	VA-guaran-teed		
1960	227.1	17.4	209.7	137.8	28.0	43.9	62.3	56.4	26.7	29.7	147.4	81.4
1961	248.6	18.7	229.9	149.5	31.5	48.9	65.6	59.1	29.5	29.6	164.3	90.4
1962	271.8	20.3	251.6	163.1	34.6	53.8	69.4	62.2	32.3	29.9	182.2	100.9
1963	297.6	22.4	275.1	179.0	37.5	58.7	73.4	65.9	35.0	30.9	201.7	113.1
1964	324.2	25.3	298.9	195.7	41.6	61.7	77.2	69.2	38.3	30.9	221.7	126.4
1965	349.5	28.2	321.3	212.0	44.2	65.2	81.2	73.1	42.0	31.1	240.2	138.9
1966	373.7	30.3	343.4	225.3	46.9	71.2	84.1	76.1	44.8	31.3	259.3	149.3
1967	396.9	32.9	363.9	238.0	50.0	75.9	88.2	79.9	47.4	32.5	275.7	158.1
1968	424.5	36.0	388.5	254.2	53.0	81.3	93.4	84.4	50.6	33.8	295.1	169.8
1969	450.5	38.4	412.1	269.0	56.5	86.6	100.2	90.2	54.5	35.7	311.9	178.9
1970	498.5	40.8	457.6	292.2	68.1	97.3	109.2	97.3	59.9	37.3	348.4	195.0
1971	544.5	43.9	500.6	318.4	76.6	105.6	120.7	105.2	65.7	39.5	379.9	213.2
1972	618.2	47.7	570.5	357.4	89.7	123.5	131.1	113.0	68.2	44.7	439.4	244.4
1973	694.2	53.4	640.7	399.8	99.0	141.9	135.0	116.2	66.2	50.0	505.7	283.6
1974	766.2	62.5	703.7	441.2	105.7	156.7	140.2	121.3	65.1	56.2	563.5	319.9
1975	830.2	68.9	761.3	483.0	105.5	172.8	147.0	127.7	66.1	61.6	614.3	355.2
1976	917.5	76.7	840.8	544.8	110.1	185.9	154.0	133.5	66.5	67.0	686.8	411.2
1977	1,049.7	88.3	961.4	638.5	118.0	204.9	161.7	141.6	68.0	73.6	799.7	496.9
1978	1,206.8	100.3	1,106.4	751.4	128.7	226.3	176.4	153.4	71.4	82.0	930.0	598.0
1979	1,381.0	120.5	1,260.5	870.2	139.4	250.8	199.0	172.9	81.0	92.0	1,061.4	697.3
1980	1,528.2	132.7	1,395.5	977.3	146.4	271.8	225.1	195.2	93.6	101.6	1,170.4	782.2
1981	1,654.6	146.7	1,507.9	1,052.6	146.4	308.9	238.9	207.6	101.3	106.2	1,269.0	845.1
1982	1,741.4	150.9	1,590.4	1,097.2	152.4	340.9	248.9	217.9	108.0	109.9	1,341.6	879.3
1983	1,942.4	153.9	1,788.5	1,217.8	171.9	398.8	279.8	248.8	127.4	121.4	1,508.7	968.9
1984	2,178.3	150.1	2,028.1	1,350.7	197.2	480.2	294.8	265.9	136.7	129.1	1,733.3	1,084.9
1985	2,439.9	125.3	2,314.6	1,548.9	213.9	551.8	328.3	288.8	153.0	135.8	1,986.3	1,260.1
1986	2,676.3	101.3	2,574.9	1,730.1	241.8	603.0	370.5	328.6	185.5	143.1	2,204.4	1,401.5
1987	2,968.8	89.9	2,878.9	1,928.5	258.4	692.1	431.4	387.9	235.5	152.4	2,447.5	1,540.6
1988	3,283.8	82.3	3,201.5	2,162.8	274.5	764.2	459.7	414.2	258.8	155.4	2,741.8	1,748.6
1989	3,534.5	79.2	3,455.3	2,369.6	287.0	798.7	486.8	440.1	282.8	157.3	2,968.4	1,929.5
1990	3,790.0	77.6	3,712.5	2,606.8	287.4	818.3	517.9	470.9	310.9	160.0	3,194.5	2,135.9
1991	3,941.7	77.7	3,864.0	2,774.7	284.1	805.2	537.2	493.3	330.6	162.7	3,326.8	2,281.4
1992	4,052.4	78.6	3,973.8	2,942.1	270.9	760.8	533.3	489.8	326.0	163.8	3,440.5	2,452.3
1993	4,183.7	79.8	4,103.9	3,101.0	267.7	735.2	513.4	469.5	303.2	166.2	3,590.4	2,631.5
1994	4,348.1	81.6	4,266.5	3,278.2	268.2	720.1	559.3	514.2	336.8	177.3	3,707.2	2,764.0
1995	4,520.7	71.7	4,449.0	3,445.7	273.9	729.4	584.3	537.1	352.3	184.7	3,864.7	2,908.6
1996	4,801.2	74.4	4,726.8	3,681.9	286.1	758.8	620.3	571.2	379.2	192.0	4,106.5	3,110.8
1997	5,114.0	78.5	5,035.5	3,916.5	298.0	821.0	656.7	605.7	405.7	200.0	4,378.9	3,310.8
1998	5,603.2	83.1	5,520.1	4,275.8	334.5	909.8	674.1	623.8	417.9	205.9	4,846.1	3,652.0
1999	6,209.5	87.2	6,122.3	4,701.2	375.2	1,046.0	731.5	678.8	462.3	216.5	5,390.9	4,022.4
2000	6,766.6	84.7	6,681.9	5,125.0	404.5	1,152.4	773.1	720.0	499.9	220.1	5,908.8	4,405.0
2001	7,450.0	88.5	7,361.5	5,678.0	446.1	1,237.4	772.7	718.5	497.4	221.2	6,588.8	4,959.5
2002	8,358.7	95.4	8,263.3	6,434.4	486.3	1,342.5	759.3	704.0	486.2	217.7	7,504.0	5,730.4
2003	9,366.7	83.2	9,283.5	7,261.4	560.5	1,461.7	709.2	653.3	438.7	214.6	8,574.4	6,608.1
2004	10,648.6	95.7	10,552.9	8,293.1	610.1	1,649.7	660.2	604.1	398.1	206.0	9,892.7	7,689.0
2005	12,116.7	104.8	12,012.0	9,449.6	675.3	1,887.1	606.6	550.4	348.4	202.0	11,405.4	8,899.2
2006	13,529.5	108.0	13,421.5	10,531.9	718.4	2,171.2	600.2	543.5	336.9	206.6	12,821.3	9,988.4
2007	14,613.1	112.7	14,500.4	11,253.2	807.8	2,439.4	609.2	552.6	342.6	210.0	13,891.3	10,700.6
2008	14,693.8	134.7	14,559.1	11,152.1	853.5	2,553.5	807.2	750.7	534.0	216.7	13,751.8	10,401.3
2009	14,449.7	146.0	14,303.7	10,962.5	865.9	2,475.2	1,005.0	944.3	752.6	191.7	13,298.6	10,018.2
2010	13,896.5	154.1	13,742.4	10,524.6	866.0	2,351.7	1,227.6	1,156.1	934.4	221.7	12,514.7	9,368.6
2011	13,571.7	167.2	13,404.5	10,282.8	866.5	2,255.3	1,368.6	1,291.3	1,036.0	255.3	12,035.9	8,991.5
2012	13,339.1	173.4	13,165.7	10,052.3	894.0	2,219.4	1,544.8	1,459.7	1,165.4	294.2	11,620.9	8,592.7
2013	13,346.5	185.2	13,161.3	9,961.6	932.1	2,267.5	3,927.2	3,832.6	3,480.8	351.8	9,234.1	6,129.1
2014	13,500.1	196.8	13,303.3	9,948.0	993.2	2,362.1	4,130.9	4,028.1	3,615.3	412.8	9,172.3	5,919.8
2015	13,876.2	208.8	13,667.4	10,080.1	1,095.0	2,492.3	4,432.7	4,326.7	3,851.3	475.4	9,234.7	5,753.4
2016	14,352.0	226.0	14,126.0	10,298.3	1,202.7	2,625.1	4,764.8	4,654.9	4,106.9	548.1	9,361.2	5,643.3
2017	14,898.3	238.1	14,660.2	10,600.3	1,309.9	2,750.0	5,079.1	4,958.2	4,344.3	613.9	9,581.1	5,642.1
2017: I	14,434.0	229.0	14,205.1	10,343.2	1,223.7	2,638.1	4,785.9	4,674.2	4,166.7	507.6	9,419.2	5,669.0
II	14,582.3	232.0	14,350.3	10,428.9	1,244.2	2,677.2	4,917.6	4,805.3	4,227.5	577.8	9,432.7	5,623.6
III	14,716.7	235.1	14,481.7	10,518.2	1,264.4	2,697.1	5,004.2	4,886.0	4,289.6	596.5	9,477.5	5,632.2
IV	14,898.3	238.1	14,660.2	10,600.3	1,309.9	2,750.0	5,079.1	4,958.2	4,344.3	613.9	9,581.1	5,642.1
2018: I	14,985.1	240.7	14,744.4	10,639.7	1,326.8	2,778.0	5,148.7	5,024.1	4,393.2	630.9	9,595.8	5,615.5
II	15,136.0	243.3	14,892.7	10,713.0	1,351.3	2,828.4	5,219.0	5,090.9	4,444.8	646.1	9,673.7	5,622.1
III p	15,269.5	245.9	15,023.6	10,809.6	1,379.2	2,834.8	5,292.3	5,162.2	4,498.6	663.7	9,731.3	5,647.3

[1] Includes Federal Housing Administration (FHA)–insured multi-family properties, not shown separately.
[2] Derived figures. Total includes multi-family and commercial properties with conventional mortgages, not shown separately.

Source: Board of Governors of the Federal Reserve System, based on data from various Government and private organizations.

End of year or quarter	Total	Major financial institutions			Other holders		
		Total	Depository Institutions [1], [2]	Life insurance companies	Federal and related agencies [3]	Mortgage pools or trusts [4]	Individuals and others
1960	227.1	156.4	114.6	41.8	11.3	0.2	59.2
1961	248.6	171.1	126.9	44.2	11.9	.3	65.3
1962	271.8	190.5	143.6	46.9	12.2	.4	68.7
1963	297.6	214.6	164.1	50.5	11.3	.5	71.2
1964	324.2	238.8	183.6	55.2	11.6	.6	73.2
1965	349.5	262.4	202.4	60.0	12.7	.9	73.6
1966	373.7	279.5	214.8	64.6	16.2	1.3	76.7
1967	396.9	296.4	228.9	67.5	19.0	2.0	79.5
1968	424.5	317.3	247.3	70.0	22.6	2.5	82.2
1969	450.5	336.6	264.6	72.0	27.9	3.2	82.8
1970	498.5	352.9	278.5	74.4	33.6	4.8	107.3
1971	544.5	389.2	313.7	75.5	36.8	9.5	109.0
1972	618.2	443.8	366.8	76.9	40.1	14.4	119.9
1973	694.2	500.7	419.4	81.4	46.6	18.0	128.8
1974	766.2	539.3	453.1	86.2	68.2	23.8	134.9
1975	830.2	576.1	486.9	89.2	80.2	34.1	139.9
1976	917.5	640.7	549.1	91.6	82.4	49.8	144.7
1977	1,049.7	735.3	638.4	96.8	87.6	70.3	156.5
1978	1,206.8	837.5	731.3	106.2	103.4	88.6	177.3
1979	1,381.0	928.6	810.2	118.4	123.7	118.7	210.0
1980	1,528.2	988.0	857.0	131.1	142.6	145.9	251.6
1981	1,654.6	1,034.1	896.4	137.7	160.8	168.0	291.7
1982	1,741.4	1,019.6	877.6	142.0	177.3	224.4	320.1
1983	1,942.4	1,108.4	957.4	151.0	188.3	297.3	348.4
1984	2,178.3	1,248.2	1,091.5	156.7	202.3	350.7	377.1
1985	2,439.9	1,368.7	1,196.9	171.8	213.7	438.6	419.0
1986	2,676.3	1,483.3	1,289.5	193.8	202.1	549.5	441.3
1987	2,968.8	1,631.5	1,419.1	212.4	188.5	700.8	447.9
1988	3,283.8	1,797.8	1,564.9	232.9	192.5	785.7	507.8
1989	3,534.5	1,897.4	1,643.2	254.2	197.8	922.2	517.1
1990	3,790.0	1,918.8	1,651.0	267.9	239.0	1,085.9	546.3
1991	3,941.7	1,846.2	1,586.7	259.5	266.0	1,269.6	560.0
1992	4,052.4	1,770.5	1,528.5	242.0	286.1	1,440.0	555.9
1993	4,183.7	1,770.1	1,546.3	223.9	326.1	1,561.1	526.4
1994	4,348.1	1,824.7	1,608.9	215.8	315.6	1,696.9	511.0
1995	4,520.7	1,900.1	1,687.0	213.1	307.9	1,812.0	500.6
1996	4,801.2	1,982.2	1,773.7	208.5	294.4	1,989.1	535.6
1997	5,114.0	2,084.2	1,877.1	207.0	285.2	2,166.5	578.2
1998	5,603.2	2,194.7	1,981.0	213.8	291.9	2,487.1	629.5
1999	6,209.5	2,394.5	2,163.5	231.0	319.8	2,832.3	663.0
2000	6,766.6	2,619.2	2,383.0	236.2	339.9	3,097.5	710.0
2001	7,450.0	2,791.0	2,547.9	243.1	372.0	3,532.4	754.7
2002	8,358.7	3,089.4	2,839.3	250.1	432.3	3,978.4	858.5
2003	9,366.7	3,387.5	3,126.4	261.2	694.1	4,330.3	954.8
2004	10,648.6	3,926.5	3,653.0	273.5	703.2	4,834.5	1,184.4
2005	12,116.7	4,396.5	4,110.8	285.7	665.4	5,711.8	1,343.1
2006	13,529.5	4,784.0	4,479.8	304.1	687.5	6,631.4	1,426.7
2007	14,613.1	5,065.5	4,738.4	327.1	725.5	7,436.3	1,385.9
2008	14,693.8	5,045.8	4,702.0	343.8	801.2	7,594.4	1,252.4
2009	14,449.7	4,779.4	4,452.0	327.4	816.1	7,651.3	1,202.9
2010	13,896.5	4,585.2	4,266.1	319.2	5,127.5	3,109.6	1,074.0
2011	13,571.7	4,450.3	4,115.7	334.6	5,033.9	3,035.6	1,051.9
2012	13,339.1	4,441.5	4,094.6	346.9	4,935.0	2,948.4	1,014.2
2013	13,346.5	4,412.5	4,046.2	366.3	4,993.2	2,774.1	1,166.7
2014	13,500.1	4,546.8	4,158.7	388.2	4,987.7	2,742.6	1,223.0
2015	13,876.2	4,804.9	4,374.2	430.7	5,036.6	2,791.6	1,243.1
2016	14,352.0	5,096.1	4,630.6	465.5	5,146.9	2,827.6	1,281.5
2017	14,898.3	5,307.8	4,801.2	506.7	5,314.9	2,973.7	1,301.8
2017: I	14,434.0	5,125.8	4,649.3	476.5	5,201.0	2,832.1	1,275.1
II	14,582.3	5,209.2	4,719.1	490.1	5,219.2	2,876.4	1,277.6
III	14,716.7	5,257.2	4,759.5	497.7	5,261.8	2,917.5	1,280.2
IV	14,898.3	5,307.8	4,801.2	506.7	5,314.9	2,973.7	1,301.8
2018: I	14,985.1	5,341.1	4,824.9	516.2	5,338.4	3,002.6	1,303.0
II ᵖ	15,136.0	5,396.2	4,868.6	527.7	5,369.8	3,054.2	1,315.7
III ᵖ	15,269.5	5,437.6	4,897.6	540.0	5,415.4	3,093.3	1,323.1

[1] Includes savings banks and savings and loan associations. Data reported by Federal Savings and Loan Insurance Corporation–insured institutions include loans in process for 1987 and exclude loans in process beginning with 1988.

[2] Includes loans held by nondeposit trust companies but not loans held by bank trust departments.

[3] Includes Government National Mortgage Association (GNMA or Ginnie Mae), Federal Housing Administration, Veterans Administration, Farmers Home Administration (FmHA), Federal Deposit Insurance Corporation, Resolution Trust Corporation (through 1995), and in earlier years Reconstruction Finance Corporation, Homeowners Loan Corporation, Federal Farm Mortgage Corporation, and Public Housing Administration. Also includes U.S.-sponsored agencies such as Federal National Mortgage Association (FNMA or Fannie Mae), Federal Land Banks, Federal Home Loan Mortgage Corporation (FHLMC or Freddie Mac), Federal Agricultural Mortgage Corporation (Farmer Mac, beginning 1994), Federal Home Loan Banks (beginning 1997), and mortgage pass-through securities issued or guaranteed by GNMA, FHLMC, FNMA, FmHA, or Farmer Mac. Other U.S. agencies (amounts small or current separate data not readily available) included with "individuals and others."

[4] Includes private mortgage pools.

Source: Board of Governors of the Federal Reserve System, based on data from various Government and private organizations.

TABLE B–45. Federal receipts, outlays, surplus or deficit, and debt, fiscal years 1953–2020

[Billions of dollars; fiscal years]

Fiscal year or period	Total			On-budget			Off-budget			Federal debt (end of period)		Addendum: Gross domestic product
	Receipts	Outlays	Surplus or deficit (−)	Receipts	Outlays	Surplus or deficit (−)	Receipts	Outlays	Surplus or deficit (−)	Gross Federal	Held by the public	
1953	69.6	76.1	−6.5	65.5	73.8	−8.3	4.1	2.3	1.8	266.0	218.4	382.0
1954	69.7	70.9	−1.2	65.1	67.9	−2.8	4.6	2.9	1.7	270.8	224.5	387.2
1955	65.5	68.4	−3.0	60.4	64.5	−4.1	5.1	4.0	1.1	274.4	226.6	406.3
1956	74.6	70.6	3.9	68.2	65.7	2.5	6.4	5.0	1.5	272.7	222.2	438.2
1957	80.0	76.6	3.4	73.2	70.6	2.6	6.8	6.0	.8	272.3	219.3	463.4
1958	79.6	82.4	−2.8	71.6	74.9	−3.3	8.0	7.5	.5	279.7	226.3	473.5
1959	79.2	92.1	−12.8	71.0	83.1	−12.1	8.3	9.0	−.7	287.5	234.7	504.6
1960	92.5	92.2	.3	81.9	81.3	.5	10.6	10.9	−.2	290.5	236.8	534.3
1961	94.4	97.7	−3.3	82.3	86.0	−3.8	12.1	11.7	.4	292.6	238.4	546.6
1962	99.7	106.8	−7.1	87.4	93.3	−5.9	12.3	13.5	−1.3	302.9	248.0	585.7
1963	106.6	111.3	−4.8	92.4	96.4	−4.0	14.2	15.0	−.8	310.3	254.0	618.2
1964	112.6	118.5	−5.9	96.2	102.8	−6.5	16.4	15.7	.6	316.1	256.8	661.7
1965	116.8	118.2	−1.4	100.1	101.7	−1.6	16.7	16.5	.2	322.3	260.8	709.3
1966	130.8	134.5	−3.7	111.7	114.8	−3.1	19.1	19.7	−.6	328.5	263.7	780.5
1967	148.8	157.5	−8.6	124.4	137.0	−12.6	24.4	20.4	4.0	340.4	266.6	836.5
1968	153.0	178.1	−25.2	128.1	155.8	−27.7	24.9	22.3	2.6	368.7	289.5	897.6
1969	186.9	183.6	3.2	157.9	158.4	−.5	29.0	25.2	3.7	365.8	278.1	980.3
1970	192.8	195.6	−2.8	159.3	168.0	−8.7	33.5	27.6	5.9	380.9	283.2	1,046.7
1971	187.1	210.2	−23.0	151.3	177.3	−26.1	35.8	32.8	3.0	408.2	303.0	1,116.6
1972	207.3	230.7	−23.4	167.4	193.5	−26.1	39.9	37.2	2.7	435.9	322.4	1,216.2
1973	230.8	245.7	−14.9	184.7	200.0	−15.2	46.1	45.7	.3	466.3	340.9	1,352.7
1974	263.2	269.4	−6.1	209.3	216.5	−7.2	53.9	52.9	1.1	483.9	343.7	1,482.8
1975	279.1	332.3	−53.2	216.6	270.8	−54.1	62.5	61.6	.9	541.9	394.7	1,606.9
1976	298.1	371.8	−73.7	231.7	301.1	−69.4	66.4	70.7	−4.3	629.0	477.4	1,786.1
Transition quarter	81.2	96.0	−14.7	63.2	77.3	−14.1	18.0	18.7	−.7	643.6	495.5	471.6
1977	355.6	409.2	−53.7	278.7	328.7	−49.9	76.8	80.5	−3.7	706.4	549.1	2,024.3
1978	399.6	458.7	−59.2	314.2	369.6	−55.4	85.4	89.2	−3.8	776.6	607.1	2,273.4
1979	463.3	504.0	−40.7	365.3	404.9	−39.6	98.0	99.1	−1.1	829.5	640.3	2,565.6
1980	517.1	590.9	−73.8	403.9	477.0	−73.1	113.2	113.9	−.7	909.0	711.9	2,791.9
1981	599.3	678.2	−79.0	469.1	543.0	−73.9	130.2	135.3	−5.1	994.8	789.4	3,133.2
1982	617.8	745.7	−128.0	474.3	594.9	−120.6	143.5	150.9	−7.4	1,137.3	924.6	3,313.4
1983	600.6	808.4	−207.8	453.2	660.9	−207.7	147.3	147.4	−.1	1,371.7	1,137.3	3,536.0
1984	666.4	851.8	−185.4	500.4	685.6	−185.3	166.1	166.2	−.1	1,564.6	1,307.0	3,949.2
1985	734.0	946.3	−212.3	547.9	769.4	−221.5	186.2	176.9	9.2	1,817.4	1,507.3	4,265.1
1986	769.2	990.4	−221.2	568.9	806.8	−237.9	200.2	183.5	16.7	2,120.5	1,740.6	4,526.2
1987	854.3	1,004.0	−149.7	640.9	809.2	−168.4	213.4	194.8	18.6	2,346.0	1,889.8	4,767.6
1988	909.2	1,064.4	−155.2	667.7	860.0	−192.3	241.5	204.4	37.1	2,601.1	2,051.6	5,138.6
1989	991.1	1,143.7	−152.6	727.4	932.8	−205.4	263.7	210.9	52.8	2,867.8	2,190.7	5,554.7
1990	1,032.0	1,253.0	−221.0	750.3	1,027.9	−277.6	281.7	225.1	56.6	3,206.3	2,411.6	5,898.8
1991	1,055.0	1,324.2	−269.2	761.1	1,082.5	−321.4	293.9	241.7	52.2	3,598.2	2,689.0	6,093.2
1992	1,091.2	1,381.5	−290.3	788.8	1,129.2	−340.4	302.4	252.3	50.1	4,001.8	2,999.7	6,416.2
1993	1,154.3	1,409.4	−255.1	842.4	1,142.8	−300.4	311.9	266.6	45.3	4,351.0	3,248.4	6,775.3
1994	1,258.6	1,461.8	−203.2	923.5	1,182.4	−258.8	335.0	279.4	55.7	4,643.3	3,433.1	7,176.8
1995	1,351.8	1,515.7	−164.0	1,000.7	1,227.1	−226.4	351.1	288.7	62.4	4,920.6	3,604.4	7,560.4
1996	1,453.1	1,560.5	−107.4	1,085.6	1,259.6	−174.0	367.5	300.9	66.6	5,181.5	3,734.1	7,951.3
1997	1,579.2	1,601.1	−21.9	1,187.2	1,290.5	−103.2	392.0	310.6	81.4	5,369.2	3,772.3	8,451.0
1998	1,721.7	1,652.5	69.3	1,305.9	1,335.9	−29.9	415.8	316.6	99.2	5,478.2	3,721.1	8,930.8
1999	1,827.5	1,701.8	125.6	1,383.0	1,381.1	1.9	444.5	320.8	123.7	5,605.5	3,632.4	9,479.4
2000	2,025.2	1,789.0	236.2	1,544.6	1,458.2	86.4	480.6	330.8	149.8	5,628.7	3,409.8	10,117.4
2001	1,991.1	1,862.8	128.2	1,483.6	1,516.0	−32.4	507.5	346.8	160.7	5,769.9	3,319.6	10,526.5
2002	1,853.1	2,010.9	−157.8	1,337.8	1,655.2	−317.4	515.3	355.7	159.7	6,198.4	3,540.4	10,833.6
2003	1,782.3	2,159.9	−377.6	1,258.5	1,796.9	−538.4	523.8	363.0	160.8	6,760.0	3,913.4	11,283.8
2004	1,880.1	2,292.8	−412.7	1,345.4	1,913.3	−568.0	534.7	379.5	155.2	7,354.7	4,295.5	12,025.4
2005	2,153.6	2,472.0	−318.3	1,576.1	2,069.7	−493.6	577.5	402.2	175.3	7,905.3	4,592.2	12,834.2
2006	2,406.9	2,655.1	−248.2	1,798.5	2,233.0	−434.5	608.4	422.1	186.3	8,451.4	4,829.0	13,638.4
2007	2,568.0	2,728.7	−160.7	1,932.9	2,275.0	−342.2	635.1	453.6	181.5	8,950.7	5,035.1	14,290.8
2008	2,524.0	2,982.5	−458.6	1,865.9	2,507.8	−641.8	658.0	474.8	183.3	9,986.1	5,803.1	14,743.3
2009	2,105.0	3,517.7	−1,412.7	1,451.0	3,000.7	−1,549.7	654.0	517.0	137.0	11,875.9	7,544.7	14,431.8
2010	2,162.7	3,457.1	−1,294.4	1,531.0	2,902.4	−1,371.4	631.7	554.7	77.0	13,528.8	9,018.9	14,838.8
2011	2,303.5	3,603.1	−1,299.6	1,737.7	3,104.5	−1,366.8	565.8	498.6	67.2	14,764.2	10,128.2	15,403.7
2012	2,450.0	3,526.6	−1,076.6	1,880.5	3,019.0	−1,138.5	569.5	507.6	61.9	16,050.9	11,281.1	16,056.4
2013	2,775.1	3,454.9	−679.8	2,101.8	2,821.1	−719.2	673.3	633.8	39.5	16,719.4	11,982.7	16,603.8
2014	3,021.5	3,506.3	−484.8	2,285.9	2,800.2	−514.3	735.6	706.1	29.5	17,794.5	12,779.9	17,332.9
2015	3,249.9	3,691.8	−442.0	2,479.5	2,948.8	−469.3	770.4	743.1	27.3	18,120.1	13,116.7	18,090.3
2016	3,268.0	3,852.6	−584.7	2,457.8	3,077.9	−620.2	810.2	774.7	35.5	19,539.5	14,167.6	18,551.0
2017	3,316.2	3,981.6	−665.4	2,465.6	3,180.4	−714.9	850.6	801.2	49.4	20,205.7	14,665.4	19,272.2
2018	3,329.9	4,109.0	−779.1	2,475.2	3,260.5	−785.3	854.7	848.6	6.2	21,462.3	15,749.6	20,235.9
2019 (estimates)	3,437.7	4,529.2	−1,091.5	2,526.5	3,620.3	−1,093.7	911.1	908.9	2.2	22,775.5	16,918.6	21,288.9
2020 (estimates)	3,644.8	4,745.6	−1,100.8	2,695.5	3,777.9	−1,082.4	949.3	967.7	−18.4	24,057.5	18,086.9	22,409.7

Note: Fiscal years through 1976 were on a July 1–June 30 basis; beginning with October 1976 (fiscal year 1977), the fiscal year is on an October 1–September 30 basis. The transition quarter is the three-month period from July 1, 1976 through September 30, 1976.

See Budget of the United States Government, Fiscal Year 2020, for additional information.

Sources: Department of Commerce (Bureau of Economic Analysis), Department of the Treasury, and Office of Management and Budget.

TABLE B–46. Federal receipts, outlays, surplus or deficit, and debt, as percent of gross domestic product, fiscal years 1948–2020

[Percent; fiscal years]

| Fiscal year or period | Receipts | Outlays | | Surplus or deficit (−) | Federal debt (end of period) | |
		Total	National defense		Gross Federal	Held by public
1948	15.9	11.4	3.5	4.5	96.2	82.6
1949	14.3	14.0	4.8	.2	91.4	77.5
1950	14.2	15.3	4.9	−1.1	92.2	78.6
1951	15.8	13.9	7.2	1.9	78.1	65.5
1952	18.5	19.0	12.9	−.4	72.6	60.1
1953	18.2	19.9	13.8	−1.7	69.6	57.2
1954	18.0	18.3	12.7	−.3	70.0	58.0
1955	16.1	16.8	10.5	−.7	67.5	55.8
1956	17.0	16.1	9.7	.9	62.2	50.7
1957	17.3	16.5	9.8	.7	58.8	47.3
1958	16.8	17.4	9.9	−.6	59.1	47.8
1959	15.7	18.3	9.7	−2.5	57.0	46.5
1960	17.3	17.3	9.0	.1	54.4	44.3
1961	17.3	17.9	9.1	−.6	53.5	43.6
1962	17.0	18.2	8.9	−1.2	51.7	42.3
1963	17.2	18.0	8.6	−.8	50.2	41.1
1964	17.0	17.9	8.3	−.9	47.8	38.8
1965	16.5	16.7	7.1	−.2	45.4	36.8
1966	16.8	17.2	7.4	−.5	42.1	33.8
1967	17.8	18.8	8.5	−1.0	40.7	31.9
1968	17.0	19.8	9.1	−2.8	41.1	32.3
1969	19.1	18.7	8.4	.3	37.3	28.4
1970	18.4	18.7	7.8	−.3	36.4	27.1
1971	16.8	18.8	7.1	−2.1	36.6	27.1
1972	17.0	19.0	6.5	−1.9	35.8	26.5
1973	17.1	18.2	5.7	−1.1	34.5	25.2
1974	17.8	18.2	5.4	−.4	32.6	23.2
1975	17.4	20.7	5.4	−3.3	33.7	24.6
1976	16.7	20.8	5.0	−4.1	35.2	26.7
Transition quarter	17.2	20.3	4.7	−3.1	34.1	26.3
1977	17.6	20.2	4.8	−2.7	34.9	27.1
1978	17.6	20.2	4.6	−2.6	34.2	26.7
1979	18.1	19.6	4.5	−1.6	32.3	25.0
1980	18.5	21.2	4.8	−2.6	32.6	25.5
1981	19.1	21.6	5.0	−2.5	31.8	25.2
1982	18.6	22.5	5.6	−3.9	34.3	27.9
1983	17.0	22.9	5.9	−5.9	38.8	32.2
1984	16.9	21.6	5.8	−4.7	39.6	33.1
1985	17.2	22.2	5.9	−5.0	42.6	35.3
1986	17.0	21.9	6.0	−4.9	46.8	38.5
1987	17.9	21.1	5.9	−3.1	49.2	39.6
1988	17.7	20.7	5.7	−3.0	50.6	39.9
1989	17.8	20.6	5.5	−2.7	51.6	39.4
1990	17.5	21.2	5.1	−3.7	54.4	40.9
1991	17.3	21.7	4.5	−4.4	59.1	44.1
1992	17.0	21.5	4.6	−4.5	62.4	46.8
1993	17.0	20.8	4.3	−3.8	64.2	47.9
1994	17.5	20.4	3.9	−2.8	64.7	47.8
1995	17.9	20.0	3.6	−2.2	65.1	47.7
1996	18.3	19.6	3.3	−1.4	65.2	47.0
1997	18.7	18.9	3.2	−.3	63.5	44.6
1998	19.3	18.5	3.0	.8	61.3	41.7
1999	19.3	18.0	2.9	1.3	59.1	38.3
2000	20.0	17.7	2.9	2.3	55.6	33.7
2001	18.9	17.7	2.9	1.2	54.8	31.5
2002	17.1	18.6	3.2	−1.5	57.2	32.7
2003	15.8	19.1	3.6	−3.3	59.9	34.7
2004	15.6	19.1	3.8	−3.4	61.2	35.7
2005	16.8	19.3	3.9	−2.5	61.6	35.8
2006	17.6	19.5	3.8	−1.8	62.0	35.4
2007	18.0	19.1	3.9	−1.1	62.6	35.2
2008	17.1	20.2	4.2	−3.1	67.7	39.4
2009	14.6	24.4	4.6	−9.8	82.3	52.3
2010	14.6	23.3	4.7	−8.7	91.2	60.8
2011	15.0	23.4	4.6	−8.4	95.8	65.8
2012	15.3	22.0	4.2	−6.7	100.0	70.3
2013	16.7	20.8	3.8	−4.1	100.7	72.2
2014	17.4	20.2	3.5	−2.8	102.7	73.7
2015	18.0	20.4	3.3	−2.4	100.2	72.5
2016	17.6	20.8	3.2	−3.2	105.3	76.4
2017	17.2	20.7	3.1	−3.5	104.8	76.1
2018	16.5	20.3	3.1	−3.9	106.1	77.8
2019 (estimates)	16.1	21.3	3.2	−5.1	107.0	79.5
2020 (estimates)	16.3	21.2	3.3	−4.9	107.4	80.7

Note: See Note, Table B–45.

Sources: Department of the Treasury and Office of Management and Budget.

[Billions of dollars; fiscal years]

Fiscal year or period	Receipts (on-budget and off-budget)					Outlays (on-budget and off-budget)											Surplus or deficit (−) (on-budget and off-budget)
	Total	Individual income taxes	Corporation income taxes	Social insurance and retirement receipts	Other	Total	National defense		International affairs	Health	Medicare	Income security	Social security	Net interest	Other	
							Total	Department of Defense, military								
1953	69.6	29.8	21.2	6.8	11.7	76.1	52.8		2.1	0.3		3.8	2.7	5.2	9.1	−6.5
1954	69.7	29.5	21.1	7.2	11.9	70.9	49.3		1.6	.3		4.4	3.4	4.8	7.1	−1.2
1955	65.5	28.7	17.9	7.9	11.0	68.4	42.7		2.2	.3		5.1	4.4	4.9	8.9	−3.0
1956	74.6	32.2	20.9	9.3	12.2	70.6	42.5		2.4	.4		4.7	5.5	5.1	10.1	3.9
1957	80.0	35.6	21.2	10.0	13.2	76.6	45.4		3.1	.5		5.4	6.7	5.4	10.1	3.4
1958	79.6	34.7	20.1	11.2	13.6	82.4	46.8		3.4	.5		7.5	8.2	5.6	10.3	−2.8
1959	79.2	36.7	17.3	11.7	13.5	92.1	49.0		3.1	.7		8.2	9.7	5.8	15.5	−12.8
1960	92.5	40.7	21.5	14.7	15.6	92.2	48.1		3.0	.8		7.4	11.6	6.9	14.4	.3
1961	94.4	41.3	21.0	16.4	15.7	97.7	49.6		3.2	.9		9.7	12.5	6.7	15.2	−3.3
1962	99.7	45.6	20.5	17.0	16.5	106.8	52.3	50.1	5.6	1.2		9.2	14.4	6.9	17.2	−7.1
1963	106.6	47.6	21.6	19.8	17.6	111.3	53.4	51.1	5.3	1.5		9.3	15.8	7.7	18.3	−4.8
1964	112.6	48.7	23.5	22.0	18.5	118.5	54.8	52.6	4.9	1.8		9.7	16.6	8.2	22.6	−5.9
1965	116.8	48.8	25.5	22.2	20.3	118.2	50.6	48.8	5.3	1.8		9.5	17.5	8.6	25.0	−1.4
1966	130.8	55.4	30.1	25.5	19.8	134.5	58.1	56.6	5.6	2.5	0.1	9.7	20.7	9.4	28.5	−3.7
1967	148.8	61.5	34.0	32.6	20.7	157.5	71.4	70.1	5.6	3.4	2.7	10.3	21.7	10.3	32.1	−8.6
1968	153.0	68.7	28.7	33.9	21.7	178.1	81.9	80.4	5.3	4.4	4.6	11.8	23.9	11.1	35.1	−25.2
1969	186.9	87.2	36.7	39.0	23.9	183.6	82.5	80.8	4.6	5.2	5.7	13.1	27.3	12.7	32.6	3.2
1970	192.8	90.4	32.8	44.4	25.2	195.6	81.7	80.1	4.3	5.9	6.2	15.7	30.3	14.4	37.2	−2.8
1971	187.1	86.2	26.8	47.3	26.8	210.2	78.9	77.5	4.2	6.8	6.6	22.9	35.9	14.8	40.0	−23.0
1972	207.3	94.7	32.2	52.6	27.8	230.7	79.2	77.6	4.8	8.7	7.5	27.7	40.2	15.5	47.3	−23.4
1973	230.8	103.2	36.2	63.1	28.3	245.7	76.7	75.0	4.1	9.4	8.1	28.3	49.1	17.3	52.8	−14.9
1974	263.2	119.0	38.6	75.1	30.6	269.4	79.3	77.9	5.7	10.7	9.6	33.7	55.9	21.4	52.9	−6.1
1975	279.1	122.4	40.6	84.5	31.5	332.3	86.5	84.9	7.1	12.9	12.9	50.2	64.7	23.2	74.8	−53.2
1976	298.1	131.6	41.4	90.8	34.3	371.8	89.6	87.9	6.4	15.7	15.8	60.8	73.9	26.7	82.7	−73.7
Transition quarter	81.2	38.8	8.5	25.2	8.8	96.0	22.3	21.8	2.5	3.9	4.3	15.0	19.8	6.9	21.4	−14.7
1977	355.6	157.6	54.9	106.5	36.6	409.2	97.2	95.1	6.4	17.3	19.3	61.1	85.1	29.9	93.0	−53.7
1978	399.6	181.0	60.0	121.0	37.7	458.7	104.5	103.2	7.5	18.5	22.8	61.5	93.9	35.5	114.6	−59.2
1979	463.3	217.8	65.7	138.9	40.8	504.0	116.3	113.6	7.5	20.5	26.5	66.4	104.1	42.6	120.2	−40.7
1980	517.1	244.1	64.6	157.8	50.6	590.9	134.0	130.9	12.7	23.2	32.1	86.6	118.5	52.5	131.3	−73.8
1981	599.3	285.9	61.1	182.7	69.5	678.2	157.5	153.9	13.1	26.9	39.1	100.3	139.6	68.8	133.0	−79.0
1982	617.8	297.7	49.2	201.5	69.3	745.7	185.3	180.7	12.3	27.4	46.6	108.2	156.0	85.0	125.0	−128.0
1983	600.6	288.9	37.0	209.0	65.6	808.4	209.9	204.4	11.8	28.6	52.6	123.0	170.7	89.8	121.8	−207.8
1984	666.4	298.4	56.9	239.4	71.8	851.8	227.4	220.9	15.9	30.4	57.5	113.4	178.2	111.1	117.8	−185.4
1985	734.0	334.5	61.3	265.2	73.0	946.3	252.7	245.1	16.2	33.5	65.8	129.0	188.6	129.5	130.9	−212.3
1986	769.2	349.0	63.1	283.9	73.2	990.4	273.4	265.4	14.1	35.9	70.2	120.7	198.8	136.0	141.3	−221.2
1987	854.3	392.6	83.9	303.3	74.5	1,004.0	282.0	273.9	11.6	40.0	75.1	124.1	207.4	138.6	125.2	−149.7
1988	909.2	401.2	94.5	334.3	79.2	1,064.4	290.4	281.9	10.5	44.5	78.9	130.4	219.3	151.8	138.7	−155.2
1989	991.1	445.7	103.3	359.4	82.7	1,143.7	303.6	294.8	9.6	48.4	85.0	137.6	232.5	169.0	158.1	−152.6
1990	1,032.0	466.9	93.5	380.0	91.5	1,253.0	299.3	289.7	13.8	57.7	98.1	148.8	248.6	184.3	202.3	−221.0
1991	1,055.0	467.8	98.1	396.0	93.1	1,324.2	273.3	262.3	15.8	71.2	104.5	172.6	269.0	194.4	223.3	−269.2
1992	1,091.2	476.0	100.3	413.7	101.3	1,381.5	298.3	286.8	16.1	89.5	119.0	199.7	287.6	199.3	171.9	−290.3
1993	1,154.3	509.7	117.5	428.3	98.8	1,409.4	291.1	278.5	17.2	99.4	130.6	210.1	304.6	198.7	157.7	−255.1
1994	1,258.6	543.1	140.4	461.5	113.7	1,461.8	281.6	268.6	17.1	107.1	144.7	217.3	319.6	202.9	171.4	−203.2
1995	1,351.8	590.2	157.0	484.5	120.1	1,515.7	272.1	259.4	16.4	115.4	159.9	223.8	335.8	232.1	160.2	−164.0
1996	1,453.1	656.4	171.8	509.4	115.4	1,560.5	265.7	253.1	13.5	119.4	174.2	229.7	349.7	241.1	167.2	−107.4
1997	1,579.2	737.5	182.3	539.4	120.1	1,601.1	270.5	258.3	15.2	123.8	190.0	235.0	365.3	244.0	157.3	−21.9
1998	1,721.7	828.6	188.7	571.8	132.6	1,652.5	268.2	255.8	13.1	131.4	192.8	237.8	379.2	241.1	188.9	69.3
1999	1,827.5	879.5	184.7	611.8	151.5	1,701.8	274.8	261.2	15.2	141.0	190.4	242.5	390.0	229.8	218.1	125.6
2000	2,025.2	1,004.5	207.3	652.9	160.6	1,789.0	294.4	281.0	17.2	154.5	197.1	253.7	409.4	222.9	239.7	236.2
2001	1,991.1	994.3	151.1	694.0	151.7	1,862.8	304.7	290.2	16.5	172.2	217.4	269.8	433.0	206.2	243.1	128.2
2002	1,853.1	858.3	148.0	700.8	146.0	2,010.9	348.5	331.8	22.3	196.5	230.9	312.7	456.0	170.9	273.1	−157.8
2003	1,782.3	793.7	131.8	713.0	143.9	2,159.9	404.7	387.1	21.2	219.5	249.4	334.6	474.7	153.1	302.6	−377.6
2004	1,880.1	809.0	189.4	733.4	148.4	2,292.8	455.8	436.4	26.9	240.1	269.4	333.1	495.5	160.2	311.8	−412.7
2005	2,153.6	927.2	278.3	794.1	154.0	2,472.0	495.3	474.1	34.6	250.5	298.6	345.8	523.3	184.0	339.8	−318.3
2006	2,406.9	1,043.9	353.9	837.8	171.2	2,655.1	521.8	499.3	29.5	252.7	329.9	352.5	548.5	226.6	393.5	−248.2
2007	2,568.0	1,163.5	370.2	869.6	164.7	2,728.7	551.3	528.5	28.5	266.4	375.4	366.0	586.2	237.1	317.9	−160.7
2008	2,524.0	1,145.7	304.3	900.2	173.7	2,982.5	616.1	594.6	28.9	280.6	390.8	431.3	617.0	252.8	365.2	−458.6
2009	2,105.0	915.3	138.2	890.9	160.5	3,517.7	661.0	636.7	37.5	334.3	430.1	533.2	683.0	186.9	651.6	−1,412.7
2010	2,162.7	898.5	191.4	864.8	207.9	3,457.1	693.5	666.7	45.2	369.1	451.6	622.2	706.7	196.2	372.6	−1,294.4
2011	2,303.5	1,091.5	181.1	818.8	212.1	3,603.1	705.6	678.1	45.7	372.5	485.7	597.3	730.8	230.0	435.5	−1,299.6
2012	2,450.0	1,132.2	242.3	845.3	230.2	3,526.6	677.9	650.9	36.8	346.7	471.8	541.3	773.3	220.4	458.3	−1,076.6
2013	2,775.1	1,316.4	273.5	947.8	237.4	3,454.9	633.4	607.8	46.5	358.3	497.8	536.5	813.6	220.9	347.9	−679.8
2014	3,021.5	1,394.6	320.7	1,023.5	282.7	3,506.3	603.5	577.9	46.9	409.4	511.7	513.6	850.5	229.0	341.7	−484.8
2015	3,249.9	1,540.8	343.8	1,065.3	300.0	3,691.8	589.7	562.5	52.0	482.2	546.2	508.8	887.8	223.2	401.9	−442.0
2016	3,268.0	1,546.1	299.6	1,115.1	307.3	3,852.6	593.4	565.4	45.3	511.3	594.5	514.1	916.1	240.0	437.9	−584.7
2017	3,316.2	1,587.1	297.0	1,161.9	270.1	3,981.6	598.7	568.9	46.3	533.1	597.1	503.5	944.9	262.6	495.2	−665.4
2018	3,329.9	1,683.5	204.7	1,170.7	270.9	4,109.0	631.2	600.7	49.0	551.2	588.7	495.3	987.8	325.0	480.9	−779.1
2019 (estimates)	3,437.7	1,698.4	216.2	1,242.4	280.7	4,529.2	684.6	652.2	54.3	601.0	651.2	533.2	1,047.0	393.5	564.4	−1,091.5
2020 (estimates)	3,644.8	1,824.2	255.2	1,295.5	269.9	4,745.6	737.9	704.3	53.1	616.0	685.2	514.2	1,107.1	478.8	553.2	−1,100.8

Note: See Note, Table B–45.

Sources: Department of the Treasury and Office of Management and Budget.

[Millions of dollars; fiscal years]

Description	Actual				Estimates	
	2015	2016	2017	2018	2019	2020
RECEIPTS, OUTLAYS, AND SURPLUS OR DEFICIT						
Total:						
Receipts	3,249,887	3,267,961	3,316,182	3,329,904	3,437,656	3,644,772
Outlays	3,691,847	3,852,612	3,981,628	4,109,042	4,529,188	4,745,573
Surplus or deficit (–)	–441,960	–584,651	–665,446	–779,138	–1,091,532	–1,100,801
On-budget:						
Receipts	2,479,515	2,457,781	2,465,564	2,475,157	2,526,542	2,695,492
Outlays	2,948,770	3,077,939	3,180,427	3,260,470	3,620,287	3,777,890
Surplus or deficit (–)	–469,255	–620,158	–714,863	–785,313	–1,093,745	–1,082,398
Off-budget:						
Receipts	770,372	810,180	850,618	854,747	911,114	949,280
Outlays	743,077	774,673	801,201	848,572	908,901	967,683
Surplus or deficit (–)	27,295	35,507	49,417	6,175	2,213	–18,403
OUTSTANDING DEBT, END OF PERIOD						
Gross Federal debt	18,120,106	19,539,450	20,205,704	21,462,277	22,775,547	24,057,463
Held by Federal Government accounts	5,003,414	5,371,826	5,540,265	5,712,692	5,856,940	5,970,595
Held by the public	13,116,692	14,167,624	14,665,439	15,749,585	16,918,607	18,086,868
Federal Reserve System	2,461,947	2,463,456	2,465,418	2,313,209	....	....
Other	10,654,745	11,704,168	12,200,021	13,436,376	....	....
RECEIPTS BY SOURCE						
Total: On-budget and off-budget	3,249,887	3,267,961	3,316,182	3,329,904	3,437,656	3,644,772
Individual income taxes	1,540,802	1,546,075	1,587,120	1,683,538	1,698,353	1,824,185
Corporation income taxes	343,797	299,571	297,048	204,733	216,194	255,161
Social insurance and retirement receipts	1,065,257	1,115,065	1,161,897	1,170,701	1,242,405	1,295,484
On-budget	294,885	304,885	311,279	315,954	331,291	346,204
Off-budget	770,372	810,180	850,618	854,747	911,114	949,280
Excise taxes	98,279	95,026	83,823	94,986	98,669	108,835
Estate and gift taxes	19,232	21,354	22,768	22,983	19,295	19,304
Customs duties and fees	35,041	34,838	34,574	41,299	69,469	48,383
Miscellaneous receipts	147,479	156,032	128,952	111,664	93,271	94,379
Deposits of earnings by Federal Reserve System	96,468	115,672	81,287	70,750	48,783	49,474
All other	51,011	40,360	47,665	40,914	44,488	44,905
Legislative proposals [1]	....	....	....	....	....	–959
OUTLAYS BY FUNCTION						
Total: On-budget and off-budget	3,691,847	3,852,612	3,981,628	4,109,042	4,529,188	4,745,573
National defense	589,659	593,372	598,722	631,161	684,568	737,886
International affairs	52,040	45,306	46,309	48,972	54,337	53,125
General science, space, and technology	29,412	30,174	30,394	31,534	33,816	34,587
Energy	6,838	3,719	3,856	2,169	3,194	3,536
Natural resources and environment	36,033	39,082	37,896	39,140	39,864	43,690
Agriculture	18,500	18,342	18,870	21,787	38,068	19,474
Commerce and housing credit	–37,905	–34,077	–26,685	–9,470	–26,394	–5,126
On-budget	–36,195	–32,716	–24,412	–8,005	–25,450	–5,256
Off-budget	–1,710	–1,361	–2,273	–1,465	–944	130
Transportation	89,533	92,566	93,552	92,785	98,907	100,889
Community and regional development	20,669	20,140	24,907	42,159	33,001	35,664
Education, training, employment, and social services	122,061	109,737	143,976	95,516	142,527	112,368
Health	482,231	511,297	533,129	551,216	600,966	615,950
Medicare	546,202	594,536	597,307	588,706	651,199	685,230
Income security	508,843	514,139	503,484	495,318	533,228	514,241
Social security	887,753	916,067	944,878	987,791	1,046,955	1,107,132
On-budget	30,990	32,522	37,393	35,752	36,327	39,766
Off-budget	856,763	883,545	907,485	952,039	1,010,628	1,067,366
Veterans benefits and services	159,738	174,516	176,543	178,856	200,458	217,521
Administration of justice	51,906	55,768	57,944	60,418	71,780	69,025
General government	20,956	23,146	23,821	23,878	26,834	31,628
Net interest	223,181	240,033	262,551	324,975	393,498	478,812
On-budget	319,149	330,608	349,063	408,784	476,241	560,431
Off-budget	–95,968	–90,575	–86,512	–83,809	–82,743	–81,619
Allowances	....	....	....	....	–677	315
Undistributed offsetting receipts	–115,803	–95,251	–89,826	–97,869	–96,941	–110,374
On-budget	–99,795	–78,315	–72,327	–79,676	–78,901	–92,180
Off-budget	–16,008	–16,936	–17,499	–18,193	–18,040	–18,194

[1] Includes undistributed allowance for empowering States and consumers to reform healthcare.

Note: See Note, Table B–45.

Sources: Department of the Treasury and Office of Management and Budget.

TABLE B–49. Federal and State and local government current receipts and expenditures, national income and product accounts (NIPA) basis, 1968–2018

[Billions of dollars; quarterly data at seasonally adjusted annual rates]

Year or quarter	Total government			Federal Government			State and local government			Addendum: Grants-in-aid to State and local governments
	Current receipts	Current expenditures	Net government saving (NIPA)	Current receipts	Current expenditures	Net Federal Government saving (NIPA)	Current receipts	Current expenditures	Net State and local government saving (NIPA)	
1968	251.4	261.7	–10.3	170.6	184.3	–13.8	92.6	89.1	3.5	11.8
1969	282.7	284.7	–2.0	191.8	197.0	–5.1	104.5	101.4	3.1	13.7
1970	285.8	319.2	–33.4	185.1	219.9	–34.8	119.1	117.6	1.4	18.3
1971	302.3	354.5	–52.2	190.7	241.6	–50.9	133.7	135.0	–1.3	22.1
1972	345.6	388.5	–42.9	219.0	268.0	–49.0	157.1	151.0	6.1	30.5
1973	388.8	421.5	–32.7	249.2	287.6	–38.3	173.0	167.4	5.6	33.5
1974	430.2	473.9	–43.7	278.5	319.8	–41.3	186.6	189.0	–2.3	34.9
1975	441.2	549.9	–108.7	276.8	374.8	–97.9	208.0	218.7	–10.7	43.6
1976	505.7	591.0	–85.3	322.6	403.5	–80.9	232.2	236.6	–4.4	49.1
1977	567.4	640.3	–72.9	363.9	437.3	–73.4	258.3	257.8	.5	54.8
1978	646.1	703.3	–57.2	423.8	485.9	–62.0	285.8	280.9	4.9	63.5
1979	729.3	777.9	–48.6	487.0	534.4	–47.4	306.3	307.5	–1.2	64.0
1980	799.9	894.6	–94.7	533.7	622.5	–88.8	335.9	341.8	–5.9	69.7
1981	919.1	1,017.4	–98.2	621.1	709.1	–88.1	367.5	377.6	–10.2	69.4
1982	940.9	1,131.0	–190.1	618.7	786.0	–167.4	388.5	411.3	–22.8	66.3
1983	1,002.1	1,227.7	–225.6	644.8	851.9	–207.2	425.3	443.7	–18.4	67.9
1984	1,115.0	1,311.7	–196.7	711.2	907.7	–196.5	476.1	476.3	–.2	72.3
1985	1,217.0	1,418.7	–201.7	775.7	975.0	–199.2	517.5	519.9	–2.4	76.2
1986	1,292.9	1,512.8	–219.9	817.9	1,033.8	–215.9	557.4	561.3	–4.0	82.4
1987	1,406.6	1,586.7	–180.1	899.5	1,065.2	–165.7	585.5	599.9	–14.4	78.4
1988	1,507.1	1,678.3	–171.3	962.4	1,122.4	–160.0	630.4	641.7	–11.3	85.7
1989	1,632.0	1,810.7	–178.7	1,042.5	1,201.8	–159.4	681.4	700.7	–19.3	91.8
1990	1,713.3	1,952.9	–239.5	1,087.6	1,290.9	–203.3	730.1	766.3	–36.2	104.4
1991	1,763.7	2,072.2	–308.5	1,107.8	1,356.2	–248.4	779.9	840.0	–60.1	124.0
1992	1,848.7	2,254.2	–405.5	1,154.4	1,488.9	–334.5	836.1	907.0	–71.0	141.7
1993	1,953.3	2,339.3	–386.0	1,231.0	1,544.6	–313.5	878.0	950.4	–72.5	155.7
1994	2,097.6	2,417.2	–319.6	1,329.3	1,585.0	–255.6	935.1	999.1	–63.9	166.8
1995	2,223.9	2,536.5	–312.5	1,417.4	1,659.5	–242.1	981.0	1,051.4	–70.4	174.5
1996	2,388.6	2,621.8	–233.2	1,536.3	1,715.7	–179.4	1,033.7	1,087.5	–53.8	181.5
1997	2,565.9	2,699.9	–133.9	1,667.4	1,759.4	–92.0	1,086.7	1,128.7	–42.0	188.1
1998	2,738.6	2,767.4	–28.7	1,789.8	1,788.4	1.4	1,149.6	1,179.7	–30.1	200.8
1999	2,910.1	2,882.2	28.0	1,906.6	1,839.7	66.9	1,222.7	1,261.6	–38.9	219.2
2000	3,139.4	3,024.6	114.8	2,068.4	1,912.9	155.5	1,304.1	1,344.8	–40.6	233.1
2001	3,124.4	3,229.4	–105.0	2,032.2	2,018.2	14.0	1,353.4	1,472.4	–119.0	261.3
2002	2,968.3	3,422.6	–454.4	1,870.8	2,142.3	–271.5	1,386.2	1,569.1	–182.9	288.7
2003	3,045.9	3,631.3	–585.4	1,895.6	2,299.7	–404.1	1,472.0	1,653.3	–181.3	321.7
2004	3,275.7	3,825.6	–549.9	2,027.7	2,428.6	–400.9	1,580.3	1,729.3	–149.0	332.3
2005	3,679.3	4,088.1	–408.7	2,304.4	2,610.3	–305.9	1,718.5	1,821.3	–102.8	343.5
2006	4,013.4	4,326.1	–312.6	2,538.3	2,765.9	–227.6	1,816.2	1,901.2	–85.0	341.0
2007	4,210.8	4,606.2	–395.4	2,667.8	2,933.9	–266.1	1,902.1	2,031.4	–129.3	359.1
2008	4,125.0	4,977.0	–852.0	2,580.7	3,211.8	–631.1	1,915.5	2,136.4	–220.9	371.2
2009	3,696.6	5,286.8	–1,590.3	2,239.5	3,488.4	–1,248.9	1,915.2	2,256.6	–341.3	458.1
2010	3,933.2	5,565.7	–1,632.6	2,444.0	3,769.1	–1,325.1	1,994.4	2,301.8	–307.5	505.2
2011	4,130.6	5,647.7	–1,517.1	2,572.8	3,814.7	–1,242.0	2,030.4	2,305.4	–275.1	472.5
2012	4,312.2	5,673.6	–1,361.4	2,700.3	3,779.0	–1,078.6	2,056.3	2,339.1	–282.8	444.4
2013	4,834.5	5,737.8	–903.3	3,139.0	3,776.9	–637.9	2,145.6	2,411.0	–265.4	450.1
2014	5,056.5	5,895.0	–838.5	3,292.2	3,894.0	–601.8	2,259.4	2,496.1	–236.7	495.1
2015	5,281.5	6,074.0	–792.5	3,446.3	4,015.2	–568.9	2,368.6	2,592.2	–223.6	533.4
2016	5,340.3	6,251.2	–910.9	3,475.5	4,140.6	–665.1	2,421.9	2,667.8	–245.8	557.1
2017	5,483.8	6,438.2	–954.5	3,558.8	4,254.2	–695.4	2,484.2	2,743.3	–259.1	559.3
2018 ᵖ		6,734.7			4,482.3			2,830.5		578.1
2015: I	5,181.1	5,962.5	–781.5	3,388.3	3,939.9	–551.6	2,318.4	2,548.3	–229.8	525.6
II	5,269.9	6,079.2	–809.3	3,446.1	4,017.7	–571.6	2,354.1	2,591.7	–237.7	530.2
III	5,268.7	6,136.2	–867.4	3,446.1	4,057.1	–611.0	2,354.6	2,611.0	–256.4	532.0
IV	5,406.3	6,118.1	–711.8	3,504.9	4,046.1	–541.3	2,447.3	2,617.9	–170.5	545.9
2016: I	5,284.4	6,172.4	–888.0	3,447.2	4,085.2	–638.0	2,376.1	2,626.1	–250.0	539.0
II	5,305.5	6,219.5	–914.0	3,448.4	4,117.3	–668.8	2,411.4	2,656.6	–245.2	554.3
III	5,369.0	6,284.5	–915.4	3,491.8	4,166.7	–674.9	2,442.6	2,683.1	–240.5	565.4
IV	5,402.2	6,328.5	–926.3	3,514.4	4,192.9	–678.6	2,457.5	2,705.2	–247.7	569.7
2017: I	5,465.9	6,387.6	–921.8	3,572.4	4,228.3	–655.9	2,455.0	2,720.8	–265.8	561.6
II	5,443.8	6,376.2	–932.4	3,538.8	4,200.3	–661.5	2,452.0	2,722.9	–270.9	547.0
III	5,524.0	6,439.3	–915.3	3,590.3	4,250.9	–660.5	2,501.0	2,755.7	–254.7	567.3
IV	5,501.4	6,549.9	–1,048.5	3,533.6	4,337.2	–803.6	2,529.0	2,773.9	–244.9	561.2
2018: I	5,413.1	6,613.4	–1,200.2	3,428.3	4,398.2	–969.9	2,564.0	2,794.4	–230.4	579.2
II	5,460.5	6,696.6	–1,236.1	3,456.2	4,449.9	–993.7	2,580.8	2,823.3	–242.4	576.6
III	5,576.8	6,768.8	–1,192.1	3,547.5	4,508.1	–960.6	2,616.3	2,847.8	–231.5	587.0
IV ᵖ		6,860.2			4,573.1			2,856.6		569.6

Note: Federal grants-in-aid to State and local governments are reflected in Federal current expenditures and State and local current receipts. Total government current receipts and expenditures have been adjusted to eliminate this duplication.

Source: Department of Commerce (Bureau of Economic Analysis).

Table B–50. State and local government revenues and expenditures, fiscal years 1956–2016

[Millions of dollars]

Fiscal year [1]	General revenues by source [2]							General expenditures by function [2]				
	Total	Property taxes	Sales and gross receipts taxes	Individual income taxes	Corporation net income taxes	Revenue from Federal Government	All other [3]	Total [4]	Education	Highways	Public welfare [4]	All other [4, 5]
1956	34,670	11,749	8,691	1,538	890	3,335	8,467	36,715	13,224	6,953	3,139	13,399
1957	38,164	12,864	9,467	1,754	984	3,843	9,252	40,375	14,134	7,816	3,485	14,940
1958	41,219	14,047	9,829	1,759	1,018	4,865	9,701	44,851	15,919	8,567	3,818	16,547
1959	45,306	14,983	10,437	1,994	1,001	6,377	10,514	48,887	17,283	9,592	4,136	17,876
1960	50,505	16,405	11,849	2,463	1,180	6,974	11,634	51,876	18,719	9,428	4,404	19,325
1961	54,037	18,002	12,463	2,613	1,266	7,131	12,562	56,201	20,574	9,844	4,720	21,063
1962	58,252	19,054	13,494	3,037	1,308	7,871	13,488	60,206	22,216	10,357	5,084	22,549
1963	62,891	20,089	14,456	3,269	1,505	8,722	14,850	64,815	23,776	11,135	5,481	24,423
1963–64	68,443	21,241	15,762	3,791	1,695	10,002	15,952	69,302	26,286	11,664	5,766	25,586
1964–65	74,000	22,583	17,118	4,090	1,929	11,029	17,251	74,678	28,563	12,221	6,315	27,579
1965–66	83,036	24,670	19,085	4,760	2,038	13,214	19,269	82,843	33,287	12,770	6,757	30,029
1966–67	91,197	26,047	20,530	5,825	2,227	15,370	21,198	93,350	37,919	13,932	8,218	33,281
1967–68	101,264	27,747	22,911	7,308	2,518	17,181	23,599	102,411	41,158	14,481	9,857	36,915
1968–69	114,550	30,673	26,519	8,908	3,180	19,153	26,117	116,728	47,238	15,417	12,110	41,963
1969–70	130,756	34,054	30,322	10,812	3,738	21,857	29,973	131,332	52,718	16,427	14,679	47,508
1970–71	144,927	37,852	33,233	11,900	3,424	26,146	32,372	150,674	59,413	18,095	18,226	54,940
1971–72	167,535	42,877	37,518	15,227	4,416	31,342	36,156	168,549	65,813	19,021	21,117	62,598
1972–73	190,222	45,283	42,047	17,994	5,425	39,264	40,210	181,357	69,713	18,615	23,582	69,447
1973–74	207,670	47,705	46,098	19,491	6,015	41,820	46,542	199,222	75,833	19,946	25,085	78,358
1974–75	228,171	51,491	49,815	21,454	6,642	47,034	51,735	230,722	87,858	22,528	28,156	92,180
1975–76	256,176	57,001	54,547	24,575	7,273	55,589	57,191	256,731	97,216	23,907	32,604	103,004
1976–77	285,157	62,527	60,641	29,246	9,174	62,444	61,125	274,215	102,780	23,058	35,906	112,472
1977–78	315,960	66,422	67,596	33,176	10,738	69,592	68,435	296,984	110,758	24,609	39,140	122,478
1978–79	343,236	64,944	74,247	36,932	12,128	75,164	79,822	327,517	119,448	28,440	41,898	137,731
1979–80	382,322	68,499	79,927	42,080	13,321	83,029	95,467	369,086	133,211	33,311	47,288	155,276
1980–81	423,404	74,969	85,971	46,426	14,143	90,294	111,599	407,449	145,784	34,603	54,105	172,957
1981–82	457,654	82,067	93,613	50,738	15,028	87,282	128,925	436,733	154,282	34,520	57,996	189,935
1982–83	486,753	89,105	100,247	55,129	14,258	90,007	138,008	466,516	163,876	36,655	60,906	205,080
1983–84	542,730	96,457	114,097	64,871	16,798	96,935	153,571	505,008	176,108	39,419	66,414	223,068
1984–85	598,121	103,757	126,376	70,361	19,152	106,158	172,317	553,899	192,686	44,989	71,479	244,745
1985–86	641,486	111,709	135,005	74,365	19,994	113,099	187,314	605,623	210,819	49,368	75,868	269,568
1986–87	686,860	121,203	144,091	83,935	22,425	114,857	200,350	657,134	226,619	52,355	82,650	295,510
1987–88	726,762	132,212	156,452	88,350	23,663	117,602	208,482	704,921	242,683	55,621	89,090	317,527
1988–89	786,129	142,400	166,336	97,806	25,926	125,824	227,838	762,360	263,898	58,105	97,879	342,479
1989–90	849,502	155,613	177,885	105,640	23,566	136,802	249,996	834,818	288,148	61,057	110,518	375,094
1990–91	902,207	167,999	185,570	109,341	22,242	154,099	262,955	908,108	309,302	64,937	130,402	403,467
1991–92	979,137	180,337	197,731	115,638	23,880	179,174	282,376	981,253	324,652	67,351	158,723	430,526
1992–93	1,041,643	189,744	209,649	123,235	26,417	198,663	293,935	1,030,434	342,287	68,370	170,705	449,072
1993–94	1,100,490	197,141	223,628	128,810	28,320	215,492	307,099	1,077,665	353,287	72,067	183,394	468,916
1994–95	1,169,505	203,451	237,268	137,931	31,406	228,771	330,677	1,149,863	378,273	77,109	196,703	497,779
1995–96	1,222,821	209,440	248,993	146,844	32,009	234,891	350,645	1,193,276	398,859	79,092	197,354	517,971
1996–97	1,289,237	218,877	261,418	159,042	33,820	244,847	371,233	1,249,984	418,416	82,062	203,779	545,727
1997–98	1,365,762	230,150	274,883	175,630	34,412	255,048	395,639	1,318,042	450,365	87,214	208,120	572,343
1998–99	1,434,029	239,672	290,993	189,309	33,922	270,628	409,505	1,402,369	483,259	93,018	218,957	607,134
1999–2000	1,541,322	249,178	309,290	211,661	36,059	291,950	443,186	1,506,797	521,612	101,336	237,336	646,512
2000–01	1,647,161	263,689	320,217	226,334	35,296	324,033	477,592	1,626,063	563,572	107,235	261,622	693,634
2001–02	1,684,879	279,191	324,123	202,832	28,152	360,546	490,035	1,736,866	594,694	115,295	285,464	741,413
2002–03	1,763,212	296,683	337,787	199,407	31,369	389,264	508,702	1,821,917	621,335	117,696	310,783	772,102
2003–04	1,887,397	317,941	361,027	215,215	33,716	423,112	536,386	1,908,543	655,182	117,215	340,523	795,622
2004–05	2,026,034	335,779	384,266	242,273	43,256	438,558	581,902	2,012,110	688,314	126,350	365,295	832,151
2005–06	2,197,475	364,559	417,735	268,667	53,081	452,975	640,458	2,123,663	728,917	136,502	373,846	884,398
2006–07	2,330,611	388,905	440,470	290,278	60,955	464,914	685,089	2,264,035	774,170	145,011	389,259	955,595
2007–08	2,421,977	409,540	449,945	304,902	57,231	477,441	722,919	2,406,183	826,061	153,831	408,920	1,017,372
2008–09	2,429,672	434,818	434,128	270,942	46,280	537,949	705,555	2,500,796	851,689	154,338	437,184	1,057,586
2009–10	2,510,846	443,947	425,521	261,510	44,108	623,850	701,909	2,542,231	860,118	155,912	460,230	1,065,971
2010–11	2,618,037	445,771	463,979	285,293	48,422	647,606	726,966	2,583,805	862,271	153,895	494,682	1,072,957
2011–12	2,598,849	446,101	478,224	307,258	48,934	585,162	733,169	2,592,466	867,508	160,299	489,259	1,075,400
2012–13	2,682,661	453,214	503,466	338,617	52,898	583,545	750,901	2,626,697	877,059	167,637	518,485	1,073,526
2013–14	2,763,644	465,317	522,013	341,357	54,611	602,851	777,496	2,714,357	905,213	161,954	546,735	1,100,455
2014–15	2,915,426	484,351	544,973	367,917	57,235	657,567	803,384	2,842,867	935,754	167,769	617,768	1,121,576
2015–16	3,008,262	503,262	558,871	376,297	54,259	690,209	825,363	2,948,039	972,906	174,990	640,860	1,159,284

[1] Fiscal years not the same for all governments. See Note.
[2] Excludes revenues or expenditures of publicly owned utilities and liquor stores and of insurance-trust activities. Intergovernmental receipts and payments between State and local governments are also excluded.
[3] Includes motor vehicle license taxes, other taxes, and charges and miscellaneous revenues.
[4] Includes intergovernmental payments to the Federal Government.
[5] Includes expenditures for libraries, hospitals, health, employment security administration, veterans' services, air transportation, sea and inland port facilities, parking facilities, police protection, fire protection, correction, protective inspection and regulation, sewerage, natural resources, parks and recreation, housing and community development, solid waste management, financial administration, judicial and legal, general public buildings, other government administration, interest on general debt, and other general expenditures, not elsewhere classified.

Note: Except for States listed, data for fiscal years listed from 1963–64 to 2015–16 are the aggregation of data for government fiscal years that ended in the 12-month period from July 1 to June 30 of those years; Texas used August and Alabama and Michigan used September as end dates. Data for 1963 and earlier years include data for government fiscal years ending during that particular calendar year.

Source: Department of Commerce (Bureau of the Census).

Table B–51. U.S. Treasury securities outstanding by kind of obligation, 1980–2018

[Billions of dollars]

End of fiscal year or month	Total Treasury securities outstanding [1]	Marketable							Nonmarketable				
		Total [2]	Treasury bills	Treasury notes	Treasury bonds	Treasury inflation-protected securities			Total	U.S. savings securities [3]	Foreign series [4]	Government account series	Other [5]
						Total	Notes	Bonds					
1980	906.8	594.5	199.8	310.9	83.8				312.3	73.0	25.2	189.8	24.2
1981	996.8	683.2	223.4	363.6	96.2				313.6	68.3	20.5	201.1	23.7
1982	1,141.2	824.4	277.9	442.9	103.6				316.8	67.6	14.6	210.5	24.1
1983	1,376.3	1,024.0	340.7	557.5	125.7				352.3	70.6	11.5	234.7	35.6
1984	1,560.4	1,176.6	356.8	661.7	158.1				383.8	73.7	8.8	259.5	41.8
1985	1,822.3	1,360.2	384.2	776.4	199.5				462.1	78.2	6.6	313.9	63.3
1986	2,124.9	1,564.3	410.7	896.9	241.7				560.5	87.8	4.1	365.9	102.8
1987	2,349.4	1,676.0	378.3	1,005.1	277.6				673.4	98.5	4.4	440.7	129.8
1988	2,601.4	1,802.9	398.5	1,089.6	299.9				798.5	107.8	6.3	536.5	148.0
1989	2,837.9	1,892.8	406.6	1,133.2	338.0				945.2	115.7	6.8	663.7	159.0
1990	3,212.7	2,092.8	482.5	1,218.1	377.2				1,119.9	123.9	36.0	779.4	180.6
1991	3,664.5	2,390.7	564.6	1,387.7	423.4				1,273.9	135.4	41.6	908.4	188.5
1992	4,063.8	2,677.5	634.3	1,566.3	461.8				1,386.3	150.3	37.0	1,011.0	188.0
1993	4,410.7	2,904.9	658.4	1,734.2	497.4				1,505.8	169.1	42.5	1,114.3	179.9
1994	4,691.7	3,091.6	697.3	1,867.5	511.8				1,600.1	178.6	42.0	1,211.7	167.8
1995	4,953.0	3,260.4	742.5	1,980.3	522.6				1,692.6	183.5	41.0	1,324.3	143.8
1996	5,220.8	3,418.4	761.2	2,098.7	543.5				1,802.4	184.1	37.5	1,454.7	126.1
1997	5,407.6	3,439.6	701.9	2,122.2	576.2	24.4	24.4		1,968.0	182.7	34.9	1,608.5	141.9
1998	5,518.7	3,331.0	637.6	2,009.1	610.4	58.8	41.9	17.0	2,187.6	180.8	35.1	1,777.3	194.4
1999	5,647.3	3,233.0	653.2	1,828.8	643.7	92.4	67.6	24.8	2,414.3	180.0	31.0	2,005.2	198.1
2000	5,622.1	2,992.8	616.2	1,611.3	635.3	115.0	81.6	33.4	2,629.4	177.7	25.4	2,242.9	183.3
2001	5,807.5	2,930.7	734.9	1,433.0	613.0	134.9	95.1	39.7	2,876.7	186.5	18.3	2,492.1	179.9
2002	6,228.2	3,136.7	868.3	1,521.6	593.0	138.9	93.7	45.1	3,091.5	193.3	12.5	2,707.3	178.4
2003	6,783.2	3,460.7	918.2	1,799.5	576.9	166.1	120.0	46.1	3,322.5	201.6	11.0	2,912.2	197.7
2004	7,379.1	3,846.1	961.5	2,109.6	552.0	223.0	164.5	58.5	3,533.0	204.2	5.9	3,130.0	192.9
2005	7,932.7	4,084.9	914.3	2,328.8	520.7	307.1	229.1	78.0	3,847.8	203.6	3.1	3,380.6	260.5
2006	8,507.0	4,303.0	911.5	2,447.2	534.7	395.6	293.9	101.7	4,203.9	203.7	3.0	3,722.7	274.5
2007	9,007.7	4,448.1	958.1	2,458.0	561.1	456.9	335.7	121.2	4,559.5	197.1	3.0	4,026.8	332.6
2008	10,024.7	5,236.0	1,489.8	2,624.8	682.9	524.5	380.2	144.3	4,788.7	194.3	3.0	4,297.7	293.8
2009	11,909.8	7,009.7	1,992.5	3,773.8	679.8	551.7	396.2	155.5	4,900.1	192.5	4.9	4,454.3	248.4
2010	13,561.6	8,498.3	1,788.5	5,255.9	849.9	593.8	421.1	172.7	5,063.3	188.7	4.2	4,645.3	225.1
2011	14,790.3	9,624.5	1,477.5	6,412.5	1,020.4	705.7	509.4	196.3	5,165.8	185.1	3.0	4,793.9	183.8
2012	16,066.2	10,749.7	1,616.0	7,120.7	1,198.2	807.7	584.7	223.0	5,316.5	183.8	3.0	4,939.3	190.4
2013	16,738.2	11,596.2	1,530.0	7,758.0	1,366.2	936.4	685.5	250.8	5,142.0	180.0	3.0	4,803.1	156.0
2014	17,824.1	12,294.2	1,411.0	8,167.8	1,534.1	1,044.7	765.2	279.5	5,529.9	176.7	3.0	5,212.5	137.7
2015	18,150.6	12,853.8	1,358.0	8,372.7	1,688.3	1,135.4	832.1	303.3	5,296.9	172.8	.3	5,013.5	110.3
2016	19,573.4	13,660.6	1,647.0	8,631.0	1,825.5	1,210.0	881.6	328.3	5,912.8	167.5	.3	5,604.1	141.0
2017	20,244.9	14,199.8	1,801.9	8,805.5	1,951.7	1,286.5	933.3	353.2	6,045.1	161.7	.3	5,771.1	112.0
2018	21,516.1	15,278.0	2,239.9	9,154.4	2,127.8	1,376.4	993.4	383.0	6,238.0	156.8	.3	5,977.6	103.4
2017: Jan	19,937.3	13,863.8	1,762.0	8,678.5	1,861.7	1,238.6	903.9	334.7	6,073.5	165.1	.3	5,768.7	139.4
Feb	19,959.6	13,898.9	1,753.0	8,684.6	1,878.4	1,246.9	904.1	342.8	6,060.7	164.7	.3	5,758.0	137.7
Mar	19,846.4	13,966.7	1,757.0	8,702.4	1,890.4	1,266.3	921.6	344.7	5,879.7	164.2	.3	5,577.2	138.0
Apr	19,846.3	13,950.5	1,742.0	8,716.7	1,902.5	1,238.7	892.9	345.8	5,895.8	163.8	.3	5,597.2	134.5
May	19,845.9	13,982.7	1,748.0	8,735.9	1,906.9	1,252.3	906.2	346.1	5,863.3	163.3	.3	5,568.5	131.2
June	19,844.6	14,009.4	1,718.0	8,758.3	1,918.9	1,261.6	908.8	352.8	5,835.1	162.8	.3	5,548.8	123.2
July	19,844.9	14,060.2	1,758.0	8,782.3	1,931.2	1,260.6	907.5	353.1	5,784.7	162.6	.3	5,505.4	116.5
Aug	19,844.5	14,093.6	1,747.9	8,788.5	1,939.7	1,276.3	922.8	353.5	5,751.0	162.0	.3	5,476.3	112.5
Sept	20,244.9	14,199.8	1,801.9	8,805.5	1,951.7	1,286.5	933.3	353.2	6,045.1	161.7	.3	5,771.1	112.0
Oct	20,442.5	14,273.7	1,855.9	8,830.1	1,963.7	1,295.4	935.9	359.5	6,168.8	161.1	.3	5,893.5	113.9
Nov	20,590.4	14,437.5	1,970.9	8,830.7	1,980.5	1,313.9	952.5	361.3	6,152.8	160.9	.3	5,875.0	116.7
Dec	20,492.7	14,480.2	1,955.9	8,849.7	1,992.5	1,327.5	966.3	361.2	6,012.5	160.4	.3	5,727.5	124.3
2018: Jan	20,493.7	14,514.5	1,966.9	8,889.2	2,004.9	1,323.1	961.9	361.2	5,979.2	159.9	.3	5,700.7	118.4
Feb	20,855.7	14,677.9	2,078.0	8,899.6	2,024.0	1,331.0	961.3	369.7	6,177.7	159.4	.3	5,902.8	115.2
Mar	21,089.9	14,945.0	2,289.0	8,924.6	2,037.0	1,349.0	977.4	371.6	6,144.9	159.0	.3	5,869.3	116.3
Apr	21,068.2	14,849.9	2,169.0	8,974.2	2,050.0	1,319.4	946.1	373.3	6,218.3	158.6	.3	5,945.6	113.9
May	21,145.2	14,939.4	2,184.0	9,002.2	2,064.4	1,335.6	961.4	374.2	6,205.8	158.2	.3	5,932.1	115.3
June	21,195.3	14,982.6	2,158.0	9,032.2	2,078.4	1,345.9	965.2	380.7	6,212.8	157.8	.3	5,943.9	110.8
July	21,313.1	15,085.3	2,205.9	9,094.9	2,092.4	1,347.8	965.5	382.3	6,227.8	157.5	.3	5,962.2	107.8
Aug	21,458.8	15,301.8	2,340.9	9,120.4	2,112.8	1,365.2	982.3	383.0	6,157.0	157.0	.3	5,895.9	103.8
Sept	21,516.1	15,278.0	2,239.9	9,154.4	2,127.8	1,376.4	993.4	383.0	6,238.0	156.8	.3	5,977.6	103.4
Oct	21,702.4	15,357.9	2,258.0	9,218.2	2,142.8	1,382.3	994.0	388.3	6,344.5	156.4	.3	6,084.1	103.7
Nov	21,850.1	15,560.1	2,389.1	9,240.4	2,158.5	1,395.9	1,007.1	388.8	6,290.0	156.2	.3	6,032.9	100.7
Dec	21,974.1	15,618.3	2,340.0	9,297.0	2,174.5	1,412.6	1,023.2	389.4	6,355.8	155.7	.3	6,101.9	97.9

[1] Data beginning with January 2001 are interest-bearing and non-interest-bearing securities; prior data are interest-bearing securities only.

[2] Data from 1986 to 2002 and 2005 forward include Federal Financing Bank securities, not shown separately. Beginning with data for January 2014, includes Floating Rate Notes, not shown separately.

[3] Through 1996, series is U.S. savings bonds. Beginning 1997, includes U.S. retirement plan bonds, U.S. individual retirement bonds, and U.S. savings notes previously included in "other" nonmarketable securities.

[4] Nonmarketable certificates of indebtedness, notes, bonds, and bills in the Treasury foreign series of dollar-denominated and foreign-currency-denominated issues.

[5] Includes depository bonds; retirement plan bonds through 1996; Rural Electrification Administration bonds; State and local bonds; special issues held only by U.S. Government agencies and trust funds and the Federal home loan banks; for the period July 2003 through February 2004, depositary compensation securities; and for the period August 2008 through April 2016, Hope bonds for the HOPE For Homeowners Program.

Note: The fiscal year is on an October 1–September 30 basis.

Source: Department of the Treasury.

[Billions of dollars]

End of month	Total public debt [1]	Federal Reserve and Intra-governmental holdings [2]	Held by private investors									
			Total privately held	De-pository institu-tions [3]	U.S. savings bonds [4]	Pension funds		Insurance compa-nies	Mutual funds [6]	State and local govern-ments	Foreign and inter-national [7]	Other inves-tors [8]
						Private [5]	State and local govern-ments					
2005: Mar	7,776.9	3,921.6	3,855.3	149.4	204.2	114.4	157.2	193.3	264.3	429.3	1,952.2	391.0
June	7,836.5	4,033.5	3,803.0	135.9	204.2	115.4	165.9	195.0	248.6	461.1	1,877.5	399.4
Sept	7,932.7	4,067.8	3,864.9	134.0	203.6	116.7	161.1	200.7	246.6	493.6	1,929.6	378.9
Dec	8,170.4	4,199.8	3,970.6	129.4	205.2	116.5	154.2	202.3	254.1	512.2	2,033.9	362.7
2006: Mar	8,371.2	4,257.2	4,114.0	113.0	206.0	116.8	152.9	200.3	254.2	515.7	2,082.1	473.0
June	8,420.0	4,389.2	4,030.8	119.5	205.2	117.7	149.6	196.1	243.4	531.6	1,977.8	490.1
Sept	8,507.0	4,432.8	4,074.2	113.6	203.7	125.8	149.3	196.8	234.2	542.3	2,025.3	483.2
Dec	8,680.2	4,558.1	4,122.1	114.8	202.4	139.8	153.4	197.9	248.2	570.5	2,103.1	392.0
2007: Mar	8,849.7	4,576.6	4,273.1	119.8	200.3	139.7	156.3	185.4	263.2	608.3	2,194.8	405.2
June	8,867.7	4,715.1	4,152.6	110.4	198.6	139.9	162.3	168.9	257.6	637.8	2,192.0	285.1
Sept	9,007.7	4,738.0	4,269.7	119.7	197.1	140.5	153.2	155.1	292.7	643.1	2,235.3	332.9
Dec	9,229.2	4,833.5	4,395.7	129.8	196.5	141.0	144.2	141.9	343.5	647.8	2,353.2	297.8
2008: Mar	9,437.6	4,694.7	4,742.9	125.0	195.4	143.7	135.4	152.1	466.7	646.4	2,506.3	371.9
June	9,492.0	4,685.8	4,806.2	112.7	195.0	145.0	135.5	159.4	440.3	635.1	2,587.4	395.9
Sept	10,024.7	4,692.7	5,332.0	130.0	194.3	147.0	136.7	163.4	631.4	614.0	2,802.4	512.9
Dec	10,699.8	4,806.4	5,893.4	105.0	194.1	147.4	129.9	171.4	758.2	601.4	3,077.2	708.9
2009: Mar	11,126.9	4,785.2	6,341.7	125.7	194.0	155.4	137.0	191.0	721.1	588.2	3,265.7	963.7
June	11,545.3	5,026.8	6,518.5	140.8	193.6	164.1	144.6	200.0	711.8	588.5	3,460.8	914.2
Sept	11,909.8	5,127.1	6,782.7	198.2	192.5	167.2	145.6	210.2	668.5	583.6	3,570.6	1,046.3
Dec	12,311.3	5,276.9	7,034.4	202.5	191.3	175.6	151.4	222.0	668.8	585.6	3,685.1	1,152.1
2010: Mar	12,773.1	5,259.8	7,513.3	269.3	190.2	183.0	153.6	225.7	678.5	585.0	3,877.9	1,350.1
June	13,201.8	5,345.1	7,856.7	266.1	189.6	190.8	150.1	231.8	676.8	584.4	4,070.0	1,497.1
Sept	13,561.6	5,350.5	8,211.1	322.8	188.7	198.2	145.2	240.6	671.0	586.0	4,324.2	1,534.4
Dec	14,025.2	5,656.2	8,368.9	319.3	187.9	206.8	153.7	248.4	721.7	595.7	4,435.6	1,499.9
2011: Mar	14,270.0	5,958.9	8,311.1	321.0	186.7	215.8	157.9	253.5	749.4	585.3	4,481.4	1,360.1
June	14,343.1	6,220.4	8,122.7	279.4	186.0	251.8	158.0	254.8	753.7	572.2	4,690.6	976.1
Sept	14,790.3	6,328.0	8,462.4	293.8	185.1	373.6	155.7	259.6	788.7	557.9	4,912.1	935.8
Dec	15,222.8	6,439.6	8,783.3	279.7	185.2	391.9	160.7	297.3	927.9	562.2	5,006.9	971.4
2012: Mar	15,582.3	6,397.2	9,185.1	317.0	184.8	406.6	169.4	298.1	1,015.4	567.4	5,145.1	1,081.2
June	15,855.5	6,475.8	9,379.7	303.2	184.7	427.4	171.2	293.6	997.8	585.4	5,310.9	1,105.4
Sept	16,066.2	6,446.8	9,619.4	338.2	183.8	453.9	181.7	292.6	1,080.7	596.9	5,476.1	1,015.4
Dec	16,432.7	6,523.7	9,909.1	347.7	182.5	468.0	183.6	292.7	1,031.8	599.6	5,573.8	1,229.4
2013: Mar	16,771.6	6,656.8	10,114.8	338.9	181.7	463.4	193.4	284.3	1,066.7	615.6	5,725.0	1,245.7
June	16,738.2	6,773.3	9,964.9	300.2	180.9	444.5	187.7	276.2	1,000.1	612.6	5,595.0	1,367.8
Sept	16,738.2	6,834.2	9,904.0	293.2	180.0	347.8	187.5	273.2	986.1	624.3	5,652.8	1,359.1
Dec	17,352.0	7,205.3	10,146.6	321.1	179.2	464.9	181.3	271.2	983.3	633.6	5,792.6	1,319.5
2014: Mar	17,601.2	7,301.5	10,299.7	368.3	178.3	474.3	184.3	276.8	1,060.4	632.0	5,948.3	1,177.0
June	17,632.6	7,461.0	10,171.6	407.2	177.6	482.6	198.3	287.7	986.2	638.7	6,018.7	974.5
Sept	17,824.1	7,490.8	10,333.2	469.6	176.7	490.7	198.7	298.1	1,075.8	628.8	6,069.2	925.5
Dec	18,141.4	7,578.9	10,562.6	513.7	175.9	507.1	199.2	307.0	1,121.8	657.3	6,157.7	922.8
2015: Mar	18,152.1	7,521.3	10,630.8	511.7	174.9	447.8	176.7	305.1	1,170.4	676.9	6,172.6	994.7
June	18,152.0	7,536.5	10,615.5	515.4	173.9	373.8	185.7	304.3	1,139.8	658.2	6,163.1	1,101.2
Sept	18,150.6	7,488.7	10,661.9	513.6	172.8	305.3	171.0	306.6	1,195.1	648.4	6,105.9	1,243.3
Dec	18,922.2	7,711.2	11,211.0	546.8	171.6	504.7	174.5	306.7	1,318.3	680.2	6,146.2	1,361.9
2016: Mar	19,264.9	7,801.4	11,463.6	555.3	170.3	524.0	170.4	315.5	1,321.7	691.9	6,284.4	1,430.2
June	19,381.6	7,911.2	11,470.4	570.3	169.0	537.1	185.0	329.8	1,336.0	710.0	6,279.1	1,354.2
Sept	19,573.4	7,863.5	11,709.9	620.4	167.5	544.3	203.3	341.2	1,506.5	721.6	6,155.9	1,449.1
Dec	19,976.9	8,005.6	11,971.3	666.8	165.8	536.4	217.8	330.2	1,593.3	717.9	6,006.3	1,736.7
2017: Mar	19,846.4	7,941.1	11,905.3	660.4	164.2	436.9	238.1	338.4	1,575.0	712.1	6,075.3	1,705.0
June	19,844.6	7,943.4	11,901.1	622.7	162.8	408.5	262.8	348.4	1,438.1	685.4	6,151.9	1,820.5
Sept	20,244.9	8,036.9	12,208.0	604.5	161.7	546.6	261.2	359.7	1,616.4	670.5	6,301.9	1,685.6
Dec	20,492.7	8,132.1	12,360.6	634.4	160.4	404.8	277.3	372.6	1,713.2	687.4	6,211.3	1,899.3
2018: Mar	21,089.9	8,086.6	13,003.3	635.2	159.0	571.4	280.9	360.4	1,880.6	675.2	6,223.2	2,217.4
June	21,195.3	8,106.9	13,088.5	670.0	157.8	593.9	277.3	223.8	1,760.7	699.0	6,214.0	2,491.9
Sept	21,516.1	8,068.1	13,447.9	690.1	156.8	613.6	279.5	223.6	1,795.9	678.8	6,225.6	2,784.1
Dec	21,974.1	8,095.0	13,879.1	....	155.7	....	....	....	....	....	6,265.2	....

[1] Face value.
[2] Federal Reserve holdings exclude Treasury securities held under repurchase agreements.
[3] Includes U.S. chartered depository institutions, foreign banking offices in U.S., banks in U.S. affiliated areas, credit unions, and bank holding companies.
[4] Current accrual value includes myRA.
[5] Includes Treasury securities held by the Federal Employees Retirement System Thrift Savings Plan "G Fund."
[6] Includes money market mutual funds, mutual funds, and closed-end investment companies.
[7] Includes nonmarketable foreign series, Treasury securities, and Treasury deposit funds. Excludes Treasury securities held under repurchase agreements in custody accounts at the Federal Reserve Bank of New York. Estimates reflect benchmarks to this series at differing intervals; for further detail, see Treasury Bulletin and http://www.treasury.gov/resource-center/data-chart-center/tic/pages/index.aspx.
[8] Includes individuals, Government-sponsored enterprises, brokers and dealers, bank personal trusts and estates, corporate and noncorporate businesses, and other investors.

Source: Department of the Treasury.

TABLE B–53. Corporate profits with inventory valuation and capital consumption adjustments, 1968–2018

[Billions of dollars; quarterly data at seasonally adjusted annual rates]

Year or quarter	Corporate profits with inventory valuation and capital consumption adjustments	Taxes on corporate income	Corporate profits after tax with inventory valuation and capital consumption adjustments		
			Total	Net dividends	Undistributed profits with inventory valuation and capital consumption adjustments
1968	101.7	37.2	64.6	26.0	38.6
1969	98.4	37.0	61.5	27.3	34.2
1970	86.2	31.3	55.0	27.8	27.2
1971	100.6	34.8	65.8	28.4	37.5
1972	117.2	39.1	78.1	30.1	48.0
1973	133.4	45.6	87.8	34.2	53.5
1974	125.7	47.2	78.5	38.8	39.7
1975	138.9	46.3	92.6	38.3	54.3
1976	174.3	59.4	114.9	44.9	70.0
1977	205.8	68.5	137.3	50.7	86.6
1978	238.6	77.9	160.7	57.8	102.9
1979	249.0	80.7	168.2	66.8	101.4
1980	223.6	75.5	148.1	75.8	72.3
1981	247.5	70.3	177.2	87.8	89.4
1982	229.9	51.3	178.6	92.9	85.6
1983	279.8	66.4	213.3	97.7	115.7
1984	337.9	81.5	256.4	106.9	149.5
1985	354.5	81.6	272.9	115.3	157.5
1986	324.4	91.9	232.5	124.0	108.5
1987	366.0	112.7	253.3	130.1	123.2
1988	414.5	124.3	290.2	147.3	142.9
1989	414.3	124.4	289.9	179.6	110.3
1990	417.7	121.8	295.9	192.7	103.2
1991	452.6	117.8	334.8	201.3	133.5
1992	477.2	131.9	345.3	206.3	139.0
1993	524.6	155.0	369.5	221.3	148.2
1994	624.8	172.7	452.1	256.4	195.7
1995	706.2	194.4	511.8	282.3	229.4
1996	789.5	211.4	578.1	323.6	254.5
1997	869.7	224.8	645.0	360.1	284.9
1998	808.5	221.8	586.6	383.6	203.0
1999	834.9	227.4	607.5	373.5	234.1
2000	786.6	233.4	553.2	410.2	142.9
2001	758.7	170.1	588.6	397.9	190.8
2002	911.7	160.6	751.1	424.9	326.2
2003	1,056.3	213.7	842.5	456.0	386.5
2004	1,289.3	278.5	1,010.8	582.2	428.6
2005	1,488.6	379.8	1,108.8	602.0	506.8
2006	1,646.3	430.4	1,215.8	755.1	460.8
2007	1,533.2	392.1	1,141.1	853.5	287.6
2008	1,285.8	256.1	1,029.7	840.3	189.4
2009	1,386.8	204.2	1,182.6	622.1	560.6
2010	1,728.7	272.5	1,456.2	643.2	813.0
2011	1,809.8	281.1	1,528.7	779.1	749.6
2012	1,997.4	334.9	1,662.5	948.7	713.9
2013	2,010.7	362.8	1,647.9	1,009.0	638.9
2014	2,118.8	407.4	1,711.5	1,096.1	615.4
2015	2,057.3	397.2	1,660.1	1,164.9	495.2
2016	2,035.0	392.9	1,642.1	1,187.4	454.7
2017	2,099.3	350.7	1,748.6	1,215.3	533.3
2018 ᵖ				1,241.7	
2015: I	2,133.7	417.5	1,716.3	1,148.0	568.2
II	2,102.5	421.9	1,680.6	1,128.9	551.7
III	2,056.6	391.5	1,665.1	1,157.4	507.7
IV	1,936.2	358.0	1,578.2	1,225.2	353.0
2016: I	1,995.2	384.4	1,610.8	1,180.2	430.6
II	2,017.7	385.5	1,632.2	1,180.9	451.3
III	2,044.6	413.0	1,631.6	1,196.3	435.3
IV	2,082.4	388.5	1,693.9	1,192.4	501.5
2017: I	2,055.9	348.0	1,707.8	1,217.7	490.2
II	2,089.5	355.8	1,733.7	1,233.3	500.4
III	2,101.1	365.2	1,735.9	1,215.5	520.5
IV	2,150.7	333.8	1,816.8	1,194.8	622.0
2018: I	2,177.3	212.0	1,965.3	1,213.2	752.1
II	2,242.3	234.8	2,007.5	1,223.0	784.5
III	2,320.5	243.7	2,076.8	1,250.6	826.2
IV ᵖ				1,279.8	

Source: Department of Commerce (Bureau of Economic Analysis).

TABLE B–54. Corporate profits by industry, 1968–2018

[Billions of dollars; quarterly data at seasonally adjusted annual rates]

		Corporate profits with inventory valuation adjustment and without capital consumption adjustment												
		Domestic industries												Rest of the world
Year or quarter	Total	Total	Financial			Nonfinancial								
			Total	Federal Reserve banks	Other	Total	Manu-factur-ing	Trans-porta-tion[1]	Utilities	Whole-sale trade	Retail trade	Infor-mation	Other	
SIC:[2]														
1968	94.3	88.6	12.9	2.5	10.4	75.7	45.9	11.4	....	4.7	6.4	....	7.4	5.6
1969	90.8	84.2	13.6	3.1	10.6	70.6	41.6	11.1	....	4.9	6.4	....	6.5	6.6
1970	79.7	72.6	15.5	3.5	12.0	57.1	32.0	8.8	....	4.6	6.1	....	5.8	7.1
1971	94.7	86.8	17.9	3.3	14.6	68.9	40.0	9.6	....	5.4	7.3	....	6.7	7.9
1972	109.3	99.7	19.5	3.3	16.1	80.3	47.6	10.4	....	7.2	7.5	....	7.6	9.5
1973	126.6	111.7	21.1	4.5	16.6	90.6	55.0	10.2	....	8.8	7.0	....	9.6	14.9
1974	123.3	105.8	20.8	5.7	15.1	85.1	51.0	9.1	....	12.2	2.8	....	10.0	17.5
1975	144.2	129.6	20.4	5.6	14.8	109.2	63.0	11.7	....	14.3	8.4	....	11.8	14.6
1976	182.1	165.6	25.6	5.9	19.7	140.0	82.5	17.5	....	13.7	10.9	....	15.3	16.5
1977	212.8	193.7	32.6	6.1	26.5	161.1	91.5	21.2	....	16.4	12.8	....	19.2	19.1
1978	246.7	223.8	40.8	7.6	33.1	183.1	105.8	25.5	....	16.7	13.1	....	22.0	22.9
1979	261.0	226.4	41.8	9.4	32.3	184.6	107.1	21.6	....	20.0	10.7	....	25.2	34.6
1980	240.6	205.2	35.2	11.8	23.5	169.9	97.6	22.2	....	18.5	7.0	....	24.6	35.5
1981	252.0	222.3	30.3	14.4	15.9	192.0	112.5	25.1	....	23.7	10.7	....	20.1	29.7
1982	224.8	192.2	27.2	15.2	12.0	165.0	89.6	28.1	....	20.7	14.3	....	12.3	32.6
1983	256.4	221.4	36.2	14.6	21.6	185.2	97.3	34.3	....	21.9	19.3	....	12.3	35.1
1984	294.3	257.7	34.7	16.4	18.3	223.0	114.2	44.7	....	30.4	21.5	....	12.1	36.6
1985	289.7	251.6	46.5	16.3	30.2	205.1	107.1	39.1	....	24.6	22.8	....	11.4	38.1
1986	273.3	233.8	56.4	15.5	40.8	177.4	75.6	39.3	....	24.4	23.4	....	14.7	39.5
1987	314.6	266.5	60.3	16.2	44.1	206.2	101.8	42.0	....	18.9	23.3	....	20.3	48.0
1988	366.2	309.2	66.9	18.1	48.8	242.3	132.8	46.8	....	20.4	19.8	....	22.5	57.0
1989	373.1	305.9	78.3	20.6	57.6	227.6	122.3	41.9	....	22.0	20.9	....	20.5	67.1
1990	391.2	315.1	89.6	21.8	67.8	225.5	120.9	43.5	....	19.4	20.3	....	21.3	76.1
1991	434.2	357.8	120.4	20.7	99.7	237.3	109.3	54.5	....	22.3	26.9	....	24.3	76.5
1992	459.7	386.6	132.4	18.3	114.1	254.2	109.8	57.7	....	25.3	28.1	....	33.4	73.1
1993	501.9	425.0	119.9	16.7	103.2	305.1	122.9	70.1	....	26.5	39.7	....	45.8	76.9
1994	589.3	511.3	125.9	18.5	107.4	385.4	162.6	83.9	....	31.4	46.3	....	61.2	78.0
1995	667.0	574.0	140.3	22.9	117.3	433.7	199.8	89.0	....	28.0	43.9	....	73.1	92.9
1996	741.8	639.8	147.9	22.5	125.3	492.0	220.4	91.2	....	39.9	52.0	....	88.5	102.0
1997	811.0	703.4	162.2	24.3	137.9	541.2	248.5	81.0	....	48.1	63.4	....	100.3	107.6
1998	743.8	641.1	138.9	25.6	113.3	502.1	220.4	72.6	....	50.6	72.3	....	86.3	102.8
1999	761.9	640.2	154.6	26.7	127.9	485.6	219.4	49.3	....	46.8	72.5	....	97.6	121.7
2000	729.8	584.1	149.7	31.2	118.5	434.4	205.9	33.8	....	50.4	68.9	....	75.4	145.7
NAICS:[2]														
1998	743.8	641.1	138.9	25.6	113.3	502.1	193.5	12.8	33.3	57.3	62.5	33.1	109.7	102.8
1999	761.9	640.2	154.6	26.7	127.9	485.6	184.5	7.2	34.4	55.6	59.5	20.8	123.5	121.7
2000	729.8	584.1	149.7	31.2	118.5	434.4	175.6	9.5	24.3	59.5	51.3	–11.9	126.1	145.7
2001	697.1	528.3	195.0	28.9	166.1	333.3	75.1	–7	22.5	51.1	71.3	–26.4	140.2	168.8
2002	797.4	640.6	265.3	23.5	241.9	375.3	78.3	–6.5	10.5	53.5	83.3	5.0	151.2	156.8
2003	955.7	796.7	302.8	20.0	282.7	494.0	123.9	4.4	13.2	56.6	87.9	28.1	179.9	158.9
2004	1,217.5	1,022.4	346.0	20.0	326.0	676.3	186.2	12.0	21.1	72.7	94.0	61.6	228.8	195.1
2005	1,629.2	1,403.4	409.5	26.5	383.0	993.9	279.7	28.4	32.4	96.0	123.3	100.7	333.5	225.7
2006	1,812.2	1,572.5	413.1	33.8	379.3	1,159.4	352.9	40.8	55.2	105.0	133.6	115.2	356.8	239.7
2007	1,708.3	1,370.5	300.2	36.0	264.2	1,070.3	321.1	23.3	49.6	102.8	119.4	120.5	333.6	337.8
2008	1,344.5	954.3	94.6	35.1	59.5	859.7	240.0	29.3	30.4	92.7	82.2	98.8	286.3	390.2
2009	1,470.1	1,121.3	362.7	47.3	315.3	758.7	164.7	21.7	23.4	88.9	107.9	87.0	265.1	348.8
2010	1,786.4	1,400.6	405.8	71.6	334.3	994.8	281.8	44.6	30.6	99.3	115.9	102.3	320.4	385.8
2011	1,750.2	1,337.7	378.4	76.0	302.4	959.3	296.0	30.6	10.2	97.2	115.1	95.7	314.5	412.6
2012	2,144.7	1,739.3	482.4	71.7	410.6	1,256.9	403.0	54.4	13.8	137.9	155.7	112.0	380.1	405.4
2013	2,165.9	1,767.1	430.7	79.7	351.1	1,336.3	446.9	45.2	28.3	146.4	153.3	137.6	378.6	398.8
2014	2,266.1	1,861.2	483.1	103.5	379.6	1,378.1	457.4	55.6	32.7	150.8	158.6	126.3	396.6	404.9
2015	2,187.0	1,784.5	437.6	100.7	336.8	1,346.9	422.5	62.2	20.1	152.1	169.2	140.4	380.4	402.5
2016	2,128.7	1,722.2	468.9	92.0	376.9	1,253.3	322.9	62.9	7.2	127.5	173.5	171.6	387.7	406.5
2017	2,136.4	1,687.5	468.7	78.3	390.4	1,218.9	292.9	59.4	3.8	111.8	162.5	148.6	439.8	448.8
2016: I	2,101.2	1,711.7	377.4	96.4	281.1	1,334.2	395.5	69.0	12.6	151.8	169.6	160.3	375.5	389.5
II	2,114.4	1,714.1	472.1	92.9	379.2	1,241.9	311.1	65.8	10.5	120.6	164.9	186.6	382.4	400.4
III	2,132.3	1,741.9	505.5	90.6	414.9	1,236.4	298.2	61.9	1.2	136.8	179.5	163.3	395.5	390.4
IV	2,166.8	1,721.0	520.4	87.9	432.5	1,200.6	286.6	55.1	4.4	100.7	179.9	176.4	397.6	445.8
2017: I	2,148.0	1,714.8	463.3	89.3	373.9	1,251.5	279.2	61.0	5.9	117.4	171.4	164.1	452.5	433.2
II	2,187.3	1,768.0	468.7	80.1	388.6	1,299.3	306.9	66.4	5.3	128.9	170.7	148.6	472.5	419.3
III	2,199.9	1,740.0	489.0	71.8	417.2	1,251.0	320.8	59.6	2.7	114.7	168.7	157.8	426.6	459.9
IV	2,010.3	1,527.3	453.7	71.9	381.8	1,073.6	264.5	50.6	1.4	86.3	139.2	124.0	407.5	483.0
2018: I	2,036.9	1,550.2	444.5	69.9	374.6	1,105.8	238.5	47.9	–1.1	88.6	155.4	148.9	427.6	486.7
II	2,107.3	1,625.2	461.6	66.6	395.0	1,163.6	267.7	54.0	–7	83.3	141.1	161.6	456.6	482.1
III	2,189.5	1,706.2	456.3	63.9	392.4	1,249.9	302.9	52.4	–2.2	117.1	164.8	162.6	452.2	483.4

[1] Data on Standard Industrial Classification (SIC) basis include transportation and public utilities. Those on North American Industry Classification System (NAICS) basis include transporation and warehousing. Utilities classified separately in NAICS (as shown beginning 1998).
[2] SIC-based industry data use the 1987 SIC for data beginning in 1987 and the 1972 SIC for prior data. NAICS-based data use 2002 NAICS.

Note: Industry data on SIC basis and NAICS basis are not necessarily the same and are not strictly comparable.

Source: Department of Commerce (Bureau of Economic Analysis).

TABLE B–55. Historical stock prices and yields, 1949–2003

End of year	Common stock prices (end of period) [1]									Common stock yields (Standard & Poor's) (percent) [5]	
	New York Stock Exchange (NYSE) indexes [2]						Dow Jones industrial average [2]	Standard & Poor's composite index (1941–43=10) [2]	Nasdaq composite index (Feb. 5, 1971=100) [2]	Dividend-price ratio [6]	Earnings-price ratio [7]
	Composite (Dec. 31, 2002= 5,000) [3]	December 31, 1965=50									
		Composite	Industrial	Transportation	Utility [4]	Finance					
1949	....	....	....	....	....	....	200.52	16.76	....	6.59	15.48
1950	....	....	....	....	....	....	235.42	20.41	....	6.57	13.99
1951	....	....	....	....	....	....	269.23	23.77	....	6.13	11.82
1952	....	....	....	....	....	....	291.90	26.57	....	5.80	9.47
1953	....	13.60	....	....	....	....	280.90	24.81	....	5.80	10.26
1954	....	19.40	....	....	....	....	404.39	35.98	....	4.95	8.57
1955	....	23.71	....	....	....	....	488.40	45.48	....	4.08	7.95
1956	....	24.35	....	....	....	....	499.47	46.67	....	4.09	7.55
1957	....	21.11	....	....	....	....	435.69	39.99	....	4.35	7.89
1958	....	28.85	....	....	....	....	583.65	55.21	....	3.97	6.23
1959	....	32.15	....	....	....	....	679.36	59.89	....	3.23	5.78
1960	....	30.94	....	....	....	....	615.89	58.11	....	3.47	5.90
1961	....	38.93	....	....	....	....	731.14	71.55	....	2.98	4.62
1962	....	33.81	....	....	....	....	652.10	63.10	....	3.37	5.82
1963	....	39.92	....	....	....	....	762.95	75.02	....	3.17	5.50
1964	....	45.65	....	....	....	....	874.13	84.75	....	3.01	5.32
1965	528.69	50.00	....	....	....	....	969.26	92.43	....	3.00	5.59
1966	462.28	43.72	43.13	47.56	90.38	44.91	785.69	80.33	....	3.40	6.63
1967	569.18	53.83	56.59	49.66	86.76	53.80	905.11	96.47	....	3.20	5.73
1968	622.79	58.90	61.69	56.27	91.64	76.48	943.75	103.86	....	3.07	5.67
1969	544.86	51.53	54.74	37.85	77.54	67.87	800.36	92.06	....	3.24	6.08
1970	531.12	50.23	52.91	35.70	81.64	64.34	838.92	92.15	....	3.83	6.45
1971	596.68	56.43	60.53	49.56	78.78	73.83	890.20	102.09	114.12	3.14	5.41
1972	681.79	64.48	70.33	47.69	84.34	83.34	1,020.02	118.05	133.73	2.84	5.50
1973	547.93	51.82	56.60	37.53	68.66	64.51	850.86	97.55	92.19	3.06	7.12
1974	382.03	36.13	39.15	26.36	53.30	39.84	616.24	68.56	59.82	4.47	11.59
1975	503.73	47.64	52.73	32.98	66.94	45.20	852.41	90.19	77.62	4.31	9.15
1976	612.01	57.88	63.36	42.57	82.54	59.23	1,004.65	107.46	97.88	3.77	8.90
1977	555.12	52.50	56.43	40.50	81.08	53.85	831.17	95.10	105.05	4.62	10.79
1978	566.96	53.62	58.87	41.58	75.38	55.01	805.01	96.11	117.98	5.28	12.03
1979	655.04	61.95	70.24	50.64	73.80	63.45	838.74	107.94	151.14	5.47	13.46
1980	823.27	77.86	91.52	76.19	76.90	70.83	963.99	135.76	202.34	5.26	12.66
1981	751.90	71.11	80.89	66.85	80.10	73.68	875.00	122.55	195.84	5.20	11.96
1982	856.79	81.03	93.02	73.63	86.94	85.00	1,046.54	140.64	232.41	5.81	11.60
1983	1,006.41	95.18	111.35	98.09	92.48	94.32	1,258.64	164.93	278.60	4.40	8.03
1984	1,013.91	96.38	110.58	90.61	103.14	97.63	1,211.57	167.24	247.35	4.64	10.02
1985	1,285.66	121.59	139.27	113.97	126.38	131.29	1,546.67	211.28	324.93	4.25	8.12
1986	1,465.31	138.59	160.11	117.65	147.54	140.05	1,895.95	242.17	348.83	3.49	6.09
1987	1,461.61	138.23	167.04	118.57	134.62	114.57	1,938.83	247.08	330.47	3.08	5.48
1988	1,652.25	156.26	189.42	146.60	149.38	128.19	2,168.57	277.72	381.38	3.64	8.01
1989	2,062.30	195.04	232.76	178.33	204.00	156.15	2,753.20	353.40	454.82	3.45	7.42
1990	1,908.45	180.49	223.60	141.49	182.60	122.06	2,633.66	330.22	373.84	3.61	6.47
1991	2,426.04	229.44	285.82	201.87	204.26	172.68	3,168.83	417.09	586.34	3.24	4.79
1992	2,539.92	240.21	294.39	214.72	209.66	200.83	3,301.11	435.71	676.95	2.99	4.22
1993	2,739.44	259.08	315.26	270.48	229.92	216.82	3,754.09	466.45	776.80	2.78	4.46
1994	2,653.37	250.94	318.10	222.46	198.41	195.80	3,834.44	459.27	751.96	2.82	5.83
1995	3,484.15	329.51	413.29	301.96	252.90	274.25	5,117.12	615.93	1,052.13	2.56	6.09
1996	4,148.07	392.30	494.38	352.30	259.91	351.17	6,448.27	740.74	1,291.03	2.19	5.24
1997	5,405.19	511.19	630.38	466.25	335.19	495.96	7,908.25	970.43	1,570.35	1.77	4.57
1998	6,299.94	595.81	743.65	482.38	445.94	521.42	9,181.43	1,229.23	2,192.69	1.49	3.46
1999	6,876.10	650.30	828.21	466.70	511.15	516.61	11,497.12	1,469.25	4,069.31	1.25	3.17
2000	6,945.57	656.87	803.29	462.76	440.54	646.95	10,786.85	1,320.28	2,470.52	1.15	3.63
2001	6,236.39	589.80	735.71	438.81	329.84	593.69	10,021.50	1,148.08	1,950.40	1.32	2.95
2002	5,000.00	472.87	583.95	395.81	233.08	510.46	8,341.63	879.82	1,335.51	1.61	2.92
2003 [3]	6,440.30	572.56	735.50	519.58	265.58	655.12	10,453.92	1,111.92	2,003.37	1.77	3.84

[1] End of period.
[2] Includes stocks as follows: for NYSE, all stocks listed; for Dow Jones industrial average, 30 stocks; for Standard & Poor's (S&P) composite index, 500 stocks; and for Nasdaq composite index, over 5,000.
[3] The NYSE relaunched the composite index on January 9, 2003, incorporating new definitions, methodology, and base value. (The composite index based on December 31, 1965=50 was discontinued.) Subset indexes on financial, energy, and health care were released by the NYSE on January 8, 2004 (see Table B–56). NYSE indexes shown in this table for industrials, utilities, transportation, and finance were discontinued.
[4] Effective April 1993, the NYSE doubled the value of the utility index to facilitate trading of options and futures on the index. Indexes prior to 1993 reflect the doubling.
[5] Based on 500 stocks in the S&P composite index.
[6] Aggregate cash dividends (based on latest known annual rate) divided by aggregate market value based on Wednesday closing prices. Monthly data are averages of weekly figures; annual data are averages of monthly figures.
[7] Quarterly data are ratio of earnings (after taxes) for four quarters ending with particular quarter-to-price index for last day of that quarter. Annual data are averages of quarterly ratios.

Sources: New York Stock Exchange, Dow Jones & Co., Inc., Standard & Poor's, and Nasdaq Stock Market.

TABLE B–56. Common stock prices and yields, 2000–2018

End of year or month	Common stock prices (end of period) [1]							Common stock yields (Standard & Poor's) (percent) [4]	
	New York Stock Exchange (NYSE) indexes (December 31, 2002=5,000) [2, 3]				Dow Jones industrial average [2]	Standard & Poor's composite index (1941–43=10) [2]	Nasdaq composite index (Feb. 5, 1971=100) [2]	Dividend-price ratio [5]	Earnings-price ratio [6]
	Composite	Financial	Energy	Health care					
2000	6,945.57	....	....	....	10,786.85	1,320.28	2,470.52	1.15	3.63
2001	6,236.39	....	....	....	10,021.50	1,148.08	1,950.40	1.32	2.95
2002	5,000.00	5,000.00	5,000.00	5,000.00	8,341.63	879.82	1,335.51	1.61	2.92
2003	6,440.30	6,676.42	6,321.05	5,925.97	10,453.92	1,111.92	2,003.37	1.77	3.84
2004	7,250.06	7,493.92	7,934.49	6,119.07	10,783.01	1,211.92	2,175.44	1.72	4.89
2005	7,753.95	7,996.94	10,109.61	6,458.20	10,717.50	1,248.29	2,205.32	1.83	5.36
2006	9,139.02	9,552.22	11,967.88	6,958.64	12,463.15	1,418.30	2,415.29	1.87	5.78
2007	9,740.32	8,300.68	15,283.81	7,170.42	13,264.82	1,468.36	2,652.28	1.86	5.29
2008	5,757.05	3,848.42	9,434.01	5,340.73	8,776.39	903.25	1,577.03	2.37	3.54
2009	7,184.96	4,721.02	11,415.03	6,427.27	10,428.05	1,115.10	2,269.15	2.40	1.86
2010	7,964.02	4,958.62	12,520.29	6,501.53	11,577.51	1,257.64	2,652.87	1.98	6.04
2011	7,477.03	4,062.88	12,409.61	7,045.61	12,217.56	1,257.60	2,605.15	2.05	6.77
2012	8,443.51	5,114.54	12,606.06	7,904.06	13,104.14	1,426.19	3,019.51	2.24	6.20
2013	10,400.33	6,353.68	14,557.54	10,245.31	16,576.66	1,848.36	4,176.59	2.14	5.57
2014	10,839.24	6,707.16	12,533.54	11,967.04	17,823.07	2,058.90	4,736.05	2.04	5.25
2015	10,143.42	6,305.68	9,343.81	12,385.19	17,425.03	2,043.94	5,007.41	2.10	4.59
2016	11,056.89	6,961.56	11,503.76	11,907.20	19,762.60	2,238.83	5,383.12	2.19	4.17
2017	12,808.84	8,235.89	11,470.58	14,220.58	24,719.22	2,673.61	6,903.39	1.97	4.22
2018	11,374.39	6,969.48	9,341.44	15,158.38	23,327.46	2,506.85	6,635.28	1.90	....
2016: Jan	9,632.70	5,743.94	9,032.22	11,778.53	16,466.30	1,940.24	4,613.95	2.33	....
Feb	9,559.53	5,530.09	8,847.72	11,526.98	16,516.50	1,932.23	4,557.95	2.38	....
Mar	10,207.38	5,931.58	9,681.17	11,795.36	17,685.09	2,059.74	4,869.85	2.23	4.20
Apr	10,436.92	6,120.84	10,601.99	12,213.31	17,773.64	2,065.30	4,775.36	2.18	....
May	10,441.00	6,175.68	10,267.72	12,418.63	17,787.20	2,096.96	4,948.06	2.19	....
June	10,489.76	5,899.18	10,707.35	12,711.06	17,929.99	2,098.86	4,842.67	2.19	4.14
July	10,785.51	6,145.11	10,470.13	13,197.22	18,432.24	2,173.60	5,162.13	2.14	....
Aug	10,764.75	6,363.23	10,480.12	12,595.43	18,400.88	2,170.95	5,213.22	2.12	....
Sept	10,721.74	6,236.63	10,787.85	12,496.06	18,308.15	2,168.27	5,312.00	2.14	4.11
Oct	10,481.89	6,279.55	10,541.10	11,686.99	18,142.42	2,126.15	5,189.14	2.16	....
Nov	10,838.46	6,729.90	11,215.51	11,669.05	19,123.58	2,198.81	5,323.68	2.15	....
Dec	11,056.89	6,961.56	11,503.76	11,907.20	19,762.60	2,238.83	5,383.12	2.08	6.15
2017: Jan	11,222.95	7,064.02	11,220.98	12,061.43	19,864.09	2,278.87	5,614.79	2.08	....
Feb	11,512.39	7,320.48	10,854.83	12,761.57	20,812.24	2,363.64	5,825.44	2.04	....
Mar	11,492.85	7,216.68	10,834.06	12,728.55	20,663.22	2,362.72	5,911.74	2.02	4.24
Apr	11,536.08	7,208.13	10,521.74	13,000.70	20,940.51	2,384.20	6,047.61	2.03	....
May	11,598.03	7,159.54	10,235.99	13,318.92	21,008.65	2,411.80	6,198.52	2.02	....
June	11,761.70	7,468.28	10,083.36	13,732.80	21,349.63	2,423.41	6,140.42	2.01	4.29
July	11,967.67	7,652.38	10,416.42	13,636.10	21,891.12	2,470.30	6,348.12	1.99	....
Aug	11,875.69	7,527.52	9,978.32	13,727.98	21,948.10	2,471.65	6,428.66	2.00	....
Sept	12,209.16	7,780.56	10,911.61	13,959.19	22,405.09	2,519.36	6,495.96	1.99	4.25
Oct	12,341.01	7,921.32	10,889.68	13,971.09	23,377.24	2,575.26	6,727.67	1.94	....
Nov	12,627.80	8,108.70	10,994.32	14,331.40	24,272.35	2,647.58	6,873.97	1.93	....
Dec	12,808.84	8,235.89	11,470.58	14,220.58	24,719.22	2,673.61	6,903.39	1.89	6.91
2018: Jan	13,367.96	8,637.58	11,843.94	15,051.71	26,149.39	2,823.81	7,411.48	1.82	....
Feb	12,652.55	8,246.24	10,625.83	14,357.41	25,029.20	2,713.83	7,273.01	1.89	....
Mar	12,452.06	8,029.25	10,863.28	14,040.86	24,103.11	2,640.87	7,063.45	1.90	4.37
Apr	12,515.36	7,995.25	11,878.26	14,198.80	24,163.15	2,648.05	7,066.27	1.95	....
May	12,527.14	7,877.77	12,056.61	14,292.95	24,415.84	2,705.27	7,442.12	1.92	....
June	12,504.25	7,781.67	12,131.49	14,464.62	24,271.41	2,718.37	7,510.30	1.90	4.51
July	12,963.28	8,097.12	12,282.46	15,409.93	25,415.19	2,816.29	7,671.79	1.85	....
Aug	13,016.89	8,109.69	11,837.21	15,887.99	25,964.82	2,901.52	8,109.54	1.82	....
Sept	13,082.52	7,979.54	12,169.73	16,299.34	26,458.31	2,913.98	8,046.35	1.81	4.47
Oct	12,208.06	7,543.04	10,915.63	15,506.53	25,115.76	2,711.74	7,305.90	1.89	....
Nov	12,457.55	7,713.77	10,478.32	16,505.42	25,538.46	2,760.17	7,330.54	1.95	....
Dec	11,374.39	6,969.48	9,341.44	15,158.38	23,327.46	2,506.85	6,635.28	2.10	....

[1] End of year or month.
[2] Includes stocks as follows: for NYSE, all stocks listed (in 2018, over 2,700); for Dow Jones industrial average, 30 stocks; for Standard & Poor's (S&P) composite index, 500 stocks; and for Nasdaq composite index, in 2018, over 3,000.
[3] The NYSE relaunched the composite index on January 9, 2003, incorporating new definitions, methodology, and base value. Subset indexes on financial, energy, and health care were released by the NYSE on January 8, 2004.
[4] Based on 500 stocks in the S&P composite index.
[5] Aggregate cash dividends (based on latest known annual rate) divided by aggregate market value based on Wednesday closing prices. Monthly data are averages of weekly figures, annual data are averages of monthly figures.
[6] Quarterly data are ratio of earnings (after taxes) for four quarters ending with particular quarter-to-price index for last day of that quarter. Annual data are averages of quarterly ratios.

Sources: New York Stock Exchange, Dow Jones & Co., Inc., Standard & Poor's, and Nasdaq Stock Market.

Corporate Profits and Finance | 699

TABLE B–57. U.S. international transactions, 1968–2018

[Millions of dollars; quarterly data seasonally adjusted]

| Year or quarter | Current Account [1] | | | | | | | | | | | | Current account balance as a percentage of GDP |
| | Goods [2] | | | Services | | | Balance on goods and services | Primary income receipts and payments | | | Balance on secondary Income [3] | Balance on current account | |
	Exports	Imports	Balance on goods	Exports	Imports	Balance on services		Receipts	Payments	Balance on primary income			
1968	33,626	32,991	635	11,918	12,301	–385	250	9,368	3,378	5,990	–5,629	611	0.1
1969	36,414	35,807	607	12,806	13,323	–517	90	10,913	4,869	6,044	–5,735	399	.0
1970	42,469	39,866	2,603	14,171	14,519	–348	2,255	11,748	5,514	6,234	–6,156	2,331	.2
1971	43,319	45,579	–2,260	16,358	15,401	959	–1,301	12,706	5,436	7,270	–7,402	–1,433	–.1
1972	49,381	55,797	–6,416	17,842	16,867	973	–5,443	14,764	6,572	8,192	–8,544	–5,796	–.5
1973	71,410	70,499	911	19,832	18,843	989	1,900	21,809	9,656	12,153	–6,914	7,140	.5
1974	98,306	103,811	–5,505	22,591	21,378	1,212	–4,293	27,587	12,084	15,503	–9,248	1,961	.1
1975	107,088	98,185	8,903	25,497	21,996	3,500	12,403	25,351	12,565	12,786	–7,076	18,117	1.1
1976	114,745	124,228	–9,483	27,971	24,570	3,402	–6,082	29,374	13,312	16,062	–5,686	4,296	.2
1977	120,816	151,907	–31,091	31,486	27,640	3,845	–27,247	32,355	14,218	18,137	–5,227	–14,336	–.7
1978	142,075	176,002	–33,927	36,353	32,189	4,164	–29,763	42,087	21,680	20,407	–5,788	–15,143	–.6
1979	184,439	212,007	–27,568	39,693	36,689	3,003	–24,566	63,835	32,961	30,874	–6,593	–285	.0
1980	224,250	249,750	–25,500	47,585	41,492	6,093	–19,407	72,605	42,533	30,072	–8,349	2,318	.1
1981	237,044	265,067	–28,023	57,355	45,503	11,851	–16,172	86,529	53,626	32,903	–11,702	5,029	.2
1982	211,157	247,642	–36,485	64,078	51,750	12,330	–24,156	96,522	61,359	35,163	–16,545	–5,537	–.2
1983	201,799	268,901	–67,102	64,307	54,973	9,335	–57,767	96,031	59,643	36,388	–17,311	–38,691	–1.1
1984	219,926	332,418	–112,492	71,168	67,748	3,418	–109,074	115,639	80,574	35,065	–20,334	–94,344	–2.3
1985	215,915	338,088	–122,173	73,156	72,863	294	–121,879	105,046	79,324	25,722	–21,999	–118,155	–2.7
1986	223,344	368,425	–145,081	86,690	80,147	6,543	–138,539	102,798	87,304	15,494	–24,131	–147,176	–3.2
1987	250,208	409,765	–159,557	98,661	90,788	7,874	–151,683	113,603	99,309	14,294	–23,265	–160,655	–3.3
1988	320,230	447,189	–126,959	110,920	98,525	12,394	–114,566	141,666	122,981	18,685	–25,274	–121,153	–2.3
1989	359,916	477,665	–117,749	127,087	102,480	24,607	–93,142	166,384	146,560	19,824	–26,169	–99,487	–1.8
1990	387,401	498,438	–111,037	147,833	117,660	30,173	–80,865	176,894	148,345	28,549	–26,654	–78,969	–1.3
1991	414,083	491,020	–76,937	164,260	118,459	45,802	–31,136	155,327	131,198	24,129	9,904	2,897	.0
1992	439,631	536,528	–96,897	177,251	119,566	57,685	–39,212	139,082	114,845	24,237	–36,635	–51,613	–.8
1993	456,943	589,394	–132,451	185,920	123,780	62,141	–70,311	141,606	116,287	25,319	–39,811	–84,805	–1.2
1994	502,859	668,690	–165,831	200,395	133,057	67,338	–98,493	169,447	152,302	17,145	–40,265	–121,612	–1.7
1995	575,204	749,374	–174,170	219,183	141,397	77,786	–96,384	213,661	192,771	20,890	–38,074	–113,567	–1.5
1996	612,113	803,113	–191,000	239,489	152,554	86,935	–104,065	229,530	207,212	22,318	–43,017	–124,764	–1.5
1997	678,366	876,794	–198,428	256,087	165,932	90,155	–108,273	261,357	248,750	12,607	–45,062	–140,725	–1.6
1998	670,416	918,637	–248,221	262,758	180,677	82,081	–166,140	266,244	261,978	4,266	–53,187	–215,062	–2.4
1999	698,524	1,035,592	–337,068	271,343	192,893	78,450	–258,617	299,114	287,981	11,134	–40,881	–288,365	–3.0
2000	784,940	1,231,722	–446,783	290,381	216,115	74,266	–372,517	356,706	338,637	18,069	–49,003	–403,450	–3.9
2001	731,331	1,153,701	–422,370	274,323	213,465	60,858	–361,511	296,977	269,447	27,530	–55,708	–389,689	–3.7
2002	698,036	1,173,281	–475,245	280,670	224,379	56,290	–418,955	286,525	263,860	22,665	–54,507	–450,797	–4.1
2003	730,446	1,272,089	–541,643	289,972	242,219	47,754	–493,890	324,374	289,657	34,716	–59,571	–518,744	–4.5
2004	823,584	1,488,349	–664,766	337,966	283,083	54,882	–609,883	416,085	362,179	53,906	–75,614	–631,591	–5.2
2005	913,016	1,695,820	–782,804	373,006	304,448	68,558	–714,245	534,215	480,317	53,898	–84,887	–745,234	–5.7
2006	1,040,905	1,878,194	–837,289	416,738	341,165	75,573	–761,716	680,830	653,928	26,902	–71,149	–805,964	–5.8
2007	1,165,151	1,986,347	–821,196	488,396	372,575	115,821	–705,375	834,983	749,977	85,005	–90,665	–711,035	–4.9
2008	1,308,795	2,141,287	–832,492	532,817	409,052	123,765	–708,726	815,567	685,918	129,649	–102,312	–681,389	–4.6
2009	1,070,331	1,580,025	–509,694	512,722	386,801	125,920	–383,774	613,249	498,089	115,160	–103,907	–372,521	–2.6
2010	1,290,279	1,938,950	–648,671	562,759	409,313	153,446	–495,225	660,949	511,948	168,221	–104,261	–431,265	–2.9
2011	1,498,887	2,239,886	–740,999	627,061	435,761	191,300	–549,699	755,937	544,853	211,084	–107,047	–445,662	–2.9
2012	1,562,630	2,303,749	–741,119	655,214	452,013	203,711	–537,408	767,972	560,497	207,475	–96,900	–426,832	–2.6
2013	1,593,708	2,294,247	–700,539	700,491	461,087	239,404	–461,135	792,819	586,842	205,977	–93,643	–348,801	–2.1
2014	1,635,563	2,385,480	–749,917	741,094	480,761	260,333	–489,584	824,543	606,152	218,391	–94,006	–365,199	–2.1
2015	1,511,381	2,273,249	–761,868	755,310	491,966	263,343	–498,525	810,073	606,464	203,608	–112,848	–407,764	–2.2
2016	1,456,957	2,208,008	–751,051	758,888	509,838	249,050	–502,001	830,174	637,151	193,023	–123,895	–432,873	–2.3
2017	1,553,383	2,360,878	–807,495	797,690	542,471	255,219	–552,277	928,118	706,386	221,731	–118,597	–449,142	–2.3
2015: I	384,030	577,355	–193,325	189,012	121,395	67,617	–125,708	201,600	149,222	52,378	–28,270	–101,600	–2.3
II	385,894	574,332	–188,438	189,078	122,113	66,965	–121,473	206,389	157,237	49,152	–24,677	–96,999	–2.1
III	377,113	569,157	–192,044	188,535	124,022	64,513	–127,531	206,188	157,172	49,016	–31,035	–109,550	–2.4
IV	364,344	552,406	–188,062	188,685	124,436	64,249	–123,813	195,896	142,834	53,062	–28,865	–99,616	–2.2
2016: I	353,330	539,770	–186,440	186,905	125,727	61,179	–125,261	199,946	154,498	45,447	–32,087	–111,901	–2.4
II	361,159	546,454	–185,295	189,118	125,922	63,196	–122,099	207,929	160,387	47,543	–28,501	–103,057	–2.2
III	371,283	556,600	–185,316	191,760	128,214	63,546	–121,770	206,389	162,480	43,909	–31,465	–109,327	–2.3
IV	371,186	565,185	–194,000	191,104	129,975	61,129	–132,871	215,911	159,787	56,124	–31,842	–108,589	–2.3
2017: I	381,138	579,484	–198,346	195,168	131,781	63,387	–134,959	217,567	164,962	52,604	–25,355	–107,709	–2.2
II	382,492	582,440	–199,948	197,252	134,004	63,248	–136,700	223,979	175,444	48,535	–33,672	–121,837	–2.5
III	387,814	584,637	–196,823	201,293	137,261	64,032	–132,791	237,632	179,410	58,222	–28,878	–103,441	–2.1
IV	401,939	614,317	–212,378	203,977	139,426	64,551	–147,826	248,940	186,569	62,371	–30,692	–116,148	–2.3
2018: I	411,442	632,244	–220,802	205,994	139,182	66,812	–153,989	256,029	194,854	61,175	–28,896	–121,710	–2.4
II	429,431	632,489	–203,058	207,537	137,365	68,452	–134,806	266,274	203,926	62,348	–28,966	–101,224	–2.0
III p	421,762	648,775	–227,012	207,635	139,279	68,356	–158,656	264,523	205,098	59,425	–25,586	–116,176	–2.4

[1] Current and capital account statistics in the international transactions accounts differ slightly from statistics in the National Income and Product Accounts (NIPAs) because of adjustments made to convert the international statistics to national accounting concepts. A reconciliation can be found in NIPA table 4.3B.

[2] Adjusted from Census data to align with concepts and definitions used to prepare the international and national economic accounts. The adjustments are necessary to supplement coverage of Census data, to eliminate duplication of transactions recorded elsewhere in the international accounts, to value transactions according to a standard definition, and for earlier years, to record transactions in the appropriate period.

See next page for continuation of table.

[Millions of dollars; quarterly data seasonally adjusted]

Year or quarter	Balance on capital account [1]	Financial account											Statistical discrepancy
		Net U.S. acquisition of financial assets excluding financial derivatives [net increase in assets / financial outflow (+)]					Net U.S. incurrence of liabilities excluding financial derivatives [net increase in liabilities / financial inflow (+)]				Financial derivatives other than reserves, net transactions	Net lending (+) or net borrowing (−) from financial account transactions [5]	
		Total	Direct investment assets	Portfolio investment assets	Other investment assets	Reserve assets [4]	Total	Direct investment liabilities	Portfolio investment liabilities	Other investment liabilities			
1968	....	10,977	5,294	1,569	3,244	870	9,928	808	3,780	5,340	....	1,049	438
1969	....	11,584	5,960	1,549	2,896	1,179	12,702	1,263	719	10,720	....	−1,118	−1,517
1970	....	9,336	7,590	1,076	3,151	−2,481	7,226	1,464	11,710	−5,948	....	2,110	−219
1971	....	12,474	7,618	1,113	6,092	−2,349	23,687	368	28,835	−5,516	....	−11,213	−9,779
1972	....	14,497	7,747	619	6,127	4	22,171	948	13,123	8,100	....	−7,674	−1,879
1973	....	22,874	11,353	672	11,007	−158	18,388	2,800	4,790	10,798	....	4,486	−2,654
1974	....	34,745	9,052	1,853	22,373	1,467	35,228	4,761	5,500	24,967	....	−483	−2,444
1975	....	39,703	14,244	6,247	18,363	849	16,870	2,603	12,761	1,506	....	22,833	4,717
1976	....	51,269	11,949	8,885	27,877	2,558	37,840	4,347	16,165	17,328	....	13,429	9,134
1977	....	34,785	11,891	5,459	17,060	375	52,770	3,728	37,615	11,427	....	−17,985	−3,651
1978	....	61,130	16,057	3,626	42,179	−732	66,275	7,896	30,083	28,296	....	−5,145	9,997
1979	....	66,053	25,223	12,430	27,267	1,133	40,693	11,876	−13,502	42,319	....	25,360	25,647
1980	....	86,968	19,222	6,042	53,550	8,154	62,036	16,918	23,825	21,293	....	24,932	22,614
1981	....	114,147	9,624	15,650	83,697	5,176	85,684	25,196	17,509	42,979	....	28,463	23,433
1982	....	142,722	19,397	12,395	105,965	4,965	109,897	27,475	19,695	62,727	....	32,825	38,362
1983	....	74,690	20,844	2,063	50,588	1,195	95,715	18,688	18,382	58,645	....	−21,025	17,666
1984	....	50,740	26,770	3,498	17,340	3,132	126,413	34,832	38,695	52,886	....	−75,673	18,673
1985	....	47,064	21,241	3,008	18,957	3,858	146,544	22,057	68,004	56,483	....	−99,480	18,677
1986	....	107,252	19,524	8,984	79,057	−313	223,854	30,946	104,497	88,411	....	−116,602	30,570
1987	....	84,058	39,795	7,903	45,508	−9,148	251,863	63,232	79,631	109,000	....	−167,805	−7,149
1988	....	105,747	21,701	4,589	75,544	3,913	244,008	56,910	86,786	100,312	....	−138,261	−17,108
1989	−207	182,908	50,973	31,166	75,476	25,293	230,302	75,801	74,852	79,649	....	−47,394	52,299
1990	−7,221	103,985	59,934	30,557	11,336	2,158	162,109	71,247	25,767	65,095	....	−58,124	28,066
1991	−5,129	75,753	49,253	32,053	210	−5,763	119,586	34,535	72,562	12,489	....	−43,833	−41,601
1992	1,449	84,899	58,755	50,684	−20,639	−3,901	178,842	20,315	92,199	56,328	....	−93,943	−43,776
1993	−714	199,399	82,799	137,917	−22,696	1,379	278,607	50,211	174,387	54,009	....	−79,208	6,313
1994	−1,112	188,758	89,988	54,088	50,028	−5,346	312,995	55,942	131,849	125,204	....	−124,237	−1,514
1995	−221	363,555	110,041	143,506	100,266	9,742	446,393	69,067	254,431	122,895	....	−82,838	30,951
1996	−8	424,548	103,024	160,179	168,013	−6,668	559,027	97,644	392,107	69,276	....	−134,479	−9,706
1997	−256	502,024	121,352	121,036	258,626	1,010	720,999	122,150	311,105	287,744	....	−218,975	−77,995
1998	−7	385,936	174,751	132,186	72,216	6,783	452,901	211,152	225,878	15,871	....	−66,965	148,106
1999	−4,176	526,612	247,484	141,007	146,868	−8,747	765,215	312,449	278,697	174,069	....	−238,603	53,938
2000	−1	587,682	186,371	159,713	241,308	290	1,066,074	349,124	441,966	274,984	....	−478,392	−74,941
2001	13,198	386,308	146,041	106,919	128,437	4,911	788,345	172,496	431,492	184,357	....	−402,037	−25,546
2002	−141	319,170	178,984	79,532	56,973	3,681	821,844	111,056	504,155	206,634	....	−502,673	−51,735
2003	−1,821	371,074	195,218	133,059	44,321	−1,524	911,660	117,107	550,163	244,390	....	−540,586	−20,021
2004	3,049	1,058,654	374,006	191,956	495,498	−2,806	1,600,881	213,642	867,340	519,899	....	−542,226	86,316
2005	13,116	562,983	52,591	267,290	257,196	−14,094	1,277,056	142,345	832,037	302,673	....	−714,073	18,045
2006	−1,788	1,324,607	283,800	493,366	549,814	−2,373	2,120,480	298,464	1,126,735	695,280	−29,710	−825,583	−17,832
2007	384	1,563,459	523,889	380,807	658,641	122	2,190,087	346,615	1,156,612	686,860	−6,222	−632,850	77,801
2008	6,010	−317,607	343,584	−284,269	−381,770	4,848	462,408	341,091	523,683	−402,367	32,947	−747,069	−71,690
2009	−140	131,074	312,597	375,883	−609,662	52,256	325,644	161,082	357,352	−192,789	−44,816	−239,386	133,275
2010	−157	958,703	349,829	199,620	407,420	1,835	1,391,042	264,039	820,434	306,569	−14,076	−446,415	−14,992
2011	−1,186	492,530	436,615	85,365	−45,327	15,877	983,522	263,499	311,626	408,397	−35,006	−525,998	−79,150
2012	6,904	176,764	377,239	248,760	−453,695	4,460	632,034	250,343	747,017	−365,327	7,064	−448,205	−28,277
2013	−412	649,587	392,796	481,298	−221,408	−3,099	1,052,068	288,131	511,987	251,949	2,222	−400,259	−51,046
2014	−45	866,523	387,528	582,676	−100,099	−3,583	1,109,443	251,857	697,607	159,979	−54,335	−297,255	67,989
2015	−42	202,208	307,058	160,410	−258,968	−6,292	501,121	509,087	213,910	−221,876	−27,035	−325,948	81,859
2016	−59	348,625	312,975	36,283	−2,723	2,090	741,529	494,455	231,349	15,725	7,827	−385,078	47,855
2017	24,746	1,182,749	379,222	586,695	218,522	−1,690	1,537,683	354,829	799,182	383,671	23,074	−331,860	92,536
2015: I	−22	348,283	88,547	221,847	42,049	−4,159	429,374	243,726	107,435	78,214	−40,197	−121,288	−19,667
II	−20	46,345	92,779	113,617	−159,175	−877	181,700	116,973	243,152	−178,425	1,701	−133,654	−36,635
III	−1	−74,432	51,137	−97,440	−27,863	−266	−37,175	69,900	−146,760	39,685	722	−36,535	73,016
IV	0	−117,988	74,594	−77,613	−113,979	−990	−72,777	78,489	10,083	−161,350	10,739	−34,471	65,145
2016: I	−58	39,781	76,062	−64,312	29,222	−1,191	152,172	158,914	−52,832	46,089	10,782	−101,609	10,350
II	0	350,387	103,425	147,012	99,761	189	368,537	186,295	4,783	177,458	608	−17,541	85,516
III	−1	40,432	95,894	−33,346	−23,759	1,642	243,723	130,934	217,768	−104,979	3,437	−199,854	−90,527
IV	0	−81,975	37,593	−13,071	−107,947	1,450	−22,901	18,312	61,630	−102,843	−7,000	−66,073	42,515
2017: I	−1	366,101	135,054	141,783	89,505	−241	429,098	112,354	160,111	156,633	−5,609	−68,606	39,104
II	0	315,922	49,976	180,700	85,095	150	445,338	97,118	263,170	85,050	9,306	−120,111	1,727
III	24,787	373,591	102,936	175,910	94,804	−61	504,082	107,107	294,275	102,701	18,600	−111,891	−33,231
IV	−40	127,135	91,256	88,301	−50,883	−1,539	159,164	38,250	81,626	39,288	777	−31,252	84,936
2018: I	−2	251,126	−139,326	304,094	86,365	−7	441,080	57,949	301,503	81,628	29,024	−160,930	−39,218
II	−5	−199,943	−68,060	−14,272	−120,679	3,068	−63,262	16,499	20,596	−100,358	−16,969	−153,650	−52,421
III p	562	132,689	76,846	72,598	−16,577	−177	151,723	122,336	12,469	16,918	−12,255	−31,289	92,966

[3] Includes U.S. government and private transfers, such as U.S. government grants and pensions, fines and penalties, withholding taxes, personal transfers, insurance-related transfers, and other current transfers.

[4] Consists of monetary gold, special drawing rights (SDRs), the U.S. reserve position in the International Monetary Fund (IMF), and other reserve assets, including foreign currencies.

[5] Net lending means that U.S. residents are net suppliers of funds to foreign residents, and net borrowing means the opposite.

Source: Department of Commerce (Bureau of Economic Analysis).

[Billions of dollars; monthly data seasonally adjusted]

Year or month	Goods: Exports (f.a.s. value)[1,2]							Goods: Imports (customs value)[6]							Services (BOP basis)	
	Total, BOP basis[3,4]	Census basis (by end-use category)						Total, BOP basis[4]	Census basis (by end-use category)						Exports[4]	Imports[4]
		Total, Census basis[3,5]	Foods, feeds, and beverages	Industrial supplies and materials	Capital goods except automotive	Automotive vehicles, parts, and engines	Consumer goods (non-food) except automotive		Total, Census basis[5]	Foods, feeds, and beverages	Industrial supplies and materials	Capital goods except automotive	Automotive vehicles, parts, and engines	Consumer goods (non-food) except automotive		
1990	387.4	393.6	35.1	104.4	152.7	37.4	43.3	498.4	495.3	26.6	143.2	116.4	87.3	105.7	147.8	117.7
1991	414.1	421.7	35.7	109.7	166.7	40.0	45.9	491.0	488.5	26.5	131.6	120.7	85.7	108.0	164.3	118.5
1992	439.6	448.2	40.3	109.1	175.9	47.0	51.4	536.5	532.7	27.6	138.6	134.3	91.8	122.7	177.3	119.6
1993	456.9	465.1	40.6	111.8	181.7	52.4	54.7	589.4	580.7	27.9	145.6	152.4	102.4	134.0	185.9	123.8
1994	502.9	512.6	42.0	121.4	205.0	57.8	60.0	668.7	663.3	31.0	162.1	184.4	118.3	146.3	200.4	133.1
1995	575.2	584.7	50.5	146.2	233.0	61.8	64.4	749.4	743.5	33.2	181.8	221.4	123.8	159.9	219.2	141.4
1996	612.1	625.1	55.5	147.7	253.0	65.0	70.1	803.1	795.3	35.7	204.5	228.1	128.9	172.0	239.5	152.6
1997	678.4	689.2	51.5	158.2	294.5	74.0	77.4	876.8	869.7	39.7	213.8	253.3	139.8	193.8	256.1	165.9
1998	670.4	682.1	46.4	148.3	299.4	72.4	80.3	918.6	911.9	41.2	200.1	269.5	148.7	217.0	262.8	180.7
1999	698.5	695.8	46.0	147.5	310.8	75.3	80.9	1,035.6	1,024.6	43.6	221.4	295.7	179.0	241.9	271.3	192.9
2000	784.9	781.9	47.9	172.6	356.9	80.4	89.4	1,231.7	1,218.0	46.0	299.0	347.0	195.9	281.8	290.4	216.1
2001	731.3	729.1	49.4	160.1	321.7	75.4	88.3	1,153.7	1,141.0	46.6	273.9	298.0	189.8	284.3	274.3	213.5
2002	698.0	693.1	49.6	156.8	290.4	78.9	84.4	1,173.3	1,161.4	49.7	267.7	283.3	203.7	307.8	280.7	224.4
2003	730.4	724.8	55.0	173.0	293.7	80.6	89.9	1,272.1	1,257.1	55.8	313.8	295.9	210.1	333.9	290.0	242.2
2004	823.6	814.9	56.6	203.9	327.5	89.2	103.2	1,488.3	1,469.7	62.1	412.8	343.6	228.2	372.9	338.0	283.1
2005	913.0	901.1	59.0	233.0	358.4	98.4	115.3	1,695.8	1,673.5	68.1	523.8	379.3	239.4	407.2	373.0	304.4
2006	1,040.9	1,026.0	66.0	276.0	404.0	107.3	129.1	1,878.2	1,853.9	74.9	602.0	418.3	256.6	442.6	416.7	341.2
2007	1,165.2	1,148.2	84.3	316.4	433.0	121.3	146.0	1,986.3	1,957.0	81.7	634.7	444.5	256.7	474.6	488.4	372.6
2008	1,308.8	1,287.4	108.3	388.0	457.7	121.5	161.3	2,141.3	2,103.6	89.0	779.5	453.7	231.2	481.6	532.8	409.1
2009	1,070.3	1,056.0	93.9	296.5	391.2	81.7	149.5	1,580.0	1,559.6	81.6	462.4	370.5	157.7	427.3	512.7	386.8
2010	1,290.3	1,278.5	107.7	391.7	447.5	112.0	165.2	1,939.0	1,913.9	91.7	603.1	449.4	225.1	483.2	562.8	409.3
2011	1,498.9	1,482.5	126.2	501.1	494.0	133.0	175.3	2,239.9	2,208.0	107.5	755.8	510.8	254.6	514.1	627.1	435.8
2012	1,562.6	1,545.8	133.0	501.2	527.2	146.2	181.7	2,303.7	2,276.3	110.3	730.6	548.7	297.8	516.9	655.7	452.0
2013	1,593.7	1,578.5	136.2	508.2	534.4	152.7	188.8	2,294.2	2,268.0	115.1	681.5	555.7	308.8	531.7	700.5	461.1
2014	1,635.6	1,621.9	143.7	505.8	551.5	159.8	199.0	2,385.5	2,356.4	125.9	667.0	594.1	328.6	557.1	741.1	480.8
2015	1,511.4	1,503.3	127.7	427.0	539.5	151.9	197.7	2,273.2	2,248.8	127.8	486.0	602.5	349.2	594.2	755.3	492.0
2016	1,457.0	1,451.0	130.5	397.0	519.6	150.3	193.7	2,208.0	2,187.6	130.0	443.3	589.9	350.1	583.4	758.9	509.8
2017	1,553.4	1,546.3	132.7	464.7	533.3	157.6	197.7	2,360.9	2,342.0	137.8	507.3	640.6	359.0	601.9	797.7	542.5
2018 P		1,672.9	141.2	538.9	562.0	158.7	206.6		2,541.7	147.5	574.9	693.2	372.2	647.8		
2017: Jan	126.7	126.1	10.9	37.3	43.6	13.4	16.4	194.4	192.7	11.1	41.5	50.9	30.9	50.6	64.7	43.9
Feb	127.2	126.6	10.6	38.1	43.1	13.3	16.6	192.6	191.0	11.2	43.3	50.9	29.0	48.9	65.1	43.9
Mar	127.2	126.6	11.2	37.2	43.6	13.0	16.5	192.4	190.7	11.1	42.6	50.8	30.2	48.9	65.4	44.0
Apr	126.8	126.3	11.4	37.6	43.6	12.6	16.0	194.1	192.6	11.4	41.6	51.6	29.8	50.4	65.4	44.1
May	127.1	126.6	11.0	37.6	43.3	12.9	16.8	193.9	192.3	11.4	41.8	52.6	29.3	49.3	65.7	44.7
June	128.6	128.1	11.4	37.7	43.9	13.5	16.5	194.5	192.9	11.4	41.1	52.9	30.2	49.1	66.2	45.1
July	128.5	127.9	11.7	37.6	44.7	12.9	15.9	193.9	192.4	11.6	40.6	53.9	29.5	48.7	66.7	45.5
Aug	128.6	128.1	11.2	36.9	45.2	13.1	16.7	194.1	192.6	11.5	40.4	53.7	30.0	49.2	67.0	45.6
Sept	130.7	130.2	11.3	39.2	44.9	13.1	16.3	196.6	195.1	11.7	41.2	54.8	29.7	49.8	67.7	46.2
Oct	130.9	130.3	10.6	41.5	44.0	12.7	16.4	199.4	198.0	11.7	42.8	55.1	29.5	50.2	67.7	46.2
Nov	134.3	133.5	10.7	41.2	46.2	13.5	16.8	204.8	203.3	11.7	44.9	56.2	30.2	52.0	68.0	46.4
Dec	136.8	136.1	10.9	42.8	47.0	13.5	16.8	210.1	208.5	11.9	45.5	57.1	30.7	55.0	68.2	46.8
2018: Jan	133.8	133.0	10.7	40.9	44.9	13.6	17.9	208.3	206.6	11.8	46.9	55.7	30.7	53.2	68.2	46.0
Feb	136.7	136.0	10.9	43.0	45.7	14.5	16.7	213.5	211.9	12.6	47.1	57.6	31.1	55.7	68.7	46.9
Mar	141.0	140.3	11.8	44.3	47.5	14.1	17.1	210.4	208.9	12.3	46.7	56.5	30.9	54.7	69.0	46.3
Apr	141.3	140.6	12.4	45.7	46.1	13.9	17.2	209.7	208.0	12.3	47.9	56.9	30.0	51.9	68.6	45.9
May	145.0	144.2	14.1	44.4	48.2	13.6	17.8	210.8	208.9	12.4	47.9	59.0	29.7	51.4	68.6	45.6
June	143.1	142.5	14.1	46.3	47.3	12.9	16.4	212.0	210.4	12.2	48.8	57.5	30.2	53.4	68.7	45.9
July	140.8	140.2	13.2	46.5	46.3	13.1	16.0	214.0	212.3	12.4	49.3	58.2	30.7	52.6	69.0	46.2
Aug	139.1	138.5	12.0	44.1	46.4	12.8	17.6	215.7	213.9	12.3	49.7	57.7	31.7	53.5	69.2	46.3
Sept	141.9	141.3	11.0	46.9	47.5	13.0	17.8	219.1	217.6	12.1	49.4	60.1	31.1	55.5	69.5	46.8
Oct	141.5	140.9	10.4	47.2	47.0	12.7	17.9	219.8	218.0	12.3	49.4	56.9	31.8	57.4	69.7	47.1
Nov P	140.3	139.7	10.4	45.9	48.4	12.3	17.0	211.9	210.2	12.2	46.0	57.3	32.1	53.1	69.5	47.3
Dec P		135.7	10.3	43.7	46.3	12.3	17.1		215.2	12.6	45.8	59.9	32.1	55.5		

[1] Department of Defense shipments of grant-aid military supplies and equipment under the Military Assistance Program are excluded from total exports through 1985 and included beginning 1986.
[2] F.a.s. (free alongside ship) value basis at U.S. port of exportation for exports.
[3] Beginning with data for 1989, exports have been adjusted for undocumented exports to Canada and are included in the appropriate end-use categories. For prior years, only total exports include this adjustment.
[4] Beginning with data for 1999, exports of goods under the U.S. Foreign Military Sales program and fuel purchases by foreign air and ocean carriers in U.S. ports are included in goods exports (BOP basis) and excluded from services exports. Beginning with data for 1999, imports of petroleum abroad by U.S. military agencies and fuel purchases by U.S. air and ocean carriers in foreign ports are included in goods imports (BOP basis) and excluded from services imports.
[5] Total includes "other" exports or imports, not shown separately.
[6] Total arrivals of imported goods other than in-transit shipments.
[7] Total includes revisions not reflected in detail.
[8] Total exports are on a revised statistical month basis; end-use categories are on a statistical month basis.

Note: Goods on a Census basis are adjusted to a BOP basis by the Bureau of Economic Analysis, in line with concepts and definitions used to prepare international and national accounts. The adjustments are necessary to supplement coverage of Census data, to eliminate duplication of transactions recorded elsewhere in international accounts, to value transactions according to a standard definition, and for earlier years, to record transactions in the appropriate period.
Data include international trade of the U.S. Virgin Islands, Puerto Rico, and U.S. Foreign Trade Zones.

Source: Department of Commerce (Bureau of the Census and Bureau of Economic Analysis).

TABLE B–59. U.S. international trade in goods and services by area and country, 2000–2017

[Millions of dollars]

Item	2000	2005	2010	2012	2013	2014	2015	2016	2017
EXPORTS									
Total, all countries	1,075,321	1,286,022	1,853,038	2,218,354	2,294,199	2,376,657	2,266,691	2,215,845	2,351,073
Europe	296,284	365,200	503,816	577,786	580,234	606,544	598,616	602,936	632,667
Euro area [1]	173,446	214,355	288,604	319,172	327,600	347,609	346,115	351,059	366,522
France	30,759	35,504	44,114	48,921	50,672	50,989	49,990	51,099	52,980
Germany	45,253	55,247	73,378	76,076	74,644	77,907	80,134	81,283	86,585
Italy	16,761	18,727	22,845	24,930	25,483	26,212	25,453	25,656	27,808
United Kingdom	73,139	83,183	102,648	115,293	108,030	119,074	124,309	122,350	126,192
Canada	203,861	245,134	303,409	356,099	364,968	374,850	336,261	321,595	341,309
Latin America and Other Western Hemisphere ..	225,116	256,066	409,201	523,576	561,468	585,359	549,554	514,863	548,526
Brazil	21,858	21,230	53,753	68,827	70,900	71,102	59,360	53,917	63,490
Mexico	127,076	142,977	188,371	244,593	256,342	271,635	268,211	261,999	276,701
Venezuela	8,810	9,068	15,784	23,958	20,568	18,045	14,904	11,171	8,788
Asia and Pacific	299,103	341,564	523,131	616,841	634,902	652,735	636,150	639,768	693,496
China	21,464	50,572	115,559	144,894	160,375	169,008	165,526	170,881	188,004
India	6,472	13,232	29,667	34,503	35,231	36,950	40,060	42,296	49,472
Japan	101,247	94,356	104,731	118,044	112,201	114,828	108,417	108,834	114,746
Korea, Republic of	34,744	38,000	55,533	62,336	64,491	66,653	65,327	64,689	73,424
Singapore	24,400	26,482	39,459	44,090	42,025	41,687	42,653	43,387	47,518
Taiwan	30,403	29,232	36,717	37,278	38,317	40,084	38,714	38,193	36,192
Middle East	28,241	48,427	70,094	94,651	100,176	101,881	101,723	98,048	96,338
Africa	17,178	23,003	40,400	46,300	49,212	52,404	41,760	36,052	36,292
Memorandum: Members of OPEC [2]	29,407	49,194	78,985	110,913	117,063	115,626	107,493	106,104	91,962
IMPORTS									
Total, all countries	1,447,837	2,000,268	2,348,263	2,755,762	2,755,334	2,866,241	2,765,215	2,717,846	2,903,349
Europe	359,670	493,933	559,596	651,331	660,838	702,465	703,264	700,730	741,593
Euro area [1]	217,211	303,692	336,152	397,488	407,245	438,198	444,052	442,411	467,402
France	40,829	47,269	54,637	58,937	61,610	64,433	64,666	63,614	66,796
Germany	74,855	109,551	111,902	141,632	147,834	157,554	157,162	148,355	153,314
Italy	31,888	40,719	38,349	48,162	49,464	53,333	55,207	56,851	62,547
United Kingdom	71,400	85,508	93,860	103,222	102,811	108,172	112,216	107,283	110,616
Canada	251,750	316,798	309,173	361,031	369,111	385,992	332,095	314,189	338,548
Latin America and Other Western Hemisphere ..	249,553	352,076	453,253	547,280	538,026	550,327	519,837	509,002	538,956
Brazil	15,384	26,389	29,343	39,319	34,809	37,851	34,663	32,362	35,011
Mexico	148,258	188,192	246,770	298,599	303,988	322,950	326,244	324,371	345,446
Venezuela	19,291	34,512	33,445	39,630	32,781	31,019	16,470	11,765	13,028
Asia and Pacific	507,225	680,901	836,903	984,908	1,004,303	1,061,705	1,094,871	1,081,812	1,157,557
China	103,433	251,556	376,735	439,832	455,524	483,677	499,058	479,244	523,708
India	12,612	23,648	44,394	59,446	62,368	67,957	69,561	71,937	76,833
Japan	164,231	160,965	147,518	176,439	171,479	168,511	163,659	165,232	171,334
Korea, Republic of	46,203	51,128	59,096	70,226	73,605	81,412	83,579	81,301	82,721
Singapore	21,360	18,799	22,733	26,185	23,539	22,657	25,058	25,004	27,214
Taiwan	44,784	41,661	41,881	46,198	45,194	48,346	48,661	46,988	50,587
Middle East	44,296	81,553	95,077	133,896	124,016	121,193	81,005	75,158	83,070
Africa	31,390	69,921	93,190	75,999	58,784	43,297	33,893	35,512	43,366
Memorandum: Members of OPEC [2]	71,068	139,431	164,837	192,233	163,732	143,029	76,913	89,578	83,012
BALANCE (excess of exports +)									
Total, all countries	−372,517	−714,246	−495,225	−537,408	−461,135	−489,584	−498,525	−502,001	−552,276
Europe	−63,386	−128,733	−55,779	−73,544	−80,604	−95,923	−104,649	−97,795	−108,926
Euro area [1]	−43,765	−89,336	−47,548	−78,316	−79,646	−90,588	−97,938	−91,352	−100,881
France	−10,070	−11,765	−10,524	−10,017	−10,938	−13,444	−14,676	−12,515	−13,816
Germany	−29,603	−54,304	−38,524	−65,557	−73,190	−79,647	−77,029	−67,072	−66,729
Italy	−15,127	−21,991	−15,504	−23,231	−23,980	−27,121	−29,755	−31,196	−34,739
United Kingdom	1,739	−2,324	8,786	12,070	5,219	10,902	12,093	15,065	15,575
Canada	−47,889	−71,663	−5,764	−4,932	−4,144	−11,142	4,165	7,406	2,760
Latin America and Other Western Hemisphere ..	−24,437	−96,010	−44,052	−23,703	23,442	35,032	29,718	5,861	9,570
Brazil	6,474	−5,158	24,410	29,507	36,091	33,251	24,697	21,556	28,479
Mexico	−21,182	−45,215	−58,399	−54,006	−47,646	−51,317	−58,033	−62,372	−68,745
Venezuela	−10,481	−25,443	−17,662	−15,672	−12,212	−12,974	−1,566	−594	−4,240
Asia and Pacific	−208,122	−339,337	−313,772	−368,067	−369,401	−408,969	−458,722	−442,044	−464,061
China	−81,969	−200,984	−261,176	−294,938	−295,149	−314,669	−333,534	−308,363	−335,704
India	−6,140	−10,416	−14,728	−24,944	−27,136	−31,007	−29,501	−29,641	−27,360
Japan	−62,967	−66,609	−42,787	−58,395	−59,277	−53,683	−55,242	−56,398	−56,588
Korea, Republic of	−11,459	−13,128	−3,564	−7,890	−9,114	−14,759	−18,252	−16,612	−9,297
Singapore	3,041	7,683	16,726	17,904	18,486	19,029	17,595	18,383	20,303
Taiwan	−14,381	−12,428	−5,163	−8,920	−6,878	−8,264	−9,947	−8,794	−14,396
Middle East	−16,054	−33,126	−24,983	−39,245	−23,840	−19,312	20,718	22,890	13,269
Africa	−14,212	−46,917	−52,790	−29,698	−9,571	9,107	7,867	540	−7,074
Memorandum: Members of OPEC [2]	−41,660	−90,237	−85,853	−81,320	−46,669	−27,403	30,580	16,526	8,950

[1] Euro area consists of: Austria, Belgium, Cyprus (beginning in 2008), Estonia (beginning in 2011), Finland, France, Germany, Greece (beginning in 2001), Ireland, Italy, Luxembourg, Malta (beginning in 2008), Netherlands, Portugal, Slovakia (beginning in 2009), Slovenia (beginning in 2007), and Spain.

[2] Organization of Petroleum Exporting Countries, consisting of Algeria, Angola (beginning in 2007), Ecuador (beginning in 2007), Indonesia (ending in 2008), Iran, Iraq, Kuwait, Libya, Nigeria, Qatar, Saudi Arabia, United Arab Emirates, and Venezuela.

Note: Data are on a balance of payments basis. For further details, and additional data by country, see *Survey of Current Business*, February 2019.

Source: Department of Commerce (Bureau of Economic Analysis).

TABLE B–60. Foreign exchange rates, 2000–2018

[Foreign currency units per U.S. dollar, except as noted; certified noon buying rates in New York]

Period	Australia (dollar) [1]	Brazil (real)	Canada (dollar)	China, P.R. (yuan)	EMU Members (euro) [1,2]	India (rupee)	Japan (yen)	Mexico (peso)	South Korea (won)	Sweden (krona)	Switzer-land (franc)	United Kingdom (pound) [1]
March 1973	1.4129		0.9967	2.2401		7.55	261.90	0.013	398.85	4.4294	3.2171	2.4724
2000	.5815	1.8301	1.4855	8.2784	0.9232	45.00	107.80	9.459	1,130.90	9.1735	1.6904	1.5156
2001	.5169	2.3527	1.5487	8.2770	.8952	47.22	121.57	9.337	1,292.01	10.3425	1.6891	1.4396
2002	.5437	2.9213	1.5704	8.2771	.9454	48.63	125.22	9.663	1,250.31	9.7233	1.5567	1.5025
2003	.6524	3.0750	1.4008	8.2772	1.1321	46.59	115.94	10.793	1,192.08	8.0787	1.3450	1.6347
2004	.7365	2.9262	1.3017	8.2768	1.2438	45.26	108.15	11.290	1,145.24	7.3480	1.2428	1.8330
2005	.7627	2.4352	1.2115	8.1936	1.2449	44.00	110.11	10.894	1,023.75	7.4710	1.2459	1.8204
2006	.7535	2.1738	1.1340	7.9723	1.2563	45.19	116.31	10.906	954.32	7.3718	1.2532	1.8434
2007	.8391	1.9461	1.0734	7.6058	1.3711	41.18	117.76	10.928	928.97	6.7550	1.1999	2.0020
2008	.8537	1.8326	1.0660	6.9477	1.4726	43.39	103.39	11.143	1,098.71	6.5846	1.0816	1.8545
2009	.7927	1.9976	1.1412	6.8307	1.3935	48.33	93.68	13.498	1,274.63	7.6539	1.0860	1.5661
2010	.9200	1.7600	1.0298	6.7696	1.3261	45.65	87.78	12.624	1,155.74	7.2053	1.0432	1.5452
2011	1.0332	1.6723	.9887	6.4630	1.3931	46.58	79.70	12.427	1,106.94	6.4878	.8862	1.6043
2012	1.0359	1.9535	.9995	6.3093	1.2859	53.37	79.82	13.154	1,126.16	6.7721	.9377	1.5853
2013	.9683	2.1570	1.0300	6.1478	1.3281	58.51	97.60	12.758	1,094.67	6.5124	.9269	1.5642
2014	.9034	2.3512	1.1043	6.1620	1.3297	61.00	105.74	13.302	1,052.29	6.8576	.9147	1.6484
2015	.7522	3.3360	1.2791	6.2827	1.1096	64.11	121.05	15.874	1,130.96	8.4350	.9628	1.5284
2016	.7445	3.4839	1.3243	6.6400	1.1072	67.16	108.66	18.667	1,159.34	8.5541	.9848	1.3555
2017	.7671	3.1910	1.2984	6.7569	1.1301	65.07	112.10	18.884	1,129.04	8.5430	.9842	1.2890
2018	.7481	3.6513	1.2957	6.6090	1.1817	68.37	110.40	19.218	1,099.29	8.6945	.9784	1.3363
2017: I	.7586	3.1402	1.3237	6.8853	1.0661	66.87	113.52	20.255	1,150.02	8.9198	1.0032	1.2399
II	.7510	3.2152	1.3446	6.8586	1.1008	64.47	111.11	18.548	1,129.92	8.8025	.9847	1.2798
III	.7899	3.1593	1.2530	6.6684	1.1755	64.27	110.95	17.811	1,131.16	8.1329	.9629	1.3089
IV	.7687	3.2491	1.2715	6.6131	1.1778	64.71	112.89	18.974	1,104.96	8.3175	.9868	1.3273
2018: I	.7859	3.2474	1.2656	6.3535	1.2289	64.38	108.27	18.717	1,071.10	8.1182	.9484	1.3920
II	.7568	3.6043	1.2907	6.3772	1.1922	67.00	109.14	19.412	1,079.64	8.6733	.9854	1.3612
III	.7315	3.9492	1.3070	6.8053	1.1629	70.11	111.50	18.945	1,120.84	8.9482	.9843	1.3030
IV	.7174	3.8061	1.3201	6.9143	1.1414	72.13	112.77	19.816	1,126.77	9.0460	.9957	1.2870

Trade-weighted value of the U.S. dollar

Period	Nominal			Real [6]		
	Broad index (January 2006=100) [3]	Advanced foreign economies index (January 2006=100) [4]	Emerging market economies index (January 2006=100) [5]	Broad index (January 2006=100) [3]	Advanced foreign economies index (January 2006=100) [4]	Emerging market economies index (January 2006=100) [5]
2000						
2001						
2002						
2003						
2004						
2005						
2006	98.6180	95.9714	99.8070	98.9402	98.3178	99.7562
2007	93.8431	90.4796	96.1330	94.2867	93.6310	95.1426
2008	90.8882	86.8919	94.1320	90.9832	90.8429	91.2060
2009	96.7742	91.1579	102.0238	95.3306	94.7051	96.1058
2010	93.0696	88.5236	97.2219	90.7766	92.0125	89.5961
2011	88.8310	83.3260	94.0635	86.2804	87.3149	85.2818
2012	91.6426	86.4375	96.5637	88.4827	90.8405	86.1746
2013	92.7779	89.0205	96.1026	88.7777	93.8352	83.9814
2014	95.6108	91.7259	99.0021	90.7991	97.0042	85.0028
2015	108.1046	106.2262	109.4944	101.2526	111.8230	91.7986
2016	113.1535	107.4023	118.2744	105.4676	113.9821	97.6114
2017	112.8357	106.9800	118.1568	104.9129	114.1351	96.4965
2018	112.0443	104.5312	119.1041	104.0657	112.2009	96.5207
2017: I	114.8194	110.7712	120.4457	108.6358	118.0443	100.0331
II	112.2865	109.1314	116.9725	105.7975	116.2253	96.4225
III	108.3938	103.6723	114.6228	102.0967	110.6292	94.2530
IV	109.4182	104.3478	116.0207	103.1217	111.6416	95.2773
2018: I	106.5139	101.1235	113.4157	100.5081	108.3846	93.2050
II	109.0914	103.6642	116.0625	103.0115	111.3112	95.3444
III	112.1177	105.9362	119.9192	105.4847	113.6095	97.9346
IV	114.1331	107.4535	122.4839	107.2587	115.4982	99.5989

[1] U.S. dollars per foreign currency unit.
[2] European Economic and Monetary Union (EMU) members consists of Austria, Belgium, Cyprus (beginning in 2008), Estonia (beginning in 2011), Finland, France, Germany, Greece (beginning in 2001), Ireland, Italy, Luxembourg, Malta (beginning in 2008), Netherlands, Portugal, Slovakia (beginning in 2009), Slovenia (beginning in 2007), and Spain.
[3] Weighted average of the foreign exchange value of the U.S. dollar against the currencies of a broad group of major U.S. trading partners.
[4] Subset of the broad index. Consists of currencies of the Euro area, Australia, Canada, Japan, Sweden, Switzerland, and the United Kingdom.
[5] Subset of the broad index currencies that are emerging market economies. For details, see *Revisions to the Federal Reserve Dollar Indexes*, January 2019.
[6] Adjusted for changes in consumer price indexes for the United States and other countries.

Source: Board of Governors of the Federal Reserve System.

TABLE B-61. Growth rates in real gross domestic product by area and country, 2000-2019

[Percent change]

Area and country	2000-2009 annual average	2010	2011	2012	2013	2014	2015	2016	2017	2018[1]	2019[1]
World	3.9	5.4	4.3	3.5	3.5	3.6	3.5	3.3	3.8	3.7	3.5
Advanced economies	1.8	3.1	1.7	1.2	1.4	2.1	2.3	1.7	2.4	2.3	2.0
Of which:											
United States	1.9	2.6	1.6	2.2	1.8	2.5	2.9	1.6	2.2	2.9	2.5
Euro area[2]	1.4	2.1	1.6	−.9	−.2	1.4	2.1	1.9	2.4	1.8	1.6
Germany	0.8	3.9	3.7	.7	.6	2.2	1.5	2.2	2.5	1.5	1.3
France	1.4	1.9	2.2	.3	.6	1.0	1.0	1.1	2.3	1.5	1.5
Italy	0.5	1.7	.6	−2.8	−1.7	.1	1.0	.9	1.6	1.0	.6
Spain	2.7	.0	−1.0	−2.9	−1.7	1.4	3.6	3.2	3.0	2.5	2.2
Japan	0.5	4.2	−.1	1.5	2.0	.4	1.4	1.0	1.9	.9	1.1
United Kingdom	1.8	1.7	1.6	1.4	2.0	2.9	2.3	1.8	1.8	1.4	1.5
Canada	2.1	3.1	3.1	1.7	2.5	2.9	1.0	1.4	3.0	2.1	1.9
Other advanced economies	3.4	5.9	3.4	2.2	2.4	2.9	2.2	2.3	2.8	2.8	2.5
Emerging market and developing economies	6.1	7.4	6.4	5.3	5.1	4.7	4.3	4.4	4.7	4.6	4.5
Regional groups:											
Commonwealth of Independent States[3]	5.9	4.6	5.3	3.7	2.5	1.1	−1.9	.4	2.1	2.4	2.2
Russia	5.4	4.5	5.1	3.7	1.8	.7	−2.5	−.2	1.5	1.7	1.6
Excluding Russia	7.5	5.0	6.0	3.6	4.2	1.9	−.6	2.0	3.6	3.9	3.7
Emerging and Developing Asia	8.1	9.6	7.9	7.0	6.9	6.8	6.8	6.5	6.5	6.5	6.3
China	10.3	10.6	9.5	7.9	7.8	7.3	6.9	6.7	6.9	6.6	6.2
India[4]	6.9	10.3	6.6	5.5	6.4	7.4	8.2	7.1	6.7	7.3	7.5
ASEAN-5[5]	5.0	6.9	4.7	6.2	5.1	4.6	4.9	4.9	5.3	5.2	5.1
Emerging and Developing Europe	4.0	4.3	6.6	2.5	4.9	3.9	4.7	3.3	6.0	3.8	.7
Latin America and the Caribbean	3.0	6.1	4.6	2.9	2.9	1.3	.3	−.6	1.3	1.1	2.0
Brazil	3.4	7.5	4.0	1.9	3.0	.5	−3.5	−3.5	1.1	1.3	2.5
Mexico	1.4	5.1	3.7	3.6	1.4	2.8	3.3	2.9	2.1	2.1	2.1
Middle East, North Africa, Afghanistan, and Pakistan	5.2	4.6	4.4	4.8	2.6	2.9	2.5	5.1	2.2	2.4	2.4
Saudi Arabia	3.4	5.0	10.0	5.4	2.7	3.7	4.1	1.7	−.9	2.3	1.8
Sub-Saharan Africa	5.6	7.1	5.1	4.6	5.2	5.1	3.3	1.4	2.9	2.9	3.5
Nigeria	8.3	11.3	4.9	4.3	5.4	6.3	2.7	−1.6	.8	1.9	2.0
South Africa	3.6	3.0	3.3	2.2	2.5	1.8	1.3	.6	1.3	.8	1.4

[1] All figures are forecasts as published by the International Monetary Fund. For the United States, initial estimates by the Department of Commerce show that real GDP rose 2.9 percent in 2018.

[2] For 2019, includes data for: Austria, Belgium, Cyprus, Estonia, Finland, France, Germany, Greece, Ireland, Italy, Latvia, Lithuania, Luxembourg, Malta, Netherlands, Portugal, Slovak Republic, Slovenia, and Spain.

[3] Includes Georgia, Turkmenistan, and Ukraine, which are not members of the Commonwealth of Independent States but are included for reasons of geography and similarity in economic structure.

[4] Data and forecasts are presented on a fiscal year basis and output growth is based on GDP at market prices.

[5] Consists of Indonesia, Malaysia, Philippines, Thailand, and Vietnam.

Note: For details on data shown in this table, see *World Economic Outlook*, October 2018, and *World Economic Outlook Update*, January 2019, published by the International Monetary Fund.

Sources: International Monetary Fund and Department of Commerce (Bureau of Economic Analysis).